EXPERIMENTAL CHILD PSYCHOLOGY

HAYNE W. REESE
University of Kansas

LEWIS P. LIPSITT
Brown University

ACADEMIC PRESS · NEW YORK AND LONDON

ACADEMIC PRESS, INC.
111 Fifth Avenue, New York, New York 10003

United Kingdom Edition published by
ACADEMIC PRESS, INC. (LONDON) LTD.
Berkeley Square House, London W1X 6BA

LIBRARY OF CONGRESS CATALOG CARD NUMBER: 75-91426

First Printing, May 1970
Second Printing, October 1970

PRINTED IN THE UNITED STATES OF AMERICA

EXPERIMENTAL CHILD PSYCHOLOGY

CONTRIBUTORS

Donald M. Baer, University of Kansas

Peter D. Eimas, Brown University

David Elkind, University of Rochester

Mitchell Glickstein, Brown University

Wendell E. Jeffrey, University of California, Los Angeles

Herbert Kaye, Emory University

Lewis P. Lipsitt, Brown University

Langdon E. Longstreth, University of Southern California

Boyd R. McCandless, Emory University

Robert Y. Moore, University of Chicago

David S. Palermo, Pennsylvania State University

Hayne W. Reese, University of Kansas

Morton Rieber, San Francisco State College

Thomas J. Ryan, Carleton University, Ottawa

Winifred O. Shepard, State University College, Fredonia, New York

James A. Sherman, University of Kansas

Einar R. Siqueland, Brown University

Joachim F. Wohlwill, Clark University

CONTENTS

PREFACE   ix

ACKNOWLEDGMENTS   xii

Chapter 1. INTRODUCTION
The Scope of Experimental Child Psychology   1
Methods of Child Psychology   12

Chapter 2. SENSORY PROCESSES
Introduction   33
Vision   35
Audition   47
Somesthesis   53
Gustation   56
Olfaction   58
Conclusions   62

Chapter 3. BASIC LEARNING PROCESSES:
I. CLASSICAL CONDITIONING
Introduction   65
Classical Conditioning Designs and Controls   68
Classical Reward Conditioning   73
Classical Aversive Conditioning   85
Age Differences in Classical Conditioning   94

Chapter 4. BASIC LEARNING PROCESSES:
II. INSTRUMENTAL CONDITIONING
Introduction   97
Instrumental Conditioning in Infants   102
Free Operant Conditioning in Children   123
Discrete-Trial Instrumental Conditioning in Children   139

Chapter 5. DISCRIMINATIVE LEARNING
Introduction   151
Discriminative Learning in Infancy   157
Discriminative Learning in Childhood   183

Chapter 6.   VERBAL LEARNING AND MEMORY
Introduction   195
Methodological Problems   196
Variables Affecting Learning   201
Memory   218
Concluding Remarks   221

Chapter 7.   TRANSFER
Introduction   223
Empirical and Theoretical Background   224
Transfer in Discrimination Tasks   230
Transfer in Paired Associate Tasks   250
Age Trend in Efficiency of Mediation   257
Summary and Conclusions   261

Chapter 8.   SET
Introduction   263
Perceptual Set   263
Performance Sets   268
Learning Sets   270

Chapter 9.   ATTENTIONAL PROCESSES
Introduction   279
The Orientation Reaction   281
Attention   286
Summary and Conclusions   309

Chapter 10.   MOTIVATION
Introduction   311
Incentive Motivation   320
Frustration   330
Conflict   338
Anxiety   342
The Motivation of Exploratory Behavior   355

Chapter 11.   PERCEPTUAL DEVELOPMENT
Introduction   363
Form Perception in Children   364
Developmental Trends in Space Perception   384
Mechanisms of Perceptual Development   391
Feedback, Reinforcement, and the Role of Experience in
    Perceptual Development   401
The Role of Motivation in Children's Perception   403
Imagery   405

Chapter 12. **EMOTIONAL DEVELOPMENT**
Introduction   411
Biogenetic Origins of Emotional Behavior in Infancy   412

Chapter 13. **LANGUAGE ACQUISITION**
Introduction   425
Phonological Development   425
Syntactic Development   436
Semantic Development   462
Theoretical Accounts of Language Acquisition   465
Summary   476

Chapter 14. **COGNITIVE DEVELOPMENT**
Introduction   479
Piaget's Developmental Theory of Intelligence   479
The Development of Concepts of Quantity, Relation, and
    Class   484
Evaluation of Piaget's Work   499
Summary   507

Chapter 15. **INTELLIGENCE: THEORY AND ASSESSMENT**
Problems of Definition   509
Theories of Intelligence   512
Intelligence Testing   519

Chapter 16. **INTELLIGENCE: DEVELOPMENT
AND CORRELATES**
Growth Trends   529
Correlates of IQ   539
Summary   569

Chapter 17. **SOCIALIZATION**
Introduction   571
Socialization and Intraindividual Characteristics   577
Theories of Socialization   583
Power and Socialization   587
Identification   600
Social Influences   609
Summary   615

Chapter 18. **BIOGENETIC FACTORS IN DEVELOPMENT**
Introduction   619
Structure and Function of the Nervous System   620
Mental Impairment   629
Nervous System Damage and Age   640

Chapter 19. **BEHAVIOR MODIFICATION: CLINICAL AND EDUCATIONAL APPLICATIONS**

Basic Principles   643
Contrast with Traditional Child Psychotherapy   653
The Problem of Proof   655
Examples of Experimental Behavior Modification   659
Summary   672

REFERENCES   673

AUTHOR INDEX   759

SUBJECT INDEX   777

PREFACE

This textbook was written for courses in experimental child psychology at the advanced undergraduate and early graduate levels. We believe it is the first book devoted specifically to experimental child psychology, even though the area has long been recognized as a distinct branch of developmental psychology.

The book is composed of original contributions from experts who agreed that an orderly, integrated presentation of the principles, methods, and findings in the field was needed. They generously agreed to permit the editors to revise, amend, and reorganize their papers, with the aim of integrating the separate contributions into a coherent whole without sacrificing the special expertise which each of the contributors brought to his task.

In preparing the volume, we devised a table of contents covering the major research topics in child psychology and then invited the contributors to participate in the project. The selected topics reflected different orientations or methodological approaches, those currently most influential being: (a) the theoretical-empirical approach, deriving from the Iowa tradition; (b) the empirical or operant approach, deriving from the work of Skinner; and (c) the organismic approach, deriving from the work of Piaget and Werner. While all three are represented in this book, they are seldom dealt with comparatively because the contributors have usually applied them to separate topics with little overlap.

An advantage of the system used in the preparation of the book is that writers require less time to prepare a paper in their own specialty areas, with the result that the volume is more thoroughly documented and up-to-date than is possible when one or two authors review all of the pertinent literature. A corollary disadvantage results from the inevitable overlap among topics covered by different authors who may hold different theoretical orientations or may emphasize different aspects of the research literature. Thus, not all contributors agree with each other, nor do the editors agree with all contributors. No doubt each will feel that some of the others have made errors of commission or omission. We hope that the disadvantage is slight, however, when weighed against the advantages, especially since the contributors turned out to be in surprising agreement on most of the main principles.

The editors actually found it unnecessary to impose a unifying theme upon the chapters because the contributors had independently achieved a consensus. The theme that runs through the text is an emphasis on cognitive processes, especially on the concept of attention, although the concept has different application in different chapters and is sometimes behavioristic and sometimes mentalistic. All authors assumed that the student will have some background in general psychology. Moreover, some benefit would be derived from having had introductory courses in child psychology and statistics, although the latter is probably not essential.

Perhaps the ordering of the chapters should be explained briefly. Chapter 2 deals with sensory processes in such a way that it provides a background for the next three chapters, on conditioning and discrimination learning. Chapters 6, 7, and 8 deal with more complex learning and transfer operations, and Chapter 9 utilizes concepts explicated in the preceding chapters in an exposition of attentional processes. Similarly, the treatment of motivation in Chapter 10 is most easily understood after reading the learning and transfer chapters. The next seven chapters—11 through 17—deal with topics that are covered in traditional developmental textbooks, but here the emphasis is on experimental research (where available) and theoretical controversy rather than on developmental norms. Chapters 18 and 19 were conceived as "frosting on the cake." Chapter 18, in particular, might reasonably have occupied an earlier position in the text, but its selected location at the end gives the topic "recency" and serves to emphasize that biogenetic factors cannot be ignored in any thorough treatment of child psychology. Moreover, the understanding of the close interaction between physiological and psychogenic factors is of paramount importance in the understanding of both neurological and behavioral aberrations. Chapter 19 uniquely demonstrates why some of the more esoteric material presented in earlier chapters, particularly those on learning, is worth studying in detail. In a sense, the final chapter represents a culmination of all that is presented earlier. The remediation of clinical and educational problems requires not only the identification of the problem, for which the material in Chapters 11 through 18 is especially relevant, but also the application of successful treatment procedures, some of which have been derived from conditioning techniques described in the initial chapters.

The introductory section of Chapter 1 ("The Scope of Experimental Child Psychology") was contributed by Hayne W. Reese, "Methodological Variations" and "Ethical Considerations" were contributed by Lewis P. Lipsitt, and the other sections are integrations of separate contributions by Reese and Lipsitt. Chapter 2 was contributed by Herbert Kaye, and Chapter 3 by Einar R. Siqueland. The contributors to Chapter 4 were Einar R. Siqueland ("Instrumental Conditioning in Infants") and Thomas J. Ryan ("Free Operant Conditioning in Children" and "Discrete-Trial Instrumental Conditioning in Children"); the introduction to this chapter is an integration of separate contributions by Siqueland and Ryan. The primary contributors to Chapter 5 were Einar R. Siqueland ("Discrimination Learning in Infancy") and Morton Rieber ("Discrimination Learning in Childhood"); "Theoretical Models and Applications" is an integration of separate contributions by Einar R. Siqueland, Morton Rieber, and Hayne W. Reese; and "Simultaneous and Successive Discrimination" is an integration of separate contributions by Rieber and Reese. Chapter 6 was contributed by David S. Palermo, except that "Imagery in Paired Associate Learning" is an integration of separate contributions by Palermo and Reese. Wendell E. Jeffrey was the primary contributor to Chapter 7; other contributors were Reese ("Transposition," "Cross-Modal Transfer," and "Age Trend in Efficiency of Mediation") and Palermo ("Transfer in Paired Associate Tasks"). Chapter 8 was contributed by Hayne W. Reese. Peter D. Eimas contributed most of Chapter 9; additional material from other contributors was inserted in some of his sections: Wendell E. Jeffrey (included in "Introduction," "Reversal, Extradimensional, and Nonreversal Shifts," and "Conclusion" of "Attention" section) and Hayne W. Reese (included in "Theory" in "Attention" section and in "The Overtraining Reversal Effect" and "Reversal, Extradimensional, and Nonreversal Shifts"); Thomas J. Ryan contributed the section on "Conditional-Stimulus Familiarization." Chapter 10 was contributed primarily by Langdon E. Longstreth; material from a separate contribution by Thomas J. Ryan is included in the discussion of secondary reinforcement; and "The Motivation of Exploratory Behavior" is an integration of separate contributions by Longstreth and Eimas. Chapter 11 was contributed by Joachim F. Wohlwill, with one section ("Imagery") contributed by Reese. Chapter 12 was contributed by Lewis P. Lipsitt, Chapter 13 by David S. Palermo, Chapter 14 by David Elkind, Chapters 15 and 16 by Winifred O. Shepard, and Chapter 17 by Boyd R. McCandless. The contributors to Chapter 18 were Mitchell Glickstein ("Introduction," "Structure and Function of the Nervous System," and "Nervous System Damage and Age") and Robert Y. Moore ("Mental Impairment"). Chapter 19 was contributed jointly by Donald M. Baer and James A. Sherman.

The editors wish to express their warm gratitude to the contributors to this book, not only for their fine and timely presentations of the material, but also for their good-humored acceptance of the editorial treatment imposed upon them. We must also mention here with sadness that Professor Richard H. Walters had agreed to write a section for the volume but his unfortunate death in December, 1967, prevented its preparation.

The editors are also grateful to their home institutions, the University of Kansas and Brown University, for generously absorbing many small expenses involved in the preparation of the book and, most importantly, for providing typists. Miss Dagmar Paden, at the University of Kansas, typed most of the extensive bibliography, and Mrs. Eunice Mabray, at Brown University, typed much of the revised text. Both did outstanding work. Finally, the editors are grateful to their many colleagues whose favorable reactions to the idea of the book inspired the sustained effort needed to bring the project to fruition.

Hayne W. Reese
Lewis P. Lipsitt

ACKNOWLEDGMENTS

BAER, DONALD M., Professor, Department of Human Development and Department of Psychology, and Research Associate, Bureau of Child Research, University of Kansas (Chapter 19, with James A. Sherman). Drs. Baer and Sherman wish to acknowledge that much of their acquaintance with the material and arguments presented in their chapter has resulted from research supported by the following agencies: National Institute of Mental Health (Grants MH 02208 and MH 11768 for the experimental analysis of social motivation), United States Office of Education (a grant to study the varieties of reinforcement inherent in preschool settings, through the National Laboratory on Early Childhood Education and the Kansas Center for Research on Early Childhood Education), and National Institute of Child Health and Human Development (Program Grant HD 00870 to the Bureau of Child Research of the University of Kansas for research in communication disorders, and Research Grant HD 02674 for the study of imitation and related complex behaviors). In addition, they acknowledge the important contributions to their chapter that have resulted from continuing interaction with their colleagues in this area of research, most particularly Drs. Barbara Etzel, Montrose Wolf, Todd Risley, Jay Birnbrauer, and Sidney Bijou.

EIMAS, PETER D., Associate Professor, Department of Psychology, Brown University (contributions to Chapters 9 and 10). Preparation of the contributions was made possible by Grant HD 03045 to Dr. Eimas from the National Institute of Child Health and Human Development.

ELKIND, DAVID, Professor, Department of Psychology, University of Rochester (Chapter 14).

GLICKSTEIN, MITCHELL, Associate Professor, Department of Psychology, Brown University (Chapter 18, with Robert Y. Moore). Drs. Glickstein and Moore wish to acknowledge their gratitude to Dr. Paul Yakovlev, of Harvard University, who graciously gave them the photographs illustrating the development of myelin in the monkey brain, and to Eileen LaBossiere, who prepared the Golgi-stained brain shown in Figure 18-1.

JEFFREY, WENDELL E., Professor, Department of Psychology, University of California, Los Angeles (contributions to Chapters 7 and 9).

KAYE, HERBERT, Associate Professor, Department of Psychology and Department of Gynecology and Obstetrics, Emory University (Chapter 2). Preparation of Chapter 2 was supported in part by Grant No. 5R01 HD 02458-02 to Dr. Kaye from the National Institute of Child Health and Human Development, in part by the United States Department of Health, Education, and Welfare Children's Bureau Maternal and Infant Care Project No. 516 to Grady Memorial Hospital, Atlanta, Georgia, and in part by the Fulton-DeKalb Medical Authority. Dr. Kaye thanks Drs. J. D. Thompson, I. J. Knopf, and L. Klein for their cooperation. He expresses gratitude to Mrs. Perry Bernard, May Ringold, and assistants Eugenia Jones and Emil Karp for typing, proofing, and picking up the pieces, and especially thanks Mrs. Josephine Brown for her critical reading of the manuscript and many valuable suggestions.

LIPSITT, LEWIS P., Professor, Department of Psychology, Brown University (Chapter 12, contribution to Chapter 1).

LONGSTRETH, LANGDON E., Professor, Department of Psychology, University of Southern California (contribution to Chapter 10). The contribution was written during Dr. Longstreth's sabbatical stay at the Newborn Psychological Research Laboratory, Pacific Biomedical Research Center, University of Hawaii. Dr. Longstreth especially thanks Dr. David H. Crowell for providing facilities and secretarial help during the writing of the contribution.

McCANDLESS, BOYD R., Professor, Department of Psychology, and Director, Educational Psychology, Emory University (Chapter 17).

MOORE, ROBERT Y., M.D., Ph.D., Associate Professor of Neurology, Department of Pediatrics and Department of Medicine; Chief, Section on Pediatric Neurology; Associate Director, Joseph P. Kennedy, Jr. Mental Retardation Research Center; University of Chicago (Chapter 18, with Mitchell Glickstein).

PALERMO, DAVID S., Professor, Department of Psychology, Pennsylvania State University (Chapter 13, contributions to Chapters 6 and 7). The contributions were written while Dr. Palermo was supported by Public Health Service Research Career Program Award HD-28, 120 from the National Institute of Child Health and Human Development.

REESE, HAYNE W., Professor, Department of Human Development and Department of Psychology, University of Kansas (Chapter 8, contributions to Chapters 1, 5, 6, 7, 9, and 11).

RIEBER, MORTON, Visiting Lecturer, Department of Psychology, San Francisco State College (contribution to Chapter 5). Preparation of the contribution was assisted by Grant No. APA203 from the National Research Council of Canada and Grant No. 133 from the Ontario Mental Health Foundation.

RYAN, THOMAS J., Associate Professor, Department of Psychology, Carleton University, Ottawa (contributions to Chapters 4, 9, and 10). The contributions were written while Dr. Ryan was holding Grant No. APB-2 from the National Research Council of Canada and Grant No. 79 from the Ontario Mental Health Foundation.

SHEPARD, WINIFRED O., Assistant Professor, Department of Psychology and Department of Education, State University College, Fredonia, New York (Chapters 15 and 16).

SHERMAN, JAMES A., Associate Professor, Department of Human Development, and Research Associate, Bureau of Child Research, University of Kansas (Chapter 19, with Donald M. Baer).

SIQUELAND, EINAR R., Assistant Professor, Department of Psychology, Brown University (Chapter 3, contributions to Chapters 4 and 5). Preparation of the contributions was supported in part by Research Grant R01 HD 03386 from the National Institute of Child Health and Human Development.
WOHLWILL, JOACHIM F., Professor, Department of Psychology, Clark University (contribution to Chapter 11).

EXPERIMENTAL CHILD PSYCHOLOGY

CHAPTER 1

Introduction

THE SCOPE OF EXPERIMENTAL CHILD PSYCHOLOGY

Introductory Considerations

Accumulated knowledge has reached such vast proportions that it is customary to divide it into content areas. It is difficult to define any specific content area, especially to define it precisely; but fortunately the definitions of the areas have only limited usefulness and are best if left somewhat vague. The reason is that much knowledge is appropriately classified into more than one area, and consequently the boundaries of a content area are more like regions than firm lines. The division of knowledge is not like the taxonomy of biology, for example, which must be relatively precise to be useful, but rather serves only to break what is known into conveniently small chunks to facilitate consumption. Therefore, the discussion that follows aims to provide only an imprecise definition or characterization of the area of experimental child psychology.

Science is one division of knowledge, psychology is one subdivision of science, and experimental child psychology is one of the content areas of psychology. Psychology is the branch of science that deals with the behavior of organisms. The adjective "biological" might be used in front of "organisms" to exclude such units as the social group, culture, and society, which are "organisms" in a figurative sense. Such "organisms" are of principal interest to cultural anthropologists and sociologists, and sometimes to psychologists. By and large, however, psychologists are interested in the individual, usually as an ideal or generalized concept and not as a specific entity. While the understanding and prediction of the behavior of relatively unique individuals is one of the ultimate goals of the human behavior scientist, the achievement of this objective is usually taken as a very useful by-product of the successful pursuit of general functional relationships.

"Behavior" includes all the activities of the organism—observable overt responses, implicit "mental" processes, physiological functions, etc. The subject matter of psychology is behavior in this broad sense. (Physiological psychologists are more likely to be interested in the *effects* of physiological functions, especially the effects on more molar behavior; physiologists are more likely to be interested in the functions as such.) Because psychology is a science, its data must come from applications of the scientific method, which consists essentially of careful observation made under precisely described conditions (see Bechtoldt, 1959).

The Concept of Development

Experimental child psychology is a branch of psychology that deals with child behavior and development. The term "development" often connotes "the notion of a system possessing a definite structure and a definite set of pre-existing capacities; and the notion of a sequential set of changes in the system, yielding relatively permanent but novel increments not only in its structure but in its modes of operation as well" (Nagel, 1957, p. 17; see also Harris, 1957). However, as Spiker (1966) has shown, these connotative meanings are not only *unnecessary*, they are also *undesirable*. "Development" implies change, or more accurately, two types of change since the trend of the definitions of "development" in the Oxford dictionary refers to unfolding and evolution. The two types of development implied by these nontechnical terms correspond at least roughly to two kinds of behavioral development identified technically as ontogenesis and phylogenesis. Ontogenesis is the development of behavior within an individual organism; phylogenesis is the evolutionary development of behavioral capacities of a species. Ontogenesis is correlated with age in individuals; phylogenesis is correlated with level of complexity on phyletic scales. However, behavioral differences between groups that are different in age (but alike with respect to variables unrelated to age) are interpreted as ontogenetic; and behavioral differences in cross-species comparisons are interpreted as phylogenetic.

The technical terms, and their synonyms ontogeny and phylogeny, which are also used, were borrowed from biology. However, since behavior—broadly defined—is the subject matter of psychology, it is to be understood that the terms refer here to behavioral development and not to morphological development. It should also be noted that the terms refer to the fact of behavioral changes, and not to the underlying processes or sources that cause the changes.

Classification of Studies of Development

The study of behavioral phylogenesis is usually called comparative psychology (e.g., Schneirla, 1957), but Munn (1965, p. 1) used the terms "evolutional" and "phylogenetic" psychology. He argued that in practice "comparative psychology" is usually limited to the study of a single species, most often the rat, and to the study of basic behavioral processes without reference to their evolution. His argument was based on the observation that the scope of many of the research reports published in the *Journal of Comparative and Physiological Psychology* was limited in this way. The argument is persuasive but—for reasons considered later—not compelling.

The study of behavioral ontogenesis is usually called developmental psychology. There could be a separate developmental psychology for each species, but behavioral ontogenesis has been subjected to systematic investigation primarily in the human species. Developmental psychology is therefore generally considered to be the study of behavioral changes associated with age changes in human individuals.

The term "genetic psychology" is sometimes used to include both developmental psychology and comparative (or "evolutional") psychology. However, the term has also been used as a synonym for developmental psychology alone and as a synonym for comparative psychology alone. Furthermore, according to Munn (1965, p. 1) students often confuse "genetic psychology" with "genetics," and mistakenly infer an emphasis on hereditary processes.

The study of behavioral ontogenesis during childhood is part of developmental psychology and is called child psychology or child development. The terms "child psychology" and "child development" were originally used synonymously (e.g., see Carmichael, 1954a, pp. *v–vi*), but more recently several kinds of distinction have been suggested. According to one distinction, child psychology is the study of child behavior, and child development is the study of behavioral ontogenesis during childhood (e.g., Gollin, 1965; Harris, 1956; McNeil, 1966). It was argued that child psychologists are interested in the child only as a subject for the study of basic behavioral processes, and that child developmentalists are interested in the child as such, the child as a developing person (e.g., Harris, 1956; Penney, 1960c).

If the argument had merit and if the terms were used consistently, then "child psychology" and "child development" could serve as rubrics for categorizing research reports on the basis of the interest or intent of the investigators. Actually, however, the distinction has not been used consistently by writers of textbooks, monographs, and research reports; therefore, the terms would serve as poor guides to the interests of investigators. Even if this were not so, categorization of research reports on the basis of the interests of investigators would be trivial. The design, outcome, and implications of a study are important bases for categorization; why the study was done is not. (The historian or social psychologist might be interested in knowing why a study was done, but not as a basis for categorizing the study into a content area.) As Spiker (1966) noted, any study demonstrating a relation between behavior and age contributes knowledge about development, whether or not the investigator himself is interested in development. The investigator "may have included the age factor only to increase the precision of his experiment—as a leveling factor" (Spiker, 1966, p. 43). His interest may be in the child only as subject, but his study can still reveal developmental laws. Furthermore, a study in which age level is not varied at all would belong in developmental psychology if its outcome were relevant to developmental theory or generated a developmental hypothesis. The Kendlers, for example, generated an important developmental hypothesis on the basis of the results of a study in which age was not varied (Kendler and Kendler, 1959). In summary, the distinction between child psychology and child development on the basis of the interests of investigators is trivial and often misleading.

Other distinctions were based on the methodological, theoretical, and philosophical preferences of investigators (see Harris, 1956; Laidlaw, 1960; Penney, 1960a, 1960c; Spiker, 1966). The preferences tended to be interrelated, but there is no logical necessity for the interrelations, and the preferences actually provide few important bases for categorization.

METHODOLOGY. The child psychologist was said to prefer the controlled laboratory setting in which independent variables are manipulated experimentally and effects on behavior are observed. The child developmentalist was said to prefer natural settings in which the effects of naturally varying conditions can be observed. The difference is between experimental and nonexperimental approaches, and the phrase "experimental child psychology" seems to have been introduced partly to emphasize this methodological difference (and partly to reduce the linguistic similarity of the terms labeling the two groups). The difference in approaches is critically important because of consequent differences in the ways results can be interpreted. Full consideration of the two approaches is postponed to a later section, in which they are discussed in the context of specific research methods. However, it can be noted here that experimental manipulation means that the researcher imposes upon the subject some treatment or condition that is identified with the independent variable, and nonexperimental manipulation means that the researcher assesses the naturally occurring or pre-experimentally acquired level of the independent variable. When the first approach is used, the researcher can be more confident that the treatment which was imposed actually caused observed behavioral changes than when the second approach is used. When the second approach is used, the researcher can seldom be sure that the assessed variable was the cause, rather than some extraneous variable associated with the assessed variable. Naturally occurring conditions do not vary in isolation; they usually covary with many other conditions, any of which could have caused the observed behavioral changes.

It is worth noting that *age* is a variable that cannot be manipulated experimentally. There is no treatment or condition that can be imposed on subjects to make them older or younger (and if there were, there would be serious objections to its use). The researcher studying the behavioral correlates of age must wait for the natural occurrence of age changes, and it is therefore impossible to obtain unequivocal evidence that age is causally related to other variables. However, this problem creates no real difficulty, because all modern developmental psychologists treat age as an index variable, not as a causal variable. As Bijou and Baer (1963, p. 198) have pointed out, ". . . a developmental analysis is not a relationship of behavior to age, but is a relationship of behavior to events which, requiring time in order to occur, will necessarily have some correlation with age." It is assumed that behavioral changes that are correlated with age are correlated with age only because the variables that cause the changes are also correlated with age.[1]

THEORY. It was said that (a) the child psychologist prefers learning theory or "general behavior theory," and the child developmentalist prefers organismic

[1] The word "cause" is being used here in a common sense way. Philosophically, age is a causally effective variable; it is an "historical" variable occurring in historical laws in psychology, and does not have the same status as "time" in the process laws of physics (see Bergmann, 1957, pp. 105, 124–130).

theories emphasizing cognition. Consequently, (b) the child psychologist sees the organism as "reactive," and the child developmentalist sees the organism as "active" (Harris, 1956; see also Stevenson, 1962). (c) The child psychologist emphasizes environmental effects; the child developmentalist emphasizes hereditary effects. (d) The child psychologist prefers to study "micro-dependent" variables, the child developmentalist "macro-dependent" variables (Penney, 1960c). (e) The child psychologist looks for continuity; the child developmentalist sees development as progression through stages. (f) The child psychologist is more interested in "explanatory" theories; the child developmentalist is more interested in "descriptive" theories.

It is true that many investigators who call themselves "experimental child psychologists" have the cluster of preferences attributed to child psychologists, but there are many exceptions. Many investigators have some of the preferences attributed to child psychologists and some of the ones attributed to child developmentalists. There is no logical necessity that an investigator studying development adopt particular theoretical preferences, nor is there any necessary relation between methodological and theoretical preferences. Therefore, theoretical preferences serve as a poor basis for distinguishing between child psychology and child development.

PHILOSOPHY. The child psychologist was said to prefer the "naive realism" adopted by most physical scientists, and the child developmentalist was said to prefer phenomenological approaches. The child psychologist prefers operational definitions, tying even inferred states or processes to observables, and the child developmentalist prefers phenomenistic terminology and analogy. The distinction is important, not because of the formal differences between the philosophies, but because of the *associated* difference in precision of terminology. ("Associated" is italicized to emphasize that the association results from historical accident, not from logical necessity. Precise terminology—or imprecise terminology—can be used by investigators having either philosophical bias.)

Finally, it was said that the child psychologist is interested in basic or "pure" research, and the child developmentalist is interested in applied research, or research on socially significant problems. The one is concerned with scientific psychology, the other with child welfare. Both kinds of concern are, of course, legitimate. They reflect a broader distinction, between psychology as a science and psychology as a helping profession; and since the dichotomy exists in developmental psychology, it might be useful to emphasize the distinction by using different labels.

Experimental Child Psychology

It is apparent that there are several approaches to the study of child behavior and development. It is equally apparent that many of the suggested distinctions between child psychology and child development have little merit, and that others are irrelevant to any useful distinction. Therefore, it does not seem worthwhile to attempt to distinguish between "child psychology" and "child development." However, it remains possible to characterize the field of experimental child psychology in such a way that it is meaningfully distinct from other branches of developmental psychology. Experimental child psychology is concerned with child behavior and development. It is characterized by preference for (a) the study of basic processes, as opposed to the "whole child," (b) basic research on theoretically significant variables, as opposed to applied research on socially significant problems, (c) the search for relations to determining variables, as opposed to norm gathering or description, and (d) the use of experimental methods, as opposed to naturalistic and other nonexperimental methods.

Whether or not any other branch of developmental psychology has *all* of the opposing characteristics is debatable, but it is certain that others share some of the positive characteristics. Russell (1957) pointed out that the methodological criterion is the only necessary one for an "experimental psychology of development," but he added that the overall orientation of "experimentalists" is characterized by more than a methodological preference. His characterization of this overall orientation was somewhat different from the above characterization of the "experimental child psychologist," suggesting that he had a more narrow conception of the experimentalist (restricting it to behaviorists) than is adopted here.

It should be emphasized that the characterization of experimental child psychology is based on *preferences,* not on absolute adherences. When necessity demands it, deviation from preference is not shunned.

PROCESS VERSUS WHOLE. In the list above, the first distinguishing characteristic of experimental child psychology is between "processes" and "whole." In the sense of "process" as a dependent variable, the distinction is between creeds rather than activities of psychologists. As Spiker pointed out, no child psychologist studies children whole, although some "look at bigger chunks of the child than do others. . . . To be able to look at the whole would require all the knowledge we do not have" (Spiker, 1966, p. 50). The distinction, then, is not between psychologists who study processes and those who study the whole, but between those who belittle the wholistic doctrine as unrealistic and those who advocate it as necessary for the understanding of the behavior and development of children.

In another sense, "process" refers to underlying mechanisms. The distinction based on this meaning is discussed later.

BASIC VERSUS APPLIED RESEARCH. Because experimental child psychology is scientific and theoretically oriented, research is aimed at problems of theoretical significance. If a problem also has social or practical significance, it may be especially interesting to the experimental child psychologist, who is, after all, a citizen as well as a scientist. However, the application of behavior modification techniques (for example) is not part of experimental child psychology, although *research* on the application of these techniques can be (see Chapter 19).

RELATIONS TO DETERMINING VARIABLES VERSUS DESCRIPTION. As indicated above, "process" can refer to the mechanism underlying observed behavior. In this sense, the distinction is between psychologists whose research is designed to reveal causes rather than only to describe behavior. It implies a strong commitment to theoretical explanation, but not a commitment to any specific theory, although it implies an uneasiness about "descriptive" theories, such as those of the Gestalt psychologists and, to some extent, Piaget (see Zigler, 1963).

EXPERIMENTAL VERSUS NONEXPERIMENTAL METHODOLOGY. Relations to determining variables can be more clearly demonstrated when experimental methods are used than when other methods are used (as explained in a later section). Therefore, the experimental child psychologist, because of his interest in discovering causes, prefers experimental methods. However, some problems are not amenable to experimentation; some variables, such as age and sex, cannot be manipulated in an experimental manner. The experimental child psychologist does not eschew research on such problems, but does recognize the inherent limitations of nonexperimentally obtained results.

The Role of Theory in Experimental Child Psychology

EXPLANATION, PREDICTION, AND UNDERSTANDING. The goal of psychology is to understand behavior. However, "understand" has a restricted meaning in science, different from the nontechnical meaning. Scientific understanding of a phenomenon means that the occurrence of the phenomenon can be explained or predicted. To ask why a phenomenon occurred, or what caused it, is to ask for an explanation. An individual fact is explained by showing that it is an instance of a law. The explanation consists of showing that the description of the fact can be logically deduced from (a) statements about the specific antecedent conditions and (b) general laws. [See, e.g., Hempel and Oppenheim (1948). For a different view, see Toulmin (1962).] The difference between explanation and prediction is temporal. If the phenomenon described has already occurred, it is *explained* by the deductive process; if it has not yet occurred, it is *predicted* by the same deductive process. Therefore, an explanation is not fully adequate unless it could have served as a basis for predicting the phenomenon (e.g., Hempel and Oppenheim, 1948).[2]

Consider an idealized and simplified example given by Bergmann (1957, pp. 75–76). The facts described are these: "This is water; this is being heated; and (later) this boils." The question is why it boiled. The explanation, in the form of a syllogism, is

(a) This is water.
(b) This is being heated.
(c) Water if heated boils.

(d) This boils.

[2] "Prediction" is used here in its strict sense. Used loosely, it is synonymous with guess or hunch, and as such is based on intuition rather than deduction. It might also be noted that just as individual facts are explained by deduction from laws, laws can be "explained" by deduction from more general laws or from a theory (e.g., Bergmann, 1957, p. 76).

Statements (a) and (b) are statements about antecedent conditions, and (c) is a law (actually it is only a schema of a law, because it is overly simplified, but the inaccuracy can be overlooked for purposes of the example). Since (d) is the conclusion deduced from the premises, and is also the description of the fact to be explained, the syllogism explains the fact. Note that if (d) is changed to "This will boil," the syllogism becomes a prediction of the fact described.

Another example, which has frequently been used in discussions about developmental psychology, has been given in the following way (e.g., Kessen, 1962, p. 67):

Q. Why did Johnny say "no" to me?
A. Because he's in the negativistic stage.

This is an elliptical way of illustrating the deductive process involved in explanation, because it contains no statements about antecedent conditions and omits two crucial general laws. One of the antecedent conditions is Johnny's age, because the general law in this case specifies an age range for the "negativistic stage" [roughly three to six years of age (see Hurlock, 1964, pp. 341–342)]. Furthermore, it is implicit in the question that the "no" seemed to be unreasonable or irrational. Otherwise the questioner would presumably not have asked. Therefore, the antecedent conditions must include a specification of the situation in which the "no" occurred. The other general law needed specifies the situations in which children in the negativistic stage say "no." The explanation, then, would take the following schematic form:

(a) Johnny is a three year old child.
(b) Johnny is in Situation x.
(c) Children in the negativistic stage say "no" in Situations x, y, and z.
(d) Children from three to six years of age are in the negativistic stage.
(e) Johnny is in the negativistic stage [deduced from (a) and (d)].
(f) Johnny says "no" [deduced from (b), (c), and (e)].

Note that (a) and (b) are statements of antecedent conditions, and (e) is a deduction about an antecedent condition. Statements (c) and (d) are laws (actually schemata of laws); and (f) is the conclusion of the syllogism and the description of the fact to be explained by the syllogism.

An explanation is sound or correct if the argument is valid (i.e., if the rules of deduction are correctly applied) and if the statements about antecedent conditions and general laws are true. However, there have been frequent objections to the kind of explanation illustrated in the examples, in which low-level laws serve as premises, on the ground that it is not "true" explanation (e.g., Toulmin, 1962, p. 49). An explanation is logically true if the deductive process is valid, whether or not the premises are true, because it is a tautology. What is really meant by the objectors seems to be that this kind of explanation is not satisfying. It appears, furthermore, that it is unsatisfying because of its lack of generality or scope (e.g., Toulmin, 1962, p. 50). The scope is limited because the premises are low-level laws. The scope could be increased by using as premises laws of greater generality, explaining, for example, not merely why Johnny said "no," but also why there is a negativistic stage and why it occurs when it does. Such an explanation would be on a higher level than the ones in the examples, and would raise the level of understanding. Looked at in this way, the objection is that the explanation is too specific and hence the level of explanation and understanding is too low to be satisfying (or perhaps too low to be interesting).

Toulmin (1962) has raised another objection, denying the deductive nature of scientific explanation. "It is the *terms* appearing in the statements at one level, not the statements themselves, which are logically linked to the statements in the level below" (Toulmin, 1962, p. 85). A prediction, according to Toulmin, is not deduced from laws, but is obtained from an application of the laws. It can be argued, however, that deduction is implicit in this kind of "application," even if the explanation or prediction makes no explicit use of deduction. As Alexander (1963, p. 113) pointed out, the philosopher of science ". . . is exposing principles and assumptions which we implicitly rely on but do not explicitly state." For example, to borrow Toulmin's illustration (Toulmin, 1962, pp. 84–85), in predicting where a particular planet will be next week from a knowledge of its present position, velocity, and so on (and a knowledge of the present positions, velocities, mutual distances, and so on, of the rest of the bodies in the system), one *applies* the laws of motion. However, deduction is used implicitly:

(a) $p_1 = f(s_0, t_1)$, where p_1 is the position of a given body in a given system at time t_1, and s_0 is the state of the system at time t_0.
(b) A is a body in System x.
(c) The s_0 of System x is m_0.
(d) $t_1 = t$.
$$\overline{\text{(e) } p_1 \text{ (of A)} = f(m_0, t).}$$

Statement (a) is the general law; (b), (c), and (d) are antecedent conditions; and (e) is the conclusion deduced. Since (e) is also the *application* of the general law, the application is deductive.

The developmental psychologist Harris (1957) also appeared to disagree with the conception of explanation as a deductive process: ". . . explanation is a matter of *describing* a phenomenon in all its relationships" (Harris, 1957, p. 7). However, Alexander (1963, Chapter 6) has shown that explanation and description are fundamentally different: ". . . a man may be guessing at an explanation and if he is giving an explanation then he is explaining, whereas a man who is guessing at a description, even if he produces a description, is not describing but guessing. Guessing and explaining are not incompatible in the way in which guessing and describing are. Looking for an explanation is not at all like trying to get a description right" (Alexander, 1963, p. 140).

THEORIES AND MODELS. In everyday language, "theory" often means a conjecture which has no well-established factual basis, or even no known factual basis at all. In this sense, it is synonymous with hunch or guess. In science, the term refers to a set of statements, including (a) general laws and principles which serve as axioms, (b) other laws, called theorems, which are deducible from the axioms, and (c) definitions relating terms to observables. A *model* is structurally separate from a theory, but functionally part of its axioms. The functions of a model include (a) providing a way of representing the phenomena dealt with by the theory and the operation of theoretical principles, (b) providing rules of inference through which new relations are deduced, and (c) providing suggestions about how the scope of the theory can be increased (see Lachman, 1960; Toulmin, 1962). A model can function, in other words, as a metaphor or analogy that represents reality and interprets the theory, as a short-cut method of deduction, and as a device showing how to apply the theory and suggesting how to extend it. It is the latter two functions that make a good model more than a simple analogy (Toulmin, 1962, p. 39).

It should be emphasized that the representational function is metaphorical. As Toulmin said in discussing the two-dimensional model of the rectilinear propagation of light, "We do not *find* light atomized into individual rays; we *represent* it as consisting of such rays" (Toulmin, 1962, p. 29). Descriptions of the model are not empirical statements; the model represents but does not describe reality. Thus, the terms true and false, which are applicable to empirical statements, are not applicable to models. Models can have greater or lesser usefulness, depending upon how well they serve the second two functions, but they cannot be true or false (Lachman, 1960). [For further discussions of the characteristics and functions of models, see Black (1962, Chapter XIII), Ferré (1963), and Reese and Overton (1970).]

Having considered the constituents of a theory, it is now possible to consider the functions of a theory. Scientific theories have two functions: (a) they organize or integrate the knowledge in some restricted area, delimited by initial and boundary conditions specified, sometimes implicitly, in the theory; and (b) they guide experimentation. The first function is to explain what is already known, by showing how the laws are deductively interrelated. The second function is to generate predictions.

Zigler (1963) has pointed out an advantage of theory in connection with research on problems that are not amenable to experimentation. Any adequate theory explains (or predicts) the phenomena which it was designed to encompass, but it may also generate predictions about experimental phenomena. "What the experimenter is saying is that if such and such holds in the real world because of the principles expounded in the particular theory under investigation, then such and such should hold in the world which the experimenter has created. This translatability is what gives theoretical import to experiments which involve phenomena which, taken in isolation, not only appear picayune but seem to have little relationship with what one observes in nature" (Zigler, 1963, pp. 352–353).

It is useful to evaluate theories in terms of their scope, precision, and deployability. The *scope* of a theory is determined by the range of phenomena dealt with; the *precision* of a theory is determined by the soundness of its explanations and accuracy of its predictions; and the *deployability* of a theory is the extent to which its model suggests new applications of the theory. Theories in developmental psychology can be categorized on the basis of their scope into a class of "grand systems" and a class of miniature theories. In general, the grand systems, such as those of Freud and Werner, have wide scope but low precision; and the miniature theories have limited scope, sometimes extremely limited scope, but great precision. It seems that the miniature theories, such as mediation theory and conditioning theory, have great deployability, in addition to precision. If a theory is successfully deployed (that is, applied in a new context), the scope of the theory increases. Therefore, it seems safe to "predict" that the miniature theories will increase in scope, and become more prevalent in developmental psychology than they have been in the past.

Many, and perhaps most, experimental child psychologists prefer miniature theories, probably because of the greater precision of these theories. Some experimental child psychologists seem to prefer to work within the framework of a global system, but often they attempt to deploy, explicitly or implicitly, some miniature theory into the larger framework.

THE CONCEPT OF STAGES OF DEVELOPMENT. Stage—or more accurately, stage of development—is sometimes considered to be a theoretical construct (see Kessen, 1962), but it seems to be more an aspect of a model than of a theory *per se*. To paraphrase Toulmin, we do not *find* behavioral development segmented into stages, we *represent* it as conveniently segmented. Recognition of this fact would have prevented much controversy about whether behavioral development is "really" saltatory or continuous.[3] One function of the stage model is to indicate when different theoretical rule systems are to be used, or what values of theoretical parameters are appropriate. It can be argued that such a model is appropriate for theories of child behavior, but not for theories of child development. The argument dissolves, however, if the theory explains (or predicts) the changes in rule systems or parametric values that occur. There are developmental laws pertaining to the sequences of stages, but there has been very little theorizing about why the stages occur at the times they do. For example, White (1965) showed that transitions in several kinds of behavior occur between the ages of five and seven years, and he proposed a theory in which the major axiom is a general law from which the several individual laws can be deduced. The general law refers to three stages, an associative stage, a transitional stage, and a cognitive stage. The law specifies not only the sequence of these stages, but also the approximate age limits of each one. The theory specifies that one kind of behavioral model (a one-stage conditioning

---

[3] "Stage" has also been used as a paraphrase for age and observation. For example, "nursery-school stage" often means "nursery-school age," the range from about three to five years of age; and "He's in the teething stage" means "he's teething." It sometimes is used as a kind of shorthand description of the environment; for example, "nursery-school stage" can imply exposure to the social and educational environment of the nursery school. [See Kessen (1962) and Reese and Overton (1970) for discussions of these and other uses of "stage."]

model) is to be used in explaining the behavior of children in the first stage, and that another model (the two-stage mediational model) is to be used in the last stage. The theory also explains why the transition occurs. However, it does not explain why the transition occurs when it does. (See Chapter 7 for a discussion of White's theory.)

The criterion for evaluating a stage model is its usefulness, not its truth or falsity. It may be useful to represent development as progressing through stages, but it is irrelevant to argue about whether or not the stage model accurately describes "real" development. When "stage" refers to a property or characteristic of a model, identifying the stage of development of a child does not in itself explain the behavior of the child; it only indicates what part of the theory should be used to explain his behavior. (As already noted, however, stage does not always refer to a model. It can be used to paraphrase age, as in "negativistic stage"; when it is used in this way, it can occur in general laws, which can be used in low-level explanations of the child's behavior.)

METHODS OF CHILD PSYCHOLOGY

Basis for Classification

Previous sections of this chapter have already suggested that the orientation adopted in this volume is that psychology is in principle like any other science and differs only in the particular subject matter to which it addresses itself. Science deals in (a) facts, or perhaps better, factual (empirical) propositions and (b) theoretical integrations of these facts which scientists devise to aid themselves in organizing their data and deducing further testable factual propositions.

Statements of fact are always either true or false, although the scientist's information about the truth or falsity of any given statement is usually incomplete. However, statements of fact do admit of an empirical test of their veracity or credibility. The primary responsibility of the scientist relates to the obligation to adduce evidence on behalf of or in refutation of empirical propositions. This point is emphasized here because the selection of methods used to test facts is to some extent arbitrary, to some extent dependent upon the personal proficiencies and preferences of the scientist, and to some extent dictated by social, technological, and humane considerations. Always, however, the outcome of a factual test must be viewed in the light of the extent to which the method used has been adequate to the task, the extent to which the method has enabled support of the proposition up for examination. One cannot simply ask, then, for a fact. The data in support of the factual proposition must be analyzed in terms of the methods used to establish it as fact. There is implicit in these remarks the assumption that one must be careful in his use of words in putting forth a factual proposition, for a complete examination of the proposition necessitates that it be translated into operational terms. "Frustration is associated with aggression" can have a number of different meanings, and the proposition

"Frustration produces aggression" has meaning beyond any of the operational translations of the former phrase. Filling out these propositions with their "real" meanings demands attention to methodology.

All psychological research is ultimately based upon observation of behavior. However, research can be based either directly or indirectly upon the observations. Reports of direct observations are sometimes called primary research; reviews of primary research are sometimes called secondary research or library research. The adjectives "primary" and "secondary" do not refer to the order of importance of the research, but to the directness of its relation to observations. Thus, primary research is directly related to observations; secondary reports are indirectly related to observations, since they are directly related to *reports* of observations.

It is important to emphasize the mutual interdependence of primary and secondary research, and the consequent lack of a difference in status. It is obvious that reviews would be impossible unless there existed primary reports to be reviewed. Perhaps less obviously, a single primary report is often best evaluated in context with other related primary reports; the full implications of a study may be apparent only through comparison with other studies. Conversely, knowing what others have done (or, in many cases, what others have *not* done) usually influences the selection of topics to be studied and the methods to be used in primary research.

Secondary Research

Reviews of primary research generally deal with relatively narrow areas of investigation. The best reviews include more than a mere recitation of the conclusions of the original investigators, and indeed often show that the original conclusions are not compelling. Critical evaluation of methods used often helps to clarify ambiguities or contradictions in the results of studies, by permitting the reviewer to give less weight to the less adequate studies and to emphasize the more adequate ones (see R. A. Gardner, 1966). The conclusions of the reviewer may turn out to be quite different from the conclusions of the individual researchers; but when they are, it is desirable for the reviewer to include more detailed discussion of methods than would otherwise be necessary (Reese, 1964).

Reviews often reveal trends that are not apparent in individual studies. The relevant observations may have been incidental to the primary interests of the investigator, or the trends may have been statistically nonsignificant in the original studies. The reviewer, seeing as he does the results of many studies, is able to detect consistencies in nonsignificant trends, which because of their consistency may suggest reliability.

A major problem for the reviewer is that most of his conclusions must be advanced as tentative rather than as established. One reason is that the studies reviewed seldom use exactly comparable methods. Another is that very few reports of nonsignificant findings are published, and it is therefore possible that for every published study on a particular topic, each showing significant positive results, there are many other unpublished studies showing nonsignificant results. This possibility is taken into account when the reviewer's conclusions are interpreted as suggestions that need to be tested by further primary research.

Primary Research

It is possible to classify primary research studies in various ways. This book is concerned with studies of child behavior and development, and therefore the discussion is limited to schemes for classifying these studies. One approach, suggested by McCandless (1967, pp. 59–64) and credited to Charles C. Spiker, is based upon the assumption that all studies with children may be categorized in terms of their positions on four dimensions: normative–explanatory, historical–ahistorical, naturalistic–manipulative, and atheoretical–theoretical. To these four can be added two others not discussed by McCandless: basic versus applied and single-subject versus group.

NORMATIVE–EXPLANATORY. The normative approach is characterized as descriptive and dealing with average ages at which various behaviors are observed; the explanatory approach seeks to discover causal relations in order to permit predictions from antecedent events to behavioral or other developmental consequences. A study of the onset of walking, which might reveal that the mean age for attainment of this behavior is 11 months in a certain society, would be an example of normative study; a study of the effects of differential training practices on the earliest age of walking would be explanatory.

HISTORICAL–AHISTORICAL. Ahistorical research deals with relationships among variables studied contemporaneously with no exploration of their origins, and historical research requires historical examination of the origins. An ahistorical study may be either normative or explanatory. In fact, all four dimensions proposed by McCandless and the two added are considered to be independent of one another.

An ahistorical study might seek to discover whether children behave differently in the classroom when their mothers are present from when they are not; an historical study might investigate whether there is a trend over time for the child's behavior to change in the classroom with repetitive presence of his mother.

NATURALISTIC–MANIPULATIVE. The third continuum ranges from the study of behavior "in the wild" or under ordinary circumstances to the study of behavior under conditions in which the circumstances under study, or at least some of them, are deliberately manipulated, usually in a controlled laboratory situation. It should be apparent that behavior in natural circumstances need be no less "controlled" than that occurring in laboratory situations; the difference is in the deliberateness with which certain conditions are made operative during the behavioral observations. Moreover, experimental manipulations of some sorts can be as well administered in a "naturalistic" classroom setting as they can in a laboratory cubicle.

A related distinction is between experimental manipulative and correlational methods. In experimental manipulative research, the independent variable is a condition that is imposed upon the subject by the experimenter. In correlational research, the independent variable is a condition that existed in the subject before the study began, and the investigator assesses its magnitude to determine whether the criterion behavior covaries with it. The study of the relation of performance to anxiety level as assessed by some test would be correlational; the study of the relation of performance to anxiety level induced by some condition imposed by the experimenter would be experimental manipulative. Most naturalistic research is correlational.

ATHEORETICAL–THEORETICAL.   Atheoretical research is designed merely to substantiate an informal observation or satisfy a particular curiosity; theoretical research entails the testing of a proposition that might be closely derived from a well-organized set of axioms.

Atheoretical research is exploratory. It is designed to answer such empirical questions as "Can X learn Y?" (e.g., "Can an autistic child be taught language?") and "What would happen if . . . ?" In theoretical research the theory is supported if the prediction is verified. The theory is not *proved* to be correct, however, because it is possible to get a true prediction from false premises. For example, suppose it is not raining, but the ground is wet. Then from the premises, "If it is raining, then the ground is wet" and "It is raining," one can deduce that "The ground is wet." The deduction (prediction) is correctly derived from the premises, and upon being checked against the facts, is found to be true. However, one of the premises ("It is raining") is false.

Failure to support an otherwise well supported theory requires more convincing evidence than further support does. Exploratory research requires more or less convincing evidence, depending upon the individual researcher, journal editors, and the reactions of colleagues.

It might be noted that if there is no adequate theory available to guide research, then all research must be exploratory.

BASIC VERSUS APPLIED.   One basis for distinguishing between basic and applied research was considered in an earlier section. On another basis, basic research is designed to add to scientific knowledge and applied research is designed to advance technology. However, the distinction is not sharp, because, for one thing, technology is sometimes called applied *science*—the science of applying scientific knowledge to practical problems. In the second place, the distinction is based, in many cases, upon the researcher's purposes, and classification on this basis is tenuous. The *outcome* of an applied study may have basic implications.

SINGLE-SUBJECT VERSUS GROUP.   The final dimension distinguishes between research involving a single subject and research involving groups of subjects. In single-subject research the performance of the single subject is often studied in many sessions and is often indexed by the rate of his responses, sometimes by the mean of a performance index obtained in blocks of observations. In group research the group is generally studied in a single session or at most in a few sessions; the interest is primarily in the group mean.

Statistical analysis of the performance of a single subject is impossible with statistical techniques presently available. Therefore, the researcher must find other ways than statistical analysis for assessing the data of a single subject. For example, he might (a) demonstrate an effect that is so strong that it is

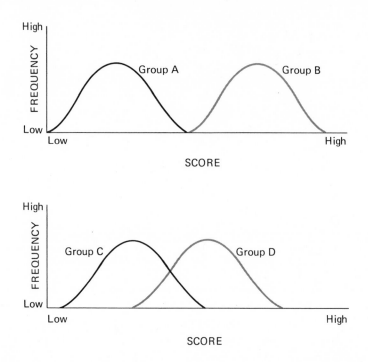

Fig. 1-1. Fictitious data illustrating need for statistical analysis. Left half: Group A and Group B do not overlap. Right half: Group C and Group D overlap.

self-evident (e.g., physiological indexes of anxiety before and after administering tranquilizing drugs), (b) demonstrate repeated reversals of the behavior with repeated reversals of the experimental condition, or (c) use other techniques (see Sidman, 1960).

Data obtained in group research generally require statistical analysis. The reason is illustrated by the fictitious data in Figure 1-1, in which the baseline represents scores of some kind and the vertical axis represents frequency (i.e., the number of subjects obtaining each score). In the left half of the figure are shown two nonoverlapping distributions of scores. That is, the best subjects in Group A have lower scores than the worst subjects in Group B. In this case, no formal statistical test is necessary (although it is customary to run

one anyway). In the right half of the figure are shown two overlapping distributions. In this case, many subjects in Group C are as good as or better than
many subjects in Group D; and the only way to determine whether the groups
as a whole differ from one another is to perform a statistical test.

Presentation of the theoretical basis of statistical analysis is beyond the scope
of this text, but one basic point needs to be explained. The purpose of statistical
analysis is to determine the probability that an observed difference between
group means could have arisen entirely as a result of chance instead of as
a result of the different treatment conditions given to the groups. If the probability is low (usually below .05), the difference between the group means is said
to be statistically significant; and it is concluded that the difference is attributable
to the difference between the treatment conditions and not to chance.

The sources of chance differences include errors of measurement, fluctuations
of organismic or subject variables affecting performance, fluctuations of environmental variables that affect different subjects differently, etc. A simple example
of error of measurement is a mistake by the observer in reading the pointer
on the measuring instrument (e.g., a galvanometer used to measure the galvanic
skin response). An example of a subject variable contributing to error, in a
study of the effect of caffeine on reaction speed, would be the drinking of
coffee by a subject just before the experiment started. Such a subject might
react quite differently to the caffeine (or placebo) administered during the
experiment if he had not already had a "dose" of caffeine. An example of an
environmental source of error could be the weather; the effects of a frustration
condition on performance might vary, for some subjects, depending upon
whether the sky is overcast and gloomy or is bright and cheerful.

In interpreting a group performance curve, a problem is to determine
how representative it is of individual curves. The problem is dramatically illustrated by the hypothetical data in Figure 1-2. The left half of the figure shows
the performance of six fictitious subjects, each of whom performs for a time
at the chance level and then jumps to the criterional level. The right half of
the figure shows the group curve, that is, the mean performance on each trial
for the combined subjects. The group curve is clearly not representative of
any of the individual curves, which are saltatory ("jump-wise").

Several techniques have been devised to yield group curves that are more
representative of individual curves. One, "Vincentizing," involves dividing the
trials or observations that occur before criterion is attained into some fixed
number of blocks (Vincent, 1912). Each subject will then have the same number
of data points, determined by the number of blocks selected by the investigator,
but different subjects may have different numbers of trials in each block. For
example, if the precriterional data in Figure 1-2 were divided into two blocks,
Subject 3 would have two trials per block (Trials 1 and 2 in the first block
and Trials 3 and 4 in the second) and Subject 5 would have three trials per
block. All of the subjects would have three data points (the two precriterional
ones and the one showing performance at criterion), and the group curve would
be saltatory, jumping from the chance level between Blocks 2 and 3. One problem with this approach is the arbitrariness of selection of number of blocks;

another, perhaps more serious problem is the arbitrariness of definition of the criterional level (Spence, 1956, p. 60).

Another technique is to plot "backward" performance curves for the group (Hayes, 1953). Rather than plotting the beginning of training at the left and continuing to the right, one plots the criterion performance for all subjects on the right and proceeds to plot performance on earlier blocks of trials toward the left. (See, e.g., Figures 9-5 and 9-6.) In performance curves plotted in the traditional way, the data points for the early trials are more reliable, in the sense of being representative of individuals, than are the data points for

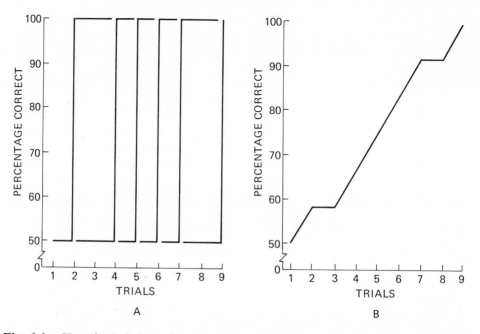

Fig. 1-2. **Hypothetical data showing how group curve can misrepresent individual curves. Left half: six individual curves. Right half: mean of these.**

later trials. The "backward" technique overcomes the defect in the later data points, but may make the data points for early trials less reliable (Hayes, 1953). The technique also subjects all precriterional data points to downward selection, making them spuriously low (Hayes and Pereboom, 1959).

Another technique is to divide the subjects into relatively homogeneous subgroups, and to plot separate curves for each subgroup (see Spence, 1956, pp. 60–61). Subgroups can be defined as homogeneous with respect to the point at which criterion was reached (e.g., Levinson and Reese, 1967), or with respect to this criterion and the rate of approach to the criterional level (e.g., Spence, 1956, p. 61), or with respect to the shape of the individual performance curves. The major problem is in the selection of a definition of "homogeneous," since different definitions will often yield different subgroupings and hence different subgroup curves.

Many investigators have used combinations of these three basic techniques. Levinson and Reese (1967), for example, formed two roughly homogeneous subgroups on the basis of trials to criterion, then plotted backward learning curves with the first two data points Vincentized (see Figure 1-3). They did not, however, assess how well these curves represented individual curves.

Another possible solution, as Spence (1956, p. 61) noted, is to plot the curves of individual subjects. The problem here, of course, is that unless some

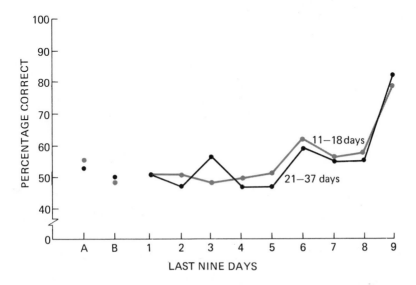

Fig. 1-3. Acquisition curves of elderly subjects requiring 11 to 18 and 21 to 37 days of training to reach criterion. The last 9 data points represent backward learning curves for the last 9 days of training; points A and B are Vincentized data points for the earlier training. (After Levinson and Reese, 1967, Fig. 18, p. 50. Copyright 1968 by the Society for Research in Child Development, Inc. Reprinted by permission.)

regularity can be detected, there can be obtained no estimate of the population effect against which individual differences must be evaluated. It is perhaps worth pointing out that researchers who study operant conditioning with single-subject designs have in fact implicitly abstracted a "group" or expected shape of learning curves from extensive examination of individual learning curves (see Chapter 4 for examples, such as the expectation that a fixed-interval schedule of reinforcement will produce a "scalloped" learning curve).

Table 1-1 illustrates the principle that all the dimensions discussed are independent of each other, using the single-subject versus group and experimental manipulative versus correlational dimensions as examples. The existence of many studies in each of the four cells of this two-dimensional table demonstrates the independence of the dimensions.

Table 1-1

Independence of Two Dichotomous Classes of Primary Studies

Dichotomy 2	Dichotomy 1	
	Experimental	*Correlational*
Single-subject	Much of operant conditioning work, including research on application of behavior modification techniques.	The classic baby biographies; *One Boy's Day* (Barker and Wright, 1951); case studies in clinical psychology; etc.
Group	Much of classical conditioning work; most of discrimination learning work; most theoretical research; performance as a function of manipulated anxiety, etc.	Much of developmental research; performance as a function of age, test score, etc.

Methodological Variations

While the system outlined above has merit in emphasizing features of developmental-behavioral investigations which provide clues as to what sort of fact the investigator was trying to uncover, it may be helpful to provide a classification system which reflects the actual methods used and gives some flavor of the types of specific variables that have been studied. Like the just-described classification system, the one utilized here contains categories that are not mutually exclusive. Moreover, all studies may be delivered into one or more of the several categories proposed here *and* may in addition be analyzed in accordance with the previous system. The methods will be classified in terms of the following categories: (a) the developmental approach, (b) the comparative approach, (c) the cross-cultural approach, (d) the ecological and ethological approaches, and (e) the experimental manipulative approach.

THE DEVELOPMENTAL APPROACH.   The developmental method of investigation is characterized by the continuous or periodic observation of behavior over time, but the temporal continuity need not reside in individual subjects. The same subjects may be studied continuously (the "longitudinal" method), or different subjects may be studied "cross-sectionally" at different ages. Each method has advantages and disadvantages. For example, longitudinal research is more costly, in both time and money, than cross-sectional research; improved technology may invalidate the observations obtained early in longitudinal research; attrition (i.e., subjects dropping out of the study) may make the longitudinal sample nonrepresentative of any interesting population; and changing interests of investigators (and funding agencies) may result in the accumulation of vast amounts of data that no one cares to analyze. These considerations might lead one to prefer the cross-sectional method, but it too has disadvantages. It is usually impossible to determine whether the differences between the age groups reflect an age difference or reflect a secular trend. (A secular trend, in this case, is one that results from changing environmental conditions. An example is given in Chapter 16.) The age groups must also be equivalent on organismic variables that are not age-related (e.g., IQ, motivational level), but this is seldom completely attained. Finally, the cross-sectional method can provide averages, or norms, but the longitudinal method can also provide *velocity* measures, and only the longitudinal method can provide data on individual differences in growth patterns.

The hallmark of the developmental approach is that the overriding interest of the investigator is in the relationship of age to the behavioral or other attributes under study. An example of the developmental approach in its simplest form is found in the detailed observations of the growth and behavior change of one child by Stern and Stern (1907). The historically important biographical observation technique sought to record items of information on individual children and often, as in the Sterns' case, the investigators' own child. The approach seeks not to "interfere" with the observed behavior but rather merely to record behavioral events as they occur. Any kind of behavioral index is a proper candidate for inclusion in such studies. Often there is, in such studies, no particular system for recording observations, no particular "target" behaviors except for those which simply happen to fascinate the observer or are deemed somehow pertinent, and often there are no provisions for examining the reliability of the observations made.

Many modern developmental investigations, such as that of Kagan and Moss (1962), while perpetuating the primary interest of early child developmentalists in the study of behavioral progression as a function of age, use rather highly refined procedures for the systematic and reliable observation of behavior and for conducting appropriate statistical tests to determine the replicability of the findings. Indeed, much of the earlier developmental work of Piaget (e.g., 1952a) was of a rather loose anecdotal sort which gave way ultimately to more systematic documentation of the developmental phenomena under observation (see Flavell, 1963). Binet and Simon (1905) also capitalized on their initially casual behavioral observations in children of different ages, some of whom were performing well in school and others of whom were doing poorly, in order to arrive eventually at the selection of test items which would be used in the Binet-Simon Scale and ultimately in the Stanford-Binet Intelligence Scales. Clearly, many sound hypotheses about child development and the precursors of later behavior have their origins in the sheer normative observation of characteristics in different-aged children.

An important by-product of the developmental approach to the study of children has been the generation of vast amounts of normative information relating to the typical or mean ages at which certain behaviors "normally" become manifest in children. For example, a study from birth to 15 months of age by Shirley (1933) showed that the typical child can hold his chest up by 2 months of age, sits with support by 4 months, sits alone at 7 months, creeps at 10 months, and pulls himself to a standing position by 12 months (see Figure 1-4). Similarly, Smith (1926) collected normative information on the development of vocabulary in children from birth to 5 years of age, which yielded the fact that by 2 years of age children already use meaningfully about 300 words in free speech, and by 5 years of age they are capable of expressing themselves with 2100 different communicable sounds, most of them with different referents. When such findings are confirmed on a sufficiently large number of subjects, they may thereafter be used psychometrically in the examination of similar behaviors

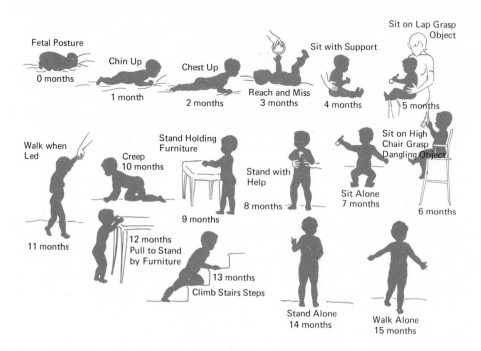

Fig. 1-4. The sequence of motor development. (From Mary M. Shirley, *The first two years: A Study of twenty-five babies,* Vol. II, Institute of Child Welfare Monograph Series No. 7. Minneapolis: University of Minnesota Press, 1933. Copyright by the University of Minnesota. Reprinted by permission.)

in other children. This in fact is the way in which developmental and intelligence tests are constructed. A child with a mental age of 3 years is one who engages in behavior characteristic of or "normal" for 3 year old children. The well-known developmental schedules of Gesell (1934) are constituted precisely of test items that reliably elicited certain responses in most children by a certain age, fewer children at ages lower than that certain age, and almost all children at ages beyond.

As interesting as developmental facts are, they do not usually provide information as to how the children under study came to behave in the way they now do. While a certain kind of functional relationship is apparent (that relating age with behavior), and while prediction is possible (for example, a 12 month old child is more likely to be capable of walking than is a 6 month old child), such developmental facts do not provide information as to *how* the children got to be in the condition we now observe.

Thompson (1962, pp. 27–31) makes an important distinction which is relevant to our understanding of the major deficiency in the developmental approach. He says that there are two principal strategies for studying child behavior and development—correlational analysis and experimental investigation. The correlational procedure describes the degree of covariation between two variables, such as age of weaning and dependency. The plotting of the number of words in children's vocabularies as a function of age capitalizes on such a correlational approach. As Thompson says: "Correlational analysis is beset with one serious inferential hazard . . . [for] . . . two variables may be highly correlated with each other on the basis of a covarying (but unknown and unmeasured) third variable. For example, the high correlation between a group-administered intelligence test and a test of academic achievement may be due to a common variable of reading ability" (p. 28). While it is of some consequence that most children do not walk at 8 months of age, and while it is comforting to know that a particular child of 8 months who does not walk has this characteristic in common with most other children, it would be somewhat more informative to know whether different training conditions result in different ages of onset of walking and whether some particular training techniques are especially facilitative of this behavior. After all, it is possible that the reason most children in a given culture do not walk until 12 or more months of age is that parents in that culture do not encourage it. Indeed, recent evidence suggests that walking occurs in other cultures much earlier than it does in the United States, and that many children can learn to read much earlier than has been previously thought possible. It is at least a teasing hypothesis that children do not characteristically read in our society until they are 6 years old simply because it has not been thought possible or desirable by parents and teachers.

As Thompson points out: "The experimental investigation . . . has the distinct advantage of permitting the child psychologist to study a given antecedent-consequent relationship at his convenience and upon demand. He need not wait for the behavior to occur by fortuitous circumstances" (p. 30). The reasons for this will be shown later.

The developmental or normative investigation has persisted in the field of child psychology for many years as the dominant research strategy. Lipsitt (1966) has suggested that, historically, the biological roots of the scientific study of child development have been responsible in part for the obsession of the field with the age correlates of behavior. After all, the age-correlate strategy worked very well for the study of morphological change in development, although even here one cannot be entirely certain that norms will remain the same from generation to generation, and one *certainly* cannot assume that norms under one cultural condition or under one set of nutritional standards will apply to others (Meredith, 1965).

Finally, it must be said that the strictly developmental approach to the study of child behavior carried with it a rather strong hereditary or maturational bias in the understanding of the determinants of behavior. Only relatively recently has the field of child psychology freed itself, largely on the basis of the mounting evidence of the importance of experiential factors in the determination of behavior, from the stultifying working proposition that intelligence is essentially a constant and immutable attribute of the human organism; this sort of hereditary bias pervaded the field at one time and fostered ". . . a rather pervasive pessimism which one can find in the psychological literature with respect to the *potentialities* of infants" (Lipsitt, 1966, p. 45). See J. McV. Hunt's *Intelligence and Experience* (1961) for an interesting historical treatment of the changing conception of intelligence.

THE COMPARATIVE APPROACH.   The child is a major source of interest to investigators concerned with the similarities and differences among species. The comparative approach in its simplest form bears great similarity to the developmental approach. The developmental study of the child seeks to relate changes in the child's behavior to age or the passage of time; the comparative approach studies behavior as a function of species membership. Researchers in this area are often interested in the comparative development, in animals and children, of motor skills, intelligence, discriminative abilities, and memory processes. Kellogg and Kellogg (1933) conducted one of the more notable studies of this sort, rearing a newborn ape in their household along with their own newborn child. Their study had similarities to the developmental diary-keeping procedures mentioned previously. Some of their observations, however, involved the implementation of special testing conditions under which repeated observations could be made in rather objective fashion. One of their procedures, for example, was a delayed reaction test in which the objective was to discover at what age the ape and child each became capable of performing a task requiring memory of discriminative stimulation previously present but now absent. They were interested in how much time could be permitted to elapse without a breakdown in discriminative performance. In a sense, this type of experiment permits the study of ontogeny and phylogeny together, with the recapitulation occurring before one's eyes.

Of course, comparative investigations often suffer from the same sorts of weaknesses as many developmental studies; records are often of an anecdotal nature, the number of subjects is small, and the home environment of most of us is rather atypical from the standpoint of the natural habitat and rearing circumstances of, for example, the ape.

Truly comparative psychological studies involving children are relatively rare. Most comparative studies are secondary research reports such as that of Harlow and Harlow (1949) in which the well-documented behavior of lower animals is compared with other independently studied behavior of children in similar situations. Often, as in the case of the Harlows, there is a theoretical integration provided between the two broad sets of data on similar processes (in this instance, relating to thinking processes) whose essence is analyzed in terms of mechanisms that are considered to be common to both or all species. Some such data purport to show, and indeed some do show, that there are commonalities among species with respect to the sensory or learning processes involved and that the phylogenetic differences between the species have their counterparts or correlates in behavior as well as in morphological attributes.

Hunter (1913) has been one of the few psychologists to implement studies of a specific psychological phenomenon in children and lower animals under conditions which allow true comparison between the different species with respect to their potentialities for engaging in the behavior under consideration. He devised a common experimental procedure for rats, dogs, raccoons, and children, in which it was possible to observe these various mammals in comparable delayed reaction discrimination learning situations. Each organism had to remember which of three doors was previously signaled (with a discriminative stimulus) as the baited (or reinforced) door. The animals were first taught to go to that door among three where a light was on. Having learned this, each subject was then tested to determine the maximum delay, from the offset of the light to the moment at which there was now opportunity to respond, which could be tolerated or "bridged." The interesting finding was that the maximum delay possible was 10 seconds, 25 seconds, 5 minutes, and 25 minutes for rats, raccoons, dogs, and children, respectively, thus providing indications that the memory duration for this particular act coincided well with the phylogenetic ordering of the species under consideration. Moreover, the study revealed that the "higher" organisms were increasingly capable of utilizing mediational techniques between the offset of the discriminative light and the opportunity to respond in order to facilitate correct (reinforced) behavior. The information yielded from this study, as well as other developmental work done with children by Hunter (1917), suggested that mammals higher in the phylogenetic hierarchy, and older relative to younger children, tend to utilize "mediating" behavioral devices that facilitate higher-level or more complex behavior.

THE CROSS-CULTURAL APPROACH. Just as the comparative approach bears certain similarities to the developmental approach, so does the cross-cultural method of study bear comparison with each of the two previous methods. The cross-cultural method is, in its most primitive form, a set of descriptive procedures applied in some fairly standardized fashion to more than one culture for comparative purposes. The cultural anthropologists, such as Margaret Mead (1946), have been responsible for most such studies. While the heritage of this field has been such as to endorse and capitalize upon casual observations of different cultures with respect to certain behavioral, familial, and other social attributes, it is interesting that Mead has proposed that cross-culture specialists should make increasing use of other more refined methodological approaches to the study of different peoples. She suggests, for instance, that test situations (constant stimulating circumstances) be devised for use with many cultures, so that the conclusions drawn about any given culture, and the children in those cultures, are less subject to observer biases and distortions.

Just as in the comparative approach researchers may utilize already existing data on animals with which to compare newly found information on child development, so also does the cross-cultural investigator sometimes utilize previous data on one culture as the norm against which to compare developmental attributes of children in another culture. Geber and her associates (Geber, 1958; Geber and Dean, 1957) have, for example, utilized the standardized test results of American and west European children to make similar observations, and to draw comparisons, on African children. Specifically, the Gesell schedules of development were utilized to arrive at developmental quotients for children born and reared in Kenya, with the result that the African children were seen to be precocious, at least during the first year of life, with respect to a number of developmental milestones such as the age of onset of crawling, climbing stairs, and walking. While Geber provided some speculative comments as to the origins of these differences, referring, for example, to the anecdotal observation that the African children seem to be handled more and played with more freely, it is impossible to determine from such data what the true antecedents of the cross-cultural differences are. One observer might wish to make a case for genetic superiority of the members of one culture over another, but another plausible interpretation is certainly that greater opportunity for learning is available in one or the other culture. The specific mechanisms and processes underlying intercultural variations in behavior probably require for complete understanding the embellishment of the cross-cultural approach with other methodologies, such as experimental manipulative procedures.

THE ECOLOGICAL AND ETHOLOGICAL APPROACHES.   The object of the ecological approach, which is the study of an organism and its development in the context of its environmental milieu, necessitates an almost purely descriptive type of study, of which Roger Barker and his colleagues have been the main proponents in the United States (Barker and Wright, 1949, 1951; Wright, Barker, Koppe, Myerson, and Nall, 1951). The object is to make a natural history of the developmental circumstances in which the child is reared. Typically, one small unit of a culture, sometimes just one family, or sometimes just child, is chosen as the target of study. Then every bit of conceivable data is collected on that social unit or that person, from the nature of the schools attended to the size of families involved, to the kinds of games that the children play. The intended result is the discovery of the subtleties of interaction between the person and his environment, and this entails elaborate descriptions of each. Indeed, an entire book may be written on one boy's day (Barker and Wright, 1951). While workers in this area have not, in general, stated just what kinds of psychological and developmental laws they are seeking, and while one tends to become rather overwhelmed with a great deal of unwieldy, unsystematized information, it is perhaps fair to say that the ultimate objective is a total or complete documentation of the behavior of individuals reared in certain specifiable circumstances. Unfortunately, observations of this sort about occurrences of behavior vary considerably from one observer to another, except perhaps when the observer is dealing with very simple, easily labeled kinds of activity such as "Johnny left his front door at 8:25 a.m., his usual time of departure on week days, heading for school."

This sort of documentation may prove a relevant source of hypotheses for future work of a more theoretical and controlled nature. Naturalistic observations are certainly an important part of one's training for clinical or educational work. From such meticulous documentation, it would be quite possible, for example, for the observation to emerge that before a given child engages in fights with other children there is a high probability that he has within the past hour been involved in a hostile exchange with his mother. Such an observation could lead to the formulation of an hypothesis to the effect that hostile interactions with mother tend to be associated with subsequent fights with peers, or better still, anger with one's parents leads to "displaced" aggression toward other children.

One may well ask whether there is no broader purpose for such ecological, almost totally descriptive studies of this sort. Actually, the ecological style of some child developmentalists bears important similarities to the naturalistic-observational studies of the ethologists (such as Hinde, 1966; Thorpe, 1956). Hinde makes a distinction between two types of description. One involves simple enumeration of behavioral events, while the other involves "description by consequence." The first type of description ". . . involves reference ultimately to the strength, degree and patterning of muscular contractions (or glandular activity, or change in some other physiological property)," while description by consequence could refer to any pattern of behavior which leads to a specified result. "Descriptions like this are normally used when the behavior involves orientation to objects in the environment, and when the motor patterns, though leading to a constant result, are themselves diverse" (pp. 9–10). A major advantage of descriptions by consequence is that ". . . they often call attention to essential features of the behaviour that may not appear in physical descriptions, such as orientation with respect to the environment, or responsiveness to external stimuli" (p. 10). Thus, the second type of description inevitably involves specification of a relationship between the behaving organism and the environment on which it acts, or a relationship between the stimulating environment, the behavior elicited, and the consequent change (if any) in the effective stimuli. It should be obvious that one can hardly engage in scientific description of behavior by consequence without encountering questions of causation and function of behavior.

Hinde (1966, pp. 12–13) further points out that once behavioral observations are made, that is, behavior is described, different behavioral events may be considered to be and might be categorized as of the same type. These types, however, can be further classified as causal, functional, or historical. Under the causal classification would be behaviors grouped together according to causal factors on which they depend, activities sharing causal factors being classified together. Functional classification sorts behaviors according to the adaptive—in the evolutionary sense—consequences served by them. Historical classification relates to similarities in patterns of behavior seeming to have a common evolution. Hinde properly points out that the classification of behavior as having either causal or functional significance may often require the experimental manipulation of a stimulus event in order to note or verify a certain behavioral consequence. (He further implies that historical classification perhaps depends more upon conjecture and surmise than on directly observable stimulus and response events.) For an interesting similar integration of descriptive and experimental approaches in the understanding of the origins and consequences of child behavior, see Bijou, Peterson, and Ault (1968). An interesting review and experimental analysis of exploration and play behavior in children, conducted in the modern ethological tradition, is provided by Hutt (1966).

THE EXPERIMENTAL MANIPULATIVE APPROACH. The experimental manipulative approach is perhaps the more rigidly objective research orientation of the outlined methods. The orientation here is more like that of "general experimental psychology" than any of the foregoing procedures. Paradoxically, while experimental manipulative studies of child behavior have been conducted with children throughout the history of the child development field, it is only within the past 20 or so years that such an approach could be considered the "vogue" in the field. Experimental manipulative procedures, however, are not without intelligent and well-meaning dissenters.

The essence of the experimental manipulative procedure is that any child behavior is a proper target in the psychologist's pursuit of credibility, but the procedures must be such that the experimenter can develop methods of recording that behavior with a high degree of reliability *and* such that the experimenter can produce the behavior under study. That is, the experimental researcher seeks to control the antecedent conditions for a given behavior. The locus of this control is usually his laboratory, but his laboratory may encompass a large area, including the public school system, a nursery school, an orphanage, a maternity ward, or the neighborhood playground. Thus, if a psychologist wishes to study the relationship between frustration as an antecedent condition and aggression as the outcome or dependent behavior, he seeks to create the frustrative circumstances in his laboratory and measure the child's aggressive responses resulting directly therefrom. If he wishes to study whether the single presentation of two words (such as "cow" and "horse") leads to faster discrimination of (differential responsiveness to) these two words than a condition of simultaneous presentation, he sets up those conditions in such a way that children are exposed to the two conditions and their behavior is compared under controlled stimulating circumstances and with the utilization of reliable response recording procedures.

Needless to say, this orientation makes the experimental child psychologist look more and more like any other research psychologist. The experimentalist equips himself with refined apparatus—to assure constant and controlled stimulating circumstances. He usually strives to use larger numbers of subjects in his experiments—merely to ensure the statistical reliability of his conclusions. He seeks stimulation from general psychological theory, even if that theory happens to be based largely on infrahuman data—merely to ensure that he has a hypothesis of some generality and import to investigate, or perhaps to ensure that he has a hypothesis at all. He seeks to become proficient in the use of words, the nature of operational definitions, and the logic of science—merely to ensure the communicability and replicability of his findings.

The critics (e.g., Harris, 1956) of the experimental manipulative approach have two major arguments. The first is that reliance upon such methods in child psychology results in the experimenter's losing sight of the unique, distinctive child through involvement with methodology, theory, statistics, and apparatus. Experimental manipulators can only reply with reassurances; most of them are in fact terribly interested in and usually tolerant of, and only occasionally annoyed with, child behavior.

The second argument is that general psychological theory does not provide the appropriate concepts and methods for the study of the child, and that the effective differences between two different amounts of reinforcement (for example) may be important to a rat but not to a child. There are two objections to this objection. The first is that it cannot be known how important any variable is to the child until the variable has been investigated, that is, until it has been treated as an independent variable and the consequent behavior has been noted. If any variables found important for infrahuman behavior are revealed as unimportant for children, then psychologists will have to accept that that is the way the world of child behavior is. But they cannot know until they have tried. A successful case in point has been the utilization of Dollard and Miller's (1950) elaborations of Hull's theory, in which these authors adapted a simple stimulus-response analysis of discrimination and generalization behavior to the learning of words (names or labels for stimuli), and thereby accounted for certain response enhancement (acquired distinctiveness) and response impairment (mediated generalization) phenomena in the learning of subsequent discriminations. These two concepts and their analysis have provided, judging from the amount and consistency of experimentation resulting, a hopeful example of the type of elaboration that may be made on simpler constructs, based in large part in this case on infrahuman data and theorizing, to account for the greater complexities in behavior of the human organism.

Second, there *is* no broad psychological theory of and for child behavior *per se*. In this respect, child psychology is said by some to be much behind (although others argue ahead of) general psychology. Until such time as we need and/or get such a theory, it seems most parsimonious to take our lead from general psychology which has met with some success in this respect, assuming for the time being that motivational and learning processes have considerable commonalities among species. For the latter point, there is some support derivable from comparative psychology and the work of the ethologists. Again, child psychology will perhaps not know the extent of its need for a theory of its own until it has empirically exhausted some of the general psychological theories which are extant.

It is often supposed, quite erroneously, that experimental manipulative techniques applied to the study of child behavior necessarily preclude the investigation of truly relevant, "real life," socially and personally significant behavior. For example, it is sometimes argued that the "love" of a child for his mother could not possibly be examined in an experimental manipulative way. The best rejoinder to this criticism is based on facts, which show that successful studies have been conducted on the effects of permissiveness on fantasy behavior of children, the effect of mother absence on the expression of anger and hostility, the effects of frustration on aggression, and the effects of exposure to aggressive adults on imitative behavior in children. Ainsworth and Bell (1969) have recently reported a study of 56 children one year of age who were introduced to a strange situation. The primary manipulations involved the programmed departure from the scene of the mother, stranger, or both. Various classes of behavior of the child were studied as a consequence of these particular manipulations. The authors indicated that the presence of the mother was found to encourage exploratory behavior, while her absence tended to depress exploration and to heighten attachment behaviors. Specifically, when the mother was absent, crying and visual search increased. Upon reunion with the mother, the children generally sought to regain and maintain proximity with the mother. The experimenters indicated that in many subjects contact- and interaction-resisting behaviors were increased during the reunion episodes, usually along with contact-maintaining behaviors. One might say that the authors conducted an experimental study of "ambivalence," apparently engendered by the existence of two conflicting tendencies on the part of the child, the first having to do with a need to approach and maintain contact, and the second relating to a tendency to "reject" the mother, perhaps out of anger with her.

Of course, there are always some observers of child psychology research who believe that whatever is experimentally manipulated and whatever is objectively studied as behavioral output from a child cannot possibly have a meaningful relationship to what transpires and is important in the "real life" of a human being. There just is no good reply to this antiscientific orientation except to point out that it is unlikely that astronauts could go to the moon if someone had not first studied the behavior of spheres rolling down an inclined plane.

Ethical Considerations

The care and treatment of human subjects is intimately related to any discussion of methodological considerations. It should be apparent that the choice of method for the study of certain human conditions is dictated by ethical restrictions on what may be done or said to subjects and what they may reasonably be requested to reveal or perform. Simply on humane grounds, a psychological researcher with children would not want to ask one child to punch another so that the behavior of the assaulted child could be studied under conditions of threat or violence. Similarly, no child should be asked for research purposes to humiliate himself through the revelation of ordinarily private information. Frequently the choice of a naturalistic-observational mode of investigation over an experimental manipulative method will be dictated by the necessity or desirability for the researcher to refrain from imposing himself inordinately upon the children under study. This very frequently, and sometimes unfortunately, results in the availability of less definitive information about certain aspects of child behavior, and this particular deficiency of knowledge is often especially noticeable in connection with psychological attributes that are of great social concern. Society would like to know much more from psychologists than can be currently known about the effects of watching particular kinds of programmed television material on children's behavior, such as aggression and other anti-social attributes, but most psychologists would be loath, even if permitted to do so, to alter very substantially or vitally the "natural" television viewing experi-ence of children. It would also be very helpful to the science of psychology and human development, as well as to those segments and institutions of our society responsible for the rearing and education of children, to know much more about the differential effects of greatly disparate environmental circum-stances, but no child psychologist would consider subjecting one member of a pair of identical twins to a deliberately educationally insufficient environment to compare the outcome with that of a sibling subjected either to an ordinary or enormously enriched milieu. Thus, it is necessary on occasion to glean the facts as precisely as possible from "experiments" made by nature or natural circumstance.

Psychologists have been much interested in the rights of subjects and the privileges of researchers. A Committee on Ethics has been assembled, for in-stance, in the Division on Developmental Psychology of the American Psycho-logical Association. This committee had the particular task of supplementing, particularly for the researcher studying children, the published Ethical Standards of Psychologists of the American Psychological Association. Such intradisci-plinary guides for the control of scientific pursuits are usually supplemented by external, societal sanctions and controls; there has been recent activity in the United States Senate to establish a National Commission on Health Science and Society "to study the ethical, legal, and social questions raised by such health science advances as organ transplants, genetic intervention, and behavior control."

A large portion of the most recent (1968) statement of ethical standards for developmental psychologists is set forth below for the edification and advice of persons interested in the pursuit of information advances in child psychology.[4]

Children as research subjects present problems for the investigator different from those of adult subjects. Our culture is marked by a tenderness of concern for the young. The young are viewed as more vulnerable to distress (even though evidence may suggest that they are actually more resilient in recovery from stress). Because the young have less knowledge and less experience, they also may be less able to evaluate what participation in research means. And, consent of the parent for the study of his child is the prerequisite to obtaining consent from the child. These characteristics outline the major differences between research with children and research with adults.

1. No matter how young the subject, he has rights that supersede the rights of the investigator of his behavior. In the conduct of his research the investigator measures each operation he proposes against this principle and is prepared to justify his decision.

[4] From *Newsletter*, American Psychological Association, Division on Developmental Psy-chology, 1968, pp. 1–3. Quoted by permission.

2. The investigator uses no research operation that may harm the child either physically or psychologically. Psychological harm, to be sure, is difficult to define; nevertheless, its definition remains a responsibility of the investigator.

3. The informed consent of parents or of those legally designated to act *in loco parentis* is obtained, preferably in writing. Informed consent requires that the parent be given accurate information on the profession and institutional affiliation of the investigator, and on the purpose and operations of the research, albeit in layman's terms. The consent of parents is not solicited by any claims of benefit to the child. Not only is the right of parents to refuse consent respected, but parents must be given the opportunity to refuse.

4. The investigator does not coerce a child into participating in a study. The child has the right to refuse and he, too, should be given the opportunity to refuse.

5. When the investigator is in doubt about possible harmful effects of his efforts or when he decides that the nature of his research requires deception, he submits his plan to an *ad hoc* group of his colleagues for review. It is the group's responsibility to suggest other feasible means of obtaining the information. Every psychologist has a responsibility to maintain not only his own ethical standards but also those of his colleagues.

6. The child's identity is concealed in written and verbal reports of the results, as well as in informal discussions with students and colleagues.

7. The investigator does not assume the role of diagnostician or counselor in reporting his observations to parents or those *in loco parentis*. He does not report test scores or information given by a child in confidence, although he recognizes a duty to report general findings to parents and others.

8. The investigator respects the ethical standards of those who act *in loco parentis* (e.g., teachers, superintendents of institutions).

9. The same ethical standards apply to children who are control subjects, and to their parents, as to those who are experimental subjects. When the experimental treatment is believed to benefit the child, the investigator considers an alternative treatment for the control group instead of no treatment.

10. Payment in money, gifts, or services for the child's participation does not annul any of the above principles.

11. Teachers of developmental psychology present the ethical standards of conducting research on human beings to both their undergraduate and graduate students. Like the university committees on the use of human subjects, professors share responsibility for the study of children on their campuses.

12. Editors of psychological journals reporting investigations of children have certain responsibilities to the authors of studies they review: they provide space for the investigator to justify his procedures where necessary and to report the precautions he has taken. When the procedures seem questionable, editors ask for such information.

13. The Division and its members have a continuing responsibility to question, amend, and revise the standards.

CHAPTER 2

Sensory Processes

INTRODUCTION

The Problem

In theories of human behavioral development, the period of infancy has received attention disproportionate to the amount of time it encompasses, partly because this period is believed to be more important than most for the understanding or predicting of later gross development. However, because the infant's operating characteristics are in many ways different from those of the adult, the actual construction of a psychology of behavior which can be generalized to infants has been accomplished only in a most general form.

For researchers interested in the earliest period of infancy, a unique set of problems has increased the difficulty of constructing more specifically adequate theories. These problems concern the sensory capacities of the young infant, and have only recently begun to be systematically attacked.

The issues to be settled concern the general questions of what forms of physical energy young infants are capable of transducing into biological energy, and how these biological energies can be employed for organizing or systematizing behavior output. Without answers to these questions, it is difficult to estimate which more molar aspects of the environment are relevant to later behavioral development.

Two empirical questions are immediately pertinent. First, What responses can the young infant emit? and second, How can these responses be used as dependent variables for assessing the characteristics of the infant's sensory processes? Without belaboring these questions, a somewhat arbitrary outline of behaviors found to be useful as dependent variables is given in Table 2-1, and the experimental procedures usually employed for studying infant sensory processes are briefly described in the next section. Most of these dependent variables may reasonably be indexed in terms of frequency, amplitude, latency, probability, rate (interresponse time), temporal patterning, and many derived measures (e.g., responses per burst in sucking, degree of change from base rate in heart rate or hormone secretion).

The Experimental Procedures

Three experimental procedures have typically been used to examine early infant sensory capacities: the *reflex, habituation,* and *conditioning* procedures.

Table 2-1

Behaviors Observed in Studies of Infant Sensory Processes

Behavior

Movement of face parts and portions of the extremities
    Lips and tongue (sucking, mouthing, yawning)
    Vocal apparatus (articulator movement, frequency characteristics of phonation or cries)
    Eyes (fixation direction and focal length of gaze, tracking)
    Eyelids (opened or closed)
    Finger and toe movement (single digits or topography of whole assemblage, e.g., spreading of toes or clinching of fist)
Movement of extremities
    Head turning (any direction)
    Arm flailing (flexion or extension)
    Leg movement (flexion or extension)
Movement of trunk
    Rolling to left or right
    Arching of back
    Whole body startle
Breathing activity
    Changes of inspiration–expiration ratio
    Oxygen (O_2) consumption factors (basal metabolism rate)
Autonomic nervous system activity
    Heart rate
    Pupillary dilation and constriction
    Blood pressure and volume
    Skin resistance and potential
Neuromuscular potential changes
    Electroencephalogram pattern
    Brain DC level
    Electromyogram
    Electroretinogram
    Evoked responses
Body chemistry
    Blood serum factors
    Hormone secretion

The reflex procedure consists of a single presentation of a stimulus, and observation primarily of a single response (or response sequence). Subsequent presentations of the stimulus might be given, but only as a reliability check or procedural replication. The necessary and sufficient stimulus for the reflex is usually one or more simple forms of energy.

The habituation procedure consists of two or more presentations of the effective stimulus. With this procedure the focus is on changes in the response over trials. The stimulus is usually presented in a regular temporal sequence, but repetition is the only critical characteristic of the procedure.

The key characteristics of the conditioning procedures are described in the introductory section of Chapter 3. In brief, in the classical conditioning procedure a conditional stimulus (CS) is presented and is followed by an unconditioned stimulus (US). The CS can be any stimulus that initially has little or no relation to the strength of the dependent (response) variable; the US is an elicitor of the relevant response. In the instrumental or operant conditioning procedure the first stimulus is a discriminative stimulus (S^D), the second is an assumed configuration of internal and external energy leading to emission of the response, and a third stimulus, which must also be presented, is the reinforcer.

The kinds of data that are obtained from the three kinds of procedure seem to be hierarchically organized, in that the most complex levels of stimulus–response relationships are observable only in the conditioning procedures, the next more primitive levels are observable in the habituation procedure, and the most primitive levels are observable in the reflex procedure. It is suggested, however, that sensory "capacities" that are revealed in the conditioning procedures must also be evident in the reflex and habituation procedures; capacities revealed in the habituation procedure must also be revealed in the reflex procedure, and not necessarily in the conditioning procedures; and capacities revealed in the reflex procedure are not necessarily revealed in the habituation and conditioning procedures. In other words, as the complexity of the observable stimulus–response relationships increases, the range of sensory capacities that can be revealed is narrowed.

Each of the traditional sensory modes (vision, audition, somesthesis, gustation, and olfaction) will be discussed, where possible, in terms of these three levels of information extraction.

VISION

Introduction

It is impossible in the space available to describe adequately the anatomy of the eye or the physics of visual energy. Both Davson (1962) and Mann (1964) have described the embryology of the visual apparatus, and Spears and Hohle (1967) have provided an extensive bibliography of recent research on "sensation" and "perception" in infancy.

The primary development of the visual apparatus begins in the first month of gestation, and the system is apparently completed in all respects, except ultimate "bulk," within the first year following birth. At birth, the moment when relevant visual experience begins, the infant's eye apparently differs in structure from the adult's in the following ways: (a) The diameter is, on the average, 5 to 10 mm smaller than the 24 to 25 mm average for adults; (b) the retinal cellular structures are not completely differentiated, although differences from mature structures are apparently minimal; (c) the macular area, including the fovea, is not yet fully pigmented; (d) the curvature of the cornea is relatively greater than in the adult, tending to produce hyperopia (the essence of which would be a blurring of near objects); and (e) the size of the pupillary opening is smaller than in the adult (at maximum constriction, about 1 mm smaller;

at maximum dilation, about 3.5 mm smaller), but the adjustment of the pupillary opening is slower.

Even though some structures within the visual system are not completely formed, it might generally be said that at birth the eye is physiologically and anatomically prepared to respond differentially to most aspects of its visual field. The characteristics of the visual field have been divided into a number of artificially unique parameters: brightness, hue, saturation, pattern, spatiality (depth), and complexity. For the naive observer, however, there is probably no visual stimulus such as a brightness without the concomitant qualities of hue, saturation, pattern, and depth; "reality" does not isolate these characteristics. Yet, it is reasonable to look at these factors as separable since the physics of light makes them operationally unique, and experimental circumstances can be arranged to show differential responding when all but one are held constant.

Brightness

REFLEX STUDIES.   Use of the reflex procedure has shown that numerous response systems covary with variation of the energy level of a given emitted electromagnetic frequency entering the pupil. Early studies by Pfister (cited by Peiper, 1963) and Sherman, Sherman, and Flory (1936) indicated that pupillary constriction occurs in the newborn in response to simple changes in light intensity, the amount of constriction increasing with age. This age factor may or may not be partly a function of growth in the size of the eye; the issue has not been resolved. The response is more sluggish in the newborn than in older infants, but the speed of the response increases as the brightness of the stimulus increases. Sudden increases in light intensity also elicit a blink reflex (Kroner, cited by Peiper, 1963) and the eye-neck reflex, which consists of quick retraction of the head (Loth, 1952).

In addition to pupillary constriction, several other responses of the autonomic nervous system have been found to be correlated with visual stimuli. However, the electroretinogram (ERG), a reflection of gross retinal activity, represents a more fruitful set of "internal" responses for monitoring operations in the visual system. Recent work by Horsten and Winkelman (1962), using relatively sophisticated equipment, led these investigators to conclude that with sufficiently intense stimulation the form of the ERG of the newborn does not differ from that of the adult. Earlier pioneering work by Zetterström (1951, 1952, 1955) had led to a different conclusion. Horsten and Winkelman found the essentially normal ERG even in prematures as small as 1600 grams, although its elicitation in these infants was erratic.[1] Dark adaptation was found to affect the size of the "beta" wave component, as did age.

Optico-kinetic nystagmus has also been used as the dependent response. It

---

[1] Prematurity is generally defined in terms of the weight or length of the baby at birth because estimates of the age at birth are subject to large error (see, e.g., Carmichael, 1954b, pp. 114–118). However, a birth weight of 1600 grams (about 3½ lb.) would indicate, very roughly, an age of 6.8 months, about 10½ weeks premature.

is movement of the eyes in the direction of movement of a moving, repetitive display (usually moving stripes) placed in front of the face, with quick return of the eyes to the initial direction of gaze. Doris and Cooper (1966) and Doris, Casper, and Poresky (1967) used a constantly moving pattern of relatively large stripes (8 degrees in width), and found age-related changes in nystagmus as a function of stripe contrast, indicating that the child becomes increasingly sensitive to contrast from birth to about two months of age. During this period the Weber ratio[2] changes from 50 percent to about 26 percent, but this change is difficult to assess within infancy or to compare with adult figures. The adult data usually indicate a need for approximately 1 percent contrast in absolute energy differences between dark and lighter stripes in order for the stripes to be seen, but there is a "trading" relationship between brightness difference and stripe width which must also be considered (Brown and Mueller, 1965).

Fixation has been shown by Watson (1924b) to occur if a stationary beam of light in an otherwise darkened room is within 20 degrees of the line of sight. Reliable tracking of a moving target is also found in a sufficiently large proportion of the population to allow this behavior to be incorporated into a number of standardized neonatal tests (Gesell, 1941; Graham, Matarazzo, and Caldwell, 1956; Rosenblith, 1961).

Numerous investigators have recorded either quieting or activation in the presence of visual stimuli of various constant intensities. Irwin and Weiss (1934a) found that in infants dark-adapted for 30 minutes, activity increased when the total illumination increased to a "very dim" level (.002 foot-candle). The activity at this level was greater than activity at more intense levels (.02 and 3.9 foot-candles). However, in a follow-up study by Irwin (1941a), still more intense levels (5, 25, and 50 foot-candles) yielded a positive relation between activity and intensity. This inverted U-shaped function undoubtedly results from antagonistic processes, but lack of knowledge about many critical behavioral characteristics makes it difficult to specify their nature.

HABITUATION STUDIES. Because of the difficulty in maintaining a fixed orientation with eyes open, it is difficult to examine the brightness dimension with the habituation procedure. Bronshtein, Antonova, Kamenetskaya, Luppova, and Syrova (1960) mentioned suppression of sucking with the first presentation of a visual stimulus to an infant, and subsequent habituation of the sucking suppression. However, the age of the infants from whom these data were collected was not indicated, and none of the attempts to replicate the habituation of suppression with very young infants has been successful (Haith, 1966; Kaye and Levin, 1963; Semb and Lipsitt, 1968).

CONDITIONING STUDIES. The conditioning procedure presents the same general problem as the habituation procedure. Although "white light" has been used

---

[2] The Weber ratio is $100 \times \Delta I/I$, where I is the initial or comparison intensity and ΔI is the minimal increase in intensity that will produce a change in response. In the present context, I is the intensity of the dark stripes and ΔI is the minimum difference in intensity between the light and dark stripes that will produce nystagmus.

as the US for classical conditioning in newborns (Wenger, 1936), it has apparently not been used successfully as a conditional or discriminative stimulus until infants are 40 days old. However, as Lipsitt (1963) suggested, the adequate techniques for demonstrating conditioning to certain CSs may still need to be worked out.

CONCLUSION.   The evidence suggests that *brightness* is available to the newborn infant as a functional psychological dimension.

Hue

It is difficult to separate responses to hue from responses to brightness because the eye differentially "accepts" similar physical intensities at different frequencies or wavelengths (Graham *et al.*, 1965). The so-called photopic and scotopic luminosity functions represent the visual efficiency of the color (cone) and noncolor (rod) receptors in reacting to monochromatic light. For the cones, efficiency peaks at about 555 millimicrons (middle green) and decreases in the lower (blue) and higher (red) ranges. This creates a difficulty in matching the brightnesses of the hues, but without this matching the study of hue discrimination is difficult and the results often equivocal.

Additional problems arise because macular pigmentation is incomplete until the infant reaches the age of five or six months. This probably means that the color spectrum is shifted and possibly altered slightly in shape during this period as the pigment creates a progressively stronger "yellow" filter. Nevertheless, it is worthwhile to examine a few of the representative studies on hue discrimination in infancy.

REFLEX STUDIES.   The reflex procedure has been used in a number of experiments. Early work by Adrian (1945) indicated that characteristics of the ERG (electroretinogram) were sensitive to hue as well as brightness. The fast component of the ERG, the "x" wave, was explored in adults by Armington and Biersdorf (1956) and was found to yield a photopic luminosity function displaced slightly toward the blue end of the spectrum. Barnett, Lodge, and Armington (1965) tested x wave differences between white and orange at different intensities and found definite indications of a photopic response in infants during the first days of life. Like Horsten and Winkelman (1962), cited above, they found the shape of the response similar to that of the adult, but reduced in amplitude.

Following the work by Peiper (1963, pp. 71–73), which indicated the photopic Purkinje phenomenon,[3] Trincker and Trincker (1955) used the eye-neck reflex to examine varying sensitivity as a function of wavelength. Both premature and full-term infants exhibited photopic luminosity functions that were similar, in many respects, to the adult function. However, the curves of light-adapted

---

[3] The Purkinje phenomenon is a shift in the point of maximal brightness in the spectrum as the eye becomes dark-adapted. Yellow and red become dimmer, green and blue brighter as the eye shifts from light (photopic) to dark (scotopic) adaptation (Best and Taylor, 1955, p. 1113).

infants were uniform regardless of age, but the curves of dark-adapted premature infants showed a shift in the peak (maximum response) toward the longer wavelengths in the first weeks, including relatively greater sensitivity to the red end of the spectrum and relatively less sensitivity to the blue end. As the infant enters his second week the peak shifts to about 550 millimicrons, but the red and blue ends of the spectrum still elicit relatively more and less response, respectively, than is found in the adult. By approximately the fourth week this has been "corrected." Since this occurs in both the full-term and the premature infant, with only slight differences in the quantitative values, it would appear that the photopic process, although initially a function of morphological integrity, probably requires visual stimulation for completion of its functional development.

Several researchers (e.g., Spears, 1964; Staples, 1932) have utilized so-called *preference* procedures, with paired comparison presentations and differential fixation time as the dependent variable indicating preference. The results using these procedures have not been uniform, and procedural problems add some difficulties to interpretation (Ames and Silfen, 1965).

HABITUATION AND CONDITIONING STUDIES.   Habituation of sucking suppression to chromatic stimuli was reported by Bronshtein *et al.* (1960). However, the documentation was not adequate, and further work is needed to provide a definitive conclusion.

Kasatkin and Levikova (1935b) used chromatic stimuli as the CS in classical conditioning, but found no stable CR until the age of three months. Brackbill (1967) pointed out that the small amount of research and the questionable adequacy of the few designs currently employed leave much yet to be done before the age at which chromaticity becomes a useful dimension for conditioning can be specified.

Acuity

Visual acuity, operationally defined, is the minimum aspect of the test object dimension that can be correctly identified (Riggs, 1965).

REFLEX STUDIES.   In several reflex studies of acuity in the newborn, the response used has been optico-kinetic nystagmus, usually with moving stripes as the repetitive display. Gorman, Cogan, and Gellis (1957), using a device suggested by McGinnis (1930), presented two stripe widths, .02 and .06 inch, at a distance of approximately 6 inches from the infant's eyes. The stripes were printed on a 42-foot sheet of paper rotated on a semitubular structure within which the infant was placed. Rotation speed was approximately 7.5 degrees per second. In the initial work nearly all infants responded to the .06 stripe, indicating acuity equivalent to a Snellen Chart rating of 20/600. (The Snellen Chart is the familiar test used by eye doctors.) Acuity of 20/600 indicates that the normal adult can see at 600 feet what the infant can see at 20 feet. Subsequent work showed that some infants responded at 20/350. This is equivalent to a minimal angle of resolution of about 20 minutes of arc, about 600 times poorer than adult acuity under optimal conditions, but somewhat more comparable to adult acuity measured under similar conditions with nystagmus as the response.

Fantz, Ordy, and Udelf (1962) used fixation on striped displays, which are preferred to totally gray surfaces, and obtained no difference in acuity at 5, 10, and 20 inches, suggesting possible accommodation to different distances. In infants under one month of age, 40 minutes of arc was the minimum preferred stimulus, decreasing to 5 minutes of arc at about six months of age.

It is difficult to compare measures of acuity based on nystagmus with measures based on other responses, because of differences in distances to the target and differences in movement speed (indeed, for some measures, such as with the Snellen Chart, the stimuli are stationary). Perhaps, then, the discrepancy between the Gorman *et al.* and Fantz *et al.* data is an artifact of the difference in procedures.

Using a test apparatus similar to the one used by Gorman *et al.* (1957), Dayton *et al.* (Dayton, Jones, Aiu, Rawson, Steele, and Rose, 1964a; Dayton, Jones, Steele, and Rose, 1964b) recorded nystagmus electrically, from electrodes on the outer canthus of the eyes and the bridge of the nose, and thus were able to distinguish tiny movements from "noise" (tremor and drift). With this more refined measure, they detected responses in some infants less than 24 hours old to line widths of only .032 inch, approximately 7.5 minutes of arc and equivalent to the Snellen notation of 20/150. Apparently, improved techniques yield more precise results. It is possible that computers will allow even finer analysis of the data, by isolating systematic trends statistically.

HABITUATION AND CONDITIONING. Neither habituation nor conditioning procedures have been used in studies of visual acuity. Although the designs would be difficult to execute in early stages of development, they appear to be worth attempting. For example, using the Fantz *et al.* (1962) procedure of recording "fixation," the attractiveness of displays of decreasing stripe width could be examined over successive trials, using a gray contrast card of equal luminance.

Form

In many respects the discussion of the previous topics has anticipated certain issues inherent in the questions of whether and at what age the developing infant responds to form. Acuity tests are based on stimuli that are, at the most gross level, *form* stimuli. However, the study of form perception requires more operations, in both defining the stimulus and relating the stimulus to the response, than does the study of the characteristics of vision described above. This is because any given portion of the visual display may have an infinite number of forms but only a single average brightness or hue. A form therefore requires some kind of gross differentiation of a portion of visual space on the basis of variations in brightness and/or hue, and these variations must have a relatively specific distribution of "density" across a set of coordinates.

From the experimenter's point of view, how one creates a form stimulus is mechanically simple and descriptively complex. The linear bounding of portions of space provides the basic operation for producing forms. However, as pointed out by Attneave and Arnoult (1956):

(a) Shape is a multidimensional variable, though it is often carelessly referred to as a *dimension*, along with brightness, hue, area and the like. (b) The number of dimensions necessary to describe a shape is not fixed or constant, but increases with the *complexity* of the shape. (c) Even if we know how many dimensions are necessary in a given case, the choice of particular descriptive terms (i.e., of reference-axes in the multidimensional space with which we are dealing) remains a problem . . . . (p. 452.)

Hake (1966) presented a partial list of characteristics that have been used in the description of form: area, perimeter, maximum segments, number of indefinitely extended straight lines, texture, ratio of perimeter to area, and regular–irregular, simple–complex, and symmetrical–asymmetrical dimensions. To this list can be added the meaningful–meaningless dimension.

Reflex Studies. The two measures most often used in the study of the control that form may have over behavior in the newborn are general orientation of the eyes and specific center of focus. Although these are apparently related, the operations for measuring them are independent. General orientation, often called fixation, has been used longer than specific center of focus, because the latter requires techniques that have only recently been developed, by Kessen and his colleagues (Hershenson, 1964; Kessen, 1967; Kessen and Hershenson, 1963; Salapatek and Kessen, 1966). More recently, innovations by Haith (1968) have modified the procedures to reduce the drudgery of data analysis, and have made these techniques economically feasible for most infant laboratories. The experimental procedure for studying these behaviors has been the reflex procedure.

The "fixation" procedure, although extensively used over 25 years ago (Ling, 1942), has only recently been developed for the study of human infants, primarily through the efforts of Robert Fantz (1958, 1965, 1967). The basic operations consist of presenting to the infant a pair of stimuli on a board several inches from his eyes. The observer sits behind the stimulus board and observes the direction of gaze of the infant. The criterion for the response may be as loose as ". . . the time during which the subject is turned in a given direction" or ". . . the time during which a given stimulus is reflected in the child's pupils." The basis of the procedure is the belief that what is "looked at" is "seen" and that the child is responding to the whole stimulus complex presented by the experimenter. In other words, when the infant responds to the stimulus, he is considered to be responding to the generic stimulus as defined by the experimenter—newsprint, circle, checkerboard, or face—and not to be responding to "irrelevant" elements.

Fantz and his co-workers have found greater fixation on "normal" than "scrambled" faces, and more on "complex" than "simple" figures in very young infants.

"Fixation" is treated as an instrumental response in the newborn, but may in fact be a respondent.[4] The unconditioned stimulus may be a mechanism operating on brightness contrast (for example). In a tropistic manner, the eyes and then the head may be "pulled" toward certain relative brightnesses in the field. The apparent "scanning"—the changes in fixation—may be precipitated by either satiation as a function of time spent oriented to a given portion of the field, or strain produced by uneven tension on the ocular muscles (or both processes).

Furthermore, our ignorance of the relative acuity of peripheral vision in the newborn makes it difficult to estimate what portions of the visual field are simultaneously capable of yielding information on form. The idea that form can be "built" from the successive incorporation of parts is to be doubted since it presupposes knowledge of the end goal. It would seem more reasonable to consider both the building of an immediate image and the recognition of whole forms to be a product of a process such as that proposed by Hebb (1949). (The theory is discussed in Chapter 15.) The *cell assembly* could be guided in its organization by, say, a contrast tropism which, because of the structure of "reality" (e.g., *geometric* or *responsive*), would increase the probability that certain responses will follow the initial movements. Thus, for generally similar structures (represented by species designation), there would be a high probability of generally uniform *phase sequences* for individuals reared in similarly relevant environs. (However, Hebb's theory suggests that the required phase sequences should not yet be developed in early infancy.)

Starting with this general approach, a first step in the analysis of the ontogeny of form perception would appear to be an examination of the exact factors "capturing" foveal fixation, and the relation of pattern parameters to foveal fixation. This work has been initiated by Salapatek and Kessen (1966), and is being extended by Salapatek and Kessen (1969).

Salapatek and Kessen recorded reflections of infrared lights from the cornea of the infant, permitting determination (within a few degrees) of where the central pupil was fixated. They recorded fixations approximately once per second. They compared the patterns of successive fixations in the presence of a solid black triangle with the patterns of successive fixations in the presence of a uniform field, and demonstrated (a) a greater dispersion of fixation along the horizontal axis than along the vertical axis in the uniform field, (b) a decrease in fixation dispersion to the triangle, and (c) concentration of fixation around the vertices of the triangle. All infants were less than eight days old, and no developmental trend was observed.

Salapatek and Kessen (1966) suggested three factors that may be responsible for the "attractiveness" of the vertices:

It is possible that the newborns respond to transitions in brightness and that the orientation toward a vertex is directed by the presence of two brightness transitions. Secondly, the infant may respond to vertices through a mechanism specifically tuned to angles. This interpretation is congruent with analyzer theories of discrimination . . . and may suggest the presence

---

[4] A respondent is an *elicited* response, controlled by the pattern of stimulation that precedes it; an instrumental (or operant) response is *emitted* with no identifiable eliciting stimulus, and is controlled by its environmental consequences (see "Introduction" in Chapter 4 and "Basic Principles" in Chapter 19).

in young infants of neurophysiological coding mechanisms analogous to the contour operators described for the visual system of cats. . . . Thirdly, it is possible that the infants were responding to an optimal level of brightness . . . that is only to be found near a vertex. (p. 166.)

More recent work by these investigators has shown that fixation is limited by simple brightness boundaries. Future work will undoubtedly deal with the probabilities of fixation as a function of contrast and movement sequences.

If the infant's behavior is under control of only parts of a stimulus display at any one time, as the Salapatek and Kessen data suggest, and if, as Hebb's theory suggests, attention to parts by the very young infant cannot initiate a phase sequence that signals the probability of a whole form, the findings of Fantz are very difficult to interpret. Recent failures to replicate some of Fantz's results with the three month old (Koopman and Ames, 1968) would indicate that interpreting his data on older infants may also be difficult. Perhaps the ontogenetic systematization of form perception is to be explained by assuming that gross fixation in a paired comparison presentation is under the control of three or more processes that have relatively independent sources and possibly very different time courses. The first could be an unconditioned response to one or more of the factors suggested by Salapatek and Kessen with respect to the attractiveness of vertices. The second could be short term conditioning occasioned by immediate preferences (Watson, 1965), perhaps under the control of such things as previous satiation and amount of movement preceding "stopping." The third could be long term conditioning which increases the probability of (a) *stopping* on a certain target (e.g., a hungry man looking longer at a picture of food than at a picture of an airplane) or (b) *searching* given displays more than others because doing so has in the past yielded some satisfaction or feedback.[5]

HABITUATION AND CONDITIONING.   For an adequate description of the development of form as a controlling stimulus, the kinds of conditioned relationships suggested above will have to be explored. Siqueland (1968a) has developed a technique for examining conditioning to form stimuli, which provides procedural flexibilities for examining satiation *to* and conditioned generalization *from* given forms. Because the sucking response is used as the dependent variable, the technique allows examination of infants from birth to about four months of age.

Habituation procedures have not yet been tested; but if good conditioning procedures are discovered, they may not be necessary.

Depth

Changes in the distance of a form from the eyes might provide differential information for the infant, as they do for the adult. Accommodation, conver-

---

[5] It is possible that a satisfactory alternative explanation can be derived from a "world hypothesis" (Pepper, 1942; Reese and Overton, in press) other than the mechanistic one assumed here, as has been done in the area of language development (see "Theoretical Accounts of Language Acquisition," Chapter 13).

gence, binocular disparity, stereoscopic vision (possibly), and motion parallax are factors capable of signaling "depth" or object distance for the human adult. To the degree that these are operative in the newborn, they may act in a similar fashion. Whether other variables (e.g., perspective, interposition, texture gradients, shadows), which act for the more mature organism, are also effective for the nonverbal infant is methodologically a moot point.

Phylogenetic comparisons of the ontogeny of depth perception have an extensive history theoretically tied to the nature–nurture issue and to aspects of the development of Gestalt theory. J. J. Gibson (1950), who has carried out some of the most important research on the relation of various aspects of the environment to depth perception, believed that the organism is able to use three-dimensional organization of form from birth, a position that requires assuming a built-in response to depth.

The issue of the presence of a sensitivity to depth is not independent of the definition of the control of behavior by patterned stimuli. The operations for testing depth sensitivity assume focusing on a form at a given distance. For certain levels of explanation, however, the control by patterned stimuli need be no more than reflexive.

Haynes, White, and Held (1965) questioned the ability of the infant under one month of age to accommodate his lens enough for the image to be reproduced sharply on the retina. Although there is a great deal of individual variability, these young infants are reported to have fairly fixed focal lengths which come more and more under control of the stimulus until, at four months, this ability is quite mature. However, Hershenson (1965, 1967) has pointed out a number of difficulties with the recording procedures, fixation elicitation, and targets employed. No other researchers have expanded or improved on these techniques, which, as employed by Haynes *et al.*, are technically quite demanding. Fantz *et al.* (1962), as mentioned above, did not find a distance effect on the acuity task, suggesting that (a) the infant was accommodating to the different target distances (5, 10, and 20 inches), (b) the targets to which the infants were responding were sufficiently large that blur was irrelevant, (c) the accommodation was such that none of the targets was in focus, or (d) the infant was responding to brightness distributions, which are only secondarily related to pattern. Furthermore, to what degree a *clear* image is a necessary condition for controlling behavior is still unknown.

Conjugate movement of the eyes would appear to be more critical than accommodation. It is hard to understand how a visual system could be functionally valuable as an information transducer unless the two eyes move together (except, of course, when one eye is inoperative), since independent scanning by the two eyes would undoubtedly yield conflicting information about distance. Apparently, conjugate eye movement does occur a large proportion of the time during which the *newborn* is either fixating or pursuing a target (Dayton *et al.*, 1964a, 1964b; Hershenson, 1965).

There is no current work on binocular disparity (the general horopter) in the developing child, nor on stereoscopic perception in the nonverbal child. There are, however, two lines of research related to the more functional properties of the relation of behavior to distance of the display. The first is that by Walk and Gibson (1961) on the so-called *visual cliff*, a *reflex* procedure created and elaborated by these investigators for the study of the ontogeny and phylogeny of depth perception. Unfortunately, the procedure is somewhat difficult to use directly with the developing human infant, because of the lack of mobility of the infant during the first five to six months. At the age of five or six months, the infant does exhibit sufficiently differentiated behavior on the "cliff" to warrant inferring possession of sensitivity to depth. However, the technique requires, even for many lower species, arbitrary decisions about the criteria for a response, and the theory elaborated by the investigators has, at this time, only potential face validity.

Table 2-2

Design and Data of Bower Study

| Condition | Stimulus | | Comment | Responses[a] |
	Side (ft.)	Distance (ft.)		
Training	1	3		—
Extinction (a)	1	3	Size and distance unchanged	103
(b)	1	9	Size unchanged, distance changed	66
(c)	3	3	Size changed, distance unchanged	54
(d)	3	9	Size and distance changed, size of retinal image unchanged	23

[a] Number of responses in extinction.

More promising for resolving the issue of early functional sensitivity to depth are the experiments of Bower (1965a, 1965b, 1967). Essentially, Bower *conditioned* infants between 70 and 85 days of age to respond with a head movement in the presence of a one-foot cube at a distance of three feet from the infant. The response by the infant produced multidimensional visual and auditory feedback, serving as reinforcement. As soon as the infant reached a stable rate of responding, extinction was given in the presence of (a) a one-foot cube at a three-foot distance, (b) a one-foot cube at a nine-foot distance, (c) a three-foot cube at a three-foot distance, and (d) a three-foot cube at a nine-foot distance. The dependent variable was the number of responses emitted during the extinction period. Table 2-2 summarizes the design and results.

If the size of the retinal image is critical, Stimuli (a) and (d) should yield similar results. In fact, they did not. Stimulus (a) evoked the largest average number of responses in extinction, Stimuli (b) and (c) evoked essentially equal numbers of responses, and Stimulus (d) evoked the fewest responses. Stimuli (c) and (d) (cube size changed) produced the greatest decrement, but there was less decrement with Stimulus (c), apparently because the distance was unchanged.

In a follow-up experiment, an attempt was made to tease out the mechanism underlying the previously indicated sensitivity to distance. One group received a binocular cue, a one-foot cube, placed on a table to signal reinforcement availability; another group had monocular exposure to the cube on the table; and a third group was shown the cube projected on an otherwise blank screen four feet away (S^D), alternated with a projection of the empty table (S^{Δ}).

Table 2-3

Design of Bower Follow-Up Study

	Stimulus[a]		
Condition	*Side (ft.)*	*Distance (ft.)*	*Comment*
Training	1	3	
Extinction (a)	1	3	Size and distance unchanged
(b)	1	9	Size unchanged, distance changed
(c)	3	3	Size changed, distance unchanged
(d)	3	9	Size and distance changed, size of retinal image unchanged

[a] Sides and distances approximate. Actual sides were 30 and 90 cm., and distances 1 and 3 meters.

As in the previous experiment, four test conditions were employed: (a) a one-foot cube at a three-foot distance, (b) a one-foot cube at a nine-foot distance, (c) a three-foot cube at a three-foot distance, and (d) a three-foot cube at a nine-foot distance. The design is outlined in Table 2-3.

The binocular and monocular groups performed essentially alike and similarly to the group in the previous experiment (even though the infants were as much as 30 days younger than in the previous experiment). However, the results for the projection group were different. The projection group emitted similar numbers of responses in test conditions (a) and (d). Apparently because the necessary contextual cues for motion parallax were lacking for this group, the infants did not differentiate the two stimuli that produced similar sizes of retinal image. However, this finding is made somewhat difficult to interpret because in the projection group Conditions (b) and (c) produced response rates quite similar to those in the binocular and monocular groups.

Nevertheless, the importance of motion parallax as a cue for depth is indicated by this research, and also by research on the visual cliff with lower animals (Walk and Gibson, 1961) and older infants (Walk, 1968). It appears, then, that sensitivity to distance cues, if not present at birth, quickly becomes one of the infant's dimensional sensitivities.

AUDITION

Introduction

Whether the newborn responds to sound in the first days of life has been a controversial question for well over a hundred years (Peiper, 1963). The issue was undoubtedly confused by the lack of experimental and statistical sophistication, and further complicated by the general naivete concerning the description of the stimulus. Peiper (1963, pp. 83–92) described the early attempts to answer this question, pointing out that the more recent studies indicate that most infants are responsive to some aspect of sound within the first few hours after birth (Graham, Clifton, and Hatton, 1968; Richmond, Grossman, and Lustman, 1953). Part of the problem revolves around whether the auditory apparatus is adequately free to respond. It is known that the ear, unlike the eye, is totally differentiated by about the sixth month of gestation (Arey, 1965, pp. 541ff). The bony labyrinth of the inner ear has assumed its maximum proportions by the fifth month (unlike the eyeball, which continues to grow after birth), and the same appears to be true for the underlying neurological structures of the brain stem which are relevant to later auditory sensitivity. The degree to which functional impairment immediately after birth may be caused by the presence of vernix caseosa (a waxy substance covering the newborn) in the external auricular passage or by mucous in the middle ear is not known, but both of these possible mechanical blockages disappear rapidly following birth.

Current evidence indicates that sound is mediated by movement of the fluid in the cochlea. The movement of the cochlear fluid is most obviously produced by oscillation of a bone, the stapes, at the entrance to the cochlea (at the round window). This oscillation is usually created by changes in the air pressure entering the ear, vibrating the tympanic membrane and transmitting the vibration frequency through the malleus and incus to the stapes. Movement of the cochlear fluid is also caused by oscillation of the whole cochlear structure by bone conduction, transmitting the vibration through an essentially rigid vibration system (Naunton, 1963). Normally, both systems are operative.

Sound stimuli are usually generated by vibrating an object in air. These vibrations set up traveling zones of rarefied and compressed air. The physical theory of auditory functioning has been developed most successfully by von Békésy (von Békésy, 1960), but a recent review of theories by Licklider (1959) describes problems of the attempts to organize the data on auditory input.

Sounds apparently have many qualities (Stevens, 1934), but physical characteristics of sound stimuli may be expressed most succinctly in terms of amplitude, frequency, and phase. *Amplitude* is the maximum difference between the pressure at rarefaction and compression, *frequency* is the number of rarefaction–compression cycles per unit time, and *phase* represents the point or degree of completion in a rarefaction–compression cycle at the moment of input. Amplitude and frequency are not directly proportional to the psychological dimensions of loudness and pitch, respectively, but are related; phase is probably most important in sound localization.

Amplitude

Amplitude is figured in arbitrary pressure units relative to a nonzero baseline. A currently popular unit is the decibel (defined as $10 \log_{10} P_1/P_0$, where P_1 is the pressure of the stimulus and P_0 equals .0002 dynes per sq. cm.).[6]

REFLEX STUDIES.   Numerous reflexes appear to be responsive to sounds (see Peiper, 1963), but differential sensitivity to amplitude has not been explored extensively. Stubbs (1934) found an increased probability of the eyeblink with increased tone intensity. The startle response increases in intensity (Stubbs, 1934) and speed (Kaye, 1968a) with increases in tone intensity. Kaye (1966) studied infants less than four days old, and found a linear relation of intensity in decibels to probability of breathing disruption.

Bartoshuk (1964) and Steinschneider, Lipton, and Richmond (1966) found differential changes in heart rate as a function of sound intensity. The relation of heart rate changes to gross body startle has yet to be studied, but Kaye (1968a) found that some startle responses in the newborn have latencies under 200 milliseconds (.2 second). This would be well within a single heartbeat cycle (200 to 600 millisecond range for most newborns in states ranging from extreme agitation to quiet), and therefore startle may be the cause of the changes in heart rate with intense stimulation. Barnett and Goodwin (1965) found the greatest heart rate acceleration when there was concomitant movement, but they found *no* correlation between tone intensity and heart rate when activity was partialled out.

Steinschneider (1967) suggested, from work by Bartoshuk, that the threshold for heart rate acceleration in the newborn is somewhere above 40 decibels. Considering that most indoor conversation has a general level above 55 to 60 decibels, it is likely that language and many other "meaningful" sounds are within the child's autonomic audibility range.

Crowell, Davis, Chun, and Spellacy (1965) reported galvanic skin responses (GSR) to some of their auditory presentations, but their data are difficult to interpret. Kaye (1964) found GSR impossible to elicit reliably during the first few days of life.

A study by Barnett and Goodman (1965) explored the relation between click

---

[6] Roughly, the sound of leaves rustling in a gentle breeze has an intensity of 10 decibels; a whisper at a distance of 4 feet, 20 decibels; sounds in a quiet street, 30 decibels; a conversational voice at 12 feet, 50 decibels; a loud peal of thunder, 70 decibels; and sounds at the pain threshold, 130 decibels (Best and Taylor, 1955, p. 1192).

intensity (peak frequency 600 to 800 cycles per second) and amplitude of the P2-N3 phase or wave of the evoked response, this being one of the major characteristics of an auditory evoked potential. The evoked potential showed a positive linear relation between the P2-N3 amplitude and sound intensity, the response being slight but present at about 35 decibels above adult waking threshold. The latency of the auditory evoked response is longer for the infant than for the adult, as is also true for the visual evoked response, and is partly under the control of prestimulus EEG rhythms, with the larger P2-N3 phases inversely related to depth of sleep. Depth of sleep was indicated by increases in the proportion of slow, high voltage waves per unit time. The law of initial values (Lacey, 1956) was found generally applicable to these findings.

Weitzman, Fishbein, and Graziani (1965) used a different index of depth of sleep, but they also found that the response level is lower and the latency greater during deep sleep than during lighter sleep.

HABITUATION STUDIES. Several studies have dealt with the habituation of response systems after repetitive auditory stimulation. In the study by Barnett and Goodman described above, 250 one-second clicks at each attenuation level were given to allow a comparison of responses as a function of repetition. The last 30 clicks yielded a lower amplitude than the first 30. However, without further operational analysis it is difficult to ascribe this decrement to the habituation process. Fatigue (change of state) would be a reasonable alternative.

Bartoshuk (1962a, 1962b) explored habituation to tone using heart rate as the dependent variable. His studies indicated that habituation was more rapid with 6-second intervals between tones than with 60-second intervals, and that dishabituation was produced by both an increase in intensity and a change in tonal pattern. Previous work by Bridger (1962) had shown that the greatest habituation rates occurred to tones with long durations and short intertonal intervals. In other words, presenting long tones at a rapid rate produces habituation more quickly than presenting short tones at a slow rate.

Graham et al. (1968) studied 20 newborns in each of 5 different groups, given a 75 decibel stimulus for 2, 6, 10, 18, or 30 seconds, with a 90-second intertonal interval. The data were interpreted by the researchers as showing a greater response to the 10-second tones than to the other tones (the response was acceleration in all cases). This inverted U-shaped function has been found in many studies of "arousal" (see Cofer and Appley, 1964, pp. 392–398). In all groups except the 2 second group, there was a decrement in response over successive presentations.

Kaye (1968a) used an extensive set of parametric manipulations of tone duration and intertonal interval, and found that short (1 second) tones with long intertonal intervals (20 seconds) produced sensitization rather than habituation. (Sensitization, although sometimes used in a theoretical sense, refers here to an increment in responding over "habituation" trials.) Longer durations and longer intertonal intervals produced habituation, and the rate of habituation increased with increasing duration and with increasing interval. Figure 2-1 shows these relations graphically. In the studies providing data on these functions,

Kaye utilized general activity (movement in a stabilimeter) as the dependent variable.

In a subsequent study, Kaye and Brown (1968) supported the contention that tonal amplitude is not the only relevant factor controlling the habituation response to tone, since they obtained dishabituation with a change in frequency. However, they did not examine dishabituation to a change in amplitude and

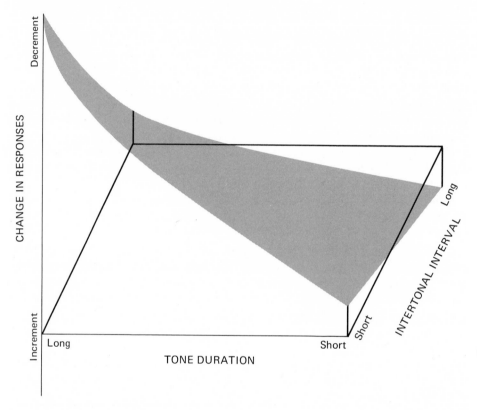

Fig. 2-1. Change in responding over an "habituation" series for a *loud* tone presented to a *quiet* baby. The graph is three-dimensional, indicating degree of change for various durations and intertonal intervals.

therefore could not describe the relative contribution of each. A percentage-of-change transformation was used by these investigators, comparing activity during five seconds of tone presentation (A) with activity during the five seconds just prior to the tone presentation (B). The average response to the initial stimulus in a 30 stimulus sequence, using the ratio of A to $A + B$, was .86 (.50 would be no change in activity level, .00 would be total suppression of activity, and 1.00 would be change from no activity to any other level of activity).

In a recent study by Kaye, Brown, and Jones (1968), independent observational ratings of pretest activity were used as approximate estimates of state.

It was found that the most active subjects suppress activity with tone onset, and quiet children become more active. This parallels the work by Rovee and Levin (1966) on the "pacification" effects of nipples for infants at different state levels.

A study by Keen, Chase, and Graham (1965) indicated that tonal habituation carries over from one day to another, even in the newborn as young as two to three days of age.

CONDITIONING STUDIES. In many learning experiments with newborns, a tone or a noise has been used as the conditional or discriminative stimulus (see Chapters 3 and 4 for reviews). However, no investigator of infant learning has used a discrimination paradigm in which the reinforced stimulus (S^D) and the non-reinforced stimulus (S^Δ) were different tones, nor has any examined generalization in the human newborn. Thus, although it appears that conditioned responses can be controlled by tones, it is not currently known which aspects of the tone are responsible for signaling response onset.

Graham *et al.* (1968) and Bartoshuk (1962b) found greater responses in their older subjects (first five days of life), but these differences were in part a function of changes in prestimulus levels.

Bronshtein *et al.* (1960) described a number of procedures for suppressing the sucking response; in one procedure with tone presentations, repeated presentations led to subsequent recovery through habituation of suppression. Kaye and Levin (1963) could neither suppress sucking nor show habituation. However, Sameroff (1968b) found that alterations in the burst length and/or interburst interval resulted from presentations of extended tones; and Semb and Lipsitt (1968) showed with a sophisticated use of *likelihood ratios* that infants who are sucking tend to continue sucking, and those at rest tend to stay at rest—the human analogue to the physical property of inertia. Kaye (1968b) obtained suppression of sucking movements in the presence of an extended tone, but did not obtain suppression of nipple sucking. This would indicate the relatively strong control of sucking by nipples and the relatively weak control of sucking by tones, a not unexpected finding.

CONCLUSION. Several response systems are responsive to tonal intensity, and it seems safe to forecast that increased sophistication in design will probably reveal a differential response to intensity with the conditioning procedure.

Frequency

The adult human ear can discern sounds between 15 cycles per second and 15,000 to 20,000 cycles per second, although the range constricts in old age. Responses to frequency are difficult to separate from responses to amplitude, especially with low and high frequencies at low intensities because the efficiency of the ear at these extremes is reduced. Thus, a tone of 50 or 15,000 cycles per second (for example) will seem to be less loud than a tone of 1000 to 3000 cycles per second if the tones are equal in physical amplitude. To match the apparent loudnesses the low and high frequency tones would have to be greater in physical intensity than tones of intermediate frequencies. However, for the adult, as the middle tones to be matched increase in intensity, the disparity at low and high frequency levels required for the match is reduced.

Stubbs (1934) used a *reflex* procedure in a study of the activity response to seven different tones varying in frequency from 128 to 4096 cycles per second. She obtained no differential responding, but it is difficult to interpret her results, in light of the response measure used, inadequate data analysis, and relatively poor stimulus control. The same is true of a study by Haller (1932), although he found a decrease in activity beyond 2048 cycles per second.

Kaye and Brown (1968), in the second half of their *habituation* study cited above, switched subjects to a second frequency of either 350 or 1000 cycles per second, depending upon which had been used in the first half of the trials. They obtained dishabituation (a recovery of the initial response) and then habituation again. If the dishabituation was not caused by the change in frequency, then it probably indicates a differential sensitivity to intensity as a function of frequency, since the physical intensities were matched.

Leventhal and Lipsitt (1964) used habituation in part to test sensitivity to frequency. The subjects were habituated to either a 200 or a 1000 cycle per second tone, and then the alternate frequency was used in an unsuccessful attempt to produce dishabituation. The trend approached statistical significance, and the investigators suggested that a weakness in their procedure may have masked the response to frequency.

No *conditioning* studies in which frequency is the relevant dimension have been carried out with the young infant, nor have any frequency generalization studies been conducted.

Responses to patterns of frequency have been examined in the newborn by both Bartoshuk (1962a) and Eisenberg, Coursin, and Rupp (1966). Bartoshuk habituated heart rate acceleration to a sequence going from 100 to 1000 cycles per second over an eight-second period, and obtained dishabituation when the sequence was reversed. Eisenberg *et al.* (1966) did not report the results of a similarly designed study they conducted, but did mention obtaining habituation to the patterned stimuli. Eisenberg (1966) speculated about the neurological properties underlying the response to patterned stimuli and its ethological significance, but there are still too few hard data to warrant construction of a theory.

Localization

In a loose observational study by Wertheimer (1961), *reflexive* head orientation to the source of a sound was found in an infant less than an hour old.

Leventhal and Lipsitt (1964) *habituated* sounds presented to one ear, and found dishabituation when the locus of the source was changed. However, Turkewitz, Moreau, and Birch (1966) found that head position prior to testing alters lateral sensitivity, and these factors must now be taken into account in any study of localization.

There have been no *conditioning* studies with sound localization as the stimulus, although Papoušek (1961) has used location confounded with differential frequency as the CS in a novel kind of conditioning design (for discussion of Papoušek's work, see Chapter 4, section entitled "Instrumental Conditioning in Infants").

Conclusions

Sound undoubtedly represents a potent stimulus for building cognitive structures and/or learning sets, especially because the young child does not need to "focus" his sensory system before he is exposed to the stimulus. It seeks him out. However, the response to sound and the control of responding through conditioning to sound require considerably more extensive experimental treatment before the processes will be well understood.

SOMESTHESIS

Introduction

Harlow (e.g., 1961), perhaps more than any other researcher, made the infant psychologist aware of the role that tactile stimulation might play as a reinforcing agent for the developing child. Pressure, pain, heat, and cold, the four major "surface" sensations in the human adult, constitute the often unified sensory mode called somesthesis. It is only within the last ten years that the sophistication of the physiology underlying differential response to these forms of stimulation has been recognized. Classical sensory physiology suggested that five different types of fibers mediated the four sensory qualities: Pacinian and Meissner's corpuscles for pressure, Krause end bulbs for cold, Ruffini end organs for heat, and the tiny free nerve endings for pain and more diffuse qualities of touch. Recent work, however, has indicated that neural patterning is crucial. The Oxford group (see Lele and Weddell, 1956) found that reports of all the somesthetic "sensations" could be obtained from stimulation of the cornea, which has only free nerve endings, when appropriate levels of stimulation were used. It would appear at this point that physiologists and physiological psychologists are just beginning to understand the underlying processes. In light of this, the following discussion will leave many questions unanswered.

Pressure, Touch, and Pain

REFLEX STUDIES. Pressure, touch, and pain sensations are difficult for the adult to separate under certain conditions (e.g., an excessively strong handshake) even with an extensive verbal or other symbolic system. For the newborn it is difficult to define the characteristics of these qualities as reflected in his immature behavior, without a certain amount of guesswork and anthropomorphizing. For example, in terms of *reflexes* the newborn's hands are apparently more sensitive than his calf (Dockeray and Rice, 1934). However, squeezing the palm quite hard will cause the infant's mouth to open without a cry, this being the Babkin reflex (Kaye, 1965; Parmelee, 1963), but pinching the toe with relatively less pressure will cause the newborn to cry immediately. Crying is also elicited by pulling the hair at the base of the scalp (Jensen, 1932). Lightly stroking the cheek or lips will turn the head in such a way that the mouth is brought toward the source of the stimulus, this being the "rooting" reflex, but applying strong pressure to the cheeks or head, tending to turn the head away, "locks" it in place (up to a point) with a pressure proportional to that of the push.

Other "setting conditions" also affect these dependent variables. For example, the sensitivity to cheek stroking (rooting) was found by Turkewitz *et al.* (1966) to be a function of the resting head position. Resting the head on one side causes ipsilateral desensitization; when the head is placed at midline for short periods, the sensitivity increases toward a level equivalent to that of the contralateral side. Many reflex movements are dependent upon different loci of tactile stimuli: the fanning of the toes to plantar stroking (the Babinski reflex), gripping an object placed in the palm (the grasp reflex), extension of the contralateral leg to pressure on the ipsilateral leg (the cross extensor reflex), and many others (see Peiper, 1963, Chapter 2; Prechtl and Beintema, 1964).

Sherman and Sherman (1925) noted a decrease in number of pinpricks necessary to elicit a response, as the child increased in age from one to about five days. Although Dockeray and Rice (1934) reported no change as a function of age, Kaye (1962) reanalyzed their data and found an age trend for all parts of the body except the thigh. (The statistical design used by Dockeray and Rice gave inordinate weight to the thigh measurements, and thus obscured the changes that had actually been obtained.)

More recent work by Graham (1956) and Lipsitt and Levy (1959) has indicated an increasing sensitivity to electric shock as a function of age over the first five days. Lipsitt and Levy found a sex difference, females being more sensitive than males. Electrical stimuli were used by these researchers because of the high degree of control potentially obtainable over the stimulus source. The Lipsitt and Levy procedure, with foot withdrawal as the dependent variable, demonstrated increased sensitivity for both longitudinal and cross-sectional age samples. However, because voltage variation was the independent variable, the decrease in threshold could have been an artifact of decreases in skin resistance, rather than a result of increases in neural sensitivity. Richter (1930) had presented skin resistance data which tended to show lower levels for older neonates; and Kaye (1964) also found a decreasing level of skin resistance, during the first four days of life. However, Kaye and Lipsitt (1964), in a further analysis, corroborated the age trend in sensitivity when differences in resistance were partialled out.

Bell and Costello (1965) used the Semmes-Weinstein esthesiometer in an attempt to duplicate the electrotactual findings. However, the stimulations were presented to the relatively insensitive heel, and the group was not particularly divergent in age extremes. (The heel was used because it gave the most reliable test-retest measures.) Not unexpectedly, he found no age differences. He did, however, further confirm both parity differences and sex differences that he had previously noted (Bell, 1963).

Kaye and Karp (1968) used plantar presentation of the stimulus with the same type of esthesiometer, and obtained a definite decrease in threshold from the first to the fourth day, but found no consistent sex difference. Kaye and Lipsitt (1964) suggested that the differences in sensitivity of males and females might be a function of the sex differences in skin histochemistry reported by Siegel (1955). This hypothesis is strengthened by the similarities between thresholds for the sexes using the esthesiometer.

Using a rather complicated design, Gullickson and Crowell (1964) attempted to manipulate changes in electrotactual threshold, by exposing subjects to various experiences with noxious stimuli. The criterion was two consecutive foot movements. The results showed a significant increase in threshold over days for the "experience" groups; the "non-experience" control group was significantly below the others on Day 3. There were no overall sex differences, and too few infants to test for sex differences in the control group alone.

The design does not appear to be complete enough to permit interpretation of the differences between groups, but the major findings are sufficiently clear. Apparently, the additional experience with noxious stimuli altered the threshold of the response to shock so that most infants became less "sensitive." Given the design and controls, this could result from two processes. First, by requiring two consecutive responses the researchers may have created—with the occurrence of the initial suprathreshold response—a "momentary" desensitization which had a recovery time proportional to age. Thus, the first response would partially desensitize the "system" to the following stimulus, progressively more so as age increased. ("Desensitization" should be taken in its broadest meaning here, to include interference from other activities that might begin as a function of the initial suprathreshold stimulus.) The second process is habituation, which Gullickson and Crowell felt contributed most importantly to their results.

HABITUATION AND CONDITIONING. *Habituation* to tactile stimulation has been indirectly described by Lipsitt (1963), in reporting a need to increase voltage levels within experimental sessions in order to maintain the occurrence of the unconditioned foot withdrawal response.

Lewis, Goldberg, and Dodd (1967b) have shown that interpreting changes in heart rate with successive tactile presentations as simple habituation is, at best, tenuous, because the changes are very much influenced by the state of the subject and certain characteristics of age.

Conditioning to a tactile CS was perhaps demonstrated by Lipsitt, Kaye, and Bosack (1966a), in the three day old, when they showed that response to a nonpreferred or nonoptimal sucking elicitor could be increased through contingent reinforcement. Earlier work by Mateer (1918) and Denisova and Figurin (1929) indicated that this mode could be employed with slightly older infants to elicit anticipatory responses.

Thermal Sensitivity

Although thermal regulation represents one of the more critical biological adaptations, and thermal variation is one of the most important vital signs, temperature change as a cue for psychological behavior has apparently been relegated to a secondary position. Thermal cues have very rarely been used as other than the stimulus for an unconditioned or reflexive response. Thermal regulation, although not at maximum efficiency in the newborn (Adamson and Towell, 1965; Bruck, 1961), reaches a relatively stable level at about $1\frac{1}{2}$ weeks, with only minor adjustments occurring slowly over the remainder of the life of the system. Except during the first day or so of life, changes in the temperature of the general environment cause appropriate compensatory changes to occur in basal metabolic rate, thus maintaining a constant internal temperature.

Increasing temperature, probably up to a limit, seems to reduce bodily activity and hence to facilitate sleep, but most of the data on comfortable sleeping temperatures for the developing child have come from gross observations, usually with temperature and tactile stimulation confounded. There are much more extensive data on the relation of temperature to sleep and activity of the premature infant, for whom these conditions are more critical (Bruck, Parmelee, and Bruck, 1962).

Jensen (1932), in his extensive examination of the sucking response, found that both excessive heat and excessive cold, approximately above 122°F and below 68°F, respectively, produced differential sucking. A number of reflexes may also be elicited by rapid changes of temperature; for example, the head is reflexively snapped back when a cold or warm stimulus is applied to the forehead.

No research has been carried out on *habituation* or *conditioning* with thermal stimuli.

GUSTATION

Although there has been controversy about whether the newborn responds differentially to selected gustatory stimuli, an overwhelming amount of data indicates that he does (see Peiper, 1963, pp. 44–49; Pratt, 1954, p. 242). The newborn appears to be amply supplied with taste buds throughout the oral mucosa. The child is perhaps no more sensitive to taste stimuli at any time in his life than at birth, although this type of qualitative estimate is most difficult to define, much less test.

The notion or theory of morphological differentiation of taste buds into ones corresponding to the four classic qualities of taste (sweet, sour, salt, and bitter) has recently been abandoned. Apparently, not only do most taste buds respond to two or more of the classes of stimuli, but the buds themselves have a complete turnover rate of once every 8 to 11 days. It appears that the taste buds are formed from the tongue epithelium, and that cells migrate toward the center and then disintegrate. A most important role in patterning the receptor potential into useful qualitative information is undoubtedly played by the first neuron connected to the taste bud. This patterning may take place in many ways (see Kitchell, 1961), but the code has not yet been broken.

Pfaffmann (1961) has pointed out that taste, because it is integrally involved in the nature and quality of appetitive reinforcement, is scientifically a potentially important sensory process to understand. Unfortunately, few studies of this process have been carried out with the newborn, for reasons that are obvious to researchers who have tried to design experiments to obtain more than superficial information on the sense of taste. First, in order to assess taste, the researcher must interfere with one of the vital activities of the infant, his feeding routine. When the researcher is giving sugar solutions or milk, the problem is reduced or eliminated; but bitter, sour, and salty solutions can be given only in small quantities. Second, even when giving sugar solutions, the researcher is producing a change in the infant's "state" while feeding him, and the change will affect the rate of response regardless of whether or not sucking is being used as the dependent variable. There is not at this time a sufficient understanding of the changes in these response parameters to permit adequate analysis of differential taste effects.

Most of the studies of taste in young animals have been reflex studies. For the human infant under normal circumstances of nutrition, the quality of taste apparently carries both its discriminative and immediate reinforcing values in a single excitation pattern. The dependent variable, loosely recorded and often photographed, has been mimetic (facial expression) responses. However, lack of reliable means for recording these complex responses, and the resulting inability to quantify them, have relegated these data to a level of secondary importance.

Canestrini (1913), using activity, breathing, and blood volume as the dependent variables, found quieting to sweet solution (up to 5% sugar) and restlessness to sour (5% vinegar) and salty (2% salt) solutions.

One set of widely cited results offers promise for a fruitful procedure. These data were gathered by Kai Jensen in 1932, but they are yet to be replicated and expanded. Jensen used a specially prepared bottle attached to a manometer and recorded changes in sucking to solutions of various tastes and temperatures. (The major temperature findings were discussed above.) Apparent differential sucking occurred to increasing salinity (.2% to .9% salt by volume), when compared with milk at 104°F (the control solution). This was not true for acid (sour) or glucose (sweet) mixtures. However, Jensen did not make full use of his data, doing no more than an "eyeball" comparison of the experimental and control solution curves. Kaye (1967), in his review of studies on the newborn's sucking response, has suggested a number of measurements that should be taken from such data.

Jensen's data suggest that the sucking response can be used as the dependent variable in testing differential response to taste stimuli. The use of a sucking device such as one constructed by DeLucia (1967) combined with a feeding system such as one suggested by Sameroff (1965) would allow the automatic feeding of a number of solutions. As Jensen (1932) and before him Nelson (1928) recommended, control solutions should be presented, but milk and distilled water are probably not the best control solutions. In the first place, recent evidence indicates that water "tastes," both physiologically and psychophysically; and in the second place, adequate controls must be constructed not only for taste but also for viscosity in short term experiments, and for caloric factors in longer term experiments.

OLFACTION

Introduction

Although olfaction and gustation are usually considered together, as the two chemoreceptor systems of the body, olfaction might be classed more appropriately with vision and audition, since the locus of the stimulus is usually at a distance from the receptor. The fact that the olfactory source cannot be immediately located without either moving or using other senses, only expands in time the ancillary behaviors often accompanying localization in other modalities.

The volatile nature of some liquids and solids produces the olfactory stimulus in the form of complex molecules which drift or are blown or inspired into the nasal cavity. There they make contact with the olfactory epithelia of the olfactory bulb, where the selective absorption to chemical "sites" on these dendrites creates the receptor potentials. Only a small amount of the air and critical gases entering the nose is likely to drift to the area of these sensory elements, but the receptors are apparently extremely sensitive. For example, "methyl mercaptan (garlic odor) is perceptible to the average person in a concentration of 1/23,000,000,000 of a milligram per cu. cm. of air. Assuming that 50 cc. of air is required for arousing an olfactory sensation, this would mean that 1/460,000,000 mg. of the substance is an effective stimulus" (Best and Taylor, 1955, p. 1220).

However, many factors seem to introduce variability into estimates of sensitivity to given olfactory stimuli in adults. For example, temperature, humidity, and altitude differentially affect volatility of liquids; some persons apparently have genetically determined sensitivities to certain odors to which others are insensitive; women react strongly to certain odors (such as musk) that are hardly noticeable to men, the response apparently being under the control of certain hormones; and immediate emotional and cognitive factors are also important determinants of odor detection.

Relative to the adult, the newborn is working with a much reduced volume of air intake (Avery and Normand, 1965) but breathes through his nose from birth and thus exposes the tiny filaments of his olfactory bulb to potential sources of stimulation. Early work in this area led to controversy over whether the newborn infant shows differential sensitivity to odors, and again, as with gustation, the methodological and statistical naivete of the early investigators make the controversial data difficult to interpret. Part of the problem revolves around the difficulty of separating olfactory from tactile properties of olfactory stimuli. The trigeminal nerve, which matures early in fetal development, sends branches into the nasal cavity where they mix with olfactory nerves. The trigeminal nerve responds nondifferentially to some chemical properties of gases. This constitutes the so-called "common chemical sense," but the separation of this sensation from olfactory sensations in the human is at best difficult. It is hard to estimate the extent to which humans distinguish the trigeminal component from olfactory components, even though the common chemical sense is thought to arouse relatively violent reflexes such as sneezing and lacrymation while olfactory sensations arouse relatively mild reactions (Best and Taylor, 1955, p. 1220). For example, both ammonia and acetic acid (vinegar) have large trigeminal components which are undoubtedly considered by most to be part of the "odor."

A partial list of some of the classes of odors includes pungent, floral, musky, fruity, minty, putrid, oily, and rancid. The list could be extended, and although numerous groupings have been suggested, there is currently no uniformly accepted classification scheme.

Quality and Quantity

REFLEX STUDIES. Standard solutions were used in several studies of early olfactory sensitivity, with mimetic expression, activity, sucking, breathing, and blood pressure changes as dependent variables. However, the problems of specifying mimetic expression, as stated above, have not been dealt with adequately; and, in general, the reflex procedure does not at this time appear to be appropriate for separating differential sensitivities to odors. Even if researchers could specify the "type" of facial expression as pleasant or unpleasant, or show that the heart rate decelerates as a reaction to some "positive" stimuli and accelerates to some "negative" stimuli, there is a tremendous number of seemingly independent stimuli in each of these broad classes. The technique for studying these differences must be much more specific.

In spite of these difficulties, the reflex procedure can provide useful data. Lipsitt, Engen, and Kaye (1963), for example, used this kind of procedure and demonstrated increasing sensitivity (decreasing response threshold) to asafetida during the first four days of life. (The response and mode of stimulus presentation are described in the discussion of Engen's research in the next section.) It might be noted that the increase in sensitivity parallels the increase in sensitivity to electrotactual stimulation, mentioned earlier (Lipsitt and Levy, 1959).

HABITUATION STUDIES. Engen and his associates, in a number of papers to be briefly described below, used the habituation procedure to examine differential responsiveness to several odors, exploring these responses in the light of more general theories of olfaction. One of the advantages of using the newborn for this research is that he has no stimulus biases or learned idiosyncrasies. The disadvantage, as in all research with the newborn, is that a reliable dependent variable must be found. Engen and his associates chose breathing disruption and activity change.

The basic technique for their experiments consisted of placing the child on a stabilimeter (Lipsitt and DeLucia, 1960) with a pneumograph around his abdomen. Changes in activity and breathing were recorded on a polygraph. One cubic centimeter of the odorant was placed in a small test tube, and a commercial cotton swab protruding from a cork wrapped in aluminum foil was placed into the solution. (In some later studies, a cotton swab wrapped on a glass rod was used.) The cotton swab saturated with odorant was placed about one-fifth of an inch (five millimeters) beneath the nostrils for ten seconds. The relevant dependent variable was observed during the ten second experimental trial and during a ten second nonodorous control trial; the experimental trial was scored as "positive" if the activity on that trial surpassed the activity on the control trial. In one study, the reliability for three independent judges was 86 percent; the two agreeing judges decided the response on the remaining 14 percent of the trials.

In the initial study (Engen, Lipsitt, and Kaye, 1963), responses on ten consecutive trials with each of two odorants, acetic acid and phenylethyl alcohol, were recorded for ten infants approximately two days of age. Half the subjects received the acetic acid trials first and the others received the phenylethyl alcohol trials first. Acetic acid elicited responses on from 80 to 100 percent of the presentations, and phenylethyl alcohol elicited responses on 25 to 10 percent of the trials, the decrease occurring on the last two presentations. With these two odorants, order of presentation had no effect.

For asafetida and anise oil, tested in the same way with a similar population, there was a sharp drop over the ten trials. When the asafetida was presented first, the initial response on Trials 1 and 2 was 100 percent, dropping to 25 percent by Trial 10. When it was presented second, the initial trials yielded 80 percent response, and the later trials 25 percent. Anise oil, when presented first, produced about 80 percent response in early trials, dropping to 10 percent by Trial 10. When presented after ten trials of asafetida, the response level started at about 15 percent and dropped to zero by the fifth trial. After the last trial with the second odor, two trials with the initial odor were given; on these trials there was 40 percent "recovery" of the response to anise and 80 percent "recovery" of the response to asafetida.

This study gave strong indication that newborns respond differentially to odors. Although acetic acid and phenylethyl alcohol odors may have trigeminal components, this is not true for the other two odorants. The 100 percent response to asafetida on Trials 1 and 2 indicated that all infants reacted to this odor; but because not all infants responded to the anise, the individual data on this odorant are difficult to interpret. However, the technique of using the odor "profile" over extended trials is a valuable methodological improvement. All four substances gave distinct profiles, which could be used tentatively to define the differential qualities of the odors. The recovery of response in the posttest trials to levels above those for the immediately preceding odor indicated that the suppression of response during the consecutive presentations was not simply a general sensory adaptation or fatigue effect.

In a further study exploring the mechanism of posttest recovery (Engen and Lipsitt, 1965), a half-anise, half-asafetida mixture was presented for ten trials to infants approximately two days of age, then either the anise or the asafetida was presented to the subject, each in a 50 percent solution with a nonodorous diluent (diethyl phthalate) making up the other 50 percent. Over the ten initial trials, response to the mixture decreased sharply. However, response to the 50 percent asafetida solution in the posttest was as great as response to the *mixture* on the initial trials, but response to the 50 percent anise solution did not show this recovery. In subsequent scaling carried out with adults, it appeared that the 50 percent concentration of anise, although weaker than the 50 percent concentration of asafetida when they were presented separately (in solution with the diethyl phthalate), was the dominant odor of the *mixture*. Perhaps when presented by itself after the mixture, then, the 50 percent anise solution was much more comparable to the mixture than was the 50 percent asafetida solution, and the lack of response to anise was due to its lack of novelty. The problem of interpretation was further complicated by differences in the initial response elicitation capacities of the two chemicals.

To solve these problems, a pair of stimuli with the following qualities is needed: First, the component odors should be different from each other in quality but equally similar to the odor of the mixture; and second, the components should be of equal response eliciting intensity. These criteria were approached with a mixture of 16.7 percent heptanol, 33.3 percent amyl acetate, and 50 percent diluent, as scaled with adults. With a procedure similar to those previously described, it was found that both the heptanol solution and the amyl acetate solution, when presented with the diluent alone, brought about a recovery of response. Again, the slightly "dominant" smell in the mixture, the amyl acetate, produced the *least* recovery, but in this experiment there was for both odors a significant return of responding. This study indicates that the decrement in response, the habituation process, is apparently more a function of a decrease in novelty than of sensory adaptation. Furthermore, the data strongly suggest that the phenomenon of habituation, as a theoretical concept, should be separated from other operations leading to response decrement.

In research following up studies by Engen (1964) and Kruger, Feldzmen, and Miles (1955), Rovee (1966) examined responsiveness to five aliphatic alcohols (propanol, ethanol, hexanol, octanol, and decanol). She found that response amplitude and rate of habituation decreased as the number of carbons in the alcohol molecule increased (3, 5, 6, 8, and 10, in the respective alcohols), and the threshold decreased (i.e., sensitivity increased) as the length of the carbon chain increased. (Since all of the alcohols used were straight-chain alcohols, the number of carbons is confounded with chain length.)

There is some evidence (see Engen, 1965) that olfactory stimulation would be more adequately provided by the long-chain alcohols than by shorter-chain alcohols at the low concentrations encountered at the threshold levels. The alcohols with the shorter chain lengths apparently have a stronger trigeminal component; at full strength these would produce immediate trigeminal and olfactory summation, but perhaps the weaker "threshold" solutions produce only olfactory stimulation. If so, then the threshold solutions of short-chain alcohols would have to be more concentrated than the threshold solutions of long-chain alcohols, explaining the obtained relation of chain length to threshold. However, this would not explain the relations of chain length to response amplitude and habituation rate, since these relations amount to relations of threshold to response amplitude and habituation rate. There seems to be no reason to expect weaker responses or faster habituation at lower thresholds.

CONCLUSIONS

Introduction

This last section relates the work on infant olfaction to the "main stream" of psychological research in this field, a goal which could do much to improve the quality of work being carried out on the other sensory qualities in infancy. For many reasons, this has not been done. First, and perhaps most important, many of the early workers were pediatricians and clinicians. They were interested in the diagnostic value of their measurements, but apparently lacked the time, inclination, or training to carry out long term programmatic research. Others who studied the newborn were anatomists, neurologists, embryologists, and geneticists, interested in problems and techniques that were only tangentially related to the directions in which behavioral research is oriented. These latter researchers, because of their naivete with respect to both psychological theory and statistics, accepted a number of gross behavioral theories that had poor empirical support and were often epistomologically unadaptable to their particular problem areas.

In contrast, many of the researchers currently studying infancy are psychologists. With their more or less common background has come a basic commonality of language and a sharing of techniques. This does not, however, negate the conclusion that there is, at this time, very little acceptable research on the development of sensory processes. Nor, for that matter, is there adequate information available on *any* aspect of the early ontogenesis of behavior. Because of the paucity of information, work in almost any area of newborn behavior has been acceptable. It is suggested that in some cases this has led to confusion that will probably take many years to untangle. However, some general statements can be made about the newborn's gross sensory abilities, and some suggestions can be made about future directions of research.

General Summary

The physiological apparatuses for many of the traditional sensory modalities are apparently in working order by the time the infant is born. Differential response has been shown at the reflex level for several dimensions of visual, auditory, tactual, gustatory, and olfactory stimuli, and to this list could be added vestibular and kinesthetic stimuli (see Spears and Hohle, 1967). Some dimensions are still in doubt. For example, it has not been adequately shown that frequency of a sound is differentiated from intensity at different frequencies, and a great deal of research must still be carried out on taste discrimination. For the most part, however, there are sufficient data on the neonate's differential response to stimuli at the reflex level to say that the infant's transducers are adequately separating energy inputs into major within-modal dimensions. Beyond this, little can be said. There are almost no data available to permit the researcher to scale intensity or quality differences, and without these it is difficult to establish general environmental priorities for training, or to interpret previous sensory experience.

"State," the general rubric covering a large complex of subject variables that affect one or more dependent variables, is apparently critical for predicting behavioral outcome. Many dependent variables show both qualitative and quantitative variations when the infant is studied at different levels of "state."

A few of the sensory characteristics of the infant are reflected at the level of the most complex experimental procedure described in this chapter, the conditioning procedure.

Future Research

Three general areas of research are important for understanding stimulus control in the newborn. First, information is needed on dependent variables that can be easily and reliably recorded. Studies currently being carried out on head movement, eye movement, and sucking should provide some of the data on expected baseline levels of activity. This would allow researchers to set up some of the more complex stimulus-response designs without the necessity of first going through the time-consuming testing of the components of the design. This would also make it possible to identify deviant subjects on a more rational basis than has heretofore been possible, and would therefore provide a firmer basis for excluding subjects *before* the experiment begins.

Second, conditioning procedures must be improved so that almost all subjects can be brought successfully under simple stimulus control, in order that finer discriminations can be tested. Ultimately, this type of procedure yields the most secure data for theory building.

Third, the relations of "state" variables to behavior must be functionally tested with both the simple and complex procedures. The infant cannot easily be placed in a given state, but when this is possible it would greatly simplify the research designs. A first step would be to examine the relations of pre-event behaviors to the stimulus-produced responses, and then to explore ways in which these relevant prestimulus levels can be manipulated.

CHAPTER 3

Basic Learning Processes:
I. Classical Conditioning

INTRODUCTION

Definition and Classification of Learning Processes

Offenbach (1966) and White (1962) listed over 1200 studies of learning in children, including work from the 1920s to the middle 1960s. It is doubtful that this literature could be summarized adequately in a single volume, and it is obviously impossible to do so in a few chapters. Therefore, the coverage in this volume is necessarily selective. It is selective in two ways: first, many of the studies are not mentioned at all, and second, many of the topics of investigation are not mentioned. However, an attempt has been made to include all of the historically important studies and all of the recent advances that have been made, and to cover all of the salient problems and issues in the area.

This chapter and the next two are concerned with the study of learning or conditioning. Although learning occupies an important role in most theories of child development, there is no single definition of learning that finds acceptance among all psychologists who use the term. The problem of demarcating "learning" as a given area of investigation is beyond the scope of this volume; the student is referred to detailed discussions of the problem in standard learning texts (e.g., Hall, 1966; Hilgard, 1956; Kimble, 1961).

Generally, learning is inferred from changes in behavior resulting from experience, practice, or training, as distinguished from changes resulting from physical growth, genetic determination, fatigue, sensory adaptation, arousal, or changes attributable to transitory physiological states. Kessen (1963) has suggested that not all changes in performance resulting from experiential precursors are "learning" and that attempts to conceptualize them as such result in theoretical vagueness. Reliance upon tenuous operational criteria, derived from studies with adult organisms, to distinguish learning from other "adaptive" processes may hinder or even preclude a careful experimental analysis of certain kinds of effects within the framework of classical and instrumental conditioning paradigms. Furthermore, the results of infant studies may indicate deficiencies in contemporary learning theories.

For example, the frequently used criterion of relative permanency for differentiating the effects of learning from the effects of other cases of behavioral change can be misleading. Campbell (1967), in a series of studies with infrahuman organisms, has shown that retention of acquired behavior varies inversely with the subject's age at time of conditioning, although acquisition and extinction of the behavior are invariant with age. Thus, if memory is quite limited in the immature organism, acquired behavioral changes that are not maintained for some arbitrarily specified duration (e.g., 24 hours) would, by definition, not be "learned." The results of Campbell's studies, together with recent studies in short term retention, suggest that the study of memory processes in young organisms is an important area of investigation; they also suggest that defining learning so that it is dependent upon relative permanency, which is arbitrarily delimited, may be overly restrictive. Woodworth and Schlosberg (1954) raised similar objections to the use of duration of behavioral change as a criterion for learning.

For these reasons, the present concern is to examine the effects of certain experimenter-specified variables on behavioral changes and to attempt to determine whether the observed behavioral changes (short term and long term, gradual and abrupt) are uniquely attributable to the learning contingencies under investigation.

The familiar distinction between classical and instrumental conditioning will be used. The prototype for classical conditioning is Pavlov's (1927) experiments in which dogs learned to salivate to a previously neutral stimulus that had been repeatedly presented shortly before food was given. Similarly, the historical prototype for instrumental learning is Thorndike's (1911) experiment in which hungry cats learned to make complex motor responses to obtain food and to escape from a puzzle box. A more frequently used prototype for instrumental learning is the free operant conditioning situation, devised by Skinner (1938), in which the rat learns to press a lever in a setting where such responses result in the delivery of food. More technical definitions will be given in later sections in which each kind of conditioning is considered in detail.

The distinction between the classical and instrumental paradigms has been of considerable theoretical interest for researchers in the field of learning, and the history of learning theories has been a series of efforts to delineate theoretically the relations between these two broad classes of learning experiments.

Attempts to differentiate between classical and instrumental conditioning in terms of the learning process involved have not been entirely successful. As a result, psychologists have relied on distinctions between the two in terms of experimental operations. The usual distinction refers to the consequences of the conditioned response (e.g., Grant, 1964; Kimble, 1961). The principle of reinforcement, or "law of effect" as Thorndike called it, means that the rewarding and punishing contingencies following responses influence the future occurrence of the responses. In classical conditioning the sequence of experimental events is independent of the subject's behavior; the experimenter has rather complete control over the stimulus events (including the reinforcements) and determines the temporal relations among these, irrespective of the subject's behavior. In contrast, in instrumental (or operant) conditioning the rewards and punishments occur as consequences of the subject's behavior; reinforcement is given only if the subject performs some arbitrarily specified response.

Both the classical and instrumental conditioning paradigms can be subdivided in terms of the functions of the reinforcing stimulus. The reinforcing stimulus can be a positive stimulus, which elicits approach behavior, or an aversive stimulus, which elicits withdrawal behavior. Classical conditioning is labeled *classical reward conditioning* if food or some other positive stimulus is used as the reinforcing, or unconditioned stimulus (US), and is called *classical defense conditioning* if the US is aversive, or noxious. In instrumental conditioning, the experimenter can strengthen a response by presenting a positive stimulus or by terminating an aversive stimulus contingent upon the occurrence of that response.

In instrumental conditioning the experimenter arbitrarily selects the response that must be made by the subject in order to obtain reinforcement. The experimenter can even select some characteristic of a single kind of response (amplitude, rate, duration, pattern, etc.) as the event leading to reinforcement. In classical conditioning the sequence of stimulus events is independent of the subject's behavior. However, some investigators have argued that although the experimental operations are different in the two paradigms, the actual behaviors and learning processes of the subject are quite similar (Grant, 1964; Kimmel, 1965; Prokasy, 1965). For example, Prokasy suggested that in classical eyelid conditioning the subject rather than the experimenter may be effectively controlling the relations between the response and the US, by timing his blinks to avoid the US.

Problems for a Developmental Analysis of Learning

In order to make statements about differences in the learning capacities of children at different age levels, it is necessary to give all of the children an equal opportunity to learn. It must be plausible to assume that the observed age differences in performance are not attributable to age differences in motivation, effectiveness of reinforcement, response or sensory capacities, etc. Children at different age levels may differ in their unconditioned responses to the specific stimulating situation. Older children may be less "emotional" in new situations and, thus, learning may be impeded or improved depending upon the specific circumstances. Furthermore, before asserting that differences in performance on a learning task reflect differences in learning *capacity*, we would need to be sure that the differences are not attributable simply to transfer of previous learning to the present learning task. Comparative psychologists, who study interspecies differences in learning capacity, have recognized that these variables influence learning and have attempted to devise research strategies to deal with the problems of controlling them. However, developmental psychologists, who face these problems when they investigate age differences in learning capacity, have seldom evidenced concern about them. Few developmental investigations of learning have been addressed to the complex problems of equating motivating and reinforcing conditions at different ages. Campbell (1967) critically examined some of these problems and addressed his research to this difficult task in a series of developmental studies with animals.

Bitterman (1960) has argued that *control by equation* is not likely to be achieved and has suggested *control by systematic variation* as an alternative. Applied to developmental studies, that is, studies of functional relations that appear to differ in children at different age levels, the essential feature of this type of control is to examine the functional relations at several levels of "contextual variables," such as motivation, reinforcement, and the other variables mentioned in the preceding paragraph. The developmental psychologist would need to determine the extent to which apparent differences between age groups are resistant to change when the training procedures are modified to reduce the differences and establish optimal levels of contextual variables for the deficient age group. Gollin (1965) has provided a more detailed discussion of the implications of this type of research strategy for developmental studies with children. The researcher studying the ontogeny of learning processes in the nonverbal, motorically immature infant is confronted with many of the problems of the comparative psychologist in addition to those unique to developmental research.

We will be concerned in the rest of this chapter with studies of classical conditioning in human infants, ranging in age from birth to three years. Virtually no work has been done on classical conditioning in older children; much work has been done with animals and human adults, but this work is outside the scope of this volume and is therefore not reviewed here. Studies of instrumental conditioning will be considered in the next chapter.

CLASSICAL CONDITIONING DESIGNS AND CONTROLS

Designs

The classical conditioning procedure is sufficiently familiar to students of psychology that a brief recitation of the essential features will suffice at this point. Classical conditioning refers to learning effects due uniquely to the contingency between a previously neutral or "conditional" stimulus (CS) and an unconditioned stimulus (US) that evokes a regular and measurable response in the organism. Conditioning is demonstrated when, as a result of the temporal pairing of the CS and US, some aspect or part of the unconditioned response (UR) to the US subsequently occurs to the CS. The part of the UR that occurs in the presence of the CS is labeled the conditioned response (CR).

In classical conditioning, the experimenter has complete control over the onset and termination of the CS and US. Several variations in the temporal spacing and ordering of these stimuli have been used; and although many of them have not been used frequently in conditioning studies with children, it is instructive to consider these variations briefly. The salient features of the variants are illustrated in Figure 3-1. In *simultaneous conditioning* the CS and US are presented and terminated at the same time; in *delayed conditioning* the CS is presented before the US and is maintained at least until the onset of the US; in *trace conditioning* the CS is presented and terminated before the onset of the US; in *backward conditioning* the CS and US are paired but the US is always presented before the CS. [Backward conditioning is difficult to obtain and has therefore often been used as a control procedure. However, Konorski (1948) considered backward conditioning to be an "inhibitory conditioning" paradigm (see below).] In *temporal conditioning* a time interval functions as

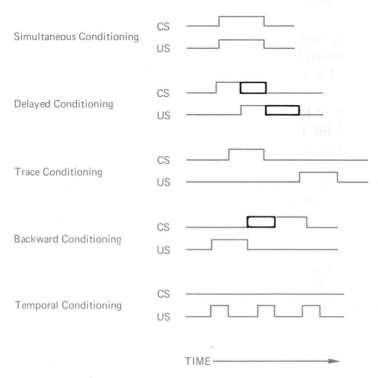

Fig. 3-1.   Classical conditioning designs. Upstrokes indicate onset; downstrokes, offset. Boxes indicate alternative procedures.

the CS; the US is presented at regular time intervals (e.g., once every 30 seconds), and the CR should occur, if the procedure is successful, at the appropriate time interval when the US is omitted.

After the learning phase, utilizing one of these conditioning procedures, an *extinction* phase is usually given. In extinction the CS is usually presented alone, with no further presentations of the US. A variant of this procedure is to present the CS and US unpaired, but this technique has not been used in extinction in any studies with infants (although it has frequently been used as a control procedure).

The delayed conditioning procedure has been used in most of the conditioning studies with infants, with the interval between CS and US subject to wide variation in different studies. Soviet investigators have frequently begun with simultaneous conditioning and then shifted to a delayed conditioning procedure over successive days. Temporal conditioning has recently been employed in two studies (Brackbill, Fitzgerald, and Lintz, 1967; Lipsitt and Ambrose, 1967), following rather limited use in previous studies of normal feeding schedules (Bystroletova, 1954; Krachkovskaia, 1959; Marquis, 1931).

Controls

Control procedures have been developed to distinguish between effects that result uniquely from the temporal relation between the CS and US and non-conditioned behavioral changes that do not result from this contingency. It is assumed that "true" conditioning is an associative relation between the CS and US, or between the CS and UR (see Lipsitt, 1963). Two effects that are frequently noted in classical conditioning but that are regarded as nonassociational are *sensitization* and *pseudoconditioning*. Sensitization is an augmentation of the response to the CS as a result of repeated exposure of the CS (with no exposure of the US). Pseudoconditioning is a general sensitization of the organism resulting from presentation of the US; after it occurs, any stimulus arouses a response that looks like a CR. Sensitization and pseudoconditioning presumably reflect a lowering of response thresholds. Before the repeated exposures of the stimulus, the particular stimulus being used as the CS may be subthreshold, too weak to arouse a response; but as a result of the repeated exposures, the threshold may be lowered and the stimulus magnitude that was previously subthreshold may be greater than the new threshold and therefore capable of arousing a response. When this occurs, the CS is no longer neutral with respect to the response that was to be conditioned; the "CS" becomes a US, because it is now capable of arousing the response without intervention of learning processes. In sensitization the threshold affected seems to be specific to the CS; in pseudoconditioning the thresholds of many different stimuli seem to be affected.

Table 3-1 gives a list of traditional control procedures used in studies of classical conditioning in infants, the purposes of these procedures, and examples of studies in which they were used. Rescorla (1967) analyzed these control procedures and suggested that some of them introduce nonassociative factors not present in the conditioning procedures (CS alone, US alone, novel CS alone) while others (US and CS unpaired, backward conditioning) shift the excitatory CS-US relation into an inhibitory relation. In America, investigators of classical conditioning processes have been concerned primarily with conditioned excitatory processes and have frequently used a control procedure that is biased toward the inhibitory side. Rescorla suggested that a control with truly random presentation of CS and US would provide the most appropriate baseline condition against which to compare both the inhibitory and excitatory kinds of conditioning relations. Jensen (1961) and Prokasy (1965) have suggested a similar control procedure for classical conditioning studies, but it has not been employed in infant conditioning studies nor has it been used frequently in classical conditioning studies with adults.

A careful examination of control procedures and their functions may be of particular significance for developmental studies of classical conditioning. Researchers in the Soviet Union (e.g., Luria, 1961) have held that young children have weak inhibitory and strong excitatory processes, but they typically have not used experimental designs that allow an assessment of these different conditioning processes. The better controlled conditioning studies with infants have

Table 3-1

Control Procedures in Studies of Classical Conditioning

Procedure	Variable controlled	Illustrative studies
CS presented alone (i.e., without any US presentations)	Sensitization (and maturation of unconditioned ability of the conditional stimulus to arouse the response)	Kaye (1967); Lintz et. al. (1967); Wickens and Wickens (1940)
Novel CS alone	Maturation effects on UR to CS	Kaye (1967); Wenger (1936)
US alone (CS presented only on test trials, on which US is omitted)	Sensitization effects of US on unconditioned response to novel CS	Brackbill et al. (1967); Kaye (1967); Wenger, (1936); Wickens and Wickens (1940)
CS and US unpaired	Sensitization, pseudoconditioning	Kaye (1965, 1967); Lintz et al. (1967); Lipsitt and Kaye (1964); Lipsitt et al. (1966a); Marquis (1931)
Backward conditioning	Sensitization, pseudoconditioning	Brackbill et al. (1967)
Trace conditioning	Sensitization, pseudoconditioning	Marum (1962)

used "between-subjects" experimental designs in which different groups are presented different CS-US contingencies (CS-US paired, versus CS-US explicitly unpaired) (Brackbill et al., 1967; Kaye, 1967; Lintz et al., 1967; Lipsitt and Kaye, 1964). That is, a conditioned inhibition group is compared with a conditioned excitation group without a baseline control against which to assess these effects.

It should be noted that these control procedures are also needed in the instrumental or operant learning paradigm. In attempts to determine which effects are uniquely attributable to the contingency of reinforcement upon the response, the issues are the same as in classical conditioning (Premack, 1965).

General Considerations

An important consideration in classical conditioning studies, in contrast to instrumental conditioning studies, is the selection of the US, because the US uniquely determines the UR (and hence the CR) in classical conditioning. The US that is selected must reliably elicit the UR and must not produce appreciable habituation over repeated conditioning trials (habituation is a decrease in reactivity). The UR is not a simple discrete response, but rather is a complex of responses from which the experimenter must choose components to be studied as the dependent variable or CR. His choice of the CR will be determined by the conditions of the experiment, the responses available for observation, and the type of equipment that he has available for refined measurement of the response. Pavlov deliberately chose to measure and record salivation and, for the most part, to ignore such aspects of the dog's behavior as licking, swallowing, and making approach movements to the food. It is generally acknowledged that the CS does not fully substitute for the US in eliciting all components of the UR, but rather serves to signal that food is about to be presented; the CR is thus seen as a component of the UR. A similar analysis of the relations between the UR and CR could be made for aversive conditioning when a noxious stimulus (e.g., shock, strong odor, or air puff) is used as a US.

The problems involved in designing a classical conditioning experiment and defining the CR have not been minor, as recent reviews of the history of cardiac conditioning (Shearn, 1961) and eyelid conditioning (Grant, 1964; Prokasy, 1965) clearly illustrate. A recently sounded note of caution bears repeating:

> One ought not to expect to get exactly the same results from sick dogs and healthy dogs, from alert dogs and drowsy dogs . . . . One cannot expect to get exactly the same results when different procedures are used; one can hardly expect to discover laws of conditioning when one's data are made up primarily of responses which are not conditioned but which are sensitized. Comparisons between different procedures and different responses are also complicated by the bewildering complexity of organismic variables. To see any order which may exist among different conditioning experiments it is necessary that the irrelevant variables be understood and brought under control. This involves a tremendous amount of methodological experimentation, and it is probable that the job has to be done anew with each different response system that is investigated. It is regrettably the case that for most response systems the basic methodological work simply has not been done. (Grant, 1964, p. 19.)

This caution has particular significance for investigators concerned with the ontogenetic study of conditioning. While the growing list of conditionable responses in the human infant testifies to the ingenuity and increased sophistication of researchers dealing with this perplexing experimental subject, the basic methodological work that would allow parametric investigation within a single response system of the infant has not been done.

Recent studies on the ontogeny of learning in infrahuman organisms point up the complexity of organismic variables confronting the developmental researcher. We will not attempt to review in detail the studies of classical conditioning in infrahuman infant organisms but can refer the student to a recent review of these studies by Zimmerman and Torrey (1965). Briefly, the available evidence from animal studies indicates that age differences in rate of conditioning reported by some investigators (Fuller, Easler, and Banks, 1950; Solenkova and Nikitina, 1960) have been found to depend more upon the response index chosen (Green, 1962), the type of CS used (Cornwell and Fuller, 1961), and the interval between the CS and US (Bykov, 1960), than upon clear differences in learning capacities (Stanley, Cornwell, Poggiani, and Trattner, 1963).

CLASSICAL REWARD CONDITIONING

Conditioned Salivation

The prototype for classical reward conditioning is the Pavlovian experiment in which the US is food and the measure of conditioning is amount of salivation. The natural extension of the Pavlovian salivary conditioning experiment was made by Krasnogorski (1907), who used swallowing as his measure of conditioning in infants. He also used "salometers" (small cups fitted over the salivary gland with tubes attached) to collect saliva. On the basis of his observations of a 14 month old infant, he concluded that accumulations of saliva accompanied the act of swallowing, and thus the amount of salivation could be estimated by the number of swallows elicited by the CS. In later experiments, Krasnogorski and his colleagues measured swallowing responses by means of a tambour placed over the thyroid cartilage. (See Razran, 1933, for a detailed description of these early conditioning studies.) On the basis of his results, Krasnogorski (1913) concluded that infants cannot acquire any conditioned responses until the fourth or fifth month of life because of a lack of functional maturity of the cortex during the first months. However, Krasnogorski's conclusions about the conditionability of the infant during the first three months of life proved, as we know now, to be premature, due largely to his choice of the response to be conditioned. Although salivation is an appropriate response for conditioning in adults and older infants, the salivary glands are not fully functional in the newborn. Also, Kasatkin and Levikova (1935a) argued that swallowing as a measurable response develops later than sucking in infants; they suggested, therefore, that sucking is a more appropriate response for conditioning studies with young infants.

Conditioned Sucking in Neonates

One of the first references to conditioned responses in the young infant is found in the work of Bekhterev and Shchelovanov, who suggested that if an infant in about the third week of life is placed in the position associated with breast feeding, searching movements will be exhibited, as well as sucking and mouth-opening responses (see Kasatkin and Levikova, 1935a). Denisova and Figurin (1929) systematically studied breast-fed infants as young as 10 days of age in the natural feeding situation. They reported that 10 of 11 infants observed began to make anticipatory sucking responses during the third week of life (21 to 27 days) as soon as they were placed in the position characteristically associated with natural feeding. They also reported, interestingly enough, that the anticipatory sucking responses to proprioceptive stimulation (position) disappeared at about 3 months of age and that anticipatory sucking subsequently occurred only as the child's face and mouth approached the mother's breast.

In the absence of the appropriate controls, caution is required in interpreting this reported "conditioning" phenomenon, but these results were the first to suggest evidence for conditioned "inhibition of delay" in infants. In his discussion of various types of internal inhibition, Pavlov wrote:

> . . . if a regular interval of sufficient duration is established between the commencement of a conditioned stimulus and its reinforcement by the unconditioned stimulus, the former becomes ineffective during the first part of its isolated action; during the second part of its action a positive excitatory effect appears, and this increases progressively in intensity as the moment approaches when the unconditioned stimulus has customarily been applied (inhibition of delay). In the above manner a continuous and most exact adaptation of the organism to its environment is effected, revealing a most delicate adjustment of the antagonistic nervous processes of the higher animals. (Pavlov 1927, p. 106.)

Pavlov's concept of inhibition of delay may seem to be misnamed, because it is not delay that is inhibited but rather the CR. The CR is inhibited or delayed until just before the customary time of presentation of the US.

Several investigators have interpreted inhibition of delay in terms of differential reinforcement of an instrumentally conditioned response (Damianopoulos, 1967; Kimmel, 1965).

The early interest of American psychologists in classical conditioning in infants was focused on the question of the conditionability of the neonate, but there have been only a few American studies of classical reward conditioning in neonates (Kaye, 1965, 1967; Lipsitt and Ambrose, 1967; Lipsitt and Kaye, 1964; Lipsitt et al., 1966a; Marquis, 1931; Wenger, 1936). A review of these studies illustrates the increasing sophistication of researchers in selecting optimal levels of contextual variables for use in investigations of conditioning. They also demonstrate an increasing refinement in the control procedures used in assessing the effects of the CS-US contingency.

Marquis's (1931) study of anticipatory sucking was the first on conditioning in the human neonate. Her study was remarkable for its rigorous experimental control of the infants' early feeding experiences over the first nine days of life; it is not likely to be replicated in contemporary research laboratories because of the usual unavailability of infants after four or five days of age. She used every feeding over the first nine days of life for her experimental conditioning sessions. Each infant had a total of 50 experimental sessions and between 100 and 250 conditioning trials. Both anticipatory and nutritive sucking were recorded by means of a balloon fastened under the infant's chin and connected to a recording device. Stabilimeter records of activity and observations of crying were also used. Marquis's conditioning procedure consisted of presenting a buzzer (CS) for five seconds before presenting the nursing bottle (US). She also presented the buzzer again after the infant had begun sucking and at "various times while the infant was sucking." Two to five pairings of the CS and US were presented during each experimental feeding. Using anticipatory sucking and decreases in activity and crying as her dependent variables, Marquis reported that seven of eight subjects on whom complete data were obtained showed evidence of conditioning. Within five days, eight of ten subjects showed anticipatory sucking and mouth opening responses to the buzzer, as well as decreases in crying and activity. Figure 3-2 shows the course of conditioning over the nine days of the study. Marquis did not present the data for her control subjects, who received buzzer presentations uncorrelated with feedings, but she reported that they did not exhibit "conditioning reactions."

Even though this control for pseudoconditioning was included, there are several reasons for caution in the interpretation of Marquis's results. Results from the control subjects were not presented nor were any statistics for the conditioning effects reported. More important to a clear interpretation of these results within a classical conditioning paradigm is that it is difficult to understand Marquis's method of presenting the CS-US contingency and to determine what interstimulus interval was used in recording "anticipatory" responses. An examination of the reported procedure indicates that it could be trace conditioning, backward conditioning, or a combination of both. Marquis reported that she stood inside a curtained compartment, outside the infant's view, during the intertrial interval. The CS (buzzer) was presented for five seconds, and then "as soon as possible after the end of the buzzer, the bottle was inserted in the infant's mouth and the buzzer rung for five sec. more after the infant started sucking" (Marquis, 1931, p. 181). Marquis recorded as CRs "the reactions after the buzzer began to sound." On the basis of the procedures reported we would expect to find evidence of trace conditioning, since the onset of the US followed the offset of the CS by some time interval of appreciable though short duration. It is not possible to determine from Marquis's report of her results whether the CR was delayed for the appropriate interval of time, but the apparent decline in the group curve after the 7th day of conditioning (see Figure 3-2) may reflect the effects of trace conditioning. Bijou and Baer (1965) have reinterpreted the results of Marquis's experiment in the context of operant conditioning; we will return to a discussion of instrumental reinforcement contingencies in classical reward conditioning later in this chapter.

Wenger (1936) criticized Marquis's experiment for its lack of adequate controls and its use of subjective response measurement procedures. In his own study, with two newborns, he obtained no evidence of conditioned sucking.

The clearest evidence for classical reward conditioning in the neonate has been provided by Lipsitt and his collaborators (Kaye, 1967; Lipsitt and Kaye, 1964; Lipsitt et al., 1966a). The results of these studies clearly illustrate the necessity for pseudoconditioning control procedures.

Lipsitt and Kaye (1964) included 10 infants, 3 to 4 days of age, in an experimental group and 10 in a pseudoconditioning control group. Both groups received 5 baseline trials in which the CS (tone) was presented for 15 seconds.

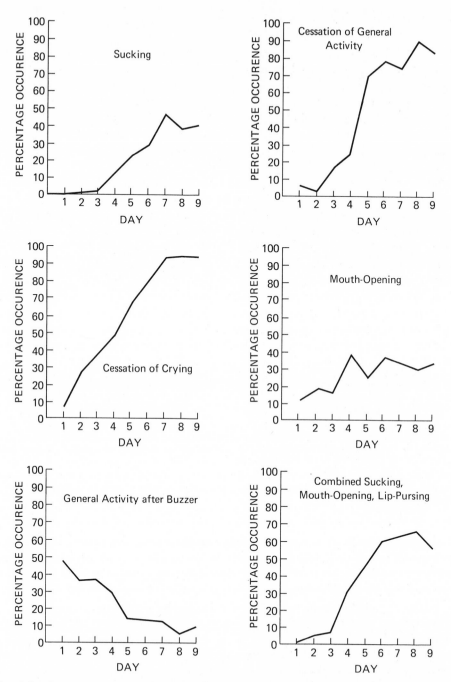

Fig. 3-2.   Percentage occurrence of different conditioning indexes (each representing number of times a given reaction occurred at the sound of the buzzer, divided by number of pairings of bottle and buzzer on each day). (From Marquis, 1931, Fig. 1, p. 487. Reprinted by permission of the author and the Journal Press.)

The experimental subjects were given 20 pairings of the CS and US (pacifier); on each trial the CS began 1 second before the US and remained on for 15 seconds, and the CS and US terminated simultaneously. Five CS-alone test trials were given (one after every fourth conditioning trial). The control group received nonpaired presentations of the CS and US for 25 trials. For this group the pacifier was presented for 15 seconds, approximately 30 seconds after offset of the CS. Thereafter, the subjects from both groups received up to 30 extinction trials. After the first 10 extinction trials, extinction was discontinued as soon as the infant failed to make a sucking response on 2 successive trials. Sucking responses to the tone were counted during training and extinction.

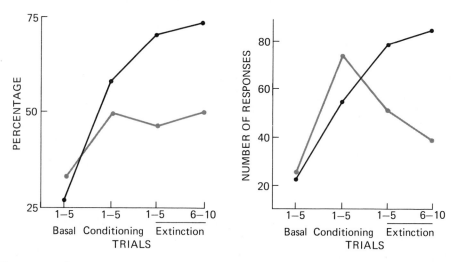

Fig. 3-3. **Classical conditioning of the anticipatory sucking response. Darker line, experimental group; lighter line, control group. Left panel: percentage of trials on which at least one response occurred. Right panel: absolute number of CRs. (From Lipsitt and Kaye, 1964, Fig. 1, p. 30. Reprinted by permission of the authors and publisher.)**

The experimental and control groups are compared in Figure 3-3, showing the percentage of CS-alone trials on which the response occurred, and the total number of responses to the CS alone. Although both groups showed an increase in sucking to tone, there was a progressive separation between the two groups over training and a significant difference between the groups during extinction trials. Lipsitt and Kaye suggested that the increased sucking to tone by the control subjects may reflect sensitization or pseudoconditioning effects. However, they concluded that conditioning was demonstrated, because the increase in sucking in the experimental group was greater and more stable than in the control group. Furthermore, the rate of response decrement over the extinction trials not shown in Figure 3-3 was greater in the experimental group than in the control group, as would be expected if conditioning occurred in the experimental group and pseudoconditioning occurred in the control group.

The results of the Lipsitt and Kaye study clearly illustrate the need for appropriate control procedures. The changes in the sucking response to tone by the control group "mocked" the type of change in response we would predict to result from "true" conditioning. The control group showed an increase in sucking over the "training" trials and an apparent decrease during "extinction." Sucking responses occur in the newborn spontaneously, in the absence of any experimentally introduced eliciting stimulus. The increase in sucking to tone by the control group may reflect habituation of an unconditioned suppression of sucking in the presence of a novel stimulus (Bronshtein and Petrova, 1952). Without appropriate control procedures such as were utilized here, we would have no basis for evaluating apparent evidence of "unstable" conditioning or of increases in conditioned-like responses.

Kaye (1967) recently attempted to answer several questions raised by Lipsitt and Kaye's interpretation of their results as demonstrating conditioning. In their study, sucking movements were recorded only during the 15 second interval in which the tone was presented, and therefore it is not known whether the effect obtained during extinction simply reflected higher overall sucking rates in the experimental group than in the control group. As Kaye observed, "If rates were rising for the experimental subjects, then attributing the differences between the treatments to the pairing of the tone and nipple was gratuitous, and the effect could be handled more parsimoniously as a phenomenon other than 'conditioning' such as 'arousal' and/or sensitization" (Kaye, 1967, p. 37). Kaye's study was largely a replication of the previous study but with additional sensitization control groups. Also, sucking responses were counted throughout the experimental session so that the frequency of their occurrence on the CS-alone trials could be compared with the frequency during the no-tone intertrial intervals. Six groups of newborns, ten per group, were studied: an experimental group (CS and US paired), a control group given nonpaired presentations of the CS and US (as in Lipsitt and Kaye's study), a CS-alone group, and three US-alone groups. Results for the last four groups—the sensitization control groups—were not reported in detail by Kaye; therefore, our discussion of this study will focus on his more detailed analysis of changes in sucking behavior in the experimental group and nonpaired control group. Except that the US duration was extended from 15 seconds to 19 seconds, the training and extinction procedures for these two groups were identical to those used in the Lipsitt and Kaye study.

The results of the Lipsitt and Kaye study were essentially replicated, but with increased differences between the experimental and control groups (see Figure 3-4). The increased differences between the groups may reflect the longer interval in which the tone and pacifier were paired in Kaye's study. The results of these studies provide clear evidence for conditioned sucking in the newborn.

In a study by Lipsitt et al. (1966a), the CS was a flexible rubber tube and the US was a five percent solution of dextrose in water. The subjects were 20 newborns. Conditioning consisted of presenting the CS for 15 seconds and delivering the dextrose solution through the tube during the last 5 seconds of this interval. An experimental group was given 6 baseline trials (tube alone),

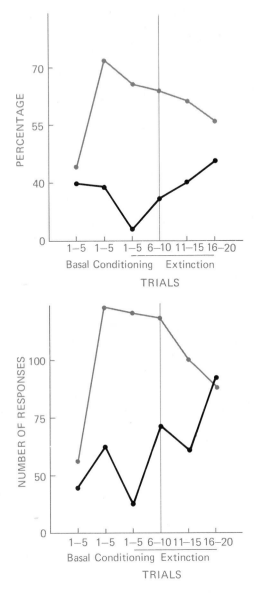

Fig. 3-4. Classical conditioning of the anticipatory sucking response. Lighter line, experimental group; darker line, control group. Top panel: percentage of trials on which at least one response occurred. Bottom panel: absolute number of CRs. (From Kaye, 1967, Fig. 12, p. 39. Reprinted by permission of the author and Academic Press, Inc.)

10 conditioning trials, 10 extinction trials, 5 reconditioning trials, and finally, 5 more extinction trials. A control group was given tube presentation trials but received the dextrose solution through a syringe 30 seconds after withdrawal of the tube. The experimental group was also presented with the syringe 30 seconds after tube withdrawal, but no dextrose solution was delivered. Both

groups had the same numbers of tube presentations, dextrose presentations, and total syringe and tube stimulations. The measure of conditioning was the number of sucking responses made during the first 10 seconds of each tube trial, and the two groups were compared on the amount of sucking over conditioning and extinction trials, relative to the amount on baseline trials. The amount of tube sucking in the experimental group increased over conditioning trials significantly more than in the control group (see Figure 3-5). The investigators interpreted the difference as a learning effect; but the experimental effect appears to have been relatively weak, and the changes in sucking behavior

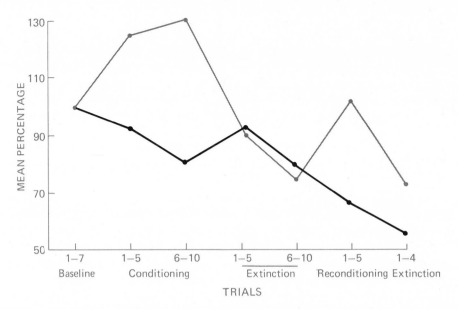

Fig. 3-5. Changes in sucking rate for experimental (lighter line) and control (darker line) groups. Mean ratio of number of sucks per trial in each period to number of sucks per trial in the baseline period. (From Lipsitt *et al.*, 1966a, Fig. 2, p. 166. Reprinted by permission of the authors and Academic Press, Inc.)

were not as stable as those obtained by Lipsitt and his colleagues in their previous studies of conditioned sucking in newborns. Stronger support for the conditioning interpretation would be provided by evidence of a residual separation between the groups during extinction, and by re-establishment of the originally obtained differences over reconditioning and subsequent extinction trials.

Conditioned Sucking in Older Infants

Denisova and Figurin (1929) developed the first laboratory procedures for studying sucking as a classically conditioned response in infants. Using a delayed conditioning procedure (see Figure 3-1), they presented a CS (visual or auditory stimulus) for 15 seconds before the onset of the US (bottle or breast feeding) and for an additional 30 seconds with the US. One conditioning procedure included all normal feedings over the first month of life, and each feeding provided the infants with a single conditioning trial. The infants were thus given five to seven conditioning trials in each 24 hours. In a second procedure one experimental feeding was given each day, and six to ten paired presentations of the CS and US (bottle) were given in each experimental feeding. Denisova and Figurin reported that conditioned sucking first appeared at 33 to 36 days of age.

Soviet studies of classical conditioning have focused primarily on age and the sensory modality of the CS as independent variables influencing the rate of conditioning in infants (Denisova and Figurin, 1929; Kasatkin, 1957; Kasatkin and Levikova, 1935a, 1935b; Kasatkin, Mirzoiants, and Khokhitva, 1953). Denisova and Figurin were the first of these investigators to study conditioning as a function of the sensory modality of the CS employed. In the study described in the preceding paragraph, they compared the effectiveness of a bell, a flashing red light, and combination of the auditory and visual stimuli as CSs. Their measure of conditioning was the occurrence of anticipatory sucking during the 15 second interstimulus interval (i.e., the interval between the onset of the CS and the onset of the US). They found that conditioned sucking to the auditory stimulus appeared earlier than to the visual stimulus and that the visual component of the compound CS was ineffective in eliciting anticipatory sucking when presented alone. These results and the results of subsequent studies by Kasatkin (Kasatkin, 1948, 1952, 1957; Kasatkin and Levikova, 1935a, 1935b) led Soviet investigators to conceptualize a developmental sequence for conditioning as a function of the sensory modality of the CS. Brackbill (1962) and Brackbill and Koltsova (1967) have provided detailed discussions of the Soviet studies that provide the basis for the developmental ranking of CSs of different sensory modalities. Although similar concepts of a hierarchical structure of sensory systems have been suggested by other investigators of learning processes in children (Renshaw, 1930; White, 1964; Zaporozhets, 1961), no clear conclusions can be reached on the basis of the classical conditioning data obtained by the Soviet investigators. It is known that conditioning depends upon such characteristics of the CS as intensity and duration, and also upon their interactions with characteristics of the US (Kamin, 1965). However, parametric investigations of such stimulus characteristics within a sensory modality have not been done with infants. An auditory stimulus may be more effective in eliciting attention than a visual stimulus simply because a visual stimulus can be avoided by change of position or eye closure while an auditory stimulus cannot be avoided by the infant.

These early Soviet studies of classical reward conditioning in infants lacked many of the controls characteristic of contemporary American studies of conditioning, and yet they represented major contributions to the refinement of experimental laboratory techniques and instrumentation of response measures. For example, automatic recording of anticipatory sucking responses was obtained by attaching under the chin of the infant a hollow rubber ball or balloon which was connected pneumatically to a recording device.

Kantrow (1937) studied conditioned sucking in infants ranging from 1.5 to 4 months of age; the study, conducted at the University of Iowa under the direction of Orvis Irwin, provides an excellent example of refined response measurement and stimulus control. A linen harness placed under the infant's chin was mechanically connected by strings to a kymograph pen, providing a graphic record of the sucking responses; a second pen recorded the onset, duration, and offset of the CS and US. The CS (a buzzer) was presented for 5 seconds before the presentation of the US (nursing bottle), and the CS and US overlapped for 15 seconds (this is the delayed conditioning procedure, illustrated in Figure 3-1). The infant was allowed to continue sucking for 15 to 20 seconds after the termination of the CS. The intertrial interval (the interval between the termination of the US at the end of one trial and the onset of the CS on the next trial) was 25 to 75 seconds long. Kantrow's measure of conditioning was the number of sucking responses that occurred during the 5 second interstimulus interval, corrected for the number of sucking responses that occurred during the intertrial interval immediately preceding the onset of the CS. Kantrow selected what she called the "critical control period" to assess conditioned sucking; this was the 5 second period in the immediately preceding intertrial interval in which the largest number of sucking responses occurred. She considered that conditioning was demonstrated when the mean amount of sucking in the 5 second CS-US interval exceeded the amount of sucking in the "critical control period." Infants received four experimental feedings a day until stable conditioned sucking was obtained. Kantrow's use of the "critical control period" assured that her conditioning effect was not attributable simply to a generalized increase in sucking over conditioning sessions but rather reflected an increased response to the auditory CS.

Subsequently, Kantrow studied extinction of the conditioned sucking response and employed an extinction criterion of three successive presentations of the CS alone without the occurrence of sucking. Although the stable increase in sucking to the CS over conditioning sessions and the subsequent decrease during extinction strongly suggest that conditioned sucking was demonstrated in this study, the lack of pseudoconditioning controls necessitates caution in interpreting these results as evidence of "true" conditioning.

The results of Soviet studies are frequently interpreted as evidence that classical reward conditioning cannot be established during the first three weeks of life (e.g., Denisova and Figurin, 1929; Kasatkin and Levikova, 1935a, 1935b; Mirzoiants, 1954). The Soviet investigators have frequently reported unstable conditioning at an earlier age, based on observations of isolated sucking responses occurring contiguously with the CS; however, the lack of appropriate controls excludes the possibility of determining whether the effects were due uniquely to the CS-US contingency.

Other Conditioned Responses

The Babkin reflex is an unconditioned mouth opening or gaping response elicited in young infants by pressure on the palms. Kaye (1965) has demonstrated conditioning of this reflex in infants from two to four days old, using arm flexion as the CS. The control groups were a CS-alone group and a US-alone group.

Lipsitt and Ambrose (1967) have recently reported evidence of temporal conditioning in newborns. The measure of conditioning was behavioral change in any of three response systems, respiration, heart rate, and motility. They used three types of stimulation successively presented to individual subjects as their US (anise oil odorant, sound of a wooden ball falling on a wooden surface, and vestibulation or rocking). Using a "within-subjects" design (each subject serving as his own control), the investigators obtained evidence of reliable temporal conditioning.

Head-turning and eye movements have been studied in the classical reward conditioning paradigm with infants beginning at 1 month of age (Kasatkin et al., 1953; Koch, 1965; Mirzoiants, 1954). Kasatkin et al. (1953) developed an apparatus for recording head movements of infants. The infant's right and left head-turning responses were recorded by means of a head harness mechanically attached to a kymograph. Using flashing colored lights positioned to the right of the infant's head as the US and various simple and complex auditory stimuli as the CS, Kasatkin and his collaborators obtained conditioned head-turning to sound by 2.5 months of age and stable conditioning by the fifth month. Koch (1965) has studied the relative effectiveness of unconditioned stimuli as a function of familiarity (mother's face, stranger's face, and changing toys) on conditioned responding in 2 and 3 month old infants. Other studies of conditioned head-turning, by Papoušek (1959, 1967a, 1967b), will be discussed in the next chapter, dealing with instrumental conditioning.

Conclusions

Sucking and related mouth movements made with no eliciting stimulus placed in the mouth have been the most frequently used responses in studies of classical reward conditioning in infants. Both the Soviet investigators and earlier American psychologists (Kantrow, 1937; Marquis, 1931; Mateer, 1918) have used anticipatory CRs (responses occurring in the CS-US interstimulus interval) as their index of conditioning. With the possible exception of Marquis, these investigators have seldom obtained clear evidence of stable conditioning in the neonate. However, later investigators studied independent groups of experimental and control subjects and compared the groups on occurrence of CRs to CS alone on test trials and extinction trials (e.g., Kaye, 1965, 1967; Lipsitt and Kaye, 1964; Lipsitt et al., 1966a). These investigators have obtained clear evidence of conditioning in neonates.

With appropriate controls, the more recent studies have demonstrated reliable conditioning effects at early ages, even though the effects are relatively unstable. Lacking these control procedures, the Soviet investigators have been forced to adopt the position that conditioning has occurred only when "stable" conditioning has been demonstrated for individual infants. Consequently, they cannot identify "unstable conditioning," and have obtained what they identify as "conditioning" only at later ages. When Soviet investigators speak of an anticipatory CR, they seem to be talking about a response characterized by a pronounced intensification of sucking to the CS. However, as Lipsitt (1963) has suggested, conditioning may actually occur earlier than the ages reported by Soviet investigators if one selects a less stringent criterion for conditioned sucking.

The studies that have demonstrated conditioning in the neonate have, in effect, compared two conditioning groups, a conditioned inhibition group (CS-US unpaired) and a conditioned excitation group (CS-US paired). Differences between the groups allow the experimenter to conclude that conditioning occurred, but the effects of the two kinds of conditioning process cannot be independently assessed without additional control groups.

Although we have classified the preceding studies with infants as investigations of classical reward conditioning on the basis of the experimenter's explicit operations, an examination of the experimental situation suggests an alternative interpretation of the "effective" stimulus and response relations, using an instrumental learning context. Although the experimenter specifies that the CS-US presentations are independent of the subject's response, the choice of interstimulus intervals and the latency of the response investigated may determine whether the temporal contiguity between the CR and US, or between the CS and UR, is maximized in the conditioning situation. We can consider such stimuli as milk, nipple, and colored lights as reinforcing stimuli and the CS as a discriminative stimulus that marks the occasions on which sucking or head movements will be reinforced (Bijou and Baer, 1965). In most classical conditioning studies, it is difficult to specify whether the response being conditioned is "effectively" controlled by the eliciting stimulus or by consequent stimulation.

Recent studies of classical conditioning in adults suggest that the temporal relation between the CR and US, and between the CS and UR, may be of considerable importance (Boneau, 1958; J. E. Jones, 1961; Kimmel, 1965; Prokasy, 1965). The frequent use of a long interstimulus interval by Soviet investigators could maximize instrumental learning contingencies. Some investigators of conditioned sucking in infants have used CS presentations as long as 15 to 20 seconds (e.g., Denisova and Figurin, 1929), and many of the Soviet investigators have progressively lengthened the interstimulus interval over the course of their conditioning procedures (e.g., Kasatkin, 1957). J. E. Jones (1961) has predicted that differences in the latency of the response to be conditioned would be influenced by the interstimulus interval that is initially used. Apparent age differences in acquisition rate may be attributable, in part, to age differences in the latency of the response to be conditioned.

Sameroff (1968a) has recently suggested that all conditioned sucking studies with infants should be classified as questionable with respect to the type of conditioning involved. His argument seems to be based on the suggestion that the mouth movement response without an oral stimulus is quite different from sucking on a nipple and that the sucking response is a prepotent response in the hungry infant. "The potentiation of this response and the inability of the investigator to truly decide what elicited the response . . . when it occurs does not make sucking an ideal response to use in studies of classical conditioning"

(Sameroff, 1968a, p. 19). The questions that Sameroff has raised are not unique to the sucking response but are problems for most of the response classes studied in the classical conditioning paradigm, including conditioned salivation (Sheffield, 1965).

CLASSICAL AVERSIVE CONDITIONING

Preliminary Considerations

The most frequently cited example of classical aversive conditioning in infants is Watson and Rayner's (1920) study of "conditioned fear" in Albert, a nine month old infant. (The study is also discussed in Chapters 10 and 12.) Although Albert responded at the outset with crying and vigorous startle responses to loud sounds, his unconditioned response to white rats, rabbits, and other furry objects was one of positive approach and manipulation. The usual report of this study cites the use of classical conditioning procedures in which the previously neutral or positive object (the rat) was paired with the primary aversive stimulus (loud noise). On subsequent presentations of the rat, Albert responded with conditioned fear responses of crying and withdrawal. Furthermore, on test trials Albert evidenced fear responses generalized to other furry objects such as a rabbit and a fur coat. However, as Church (1966) has observed, a careful examination of Watson and Rayner's training procedures indicates that this experiment is a study of instrumental conditioning, and not of classical conditioning. The primary aversive stimulus (loud noise) was not made contingent upon the occurrence of the CS (white rat) but rather upon Albert's response of touching the rat. Evidence for instrumental escape and avoidance responses is found in Watson and Rayner's report that conditioned fear responses were not evoked as long as Albert had his thumb in his mouth. Evidently, Albert learned to put his thumb in his mouth when the CS was presented. Strictly speaking, then, the Watson and Rayner study is one of the few experimental studies of punishment in the infant research literature, rather than the first of many studies of classical aversive conditioning.

A study that is not strictly relevant in this chapter, because of the age of the subjects, was conducted by Spelt (1948). The subjects were human fetuses in utero, ranging in age from seven to nine months from conception. A loud clapper was the US, and vibrotactile stimulation served as the CS. On test trials, as few as 15 paired stimulations resulted in movements to the tactile stimulus when presented alone, according to Spelt. As many as 5 to 11 successive CRs were obtained, and it was reported that one fetus exhibited retention over an 18 day period. The behavior of control subjects, although given too few trials to constitute a truly adequate test, suggested that response to the vibrotactile stimulation did not develop as a function of sheer passage of time. Moreover, the conditioning procedure was applied to nonpregnant females with the result that no conditioned-like abdominal responses occurred. Although complications in the research design render the Spelt results difficult to interpret (see Lipsitt,

1963, p. 151), the demonstration of an acquisition and extinction effect in the same subjects suggests that replication of the prenatal conditioning phenomenon would probably produce positive effects.

The early studies of aversive conditioning in infants involved a direct extension of Bekhterev's (1913) general procedures for establishing what he called "associative reflexes" in dogs. Shock to the dog's foot or leg initially elicits withdrawal or "protective" reflexes; Bekhterev studied the development of similar withdrawal responses to previously neutral stimuli that had been paired with shock.

Marinesco and Kreindler (1933), using a modification of Bekhterev's procedures, performed an extensive series of conditioning experiments with infants from 25 days to 3.5 years of age. Shock to the infant's foot served as the US; the CS was the sound of a metronome. Foot movements were recorded by means of a thread attached to the subject's limb and connected to the marker on a kymograph through a pulley system. Graphic records of conditioned and unconditioned limb movements were obtained, and event markers recorded the onsets and durations of the CS and US. The stimulus durations used in these studies were extremely long; the CS was presented for 50 seconds before the onset of a 20 second US. Classical conditioning studies have generally shown that the frequency of conditioned responding increases with increasing intensity of the US, and results of recent avoidance conditioning studies suggest that increasing the duration of the US increases its "intensity" (Church, LoLordo, Overmier, Solomon, and Turner, 1966; Overmier, 1966). Furthermore, the studies of aversive conditioning with adults suggest that a shorter CS-US interval results in a faster rate of conditioning (Hall, 1966; Kimble, 1961). Marinesco and Kreindler reported no success in conditioning infants at 25 days but their method of presenting data does not permit a determination of the degree of success they had with infants below 2 years of age. Many infants were seen over several conditioning sessions, and evidence for retention of conditioned responses was found when infants were tested several months after original conditioning. Furthermore, Marinesco and Kreindler demonstrated, clearly for older children, many of the phenomena of conditioning disclosed in experiments by Pavlov (1927) and Bekhterev (1913) with infrahuman organisms.

Jones (1930) has reported conditioning of the galvanic skin response in nine month old infants to combinations of auditory, visual, or tactile stimuli, with shock as the US. The US was presented for ten seconds and a ten second interstimulus interval was used. The only control procedure used by Jones was a CS-alone group (novel CS control) to test for maturational changes in response to the CS.

Aversive Conditioning in Neonates

Studies of classical aversive conditioning with infants in the neonatal period have produced negative findings (Morgan and Morgan, 1944; Rendle-Short, 1961; Wickens and Wickens, 1940) or, at best, equivocal results (Lipsitt, 1963; Wenger, 1936).

Wenger (1936) was the first investigator to report successful classical avoidance conditioning in the newborn. Although Wenger's study lacked the appropriate control groups needed to support his conclusion of eyelid and foot withdrawal conditioning, his otherwise rigorous laboratory techniques, including careful recording of response measures, provided an excellent example which subsequent investigators have not always followed. His independent variables were controlled and recorded mechanically, and responses were recorded polygraphically or by independent observers. In his first experiment, Wenger studied the eyeblink response, using as the US a .45 second flash of a 100 or 200 watt light. The CS was a 3 second vibratory stimulus to the subject's foot. Wenger reported that conditioning occurred after an average of approximately 205 trials and 5 days of training. By the ninth and final day of conditioning, three experimental subjects responded to the CS 69 percent of the time, on the average; six control subjects, who were tested with CS alone (novel CS) on the ninth day, responded an average of only 29 percent of the time. In a second study, Wenger reported conditioned foot withdrawal in three of five infants, for whom the CS was a high-pitched (1084 cycles per second) tone and the US consisted of electrotactual stimulation of the toe. In addition to a CS-alone group tested on the ninth postnatal day, a second control group of four infants was given US alone (30 shocks per day for 7 days) and then tested for responses to the CS on the ninth day. Although the latter control group gave several responses to the tone, Wenger concluded that conditioning was evidenced because the experimental group gave more responses. Wenger did not report statistical significance levels, and it would appear that only slight differences between the groups were obtained in this study. Furthermore, Wenger's control procedures were inadequate for assessing the effects of the CS-US contingency. The subjects in the control groups were tested for response to a novel stimulus (CS), but the experimental subjects received a CS they had experienced many times.

Wickens and Wickens (1940) followed up Wenger's study and used similar conditioning procedures, but included larger numbers of subjects in the experimental and control groups. Unfortunately, however, they did not utilize the recording techniques developed by Wenger. The CS was a buzzer, and the US was a strong shock to the right foot, eliciting foot withdrawal. For the experimental group the CS was initiated .25 second before the onset of a .25 second shock, and the CS and US terminated together. Conditioning trials were given on the first 3 days, 12 per day for a total of 36 trials. After the last conditioning trial on the third day, extinction began, with presentations of the CS alone (i.e., without any further presentations of the US). Extinction trials were continued on the fourth day until the subject met an extinction criterion of three successive failures to respond to the CS. A CS-alone control group and a US-alone control group were also tested. The CS-alone group received 12 trials of buzzer alone on the first day and was tested for occurrence of withdrawal response to buzzer during the extinction test on the third day. The US-alone group received 12 shocks per day for 3 days (after an appropriate number of buzzer trials on the first day), then the extinction test. Although only 1 of 12 subjects in the CS-alone group responded to the buzzer on extinction trials, 9 of 12 subjects in the experimental group and 11 of 12 in the US-alone group made foot withdrawal responses to the buzzer on extinction trials. The similarity of responsiveness to the buzzer in the experimental group and the pseudoconditioning (US-alone) control group implies that pseudoconditioning occurred in both groups. Apparently, the mere presentation of the US in these groups produced a general sensitization to stimulation, with the result that leg withdrawal responses occurred when the buzzer was presented on the test trials.

Alternative interpretations are possible, however. As already emphasized, it can be argued that the US-alone control is not appropriate for assessing the effects of Pavlovian conditioning, because the group given this control treatment has had less experience than the experimental group with the CS in the experimental situation before extinction begins. Furthermore, not everyone agrees that pseudoconditioning effects are nonassociational or truly *pseudo*learning effects. It has been argued that the CS and US in the experimental situation may have much in common, in that both occur in the same surroundings and both may have sharp onsets and offsets (e.g., Grant and Dittmer, 1940). If so, then the similarity of performance in the experimental and US-alone groups in the Wickens and Wickens study could be interpreted as indicating that *conditioning* occurred in both groups.

Wickens and Wickens (1942) hypothesized that apparent pseudoconditioning is actually true conditioning, and they tested this hypothesis in a study with rats that were trained to escape shock. The shock came on suddenly for one group and gradually for another. Each of these groups was subsequently subdivided and tested with a light that came on either suddenly or gradually. Thus, two groups were tested with similar onsets of shock and light (both sudden or both gradual), and two groups were tested with dissimilar onsets of the two stimuli (one stimulus with sudden onset, the other gradual). The results clearly supported the hypothesis; 15 of 19 animals with similar onsets showed pseudoconditioning but only 3 of 18 animals with dissimilar onsets showed pseudoconditioning.

Studies of pseudoconditioning as a generalization phenomenon could have important implications for understanding the early forms of learning in the developing organism, since there is some evidence of an inverse relation between stimulus generalization and age (Mednick and Lehtinen, 1957; Tempone, 1965). Unfortunately, however, there has been very little experimentation on pseudoconditioning. The learning interpretation of the pseudoconditioning effect obtained in the Wickens and Wickens study with newborns would therefore require additional controls to assess the possibility of stimulus generalization.

Another aspect of the Wickens and Wickens conditioning procedure provides the basis for speculation about a possible influence of instrumental reinforcement contingencies. Like many other investigators working with infants, Wickens and Wickens tried to control the activity levels of the infants at the time of stimulation. They reported, "An attempt was made to stimulate the infant only when his activity level corresponded with stages three to five of Wagner's criteria of sleep, i.e., when it was neither crying nor highly active and yet not in an extremely deep sleep" (p. 95). Therefore, awake infants were given aversive stimulation during periods of low activity but not during periods of high activity. With extended training under such reinforcement contingencies, involving "punishment" of low activity, there should be a general increase in activity level over experimental sessions and consequently an increased likelihood that limb activity would coincide with the CS. The coincidental response would be interpreted, erroneously, as a CR (in the experimental group) or as a pseudoconditioned response (in the control group). Therefore, although the experimenter presents the US independently of the subject's response to the CS, he must also guard against presenting the CS (and hence the US) contingently upon the subject's behavior in order to avoid *instrumental* contingencies.

A study of classical aversive conditioning by Marum (1962) included important refinements of control procedures and was the first study of its kind to control frequency of exposure to both the CS and US. Marum used a trace conditioning control group to hold the total amount of stimulation constant for the experimental and control groups. In trace conditioning the CS is terminated before the onset of the US (see Figure 3-1). If the interstimulus interval is long enough, no conditioning can occur and the procedure can serve as a pseudoconditioning control. If it is not long enough, conditioning can occur (e.g., Marinesco and Kreindler, 1933). Figure 3-6 shows Marum's apparatus for recording foot withdrawal activity and general body movement. The infant wore a boot that was attached to a rod containing a universal joint, thus permitting unrestricted movement of the leg in all planes. The rod contained a light-sensitive resistor, and changes in resistance caused by movements of the leg were transmitted to a polygraph pen. Marum adjusted the intensity of the US (shock) for each subject, using a psychophysical procedure developed by Lipsitt and Levy (1959), and made the effective intensity of the US constant for all subjects. Further adjustments in the intensity were made during training to compensate for adaptation to the US. The CS (tone) was presented for 2.5 seconds, and the US for 2 seconds. For the experimental group the onset of the US followed the onset of the CS by .5 second; for the control group the onset of the US followed the *offset* of the CS by 7.5 seconds. Conditioning procedures began on the first day of life, and subjects were given 25 trials a day for 4 consecutive days. Every fifth trial was a test trial on which the CS alone was presented. Figure 3-7 shows the total number of responses given by each of the two groups on test trials over the 4 day period. The experimental group gave significantly more responses than the control group over the entire period. However, evidence for classical aversive conditioning would require an increasing separation between the groups over the 4 days of conditioning. Although an apparently increasing separation is seen in Figure 3-7, this effect was not statistically reliable.

Subsequent attempts by Lipsitt and colleagues (see Lipsitt, 1963) to obtain classical aversive conditioning in newborns with shock as the US were not successful. These studies are usually cited as failures to obtain classical conditioning in newborns (Brackbill, 1967; Sameroff, 1968a). Marum's results provide, at best, equivocal evidence for classical aversive conditioning, but it should be noted that the subsequent experiments cited by Lipsitt involved shorter conditioning periods than the Marum study, and, possibly of greater importance, longer interstimulus intervals. Results of aversive conditioning studies with adults strongly suggest that the most effective interstimulus interval is approximately .5 second (Hall, 1966; Kimble, 1961).

On the basis of the available data we would conclude that aversive conditioning has not been clearly demonstrated in the human newborn. However, with few exceptions (see Lipsitt, 1963), these investigations have not included controls

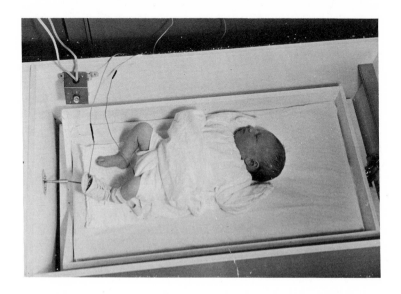

Fig. 3-6.   Neonate in stabilimeter, with electrodes attached for delivery of US and with boot attached for recording leg withdrawal movements. Monitor light signals when US is delivered. (From Marum, 1962, Fig. 1, p. 11. Reprinted by permission of the author.)

for differences between the experimental and control groups in total amount of stimulation. Studies in which the CS- and US-alone control procedures were used can be criticized as lacking the appropriate control methods for assessing effects due uniquely to the CS-US contingency. Future investigations should include control procedures that allow the investigator to examine both conditioned excitation and conditioned inhibition.

The use of classical aversive conditioning procedures to study conditioned emotional responses would add greatly to our knowledge of conditioned fear and anxiety in the developing infant, but a great deal of methodological work on the infant's unconditioned responses to aversive stimulation is needed first.

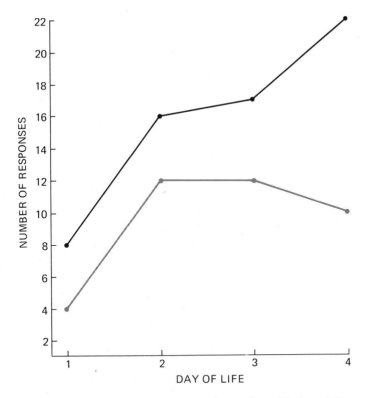

Fig. 3-7. Number of conditioned responses obtained in blocks of 5 test trials on each of 4 conditioning days. Darker line, experimental group; lighter line, control group. (From Marum, 1962, Fig. 3, p. 17. Reprinted by permission of the author.)

Difficulties in identifying and measuring reliable indexes of the infant's unconditioned autonomic response to aversive stimulation should not be underestimated, but respiration and heart rate may prove to be useful indexes for future studies of aversive conditioning (Polikanina, 1961).

Eyelid Conditioning

The eyeblink has been the most frequently used response in Soviet investigations of aversive conditioning in infants. Kasatkin studied eyelid conditioning to an auditory stimulus in infants, beginning at 25 days of age, and obtained somewhat stable conditioning by 39 days of age (see Brackbill and Koltsova, 1967). Zonova obtained stable eyelid conditioning to a visual CS (colored lights) in infants who were 2 months old at the start of conditioning (see Brackbill and Koltsova, 1967). Janos (1965) obtained stable conditioned eyeblinks to an auditory stimulus in infants 3 weeks and 8 weeks old.

The use of the eyeblink response in studies of aversive conditioning with infants has a number of advantages over the use of responses to electric shock. The unconditioned eyeblink can be reliably elicited by very mild forms of aversive stimulation, such as a light puff of air and a flash of light. In addition, recent developments in instrumentation allow reliable recordings of URs and CRs in even the young infant. Brackbill (1962) has provided a bibliography of Soviet studies of eyelid conditioning, and a description of an apparatus developed by Koltsova and colleagues which is suitable for use with children above 18 months of age.

More recently, Lintz and Fitzgerald (1966) have described an apparatus, modeled after one developed by Kasatkin, that can be used with younger infants. The frequency, duration, and amplitude of the eyeblink are recorded by means of a magnetic detector fastened to the subject's upper eyelid. This apparatus was used by Lintz, Fitzgerald, and Brackbill (1967) in an eyelid conditioning study with infants ranging from 33 to 133 days of age. The CS was a loud (65 decibel) tone, presented 1 second before the onset of a .3 second air puff to the infant's right eye. The subjects were given approximately 25 trials each day, with CS-alone test trials randomly interspersed among the conditioning trials in a 1 to 3 ratio. Conditioning continued until the subject reached a criterion of 9 CRs on 10 successive test trials. The main control group received the same total number of CS and US presentations as the experimental group, but the presentations were unpaired. Another control group, tested in a single session, was given only the CS; and a "no-stimulus" control group was included to measure spontaneous blinking. The investigators reported that all of their experimental subjects reached the conditioning criterion, but no subject in the control groups approached criterion.

Pupillary Conditioning

Brackbill *et al.* (1967) obtained temporal conditioning of pupillary dilation and pupillary constriction in infants from 26 to 86 days of age. (In temporal conditioning, *time* is the CS.) The experiment included six experimental groups and four control groups. The experimental groups were equally divided between conditioned dilation and constriction procedures, using change in illumination as the US (onset of illumination for constriction conditioning and offset for dilation conditioning). The experimental groups received 32 conditioning trials, with 9 randomly interspersed test trials of CS alone, followed by 35 extinction trials. The design of the study is summarized in Table 3-2. For the temporal conditioning group (time alone), the US was presented for 4 seconds, with a constant intertrial interval of 20 seconds. The time plus tone group had the same procedure, except that a loud (65 decibel) tone was presented simultaneously with the 4 second US. The tone conditioning group was given a 5.5 second tone, which preceded the onset of the 4 second US by 1.5 seconds, and the intertrial interval ranged from 10 to 30 seconds (mean = 20 seconds). The control groups for tone conditioning received backward conditioning, and the control groups for temporal conditioning received randomly spaced presentations of the US. No evidence of conditioning was obtained in any of the control groups; the results for the temporal conditioning groups and the compound CS (time plus tone) groups indicated both conditioned constriction and conditioned dilation. Paradoxically, no evidence of pupillary conditioning was obtained in the tone CS group. This result is difficult to interpret in light of the results of the previously cited study of eyelid conditioning with infants of approximately the same age. Furthermore, Kasatkin reported that Soviet studies have shown stable conditioning of most responses to auditory stimuli by 35 days of age (see Brackbill and Koltsova, 1967).

Table 3-2

Design of Temporal Conditioning Study[a]

Condition	CS	Procedure
Temporal conditioning	Time (20 seconds)	4 second US presented every 20 seconds
Compound CS	Time plus tone	4 second US presented simultaneously with 4 second tone every 20 seconds
Tone	Tone	5.5 second CS presented 1.5 seconds before 4 second US; intertrial interval 10 to 30 seconds
Control for tone condition	Tone	Backward conditioning (US presented before CS)
Control for temporal conditioning	—	4 second US presented at intervals randomly varying between 10 and 30 seconds

[a] Brackbill *et al.* (1967).

We should note that the rapid and uniform conditioning of both pupillary constriction and dilation in infants is somewhat surprising in light of the conflicting results that have been obtained in pupillary conditioning studies with adults. In general, there has been notably more success in conditioning the pupillary response when electric shock is used as the US than when change in illumination is the US (Kimble, 1961). Young (1965) has argued that sensory feedback is an essential component of conditioning and that it is missing in pupillary constriction; therefore, he has stated that conditioning of the constriction response cannot occur. Some investigators have pointed out that pupillary dilation occurs as part of the generalized emotional response to noxious stimulation, and have assumed that it is this response that becomes conditioned to shock. Although further studies of pupillary conditioning are needed, the results of the study by Brackbill *et al.* indicate that pupillary constriction and dilation can be temporally conditioned in young infants. Contrary to the findings of Soviet investigators (Kasatkin, 1957), these investigators found that age differences within the range from 26 to 86 days did not appear to influence rate of conditioning.

AGE DIFFERENCES IN CLASSICAL CONDITIONING

Many investigators, beginning with Mateer (1918), have reported a positive correlation between chronological age (CA) and the speed of establishing stable conditioning (i.e., conditioning is faster in older infants than in younger infants). Studying subjects from 1 to 7.5 years of age, Mateer obtained a substantial correlation of .57 between CA and speed of attaining a conditioning criterion (two successive anticipatory mouth-opening responses). Mateer concluded that within the range from 1 to 4 years of age, the speed of conditioning increases with increasing age, but that there is no relation between speed of conditioning and age thereafter. Morgan and Morgan (1944), studying eyelid conditioning in infants from 5 to 75 days of age, reported that no infants under 53 days of age reached the conditioning criterion (10 successive CRs within 100 trials), while only one subject over 66 days of age failed to meet this criterion. Similarly, Rendle-Short (1961) reported that infants under 6 months of age failed to acquire a conditioned eyeblink response within 20 trials, and that after 6 months of age conditioning required progressively fewer trials. Similar correlations between age and rate of conditioning have been obtained with infants over the first 4 months of life in studies of conditioned sucking (Kasatkin and Levikova, 1935a, 1935b), and in studies of the conditioned eyeblink (Janos, 1959). The Soviet investigators have generally found a substantial relation between CA and speed of conditioning (see Brackbill, 1967). However, Brackbill et al. (1967) obtained no evidence of differences in rate of pupillary conditioning in infants from 26 to 86 days of age. In addition, most investigators have failed to find evidence of reliable age differences in rate of extinction and in speed of conditioned differentiation (Janos, 1959; Kasatkin and Levikova, 1935b; Rendle-Short, 1961).

Briefly summarized, the evaluation of these reported age differences in rate of conditioning is that classical conditioning in infants provides little basis for concluding that differences in learning *capacities* have been demonstrated. Differences due to the effects of variations in motivation, reinforcement, and unconditioned response capacities have not been systemically explored in any of these studies. There is no *a priori* basis for determining whether the motivating effects of shock, air puff, food, or visual stimulation vary with age or remain constant. Animal studies have shown large differences in the effects of food deprivation in animals of different ages (Campbell and Cicala, 1962; Williams and Campbell, 1961). There is ample evidence to suggest that sensory thresholds for the newborn change over the first days of life (Kaye, 1964b; Lipsitt and Levy, 1959; Lipsitt et al., 1963). With few exceptions (Brackbill et al., 1967), investigators have not examined the age groups studied for evidence of differential changes in their URs to the US over conditioning trials. Green

(1962) has shown differential changes over trials in the UR of rhesus monkeys to shock as a function of age; all age groups initially showed a sharp increase over trials in activity to shock as a US, but after the third day of conditioning the youngest group showed a marked decrease in activity to shock and typically responded by freezing and crouching. By using a "combined" index of conditioned responding (including both increased activity and decreased activity), Green obtained evidence that the development of conditioned responding was similar in all of his age groups. Such results suggest that evidence for the relation of rate of conditioning to age may depend in part upon the particular index of conditioned responding chosen. The major task confronting investigators of learning processes in infants is one of systematically attempting to control, equate, or assess the effects of differences in motivation, reinforcement, and response requirements of these conditioning situations for infants of different ages.

CHAPTER 4

Basic Learning Processes:
II. Instrumental Conditioning

INTRODUCTION

In contrast to classical conditioning, in which the unconditioned stimulus (US) uniquely determines the response that is to be associated with the conditional stimulus (CS), in instrumental conditioning the experimenter selects the response to be reinforced. That is, in classical conditioning the experimenter selects a *stimulus* (US) that elicits a particular response in which he is interested; in instrumental conditioning the experimenter selects a *response* of interest and observes how frequently it occurs without attempting to identify the eliciting stimulus (or stimuli).

The response in classical conditioning is sometimes called "respondent," because it is *elicited;* the response in instrumental conditioning is sometimes called "operant," because it seems to be emitted with no identifiable eliciting stimulus. Skinner (1937) has diagrammed the instrumental learning situation in the following way:

$$\text{s}\underline{\qquad}R_0\underline{\qquad}\rightarrow S_1\underline{\qquad}R_1$$

The child emits a response, R_0, to a stimulus, s, that is often assumed to be internal but is actually unidentified. Other stimuli, S_1, are presented to the subject, but only after occurrences of R_0. The response, R_1, to S_1 is a consummatory response, and the occurrence of the S_1—R_1 sequence is reinforcing. Learning is dependent upon the contingency between R_0 and S_1—R_1, and results in an increased probability or rate of emission of R_0.

Positive reinforcers and *negative reinforcers* are two classes of stimulus consequences (S_1) that affect the strength of R_0. An increase in response strength occurs when the response is followed by a positive reinforcer (positive stimulus) and when the response is followed by termination or avoidance of a negative reinforcer (aversive stimulus). There are two classes of stimulus consequences that weaken the response; these are labeled *punishment* operations. A decrease in response strength occurs when the response is followed by an aversive stimulus and when the response is followed by termination of a positive stimulus.

Hilgard and Marquis (1940) and Woodworth and Schlosberg (1954) classified instrumental conditioning experiments as involving reward training, escape training, avoidance training, and secondary reward training, and Kimble (1961) added punishment and omission training (see Table 4-1).

The primary effect of response-contingent reinforcement is to strengthen and intensify some aspect of the preceding response. Subsequently, in the absence of further reinforcement the conditioned response (CR) becomes weaker and gradually declines in frequency of occurrence. Typically, these effects of reinforcement are divided into *conditioning* and *extinction*. Conditioning refers to the strengthening of behavior by reinforcement, and extinction refers to the subsequent decline of the behavior when reinforcement is discontinued. An important characteristic of reinforcement is that its effects may be reflected in rapid acquisition of the CR. However, a CR, in contrast to responses produced

Table 4-1

Classification of Instrumental Conditioning Designs

Design	General procedure
Reward training	Response followed by positive reinforcer
Secondary reward training	Response followed by stimulus previously associated with positive reinforcer
Escape training	Response followed by termination of negative reinforcer
Avoidance training	Response prevents occurrence of negative reinforcer
Punishment training	Response followed by negative reinforcer
Omission training	Response followed by withdrawal of positive reinforcer

by nonspecific arousal effects, should also show evidence of persistence following termination of reinforcement.

Discrete-Trial, Free Operant, and Restricted Operant Methods

It is useful to distinguish discrete-trial, free operant, and restricted operant instrumental learning situations. These methods differ in experimental procedure, definition of a trial, and response measure used to assess learning.

The discrete-trial procedure most closely parallels the classical conditioning procedure, in terms of the response measure used and the definition of a trial. The experimenter presents a CS and allows the subject a certain amount of time in which to make the desired response. The trial is terminated immediately if the subject makes the appropriate response, otherwise when the fixed time interval has elapsed. Learning can be assessed with several response measures. Increased response frequency and decreased response latency over conditioning trials can be used as measures of learning. (Response latency is the time between the presentation of the CS and the occurrence of the response.) The data from studies using the discrete-trial procedure are usually presented as group means, such as mean frequency or mean latency over successive blocks of trials or mean number of trials required to reach an arbitrarily selected learning criterion (e.g., ten successive correct responses). A study by Papoušek (1967a) on conditioned head-turning provides an example of the use of the last response measure with the discrete-trial procedure. He required infants to respond with a 30 to 45 degree rotation of the head to the left within 10 seconds after a buzzer had sounded. Results were reported in terms of the mean number of training trials required to obtain a criterion of five consecutive responses in one daily session of ten trials.

In the free operant learning situation the experimenter does not use discrete trials, but rather places the subject in an experimental situation in which he is free to make as many responses as time permits. Thus, in the free operant situation the response of the subject does not result in his being displaced in time or space from the locus of his subsequent response. Practical considerations in the choice of a response to be studied with the free operant conditioning paradigm have been summarized by Ferster (1953). The optimal free operant is a response that requires little muscular exertion, results in minimal temporal and spatial displacement of the organism, and is subject to a wide range of rates of occurrence. The typical measure of learning is the frequency of responding or number of responses per unit of time. A study by Weisberg (1968) with two year old infants, on the effects of intermittent reinforcement on acquisition and extinction performance, provides an example of a direct extension of the free operant paradigm for use with infants. Following a pretraining procedure designed to adapt infants to the experimental apparatus, infants were trained to press a lever for cookie reinforcement, and response rate was studied during acquisition and extinction as a function of reinforcement schedules.

The restricted operant or controlled operant method represents a combination of the free operant and discrete-trial methods. The subject remains in the situation, but his ability to respond is curtailed in some way. For example, the manipulandum can be removed from the experimental situation after each response; each presentation of the manipulandum would constitute a new trial. Or the experimenter can remove the manipulandum after a fixed time interval and use as his response measure the number of responses occurring during each presentation of the manipulandum. The procedure also allows the experimenter to obtain response latency measures, as well as rate measures, over successive trials. Two studies by Spiker (1956a, 1956d) with preschool children perhaps illustrate the restricted operant procedure. However, rather than removing the manipulandum to terminate each trial, Spiker withdrew a response signal or CS (a light). Only responses that occurred while the CS was on were reinforced. The performance measure was the number of responses during each CS interval.[1] A study by Feldstone (1966) provides another example. On each trial one group was rewarded after making a fixed number of responses and another group

---

[1] Spiker's procedure closely resembles the "discriminated free operant" procedure, in which reinforcement is given for responses that occur in the presence of one stimulus (S^D) and not for responses that occur in the presence of another stimulus (S^Δ). The S^Δ can be the absence of S^D. The CS in Spiker's study can be considered to be an S^D and the absence of the CS an S^Δ, because the subjects were allowed to respond to the manipulandum during the intertrial interval and these responses were not rewarded.

was rewarded after a fixed interval of time. As in Spiker's studies, the manipulandum was not physically removed between trials. The performance measure was response speed.

This chapter will deal with operant and discrete-trial instrumental conditioning in infancy and childhood. An important distinction between these techniques has been the focus of operant research upon individual behavior and discrete-trial research upon group or average behavior. The operant researcher typically conducts an experimental analysis of individual behavior. If a certain manipulation does not produce the desired effect upon the child's behavior, the experimenter sets about discovering what additional environmental changes will bring about that behavior. Thus, it is common to see procedural changes one or more times during the course of experimentation with a given individual until his behavior is brought under environmental control. In discrete-trial research, manipulations are performed on groups of individuals, and once specified, the procedure is not altered. Statistical comparisons of average performances may reveal significant differences between groups even though several individuals may have deviated markedly from their group mean. Similar statistical comparisons are usually not necessary in operant conditioning since the behavior has either been brought under environmental control or it has not.

Both the operant and discrete-trial researcher assume that individual differences in behavior are attributable to varied genetic and experiential backgrounds. The strategy in operant research is to change environmental stimulation to whatever extent is necessary to gain control of each individual's behavior. In discrete-trial research, individuals and hence individual differences are randomly assigned to groups in order to assess the effect of some selected variable upon behavior. It is typically assumed that eventually enough variables will be discovered to allow prediction and control of individual behavior. Thus, both approaches have the same eventual goal.

Two further points should be noted. First, because of its concentration upon individual behavior, operant research has provided a much greater contribution toward the everyday application of research findings (see Chapter 19). Discrete-trial research, because of its variable-oriented approach, has contributed more toward the development of behavior theory. Second, the characteristic interests of those engaged in operant and discrete-trial research are determined by the investigators themselves and *not* by the techniques. One could employ the free operant method to investigate group differences or the discrete-trial method for individual control.

Schedules of Reinforcement

Reinforcement may be administered according to a continuous or an intermittent schedule. However, very few data have been gathered on the long term employment of CRF (continuous reinforcement) in the free operant situation, because response rate is not under the control of the experimenter and consequently the subjects receive many reinforcements and satiate quickly. The main use of CRF has been to build up response strength before the introduction of some other schedule of reinforcement. The various schedules used are defined below and in Table 4-2.

Intermittent schedules can be subdivided into *ratio* and *interval* schedules. Ratio schedules prescribe that a certain number of responses must be emitted before a reinforcement will be delivered. The ratio may be fixed (FR) or variable (VR). On an FR 5, for example, every fifth response will be rewarded.

Table 4-2

Glossary of Terms Referring to Schedules of Reinforcement

Schedule	Symbol	Definition
Continuous	CRF	Every response reinforced
Intermittent		
Fixed Ratio	FR[a]	Every nth response reinforced
Variable Ratio	VR[a]	On the average, every nth response reinforced
Fixed Interval	FI[a]	Reinforcement only for first response after time interval of x duration has elapsed
Variable Interval	VI[a]	Reinforcement only for first response after time interval averaging x duration has elapsed
Extinction	Ext	No responses reinforced
Multiple[b]		
Multiple	Mult	Two or more separate schedules, each with a different S^D, each in effect for predetermined time period
Chain	Chain	Same as Mult, except each in effect until S responds appropriately
Tandem	Tandem	Same as Chain, but with no differential S^Ds
Differential		
Differential Reinforcement of Low Rates	DRL	Response is reinforced only if some specified amount of time has elapsed since last reinforced response
Differential Reinforcement of Other Response	DRO	Response reinforced is other than response of primary interest

[a] A number follows the symbol to specify the ratio (n) or interval (x).
[b] Symbols follow to specify the components of the multiple schedule.

On a VR 5, the child will receive a reinforcement on the *average* for every 5 responses; for example, 25 responses will lead to 5 reinforcements, 1 of which may be delivered after 2 responses, 1 after 4 responses, 1 after 5, 1 after 6, and 1 after 8 responses.

Interval schedules prescribe that a certain amount of time must elapse before the next response will be reinforced. The interval may be fixed (FI) or variable

(VI), that is, it may be constant in duration or variable around some average. However, reinforcements do not arrive automatically at the termination of intervals but follow the first postinterval response. On an FI 15 sec., for example, an interval of 15 seconds must elapse before the next response produces reinforcement. On a VI 15 sec., a variable interval averaging 15 seconds over a series of intervals must elapse before the next response produces reinforcement. It is customary to omit the time unit when it is minutes; thus, FI 2, for example, means FI 2 min. (In an interesting extension of interval scheduling, reinforcement is delivered at the end of an interval irrespective of the organism's behavior. In this situation, the reinforcement strengthens whatever behavior is occurring at the time. This kind of scheduling has been shown to produce "superstitious" behavior in infrahumans but has yet to be investigated with children.)

Each kind of schedule has been found to have a particular kind of effect upon rate of responding in infrahumans (e.g., Ferster and Skinner, 1957; Reynolds, 1968, p. 62), and it is of interest to determine whether similar or unique schedule effects are evident in children.

INSTRUMENTAL CONDITIONING IN INFANTS

Special Considerations in Studies with Infants

The study of instrumental learning in infants confronts the researcher with several problems. The majority of the tasks used with adults and infrahuman organisms require locomotive or manipulative skills that are absent or extremely limited in the infant. Therefore, the first problem facing the researcher is one of developing learning tasks that are suitable to the infant's limited response repertoire. Historically, the immature neuromuscular status of the young infant has been a barrier to extensive use of instrumental learning procedures, and research in this area is of recent origin. The researcher must address himself to special problems of selecting dependent and independent variables appropriate to the instrumental learning paradigm; he must find responses that the infant has sufficient motor coordination to emit reliably, and must identify stimuli that are potentially reinforcing for the infant.

Reinforcers for Instrumental Learning in Infants

The identification of effective reinforcers that can be used in studies of instrumental learning in infants has posed a challenge to researchers studying the development of early learning processes. There has been no easy solution to the problem of finding stimuli that can support the behavior of infants over the relatively long period of time required for an experimental analysis of the variables that are of interest to the experimenter. Usually, the experimenter does not have control over the infant's feeding schedule and cannot employ the kind of deprivation procedures that are common in learning studies with infrahuman organisms. For obvious reasons, the investigator of learning in infants cannot use negative reinforcers that require strong aversive stimuli to maintain their effectiveness. Despite these problems, effective reinforcement procedures have been developed for use in learning studies with infants.

APPETITIONAL REINFORCERS. Food and water, the most frequently used positive reinforcers with infrahuman subjects, have been employed in learning studies with infants. The food stimuli that have been used in studies of discrete-trial and free operant learning in infants include milk (Papoušek, 1967b; Seltzer, 1968; Siqueland, 1964), sugar solution (Siqueland and Lipsitt, 1966), candies (Bijou, 1957b; Munn and Stiening, 1931; Warren and Brown, 1943), cookies (Skeels, 1933; Weisberg and Fink, 1966), fruit (Gellermann, 1933b), sugar, jam, and honey (Ling, 1941; Myers, 1908; Valentine, 1914), and raisins (Jackson, Stonex, Lane, and Dominguez, 1938). One problem with the use of food reinforcers is that the experimenter has minimal control over deprivation conditions. Hospital and institutional research settings provide some control over feedings, but except in one study (Siqueland and Lipsitt, 1966), deprivation conditions have not been experimentally manipulated. Candy has been the most typical and durable reinforcer in learning studies with older children, but increased concern of parents, school personnel, and researchers about the effects of carbohydrates on tooth decay has reduced the popularity of candy rewards.

SOCIAL REINFORCERS. Some of the earliest studies providing evidence of operant conditioning in infants, as well as more recent studies, have shown that adult social behaviors are effective as reinforcing stimuli; but there have been no studies comparing the reinforcing effectiveness of the various components of social behavior—physical contact with the infant, talking to him, and smiling at him. The results of a recent study of conditioned smiling (Etzel and Gewirtz, 1967), using social reinforcement but excluding the component of physical contact, indicate that the combination of visual and auditory stimulation from an adult is sufficient to obtain reliable reinforcement effects in infants.

In a study of conditioned smiling in three month old infants, Wahler (1967) used a within-subjects design to compare the reinforcing effectiveness of mothers and strangers as dispensers of visual, auditory, and tactual stimulation. The infants received two 15-minute conditioning procedures, separated by 1 or 2 days. The conditioning procedures consisted of 5-minute baseline, conditioning, and extinction phases. The reinforcer included visual, auditory, and physical stimulation of the infant. Each infant was tested with both mother and stranger as reinforcing agents, the order of these conditions being counterbalanced across subjects. Reliable increases in smiling occurred during conditioning when the infant's mother dispensed reinforcement but not when the female stranger served as the reinforcing agent. The ineffectiveness of adult strangers as reinforcing agents is difficult to interpret in light of the results of previous studies, but procedural differences may account for the discrepancies between Wahler's results and those of the previous studies. For example, Brackbill (1958) picked up the infant and jostled and patted him for 30 seconds; Wahler limited the physical contact to a light touch of the experimenter's hand to the infant's chest. Unfortunately, these reinforcement parameters have not been investigated within a single study. Differences in results may also reflect differences in past histories of subjects with "strange" adults as sources of exteroceptive stimulation and nutritive reinforcement. At any rate, these studies show that the young infant is highly sensitive to social reinforcers and that social reinforcement is effective in strengthening and maintaining a number of responses. It is important that future studies delineate the most effective components of social reinforcers and further explore the role of social agents as dispensers of complex auditory, visual, and physical stimulation.

AUDITORY AND VISUAL REINFORCERS.   Numerous studies with infrahuman organisms have shown that certain classes of visual and auditory stimuli have reinforcing properties and that the effectiveness of these stimuli as reinforcers is influenced by satiation and deprivation conditions. Similar results have been obtained in studies of visual and auditory reinforcement in children (Cantor and Cantor, 1964, 1966; Odom, 1964; Stevenson and Knights, 1961). Visual and auditory stimuli have been shown to be effective reinforcers in a number of free operant studies of manipulative behavior in infants from four months to five years of age (Caron, 1967; Friedlander, 1967; Levinson and Levinson, 1967; Lipsitt, 1963; Lipsitt, Pederson, and DeLucia, 1966b; Rheingold, Stanley, and Cooley, 1962; Rheingold, Stanley, and Doyle, 1964; Simmons, 1964; Siqueland, 1966, 1968a; Siqueland and DeLucia, 1969).

There have been few studies of operant conditioning in infants using auditory feedback alone as a reinforcing stimulus. Smith and Smith (1962) obtained no conditioning in infants ranging from 4 to 22 months of age when a 2 to 3 minute presentation of recorded nursery songs was paired with panel touching. Weisberg (1963) obtained no conditioning in 3 month old infants when a door chime was paired with vocalizations by the subjects. However, the studies demonstrating the effectiveness of social reinforcement, which has an auditory component, suggest that auditory reinforcers are not always ineffective. Support for this suggestion has been obtained in studies of acquired color discrimination in older infants. Presentation of a two-tone door chime contingent upon correct responses was an effective reinforcer in training color discrimination in 12 month old infants (Simmons 1964; Simmons and Lipsitt, 1961); and a buzzer was effective in 8 month old infants (Lipsitt, 1963).

The results of a study by Friedlander (1967) suggest that auditory preferences can be measured in infants 11 to 13 months of age. Stable preferences were obtained when the infants were allowed to choose between two recordings of voices different in identity of speaker (mother and stranger), amount of inflection, number of speakers, and redundancy of message. Although this was an exploratory study of infant auditory preferences, the techniques developed by Friedlander offer considerable promise for future studies of auditory reinforcement and selective listening in preverbal infants.

Another technique for studying auditory reinforcers in infants as young as ten weeks of age is suggested by the results of two studies reported by Watson (1966). Watson used auditory and visual stimuli to reinforce spatially discriminated eye fixations (left versus right fixations). Two white circles were presented against a black background while the infant was lying in a bassinet. The circles were 3 inches apart, and were presented on the ceiling of the bassinet 12 inches above the infant's eyes. The visual reinforcer was a red face projected on one of the circles, and the auditory reinforcer was a soft, moderately pitched tone (approximately 1000 cycles per second). During conditioning sessions the subjects received reinforcement for fixating either the left or right circle. Watson found that rewarding a fixation response had a considerable effect on the next fixation if the second fixation occurred between 3 and 5 seconds after the first. However, if the second fixation occurred either earlier or later than these limits, the reinforcer had a negligible effect on the second fixation. Further research along these lines, with conditioning procedures of longer duration and with a greater variety of comparisons between visual and auditory reinforcers, should be fruitful.

Visual stimuli have been effective reinforcers in conditioning studies of nonnutritive sucking (Siqueland, 1966; Siqueland and DeLucia, 1969; Stern and Jeffery, 1965), head-turning (Caron, 1967; Koch, 1965; Levinson and Levinson, 1967), and manipulative responses (Lipsitt, 1963; Lipsitt et al., 1966b).

Recently reported studies of conditioned sucking (Siqueland, 1968b; Siqueland and Delucia, 1969) have shown that visual stimuli are effective reinforcers for infants as young as three weeks of age. The reinforcement procedure used in these studies—"conjugate reinforcement"—was one suggested initially by Lindsley, Hobika, and Etsten (1961). Conjugate reinforcement involves continuous presentation of a stimulus whose intensity is contingent upon the subject's response rate, such that the intensity varies directly and immediately with rate. Conjugate visual and auditory reinforcement seem to have ethological validity, in that they parallel the more naturally occurring stimulus feedback that the infant has received as a function of his response output. Conjugate reinforcement allows the subject to maintain the reinforcing stimulus for an indefinite period of time. In contrast to episodic schedules of reinforcement, which provide stimuli having discrete onsets and offsets, the conjugate type of contingency provides readily discriminable, but graded, changes in the intensity of the stimulus as a result of momentary changes in the subject's response rate.

In a study of four month old infants, with high-amplitude sucking as a dependent variable, Siqueland (1966) showed that the effectiveness of visual stimuli as reinforcers is diminished by preconditioning familiarization procedures, just as with infrahuman organisms and older children. The infants were divided into four groups: novel reinforcement group, familiarized reinforcement group, novel withdrawal group, and familiarized withdrawal group. For all four groups 1 minute of baseline sucking was observed, followed by 2 minutes of stimulus exposure (constant exposure to a set of four chromatic stimuli irrespective of sucking), 8 minutes of sucking-contingent visual stimulation, and finally 4 minutes of extinction. The reinforcing stimuli were identical for all four groups, and consisted of four replications of four chromatic slides, presented for 30 seconds. During the stimulus exposure phase, the familiarized groups were exposed to the set of four visual reinforcing stimuli, and the novel groups viewed a different set of four chromatic slides. During conditioning in the reinforcement groups, high-amplitude sucking activated the light source in a slide projector and reinforcement consisted of an opportunity to view the projected visual stimuli; in the withdrawal groups high-amplitude sucking turned off the projector light, removing the projected visual stimuli. Thus, during conditioning, high-

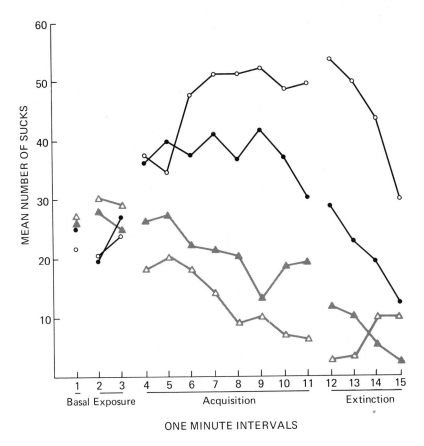

Fig. 4-1. Comparison of mean sucking rates for the four experimental groups over baseline, stimulus exposure, conditioning, and extinction phases. Open circles, novel reinforcement group; closed circles, familiarized reinforcement group; open triangles, novel withdrawal group; closed triangles, familiarized withdrawal group. (From Siqueland, 1966. Reprinted by permission of the author.)

amplitude sucking resulted in the presentation or withdrawal of familiar or novel visual stimuli. As shown in Figure 4-1, the reinforcement groups (dark lines) responded at higher levels during acquisition and extinction than the withdrawal groups (light lines). In the presentation condition (reinforcement groups) the novel group (open symbols) sucked at higher rates than the familiarized group (closed symbols). However, withdrawal of familiar visual stimuli resulted in less suppression of high-amplitude sucking than withdrawal of novel visual stimuli. An interaction between familiarization and training procedures was also obtained during extinction: In the novel withdrawal group the sucking rate, which was suppressed during the training phase, recovered during extinction. Sucking was weakened by the withdrawal of the visual stimuli, but recovered quickly when the contingency between stimulus withdrawal and sucking was terminated.

The results of these studies on sensory reinforcement suggest that effective reinforcement is not limited to a restricted class of stimuli in the infant's environment. In addition to nutritive reinforcers, there may be classes of stimuli in each sensory modality that are effective in strengthening instrumental behaviors of the infant. Berlyne (1966) has suggested that any stimuli that are effective in "capturing the subject's attention" can have reinforcing value in suitable circumstances. An important problem for future studies is the specification of the stimulus parameters that distinguish positive from negative reinforcing stimuli, and distinguish reinforcing from nonreinforcing stimuli, in each of the sensory modalities.

NEGATIVE REINFORCERS.   In instrumental escape learning an aversive stimulus terminates when the correct response is made. In avoidance learning a CS precedes the onset of the aversive stimulus, and if the subject makes the correct response before the onset of the aversive stimulus, the aversive stimulus is forestalled. Although these are familiar learning situations in the natural environments of many children, escape and avoidance learning have rarely been studied in infants and children in the experimental laboratory. The obvious difficulty confronting the researcher is that of finding mildly aversive stimuli that reliably elicit withdrawal responses but also are minimally stressful to the child and parents.

One of the few examples of instrumental escape and avoidance conditioning is a study by Polikanina (1961) with 14 newborns, born 1 to 3 weeks prematurely. An ammonia vapor was used as the unconditioned aversive stimulus and a low-pitched tone (500 cycles per second) as the CS. In the initial conditioning session the CS preceded the US by 2 to 3 seconds, but the interstimulus interval was progressively lengthened to 10 to 15 seconds. The CRs were anticipatory autonomic and motor responses (respiration, heart rate, drawing back the head). Although this study is typically described as a classical conditioning experiment, Polikanina clearly indicated that the infant's motor response was instrumental in terminating and avoiding the aversive odor. Occurrence of the motor response in the presence of the US terminated the US, and anticipatory motor responses occurring in the interstimulus interval resulted in omission of the US presentation. Polikanina reported that conditioned changes in respiration occurred first; conditioned cardiac and head movement responses occurred later. Six to seven trials were given each day, and conditioning of both the autonomic and motor responses was obtained by the second week of life.

Marum (1962) failed to obtain evidence of conditioned avoidance in newborns when shock served as the US and a tone as the CS. Anticipatory leg withdrawal responses made at any time during a four second CS-US interval terminated all stimulation. The infants were given two 25 trial conditioning sessions in one day.

There have been few studies with infants on the effects of punishment (i.e., presentation of an aversive stimulus contingent upon the subject's response). Clayton and Lipsitt (Lipsitt, 1963) obtained no conditioning in newborns who received mild shock contingent upon a panel-kicking response. However, punishment in the form of the sudden onset of a loud auditory stimulus effectively suppresses reaching and touching behavior in older infants (Valentine, 1930; Watson and Rayner, 1920).

An alternative punishment technique, the withdrawal of positive stimuli contingent upon some response, has been suggested by Bijou and Baer (1967) for work with infants, and has been used successfully with preschool children (Baer, 1960, 1962a). Siqueland (1966) has shown that high-amplitude non-nutritive sucking is weakened when projected visual stimuli are withdrawn upon the occurrence of high amplitude sucks, but the punished response reappeared when the stimulus withdrawal procedure was terminated (see Figure 4-1). Baer (1962a) obtained similar results in preschool children. Despite the frequent use of this type of punishment technique in the child's natural environment, it has received very little attention in the experimental literature. The effects of punishment and negative reinforcement, using the removal of positive stimuli as an aversive event, deserve further study by developmental psychologists.

Instrumental Learning in the First Four Weeks of Life

A series of learning studies with infants from birth to eight months of age by Papoušek (1959, 1967a, 1967b) represents a major contribution and methodological advance in the study of early instrumental learning. Conditioning, extinction, reconditioning, and discrimination learning were studied with differentiated head-turning as the dependent variable. Polygraphic records of head-turning were obtained by means of a special head cradle apparatus (Papoušek, 1967b). The conditioning procedure consisted of presenting a CS (bell) for 10 seconds and reinforcing the infant with milk from a nursing bottle if the subject responded with a left head-turn within the 10 second time interval. The response criterion was a left turn, from midline position, in excess of 30 to 45 degrees. The trial was terminated with reinforcement as soon as the subject responded and the CS continued for one to two seconds after the infant started sucking. Papoušek also used a special training or response shaping procedure if the criterion head-turn did not occur within the 10 second interval. After 10 seconds the experimenter attempted to elicit the left turn by tactile stimulation of the left cheek[2]; if the response could not be elicited in this way the experimenter manually turned the subject's head. Reinforcement was given on each trial following the occurrence of an emitted, elicited, or forced head-turn. Each training session consisted

---

[2] In young infants stimulation of the cheek is a US for head-turning toward the side stimulated. The response is sometimes called the "search reflex" or "rooting reflex."

of 10 trials; a criterion of 5 consecutive responses within one session was used to indicate the establishment of conditioned head-turning. Highly significant differences in the number of trials to attain criterion were found for the three age groups studied: newborns, 3-month-old infants, and 5-month-old infants. Although the newborns, as compared with the two older groups, required more trials to reach criterion, conditioning was demonstrated in most of them during the 28 days of the neonatal period. Four of the 14 newborns reached criterion within 12 days of training. These results provided the first clear evidence of instrumental learning within the first weeks of human life. A learning interpretation of Papoušek's findings is strengthened by the results of the extinction and reconditioning training. Newborns required an average of 26.8 nonreinforced trials to meet an extinction criterion of 5 consecutive trials without a CR to the CS. By subsequently re-establishing the response with reconditioning procedures, Papoušek showed that the head-turning response was reliably influenced by the reinforcement contingency. No significant age differences were obtained in extinction and reconditioning.

The increase in speed of conditioning with increasing age at the start of conditioning was interpreted by Papoušek as evidence of differences in learning capacities at the different age levels. However, a careful examination of Papoušek's procedures and results raises serious questions about this interpretation. The study suffered from all the problems of equating age groups for motivation, sensory capacities, and response capacities that have plagued both comparative and developmental investigations. Specifically, Papoušek's carefully detailed observations suggest that the response requirements of his instrumental task were markedly different for the three age groups; the two older groups of infants had a relatively high baseline of spontaneously emitted criterion responses, but the newborns rarely emitted a left-turning response in excess of 30 degrees. Papoušek observed, ". . . marked signs of this lack of coordination are observed in less than 1% of the older subjects, but they are present in 50% of the newborns" (Papoušek, 1967a, p. 272). His special training or response shaping procedures were required with most of the newborns, but they were rarely needed with the older infants. Also, the selection of a left head-turn as the CR imposed an additional handicap upon the newborn infants. Several investigators have demonstrated that the newborn infant has a strong unconditioned bias for right head-turning responses relative to left-turning responses (Papoušek, 1959; Siqueland and Lipsitt, 1966; Turkewitz, Gordon, and Birch, 1965).

We can have little confidence that the reported differences in acquisition rates for the respective age groups were not seriously confounded by marked differences in the unconditioned response capacities of these groups. Newborn infants may have had minimal exposure to the response-reinforcement contingency during the earlier training trials because of their extremely low baseline frequency of emitted criterion responses. Reinforcement for this group was almost always contingent upon response to tactile stimulation, but in the older groups it was almost always contingent upon emitted responses in the presence of the CS. One way to assess the effects of differences in unconditioned response capacities on learning rates would be to vary systematically the response requirements of the instrumental learning task within each age level. To equate the response requirements for different age levels, the experimenter might attempt to select a response criterion appropriate to the unconditioned baseline level of each age group. For example, a 20 degree head-turn for the newborn may be comparable to an 80 degree turn for the 5-month-old infant when differences in unconditioned baseline levels of responses are taken into consideration. It appears from Papoušek's observations that the response criterion used in his studies made greater demands on the limited response repertoire of the newborn infants than it did on the repertoire of the older infants; his measure of conditioning therefore provided a conservative estimate of the learning capacity of the newborn infant.

Instrumental learning in newborns was also studied by Siqueland and Lipsitt (1966), who showed that reinforcement contingencies increased the occurrence of a response that is usually classified as a respondent in infants. The study represented a departure from the usual conditioning paradigm in that a stimulus that is typically considered a US (tactile stimulation of the cheek) served as the CS, and reinforcement (5 percent dextrose via nipple) was made contingent upon the subject's turning his head in the presence of the CS and in the direction of the CS. In the first of three studies, 18 experimental and 18 matched control infants were compared over conditioning and extinction trials. The infants were presented with conditioning and extinction trials on which a 3 second tactile stimulus followed the onset of a 5 second buzzer by 2 seconds. For the experimental group, reinforcement was contingent upon the occurrence of an ipsilateral head-turn (i.e., a turn in the direction of the tactile·stimulus). The control subjects received the same number of dextrose presentations during training, but the nipple-dextrose presentations always occurred 8 to 10 seconds after termination of the buzzer-tactile stimulus, and were given irrespective of whether head-turning responses occurred during the CS interval. It should be noted that the control procedure assured that infants in the control group never received immediate reinforcement for turning to tactile stimulation. The results of the study are shown in Figure 4-2. The contingent reinforcement group gave significantly more responses than the control group during both training and extinction. The increasing separation between the two groups across training trials indicates conditioning of the instrumental head-turning response in the experimental group. (Siqueland and Lipsitt used discrimination training procedures in subsequent studies, the results of which are discussed in the next chapter.) The results of the Siqueland and Lipsitt studies raise some important issues with respect to learning processes in young infants. Specifically, they suggest that components of unconditioned responses may be influenced or shaped by reinforcement contingencies in the infant's environment. Responses that are initially controlled by antecedent (eliciting) stimuli may be progressively elaborated as a function of the infant's adaptive interactions with relevant reinforcement contingencies.

Recent studies of sucking behavior suggest that sucking is rapidly modified by reinforcement contingencies (Sameroff, 1968b). Sameroff has shown that when nutritive consequences are made experimentally contingent upon the "suc-

tion" (negative pressure) or "expression" (positive pressure) components of
the sucking response in newborn infants, these components can be modified.
He developed an experimental nipple and nutrient delivery system that permitted
independent measurements of these components, and that allowed delivery of
the nutrient as a function of the occurrence of either component of the sucking
response. He studied 30 infants, 2 to 5 days of age, during 2 feedings separated

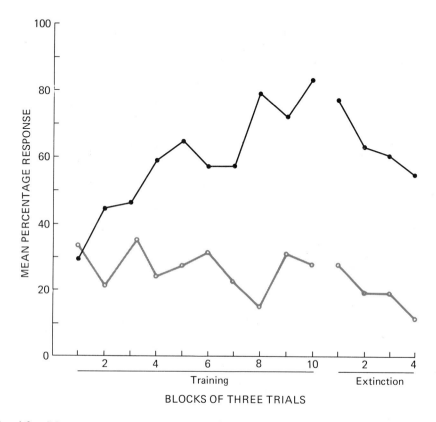

Fig. 4-2. Mean percentage responses to eliciting stimulus during training and extinction trials for experimental (closed circles) and control (open circles) groups. (From
Siqueland and Lipsitt, 1966, Fig. 1, p. 360. Reprinted by permission of the authors
and Academic Press, Inc.)

by 4 hours. Sameroff was cautious in interpreting changes in the components
of the sucking response resulting from this procedure as *learned* behavior because the changes occurred rapidly (within the first minute) and were not
reliably reflected in posttest measures of non-nutritive sucking. A clear interpretation of the changes in the components of the sucking response as conditioning requires evidence for residuals of the response following the termination
of reinforcement (i.e., during extinction).

Siqueland (1968a) has recently shown that head-turning in newborns can be operantly conditioned and that intermittent reinforcement during acquisition training, as compared with continuous reinforcement, results in more responding during extinction. Polygraphic records of head-turning were obtained by means of an apparatus described by Siqueland and Lipsitt (1966). Briefly, the apparatus consisted of a potentiometer circuit, which recorded changes in potential resulting from rotations of the infant's head about the horizontal axis, and a flexible shaft that connected a light plastic headpiece with the potentiometer circuit and allowed the infant complete freedom of head movements. A 10 degree head-turn was selected as the criterion response; the reinforcer was a 5 second presentation of a non-nutritive nipple. Three groups of neonates were given equal numbers of reinforcements but in different patterns. In one group every criterion response was reinforced (continuous reinforcement group); in a second group every third response was reinforced (fixed ratio group); and in the third group a response was reinforced only if it was emitted after the infant had maintained his head position for 20 seconds without emitting a criterion response (pause group). Figure 4-3 shows the mean number of responses emitted by each of the three groups during two extinction periods. The first extinction period was initiated after 30 reinforcements had been given, and the second was initiated after an additional 15 reinforcements had been given. The intermittent reinforcement (fixed ratio) group gave reliably more responses than the continuous reinforcement group, and the pause group, in which head-turning delayed reinforcement, gave the fewest responses over each of the extinction periods. The results of this study show that operant conditioning can be demonstrated in infants during the first days of life and that intermittent reinforcement effects similar to those obtained in adults and infrahuman organisms can be obtained in newborn infants.

Seltzer (1968), in his doctoral thesis, studied acquisition and extinction of high amplitude sucking in 10-day-old infants as a function of reinforcement schedules. The amplitude criterion for the CR was determined individually for each infant on the basis of his non-nutritive sucking baseline. For each infant, Seltzer selected as the criterion response a sucking amplitude that represented approximately 10 percent of the infant's total sucking rate during a one minute baseline period. Delivery of the nutrient (.1 cc of milk) was contingent upon the occurrence of sucking responses that were at least as strong as the criterion amplitude. The sucking device used by Seltzer, and described by DeLucia (1967), provided recordings of all sucking responses and a count of the criterion-amplitude sucks. Conditioned sucking responses were counted automatically and reinforcement was delivered according to various reinforcement schedules. All subjects received a total of 50 reinforcements during training; three groups were given either continuous reinforcement, then intermittent reinforcement (CRF-FR), intermittent reinforcement then continuous reinforcement, (FR-CRF), or continuous reinforcement throughout (CRF-CRF). The two groups that received two different schedules of reinforcement during training were given 25 reinforcements on each schedule. With the intermittent schedule (FR) every fifth response was followed by reinforcement. The three groups were compared over five minutes of extinction following their respective training schedules.

Figure 4-4 shows the results: The graph on the left shows the mean frequencies of CRs over the five minutes of extinction; the graph on the right shows the extinction rates for each group. In the latter graph the slopes of the extinction curves for the three groups have been equated for differences in terminal response rate. Reliable extinction effects and significant differences between the

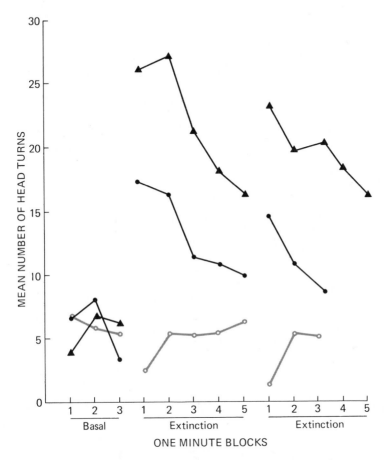

Fig. 4-3. Comparison of mean response frequencies for the three reinforcement schedule groups over baseline and extinction phases. Dark triangle lines, ratio group; dark circle lines, CRF group; light circle lines, pause group. (From Siqueland, 1968a, Fig. 2, p. 435. Reprinted by permission of the author and Academic Press, Inc.)

three groups were obtained with both response measures. The CRF-FR group gave more conditioned sucking responses during extinction than the other two groups, and demonstrated greater stability of conditioned sucking over time.

These results indicate that development of sucking in the newborn, like head-turning to tactile stimulation (Siqueland and Lipsitt, 1966), may reflect the effects of the infant's adaptive interactions with reinforcement contingencies in his environment. Furthermore, Seltzer's results indicate that the conditioned components of the sucking response, a response that is initially closely tied to an eliciting stimulus, are amenable to control by reinforcement schedules. The extinction behavior of newborns showed that intermittent reinforcement of sucking resulted in greater resistance to extinction than continuous reinforcement, and response rate changes during extinction were similar to those obtained

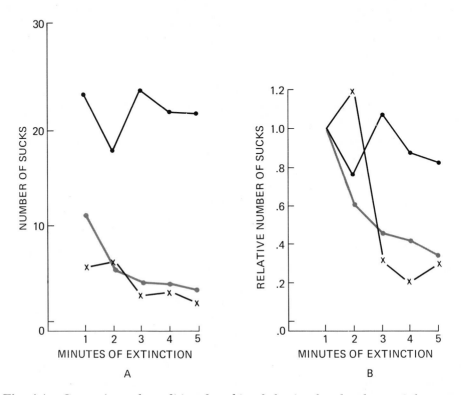

Fig. 4-4. Comparison of conditioned sucking behavior for the three reinforcement schedule groups over the five minute extinction phase. Dark circle line, CRF-FR; light circle line, FR-CRF; cross line, CRF-CRF. (A) Mean number of sucks in 1 minute blocks. (B) Mean responses in 1 minute blocks expressed as proportion of responding in first extinction minute. (From Seltzer, 1968. Reprinted by permission of the author.)

in studies of free operant conditioning. The investigations by Seltzer and Sameroff are in the tradition of earlier studies of instrumental conditioning in the development of non-nutritive sucking (Blau and Blau, 1955; Brodbeck, 1950; Davis, Sears, Miller, and Brodbeck, 1948). However, refinements in response measurement and experimental procedures now permit researchers to study the effects of differential reinforcement superimposed on a reflexive response and to analyze progressive changes in both the conditioned and unconditioned components of that response.

Clayton and Lipsitt (Lipsitt, 1963) studied instrumental punishment in newborn infants, using a "yoked-control" procedure. In the yoked-control procedure, subjects are run in pairs. The experimental subject receives reinforcers contingent upon his own responses; the paired control subject receives reinforcers whenever the experimental subject does, regardless of the responses of the control subject. With this arrangement the experimental subject's behavior instrumentally controls the reinforcing stimulation while the control member of the pair receives the same amount and pattern of stimulation but the stimulation is independent of his behavior. In the Clayton and Lipsitt study, one newborn infant in each pair received a very mild shock each time he kicked a panel while the second newborn in the pair received the same number and pattern of shocks on a noncontingent basis. This is a study of instrumental punishment, since aversive stimulation was contingent upon the occurrence of the response (panel kicking). The investigators obtained no evidence of conditioning, but possibly the failure resulted from interference; the unconditioned response to aversive stimulation is an increase in activity, which would interfere with the response to be conditioned (reduction in kicking).

IMPLICATIONS.   These studies represent a departure from the usual classification of respondent and operant conditioning. Careful experimental analysis of the responses of the newborn, with the kinds of reinforcement procedures used in these studies, may allow the developmental psychologist to specify which response systems are rather strictly reflexive and resistant to modification, and which are subject to multiple control by both eliciting and reinforcing stimuli. The question of multiple control of response systems in the newborn may be closely relevant to the question of how the infant progresses from being a highly reflexive organism to an adaptive organism subject to control by reinforcing events in the environment. These recent studies show that considerable response modification or learning can occur over the first days of human life. An important issue for future studies of instrumental conditioning in newborns is the question of the stability or retention of these instrumental behaviors. With the exception of Papoušek's work, instrumental conditioning studies with newborns have involved relatively brief conditioning procedures, and retention of the obtained changes in behavior has been studied over only brief intervals, usually within a single experimental session.

Instrumental Learning by Older Infants

The major task of identifying the response systems of the developing infant that are amenable to operant control has been attacked by a number of investigators in recent years. Instrumental studies with infants in the first year of life have shown that reinforcement operations can influence a variety of behaviors, including smiling (Brackbill, 1958; Etzel and Gewirtz, 1967; Wahler, 1967), vocalization (Rheingold, Gewirtz, and Ross, 1959; Weisberg, 1963), nonnutritive sucking (Seltzer, 1968; Siqueland, 1966, 1968a), kicking (Lindsley, 1963), manipulative responses (Friedlander, 1967; Lipsitt, 1963; Lipsitt *et al.*, 1966b; Rheingold *et al.*, 1962; Simmons, 1964), eye fixation (Watson, 1966), and head movements (Bower, 1964, 1965b, 1966b; Caron, 1967; Levinson and Levinson, 1967).

With infants under six months of age, researchers have been most successful when they have used learning tasks that require the infant literally to "use his head," producing eye movements, head movements, sucking, vocalizations, and smiling responses. By six months of age the infant has developed sufficient motor coordination to manipulate attractive objects if he is positioned in a specially designed infant seat (Rheingold *et al.*, 1962), and by eight months of age the infant can sit unsupported and respond on panel-pressing and cord-pulling tasks (Lipsitt, 1963). Measures of the operant rates of manipulative responses have been obtained by a number of investigators who have tailored their experimental situations to capitalize on the rapidly developing motor skills of infants from one to three years of age (Bijou, 1957b; Lovaas, 1961; Pumroy and Pumroy, 1961; Rheingold *et al.*, 1964; Simmons, 1964; Simmons and Lipsitt, 1961; Warren and Brown, 1943; Weisberg and Fink, 1966; Weisberg and Tragakis, 1967).

The most common experimental design used in these studies has been the *baseline* technique, in which the experimenter first measures the operant level of the response—the baseline or spontaneous rate of emitting the response—then presents a reinforcing stimulus contingent upon the response (conditioning), and finally makes the reinforcer no longer contingent upon the response (extinction). Most studies have shown reliable increases in response rate during conditioning and decrements during extinction. Despite the predictable changes in response rate over conditioning, there are obvious limitations in this design. In operant studies, it is important to distinguish between changes in response rate that are attributable to the response-reinforcement contingency and changes in behavior that are independent of this association between response and consequent stimulation. Unconditioned changes in response rate may occur as a result of changes in the subject's arousal level or "state" following the presentation of a positive or aversive stimulus. Changes in arousal may result in sizable shifts in the frequency of unconditioned responses. For example, crying and smiling are incompatible responses, and smiling may increase in frequency simply because an incompatible crying response has been disrupted by the presentation of an attractive visual stimulus. Thus, the change in smiling, though correlated with the experimenter's presentation of some reinforcer, may not involve any direct associative or learning process.

It can be argued that in operant conditioning experiments, in which the experimenter presents stimuli contingent upon a response, the presentation of the reinforcing stimuli is in fact eliciting the behavior and any increase in the frequency of responding is attributable to the eliciting properties of the reinforcing stimuli. The problem of distinguishing between these unconditioned behavioral changes and the response changes that are uniquely attributable to the association between response and reinforcing stimuli has been discussed by Rheingold *et al.* (1959). A brief discussion of their study and a subsequent study by Weisberg (1963) will illustrate the problem and one type of control procedure that allows a clear demonstration of operant conditioning.

Rheingold *et al.* (1959) used the baseline technique to study operant conditioning of vocalization in three month old institutionalized infants. The infants were studied for 6 days, 2 days of baseline assessment, 2 days of conditioning, and finally 2 days of extinction. Observations were made in 3-minute periods separated by rest intervals. On each of the 6 days there were 9 observation periods. During the baseline phase the experimenter leaned over the crib with an expressionless face and looked at the infant for a total of 18 3-minute periods. During the conditioning phase each vocalization by the infant was reinforced by the experimenter (smiling, touching the infant's abdomen, and saying "tsk, tsk, tsk"). During the extinction phase the experimenter leaned over the crib with an expressionless face and made no response to the subject's vocalizations. The frequency of vocalizations during conditioning rose above the baseline level, and subsequently during extinction returned to the baseline level. The baseline average was about 14 vocalizations in each 3-minute period. By the second day of conditioning the vocalization rate had increased to 25, an increase of 86 percent over the baseline level. On the first day of extinction the rate decreased to 17 responses and on the second day to 15. Despite the reliable changes in response rate over the conditioning and extinction phases, the conclusion that vocalizations were operantly conditioned is equivocal because these changes could have resulted from increased elicitation of smiling by the reinforcing stimulus (the experimenter's actions). The appropriate controls required to reject the elicitation interpretation of these results were discussed by Rheingold *et al.* (1959), and Weisberg (1963) subsequently repeated the experiment with the necessary controls added.

With four independent groups of subjects, Weisberg compared the effects of contingent and noncontingent presentation of two classes of reinforcing stimuli—adult social reactions similar to those in the study by Rheingold *et al.,* and an auditory stimulus (a door chime). In addition to these four primary groups, two groups were utilized for extended baseline observations, one group with the experimenter present and the other with the experimenter absent (see Table 4-3). Three month old institutionalized infants were studied for 8 days, 4 days of baseline assessment, 2 days of conditioning, and 2 days of extinction. There were 2 10-minute observation periods each day. During the baseline phase the experimenter observed each infant from behind a partition on the first 2 days and sat facing the infant with an expressionless face on the next 2 days. The conditioning phase, on Days 5 and 6, involved essentially the same procedures as used by Rheingold *et al.* On Days 7 and 8 the contingent social and auditory stimulation groups were given extinction with the experimenter present. The noncontingent social and auditory stimulation groups continued to receive the stimulation on Days 7 and 8. There were no changes in the conditions for the extended baseline groups over the 8 days.

The two contingent stimulation groups were included to provide an assessment of the relative effectiveness of adult social behavior and the door chime as reinforcers; the two noncontingent groups provided a control for possible eliciting effects of these stimuli; and the extended baseline groups permitted an assessment of possible changes in operant levels of vocalization in the presence and absence of an adult's face. Weisberg's results clearly supported the operant conditioning interpretation of Rheingold *et al.* The only group that showed a reliable increase in rate of vocalization during conditioning was the group given contingent social reinforcement. In the baseline phase this group averaged approximately 11 responses per ten minute period; in the conditioning phase the rate increased to 31 responses; and in the extinction phase it dropped to about 20 responses. The results rule out the interpretation of increased vocalization as a product of arousal or specific eliciting effects of the reinforcing stimulus.

Although not without problems, a control procedure in which noncontingent or random stimulation is presented provides data for assessing unconditioned effects that might be produced by the successive presentation of the reinforcing stimulus. It should be noted, however, that a control procedure in which stimula-

Table 4-3

The Weisberg Design[a]

Group	Reinforcement	Reinforcer	Special feature
1	Contingent	Social	Experimenter present during extinction
2	Contingent	Auditory	Experimenter present during extinction
3	Noncontingent	Social	Noncontingent reinforcement in both conditioning and extinction phase
4	Noncontingent	Auditory	Noncontingent reinforcement in both conditioning and extinction phase
5	—	—	Baseline only, with experimenter present throughout
6	—	—	Baseline only, with experimenter absent throughout

[a] Weisberg (1963). See text for further explanation.

tion is not only noncontingent but also *truly random* may not produce the same baseline rate as a control procedure in which response and reinforcement are explicitly unpaired. The latter procedure amounts to differential reinforcement for not responding (DRO) and should produce "conditioned inhibition of response" (Siqueland, 1968a). The previously discussed study by Clayton and Lipsitt (Lipsitt, 1963) using the yoked-control procedure provides an example of the truly random stimulation control.

In addition to the use of noncontingent stimulation and DRO controls in between-subjects experimental designs, in which each treatment is given to a different group, researchers may use these control conditions in within-subjects designs, in which a group receives more than one treatment. Individual subjects can be given, at different times, contingent, noncontingent, and DRO stimulation. Such procedures were used in two recent experiments in which individual infants were studied in daily experimental sessions from the age of two weeks to the age of three months (Heid, 1965; Sheppard, 1967).

Another example of a within-subjects control is provided in a study by Rheingold *et al.* (1962). The response was manipulation of a small sphere mounted on an adjustable rod; the reinforcing stimulation was the projection of brightly colored, moving geometric forms on a screen in front of the infant. Response rates in each infant were observed under conditions of both contingent and noncontingent visual stimulation. The investigators reported preliminary results showing that some infants responded at higher rates during the contingent phase than during the noncontingent phase.

All too frequently, control procedures have not been included in studies of operant conditioning; experimenters have too often relied exclusively on the use of the baseline technique. Stronger evidence for operant control has been provided by studies in which infants are required to make a highly differentiated response within a general class of motor behavior and in which the effectiveness of the reinforcer in "shaping" a response specified by the experimenter is demonstrated.

Reinforcement influences not only the rate but also the specific "topography" of responses. Topography refers to the physical components that constitute the specified operant. Reinforcement may modify the form, duration, amplitude, and pattern of a response. The experimenter can consistently reinforce one topographical variation of a larger response class and progressively strengthen that response by his selective reinforcement procedures. Several investigators (Sameroff, 1968b; Seltzer, 1968; Siqueland, 1966) have shown that sucking amplitude can be shaped by reinforcement. In head-turning studies investigators have differentially reinforced directional head movements, requiring infants to make a left-right response discrimination (Caron, 1967; Siqueland, 1964). Watson (1966) obtained some evidence for spatially differentiated eye fixation responses in 9 and 14 week old infants. With older infants a multiple response apparatus can be used to deal with the problem of "attractive" manipulanda eliciting high levels of baseline responding. Presenting infants with two or three response manipulanda has allowed investigators to demonstrate the effectiveness of reinforcers in shaping spatially discriminated lever-pressing responses when relative response frequency (Lipsitt, 1963; Simmons, 1964) and relative response duration (Friedlander, 1967) are used to index conditioned responding. Lovaas (1961), in a study of verbal conditioning in older infants, used trinkets to reinforce aggressive verbal responses in one group of subjects and nonaggressive verbalizations in a second group. Both groups showed a reliable increase in rate of occurrence of the reinforced class of verbalizations, demonstrating that the reinforcement procedures were effective in changing the relative frequencies of these two classes of verbal responses. Evidence for progressive response discrimination resulting from selective reinforcement contingencies, and subsequent extinction of this discrimination, provides strong evidence for operant control of responding.

Recent attempts have been made to establish reinforcement control over operants that were initially too weak to permit instrumental reinforcement. If the baseline rate is extremely low, the response occurs so rarely that there is virtually no opportunity to introduce the response-reinforcement contingency. In recent studies of conditioned smiling (Etzel and Gewirtz, 1967) and head-turning (Caron, 1967), the experimenters found it necessary to institute a response shaping procedure with some infants, who initially evidenced low operant levels of the response. The experimenter elicited the desired response prior to reinforcement and then shaped the response by reinforcing gradual approximations to the desired response.

A study by Etzel and Gewirtz on conditioned smiling in a 6 week old infant and a 20 week old infant provides an example of this kind of response shaping procedure. Initially, high levels of crying, which is incompatible with smiling, required the experimenters to elicit the smiling response by presenting the infant with a shiny metal saucer. The smiling response was shaped by reinforcing successive approximations of the elicited response to the desired response; once the smile met the criterion of "a broad, full smile," the eliciting stimulus was discontinued and the response was regularly maintained by the reinforcer. The initial response shaping procedure used by Etzel and Gewirtz is similar to the procedure used by Siqueland and Lipsitt (1966), in that reinforcement contingencies were employed to strengthen components of an "elicited" response. However, the procedures used by Etzel and Gewirtz went a step further in bringing the response under operant control. Smiling, a response that initially required an eliciting stimulus for its occurrence, became detached from the eliciting stimulus and was thereafter maintained by the reinforcement contingencies in the absence of the original eliciting stimulus. Gewirtz (1969) and Bijou and Baer (1965) have discussed a conceptual framework for analyzing the effects of reinforcement on classes of "elicited" behaviors. The adaptive function of early reflexes and the influence of reinforcement contingencies on the subsequent modification of these reflexes may prove to be important topics for future studies of instrumental learning in young infants.

SCHEDULES OF REINFORCEMENT.   A few studies have dealt with the effects of intermittent reinforcement schedules on the acquisition and extinction of behavior in older infants. (See Table 4-2 for descriptions of the various schedules.)

Acquisition and maintenance of behavior under FR schedules have been obtained in children from 2 to 5 years of age, with visual-auditory reinforcement (Rheingold et al., 1964), and in infants from 1 to 2 years of age, with food as the reinforcer (Weisberg and Fink, 1966). In both studies, the subjects were initially trained with continuous reinforcement and progressively advanced to short FR schedules. Within 4 to 9 sessions, Weisberg and Fink established stable responding under FR 10 in 4 infants and FR 15 in another infant. Fifteen of 20 subjects in the study by Rheingold et al. showed sensitivity to ratio control, as reflected by increased response rates with increased ratios. In subjects under 3 years of age, the median ratio that exerted effective control was 3, and in the older subjects it was 10. However, this apparent age difference was not statistically reliable. In both of these studies the subjects' FR performance was consistent with FR performance characteristically obtained in infrahuman organisms and older children, showing a high and constant run of responses without pauses, followed by brief pauses at the delivery of reinforcement. Figure 4-5 shows the typical FR performance curve.

Sheppard (1967) recently reported the results of a study with a single infant in daily 20 to 30 minute experimental sessions over the first 3 months of life. His findings suggest FR control of conditioned vocalizations within the first 30 days of life. The subject also showed progressive increases in conditioned kicking rates as the schedule was shifted from CRF to FR 5. Vibratory stimulation of the infant's right hand served as the reinforcer for vocalization, and a complex visual-auditory reinforcer was used for the kicking response.

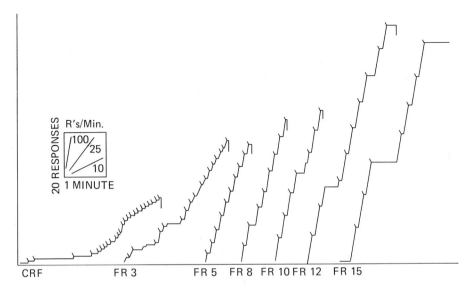

Fig. 4-5. Effect of increasing FRs on the responding of a boy 2.8 years old. The vertical axis is cumulative number of responses, and the baseline is time; each diagonal "notch" indicates delivery of a reinforcement; the curves are displaced to save space; the slope of any segment can be interpreted as response rate, as shown in the insert; flat segments indicate pausing. (From Rheingold *et al.*, 1964, Fig. 1, p. 319. Reprinted by permission of the authors and Academic Press, Inc.)

Studies of interval reinforcement schedules with infants below 3 years of age have been scarce (Stoddard, 1962; Warren and Brown, 1943; Weisberg and Tragakis, 1967). Investigators interested in the development of temporal discrimination have used a special type of interval schedule. In contrast to schedules that shape and maintain high response rates, DRL schedules (differential reinforcement of low rates) limit the rate of responding that precedes the reinforced response. The subject must wait a minimum amount of time between responses or responses will not be reinforced. Stoddard investigated timing behavior in children from 2 to 10 years of age with DRL schedules of 10 and 20 seconds (the subject is required to wait a minimum of 10 or 20 seconds between reinforced responses). All subjects, including two below 3 years of age, learned to space their responses in accordance with the DRL schedule used. Weisberg and Tragakis studied DRL performance in infants ranging from 15 to 41 months of age, and found that DRL 10 sec. and DRL 18 sec. produced and maintained low response rates which revealed temporal conditioning comparable to that in animals and adults. These studies suggest that DRL schedules may provide a valuable research tool for studying the process by which children discriminate time intervals.

The course of extinction following each of these schedules of reinforcement is influenced by the previously maintained response pattern. Most investigations with older children and adults, using number of responses per unit time or number of responses to cessation of responding as the dependent variable, have demonstrated the so-called intermittent reinforcement effect, that is, more responding in extinction following intermittent reinforcement than following CRF (Bijou, 1957b; Carment and Miles, 1962; Kass, 1962; Kass and Wilson, 1966; Lewis, 1960). The results of infant studies are generally in agreement with these findings. Studies with newborns (Seltzer, 1968; Siqueland, 1968a), four month old infants (Brackbill, 1958), and three year olds (Bijou, 1957b) have shown that subjects given intermittent reinforcement respond more during extinction than subjects who receive CRF. Both Bijou and Brackbill trained their intermittent reinforcement groups on VR schedules; Siqueland and Seltzer both used FR schedules. Except in one study (Brackbill, 1958), the number of reinforcements was held constant and the number of responses was free to vary. In the Brackbill study, the intermittent reinforcement group gave more responses than the CRF group despite the greater number of reinforcements received by the CRF group. The results are therefore somewhat ambiguous, because in older infants, at least, there is a positive correlation between number of previously reinforced responses and resistance to extinction (Pumroy and Pumroy, 1961; Siegel and Foshee, 1953). Comparative studies by Gonzalez, Eskin, and Bitterman (1962, 1963) have shown that equating frequency of reinforcement across subjects is important in demonstrating intermittent reinforcement effects across species. Despite differences in the age of subjects, responses investigated, number of reinforcements and responses, and type of reinforcers used in studies with infants, more responding during extinction followed intermittent than continuous reinforcement.

The effects of extended FR and DRL training on extinction performance of 1- to 2-year-old infants have been examined in two studies by Weisberg and collaborators (Weisberg and Fink, 1966; Weisberg and Tragakis, 1967). The degree to which the extinction performance of individual subjects paralleled the performance of other organisms under these schedules was dependent upon the stability and type of performance pattern obtained during conditioning.

Summary and Future Directions

Instrumental conditioning studies have shown that the human infant from the first days of life is an active, adaptive organism as well as a reflexively reacting organism. The infant's sensitivity to control by a wide variety of reinforcement contingencies suggests that instrumental learning plays an important role in the child's adaptive interactions with his environment. Unfortunately, most learning studies with infants have tended to be of an exploratory nature, designed to determine whether a given response can be classically or operantly conditioned in infants, whether the infant behaves like the adult in acquisition and extinction, whether particular stimuli function as reinforcers for the infant, and so on. Despite the frequently reported positive correlations between learning rate and age, there is no unequivocal evidence of ontogenetic differences in *capacity* for simple classical and operant conditioning. Differences obtained between different age groups are frequently equivocal because of failure of the investigator to control for differences in motivation, reinforcement, response capacities, and past learning histories. By selecting conditioning procedures that are optimal for the motorically immature and nonverbal infant, investigators have begun systematic study of learning parameters that may influence the ontogeny of learning over the first years of life.

Investigators of learning in infants have given little attention to the problem of the relations between classical and instrumental conditioning. A recent review of research generated by two-process learning theory has raised a number of important questions for researchers interested in the study of the ontogeny of learning (Maier, Seligman, and Solomon, 1968). Specifically, studies with both human adults and infrahuman organisms suggest that past classical conditioning histories with aversive and appetitive stimuli can have disruptive or facilitative effects on subsequent instrumental behavior. Although artificial experimental environments have shown the young infant to be susceptible to instrumental conditioning, much of the young infant's real-life learning is of the classical conditioning variety. Studies of escape and avoidance conditioning have shown that the effects of a contingency between a CS and US on subsequent instrumental learning are dependent upon whether instrumental responding was established prior to experience with the classical contingency. These well-demonstrated order effects in the relations between Pavlovian conditioning and instrumental behavior may have important implications for the development of instrumental adaptive behaviors in the human infant.

FREE OPERANT CONDITIONING IN CHILDREN

Acquisition

SINGLE SCHEDULES OF POSITIVE REINFORCEMENT. The various schedules of intermittent reinforcement that have been used in studies with children are described in Table 4-2. The first reported study of operant conditioning in children, by Warren and Brown (1943), is mainly of historical interest. Children two to five years old participated for 15 22-minute sessions in a task that involved pushing a lever to obtain candy. The sequence of events over the 15 sessions included adaptation days, acquisition under CRF, extinction, reacquisition under

CRF, shift to FI 15 sec., and finally re-extinction. A comparison of response rates under CRF and FI 15 sec. would not be meaningful, because extinction and reconditioning sessions intervened between these schedules. Under both schedules, however, high drive subjects (children who ate all their candy quickly) responded at a fairly constant rate and weak drive subjects (those who ate little or no candy within the session) exhibited irregular response curves in which rapid responding alternated with periods of no response at all (see Figure 4-6). None of the subjects conditioned rapidly. Instead, the general pattern was to begin with slow irregular rates, shift to rapid rates, then level off

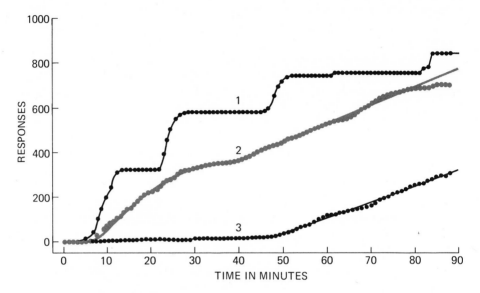

Fig. 4-6. Cumulative number of responses during the initial CRF conditioning sessions. The irregular curve (1) is for a weak drive subject; the more regular curves (2 and 3) are for subjects with stronger drive. (From Warren and Brown, 1943, Fig. 1, p. 188. Reprinted by permission of the authors and the Journal Press.)

at a constant rate. It seems likely that the subjects were at least initially somewhat apprehensive in the special experimental room; if so, extra adaptation training might have resulted in more regular response rates during the earlier conditioning periods.

Surprisingly, over a decade passed before it was ardently proposed that extensive and systematic research be conducted with children employing the free operant response (Bijou, 1955, 1957a). There are several important considerations involved in developing a plan for such research. These include (among others) (a) choosing a simple methodology that will allow considerable control of experimental variables; (b) selecting an uncomplicated voluntary response, the initiation and termination of which are accomplished in a brief time period; (c) devising an apparatus that elicits a large number of responses, to increase the likelihood of getting useful comparisons of response rates, especially when resistance to extinction is examined; (d) selecting appropriate reinforcers; (e) minimizing adult influence through verbalization or physical presence; and (f) arranging initial play sessions with the child to reduce any disrupting effect of emotionality in the experimental sessions.

Complying with these general principles, investigators have studied schedule effects in infants and normal and retarded children. Most reports include detailed accounts of the conditioning techniques employed initially and further developed over training.

Long, Hammack, May, and Campbell (1958) investigated FR, FI, and VI schedules in 200 normal four to eight year old children. Information was

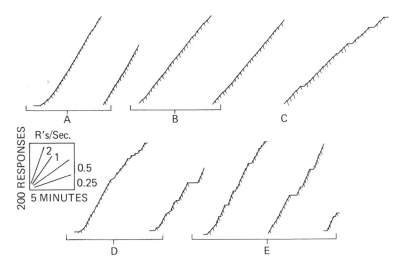

Fig. 4-7. First-session records of five children on FR 15. All are FR-like curves. As the session progresses the decline in overall rate for Subjects C, D, and E is evident. (From Long, Hammack, May, and Campbell, *Journal of the Experimental Analysis of Behavior*, 1958, *1*, 315–339. Fig. 1, p. 317. Copyright 1958 by the Society for the Experimental Analysis of Behavior, Inc. Reprinted by permission.)

gathered on FR schedules ranging from FR 5 to FR 150. With trinkets as reinforcers, almost all subjects developed response rates resembling those of infrahuman subjects receiving primary reinforcement (e.g., food, water). The response rate curve exhibited a pause after reinforcement, followed by a fairly rapid and constant rate of responding until the ratio was run off (see Figure 4-7). This typical curve obtained with FR was not evident, however, if the initial ratios employed were either too small or too large. (This finding calls into question the frequently used technique of starting with very small FRs or CRF in attempting to establish the response.) The use of schedules of FR 20 or less in the first session increased the length of the postreinforcement pauses by the end of the session (see curves of Subjects C, D, and E in Figure 4-7). Prolonged use of small ratios resulted in a deterioration over sessions in the response rate for all subjects. The decline in the reinforcing effect of trinkets may be overcome by substituting reinforcers, increasing the time between sessions, doubling the number of reinforcements given, or reducing the size of the ratio (e.g., from FR 90 to FR 25, as shown in Figure 4-8). When the ratio in the first sessions was too high (FR 60 or greater), ratio-like behavior did not develop even after 17 sessions. However, good schedule control over response rate was obtained with ratios as high as FR 90 or FR 100 if (a) sufficient schedule control had been developed first with smaller ratios, (b) the shift to increasingly larger ratios had been gradual, and (c) the subject had not become satiated for trinket reinforcers.

Spradlin, Girardeau, and Corte (1965) also employed gradually increasing FR schedules with severely retarded subjects (7 to 19 years old). Various foods and liquids were used as reinforcers. All subjects exhibited typical high-rate

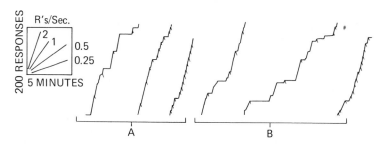

Fig. 4-8.   Effect of reduction of FR 90 to FR 25 in two subjects (A and B). Note the increase in response rate and near elimination of pausing and negative curvature. (From Long, Hammack, May, and Campbell, *Journal of the Experimental Analysis of Behavior*, 1958, *1*, 315–339. Fig. 8, p. 322. Copyright 1958 by the Society for the Experimental Analysis of Behavior, Inc. Reprinted by permission.)

FR behavior at some time during the experiment. In the records of several subjects, the pauses were relatively long, possibly because no deprivation conditions were in effect. If the ratio reached too high a limit, such as beyond FR 650, response rate deteriorated. In another study with retardates (9 to 21 years old), high stable rates of responding on a metal bar were obtained under various FR schedules (Orlando and Bijou, 1960).

Relatively less attention has been given to the effect of VR schedules upon response acquisition. Orlando and Bijou (1960) noted that VR schedules produced rates of responding that were roughly proportional to the size of the ratio. Short pauses in responding occurred, but they were infrequent and, unlike those found with FR schedules, were random with respect to time of reinforcement (see Figure 4-9).

Gaining schedule control over a child's behavior has been more difficult with FI than with other intermittent schedules. Infrahumans under FI control exhibit pauses (somewhat longer than under FR) following reinforcement and then a scallop, that is, relatively gradual acceleration in response rate until a terminal

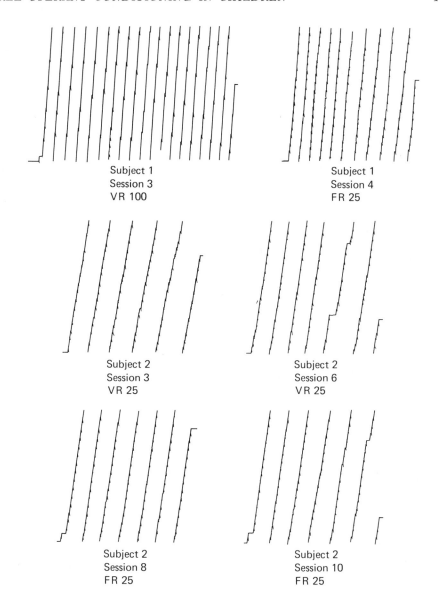

Subject 1
Session 3
VR 100

Subject 1
Session 4
FR 25

Subject 2
Session 3
VR 25

Subject 2
Session 6
VR 25

Subject 2
Session 8
FR 25

Subject 2
Session 10
FR 25

Fig. 4-9. Cumulative records showing VR and FR performances of two subjects in different sessions. (From Orlando and Bijou, *Journal of the Experimental Analysis of Behavior*, 1960, 3, 339–348. Fig. 1, p. 341. Copyright 1960 by the Society for the Experimental Analysis of Behavior, Inc. Reprinted by permission.)

rate is attained. Long *et al.* (1958) found that some children's response rates were never controlled by the FI schedule. Orlando and Bijou (1960) and Spradlin *et al.* (1965) found that scalloping was infrequent, although the few retarded subjects who did show the scallop did so consistently (Orlando and Bijou, 1960; see Figure 4-10). In many normal subjects, the FI scallop was transitory, appear-

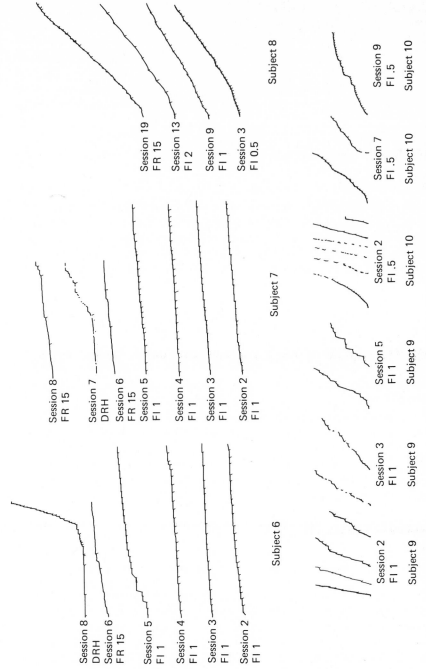

Fig. 4-10. Cumulative records showing the variety of performances produced in retarded subjects under FI. Subject 8 shows scalloping on a variety of FI schedules. Subject 9 shows weak FI control with irregular rate and pause distribution. (From Orlando and Bijou, *Journal of the Experimental Analysis of Behavior*, 1960, 3, 339–348. Fig. 4, p. 345. Copyright 1960 by the Society for the Experimental Analysis of Behavior, Inc. Reprinted by permission.)

ing for a time and then disappearing never to return (Long *et al.*, 1958). When the FI scallop did occur, deviations were often imposed upon it. For example, some subjects responded continually through several intervals, pausing only after several reinforcements had been obtained; some subjects exhibited additional acceleration or deceleration within the scallop.

Long *et al.* reviewed the procedures found to be successful in establishing FI-like behavior. These included the following: (a) Starting the subject on VI 30 sec. and shifting to FI 1 or (b) beginning on FI 1 without previous experience with intermittent reinforcement. Subjects who were started on either FI 30 sec. or small FRs before being shifted to FI 1 showed delayed development of FI-like behavior. (c) In some cases a shift from FI 1 to FI 2 led to FI-like behavior, oddly enough; however, several subjects refused to remain in the experimental room under the longer interval. (d) Changing the reinforcement procedure also had the effect of producing more regular post-reinforcement pauses. The change consisted of projecting a picture on a screen while the subject responded. In addition to the regular reinforcement—a penny or a trinket—the picture was changed at the termination of the reinforcement interval. There are several possible reasons for the success of this manipulation in establishing FI-like behavior: Changing the pictures may have constituted additional reinforcement; the subject may have tired of the picture over time and performed at a high terminal rate in order to get rid of it; presenting a new picture may have led to more regular post-reinforcement pauses simply because the subject stopped to look at the picture instead of operating the manipulandum; or the picture may have provided a better stimulus basis for the subject to make the temporal discrimination necessary under an FI schedule. All four of these possibilities should be investigated in future studies.

Under VI schedules, both retardates (Orlando and Bijou, 1960) and normals (Long *et al.*, 1958) have developed fairly high and constant rates of responding. In some instances, there is random pausing under VI schedules, especially if the schedule contains too few short intervals. Orlando and Bijou (1960) reported that VI performance was almost identical to VR of a comparable value. A good procedure for use in experiments comparing these schedules would involve the yoked experimental control. With such a procedure, two subjects are run simultaneously on separate response devices. One subject is reinforced on a VR schedule, and as soon as reinforcement is delivered the second subject's next response is also reinforced. Thus, the second subject is on a VI schedule, and comparisons of VR and VI can be made with the total number of reinforcements held constant and with the times of delivering reinforcements approximately constant. In pigeons a constant rate of responding develops under each schedule but the rate is considerably higher for VR (Reynolds, 1968). There is a need for similar investigations with children.

With the simple schedules discussed so far, there are clear relations between the type of schedule employed and the child's behavior. In some cases differences between performance under the various schedules are as distinct as with infrahumans, and in other cases schedule control is not as strong with human subjects. The investigator who employs child subjects has several complicating factors to deal with. His subjects do not arrive at the laboratory after having been deprived of food for 22 hours, and his subjects have had several years of reinforcement history that might increase the difficulty of establishing schedule control. Two possible plans of attack upon the problem of establishing schedule control might be (a) to focus upon the development of new techniques for shaping the behavior in question, or (b) to employ social reinforcers following periods of social deprivation. Even relatively brief deprivation has been shown to lead to increased effectiveness of social reinforcers (e.g., Stevenson, 1965).

COMPLEX SCHEDULES. An ultimate understanding of the relation between a child's past history of reinforcement and his present behavior necessitates investigations of the effects of schedules relatively more complex than those discussed above. Several complex schedules have received at least preliminary study. The use of multiple schedules provides one example (see Table 4-2 for definitions).

A multiple schedule (Mult) consists of two or more separate schedules, each of which is associated with a different discriminative stimulus (S^D). (If one of the schedules involves extinction, the discriminative stimulus is labeled S^Δ.) Each schedule is put into effect for a particular time period in an attempt to bring the subject's behavior under control of the separate S^Ds. The two schedules may be presented in an alternating or random manner. The dependent variable is rate of response under each S^D. Investigations with multiple schedules provide information on the acquisition of discriminations and on the interaction of particular schedules with other features of the environment. It is quite possible that behavior under any schedule when presented singly may differ significantly from behavior under the same schedule in a multiple arrangement.

Techniques have been developed for investigating multiple schedules in normal and retarded children. Long (1959) employed a Mult FI FR schedule with 32 preschool children. Most were begun on Mult FI 1.5 FR 10, or Mult FI 2 FR 10. Only 18 of the subjects ever showed any evidence of multiple control, and none had been brought under multiple control after approximately eight sessions. Multiple control was finally obtained in 14 subjects by introducing procedural changes. These included using a different reinforcer with each of the two schedules, changing the response manipulandum, and satiating subjects with 25 trinkets prior to the experimental session. In another study, Long (1962) established multiple control in six subjects (four to seven years of age) without the use of any additional techniques. Additional techniques were useful, however, in establishing control in other subjects. Presenting the FR component until four to six reinforcements had been obtained led to strong control in four to five sessions. Increasing the size of FR seemed to make the schedules more discriminable and aided control especially in subjects with initially high rates of responding. Strong control during FI was established in some subjects by the addition of differential reinforcement of low rates of responding (DRL) to the FI schedule. Under a DRL schedule, a response leads to reinforcement only if some specified amount of time has elapsed since the last reinforced response. A response made before the time period has terminated does not lead to reinforcement and resets the timer measuring the required pause. The process was not that simple, however, because adding DRL to FI resulted in an initial delay of reinforcement. Therefore, the FIs had to be temporarily reduced. For example, a subject might begin on Mult FI 1.25 FR 10; when a DRL requiring one second pauses is added, the FI is reduced to 30 sec. The FI can then be gradually increased as control develops. Another procedure that aided the establishment of multiple control under Mult FI FR was a temporary shift to a different schedule, for example, Mult DRL FR, or Mult FR Ext (extinction). Finally, a procedure that was highly effective in producing control involved the addition of an "external clock" to FI. In general, an external clock is any method used to signal the passage of time. In Long's study it was the withholding of the S^D for FI during the first 20 to 25 seconds of FI.

Multiple control has also been successfully established with Mult FR Ext, Mult DRL Ext, Mult DRO FR (Long, 1962), and Mult VR Ext (Bijou, 1961). (The DRO schedule—*differential reinforcement of other response*—is one in which the response that is reinforced is *other* than the response of primary interest. For example, to produce a slow rate of responding the experimenter could use DRL, reinforcing only responses with latencies greater than some specified value, or could use DRO, reinforcing *not* responding.) Under DRO, the subjects were reinforced for not operating the manipulandum when a particular S^D was presented. Long found that DRO was particularly effective with subjects who performed at an initially high rate or who presented such problems in the laboratory as not remaining in the experimental room.

In a series of investigations with retarded subjects, the initial rate was evaluated and subjects with either initially high or initially low rates were identified (Bijou and Orlando, 1961; Orlando, 1965; Orlando and Bijou, 1960). When one component of the multiple schedule is extinction, the evaluation of the initial rate serves two important functions. First, since it may take considerable time to establish extinction to S^Δ in a high-rate subject, early detection of high rates warns the experimenter to avoid dispensing any more reinforcements than necessary, permitting him to bring the subject quickly to the next phase of the experiment. Second, if training on low rates of responding to S^Δ is undertaken when initial rates are generally low or are weakened by the schedule in force, then extinction may develop even for S^D. To avoid this, an increasing ratio schedule may be employed to strengthen response rate before undertaking any training with S^Δ.

A key feature of the Bijou and Orlando procedure involved a phase called *pause building*, the purpose of which was to strengthen response withholding for increasing periods of time in the presence of S^Δ while maintaining prompt responding with the onset of S^D. The technique consisted of employing a DRL contingency in the presence of S^Δ. Thus, rapid responses to S^Δ were not reinforced and in addition delayed the presentation of S^D for a specified amount of time. As training progressed, the pause in responding required during S^Δ was gradually increased. Early in the pause building phase, each response to S^D brought a reinforcement (CRF) and terminated S^D; later, the S^D periods were also lengthened.

Orlando (1965) introduced modifications into the pause building phase to overcome two major defects. First, some subjects in the Bijou and Orlando study developed a tendency to give a single response whenever S^D was presented. Perhaps the single reinforcement with each S^D presentation became itself a discriminative stimulus for pausing, since it was always followed by S^Δ. This failure to maintain S^D rate while establishing stimulus control led to extinction when subjects were transferred to the final multiple schedule. A second defect was a general depression of response rate during the pause building phase, with little or no stimulus control established. It seemed as though for some subjects the pause building phase was functioning as a simple DRL schedule without any regard to stimulus conditions.

The details of Orlando's modifications will not be presented here. Essentially, the conditions ensured that rate was maintained during establishment of stimulus control, and the duration of the pause required during S^Δ was not increased unless stimulus control was developing. Several older retarded subjects still failed to be shaped under the modified procedure, mainly because of high resistance to extinction to S^Δ. However, establishment of stimulus control was aided by the introduction of further modifications, such as giving demonstrations by the experimenter, presenting a loud noise for response during S^Δ, and changing the positive reinforcer for responses during S^D. The ultimate success in establishing multiple control suggests that often the failure of mentally retarded subjects to acquire appropriate behavior in learning situations may actually be due to inadequate shaping procedures or ineffective reinforcers rather than some general learning deficit.

Additional complex schedules that have received exploratory study with young children (four to seven years old) are *chained* and *tandem* schedules (Long, 1963). In a chain, as in any multiple schedule, different discriminative stimuli are associated with different schedules. Appropriate behavior during presentation of the S^D associated with the first schedule is not reinforced, but brings the other S^D and the other schedule into operation. For example, during DRL in Chain DRL FR, a response with a latency greater than some predetermined value terminates the S^D for DRL and initiates the S^D for FR. During FR, the subject can run off the ratio at any rate and acquire a reinforcement. Long (1963) found that both Chain DRL FR and Chain DRO FR almost always produced strong schedule and stimulus control, but with Chain FI FR additional procedures were needed to establish strong control (see Figure 4-11). These included (a) first establishing schedule and stimulus control with either Chain DRL FR or Chain DRO FR and then switching to Chain FI FR; (b) increasing the size of the FR component; and (c) adding an external clock to the FI component.

A tandem schedule is like a chain except that no separate S^D is associated with each schedule. Thus, on Tandem FI FR the stimulus light remains constant throughout the session, except for the few seconds during reinforcement delivery. Long (1963) was unable to produce regular or repeatable patterns of responding with Tandem FI FR unless additional procedures were employed, such as adding an external clock to the FI component or first establishing control on Tandem DRO FR before switching to Tandem FI FR. Long found evidence of both

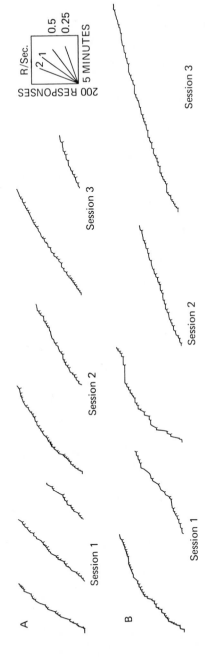

Fig. 4-11. The development of stimulus control in two subjects (A and B) on Chain DRL FR schedules. The DRL varied between and within sessions. (From Long, *Journal of the Experimental Analysis of Behavior,* 1963, *6,* 459–472. Fig. 1, p. 460. Copyright 1963 by the Society for the Experimental Analysis of Behavior, Inc. Reprinted by permission.)

stimulus and schedule control in switching from Chain FI FR to Tandem FI FR. When the constant stimulus in the tandem schedule had been the S^D for FI in the chain schedule, the switch in schedules produced a decrement in overall response rate, suggesting that stimulus change can be an important controlling factor. When the constant stimulus in the tandem schedule had been the S^D for FR in the chain, the response rates in the tandem approximated those produced in the chain, suggesting that schedule also operates as a controller of rate pattern.

Research on complex schedules has just begun with child subjects. An interesting and promising field of investigation awaits the ambitious researcher on the following complex schedules that have been studied with infrahumans: (a) conjunctive schedules—a single response is reinforced only if the subject meets the requirements of two (or more) schedules; (b) alternative schedules—a response is reinforced when either of two (or more) requirements of different schedules are met; (c) interlocking schedules—a response is reinforced after a certain number of responses, but the number increases (or decreases) the longer the time since the last reinforced response; (d) concurrent schedules—reinforcing two (or more) responses according to two (or more) schedules at the same time.

ESCAPE AND AVOIDANCE.   The crucial area of escape and avoidance conditioning in children was long ignored because of possible ethical problems in the use of noxious stimulation. Although knowledge gained from this kind of research with animals has been useful to child researchers, the types of noxious stimuli employed in work with animals—electric shock and air blasts, for example—seemed too drastic for work with children. Actually, however, the only requirement for initiating this kind of research with children was the development of scientifically useful techniques that would not violate ethical standards. In two relevant experiments Baer (1960, 1962b) employed the temporary withdrawal of positive reinforcement as the aversive stimulus, and studied the development of behavior that prevented withdrawal of the positive state of affairs. In the first study, four to six year old children were brought into a playroom and seated at a table. The table contained a lever by the subject's right hand. On the first day, the operant level of lever pressing was measured while the subject watched two or three seven-minute cartoons. On the second day, the cartoon was interrupted after the first minute and remained off until the subject pushed the lever. Further interruptions were programmed by the subject's responses on one of two schedules. Sixteen subjects were maintained on an escape-avoidance schedule. Responses made during cartoon interruption were escape responses, which served to terminate the interruption; responses made during cartoon presentation were avoidance responses, which served to delay the interruption for n seconds. A burst of responses would *not* lead to an accumulation of noninterruption time but only recycled the next interruption for n seconds after the last response. Under this escape-avoidance schedule, responding came increasingly under control of the escape contingency and showed decreasing sensitivity to the avoidance contingency. (It is possible that the use of a discriminative stimulus to indicate onset of the interruption would have facilitated acquisition of avoidance responding.) Additional subjects were maintained on an "escalator" schedule in which time could be saved up. That is, each response added a fixed number of seconds to the interval before the next interruption. Initial responses were exclusively to the escape contingency with rapid bursts of responses ending first in a plateau and eventually in reinforcement withdrawal. By the sixth session, response rate was relatively smooth, plateaus were rare, and reinforcement was rarely withdrawn although withdrawal may have been only a few seconds away (see Figure 4-12). Cartoon withdrawal appears to be sufficiently aversive that subjects will acquire an avoidance response when appropriate schedules are used.

In Baer's (1962b) second study, the subjects sat facing a mechanical cowboy puppet. At the onset of a light (S^D) the puppet raised its head and talked to the child. Turning on the light and keeping the puppet talking depended

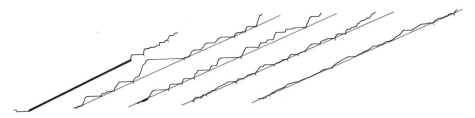

Fig. 4-12. Developing response under the "escalator" schedule of reinforcement withdrawal. The straight diagonal lines indicate minimal rate for avoiding interruptions. (From Baer, *Journal of the Experimental Analysis of Behavior*, 1960, *3*, 155–159. Fig. 2, p. 158. Copyright 1960 by the Society for the Experimental Analysis of Behavior, Inc. Reprinted by permission.)

upon the subject's responses (lever pressing). Withdrawal of reinforcement (lowering of puppet's head and cessation of talking) was programmed according to the escalator schedule. Avoidance behavior developed, especially in children rated by teachers as attention-seekers.

The techniques introduced by Baer should stimulate further investigation employing aversive stimulation. A possible extension of this research might lead to studies of "conditioned response-suppression," widely studied with animals but seldom with children. The term refers to suppression of response rate during the presence of a cue previously associated with punishment. The phenomenon could be studied in children by using Baer's techniques: The child presses a bar for reinforcements and simultaneously watches cartoons. Once behavior has stabilized, a tone or some other neutral stimulus is introduced for a fixed time period, after which the cartoon is interrupted briefly. Conditioned suppression would be evident if there was a suppression of response rate during the tone as compared with equal time periods before and after the tone. In addition to providing further extensions of animal work to humans, research on conditioned suppression might yield clues about what happens to a child's behavior when his mother says something like, "Wait till your father comes home. He's going to punish you."

Extinction

REINFORCEMENT SCHEDULES.   Although some extinction data are available from studies of multiple schedules, the effect of reinforcement schedule upon extinction of free operant responses has been much less extensively studied than the effect upon acquisition. The data that are available do not provide a consistent body of evidence but rather one that leads to suggestions for needed research.

In a study mentioned previously, Warren and Brown (1943) extinguished lever pressing during the seventh and eighth days of the experiment. On the four previous days, the subjects had been on CRF. Extinction on Day 7 was complete by the middle of the 20-minute session. At the beginning of Day 8 the subjects showed spontaneous recovery, that is, some re-emergence of the response, but re-extinction was rapid. After reacquisition under CRF on Day 9, the response was maintained on FI 15 sec. on Days 10 to 13, then the response was extinguished again. Extinction following intermittent reinforcement was faster than extinction following CRF. Rapid extinction following intermittent reinforcement appears incongruous with the abundant literature on infrahumans and humans, which generally extinguish more rapidly after CRF than after intermittent reinforcement. It is possible that rapid extinction occurred simply because the extinction periods following intermittent reinforcement were the third and fourth extinctions that the subjects had experienced, while those following CRF were the first and second. It has been shown that successive extinction periods lead to faster extinction (Pumroy and Pumroy, 1961).

However, greater resistance to extinction following CRF is not an isolated finding and has been demonstrated in a study that included several different intermittent schedules. In this study, by Pumroy and Pumroy (1961), nursery school children acquired a ball-dropping response under $16\frac{2}{3}$, $33\frac{1}{3}$, 50, or 100 percent reinforcement schedules. Each child acquired the response under each schedule, with two-minute extinction periods intervening. The four schedules were arranged into the 24 possible orders, and two children were assigned to each order. The number of reinforcements was held constant at three trinkets during each reinforcement period. The greatest number of extinction responses was made by subjects in the 100 percent condition (489), followed by the 50 percent (481), $33\frac{1}{3}$ percent (463), and $16\frac{2}{3}$ percent (419) conditions. An additional finding was that successive extinction periods led to progressively fewer responses during extinction. Hence, the Warren and Brown finding of greater resistance to extinction following CRF as compared with FI 15 sec. may be a reliable schedule effect or it may have occurred because extinction following FI came after extinction following CRF. The fact that the duration of the extinction period in the study by the Pumroys was only two minutes may also be of major importance. Perhaps using a longer extinction period or allowing subjects to respond until they quit would have led to entirely different results. It should also be noted that in both of these studies the schedules were manipulated within subjects rather than in separate groups, which may lead to unique extinction effects.

Additional data on resistance to extinction following an FI schedule have been provided by Bijou (1958), although only four subjects were included. One subject performed a lever-pressing task on FI 60 sec., two on FI 30 sec., and one on FI 20 sec. The manner of delivering reinforcements is worth mentioning. Plastic trinkets were delivered in Intervals 1, 2, 4, 7, 11, 15, and 19, and only the sound of the dispenser motor occurred in the other intervals. Note that as training progressed an increasing number of intervals elapsed between delivery of the trinkets. Such a procedure might be useful for conducting training over a relatively long session while keeping down the total number of reinforcers. The rate of responding in extinction was found to be directly related to the size of the fixed interval, that is, the subject on FI 60 sec. had the greatest rate and the subject on FI 20 sec. had the lowest. Unfortunately, a CRF condition was not included, but since CRF is actually an FI 0 schedule, the implication of these data is that the lowest rate of responding in extinction would have been obtained under CRF. Further studies are needed to clarify this matter.

In two experiments Bijou (1957b) compared resistance to extinction following VR and CRF training. Preschool children performed the ball-dropping task and received trinkets on either a 20 or 100 percent reinforcement schedule. Six reinforcements were administered to each group. In order to keep the total number of reinforcements constant, 30 trials were administered to the 20 percent group. Each response was followed by a 1 second motor hum from the trinket dispenser. During a 3.5 minute extinction period, the 20 percent group produced more responses (Mean = 22) than the 100 percent group (Mean = 15.3), but the difference was not statistically significant. A follow-up experiment was similar in design except that the motor hum was accentuated by a buzzer. The mean number of extinction responses was significantly greater for the 20 percent group (26.2) than for the 100 percent group (13.0).

This finding was replicated in a study by Kass and Wilson (1966) in which number of trials rather than number of reinforcements was held constant. Six and seven year old children pulled a slot machine handle and were reinforced with pennies on either a VR ($33\frac{1}{3}$ percent) or a CRF (100 percent) schedule. Subgroups received either 3, 9, 21, 45, or 60 training trials. Following training, extinction began without warning. The subjects played until they quit or until either 20 minutes or 400 extinction trials had expired. Extinction was more rapid in the CRF (100 percent) group than in the VR ($33\frac{1}{3}$ percent) group, irrespective of the number of training trials.

The only investigation on the relative effects of CRF and FR schedules on resistance to extinction was conducted by Cowan and Walters (1963). The operant response involved hitting a clown, and the subjects performed in extinction until they voluntarily stopped. All subjects performed 18 acquisition responses under one of three schedules. Children who received CRF in acquisition were the least resistant to extinction, children reinforced on FR 3 were intermediate, and children reinforced on FR 6 were the most resistant to extinction.

Amount of Reinforcement and Amount of Training. Complications arise in the design and interpretation of experiments relating reward schedule to resistance to extinction. For example, in the Cowan and Walters study the subjects in the three reinforcement groups performed the same number of acquisition responses; therefore, they differed not only in terms of reward schedule but also in terms of number of reinforcements. Poorer resistance to extinction following CRF training may have been due as much to satiation as to schedule effects.

Siegel and Foshee (1953) investigated the relation between amount of reinforcement and extinction. Four groups of preschool children performed a lever-pressing response for candy reinforcers. The various groups won either 2, 4, 8, or 16 candies on a CRF schedule followed immediately by a 3-minute extinction period. A direct relation between resistance to extinction and amount of reinforcement was obtained; the median numbers of extinction responses for the four reinforcement groups were 10.0, 29.0, 49.5, and 99.5, respectively. A similar finding was obtained by Pumroy and Pumroy (1961). Four amounts of reinforcement (1, 3, 5, and 7 trinkets) were employed in a within-subjects design. As in their reinforcement schedule study, 24 possible permutations were arranged and two subjects were assigned to each. The numbers of responses during the 2-minute extinction periods were 368, 419, 446, and 435 for 1, 3, 5, and 7 trinkets, respectively. Thus, there was no support from these two studies for the contention that subjects who receive greater amounts of reinforcement during acquisition show decreased resistance to extinction because of satiation effects. However, two points must be noted. First, there may be a curvilinear relation between amount of reinforcement and extinction performance; studies employing greater ranges of amounts of reinforcement are needed to test this possibility. Second, in order to allow subjects to obtain larger amounts of reinforcements, the procedures of the studies by Siegel and Foshee and the Pumroys also entailed having the high-amount groups perform more acquisition responses than the low-amount groups. Thus, amount of training, although not itself a manipulated variable, was confounded with the manipulated variable, and the studies therefore provide only ambiguous data on the effects of amount of reinforcement.

As previously noted, Kass and Wilson (1966) found that extinction proceeded faster, the greater the number of acquisition trials. On the basis of this finding, several previous findings may be reassessed. Extinction performance in Bijou's (1957b) 20 percent reinforcement group may have been weakened by the extra training given to equate amount of reinforcement with the 100 percent condition. A similar argument may be raised with respect to the high reinforcement groups in the studies by Siegel and Foshee and the Pumroys. However, this reassessment may be of dubious merit since the studies reviewed differed so widely in terms of subjects, response situations, types of reward, experimental designs (between-subjects versus within-subjects), and definitions of extinction. It should by now be apparent that extensive investigations of the interactions between reinforcement schedule, amount of reinforcement, and amount of training must be conducted with common procedures before these complexities can be clarified.

PUNISHMENT.   Baer (1961) showed that punishment can speed up the extinction process. Preschool children learned to press a lever to win peanuts while watching cartoons. During extinction, lever presses were no longer reinforced with peanuts. In addition, for a punishment group each response turned off the cartoons for two seconds. This procedure reduced sharply the number of extinction responses. When the cartoons were completed and no further punishment was possible, the experimenter waited for a two-minute interval during which the subjects were free to respond. The punishment group did not show any tendency to resume responding. Spontaneous recovery was assessed in a second session, during which lever presses were neither reinforced nor punished. Spontaneous recovery of the extinguished response was shown only by the subjects in the control group. In a third session, punishment was again not administered; the subjects were told that cartoons would not be shown and that they

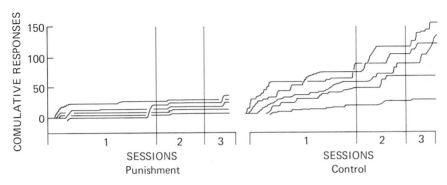

Fig. 4-13.   Cumulative response curves of individual subjects in punishment and control groups (five subjects per group). (From Baer, 1961, Fig. 1, p. 71. Copyright 1961 by the Society for Research in Child Development, Inc. Reprinted by permission.)

were free to play with the lever or a toy. During this session, the punishment subjects directed their play to the toy rather than to the lever far more than the control subjects. Thus, the effect of the punishment condition was both strong and persistent (see Figure 4-13).

DISCRETE-TRIAL INSTRUMENTAL CONDITIONING IN CHILDREN

Acquisition

REINFORCEMENT SCHEDULES.   The effect of reinforcement schedules in discrete-trial tasks began to receive attention relatively later than in the free operant situation. Now, however, research with this technique is quite active. In the discrete-trial studies the experimenter controls the onset of a stimulus that indicates to the subject that a single response may now be made.

Bruning (1964) required kindergarten children to move a lever in order to win candy. Half of the subjects were rewarded on a random 50 percent schedule, and the rest received 100 percent reinforcement. Similarly, Ryan and Moffitt (1966) gave preschool and kindergarten children 56 trials on a lever-pulling device. Half of each age group received a marble for each pull (100 percent); the other half was rewarded on a 50 percent schedule. The marbles were later traded for a toy. In both investigations intermittent reinforcement produced significantly faster movement speeds than continuous reinforcement. A similar finding was obtained by Semler and Pederson (1968), using a within-subjects

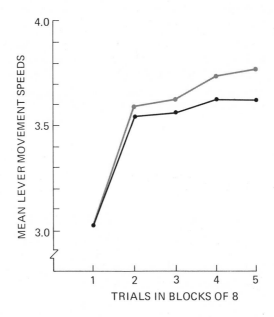

Fig. 4-14. Lever movement speeds in the S_{50} (light line) and S_{100} (dark line) conditions. (From Semler and Pederson, 1968, Fig. 1, p. 286. Reprinted by permission of the authors and the Psychonomic Society, Inc.)

design. They gave first grade children 40 trials on a lever-pulling apparatus, 20 trials with each of two stimulus lights, S_{100} and S_{50}. All responses to S_{100} were rewarded with a marble; for S_{50}, reward was on a random 50 percent schedule. Movement speed was faster to S_{50} than to S_{100} (see Figure 4-14).

These data are consistent with the data of studies with animals and adults. The usual interpretation is that nonreward leads to a frustration-produced increment in drive level. As an alternative to this motivational interpretation, it is possible that vigorous performance under an intermittent reward schedule is attributable to subjects' having learned in the past to try harder, that is, to respond more vigorously, if they fail to attain some goal. However, this associative interpretation is not altogether consistent with the results of several experiments. Pederson (1967) eliminated the possibility that subjects might pull harder because they thought the marble was stuck on nonreward trials. Instead of receiving no marbles on these trials, the 50 percent group received valueless marbles (ones that could not be traded for a toy), yet still responded more vigorously. Other studies have shown that nonreward of one response enhances the vigor of the immediately following response (Penney, 1960b; Ryan, 1965) even though the latter response is always rewarded. Moreover, evidence for the temporary nature of the arousal produced by a nonreward has also been obtained (Watson and Ryan, 1966).

Three investigations have dealt with response speeds under various schedules of intermittent reward and continuous reward. Ryan (1966) divided preschool and kindergarten children into six reinforcement groups (100, 83, 66, 50, 33, and 17 percent) and administered 54 trials on a lever-pulling task. The intermittent-reward groups had faster response speeds than the continuous-reward group. In addition, asymptotic speeds were shown to be an inverted U-shaped function of percentage reinforcement, with fastest responding produced by intermediate percentages of reinforcement. In a second study (Ryan and Voorhoeve, 1966) kindergarten subjects were divided into six reinforcement groups (100, 70, 50, 30, 10, and 0 percent). The results were strikingly similar to those obtained by Ryan (1966); and the results of both studies compare interestingly with the results of similar experiments with rats (Weinstock, 1958; see also Spence, 1960, Chapter 6, p. 103), as shown in Figure 4-15. In a third study (Ryan, Orton, and Pimm, 1968), similar in design, the inverted U-shaped function was obtained in children from Grades 2, 4, and 6, but not in college freshmen or elderly subjects. It was suggested that nonreward for adult subjects is more likely to elicit various problem solving behaviors than to elicit frustration. In support of this contention, the college students and the elderly subjects were significantly more variable in response speeds than were the young children.

Several other studies have shown that children can learn to anticipate reward conditions. Rieber and Johnson (1964) trained kindergarten children on a lever-pulling task under one of two treatments. One group was given intermittent reinforcement on an alternating (nonrandom) schedule, with separate discriminative stimuli (red or yellow light) associated with reward and nonreward. Another group was given continuous reinforcement; the light colors alternated, but of course not with reward and nonreward, since all responses were rewarded. Within a few trials, the intermittent-reinforcement subjects were responding more rapidly on reward trials than on nonreward trials. Presumably, once subjects had learned the schedule, presentation of the light signalling nonreward elicited anticipatory frustration and hence produced slower speeds, and presentation of the light signalling reward elicited expectancy for reward and hence faster speeds (see Chapter 10 for further discussion of frustration and expectancy effects). On reward trials, the speeds of the intermittent- and continuous-reinforcement groups did not differ significantly. This last finding contrasts with the previously discussed finding that subjects given intermittent reward on a random 50 percent schedule respond more rapidly than continuously rewarded subjects. It should be fruitful to investigate factorially the effects of alternating versus random intermittent reward with discriminative versus irrelevant stimuli.

Fastest response speeds should be obtained with random intermittent reward when the stimulus lights are not related to the reward conditions.

In two experiments (Longstreth, 1966a), one with second and third grade children and one with retardates, responses to one intensity of light (S^D) were

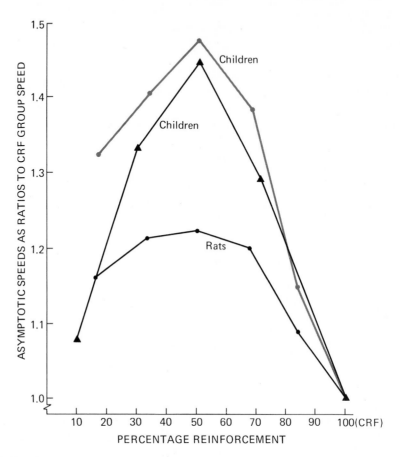

Fig. 4-15. Asymptotic movement speed as a function of percentage reinforcement in children (Ryan, 1966; Ryan and Voorhoeve, 1966) and in rats (Weinstock, 1958). Light circle line, Ryan; triangle line, Ryan and Voorhoeve; dark circle line, Weinstock. (From Ryan and Voorhoeve, 1966, Fig. 2, p. 194. Reprinted by permission of the authors and Academic Press, Inc.)

reinforced and responses to another intensity (S^Δ) were not. During training, each light was presented separately 18 times. Response speed and response amplitude were greater in the presence of S^D than S^Δ. (For further discussion of these and related studies, see Chapter 10.)

DELAYED REINFORCEMENT. It was suggested by Spence (1956, pp. 153–154) that processes operating in extinction may also operate under conditions of delayed reinforcement. Having made a response, a child may engage in certain behaviors such as looking around or speaking to the experimenter while waiting for a delayed reward to arrive. Such responses, occurring as they do in the same stimulus complex in which the instrumental response is emitted, may become associated with the general experimental situation and serve as a source of competition for prompt execution of instrumental responses on later trials. In addition, the delayed reward may arrive while the competitional behavior is occurring, thus adding further strength to the probability of recurrence of the competitional behavior.

Rieber (1961a) assessed the extent to which interference was related to the similarity between cues present during the delay interval and cues used to elicit the response. A light served as a signal to move a lever through a 15 inch excursion, and each lever press led to delivery of a trinket. The subjects were

Table 4-4

Conditions in Studies of Delay of
Stimulus Offset and Delay of Reward[a]

Condition	Stimulus Offset	Reward
I-I	Immediate	Immediate
I-D	Immediate	Delayed
D-D	Delayed	Delayed
I	Immediate	No reward
I-Dv	Immediate	Varied

[a] See text for explanation.

three groups of kindergarten children. For Group I-I both light offset and trinket delivery occurred immediately upon termination of the response. For Group I-D light offset was immediate but trinket delivery was delayed 12 seconds on each trial. For Group D-D, light offset and trinket delivery were both delayed for 12 seconds; it was expected that interference would be greatest in this group. Table 4-4 summarizes the treatment conditions (and other conditions used in studies discussed later). "Starting" speeds and "movement" speeds were measured separately. Starting speed is the time between the onset of the signal and the beginning of the response; movement speed is the time required for completion of the response after it begins. The starting speeds of Group I-I were significantly faster than those of Group I-D, and were significantly faster in both of these groups than in Group D-D. The movement speeds were not significantly different in Groups I-I and I-D, but were significantly faster in Group I-D than in Group D-D. Faster starting speeds for the I-I condition than for the I-D condition have also been shown in first grade subjects with a 12-second delay interval (Rieber, 1961b) and in preschool subjects with a 14-second delay interval (Sheikh, 1967). A comparable finding was obtained with a 7-second delay although the difference was not statistically significant (Estes, 1963).

The data from Rieber's (1961a) investigation offer support for the response competition notion; but since delayed reward interfered predominantly with the starting response, a further assumption is needed. It can be assumed, after Spence (1956, pp. 116–118), that response competition is likely to have a greater effect on the initiation (starting) than the execution (movement) of an instrumental response. Some support for this assumption has been provided by Rabinowitz (1966). Kindergarten subjects performed a lever-pulling response under the I-I condition, or under a condition in which light offset was immediate but no marbles were delivered (Group I). Since the two groups did not differ in terms of opportunities for competing responses to develop, no difference was expected—and none was obtained—between the mean starting speeds of the two groups. Group I-I did, however, move the lever significantly faster than Group I. Rabinowitz concluded that response competition is more likely to affect starting speed and incentive motivation is more likely to affect movement speed. It would follow that the I-D and D-D conditions should produce slower starting speeds than the I condition, because of response competition, but faster movement speeds, because of higher incentive motivation. The I-D and D-D conditions were included in the study by Rabinowitz, but they were apparently not compared with the I condition.

Rieber (1961b) provided information on the effect of shifting reward conditions. First grade children responded on the lever-pulling task under four conditions. The data for two groups, I-I and D-D, replicated the earlier findings in that starting speeds were significantly faster under the condition of immediate reward. For two other groups, reward conditions were reversed midway through training. Switching from delayed to immediate reward led to increased starting speeds; however, even after 15 trials, starting speeds were still slower than in Group I-I, indicating that competing responses acquired under delay resist any rapid extinction. A switch from immediate to delayed reward led to a decrement in starting speeds. This drop in speed occurred not gradually but sharply (see Figure 4-16), introducing the possibility that frustration-produced competing responses may play some role at least on the early postshift trials. No significant group differences in movement speed were obtained in this study.

Estes (1963) studied the effect of a varied delay of reward. The groups of immediate interest are I-I and I-Dv; in the latter condition, stimulus offset was immediate, and reward was immediate on a random half of the trials and delayed for 14 seconds on the other half. Starting speeds in Group I-Dv were slower than in Group I-I, but movement speeds were faster. Estes suggested that frustration-produced competing responses in the varied delay group (I-Dv) depressed the starting speeds. He also argued that subjects must have overcome the competition by the time the movement measure is taken, and that fast movement speeds for a varied delay group are due to frustration-produced drive. Terrell and Ware (1963) obtained evidence, with kindergarten and first grade children, that also suggested that delayed reward may produce frustration. Early in training, measures of the galvanic skin response indicated greater emotionality under delayed than under immediate reward conditions. However, the frustration interpretation seems weak when applied to studies in which the delay of reward was constant, because in none of these were movement speeds faster under conditions of delayed reward. It is possible that the effect of constant delay results from the acquisition of interfering responses and that the effect of varied delay results from frustration drive.

ESCAPE AND AVOIDANCE. The study of avoidance conditioning in young children requires finding a stimulus that is (a) definitely unpleasant to most children without producing severe fright, (b) precisely reproducible, (c) apparent to the child even if he does not pay close attention to it, (d) continuous or repeti-

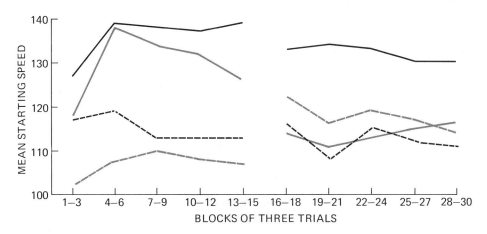

Fig. 4-16. Mean starting speeds. Dark solid line, I-I; dark dashed line, D-D; light solid line, I-I to D-D; light dashed line, D-D to I-I. The shift from I-I to D-D and from D-D to I-I followed Trial 15. (Figure 1 from Rieber, M. Shifts in response-reward interval and its effect upon response speed. *Psychological Reports*, 1961, 9, 393–398. Reprinted with permission of author and publisher.)

tive so that the child can avoid it by making the appropriate response, (e) able to be avoided only by the appropriate response, and (f) somewhat removed from everyday experience so that responses to it are more likely to be dependent upon experience in the experimental situation than upon other experiences. Robinson and Robinson (1961) tested and discarded a number of possible aversive stimuli; they found that the one best meeting these specifications was a moderately loud, high-pitched pure tone (2300 cycles per second at 50 decibels). The aversiveness of this stimulus was supplemented in their study by comments from the experimenter and by having the tone interrupt a tape of popular children's music, stories, and songs that played continuously except when interrupted by the tone. The apparatus is illustrated schematically in Figure 4-17. Preschool children in one group were given a 20-minute session in the experimental room in order to adapt them to the CS before the aversive US was introduced. During adaptation, the red lights were turned on at 10-second intervals and remained on for 6 seconds unless turned off by the subject. Another group received no adaptation training.

In the first avoidance conditioning session, the subjects were informed that loud noises would come on but could be turned off (escape response) or prevented (avoidance response) by pulling the manipulandum while the lights were on. The intertrial interval was 10 seconds; the CS-US interval was 1.5 seconds. Most subjects acquired the avoidance response rapidly, although the adapted group took slightly longer. The adapted subjects had experienced the lights in the absence of the aversive stimulus, and perhaps had learned that the combination was not invariable; also the experimenter had not encouraged them to respond when the lights were presented without the tone.

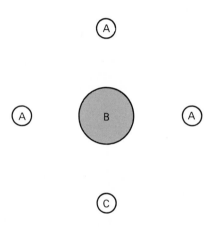

Fig. 4-17. Schematic drawing of apparatus used by Robinson and Robinson. (A) Dim red lights used as CS. (B) Speaker. (C) Response manipulandum. (After Robinson and Robinson, 1961, Fig. 1, p. 21.)

A noxious tone was also used as an aversive stimulus by Penney and Croskery (1962). High anxious and low anxious children from Grades 3 and 4 were instructed that noises were going to come on but could be turned off (escaped) or prevented (avoidance response) by pulling a lever. For half of the high anxious and half of the low anxious children the US was a 65 decibel tone; for the rest of the children it was a 98 decibel tone (see footnote 6 in Chapter 2 for a rough decibel scale). On each trial the US came on 1.5 seconds after the CS (a green light) unless an avoidance response was made. The avoidance response was defined as a complete lever pull after the onset of the CS but before the onset of the US. If no avoidance response occurred, the CS and US remained on until the subject pulled the lever. More avoidance responses were made by the low anxious than high anxious subjects, especially with the 98 decibel US (although the effect of US intensity did not attain statistical significance).

A possible explanation of the faster avoidance learning in the low anxious subjects is that lever pulling in the presence of the US was established by the instructions as the dominant response in the experimental situation; and therefore in order to acquire the avoidance response, the subject had to react to the CS and inhibit the dominant tendency to wait for the tone to come on before pulling the lever. As will be explained in Chapter 10, high drive—including high anxiety—makes the dominant response tendency even more dominant. Thus, the tendency to wait and respond to the tone would be greater in the high anxious subjects and would consequently interfere more with acquisition of the avoidance response.

If this explanation is correct, then reaction to the tone, that is, escape responding, should be faster in high anxious than low anxious subjects. Partial support for this prediction was obtained by Penney and McCann (1962). High and low anxious children in Grades 3 and 4 performed on a lever-pulling task. Only escape responses were possible, because there was no CS to serve as a warning signal that the tone was about to come on. The instructions indicated that pulling the lever would terminate the tone. For half of the subjects in each anxiety group the US was a 65 decibel tone; for the other half it was a 98 decibel tone. Escape responding was significantly faster in the high anxious than low anxious subjects, but only with the 65 decibel US. High anxious subjects were slower than low anxious subjects with the 98 decibel US, but only in the first block of trials. Perhaps very loud tones elicit competing tendencies that adapt relatively quickly in low anxious subjects and relatively slowly in high anxious subjects.

This interpretation would be supported by evidence that (a) high anxious subjects eventually respond to a loud tone faster than low anxious subjects, or (b) low anxious subjects do in fact adapt relatively quickly to a loud tone. Training beyond 20 trials would be needed to obtain evidence of the first kind. Evidence of the second kind has been provided by Penney and Kirwin (1965), for high and low anxious children from Grades 4 and 5. Half of each anxiety group received US adaptation training, consisting of 15 5-second presentations of an 84 decibel tone; the other subjects received no adaptation training. Adaptation training had no effect upon the escape latencies of the high anxious subjects, but adapted low anxious subjects exhibited slower escape responses than nonadapted low anxious subjects. Although the data are in agreement with the differential adaptation hypothesis, some complicating factors must be dealt with in future research. First, the adaptation effect was evident only in the first block of trials. One explanation of this may be that the nonadapted low anxious subjects adapted during this block of trials. A second complicating factor is that the relatively high intensity tone (84 decibels) produced no significant differences between the escape latencies of the high and low anxious subjects, thus failing to replicate results of the Penney and McCann study.

Extinction

REINFORCEMENT SCHEDULES.   The relation between schedules of reinforcement and resistance to extinction in discrete-trial studies is not altogether clear. Lewis

(1952) trained young children (6.5 to 7.5 years old) to push buttons to turn on lights. All subjects were given 20 toys at the beginning of the session and were informed that they would win another toy if a red light appeared but would lose one if a blue light appeared. Three groups received ten acquisition trials under conditions of 100, 60, or 50 percent reward. These three groups, and a group that received no acquisition trials (0 percent), were then put into extinction (blue light only) with the instruction that they could quit whenever they wanted. The two intermittent reward groups exhibited greater resistance to extinction than the 100 percent and 0 percent groups, which did not differ from one another. These data were explained in terms of Sheffield's (1949) hypothesis that the aftereffects of each trial become part of the stimulus complex for the next trial. In the 50 and 60 percent conditions, responses on reinforced trials are made in the presence of the aftereffects of both success and failure, and therefore the intermittently rewarded subjects become accustomed to continue responding after nonreinforcement. Since the aftereffects are homogeneous during acquisition under 100 percent reward, responses will be relatively weak in extinction because the aftereffects of each extinction trial markedly differ from those present during acquisition. The 0 percent subjects experience only nonreinforcement and hence also extinguish relatively quickly.

Kass (1962) had 4 to 11 year old children perform on a simulated slot machine for pennies, which could later be traded for prizes. Responses were rewarded on either 0, $16\frac{2}{3}$, $33\frac{1}{3}$, 60, 80, or 100 percent schedules in different groups. Extinction continued until the subject quit or until 370 extinction trials had been given. Resistance to extinction was found to decrease with increasing percentage reinforcement. These results were interpreted in terms of the "discrimination hypothesis": Extinction progresses more slowly as the discrimination between the acquisition and extinction situations becomes more difficult (e.g., Bitterman, Fedderson, and Tyler, 1953). The 0 percent group in the study by Lewis did not behave like Kass's 0 percent group, probably because of procedural differences. Lewis's 0 percent group received no acquisition trials, but Kass gave his 30 acquisition trials. Also, in Lewis's study it cost the subjects one toy per trial to stay, while in the Kass study subjects were only nonrewarded (they had also been told that the machine was full of pennies which they were to try to get).

The data of another series of studies complicate matters. Instead of being allowed to quit at any time during extinction, the subjects were given fixed numbers of extinction trials. In a study by Bruning (1964) both 50 and 100 percent groups increased rather than decreased response speeds on 12 extinction trials. There was a nonsignificant tendency for this increase to be *greater* in the 100 percent group. In a follow-up investigation, Rosenbaum and Bruning (1966) gave 30 extinction trials. Still the subjects did not decrease speeds in extinction, and in fact the 100 percent group showed a significant increase in response speed during extinction. It was suggested that special frustrative effects might play some role in this situation. In the 100 percent condition, subjects might quickly realize that rewards are no longer being delivered and might be showing their frustration at not being permitted to leave.

Ryan and Voorhoeve (1966) presented data that complicate matters still further. Each of five reinforcement groups (100, 70, 50, 30, 10 percent) was divided into two subgroups, one given an additional 30 acquisition trials and the other given 30 extinction trials. Over extinction training, slower response speeds for the extinction as compared with the nonextinction groups became evident. These data were complicated by the fact that the 30 percent group increased speed in extinction, the 70 percent group decreased speed, while the 100, 50, and 10 percent conditions showed no change in performance over extinction. Neither the aftereffects hypothesis, the discrimination hypothesis, nor the frustration hypothesis can explain these results.

Johnson (1966) trained normal and retarded children on a lever-pulling task under either continuous reward or alternating intermittent reward. Response speeds decreased significantly during the 20 extinction trials given, but not differentially for the two reinforcement groups. Thus, when subjects have not been told they can leave the lever-pulling task when they wish, difficulty has been encountered in attempts to demonstrate the intermittent reinforcement effect (i.e., relatively greater resistance to extinction in intermittently rewarded subjects). Since the effect is reliably demonstrated when subjects may quit at will, it seems apparent that the role played by instructions must become a matter for further study.

CHAPTER 5

Discriminative Learning

INTRODUCTION

The Problems

The problem of how one learns to make choices between stimulus objects in his environment and to use features of stimuli as cues for adaptive behavior is a concern of psychologists interested in the development of discriminative behavior. Studies of discrimination learning encompass a wide variety of experimental situations which often have only one thing in common: presentation of two or more stimuli, to each of which appropriate responses must be learned. An eight month old infant, for example, distinguishes his mother from other adult females, as evidenced by his smiling in response to the approach of his mother and failing to smile, or even crying, in response to an unfamiliar female. A child is said to discriminate between two stimuli when he responds differentially to them. Discrimination learning studies are specifically concerned with the problem of how the child acquires such differential responses to different stimuli.

Literally, discrimination learning refers to the acquisition of the ability to differentiate among two or more highly similar stimuli; but only rarely have discrimination tasks been employed to study such learning. Studies of such learning are generally referred to as experiments in *perceptual discrimination learning*. There is a second category, composed of investigations in which discrimination learning tasks are used for the study of the ability of children to formulate and utilize abstract concepts. These will be referred to here as studies of *conceptual discrimination learning*. Discrimination learning tasks have usually been employed for a third purpose: as tools for the study of the variables affecting choice behavior. Most of the studies of discrimination learning have been concerned with the variables affecting the speed with which children learn to respond to a single stimulus dimension embedded in a complex composed of stimuli varying along a number of other dimensions. Experiments that are addressed to aspects of this problem will be referred to here as studies of *dimensional discrimination learning*. This chapter will be concerned, for the most part, with this kind of investigation.

Before delving into an exposition of dimensional discrimination learning and the variables that affect this process, we will briefly consider all three categories and the types of experimental procedures that distinguish one from the other.

PERCEPTUAL DISCRIMINATION LEARNING. Although there is a considerable amount of evidence that perceptual thresholds are not absolute for any individual, but are dependent upon practice (see Gibson, 1953), studies of children's perception have, by and large, ignored learning variables. An exception is found in a study reported by Wolner and Pyle (1933), who challenged the widely held assumption that pitch discrimination in children is little affected by practice. They selected seven children from the fifth, sixth, and seventh grades who showed extremely poor ability to discriminate pitch and exposed them to training in pitch discrimination. Following an unspecified number of hours of practice during a three month period, all of the children could differentiate among each of 49 semitones in a range of four octaves. More remarkably, four of the children had learned to discriminate differences as small as one-half cycle per second. Other studies of perceptual discrimination learning have been concerned with determining the relation between the age of children and their ability to distinguish among colors (e.g., Cook, 1931), shapes (e.g., Ling, 1941), and sizes (e.g., Welch, 1939b).

CONCEPTUAL DISCRIMINATION LEARNING. Conceptual discrimination learning includes studies of the ability of subjects to acquire and utilize concepts or rules about the stimuli to which they are responding. For example, in one kind of study (reviewed by Reese, 1963a), two stimuli that differ in several ways are presented and responses to one are always reinforced. After some appropriate number of trials, two new and different stimuli are presented; this procedure is usually continued until the subject takes no more than one trial to learn which of two new stimuli is the correct stimulus. What is learned in this situation may be the rule "win-stay, lose-shift" rather than a response to any particular attribute (see Chapter 8, section entitled "Learning Sets").

Oddity problems also exemplify conceptual discrimination learning. In a typical example (Martin and Blum, 1961), three stimuli were presented on each trial. Two were identical to each other, and one was different. The subjects learned to choose the odd one since it was the only one associated with reinforcement.

Probability learning studies also come under this heading. Brackbill, Kappy, and Starr (1962b) studied probability learning in children as a function of magnitude of reward. The test consisted of a deck of cards, each with a picture of either a dog or a cat printed on it. Seventy-five percent of the cards had one picture, and the rest had the other. As the cards were turned over, one at a time, the children predicted which picture would come up next. The rule or concept that had to be learned was always to predict that the more frequent picture would appear since that response resulted in maximum reinforcement.

A more clear-cut example of conceptual discrimination can be seen in studies of single and double alternation. Hunter and Bartlett (1948) asked children of various ages to guess which of two boxes, identical in every respect except their position, contained a piece of candy. The candy was placed in the left box on the first two trials, the right box on the next two, the left box on the next two, and so on until the child learned the rule of double alternation.

There are other variations of the conceptual discrimination task, but the foregoing examples should serve to identify the kinds of studies that fall into this category. In essence, this category differs from the other two categories in that it includes studies dealing not with stimulus dimensions *per se* but rather with abstractions or rules based on the stimuli.

DIMENSIONAL DISCRIMINATION LEARNING. The category of dimensional discrimination learning includes studies that assess the ability of children to make consistent differential responses to two or more values along a single stimulus dimension when the stimuli vary in more than one dimension. A basic assumption in these studies is that the child is fully capable of perceiving the differences among the stimuli presented. What he apparently has to learn is to identify the dimension that has been arbitrarily chosen as the relevant one and to make the appropriate choice responses to different values along that dimension.

One of the simplest types of dimensional discrimination problem involves color discrimination. Calvin and Clifford (1956) presented two stimulus cards, one dark green and the other blue, covering two identical cups. A reward was always hidden under one of the colors. The position of the cards varied from trial to trial, and the child's task was to learn to choose the color under which the reward was concealed. This task, then, involved two dimensions: color and position. The fact that it took a median of 40 trials for first grade children to achieve solution might indicate that they were having some difficulty in telling the two colors apart. The investigators reported, however, that when the children were questioned at the end of the experiment, all could identify which card was blue and which was green. Apparently, the children learned slowly because they conceptualized both cards as "colored" instead of conceptualizing one as "blue" and the other as "green," and therefore failed to attend to the difference between the colors. If so, the children were probably basing their choices on the positional dimension; or they were responding randomly. Findings of this kind have led investigators to explore the roles that language and attention play in the acquisition of dimensional discriminations. These variables are discussed in greater detail in Chapters 7 and 9.

Investigations of dimensional discrimination learning have also dealt with discriminanda that vary along more than two dimensions. In some cases (e.g., Hill, 1965), all dimensions are relevant (correlated with reinforcement); and in others (e.g., Gellermann, 1933b; Suchman and Trabasso, 1966b), only one of the several dimensions is consistently associated with reinforcement.

Since perceptual discrimination learning is considered in Chapters 2 and 11 and conceptual discrimination learning is considered in Chapters 7 and 8, the rest of this chapter will be devoted to a more detailed examination of dimensional discrimination learning in children. This kind of task has proved to be a very useful paradigm for analyzing simple choice behavior.

Theoretical Models and Applications

Many theories have been proposed to explain the process of discrimination learning, but only three kinds of theoretical models have been used. Figure 5-1 illustrates these three basic models. In the one-stage model, the choice response and inhibition of the choice response are directly conditioned to the stimuli. In the two-stage "mediation" model, the choice and inhibitory responses are conditioned not only to the stimuli but also to labels associated with the stimuli. The subject is responding not only to what he sees but also to the way he conceptualizes what he sees. According to this model, prejudiced individuals (for example) are responding to the label they use to classify an individual

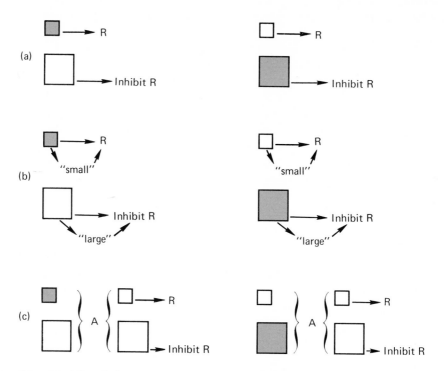

Fig. 5-1. Models of discrimination learning with two-dimensional stimuli. Size is relevant and brightness irrelevant. Responses to the small stimulus are rewarded, responses to large nonrewarded. (a) One-stage model. (b) Two-stage model with verbal mediation (by the words "small" and "large" labeling the sizes). (c) Two-stage "attention" model. The situational cues arouse selective attention (A) to size, and therefore the size difference is perceived and the brightness difference is not. Selective attention may be a purely perceptual mechanism or may be mediated by verbalization labeling the dimension. (See Figure 9-2 for a more detailed two-stage attention model.)

into some ethnic, religious, or other group, rather than to the individual as such. In the two-stage "attention" model, the responses are conditioned to stimulus components that are attended to; and the subject learns nothing about the other components, which are ignored. For example, a subject could discriminate between the two triangles in Figure 5-2 by attending to the length of the baselines and might entirely fail to notice the size of the angle at the apexes.

For present purposes, it is sufficient to note that the speed of learning should be greater with either kind of two-stage process than with the one-stage process, because mediation permits the subject to provide himself with extra training through rehearsal between trials and selective attention prevents distraction by irrelevant aspects of the situation. The different models have important differences in implications about the transfer of responses to new situations, but these are considered in later chapters (especially Chapters 7 and 9) and need not be considered here.

In discrimination learning studies, the experimenter usually presents the subject with two discriminative stimuli (S^Ds); responses to one stimulus (S^+) are reinforced, and responses to the other stimulus (S^-) are not reinforced.[1] In *simultaneous discrimination learning*, two or more stimuli are presented on each trial or in each time block, and the subject is required to choose or approach S^+ (the correct stimulus) in the set of simultaneously presented stimuli. In *successive discrimination learning*, only one of the S^Ds is presented on each trial or in each time block, and the subject is required to respond differentially to S^+ and S^-.

In studies of discrimination learning with infants, investigators have used both discrete-trial and free operant procedures, which are discussed in Chapter 4.

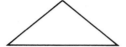

Fig. 5-2. **Discrimination between triangles. A subject could discriminate on the basis of the baseline length and might fail to notice the sizes of the apical angles.**

In both situations, reliable differences in response to the S^Ds indicate an acquired discrimination between these stimuli. The discrete-trial procedure typically involves one response made to one stimulus. Many child studies have used adaptations of familiar animal discrimination procedures, employing techniques previously used with rats (Y and T mazes), nonhuman primates (Wisconsin General Testing Apparatus), and dogs (Pavlovian differential conditioning). To ensure that discriminative responding by the subject is controlled by the experimental stimuli in question, the experimenter must take care to control for position and sequential effects in his presentation of the S^Ds. To control for position bias and to minimize the formation of position habits in a simultaneous form discrimination problem (for example), the experimenter must randomize the relative positions of the S^Ds over successive trials. Typically, experimenters use a special order of stimulus-pair presentations prepared by Gellermann (1933a) to prevent better-than-chance performance through positional responding.

The typical procedure in studying free operant discrimination learning is to present one stimulus in the presence of which the operant response will be reinforced (S^+) and another in the presence of which the response will not be

---

[1] Some writers use the symbols S^D and S^Δ instead of S^+ and S^-.

reinforced (S⁻). The subject may make more than one response in the presence of the S^{D}s; the prevailing S^D is not removed following the occurrence of a single response, as it is in the discrete-trial procedure. The formation of the discrimination is studied over time. Discrimination is indicated by an increasing difference between the subject's response rates in the presence of the two stimuli. In operant discrimination procedures, typically, the successive stimulus presentation method is used, and separate schedules of reinforcement are paired with each of the different S^{D}s. Each S^D is presented for a specified time period in an attempt to bring response rates under the control of the separate S^{D}s. To control for sequential effects, the S^{D}s are usually presented in a random order. By the use of differential reinforcement, the experimenter attempts to demonstrate that the prevailing S^{D}s have acquired control over the subject's responding.

A higher probability of response in the presence of a stimulus that is correlated with reinforcement (S⁺) than in the presence of a stimulus that is not correlated with reinforcement (S⁻) is typically cited as evidence of an acquired stimulus discrimination. However, Jenkins (1965b) has argued that the usual procedures of operant conditioning may not provide a valid measure of stimulus discrimination. Specifically, he suggested that the conditions in common use in operant studies allow the effects of antecedent reinforcement and nonreinforcement on response probability to be confounded with the effects of the S^{D}s on response probability. Operant conditioning procedures with maintained presentations of the S^D and unrestricted responding in the presence of the prevailing S^D allow reinforcement and nonreinforcement to develop differential cue functions: One reinforcement (in the presence of S⁺) predicts an interval during which other reinforcements will follow, and one nonreinforcement (in the presence of S⁻) predicts an interval in which other responses will also be nonreinforced. In contrast to discrete-trial procedures, in which response measures are discontinued after the occurrence of a single reinforcement or nonreinforcement, thus differentiating the S⁺ and S⁻ trials, free operant procedures result in the confounding of the controlling effects of the experimental stimuli with the controlling effects of stimulation produced by reinforcement and nonreinforcement. Thus, differential responding obtained during acquisition in the typical free operant situation cannot be unequivocally attributed to the experimental stimuli in question. However, differential responding during extinction and during generalization testing unequivocally indicates control by the experimental stimuli. During extinction, reinforcement is no longer given and, hence, cannot provide differential stimulation; and, during generalization testing, a weakened probability of responding can be explained only on the basis of control by the experimental stimuli (see Guttman and Kalish, 1956). It will be important to keep these considerations in mind in evaluating studies of discrimination learning.

Much of the learning that takes place in early childhood involves choosing the relevant aspects of a stimulus complex and responding appropriately to them. For example, the acquisition of word meanings, at least in part, can be analyzed as a process in which the child is required to attach labels to objects and events in his environment. In order to use words appropriately, the child must sort out the distinguishing features of a given object from those which are common as well to other objects. When young children are first learning to speak, they commonly make errors such as calling a horse "doggie." In essence, this error is an instance of an incomplete dimensional discrimination. The child may have learned to respond with the word "doggie" to the sight of any four-legged objects that move; but, although the attributes of four leggedness and motion are certainly relevant, they do not completely define the distinguishing characteristics of dogs. Before the child can use the label appropriately, he must learn to attend to other relevant dimensions such as size, surface texture, and proportion of body parts. The acquisition of many words, then, depends upon a process quite similar to that observed in laboratory experiments on dimensional discrimination learning. (For more complete discussion and evaluations of this kind of analysis, see Chapter 13, section entitled "Theoretical Accounts of Language Acquisition," and Chapter 14, introductory part of section entitled "The Development of Concepts of Quantity, Relation, and Class.")

The same holds true for learning to read letters. Reversal of the letters b and d is a very common error made by children just learning to read (see Chapter 11, section entitled "Form Perception in Children"). These symbols are identical in all respects except that they differ in orientation. Children who fail to discriminate consistently among them are failing to attend to the distinguishing dimension of orientation. Gibson (1965) stated, in a provocative discussion of the factors affecting the process of learning to read, "The most relevant kind of training for discrimination [of letters] is practice which provides experience with the characteristic differences that distinguish the set of items" (p. 1069).

Dimensional discrimination learning tasks, which are prototypes for much of children's everyday learning, are used in controlled laboratory situations to study many variables that influence the course of learning. Included among these are age, intelligence, and socioeconomic background, as well as the effects of reinforcement conditions such as reward versus punishment, and intermittent and delayed reward.

The learning process itself has been subjected to close scrutiny in investigations of the role of verbal mediation, attention, and hypothesis testing as determinants of discrimination learning. Other factors, such as the method of stimulus presentation and children's dimensional preferences and response sets, have been the subject of a number of studies. The remaining sections of this chapter summarize the methods and results of studies in which dimensional discrimination learning tasks have been used for the exploration of the effects of these variables.

DISCRIMINATIVE LEARNING IN INFANCY

The distinction between perceptual and dimensional discrimination learning is important, but has too seldom been made explicit, especially in studies with infants. Perceptual discrimination tasks, as already noted, are designed to determine whether differential responses *can* be learned with particular stimuli, to assess the organism's capacity to discriminate in the perceptual sense. Infant studies with this primary aim were reviewed in Chapter 2. Dimensional discrimination tasks start with the implicit assumption that the stimuli are perceptually discriminable, and focus on either the learning process *per se* or on conditions affecting that process. Infant studies with this primary aim are reviewed here. However, many of the infant studies are ambiguous in terms of the experimenter's intent; it is not always clear whether the purpose was to determine whether perceptual discrimination is possible or whether discrimination *learning* is possible at these young age levels. We will also find, in the review that follows, that too few of these studies were designed to permit the investigator to determine precisely which aspects of the stimuli controlled the responses, once discrimination learning was successfully established.

Differential Conditioning in Infants

Differential conditioning, also called conditioned discrimination, is a direct extension of the classical conditioning paradigm, but involves the successive presentation of two or more stimuli with the unconditioned stimulus (US) paired with only one of them. To achieve differentiation, the experimenter typically presents the conditional stimulus (S$^+$) in a temporal relation with the US (e.g., food). After the conditioned response (e.g., anticipatory salivation or sucking) is clearly established to the S$^+$, a negative stimulus (S$^-$) not followed by food is introduced and alternated with presentations of the S$^+$.

Differential conditioning of infants by Soviet investigators has followed the experimental prototype described by Pavlov (1927). Pavlov reported two differentiation experiments in which visual and auditory discriminations were studied in dogs. In both experiments the conditioned salivary response had been established to S$^+$ prior to the initial introduction of S$^-$. Pavlov reported that the initial presentation of S$^-$ resulted in a low level of conditioned salivation due to competing investigatory responses. The "investigatory" or "orientation" reaction occurs whenever novel or ambiguous stimuli are presented during the process of conditioning and discrimination, resulting in interference with the conditioned response (see Chapter 9). Two stages of differential conditioning can be distinguished. After a few trials of random presentations of S$^+$ and S$^-$, a stage of wide generalization is observed; many stimuli elicit the conditioned response. With further training the differential conditioning is established, and the development of the discrimination with successive trials is reflected by the difference in occurrence of the conditioned response on the S$^+$ and S$^-$ trials.

Soviet investigators have reported conditioned visual, auditory, and tactile discriminations with a variety of response measures in infants by the second and third months of life. Unfortunately, only descriptive accounts of their results are provided; and the reports of these studies are incomplete with respect to specification of controls, experimental procedures, and discrimination learning criteria.

Following the establishment of conditioned anticipatory sucking to a tone with three infants between 35 and 45 days of age, Kasatkin and Levikova

(1935a) obtained "stable" conditioned differentiation between the tone and a bell by 2 to 3 months of age. They reported that some of their subjects differentiated the S⁻ from the S⁺ on the first presentation of the new auditory stimulus. Apparently, other infants showed evidence of stimulus generalization over the early trials of differentiation training. Subsequently, these investigators trained the infants to discriminate between two pipe organ tones of the same octave but separated by five steps. In another experiment, Kasatkin and Levikova (1935b) reported conditioned color discrimination in infants between 3 and 4 months of age. Again, stable conditioned sucking to colored lights (red or yellow) was established prior to the first presentation of S⁻ (green light) and the initiation of differentiation training. In this study, generalization of the conditioned response was observed on the initial S⁻ trials, but conditioned differentiation was obtained with further training.

Auditory and visual differentiation has been obtained by a number of investigators with infants in the first 4 to 5 months of life (Janos, 1959; Nichaeva, 1954; Rendle-Short, 1961; Tomka, see Brackbill and Koltsova, 1967; Vakhrameeva, 1964). With few exceptions (Kasatkin and Levikova, 1935a; Vakhrameeva, 1964), investigators have not found a significant relation between age and rate of acquired differentiation in infants during the first year of life.

Despite the successful demonstration of differentiation in several sensory modalities with classical conditioning procedures, several important developmental issues have not been systematically analyzed. The concept of inhibition has served an important function in the analysis of instrumental discrimination learning (Luria, 1961; Terrace, 1966), and Luria has suggested that the preverbal child's main problem in the conditional type of learning task is a lack of inhibitory mechanisms (see also White, 1965). Conceptual and experimental analyses of independent inhibitory and excitatory effects are important tasks for future investigations of discrimination learning in infants. Jenkins has discussed Pavlov's concept of differential inhibition as a basis for distinguishing "the absence of an inhibitory effect from the absence or reduction of an excitatory effect . . ." (Jenkins, 1965a, p. 56).

The bare fact that an animal has learned a "go/no-go" discrimination with say, S_1^+ and S_2^-, does not in itself [however] provide evidence of inhibitory control. One can equally well assume the animal to be operating by any one of the following: 1. Respond if S_1; otherwise, do not respond. 2. Do not respond if S_2; otherwise respond. 3. Respond if S_1; and do not respond if S_2. The first rule entails only excitatory control, the second, only inhibitory control, the third, a combination of the two. (Jenkins, 1965a, p. 56.)

As Jenkins and Harrison (1962) have suggested, to determine whether a subject has learned to respond to S⁻, it is necessary to vary the value of S⁻ along some stimulus dimension and to determine whether the subject's tendency to respond to S⁻ is affected. Studies of operant discrimination with infrahuman organisms showed gradients of inhibition during a subsequent generalization test (Honig, Boneau, Burstein, and Pennypacker, 1959; Jenkins and Harrison, 1962), but these were rather shallow when compared with excitation gradients on the S⁺ continuum. Conditioned inhibition and excitation in infants have not been independently assessed using typical differentiation and instrumental discrimination learning tasks.

Discrimination Learning in the First Six Months of Life

The paucity of instrumental discrimination learning studies with infants during the first six months of life attests to the methodological problem confronting researchers working with a motorically immature and preverbal organism. Discrimination learning studies with infants in this age group have been limited to the work of four or five investigators and all but a couple of these studies used the head-turning response as the dependent variable.

DISCRETE-TRIAL PROCEDURES. Evidence of a learned spatial discrimination has been obtained with infants as young as ten weeks of age with eye fixation as the dependent variable (Watson, 1966). Visual and auditory stimuli were used to reinforce spatially discriminated eye fixations (i.e., left vs. right position). The experimental procedures are described in Chapter 4.

Experiments by Papoušek and by Siqueland and Lipsitt are the only studies of discrimination learning in infants during the first month of life; they provide examples of the discrete-trial successive discrimination learning task. Siqueland and Lipsitt presented infants with a "go/no-go" successive discrimination problem; the successive or patterned discrimination problem employed by Papoušek required infants to choose the correct response (right vs. left turn) on each trial. In the latter study reinforcement was available on every trial contingent upon the correct position response. These studies clearly support the conclusion that infants are capable of learning an auditory discrimination in the first three months of life.

An important series of longitudinal studies with infants from birth to eight months of age by Papoušek (1959, 1967a, 1967b) provided a major methodological break-through and clearly demonstrated auditory discrimination in an instrumental learning task with infants as young as three months of age. A detailed account of Papoušek's training procedures and experimental design (involving three age groups) is given in Chapter 4. Following evidence of stable conditioning of a left head-turning response to a tone a second stimulus, a buzzer, was introduced. The infant continued to be reinforced with milk for left turns on the tone trials, but was now required to turn to the right on buzzer trials to receive milk reinforcement. The infants received daily sessions of ten training trials, including five tone and five buzzer trials presented randomly, and attainment of six consecutive correct responses was taken as criterion for the establishment of discrimination learning. In the youngest group such learning occurred at three months of age and reversal of the discrimination was obtained at four months. Papoušek reported that a significant relation between rate of discrimination learning and age was obtained when he compared the performance of his three age groups in the discrimination learning task (see Figure 5-3).

Clear evidence of auditory stimulus control of differential head-turning was demonstrated by two reversals of the originally acquired discrimination (Figure

5-3). Infants who started the series of learning procedures at three and five months learned the reversal more rapidly than subjects who started as newborns. The two younger groups, but not the oldest group, learned the reversal discrimination more rapidly than the original discrimination. This study provides the only evidence of a savings effect with infants below one year of age. All three groups performed equally well on the second reversal problem and the two younger groups again showed a savings effect. The failure of the oldest group (six month

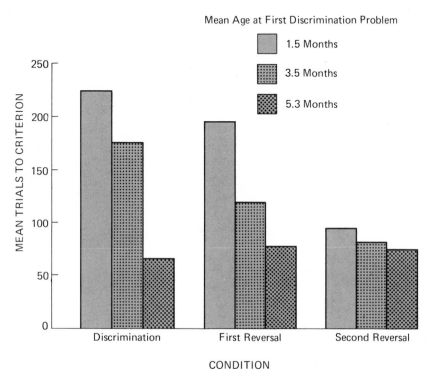

Fig. 5-3. Comparison of three age groups on mean number of trials to criterion on original discrimination problem and subsequent reversal problems. (Adapted from Papoušek, 1967b, Table 10-1, p. 257.)

old infants) to demonstrate further savings on the reversal problems may have reflected a ceiling effect.

The age differences in rate of acquisition of the discrimination may have been due to differences in unconditioned response bias or preference in the respective age groups. Several studies with older children have suggested that position and perseveration response tendencies, which interfere with acquisition in a two-choice discrimination task, vary with the age of the child (Jeffrey and Cohen, 1965; White, 1964). For example, White reported that it is difficult to teach a discrimination to $2\frac{1}{2}$ to 3 year old children because of strong position habits. Age differences in such unconditioned response biases have not been systematically analyzed in infants during the first 2 years of life. However, the interfering effects of head position preferences in the young infant were discussed in our earlier analysis of Papoušek's procedures in Chapter 4.

Siqueland and Lipsitt (1966) have reported evidence of discrimination learning in the newborn. Using differential head-turning as the dependent variable, they extended their experimental procedures, which proved successful in a study of instrumental conditioning (previously described in Chapter 4), to investigate discriminative behavior in two to four day old infants. Two groups of infants were subjected to procedures designed to assess the effect of differentially reinforcing two responses, left head-turns and right head-turns. Two different auditory stimuli were presented; tactile stimulation to one side of the infant's face was paired with a buzzer and stimulation to the other side was paired with a tone. As in the previous experiment by these investigators, tactile stimulation to the infant's cheek overlapped the last three seconds of a five second auditory stimulus. For the experimental subjects, reinforcement (dextrose solution) was presented following ipsilateral (same-side) turns to the positive stimulus (S^+), but not following ipsilateral turns to the negative stimulus (S^-). Control subjects were individually matched with experimental subjects on total number of reinforcements over training trials, but the dextrose presentations were given eight to ten seconds following the auditory-tactile stimulus. Both the experimental and the control group received 6 baseline trials, 48 "training" trials, and 36 "extinction" trials, and the two groups were compared on changes in differential head-turning over the training and extinction trials.

A reliable increase in responding to S^+ was obtained in the experimental group, shifting from a baseline response probability of .18 to a probability of .73 by the end of training. In contrast, the control group showed a decrease in responding to S^+ over the "training" trials. Also, both groups showed a decrease in occurrence of ipsilateral responses on S^- trials during training. These data clearly demonstrate discrimination learning in the experimental group. Reliable evidence for extinction of the acquired discrimination was also obtained.

The results of this experiment indicate that reinforcement operations can result in differential head-turning in newborn infants. However, even though the discrete-trial procedure was used, it is not possible to specify what the effective controlling stimulus was. Both S^+ and S^- were compound stimuli, with auditory (buzzer and tone) and tactile (left and right cheek) stimulation confounded. Since head-turns in the direction of tactile stimulation were reinforced, the infants could have solved the problem as a simple position discrimination.

In a subsequent study, these investigators gave infants an auditory discrimination task, using a similar experimental procedure. The two auditory stimuli served as positive and negative cues for reinforcement of ipsilateral turns to tactile stimulation presented to the infant's right cheek only. Turns to right-sided stimulation in the presence of one auditory stimulus were reinforced, but right turns to the same tactile stimulus in the presence of the other auditory stimulus were never reinforced. Following this initial training procedure, reversal training was instituted so that turning to the previous S^+ was extinguished and responding to the previous S⁻ was reinforced. The response criterion in this experiment was the occurrence of a 10 degree ipsilateral movement.

A head-turning apparatus provided instrumentation and recording of head movements. A photograph of the apparatus is shown in Figure 5-4. As seen in the photograph, the apparatus consisted of a lightweight plastic headpiece which rested on the subject's temples and connected to a potentiometer circuit by means of a flexible shaft. This apparatus provided polygraphic recording

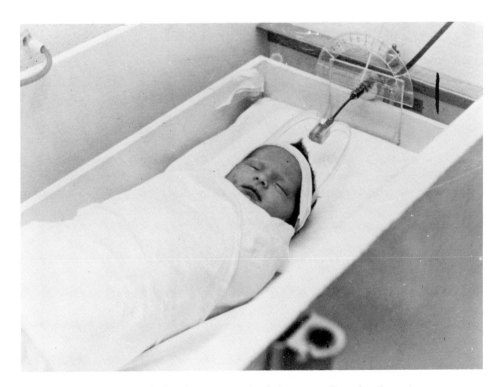

Fig. 5-4. Neonate with headpiece attached for recording head-turning responses. (From Siqueland and Lipsitt, 1966, Fig. 3, p. 367. Reprinted by permission of the authors and Academic Press, Inc.)

and measurement of lateral head movements about the horizontal axis. A sample polygraphic record is shown in Figure 5-5. The sample record shows two continuous minutes of recording obtained from one infant over the last block of training trials. Four trials are shown in the record, two buzzer-touch presentations and two tone-touch presentations, one every 30 seconds. The event markers on the first line show the onset of the 5 second auditory stimuli and the overlapping 3 second tactile stimulus. The second and third lines show analogue records of lateral head movements and respiration, respectively. Downward deflections of the polygraph pen indicate head movement to the right of a midline position and upward deflections indicate left head-turns.

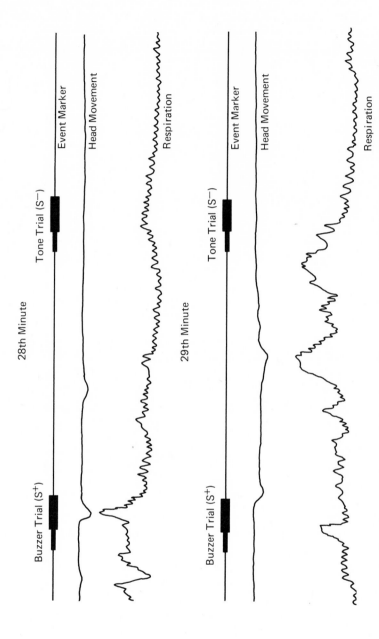

Fig. 5-5. Polygraph record showing comparison of response (right head-turns) to positive and negative stimuli by one infant over successive trials. (From Siqueland and Lipsitt, 1966, Fig. 4, p. 369. Reprinted by permission of the authors and Academic Press, Inc.)

Sixteen newborns were divided into two groups; the tone was the S⁺ and the buzzer the S⁻ for one group, and for the other group the cue functions of the two auditory stimuli were reversed. All infants received 60 training trials (30 with S⁺ and 30 with S⁻), followed by 60 reversal trials, 1 trial every 30 seconds. As in the previous experiment, stimulus presentations consisted of tactile stimulation (right cheek) overlapping the last 3 seconds of the 5 second auditory stimulus. Reinforcement was contingent upon a 10-degree head-turn to the right. Reinforcement was the presentation of .2 cubic cm. of a dextrose solution via a 4-second presentation of a nipple. The results of this study, shown in Figure 5-6, indicate that newborns learned the discrimination problem. The figure shows

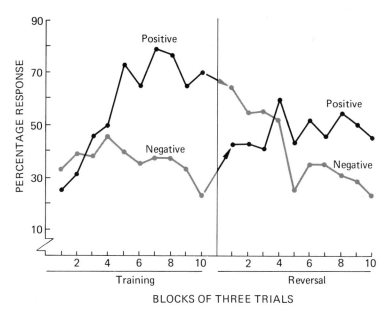

Fig. 5-6. Comparison of percentage responses to positive (dark line) and negative (light line) stimuli during training and reversal trials. (From Siqueland and Lipsitt, 1966, Fig. 5, p. 370. Reprinted by permission of the authors and Academic Press, Inc.)

the mean percentage of right turns to S⁺ and S⁻ over training and reversal trials. Statistical analysis of the results indicated that head-turning to S⁺ increased reliably over training, and responding to S⁻ showed negligible change. During reversal training, the primary effect was a decrease in responding to S⁻ (previously S⁺) over trials; responding to S⁺ (previously S⁻) showed no change.

The Siqueland and Lipsitt experiments indicate discrimination learning in the newborn in a discrete-trial "go/no-go" discrimination problem. As previously indicated, the absence of increased responding to S⁻ does not provide evidence of inhibitory control. However, these investigators noted, during the course of training, that there was an apparent increase in the occurrence of contralateral head movements on the S⁻ trials. An analysis of this effect showed that the ratio of ipsilateral to contralateral movements to the tactile stimulus in the presence of S⁺ increased over training trials, shifting from .70 to .90. However, response ratios in the presence of S⁻ decreased from .72 to .50 over training trials. This change in response to S⁻ reflected a sharp increase in contralateral head-turns over the last four blocks of training trials. These effects are shown in Figure 5-7, which presents the mean response differentiation ratio (number of ipsilateral responses divided by total number of ipsilateral and contralateral

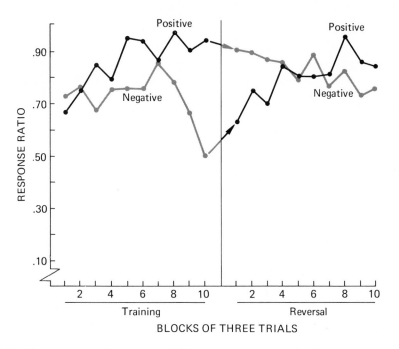

Fig. 5-7. Comparison of response differentiation ratios (number of ipsilateral responses divided by total number of ipsilateral and contralateral responses) to positive (dark line) and negative (light line) stimuli during original training and reversal trials. (From Siqueland and Lipsitt, 1966, Fig. 6, p. 372. Reprinted by permission of the authors and Academic Press, Inc.)

responses) to S⁺ and S⁻ during training and reversal trials. The shift in the differentiation ratio to S⁺ (previously S⁻) on reversal training trials reflects a decrease in contralateral responses.

Although these results are at best only suggestive, the increased occurrence of contralateral head-turns to S⁻ may reflect a type of conditioned inhibition in the newborn. Recent results obtained in studies of free operant discrimination learning with infrahuman organisms suggest that during the course of discrimination training, the S⁻ may function as an aversive stimulus (Terrace, 1966). The tactile stimulus in the presence of the negative auditory stimulus may have acquired aversive properties for the subject, and the contralateral response may reflect an active escape response that terminates the conditioned aversive stimulus.

The type of discrimination learning experiences provided for the infant in the normal feeding situation may not be much different from the experimental prototypes used in the later experiment by Siqueland and Lipsitt. The breast-fed infant may learn to respond in one way to tactile stimulation when it is presented in the context of complex visual and postural cues signalling that reinforcement is forthcoming, and to respond in another way to the same tactile stimulation in the presence of other stimulus complexes. Thus, an infant one month of age may demonstrate a higher probability of ipsilateral head-turns to a tactile stimulus when he is held in the feeding position at the mother's breast than when he is lying supine in his crib. Naturalistic observations by Denisova and Figurin (1929) on the development of anticipatory sucking in the feeding situation suggest that this type of discrimination learning occurs in the normal feeding situation.

FREE OPERANT PROCEDURES. Free operant discrimination learning procedures have found limited use in studies with infants in the first six months of life. The simplest simultaneous discrimination problem involves a spatial discrimination. For example, in visual choice discrimination the subject may be required to select the right one of two identical objects. Two investigators (Caron, 1967; Siqueland, 1964), using a modification of the operant conditioning procedure, have obtained evidence of spatial discrimination with infants at four months of age. Although rate of differential head-turning (right and left turns from a midline position) was the dependent variable in these studies, reinforcement was presented in such a way that the subject's head was returned to midline position at the termination of the reinforcing stimulus. Thus, the operant task in these studies is similar to a simultaneous spatial discrimination problem, in that the infant had to learn to make a spatially discriminated head movement prior to reinforcement.

An example of this type of conditioning procedure is seen in the study of differentiated head-turning by Siqueland (1964). The apparatus in this study consisted of a reclining seat with an attached headpiece for recording head movements polygraphically. The apparatus is similar to the one used in the Siqueland and Lipsitt study (1966). The infant was placed in a white experimental chamber. The chamber, open on one side with the subject facing the back, provided the infants with an environment devoid of distracting stimuli. The experimenter stood behind the subject, and during conditioning a nursing bottle was presented from behind the subject. After the presentation of the bottle, the subject was returned to midline; and the bottle was withdrawn from the midline position. An eight minute training procedure consisted of a one minute baseline, three minutes of conditioning, two minutes of extinction, and a two minute reconditioning period. Reinforcement consisted of presenting the bottle for three seconds. There were three groups of infants. Group R⁺ was given reinforcement following each right turn of 45 degrees. To provide a control for arousal effects of milk presentation on differential head-turning, individual subjects in Group C were matched with subjects in Group R⁺ for number of reinforcements over training, but the reinforcements were not contingent upon head-turning. A third group, Group L⁺, was reinforced for left head-turns of

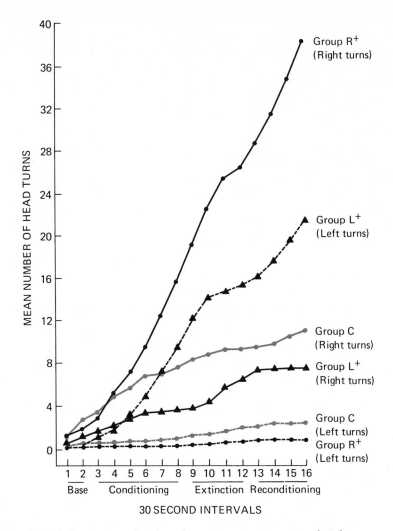

Fig. 5-8. Cumulative curves showing the mean response rate of right turns and left turns, for three experimental groups, for 30-second periods during baseline, conditioning, extinction, and reconditioning phases. (From Siqueland, 1964, Fig. 1, p. 224. Reprinted by permission of the author and the Psychonomic Society, Inc.)

45 degrees. The mean cumulative head-turns, both left and right, for each of the three groups are shown in Figure 5-8. There were no reliable differences among the three groups during baseline for either left or right head-turns. Group R⁺ and Group L⁺ both showed significant acquisition and extinction effects for

the reinforced response: an increase and subsequent decrease in right and left head-turns, respectively. No reliable changes in the nonreinforced response were obtained in these two groups. Group C showed no evidence of reliable changes in differentiated head-turning.

Similar results, showing the effects of visual reinforcement on differentiated head-turning, were obtained by Caron (1967). Using a design in which each individual subject served as his own control, Caron demonstrated both acquisition and extinction of spatially differentiated head movements. Subsequently, a reversal of the spatial discrimination was presented to some of the subjects. To the extent that these procedures can be treated as constituting a simultaneous choice discrimination problem, the results provide some evidence for simple spatial discrimination in the four month old infant. Evidence of stable differential head movements resulting from reinforcement procedures within a relatively brief training procedure suggests that spatial discrimination problems are readily solved by the young infant.

The strongest evidence for operant discrimination learning in young infants has been provided by Bower (1964, 1965a, 1965b, 1967). In two studies Bower used head-turning as the operant response, and in a third he used high amplitude sucking. Differential response rate in the presence of S^+ and S^- was the dependent variable.

In the first study Bower (1964) developed a discrimination training and generalization testing procedure. Nine infants from two to three months of age served as subjects. The subject was placed in a crib inclined at a 45 degree angle with his head positioned between two pads. The left pad was attached to a microswitch; movement of the head to the left closed the microswitch and stepped a cumulative recorder. The S^+ was a one foot cube made of white paper, placed on a table three feet from the infant's eyes. The reinforcing stimulus was the appearance of the experimenter from below the table "peek-a-booing" at the infant for 15 seconds. During initial training, the S^+ was the white cube; and S^- was the table with cube absent. Although acquisition data were not given in the brief report of this study, Bower stated that discriminative control of head-turning was established.

The results of stimulus generalization tests with four stimuli were reported, but it is difficult to compare these results with the findings of typical generalization studies. Instead of testing for evidence of stimulus generalization along a single stimulus continuum, as is typically done, Bower compared response rates to the training stimulus (S^+) with rates to three other stimuli that differed from S^+ on two dimensions, size and distance. A generalization gradient was apparently obtained, but clearer evidence of generalization gradients might be obtained by testing on several values of a single stimulus dimension (size or distance). (See Table 2-2 and the accompanying textual material for further discussion of this study and related work by Bower.)

The generalization data obtained by Bower suggest that the infants were responding to differences in both stimulus size and stimulus distance. However, the effects reported may have been obtained because some subjects were responding to stimulus size and others to stimulus distance, but with varying magnitudes. This possibility cannot be evaluated from the reported data, because no indication was given as to whether the group means reflected the responsiveness of individual subjects to the various generalization stimuli. Reynolds (1961) demonstrated, in a study of discrimination learning with pigeons, that different aspects of a complex S+ acquire control over responding in different subjects. Questions about the nature of the training conditions necessary for establishing control along several dimensions have not yet been answered. Bower's results do not necessarily indicate that differential reinforcement with respect to the size and distance dimensions was necessary to demonstrate the control of these dimensions during generalization testing; these dimensions may have been prepotent because of innate factors.

Bower (1966a, 1966b) has also studied shape and orientation discrimination, using a similar type of generalization testing procedure. In experiments with two month old infants, training procedures similar to those of the previous study were employed. In one experiment, a group of nine infants was given three successive generalization tests following free operant discrimination training. During the initial discrimination training, head-turning was reinforced on a variable ratio schedule in the presence of S+ (rectangular board presented at a 5° counterclockwise orientation). Differential reinforcement training was given in the presence and absence of the S+. During three successive generalization tests, each subject was presented four orientations (5°, 15°, 30°, or 45° counterclockwise) of the following: (a) rectangular board, (b) trapezoids casting the same retinal image as the rectangles shown in a frontoparallel plane, and (c) rectangle with one edge not exposed. Each stimulus in the three generalization conditions was presented 30 times in a random order for five-second periods. During the generalization testing procedures the S+ (5° orientation) was reinforced on a continuous schedule, and therefore differences in response to the S+ relative to the three test stimuli would not provide evidence of stimulus discrimination. The use of continuous reinforcement prevents interpreting performance differences among the stimuli as reflecting acquired stimulus control; differences in response rates in the presence of the stimuli may reflect a confounding of the effects of antecedent reinforcement–nonreinforcement with the effects of the test stimuli (Jenkins, 1965b). Bower reported the results in terms of proportions of responses made to the test stimuli relative to the number of responses to the S+ in each of the three generalization measures. The proportions of responding to the test stimuli are shown in Table 5-1. Although Bower suggested that discrimination performance under (a) was poorer than under (b) and (c), his statistical analysis does not allow a conclusion that discrimination was unequivocally demonstrated. Statistical tests for reliable overall differences in performance to the three test stimuli within each generalization test condition were not reported. While the apparent differences in response proportions in (b) as a function of orientation of that stimulus provide suggestive evidence of acquired orientation discrimination, the statistical reliability of this apparent generalization effect was not reported.

Recent developments in the use of operant conditioning techniques, in which visual stimuli have been shown to be effective reinforcers when high amplitude nonnutritive sucking is treated as the operant response, may provide flexible and efficient procedures for studying operant discrimination learning in the young infant (Siqueland, 1966; see also Chapter 4). Rank (1968) has shown that auditory stimuli (female voice and music) are also effective as reinforcers of high amplitude nonnutritive sucking in the four month old infant. Visual and auditory stimuli, used as reinforcers of the sucking response, can provide considerable flexibility in the study of discrimination learning.

Bower (1967) has recently attempted to extend this type of operant conditioning technique with the sucking response to the study of form discrimination. His dependent variable was high amplitude sucking, and the reinforcer was a 10 second presentation of a movie showing older children at play. The projection screen was 15 inches from the subject's face at a 45 degree angle to his

Table 5-1

Proportions of Responding on Generalization Tests[a]

	Anticlockwise orientation		
Test stimulus	*15°*	*30°*	*45°*
(a) Rectangular board	1.04	.98	.90
(b) Trapezoid	.70	.64	.55
(c) Rectangle with one edge not exposed	.86	.78	.77

[a] After Bower (1966a, Table 1, p. 833). "Proportions of responding" is defined in text.

line of vision. A pegboard, illuminated by fluorescent tubes at the top and bottom (luminance of 52 foot-lamberts) and parallel to the infant's line of sight, was used to expose the positive stimulus, for one group a triangle with a black bar placed over it and for the other group a series of three black disks. As in the previous studies by Bower, subjects were given differential reinforcement in the presence and absence of the S⁺. The S⁻ consisted of offset of the pegboard lights and thus the withdrawal of the triangle or black disks. Differential reinforcement procedures were begun on the second day of training and consisted of a progressive lengthening of the S⁻ period. During the initial acquisition and discrimination training, every third suck on the average was reinforced (VR 3). Within one session the S⁻ period was progressively lengthened from 1 to 60 seconds, and Bower reported that none of the infants emitted a single response in the presence of the S⁻. The progressive lengthening of the S⁻ period is similar to the type of fading procedures suggested by Terrace (1963).

The rather remarkable level of stimulus control over operant sucking in one month old infants is difficult to interpret in light of Bower's training procedures.

In original training the offset of the pegboard lights immediately preceded the presentation of the visual reinforcer and the lights remained off for the duration of the ten-second reinforcement period. Thus, the same stimulus event (offset of pegboard lights) served as a signal for reinforcement presentation and also served as the S⁻ during discrimination training. Bower reported that a discrimination test was given during the terminal minute of the second day of training. The test consisted of extinguishing the pegboard lights during the terminal minute. He reported, "none of the infants emitted a single response during the test" (Bower, 1967, p. 75). Although this effect was taken as adequate evidence of discrimination, quantitative data with respect to acquisition of the discrimination were not reported.

Bower also gave generalization tests, but as in the earlier work clear evidence of generalization along a single stimulus dimension does not seem to have been demonstrated.

These studies by Bower, with infants from one to four months of age, suggest that head-turning and sucking may provide the researcher with response measures that can be profitably investigated in free operant discrimination tasks with young infants.

Discrimination Learning in the 6 to 12 Month Infant

DISCRETE-TRIAL PROCEDURES.   By six to eight months of age the infant's rapidly developing manipulative skills have allowed the adaptation of more traditional types of learning tasks to the study of discrimination problems. Some of the earliest attempts to demonstrate simultaneous two-choice discrimination learning with individual infants in the first year of life met with negligible success. Meyers (1908) presented his six month old daughter with a color discrimination problem (red and blue blocks). Choice of the red block was reinforced with a lick of honey and the infant was given 12 trials each day for four days. No evidence of learning was obtained on the color discrimination task and the infant also failed to learn a brightness discrimination problem at nine months of age. Valentine (1914) failed in an attempt to train a color discrimination when he presented his eight month old son with a choice between blue and green wools and reinforced picking the blue wool with the presentation of jam.

Experimental procedures developed by Ling (1941) have provided some of the best evidence of discrimination learning with infants in the second half of the first year of life. Infants from 8 to 14 months of age were studied in a discrete-trial two-choice discrimination task. They were tested while sitting in a crib and were presented with a gray tray containing yellow blocks (circle, cross, triangle, square, and oval). The tray was presented so that the infant could easily reach the blocks, and stimulus pairs were presented with order and position randomized. Within a given form discrimination problem, the positive stimulus could be removed from the tray by the infant, but the negative stimulus was locked to the tray. The removable positive stimulus was coated with a saccharine solution, providing a sweet taste reward when the infant brought the form to his mouth. The learning criterion on each problem was 8 correct out of 10 choices. The same positive stimulus, circle, was maintained over 27 of the discrimination problems, while the negative stimuli changed in form, size, orientation, and number. After the problems had been learned, the subjects were given reversal training in which the previously positive form was now the negative form and *vice versa*. The infants required approximately 30 to 35 trials to learn the first discrimination problem, and savings were noted on each of the subsequent problems. The reversal problems were learned in approximately half the number of trials required to reach criterion on the corresponding original problems. This study provides some of the most convincing

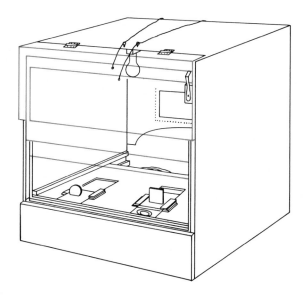

Fig. 5-9. Modification of Wisconsin General Testing Apparatus. (From Weisberg and Simmons, 1966, Fig. 1, p. 101. Reprinted by permission of the authors and the Journal Press.)

evidence of discrimination learning in the discrete-trial problem in infants one year of age and under.

Recent investigators (Hill, 1962, 1965; Weisberg and Simmons, 1966) have used modifications of the Wisconsin General Testing Apparatus to study object discrimination in one year olds. Figure 5-9 shows one of these modified apparatuses. It is important to note that these investigators found it necessary to develop special shaping procedures in an attempt to orient their infants to the simultaneous choice task. For example, in the first stage infants were trained to pick up the reinforcer (candy or cookies) from the stimulus tray. Next, the reinforcer was placed in the food well with the stimulus objects behind the food well. A third step in the shaping process consisted of placing the reinforcer in the food well with the stimulus objects only half covering the reinforcer.

Next, the subjects were trained to slide the stimulus object back to obtain the reinforcer. Following this progression of successive steps, infants were given the typical two-choice simultaneous discrimination problem. Such shaping procedures are common in studies with monkeys, but are seldom used in studies with older children.

Hill found that 8 of 15 infants learned an object discrimination (green triangle and red cylinder) with a median of 36 errors. Receiving 20 trials each day, 7 of Hill's infants failed to reach a criterion of 10 successive correct responses within 100 trials. In a similar type of object discrimination problem, Weisberg and Simmons reported that 3 of 8 infants failed to learn the problem.

These results indicate that some one year old children are able to learn an object discrimination problem. Hill also analyzed response strategies and concluded that one year old children tend to respond with consistent position preferences. Approximately 70 percent of the responses of these children reflected position preferences. Failure of some subjects to learn the object discrimination problem may have resulted from the effects of intermittent reinforcement of a dominant position response. At the present time there is little empirical evidence about stimulus preferences in infants. Studies with older children indicate that form is the more salient cue in form–color discrimination problems (Suchman and Trabasso, 1966b). If infants are responding initially on the basis of the more salient stimulus dimension in a multidimensional discrimination task, the effects of intermittent reinforcement on these initial stimulus dimension preferences may account for the failure of some subjects to learn to attend to the relevant stimulus dimensions.

FREE OPERANT PROCEDURES. Studies of color discrimination with 8 and 12 month old infants have been conducted by Simmons and Lipsitt (Lipsitt, 1963; Simmons, 1964; Simmons and Lipsitt, 1961). They developed an operant discrimination apparatus in which the subject was presented with two six-inch wooden panels as manipulanda (Simmons and Lipsitt, 1961). Windows in the middle of the panels allowed presentation of different colored lights as discriminative stimuli. Responding to the correct colored panel (S^+) was reinforced with the presentation of a door chime. Their initial experiment consisted of an eight minute experimental session, divided into four two minute phases. Responding to a red light (S^+) was reinforced, and responses to a blue light (S^-) were never reinforced. The positions of the S^+ were counterbalanced over the first two phases of the experiment. During the third two minute phase both panels were S^- (i.e., both were blue and no reinforcement was given), and during the fourth phase the S^+ was again paired with one of the panels and reinforced with presentation of the door chime. The results indicated that the subjects responded more to the reinforced color than to the nonreinforced color during the differential reinforcement phases of the experiment.

Unfortunately, we cannot conclude that the differential response rates to the S^+ and S^- in this experiment provide clear evidence of an acquired *color* discrimination. With the use of continuous reinforcement during acquisition training, the S^Ds and the context of reinforcement and nonreinforcement were highly correlated. Reinforcement tracking, independent of the discriminative stimuli, could have produced the effects obtained. Within each time block, response to either the left or the right panel was reinforced, and following the initial response and its reinforcement or nonreinforcement all subsequent responding could have been determined by the differential reinforcement probability for the rest of the period. In order to obtain an unequivocal measure of discriminative control, it is necessary to have a measure of differential response to experimental stimuli under conditions which differ only with respect to the discriminative stimuli in question. One method of eliminating the confounding effects of reinforcement context is to use a control group in which position of the panels alone (independent of color) differentiates reinforcement probability. A second method is to test for evidence of discriminative control during extinction (i.e., with no further differential reinforcement).

In subsequent studies of color discrimination with a multiple response these investigators have used both kinds of control procedure. Using the two-panel discrimination apparatus already described, Simmons (1964) studied color discrimination learning in 12 month old infants. One group was reinforced for responding to the red light, and another group for responding to the blue light. The reinforcer, as in the previous study, was the door chime. A 1-minute baseline measure was obtained in which the blue and red lights were presented on the right or left response panels for 30-second periods. During a 4-minute discrimination training period, continuous reinforcement was in effect during the first 2 minutes and an FR 2 reinforcement schedule was used during the last 2 minutes. The right-left positions of the colored lights were changed each minute. The third phase of the experiment was a 2-minute extinction period with the positions of the stimuli switched at the end of 1 minute. The results are presented in Figure 5-10, which shows the mean cumulative responses to S+ and S− for the two groups. Statistical analysis of the results indicated that differential responding to the S+ and S− increased from the beginning to the end of the training period.

Lipsitt (1963) has provided evidence of color discrimination in eight month old infants, using a design to control for the effects of reinforcement tracking in the absence of differential colors paired with the reinforced panel. To minimize the tendency of infants to strike the two panels simultaneously, a three-panel apparatus was developed. The apparatus is shown in Figure 5-11. The apparatus was equipped with a mechanism that prohibited reinforcement when more than one panel was pressed. The middle panel was available for responding but was never reinforced. One group of infants was presented a red-green discrimination problem, half of the subjects reinforced for responding to the red stimulus and the other half for responding to the green stimulus. The middle panel was always negative; the positive stimulus was switched between the left and right panels according to a prearranged random sequence. Thus, in each time block, the subjects were presented with two negative stimuli and one positive. A control group received the same randomized sequence of shifting of the reinforced panel, but no differential colors were paired with the availability of reinforcement; all three response panels were the same color, the color changing over the successive time periods. Thus, differences between the red-green discrimination group and the control group in differential responding to the reinforced and nonreinforced panels provided a measure of acquired color discrimination. The two groups received six minutes of differential reinforcement

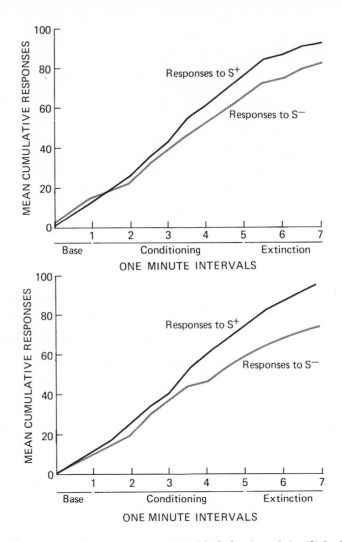

Fig. 5-10.   Mean cumulative responses to S⁺ (dark line) and S⁻ (light line). Upper figure: blue positive; lower figure: red positive. (From Lipsitt, 1963, Fig. 8, p. 180. Reprinted by permission of the author and Academic Press, Inc.)

training under the above conditions. From the first to the sixth minute of training the discrimination ratio (responses to S^+ relative to total responses) for the color group increased from .27 to .60, while the ratio for the control group shifted from .38 to .49. The color group showed a reliable increase in relative response to the S^+, while the control group did not.

The studies by Simmons and Lipsitt suggest that the multiple-response operant discrimination task provides a useful experimental procedure for the study of discrimination learning in infants under one year of age. The major problem with this procedure is in providing the appropriate opportunity for a measure

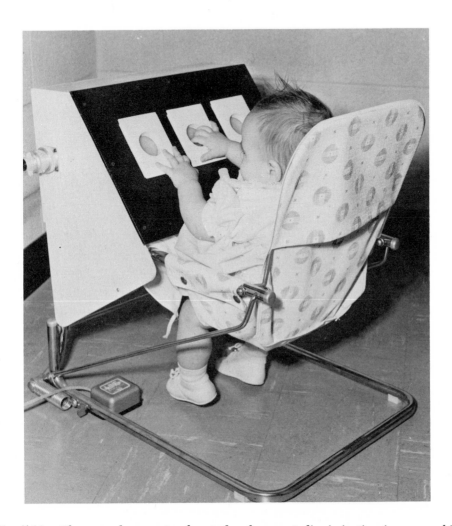

Fig. 5-11. Three-panel apparatus for study of operant discrimination in young children. Colors appear in windows on panels. Depression of "correct" panel produces buzzer sound. (From Lipsitt, 1963, Fig. 9, p. 181. Reprinted by permission of the author and Academic Press, Inc.)

of discriminative control independent of the confounding effects of the reinforcement context. The type of apparatus developed by Simmons and Lipsitt may also lend itself to discrete-trial simultaneous discrimination problems in which the panels could be withdrawn or blacked out following each choice response.

Discrimination Learning in the Second Year of Life

A review of the literature on discrimination learning leads to the conclusion that children in the second year of life have been the most neglected age group in studies of learning. This neglect does not seem to reflect major methodological problems in devising research strategies, but rather a problem with respect to availability of subjects for research. The editor of a major journal in child development (Siegel, 1967) recently noted that not a single study with children between one and three years of age appeared in the journal in 1966. The paucity of studies with this age group would seem to indicate that researchers have not found ways of obtaining subjects who are conveniently accessible for psychological research in our society.

Most studies of discrimination learning with children in this age group have used the discrete-trial two-choice problem; free operant techniques have been infrequently used.

FORM DISCRIMINATION.   In one of the earliest investigations of form discrimination with infants, Munn and Stiening (1931) presented a 15 month old boy with a series of two-choice simultaneous discrimination problems. The discrimination apparatus consisted of a box with two doors on the front face. Two-dimensional block forms on a white background were mounted on the doors of the box. When the child chose the "correct" form, he found a piece of chocolate in the compartment behind the correct stimulus. In six of eight discrimination problems the same form was the positive stimulus. Changes in the position, orientation (45 degree or 90 degree rotation), or size of both positive and negative stimuli, and changes in the form of the negative stimulus had only a very slight effect on the discrimination performance of the child.

Gellermann (1933b, 1933c) studied form discrimination with 2-year-old children using a Yerkes alley technique. The subject sat in a chair facing stimulus forms mounted by doors on a platform. Under the correct door was hidden a food reinforcement. Using a criterion of ten consecutive correct choices, Gellermann initially trained a form discrimination with a star as the positive stimulus and a circle as the negative stimulus. On a series of nine subsequent discrimination problems the subjects were presented with both new form and new orientation discrimination problems. In the course of learning a difficult discrimination, all subjects at one time or another traced the outline of the forms with a finger. Changes in the subject's head orientation also occurred with rotation of triangles in the orientation discrimination problems. These observations suggest that the use of proprioceptive cues may be an intrinsic part of the child's behavior on a discrimination learning task.

A direct application of the T-maze technique was recently employed by Henning and Hayweiser (1968) in a study of form discrimination in children from 15 to 38 months of age. A child-size T-maze was constructed of the following dimensions: The stem of the maze was 8 feet long, each of the arms was 4 feet long, the walls were 3 feet high, and the alleys were 2 feet wide. Stimulus cards were mounted on doors opening outward at the end of each maze arm.

The differential cues at the end of each arm required the subject to pause at the choice point and look both ways. All subjects learned a triangle versus circle discrimination problem with the triangle as the positive stimulus (the form cues were not counterbalanced over subjects). The reward was "finding the toy" (a red stuffed elephant); the negative stimulus door was locked. Following each correct response the toy was exchanged for a sugar pellet and the experimenter responded "very good, you found the toy right away." Subjects received 10 trials each day and were trained to a criterion of 5 consecutive correct choices or 8 correct out of 10 choices in a single session. One week after attaining criterion, the subjects were tested for retention and subsequently were trained on a form reversal problem. Seven of the 28 subjects were terminated short of 110 trials because of "extreme emotionality and fearful behavior" in the experimental situation or because of irregular attendance. Fifteen of the remaining 21 subjects met the relatively weak learning criterion within approximately 110 trials. Of those who learned the original form discrimination problem, 12 subjects demonstrated retention of the discrimination when they were tested one week later. However, only 5 of these children learned the reversal problem within 3 or fewer sessions. In the absence of evidence of reversal learning, it is not possible to conclude unequivocally that choice behavior in the T-maze was influenced by the differential reinforcement of the form cues. Because of the experimenter's focus on individual differences in discrimination learning, the typical method of counterbalancing the positive and negative form cues between subjects was not employed.

Learning or not learning the original discrimination problem was related to neither IQ nor chronological age, although the relation to mental age approached statistical significance. This study provides the only example of a discrimination learning procedure in which locomotor responses were employed with children under three years of age.

Skeels (1933) devised a simplified simultaneous discrimination task by presenting children with a form board in which individual forms were recessed. The form board with the recessed forms (cubes, spheres, crosses, etc.) provided the subject with a four-choice simultaneous discrimination task. When the child lifted the correct form block, he found a cookie. Skeels studied 41 children ranging from 15 to 46 months of age. In the initial discrimination problem the circle was the correct form. After the subject had reached criterion performance on the first problem, he was told that the reward was no longer under the circle but under another of the form blocks. On successive problems each of the four form blocks was the positive stimulus. Skeels reported that the older subjects (mean CA 37 months) took 4.1 trials to reach criterion on the first problem and 3.2 to meet criterion on the second form problem. In contrast, the younger subjects (mean CA 26 months) took 1.3 trials to reach criterion on the first problem and 27.3 trials on the second problem.[2]

[2] The ease of solving the first problem, especially in the younger group, strongly suggests a form preference, since the circle was positive for all subjects in this problem. The study is flawed in that form preferences were not counterbalanced; a better procedure would have been to have different forms positive in different subgroups.

SIZE DISCRIMINATION.   Size discrimination has been studied by several investigators with children under three years of age (Graham, Ernhart, Craft, and
Berman, 1964; Hicks and Stewart, 1930; Hunter, 1952; Thrum, 1935; Welch,
1939b). Hicks and Stewart (1930) tested 40 subjects between two and five
years of age, with 10 in each age group, on a discrimination problem requiring
selection of the "middle-size" box from a set of three randomly positioned boxes.
Four sets of three boxes differing in size were used as the training stimuli.
Nine of the 10 subjects in the two year old group failed to learn the initial
discrimination problem, but all subjects in the other three age groups learned
all four problems with decreasing numbers of errors to criterion over the successive problems.

Welch (1939b) was unable to demonstrate size discrimination in infants
below 16 months of age. Tests for "larger," "smaller," and "middle-size" discrimination with three year old children indicated that only 20 percent solved the
"middle-size" discrimination problem.

Thrum (1935) found that children from two to four years of age made more
errors in selecting the "larger" than the "smaller" sized stimuli. Hunter (1952)
trained children 23 months of age and older to choose the larger (or smaller)
of a pair of boxes varying in size to find a raisin concealed under the correct
sized box.

Despite the variety of experimental procedures that have been devised to
study discrimination in the simultaneous two-choice situation with infants over
the first three years of life, the studies have at best provided only demonstration
data on isolated visual discrimination problems. A program for explaining the
choice behavior by means of a systematic analysis of the relevant controlling
conditions and the controlling stimulus class or dimension has not yet begun.

FREE OPERANT DISCRIMINATION LEARNING.   A study by Weisberg (1968) provides one of the few examples of the use of the operant conditioning technique
with infants in the second year of life. Weisberg gave 8 infants, 15 to 25 months
of age, a visual discrimination problem with differentially reinforced lever
pressing in the presence of "steady" and "flashing" lights. For half of the subjects
the positive stimulus was the steady light, and for the other half it was the
flashing light (flashing at one cycle per second rate). Responding in the presence
of the S+ was reinforced on either a variable interval (VI 15 sec. or VI 25 sec.)
or a variable ratio (VR 15) schedule. Schedule conditions in the presence
of the S− included extinction, differential reinforcement of other behaviors
(DRO), or a combination of both. During training sessions, the child sat
strapped in a high chair facing a "snack" dispenser. A lever extending from
the food dispenser was within easy reach of the seated child. The discriminative
stimuli were provided by a light source mounted slightly above and to the
left of the response manipulandum. During the early stages of discrimination
training the S+ duration was three times longer than the S− duration, but the
difference between these time intervals was gradually reduced over training
sessions until they were approximately equal. Discriminative behavior in the
first and last half of each training session was assessed by the computation of

"discrimination indexes" (Sadowsky, 1966). The discrimination index is the ratio of S⁺ responding relative to total S⁺ and S⁻ responding, corrected for the disproportional amount of time devoted to S⁺ and S⁻. The discrimination indexes of Weisberg's eight subjects during the last half of the last training session ranged from .76 to 1.00 (median, .87). These terminal discrimination indexes indicate that differential reinforcement in the presence of S⁺ and S⁻ exerted the predicted control over lever pressing by preverbal children.

Subsequent postdiscrimination generalization gradients obtained by Weisberg provide some of the first unequivocal evidence of discriminative control in a free operant discrimination problem with children under two years of age. The generalization tests were given during two extinction sessions with an interpolated session of discrimination training. During generalization testing eight stimuli, including the two training stimuli and six flickering lights ranging from 2 to 10 cycles per second, were presented for 30 seconds each. The obtained generalization gradients indicated greatest responsiveness to the S⁺ for all subjects. The gradients were steeper following the interpolated discrimination training session, consistent with generalization measures obtained from adult infrahuman organisms (Jenkins and Harrison, 1962; Terrace, 1966). Weisberg reported that the difference between the relative response rates to the positive and negative training stimuli was as great during generalization testing as during the last training session. Thus, the confounding effects of order of reinforcement schedules and reinforcement-nonreinforcement context were ruled out as controlling variables (see Jenkins, 1965b). These findings provide clear support for the conclusion that the two exteroceptive stimuli (varying in flicker frequency) acquired control over the operant response rates.

Except for Bower's study with younger infants and Weisberg's study with children in the second year of life, there have been almost no studies with the more typical free operant successive discrimination problem. Heid (1965) and Sheppard (1967) were unable to establish discrimination learning in single infants over the first weeks of life. Using kicking and vocalization as the operant responses, these investigators attempted to establish multiple schedule control with the typical successive discrimination procedure. They reported that high rates of responding and emotional behavior (crying) were obtained during the extinction (S⁻) and DRO components of the schedule.

Apparently, the introduction of extinction following the initial shaping and strengthening of the operant response elicited emotional behavior, which interfered with the development of stable discriminative performance. In infrahuman organisms S⁻ seems to become an aversive or inhibitory stimulus following the traditional training procedure (Terrace, 1964, 1966). Problems in demonstrating discriminative control in the typical free operant discrimination task with infants may reflect deficiencies in inhibitory control with young infants. As previously mentioned in this chapter, Luria (1961) has speculated that the young child's problem in the conditional type of learning task reflects a "lack of inhibitory mechanisms."

The most stable discrimination performance has been obtained when the required response to the negative stimulus is incompatible with the response to the positive stimulus (Lipsitt, 1963; Simmons and Lipsitt, 1961; Papoušek, 1967a, 1967b; Weisberg, 1968). Sheppard (1967), after failing to obtain evidence of differential responding to the positive and negative stimuli in the successive discrimination task, presented the infant with a two-response situation. His research strategy involved achieving control over two distinctive operant responses, leg kick and vocalization, and then progressively integrating these two responses using concurrent multiple schedules with reinforcement continuously available to the infant. Reinforcement and extinction were reciprocal operations: The stimulus correlated with reinforcement (S^+) for one response was correlated with extinction (S^-) for the other response, and *vice versa*. With reinforcement conditions alternating every 5 minutes within a 20 minute training session and responding maintained on a fixed ratio schedule (FR 3), differential responding in the presence of the discriminative stimuli for both vocalization and leg kicking developed over the course of nine daily sessions. Unfortunately, the lack of extinction or generalization measures in the Sheppard study prevents an unequivocal interpretation of his results as evidence for discriminative control. However, his results showing differential responding in infants in the two-response operant discrimination task are consistent with the findings of other investigators.

As previously suggested in this chapter, the conceptual and experimental analyses of independent inhibitory and excitatory effects are important tasks for future developmental studies of discrimination learning in young children. Procedures for independent assessment of gradients of inhibition and excitation during postdiscrimination generalization tests have been suggested by Jenkins and Harrison (1962).

Summary

So far in this chapter we have reviewed studies of discrimination learning in infants over a variety of discrimination problems. Generally, discrimination learning studies with infants have not gone far beyond simple demonstrations showing evidence of an acquired discrimination in the types of discrimination tasks employed with older children and infrahuman organisms. Frequently, the appropriate controls for demonstrating the effects of the discriminative stimuli on response probability independently of the effects of reinforcement context, stimulus preferences, or response biases have been lacking. However, isolated studies have shown that some infants are capable of solving auditory and visual discrimination problems within the first weeks of life when confronted with the typical discrete-trial and free operant learning tasks. The important task of explaining choice behavior in infants by means of a description of the relevant controlling conditions awaits further experimentation.

The effects of position habits in the two-choice discrimination task may account for the marked within-subject variability obtained in a number of the studies discussed. However, with few exceptions (Graham *et al.*, 1964; Hill, 1965) investigators have not attempted systematic analyses of the effects of response biases and strategies in studies of discrimination learning in infants. The typical method of randomizing the position of the correct response may not be particularly effective in eliminating position responding in subjects for whom position response tendencies are dominant (White, 1964). Experimental arrangements which discourage the development of a position habit have not been explored.

An aspect of the discrimination task that has often been neglected by investigators of discrimination learning in the classical S-R or behavioristic tradition has been the question of the discriminability of the discriminative stimuli employed. Typically, experimenters have used easily discriminable stimuli in hopes of highlighting the learning process *per se*. However, clear evidence of the effects of selective attention or stimulus saliency on learning speed in discrimination problems has been obtained in studies with older children (Shepp and Zeaman, 1966; Suchman and Trabasso, 1966b). Discrimination learning studies with the young infant which focus on the effects of these stimulus variables would provide an important contribution to a developmental analysis of discrimination learning. The progressive refinement in experimental methodologies reviewed in this chapter suggests that variables that have a part in determining the controlling stimulus class can be systematically analyzed in discrimination learning studies with the young infant.

DISCRIMINATIVE LEARNING IN CHILDHOOD

Dimensional Preferences

The vast majority of the research on dimensional discrimination learning in children has utilized visual presentation of stimuli. Little information is available on the comparative difficulty of visual, tactile, and auditory discrimination learning, probably because of the methodological problems involved in equating the perceptual discriminability of stimuli across modalities.

The visual mode contains a number of dimensions, such as size, color, and shape or form, along which stimuli can vary. Some of these dimensions appear to "stand out" more than others, and the degree to which they do depends upon the age of the child, among other things. In a comprehensive study of the relative difficulty of the dimensions of size, color, form, and number for children between the ages of three and six years, Lee (1965) reported that the younger children found form discriminations most difficult, with size, and then number less difficult. Stimuli differing in color were the easiest. Older children, however, found form to be the easiest dimension to discriminate, with color next, and size and number tied as the most difficult dimensions. The experimenter hypothesized that form was easiest for five and six year olds because children of these ages are in kindergarten and are concentrating their efforts on learning the alphabet, a task that forces the child to pay attention to relatively minute differences in form while ignoring color and size differences. A similar "environmental" account is reasonable for the dominance of color at the ages of three to four years, when parents are most likely to point to and label colors for their children.

Although age trends for dimensional preferences exist, there are wide individual differences. These explain, in part, why some children learn a discrimination task more rapidly than others. If the dimension arbitrarily chosen by the experimenter as the to-be-reinforced one coincides with a child's preference, learning will tend to be considerably facilitated (Heal, Bransky, and Mankinen, 1966; Suchman and Trabasso, 1966b). Dimensional preferences exhibited by young children vary from one culture to another (Greenfield, Reich, and Olver, 1966), emphasizing the importance of considering these preferences in interpreting cultural and subcultural (socioeconomic) differences in "learning ability."

Simultaneous and Successive Discrimination

In discrimination learning situations, stimuli can be presented in either of two ways. The most popular method entails the simultaneous presentation of two or more stimuli; the child is required to choose one, regardless of its spatial position on any given trial. The alternate procedure is to present the stimuli successively so that only one is available on each trial; the child learns to make a differential position response to each stimulus. Although these two techniques differ from each other in a number of ways, the important distinguishing characteristic may be whether or not the task provides the child with an opportunity to make direct comparisons among the stimuli, an opportunity afforded only by the simultaneous method (see Reese, 1968, pp. 80–98; Rieber, 1966b). The empirical question of which method is more conducive to learning does not have a simple answer.

SEPARATION OF STIMULUS AND RESPONSE LOCI. As early as 1928, Heidbreder compared the relative difficulty of the two methods and reported that successive presentation was more difficult for both children and adults. More recently, however, Lipsitt (1961) found that the effectiveness of the two methods appears to depend upon the locus of the response. He found that the successive problem was learned more rapidly than the simultaneous problem when the response units and stimulus apertures were separated—except when the stimuli were highly similar, as discussed below. When the response was to the source of stimulation, however, the opposite result was obtained. In the latter condition, with no separation between the stimulus and response loci, the simultaneous problem was learned very rapidly, and the successive problem was not solved at all by most of the subjects. This finding is not so puzzling when considered in conjunction with evidence reported by Calvin (1955) and Rieber (1966b) that stimuli presented simultaneously may be perceived as a single stimulus configuration, rather than as several unique cues. Under these conditions, requiring the child to respond directly to one of the stimuli should serve to emphasize its uniqueness. Once the several stimuli are perceived as separate cues, the advantage of the simultaneous method—permitting direct comparison—can be realized.

Additional research is needed, however, to identify the factors that enhance the salience of cues presented simultaneously, because contradictory data have been obtained. In other studies in which there was no separation between the stimulus and response loci (Horowitz, 1965; Price and Spiker, 1967; Shepp, 1962), the simultaneous problem was easier than the successive problem, replicating Lipsitt's result with unseparated loci. However, in other studies in which the stimulus and response loci were *separated,* the simultaneous problem was solved as rapidly as the successive problem (Erickson and Lipsitt, 1960, 3 sec. delay; Jackson and Jerome, 1940, 1943) or more rapidly (Erickson and Lipsitt, 1960, 0 and 6 sec. delay; Horowitz, 1965; Horowitz and Armentrout, 1965), contradicting Lipsitt's result with separated loci. Jeffrey (1961) also found that the simultaneous problem was easier than the successive problem, apparently with unseparated loci in the simultaneous problem and separated loci in the successive problem.

PROBLEM DIFFICULTY. Lipsitt (1961) suggested that factors that increase the difficulty of a simultaneous discrimination may increase the difficulty of the successive discrimination more. Erickson and Lipsitt (1960) obtained corroborative evidence: Delay of reward increased the difficulty of the successive discrimination more than that of the simultaneous discrimination (see also Hockman and Lipsitt, 1961). Perkins, Banks, and Calvin (1954) found no differential effect of delay of response on the difficulty of the simultaneous and successive problems, but there was probably a floor effect in the successive problem, obscuring any possible differential effect of delay. (There may also have been confounding of separation of stimulus and response loci with problems. In the simultaneous problem there appears to have been no separation, but in the successive problem there was clearly some separation.)

Lipsitt (1961) found that with the stimulus and response loci separated, the successive problem was easier than the simultaneous problem when the stimuli were distinctively different from one another or were moderately similar to one another, but when the stimuli were highly similar to one another the simultaneous problem was easier than the successive problem. Increasing stimulus similarity generally increases the difficulty of simultaneous discrimination, as it did in Lipsitt's study, but it increased the difficulty of the successive discrimination even more, producing the reversal in relative difficulty levels. Loess and Duncan (1952) obtained the same effect of stimulus similarity: The successive problem was easier than the simultaneous problem (but not significantly so) when the stimuli were more distinctively different from one another, and the simultaneous problem was easier than the successive problem when the stimuli were more similar to one another. However, Rieber (1966b) found no effect of stimulus similarity. Spiker and Holton (1959, Exp. I) found that increasing stimulus similarity increased the difficulty of a successive problem, but they did not run a simultaneous discrimination condition.

Position is an irrelevant cue in the simultaneous problem and is a relevant cue in the successive problem. Therefore, conditions that direct attention toward the positional cues should interfere with simultaneous discrimination and facilitate successive discrimination, and conditions that result in inattentiveness to positional cues should facilitate simultaneous discrimination and interfere with successive discrimination. Spiker (1963a, pp. 260–261) found that confounding irrelevant cues with position interfered with performance on the simultaneous problem, and Price and Spiker (1967) obtained the same effect and, further, obtained facilitation of performance on the successive problem. Shepp (1962) increased the discriminability of the positional cues by associating the positions with different incentives. In the experimental groups, the correct object in one position was baited with one kind of incentive, and in the other position was baited with another kind of incentive. In the control groups, there was no differential placement of the incentives. The simultaneous problem was learned more rapidly than the successive problem; but the experimental group was inferior to the control group on the simultaneous problem, and was superior to the control group on the successive problem, as expected. The differential effect of attentiveness to positional cues on the difficulty of the simultaneous and successive problems contradicts Lipsitt's suggestion. Rieber (1966b) also obtained evidence that selective attention to the discriminative cues can be manipulated to determine the relative ease of solving the two kinds of problem.

MOTIVATIONAL VARIABLES. Erickson (1959) and Horowitz and Armentrout (1965, Studies I and II) found that level of manifest anxiety is irrelevant to the difference between simultaneous and successive discrimination learning. They had expected that anxiety would facilitate simultaneous discrimination and interfere with successive discrimination learning, because the simultaneous discrimination is an "easy" problem and the successive discrimination is a "hard" problem (see Chapter 10, section entitled "Anxiety").

The nature of the reinforcer may have an effect. Lipsitt (1961) used a nonsocial reinforcer in his study with separated loci of stimulus and response, in which successive learning in fourth graders was superior to simultaneous learning, and used social reinforcers in the study with unseparated loci, in which simultaneous learning was superior to successive. Horowitz and Armentrout (1965, Study I), testing fourth graders, found that the superiority of simultaneous over successive discrimination learning was greater when a social reinforcer was used than when a nonsocial reinforcer (buzzer) was used, in line with Lipsitt's data; and Horowitz (1965) obtained similar effects in kindergarten and Grades 1 through 5, and in mentally retarded subjects. (In the sixth grade, the superiority of simultaneous learning over successive was greater with the nonsocial reinforcer than with the social reinforcer, reversing the trend for the other grade levels.)

Horowitz suggested that with separated loci, the buzzer she used as a nonsocial reinforcer might have drawn the subject's attention to the response button, since the reward was coincident with the response. The buzzer, then, would have emphasized the positional cues and disrupted comparison of the discriminative stimuli. Within-trial stimulus scanning is more crucial to learning the simultaneous problem than the successive problem, as Horowitz (1965, p. 18) and Bitterman (e.g., Bitterman and McConnell, 1954) have pointed out; and the effects of attentiveness to position have already been discussed. Therefore, the use of an auditory nonsocial reward should facilitate successive discrimination and interfere with simultaneous discrimination.

Lipsitt's nonsocial reward was a light. The need to look at the light for reinforcement information should, as Horowitz (1965) pointed out, distract attention from both kinds of cue, and should therefore interfere with simultaneous discrimination more than with successive discrimination. However, Horowitz suggested that this reasoning does not explain why Lipsitt's group with unseparated stimulus and response loci and with social reinforcement should have performed so poorly. More research is therefore needed to provide a definitive solution to the problem.

Conditions of Reinforcement

POSITIVE AND NEGATIVE REINFORCEMENT. Much research has been focused on the relative effectiveness of reward and punishment on discrimination learning in children. Unfortunately, the picture that emerges is far from complete. J. T. Spence, who has done a number of studies on this problem, summarized the literature in the following way:

> As investigations in this area of response-contingent reinforcers continue . . . it is becoming increasingly apparent that reinforcers do not have a simple set of properties that affect performance in a uniform manner, but may play a number of complex roles, depending on such variables as the characteristics of the subjects, the task, the nature of the reinforcers themselves, and the precise manner in which they are introduced into the situation. Thus it should perhaps not be surprising to find that seemingly minor procedural variations among studies often produce quite different empirical results. (Spence and Segner, 1967, p. 37.)

It is with this caution in mind that some of the findings on positive and negative reward will be reviewed.

When verbal reinforcement is utilized in a discrimination task, it can be administered in any of three ways. The child can be told "right" for correct choices and nothing for incorrect choices (the so-called "Right-Blank" condition), "wrong" for each incorrect choice and nothing for correct choices, or "right" and "wrong" for correct and incorrect choices, respectively. If the child is not explicitly told the meaning of no response (*blank*), he tends to perform more poorly under the Right-Blank condition than under either of the other two reinforcement combinations (Curry, 1960; Meyer and Seidman, 1960). When the child is explicitly told the meaning of *blank*, this difference disappears (Spence, 1966), leading to the conclusion that under the Right-Blank condition, the child interprets *blank* as meaning "right."

When nonverbal reinforcers such as candy and punishment are used, punishment only and the reward-punishment combination are more effective than reward only (Brackbill and O'Hara, 1958; Penney and Lupton, 1961). These latter findings are limited by data obtained by Terrell, Durkin, and Weisley (1959), who found that middle class children learn better with nonmaterial rewards (a light flash indicating correct responses), while lower class children learn better when candy is given for correct responses. It was Spence and Segner's (1967) failure to replicate this social class difference that prompted their conclusion quoted above.

At present, few if any conclusions can be drawn from the evidence available on the differential effects of reward and punishment. Definitive statements must await more intensive research in the area.

DELAY OF REWARD.   Intuitively, one might expect that a delay in the reinforcement of correct responses during discrimination learning should have a deleterious effect, but the available evidence is equivocal. Much effort has been devoted to research on this issue. Of 14 studies published since 1960, 8 showed

Table 5-2

Summary of Studies of the Effects of Delay of Reward on Discrimination Learning

Detrimental effects		No effect	
Study	*Age level (years)*	*Study*	*Age level (years)*
Terrell & Ware (1961)	about 5–6	Brackbill *et al.* (1962a) Exp. 1	5–6
Ware & Terrell (1961)	about 5–6	Hockman and Lipsitt (1961) Simple task	8–10.5
Hetherington & Ross (1967)	5–8	Erickson and Lipsitt (1960)	about 9
Hetherington, Ross, & Pick (1964)	6–7	Brackbill *et al.* (1962a) Exp. II	9–10
Ross, Hetherington, & Wray (1965)	6–7	Brackbill and Kappy (1962)	9.4
Setterington & Walters (1964)	7	Etzel and Wright (1964)	9–11
Fagan & Witryol (1966)	7–9		
Wright & Smothergill (1967)	about 8		
Hockman & Lipsitt (1961) Difficult task	8–10.5		

significant learning decrements associated with delay, 5 showed no differences, and the remaining one showed that delay had no effect on a simple task but did retard the learning of a difficult one (see Table 5-2). There have been no studies in which delay facilitated learning, but one research group (Brackbill and Kappy, 1962; Brackbill, Bravos, and Starr, 1962a) has consistently found improved *retention* as a result of delayed reinforcement during discrimination learning.

Interestingly enough, the ages of the children tested in the studies showing detrimental effects of delay ranged from 5 to 9 years (excluding the Hockman and Lipsitt study, which showed this result only on a difficult task). In four of the five studies showing no effect of delay, the children were between 9 and 11 years old; the exception was the first of the two experiments by Brackbill *et al.* (1962a), with 5 and 6 year old children. It might be noted that Hockman and Lipsitt's subjects overlapped these two age groups, perhaps accounting for the relevance of task difficulty in their study.

Terrell (1965), in an earlier review of studies of delayed reinforcement effects, suggested that age differences might account for the discrepant findings, and studies that have appeared since tend to bear him out. Terrell assumed that delay is detrimental when the child makes inappropriate, competing responses during the delay interval, because these responses interfere with learning. Older children, he reasoned, "are better able to neutralize the effects of competing irrelevant elements in the learning environment" (p. 135), thus negating the effects of delay. Evidence that competing responses are the basis for the detrimental effects of delay in children can be found in a number of studies (Fagan and Witryol, 1966; Hockman and Lipsitt, 1961; Rieber, 1961a; Ross, Hetherington, and Wray, 1965).

However, response competition is by no means the only explanatory mechanism that has been proposed. Ware and Terrell (1961) and Rieber (1964a) hypothesized that delay of reward produces frustration, which in turn interferes with learning. Brackbill and Kappy (1962) and Brackbill *et al.* (1962a) explained the facilitative effects of delay on retention by suggesting that when a reward is not administered immediately, the child engages in relevant covert responding, such as saying the name of the stimulus to himself while waiting for the reward. This practice during the delay period would establish covert mediating responses that would facilitate later retention. Just why such practice should not facilitate learning, as well as retention, remains unclear.

INCENTIVES. In attempting to determine the relative effectiveness of different types of incentives, Terrell and Kennedy (1957) utilized a task in which children had to learn to choose the larger element in each of three different pairs of three-dimensional geometric figures. Depending upon the experimental condition they were assigned to, the children experienced either praise, reproof, candy, token, or a flash of light as reinforcement. The results indicated that the light-flash condition produced the slowest learning. In a similar study, Terrell (1958) failed to replicate these findings; the light-flash condition proved to be more facilitating than a candy reward. The apparent contradiction was resolved in a third investigation, by Terrell *et al.* (1959). They pointed out that there was a clear difference in the socioeconomic backgrounds of the children in the two earlier experiments, and this difference could have produced the difference in the findings. The children in the first study, in which light-flash was a weak incentive, came from a predominantly rural background; the children in the second study came from middle class homes. Subjecting this hypothesis to an empirical test, they carefully selected two groups differing in socioeconomic background, and tested with candy versus light-flash. As predicted, children from lower class homes learned faster with a material (candy) incentive, and those from wealthier families did better with a nonmaterial reward (light-flash).

Apparently, groups of children from different backgrounds do not value incentives in the same way; but there are also important differences among individuals from the same type of background. Bisett and Rieber (1966) asked children from an urban lower socioeconomic area to rank their preferences for eight incentives, ranging from paper clips to pennies, and then assigned half to their most preferred choice and the other half to their least preferred choice. The task was a simple discrimination problem in which responses to one position, left or right, were reinforced only one-third of the time and responses to the other position were never reinforced. The child's task was to discriminate between the position that was never rewarded and the one that was intermittently rewarded. Children who had been assigned to the preferred-incentive group learned the discrimination task more readily than children in the nonpreferred-incentive group. The same relation between incentive value and performance seems to have been obtained in a probability learning task, but only in older children (Stevenson and Hoving, 1964). In younger children, probability learning seems to be better with weak incentives than with strong incentives (Stevenson and Hoving, 1964; Stevenson and Weir, 1959b). One explanation for the discrepancy is that in the probability learning studies the two age groups may not have valued the incentives in the same way. In these studies the investigators *assumed* that certain objects had greater incentive value than others, without offering any empirical evidence; but Bisett and Rieber had found significant effects of age (and sex) of the subjects on the ranking of incentives (see Table 5-3). It is therefore possible that what was a weak incentive for the older group may have been a strong incentive for the younger group.

Miller and Estes (1961) measured the effect of a large difference in incentive value on the learning performance of nine year olds in a situation that required discrimination between drawings of faces differing only in the height and spacing of the eyebrows. The children were divided into three groups which received for each correct response half a dollar, one cent, or only knowledge of results. No difference was found between the half-dollar and one-cent groups, and both of these groups were *poorer* in learning than the knowledge-of-results group. To explain these findings, which are counter to common sense, the investigators suggested that the monetary incentives distracted the children from the discrimination task, as evidenced by the fact that children in the money groups tended to "gloat, count, and worry" about the money.

Dimensional discrimination learning requires that the subject pay attention to the dimension that the experimenter has arbitrarily chosen to correlate with reward. When several irrelevant dimensions are present, increased incentive motivation may serve to reduce the number of irrelevant cues that the subject will respond to, or it may narrow attention to such an extent that even the relevant cues are ignored (Easterbrook, 1959). Smock and Rubin (1964) measured the effect of incentive conditions on the ability of 9 through 12 year olds to recognize complex forms presented tachistoscopically.[3] Accuracy of recognition was facilitated by the use of stronger incentives. This finding was inter-

---

[3] The tachistoscope is an apparatus that permits exposure of a stimulus for very brief durations, as short as a few milliseconds.

Table 5-3

Preferences for Reward Objects[a]

Object	All children	Boys 6–7	Boys 10–11	Girls 6–7	Girls 10–11
Jewelry	1	2	3	1	1
Pennies	2	4	2	2	2
Cars	3	1	1	5	4
Beatle Cards	4	5	5	3	3
Trinkets	5	3	4	4	5
Marble Chips	6	7	7	6	6
Washers	7	6	6	7	8
Paper Clips	8	8	8	8	7

[a] "Preference" is rank order of mean number of choices, from most frequently chosen (1) to least frequently chosen (8). (Based on Bisett and Rieber, 1966, Table 1, p. 202.)

preted as evidence that incentive motivation "served to increase the efficiency of utilization of available relevant cues" (p. 116). This would suggest that incentives should facilitate discrimination learning, but as can be seen from the preceding summary, the findings are by no means unequivocal.

Subject Variables

AGE. It comes as no surprise that learning during childhood improves with age. Studies that simply report this fact, without delineating the accompanying behavioral variables, contribute little to an understanding of the phenomenon. However, investigators who pay close attention to differences in learning behaviors exhibited by children of different ages can provide clues about the variables responsible for age related changes in learning efficiency. An early example of this approach is a study reported by Heidbreder (1928), who analyzed the discrimination learning of children ranging in age from three years to young adulthood. On the basis of careful observations of their learning performance, Heidbreder concluded that younger subjects, in contrast with older ones, were more likely to attend to irrelevant aspects of the task, to engage in irrelevant speech and motor behavior, to act on the basis of subjective dimensional preferences, and to achieve solution gradually rather than suddenly, and were less likely to verbalize their reasons for particular choices or even to recognize the solution of the problem as a definite event.

A large number of studies have replicated the developmental fact that learning efficiency in children increases as they get older, but only recently has the emphasis shifted to a systematic analysis of the changes in the learning process *per se* as a function of age. Suchman and Trabasso's (1966a) finding that preferences for (and consequently attention to) color, form, and size dimensions change with age illuminates one factor underlying developmental trends in learning. Not only do stimulus preferences change with age, but so does the manner in which children scan stimuli. Braine (1965) reported that three year olds tend to orient toward the top of a figure while five year olds use the bottom as their focal point. Looking at other age changes in perceptual ability, Pollack (1965) found that hue detectability thresholds remained fairly constant as children grew older, but sensitivity to contour changes increased with age during childhood (Pollack, 1963).

These and other stimulus factors account for only part of the age-related differences in learning. Quite often the choice behavior of children is determined by response tendencies or sets that are independent of the stimuli present in the task, and that interfere with learning. The nature and strength of these response sets appear to vary with age. Jeffrey and Cohen (1965) studied three and four year old children in a two-choice task in which a reward was given on every trial, regardless of the choice made. This procedure permitted an assessment of response sets unaffected by differential reinforcement. Almost all the three year olds exhibited strong perseveration tendencies; that is, they repeatedly chose the same side. Less than 2 percent of their responses involved alternations of choices. Four year olds rarely perseverated; instead, they alternated more than 75 percent of their responses. Using a similar test procedure, Rieber (1966a) reported that alternation still accounted for most of the responses made by seven to nine year olds. However, ten year olds (Shusterman, 1963) showed no preferences for either response pattern. Similar trends have been found by Weir (1967) in both two- and three-choice situations. No doubt these response sets are important determinants of children's learning ability at different ages.

When a child is just beginning to acquire language, this skill serves primarily as an aid to communication with others. Not until the age of five or six years do words clearly begin to serve as self-generated cues which the child can use to mediate or direct his motor responses. It is the onset of the directive function of language which many investigators (Kendler and Kendler, 1962; Luria, 1961; Reese, 1962c) have regarded as the primary factor responsible for many of the age-related changes in learning ability. White (1965), after reviewing a wide variety of findings which point to a qualitative change in the learning ability of children between the ages of five and seven, postulated a two-stage developmental model for learning. According to this, children below five years of age are assumed to learn discrimination problems in an associative manner, much in the same way that rats and other infrahumans do. After approximately the age of seven years, children become capable of learning in a cognitive fashion and employ internal language to mediate their responses. However, once cognitive functioning is acquired it does not obviate associational, or S-R learning; certain conditions can still elicit the more primitive learning process. A more detailed analysis of the role of verbal mediation in discrimination learning is given in Chapters 7 and 9.

INTELLIGENCE. Traditional measures of intelligence employ the concepts of chronological age (CA), mental age (MA), and IQ. We have just noted that CA is highly correlated with learning ability, but it is possible that the relevant variable is the child's MA rather than how old he is chronologically. Among children with an average IQ, MA and CA are by definition highly related, but for children with a high or low IQ there is a difference between MA and CA. For example, a ten year old retarded child may have an MA of only five years. It is quite apparent that such a child would not be able to learn as well as the average ten year old and, in this case, CA is a poor predictor of learning ability. The important question is, would such a child be able to learn as well as his match in mental age, that is, an average five year old child?

Many studies have been devoted to research on this question. In reviewing 18 investigations involving children with the same MAs but different CAs, Zeaman and House (1967) found that 9 of them showed that younger (and therefore higher IQ) children performed better on discrimination learning tasks, 6 showed no differences related to age, and the remaining 3 were equivocal, with the direction of the findings dependent upon the learning measures employed. Zeaman and House concluded that the basis for the discrepant findings could be traced to differences in the difficulty level of the tasks employed by the various investigators: "The entire assemblage of data, both positive and negative, can be handled by the following assumption: *at least a low positive correlation exists between IQ (with MA controlled) and performance in visual discrimination tasks when a wide range of IQ's is sampled and tasks of intermediate difficulty are used*" (p. 198).

It is important to note, however, that all 18 studies were concerned only with differences between normal and mentally retarded children, matched on MA. A statement about the relationship between IQ and learning, when children of higher than average intelligence are compared with normals, might be quite a different one. There is very little information available about the relative performance of children in higher IQ categories.

An insight into the complexity of the relationship between above average intelligence and learning ability can be gained by examining the research of Osler and Trautman (1961). They tested children, ranging in age from 6 to 14 years, in a two-choice dimensional discrimination task in which pairs of stimuli were presented simultaneously.

For one group of subjects, the positive member of the stimulus pair consisted of two black dots whose position varied from trial to trial. The negative member was composed of one, three, four, or five dots, positioned randomly. This meant that the stimulus pairs varied in only two dimensions, position and number, and number was the relevant one. Another group of subjects was given a task in which the stimuli varied along a large number of dimensions. Drawings of multicolored objects were used instead of black dots, but the positive stimuli always contained two objects and the negative ones had one, three, four, or five. Children with normal IQs (mean of 101) performed equally well in these two kinds of task. In contrast, children with high IQs (mean of 120) did better than normals on the two-dimensional task but much poorer than normals on the multidimensional task. The investigators interpreted these results as evidence that brighter children formulate and test hypotheses in the process of learning the task, while normal ones learn in an associative, S-R manner. It is possible, however, that children at both IQ levels test hypotheses, but that in the multi-dimensional task the more intelligent children are not satisfied with as simple a solution as number and continue to test more complex possibilities, overlooking the fact that they had hit upon the correct solution. The bidimensional task is less likely to encourage the generation of complex hypotheses, and the correct solution is readily apparent, especially to the brighter child. In any case, the ability to solve discrimination learning tasks appears to be related to intelligence, although the nature of this relationship is intricate and only partially explored.

CHAPTER 6

Verbal Learning and Memory

INTRODUCTION

Experimental research on the learning of verbal materials has a long and continuous history in psychology, beginning with the work of Ebbinghaus (1885). Until recently, few studies by child psychologists have dealt with the theoretical issues in this field, but the amount of pertinent research with children has begun to increase. In 1964 Keppel reviewed the child research and concluded that it had provided little of consequence to a theoretical understanding of the traditional problems in the area of verbal learning (Keppel, 1964). The conclusion was based not so much on the relative scarcity of research as on the remarkable similarity of results to the results of studies with adults. Keppel argued that developmental studies have little likelihood of contributing to a theory of verbal learning unless the theory includes developmental variables. The fault, he suggested, is not only with the child research, but with the traditional theories in the area as well. He proposed that if verbal learning theories were extended to cover the entire age range, they would generate questions that could be answered only by studying verbal learning at appropriate age levels below the adult level.

Four years after the Keppel review, Goulet (1968b) re-examined the literature from a somewhat different point of view. While Keppel was more interested in traditional problems, Goulet focused upon the kinds of verbal learning research that could contribute to both developmental theory and a theory of verbal behavior. It was Goulet's thesis that most of the child research had been descriptive, and that child psychologists should now initiate research to test theoretical hypotheses about the relations between verbal learning processes and maturational variables. He generated a number of researchable possibilities by showing that certain data and associated theories for verbal learning in adults have developmental implications.

Goulet suggested that the paired associate learning task, described in detail later, is particularly appropriate for the examination of learning processes and their developmental characteristics because the difficulty of the task can be manipulated easily and yet it is possible to analyze the task, whatever its difficulty, into individual stimulus and response components for theoretical purposes. The paired associate task may be used for the study of individual stimulus-response units, interactions among the stimulus-response units within a list, discrimination learning, and transfer of learning with or without mediation built into the design. The materials utilized in the task may range from consonant-vowel-consonant (CVC) nonsense syllables through pictures to sentences. Finally, the task may involve the usual anticipation method, in which the subject is required to anticipate each successive response as its stimulus is presented, or the task may consist of a series of study–test trials in which the subject is presented with the entire list to study and then is given a test with only the stimuli presented, followed by another study trial and test trial, and so on. Thus, the difficulty of the task can be adjusted for different age levels, and the basic procedure is amenable to modifications of the paradigm, stimulus materials, and task requirements. The versatility of the paired associate task makes it ideal for studies of a wide variety of theoretically important problems.

Goulet cautioned that some methodological problems face the developmental psychologist that do not concern those working with the college student. For example, the amount of nonspecific transfer (see Chapter 8) and the degree of first-list learning may vary with age level. Such problems as these are serious and must be given careful consideration in the designs of studies of recall and transfer. However, Goulet's analysis makes it clear that these kinds of problems are surmountable.

As already noted, Keppel found little child research bearing upon theoretical problems of verbal learning; but his review came at a time when research in this area was just beginning to expand extensively. Nevertheless, although Goulet's analysis was somewhat more optimistic and broader in scope, it remains true that the majority of the empirical and theoretical problems that engage those primarily identified with the field of verbal learning have not caught the imagination of those interested in the verbal behavior of children. There is, for example, little work with children on the problems of intralist similarity, serial learning, verbal discrimination learning, interlist similarity and transfer, degree of first-list learning and transfer, retroactive and proactive interference, or short term memory. Many of these problems are of central concern to those primarily interested in verbal learning who use the college sophomore as their laboratory subject. Child psychologists have not completely ignored these problems, but as will be seen, they have focused more attention on mediation, the influence of word associations on verbal tasks, and long term memory. Later in this chapter the problems of paired associate learning that have been studied most extensively will be considered in some detail and an overview taken of the variety of research interests, problems, and theoretical issues with which those working with children have grappled. The discussion will be limited to the variables that affect the acquisition of a single list. Studies of multiple-list learning, in which the concern is with the influence of the acquisition of one list upon the acquisition of another list, are considered in Chapter 7 (section entitled "Transfer in Paired Associate Tasks"). First, though, the more important methodological problems in studies of paired associate learning must be considered.

METHODOLOGICAL PROBLEMS

The paired associate task typically consists of the presentation of a list of n pairs of items, one pair at a time in different random orders, until the subject has reached some criterion, usually two or three consecutive errorless runs through the list. Characteristically, the list is presented on a memory drum; a given stimulus item is exposed for two or three seconds in one window and then a shutter opens to expose the response item in another window, usually to the right of the stimulus window. After two or three seconds both items are removed and the next stimulus is shown immediately. At the end of the list a four to six second blank is presented and then the pairs are presented in a new order. This procedure is referred to as the *anticipation method* because the subject is expected to learn to anticipate the response upon each presentation of the stimulus, before the response item is exposed.

For some kinds of problems it is advantageous to use the *study–test procedure* rather than the anticipation method. The subject is shown the list of stimulus and response items together for study and then is presented with only the stimuli for a test. Thus, a trial consists of two presentations of the items, one to study the pairs in the list and the other to test for retention of the response to each stimulus.

It is assumed (Underwood and Schulz, 1960a), and there is ample evidence to support the assumption, that with both methods the learning process involves two stages. First, the subject must learn what the responses are—what is included in the universe of possible responses. Then he must learn which response goes with each stimulus. In the response learning stage, the problem is primarily one of "response integration." If the response is the CVC (consonant-vowel-consonant) trigram NAF, for example, the subject will have to integrate the three letters into some sort of unit (otherwise there are three responses) in order to be able to store it for recall, which is a prerequisite of learning to give that response to a particular stimulus. One way of accomplishing the response integration in this example would be to code the response as FAN (i.e., reverse the first and last letters to form a word) which for most persons is an integrated response because it is a word well learned prior to entering the task. Coding of this sort has been studied in adults (e.g., Underwood and Erlebacher, 1965) but not in children.

Once the response has been integrated, however that is accomplished, the subject must learn which stimulus is paired with that response and be able to recall the response whenever the stimulus is presented. The major concerns of those interested in paired associate learning center on factors that influence the response integration and associative hook-up stages. However, many frequently used research designs do not allow one to separate the two stages in the analysis of results, and therefore results are presented as if only one learning process were involved. This is not a serious problem in studies with adults when real words are used as response items; the response integration stage is completed when the adult subject has seen the list of response words once, because the words are already integrated and available for recall, and therefore the associative hook-up stage is virtually the only effective stage. In studies with children, however, special care must be taken to select words that are already integrated units for the age group under study, or the investigator must utilize a research design that permits analysis of both stages of the learning process. This kind of design should be used whenever the response materials are not already integrated, that is, when they are nonsense materials or, for children, low frequency words.

Normative Data

The speed of verbal learning in college students is markedly affected by the extent of natural language association between the stimulus and response items (e.g., Postman, 1962) and by such characteristics of the individual stimulus and response items as their frequency (e.g., Hall, 1954), meaningfulness or association value (e.g, Noble, Stockwell, and Pryer, 1957), concreteness (Paivio, 1967b), and pronounceability (e.g., Underwood and Schulz, 1960a). It would be difficult or impossible to conduct methodologically sound studies on certain kinds of problem, or to compare the results of studies using different materials, without normative data on characteristics such as these. Pertinent normative data for college students are readily available; but one of the problems in research on children's verbal learning is the dearth of pertinent normative data for child populations.

Until very recently, the only normative data for children were frequency and word association norms. Furthermore, only limited frequency norms were available and the word association norms collected before 1961 were misleading. In studies with college students, frequency is usually manipulated by consulting the Thorndike-Lorge word count, which was obtained from printed materials read by adults (Thorndike and Lorge, 1944). Thorndike and Lorge included a count of words in juvenile books but the data were based upon a small amount of material and stable counts were available for relatively few words. There are other sources of word frequency counts for children (e.g., Rinsland, 1945), but these counts are so far out of date that the sources are no longer in print. Until new counts become available, the Thorndike-Lorge count must be used, even though it also is out of date even for adults.

Many studies with children have used the Woodrow and Lowell (1916) word association norms, but these norms clearly do not represent the associative hierarchies of present day children, as Palermo and Jenkins (1965) pointed out (see also Koff, 1965). Within the past several years, up-to-date word association norms for children have been collected by Castaneda, Fahel, and Odum (1961), S. S. Shapiro (1964b), Entwisle (1966), and Palermo and Jenkins (1964b, 1966). The Castaneda et al. and S. S. Shapiro norms were based upon continued associations to the stimuli, that is, the subjects gave several responses to each stimulus; the Entwisle and Palermo and Jenkins norms were based upon discrete word associations, that is, the subjects gave a single response to each stimulus. The Entwisle norms were based upon the responses of children from kindergarten through fifth grade and have the advantage that the sample was stratified for socioeconomic level and intelligence. The Palermo and Jenkins norms were based upon the largest sample of subjects and stimulus words. A pool of 200 stimulus words was drawn from high frequency words and included words from all grammatical classes. The sample consisted of 50 boys and 50 girls in each of the grades from 1 through 4, using aural presentation methods, and 250 boys and 250 girls in each of the grades from 4 through 8, and in Grades 10 and 12, using written materials.

The norms indicate that popular responses, diversity of responses, number of idiosyncratic responses, contrast responses, and responses in the same grammatical class as the stimulus (paradigmatic responses) have increased markedly over the time span from 1916 to 1961. First grade children tend to give a large number of noun responses regardless of the stimulus word, but with increasing age children tend to give fewer syntagmatic or heterogeneous responses (i.e., responses in a different grammatical class from the stimulus word) and to give more paradigmatic responses and contrast responses (Entwisle, 1966; Palermo, 1963; Sullivan and Moran, 1967). In addition, there is a greater commonality of responding as children grow older. Superordinate responding (e.g, responding *animal* to *lion*) increases from Grade 1 to Grade 6 and then steadily declines (Palermo, 1965; Palermo and Jenkins, 1963).

Analyses of the developmental trends in the normative data clearly show that the use of adult word association norms for studies with children is inappropriate (Di Vesta, 1964a, 1964b, 1966; Entwisle, 1966; Palermo, 1963; Sullivan and Moran, 1967). Age-appropriate word association norms must be used.

Many experimental problems require the use of nonword stimuli such as pictures, nonsense syllables, or paralogs (two-syllable nonsense words). In work with children below the fourth grade level, it is ordinarily necessary to use pictures as stimulus and response materials when the materials are presented visually, as they usually are, because the children's reading skills are not well enough developed for paired associate learning with printed words. No normative data on pictorial stimuli and paralogs are available for child populations. Gaeth and Allen (1966a), however, have obtained association values for CVC and CCC (consonant-consonant-consonant) trigrams for children in Grades 4 through 6. The correlation between the values obtained for children and values for college students reported by Archer (1960) ranged from .83 to .88. Similarly, in a study of meaningfulness of CVC trigrams, S. S. Shapiro (1964a) obtained correlations of .88 to .96 between the values for children and the values reported by Noble (1961) for adults.[1] These correlations indicate that the association values for children at least as young as approximately nine years are relatively the same as those for adults, and suggest that the adult norms may be used in studies with children at least nine years old with reasonable confidence. Contrasting the developmental trends of word associations and meaningfulness for real words with the trends for trigrams suggests that normative data for children are crucial when real language materials are used, but that one takes few risks in using adult norms for trigram materials.

Aural Procedures

In most studies with adults verbal materials have been presented visually on a memory drum. Only recently has any attention been given to aural presentation (e.g., Schulz and Martin, 1964). Those working with young children, how-

---

[1] Both meaningfulness and association value of stimuli are obtained by asking subjects to indicate, by one of several procedures, whether the stimuli evoke word responses. The two procedures are treated here as equivalent although there is some controversy over the issue (see Noble, 1962).

ever, are limited to pictorial materials unless aural presentation methods are employed. Several investigators have recently attempted to determine the feasibility of using aural methods with children. Budoff and Quinlan (1964) found that aural presentation led to more rapid learning than visual presentation in second graders. S. S. Shapiro (1966), Klinger and Palermo (1967), and S. I. Shapiro and Palermo (1968) demonstrated that the aural procedure may be used with children in Grades 1 through 4. S. I. Shapiro and Palermo, however, reported that when the stimuli were nonsense syllables, the procedure did not work in the first grade and did not work well even in the fourth grade. This is a surprising finding since visually presented nonsense syllables have been used as stimuli without difficulty in several studies (e.g, Nikkel and Palermo, 1965). Since we know that meaningfulness may affect rate of paired associate learning (see Goss and Nodine, 1965), the results of the S. I. Shapiro and Palermo study imply that the meaningfulness or association value of nonsense syllables may be very low in the first through fourth grades, especially when the materials are presented aurally. Further research is needed to clarify this issue.

Presentation Time

For college students the rate of presenting verbal materials in paired associate and serial learning tasks affects the rate of learning if the number of trials to criterion is used as a measure, but total time to learn the list remains relatively constant (Bugelski, 1962; Bugelski and Rickwood, 1963; Keppel and Rehula, 1965). Thus, if it took 30 trials to learn a ten item list presented at a 2:2 rate (i.e., 2 second presentation of stimulus and 2 second presentation of stimulus and response), it would take only 20 trials to learn a ten item list presented at a 2:4 rate; the total time spent in learning the list would be 20 minutes in both cases.

This finding was not obtained by Heckman (1966), however, in normal and retarded children. Heckman found that as presentation time increased, the total time to learn also increased. Ring (1965) also obtained different findings, but did not replicate Heckman's result. Heckman and the investigators cited in the preceding paragraph varied the joint presentation interval—the interval during which the stimulus and response are presented together—but Ring varied the anticipation interval—during which the stimulus is presented alone. Her subjects were normal and mentally retarded children 13 to 15 years old. The data for the normal subjects were consistent with the findings of the studies with adults; total time to learn was about the same with a two second anticipation interval as with a four second anticipation interval. The retarded children, however, took a longer time to learn as well as more trials to learn with the shorter anticipation interval. The retardates took longer to learn with the shorter interval but learned as rapidly as the normal children with the longer interval (see also Ring and Palermo, 1961).

Price (1963) examined the influence of different anticipation intervals on paired associate learning in preschool children. For the first six trials of the task, half of the subjects had a two second anticipation interval and the other half had a six second anticipation interval. On the next six trials all subjects had the six second anticipation interval. Price found that the longer anticipation interval facilitated performance although it did not appear to affect learning. The performance of both groups was equal on the seventh trial, when the anticipation interval was six seconds for both groups.

Bugelski (1962) has suggested that the longer joint presentation of the stimulus and response facilitates the formation of mediators which aid in the associative hook-up stage of paired associate learning. If Bugelski is correct, the results of the studies in which joint presentation time was varied suggest that children may be less facile than adults in the use of such mediators. Increasing the time available for the formation of mediators increases only the total time children spend in the task. Perhaps children do not have as many mediators available for use, or perhaps they do not employ the strategy of using mediators in this kind of task. Spiker (1960) obtained evidence supporting the latter alternative. He demonstrated that if fifth grade children are instructed on methods of using mediators to link the stimulus and response items, they learn more rapidly than children given no such instruction. That they benefit from the instruction indicates that they are capable of using this strategy of learning but do not ordinarily do so. (However, it is possible that both alternatives are correct. If children had fewer available mediators, they might well not prefer to use a mediation strategy.)

The results of the studies in which the anticipation time was varied suggest that children need more time to make the response quickly enough to get credit for correct performance. The children with the two second anticipation interval in Price's study had apparently learned the responses as well as the children with the six second interval, as was shown in their equivalent performance when the interval was lengthened to six seconds. Similarly, in the studies by Ring and by Ring and Palermo, the retardates were able to perform as well as the normals when the anticipation intervals were long enough. Variation of the anticipation interval, therefore, does not involve the same processes as variation of the joint presentation interval.

VARIABLES AFFECTING LEARNING

The distinction between the methodological problems discussed in the previous section and the variables affecting learning which will be discussed here is an artificial one. However, knowing the normative characteristics of the materials to be used and knowing reliable techniques for presenting the materials provide a base against which manipulations of the learning situation may be evaluated. For example, the normative data on association values of trigrams make possible the manipulation of meaningfulness of response members in the paired associate task for both children and adults.

It should be noted that when the selection of the materials to be used is based upon normative data, the interpretation of results is limited by certain assumptions required for the use of normative data. One assumption is that the normative values are valid for every subject. However, the norms are group averages, which often do not reflect the behavior of individual subjects accurately. Other assumptions deal with the development of the characteristics of the verbal materials. For example, it might be assumed that verbal materials are rated as more meaningful or as having more associations because they have been involved in more previous learning experiences. The prediction might then be made, on the basis of some theory, that such a past history will affect paired associate learning in some specified way. There would be no problem if the experimental results came out right; but if the prediction was not verified, it would not be known whether the theory that generated the prediction was incorrect or the assumption about the norms was incorrect. Ideally, it would be preferable to build in the desired characteristics of verbal materials experimentally, perhaps by establishing a particular past history. Unfortunately, it would usually be too time consuming to use this procedure, and often it would be impossible or unethical to use it, which is why normative data are used so frequently.

Word Association Strength and Paired Associate Learning

Free association norms provide a frequency distribution of responses to each stimulus word included in the test. It is usually assumed that these frequency distributions reflect the "habit family hierarchy" for each stimulus word; that is, words that are frequently given as responses to a stimulus word are assumed to be higher in this hierarchy than words that are given less frequently. However, the norms reflect the frequency distribution of people who have given a particular response to a stimulus word, and not the strength of association for single subjects. Therefore, it does not seem to be reasonable to assume that the association of a response given by a large number of people to a particular stimulus is stronger for an individual person than the association of a response given by fewer people to that stimulus word. However, this assumption is in fact made, and, surprisingly, it seems to fit some of the experimental data.

Several experimenters have attempted to verify the hierarchy assumption; but only partial support has been obtained with adult subjects. Postman (1962) and Martin (1963) found no effect of word association strength when high frequency words were used, but higher word association strength facilitated learning when low frequency words were used. Underwood and Schulz (1960b) found a positive relation between learning rate and association strength when restricted word associations were used.[2] The difficulty of demonstrating effects of association strength in adults is attributable to the rapidity of the learning when the stimulus and response words have any degree of association strength according to free association norms. The learning is so rapid that no difference can be demonstrated with the usual measures of learning—number of correct

---

[2] Restricted word associations are obtained by requiring the subjects to restrict their responses in some specified way. In the Underwood and Schulz (1960b) study, the responses were restricted to adjectives descriptive of the stimuli (Underwood and Richardson, 1956). Riegel has reported restricted association norms for children (e.g., Riegel, 1965).

responses and trials to criterion. However, S. I. Shapiro (1968) used a more sensitive measure, latency of responding, and was able to demonstrate an effect of association strength in college sophomores, using high frequency words.

Since children have had less experience than adults with language, it might be expected that the word association norms for children would be more sensitive to differences in association strength and that no associations would be as strong for children as for the highly verbal college sophomore. Support for this argument has been found in several studies of paired associate learning in children, taking word association strengths from a number of different sets of norms (e.g., Castaneda *et al.*, 1961; McCullers, 1961; S. S. Shapiro, 1965; Wicklund, Palermo, and Jenkins, 1964). In the most extensive examination of the problem, Wicklund, Palermo, and Jenkins found that rate of paired associate learning was quite sensitive to variations in word association strength in fourth grade children. Wicklund (1964) demonstrated similar effects of association strength in sixth, eighth, and tenth grade children as well as fourth grade children. There was a tendency for the effect to decrease with age, but association strength still had a potent effect in the tenth grade, even though it has seldom been shown to influence performance at the college level.

Since association strength does have a demonstrable effect in children, numerous other kinds of studies are possible when children are used as subjects which are not possible when the subjects are college students. For example, McCullers (1963, 1967) has demonstrated that associations between stimuli within a list, between responses within a list, and between stimuli and responses within a list produce predictable interference and facilitation within the list. To take a simple example, interference should occur in learning a list that includes the pair *table-cloud* and the pair *sky-chair* because there is a strong tendency to give the response *chair* to the stimulus *table* and the response *cloud* to the stimulus *sky*. On the basis of the natural language associations among these words, it is possible to predict the amount of interference and the types of errors that should occur in learning a list constructed in this way. A list composed of such pairs can be conceived to be a conflict situation. Castaneda (1965) has explored the experimental data and theoretical possibilities for the study of conflict using such lists in paired associate tasks (for discussion, see section entitled "Conflict," Chapter 10).

If Stimulus *A* tends to elicit Response *B*, and Response *B* has stimulus characteristics that tend to elicit Response *C*, then an association between *A* and *C* could be mediated by *B*.[3] Jarrett and Scheibe (1963) have proposed a model which states that the product of the associative probabilities of two pairs of words, *A-B* and *B-C*, predicts the rate of learning a pair, *A-C*, which has no direct associative connection. Consider, for example, a list composed of directly associated pairs of words, *A-B*, in which *A* has a normative probability of,

---

[3] "Mediation" and its cognates refer to any situation in which a response—called a mediator—intervenes between the initial stimulus and the final response and at least potentially influences the final response. The concept is discussed further in the sections entitled "Transfer in Paired Associate Tasks" and "Age Trend in Efficiency of Mediation," Chapter 7.

say, .20 of eliciting B, and a list composed of pairs of words, A-C, which are not directly associated but are indirectly associated in that A elicits D with a probability of .50 and D elicits C with a probability of .40. The product of the probabilities in the A-C list (.50 × .40) is the same as the probability in the A-B list (.20), and therefore the lists should be learned at the same rate. Palermo and Jenkins (1964a) confirmed this expectation in a study with children. Thus, with children, it is possible to predict the relative rate of learning directly associated pairs, as indicated previously, and in addition it is possible to predict the relative rate of learning pairs in a mediation situation, basing the predictions upon the association strengths of the individual links in the mediational chain.

In addition to its effect on paired associate learning, word association strength has also been shown to have an effect on associative generalization, verbal discrimination learning, and tachistoscopic recognition. Associative generalization means that an instrumental response learned to a word tends to generalize to associates of the word. The phenomenon has been demonstrated in both adults (Mink, 1963) and children (Hall and Ware, 1968; Palermo, 1963). Since generalization of a response occurs from a word to its associates, it is not surprising that discrimination learning involving word pairs is more difficult if the word pairs are associated than if they are not associated (Palmero and Ullrich, 1968). Finally, if a word is used as a fixation point in a tachistoscopic recognition task, recognition thresholds are lower for the target words if they are associatively related to the fixation word than if they are not associated with the fixation word (Gallagher and Palermo, 1967).

Imagery in Paired Associate Learning

It has already been noted that children's paired associate learning is more rapid if the words are presented aurally than if they are presented visually. Another approach to the mode of presentation has centered about the use of pictorial versus word stimuli. In some experiments the materials have been presented as pictures, in other studies the subjects have been instructed to imagine pictures of the stimuli, and in still other studies the materials have been word stimuli with different image-arousing capacities.

It has been demonstrated that it is easier to learn a paired associate list when the stimuli and responses are pictures than when they are words representing the pictures, for both adults (e.g., Paivio and Yarmey, 1966) and children (Cole, Sharp, Glick, and Kessen, 1968; Rohwer, Lynch, Levin, and Suzuki, 1967a). Brooks (1967) has shown that reading can interfere with visual imagery in college students in certain situations, apparently because reading and visual imagery involve the same internal visual mechanisms and therefore conflict with one another. The assumption that this kind of conflict occurs in paired associate learning when the stimuli are printed words and not when they are pictures would explain the superiority of pictures as stimuli.

Several researchers have used instructions designed to induce subjects to create images that would facilitate the association of a stimulus with a response. Miller,

Galanter, and Pribram (1960), Wood (1967, Exp. I), Bugelski, Kidd, and Segmen (1968), and Bugelski (1969), among others (see Paivio, 1967a, 1969), showed that instructing college students to form bizarre associations or visual images of interactions between stimulus and response items facilitated paired associate learning with meaningful materials; and Spiker (1960) and Martin, Cox, and Bulgarella (1966) demonstrated the same effect in elementary school children.[4] In addition, Bugelski (1969) found that the use of imagery prevented the occurrence of proactive and retroactive interference, although Wood (1967, Exp. III) obtained significant proactive interference even with the use of imagery (see section entitled "Transfer in Paired Associate Tasks," Chapter 7, for definitions and a discussion of these kinds of interference). In all of these studies, however, the subjects were given instructions in which the examples used were verbal, not visual. For example, Spiker (1960) instructed his subjects to learn the pair *boat-cake* by imagining a "boat made of cake." Bugelski used numbers as stimuli, but first taught the subjects a rhyming code for the number—*one-bun, two-shoe, three-tree*, etc.—then instructed them to form visual images containing the response word and the code for the number (Bugelski, 1969; Bugelski *et al.*, 1968). For example, the instructions might be to learn the pair *one-window* by imagining a hot-cross bun in a window.

Since the instructions gave only verbal examples, it is possible that they did not result in the use of visual imagery, but rather resulted in the subjects' forming phrases or sentences containing the stimulus and response terms. There are three reasons for assuming that phrases or sentences were used instead of visual images.[5] First, verbalization aids long term memory more than visualization does (e.g., Foster, 1911; Jenkin, 1935; Kurtz and Hovland, 1953; McGeoch, 1942), although visualization may be a superior aid to short term memory (see Paivio, 1967a). Verbal coding, especially coding into sentences, has long been an established method of learning serial lists, such as the notes of the scale ("FACE" and "Every good boy does fine") and the cranial nerves ("On old Olympus' tiny top a Finn and German viewed some hops"), and of learning correct spelling (for example, "A rat in Tom's house might eat Tom's ice cream" is reported to be an effective mnemonic for the spelling of "arithmetic"—and it might be noted that for the teacher, "arithmetic" is an excellent mnemonic for the correct word order in the mnemonic sentence). [See Hunter (1964, Ch. VIII) and Manis (1966, pp. 22–24) for discussions of mnemonic systems based on this kind of coding.] The efficiency of the technique has also been demonstrated experimentally (Rohwer, 1967, Exp. III). Second, theorists have usually assumed that cognitive processes, including memory, are primarily verbal and

---

[4] Paivio and his students have conducted most of the research on the effects of nonverbal imagery on paired associate and serial learning, primarily with college students as subjects. Much of their work has been summarized elsewhere (see Paivio, 1967a, 1969) and is therefore not covered in detail here.

[5] There is possibly a fourth reason: Wood (1967) found that instructing college students to use imagery produced no more facilitation than instructing them to use a verbal mediator. However, Paivio (1967a, 1969) has reported that college students adopt the more efficient technique regardless of which they are instructed to use.

only rarely and inefficiently visual (see Reese, 1965b; Uznadze, 1966, p. 230). Third, there seems to be no theoretical reason to assume that visually organized material should be any easier to remember than verbally organized material. The occurrence of dreams indicates that thinking can be visual; but it is very difficult to re-create dreamed images or even to describe them verbally. It would be reasonable to expect, then, that even if visual imagery can facilitate memory, it should be less effective than verbalization.

In spite of these arguments against assuming that imagery is an effective mnemonic (i.e., memory aid), there is anecdotal evidence that subjects in the *one-bun, two-shoe* task actually use imagery and not words (Bugelski, 1969). To illustrate the nature of the evidence, the reader might ask another student to form visual images of paired associates (e.g., bun in window), and then question him about the detailed contents of the image. Typically, if the questioner attempts to suggest details (e.g., by asking, "The shoe laces were tied, weren't they?"), subjects not only deny the suggestions, but also add many other details, as would be expected if they really experienced images. Reported images contain irrelevant details, but phrases or sentences that might have been used would likely be devoid of irrelevant details. In fact, "the bun is in the window" is likely to be a better verbal mnemonic than "the steaming hot-cross bun is on a blue plate on the sill of an open window with no curtains," which contains the kinds of irrelevant detail expected in a visual image, but which contains so many words that memory is likely to be impaired. Relatively complex sentences can facilitate paired associate learning (Milgram, 1967a), but probably produce less facilitation than simpler sentences (Rohwer, 1967, Exp. VI). Furthermore, many subjects report the use of imagery (see, e.g., Brooks, 1967; Paivio, 1967a), and there are cases of phenomenal memory feats that are reportedly based on imagery (see Hunter, 1964; Katona, 1964).

The problem of whether or not imagery is the mnemonic is complicated by the rather loose way in which the term *imagery* has been used. It "may be visual, auditory, or of any other sensory modality, and also purely verbal" (Holt, 1964). The term "verbal imagery" has been used (see Reese, 1965b), but usually without a clearly specified referent. [Dallenbach (1927) used the term and defined it clearly, but he used it to mean auditory imagery of words—imagined hearing of words—and visual imagery of words—imagined reading of words.] The term *verbal context* was also used (McGeoch, 1942), and seems to carry the meaning of *phrase* and *sentence* as used above. Therefore, in the rest of this section, the distinction is made between *imagery* and *verbal context* as mnemonics. The problem, then, is to determine whether imagery or verbal context is a superior mnemonic device.

An ideal experimental task to determine which process is a superior aid to memory would require starting with a population of subjects who do not spontaneously use either imagery or verbal context, and to provide images to one group, verbal contexts to another group, and neither kind of mnemonic to a control group. Unfortunately, it is doubtful that the treatments would be effective in the required kinds of population (which might consist of lower animals or severely retarded children, for example). However, Reese (1965b) used a procedure designed to maximize the probabilities that one or the other kind of mnemonic would be used. One group of preschool children was shown pictures of interactions between the stimulus and response terms in each pair; if remembered, the pictures would be images. Another group was given sentences describing the same interactions, but was not shown pictures of the interactions; if

A   B   C

Fig. 6-1. Examples of pictorial materials used by Reese (1965b). A, Stimulus items; B, response elements; C, compounds. (Previously unpublished material.)

remembered, the sentences would provide verbal context. A third group was given both the sentences and the pictures of interactions; and a control group was given neither the sentences nor the pictures of interactions. The control group was given the task as a standard paired associate problem, with the stimulus and response items presented as isolated elements. Examples of the pictorial materials used are shown in Figure 6-1; the verbal materials used are listed in Table 6-1. All subjects were given the stimulus items as elements, both visually (as shown by the examples in Figure 6-1,A) and verbally (Column 1, Table 6-1). The control and "verbal context" groups saw the response items as elements (Figure 6-1,B), and the "imagery" and "combined" groups saw them as compounds (Figure 6-1,C). The control and "imagery" groups heard the response items as elements (Column 2, Table 6-1), and the "verbal context" and "combined" groups heard them as compounds (Column 3, Table 6-1).

The method is what Woodworth (1938) called "learning by the eye or the ear," and, as he pointed out, it contains the flaw that subjects might verbalize descriptions of the interactions they see pictured, or they might visualize pictures of the interactions they hear described. However, since young children are less facile than older children in language skills, they should be less efficient at

Table 6-1

The Verbal Materials Used by Reese (1965b)[a]

Stimulus	Response	
	Element	Compound
Cat	Umbrella	The cat is carrying the umbrella
Rabbit	Corn	The rabbit is eating the corn
Dog	Scissors	The dog is balancing the scissors on his nose
Fish	Telephone	The fish is talking on the telephone
Chicken	Flag	The chicken is carrying the flag

[a] The table gives verbalizations by experimenter. Based on tabular and textual material from Reese (1965b, Table 2, p. 293).

this kind of "crossover" behavior than older children; and, therefore, one mode of presentation should be inferior to the other at the younger age level and the modes should be about equally effective at older age levels.

The results of Reese's experiment are presented graphically in Figure 6-2, where it can be seen that the control group, given the standard paired associate task, required more trials to learn than the groups given the visual or verbal interactions. As expected, the visual interaction condition (the imagery condition) was less effective at the youngest age level than the verbal interaction (verbal context) condition, suggesting that the beneficial effect of the visual condition is produced only when children verbalize descriptions of the interactions they see depicted. However, although the control group was significantly inferior to the three experimental groups, the obtained age trend in the effectiveness of the visual condition was not statistically reliable; there were no significant differences among the three interaction groups. Hence, the statistically justifiable conclusion is that imagery and verbal context worked equally well in facilitating paired associate learning.

Milgram (1967b), in a somewhat better controlled study, found that verbal context was superior to visual compound, and both were superior to control. The mean numbers of trials required by these groups to attain the learning criterion are presented graphically in Figure 6-3. (The apparent asymptotes in the curves for the two compound conditions at seven years of age are ambiguous, because Milgram varied the length of the paired associate list across age levels, in an attempt to maintain a uniform level of problem difficulty.)

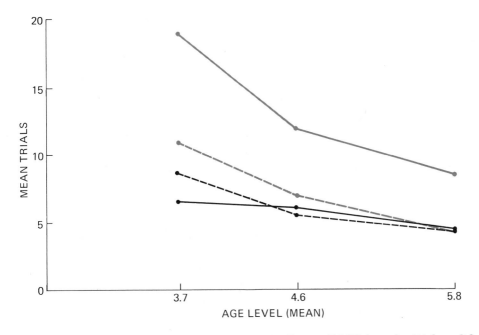

Fig. 6-2. Verbal context and visual imagery in Reese (1965b) study. Light solid line, control; dark solid line, verbal context; light dashed line, imagery; dark dashed line, combined. "Mean trials" are the antilogs of mean log trials. (Data previously unreported.)

Milgram's data and the nonsignificant trend in Reese's data support the conclusion that "facilitation in a visual compound condition probably depends upon covert encoding of the pictured interaction in verbal form" (Milgram, 1967b, p. 602). The younger child is presumably less able to do this than the older child and adult. However, a second possible explanation is that the young child is able to encode visually but is less adept at decoding visual images verbally. Since the task requires overt verbal responses, the memory code—whether visual or verbal—must mediate overt verbal responses. The inferior performance of younger children in the visual condition is an inferiority in producing these overt verbal responses. It may be that the younger children in the visual condition do in fact encode visually, but they may experience ". . . greater difficulty than . . . adults in retrieving the verbal response from a nonverbal memory image. This analysis implies that the development of verbal skills with increasing age and education is accompanied by increasing skill in translating from nonverbal images to verbal modes of cognitive representation where the overt task requires such transformation" (Dilley and Paivio, 1968, p. 239).

A third possibility is that young children have poorer visual memory than auditory or verbal memory. However, as Dilley and Paivio pointed out, this alternative "would run counter to Bruner's (1964) view that the young child's thinking is predominantly iconic [i.e., based on organized images and percepts rather than words or symbols]" (Dilley and Paivio, 1968, p. 239).[6]

Paivio (1967a) has shown that college students prefer to use images to encode concrete material, such as used in the Reese and Milgram studies, and prefer

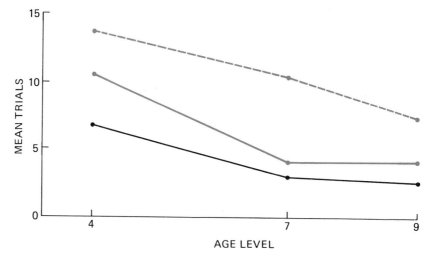

Fig. 6-3. Verbal context and visual imagery in Milgram (1967b) study. Light dashed line, control; light solid line, imagery; dark line, verbal context. (Drawn from data in Milgram, 1967b, Table 1, p. 601.)

to encode abstract material verbally. Paivio concluded that the more efficient method of encoding is the one preferred in each case (see also Paivio and Yuille, 1968). This suggests as a fourth possible explanation of the difference between visual and verbal encoding in young children that visual encoding is not used as often even when the materials make it a readily available system. That is, some subjects in the visual condition may encode visually but others may fail to utilize the visual material provided and may encode as though they were in the control condition. The latter subjects would cause the group mean to regress toward the mean of the control group. This explanation requires further assumptions to explain why the young child should fail to make use of the visual materials provided.

[6] The assumption that imagery is the prelinguistic mode of thinking has also been made by other theorists (e.g., Cameron and Magaret, 1951, pp. 106–107).

In addition to the four possibilities already discussed, a fifth is that the visual materials used in the Reese and Milgram studies did not provide adequate visual images for the young children. The materials used by both Reese and Milgram were line drawings (filled in, in Milgram's study, with colored pencil but completely unadorned in Reese's study), and were devoid of most of the kinds of irrelevant detail that are typically reported by older children and adults to be present in imagery (see Bugelski, 1969). These apparently irrelevant details may in fact be essential components that make images effective mnemonics, and the young child may be unable to generate them spontaneously. Revising a theory proposed by Huey in 1908, Bugelski (1968) argued that reading for sense is a matter of arousing feelings and images. It consists of generating a series of images that are integrated with one another, accompanied by associated feelings and emotional states. It follows that a child may fail to comprehend written material because it arouses no integrated imagery; similarly, it may be that the young child fails to "read" the kinds of pictorial material used by Reese and by Milgram. Salient details of a picture might arouse images, but the depicted interaction may generate no imagery. Bugelski's analysis implies that unless the images are integrated, they produce no *meaning* and hence produce no facilitative effect.

To summarize, the alternative explanations of the inferior performance of younger children in the visual condition are that it results from (a) inferior ability to encode visual material into verbal form; (b) inferior ability to decode visual memory images into verbal form; (c) inferior memory of visual images; (d) failure to use the imagery system; or (e) inferior ability to encode visually when the materials are stark drawings devoid of irrelevant detail.

Jensen and Rohwer (1963a, 1963b, 1965) have reported a series of experiments in which they have found marked facilitation in paired associate learning when subjects are asked to formulate sentences containing the stimulus and response words before the actual paired associate learning begins. The general procedure is to have the subject make up a sentence for each pair of words in the list on the first trial. The only restriction on the sentences is that they contain the names of the two pictures in the pair. After the initial sentence-forming trial or—for the control group—naming trial, the procedure is the same as in any paired associate task and the experimenter says nothing further about the sentences. These studies have been conducted with child and adult retardates as well as with normal children, and in all cases this kind of prelearning experience has produced much more rapid learning than the usual paired associate procedure. In the most recent study, the effect was demonstrated in children from 5 to 17 years of age, and was shown to increase in magnitude with increasing age. No facilitating effect of sentences was found in serial learning.

Rohwer (1967) reported an impressive series of experiments, most with elementary school children, on the kinds of verbal context that facilitate paired associate learning. He used the study–test method, in which the stimulus-response pairs are presented on study trials and the stimulus items are presented alone on test trials to assess retention of the response items. On the study trials, the pairs were presented one at a time for four seconds each. In the control

condition, the stimulus and response items in each pair were presented as isolated elements, as illustrated by the examples in the first part of Table 6-2.
In "verbal context" conditions, the items were connected by conjunctions, prepositions, or verbs, with grammatical fillers added, but the stimulus and response
words were capitalized and underlined so that the subject could identify them
easily. Examples of conjunctive phrases are given in the second part of Table
6-2, prepositional phrases in the third part, and sentences (verb connectives)
in the last part. A subject in the group given sentences, for example, would
see sentences like the ones in the last part of Table 6-2, presented one at a
time, each for four seconds. On the test trial the subject would see only the

Table 6-2

Examples of Verbal Materials Used by Rohwer (1967) [a]

Condition	Sample items
Control	DOG GATE
	ROCK BOTTLE
Conjunction	the DOG and the GATE
	the ROCK or the BOTTLE
Preposition	the DOG on the GATE
	the ROCK behind the BOTTLE
Verb	the DOG closes the GATE
	the ROCK breaks the BOTTLE

[a] Based on Rohwer's Table 13 (Rohwer, 1967, p. 56).

stimulus word (the first underlined word in the sentence), and would be required to supply the missing response word. (In some of the experiments,
Rohwer used variations of the general procedures outlined here.)

Rohwer found that presenting the stimulus and response items in a conjunctive
phrase had no facilitating effect; but presenting the items in a prepositional
phrase or in a sentence facilitated performance, and prepositional phrases were
almost as effective as sentences. The verb in the sentence can imply little or
no action (e.g., "ROSES like RAIN" produced as much facilitation as "ROSES
drink RAIN"), but the verb must specify a meaningful relation between the
stimulus and response items (e.g., "ROSES like HATS" and "ROSES drink
HATS" produced no facilitation).

The facilitating effect of using a verb to connect the stimulus and response
items is not attributable to the presentation of the materials in sentences as
opposed to phrases, since prepositional phrases were almost as effective as verb

connectives. Furthermore, when a conjunctive phrase was embedded in a complete sentence, the verb connective was still superior (e.g., "the ROCK hit the BOTTLE and him" was more effective than "the ROCK and the BOTTLE hit him").

Rohwer also examined the effects of different pictorial methods of presenting the material. In one study he used the four methods of verbal presentation illustrated in Table 6-2 and three methods of pictorial presentation. [Reported by Rohwer (1967, Exp. IX) and Rohwer et al. (1967b). See also Rohwer and Lynch (1967).] The pictorial methods were with isolated elements (control condition), with the elements isolated but spatially located in a way consistent with the prepositional phrase, and with an animated film strip showing the action described in the sentence. In this study the subject saw the pictorial material, depicting one stimulus-response pair on each trial, while the experimenter read aloud the appropriate verbal material. Consider two examples, using the pairs shown in Table 6-2 to illustrate the procedure. (a) A subject in the group given the Action pictures and the control verbalizations would see on one trial an animated film strip showing a dog moving toward and then closing a gate, and at the same time he would hear the experimenter say, "dog [pause] gate." On another trial he would see a rock break a bottle while the experimenter said, "rock [pause] bottle." (b) A subject in the group given Locational pictures and prepositional phrases would see on one trial a still slide showing the dog on top of a gate and would hear the experimenter say, "the dog on the gate." On another trial he would see a still picture showing a rock behind a bottle while hearing the experimenter say, "the rock behind the bottle." On the test trial, subjects from all groups would see only the stimulus item while the experimenter said aloud the stimulus word.

The results of the study are presented graphically in Figure 6-4. With Still pictures, only Sentences produced facilitation; and with Action pictures, there was facilitation in all four verbal conditions. Locational pictures produced an intermediate amount of facilitation with all four verbal conditions. Thus, Action pictures had an effect like Sentences. Rohwer recognized the possibility that subjects might spontaneously verbalize sentences about the Action pictures, but he rejected this crossover interpretation on the grounds that there was no age difference in the effect of the Action pictures (in Grades 1, 3, and 6), and that Sentences were no more effective than Action pictures. He argued, as did Reese, that increasing verbal facility with increasing age would increase the likelihood of the crossover, and that sentences provided by the experimenter would facilitate more than self-generated sentences.

Rohwer repeated part of the last study with preschool-aged subjects, and obtained similar results. The Action condition and the Sentence condition facilitated performance, compared with the Still condition and the control verbal condition.

Context seems to affect retention because of an effect at the time of input, rather than at the time of retrieval, and in this way seems to differ from the clustering effect obtained in free recall (see section entitled "Memory," this chapter). Rohwer concluded that verbal mediation theory does not adequately explain the context effects. The main problems are that traditional mediation theory requires the assumption of learned associations between the stimulus and mediator and between the mediator and response, and fails to explain why certain kinds of connections work better than other kinds. Similarly, to say that the different kinds of context are differentially effective in "organizing" the material, in the Gestalt sense, does not solve the problem, because it fails to explain why organized material is retained better and why different kinds of connection are differentially effective in this respect. Rohwer suggested that

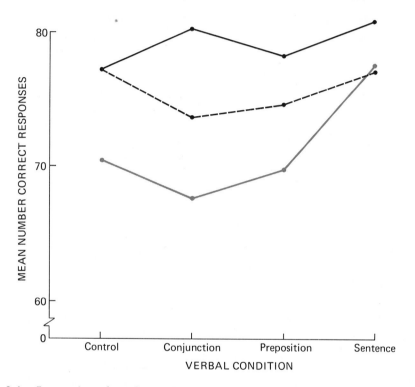

Fig. 6-4. Interaction of methods of verbal and visual presentation of paired associates: Rohwer study. Dark solid line, action; dashed line, locational; light line, still. (Drawn from data in Rohwer, 1967, Table 15, p. 64.)

further research should be directed at "the question of the form of memory storage in learning, at the question of the nature of the processes that produce these forms of storage, and at the question of the temporal locus of these processes" (Rohwer, 1967, p. 97).

One theory to account for the results of imagery studies was first advanced by Lambert and Paivio (1956). These authors argued that the stimulus items in a paired associate task function as "conceptual pegs" for the response to be learned. The efficiency of the conceptual pegs is a function of the imagery they can arouse. Imagery, in turn, is assumed to mediate response recall (Paivio, 1963). The theory is similar to the memory "plan" which according to Miller *et al.* (1960) is used as a code to aid in retrieval of items. Since pictures directly evoke images, they would be expected to be superior stimuli for learning than words. Furthermore, if words are scaled for image-evoking capacity, one would expect differences in learning rate as a function of the degree to which the words are capable of evoking images.

While such a theory does little to account for why images should be particularly good mediators or "pegs" on which to hang other responses, it is capable of accounting for much of the data (see Reese, in press). It makes a straightforward prediction about the effects of pictures versus words as stimuli in a paired associate task, and it accounts for the finding that nouns, particularly concrete nouns, as stimuli lead to faster learning than adjectives for both children (Paivio, 1963) and adults (Paivio, 1965). Since nouns are generally more concrete than adjectives, and concrete words are more likely to evoke images, it is easier to learn noun-adjective pairs than adjective-noun pairs. Furthermore, Paivio, Yuille, and Smythe (1966) found that concrete nouns as stimuli facilitated learning more than abstract nouns, although the effect was not as great with children as with adults (Paivio and Yuille, 1966).

Considering the Spiker, Reese, Milgram, and Rohwer *et al.* studies, it would appear that the verbal instructions and the picture or grammatical relationships connecting the stimuli and the responses aid in producing imagery. Essentially, these experimenters have forced the subjects to formulate images, or conceptual pegs in Paivio's terms, which facilitate learning. It is worth noting in this connection that when the stimuli and responses were merely linked by a conjunction, for example, "fork *or* cake," "towel *and* plate," in the Rohwer *et al.* study, no facilitation was observed over a control group given no instructions. The conjunction does not force an image in which the response is "pegged" to the stimulus as the verb does when the fork *cuts* the cake or the towel *wipes* the plate.

While neither Jensen nor Rohwer has considered the conceptual peg hypothesis seriously, it would seem quite plausible that the syntactic frames within which the words to be learned in these tasks are embedded could easily be scaled for imagery and related to performance in the paired associate task. Intuitively, it would seem that nouns related by verbs would have more image-evoking capacity than nouns related by conjunctions; but although performance in the paired associate task does fit with this intuitive guess, one would prefer to use theory rather than intuition in explaining the data. It might be possible, when using the Jensen-Rohwer procedure, to predict the relative rates of learning for individual subjects from the type of sentence they construct to relate the stimulus and response words before the paired associate task begins.

There are some limitations that might be noted with respect to the research in this area. Most of the studies have used only noun stimuli and noun responses in the learning task. It has been demonstrated that learning varies as a function of the part of speech of the stimulus and response members (e.g., Glanzer, 1962; S. I. Shapiro and Palermo, 1967), and it is certainly conceivable that the grammatical class of the words to be associated may interact with other variables in these tasks. It should also be noted that Paivio and his co-workers have shown that the effects of imagery result primarily from manipulation of the characteristics of the stimulus items; less effect is found when the imagery characteristics of the response items are manipulated (e.g., Paivio, 1967b, 1969; Paivio and Yuille, 1968). These effects are opposite to the effects of manipulation of the meaningfulness of the stimuli and responses. The manipulation of response meaningfulness has a substantial effect but manipulation of stimulus meaningfulness has much less effect (Goss and Nodine, 1965). Any theory attempting to account for paired associate learning must take these two facts into consideration.

Other Variables Influencing Paired Associate Learning

This section covers a number of studies, all conducted with children, that do not fit together in any systematic way. Not all have led to new insights into learning or developmental processes, but some have made important contributions, and as a group they indicate the diversity of problems that have been investigated.

INTERMITTENT REINFORCEMENT. Several investigators have examined the effect of presenting the response member of the pair with less than 100 percent of the stimulus presentations. The basic assumption is that the paired associate task may be conceptualized as a classical conditioning task with the stimulus word as the conditional stimulus, the response word as the unconditioned stimulus, and the overt response as the unconditioned response. Presentation of the response word is analogous to reinforcement in classical conditioning (Goss, Morgan, and Golin, 1959). Therefore, the procedure of omitting the presentation of the response item following some percentage of the presentations of the stimulus item is analogous to the intermittent reinforcement procedure in classical conditioning.

In children, the performance level declines as the percentage occurrence of the response member declines, but the percentage reduction in the performance level is not necessarily the same as the percentage reduction of reinforcement (e.g., Carroll, 1966; Carroll and Penney, 1966; Goss, 1966; S. S. Shapiro, 1965, 1966). The magnitude of the effect seems to be inversely related to age (Goss, 1966) and to the initial association strength of the pairs (Carroll and Penney, 1966). The data of at least two of the studies suggest that the effect of reducing the percentage occurrence of the response is attributable to interference with the response integration stage of the task (Carroll, 1966; Carroll and Penney, 1966).

ASSOCIATIVE SYMMETRY. Another study, which was based on the assumptions about the relation between the paired associate task and classical conditioning, pertains also to the Asch and Ebenholtz (1962) hypothesis of associative symmetry. If the stimulus word is considered to be a conditional stimulus and the response to be an unconditioned response, as in classical conditioning, it would not be expected that "backward" or R-S learning (as well as S-R learning) would occur in the paired associate task. However, Asch and Ebenholtz have argued that when an association is established between S and R, there is simultaneously formed an equally strong association between R and S. Support for this view has been obtained in short term memory tasks (Murdock, 1962) and the paired associate task (e.g., Murdock, 1966). However, Palermo (1961) found that in a paired associate task with fourth and sixth grade children, the strength of the R-S associations at the end of learning was only about half as great as the strength of the S-R associations. This result seems to support neither the classical conditioning nor the associative symmetry model. It should be noted, however, that since the subject is required to learn the response and is not required to learn the stimulus in the paired associate task, it may well be that associative symmetry cannot be evaluated by asking for stimulus recall since the nominal stimulus presented by the experimenter may not be the functional stimulus for the subject (Underwood, 1963).

MEANINGFULNESS OF CVC RESPONSES. Two studies have dealt with performance as a function of the association value or meaningfulness of CVC nonsense syllables used as response members of the list. Palermo, Flamer, and Jenkins (1964) used the adult association values reported by Archer (1960), and Gaeth and Cooper (1967) used the Gaeth and Allen children's association norms (1966a). In both experiments rate of learning increased as the association value of the responses increased, although the correlation between performance on individual trigrams and association value of the trigrams was very low (.16) in the Gaeth and Cooper study.

STIMULUS SIMILARITY. Gaeth and Allen (1966b) investigated the problem of intralist similarity of the stimuli in a paired associate task. They found that the performance of children in Grades 4, 5, and 6 was influenced in essentially the same way as adult performance when formal similarity (letter duplication) and meaningful or conceptual similarity were varied. Formal similarity interferes with learning when the materials are low in meaningfulness; conceptual similarity interferes when the materials are meaningful words.

SUBJECT VARIABLES. A few studies provide data on the relationship of subject variables to paired associate learning. As might be expected, older subjects learn more rapidly than younger subjects, although the paired associate task is not very sensitive to this variable. For example, several investigators who presented equivalent lists to groups of children differing in age by several years found no significant learning differences (McCullers, 1961; Palermo, 1961; S. S. Shapiro, 1965, 1967). Comparisons of normal and retarded children of equal mental age have sometimes shown no differences in acquisition (e.g., Ring and Palermo, 1961) and retention one week or one month later (e.g., Cantor and Ryan, 1962), but contradictory results have been reported for both learning (e.g., Iscoe and Semler, 1964) and retention (e.g., Hermelin and O'Connor, 1964; Vergason, 1964). In an extensive study of the correlates of paired associate learning, McCullers (1965) reported that fourth, fifth, and sixth grade children's performance is positively correlated with scores on tests of IQ, reading, vocabulary, and school achievement. Otto (1961) also reported a positive correlation between paired associate learning and reading skill in the second, fourth, and sixth grades.

MEMORY

Memory has been studied with two somewhat arbitrarily categorized and relatively independent experimental paradigms which reflect different histories and theoretical orientations. On the one hand, those who have been primarily concerned with paired associate learning have tended to focus their attention upon the acquisition of paired associate lists, the effects of learning one list upon the learning of another, and the forgetting of what was learned in such lists as a function of proactive and retroactive interference. On the other hand, another group of researchers has been less interested in paired associate learning and has focused attention upon the variables that influence the recall of a list of single items and the organization of the items in recall. Cutting across this dichotomy is a more recent dichotomy that involves a concern with long term and short term memory. A recent surge of interest in short term memory, which seems to differ in some ways from long term memory, has produced a good deal of research on whether an interference theory proposed to account for long term memory also accounts for short term memory.

It is rather surprising to find that most child psychologists have shown a marked lack of interest in most of the problems of memory that have been attracting the attention of so many other researchers in the past few years. Only a few studies of retroactive and proactive interference in children have been reported (for discussion of these, see section entitled "Transfer in Paired Associate Tasks," Chapter 7). Nor have researchers working with children shown much interest in short term memory, despite the fact that results obtained by Atkinson, Hansen, and Bernbach (1964) showed that research in this area is feasible with preschool children and that differences in short term memory of children and adults may exist. (See Belmont and Butterfield, 1969, for a review of the available data.) Maccoby and Hagen (1965) did use a variation of the Atkinson *et al.* procedure for the study of the recall of task-relevant and task-irrelevant materials as a function of distraction and age. They found that short term memory tended to increase with age and was impaired by distraction.

However, there has accumulated a body of research on organizational factors in recall by children. Bousfield, Esterson, and Whitmarsh (1958) published a developmental study of "clustering" in recall as a part of a larger program of research on the organization and recall of randomly presented semantically related words. The general procedure used in the Bousfield studies (e.g., Bousfield and Cohen, 1955) was to construct a 40 word list composed of 4 categories of 10 words each. The categories might include 10 names of flowers, 10 automobiles, 10 countries, and 10 occupations, all randomly intermixed within the list. "Clustering" refers to a tendency to recall the list in groups or clusters of semantically related words, as opposed to recalling the words in a random order.

Bousfield *et al.* found that third and fourth grade children cluster by semantic category, and the tendency to cluster as well as the total recall increases with age. Rossi (1964) examined the same problem with 5, 8, and 11 year old children. He used a 20 picture list of 5 animals, 5 clothing items, 5 foods, and 5 parts of the body. Half of the subjects in each group had the mediating superordinate terms *animal, food, clothing*, and *body* included in the list in place of one of the instances of each category. In contrast to an earlier study by Goodwin, Long, and Welch (1945), in which superordinate words facilitated the recall of subordinate words, the superordinate name did not influence the amount of clustering in the Rossi study. There was, however, a significant increase in clustering from 5 to 11 years of age.

Rossi (1963) has also presented data that suggest that the amount of clustering in recall by retarded children is a function of mental age, although Osborn (1960) found no differences between normal and retarded children. Osborn presented pictures with verbally presented names while Rossi presented only the names, possibly accounting for the difference in results. The question of relative amounts of clustering in normal and retarded children is complicated further by the results of a study by Gerjuoy and Spitz (1966). In this study, adolescent retardates and normal 9 year old children of equal mental age did not cluster above chance when the total number of words recalled was taken into account. Evidence for clustering in normal children was not obtained before the age of 14 years.

In another study, Rossi and Rossi (1965) reported significant clustering in children as young as two years of age. The amount of clustering increased with age from two to five years. In addition, increases in clustering were observed over the three presentation trials that were given. The authors commented that the two years olds "use clustering as an almost exclusive technique for recall." It is obvious that additional research is needed to reconcile the differences between the findings of Gerjuoy and Spitz and those of Rossi. The data of the Rossi and Rossi study and a study by Rossi and Wittrock (1967) were interpreted as indicating that the tendency of preschool children to cluster is far greater than the tendency to recall in the serial order in which the items were presented. The comparisons made were inappropriate, however, since the chance probability of clustering in these studies was far greater than the chance probability of serial ordering. This problem was not taken into account in the two research reports.

Laurence (1967) has recently demonstrated that a list composed entirely of related words (e.g., animals) is recalled better than a list of unrelated words. She presented two lists of related words and two lists of unrelated words for four trials each to subjects varying in age from 5 to 73 years. There was an increase with age in recall of both kinds of lists up to the college age and all groups recalled the related list better than the unrelated list.

Another approach to the problem of clustering and recall was suggested by Jenkins, Mink, and Russell (1958). They found that if a list is constructed of stimulus and response words from word association norms, subjects recall the words in associated clusters and the amount of clustering is a positive function of the association strength between the stimulus and response words. Wicklund, Palermo, and Jenkins (1965) obtained similar results in two experiments with fourth grade children. Clustering was found to be a function of the strength of association between the words and to be independent of serial order of presentation and frequency of the words. The amount of clustering, however, was considerably less than obtained with college students. Children cluster in recall but are less likely than college students to cluster on the basis of association strength built into the list. Willner (1967) obtained similar results over the age range from second grade to college with a somewhat different measure of association strength.

The studies of conceptual and associative clustering discussed thus far have dealt with the tendency of subjects to discover the special characteristics of the list and to use these special characteristics in the organization of their recall of the list. Tulving (1962) has pointed out that regardless of the characteristics of the list, subjects do organize the list in some way to facilitate their recall of the list. He has shown that in recall protocols for a series of trials, there is a consistency in the clustering of words, which he has called *subjective organization*. If a subject recalls two or more words together on one trial, there is a tendency for him to recall those same words together on other trials. Tulving has argued that performance, measured in terms of total recall, is a function of the amount of subjective organization exhibited.

Laurence (1966) investigated subjective organization developmentally. She presented 16 unrelated high frequency words for 16 trials to children 5, 6, 8, and 10 years of age, to college students, and to an older group of persons 73 years of age. There were significant increases in total recall over trials and over age groups up to the college level. There was no interaction between age and trials, however, since each age group reached a different stable asymptotic level on about the eighth to tenth trial and the maximum performance or asymptote increased with age. The amount and variability of subjective organization were greater for the adult groups than for the child groups, and the amount of subjective organization also increased more over trials for the adult populations. There were no differences among the four child groups on these measures. The child populations showed some subjective organization and some increase over trials, but clustering was far less than in the adult groups. As Tulving found for his college students, there was a high positive correlation between subjective organization and total recall for the adult group and for the 8 and 10 year old groups. There was no correlation, however, between subjective organization and total recall for the two youngest groups. The 6 and 8 year old children were retested one year later and no change in these results was apparent.

The results of this experiment do not fit with Tulving's notions about the dependence of performance upon subjective organization. Total recall increased with age among the child groups but subjective organization did not and there was no correlation between total recall and subjective organization for the two youngest groups. When a correlation did appear between total recall and subjective organization, there was no dramatic increase in total recall. Obviously there is an important developmental–theoretical problem here.

Mandler and Stephens (1967) approached the problem of organization and recall with a slightly different technique. They asked second, fourth, sixth, and eighth grade children to recall a list of 15 unrelated words after they had sorted them into categories. Half of the subjects in each grade sorted the words into self-determined categories until they were able to do so in the same way twice in succession. The other half of the children had to learn to sort the words in accordance with the categories of the experimental subjects. The "free" categorization groups made fewer errors in categorizing and took less time and fewer trials to categorize than did the "constrained" groups. The free groups also clustered by category more than the constrained groups. All measures of categorization increased with age, and total recall and clustering in recall increased with age. In addition, there was an increasing tendency with age to categorize on the basis of part of speech.

CONCLUDING REMARKS

It is clear that child psychologists, as a group, have not been particularly interested in most of the traditional experimental and theoretical problems of interest to researchers who devote most of their laboratory efforts to verbal learning. Even the theoretical implications of developmental research in the verbal behavior area have been largely ignored. In essence, child psychologists have merely dabbled now and then in the area and the methodological naivité of dabblers has often been painfully evident. As Goulet (1968b) has pointed out, however, there are many possibilities in the area and the laboratory tasks are ideally suited to use with children, although some care must be taken to modify a few of the techniques and procedures to adapt them to the subjects being used.

There are many untouched problems which appear to be fruitful areas of research. For example, young children cannot learn a paired associate list in as few trials as older children. There are numerous possible reasons for such an obvious fact, but little understanding of why it should be so. Perhaps the basic assumption has been that this fact is attributable to biological changes that occur within the organism. The young child is not as "mature" as the older child, and therefore cannot learn as rapidly. Such a statement, however, merely suggests that maturation is a physiological problem out of the realm of the psychologist's purview. Labeling and ignoring the problem is of little developmental interest or value. While it is certainly possible that physiological changes may underlie some behavioral changes, the developmental questions relating to the behavioral manifestations are still of importance. For example, in the paired associate task it would be of theoretical interest to know whether learning differences are attributable to failure of the younger child in the response integration stage of learning, the associative hook-up stage, or both.

If impairment of one of these stages of learning is the primary determinant of developmental differences in learning, then one would wish to know which variables affect the processes associated with that stage of learning.

Another question of developmental importance relates to whether the performance of the child in various learning tasks is depressed because of variables affecting acquisition or because of variables affecting memory. It is possible that the performance differences in verbal behavior tasks do not result from slower learning by the younger child than by the older child, but rather from a failure of the younger child to remember what he has learned. Questions about both short and long term memory and the relation of memory to the acquisition processes are therefore of developmental interest. Although no one has systematically examined the characteristics of memory in children, there are a number of suggestions in the literature indicating that developmental studies would add immensely to the understanding of memory processes. The results of the Atkinson *et al.* study of short term memory and the Laurence study of subjective organization, as well as the Koppenaal, Krull, and Katz (1964) study of retroactive and proactive inhibition (discussed in the next chapter), all point to research in memory as an unusually fruitful area for significant contributions from those interested in child behavior.

Finally, the fascinating questions associated with the studies of the effects of mental imagery and language syntax on learning suggest that the procedures of the verbal learning laboratory may well help in the attack upon the problems associated with the understanding of language development. If that is the case, child psychologists can hardly afford to neglect this research area any longer.

CHAPTER 7

Transfer

INTRODUCTION

In its broadest sense, *transfer* refers to the "influence of previous experiences on current performance" (Underwood, 1949, p. 637). Interest may range from the effect of one reinforced response on the occurrence of the next, to the influence of letter recognition drill on learning to read, or training in a computer-controlled flight simulator on the ability to fly an airplane. In evaluating transfer it is more precise to speak of positive or negative transfer effects, but the terms transfer (facilitation) and interference are more common.

Psychologists have studied the effects of transfer and the conditions that promote positive or negative transfer, and at least equally importantly have attempted to identify the mechanisms of transfer, that is, to determine which particular consequences of experience bring about the influence on performance. Because much of the research on transfer was conducted within the framework of learning theory, the solution to this latter problem seemed to be obvious. It is habits or S-R (stimulus-response) associations that transfer. In this narrow context, the specification of conditions for transfer was also clear. The more comparable the stimulus conditions of the training and test situations are, the more equivalent the test trial will be to the previous training trial, and hence if the learned response is appropriate to the test situation, the more one would expect previous training to *facilitate* subsequent performance. The converse is not true, however. If stimulus conditions are completely dissimilar, one does not obtain negative transfer, because no relevant response is likely to be evoked and thus there will be no transfer at all. But then what does produce interference or negative transfer? Interference appears to be primarily a function of the appropriateness of the response to the test situation. If the response that has been learned in the training situation is inappropriate in the transfer test, then the occurrence of that response may interfere with the acquisition of the correct response. Gibson (1940) stated these relationships very succinctly as follows: (a) if the responses are *identical*, facilitation is obtained, its magnitude increasing with stimulus generalization (stimulus similarity); (b) if responses are *different*, interference is obtained, its magnitude increasing with stimulus generalization.

Verbal paired associate learning lends itself particularly well to the manipulation of the similarity of both stimuli and responses and thus has provided an obvious testing ground for hypotheses regarding variables affecting transfer.

The ready availability of college students as subjects, and the relative ease with which verbal learning studies can be conducted, have led to a large amount of research and considerable sophistication regarding the variables affecting transfer in paired associate learning.

The study of transfer has been particularly popular in child psychology, but in contrast with the emphasis on paired associate tasks in research on transfer in adults, the emphasis in the child research has to a great extent been on the transfer of discrimination learning, although a few studies of paired associate transfer in children have been reported. (See Chapter 5 for definition and systematic discussion of discrimination learning, and Chapter 6 for discussion of paired associate learning.) In this chapter the child research on transfer in both kinds of task is discussed, except for research on "discriminative shifts," which is discussed in Chapter 9.

In the decade from 1930 to 1940 research on discrimination learning was directed primarily toward establishing the discriminative capacity of infants and children, with some interest in the cues that were most likely to be utilized when multiple cues were present. Most of this research was relatively crude by present standards, yet research of this kind had not been replicated until very recently, when the current emphasis on the role of observing responses and attentional mechanisms in transfer began to emerge. Before considering these studies, however, it is important to review a body of research that bulks large in the history of ideas regarding transfer in children because it provides a new foundation and more sophisticated methodology for the current interest in what may otherwise be considered older issues of psychology.

EMPIRICAL AND THEORETICAL BACKGROUND

Cue-Producing Responses

The greatest impetus for systematic research on transfer in children was provided by some provocative hypotheses in a book by Miller and Dollard (1941), subsequently elaborated in a later book by the same authors (Dollard and Miller, 1950). Miller and Dollard were particularly concerned with the kinds of behaviors, often uniquely human, that are commonly assumed to reflect "higher mental processes." The simple association concepts that accounted quite adequately for much of the behavior of lower animals were inadequate to account for man's ability to solve complex problems without overt trial and error, his ability to respond in an equivalent manner to stimuli with widely discrepant perceptual features, and his superiority in making delayed responses—that is, responses based upon a stimulus that is no longer present at the time the responses are made. To account for these behaviors Miller and Dollard utilized the concept of "cue-producing responses." These are responses, usually verbal labels, that serve to mediate or transfer behavior from one stimulus to another. Counting is one example of the use of such responses. Although a dollar bill and ten dimes present completely dissimilar perceptual cues, after counting the dimes we accept them as the equivalent of the dollar bill if our count reaches the predetermined appropriate number such that a common label is evoked.

Racial problems are thought by some to be intensified by the expectancies and emotional responses that may be attached to certain labels. Although an individual's physical features provide a very poor basis for predictions regarding the likelihood that he will be a good or bad neighbor, nevertheless, given a cue such as skin color that evokes a label to which a standard set of responses has been conditioned, these responses may transfer, no matter how inappropriately.

There are other situations in which labels may perform a more constructive role. For example, if Mr. Jones is introduced as a professor of history, the ensuing conversation is likely to be different from the conversation that would ensue if he were introduced as the artist who painted the picture hanging on a nearby wall. The label in this instance transfers some very relevant behaviors.

Cue-producing responses are not necessarily always verbal. One may make comparisons of quantity among two sets of objects dissimilar in size or appearance by pairing the objects, one with the other. If all objects from one set can be paired with objects from the other set, the numbers of objects in the two sets are identical. The widths of a door and of a desk may be compared by marking a stick held alongside one and then by placing it against the other. The weights of objects may be compared by placing them on a balance. If the pans remain level, one accepts the two quantities as equivalent. These are only a few examples of a variety of operations that can provide cues to mediate or transfer behaviors that would not occur on the basis of the immediate perceptual cues of the objects involved. In other situations a specific postural adjustment or the response involved in observing might provide appropriate cues.

Language, nevertheless, remains our richest and most convenient source of cue-producing responses, and even in the above situations is quite likely to supplement the nonverbal operations. Furthermore, it appears highly reasonable that language, often identified as man's most distinguishing characteristic, should also account for his problem-solving superiority. It therefore seems to be a highly appropriate and promising topic for investigation by the child psychologist.

From birth to adolescence the child changes from being less adequate than most infrahuman animals at solving problems, to almost full adult competence. Clear superiority of the child to other primates, such as the chimpanzee, does not appear until four or five years of age, the time at which he is presumably first beginning to use language effectively. Thus, it is important to evaluate the precise role that language may play in problem-solving behavior.

Two studies that were completed before the publication of Miller and Dollard's book are particularly relevant to their hypotheses. One was an investigation of transposition by Kuenne (1946). (Transposition is transfer that appears to result from responding to relations among stimuli rather than to an absolute quality of a stimulus. See section entitled "Transposition," this chapter, for details.) Kuenne obtained a correlation between verbalization of size relations and transposition, which has been taken as support for the proposition that the verbal response mediated the transfer of a relational response.

The other study, by Birge (1941), provided the principal experimental basis for much of Miller and Dollard's argument regarding the cue-producing function of language. It will be discussed at some length because it was never published and because so many subsequent studies involved only minor variations in procedure.

Birge's subjects were third, fourth, and fifth grade elementary school students who participated individually in three distinct phases of the experiment (see Figure 7-1). In Phase 1, each child was shown four boxes, identical except for different nonsense shapes drawn on their covers, and was required to learn to call one pair of boxes by the nonsense name "towk" and the other pair by the name "meef." Thus, although the boxes all differed in terms of the shapes on their tops, each box shared a name with one other box.

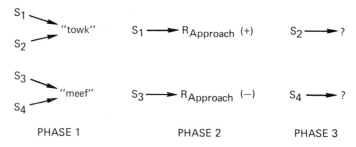

Fig. 7-1. The three phases in the Birge (1941) experiment.

In the second phase only one "towk" and one "meef" box were presented, with candy always found in "towk" and never in "meef" regardless of their spatial position, which varied over trials. After the child had learned to reach consistently for "towk," he was presented with the second pair of boxes. This was the test phase, to determine whether the children would respond in a consistent manner to this new pair. There was no basis for predicting any transfer from stimulus generalization because the nonsense figures were quite dissimilar to one another. Furthermore, how the stimuli were named varied among subjects so that any likelihood of transfer on the basis of stimulus generalization would be balanced over subjects.

The outcome can be reported only after one other aspect of the situation is described. There were four groups in the experiment, required to verbalize in different phases as shown in Table 7-1. Only the first two groups—the only ones required to verbalize during the training phase (Phase 2)—had transfer scores significantly greater than chance level. Thus, although naming did contribute to transfer, it did so only under certain circumstances. More precisely, it was critical that naming occur during Phase 2, when the association of a cue, the reaching response, and candy was taking place.

Dollard and Miller (1950, p. 104) proposed that there are three levels of generalizations and discriminations. The first includes "those based on innate similarities and differences"; the second, "those in which innate similarities or differences are enhanced by appropriate labels or cue-producing responses"; and the third, "those in which labels or other cue-producing responses mediate the transfer of already learned responses." Dollard and Miller used the Birge experiment as an example of the second level, involving acquired equivalence and distinctiveness of cues. That is, the figures that were given the same names were presumed to have become more similar by virtue of the common stimuli (labels) that, once learned, were part of the stimulus complexes. Likewise, the stimuli to which dissimilar names were applied became more distinctive. Birge's data, however, do not support this interpretation. The group that did not use names

Table 7-1

The Verbalization Groups in the Birge (1941) Experiment

	Verbalization of "towk" and "meef"			
Group	Phase 1	Phase 2	Phase 3	Transfer[a]
1	Required	Required	Required	85
2	Required	Required	Not required	77
3	Required	Not required	Required	62
4	Required	Not required	Not required	54

[a] Percentage of group choosing critical box in Phase 3.

after training in Phase 1 (Group 4) showed no evidence of transfer. Nor was there any transfer when the names were used in the transfer test if they had not been used in Phase 2, when the approach response was learned (Group 3). Thus, it would appear that Birge's study is better taken as an example of the third level, that is, as an example of mediated generalization, rather than the second level of acquired equivalence and distinctiveness of cues, because transfer did not occur unless there was training directed specifically toward connecting the instrumental reaching response to the cue-producing response (the label).

Stimulus Predifferentiation

Before describing additional research along these lines it is necessary to consider an alternative to the acquired equivalence-distinctiveness explanation for the effects of labeling, since potential alternative explanations dictate the control conditions that are required for an adequate test of a specific hypothesis. In a theory of verbal learning, Gibson (1940) proposed that the process of learning to associate different responses to different stimuli reduces the amount of generalization among the stimuli, that is, differentiates the stimuli. Thus, learning different labels for different stimuli differentiates the stimuli, and the stimuli could be said to be *predifferentiated* in any subsequent learning situation in which they appeared. The more dissimilar the labels, the more readily the predifferentiation would occur; but in contrast to the acquired distinctiveness of cues notion, once predifferentiation had occurred the labels would no longer serve any important function. In other words, the effect was assumed to result from altered perception, perhaps attributable to observing responses and attention, rather than to result from the addition of cues.

A study by Gagné and Baker (1950) was designed to demonstrate the effects of stimulus predifferentiation. In a two-phase study, experimental subjects first learned to associate labels (letters) with four different stimuli presented successively, for 8, 16, or 32 trials, then learned to associate push buttons with the same stimuli. A control group learned only the button-pushing response. The experimental, pretrained subjects were significantly superior on the button-pushing task to the control subjects, who were given no pretraining. Note that the control group had no warm-up experience, that is, no experience with either the stimuli or the experimental situation prior to the test task. (Warm-up could have been controlled, for example, by having the control subjects learn to label an irrelevant set of stimuli. For further discussion, see Chapter 8.) Therefore, warm-up rather than stimulus predifferentiation could have produced the superior performance of the experimental subjects; if it did, the group difference should have disappeared relatively quickly, since warm-up would quickly develop in the control group during training on the button-pushing task. However, the fact that there was still a difference between the experimental and control groups after 60 trials on the button-pushing task, suggests that factors other than warm-up were critical. Even so, it is impossible to determine whether the facilitation on the button-pushing task resulted from predifferentiation or acquired distinctiveness.

According to the acquired distinctiveness hypothesis, the labels must continue to occur in order to contribute to the distinctiveness of the stimuli; but according to the predifferentiation hypothesis, the role of the labels ends at the end of pretraining. Since it is possible that the labels continued to occur at a covert level in the transfer task, the two hypotheses seem to provide equally tenable explanations of the Gagné and Baker results. Actually, however, the stimuli were quite distinctive to begin with—red and green lights occurring in well-separated positions—and therefore it is unlikely that there was much predifferentiation to be done, or distinctiveness to be added. It is more likely that having learned to associate the letters (V, M, J, and S) with the lights, the experimental subjects used the letters for between-trial rehearsal, for example, "V goes with upper left, M with upper right." Such activity would most certainly facilitate performance on the transfer tasks.

Jeffrey (1953) designed a study to compare more specifically the acquired distinctiveness and predifferentiation hypotheses. He reasoned that if nonverbal motor responses were used in place of verbal labels, it should be possible to ensure that the responses did not occur after the pretraining phase. If this were possible, then facilitation in a group so treated would support the predifferentiation hypothesis, and failure of this group to show transfer would support the acquired distinctiveness hypothesis.

In a five-stage design, illustrated in Table 7-2 for just one counterbalancing group in one condition, all children were first trained either to push or to pull a lever on the appearance of a black or white stimulus patch. Next, Stage 2 was a test for generalization to a gray stimulus that had been carefully chosen to produce maximal conflict. In Stage 3, the children learned two cue-producing responses to the three stimuli. Half of the subjects learned to make the same cue-producing response to gray as to white, and the other half learned to make

Table 7-2

Basic Design of the Motor Mediation Condition in the Jeffrey (1953) Experiment

Stage 1 (Motor training)	Stage 2 (Test 1)	Stage 3 (Attaching mediator to stimuli)	Stage 4 (Attaching test response to mediator)	Stage 5 (Test 2)
S_B——R_{push}	S_B——R_{push}	S_B——R_{right}	S_B——R_R–S_R——R_{push}	S_B——R_R–S_R——R_{push}
S_W——R_{pull}	S_W——R_{pull}	S_W——R_{left}	S_W——R_L–S_L——R_{pull}	S_W——R_L–S_L——R_{pull}
	S_G——?	S_G——R_{left}		S_G——R_L–S_L——?

the same cue-producing response to gray as to black. Group 1 learned verbal cue-producing responses, "white" and "black"; Groups 2 and 3 learned motor cue-producing responses, turning the lever 45 degrees to the left to one stimulus and 45 degrees to the right to the other two, or *vice versa*. These second two groups were treated differently only in the fourth stage. It was in Stage 4 that the link between the cue-producing response and the original instrumental pushing or pulling response was established in the verbal label group (Group 1) and one of the motor "label" groups (Group 2). For example, if a subject had learned to push to white in Stage 1, and turn left to white in Stage 3, he now learned to associate left turn and push and to associate right turn and pull, thus associating the push-pull test response with the turning response or label. For the other motor "label" group (Group 3) the turning response was no longer permitted. This group was given only more trials of pushing and pulling to white and black.

In the final test situation (Stage 5), the gray stimulus was presented again. The children of Groups 1 and 2 would be expected to respond to the gray stimulus with the cue-producing response that had been attached in Stage 3, followed by the push-pull response that had been associated with that cue-producing response in Stage 4. However, if Group 3 showed similar transfer even though the test response had never been associated with the "label" learned in Stage 3, this would support the predifferentiation hypothesis and the transfer of the other two groups could be attributed to the same mechanism.

As is so frequently the case with experiments that are expected to provide a critical test of a hypothesis, the results were somewhat ambiguous. Each group differed from the others. The verbal mediation group (Group 1) showed the most transfer; the motor mediation group (Group 2) showed the next most; and the "predifferentiation" group (Group 3) showed the least. Nevertheless, this last group did show a significant change in transfer from pretest to posttest in the appropriate direction. Therefore, on the basis of the performance of this last group one is forced to conclude either that predifferentiation was a factor or that even with a nonverbal motor response, incipient movements might occur, as in subvocal speech, and provide either a mediator or an enhancing stimulus. It should be noted, however, that the transfer effects in this last group were slight in comparison with those that resulted from mediation training, and thus the weight of the evidence indicates the importance of the cue-producing function of the responses.

TRANSFER IN DISCRIMINATION TASKS

Acquired Distinctiveness and Equivalence of Cues

ACQUIRED DISTINCTIVENESS.   After the Jeffrey study, a number of studies appeared that concentrated on identifying the mechanism involved specifically in the acquired distinctiveness of cues paradigm. Whereas the design of the Birge and Jeffrey studies was a three-stage mediation paradigm that assured the association of the transfer response with the cue-producing response, the designs of these later studies followed the two-stage paradigm more common in transfer research.

A series of studies by G. N. Cantor (1955), Norcross and Spiker (1957), and Spiker and Norcross (1962) is of particular interest because the stimuli—line drawings of children's faces—were similar, though not identical, from experiment to experiment. Furthermore, these studies represent a concerted effort to demonstrate that transfer results from acquired distinctiveness of cues rather than predifferentiation. The Norcross and Spiker (1957) experiment provides a good example of this research and of the problems of control inherent in such experiments (see also Spiker, 1956c).

The stimuli were drawings of two boys' faces and two girls' faces, differing in the way the hair, eyes, and mouth were drawn. The boys' faces are shown in Figure 7-2. Seventy preschool children were divided into two age levels and assigned to three different training groups. The groups had the same transfer task, in which the girls' faces were used as stimuli, but had different preliminary tasks. One group learned initially to call the two girls' faces by the names Jean and Peg. This was the "relevant training group," that is, the group given the treatment expected to produce acquired distinctiveness. The other two groups were control groups. To control for warm-up effects, one group learned in Phase 1 to name the two boys' faces Jack and Pete. This was irrelevant to the transfer task, in that the boys' faces were used, but provided comparable learning experience other than contact with the relevant stimuli. The second control group was shown the girls' faces two at a time in Phase 1; on some trials identical pictures of one face were presented, on other trials identical pictures of the other face were presented, and on still other trials the two different faces were presented together. The children in this group were required to say whether the two faces presented on a trial were the same as or different

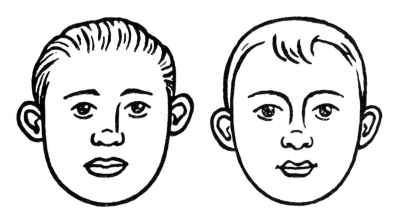

Fig. 7-2.   The boys' faces used in the Norcross and Spiker (1957) experiment.

from one another. This training was presumed to require the children to attend to differences between the stimuli without associating distinctive labels with them. Pretraining continued in each group until a criterion of 12 successive correct responses was met.

For the transfer task the girls' faces were attached to the front surfaces of wooden boxes, presented two at a time as in the Birge experiment. Each child was given 30 presentations of these two boxes with a marble consistently present under one. In case of error the experimenter pointed to the box containing the marble but the child was not permitted to obtain the marble.

The pretraining tasks were equal in difficulty, but had different effects on the transfer task. The mean correct responses in the 30 trials on the transfer task for the relevant, irrelevant, and same-different groups were 22.5, 19.0, and 18.2, respectively. The mean for the relevant labeling group differed significantly from the means of the other two groups, which did not differ significantly from each other. Although these data provide conclusive evidence that labeling the relevant stimuli has a facilitative effect beyond warm-up, the "same-different" control does not necessarily assure the development of observing or attending responses comparable to those that may result from labeling training. The response of recognizing sameness or difference is a relatively easy one and probably requires less in the way of information processing than does associating specific responses with specific cues.

A particularly surprising result of the Norcross and Spiker experiment is that the children in the two control groups had as much difficulty as they did. The stimuli, as can be judged from the examples in Figure 7-2, were readily discriminable on the basis of several cues; and if labels were helpful, children might provide their own, not necessarily proper names but possibly labels of distinctive features. Most adults would probably respond immediately to these stimuli with such responses as "straight hair," "small mouth," or the like; and even if they did not do this as they saw the stimuli, they might at least apply such terms if asked to describe the stimuli, even in the absence of the stimuli. It is known, however, that young children are not as likely to apply or utilize labels as are older children, a condition Reese (1962c) has referred to as a mediational deficiency. Flavell, Beach, and Chinsky (1966) suggested that this deficiency represents not only a failure of younger children to utilize language in problem solving but also a general lack of cognitive maturity, that is, a failure to attack learning problems appropriately. (For further discussion, see section entitled "Age Trend in Efficiency of Mediation," this chapter.)

Spiker (1956e, 1960, 1963b) has suggested as an alternative to both the acquired distinctiveness and predifferentiation hypotheses that labels may facilitate learning or transfer because they provide devices that can be used in rehearsal. Adults are likely to use labels in this manner. In the absence of the stimuli they may say, "Jean had the marble," or "The left button goes with Jean." They may also use imagery for purposes of rehearsal, for example, they may "see" the face on the button. There are apparently individual differences in the degree to which one mode or the other is used, and it is unfortunate that so little research has been done on these possibilities, because they seem to be very important to an understanding of transfer. (For discussion of imagery in paired associate learning, see section entitled "Variables Affecting Learning," Chapter 6.)

In a second study, Spiker and Norcross (1962) made a special effort to equate the pretraining experience of the attention (same-different) and labeling groups, first by having the attention group spend as much time on the pretraining task as the labeling group, and also by having one attention group make the same-different comparisons with the stimuli presented successively. A successive same-different discrimination forces a comparison in the absence of one of the two stimuli, and therefore seems to require a different process from that required in a simultaneous comparison. (What is compared with the second stimulus in a successive comparison is a question that has too long been ignored. What does it mean to say one "remembers" a stimulus? More will be said about this question later.) Nevertheless, the successive same-different judgment appears to come closer to requiring the type of perceptual or encoding response that is inherent in the labeling training; if so, it would provide a more adequate control for attending responses.

It is important to remember the precise purpose of this control group. The experimenters' intent was to show that for transfer to occur it is critical that the label become part of the stimulus complex. Because the predifferentiation hypothesis suggests that the label is unnecessary, they wanted to make certain that another group was given equal "experience" with the stimuli, but that the stimuli remained unlabeled in this group. It is difficult to determine whether the successive same-different judgment does actually accomplish this purpose.

The experimenters also equated the number of exposures to the stimuli for all groups by pairing each child in the same-different groups with a child in the labeling group and then continuing the training of the same-different child for as many trials as it took the paired labeling child to attain a criterion of 12 consecutive correct responses. These added trials do not necessarily ensure that additional learning occurred, and in fact the same-different discrimination even with successive presentation was considerably easier than learning to label. Intuitively, it seems that an easier task must require less differentiation of the stimuli than a more difficult task does.

The results of the Spiker and Norcross study showed that the successive same-different discrimination did not produce any more transfer than the simultaneous same-different training and, in agreement with the results of the earlier experiment, both same-different groups took significantly longer to reach criterion on the transfer task than the labeling group. Careful analysis of the transfer task data, however, indicates that the performance of the labeling group does not provide strong support for the acquired distinctiveness hypothesis. If the labeled stimuli were actually more distinctive at the end of pretraining, then the labeling group should show superior performance from almost the very beginning of the transfer task. As can be seen in Figure 7-3, this result was not obtained. Although all groups would indeed be expected to start performing at a chance level, as they did, no consistent differences appeared until the last three blocks of trials and only in the last two blocks did the labeling group differ significantly from either of the other groups. As Spiker and Norcross suggested, one cannot rule out rehearsal as an explanation for these data; and in fact such an explanation fits the data better than either the acquired distinctiveness or predifferentiation interpretation. The reason is that rehearsal functions like extra training trials; the subject gives himself these extra trials by rehearsing during the intervals between the formal training trials (Spiker, 1960).

A similar result was obtained in children by G. N. Cantor (1955) and in college students by J. H. Cantor (1955); the curves of the experimental and control groups diverged, with little difference in the early trials. However, in other studies with children (Reese, 1961a) and college students (Dysinger, 1951; McAllister, 1953; McCormack, 1958), the effect appeared very early in the transfer task, as the acquired distinctiveness hypothesis requires.

ACQUIRED EQUIVALENCE. Additional research on the issues discussed above has dealt with the acquired equivalence hypothesis. Of particular interest is a study by Reese (1960). He used three pairs of stimuli—two reds, two greens, and two blues—that had previously been demonstrated to be equally difficult to discriminate within pairs. In a pretraining session, different amounts of labeling training were given with each pair, and different groups of subjects learned low similarity, medium similarity, and high similarity labels. Figure 7-4 shows performance on the transfer task as a function of the three levels of similarity of the labels and the three levels of pretraining. Considering, first, only the medium similarity group, one sees that with a medium amount of pretraining

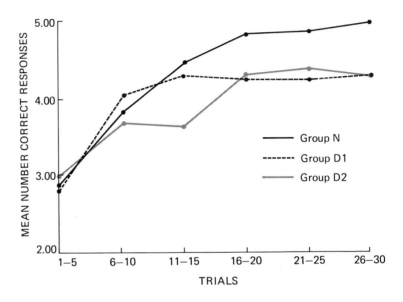

Fig. 7-3. Transfer task performance in the Spiker and Norcross study (1962). Dark solid line, labeling group; dashed line, same-different group; light line, same-different group with successive stimulus presentations. (From Spiker and Norcross, 1962, Fig. 1, p. 862. Copyright 1962 by the Society for Research in Child Development, Inc. Reprinted by permission of the authors and publisher.)

there was indeed interference, as predicted by the acquired equivalence hypothesis, but with additional pretraining this interference disappeared and positive transfer was obtained.

This shift from interference to positive transfer with increased pretraining suggests an alternative to the acquired equivalence explanation. It is well known from studies of verbal learning that when similarity among either response or stimulus items is high, learning is retarded. Thus, for any fixed number of trials in the Reese experiment, it is likely that the distinctive label group learned more than the similar label groups. If so, facilitation would be expected with distinctive labels but not with similar labels. With sufficient training to establish the appropriate associations, similar labels would no longer result in interference, but in positive transfer. Thus, Reese would predict that if the group with the highest similarity labels were given more pretraining than was used in his experiment, positive transfer would be obtained in this group also. The precise source of the interference in the early part of learning is not entirely clear (see Reese, 1960; Spiker, 1963b), but it is clear that once similar cues are well associated with the stimuli, interference no longer results. Therefore, this experiment does not support the acquired equivalence hypothesis, which would assume that the similar labels would continue to influence transfer adversely, unless one assumes that similar labels become differentiated during the process of learning to associate them with stimuli. Although this is definitely possible, it is then equally possible that the cues with which the labels are being associated are going

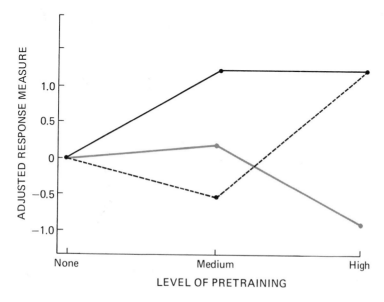

Fig. 7-4.   Facilitation (positive values) and interference (negative values) as a function of level of pretraining and similarity of stimulus labels in the Reese (1960) study. Dark solid line, low similarity; dashed line, medium similarity; light line, high similarity. (From Reese, 1958, Fig. 1, p. 27. Reprinted by permission of the author.)

through a similar process, and the argument would agree more with the predifferentiation hypothesis than the acquired equivalence hypothesis.

In an excellent review of the research on transfer of stimulus pretraining, in which the best evidence for the acquired distinctiveness and acquired equivalence hypotheses is marshalled, Cantor (1965, p. 56) concluded: ". . . we are not likely to find that any of the hypotheses are either 'correct' or 'incorrect.' Rather, we will probably find that the particular stimuli, responses, and designs used will determine the relative importance of verbal cues and observing responses."

More generally, it should be noted that in much of the research involving stimulus pretraining with children the stimuli presented no great discriminal challenge, at least as far as the receptors are concerned. In many instances there were discrete stimulus attributes that could be selected readily, and even when the stimuli were from a single stimulus dimension, differentiation could have hardly challenged the limits of the receptors. Thus, one suspects that other variables, such as learning set formation and cue selection or attention, may be rather critical variables in the studies reviewed so far. (Learning set is discussed in Chapter 8; attention is discussed in the next section and more fully in Chapter 9.)

In spite of the difficulty of providing independent measures of observing responses or attention, there has been a considerable increase in research on this topic over the last several years. It is hardly a new topic in psychology, but interest in it had been submerged by research within the models discussed above.

Stimulus Predifferentiation

Predifferentiation requires a different learning model from that considered in relation to the acquired distinctiveness and equivalence of cues. Rather than assuming that all stimuli are undiscriminated until differential responses are attached, one can assume a separate process of a perceptual or attentional nature that at least partially precedes the associative process. This is not a new idea but it had been more popular among people concerned with perception and physiological psychology than with learning theorists, and it therefore seldom influenced the research on discrimination learning and transfer. There are, however, a number of theories that represent only slight variations on the basic idea. Predifferentiation within an attention model is presumed to result from the occurrence of any operation that causes the subject to interact with the cues. Learning distinctive labels for stimuli would provide a particularly effective basis for stimulus predifferentiation because of the ease of making the responses and because the responses are less likely to interfere with responses to be learned in transfer even if they continue to occur. The labels are important, however, because they provide the occasion for predifferentiation and not because of any differential cue value.

In spite of the potential efficiency of language, possibly the best support for the predifferentiation hypothesis comes from Lawrence's (1949) research on rats. Although he spoke of acquired distinctiveness of cues, his concern was not with response-produced stimulation but with whether learning to attend to specific cues in one type of situation would transfer to another situation. For example, would training rats to discriminate black from white in a simultaneous task facilitate their learning the same discrimination in a successive task? The responses to be learned were not the same in the two tasks. In the simultaneous task the rat learned to approach one stimulus, and was equally often rewarded for turning right or left; in the successive task the rat learned to turn right to one stimulus and left to the other. Thus, there could not be any transfer of the instrumental response from the first task to the second. Since Lawrence obtained evidence of facilitation, a predifferentiation or attention explanation appears appropriate. That the subjects were rats makes it unlikely that any sort of symbolic responses could have occurred and served a cue-producing function. More recent research, by Wagner, Logan, Haberlandt, and Price (1968), provides even stronger evidence for an attention explanation. They found that a cue element that was only partially correlated with reinforcement tended to be utilized only if no other available cue element was more highly correlated with reinforcement, rather than in proportion to its correlation with reinforcement as would be predicted by a single-stage S-R theory (see Figure 5-1 for the model of a single-stage theory).

In a study with human adults, Kurtz (1955) demonstrated that when compound stimuli were used, the same training procedures could lead to positive or negative transfer depending on whether the cue dimension utilized in pretraining was the same as or different from the dimension that was critical in the transfer task. When the cue to which responses were reinforced in pretraining was irrelevant in the transfer task, transfer was delayed, presumably because of continued attention to the wrong cue. Kurtz assumed that it is observing responses that transfer, that is, cue selection responses, which he defined as "any response which, when made to one or the other of a given pair of stimulus complexes which are different, consistently results in distinctive stimulation from those two complexes" (Kurtz, 1955, p. 290). Thus, he did not suggest or require that this response be a gross receptor orienting response, nor did he suggest that its importance lies in its cue properties. Rather, he proposed that it is a response that results in distinctive stimulation from two or more stimuli. There is a certain vagueness in this definition—because no identifiable or measurable response is indicated—which is likely to make the S-R psychologist uncomfortable. However, even in the acquired distinctiveness paradigm, which has been popular with S-R psychologists, the identified response that produces the enhancing cues is often not an *observed* response but is only a *presumed* response, such as subvocal speech, and no one has ever unequivocally demonstrated its occurrence during a transfer task.

Zeaman and House (1963) proposed a two-stage theory of discrimination learning that has had considerable influence on research on transfer. According to the theory, the first stage involves an attentional process, identifying the relevant stimulus dimensions, and the second stage involves an instrumental learning process, associating the response with specific values on these dimensions. (The theory is discussed in detail in Chapter 9, in the section entitled "Attention." The data from studies of "discriminative shifts" are also discussed there, even though these are transfer conditions, because of their particular relevance to the Zeaman and House theory.)

This two-stage or two-link theory obviously differs from two-link theories involving cue-producing responses in that it does not assume an articulate organism. Furthermore, it is of particular interest that Zeaman and House spoke specifically of attention rather than of observing or receptor orienting responses. The latter terms have the advantage of suggesting a potentially measurable response, while attention suggests cue selection activities at a nonobservable level. In short, it has mentalistic connotations. When Kurtz defined observing responses as "any response . . . which consistently results in distinctive stimulation from those two complexes," it is very likely that he was not really concerned with receptor adjusting responses but rather with cue selection involving central nervous system mechanisms, or attention; but when Kurtz made this statement, in 1955, "attention" was not a popular term in the *Journal of Experimental Psychology*, where his report was published.

Transposition

THE EXPERIMENTAL PROBLEMS.   Any kind of transfer that appears to result from responding to relations among stimuli, as opposed to absolute stimulus qualities, is called *transposition*. For example, suppose that a subject is given a discrimination learning problem with two stimuli having areas of 4 and 8 square inches, that he is taught to choose the 8 square inch stimulus, and that he is then given a test with two stimuli having areas of 8 and 16 square inches. The subject can choose the 8 square inch test stimulus, which is the same absolute size as the positive training stimulus, or he can choose the 16 square inch test stimulus, which is the same *relative* size as the positive training stimulus. The latter choice would be a transposition response, because it appears to be based on the size relation.

It is important to note that it is not asserted that transposition *actually* indicates relational responding, but only that it *appears* to indicate relational responding. The reason for characterizing transposition in this cautious way is that when the term is used properly, it refers to an empirical fact, the occurrence of transfer, and not to the mechanism that causes the transfer. Saying that transposition actually indicates relational responding would be making an assumption about the underlying mechanism.

The identification of transposition as a kind of transfer distinct from other kinds resulted from the historical importance of transposition to Gestalt psychologists. They interpreted it as actually demonstrating relational responding, and hence as demonstrating the existence of a stimulus property—the relation—whose existence was denied by associationistic psychologists (see Reese, 1968). The ensuing controversy generated a large amount of research on transposition, and it has therefore continued to be treated as a distinct kind of transfer.

Transposition has usually been studied in two-stimulus and intermediate-stimulus problems in which the stimuli vary along a single dimension, as illustrated in Table 7-3. In the sample problems in Table 7-3, the stimuli in Set C are presented during training, and responses to Stimulus 5 are rewarded. After the subject learns to choose Stimulus 5 consistently, he is presented with one of the other stimulus sets as a test for transposition. *Transposition* is the choice of the test stimulus that has the same relative size as the positive training stimulus; an *absolute* response is the choice of the test stimulus that is the most similar in absolute size to the positive training stimulus; and an *error* is any other choice.

The difference or "distance" between two stimulus sets is measured in terms of "steps." For example, Sets B and D (in Table 7-3) are each one step from

Set C, and Sets A and E are each three steps from Set C. One-step tests are sometimes called "near" tests, and tests with greater separations are called "far" tests.

SURVEY OF THEORIES AND DATA. The theoretical and empirical material selected for discussion in this section represents only a small part of the literature on transposition. The survey is based on Reese's (1968) comprehensive review of the literature dealing with the problem, and therefore documentation of the empirical generalizations is by and large omitted (for references, see Reese, 1968; see also Riley, 1968, Ch. III).

Table 7-3

Sample Unidimensional Transposition Problems[a]

Problem	Stimulus set	Stimuli	Test-trial responses[b]		
			Trans.	Abs.	Error
Two-stimulus	A	1,2	2	2	1
	B	3,4	4	4	3
	C	4,5	—	—	—
	D	5,6	6	5	—
	E	7,8	8	7	—
Intermediate-stimulus	A	1,2,3	2	3	1
	B	3,4,5	4	5	3
	C	4,5,6	—	—	—
	D	5,6,7	6	5	7
	E	7,8,9	8	7	9

[a] Assume training on Set C with Stimulus 5 positive. The stimuli are ordered on some dimension, and are numbered in order of increasing magnitude. (From Reese, 1968, Table 1-1, p. 14. Reprinted by permission of the author and Academic Press, Inc.)

[b] Trans., transposition; Abs., absolute.

The Gestalt theorists, as already mentioned, explained transposition as resulting from relation perception. Other theorists attempted to show that the phenomenon can be explained without assuming relational responding. Spence (1937, 1942), for example, used principles of conditioning and generalization to account for transposition, assuming that only the absolute properties of stimuli are sensed. According to his theory of two-stimulus transposition, the positive training stimulus (Stimulus 5 in the example in Table 7-3) acquires a tendency to evoke an approach response as a result of the reinforcements of this response during training; and the negative training stimulus (Stimulus 4 in the example) acquires a tendency to inhibit the approach response as a result of the non-reinforcements received during training. These two tendencies generalize to other stimuli, but the generalized tendency becomes weaker as the similarity to the training stimuli decreases. These assumptions are illustrated in Figure 7-5, in which the height of each curve represents the strength of the generalized tendency.

Spence assumed that the net response-evocation potential of any stimulus is determined by the difference between the excitatory and inhibitory tendencies of the stimulus, including conditioned tendencies and generalized tendencies.

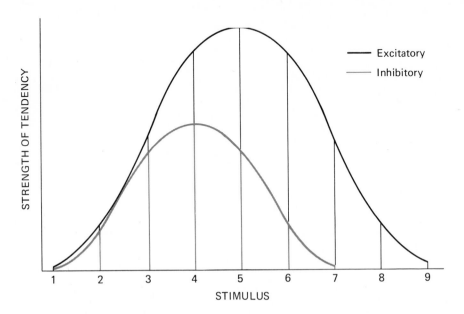

Fig. 7-5. Generalization of excitatory and inhibitory tendencies in two-stimulus problems: Spence's (1942) assumptions. (From Reese, 1968, Fig. 9-2, p. 275. Reprinted by permission of the author and Academic Press, Inc.)

In Figure 7-5, the dark portions of the vertical lines represent the differences between the excitatory and inhibitory tendencies of the stimuli.

When two stimuli are presented simultaneously, the subject will tend to approach the one having the greater net response-evocation potential, and the strength of the tendency to approach this stimulus is determined by the amount by which its net response-evocation potential exceeds the net response-evocation potential of the other stimulus. Comparison of the dark portions of the vertical lines in Figure 7-5, representing the net response-evocation potentials, indicates that the theory predicts transposition in Sets B and D (3 vs. 4 and 5 vs. 6), it predicts absolute responses in Set E (7 vs. 8), and it predicts chance-level responses in Set A (1 vs. 2). The theory, then, predicts a decline in transposition with increasing separation between the training and test sets. This decline is referred to as the "distance effect."

To deal with intermediate-stimulus transposition, Spence (1942) added an assumption about the way the inhibitory potentials of the two negative stimuli combine.[1] The dashed line in Figure 7-6 represents the combined or net inhibitory tendency, and the dark portions of the vertical lines represent the differences between excitatory tendency and net inhibitory tendency. Comparison of these portions shows that the only set in which the intermediate stimulus should be chosen is the set used in training (Stimuli 4, 5, and 6). In the other sets, the stimulus that is most similar in absolute size to the positive training stimulus has the greatest net response-evocation potential, and therefore the theory pre-

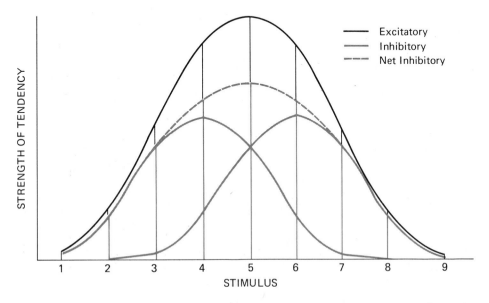

Fig. 7-6. Generalization of excitatory and inhibitory tendencies in intermediate-stimulus problems: Spence's (1942) assumptions. (From Reese, 1968, Fig. 9-4, p. 278. Reprinted by permission of the author and Academic Press, Inc.)

dicts that no intermediate-stimulus transposition should occur. Only absolute responses should occur.

The predictions of Spence's theory differ from the predictions of Gestalt theory in many ways, two of which are implied in the foregoing presentation. Spence's theory predicts a distance effect in the two-stimulus problem and predicts that no transposition will occur in the intermediate-stimulus problem. Gestalt theory predicts consistent transposition in both problems, with no distance effect as long as the relational cues remain invariant.

[1] With reference to the example in Table 7-3, the assumption would be that the net inhibitory tendency of Stimulus a is equal to $I_4 + I_6 - (I_4 \times I_6)/H_5$, where Stimulus a is any stimulus in the series, I_4 is inhibition generalized from Stimulus 4 to Stimulus a, I_6 is inhibition generalized from Stimulus 6 to Stimulus a, and H_5 is excitatory tendency generalized from Stimulus 5 to Stimulus a.

Spence designed his theory to account for transposition in nonarticulate subjects, that is, in subjects lacking an appropriate linguistic repertoire. Kuenne (1946) extended the theory to include articulate subjects, proposing that the performance of nonarticulate subjects conforms with Spence's predictions, but that the performance of articulate subjects is controlled by mediation. For example, if a child labels the stimuli "larger" and "smaller," he learns during training to avoid the stimulus that he calls "smaller" and to choose the one he calls "larger" (in the sample two-stimulus problem in Table 7-3). During the tests, he should continue to avoid any stimulus that he labels "smaller" and should continue to choose any that he labels "larger." It might be noted that the predictions of the mediation model are the same as the predictions of Gestalt theory. This is reasonable, since the child cannot label the relative sizes unless he can perceive and respond to them.

Kuenne tested these predictions in a study of two-stimulus transposition in young children, and obtained generally confirmatory results. The distance effect was obtained in "nonverbal" children (who were unable to name the relative sizes), and consistent transposition was obtained in most of the "verbal" children (who were able to name the relative sizes). She noted, however, that some of the verbal children, especially the youngest ones, behaved as though they were nonverbal, exhibiting the distance effect. On the basis of this finding, she suggested that there may be an early stage of development in which available mediators are not used effectively.

Reese (1961c) compared the performance of verbal and nonverbal children on the intermediate size transposition problem, and obtained two results that were contrary to the predictions. First, the nonverbal children showed the distance effect, instead of exhibiting only absolute responses as predicted by Spence's theory. This result can be explained by a theoretical assumption first suggested by Washburn (1926) and more recently proposed by other investigators (e.g., Stevenson and Bitterman, 1955).

Washburn suggested that the occurrence of transposition may indicate that the subject has failed to notice any difference between the training and test situations. If two situations are not discriminably different from each other, the subject responds to them in the same way. He transposes, not because of relation perception nor absolute generalization, but because of faulty perception. Any condition that makes the two situations more easily discriminable should reduce transposition. Since increasing the difference between sets of stimuli should make the sets more discriminable, the hypothesis explains the distance effect on transposition, in both two-stimulus and intermediate-stimulus problems. That is, on the assumption that many subjects fail to notice the change in stimuli from training to the one-step test, and that most do notice the change in stimuli from training to more distant tests, the hypothesis predicts distance effects in both kinds of problems.

The explanation seems to be especially reasonable because it has been demonstrated that subjects who report noticing the change in stimuli transpose less than subjects who do not report noticing the change, as the hypothesis predicts. Furthermore, short delays between the end of the training period and the beginning of testing increase transposition. Presumably, the subject's memory of the exact absolute sizes becomes hazy during the delay, making it less likely that he will notice the change in stimuli. (Long delays may reduce transposition, but this is not inconsistent with the explanation of the effect of short delays, because it is to be expected that if the memory trace fades too much, the discrimination is lost and therefore transposition cannot occur.) Still further supporting evidence is that increasing stimulus similarity increases transposition, especially on one-step tests and especially when the test is not delayed. When similar stimuli are used, the one-step shift represents a smaller shift in absolute sizes than when distinctively different stimuli are used, and the smaller shift should be harder for the subject to detect.[2]

The second contradictory finding in the Reese study was that the verbal children also exhibited the distance effect, instead of transposing consistently as predicted by mediation theory. The subjects were young children, and therefore this result can be explained on the basis of Kuenne's suggestion. The young verbal subjects, or at least some of them, could have been in the developmental stage in which available mediators are not used effectively. If so, they would be expected to behave as they did; that is, like nonverbal children they should exhibit the distance effect on the basis of the Washburn hypothesis.

The hypothesis explains Reese's finding that nonverbal children exhibit the distance effect in the intermediate-stimulus problem. This finding is typical of studies of intermediate-stimulus transposition in young children. However, the hypothesis by itself does not explain another typical finding: Absolute responses do not predominate over transposition responses at any distance in the two-stimulus problem, but they are usually predominant in the intermediate-stimulus problem when transposition fails to occur. That is, in two-stimulus problems the minimum amount of transposition obtained is at the chance level; but in intermediate-stimulus problems the minimum amount of transposition is well below the chance level, and subjects who do not transpose shift to absolute responses (rather than to random responses or to "error" responses).[3] Washburn's hypothesis does not explain these patterns of absolute responses because the hypothesis is concerned only with the occurrence of transposition, and not with what happens when transposition does not occur. If Spence's theory is accepted, then the predominance of absolute responses in the intermediate-stimulus problem is explained, since his theory predicts that they will occur; but his theory also predicts a predominance of absolute responses at some distance

[2] Spence did not consider the delay variable, but his theory predicts the effect of stimulus similarity. Gestalt theory explains the effect of delay, but did not deal with stimulus similarity (see Reese, 1968).

[3] The generalization about two-stimulus problems does not hold true when (a) the differences between the stimuli are extremely large, for example, when the training stimuli are black and middle-gray and the test stimuli are middle-gray and white, nor (b) the training or testing procedure used emphasizes the absolute qualities of the stimuli. In both cases, absolute responses predominate. The generalization about intermediate-stimulus problems may not hold true when the relative stimulus differences within a set are not constant, for example, when the subject is trained with Stimuli 1, 2, and 8 and is tested with Stimuli 1, 2, and 3 (see Zeiler, 1963).

in the two-stimulus problem, and therefore some additional assumption seems to be required.

There is another finding that is not explained by Spence's theory, even with Washburn's hypothesis added. There have been a few studies of transposition at extreme distances, beyond five or six steps. In some of these studies, it has been found that the frequency of transposition responses at extreme distances is greater than the chance level and is greater than at moderate distances, even in nonverbal children. Thus, the frequency of transposition responses decreases from one step through moderate distances, then increases again at extreme distances. In the intermediate-stimulus problem the effect is particularly striking, because children typically transpose only at one step and at extreme distances, and not at moderate distances. ["Typically" means that standard methods of training are used. Multiple-problem training and verbal training can produce intermediate-stimulus transposition even at moderate distances (see Reese, 1968).]

Reese (1968) suggested that this finding must be interpreted as indicating that both absolute and relative stimulus qualities determine responses. At one step in two-stimulus problems, the generalized absolute response tendency does not conflict with the relational response tendency, since both Spence's theory and Gestalt theory predict one-step transposition. However, at moderate distances, the two tendencies come into conflict, since Spence's theory predicts absolute responses and Gestalt theory predicts transposition. At these distances, there should be about equal numbers of absolute responses and transposition responses in the two-stimulus problem. At extreme distances, beyond the range of absolute generalization, conflict disappears because there is no generalized absolute response tendency, leaving only the relation to determine responses, and transposition should increase in frequency.

At one step in intermediate-stimulus problems, transposition occurs if the subject fails to notice the change in stimuli. Since absolute responses replace transposition responses at moderate distances, it appears that the generalized absolute response tendency is stronger than the tendency to respond relationally. This is reasonable, because the perception of the intermediate-stimulus relation should be more difficult, and therefore less common, than the perception of two-stimulus relations, especially in young children. [The effects of multiple-problem training and verbal training can be explained by assuming that these procedures emphasize the relational cues and increase their effectiveness (see Reese, 1968).] At extreme distances, beyond the range of absolute generalization, responses should be random in subjects who have not perceived the intermediate-stimulus relation, and transposition should occur in those who have perceived the relation. In both cases, there should be more transposition than at moderate distances, where transposition responses are well below the chance level in frequency.

To summarize, the theory includes (a) Spence's theory, to explain the trend in absolute responses in the intermediate-stimulus problem; (b) assumptions about relation perception, to account for the data on absolute responses in two-stimulus problems and to account for the increase in transposition at extreme distances in both kinds of problem; (c) Washburn's hypothesis, to account for the occurrence of intermediate-stimulus transposition at one step in nonverbal children; (d) Kuenne's hypothesis, to account for the consistent transposition obtained in older verbal children; and (e) Kuenne's suggestion about stages in the use of verbal cues, to account for the distance effect obtained in younger verbal children.

There are several possible explanations of the age difference in the effects of verbalization. The one that is most consistent with the available data is that in older children, verbal cues mediate instrumental choice responses, as in the acquired equivalence of cues; but in younger children, verbalizing labels for the relative sizes serves to direct attention toward the relational cues and away from the absolute cues. Young verbal children would be expected to transpose more than nonverbal children, not because of mediation of transposition responses but because of increased attention to relational cues. However, since selective attention would reduce but not eliminate the effects of absolute cues, the distance effects would still be expected in young verbal children.

The effect of verbalization on transposition seems to be reflected in four additional findings: (a) older children transpose somewhat more than younger children; (b) more intelligent children transpose somewhat more than less intelligent children; (c) girls may transpose somewhat more than boys; and (d) children who learn the initial discrimination rapidly transpose somewhat more than children who learn it more slowly. All four findings can be explained by the relation between verbalization and transposition, since verbal children, relative to nonverbal children, are likely (a) to be older, (b) to be more intelligent, (c) to be female, and (d) to learn more rapidly. The relation of verbal ability to age and intelligence is obvious. The relation to sex results from the superiority of girls over boys in language skills (see McCarthy, 1954). The relation to learning speed presumably results from the acquired distinctiveness of cues.

Delayed Reactions

A very old problem used in the study of mediation is the delayed reaction experiment. The issue is how one responds to a cue that is no longer present. For example, if you saw a five dollar bill dropped in one of two identical boxes, you would have no great difficulty choosing the box that had the bill in it once you were permitted to do so, whether you were required to wait 10 minutes, 30 minutes, or even overnight. Such a task seems so simple to us that we hardly stop to think that there is a problem involved. But how do we do it? We remember, but what information is stored, and how is it stored? Language is again an obvious possibility. We remember that the bill is "in the box on the right." If verbalization is required, however, then nonarticulate animals should not be able to perform adequately in a similar test situation. Indeed, rats do not perform very well with delays of more than a few seconds, particularly if not permitted to retain a postural adjustment, such as orientation toward the baited box, during the delay interval. Over the years research has indicated that delayed reactions may be possible in lower animals only for relatively brief periods of time, and typically only when bodily orientation is not grossly disturbed. An ingenious experiment with the octopus demonstrated that even very brief delays were not bridged when the octopus was forced to ooze through a centrally placed hole rather than allowed to swim down an alley to turn toward the site where it had previously seen a crab (Schiller, 1949). However, higher level animals, such as monkeys and chimpanzees, or even raccoons, do very well in delayed response situations. Indeed, in one experiment the performance of chimpanzees on a multiple delayed reaction test was rather amazing (Tinklepaugh, 1932). Ten rooms were prepared by placing on the floor of each room two containers. These were about four to five feet apart and about six feet from where the chimpanzee was to be positioned. The chimpanzee was brought to each room, seated at the designated spot, and allowed to observe a piece of banana being dropped into one of the two boxes. Then without being allowed to retrieve the food, he was led to a second room and the procedure was repeated except that the position of the baited box was randomized. After going through all ten rooms he was taken back to each and was permitted to retrieve the food. Two chimpanzees achieved 90 percent accuracy on this task, a performance that fairly closely approximates that of human adults in a similar situation. When the chimpanzees were returned to the rooms in the reverse order to that in which they saw them baited, their performance was not adversely affected. Also, the chimps showed evidence of dissatisfaction if a piece of lettuce was substituted for the original piece of banana during the delay interval. Monkeys could not perform with such accuracy even on a five-room series.

How do the chimpanzees do so well? To say that they remember begs the question. Unfortunately, too little systematic information is available on the processes involved in this sort of memory task to allow a conclusive answer. It is clear that the organism must be capable of encoding the information in some way and of storing it for considerable periods of time. Motor sets and verbal behavior may be used for these purposes, but neither motor sets nor verbal behavior are necessary for higher level organisms to respond correctly after relatively long periods of time. However, although the chimpanzees performed exceedingly well in the ten-room problem when position was to be remembered, they would do much more poorly if color or form were the critical cue and the boxes were rearranged during the delay. More precise information regarding such differences as this could be helpful in defining the mechanisms involved, although it is possible that any difference between learning with spatial and nonspatial cues would disappear if an appropriate attention set could be assured through pretraining with a suitable learning set procedure.

Spiker (1956e) demonstrated that children who learned different names for two stimuli performed better in a delayed reaction experiment involving these stimuli than children who had had only same-different discrimination training. Although an acquired distinctiveness effect could explain this result, Spiker noted that 9 of 27 subjects spontaneously verbalized the name of the baited box during the delay periods, and he suggested that the subjects who had learned names used them during the delay period to rehearse the choice to be made following the delay period.

Another kind of transfer that is of particular interest because of its implications for perceptual or cognitive structures that go beyond simple S-R connections is cross-modal transfer.

Cross-Modal Transfer

The influence of experiences with stimuli presented in one sensory modality upon responses to stimuli presented in another modality is called cross-modal or intersensory transfer. An example is illustrated in Figure 7-7; students seldom have trouble deciding which of the designs shown should be called "malooma" and which should be called "takete" (Köhler, 1929). Similarly, they should have little trouble deciding which design represents Khachaturian's *Sabre Dance* and which represents Debussy's *Clair de Lune,* provided they know or can hear these compositions (see Osgood, Suci, and Tannenbaum, 1957, pp. 20–24; Will-mann, 1944). These are examples of transfer between the auditory and visual modalities.

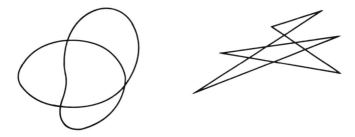

Fig. 7-7.   According to Köhler, it is easy to decide which design to call "malooma" and which to call "takete." (After Köhler, 1929, Figs. 18 and 19, p. 243.)

Another example is transfer between the visual and olfactory modalities. Schiller (1935) trained fish on a discrimination learning problem involving bright and dim lights, then tested for transfer with the compartments unilluminated but infused with musk or indol. Human observers report that musk has a "bright" odor and indol has a "dark" odor. The fish that had been trained to select the brightly lit compartment chose the compartment infused with musk, and the ones trained to select the dim compartment chose the one infused with indol (see Reese, 1968, pp. 217–224, for a review of this study and other studies of cross-modal transfer; see also Pick, Pick, and Klein, 1967, pp. 214–218).

Two experiments by Blank and Bridger (1964) provide additional examples, and illustrate procedures used with children. In one experiment, the children were given a series of problems in each of which one object was presented haptically (that is, the object was hidden from sight but could be touched) and two objects were presented visually. The subject's task was to identify which of the objects presented visually was identical to the object presented haptically. For example, the subject might be shown a cylinder and a triangle and asked to tell which is the same as a cylinder which he is allowed to feel but not to see. (According to Blank and Bridger, the transfer in this kind of task involves "cross-modal equivalence.") In the second experiment, the subjects were required to learn a two-stimulus discrimination with the stimuli presented in one sensory modality, and were then given a transfer problem with two other stimuli presented in another modality. The stimuli were one versus two flashes of light (visual modality) and one versus two auditory beeps. For example, the first problem might require learning that the object emitting two flashes of light is the one to be chosen, rather than the object emitting one flash; if transfer occurs, the object emitting two sounds should be chosen instead of the object emitting one sound. (This kind of transfer involves "cross-modal concepts," according to Blank and Bridger.)

There have been relatively few studies of cross-modal transfer, especially in species below the primate level. However, the available evidence suggests that there are both phylogenetic and ontogenetic trends. The transfer seems to decline with increasing phylogenetic level, since it occurs in fish and rats but occurs rarely in monkeys and young children; but at the human level the phylogenetic trend is superseded by an ontogenetic trend, and the transfer increases with increasing age in children.

Another phenomenon, which is sometimes classified as a kind of cross-modal transfer, is synesthesia. Synesthesia occurs when a stimulus is experienced as a sensation in the modality excited and simultaneously as a sensation in another modality. Technically, synesthesia does not fit the general definition of cross-modal transfer, because although sensations are experienced in two different sensory modalities, stimulation is presented in only one modality. However, as will become apparent, synesthesia has implications for the theoretical interpretation of cross-modal transfer. An example of synesthesia is "colored hearing," in which tones are heard as tones and seen as colors.

Direct evidence of the occurrence of synesthesia cannot be obtained, because the phenomenon involves subjective experiences, which are not objectively observable. However, verbal reports provide indirect evidence. Much of the evidence of synesthesia in young children is anecdotal, based on spontaneous remarks made by children in uncontrolled situations; but in spite of the caution with which such evidence must be treated, three conclusions seem to be justified.[4] (a) Synesthesia occurs in some children. However, it is not clear what proportion of children experience the phenomenon. (b) Synesthesia occurs less frequently as the child grows older. (c) There is consistency within individuals in the nature of the experience, but little consistency between individuals. That is, if a person has synesthetic experiences, they tend to take the same form every time; but the form of the experience may be different in different persons (see Werner, 1948).

According to Lindworsky (1931), synesthesia results from association between a sensation and an image; when sensory stimulation produces the sensation,

---

[4] Additional conclusions are justified but seem to have no direct relevance to child psychology. For example, vision is the only sensory modality that interacts synesthetically with all other modalities (McKellar, 1957).

the sensation arouses the image. For example, in colored hearing, the sensation of a tone produces the image of a color. The assumption that the aroused experience is an image, rather than a sensation, is consistent with Müller's doctrine of the specific energies of nerves, which states that "a nerve end when stimulated at all always gives rise to its own peculiar sensation" (Pillsbury, 1934, p. 201). If the assumption were that the aroused experience is a sensation, it would be inconsistent with this doctrine. However, the assumption that it is an image raises another problem, because it is experienced not as an image but as a sensation. Historically, psychologists were concerned with how a person can tell whether a particular subjective experience is a sensation or an image—How does one know that he is seeing a book and not imagining it? Many of the suggested solutions proposed that the image is distinguishably different from the sensation because the image is weaker or less vivid. In synesthesia, however, the reported "images" are very vivid and are as intense as sensations. Lindworsky recognized this problem, but took it as evidence against the notion that vividness distinguishes images from sensations.

Lindworsky seems to have assumed, in addition, that the association is usually innate, since he said that synesthesia seldom results from the association of accidentally simultaneous experiences. However, Osgood suggested that synesthesia is a product of learned associations (Osgood, 1953, pp. 124, 642–646). This account is similar to Lindworsky's, in that it assumes that a sensation produced by stimulation in one modality arouses an associated image of sensation in another modality; but it differs from Lindworsky's in assuming that the mediating link is a *learned* association.

Another possibility, apparently first suggested by Aristotle, is that there is a supermodal system—a "deeper-lying faculty," the *sensus communis*—which is stimulated by certain kinds of qualities (Strong, 1891, pp. 195–196). According to this interpretation, the synesthetic experience involves actual sensations, and not images.

Werner (1948) also assumed that actual sensations are involved, and that they result from a "primitive organic unity" of the senses. Stimulation in one modality can produce sensations in other modalities because of this unity. The notion is inconsistent with the doctrine of specific energies of nerves; but it is argued that the specificity is lacking in primitive organisms, including young children, and that it develops both phylogenetically and ontogenetically. Synesthesia, then, is characteristic of primitive organisms, including young children, but decreases with increasing phylogenetic level and, in humans at least, with increasing ontogenetic level.

Only Werner's theory explains why synesthesia declines with increasing age level. Furthermore, if it is assumed that cross-modal transfer results from synesthesia, his theory explains why cross-modal transfer is greater in rats and fish than in monkeys, since rats and fish are phylogenetically more primitive than monkeys are. However, this interpretation of cross-modal transfer fails to explain why the transfer increases with increasing age level in children, because synesthesia decreases with increasing age level. It may be that Werner's theory provides the correct interpretation of the phylogenetic trend in cross-modal transfer, and that one of the other theories of synesthesia provides the correct interpretation of the ontogenetic trend. Especially if the association between sensations and images is learned, as Osgood assumed, one would expect an increase with increasing age level. But if a learned association underlies cross-modal transfer in children, there is no reason to assume that the association must be between a sensation and an image. Association between sensations and verbalizations could also account for cross-modal transfer, as Blank and Bridger (1964), among others, have pointed out. In keeping with modern terminology, which avoids such mentalistic terms as "sensation" whenever possible, the assumption can be made that the association is between *stimuli* and images or words.

To summarize, the data are scanty, but suggest a decreasing phylogenetic trend in cross-modal transfer, superseded by an increasing ontogenetic trend in children. The explanation is tentative because of the tentativeness of the empirical generalizations. The suggested explanation is that the phylogenetic trend results from the phylogenetic trend in the unity of the senses; and the ontogenetic trend results from an ontogenetic trend in the learning of associations between stimuli and images or words.[5]

There is another kind of cross-modal transfer, usually called cross-modal integration, which is entirely different from the kinds discussed above. Cross-modal integration refers to the effect of experience or stimulation in one modality upon responsiveness (not specific responses) in another modality. For example, blind children are retarded in development in the tactile-kinesthetic modality (Menaker, 1966), indicating that normal development in the latter modality requires cross-modal integration with visual experience. A similar phenomenon has been demonstrated in cats (e.g., Held and Hein, 1963). Another example is provided by Hartmann's reference to the Dane, Bartholinus, who ". . . reported as far back as 1669 that partially deaf persons could hear better in the light than in the dark . . ." (Hartmann, 1942, p. 179). Cross-modal integration seems to have a physiological basis, but the specific mechanisms or processes involved have not yet been identified.

TRANSFER IN PAIRED ASSOCIATE TASKS

So far in this chapter, transfer in discrimination problems has been considered. Now consideration will be given to transfer between paired associate lists—the influence of the acquisition of one list upon the acquisition of another list. First the classical transfer paradigms involving paired associate tasks are considered briefly, then the paired associate paradigms used in the study of mediation. (See also reviews by Battig, 1966; Kjeldergaard, 1968.) Little child research has been done with the classical transfer paradigms, but much has been done with the mediation paradigms.

[5] Soviet researchers have found that perceptual set can transfer cross-modally, and is more common in older children and adults than in preschool children (see discussion in section entitled "Perceptual Set," Chapter 8). These findings suggest a cognitive basis, at least for this kind of cross-modal transfer.

Classical Problems

The classical transfer paradigms with paired associate lists involve learning an A-B list followed by learning an A-C, A-Br, C-B, or C-D list (see Table 7-4). In the A-B A-C paradigm, for example, the subject learns a list composed of A (stimulus terms) and B (response terms) and then is presented a list in which the stimulus terms are the same (A) but the response terms (C) are new. In the A-B A-Br condition, the stimulus and response items are the same in the A-Br list as in the A-B list but they are re-paired, that is, the responses are paired with different stimuli. All of the transfer conditions tend to produce negative transfer relative to the A-B C-D condition, which is frequently used as the baseline for zero transfer since there is no relation between the stimuli and responses in the two lists. The amount of negative transfer is generally least for

Table 7-4

Classical Paired Associate Designs for the Study of Transfer

Condition	List 1	List 2	Order of interference[a]
Classical interference	A-B	A-C	2
Associative interference	A-B	A-Br	1
Classical interference from backward associations	A-B	C-B or B-C	3
Control	A-B	C-D	—

[a] Typical order from most (1) to least (3) interference produced.

the A-B C-B condition, greater for the A-B A-C condition, and maximal for the A-B A-Br condition (e.g., Twedt and Underwood, 1959).

In an analysis of the transfer paradigms listed in Table 7-4, Martin (1965) argued that the order of interference produced is attributable to the effects of (a) response availability, which should facilitate transfer in the A-B C-B and A-B A-Br conditions but not affect transfer in the other two conditions; (b) forward associations, which should interfere with transfer in the A-B A-C and A-B A-Br paradigms but not affect transfer in the A-B C-D and A-B C-B conditions; and (c) backward associations, which should interfere with transfer in the A-B C-B and A-B A-Br conditions but not affect transfer in the A-B A-C and A-B C-D conditions. As Martin pointed out, the relative effects of the three variables can be manipulated by varying the characteristics of the materials, the amount of learning, and other aspects of the task. It should also be noted that the analysis of these paradigms is concerned with the specific transfer effects of one list upon another; nonspecific transfer effects (see Chapter 8) are irrelevant but are controlled because these effects are common to all of the paradigms and are therefore automatically subtracted out of comparisons.

As both Keppel (1964) and Goulet (1968b) pointed out, child psychologists have contributed very little to the literature in this area. There have been a few scattered studies, but certainly no systematic efforts have been made. Gladis (1960), for example, studied *A-B C-B* transfer in third, fifth, and seventh grade children. She obtained negative transfer in third grade children but positive transfer in fifth and seventh grade children. Second-list learning, which occurred five minutes, two days, or two weeks after first-list learning, was independent of the amount of time between the lists, but each list included only five pairs and the task may have been too easy to show an effect of time. As a study of transfer, the experiment is not particularly informative, because no *C-D* control list was used and no other transfer lists were included.

Boat and Clifton (1968) studied *A-B B-C* transfer with the appropriate control (*A-B D-C*) included, and obtained significant interference in the experimental group. The subjects were four years old. Daehler and Wright (1968), however, obtained no significant interference in first graders (*A-B C-A* versus *A-B C-D*).

Spiker (1960) conducted a series of three experiments in which fifth and sixth grade children learned an *A-B* list followed by a list composed half of *C-D* pairs and half of *A-C* pairs. In the first experiment, fifth grade children were given either 6 or 15 trials on the *A-B* list. Increasing the amount of first-list learning increased the amount of interference; there was no difference between *C-D* and *A-C* learning in the 6-trial group, but there was interference with *A-C* learning, relative to *C-D* learning, in the 15-trial group. Instructions to rehearse or use mnemonics during first-list learning were given in the second two experiments, and produced the same effects as increasing first-list practice.

Finally, one other study should be mentioned here, in which an *A-B C-B* transfer task was used to determine what developmental differences in transfer might occur as a function of the relation between the *A* and *C* items. Rice and Di Vesta (1965) used a transfer task in which the stimuli of the second list were homonyms, antonyms, or synonyms of the first-list stimuli and the responses were nonsense syllables. The subjects were third, fifth, and seventh grade children and college students. The results indicated that the basis for generalization or transfer shifted from physical stimulus similarity (homonyms) at the younger ages to semantic similarity at the older ages. All groups generalized to the homonyms; semantic transfer was not shown by the third grade children but became increasingly apparent in the three older groups.

The negative transfer in the learning of the second list in the *A-B A-C* condition is referred to as "classical interference." When memory is tested in this design, interference with retention of the second list is called "proactive interference" (*A-B, A-C*, rest, recall *A-C*), because the first-list learning presumably produces the interference with second-list recall. Interference with retention of the first list is called "retroactive interference" (*A-B, A-C*, recall *A-B*), because the second-list learning is presumed to have interfered with retention of the first-list associations. (Some psychologists have argued that "reproductive interference" would be a better term, since "retroactive" seems to imply action toward the past, but the phrase has never become popular.) As pointed out in Chapter 6 (section entitled "Memory"), there has been little research on retroactive and proactive interference effects in children's paired associate learning. There were a few studies done in the 1930s (e.g., Houlahan, 1937; Lahey, 1937; Matousek, 1939) but, as Keppel (1964) has noted, in light of present knowledge of methodology, the results of those studies are not very helpful. More recently there has been some interest in retroactive interference in retarded as compared to normal subjects, but little has been found to suggest that the two populations differ very much in forgetting (e.g., Cassell, 1957; McManis, 1967).

House, Smith, and Zeaman (1964) studied transfer of learning to learn in retardates. ("Learning to learn" is a nonspecific source of transfer. See section entitled "Learning Sets," Chapter 8, for further discussion.) Subjects approximately 12 years old with a mean IQ of 52 learned 10 successive paired associate lists and recalled each list 24 hours later. A significant decrease in errors to criterion was observed from first- to tenth-list learning, indicating that learning to learn did transfer over the series of lists. In addition, evidence for proactive interference was found in a significant decrease in the amount recalled after 24 hours from the first to the tenth list.

One rather extensive study in this area is particularly worthy of note. Koppenaal *et al.* (1964) were interested in testing the implication of interference theory (Postman, 1961; Underwood and Postman, 1960) that forgetting of laboratory-acquired paired associate lists is attributable to interference from verbal material learned before entering the laboratory. Assuming that young children have had less opportunity than older children to acquire verbal habits and that those that have been acquired are weaker, Koppenaal *et al.* argued that there should be an increase with age in the forgetting of verbal materials learned in the laboratory. In three experiments, four, five, and eight year old children learned an *A-B* list of four pairs, followed by an *A-C* list of four pairs, and then were given a test for recall of the responses 24 hours later. One group at each age level was required to recall the first-list responses, to provide a measure of retroactive interference; another group was required to recall the second-list responses, to provide a measure of proactive interference; a third group was required to recall the responses of both lists; and a control group which learned only a single list was required to recall the responses of that list.

The results are of particular interest because the performance of the eight year old children was quite comparable to the performance of college students in that considerable interference was exhibited in all measures of recall. However, the five year old children did not exhibit proactive interference and the four year old children exhibited neither proactive nor retroactive interference. None of these differences was obtained, however, in experienced subjects, who had had previous laboratory experiences with paired associate learning. While these data raise a number of problems for future research in this area, the experiment provides an excellent example of the contribution that might be made to the understanding of verbal behavior by research directed toward theoretical questions that may be answered by employing children as subjects.

With the exception of the Koppenaal *et al.* study, there is no evidence that the use of children has been seen as useful to the understanding of retroactive and proactive interference.

Mediation

While little work has been done with children in the traditional transfer paradigms, many studies of mediation have been conducted. "Mediation" refers to the intervention of some process between the initial stimulating event and the final response. More specifically:

A temporal sequence of stimulus-response events in which a mediating response and stimulus may be distinguished can be represented as $S_{Initiating}$——$R_{Mediating}$ $\sim$ $S_{Mediating}$——$R_{Terminating}$ . . . . Ideally, two criteria must be met in order for responses and the stimuli they produce to be considered mediating responses and stimuli. The first criterion is the observation of or grounds for inferring the occurrence of one or more responses subsequent to the initiating stimulus and before the terminating response. The second criterion is the demonstration that such temporally intermediate responses and stimuli have actual or potential facilitative or inhibitory effects on one or more measures of the occurrence and strength of the terminating response. (Goss, 1961, footnote 3, pp. 249–250.)

Three basic paradigms have been used to demonstrate mediation effects in the paired associate situation (Jenkins, 1963). These paradigms are listed in Table 7-5 and are described below.

Table 7-5

Paired Associate Designs for the Study of Mediation

Name of design	Symbolic representation of design
Chaining	
Mediated facilitation	A-B, B-C, A-C
Mediated interference	A-B, B-C, A-Cr
Response equivalence	B-A, B-C, A-C
Stimulus equivalence	A-B, C-B, A-C
Typical control	A-B, D-C, A-C

The first paradigm has been referred to as the chaining model. The subject is required to learn a series of lists of paired words; each successive list has as its stimuli the responses of the previous list, except that the final list, which is the test for mediation, is composed of the stimuli of the first list and the responses of the last preceding list. In the three-stage paradigm, the subject learns A-B, then B-C, and finally A-C or A-Cr. (In A-Cr, the C responses are scrambled—"reversed"—in such a way that mediated C responses are incorrect.) It is assumed that learning of the pairs in the final list is influenced by the mediating *B* term which links the *A* and *C* terms as a result of the learning in the previous lists. Thus, the subject has an acquired sequential chain of associations from *A* to *B* to *C*, which facilitates *A-C* learning and interferes with *A-Cr* learning.

The second type of design has been referred to as the response equivalence paradigm. The subject is required to learn several different responses to the same stimulus; as a result, these responses become equivalent in the sense that presenting one as a stimulus will tend to elicit the others as responses. In the three-stage paradigm, the subject learns *B-A*, then *B-C*, and finally *A-C*. Mediation is tested in the *A-C* list. Again it is assumed that learning the *A-C* pairs in the final list is influenced by the mediating *B* term, which is associated with both the *A* and *C* terms by the previous list learning.

The third type of design is known as the stimulus equivalence paradigm. Here the subject is required to learn the same response to several different stimuli. The task is quite similar to the response equivalence task except that the equivalence is developed on the stimulus side. The stimuli come to have equivalence in the sense that presenting one as the stimulus will tend to elicit the others as responses. In the three-stage paradigm, the subject learns *A-B*, then *C-B*, and, as in the previous paradigms, he is tested for mediation on an *A-C* list. Once again, it is assumed that the *B* term acts as a mediator. In this case, the occurrence of mediation requires both R-S and S-R associations during the learning of the previous lists. When the *A* term is presented in the third list it is assumed to lead to the overt or covert occurrence of *B* by virtue of first-list learning, and the *B* term is assumed to elicit the correct *C* term by virtue of backward (R-S) second-list learning.

The last type of design is a typical control condition, in which no mediating link between *A* and *C* in the test list is learned in the first two lists.

The theoretical analyses of all of these three-stage paradigms have received strong experimental support with adults (see Horton and Kjeldergaard, 1961). In addition, there is evidence to support the mediation interpretation when even more associative links are involved (Russell and Storms, 1955). The materials used in these experiments have included words of high and low frequency, trigrams, and combinations of these. While the literature on mediation with adults is quite extensive, the experiments with children have in many ways been much more impressive, largely because the mediation effects are not limited to the early trials of the transfer task, as they usually are in studies with adults.

Evidence of mediation is usually evaluated by comparison of the *A-C* and *A-Cr* chaining conditions with a control condition which varies from study to study but always precludes a mediating response. It is assumed that the *A-C* pairs test for mediated facilitation and the *A-Cr* pairs test for mediated interference, relative to the control pairs. Thus, most studies provide two tests of the mediation effects, a test of mediated facilitation and a test of mediated interference. Two kinds of list designs have been used. In mixed list designs all three kinds of pairs are included in a single test list; in unmixed list designs separate test lists of facilitation, interference, and control pairs are used.

In one of the early studies with children, conducted by Norcross and Spiker

(1958), the chaining paradigm was used with kindergarten and first grade children. The stimuli and responses were unrelated pictures, and were presented in a mixed list. There was clear positive transfer in the facilitation condition but the interference condition did not produce significant negative transfer. A second experiment by Norcross and Spiker (1958) involved only the control and interference conditions, again in a mixed list, and showed significant negative transfer. Several other studies have provided similar results with this chaining paradigm (Berkson and Cantor, 1960; Boat and Clifton, 1968; Clifton, 1966; Nikkel and Palermo, 1965; Wismer and Lipsitt, 1964; Wu and Lipsitt, 1965). Most of these studies have involved older grade school children, although Berkson and Cantor also demonstrated mediation effects in retarded subjects, and Boat and Clifton demonstrated the effects in four year olds. Nikkel and Palermo

Table 7-6

Design of the Flamer (1965) Study[a]

Group	List 1	List 2	List 3
Facilitation	B-C	A-B	A-C
Warm-up	B-C	D-E	A-C
Classical interference	B-C	A-E	A-C
Mediated interference	B-C	A-Br	A-C
Re-pairing	B-C	A-Cr	A-C

[a] Half of each group learned List 1; the other half were assumed to have learned it pre-experimentally (from norms). The symbols *A* and *D* represent unrelated CVC syllables; *B*, *C*, and *E* are words; *B* and *E* are unrelated.

actually gave only two lists (*B-C* and *A-C*), assuming the first list associations on the basis of word association norms. Evidence of mediation using a variant of the chaining paradigm—*B-C*, *A-B*, *A-C*—has also been obtained (Daehler and Wright, 1968; Nikkel and Palermo, 1965; Odom, 1965, Rieber, 1964b).

One of the most comprehensive studies with children was conducted by Flamer (1965) with the *B-C*, *A-B*, *A-C* design. Flamer was concerned with two problems, the effect of assuming the first-list associations from word association norms as opposed to presenting these associations to be learned in the laboratory and the effect of the type of control condition used in the experiment. The unmixed list design was used. Half of the subjects studied a list of *B-C* word pairs, which were already associated according to word association norms; the other half began with the second list, and it was assumed on the basis of the word association norms that the *B-C* link had already been learned. As shown in Table 7-6, the second list varied for different groups. One group received an *A-B* list, which should facilitate List 3 (*A-C*) learning; another group received a "warm-up" list (D-E), in which neither the stimulus items nor the response items were relevant to the third list; a third group received a classical interference list (A-E), in which the stimuli were the same as in the third list but the responses were different and unrelated to the third list responses; a fourth group received a mediated interference condition (A-Br), in which the pairs were associatively relevant to the third list but incorrectly paired; and finally a fifth group was given a list in which the stimuli and responses were the same as in the third list but re-paired (A-Cr).

The results of this study indicated that training on the associates had only a slight effect upon performance and that the effect was limited to the mediated interference condition. Greater interference was obtained when the associated pairs were actually practiced than when the association was merely assumed from the word association norms. This is an important finding because mediated interference effects are seldom as strong as facilitation effects in studies of mediation.

The order of the groups on the transfer task (List 3), from best to poorest, was as follows: facilitation, warm-up, classical interference, mediated interference, and re-pairing. These results, for sixth grade children, expand and support the findings of Jenkins, Foss, and Odom (1965) for adults and provide very clear and strong support for mediation theory.

Experimental support for the assumptions underlying the stimulus equivalence and response equivalence paradigms has not been as extensive. Two studies have shown mediation in the stimulus equivalence paradigm. In one study the associations were experimentally established (Palermo, 1962), and in the other, one link in the associative chain was assumed from word association norms (S. I. Shapiro and Palermo, 1968). The response equivalence paradigm has been demonstrated to produce facilitation of learning in one study (Palermo, 1966).

It might be noted here that mediation effects have also been demonstrated in a number of tasks which are related to verbal paired associate tasks but in which other kinds of materials and procedures have been used. Eisman (1955) and Di Vesta (1962) have both used the mediation paradigm to demonstrate the development of attitudes and preferences. In addition, Di Vesta and Stover (1962) have shown that evaluative meaning can generalize to new verbal materials via mediation.

AGE TREND IN EFFICIENCY OF MEDIATION

The period from five to seven years of age is a transitional stage in child development. Before the transition, mediation rarely occurs spontaneously; after the transition, mediation is the typical mode of responding. Most of the experimental work on mediation has dealt with extremely simple mediators, such as single words and images, but it should be noted that all cognitive processes meet Goss's (1961) two criteria of mediators—intervention between initial stimulus and terminal response, and effect on the occurrence or strength of the terminal response—and can therefore be classified as mediators. However, they are much more complex mediators than the ones studied experimentally, as Reese (1965a) pointed out.

Mediation could not occur if potential mediators were unavailable in the child's repertoire. Presumably, the lack of potential mediators accounts for some of the deficiency in mediation in children in the pretransition stage, particularly before the age of three years. However, especially near the end of the pretransition stage, around the age of four or five years, it has been demonstrated that mediation may fail to occur even when potential mediators are present in the child's repertoire. In this case, there are several possible reasons for a failure of mediation to occur. Examination of the mediation paradigm, in the paragraph quoted from Goss in the preceding section, shows that there are three associations involved in the chain. First, the initial stimulus must elicit the mediating response; second, the mediating response must produce a "mediating" stimulus of some kind; and third, the mediating stimulus must elicit the terminal response. If any one of these associations is broken, mediation cannot occur.

Flavell *et al.* (1966) have proposed the term "production deficiency" to refer to a breakdown of the first association—failure of the initial stimulus to elicit the mediating response—and the term "mediation deficiency" to refer to a breakdown of the last association—failure of the mediating stimulus to elicit the terminal response (see also Maccoby, 1964a). No theorist has considered the possibility of a breakdown of the middle association, perhaps because this association is assumed to be "given," or perhaps because a breakdown of this association would usually be experimentally indistinguishable from a breakdown of the last association. (Under appropriate conditions the mediating response and mediating stimulus can be made observable. For example, if the mediating response is vocal, the subject can be instructed to vocalize aloud, producing an overt mediating response and mediating stimulus. However, the mediator is usually covert.)

Production and mediation deficiency are usually inferred from observation of the terminal response, since the mediating response is usually not directly observable. For example, if mediation is predicted to facilitate the performance of an experimental group (as in the mediated facilitation design—A-B, B-C, A-C—in paired associate learning) relative to the performance of a control group (A-B, D-C, A-C), mediation is inferred to have occurred if the predicted facilitation is obtained, and is inferred to have failed to occur if the predicted facilitation is not obtained. However, in many designs the inference is not necessarily justified. For example, in the intermediate-stimulus transposition design, mediation is predicted to increase transposition (see section entitled "Transposition," this chapter). Experimentally, the performance of children who have the concept of middle-sizedness is compared with the performance of children who lack this concept. When these two groups differ in the predicted way, mediation is inferred to have occurred in the verbal group; and when the two groups do not differ from one another, mediation is inferred to have failed to occur in the verbal group. However, as Zeiler (1967) pointed out, the failure to obtain the predicted superior performance in the verbal group could result from errors in labeling. Suppose that a child is trained with stimuli having areas of 2, 4, and 8 square inches, and that he correctly labels the middle-sized one. Theoretically, he learns during training to choose the stimulus which he labels "middle-sized." Now suppose that he is tested with stimuli having areas of 4, 8, and 16 square inches. If he labels the 8 square inch stimulus "middle-sized," and if the label mediates the choice response, he will transpose. If, however, he labels the 4 square inch stimulus "middle-sized," and if the label mediates the choice response, he will fail to transpose; since normally the labeling will be covert, the experimenter will have observed only that a "verbal" child failed to transpose, and will infer that mediation failed to occur even though it actually did occur. This kind of error, called a "production error," does occur in young children, according to Zeiler.

Theoretically, there may also be "mediation errors"; the mediating stimulus elicits a response, but not the trained response. Such errors would be fairly readily observable in a paired associate task, but probably not in tasks with limited response possibilities, such as the transposition task.

So far, we have considered four possible causes of the apparent failure of young children to utilize potential mediators. First, there may be a production deficiency, a failure of the mediating response to occur at all. Second, there may be a production error, elicitation of the mediating response by an inappropriate stimulus. Third, there may be a mediation deficiency, a failure of the mediating stimulus to elicit the terminal response. Fourth, there may be a mediation error, elicitation of an inappropriate terminal response by the mediating stimulus. Production and mediation deficiency occur when the stimulus has a low probability of eliciting the response, presumably because the stimulus-response association has not been learned well enough or because the subject is not "set" to perform in that way. (The "set" would be the kind of performance set identified as "technique" in Chapter 8.) Production errors occur when an inappropriate stimulus has a greater probability of eliciting the mediating response than does the appropriate stimulus, and mediation errors occur when the mediating stimulus has a greater probability of eliciting an inappropriate response than of eliciting the appropriate response. These errors might result from transfer from previous learning situations.

White (1965) suggested a fifth cause of the apparent failure of mediation in young children. He pointed out that a mediated response must have a longer latency than an associative response, and that in any situation in which the initial stimulus has a tendency to elicit a mediating response *and* a tendency to elicit some terminal response associatively, the mediated response will not have time to occur before the associative response unless the associative response is inhibited. If the inhibition does not occur, the initial stimulus initiates a covert mediating response and an overt associative response; but the occurrence of the overt associative response terminates the trial. Therefore, it is not that mediation does not occur in the pretransition stage, but that it does not occur *in time*. In White's view, the transition is from an "associative" level of functioning to a "cognitive" level. White considered the development of the ability to inhibit the first-available, associative responses to be the mechanism underlying the transition from the associative to the cognitive stage. In his view, the failure of mediation to occur is but one manifestation of the young child's failure to inhibit first-available responses, a view which he documented by listing other transitions that occur in the same period from five to seven years of age.

The concepts of associative and cognitive levels of functioning resemble the concepts of "impulsive" and "reflective" cognitive styles (Kagan, Moss, and Sigel, 1963). The impulsive style is characterized by short latency responses and a high error rate; the reflective style is characterized by longer latency responses and a low error rate. Impulsives respond quickly but inaccurately; reflectives respond more slowly and accurately. It is tempting to try to coordinate the concepts, but there are differences that remain to be resolved before such a coordination would be justified. For example, (a) special training can result in a shift from the associative to the cognitive level of functioning, but appears to be ineffective in changing the cognitive style of an impulsive child; (b) the shift from the associative to the cognitive stage is closely correlated with age, but hints of both impulsivity and reflectivity can be detected in infancy (see discussion by Reese, 1968, pp. 262–263). White's concepts also resemble Uznadze's concepts of "impulsive" and "objectivated" levels of behavior (Uznadze, 1966, pp. 110–119). Examples of impulsive behavior are ". . . the instinctive activity of an animal, or habitual, mechanised human activity . . ." (Uznadze, 1966, p. 113). When some obstacle arises during the course of impulsive behavior, the behavior is disrupted because the obstacle changes the stimulating situation. The disruption is followed by inhibition of impulsive behavior and the occurrence of an "act of objectivization," which is identified as selective attention directed toward the obstacle.

Finally, Jeffrey (1965) suggested that the apparent deficiency in mediation may result from the use of inappropriate or inefficient mediators. It is not a "production error," because the mediator is aroused by the appropriate stimulus. The child's strategy is correct, but his tactics are unsound; hence, this source of the deficiency in performance might be called a "tactical error." For example, suppose a child is to learn to choose a red card in a red-green discrimination problem. If he labels both cards "colored card," mediation will interfere with performance. His strategy—using verbal labels—is good; but he has made the tactical error of using the same label for both stimuli. Calvin and Clifford (1956) and Calvin, Clancy, and Fuller (1956) obtained results that can be explained by assuming that this kind of error occurred.

The evidence on the deficiency in mediation in young children comes from two kinds of source: studies which provided evidence serendipitously, and studies specifically designed to investigate the deficiency. Reese (1962c) reviewed studies of the first kind (see also Kendler, 1964; Luria, 1957; Maccoby, 1964a; Reese, 1968, pp. 257–263; White, 1965), and clearly demonstrated that the deficiency exists [but see Youniss and Furth's (1963) argument and Reese's (1963d) reply]. The deficiency has been observed in studies of perceptual set (Reese, 1963b, 1963c; Reese and Ford, 1962), transposition (Marsh and Sherman, 1966; Potts, 1968; Reese, 1962a), discriminative shift (see review by Kendler, 1964; Silverman, 1966, failed to obtain the deficiency in this situation), paired associate learning (Milgram, 1967a),[6] lever pressing (Birch, 1966), and short term memory (Hagan and Kingsley, 1968).

There is evidence that the deficiency results largely from a production deficiency (Corsini, Pick, and Flavell, 1968; Flavell *et al.*, 1966; Griffiths, Shantz, and Sigel, 1967; Keeney, Cannizzo, and Flavell, 1967; Milgram, 1967a; see also Flavell, 1970), although mediation deficiency apparently also occurs (Potts, 1968; Reese, 1968). The extent to which production errors, mediation errors, failures to inhibit associative responses, and "tactical errors" occur and contribute to the performance deficiency of young children remains to be investigated. Imaginative research has been conducted, as exemplified by the ingenious techniques developed by Flavell and his co-workers to allow direct observation of verbal mediators (Flavell *et al.*, 1966) and nonverbal mediators (Corsini *et al.*, 1968), and it is to be hoped that this exciting area will attract further creative effort by future investigators.

SUMMARY AND CONCLUSIONS

It should be clear that the problem of transfer is a fundamental and pervasive one in psychology. Concentrated attention on investigating the mechanisms of transfer should provide insights of broad import to child psychology because of their implications for the more general effects of specific experiences on behavioral development.

It has been seen that verbal behavior has provided the focus for much of the research on transfer, but that for the most part this research has pointed increasingly toward the need to include other variables such as attention, as well as other types of symbolic processes. One should not belittle the role of language at a practical level for without question language can serve very important functions. Nevertheless, it is obviously not the only stuff of which symbolic processes are made. Indeed, it may be the potential for the formation of other symbolic processes that permits the development of language rather than the reverse. Future researchers might profitably pay more attention to processes such as imagery, which are for the most part known to us only through introspection. There is much exciting research to be done at this level, given the development of adequate methodology.

Meanwhile, there are some practical implications of what is already known. First, transfer is readily demonstrated as characteristically broader than one would expect, while interference is difficult to demonstrate. It seems that the more children are encouraged to do, the more capable they are likely to be. Second, tasks that children seem unable to perform are likely to be solvable after pretraining that assures (a) comprehension of the problem, that is, acquisition of the appropriate learning set, and (b) attention to the appropriate cues.

[6] Boat and Clifton (1968) obtained mediated facilitation in four year olds in the paired associate situation, but no older subjects were tested and it is therefore not possible to determine whether there may have been a *relative* deficiency. However, their results indicate that there may sometimes be a *deficiency* rather than a *lack*.

Third, one must not overlook the problem of motivation. Although that is a topic of another chapter (Chapter 10), it should be noted here that children's motivation is very strongly controlled by certain kinds of tasks and certain kinds of stimuli. Knowledge of these controlling variables can be put to good use in managing children's problem-solving behavior.

Children exhibit less proactive interference in laboratory learning tasks than adults, as Koppenaal *et al.* demonstrated. This developmental trend is predicted by interference theory. However, one would expect to find individual differences resulting from several years of different everyday nonlaboratory learning experiences, but Koppenaal *et al.* demonstrated that if these are present, they are apparently wiped out by experience in the one laboratory learning task. The latter finding poses a problem for interference theory. Koppenaal *et al.* also demonstrated developmental changes in retroactive interference, since there appeared to be no retroactive interference in the youngest group. Interference theory gives no hints as to why this developmental trend should occur.

CHAPTER 8

Set

INTRODUCTION

As indicated in Chapter 7, it is a well-established principle in psychology that past experience can influence the way a person presently responds to a situation. This influence—or transfer—is said to be *specific* when the source is an associative connection between specific stimuli and specific responses, as in most of the paradigms discussed in Chapter 7. Transfer is said to be *nonspecific* when it results from any other source. Transfer is attributed to these other sources when (a) the stimuli or stimulus values used in the transfer task are different from the stimuli or stimulus values used in the training task, provided they are sufficiently different that transfer cannot reasonably be attributed to stimulus generalization (a source of specific transfer), or (b) the values are the same, but the transfer cannot be explained by the laws of associative transfer. These assertions will be clarified in the discussions that follow.

Nonspecific transfer is sometimes referred to as an effect of *set*. The occurrence of set effects is well established, but there is disagreement about what causes the effects. One problem is that there has been disagreement about what it is that is supposed to be influenced by a set. Another is that psychologists have tended to use the term rather loosely. To take a few examples: (a) Learning an easy discrimination facilitates the later learning of a difficult discrimination (e.g., Spiker, 1959); one explanation is that the subject acquires in the easy problem a "set to discriminate" or "discrimination set" (Cantor, 1962). (b) Warm-up has been called a "performance set" (see below). (c) A tendency to respond to questionnaire items in some consistent but inappropriate way is called a "response set." (d) Learning how to solve problems of a particular kind is called "learning set" (see below). In short, whenever the source of the influence of past experience is not known, it has generally been called some kind of "set."

Set effects can be grouped into three categories: perceptual sets, performance sets, and learning sets. Examples of these are described and discussed in the sections that follow.

PERCEPTUAL SET

Past experience can influence the perception of or response to a present situation. This influence is attributed to *perceptual set*. Examples abound in everyday life as well as in laboratory demonstrations. To cite a few, a hungry man is disposed to look for food; a person's past experience—or life history—influences the way he interprets the relatively ambiguous pictures in the Thematic Apperception Test and the inkblots in Rorschach's test; a weight seems lighter if it is lifted after a series of heavier weights have been lifted; being instructed that a particular class of words will be presented tachistoscopically increases the recognizability of words of that class, but not the recognizability of words of other classes.

According to one interpretation, perceptual set influences the percept itself; that is, the situation is perceived in a different way because of the past experience. According to a second interpretation, set influences the response to the situation, or memory of the situation, but has no effect on the actual perception of the situation. The disagreement, in other words, is about whether set affects the percept or only the response (see Haber, 1966).

The phenomena mentioned above, and identified as examples of perceptual set, are sometimes classified as examples of "cognitive set" (e.g., Bugelski and Alampay, 1961). There have been few studies of the effects of perceptual or cognitive sets in children, and especially few in which the set was experimentally induced.

Soviet researchers have investigated a perceptual set that involves an illusory size relation (see Uznadze, 1966). The set is induced by giving training trials in which a large ball is placed in one of the subject's hands and a smaller ball is placed in his other hand. (In some of the experiments other methods of inducing the set were used, for example, presenting a large and a small circle tachistoscopically.) The larger ball is always presented in the same location, in the right hand, for example. On test trials, the balls presented are equal in size. The illusion induced seems in some cases to be an "assimilative" illusion—the ball in the right hand appears to be larger—and in other cases to be a "contrast" illusion—the ball in the left hand appears to be larger. The set can transfer cross-modally, that is, it can be induced in, say, the haptic (touch) modality and can transfer to the visual modality. This cross-modal transfer, however, is less common in preschool children than in older children and adults (see Uznadze, 1966, pp. 33–35, 83–84, 141, 212–213). The set seems fairly clearly to have a cognitive basis.

A series of experiments by Reese is illustrative of the problems involved in child research on perceptual set, even though it allows no firm conclusion to be drawn about the nature of the causal mechanisms involved. The background of the studies was provided by an experiment by Bugelski and Alampay (1961) with college students as subjects. The subjects in their study were given a set-inducing experience, involving for one group the presentation of from one to four unambiguous drawings of animals—dog, cat, etc.—and for another group the presentation of one to four unambiguous drawings of human faces—child, man, woman, etc. Then the subjects were shown the ambiguous drawing illustrated in Figure 8-1.[1] Subjects who were set to see animals should report seeing

[1] Bugelski had prepared the ambiguous figure shown in Figure 8-1 "to illustrate the bias of some psychologists who view men as rats or vice versa" (Bugelski and Alampay, 1961, footnote 2, p. 205).

a mouse or rat, and subjects set to see human faces should report seeing a bald-headed man (wearing large glasses). Bugelski and Alampay found that the sets were successfully induced by the exposure of even one unambiguous figure.

Theoretically, on set-inducing trials the subject identifies the conceptual class exemplified by the unambiguous figures—"animals" or "faces" in this case—and the concept becomes conditioned to some "ready signal" such as the removal

Fig. 8-1. Bugelski's "rat-man" ambiguous figure. (From Bugelski and Alampay, 1961, Fig. 1, p. 206. Copyright 1961 by the Canadian Psychological Association. Reprinted by permission of the authors and publisher.)

of the previous picture or the introduction of the next picture. The concept then functions as an "expectancy," and may affect either the percept of the ambiguous figure or the verbal response used to label the ambiguous figure (see Haber, 1966, especially p. 338; Reese, 1963b). The concept is assumed to serve as a mediator of the subsequent behavior, whether the subsequent behavior is perceptual or verbal.

There is evidence that young preschool children who possess concepts that are relevant to a problem often behave as though they lacked these concepts. Reese (1962c) has referred to this phenomenon as a "mediational deficiency" in young children (see section entitled "Age Trend in Efficiency of Mediation," Chapter 7). On the assumption that mediation is necessary for the occurrence of the perceptual set effect and on the basis of the known mediational deficiency in young preschoolers, Reese (1963b) predicted that the kind of set effect demonstrated by Bugelski and Alampay should be weaker in young preschool children than in older children. The subjects used to test the prediction were younger and older preschool children, kindergarten children, and first and second grade children. They were divided into three groups, one given set-inducing trials with six unambiguous drawings of animals, one given set-inducing trials with six unambiguous drawings of human faces, and one given control trials with six unambiguous drawings of inanimate objects (telephone, key, ship, etc.). Bugelski's "rat-man" figure was used to assess the effect of set. The results supported the prediction; there was no significant set effect at the youngest age level, and there were significant set effects at the older levels.

Two possible causes of the failure to obtain a set effect at the youngest age level, aside from mediational deficiency, are that the six set-inducing trials were too few to be effective at this age level, or that they were ineffective because the children failed to identify the conceptual class. To test these possibilities, Reese (1963c) trained three groups of young preschoolers, one with the same six unambiguous drawings of human faces used in the first study, one with these six set-inducing drawings and six additional ones exemplifying the same conceptual class, and one with the six faces each identified as a "person" by the experimenter. The first condition replicates one of the conditions of the first experiment, the second condition doubles the amount of training, and the third condition explicitly identifies the conceptual class. Reese found that the differences among the groups were small and statistically insignificant. (There were 36 children in each group; the set effect was exhibited by 24 in each of the first two groups and by 26 in the third group.) Therefore, it can be concluded that neither increasing the amount of training nor identifying the conceptual class affected the strength of the set effect at the preschool level. However, with respect to the latter part of the conclusion, it should be emphasized that what was demonstrated was that the *experimenter's* verbalization of the name of the conceptual class did not influence the set effect. It was not demonstrated that verbalization of the concept by the child himself would be ineffective.

In an attempt to obtain more direct evidence on the child's spontaneous identification of the conceptual class exemplified by the set-inducing figures, Reese and Ford (1962) gave preschoolers the same human-set and animal-set conditions as used in the first study, except that after the training series had been given and before the ambiguous figure was shown, the child was asked to guess what the next picture would be. The purpose of the study was defeated by the subjects, all but one of whom gave as expectancies specific members of a conceptual class rather than the name of the conceptual class. However, it was found that 80 percent of the children with expectancies consistent with the induced set also reported percepts that were consistent with the set, but only 38 percent of the children with expectancies inconsistent with the induced set reported percepts that were consistent with the set. If it is assumed that the expectancies were mediated, then even though the expectancies stated were, almost without exception, not names of conceptual classes, it can be concluded that the children whose expectancies were consistent with the set-inducing training did in fact identify the conceptual class during training. This would explain why many more of these children reported consistent percepts than did the children whose expectancies were inconsistent with the set-inducing training, and it further suggests that the cause of the relatively weak set effect in young children is a failure to identify the conceptual class. It may be that the reason no facilitation of the set effect was obtained in the previous study when the experimenter identified the conceptual class for the child was that the child failed to attend to the instructions. (Experimental child psychologists are in general agreement that young children are prone to do this.)

In the final study in the series, Reese (1965a) attempted to induce children to utilize verbal mediators spontaneously, by first giving a kind of learning task that theoretically required mediation and then giving the perceptual-set task. The results were ambiguous, because although the trained group exhibited a stronger set effect than a control group, the obtained difference was not statistically significant.

To summarize, training designed to induce a perceptual or cognitive set is less effective in younger children than in older children, apparently because many of the younger children do not spontaneously identify the conceptual class of which the training figures are members.

The theoretical rationale of the Reese studies involved the assumption that the effect of the set is on responses rather than on percepts. Haber (1966) concluded that both kinds of effect can occur; but he suggested further that the effect on response probabilities, which is the effect assumed by Reese, can be attributed to a reorganizing effect of set on memory. It is possible to conceptualize both kinds of effect—on responses and on percepts—as results of the same underlying process. It can be assumed that the sensory input is stored, unanalyzed, in short term memory, which persists only briefly, and that it can be retrieved from short term memory only through a coding process. This process may be verbal—in the form of a label describing the input—or perceptual—in the form of a memory image, usually a visual image. Assuming that the effect of set is on the coding process would explain the effect on responses and on percepts. An ambiguous input can be verbally encoded in several ways, but if the stimulus figure is appropriately constructed, only one way of encoding is consistent with the set or expectancy, and therefore the probability of actually encoding in this one way is enhanced. Similarly, the ambiguous input is consistent with several unambiguous memory images, but one image is consistent with the set and therefore has an enhanced probability of occurring as the encoded or remembered input. Whether verbal or perceptual encoding will occur or, for that matter, whether both kinds of encoding will occur simultaneously, may depend upon the availability of appropriate "codes" of each kind for the particular stimulus used.

The mechanism by which set affects the encoding process might be selective attention. As noted in Chapter 11 (section entitled "The Role of Motivation in Children's Perception"), motivation and needs affect perception, perhaps because of some kind of attentional process. The same kind of mechanism seems to underlie "preparatory sets," which are induced by instructions. For example, Maccoby and Konrad (1967) presented two messages simultaneously, one read by a man and the other by a woman, and instructed the subjects to report one of the messages, either the man's or the woman's. The instruction was given either before the messages were delivered or immediately after they were delivered. The effect of preparatory set was demonstrated, since it was found that the instruction was more effective when it was given before the messages than after the messages. The investigators interpreted the results in terms of central attentional processes.

These attentional processes, and the way they might produce the set effect, seem to fit Sokolov's theoretical model for the orientation reaction, which is discussed in detail in Chapter 9.

PERFORMANCE SETS

The performance sets that have been identified are (a) warm-up, (b) the development of exteroceptive observing responses, (c) the development of internal attentional responses, (d) the reduction of emotionality, (e) the development of appropriate "techniques," and (f) discrimination set (see Bugelski, 1956; Miller, 1948; Spence, 1960).

Warm-Up

Warm-up is the development of postural adjustments that facilitate performance, according to Kimble (1956), and should be most important in tasks involving motor responses, particularly when fast reactions are required. (Postural adjustments that are inappropriate could presumably be acquired, and would interfere with performance; but then the transfer would not be called "warm-up.") It presumably also includes learning the rhythm of stimulus presentations—learning when to look—and "getting with" other aspects of the experimental situation (see Irion, 1948). The training and transfer tasks need not be the same; guessing colors presented at random, for example, can facilitate performance on a verbal paired associate task (Thune, 1950).

Observing and Attentional Responses

Observing and attentional responses are considered in other chapters (Chapters 7, 9, and 11, particularly), but it might be noted here that attentional responses can be verbal—verbal responses that classify stimulus elements or identify stimulus dimensions (see, e.g., D. M. Johnson, 1961; Kendler, Kendler, and Learnard, 1962; Luria, 1961; Reese 1962c; Simon and Newell, 1962).

Emotionality

The reduction of emotionality should facilitate performance for two reasons, according to Spence (1956, 1960). First, as sources of drive, emotions increase the relative differences among the reaction potentials in the response hierarchy, and therefore interfere with performance when an incorrect response is dominant (see Chapter 10, section entitled "Conflict"). Reduction of emotionality would reduce the relative dominance of the incorrect response. Second, as sources of internal stimulation, emotions may produce responses that compete with the instrumental responses; even if the correct response is dominant in the unemotional state, it may not be dominant in the emotional state because of these competing responses (see Reese, 1961b). Interference would be reduced by extinguishing the competing responses aroused by the emotion, or by reducing emotionality and hence the stimuli that would elicit the competing responses.

For example, if a child is confronted with a difficult discrimination learning problem, he will make a large number of errors on the early trials. Theoretically, each error is a failure and frustrates the child. The built-up frustration may evoke a withdrawal response, and since the child cannot learn the discrimination if he leaves the scene, the frustration-produced response would interfere with performance on the task (see, e.g., Spiker, 1956b; Steigman and Stevenson, 1960; Stevenson and Pirojnikoff, 1958). Preliminary training that reduced the emotional reaction to the early failures would therefore facilitate performance.

Techniques

"Technique" is used here to mean "problem-solving strategy." It refers to the way a subject goes about solving a problem of a particular type; for example, "use verbal mnemonics" (e.g., Milgram, 1967a), "form images of interactions between stimulus and response items," "rehearse between trials," "formulate and test hypotheses." Over a series of problems, a subject might try a variety of techniques. If he shifts to more appropriate techniques, his performance will improve.

Discrimination Set

Discrimination set may be a "technique" or it may be the same as selective attention. The concept of discrimination set has been invoked to explain why training on an easy discrimination facilitates learning a difficult discrimination, a phenomenon demonstrated in children by Barnett and Cantor (1957) and Spiker (1959), among others (see Cantor, 1962; the phenomenon is discussed further in the next chapter). If discrimination set is the same as attention, then the assumption made is that the appropriate attentional responses develop earlier in an easy discrimination problem than in a difficult one (Spiker, 1959). This assumption explains the effect if the stimuli in the two tasks differ on the same dimensions, as they did in Spiker's study. If the relevant dimensions of the first task are present but irrelevant in the second task, the transfer of attentional responses would result in interference with performance, since attention to an irrelevant dimension would interfere with observation of the relevant dimensions. Interference has been obtained in this condition (e.g., Bensberg, 1958; Kurtz, 1955), further supporting the assumption. However, if the stimuli in the two tasks differ on different dimensions, as they did in Barnett and Cantor's study, the attentional responses developed in the first task would be irrelevant in the second task, and there could be no facilitation of performance from this source. The transfer in this case could result from the reduction of emotionality. This source could also explain Spiker's results, but not the results of Bensberg and Kurtz.

If the discrimination set is a "technique," then it would be unnecessary to invoke the emotionality principle to explain Barnett and Cantor's data. As a "technique," discrimination set would explain their results and Spiker's results, but it would fail to explain the Bensberg and Kurtz results. Whatever the correct explanation might be, it is clear that discrimination set is not a unique source of transfer, since the transfer that is attributed to discrimination set is actually attributable to other sources.

Conclusions

It should be apparent that attributing transfer to "performance set" is not a useful explanation unless the particular performance set and its presumed mode of operation are specified. The term "performance set" covers a heterogeneous group of mechanisms, which operate in different ways to produce their effects. The only common characteristics are that all are nonspecific with respect to particular stimulus values, and all but one can develop in one kind of task and transfer to a different kind of task. Technique is the exception. Discrimination set is not an exception if it is actually the same as selective attention; as a technique it would be an exception, requiring that both tasks be discrimination problems. Furthermore, although attentional responses can tranfer when the specific stimulus values are different, they cannot transfer unless the transfer task involves at least one dimension that is the same as in the training task. However, the dimension that is the same can be irrelevant—position, for example, in an object discrimination problem—since learning to ignore an irrelevant dimension would facilitate learning what is relevant. Similarly, the only constant "dimension" underlying transfer of observing responses can be the loci at which relevant stimuli appear, irrespective of what the stimuli are.

LEARNING SETS

The terms *learning set* and *learning to learn* have been used to refer to improvement in performance across a series of problems that have a common basis of solution but different stimuli. Specific kinds of learning sets are identified by reference to the kind of problems in the series. For example, discrimination learning set refers to improvement over a series of discrimination learning problems, and reversal learning set refers to improvement over a series of reversal problems. In each example, there is a common basis of solution—learning to choose one object and to avoid the other or learning to reverse a choice immediately after it is nonreinforced. A different set of stimuli is used for each problem in the series. For example, the series might include a horizontal-vertical discrimination, a red-green discrimination, a square-circle discrimination, and others. Since new stimuli are used on each new problem, associative transfer seems to be ruled out as a source of the interproblem improvement; the extent of the contribution of performance sets will be considered later.

Discrimination Learning Set

Instead of a general survey of the research on learning sets, detailed consideration will be given to one kind. The one most appropriate for detailed consideration is discrimination learning set, since it has been more extensively investigated than the others. [See Reese (1963a) for a review of discrimination learning-set studies with children, and Reese (1964) for a review of the studies with rhesus monkeys.]

In typical discrimination learning-set studies, subjects are given some small fixed number of trials on each problem, instead of enough trials to attain a learning criterion. A pair of stimulus objects is presented for the selected number of trials, and the left-right position of the correct object is varied from trial to trial; then a new pair of objects is introduced to initiate the next problem and the fixed number of trials is given; then another new pair is introduced, and the procedure continues, typically, until enough problems have been given to indicate learning set. Many investigators have continued to introduce new problems until the subject is able to solve each new discrimination in a single trial. Whether the subject guesses correctly and chooses the correct object on the first trial of the new problem, or guesses incorrectly and chooses the incorrect object, he will choose the correct object on the remaining trials of that problem. Since one-trial learning has been called "insight" (e.g., Köhler, 1925), it could be said that learning set culminates in insightful learning.

A detailed example will illustrate the procedure in typical studies of discrimination learning set. Levinson and Reese (1967) manufactured a thousand "junk" objects by first collecting numerous pieces of scrap lumber, broken toys, strips of metal and rubber, tin cans, and other junk, then haphazardly spraying the heap with various colors of paint, and finally nailing or gluing together randomly selected pieces. The thousand objects were divided into five hundred pairs, using a table of random numbers, and one object in each pair was selected as the "correct" object by a coin toss. Thus, the construction of the objects was haphazard, the pairing was random, and the designation of correct objects was random. A given pair of objects was used in only one discrimination problem. Therefore, there was no physical attribute of the stimuli that could serve as a systematic basis of solving the problems.

Four trials were given on each problem; one pair of objects was presented for four trials, then the next pair for the next four trials, and so on until the subject attained a learning-set criterion. The criterion was a sequence of five problems on which a total of no more than one error occurred, exclusive of errors on the first trials. That is, on the five criterional problems, there were five first trials, five second trials, five third trials, and five fourth trials, and the criterion allowed no more than one error out of the 15 responses on the second, third, and fourth trials. The five first trials were not counted, since on these trials a subject can be correct only by chance.

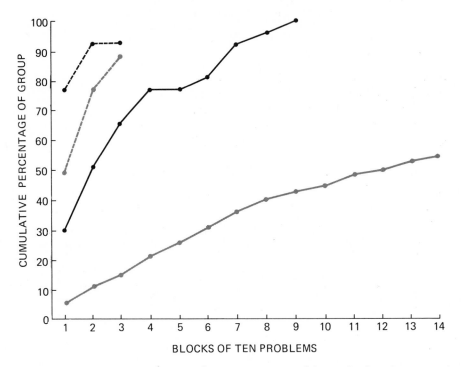

Fig. 8-2. Cumulative percentage of age groups reaching criterion in successive blocks of problems. Dark dashed line, college; light dashed line, fifth grade; dark solid line, preschool; light solid line, aged. (From Levinson and Reese, 1967, Fig. 27, p. 64. Copyright 1967 by the Society for Research in Child Development, Inc. Reprinted by permission of the authors and publisher.)

Levinson and Reese used the procedure with preschool children, fifth graders, college freshmen, and several samples of old people ranging in age from 61 to 97 years. Figure 8-2 shows the percentage of each group reaching criterion in each successive block of 10 problems. The efficiency of learning-set formation increased from the preschool to the college level, then declined sharply in old age. (However, there were marked differences among the different samples of old people, apparently largely because of differences in the amount of social and intellectual stimulation available to them.) The median number of problems required to attain the learning-set criterion (including the five criterional problems) was 20.4 at the preschool level, 10.8 at the fifth grade level, 6.7 at the college level, and about 120 at the old-age level.

There were other differences among the age groups, but these were highly technical differences and need not be discussed here. However, one salient finding that needs to be considered was a striking similarity across age groups in the shape of the learning-set acquisition curves. Levinson and Reese divided the subjects at each age level into relatively homogeneous subgroups on the

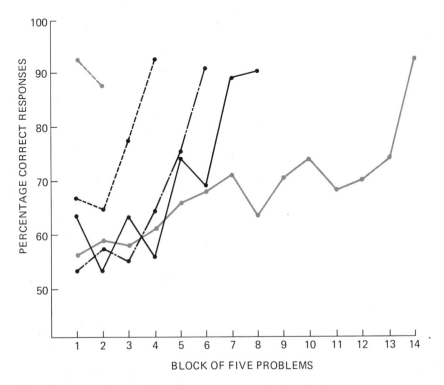

Fig. 8-3. Learning-set acquisition curves of preschool criterion-reference subgroups (combined Trials 2, 3, and 4). Light dashed line, 10-problem subgroup; dark dashed line, 20; dark broken line, 30; dark solid line, 40; light solid line, 70. (From Levinson and Reese, 1967, Fig. 3, p. 13. Copyright 1967 by the Society for Research in Child Development, Inc. Reprinted by permission of the authors and publisher.)

basis of the number of problems required to attain the learning-set criterion. (This is the so-called criterion-reference method of forming homogeneous subgroups, and is discussed briefly in Chapter 9.) Figure 8-3 shows the performance of the preschool subgroups in blocks of five problems. The curves appear to have two phases, an early phase in which performance improves only gradually and a second phase in which performance improves rapidly. The subgroups differ in the duration of the first phase, and do not differ in the second phase. [Similar curves were obtained by Hill (1965) and Harter (1965, 1967) at the preschool level.] In general, the same kinds of two-phase curves were obtained at every age level, and at every age level the subgroups differed in the duration of the first phase and did not differ in the second phase.

Reese (1965a) studied discrimination learning set in preschool children, but trained them to a criterion of five consecutive correct responses (excluding the first-trial response) on each problem before proceeding to the next problem. New problems were continued until the subject attained a learning-set criterion of five consecutive problems including at least three solved in the minimum possible number of trials (six trials) and the other two solved with no more than one error on each (excluding first-trial errors). The subjects required a median of 5.9 problems to attain the learning-set criterion, including the 5 criterional problems; therefore, learning one problem to criterion resulted, on the average, in the formation of a learning set.

In contrast to children, whose learning-set acquisition is rapid even with only four trials per problem, monkeys generally require well over a hundred problems to attain the level of one-trial learning, and no subprimate species has ever been demonstrated to be capable of attaining this level of performance (Harlow, 1959).[2] There appears to be a qualitative discontinuity between the subprimate and primate levels, and a quantitative discontinuity within the primate level between subhuman and human species. Therefore, it seems reasonable to assume that there are two kinds of source of interproblem improvement in learning-set tasks. One, presumably operating at all phylogenetic levels, is performance set; the other, apparently operating only at the primate level but operating there with varying effectiveness, is symbolic processing (see Reese, 1963a).[3]

There are two reasons for assuming that the interproblem improvement in performance in subprimates is attributable to performance sets. First, the asymptotic levels of performance attained by subprimates are well below the level of one-trial learning; and second, the interproblem improvement generally develops relatively rapidly. The specific performance sets involved might be warm-up, the development of appropriate observing responses, learning to ignore position (an attentional response), learning to search for and compare the distinctive features of the stimuli (a kind of "technique"), and the reduction of emotionality. These would be expected to develop relatively rapidly, but would not be expected to produce one-trial learning. It may be that the first-phase improvement in the curves of homogeneous human groups reflects largely the influence of the same kinds of performance sets, and they presumably affect the performance

[2] Subprimate species studied include cats (Meyers, McQuiston, and Miles, 1962; Warren, 1959; Warren and Baron, 1956; Warren and Kimball, 1959), raccoons (Johnson and Michels, 1958; Michels, Pustek, and Johnson, 1961; Shell and Riopelle, 1957), pigeons (Zeigler, 1961), and rats (Koronakos and Arnold, 1957; Lawrence, 1952; Wright, Kay, and Sime, 1963). The best subprimates are raccoons. Johnson and Michels (1958), for example, found that after learning each of 8 problems to criterion, raccoons solved each of the remaining problems in a median of 12 trials, the minimum possible number of trials to criterion. However, the percentage correct responses on Trials 2 through 12 of each problem seemed to be asymptotic at about 80 percent, and Trial 2 performance was no better than 70 to 75 percent correct by the end of training.

[3] A third possible source of the interproblem improvement is associative transfer, but the explanation is much too technical to warrant consideration here (for details, see Reese, 1964).

on early problems in subhuman primates. (However, no investigator has ever reported curves for homogeneous subgroups of monkeys.)

There are two theories that include an assumption of symbolic processing. According to Restle's theory (1958, 1960, 1962), there are three kinds of cue in the learning-set situation. There are "type-*c*" cues, which are irrelevant in all problems; "type-*b*" cues, which are relevant in a single problem but not across problems; and "type-*a*" cues, which are relevant in single problems *and* across problems. The type-*c* cues are "invalid," that is, never consistently reinforced, and therefore the subject eventually ceases to respond to them. The type-*a* and type-*b* cues are valid, but since the type-*a* cue is valid in all problems and the type-*b* cues are valid only in single problems, the subject eventually stops responding to the type-*b* cues and responds only to the type-*a* cue. In a typical study, the type-*c* cues would be apparatus cues, room cues, and the like; and the type-*b* cues would be the specific shape, color, size, composition, complexity, and so on, of a particular stimulus object.

The type-*a* cue in the learning-set situation is abstract; it is "the object just rewarded." On the first trial of a problem, a well-trained subject learns which cue is the type-*a* cue, and he chooses it on the subsequent trials of that problem. Since the type-*a* cue is abstract, it can be utilized only by subjects that are capable of abstraction. There are experimental demonstrations of abstraction in monkeys (e.g., Hicks, 1956; Stone, 1961) and even in pigeons (Herrnstein and Loveland, 1964), as well as numerous demonstrations of abstraction in humans. However, as Klüver (1933, p. 328) pointed out, it is one thing to determine whether or not a given animal is *capable* of abstraction, and another thing to find out whether or not the animal *tends* to respond to abstractions. The slower development of learning set in monkeys than in men could be attributable to slower development of the abstraction (the type-*a* cue) or to slower development of a tendency to respond to the abstraction, or to both factors.

The other relevant theory of learning-set acquisition was developed by Levine (1959, 1963). Levine devised a method of analyzing performance in learning-set tasks into systematic sequences of responses. These sequences, which he called "hypotheses," are analyzed on the basis of whether the first-trial response is correct (a "win") or incorrect ("lose"), whether the response is to an object or to a position, and whether the response on the second trial is to the same object or position as the first-trial response ("stay") or to the other object or position ("shift"). There are eight possible combinations of these three dichotomies, as shown in Table 8-1. Using appropriate equations (see Levinson and Reese, 1967), the investigator can determine the relative frequency of occurrence of each of these eight systematic response patterns. Once having determined them, however, the investigator has only a behavioral *description*, albeit a good one, and not an *explanation* of the behavior. The theoretical problem is to explain why the subject exhibits a particular response pattern and why he shifts from one to another.

To exemplify the problem: it would be correct to say, "the subject has a win-stay-position, lose-stay-position hypothesis because he consistently chooses the left position"; but it would be incorrect to say, "the subject consistently chooses the left position because he has a win-stay-position, lose-stay-position hypothesis." The first statement correctly implies that the hypothesis describes the behavior; the second statement incorrectly implies that the hypothesis *explains* the behavior.

Levine recognized the theoretical problem and proposed that there are internal mediating processes that produce the overt patterns of behavior. For example, if the processes are verbal, the subject might exhibit the win-stay-position, lose-stay-position hypothesis *because* he says to himself something like "always choose the one on the left." However, the processes need not be verbal (although it is difficult to conceptualize what they might be if they are not). Therefore,

Table 8-1

The Possible Response Patterns in Levine's Model[a]

Response pattern	Behavior described
Win-stay-object, lose-shift-object	Problem solution
Win-shift-object, lose-stay-object	Opposite of problem solution
Win-stay-object, lose-stay-object	Stimulus preference
Win-shift-object, lose-shift-object	Stimulus alternation
Win-stay-position, lose-shift-position	Solution to a position discrimination
Win-shift-position, lose-stay-position	Opposite of solution to position discrimination
Win-stay-position, lose-stay-position	Position preference
Win-shift-position, lose-shift-position	Position alternation

[a] Adapted from Levine's (1959, 1963) two-trial model.

the required processes might occur in monkeys; but as with Restle's theory, one would need to assume that monkeys acquire these processes more slowly than men do, or more slowly develop a tendency to use them.

The descriptive part of Levine's model is essentially an elaboration of a method of analysis developed by Harlow (1950, 1959). Harlow identified some of the response patterns included in Table 8-1 and some additional ones not included in Levine's system (see Levinson and Reese, 1967). He proposed that learning-set acquisition consists of the elimination of incorrect patterns, which he called "error factors." However, the model was entirely descriptive, as Reese (1964) pointed out.

The ontogenetic trends, which have been obtained in monkeys as well as humans (see Harlow, 1959), could be explained by assumptions analogous to the ones explaining the phylogenetic trends. Very young subjects may exhibit interproblem improvement resulting entirely from performance sets; as age increases, at least to early adulthood, the ability to formulate or utilize symbolic processes presumably improves, accounting for the more efficient learning-set formation. Deterioration of these abilities in old age could account for the observed decline in efficiency of learning-set formation in old age.

Oddity and Reversal Learning Sets

There are other kinds of learning set than discrimination learning set: for example, "oddity learning set" (e.g., Butterfield and Butterfield, 1967; Lubker and Spiker, 1966; Martin and Blum, 1961) and "reversal learning set" (e.g., Harlow, 1949). In the oddity learning-set situation, each problem involves the presentation of three stimuli, two identical to each other and the third different. The subject must choose the odd stimulus. In reversal learning set, two-stimulus discrimination problems are used, but after the subject has learned one (or has been given some fixed number of trials on one), the reward contingencies are reversed and the subject must choose the previously incorrect object and avoid choosing the previously correct object.

There have been relatively few studies of these kinds of learning set, particularly in children; but it appears to be necessary to assume some kind of symbolic processing to account for the available data, which will not be reviewed here.

Other Learning Sets

Harlow suggested that there may be "social-emotional learning sets":

Each contact the monkey has with a human being represents a single specific learning trial. Each person represents a separate problem. Learning to react favorably to one person is followed by learning favorable reactions more rapidly to the next person to whom the monkey is socially introduced. Experience with additional individuals enables the monkey to learn further how to behave with human beings, and eventually the monkey's favorable reactions to new people are acquired so rapidly as to appear almost instantaneous. (Harlow, 1949, p. 64.)

It has also been suggested that imitation is a kind of learning set.

The concept has also been invoked to explain improvement in paired associate learning (e.g., Duncan, 1960; House *et al.*, 1964), serial learning (e.g., Hilgard, 1951, p. 553), and language development (e.g., Simon and Newell, 1962). As in the more typical learning-set situations, discussed in the preceding sections, practice on a series of problems in these situations results in interproblem improvement in performance. The term *learning to learn* has generally been used to refer to the improvement in these situations, and although it is a synonym of *learning set*, it provides a convenient label to distinguish these situations from the standard situations.

The "learning-to-learn" situations differ from the standard learning-set situations in three important ways. First, in the standard situations there are two possible responses—approach versus avoidance or nonapproach (or "stay" versus "shift," in Levine's system); but in the learning-to-learn situations there are multiple response possibilities. Second, learning set is expected to culminate in one-trial learning in the standard situations; but in the learning-to-learn situations the asymptotic level is expected to be well below the level of one-trial learning, and in fact one-trial learning may be impossible under normal circumstances.[4] Third, in the standard situations the assumed symbolic processes are relatively simple, and they are directly concerned with specific stimuli and specific responses; for example, the subject learns that *that* object is a type-*a* cue, or he learns to stay with *that* rewarded object or to avoid *that* nonrewarded object. However, in the learning-to-learn situations, there is no analogous simple process. For example, in a series of paired associate problems, the problem solution is "learn which response goes with which stimulus." Not only is this "solution" usually given in the instructions by the experimenter, but also it makes no reference to specific stimulus-response associations. The subject in a paired associate task might learn that forming images of interactions between the stimulus and response terms is an effective mnemonic, but "form images of interactions" is a *technique,* a performance set, and not a learning set.

Therefore, the most reasonable interpretation of the interproblem improvement in the learning-to-learn situations is that it results from the operation of the performance sets discussed earlier in this chapter.

---

[4] Not all one-trial learning results from learning set. Jarvik (1953) obtained one-trial learning on the first problem given to experimentally naive monkeys by associating the negative stimulus with a strongly noxious taste on a pretraining trial. However, the aversion was highly specific since it did not transfer from the negative stimulus (a piece of bread colored red or green) to a similar stimulus (a metal plaque painted red or green).

CHAPTER 9

Attentional Processes

INTRODUCTION

During the early years of experimental psychology, *attention* was considered a basic process, and attracted much experimental effort as well as theoretical speculation as to its nature and function. It had been clearly recognized that at any moment in time an organism's sensorium is exposed to an extremely large number of stimuli emanating from the environment and yet the organism apparently perceives and responds to only an extremely small proportion of these stimuli (e.g., James, 1890; Mach, 1886; see Spearman, 1937, pp. 133–147, for a brief history of the concept of attention in psychology). The organism, in effect, is acting selectively upon the totality of stimulation. It is this active selective process that William James, among others, called *attention*—a process whose absence from the organism's repertoire would render all experience "an utter chaos." One need consider only a single example to realize the validity of this argument and the adaptiveness of attentional processes. Imagine an organism that is always equally receptive and responsive to all stimulation arriving at the various sensory organs. Imagine now this same creature attempting to maneuver an automobile along a modern high speed turnpike. Attraction and response to stimuli such as the beauty of the passing scenery, a flight of birds overhead, the pressure of clothing, or the sound of an airplane will lead shortly to disaster. Survival in this and other less dramatic situations obviously depends upon a selective mechanism with respect to reception of and response to surrounding stimuli.

Despite the apparent necessity of assuming attentional processes to account for behavior, the concept of attention became unpopular after the rise of behaviorism, early in the twentieth century. The reasons for the unpopularity of the attention concept are not trivial. The strength of behaviorism was in its revolt against the use of explanatory concepts that could be inferred only from the behavior they were to explain. Older, instinct theories were particularly good examples of the inadequacy and uselessness of such an approach (see Chapter 10). Stimulus-response psychology was committed to assuming no stimulus effect unless there was an observable response. Thus, the concept of overt observing responses was popular, because eye or head movements are potentially recordable and a cue-selection process at that level would be objectively measurable. Indeed, White and Plum (1964) photographed eye movements in a discrimination task, and their results lent support to a two-process type of discrimination learning theory (see Figure 5-1 and accompanying discussion in Chapter 5). That is, the amount of visual attention to the stimuli increased markedly just as a subject began to make correct responses consistently, indicating that the process of choice learning is dependent upon an initial process of attention to or observation of the relevant cues (see also Reese, 1968, pp. 82–83). Attention is unfortunately not always so readily measured, particularly for such stimulus dimensions as pitch and color, and indeed, one might argue that attention, defined as a selective process, was not directly measured in the White and Plum study. However, the fruitfulness of the concept of attention is not often disputed today and, moreover, it is becoming more widely recognized as a necessary theoretical construct for a complete understanding and explanation of behavior.

As implied in the preceding paragraph, attention has recently again become a meaningful experimental and theoretical topic for psychologists. There are several reasons for this revival of interest. First, there were important discoveries in the field of neurophysiology that are related to attentional processes (e.g., Hernández-Peón, Scherrer, and Jouvet, 1956). Second, there was a growing recognition of the experimental work on the orientation reaction begun by Pavlov and continued to the present by numerous other psychologists and physiologists in the Soviet Union [Sokolov (1963a) has provided a thorough review of this work]. Third, there has been an increased awareness by child psychologists that attention or attention-like concepts are necessary for an understanding of the basic cognitive functions of children (e.g., Berlyne, 1960; Zeaman and House, 1963). Contained in each of these divergent approaches to the problem of attention is the conception of the organism as "an active selector of stimuli rather than a passive recipient of stimulus impingements" (Bakan, 1966, p. iii).

Our review of the experimental and theoretical literature on attentional processes in children will cover three topics: (a) the orientation reaction and its role in governing simple and complex behavior, (b) the role of attention in discrimination learning and transfer, and (c) exploratory behavior and its relation to the development of intelligent behavior. For convenience, each of these topics will be considered separately, the first two in this chapter and the third in Chapter 10.

The order in which these topics are discussed reflects the increasing complexity of the behavior, the simplest being the orientation reaction and the most complex being exploratory behavior. The role of attention in discrimination learning falls somewhere between these two, though probably very much closer to exploratory behavior than to the orientation reaction. The amount of space devoted to each topic reflects the amount of empirical research with children and the degree of theoretical sophistication about each topic. By these criteria the relation between discrimination learning and attention warrants the greatest emphasis, and the remaining topics deserve approximately equal consideration.

THE ORIENTATION REACTION

Definition and Theory

If an animal is presented a new stimulus, there is initiated a set of responses that define the orientation reaction and that have been interpreted to indicate the organism's awareness of stimulation and readiness to respond. This set of responses may include any or all of the following reflexive reactions: (a) pupil dilation, (b) a turning or orienting of the head toward the source of stimulation, (c) momentary arrest of ongoing activity and general increase in muscle tonus, (d) changes in electroencephalographic recordings, the most noticeable and reliable being blocking of the high amplitude, low frequency alpha waves, (e) vasoconstriction in the limbs and vasodilation in the head, (f) momentary arrest of respiration, (g) a change in the galvanic skin response (GSR), and (h) changes in heart rate, these being either acceleration or deceleration depending upon species, developmental level, and initial heart rate. The orientation reaction may also include some kind of selective attention mechanism (Berlyne, 1960, Ch. 4; 1963, pp. 177–178; Jeffrey, 1968; Milerian, 1957; Sokolov, 1957; Zaporozhets, 1957); but more will be said about this in the concluding section of the chapter. All of these reactions are considered in one way or another to prepare the organism for further reception of stimulation and for response to this stimulation. For example, the increase in pupil size results in greater sensitivity of the eye, and the increase in muscle tonus coupled with arrest of ongoing activity prepares the organism for a new response.

With repeated presentation of the new stimulus, the orientation reaction habituates, that is, grows weak or disappears. This habituation is taken to indicate a decreased awareness of or attention to the stimulus and consequently a lower likelihood of responding to it. There is usually a consistent pattern or course of habituation. First, there is a gradual fading of the various response components of the orientation reaction. Next, there is a period of drowsiness, during the latter portions of which there is paradoxically a return of the orientation reaction. Finally, there is a stage of secondary habituation of the orientation reaction, after which the subject eventually falls asleep. This pattern of habituation is the characteristic product of repeated stimulation with almost all classes of stimuli, the most important exception being stimuli that have special significance to the subject, that is, conditional stimuli or, to use the terminology of Soviet psychologists, signal stimuli. These stimuli include a person's name and phrases such as "Watch out!" and "Help!" Significantly more presentations of these stimuli are needed before habituation occurs if, indeed, it occurs at all.

There have been numerous attempts to explain the orientation reaction and its habituation. Perhaps the most comprehensive model is one proposed by Sokolov (1960). This "neuronal or nervous model," as Sokolov named it, is shown in schematic form in Figure 9-1. Afferent stimulation is registered in the cortex after passage along the sensory tracts. According to Sokolov, "The model postulates a chain of neural cells which preserve information about the intensity, the quality, the duration, and the order of presentation of the stimuli" (Sokolov, 1960, p. 205). The information coming from stimulation at the present moment is analyzed and compared with the stored neuronal models of past stimulation. The analysis and comparison processes have two possible outcomes: (a) The stimulus does not match any presently existing model and the orientation reaction occurs; that is, impulses are sent from the cortex to the reticular formation and impulses from excitation of the sensorium are permitted to reach the reticular formation via the afferent collaterals initiating the orientation reaction. (b) The stimulus matches an existing neuronal model and the orientation

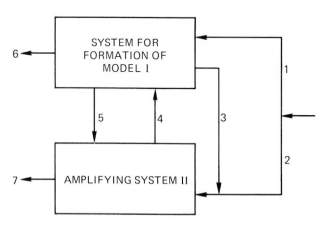

Fig. 9-1. Schema for the orientation reaction. I. Cortical modeling system. II. Reticular formation (RF) or amplifying system. 1. Specific pathway from sense organs to the modeling system. 2. Nonspecific pathway from sense organs to collaterals to RF. 3. Inhibitory pathway from modeling system to synaptic connection between collaterals and RF. 4. Ascending activating influences from RF to cortical modeling system. 5. Pathway from cortex to RF signaling nonconcordance between existing models and input. 6. Pathway to specific responses (these are often learned or habitual responses). 7. Pathway to the vegetative and somatic components of the orientation reaction resulting from stimulation of the RF. (From Sokolov, 1960. Reprinted by permission of the author and Josiah Macy, Jr., Foundation.)

reaction is blocked. This blocking results from failure of the reticular formation to receive impulses from the cortex and, more importantly, from the sensorium. Impulses from the cortex to the afferent collaterals block or inhibit the conduction of the nonspecific effects of sensory stimulation to the reticular formation.

With repeated stimulation by a once new stimulus, a neuronal model of this stimulus will be formed and stored. Thus future presentations of the same stimulus will no longer register as not matching any existing model and the orientation reaction will not occur. With these assumptions Sokolov was able to account for the initial stage of habituation. Sokolov (1963b) assumed, following Pavlov, that with further repetitions of the stimulus, neural activity in the cortex itself becomes inhibited, leading to the drowsy state. In this state, the cortex is no longer capable of sending the impulses that would block or inhibit the conduction of afferent stimulation to the reticular formation via the afferent collaterals, and the orientation reaction recurs. With even further stimulation, inhibition in the cortex increases and spreads to lower centers, including the reticular formation, resulting in secondary habituation and finally a state of sleep.

Evidence for the Neuronal Model

In Sokolov's neuronal model considerable emphasis is placed upon the role of analyzing processes in the cortex. It is assumed that attention is a high-level central process, or at least certain components of attention are. The problem now is to ascertain whether this assumption of cortical involvement is warranted by the existing data and, further, whether the data support the neuronal model itself. The most directly relevant evidence comes from neurophysiology. First, there are data, summarized by Lynn (1966), suggesting the existence of three types of cortical cells whose functions correspond to the functions of the analyzer: (a) afferent neurons that always respond to the stimulus even after repeated presentation; (b) "extrapolatory" neurons that begin to respond only after repeated presentation of the stimulus; (c) "comparator" neurons that respond to novel or new stimuli. The afferent neurons provide the means by which external stimulation is always recorded cortically and is thus able to be analyzed. The extrapolatory and comparator neurons provide the capability of processing stimulus information into categories of "same" or "different," which in turn leads to inhibition or release of the orientation reaction. Thus, the neurophysiological evidence is consistent with the assumption of a cortical or central analyzing system. However, the assumptions about inhibition of the cortex are less well documented. There is some evidence for irradiation or spread of inhibition in the cortex, but this spread is generally conceded to be restricted to the sensory area being stimulated. Consequently, exactly how we are to explain why repeated stimulation leads to the recurrence of the orientation reaction and then sleep remains a mystery at present. Further difficulty for the model is encountered when an attempt is made to explain the extremely slow habituation of "signal" stimuli. Nevertheless, the model seems to have considerable validity.

Additional evidence favoring the neuronal model is obtained from studies relating developmental and phyletic variables to the orientation reaction. Lynn (1966) has summarized the Soviet literature on these topics. Orientation reactions are typically more pronounced but habituate more readily in higher than in lower species. For example, habituation of visual and auditory stimuli requires 20 trials in dogs, 15 to 40 trials in pigeons, and from 53 to 173 trials in carp. In a comparison of monkeys and dogs, the latter were found to habituate more slowly. These data are in agreement with the hypothesis of cortical mediation of habituation; the more highly developed the cortex, the faster the occurrence of habituation, as Sokolov's model demands. Also in agreement with this conclusion, the speed of habituation increases ontogenetically, in both animals and humans. For example, Lynn (1966) found that 3 to 4 year old girls failed to habituate to a 500 cycle tone in 60 trials, while young women, 18 to 21 years of age, did so in a mean of 23 trials. Additionally, it has been demonstrated in the dog that full development of the orientation reaction and its habituation correspond closely with maturation of the cortex. Similar data are available from studies of human infants and children. There is a gradual change in the form of the orientation reaction with age, presumably a function of increasing cortical control with development.

A final study to be considered in support of a central analyzing mechanism was reported by Voronin and Sokolov (1960). They presented to their subjects a group of semantically similar but phonetically different words until there was no evidence of alpha rhythm blocking as measured by electroencephalographic recordings. Next, they presented a word differing in meaning and obtained a pronounced orientation reaction. Such fine discriminations demand cortical involvement and are frequently lost as a result of cortical injury.

The Orientation Reaction and Learning

In addition to providing basic data on the orientation reaction itself, Soviet researchers have examined its role in the learning and transfer of simple and complex habits. Sokolov (1960) has demonstrated that instrumental conditioning proceeds most rapidly when the conditional stimulus (CS) evokes an orientation reaction of intermediate magnitude. The suggested explanation is that awareness of the CS is necessary, and therefore an orientation reaction must occur, but too strong an orientation reaction to the CS interferes with the conditioned response. Other Soviet psychologists, especially Zaporozhets and his associates (see Zaporozhets, 1961), have attempted to determine how conditioning the orientation reaction in children affects their solution of complex problems. In one study, children three to six years of age were tested on the transfer of pretraining on a table-model maze. One group was pretrained by having the experimenter demonstrate the correct path. The children in a second group had their attention directed to the choice points and were made to follow each path of the maze visually and tactually. After pretraining, the maze was rotated 180 degrees and each subject had to find the correct course. Transfer was considerably greater in the second group than in the first group; it was enhanced, according to Zaporozhets, by the conditioning of the orientation reaction, although the differences were more marked in younger children, three to four years of age, than in older children, five to six years of age.

In a second experiment, children between the ages of three and seven years were instructed to make two different motor responses to two different compound stimuli, a bright red circle centered on a pale yellow background and a bright green circle on a light gray background. The children in one experimental condition were instructed to respond on the basis of the strong stimuli (the bright central colors), and those in a second condition were instructed to respond on the basis of the weak stimuli (the pale background colors). After practice had been given, the cues were interchanged as follows: the background color of each pattern was paired with the central color of the other pattern. Transfer of training was then evaluated. The children originally trained to respond to the strong cues continued to do so; but the children, especially the younger ones, trained to respond to weak cues frequently responded on the basis of the strong cues. Only 45 percent of the three and four year old children were able to transfer their responses on the basis of the weak cues; about 80 percent of the older children were able to do so. These results were interpreted to indicate that the conditioning of attention or orientation reactions can occur and mediate voluntary behavior. The results also indicate that younger children have considerable difficulty in overcoming a tendency to respond to strong cues in the environment; they often fail to inhibit an instrumental or voluntary response to the first (strong) cue eliciting the orientation reaction or attention. This, according to Soviet psychologists, is most likely a function of weaker inhibitory processes or greater distractibility found in younger or developmentally less mature children. (See also the discussion of White's theory in the section entitled "Age Trend in Efficiency of Mediation," in Chapter 7.)

Unfortunately, much of the Soviet literature is available in English only in summary form, and even in fully translated works many details of procedure are not reported (e.g., Uznadze, 1966). Furthermore, the Soviet writers have a tendency to use technical terms differently from American writers, and seem to inject interpretation into what otherwise appear to be factual statements. For example, instructing a child to respond on the basis of a particular cue is often described as conditioning an orientation reaction to that cue. While it may be true that the instruction has that effect, American writers would prefer to describe the procedure in that way in the introduction or discussion section of a report, and to describe it factually in the section on methods. Therefore, it is often difficult to evaluate the reported findings of the Soviet research. However, as will be shown in a later section, the conclusion that attention to particular cues or features of the environment can mediate the acquisition and transfer of problem solution is also supported by better controlled studies on discrimination learning in children.

CONDITIONAL STIMULUS FAMILIARIZATION. Berlyne (1960) suggested that a CS loses its effectiveness as it loses its novelty, that is, as it becomes *familiar*. In the first direct test of this suggestion, Cantor and Cantor (1964) trained kindergarten children on a lever-pulling task under different CS conditions. Before the task started, one group was familiarized with a light and another group with a buzzer. Familiarization consisted of the subject's sitting inactively but attentively before the apparatus for 40 two-second presentations of the stimulus. Five seconds elapsed between stimulus presentations. Following familiarization, the subjects were given 50 reinforced conditioning trials. The light served as CS on half the trials and the buzzer on the other half. Starting speeds were found to be faster to the novel (unfamiliarized) CS than to the familiarized CS. There was no effect of CS familiarization on movement speed.

Cantor and Cantor (1965) obtained the same effects in preschool children, using a red and a green light; and Cantor and Cantor (1966) showed that the effects can be obtained with as few as five familiarization presentations.

Several possible explanations of the effects of CS familiarization have been proposed and tested:

(a) The effects result from instructions to attend but not respond to a stimulus during familiarization, producing a set to attend and not respond. The set would interfere with prompt initiation of the response. This possibility was tested by Bogartz and Witte (1966); during familiarization the subject had to make the same response to the stimulus as he would later make to both the familiar and novel stimulus. The effects were obtained, eliminating this interference hypothesis.

(b) The effects result from the "surprisingness" of the novel stimulus, surprise somehow increasing motivation (see Chapter 10 for a discussion of this source of motivation). Witte (1967) tested this possibility by presenting both stimuli during familiarization, one for 4.5 seconds per presentation and the other for 1.5 seconds per presentation. The CS familiarization effect was obtained, in that the stimulus presented for the longer durations during familiarization was a less effective CS than the other stimulus (on early trials; the effect disappeared on later trials, as should be expected since the other stimulus should become familiar relatively quickly during the test trials).

(c) The effects result from habituation of the orientation reaction to the familiarized stimulus, resulting in decreased attentiveness to this stimulus. This explanation accounts for the findings of Cantor and Cantor that CS familiarization affects starting speeds and has no effect on movement speeds, findings that were also obtained by Bogartz and Witte (1966). Once the response has been initiated, differences in attention to the stimuli can have no further effect.

(d) Witte and Cantor (1967) obtained the CS familiarization effect on both starting speeds and movement speeds, but in their study the response was made to stimulus *offsets* rather than to stimulus onsets. Witte and Cantor suggested that novel stimuli have motivational properties that facilitate responding, and that their procedure allowed sufficient time for the novelty-produced motivation to develop, thus facilitating both starting and movement speeds to the novel stimulus.

It seems likely that both of the last two processes discussed are effective, especially if it is assumed that the motivational change produced by novel stimulation has a relatively long latency (as Witte and Cantor assumed). The motivational interpretation accounts for the effect of familiarization on movement speed in the Witte and Cantor study, but fails to account for the data of the studies in which familiarization affected starting speeds but not movement speeds. The habituation explanation accounts for the latter.

ATTENTION

Theory

BACKGROUND. Psychologists have long realized that in order for an organism to make a discriminative response, it is necessary that the relevant aspects of the stimulus array be received (at least at the level of the sense organs); but it has been only recently that learning theorists have attempted to deal directly with the reception and selection of stimuli. In the area of animal discrimination learning, several theorists have emphasized the role of peripheral observing responses, which is to expose the cues to the sensorium of the animal (Reid, 1953; Spence, 1956, 1960, Ch. 22; Stollnitz, 1965; Wyckoff, 1952). Lawrence stressed a selective type of response to the relevant dimension (Goodwin and Lawrence, 1955; Lawrence, 1949, 1950). The animal must first "identify" or in some manner react to a *dimension,* and this reaction is followed by an instrumental response to a particular value on the identified dimension. More recently, Sutherland (1959) and Lovejoy (1966) have constructed theoretical models, which, like the observing-response models and Lawrence's model, involved two stages of acquisition, but which for the first time explicitly involved a hypothesized central selective process equated with attention (see also Sutherland, 1964a, 1964b; Sutherland, Mackintosh, and Mackintosh, 1963).

The attentional response is not the same as the overt observing response (see H. H. Kendler and Kendler, 1966; Mackintosh, 1965b). Both kinds of response result in what Mandler (1962) called "stimulus learning," but he would apparently not classify them together, as the Zeamans sometimes seem to do (e.g., House and Zeaman, 1962). Mandler would probably classify the attentional response with the "cognitive structures" which he described.

According to Berlyne (1960, Ch. 3), attention is widely believed to consist of two processes, one determining alertness or vigilance and the other determining selective attention. McNamara and Fisch (1964) also believed that attention consists of two processes, "span of attention" and a "scanning" process, which seem to be the same as the processes identified by Berlyne. There is a considerable literature on vigilance and span of attention, especially in human adults, but the rest of this chapter will be concerned only with the selective aspects of attention. In particular, the role of the selective aspect of attention in discrimination learning and transfer in children is discussed.

THE ZEAMAN AND HOUSE THEORY. There are several attention theories dealing specifically with discrimination learning. However, only one of these, the theory of Zeaman and House (1963), is considered in the rest of this section, partly because space does not permit detailed consideration of all of the theories and partly because the Zeamans' theory is directly relevant to child research. Unless otherwise specified, the phrase "attention theory" refers, in the rest of this section, to the Zeamans' theory.[1]

Zeaman and House theorized that discrimination learning requires a chain of two responses. The first is a central mediating response, identified with attention, to the relevant stimulus dimension; and the second is an instrumental response of approach to one of the outcomes of the attentional response—the

---

[1] A theory proposed by the Kendlers is also relevant, and is discussed later in this chapter. It differs from the Zeamans' theory mainly in assuming that the attentional response is usually verbally directed.

positive discriminandum.[2] The theoretical position was set forth in terms of a probability model, which will be described in some detail before the supporting evidence is considered.

It should be noted first that the attention theory was designed primarily to account for the data of two-choice simultaneous discriminations and certain transfer operations. However, it is possible to extend the model to account for data from other learning situations, such as successive discriminations and concept formation tasks, as well as other transfer operations not analyzed in the original presentation of the theory, for example, the "optional shift" paradigm considered later.

Consider the following example of a two-choice simultaneous discrimination. On Trial 1 the subject sees a red square and a green triangle, with red square the positive pattern. On Trial 2 he sees a green square and red triangle and now choice of the green square is reinforced. On successive trials the two arrays are randomly alternated, and the left-right position of the positive stimulus also varies at random. It is obvious that form is the relevant dimension, since one of the forms, the square, is consistently positive and the other, the triangle, is consistently negative, but no color or position is consistently positive or negative. *Dimensions* are defined as ". . . broad classes of cues having a common discriminative property" (Zeaman and House, 1963, p. 168). There are two cue values on each of the irrelevant dimensions, red and green and left and right, and each of these values is reinforced 50 percent of the time on a random basis. Learning is considered to have occurred when the subject consistently selects the stimulus pattern that contains the square, whether it is on the right or left and whether it is red or green. How this consistent selection or learning occurs is the substance of attention theory.

The model and the stimulus situation can be represented in terms of a probability tree, as shown in Figure 9-2. The symbol S^* represents the set of relevant and irrelevant dimensions; in terms of the example above, S^* includes one relevant dimension, form, and two irrelevant dimensions, color and position. The symbol $Po_{(1)}$ represents the probability of attending to form, designated O_1; $Po_{(2)}$ and $Po_{(3)}$ represent the probabilities of attending to color (O_2) and position (O_3), respectively. Attention to a dimension has the property of making visible the particular stimulus values or cues on this dimension. Thus, if an attentional response is made to form, the subject sees square and triangle, represented by s_1 and s_1'. The symbol $Pr_{(1)}$ is the conditional probability of making the instrumental response (R_1) to s_1 (the square), and $1 - Pr_{(1)}$ is the conditional probability of making the instrumental response to triangle (R_1'). The symbols G and G' represent reward and nonreward. The diagram shows that on each trial the three stimulus dimensions compete for attention just as the cues

---

[2] In the original presentation of the attention theory, Zeaman and House (1963) often referred to the attentional response as an observing response (see Figure 9-2). However, "observing response" usually means a peripheral response, while "attentional response" usually carries the idea of some central selective process. Since Zeaman and House believed the mediating response to be central and selective, the phrase attentional response is used here.

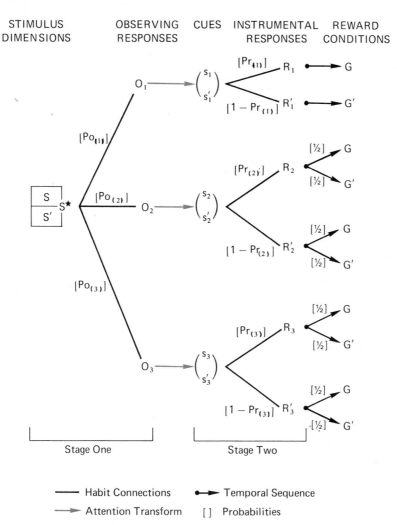

Fig. 9-2.   Probability tree of Zeaman and House's basic one-look model. The branches represent all the possible events that can occur on a single trial with a stimulus complex consisting of three dimensions. [Adapted from Zeaman and House, 1963, Fig. 5-8, p. 170. From *Handbook of Mental Deficiency*, N. R. Ellis (Ed.). Copyright 1963 by McGraw-Hill, Inc. Reprinted by permission of the authors and publisher.]

within a dimension compete for choice after attention is directed to that dimension. This competition was made explicit by the Zeamans, since they hypothesized, in their original "one-look" model, that on any trial, attention may be directed to only a single dimension. The actual dimension to which attention is directed and the cue to which a choice response is made are determined for each subject on every trial by the probabilities of attending to the various dimensions ($Po_{(1)}$, $Po_{(2)}$, and $Po_{(3)}$) and the probabilities of choice of each of the cue values ($Pr_{(1)}$, etc.).

It is apparent from the diagram that in the example given earlier, reinforcement will occur on every trial only if the subject consistently attends to form and subsequently chooses the square. This pattern of responding and its culmination in reinforcement operationally define the criterion of learning. Attention to either of the irrelevant dimensions, regardless of which cue is selected, will always lead to chance performance, that is, reinforcement of 50 percent of the choice responses, and by definition not to learning. The model in essence demands that in order for learning to occur subjects must make the appropriate mediating attentional response and then the appropriate instrumental response.

It is possible to obtain the probability (P) of the correct instrumental response on any trial by summing the branches of the tree leading to G. The result of this summation yields the basic equation:

$$P = Po_{(1)}Pr_{(1)} + .5(1 - Po_{(1)}) \tag{1}$$

on the assumption that the three attentional responses (to O_1, O_2, and O_3) are mutually exclusive and exhaustive (so that $Po_{(1)} + Po_{(2)} + Po_{(3)} = 1$, and hence $Po_{(2)} + Po_{(3)} = 1 - Po_{(1)}$). The value of P is the dependent variable in the system and, it should be noted, its computation does not take into account why the subject was correct, that is, whether by attending to the relevant dimension and making the correct choice or by attending to an irrelevant dimension and being lucky. Given this equation, the problem is to compute the changes in P over trials as a function of the sequence of events. While the derivation of these changes in P over trials will not be given in any great detail here, some appreciation and understanding of the mechanics of the model can be obtained by consideration of what happens to $Po_{(1)}$ and $Pr_{(1)}$ as a function of the possible events on any one trial.

In agreement with traditional learning theorists, Zeaman and House assumed that a trial ending in reinforcement results in increments (acquisition) in the probabilities of making both the attentional and instrumental response occurring on that trial, and that nonreinforcement leads to decrements (extinction) in the probabilities of making these responses. For example, if the subject attends to the relevant dimension and makes the correct instrumental response, then $Po_{(1)}$ and $Pr_{(1)}$ increase. This sequence of events is shown in the first row of Table 9-1. If the relevant dimension is attended to but the incorrect instrumental response occurs, and consequently nonreinforcement occurs, as shown in the second row of the table, $Po_{(1)}$ and $Pr_{(1)}'$ diminish. However, $Pr_{(1)}$ *increases*, because there are only two possible instrumental responses, R_1 and R_1', and their combined probabilities must sum to unity. (For any pair of mutually exclusive and exhaustive events, a drop in the probability of one event must be matched by an equal rise in the probability of the other event.) Consider now what happens when a subject attends to an irrelevant dimension. Since the relevant cues are not exposed or responded to, there can be no change in $Pr_{(1)}$. However, if the subject is fortunate and is reinforced while attending to an irrelevant dimension (as will occur in 50 percent of such instances), then the probability of attending to that irrelevant dimension will be enhanced while the probability of attending to all other dimensions, including the relevant dimension, will be decreased. (Again a set of mutually exclusive and exhaustive events is involved, as already noted; therefore, a change in the probability of one event must be matched by opposite changes in the probabilities of the other events.) If the subject is unlucky and is not reinforced, then the Po of the observed irrelevant dimension goes down, and all other Po's go up. From the events described in Table 9-1, it can be readily deduced that $Pr_{(1)}$ will attain unity faster than $Po_{(1)}$. The reasons for this are simply that $Pr_{(1)}$ never undergoes extinction directly or indirectly, while $Po_{(1)}$ may on occasion undergo both direct and indirect extinction. Direct extinction of $Po_{(1)}$ occurs through choice of the

Table 9-1

Changes in $Po_{(1)}$ and $Pr_{(1)}$ as a Function
of the Possible Sequence of Events

Event	Change in $Po_{(1)}$	Change in $Pr_{(1)}$
O_1R_1G	+	+
$O_1R_1'G'$	−	+
O_2R_2G	−	0
O_2R_2G'	+	0
$O_2R_2'G$	−	0
$O_2R_2'G'$	+	0
O_3R_3G	−	0
O_3R_3G'	+	0
$O_3R_3'G$	−	0
$O_3R_3'G'$	+	0

incorrect cue on the relevant dimension, and indirect extinction of $Po_{(1)}$ occurs through fortuitous reinforcement of responses to irrelevant dimensions.

Given these rules and some additional assumptions concerning the rates (θ's) of acquisition and extinction for both responses, high speed digital computers can be used to obtain theoretical curves of discrimination learning for groups of "stat-children." "Stat-children" are hypothetical children whose Po's, Pr's, and θ's have predetermined assumed values and whose performance is calculated by a computer programmed, in this instance, to behave according to the assumptions of attention theory. The performance of "stat-children" will shortly be compared with the performance of the more usual variety.

A further assumption is necessary if attention theory is to be applicable to certain transfer situations. This assumption is simply that the attentional and instrumental responses learned during the acquisition of one discrimination can transfer to new discrimination learning situations.

Before considering the relevant data, it might be instructive to summarize the major theoretical assumptions: (a) Discrimination learning requires the acquisition of a chain of two responses, one attentional and the other instrumental. (b) On any one trial, attention is directed to a single dimension. (c) Both attentional and instrumental responses can undergo acquisition and extinction through reinforcement and nonreinforcement. (d) The probability ($Pr_{(1)}$) of the correct instrumental response reaches asymptote faster than does the probability ($Po_{(1)}$) of making the relevant attentional response. (e) Given the proper stimulus conditions, both attention and the instrumental response will transfer across problems.

Evidence for Attention Theory

SHAPE OF THE DISCRIMINATION LEARNING FUNCTION. Hayes (1953), Spence (1956), and Zeaman and House (1963), among others, have noted that plotting

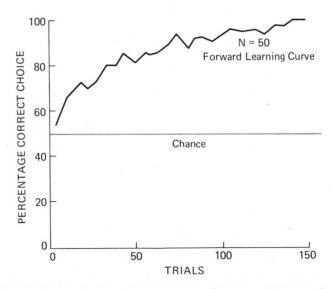

Fig. 9-3. Average discrimination learning curve of group of 50 retardates. [Zeaman and House, 1963, Fig. 5-2, p. 161. From *Handbook of Mental Deficiency*, N. R. Ellis (Ed.). Copyright 1963 by McGraw-Hill, Inc. Reprinted by permission of the authors and publisher.]

percentage correct choices as a function of trials for a large group of subjects may obscure characteristics of the learning curves of individual subjects. One method of overcoming this possibility is to plot mean curves for groups of homogeneous subjects, rather than one curve for the total sample of subjects. A homogeneous group may be defined as such by various criteria, for example, number of days to attain the learning criterion, developmental level, or type of discriminative task.

Using a simple discrimination learning task requiring the child to push aside one of two stimulus objects in order to find a reward underneath, Zeaman and House obtained rather conventional learning curves, as illustrated in Figure 9-3. Because these were retarded subjects, learning was highly variable; some children learned rapidly, others required a very large number of trials given over several days. The concern of Zeaman and House about these differences in learning rate led them to group the data on the basis of the day on which

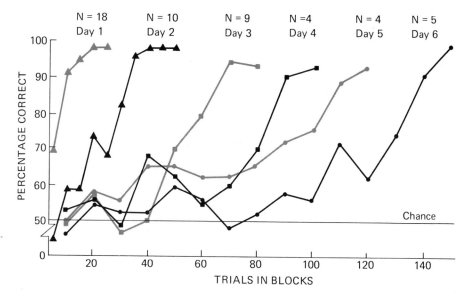

Fig. 9-4.   Learning curves of subgroups requiring various numbers of training days to reach criterion. The number of subjects in each subgroup appears at top. [Zeaman and House, 1963, Fig. 5-3, p. 161. From *Handbook of Mental Deficiency*, N. R. Ellis (Ed.). Copyright 1963 by McGraw-Hill, Inc. Reprinted by permission of the authors and publisher.]

the learning criterion was met. As can be seen in Figure 9-4, the curves showing these grouped data had a quite different form from the group curve in Figure 9-3. The performance of the children who took more trials to learn remained near the chance level over a considerable part of the training period, until some point at which the percentage correct choices ascended at a rate roughly equivalent to that of the children who reached criterion earlier. Thus, "the difference is not so much the rate at which improvement takes place, *once it starts*, but rather the number of trials for learning to start" (Zeaman and House, 1963, p. 162). This finding is illustrated more dramatically when the curves are redrawn as "backward learning curves," as shown in Figure 9-5. To produce these, rather than plotting the beginning of training at the left and proceeding to the right, one plots the criterion performance for all subjects on the right and proceeds to plot performance on earlier blocks of trials toward the left.[3]

Zeaman and House interpreted these results as reflecting the two different processes in discrimination learning. The initial portion of the curve was presumed to be controlled by the attentional process, and the rapidly ascending portion by the associational or instrumental learning process. Interestingly enough, similar conclusions were arrived at when backward learning curves were plotted for retarded subjects grouped according to mental age (MA) or type of discriminative task, that is, whether trained on a "junk" discrimination,

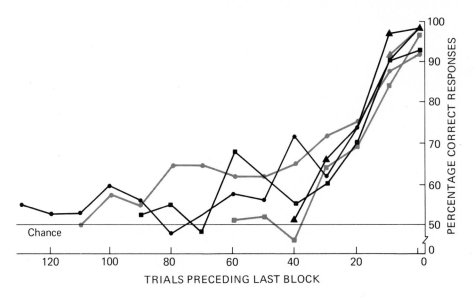

Fig. 9-5. The curves of the subgroups in Figure 9-4 redrawn as backward learning curves. The contrast in form of these curves and the average learning curve (Figure 9-3) is marked. [Zeaman and House, 1963, Fig. 5-4, p. 162. From *Handbook of Mental Deficiency*, N. R. Ellis (Ed.). Copyright 1963 by McGraw-Hill, Inc. Reprinted by permission of the authors and publisher.]

a color-form object discrimination, or a color-form pattern discrimination. The shapes of these functions varied from a sharply rising negatively accelerated function to ogival (S-shaped) functions with increasing lengths of the initial portion of the curve. The change in the shape of the learning functions was

[3] In general, the validity of the early portions of backward learning curves can be questioned, because the usual method of construction may make the data points for early trials less reliable than the data points for later trials (Hayes, 1953) and because it subjects all precriterional trials to downward selection (Hayes and Pereboom, 1959). Emphasis on the early portions of such curves is therefore generally unwarranted. However, the Zeamans have used the convention of ceasing to plot the backward curve when the median subject no longer provides data. There is a progressive loss of data, but emphasis on the early portion of the curve is justified with some slight caution. The potential selection errors do not affect the interpretation of the later phase in which the learning is rapid.

orderly and was correlated with decreasing MA and increasing problem difficulty.

In their computer simulation of children's discrimination learning, the Zeamans obtained reasonably good approximations of the obtained learning curves by systematically varying the initial probability of attending to the relevant dimension, and by varying the assumed number of irrelevant dimensions. High initial probabilities, of about .5 or greater, produced negatively accelerated functions; low initial probabilities, of .1 or less, produced ogival functions. Increasing the number of irrelevant dimensions influenced the length of the initial portion of the curve but not the rate of the final rise to asymptote. Of primary importance, it was demonstrated that group differences in learning rate can be explained without assuming individual differences in learning rate parameters; slow learners may simply have low probabilities of initially observing certain dimensions that the experimenter has designated as relevant.

A good example of how variations in the initial probabilities of attending to the relevant dimension can account for the actual performance of retarded children has been provided by Shepp and Zeaman (1966). They trained retarded children on either a brightness or size discrimination, with varying degrees of physical difference between the positive and negative stimuli. As would be expected, subjects trained on an easy discrimination (large physical difference) learned significantly faster than comparable subjects trained on a difficult discrimination (small physical difference). This effect is shown clearly in Figure 9-6(A). However, as Figure 9-6(B) shows, the difference in the rate of learning was not in the later portions of the learning curves but rather in the initial portions. Moreover, by the use of stat-children it was possible to approximate these varying functions solely on the basis of variation in the initial probability of observing the relevant dimensions. The comparability of the obtained and theoretical curves can be observed by examination of Figures 9-6(A) and 9-6(C).

Thus, from the basic assumptions of attention theory, it is possible to generate learning curves that approximate quite closely the learning curves obtained with homogeneous groups of subjects. This can be accomplished despite the wide variation in the shapes of the obtained learning curves, ranging from negatively accelerated curves to ogival curves with elongated initial portions. This is a major theoretical accomplishment.

TRANSFER ALONG A CONTINUUM. In attempting to train rats on a difficult brightness discrimination, Lawrence (1952) found that it is more efficient to train them first on an easy discrimination on the same stimulus dimension than to give all of the training trials on the difficult discrimination. The same result has been obtained in adult humans (Baker and Osgood, 1954; Marsh, 1967) and children (Spiker, 1959). Attention theory can explain this result, in the following way: If it is assumed that the initial probability ($Po_{(1,0)}$) of attending to a relevant dimension is related to the physical difference between the positive and negative stimuli (see Shepp and Zeaman, 1966), then with small physical differences $Po_{(1,0)}$ should be small and learning should require a large number

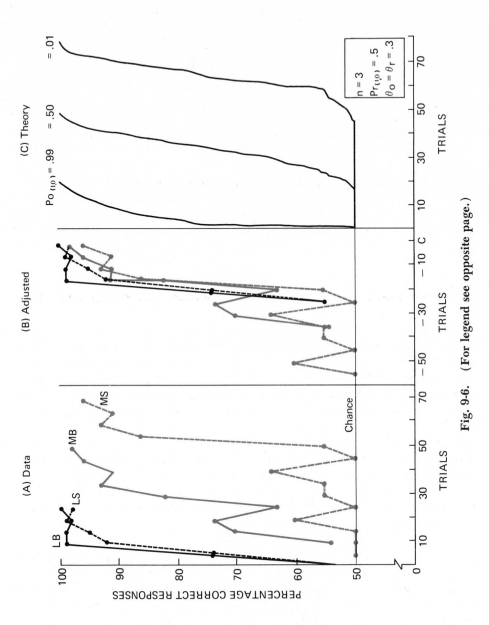

Fig. 9-6. (For legend see opposite page.)

of trials. However, with large differences $Po_{(1,0)}$ should be relatively great and learning should proceed rapidly, resulting not only in an increase in the number of correct choices but in an increment in $Po_{(1)}$. After this learning, when subjects are transferred to a second problem in which the same dimension is relevant, they are predicted to attend to this same dimension despite the smaller physical difference between the two discriminanda. In other words, the attentional response learned in Problem 1 should transfer to Problem 2 and, being quite high in probability, should result in rapid learning.

In a study involving three matched groups of retarded children, House and Zeaman (1960) tested this explanation and at the same time tested the assumption that the mediating attentional response is a response to a dimension. Pattern discriminations are known to be more difficult for children than object discriminations (e.g., House and Zeaman, 1960; Stevenson and McBee, 1958). Consequently, Group 1 was given 500 trials on a color-form *pattern* discrimination—a difficult discrimination—and Group 2 was first trained on a color-form *object* discrimination for a maximum of 250 trials and then shifted to a color-form *pattern* discrimination, again for a maximum of 250 trials. The particular cue values, for example, red square and green circle, were the same in both problems. Group 3 was given training identical to that of Group 2, except that the cue values used in the first problem were different from the ones used in the second problem, although the dimensions were the same. The results were that only 4 of 19 subjects in Group 1 learned the difficult discrimination, while 13 of 19 and 14 of 22 subjects in Groups 2 and 3 did so. These data indicate that attentional responses acquired during an easy discrimination will transfer to a difficult discrimination. Additionally, the performance of Group 3 shows that attentional responses are dimensional, since transfer in this group was not limited by particular cue values. With errors to criterion as the performance measure, Group 2 was significantly superior to Group 3, presumably because the subjects in Group 2 had the advantage of instrumental as well as attentional response transfer.

Intradimensional and Extradimensional Shifts. Two transfer paradigms that provide a critical test of attention theory by arranging for differential control

---

Fig. 9-6. (A) Backward learning curves. Medium (light solid line) and large (dark solid line) brightness difference; medium (light dashed line) and large (dark dashed line) size difference. (B) Same curves moved to the right to terminate on criterion day, represented by C on baseline. (C) Theoretical curves. Mean stat-children performances under indicated parameter conditions (n, number of inferred dimensions competing for attention; $Po_{(1,0)}$, probability of attending to relevant dimension at the start of each problem; $Pr_{(1,0)}$, conditional probability of choosing the positive cue at the start of training, given that attention has been directed toward the relevant stimulus dimension; θ_0 and θ_r, learning rate parameter for attentional and instrumental responses, respectively). (From B. E. Shepp and D. Zeaman, "Discriminative learning of size and brightness by retardates." *Journal of Comparative and Physiological Psychology,* 1966, 62, 55–59. Copyright 1966 by the American Psychological Association, and reprinted by permission of the authors and publisher.)

of the initial probability of attending to the relevant dimension are the *intra-dimensional* and *extradimensional* shift paradigms. The subjects are administered, after attaining criterion on the original problem, a second problem with the same dimensions but with new cues from all of the dimensions (except position). Examples are shown in Table 9-2. In the original problem, form is the relevant dimension, with square positive and triangle negative, and color (red and green) and position (left and right) are irrelevant and variable. In the intradimensional shift, form is still the relevant dimension, with circle positive and cross negative (or the converse); color (yellow and blue) and position (left and right) remain irrelevant. If attention to a dimension transfers, then at the beginning of the intradimensional shift the probability of attending to

Table 9-2

Sample Stimulus Arrangements for Original Learning and Discriminative Shifts[a]

Trial type	Original learning		Intradimensional shift		Extradimensional shift		Reversal shift		Nonreversal shift	
	Pos.	Neg.	Pos.	Neg.	Pos.	Neg.	Pos.	Neg.	Pos.	Neg.
1	red square	green triangle	yellow circle	blue cross	yellow circle	blue cross	green triangle	red square	green square	red square
2	green square	red triangle	blue circle	yellow cross	yellow cross	blue circle	red triangle	green square	green triangle	red triangle

[a] Pos. indicates rewarded stimulus compound; Neg. indicates nonrewarded stimulus compound. Positions of the compounds are not indicated in the table. See Shepp and Turrisi (1966) for detailed descriptions, and Slamecka (1968) for discussion of biases.

the relevant dimension, form, should be high as a result of transfer of the previously acquired attentional response. There should be no effective transfer of instrumental responses, since new values on the dimensions are introduced and any systematic transfer arising from stimulus generalization is eliminated by random selection of the positive cue to be used for each subject. In the extradimensional shift the previously irrelevant dimension, color, is made relevant, with yellow positive and blue negative (or the converse). The initial probability of attending to this dimension should be quite low and, indeed, actually suppressed by the strong competing attentional response to form. Consequently, since there should be no effective transfer of instrumental responses, intradimensional shifts should be learned more rapidly than extradimensional shifts.

Intradimensional shifts are learned more rapidly than extradimensional shifts by retarded children (Campione, Hyman, and Zeaman, 1965; House and Zeaman, 1962) and deaf children (Youniss, 1964), by normal preschool children (Dickerson, 1966; Mumbauer and Odom, 1967; Trabasso, Deutsch, and Gelman, 1966,

Exp. 2) and older children (Eimas, 1966a; Furth and Youniss, 1964; Morse and Shepp, 1967; Youniss, 1964), and by adults (Isaacs and Duncan, 1962). That this is a real effect is affirmed by the large number of confirming studies, an affirmation all too rare in the psychological literature. In the only two studies in which intradimensional shifts were not learned more rapidly than extradimensional shifts by children (House and Zeaman, 1962; Trabasso et al., 1966, Exp. 1), original training was given with no irrelevant dimension except position. When this procedure is used, it is likely, as House and Zeaman (1962) suggested, that novelty of the irrelevant cues introduced in the transfer task attenuates the difference between the two shift conditions. However, the difference was obtained in other studies in which novelty was not controlled (Furth and Youniss, 1964; House and Zeaman, 1962, retarded group; Isaacs and Duncan, 1962). (In the other studies cited above, novelty was controlled by using the kinds of stimulus arrangements shown in Table 9-2.)

This effect has considerable generality not only across developmental levels but also across phylogenetic levels. Faster intradimensional shift acquisition has been obtained in rats (Shepp and Eimas, 1964), and rhesus monkeys (Rothblat, 1967; Shepp and Schrier, 1969). Thus, it appears likely that attention theory, originally proposed to describe discrimination learning in children, may be directly applicable to similar behavior in infrahuman organisms.

As noted earlier, attention theory predicts that the instrumental response probability ($Pr_{(1)}$) reaches asymptote more rapidly than the probability of attending to the relevant dimension ($Po_{(1)}$). Hence, if the criterion of learning on the original problem is not overly stringent, additional training may reasonably be expected to increase $Po_{(1)}$. The predicted result of this increment would be to facilitate the learning of intradimensional shifts and to retard even more the acquisition of extradimensional shifts; therefore, the difference between the two shift conditions should increase with increasing amounts of original training.

In a direct test of these predictions, Shepp and Turrisi (1969) gave three groups of retarded children either 0, 100, or 300 percent overtraining on the original discrimination problem. For example, if in original training 50 trials were required to attain criterion, then an additional 50 or 150 trials would be administered to the 100 and 300 percent overtraining groups, respectively. Half of each group was given an intradimensional shift and the other half was given an extradimensional shift. It was found that the intradimensional shift was facilitated by overtraining and the extradimensional shift retarded, resulting in an increasing difference between the two shift conditions with increasing amounts of original training.

Eimas (1966a), however, found that although overtraining facilitated the acquisition of intradimensional shifts in kindergarten and second grade children, it also facilitated the acquisition of extradimensional shifts, contrary to the effect on extradimensional shifts obtained by Shepp and Turrisi. It is possible to explain Eimas's finding within the confines of attention theory (Zeaman and House, 1963, pp. 178–180), but the theory does not provide an explanation of the discrepancy between the Eimas and the Shepp and Turrisi findings. Examination of the literature on the effects of overtraining on extradimensional shifts reveals some consistency in the findings. Overtraining interferes with extradimensional shifts in retarded children (Heal, 1966; Ohlrich and Ross, 1966), but has essentially no effect in normal children (Furth and Youniss, 1964; Heal, 1966; Marsh, 1964; Tighe and Tighe, 1965), the one exception being in the study by Eimas (1966a) described above. With adult populations, overtraining has tended to facilitate extradimensional shifts (Caul and Ludvigson, 1964; Guy, Van Fleet, and Bourne, 1966). Why there should be this interaction between age (or intelligence) and the effect of overtraining on extradimensional shifts is certainly not clear. Systematic studies investigating these variables are obviously needed.

THE OVERTRAINING REVERSAL EFFECT. In a *reversal* transfer task, the dimension that was relevant in original learning remains relevant, but the previously positive value is made negative and the previously negative value is made positive (see Table 9-2). Overtraining has often been found to increase the speed of reversal learning.[4] However, since it does not always have this effect, several theorists have attempted to determine the conditions under which it is and is not obtained. Theios and Brelsford (1964) and Theios and Blosser (1965) suggested that the different results may depend on the magnitude of the incentive used. However, Sperling (1965a) concluded that incentive magnitude is effective in position discriminations but not in discriminations in which some other dimension is relevant; and she summarized evidence supporting this conclusion (Sperling, 1965b), although contradictory data have been reported (Cakmak, 1965; Clayton, 1965). Clayton (1965) suggested that the effect of incentive magnitude results from a confounding of this variable with drive level, and presented experimental evidence in support of this view. Mackintosh (1965a) concluded that overtraining affects reversal learning only when the relevant dimension is not prepotent, that is, when the initial Po is relatively low. (See Lovejoy, 1966, for an explicit mathematical treatment of this effect.)

It has been suggested that the effect of overtraining on reversal learning results from enhancement of the probability of acquiring a "response of discriminating" (Reid, 1953). Another suggested explanation is that overtraining increases the discriminability of the change in reinforcement that occurs when the reward contingencies are first reversed (Capaldi and Stevenson, 1957; Youniss and Furth, 1964a). However, these explanations suffer from either a lack of supporting evidence or from contradictory evidence (e.g., Paul, 1965b).

Attention theory can explain the overtraining reversal effect, in the following way: Since $Pr_{(1)}$ is usually very near asymptote when criterion is reached, additional training will usually result in negligible increments in this probability; but since $Po_{(1)}$ is usually considerably below asymptote at criterion, overtraining will usually increase its value appreciably. When reversal begins, the subjects will make a number of perseverative errors, but the probability of attending

---

[4] For reviews of the relevant experimental literature and discussions of explanatory mechanisms that have been proposed, see Blum and Blum (1949), Paul (1965a), Warren (1965), Sperling (1965a, 1965b), Mackintosh (1965b), Lovejoy (1966), and Shepp and Turrisi (1966). See also R. A. Gardner (1966), who criticized the method used in some of the reviews of the relevant literature.

to the relevant dimension will not be reduced to as low a magnitude as it would be had no overtraining been given. Hence, after overtraining, attention will not tend to shift to irrelevant dimensions. Reversal learning after overtraining is predicted to be characterized by a number of initial errors followed by rapid acquisition of the new response. After criterional training, reversal learning will be marked by slightly fewer consecutive errors, but then by a series of responses to irrelevant cues, and finally by acquisition of the appropriate instrumental response. Overtraining, according to attention theory, prevents the phase of responding to irrelevant dimensions and therefore facilitates reversal learning.

In a study designed to test these predictions directly, Eimas (1969b) trained third grade children on a successive discrimination and its reversal in an apparatus that permitted the independent assessment of observing responses (attention) and instrumental responses. In order to obtain criterion it was necessary for the children to learn which observing response displayed the relevant information and then to learn which instrumental response was associated with each of the two relevant cues. The children were trained to criterion or to criterion plus 25 overtraining trials. The overtrained subjects learned the reversal problem significantly faster, despite their making reliably more perseverative errors. The facilitation of reversal learning was primarily a function of the overtrained subjects' making significantly fewer irrelevant observing responses, just as predicted by attention theory.

In another ingenious test of the assumptions of attention theory that the attentional response is directed to dimensions and that overtraining facilitates reversal learning by enhancing this response, Campione *et al.* (1965) trained three matched groups of retardates on a color or form discrimination. After attaining criterion, Group R was given a reversal shift. Group ID was given 100 overtraining trials, then an intradimensional shift, and finally a reversal shift with the relevant cues of the intradimensional shift. Group ED received the overtraining, then an extradimensional shift, followed by a reversal shift with the relevant cues of the extradimensional shift. A summary of the training conditions is given in Table 9-3. Group ID had the same relevant dimension during all four stages of training, but the overtraining trials were with stimulus values not present in the reversal shift. Group ED had the same amount of training as Group ID, but the overtraining trials were not only with different values but also with a relevant dimension different from that of the reversal shift. According to attention theory, the overtraining in Group ID should facilitate reversal by increasing $Po_{(1)}$, and hence Group ID is predicted to be superior to Group R, which was given no overtraining. The theory also predicts that the overtraining in Group ED should have no effect on reversal, because this group was not given overtraining with the dimension that was relevant in the reversal stage (and Stage 3). These predictions were confirmed, as shown in the last column of Table 9-3. Reversal is facilitated not by overtraining *per se*, but by overtraining on the dimension relevant in the reversal shift. These data strongly support the contention that the determining agent of the effect of overtraining on reversal is the attentional response and that this response is directed toward a dimension.

Other studies with children have yielded the effect, but with the more conventional methods of training, that is, with identical stimulus values during original learning, overtraining, and reversal training. For example, Eimas (1966b) found this effect with second graders, using color and form discriminations; moreover, the magnitude of the effect tended to increase with an increase in the number of variable irrelevant dimensions, replicating earlier findings with rats (Mackintosh, 1963). Cross and Tyer (1966) and Youniss and Furth (1964a, 1964b) obtained the effect in children ranging in age from four to eight years. Negative evidence, either no effect of overtraining or a reversed effect, has also been reported (e.g., Eimas, 1966b, Exp. 2; Stevenson and Weir, 1959a). However, in the majority of the studies yielding negative evidence, the relevant dimension was

Table 9-3

Overtraining and Discriminative Shifts[a,b]

Group	Stage 1	Stage 2	Stage 3	Stage 4	Stage 4 errors
R	Original learning	—	—	Reversal of Stage 1	11.78
ID	Original learning	Overtraining	ID shift	Reversal of Stage 3	5.71
ED	Original learning	Overtraining	ED shift	Reversal of Stage 3	14.58

[a] From Campione, Hyman, and Zeaman (1965). Reprinted by permission of the authors and Academic Press, Inc.
[b] See text for explanation of symbols.

position. Position is a highly preferred and easily discriminated dimension, suggesting a very high probability of attention. If so, then as Mackintosh (1965a) suggested, the Po for position at criterion would be essentially asymptotic, precluding any effect of overtraining on Po and hence on reversal learning.

REVERSAL, EXTRADIMENSIONAL, AND NONREVERSAL SHIFTS. The transfer paradigm to be considered next is one that compares the rates of acquisition of three shifts: reversal, extradimensional, and nonreversal. Examples of these shifts are given in Table 9-2. It is apparent that the nonreversal shift is really a modified extradimensional shift. However, the necessity for maintaining the distinction will be made clear below (see also Shepp and Turrisi, 1966).

These shifts will first be considered from the viewpoint of attention theory, and then from the viewpoint of the Kendlers' mediational model of discrimination learning and transfer (Kendler and Kendler, 1962). In attention theory, a *reversal* shift provides positive transfer of the attentional response and negative transfer of the instrumental response, as noted in the preceding section. The *extradimensional* shift provides negative transfer of the attentional response and no transfer of the instrumental response (as noted previously). The *nonreversal* shift, however, provides zero transfer of both responses. The basis for this assertion is the assumption that a necessary condition for an attentional response to a dimension is that there be at least two values on the dimension (Shepp and Turrisi, 1966). As can be seen in Table 9-2, on any one nonreversal shift trial there is but a single value from the previously relevant dimension, thus precluding an attentional response to this dimension and obviously also precluding a differential instrumental response to the values on this dimension. According to this line of reasoning, extradimensional shifts should be more difficult than nonreversal shifts, because the former involve one kind of negative transfer and the latter involve no negative (nor positive) transfer. Dickerson (1967) confirmed this prediction in a study with kindergarten children.

Predictions about the relative acquisition rates of all three shift conditions are more difficult to make. Indeed, no rigorous predictions can be deduced from attention theory until weights are assigned to attentional responses and instrumental responses to make explicit the relative importance of their transfer. If the two are of equal importance, then reversal shifts should be learned at the same rate as nonreversal shifts and more rapidly than extradimensional shifts, because in the first the positive transfer of the attentional response is canceled by the negative transfer of the instrumental response, in the second there is zero transfer of both, and in the third there is negative transfer of the attentional response. If attentional response transfer is of greater importance, then reversal shifts should be more rapid than both extradimensional and nonreversal shifts, because only reversal shifts (among the three under consideration) involve positive transfer of the attentional response. Finally, if instrumental response transfer carries greater weight, then reversal shifts should be acquired more slowly than nonreversal shifts; and depending upon exactly how much weight the instrumental response transfer carries, reversal shifts may be acquired more rapidly or more slowly than extradimensional shifts, or even at the same rate. Since the relative weights are at present unknown, it is obvious that comparison of these shift conditions can provide no critical tests of the assumptions of attention theory.

The Kendlers' mediational model generates predictions that are quite different from the predictions of attention theory, and generates quite different predictions depending upon the developmental level of the organism. Articulate organisms are assumed to mediate, using some form of covert verbal representational response,[5] but nonarticulate organisms, including young children and animals, are assumed not to mediate and to form only simple stimulus-response associations (in accordance with some single-stage model, such as discussed in the introduction to Chapter 5). There are thus two sets of predictions, one for articulate organisms and one for nonarticulate organisms, about the rates of acquisition of the three discriminative shifts. Articulate organisms are predicted to learn reversal shifts more rapidly than nonreversal and extradimensional shifts.

[5] The Kendlers have at times argued that the mediating response need not be verbal but in fact may be perceptual. In either case, however, the availability of this response was always assumed to be related to both phyletic and ontogenetic level.

In a reversal shift the mediating response acquired during original learning is still appropriate and, thus, all that must be learned is a new instrumental response; but extradimensional and nonreversal shifts require the acquisition of both a new mediating response and a new instrumental response. Hence, the latter two shifts should be learned more slowly than the reversal shift.

Nonarticulate (nonmediating) organisms, however, are predicted to find reversal shifts more difficult than the other two shifts. A nonarticulate organism is predicted to acquire a choice response more quickly to one of the cues of the previously irrelevant dimension, because responses to these cues were reinforced 50 percent of the time during original training, while responses to the negative cue on the previously relevant dimension were never reinforced during original training.[6]

Since attention theory is capable of predicting any set of results with respect to these three shifts, rates of acquisition cannot be used as a critical test between attention theory and the mediational model of the Kendlers. However, since attention theory includes no assumptions about the availability of mediating attentional responses at different developmental levels, changes in the relative rates of acquisition with increasing developmental level may be taken as probative evidence for the Kendlers' position (provided the changes are of the predicted kinds). The evidence, unfortunately, is contradictory. Kendler and Kendler (1959) and Kendler, Kendler, and Wells (1960) found reversal shifts to be more difficult than nonreversal shifts for nursery school children and for slow learning and presumably nonmediating kindergarten children; and for fast learning, presumably mediating kindergartners, the reversal shift was easier than the nonreversal shift, as it is for adults (e.g., Harrow and Friedman, 1958). (See, however, Shepp and Turrisi, 1966, for a critique of these findings.) Infrahuman organisms have been found to behave like young children in that they learn nonreversal shifts more rapidly than reversal shifts (Kelleher, 1956). However, House and Zeaman (1962) and Ohlrich and Ross (1966) found faster reversal than extradimensional shift acquisition in retarded children, who may reasonably be assumed to be deficient in the use of verbal mediators. As Ohlrich and Ross noted, this finding may have been due in part to overtraining, which provided greater opportunity for the acquisition of the mediating response. Overtraining has also been shown to facilitate a reversal shift relative to a nonreversal shift in normal six to seven year olds (Tighe and Tighe, 1965) and rats (Mackintosh, 1962). Even more difficult for a verbal mediation theory to explain are the results of a study by Dickerson (1966)

---

[6] There is some evidence, from a study with rats (Wagner *et al.*, 1968), against the assumption that the cues that were 50 percent rewarded would be preferred (the study is discussed in Chapter 7, under "Stimulus Predifferentiation" in the section entitled "Transfer in Discrimination Tasks"). Furthermore, although the reasoning that generates the prediction makes intuitive sense, a recent theoretical paper by Wolford and Bower (1969) demonstrated that reversal shifts will not always be learned slower than nonreversal shifts. Working specifically from Spence's (1936) single-stage model of discrimination learning, the authors showed that under some conditions reversal shifts can be learned more quickly than nonreversal shifts. How the Kendlers might incorporate these findings into their model of development is beyond the scope of this chapter.

demonstrating faster reversal than nonreversal shift learning in normal four year old children without overtraining (see also Saravo, 1967). An additional difficulty is the finding of Fritz and Blank (1968) that the difficulty of the reversal shift, relative to the nonreversal shift, depends on whether or not an irrelevant dimension is included during training. Reversal was faster when no irrelevant dimension was included, and slower when an irrelevant dimension was included.

It is apparent that there is no clear decision as to which theoretical position is more adequate. On the one hand, attention theory must come to grips with findings of both phyletic and ontogenetic differences in the rates of shift acquisition. The mediational model of the Kendlers, on the other hand, must be able to explain effects that could occur only by the use of mediating responses in subjects presumably too young or too retarded to be at all proficient in the use of mediating responses. Whether suitable modifications of the models can be made is, at present, a moot question.

OPTIONAL SHIFTS. The final transfer situation to be considered is the optional shift. The upper portion of Figure 9-7 illustrates the usual procedure. Subjects are trained on an initial discrimination with one relevant visual dimension and one variable irrelevant visual dimension, size and brightness, for instance. Position is irrelevant and variable throughout all stages of training. After criterion is reached, subjects are transferred to the second or optional shift problem which has both size and brightness relevant and redundant (i.e., confounded). This problem can be solved as a reversal shift or as a nonreversal shift. In order to determine the subject's basis for solution, test trials are administered during the third stage of training. Interspersed with the test trials are additional optional shift trials to maintain the pattern of responding learned during Stage 2. If on eight or more of ten test trials, a subject responds to the small gray stimulus (in the example in Figure 9-7), it may be inferred that a reversal shift has occurred; the subject is ignoring brightness and responding to the opposite value of the initially relevant size dimension. The occurrence of eight or more responses to the large black stimulus defines a nonreversal shift; the subject is ignoring size differences and responding to brightness, the irrelevant dimension of the initial discrimination.

In the terminology of attention theory, the optional shift problem may be described as a discrimination in which two dimensions compete for attention; one, the originally relevant dimension, has a high Po, and the other, the previously irrelevant dimension, has a low Po. The expectation is that attention will be directed to the old relevant dimension and maintained unless it extinguishes prior to acquisition of the reverse instrumental response, in which case attention will shift to the old irrelevant dimension. The former situation describes a reversal shift and the latter a nonreversal shift.

Overtraining on the initial discrimination would presumably strengthen the mediating attentional response and increase the number of reversal shifts. Similarly, if the Po of the old irrelevant dimension could be enhanced, then the number of reversal shifts should decrease. One method of accomplishing the latter is suggested by the experimental findings of Zeaman and House (1963).

They demonstrated that novelty is a strong determinant of attention, and that
novel cues could be created by the sudden introduction of two values along
a stimulus dimension after training with only a single value. The lower portion
of Figure 9-7 illustrates this technique. A single value of brightness, that is,
a constant irrelevant dimension, is used during initial training; in the optional
shift problem a second value of brightness is suddenly introduced. If novelty

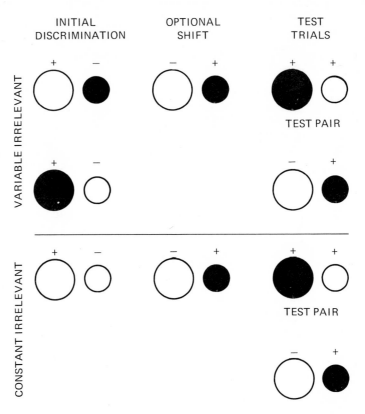

Fig. 9-7. Sample stimuli for optional shift studies. See text for explanation. (White
represents gray.) (From Eimas, 1967. Reprinted by permission of the author and
Academic Press, Inc.)

is created and attracts attention, then the number of reversal shifts should be
less than following initial training with a variable irrelevant dimension.

In an experiment with second and fourth graders, Eimas (1967) tested the
effects of enhancing either the relevant or irrelevant dimension of the initial
discrimination. For half of the subjects the initial discrimination problem had
a variable irrelevant dimension, as illustrated in the top half of Figure 9-7;
and for the other subjects, the initial problem had a constant irrelevant dimension, as illustrated in the bottom half of Figure 9-7. Half of each of these groups
was given no overtraining and the other half was given 50 overtraining trials

on the first problem. The results are presented in Table 9-4, and may be summarized as follows: (a) more reversal shifts were made after variable irrelevant training than after constant irrelevant training; (b) overtraining increased the number of reversal shifts after variable irrelevant training but decreased the number of reversal shifts after constant irrelevant training; (c) fourth graders made more reversal shifts than second graders but only after training under constant irrelevant conditions. If one were to make the simple assumption that the degree of novelty is a direct function of the amount of constant irrelevant training, then the decrement in reversal shifts after overtraining in this condition is readily

Table 9-4

*Percentage of Each Group Making Optional
Reversal Shifts*[a]

Grade level	Irrelevant dimension	Overtraining	
		0 Trials	50 Trials
2	Variable	75	96
	Constant	45	25
4	Variable	86	96
	Constant	68	47

[a] From Eimas (1967). Reprinted by permission of the author and Academic Press, Inc.

explained, and the results (with the age effect excepted) support attention theory.

The significant age effect is not expected from the assumptions of attention theory, since Zeaman and House did not posit any relation between the ability to utilize mediating attentional responses and developmental level. Indeed, the obtained age difference may reflect simply a greater control of novelty over attention in younger children. However, other investigators have hypothesized a direct relationship between developmental level and ability to use mediating responses in the control of instrumental behavior (e.g., Kendler and Kendler, 1962; Kendler *et al.*, 1962; Kuenne, 1946; Luria, 1957; Reese, 1962c). Furthermore, Kendler *et al.* (1962), T. S. Kendler and Kendler (1966), and Jeffrey (1965) used standard procedures and found the percentage of reversal shifts to increase with age. However, Smiley and Weir (1966) and Tighe and Tighe (1966) obtained a high percentage of reversal shifts, from 75 to 100 percent, in children as young as three to five years, ages at which the mediating response should be weak and the percentage of reversal shifts relatively small. Exactly how attention theory might explain this often found effect of age is not readily apparent.

One-Look versus Multiple-Look Attentional Models

An assumption of the basic one-look attentional model (which is the one discussed so far) is that just prior to the choice of an instrumental response, subjects attend to a single dimension. It is possible, of course, that children may attend to more than one dimension and utilize the resulting cues in determining their instrumental response. It should be noted that both one-look and multiple-look models account equally well for the experimental studies discussed in the previous sections and that the one-look model was adopted initially by Zeaman and House because of its simplicity.

The experimental evidence shows unequivocally that subjects can attend to more than one relevant dimension and that compound as well as individual dimensions can provide effective cues. The evidence has come from a variety of subject populations, including college students (Braley, 1962; Braley and Johnson, 1963; Guy et al., 1966), normal and retarded children (Crane and Ross, 1967; Eimas, 1964, 1965, 1969a; House and Zeaman, 1963), rats (Babb, 1957; Mackintosh, 1965b; Sutherland and Holgate, 1966), and pigeons (Terrace, 1963), and the studies have dealt with a variety of experimental problems, including incidental learning, discrimination learning, and transfer. In agreement with the evidence from these studies, Reese (1968, Ch. 11) concluded that in the transposition situation, subjects can attend simultaneously to absolute and relative cues.

Conclusion

In this chapter and in Chapter 7 it has been demonstrated that most of the evidence from studies of discrimination learning and transfer in children and, in numerous instances, infrahuman organisms supports the basic assumptions of attention theory. Briefly, these assumptions include the following: (a) discrimination learning consists of the acquisition of a chain of two responses, one attentional and the other instrumental; (b) both responses transfer across problems; and (c) the attentional response is dimensional, is selective, though often directed to more than one dimension, and is found across a wide range of developmental levels. In addition, Zeaman and House have argued that the attentional response is a central process:

A stimulus cannot be judged novel except in relation to a prior series or background of non-novel (familiar) stimuli. But such a judgment must require that the subject have some trace, record, or engram of previous (familiar) stimuli to contrast with the present novel cue. If seeing novelty requires some record of previous stimulation, then the previous stimulation must have gotten past at least the peripheral stages of sensory reception. We are forced to conclude that subjects . . . are . . . storing information somewhere. Attention is, therefore, a central process. (Zeaman and House, 1963, p. 200.)

Some of Jeffrey's earlier research (1958a, 1958b, 1968) makes particularly good sense within the context of attention theory. Jeffrey assumed that certain discriminations that were reported to be difficult or impossible for young children were actually within the sensory capacity even of infants and therefore must represent a "problem solving" deficiency. He explored various procedures and found that certain testing or learning procedures frequently confused the issue of discriminative capacity with other variables that interfered with the children's performance. For example, the question of whether a child can discriminate the small letter "d" from "b" will be answered differently depending on whether (a) he is required to press a button under one of the letters regardless of its position when the two are presented simultaneously, (b) he has to learn to press a button on the left when "b" is present and to press a button on the right when "d" is present, or (c) he must learn the vocal label "dee" for one and "bee" for the other. Each is a different problem for the child though not for the adult. Furthermore, children are often quite able to make certain discriminations under optimal conditions; and there may be positive transfer to a previously more difficult task once the child presumably has learned to attend to the appropriate cues in a simpler task. Therefore, developmental statements about discriminative capacity should be made with care. Although this work has been insufficiently systematic to establish all the relevant variables, two things have become increasingly clear. The first is that children often either do not understand or else ignore the instructions given in problem-solving experiments, and the second is that one should not take for granted that the child is attending to the appropriate cues or that he will necessarily do so as learning progresses. Thus, one can conclude that transfer will be aided by any pretraining procedures that establish learning sets that help define the problem for the child or that increase the likelihood of his attending to the appropriate cues.

SUMMARY AND CONCLUSIONS

From the review of the orientation reaction and its role in the formation of learned responses the following conclusions seem reasonably well established: the orientation reaction is (a) a set of reflexive responses to changes or features of importance in the environment, (b) a result of central analyzing processes, (c) an indicator of an organism's awareness of stimulation and readiness to respond to it, and (d) readily conditionable to neutral cues and therefore a potential mediator for the establishment of complex voluntary responses.

In attempting to relate the orientation reaction to attention, some writers (e.g., Zaporozhets, 1961) have gone so far as to equate the two, using them interchangeably. However, if the definition of attention is limited to some active selective process, then the orientation reaction must be classified as different from, though obviously related to, attention (e.g., Jeffrey, 1968). In keeping with this position, the registering of stimuli as evidenced by the orientation reaction can be considered a first and necessary condition for attention. However, the presence of an orientation reaction does not necessarily imply that the subject has acted selectively upon the stimulus input nor, more importantly, that he has obtained specific information or knowledge about the nature of the stimulus. The selective scanning of information has been defined here as attention, while the identification of the selected information, as to what it is or is not, would seem to be the function of perception. This view that attention mediates between our initial reception of stimuli and higher mental processes is compatible with the Zeaman and House model of discrimination learning. In their theoretical system, attention is a central selective response, intermediate between the external stimulus array and the instrumental response. Like the orientation reaction, it can be conditioned.

The vast majority of the data on discrimination learning and transfer in children support the assumption that some form of mediational process is necessary for learning and transfer, and that it is often tenable to equate this mediational process with attention. The results of these studies with children are also in accord with the view that attention as a mediating process may be found in children as young as three and four years of age. Children younger than this, indeed even neonates, show evidence of selectivity in their responses to stimulus arrays, but whether they are able to use these selective responses to mediate other forms of behavior is at present not known.

Finally, it should be noted that the orientation reaction and exploratory behavior, which is discussed in Chapter 10, are often directed toward the same types of external stimulation. Furthermore, these same stimuli more often than not produce profound effects on the discrimination learning of children. For example, there are the marked effects of novelty upon optional shifts and upon intradimensional and extradimensional shifts. Novel cues have also been found to facilitate the initial discrimination learning of retarded children (Zeaman, House, and Orlando, 1958), as does increasing the complexity of the relevant cues.

Despite numerous differences, the behavioral phenomena reviewed in this chapter, and exploratory behavior, can all be viewed as patterns of behavior that are strongly determined by attention or attention-like processes. That is, these behavioral phenomena reflect the child's persistent searching and scanning of his environment and his reaction only to selected portions of the available stimulation.

CHAPTER 10

Motivation

INTRODUCTION

Definition of Motivation

A fundamental prerequisite for learning and performance is that the organism be motivated. For example, Pavlov (1927) trained dogs to salivate to the sound of a metronome by delivering meat powder a few seconds after onset of the metronome, but found that a necessary condition for efficient learning of the salivary response was that the dogs be hungry, that they be deprived of food for some time prior to the conditioning trials. After the completion of learning, the hungry dog salivates profusely when it hears the metronome, but if the animal is fed to satiation before presentation of the conditional stimulus, a re-markable degree of "forgetting" appears and the dog might salivate only a few drops or not at all. Actually, the animal has not "forgotten" what it previously learned, since the re-introduction of hunger would reinstate the learned behavior; the animal "knows" what to do all along; it just does not *perform* when not hungry.

Hunger is thus seen to be important both as a condition for *learning* and as a condition for later *performance*. Particularly because of its role in perform-ance, hunger is called a source of motivation: any condition that facilitates the performance of a previously developed response (either learned or instinc-tive) is often called a source of motivation (e.g., Brown and Farber, 1968). The word "often" is used because psychologists have disagreed about the best definition of motivation. The suggested definition is probably the most frequently used, however, and it has the added advantage of being consistent with the definition appearing in the most highly developed motivational theory available, Hull's behavior theory (Hull, 1943, 1952). The interested reader is referred to Brown for a lucid discussion of different definitions of motivation (Brown, 1953).

Motivation, as defined above, is often said to have an "energizing" function; it transforms what an animal has learned (or inherited as instinct) into perform-ance. This basic function leads to Hull's fundamental equation relating the three concepts (i.e., performance, motivation, and learning). In Hull's system, the result of learning is a habit, for example, a habit to salivate in the presence of the sound of the metronome. This habit, this physiological connection between the afferent neural representation of the metronome and the efferent representation of salivation, is transformed into observable performance by the action of motivation or drive. Drive (D) and habit (sHr) combine to produce performance (sPr). Hull guessed that the form of the combination is multiplicative, a guess that has withstood many subsequent experimental tests. Thus, his fundamental equation relating the three concepts is

$$sPr = +f(D \times sHr) \tag{1}$$

This equation is to be understood as follows: the performance (P) of a given response (r) in the presence of a given stimulus (s) is a positive function (+f) of the amount of drive present at that time (D) times the strength of the habit (H) to perform that response (r) in the presence of that stimulus (s). If the value of D is measured in terms of the number of hours of food deprivation, and the value of sHr in terms of the number of previous training trials, then it can be seen how a quantitative prediction about performance is possible.

Hunger is, of course, not the only source of motivation. Thirst possesses the same energizing function as hunger, and thus fits the definition of motivation. Another source of motivation is pain, operationally defined in many different ways: too low or too high a temperature, a blast of air from an air nozzle, a blow on the head from a rolled-up newspaper, electric shock, etc. All of these procedures have been used by experimental psychologists studying animal learning; and in fact hunger, thirst, and pain are the dominant three drives in terms of frequency of usage in work on animal learning.

These drives, and the sex drive, also appear to be dominant in another sense. If the whole spectrum of animal behavior in all its natural habitats is considered, most of it seems to be energized by these four drives. The mouse in the cellar, the chicken in the henyard, the fish in the stream, the lion in the bush country— What drives would motivate behavior if these four were removed? Because of the evolutionary relation between man and beast, many psychologists assumed that these drives must account for a significant portion of human behavior too. But immediately a baffling problem arose, which will now be examined.

The Problem of Human Motivation

Like animals, humans must be motivated if they are to be active—if they are to learn and perform. Since they are vulnerable to the same pangs of hunger and thirst, the same pain of bodily injury, and the same sexual urges, it seems natural to assume that human behavior is energized by the same drives as animal behavior. However, it is not, except perhaps in the most primitive societies. Most American children, for example, spend much of each day either playing or going to school. These behaviors usually occur in the absence of deprivations of such things as food and water. The children eat a hearty breakfast, drink a large glass of orange juice, go to the toilet, and then run outside and engage in vigorous play activity. They are not hungry, thirsty, nor prodded by painful stimuli, nor is there any reason to suppose that they are motivated by sexual needs. Wherein lies the motivation for such activity? Adults too spend much time engaged in behavior far removed from the satisfaction of such drives. Witness the research scientist who abandons more profitable activities, which would earn him more money to spend on food, shelter, etc., in order to pursue a line of inquiry that nets him little, and often imperils his health, who "exists" rather than "lives," according to his perplexed fellow man. At a less extreme level, consider the commonplace adult activities of an evening's poker game, a morning's walk, a tennis match, reading a book. These activities are also far removed from the basic animal drives.

Such "unmotivated" behavior has also perplexed psychologists. Harlow, for example, wrote:

> Motivationally, man is a strange, if not bizarre, creature: he is the only known organism to arise in the morning before he is awake, work all day without resting, continue his activities after the diurnal and even the crepuscular organisms have retired to rest, and then take narcotics to induce an inadequate period of troubled sleep. But lest we decry man's motivational mechanisms we should point out that without them we would not have the steam engine, the electric light, the automobile, Beethoven's Fifth Symphony, Leonardo da Vinci's undigested "Last Supper," gastric ulcers, coronary thrombosis, and clinical psychologists. Indeed, we might well regard this aggregate as the human motivation syndrome. (Harlow, 1953, p. 24.)

Similarly, Berlyne wrote:

> The cases that raise the most acute motivational problems . . . are those in which perceptual or intellectual activities are engaged in for their own sake . . . . In these cases, none of the more conspicuous kinds of motivation and reward may be in evidence . . . . The result is what we normally classify as play or, to use a more technical and comprehensive term, "ludic behavior" (Latin *ludare,* to play). (Berlyne, 1960, p. 4.)

How have psychologists attempted to solve the riddle of human motivation? The next section presents a brief history of the major attempts.

Past Attempts to Solve the Human Motivation Problem

By way of overview, it may be said that there have been at least three major movements in the attempts to account for human behavior without placing a heavy explanatory burden on the animal drives. The first movement, relying on the concept of *instinct*, began in the late 1800s, and died in the 1930s, only to be resurrected in the 1950s. It was replaced by the notion of *psychological (learned) needs*, which became a prominent wave of thought in the late 1920s and 30s, began to die off in the 1940s and 50s, but is not yet completely extinct. Beginning in the 1940s and reaching peak strength in the mid-1960s is the third wave, relying heavily on the notion of *secondary (learned) reinforcement*. This last movement is still strong at the time of this writing, yet it appears that the bell has begun to toll for it too—but that is getting ahead of the story.

THE RISE AND FALL OF INSTINCT.   Darwinism probably provided the instinct movement with its initial impetus. Faced with incontrovertible evidence of the evolutionary relation between different life forms, it became an easy step to assume that man, being just another animal, was controlled in the same fundamental way, through the manifestation of instincts. Psychologists soon began attributing a long list of instincts to man. William James, in his classic *Principles of Psychology* (James, 1890, Vol. II), listed the following as human instincts: locomotion, vocalization, imitation, rivalry, pugnacity, sympathy, fear, cleanliness, modesty, jealousy, and on and on. Thirty years later the tradition was being continued by McDougall, who added to the list a number of other names, such as flight, repulsion, and self-abasement (McDougall, 1923).

The problem with this movement was that many psychologists began to confuse *naming* a phenomenon with *explaining* it. Whenever a bit of behavior was spotted for which there was no existing explanation, it was "explained" by postulating an underlying instinct. However, the only empirical evidence for the existence of the instinct was the occurrence of the behavior it explained.

It was not long before the uncritical use of the concept in this fashion drew heavy criticism. Holt, in criticizing the circularity of such reasoning, wrote:

> . . . man is impelled to action, it is said, by his instincts. If he goes with the fellows, it is the "herd instinct" which activates him; if he walks alone, it is the "anti-social instinct"; if he fights, it is the instinct of "pugnacity"; if he defers to another, it is the instinct of "self-abasement"; if he twiddles his thumbs, it is the thumb-twiddling instinct; if he does not twiddle his thumbs, it is the thumb-not-twiddling instinct. Thus everything is explained with the facility of magic-word magic. (Holt, 1931, p. 4.)

Other psychologists shared this objection (e.g., Dunlap, 1919; Kuo, 1924), and instincts fell out of fashion until a much more rigorous and restricted version of the concept was revived in the 1950s (Beach, 1955).

THE RISE AND FALL OF PSYCHOLOGICAL NEEDS.   A replacement for instinct was not long in coming. Indeed, some of those responsible for its death were also responsible for its replacement. Writing in 1924, John B. Watson, the founder of behaviorism, said:

> There are . . . for us no instincts—we no longer need the term in psychology. Everything we have been in the habit of calling an "instinct" today is a result largely of training—belongs to man's *learned behavior*. (Watson, 1924a, p. 74.)

The energy for behavior was also assumed to be a result of learning. Psychological or learned needs were assumed to provide the motivation, and long lists of such needs were drawn up to replace the forbidden instinct lists. Man no longer had a pugnacious *instinct*, he had *learned a need* to be pugnacious.

Henry A. Murray epitomized the practice with his need list of 1938 (Murray, 1938), but as late as 1963 a similar list was presented in one of the leading child development textbooks of the day:

.

.

.

Hostility. This motive refers to the desire to hurt, injure, destroy or cause pain to an individual or object.
Dominance. This is the desire to influence or control others and to resist the demands of other people.

.

.

.

Affiliation. This motive is the desire to form friendships and associations with other people.
Mastery. This motive refers to the child's desire to develop skills which allow him to control aspects of his environment . . . . (Mussen, Conger, and Kagan, 1963, p. 141.)

And so on for a number of other needs, or "motives."

Learned needs began to be used in the same circular way as had instincts, and critics again warned against the same old word magic. Furthermore, there were those who assumed that because a person *said* he had a certain need or desire, he actually *had* it. Warning of these perils, Brown wrote:

Human subjects are prolific in their use of phrases like "I *want* that object" or "I *desire* this" or "I *need* those." Since the subject *says* he has a multitude of needs, and since he did not say so at birth, the unwary psychologist . . . is likely to conclude that each such statement demands the postulation of a corresponding acquired motive . . . . (Brown, 1953, p. 10.)

The fallacy, of course, is that the verbalization may be simply a component of the performance tendency (sPr) which is to be explained in the first place.

Faced with these difficulties, and with a growing awareness that the hypothesized needs remain mere guesses unless the details of their development are empirically determined, there has been less and less reference to psychological needs in recent years. At the same time, an increasing frequency of usage of the concept of *secondary reinforcement* has occurred, as described in subsequent paragraphs.

THE RISE OF SECONDARY REINFORCEMENT. Beginning with Skinner in 1938 and Hull in 1943, the concept of secondary reinforcement has grown in importance until it has overtaken the role of primary reinforcement (e.g., food, water, pain reduction) in explanations of behavior. An understanding of the concept may be gained by referring to the role of the primary drives in animal learning. Not only does the animal have to be hungry, for example, *before* the to-be-learned response, it also has to receive food *after* the response; not only does it have to be thirsty, it also has to receive water after the response; pain has to be followed by pain reduction. Food, water, and pain reduction are called *reinforcers* or *rewards* because the animal seeks them and because responses that precede them are learned. Furthermore, they are called *primary* rewards for the same reason hunger, thirst, and pain are called primary drives; they are not dependent upon past learning for their effectiveness.

A secondary reward is dependent upon learning. An object becomes a secondary reward, according to Skinner and Hull, as a result of temporally contiguous pairings with an already established reinforcer, either primary or secondary (Hull, 1943; Skinner, 1938). After enough such pairings, the animal learns some response (the nature of which will be discussed later) that imparts to the object a reinforcing function similar to that of the reinforcer with which it was originally paired.

Just as the primary drives cannot account for all of human learning and performance, neither can their associated primary rewards. If a human being seldom suffers from strong pangs of thirst, water can hardly be a frequent source of reward. It does not require a strong imagination, however, to think of many originally neutral objects that have been systematically paired with primary rewards, especially during childhood. Perhaps, then, these objects have become secondary rewards; if so, their later occurrence might account for much of human learning.

Consider, for example, some of the cues that may be paired with feeding an infant and changing its diapers, primary reward events that occur with some frequency during the early years.[1] While these caretaking routines are being carried out the mother repeatedly utters words of love to the infant, such as "Momma loves you," "Good morning, Sweetheart," "That's a good girl." Perhaps, then, the sounds become "good sounds" to the infant, and later he "works" for them by learning responses that are followed by social approval. Other cues can then be paired with social approval, and they too should become secondary rewards. Thus, the teacher gives social approval for a well-performed recital in class, and records a grade of "A." Given enough such pairings the mark itself becomes a reinforcer, and then the child will work for high grades. By a similar process the child learns responses that are followed by gold stars, money, hugs, boy scout medals, ribbons, and so on.

Few psychologists doubt the reality of secondary reinforcement as an important cause of learning. The leading textbooks in learning and motivation endorse it:

It has received experimental confirmation many times. (Cofer and Appley, 1964, p. 474.)

It is obvious from the studies which have been cited that neutral stimuli may acquire the capacity to serve as a reinforcing stimulus. (Hall, 1966, p. 129.)

The fact that some forms of reinforcement are secondary or learned, is well established. (Kimble, 1961, p. 167.)

[1] The young infant is fed six to eight times a day, and needs well over a dozen diaper changes—the average numbers of defecations and micturations per day have been estimated to be 4.7 and 18.6, respectively (Halverson, 1940). Other recurrent caretaking encounters, such as bathing, playing, and soothing, further increase the daily number of "learning trials."

Many of man's most potent reinforcing stimuli are ones which would have no special reinforcement value unless man had received training that made them reinforcing. (Staats, 1968, p. 429.)

There is experimental evidence to show that new conditions can acquire the properties of reinforcers that they did not originally possess. (Travers, 1963, p. 78.)

Convinced of the reality of secondary reinforcement, child psychologists were quick to use the concept as the theoretical workhorse in their explanations of childhood learning, and this trend continues at the present time. Psychologists of the Skinnerian outlook seem especially prone to such reasoning. Any object—a stick, a stone, a flashing light, a "yes" from the experimenter, or just a gutteral "hm-mm"—is automatically labeled a secondary (or conditioned) reinforcer if it affects the frequency of a preceding response. In discussing attempts to control autistic children, for example, Ferster wrote:

The sound of the candy dispenser preceding the delivery of candy served as a conditioned reinforcer . . . . With further training, the delivery of a coin (conditioned reinforcer) sustained the child's performance . . . . Still later, coins sustained the child's performance even though they had to be held for a period of time before they could be cashed in . . . . Even longer delays of reinforcement were arranged by sustaining behavior in the experimental room with a conditioned reinforcer as, for example, a towel or a life jacket which could be used later in the swimming pool . . . . (Ferster, 1961, p. 441.)

If one reads such literature carefully, it becomes apparent that many psychologists are now using the concept in the same circular way that instinct and learned need were once used. If a response was learned, any object that systematically followed it is automatically labeled a secondary reinforcer on that basis alone, and then the circle is completed by referring to the object to explain the learning of the response in the first place: The child learned to push the lever because the response was followed by the life jacket, which was a secondary reinforcer. It was known to be a secondary reinforcer because the response was learned. Longstreth has reminded psychologists of the circularity involved in such reasoning, in a paper presented at a recent meeting of the Society for Research in Child Development (Longstreth, 1967).

THE (PROBABLE) FALL OF SECONDARY REINFORCEMENT. It is Longstreth's contention that not only is the concept of secondary reinforcement often used in a circular way that robs it of scientific meaningfulness, but even more seriously, there is only sketchy evidence supporting the reality of the phenomenon in the first place. Neither animal nor human data provide consistently clear supporting evidence. Both levels of data will be examined briefly in order to provide an understanding of the basis for the indictment.

A peculiarity of the typical Skinner box has been used many times in presumed demonstrations of secondary reinforcement in animals. When a rat presses the lever in a Skinner box, an audible click is heard as the food mechanism ejects a pellet of food into the animal's food tray. Thus, the click should become a secondary reinforcer because it is temporally paired with receipt of food.

To test for its secondary reinforcing function, rats are first trained as described, and then randomly divided into two extinction groups. Neither group obtains food pellets during the extinction phase, but one group hears the click following each response, and the other group does not—the delivery mechanism is turned off. It is found that the click group is more resistant to extinction, confirming the prediction and thus providing support for the concept; the click provides secondary reinforcement for each response, and thus extinction is retarded.

In recent years this interpretation has been so vigorously attacked that even some of its original adherents have publicly recanted. Bugelski, who was one of the first to demonstrate it (Bugelski, 1938), wrote 18 years later, "To select out the click and glamorize it into a 'secondary reinforcer' is totally unnecessary, gratuitous, and theoretically harmful" (Bugelski, 1956, p. 271). The reason is that during training the click is not only paired with food, but also precedes the next lever press, which occurs a few moments later. It therefore could become a conditional stimulus (CS) for lever pressing. If it did become a CS, its presentation during extinction would retard the extinction process because it continues to *elicit* further responses, not because it reinforces previous responses. This "elicitation problem" of operant conditioning is now well known, and such studies are seldom appealed to when the question of secondary reinforcement is considered. Indeed, the same problem is encountered with the food itself. Jenkins showed that presentation of a food pellet after the rat had been "extinguished" resulted in a prompt resumption of lever pressing (Jenkins, 1965b), and Spradlin *et al.* demonstrated the same phenomenon in children (Spradlin, Girardeau, and Horn, 1966).

A study which is free of this criticism was reported by Saltzman, and it is cited more frequently than any other as a clear demonstration of the phenomenon in animals (Saltzman, 1949). [For examples of typical evaluations of the Saltzman study, see Hall (1966), Kimble (1961), and Myers (1958).] Saltzman first trained rats to run down a gray alley to a goalbox that was sometimes black and sometimes white. Whenever the goalbox was one color (black for some rats, white for others), there was food in it; whenever it was the other color, it was empty. After about 20 runs to each goalbox, the rats were presented with a T-maze problem. If they turned in one direction, the arm terminated in a black goalbox; if they turned in the other direction, it terminated in a white goalbox. Both goalboxes were empty. The rats could not see either goalbox until after they turned, and thus goalbox color could not possibly have elicited one turn in preference to the other, eliminating the elicitation problem. The rats learned to make the turn which terminated in the goalbox color previously paired with food. Of 15 test runs, about 10 were in the predicted direction, significantly more than the chance number (7.5).

It is difficult to argue with these results on methodological grounds—the study seems to demonstrate clearly the operation of secondary reinforcement. Because it is such a crucial study, Lieberman essentially repeated it in 1967 to reaffirm the results; but she found no evidence for secondary reinforcement, in spite of the fact that she paired the goalbox color with food more often than Saltzman had, and used a larger reward (Lieberman, 1967). Therefore, although the methodology of the Saltzman study seems straightforward (but see Lieberman's criticisms), the results themselves are now open to question, since they could not be repeated.

The evidence is no better at the human level; there seems to be not one study which is free of methodological difficulties. To be sure, several investigators have *said* they found clear evidence of secondary reinforcement, but a careful examination of the procedures employed has always turned up a flaw of one kind or another.

In a representative study, Myers (1960) presented children with a clown's face that could be used to obtain candy. The children were told to press the nose, which resulted in the appearance of a token in the mouth. The token was to be inserted in a slot in the ear and the nose then pressed again. This resulted in the appearance of a piece of candy, which could be eaten. The sequence, then, was press → token → insert token → press → candy. Since the token appeared just before the candy, it should have acquired secondary reinforcing properties. To test for this possibility, two extinction conditions were used. Half of the subjects received the token but did not obtain candy. The sequence for these subjects consisted of press → token → insert token → press → press → press → etc. The other half did not receive the token; the sequence consisted simply of press → press → press → etc. The mean number of responses for each group during a 200 second extinction period was determined. The first group pressed significantly more often than the second group, leading the investigator to conclude, "The results clearly indicate that tokens can be established as strong secondary reinforcers for preschool children" (Myers, 1960, p. 177).

Careful scrutiny of the design of this study reveals that it is vulnerable to the same elicitation problem as the Skinner box studies. It need only be observed that during training the token preceded the next nose press and consequently could have become a cue eliciting the next nose press. Its absence during extinction would therefore facilitate extinction since one of the cues eliciting the press response was missing. As with the click in the Skinner box, it is not necessarily true that the token *reinforced* the previous press response; but possibly it *elicited* the next one. The investigator herself apparently recognized this possibility a year later; in reporting a highly similar experiment (with the same flaw), she wrote, "The Sr [secondary reinforcer], when administered in extinction, seemed to release the additional behavior in the chain . . ." (Myers, Craig, and Myers, 1961, p. 771). Obviously, if it "released" the next response, there is no need to assume it reinforced the previous response. It is theoretically unjustifiable to appeal to a questionable principle (secondary reinforcement) when an established principle (the eliciting property of a conditional stimulus) will account for the phenomenon under study. It is on this matter of theoretical parsimony that part of the present critique is based: many studies purporting to demonstrate secondary reinforcement have not employed control conditions which allow one to rule out more parsimonious interpretations.

Of the large number of attempted demonstrations of secondary reinforcement with children, a number have yielded negative results (e.g., Donaldson, 1961; Estes, 1960; Fort, 1961; Hall, 1964; Kass and Wilson, 1966; Kass, Wilson, and

Sidowski, 1964; Loeb, 1964; Longstreth, 1960, 1966a, 1966b; Mitrano, 1939; Myers *et al.*, 1961), and of those reporting positive results, all are subject to serious methodological criticisms (e.g., Fort, 1965; Leiman, Myers, and Myers, 1961; Myers, 1960; Myers and Myers, 1962, 1965; Myers and Myers, 1963a, 1963b, 1964; Sidowski *et al.*, 1965). It is for these reasons that Longstreth has questioned the empirical basis of the concept.

But if secondary reinforcement is at best a dubious explanatory concept, how is one to account for all its *apparent* manifestations—pats on the head, gold stars, school grades, grunts of recognition and affection, and so on, not to mention towels and life jackets? As will be shown, some of the effects can be accounted for in terms of *incentive motivation, frustration,* and *conflict;* these concepts account for its motivational effects. There are also associative effects, as yet little understood. That is, so-called secondary reinforcers elicit certain responses that have been conditioned to them in the past, as well as supply the motivational energy to perform them. This associative function will be discussed more fully later.

INCENTIVE MOTIVATION

Children and adults alike are almost continually "expecting" or "anticipating" something—to eat at noon, to get an A in math, to marry Joan, to go to Hawaii this summer for a vacation, etc. The object or event "expected" is conventionally called a reinforcement or reward, and there is accumulating evidence that expectations of reward result in increases in motivation, or drive. The high frequency of occurrence of such expectations makes them potentially important sources of human motivation, just as the low frequency of hunger, thirst, and pain relegates these primary drives to a position of lesser importance.

What are expectations, and what elicits them? Put abstractly, one "expects" or "anticipates" an object or event Y when one responds to another object or event X as though it were Y. In this sense, it can be said that Pavlov's dogs were taught to *expect* meat powder when they heard the metronome, since they responded to the metronome with salivation, the response originally elicited only by meat powder. A stimulus that elicits expectations of reward can be called an *incentive stimulus.*

Classical conditioning may well be the fundamental way of learning expectations. A reward (US) is systematically preceded by a neutral stimulus (CS) which gradually comes to elicit part of the unconditioned response (UR). It may then be said, as a matter of definition, that the CS elicits an expectation, defined as the CR, of the US. Thus, a child "expects dinner" when presented with the word *dinner* at about 6 *p.m.* by his *mother* in his *home,* because this stimulus pattern has systematically preceded dinner in the past, and therefore elicits responses previously elicited only by the dinner itself, such as sitting down at the table, picking up a fork or knife, and even salivating (if it were measured).

Likewise, if the teacher says, "You did very well on your math exam today," an expectation of an A is elicited, since in the past such statements have regularly preceded an A mark on the exam paper. In this case, the nature of the expectation is more difficult to specify, since the responses elicited by the A itself may be unknown, or if known, may be subtle and hard to observe. Perhaps they consist partly of a pleasant emotional response, or of "excitement." Components of these responses constitute the "expectation" subsequently elicited by the teacher's verbalization. Since such responses are hard to observe and measure, they may be ignored, and the expectation defined simply in terms of stimulus events: X elicits an expectation of Y, by definition, if X has systematically preceded Y in the past, and the greater the number of pairings, the greater the expectation. No mention is made of the nature of the expectation at all. Such a stimulus definition is to be contrasted with the previously described response definition, which includes an actual description of the expectative response. The response definition is the better one, since it objectifies what the stimulus definition merely assumes.

What is the evidence, then, that an incentive stimulus increases motivation? Referring back to the definition of motivation given earlier, the question may be rephrased: What is the evidence that an incentive stimulus facilitates the performance of a previously developed response (either learned or unlearned)? To answer this question, it is necessary first to select one of the two operational definitions of an incentive stimulus, and then to impose conditions upon the subject which fulfill the requirements of the definition. Having thus established the occurrence of a reward expectation, one then presents a stimulus (S) to which a response (R) has already been developed, and the strength of which is known. If the presentation of S simultaneously with the occurrence of an expectation results in facilitation of the reference response R, then the question is answered affirmatively; the expectation functioned as a source of motivation.

There is convincing evidence at the animal level that expectations of reward increase drive. Marx and Murphy carried out an experiment of the type described, using rats as subjects (Marx and Murphy, 1961). First, a buzzer was directly paired with food consumption 90 times for experimental rats, but never for control rats, which received the same number of feedings and buzzer presentations, but unpaired. Then a reference response was developed in all rats by giving them 10 reinforced runs down an alley to a goalbox. Finally, test trials were given; on certain trials the buzzer was sounded in the startbox, just as the rat started to locomote down the runway. Speeds on these trials were compared with speeds on buzzer-off trials. It was found that the sound of the buzzer increased running speeds in experimental rats, but not in control rats. This facilitation was observed on the very first set of test trials, thus precluding the possibility that some response learned during the test trials themselves facilitated running.

Other animal studies have produced similar results. For example, Weinrich et al. showed that an incentive stimulus paired with reward during a lever-pressing task later facilitated chain pulling in another task (Weinrich, Cahoon, Ambrose, and Laplace, 1966), and Bacon and Bindra showed that a tone directly paired with water consumption later facilitated the acquisition of a running response (Bacon and Bindra, 1967).

In a study with preschool children, Longstreth used a procedure analogous to the Marx and Murphy procedure (Longstreth, 1962). The reference response was locomotion down a 12 foot carpet from a chair to a goal unit. The time taken to traverse the carpet was recorded. Six preliminary trials were given to establish the response speed prior to the introduction of incentive motivation. The subject was simply told to "go down the carpet and push the button whenever the light comes on." On half of these trials, a red light signaled the onset of the trial, and on the other three trials a blue light was used. Following the six trials, one color was associated directly with reward and the other was not. The subject stood in front of the goal unit and was required to name the color of the light when it came on. Each light was presented eight times, in a random order. Immediately after each presentation of the red light, goal box doors beneath the light sprang open, revealing a single piece of candy. The subject was told he could eat it immediately. Following presentation of the blue light, nothing happened—the goalbox doors remained closed, and the subject received no candy.

It was assumed that following this training, the subject had learned to respond to the red light, but not to the blue light, with expectations of candy. If these expectations increased drive when elicited, there should be increased locomotor speeds to red, but not to blue, when the subject was again asked to sit in the chair and "go down and push the button when the light comes on." Four such test trials were given, two to the red light and two to the blue light. Half of the subjects were presented first with the red·light and then with the blue light; the order was reversed for the remaining subjects. The results are presented in Figure 10-1, in terms of mean running speeds during the preliminary trials and the test trials. It can be seen that the prediction was supported; speeds to the two colors were very similar during preliminary trials, but the incentive training resulted in a much larger increment in speeds to the red light than in speeds to the blue light.

In a more recent study (Longstreth, 1966a), children were instructed to turn a joystick response handle to the left whenever a light was activated in the stimulus aperture. Springs returned the handle to a vertical position following each response, and amplitude of the response was automatically recorded on a polygraph. The joystick response turned the light off, and the next light automatically came on two seconds later. The lights varied in intensity, and progressed from either dim to bright (for half of the subjects) or from bright to dim (for the other subjects) in four steps. The response to the fourth light (S_4) was followed by ejection of a marble into a container, and the subject was instructed to place each marble on a marble board containing 63 holes. The instructions stated that when all the holes were filled with marbles, the subject could have a large Christmas package (which was visible behind the last marble hole). The task was thus a sequential one in which the subject was informed of how close he was to the goals in two ways: first, the marble board showed him how near he was to the package at the end, and second, the light intensity showed him how near he was to each marble—the first light

(S_1) showed him that he was far, and the fourth light (S_4) showed him that a marble was imminent.

It was predicted that S_4 would come to elicit whatever responses were originally elicited by receipt of a marble, and thus to elicit expectations of marbles; S_3 should function in a similar way but to a lesser extent, unless the subject developed a sharp discrimination between the light intensities. Barring the latter possibility, a gradient of marble expectations should develop, the strongest

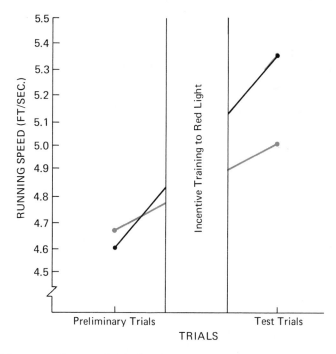

Fig. 10-1. Mean speeds to red (darker line) and blue (lighter line) stimulus lights before and after direct pairing of red light with candy. (Drawn from data presented by Longstreth, 1962, Fig. 1, p. 399.)

elicited by S_4 and the weakest by S_1. If these expectations contribute to drive, any concurrent response should be facilitated. Since the joystick response occurred directly after each light presentation, it occurred concomitantly with marble expectations, and therefore its amplitude should have been greatest to S_4 and least to S_1.

Figure 10-2 presents the amplitude data for various training trials, separately for each of the four light intensities. The lighter line is for a group not yet discussed, an intermittent-reinforcement group which received a marble after S_4 only 54 percent of the time. The darker line, for the 100 percent group, shows decreasing amplitude from S_1 to S_3, and then increased amplitude to S_4. The decrease from S_1 to S_3 probably reflects the acquisition of postural and muscular orientations toward the joystick which resulted in a smoother, more efficient, less clumsy response. These orientations were lost after each sequence, since the subject had to release his grip on the joystick to pick up the marble and place it on the marble board. Of more theoretical interest is the increased amplitude to S_4. One would expect this response to be the most efficient, and thus the weakest, but an increment is observed instead. This may be interpreted

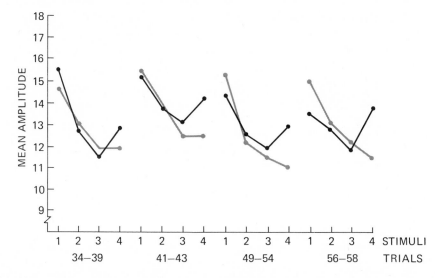

Fig. 10-2. Mean response amplitude (in millimeters) over the last half of training for the two reinforcement schedules, separately for the four responses within a trial. Darker line, 100 percent; lighter line, 54 percent. Each mean is based on the median value of blocks of three trials following reinforced trials. (From L. E. Longstreth, "Frustration and secondary reinforcement concepts as applied to human instrumental conditioning and extinction." *Psychological Monographs*, 1966, *80*, No. 11. Copyright 1966 by the American Psychological Association. Reprinted by permission of the author and publisher.)

to mean that S_4 elicited marble expectations much stronger than those elicited by S_1, S_2, and S_3, and that the resulting increase in drive energized the joystick response, resulting in greater amplitude. The absence of an increment for the intermittent-reinforcement group suggests that marble expectations in this group were much weaker, a suggestion for which there was independent evidence.

Marble expectations were actually observed in this study, albeit serendipitously. It was noted that 11 subjects consistently turned their heads away from the stimulus window and toward the marble hose whenever S_4 was presented. Two of these subjects even placed their hand under the hose, to catch the marble before it landed in the receptacle. Both of these responses are clear instances of marble expectations in the literal sense; they were originally elicited by the marble itself, and later became conditioned to a preceding cue, S_4.

There were three important findings about the behavior of these 11 subjects.

First, the expectations were seldom observed in response to S_1, S_2, or S_3, thus confirming the assumption that marble expectations would be most strongly conditioned to S_4. Second, 10 of the 11 subjects were from the 100 percent reinforcement condition, and only one from the 54 percent condition, thus confirming the assumption that marble expectations were weak in the intermittent-reinforcement condition. Third, 8 of the 11 subjects manifested clear increases in amplitude to S_4, significantly more subjects than would be expected by chance. Thus, marble expectations to S_4 were directly associated with increased amplitudes to S_4, precisely as predicted by incentive motivation theory.

An alternative interpretation of these results is that the amplitude of the response to S_4 was greatest simply because it had been reinforced the most promptly with a marble, and therefore had the greatest habit strength. In order to distinguish between these two possible interpretations, the light must be paired with marbles in the *absence* of the joystick response, just as in the Longstreth candy study in which the red light was paired with candy in the absence of the locomotor response. If the amplitude of the joystick response is increased upon subsequent presentation of the incentive light, it would be difficult to interpret such a result in terms of habit strength changes because there would have been no opportunity for such changes to occur. Gilbert (1968) carried out just such a study with first and second grade children, and obtained the results predicted by incentive motivation theory.

To summarize, there is ample evidence that reward expectations increase drive at the animal level (see Bindra, 1968, for a recent review), but there is much less evidence at the child or human adult level, the Longstreth and Gilbert studies furnishing some of the strongest support. It is not that there is contradictory evidence, but that few investigators have looked for such a function. However, as more attempts are made to isolate its drive function, reward expectation will almost surely be found to be a pervasive source of human motivation. How else is one to explain the energizing of behavior in a child presented with an incentive stimulus; the jumping, screaming, and hand clapping, for example, when he is told "Jerry just called and asked you to go swimming with him," or when he is told "The postman left a package for you"? Such excitement presents *prima facie* evidence (albeit anecdotal) of the motivating role of reward expectations.

Incentive Motivation and Secondary Reinforcement

As mentioned earlier, incentive motivation may well account for some of the apparent reinforcement effects of such so-called secondary reinforcers as social approval, coins, and academic grades. The argument will now be examined in more detail.

Consider social approval. According to the notion of secondary reinforcement, children tend to learn responses followed by social approval faster than responses that do not have this consequence, everything else remaining constant, because of the past pairing of social approval with all sorts of established rewards. One might say, for example, that a girl wears dress A (i.e., makes response A, R_a) in preference to dress B (i.e., R_b) because in the past her friends have responded with social approval when they saw her in dress A and not when they saw her in dress B. She has a stronger habit for R_a than for R_b, and since both are multiplied by whatever motivation she has when the alarm rings

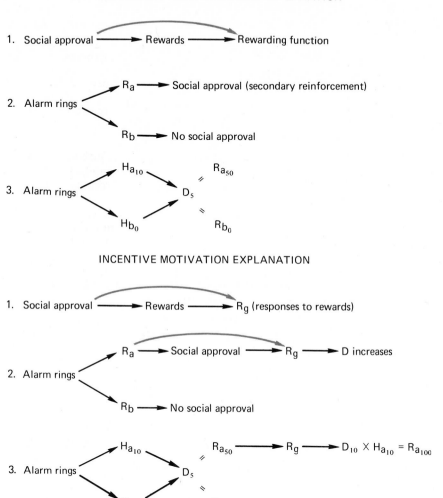

Fig. 10-3. Two explanations of why social approval strengthens a preceding response, R_a.

in the morning, the performance of R_a is greater than that of R_b, and so R_a occurs. This line of reasoning is summarized in the top half of Figure 10-3 in three distinct steps. First, social approval is paired with various rewards, and thus acquires the rewarding function of these stimuli; that is, it becomes a secondary reinforcer. Second, when the alarm clock arouses R_a, the response is followed by the social approval of peers and friends; but when the alarm clock arouses R_b, the response is not followed by social approval. Therefore, the habit between the alarm ring and R_a (H_a) becomes stronger than the habit between the alarm ring and R_b (H_b), as indicated by the arbitrary values of 10 and 0. When these habits are energized by whatever drive (D) is present, the performance strength of R_a is greater than that of R_b (Step 3).

According to the incentive motivation argument, in contrast to the secondary reinforcement position, the result of pairing social approval with reward is *not* its acquisition of a reinforcing function, but rather its conditioning to some of the same responses originally elicited by rewards (call these responses R_g—goal responses). This assumption is indicated by the lighter line in Step 1 in the bottom half of Figure 10-3. Next, since R_a is followed by social approval, it also comes to elicit R_g, as indicated by the lighter line in Step 2. Since R_g increases drive (being, by definition, a reward expectation), total drive level is higher when R_a occurs than when R_b occurs, as indicated by the arbitrary values of 10 and 5 in Step 3. Note that R_a and R_b have the *same* habit strength (arbitrarily set at 10), since social approval is not assumed to be a secondary reinforcer and therefore is not assumed to affect habit strength. When the alarm rings, whatever drive is present activates both H_a and H_b, and R_a and R_b have equal probability of occurring. If R_a starts to occur, however, R_g is elicited and drive is increased (from 5 to 10), which increases the performance strength of R_a (to 100) above that of R_b (50). Therefore, R_a is more likely *to be completed* than R_b.

The incentive motivation argument thus accounts for the same facts as the secondary reinforcement argument, with little loss in theoretical parsimony. It is an instructive exercise to take other examples of performance presumably controlled by secondary reinforcement and to reanalyze them in terms of incentive motivation. There seem to be few examples that do not readily yield to the analysis.

Other Incentive Effects

A series of studies by Nunnally and his associates suggests that reward expectations have effects in addition to drive effects (Nunnally and Faw, 1968; Nunnally, Duchnowski, and Knott, 1967a; Nunnally, Duchnowski, and Parker, 1965a; Nunnally, Knott, and Duchnowski, 1967b; Nunnally, Stevens, and Hall, 1965b; Parker and Nunnally, 1966). A typical procedure used consists of exposing children to a spin-wheel game in which the pointer stops at nonsense words. Two words (e.g., ZOJ and KEB) are distributed around the perimeter of the spin wheel with equal frequency, and are the targets of the pointer. A third word (e.g., MYV) is attached to the pivot of the pointer, and thus is never pointed at but is exposed. The children are given a series of trials in which the experimenter spins the pointer. If it stops at, say, ZOJ, the subject gets a piece of candy or a penny. If it stops at the other word, the subject gets nothing. The former word is thus the "rewarding" word, and the latter word is called the "frustrating" word.

After a number of spins, the three words are presented to the subject in various test situations. In the "Treasure Hunt" test, the subject is presented with 18 identical white boxes, with each of the words on 6 of the boxes. He is told that there is a quarter in one box, that he gets 12 choices, and that if he chooses the correct box he may keep the quarter. With this test it has been consistently found that subjects choose the boxes with the rewarding name on them more frequently than the other boxes. In the "Guess Who" test, the subject is shown three identical stick figures, each with the name of one of the three words. He is asked a series of questions, such as "Who has the most friends?" "Who would you like to sit next to in school?" (positive questions) "Who is mean to animals?" "Who don't you like?" (negative questions). For each question the subject must pick one of the stick figures. The "score" for each figure is the number of positive choices minus the number of negative choices. It has been found that the stick figure with the rewarding name gets the highest score (i.e., the most positive choices and the fewest negative choices) and the figure with the frustrating name gets the lowest score. Finally, in the "Looking Box" game the subject confronts six windows he may look through; under each window is a button that may be pressed to illuminate an object within. Pressing a button also turns on a hidden clock, providing an automatic measurement of how long the subject looks in each window. Each of the three words is in two of the windows. It has been found that subjects spend more time looking at the rewarding word than at the other two.

Nunnally's experiments thus show that stimuli paired with incentives are chosen more frequently when a further reward is possible; they elicit more positive verbal evaluations, even though the evaluations say nothing about the previous rewards; and they elicit a visual attentional preference. The experiments have also shown that these tendencies may develop very rapidly, in less than five trials in one study (Gilbert also found rapid development of incentive motivation in his study), that they develop more rapidly with a 100 percent reward schedule than with an intermittent reward schedule (also found to be true of reward expectations by Longstreth, 1966a), and that they persist for at least five weeks.

How are these facts to be interpreted? It would seem as though some sort of generalized approach response is developed which manifests itself in various ways. Just as the children "approached" or *reached toward and picked up* the candy and pennies, they later came to react in similar ways to the associated words alone (i.e., they *chose* the words in various contexts). Perhaps the habit to choose the candy and pennies became conditioned, through pairing, to the associated words. It is apparent, then, that stimuli paired with rewards can develop a steering (habit) function as well as a motivating function. Both were probably active in these studies; the habit to choose the rewarding word may have been energized by the incentive motivation which was a result of reward expectations elicited by that word.

Witryol has shown that at least one of the responses measured by Nunnally, the attentional response, generalizes to other stimuli (Witryol, Lowden, and

Fagan, 1967). Children paid more attention not only to the specific stimuli paired with reward, but also to other stimuli that varied along the same dimension. This attentional factor also facilitated the learning of discriminative motor responses, thus showing that generalized attentional responses led to the learning of still other habits that facilitated problem solution.

Level of Aspiration Studies

People develop expectations not only about objects and events, but also about their own behavior. A group of studies called *level of aspiration* studies is relevant here, since the procedure involves asking the subject to state his expectation concerning his own impending behavior. The manipulated variable has usually been the degree to which his subsequent performance actually matches his stated expectation. For some subjects performance is made to appear much worse than expected, for other subjects the reverse holds, and for still other subjects the expectations are made to appear to be accurate. The question is whether or not subsequent expectations are affected by the previous correspondence (or lack of correspondence) between expectations and outcomes.

The answer is that two things happen. First, successful performance (better than expected) tends to raise subsequent expectations, and poor performance (worse than expected) tends to lower subsequent expectations. Second, failure produces greater variability of subsequent expectations than does success. That is, following failure a subject is likely to become somewhat "irrational," either lowering his expectations an unrealistic amount or raising them too high.

It is implicitly assumed in these studies that one's expectations concerning his own behavior actually affect that behavior. However, there is practically no evidence to support this assumption, partly because most investigators have not even tested it. Rather, they have been content to demonstrate that performance feedback affects expectations, and have been willing to *assume* that the converse is also true. To determine whether expectations *do* affect performance, performance as well as expectations must be measured. One recent study in which performance was measured showed no relation; verbalized expectations of performance did not affect subsequent performance (Cottrell, 1967).

In two other studies, however, a relation was found; initial success on an anagram task not only raised expectations, but also resulted in improved performance; initial failure had the opposite effects (Feather, 1966; Feather and Saville, 1967). In a third study still under way at the time of this writing, Lundgren obtained preliminary evidence that in first and second grade children, high grades for test performance (alphabet printing) maintained the amount of time spent in independent study, and low grades resulted in a dramatic drop in study time (Lundgren, 1968). If it is assumed that grades affect performance expectations, then these results show that such expectations were associated with subsequent time spent studying. Since the total group numbered only ten, however, final judgment must be withheld until the study is completed.

FRUSTRATION

Just as children and adults are frequently anticipating rewards, so are they frequently being disappointed, when the expected reward does not occur or is delayed. Nonconfirmation of a reward expectation is often called a *frustration event,* and there is convincing evidence that such events contribute to drive in both animals and humans. To put it more operationally, if a reward expectation is not followed by the reward in its usual temporal-spatial location, facilitation of concurrent responses will occur. It can be seen that the procedure for testing this assertion is similar to the procedure employed in testing the drive function of any condition; a reference response is elicited in the presence of frustration, and if it is facilitated as compared to its strength in the absence of frustration, the assertion is verified.

Amsel and Roussel (1952) were the first to make an explicit test of this assertion. Reward expectations were conditioned to an alley and goalbox by rewarding hungry rats with food for running down the alley to the baited goalbox. A reference response was developed on the same trials by allowing the rat to leave the goalbox and enter a second alley, at the end of which was another baited goalbox. After locomotor speeds in this second alley had stabilized, the effects of frustration were determined by removing the food in the first goalbox; the rat presumably expected food, but it found none and was therefore frustrated. Speeds in the second alley were greater on these trials than on control trials on which the first goalbox was baited, clearly confirming the prediction. A number of subsequent studies supported the original findings (see reviews by Amsel, 1958, 1962) and also ruled out most alternative explanations.[2]

Comparable results have been obtained in studies with children (Gilbert, 1968; Haner and Brown, 1955; Holton, 1961; Longstreth, 1965, 1966a, 1966b; Moffitt and Ryan, 1966; Watson and Ryan, 1966; see Ryan and Watson, 1968, for a review). The Haner and Brown study is of particular interest not only because of its chronological priority, but also because it shows that the reference response need not be the same as the response leading to frustration. (In the Amsel situation, a locomotor response leads to frustration and a locomotor response is used to measure the drive effects of frustration.) Children were asked to place marbles in 36 holes of a marble board in order to win a prize. However, the marbles suddenly disappeared into the box below the board at varying distances from the end (after 9, 18, 27, 32, or all 36 marbles had been placed). After the subject had placed, say, 8 marbles, he anticipated having 9 marbles while placing the ninth one; but instead there were none, thus producing frustration. Coincident with each frustration event a buzzer sounded and the subject

---

[2] For example, it was argued that the effect could have resulted from depressed hunger on trials following reward in the first goalbox; speeds on so-called frustration trials were greater not because of frustration drive, but because of greater hunger drive (Seward, Pereboom, Butler, and Jones, 1957). This explanation was contradicted when it was shown that a group *never* rewarded in the first goalbox did not run as fast in the second alley as subjects who were frustrated (Wagner, 1959).

was instructed to turn it off before resuming the marble task. The buzzer was turned off by a lever press, the amplitude of which was recorded. It was found that the amplitude of the lever press increased, the closer the subject was to the end of the task at the time of frustration. If it is assumed that expectations of successful marble placements increased as the subject neared the last hole, then it may be argued that frustration drive should also have increased as the subject neared the end, and the reference response (the lever press) should therefore have shown more and more facilitation as the end was approached. Since precisely this result was obtained, the argument was supported.

Recall that in Longstreth's joystick experiment, children responded to a sequence of four light intensities in order to earn a marble at the end of each sequence, and that marble expectations were eventually conditioned to S_4. Recall also the 11 children who looked in the direction of the marble hose upon presentation of S_4, and the associated intensification of the joystick response. Frustration was introduced into this study by not presenting the last two marbles of the 63 required for the prize. Furthermore, frustration occurred at different points in the light sequence. For one group, only the first stimulus (S_1) was presented; instead of being followed by S_2 to S_4, S_1 reappeared, and continued to do so until the response extinguished. The subjects, then, never discovered that S_4 was no longer followed by a marble, since they never saw S_4 again. The lack of marble expectative responses to S_1 leads to the prediction that this group should have responded with weak frustration when S_1 was not followed by S_2 and eventually by a marble. Thus, subsequent joystick responses should not have been facilitated very much over those observed during training.

Another group was presented with the entire sequence, and was frustrated following S_4. Since S_4 elicited strong marble expectations, this group should have responded with strong frustration drive. Thus, subsequent joystick responses should have increased in amplitude as compared to those of the training trials.

Figure 10-4 shows the results for these two groups, at the end of training (prior to frustration) and during successive fifths of extinction. The prediction was clearly confirmed; the group frustrated after S_1 showed no consistent change in response amplitude, but the group frustrated after S_4 showed a strong intensification of response amplitude. This intensification occurred after the very first frustration event, as would be predicted if a sudden shift in motivation was involved.

Ford (1963) obtained evidence that the amount of frustration produced in children by failure is related to their expectancy for success, but the relation may be nonmonotonic. Gilbert's previously mentioned study of incentive motivation, using the same apparatus as used by Longstreth, also had frustration conditions, designed to provide parametric evidence on the relation between reward expectation and frustration drive in children. There was a rough correspondence between the presumed strength of the marble expectative responses and subsequent frustration drive strength; but the relation was not perfect (see Gilbert, 1968, for a possible explanation). More such studies are needed to provide definitive evidence about the relation between these variables.

Amsel's Theory of Frustration and Some Further Predictions

According to Amsel's theory, frustration, like pain, is aversive (Amsel, 1958, 1962); it elicits an emotional response, R_f, which increases the organism's drive level. This R_f can be conditioned to neutral stimuli, just as the pain-induced emotional response, R_e, can be conditioned (e.g., Miller, 1951); hence, there may be *conditioned frustration*, just as there is conditioned fear (Miller, 1951). Amsel has used the notion of conditioned R_f to account for several phenomena

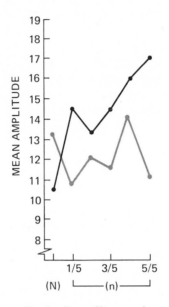

Fig. 10-4. Mean response amplitude (in millimeters) at the end of training (N) and for fifths of extinction (n), for (darker line) group frustrated after S_1 and (lighter line) group frustrated after S_1. (From L. E. Longstreth, "Frustration and secondary reinforcement concepts as applied to human instrumental conditioning and extinction." *Psychological Monographs*, 1966, *80*, No. 11. Copyright 1966 by the American Psychological Association. Reprinted by permission of the author and publisher.)

associated with instrumental conditioning. Indeed, it is the capacity of his theory to account for a variety of phenomena by a single set of relatively few and simple assumptions that makes it so attractive from a scientific point of view.

Two of the phenomena accounted for are related to acquisition and extinction effects of intermittent reinforcement. During acquisition, animals intermittently reinforced in the instrumental reward situation first perform less well than animals reinforced 100 percent of the time, but finally perform better. Thus, rats for which the goalbox is empty on a random 50 percent of the trials first run more slowly, then faster, than rats rewarded on every trial. During extinction, when the frequency of reinforcement is reduced to zero for both groups, the intermittently reinforced rats manifest much greater resistance to extinction, running faster and for more trials.

Amsel accounted for both of these effects by assuming, first, that R_f becomes conditioned to the cues preceding nonreinforcement. Intermittently reinforced subjects, which are exposed to frustration during late acquisition trials (but not during early trials, since expectations of reward would then be weak), learn to expect nonreinforcement as they locomote down the alley, that is, R_f becomes conditioned to the alley cues. Since R_f contributes to drive, these subjects are under higher total drive on late acquisition trials than are continuously reinforced subjects, and therefore run faster. (The reason they run slower on early trials is perhaps that they have weaker incentive expectations, and thus lower drive level, than continuously reinforced subjects.) The onset of extinction results in the occurrence of R_f in both groups, and in the subsequent elicitation of conditioned R_f in the alley. However, the intermittently reinforced subjects have already learned to continue with the locomotor response in the presence of conditioned R_f, while the continuously reinforced subjects have not. The latter subjects are therefore faced with a new cue which, if anything, elicits avoidance responses rather than approach responses. Therefore, continuously reinforced subjects extinguish first.

Turning to child behavior, Longstreth was apparently the first investigator to ask whether children can learn to be frustrated; that is, whether conditioned frustration can be developed (Longstreth, 1965). With the same apparatus as previously described, a joystick response was conditioned to two light intensities, then one light intensity was followed by frustration while a buzzer sounded. After three such pairings of the buzzer with frustration (interspersed with rewarded, no-buzzer trials), test trials were introduced. These consisted of light presentation concurrent with buzzer onset, but no frustration. Response amplitude on the test trials was found to be greater than in a group that had been presented with the same number of frustrations and buzzer occurrences, but unpaired rather than paired. Since the experimental subjects responded to the buzzer alone as they had previously responded to frustration, the results demonstrate conditioned frustration.

Having established that frustration can indeed be conditioned in children, and in a few trials at that, Longstreth next asked whether the acquisition and extinction effects of intermittent reinforcement could also be produced in children. Accordingly, for one group of children the joystick response was reinforced (with marbles) 54 percent of the time, and for another group it was reinforced 100 percent of the time. After 61 trials, extinction was introduced, and the subjects were allowed to continue responding until they met an extinction criterion of a 60 second response latency (training latencies were seldom more than 2 seconds). Both effects were found; intermittently reinforced children, relative to continuously reinforced children, manifested slower response speeds during early acquisition trials but faster final speeds (see Figure 10-5), and were more resistant to extinction, requiring an average of 264 trials to reach the extinction criterion as compared with 147 trials for the continuous-reinforcement group. Furthermore, of the 11 subjects who responded to S_4 with marble expectations during training, 9 extinguished faster than would be expected by chance. Likewise, 16 of 23 subjects who manifested increased joystick amplitude to S_4 during training extinguished faster than would be expected by chance. Thus, reward expectations as well as the continuous reinforcement schedule were predictive of rapid extinction, precisely as suggested by Amsel's theory. Other studies of the effects of intermittent reinforcement, and its presumed

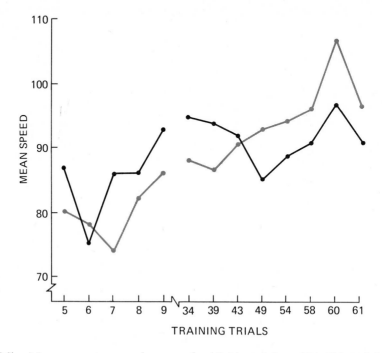

Fig. 10-5. Mean response speeds on early (5–9) and late (34–61) training trials, for (darker line) continuous-reinforcement group and (lighter line) intermittent-reinforcement group. Each of these trials was preceded by a reinforced trial in both groups. (Drawn from data presented by Longstreth, 1966a, Fig. 10, p. 18.)

relation to frustration, are discussed in Chapter 4, in the section entitled "Discrete-Trial Instrumental Conditioning in Children."

Secondary Reinforcement, Incentive Motivation, and Frustration

The concepts of secondary reinforcement, incentive motivation, and frustration are closely interrelated, tied as they all are to the notion of reinforcement. In this section, an attempt will be made to clarify their definitions and functions. Table 10-1 will assist in this process. It briefly describes the conventional definition and assumed function of each concept.

All three concepts share the stimulus definition of pairing a cue with a reward (see Amsel, 1968; Lott, 1967). The only difference between them is concerned with another condition, namely, that the reward must be omitted in order to meet the operations defining a frustration stimulus. With secondary reinforcement and incentive stimuli, it makes no difference whether the reward is omitted or not; for example, a buzzer paired with the eating of food is subsequently a secondary reinforcer or incentive stimulus whether or not it is presented with food. It is well to keep in mind, however, that the *functions* of secondary reinforcers and incentive stimuli are usually determined by presenting the cue in the absence of reward, thus meeting the definition of a frustration stimulus.

Table 10-1

Conventional Definitions and Assumed Functions of Stimuli Paired with Rewards

Concept	Stimulus definition	Assumed function
Secondary reinforcing stimulus	Cue regularly paired with reward, then presented with or without reward	Strengthens previous responses (learning)
Incentive stimulus	Cue regularly paired with reward, then presented with or without reward	Increases drive level, strengthening concurrent or immediately subsequent responses
Frustration stimulus	Cue regularly paired with reward, then presented without reward	Increases drive level, strengthening concurrent or immediately subsequent responses

In the actual test situation, then, the stimulus definitions of the three terms are often identical.

This is an intolerable state of affairs from a scientific point of view. Things with the same definition should have the same name. To call the same situation by different names is only to invite confusion, unless it is explicitly recognized that the names are exact synonyms. Such is not the case in the present discussion, as is clearly revealed by noting the different functions attributed to the three concepts. A secondary reinforcing stimulus causes learning of preceding responses; incentive and frustration stimuli do not, but rather increase subsequent drive level. Thus, the same situation is not only variously named, but has various properties (functions) assigned to it depending upon the name employed. The situation is thus hopelessly ambiguous. How can this confusion be reduced? One partial solution has already been suggested in the sections dealing with secondary reinforcement. It was concluded that since there is little evidence to support the presumed function of a secondary reinforcer in the first place, the term should be dropped. It is therefore tentatively striken from Table 10-1, and attention is concentrated on the other two concepts.[3]

The definitions of these two concepts can be sharpened and made more distinctive. An incentive stimulus can be defined as one that regularly precedes a reward, and thus always occurs in the *absence* of the reward; a frustration stimulus can be defined as one that develops in the *presence* of a reward, since it must have been spatially and temporally contiguous with reward during training, but one that is then presented without the reward. Consider an alley leading to a baited goalbox. As perceived from the alley, the goalbox is an incentive stimulus, since as viewed from this vantage point the stimulus input it produces has always been followed by reward. The same is true of the alley, thus qualifying it, too, as an incentive stimulus. But when the subject enters the goalbox and searches for the (absent) reward, the goalbox as then sensed is a frustration stimulus, since it has previously been paired with reward and now is not. The alley as viewed from the goalbox would also be a frustration stimulus, since this stimulus input has also previously been paired with reward.

This analysis clarifies a subtle problem inherent in Amsel's treatment of frustration theory. Amsel has theorized that the reason a previously rewarded but now nonrewarded stimulus situation causes frustration is that the anticipatory goal responses are blocked: the goal expectations are not allowed to follow their usual course, which involves interaction with the goal (reward) itself. Accordingly, a rat running down an alley to a baited goalbox, or a child walking to the dinner table, would be exposed to frustration, since these stimuli were previously paired with reward and hence elicit expectations of reward in the absence of reward. But from a common sense point of view, why should there be frustration? The rat never found food in the alley, nor did the child ever find food in the hallway as he walked to the dining room. Indeed, either organism might be "surprised" to find the food "moved up" to the novel locations, and perhaps consummatory responses would not even be elicited. As a matter of fact, Stolz and Lott (1964) found just this to be the case when the food was

---

[3] It is possible to give secondary reinforcement a unique definition so that it can be retained in the table. Longstreth suggested that it be defined as the presentation of a cue previously paired with reward and then presented alone in a context that otherwise elicits no reward expectation (Longstreth, 1964). The idea was that with no reward expectation preceding the appearance of the secondary reinforcer, there could be no frustration and therefore a secondary reinforcing function might appear. In other words, a "surprise" secondary reinforcer in a situation where the subject expected nothing might be reinforcing. Although Longstreth reported data that were consistent with this definition, his subsequent pessimism about the concept in general led him to abandon this line of thought. Another possibility has to do with timing. Perhaps secondary reinforcement effects are difficult to obtain (assuming correct methodology) because of the opposing effects of frustration. After all, on test trials the assumed secondary reinforcer is presented alone, and this procedure fits the definition of frustration. If the assumed secondary reinforcer could be removed soon enough to "short circuit" the frustration reaction, perhaps a secondary reinforcement function would emerge. This would require varying the time of exposure to the assumed secondary reinforcer, a procedure that typically has not been used.

placed in the alley instead of in the goalbox: the hungry rats literally waded through it in order to eat the same kind of food in the goalbox. Similarly, Jensen (1963) found that rats trained to press a lever for food pellets ignored pellets placed directly in the foodcup and chose to press first and then to eat. Consistent with these observations is the fact that with extended training, anticipatory goal responses tend to drop out during the early part of the CS-US interval, clustering instead around the time of presentation of the US. Pavlov called it "inhibition of delay" (Pavlov, 1927), and more recently it has been reported by several investigators working with dogs (e.g., Ellison, 1964; Shapiro and Miller, 1965; Sheffield, 1965). Longstreth (1966a) observed a similar phenomenon with children, reporting first the development of a goal gradient early in training and then its disappearance with further trials. He speculated that perhaps the subjects became so "sure" of the impending reward that all attendant emotion habituated, leaving a flat gradient. The implication is that with enough training, subjects will learn *not* to anticipate the goal until at the time and locus of its usual occurrence. With the disappearance of goal expectations, there can be no anticipatory frustration according to Amsel's theory, and thus the theory is seen to fit with common sense after all.

If it is argued that a stimulus must elicit goal expectations in order to function as an incentive stimulus, then it follows from the previous analysis that stimuli signaling a reward may *lose* their incentive functions as training continues. Consequently, there may be some intermediate number of trials where stimuli acquire maximum incentive value. Considerably more research is required to explore this possibility.

Having differentiated between the definitions of an incentive stimulus and a frustration stimulus, it may next be asked if there is a way of differentiating between their functions. Both energize behavior, as indicated in Table 10-1. But are there differential functions? Some theorists have suggested a function differentiating between incentive stimuli and frustration stimuli. The suggestion is that incentive drive is pleasant, and frustration drive is unpleasant, or aversive. *Pleasantness* is operationally defined in terms of approach responses; *aversiveness* is operationally defined in terms of avoidance or escape responses. Therefore, the suggestion amounts to an assertion that incentive stimuli tend to be approached and that frustration stimuli tend to be avoided. The assertion has ample empirical support (see Bindra, 1968, for a review of some of the evidence). It appears, then, that the two concepts have different associative functions, with respect to approach and avoidance behavior, but have a common energizing function.

The revised analysis is presented in Table 10-2. The cue is called an incentive or frustration stimulus, depending upon (a) the amount of time elapsing between the occurrence of the cue and the occurrence of the reward, and (b) the context in which the cue is subsequently presented (with or without reward). The concepts have in common an energizing function, but different associative functions. This revision seems to do violence to a minimum of data and to inject a maximum of clarity into the definitions and functions of incentive and frustration stimuli.

Table 10-2

Revised Definitions and Assumed Functions of Stimuli Paired with Rewards

| | | Assumed functions | |
Concept	Stimulus definition	Drive	Associative
Incentive stimulus	Cue which has regularly preceded reward	Increases drive level, strengthening concurrent or immediately subsequent responses	Tends to elicit approach responses in direction of the incentive stimulus
Frustration stimulus	Cue which has regularly accompanied reward spatially and temporally, then is presented without reward	Increases drive level, strengthening concurrent or immediately subsequent responses	Tends to elicit avoidance responses, away from the frustration stimulus

CONFLICT

The simultaneous arousal of two or more incompatible response tendencies is called *conflict*. Conflicts are part of life: some are trivial, such as not knowing which tie to put on in the morning, or which pie to choose for dessert; some are not so trivial, such as being unable to decide whether to stop or not as one approaches a yellow traffic light, or wanting to say both "yes" and "no" to the insurance salesman; and some are downright crucial, such as whether to have the advised operation or not, whether to quit smoking or not, or whether or not to get in the car with the "nice man" who says he is daddy's friend and will drive you home.

One of the consequences of conflict is indecision; the victim "freezes," unable to "make up his mind." This property of conflict has been demonstrated many times, both in animals (e.g., Miller, 1944) and in humans (e.g., Worell and Castaneda, 1961). The blocking of responses is usually explained in associative terms—the tendency to make one response blocks the occurrence of the incompatible response. Miller's theory of approach-avoidance conflict has successfully accounted for a number of such associative effects (Miller, 1944).

Recently, evidence has begun to accumulate suggesting a motivational property of conflict. Careful measurement indicates that reference responses occurring immediately after the blockage of incompatible responses are often energized as though drive were increased. In one of the first studies providing such evidence, Worell and Castaneda (1961) told college students to select the brighter (or dimmer) of two lights by removing their hand from a start platform and gripping one of two handles as soon as the lights were presented. Both reaction time, from the onset of the lights until the subject's hand left the start platform, and strength of gripping the handle were measured.

Conflict was manipulated by varying the intensities of the two lights. For one group the intensities were easily discriminable, involving little conflict as to which one to choose. For another group the intensities were close together, and it was difficult to choose one as brighter (or dimmer) than the other. The results revealed both associative and drive effects of conflict; the high conflict group, relative to the low conflict group, manifested slower reaction speed, thus showing the usual blocking effect, but greater grip pressure, as shown in Figure 10-6. (The figure shows the results for the first eight trials; the results were essentially the same on the other trials.) Presumably, the energizing function perseverated and energized whatever selective response was

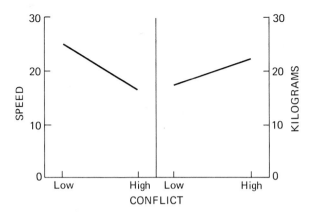

Fig. 10-6. **Mean speed and grip pressure as a function of conflict. (From Worell and Castaneda, 1961. Reprinted by permission of the authors and the Journal of Personality.)**

made. Similar evidence has been obtained in other studies (Berlyne, 1961; Steigman, 1964; Worell and Castaneda, 1961).

It is particularly interesting to note that Longstreth obtained precisely the same effects with frustration. In the previous descriptions of his experiments with children, it was noted that nondelivery of an expected marble intensified the immediately following joystick responses. Reaction speeds were also measured, from the onset of the stimulus light to the occurrence of the joystick response, and it was found in several of these studies that frustration produced a decrement in response speed on the subsequent trials, along with the increment in amplitude (e.g., Longstreth, 1966a; see also Ford, 1963).

The similarity of results with conflict and frustration implies a common condition. Recall that frustration is presumably aversive, and therefore elicits avoidance response tendencies, that is, tendencies to withdraw from the source of the frustration. Such tendencies are incompatible with the instrumental response; the subject cannot avoid the joystick and simultaneously respond with it. A state of conflict would therefore exist between these two response tendencies, and thus it becomes apparent that the common element in the two situations is conflict. The decrement in speed of initiation of the joystick response reflects its temporary blockage by the avoidance response tendency, and the subsequent increment in amplitude reflects either the drive function of frustration or the drive function of conflict.

Perhaps, then, frustration always involves conflict, between avoidance tendencies and tendencies to continue responding, and perhaps the concept of frustration drive is superfluous. Theorists have considered this possibility before (e.g., Brown and Farber, 1951, 1968).

However, it seems on both logical and empirical grounds that the concepts must remain separate. Logically, one could just as well argue that conflict drive is superfluous, since conflict always involves frustration. It need only be noted that since conflict produces response blockage, the consequences of the correct response are necessarily delayed. If these consequences are rewarding, and presumably they are or the response would not have been learned in the first place, then the delay meets the definition of frustration—an expected reward is not forthcoming. Therefore, the presumed drive function of conflict could be attributed to the frustration produced by the delay of the reward.

Aside from the logical argument, there are empirical data that suggest that conflict drive may be independent of frustration drive. In the Castaneda experiments, for example, there was no consequence of the grip response that was obviously rewarding. The response was not learned as a result of rewards; rather, it was *elicited* as a result of the instructions. Furthermore, there was no feedback informing the subject whether his choice was correct or incorrect; the lights terminated regardless of his response, and the experimenter told him nothing. Therefore, even the reward of knowing he responded correctly (presuming that such knowledge is rewarding) was denied him, making it doubtful that the delay of such feedback could be frustrating. Neither was the subject told that speed was important, or even that it was being measured. He was simply told that the experiment dealt with "accuracy of visual discrimination." Therefore, there is little likelihood that speed itself was a goal, nor that slow speeds were frustrating. Finally, there was actually no delay anyway; subjects exposed to the difficult discrimination problems never experienced the easy problems, and thus did not have an opportunity to develop expectations of a fast response or of immediate feedback. With no such expectations, slow responses and delayed feedback could not be frustrating, by definition. For all these factual reasons, it is doubtful that frustration was involved in the Castaneda studies, thus justifying the assumption of another drive source, conflict.

More recently, Castaneda and his colleagues have shown that conflict has the same effect on verbal responses in children as other drive sources (see Castaneda, 1965). Several studies have shown that verbal habits are energized according to the same rules as motor habits. Thus, if a subject has learned to respond to the stimulus word *tree* with the word *water*, and if drive is increased by, say, anxiety or incentive motivation, *tree* elicits *water* with increased certainty. Castaneda and his colleagues used such verbal paired associates as the reference responses in their tests for conflict-produced drive. Specifically, conflict was produced by either presenting another stimulus word that elicited two response tendencies, only one of which was correct (such as *fire* eliciting both *hot* and *burn*), or presenting a discrimination problem that elicited two equal and incompatible response tendencies (such as presenting two squares of equal area and asking the subject to point to the larger one). Immediately after the conflict experiences, the subject was given a different stimulus word, which elicited only one dominant response tendency, and the correctness of this reference response was noted. The result was that the probability of occurrence of the correct reference response was greater after the conflict than on control trials on which there was no preceding conflict. Since the effect of conflict on these verbal responses was the same as the effect of other sources of drive, it was concluded that conflict too is a source of drive.

Furthermore, these studies demonstrated another drive effect. To understand it, Hull's equation must be reconsidered. Suppose that two habits are conditioned to a stimulus instead of one. Since drive multiplies both, there is a tendency to perform both. The one more likely to occur is the one with the stronger P value, and the greater the difference between the two P values, the greater the probability that the stronger one will occur. This prediction is derived mathematically by writing a separate equation for each response and then subtracting the two from each other, as follows:

$$sPr_1 = +f(D \times sHr_1) \tag{2}$$

$$sPr_2 = +f(D \times sHr_2) \tag{3}$$

Subtracting,

$$sPr_1 - sPr_2 = +f(D \times sHr_1) - +f(D \times sHr_2) \tag{4}$$

Factoring,

$$sPr_1 - sPr_2 = +f[D(sHr_1 - sHr_2)] \tag{5}$$

If sHr_1 is greater than sHr_2, then sPr_1 is greater than sPr_2, and the greater the value of D, the greater this difference and therefore the greater the probability of performance of R_1. If R_1 is "correct," then increased D "improves" performance; but if R_1 is "incorrect," increased D "worsens" performance. Thus, an increase in drive is not always beneficial; it is beneficial only when the strongest habit being energized is a correct habit. In all the experiments considered so far, this has been the case, and hence increased drive has always improved performance. In the verbal learning studies by Castaneda and his colleagues, however, there were also conditions in which the strongest habit was *incorrect*. According to Hull's equation, performance in these conditions should be worsened by conflict, if conflict increases drive.

The conditions were created by choosing a low frequency associate as the correct response to a simulus word, on the assumption that such words have weaker habit connections than more frequently occurring associates. For example, *sit* is seldom given as a free associate to the stimulus word *night*, but *day* is often given. If *sit* is selected as the correct response to *night* in a paired associate task, a person under low drive should perform better than a person under high drive, since the latter person has a greater P difference in favor of *day,* and thus should be more likely to say *day.* Castaneda found that when such trials immediately followed conflict, the predicted errors occurred, confirming Hull's equation and the assumption that conflict increases drive.

A Retrospective Comment about Incentive Motivation and Frustration

In retrospect, it can be seen that Castaneda's procedure could also be used to test for detrimental drive effects of incentive motivation or frustration. That is, it would be predicted that performance on a "difficult" task (i.e., one in which the correct habit is weaker than an incorrect habit) would be impaired by the induction of incentive motivation or frustration. Neither of these predictions appears to have been adequately tested yet, with either animals, children, or human adults. Gold tested the frustration-impaired performance prediction with rats, but obtained equivocal results (Gold, 1960). Glucksberg performed an experiment with adults which could be interpreted as testing the incentive motivation-impaired performance prediction (Glucksberg, 1962). He found that promises of a possible monetary reward improved performance on easy tasks, but impaired performance on difficult tasks. If it is assumed that promises of a monetary reward elicited expectations, then his results fit the incentive motivation prediction. There is an opportunity here for several exciting research projects for those with the ingenuity to devise the appropriate experimental conditions.

ANXIETY

Anxiety has been the workhorse of motivation theorists ever since the fall of "psychological needs" as a respectable explanatory device. There are at least two important reasons. First, there is the undeniable *experience* of anxiety. Although one may not know just what the experience is in other people, just as he cannot know their experience of *red,* for example, almost everyone admits to his own feelings of fear, apprehension, tension, and anxiety. Second, there is a good deal of experimental evidence, both with animals and humans, that supports the notion that anxiety is a source of motivation.

The most straightforward procedure for experimentally investigating the drive property of anxiety is the same as previously described for other hypothesized drive sources; a reference response is elicited in the presence and absence of anxiety, and if it is stronger in the presence of anxiety, then by definition anxiety is a drive source.

Definitions of Anxiety

How does one know when an anxiety response has occurred? What is its operational definition? One definition states that any aversive stimulus elicits anxiety (Miller, 1951). Since aversiveness is response-defined, either in terms of escape responses (e.g., shock is aversive because animals perform escape responses when it is presented) or physiological responses (e.g., shock elicits a galvanic skin response, changes in heart rate, etc.), anxiety is also response-defined.

Many studies show that the physiological responses that define aversiveness are conditionable to preceding neutral stimuli, in both animals and humans. For example, Figure 10-7 shows the mean galvanic skin response (GSR) in children to one stimulus paired with shock (test stimulus) and to another stimulus not paired with shock (control stimulus). Note the increasing magnitude

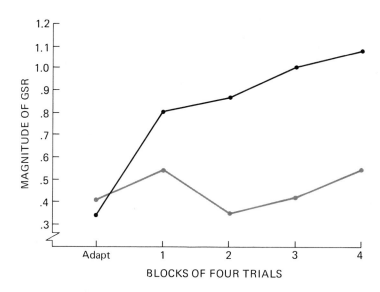

Fig. 10-7. Mean GSR to test (darker line) and control (lighter line) stimuli. (From W. W. Grings, R. A. Lockhart, and L. E. Dameron, "Conditioning autonomic responses of mentally subnormal individuals." *Psychological Monographs*, 1962, 76, No. 39. Copyright 1962 by the American Psychological Association. Reprinted by permission of the authors and publisher.)

of GSR to the test stimulus. Thus, it is well established that anxiety can be conditioned or learned, and one can therefore speak of either unconditioned (unlearned) anxiety (if the stimulus is aversive) or conditioned (learned) anxiety (if the stimulus is not aversive but has been systematically paired with an aversive stimulus in the past).

The definition of anxiety in terms of aversive stimuli has not been widely used in research with children, for obvious ethical reasons. Of course, there is the famous experiment by Watson and Rayner (1920) in which Albert, a one year old infant, was conditioned to fear a white rat by pairing it with an aversive stimulus (the unexpected noise of a bar and triangle) until signs of anxiety initially elicited by the noise (cringing, whining) began to be elicited by the white rat. However, this study (it is hardly an *experiment,* since there was no control condition) does not demonstrate the drive property of anxiety, but only its conditionability (even this demonstration is weak because of the lack of a control condition). (The study is also discussed in Chapters 3 and 12.)

Anxiety-Produced Drive in Adults

There are a number of studies with human adults in which these definitions have been used to test the drive property of anxiety. For example, Chiles (1958) tested the drive property of unlearned anxiety by eliciting verbal reference responses in the presence and absence of preceding electric shock. Specifically, the subjects were asked to learn verbal paired associate lists, including some items that were so easy that it could be assumed that the correct habit was the strongest one from the beginning of the task (e.g., the subject had to choose between *serene* and *rugged* as the response to *tranquil,* and *serene* was correct) and other items for which it could be assumed that an incorrect habit was initially the strongest (e.g., the subject had to choose between *serene* and *rugged* as the response to *peaceful,* and *rugged* was correct). Between trials, experimental subjects were shocked while control subjects were simply presented with a buzzer. The question was, Would the fear elicited by the shock act as a drive source on the immediately following verbal responses? Utilizing Hull's equation of the relationship between performance, drive, and habit, it was predicted that shock should facilitate performance on the easy items and impede performance on the difficult items. It was also predicted that after the difficult items were learned to the point where it could be assumed that the correct habit was dominant (i.e., after they became "easy" items as a result of learning), performance on them would also be facilitated by preceding shock. All three predictions were clearly confirmed, providing strong support for the assumption that unlearned anxiety is motivating.

The drive property of learned anxiety has also been demonstrated in adults. In one study (Ross, 1961), a light was paired with shock; to test the drive property of the anxiety that was presumably conditioned to the light, the light was occasionally followed by a puff of air to the eye, which elicited a reflex blink, the reference response. It was found that the amplitude of the blink response was greater when preceded by the light, demonstrating the drive property of learned anxiety. Similar results were reported by Meryman (1953) and Spence and Runquist (1958).

Social Elicitation of Anxiety

A final series of studies with adults must be mentioned because of its implications for child development. In this series of studies, Berger first showed that the sight of a person reacting to apparent shock functioned as an aversive stimulus to an observer, since a GSR was elicited in the observer (Berger, 1962).

He then tested the drive property of this kind of stimulus, using a reaction-time response as the reference response (Li Lollo and Berger, 1965). That is, subjects were asked to press a button as fast as possible after a signal was presented. For some subjects, a second "subject" (really a stooge) was presumably shocked at the same time the signal was presented. Electrodes had been attached to her arm (all subjects were female) and she jerked it as if in pain simultaneously with presentation of the reaction-time stimulus. For control subjects, the stooge was present, but one of the essential ingredients was missing; she did not jerk her arm (Control Group 1), or she jerked it "voluntarily," but with no implication that it had been shocked (Control Group 2), or both ingredients were missing—no shock and no arm movement (Control Group 3).

The results were that the experimental subjects, exposed to the arm jerk of the stooge as a result of presumed shock, exhibited significantly faster reaction speeds than the three control groups, which did not differ from one another. Furthermore, the difference did not appear on the first trial, but appeared full blown on the second trial and all succeeding trials. This is precisely what would be expected from an anxiety drive, since the button press on the first trial occurred simultaneously with the stooge's arm jerk, and therefore *prior* to the elicitation of anxiety, which has a latency of at least one second. Faster reaction times on succeeding trials were therefore apparently due to the perseverating effects of anxiety from previous trials.

The importance of these studies is in their clear indication that (a) observations of negative emotional manifestations in others elicit anxiety in the observer, and (b) this anxiety energizes concurrent responses. If the same relations hold for children, and there is no reason to believe otherwise, then it can be seen how important the emotional manifestations of parents, teachers, and peers might be. Even a nonpunitive parent, who elicits little pain-aroused anxiety in her child, nor even learned anxiety through the use of scoldings and threats, may nevertheless be responsible for important conditioning of emotional responses. A mother, for example, may react with fear and anguish when she sees her son thrown to the ground by a peer. The child, although unhurt and undisturbed, may respond with anxiety to his mother's emotionality. If such a sequence is repeated with any frequency, the child's anxiety may soon become conditioned to preceding cues; he may soon begin to feel anxious when "rough-housing" or wrestling with peers, and the increment in drive may energize avoidance behavior. Such learning may thus sow the seeds of passivity or dependency or femininity in later personality development, particularly if it is embellished by similar occurrences in related activities. Indeed, in the Fels study of personality development from birth to adulthood it was found that maternal protectiveness, reflecting overconcern for the child, was predictive of passivity, dependency, and femininity in both boys and girls (Kagan and Moss, 1962). Such learning may also account for the fact that children tend to exhibit the same fears as their mothers (e.g., Bandura and Menlove, 1968; Hagman, 1932), but tend to recover from such fears when the mothers later exhibit nonfearful responses to these stimuli (Jersild and Holmes, 1935).

Social Inhibition of Anxiety

Although there are no child studies similar to the Berger adult studies, the opposite procedure has been investigated with children. That is, if anxiety can be learned by observing emotional behavior in others, perhaps it can also be *reduced* by observing *calm* behavior in others.

Jones first discovered the possibility of such a phenomenon in her famous study of Peter, a three year old boy who happened to be attending a nursery school where Jones was carrying out experiments (Jones, 1924). It was noticed that Peter was afraid of a white rat and a white rabbit, although the origins of the fears were unknown (Peter was not Albert, contrary to the suspicions of some students). It was decided to attempt to weaken the fear of the rabbit in the following way. Every day, Peter and three other children were brought together to a special room to play. The three other children were chosen because of their complete absence of fear of the rabbit. At first the rabbit was introduced into the room for only a short time, and at some distance from Peter. As the days went on, however, it was kept in the room for longer and longer periods of time, and was moved closer and closer to Peter. On test days, Peter and the rabbit were brought together alone, in order to measure his avoidance and fear of the rabbit. Over a period of months, the following notes were recorded (only a sample is presented here):

A. Rabbit anywhere in the room in a cage causes fear reactions.

D. Rabbit three feet away in cage tolerated.

G. Rabbit touched when experimenter holds it.

M. Holds rabbit on lap.

Q. Lets rabbit nibble his fingers.

What actually happened to Peter? Presumably the presence of the three fearless children was crucial, since their calmness elicited similar behavior in Peter, thus dampening his fear, and eventually extinguishing it completely. "Social counterconditioning" might be a good label for such a procedure, but "modeling" or "imitation" might also be used (see Chapter 17, section entitled "Identification"). "Vicarious extinction," a label used by others, seems to be clearly inappropriate, since it implies that the observer is merely observing, with no concomitant responses—probably an impossible state of affairs.

The case of Peter is no more convincing than the case of Albert, because of the lack of control conditions. For example, perhaps the fear would have weakened anyway, with or without the three fearless children (for other criticisms of the study, see Chapter 19, section on "Basic Principles"). Bandura and his colleagues have carried out two carefully controlled experiments of the same type (Bandura and Menlove, 1968; Bandura, Grusec, and Menlove, 1967b). They asked if a child's fear of dogs could be weakened by observing the behavior of fearless peers. First, children with a chronic fear of dogs were identified by questioning a large group of parents. Those so identified were then given an individual "test" in order to obtain a more precise measurement of the amount of such fear. The test consisted of exposing to the child a brown cocker spaniel confined in a playpen. The child was asked to go through a series of 28 steps, each involving more intimate interaction with the dog than the previous steps. Thus, the child was asked to walk up to the playpen, to

Table 10-3

Treatment Groups in Social Counterconditioning Study[a]

| | Treatment | | |
Group	Model	Dog	Party
Model-positive	Present	Present	Present
Model-neutral	Present	Present	Absent
Exposure-positive	Absent	Present	Present
Positive	Absent	Absent	Present

[a] Bandura *et al.* (1967b).

touch the dog, to pet it, to open the playpen door, etc., until the last steps involved remaining alone in the room with the dog, feeding it biscuits, rolling it over and scratching its stomach, etc. The child was scored in terms of the number of these steps he carried out, the highest score thus reflecting the least avoidance of the dog (and presumably the least fear).

After the test the children were divided into four groups of 12 children each, with the groups matched on amount of fear of the dog. Each group was subjected to a different type of social counterconditioning, summarized in Table 10-3 and described below. One group, the *model-positive* group, went to a "birthday party" in groups of four, twice a day for four consecutive days. Each party included games, prizes, cookies, hats, balloons, stories, etc. Toward the end of each party a four year old child entered the room, accompanied by an adult and the cocker spaniel. The boy was unknown to most of the children. He played with the dog, ignoring the other children. At first he played cautiously with the dog, but by the last "party" he was completely casual, hugging her, scratching her stomach, giving her milk from a baby bottle, etc.

Children in the *model-neutral* group were treated the same way, except that the parties were omitted. Instead, the children simply sat at a table and watched the model perform. In terms of its emotional tone, the situation was thus more "neutral" than "positive."

The *exposure-positive* group went to the parties, and the dog was present, but the model was absent, and no one interacted with the dog. These children were thus exposed to the dog in a positive context, but did not observe a peer

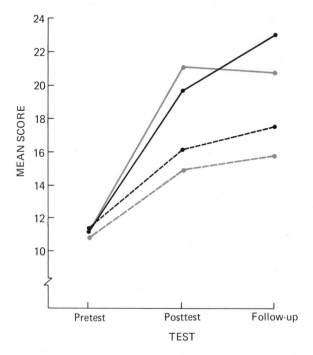

Fig. 10-8. Mean test scores reflecting fear reduction in model-positive (dark solid line), model-neutral (light solid line), exposure-positive (light dashed line), and positive (dark dashed line) groups. High scores reflect low fear. (From A. Bandura, J. E. Grusec, and F. L. Menlove, "Vicarious extinction of avoidance behavior." *Journal of Personality and Social Psychology*, 1967, 5, 16–23. Copyright 1967 by the American Psychological Association. Reprinted by permission of the authors and publisher.)

calmly interacting with the dog. The fourth group, the *positive* group, attended the parties, but there was no dog *nor* model. This control group made it possible to determine if there were any beneficial effects produced by the parties *per se,* in the absence of the dog.

On the day after the last treatment, the children were given the 28-step fear test again, and a month later they were given a follow-up test to determine if the effects would last that long. The results of the three tests (the pretest, posttest, and one-month follow-up test) are presented in Figure 10-8, showing the mean score for each group. The results are clear-cut. First, all groups showed some improvement, probably as a result of successive exposures to the

dog during the test sessions themselves. Second, exposure to the model interacting with the dog resulted in much more improvement than no exposure to
the model, regardless of whether or not the modeling was done in conjunction
with the "birthday parties." Third, the effects perseverated for at least one month.
Finally, not shown in the figure is that these effects were as strong when a
second, strange dog was used during the test sessions.

The Bandura studies show quite clearly that social counterconditioning is
effective with children's fears (of dogs, at least). Presumably, the calmness
of the model counters the child's fear of the dog, thus weakening it to the
extent that the child himself can interact with the dog. There is another control,
however, that would strengthen this argument considerably. What would have
happened if the model, although not hurt by the dog, was nevertheless quite
emotional as he interacted with the dog? Such a situation would provide the
observer with the information that the dog does not hurt children, but the
calmness of the model would be missing. Would the information alone be sufficient, or would it be necessary that it occur concurrently with an absence of
anxiety on the part of the model? The fact that the birthday parties made
no difference in the Bandura study would suggest that perhaps the information
alone is enough, since the birthday parties were also intended to reduce anxiety.
Perhaps someone will add this control group in future work, thus clarifying
the situation.

Test Anxiety

Because of the ethical problems that would be involved in experimental attempts to induce anxiety in children, there are practically no experiments that
are the converse of the Bandura experiments. It is possible, however, to obtain
groups of children who differ in level of anxiety for reasons unknown and beyond
the control of the investigator, and then to capitalize on such "natural groups"
to examine the effects of anxiety. The anxiety would be a subject variable rather
than an experimental variable; it is not manipulated, it is found.

Two "anxiety tests," developed by different groups of investigators, are available. Since one, the Yale scale, has not been used specifically to test for drive
effects, it is not further discussed here. (See Hill and Sarason, 1966, for a representative study.) The other, the Children's Manifest Anxiety Scale (CMAS),
was intended to provide a score reflecting anxiety level in children (Castaneda,
McCandless, and Palermo, 1956a; Castaneda, Palermo, and McCandless, 1956b).
Its rationale was derived from that of the Manifest Anxiety Scale (MAS), a
previously developed test intended to measure anxiety in adults (Taylor, 1951,
1953).

In the development of the MAS, five clinical psychologists were asked to pick
from approximately 200 items those which seemed to be indicative of chronic
anxiety. The first version of the test included 65 items which four of the five
judges independently picked, combined with some buffer items (to hide the
nature of the test) and some "lie" items (items to which the answer "yes"
is usually false, such as "I have never gotten angry at anybody"). Some of

the anxiety items (and the answers indicative of anxiety) are, "I have very few headaches" (false); "I practically never blush" (false); "I have nightmares every few nights" (true); "I am very confident of myself" (false). The main assumption underlying the test is that "scores on the scale are in some manner related to emotional responsiveness, which, in turn, contributes to drive level" (Taylor, 1956, p. 306). Exactly the same logic underlies the CMAS, which is simply a revision of the MAS to make the wording understandable to children (but with the buffer items omitted).

What is the evidence that CMAS scores conform to the assumption? If different scores reflect different levels of anxiety, and therefore different levels of drive, then they should be related to the strength of reference responses in the same way as are established sources of drive. (a) In situations involving a single habit, children with high CMAS scores should exhibit a stronger response than children with low CMAS scores. In situations involving more than one habit, high CMAS scores (b) should be predictive of a greater proportion of correct responses than low CMAS scores if the dominant habit is correct, and (c) should be predictive of a smaller proportion of correct responses if the dominant habit is incorrect. How well do the facts fit these three predictions?

Concerning the first prediction, that of facilitation of a single response in a situation where there is little or no competition from other response tendencies, relevant data must be obtained from MAS studies, because the CMAS has not been used in such situations. The first study in which the MAS was used showed that conditioned eyelid responses were more frequent in subjects with high MAS scores than in subjects with low MAS scores (Taylor, 1951). Since this result has been obtained a number of times (for reviews of the studies, see Cofer and Appley, 1964, p. 704; Spence, 1964), and since exactly the same result is obtained when other drive sources (e.g., intensity of the US, or threat of shock) are manipulated in eyelid conditioning studies, the first prediction has received ample support, at least with respect to the MAS.

The second and third predictions have received support with both the MAS and CMAS (see, however, the review by Goulet, 1968a, for a discussion of the complexities involved when paired associate tasks are used). A CMAS study is illustrative (Castaneda, 1961). The learning task consisted of selecting one of eight push buttons to turn off one of eight lights. The lights and buttons were arranged in parallel horizontal rows, with a button directly underneath each light, as shown in Figure 10-9. The arrows indicate the correct button for each light. Note that for four lights the correct button is directly underneath, and for the remaining lights the correct button is adjacent. Previous studies indicate that with an apparatus of this kind, subjects usually have a strong initial tendency to push the button directly underneath an activated light. The strongest habit to each light, in other words, is to push the button immediately below. Since this is the correct habit for four of the lights, high drive should facilitate performance on these lights (indicated by DHC in Figure 10-9). For the other four lights, however, this habit is incorrect (DHI), and therefore high drive should be detrimental to performance on these lights.

Two groups of fifth graders were selected, one group with high CMAS scores

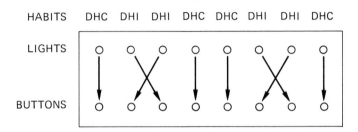

Fig. 10-9. Diagram of the apparatus used in the Castaneda study. The arrows show which button was to be associated with each light, and were not actually drawn on the apparatus. DHC, dominant habit correct; DHI, dominant habit incorrect.

(at or above the 80th percentile) and the other with low CMAS scores (at or below the 20th percentile). Each subject was tested individually, with instructions to turn off whichever light came on by pushing the correct button. Each of the 8 lights was presented 10 times, yielding a total of 80 trials.

Table 10-4

Effects of Anxiety in DHC and DHI Conditions[a,b]

| | | Anxiety level | |
Measure	Condition	Low	High
Correct responses	DHC	5.1	6.0
	DHI	3.1	1.8
Dominant habit errors[c]	DHI	4.1	5.1
Random errors[c]	DHI	2.7	2.8

[a] Castaneda (1961).
[b] DHC, dominant habit correct; DHI, dominant habit incorrect.
[c] Data only for DHI condition are presented because all errors in DHC condition are necessarily random errors.

Table 10-4 presents the results for the first 20 trials. (The results were essentially the same on the other trials.) The data in the first two rows show close conformity to theoretical predictions; the high-anxious group was superior to the low-anxious group in the DHC condition, and inferior in the DHI condition. The study also provided a more stringent test of the underlying theory than simple confirmation of the major predictions. According to the theory, the dominant habit (pushing the button directly underneath the light that is on) is energized by anxiety drive, and is therefore stronger in high-anxious subjects than in low-anxious subjects. Consequently, the inferior performance of the high-anxious subjects in the DHI condition should have resulted from performance of the dominant habit, that is, from erroneously pushing the button directly underneath the activated light. However, the inferior performance of these subjects in the DHI condition *could* have resulted from other kinds of errors, "random" errors not predicted by the theory. The last two rows of Table 10-4 show the mean numbers of dominant habit errors and random errors made by the groups in the DHI condition. Exactly as predicted, dominant habit errors were more frequent in the high-anxious group than in the low-anxious group, and random errors were about equally frequent in the two groups, providing additional confirmation of the theory.

A Word of Caution

In spite of the impressive evidence that supports the CMAS-anxiety-drive assumption, there are reasons for caution, and even doubt. The apprehension does not result from contradictory data, although some exist for both the MAS and the CMAS, but rather from the nature of the tests themselves. The problem is that children who differ in CMAS scores differ in other respects as well, and it may be these other differences that account for the effects attributed to drive. For example, CMAS (and MAS) scores are often found to be negatively correlated with IQ scores and school achievement (e.g., Horowitz and Armentrout, 1965; Reese, 1961b). They are also negatively correlated with social desirability scores (e.g., Lunneborg, 1964), indicating that the child who obtains a high CMAS score tends to be less aware of the socially approved answer to CMAS items. The accompanying "lie scale," which presumably identifies subjects who are most likely to lie about their anxiety symptoms, has also been seriously questioned, with respect to both its validity and reliability (Rie, 1963). Furthermore, Kimble and Posnick (1967) noted that many of the scale items contain expressions such as "quickly," "often," "frequently," and "a great deal of." They wrote new items containing these phrases *but with no reference to anxiety;* for example, "I often sweat" might be rewritten "I often go to the movies." Scores on the two sets of items were found to be highly correlated (.84 and .74 in two groups), indicating a high similarity of answers whether the items referred to anxiety symptoms or not. Obviously, then, something other than the anxiety content was a determinant of the answers to the items. Finally, Lipsitt (1958) obtained data suggesting that the CMAS may measure, at least in part, a tendency toward self-disparagement, which does not necessarily have drive properties.

What, then, is reflected in different CMAS scores—anxiety, IQ, achievement habits, lack of knowledge of socially desirable answers, sensitivity to the phrases identified by Kimble and Posnick, self-disparagement, other unknown factors, or some complex combination of some or all of these possibilities? All that is certain is that more than anxiety differences are involved. The problem of confounding is impossible of solution when the only difference between groups is based on a subject variable, because there can never be even reasonable assurance that the groups are equated in all other ways. This is a characteristic problem when a nonexperimental methodology is used (see Chapter 1) and probably because studies using the MAS or CMAS are necessarily nonexperimental they are decreasing in frequency.

Anxiety and Psychological Needs

Anxiety is so readily conditionable and seems so pervasive that it has become a basic concept in many theories of human behavior; indeed, some psychologists have even suggested that it is the basis of many or all so-called psychological needs (e.g., Brown, 1953). Consider the "need for social approval," which has already been analyzed in terms of secondary reinforcement and incentive motivation. The phenomenon to be explained is the repetition (perhaps learning) of responses that have previously been followed by social approval.

The crucial assumption is that the absence of social approval is often accompanied by pain and social disapproval. There are many forms of social disapproval, for example, social isolation. Social isolation is often paired with pain during infancy, as when the unattended infant has soiled and irritating diapers or feels the pain of boredom, unstretched muscles, or an air-filled stomach. Scolding, frowns, insults, and other more symbolic forms of social disapproval are also often paired with pain, because they often accompany, for example, a spanking by a parent or a shove or blow by a peer. Vocal social disapproval, even in the absence of punishment, may be anxiety arousing if it is loud enough. It is well known that an unexpected loud noise elicits a startle response as well as other signs of anxiety. Thus, a loud "No!" is frightening whether or not it is paired with punishment or anything else.

The frequent pairing of social disapproval and pain is assumed to result in the conditioning of anxiety to social disapproval *per se*. The anxiety elicits and motivates avoidance of social disapproval; but social approval always indicates the absence of social disapproval, and since the avoidance of social disapproval involves responses that are followed by social approval, the outcome appears to be a "need for social approval."[4] According to the anxiety analysis, the responses would be repeated whether they were followed by social approval or not, so long as they were followed by the termination of social disapproval. To put it more generally, if the termination of social disapproval were systematically followed by the appearance of rainbows, a "need for rainbows" would not be the best possible explanation of the appearance that people were "chasing rainbows." Anxiety reduction would provide a simple and sufficient explanation.

There is experimental evidence that responses followed by social approval

[4] Contrary to what might be expected, social acceptance is not necessarily negatively correlated with social rejection (Phillips and Devault, 1955), and therefore social approval may not seem *always* to indicate the absence of social disapproval. However, social approval must always indicate the absence of social isolation, one of the forms of "social disapproval." A child need not be socially *rejected* in order to be socially isolated—it may be that his presence is simply not noticed—but the effect is the same.

tend to be repeated, and that preceding social isolation enhances this effect (Erickson, 1962; Gewirtz and Baer, 1958a, 1958b; Gewirtz, Baer, and Roth, 1958; Hill and Stevenson, 1964; Landau and Gewirtz, 1967; Lewis, 1965; Rosenhan, 1967; Stevenson and Odom, 1961, 1962; Walters and Parke, 1964; Walters and Ray, 1960). While both of these facts are consistent with the anxiety explanation, they do not rule out the "need for social approval" explanation. There have been very few attempts to determine whether or not social isolation elicits anxiety, or whether or not social approval reduces anxiety, and this information is crucial. If social isolation did not elicit anxiety, then since it enhances the effectiveness of social approval, the effect of social approval would clearly not be attributable to anxiety reduction.

Walters and his associates produced the only available evidence (Walters and Karal, 1960; Walters and Parke, 1964; Walters and Ray, 1960). They found that (a) an anxiety-arousing situation is much more conducive to the learning of responses followed by social approval than is a social isolation situation (in one study, presence or absence of social isolation made no difference at all); and (b) social isolation does not result in changes in a physiological index of anxiety (finger temperature), but a strange adult with "cold" manners (socially disapproving) does. Both of these findings, and others, led Walters and his associates to conclude that the anxiety interpretation is the more reasonable one.

The issue, however, remains open. The crucial experiment would seem to be one in which one group of children is treated in such a way that social disapproval and social isolation are never associated with pain or other sources of anxiety. If these children, in a subsequent learning task, do not repeat responses followed by social approval, and if children for whom social disapproval and isolation have been paired with anxiety arousal do repeat the socially approved responses, then the case for anxiety would be solid indeed. Perhaps someone will actually devise a way of carrying out such an experiment, although the obstacles seem formidable.

This discussion has been limited to the "need for social approval," but the same analysis in terms of anxiety applies to many other "psychological needs" as well. A "need for money," for example, may be a fear of poverty; a "need for knowing," a fear of the unknown; a "need for religion," a fear of death; a "need for achievement," a fear of failure. The analysis of psychological needs in terms of anxiety should now be clear. As Longstreth has said, "A child or adult will appear to have a 'need' for something (call it 'X') to (1) the extent that the absence of X has been associated with anxiety, and (2) to the extent that the presence of X has been associated with reduction in anxiety and/or increases in other pleasant emotional responses" (Longstreth, 1968, p. 215, italics deleted). Such an analysis has far-reaching implications for child rearing, because parents play a major role in determining what situations are to be paired with anxiety, and what responses are to be followed by a reduction in anxiety.[5]

---

[5] Some psychologists (e.g., McClelland, Atkinson, Clark, and Lowell, 1953) have argued that anxiety cannot be the basis of "psychological needs" because there are some people with congenital insensitivity to pain who nevertheless have normal personalities, including the

THE MOTIVATION OF EXPLORATORY BEHAVIOR

Introduction

Berlyne (1960, 1963), among others, has noted that phylogenetically higher organisms devote considerable amounts of time and energy to exploration, manipulation, and investigation of their environments. Even casual observation of the behavior of primates is sufficient to convince the layman (though perhaps not the scientist) of the validity of Berlyne's remarks. Moreover, this form of behavior occurs in the absence of such primary drives as hunger and thirst and hence cannot be considered merely the active search for biologically needed substances. Exploratory behavior is also maintained throughout the life of the organism despite the lack of any apparent survival value and despite the absence of any of the usual reinforcements. The problem is to account for the initiation and maintenance of exploratory behavior, and to do so, if possible, within the confines of traditional behavior theory.

Exploratory behavior, regardless of whether it takes the form of receptor-adjusting, locomotor, or investigatory responses, is defined as ". . . behavior with the sole function of changing the stimulus field, whereas the stimulus-introducing function is present in other kinds of behavior but secondary to other biological functions" (Berlyne, 1963, p. 288). Given this definition, the orientation reaction (discussed in Chapter 9) may be classified as an example or kind of exploratory behavior, since it orients the subject to a new stimulus or feature of the environment. In some respects the attentional response, hypothesized by Zeaman and House (1963) to mediate discrimination learning, may also be viewed as a form of exploration, since it too changes the stimulus field, although by elimination or selection of stimulation rather than by the addition of stimuli (see section entitled "Attention," Chapter 9).

Specific Exploration

According to Berlyne, exploratory behavior is controlled by internal states of the organism as well as by external environmental events. The most important class of external determinants of exploratory behavior includes what Berlyne has called the *collative properties* of stimuli. These are stimulus properties that require comparison or collation of information in order to be effective; they include such properties as novelty, surprisingness, incongruity, complexity, and uncertainty. Berlyne has hypothesized that these aspects of the environment

---

usual "needs" (Cohen, Kipnis, Kunkle, and Kubzansky, 1955; McMurray, 1950). However, there are numerous causes of anxiety in addition to pain. Unexpected noise has already been mentioned, and to this should be added unexpected stimuli of any sort, as well as frustration and conflict. There is evidence that all these situations elicit anxiety, or *arousal* to use a more general term, and people with congenital insensitivity to pain are not exempt.

have in common the ability to produce conflict within the organism, and that the conflict induces heightened arousal, which motivates exploratory behavior. The reinforcement for this behavior is provided by reduction of arousal through resolution of the conflict. With the equation of arousal and drive Berlyne (1960, 1963) has constructed a motivational system for the initiation and maintenance of exploratory behavior based on the Hullian concepts of drive induction and drive reduction. While this model in its simplest form is unable to account for some varieties of exploratory behavior, suitable elaborations provide a systematic explanation of much of exploratory behavior long felt to be outside the realm of behavior theory.

To understand how collative properties induce conflict and how exploratory behavior reduces it, consider first the induction of conflict, using novelty and uncertainty as examples. Novel stimuli are so classified if they differ from previously experienced stimuli along one or more dimensions. The difference is usually one of degree rather than kind. Consequently, when novel stimuli are suddenly presented, responses appropriate to the familiar stimulus will be evoked, often covertly, by stimulus generalization. In addition, responses appropriate to the novel stimulus itself will be evoked. While some of the responses may be compatible, a certain portion will undoubtedly be incompatible. It is this incompatibility between responses that operationally defines conflict.

Uncertainty is present when one is required to classify a stimulus pattern as one of n alternative kinds of stimulus patterns. As the number of alternatives increases, so does stimulus uncertainty. Since each stimulus has a unique response and only one response may be made at a given moment, the responses are incompatible. Conflict is created, and increases with the number of alternative incompatible responses. Similar reasoning is used to demonstrate the conflict-inducing ability of the remaining collative properties.

Alleviation of this stimulus-induced or "perceptual" conflict may be accomplished most effectively by approaching and exploring the source of stimulation. While this sequence of events may lead initially to a transitory increase in arousal, prolonged exposure will culminate in drive reduction in the following ways: first, novel stimuli will habituate with prolonged exposure and thus lose their conflict-inducing property; and second, conflict arising from complex, uncertain, or incongruous stimuli can be resolved if the subject extracts sufficient information from the stimuli to be able to make an appropriate identifying response. This form of exploratory behavior has been designated "specific" exploration.

Experimental evidence confirming the basic assumption that conflict induces heightened arousal (drive) has already been considered (in the "Conflict" section of this chapter). Over the past two decades, Berlyne and his students have gathered considerable data to support his motivational approach to exploratory behavior. However, due to limitations of space, the review given here must be selective rather than exhaustive.

Given that stimuli high in collative properties or perceptual conflict produce higher states of drive, then when confronted with such stimuli subjects are predicted to require greater stimulus exposure or exploration time to resolve the conflicting response tendencies. In a series of experiments with subjects ranging from infants to college students, Berlyne demonstrated that specific exploration time increases with the complexity, incongruity, novelty, and uncertainty of the stimuli. For example, infants (3 to 9 months old) were found to look longer at the more complex pictures in two of three tests (Berlyne,

Table 10-5

Summary of Selected Studies on Perceptual Curiosity

Collative property investigated	Subjects	Effect of increments in collative property on behavior			
		Fixation time	Exploration time	Reaction time	GSR changes
Complexity	3–9 mo. infants	Increase[a]	—	—	—
	5 yr. children	—	No effect[b]	—	—
	Undergraduates	Increase[c]	Increase[b]	—	—
	Adults	—	Increase[d]	—	No effect[d]
Novelty	5 yr. children	—	No effect[b]	—	—
	Undergraduates	Increase[c]	Increase[b]	—	—
Incongruity	Undergraduates	Increase[c]	Increase[b]	—	—
	Adults	—	Increase[d]	—	No effect[d]
Uncertainty	10 yr. children	—	—	Increase[e]	—
	12 yr. males	—	—	Increase[e]	—
	Undergraduates	—	—	Increase[e]	—
	Young adults	—	—	—	Increase[f]
Intensity	3–9 mo. infants	No effect[a]	—	—	—
Conflict	Young adults	—	—	—	Increase[f]
Surprisingness	Young adults	—	—	—	Increase[f]

[a] Berlyne (1958a) (behavior observed was first fixation time).
[b] Berlyne (1957a) (behavior observed was no. of stimulus exposures).
[c] Berlyne (1958b).
[d] Berlyne and Lawrence (1964).
[e] Berlyne (1957b).
[f] Berlyne (1961).

1958a); college students were found to spend greater amounts of time exploring stimuli that were high in complexity, incongruity, or novelty (Berlyne, 1957a, 1958b; Berlyne and Lawrence, 1964); and increased reaction times were demonstrated in children (10 to 12 years of age) with increasing uncertainty (Berlyne, 1957b). A summary of these studies is presented in Table 10-5.

Epistemic Curiosity

A second, perhaps higher form of exploratory behavior is "epistemic curiosity." This form of activity has the aim not only of obtaining stimulus information to reduce relatively short term conflict but also of acquiring knowledge, by which is meant ". . . information stored in the form of symbolic responses that can guide behavior on future occasions" (Berlyne, 1966, p. 31). Epistemic curiosity is motivated not by perceptual conflict but by conceptual conflict, that is, conflict generated by incompatible symbolic responses, such as thoughts, beliefs, and attitudes. This state arises when a person is confronted by stimulus situations that provide some evidence for a number of incompatible thoughts or beliefs but not sufficient evidence to determine which of the evoked symbolic responses is the appropriate or correct one. The incompatibility of symbolic responses can be resolved only by obtaining enough additional information to permit one response to become dominant. There seem to be only two studies of epistemic curiosity in children; increments in curiosity and knowledge-seeking behavior accompanied increments in situational uncertainty, as the theory predicts (Berlyne, 1962; Berlyne and Frommer, 1966).

Diversive Exploration

Another kind of exploratory behavior is "diversive" exploration, which is aroused in situations in which the degree or magnitude of stimulation in the environment is excessively low. Berlyne (1960) assumed that drive is increased in these situations. Berlyne argued, in effect, that there is an optimal level of stimulation and that marked deviations in either direction give rise to aversive levels of arousal or drive. The relation, then, between arousal level and sensory stimulation is U-shaped. Alleviation of arousal induced by too little stimulation, a situation analogous to boredom, is attained by exploratory activity that produces new or more complex situations in the environment.

Few would deny that boredom is an aversive state of affairs, and that it goads the individual into action until it is reduced.

> Catfish had been arrested on car-stealing charges before . . . , and he had served time in a reformatory . . . . he had been arrested again—on another car-stealing charge . . . . How did he explain the high crime rate in the Negro areas? Why had he himself got into trouble in the first place?
>
> "I was *bored*, man, just plain *bored*. On the streets a man can get so bored he just don't know what to do." (Alsop, 1968, p. 18.)

What produces boredom, and how is it reduced? The dull pains of boredom seem to become apparent when two conditions are present: (a) the person is awake and alert, and (b) there is "nothing to do."

Wakefulness is largely involuntary and cyclical. It is part of man's sleep cycle, one of the circadian (24 hour) rhythms of bodily processes. An infant spends only about one-third of the day awake; a man doubles this figure, staying awake about two-thirds of the day. It is during this period of wakefulness that the first precondition of boredom may be met. "Nothing to do," the second precondition, is more technically termed *stimulus deprivation;* it includes "nothing to experience" as well as nothing to do. Stimulus deprivation refers to an unchanging environment, one in which sameness from moment to moment is the dominant theme. One's bedroom at night, with the lights off and the normal "sounds of the city" absent, is an example of mild stimulus deprivation.

Like any aversive state, boredom should energize behavior; and responses followed by a reduction in boredom should be learned. To an observer it would appear that the individual is "seeking novelty" or that he is "curious." Indeed, a drive of "curiosity" has often been assigned to humans on just this basis (see, e.g., Berlyne, 1960; Kendler, 1963). Within the present context, however, curiosity is only the name for behavior that is motivated by boredom, and the resulting increase in stimulus variation is more accurately viewed as a reduction of stimulus deprivation. Thus, the hypothesized chain of events is *wakefulness + stimulus deprivation → boredom → activity → stimulus variation.*

Anecdotal reports from parents confined with a child no longer attracted by the available amusements support the hypothesis that stimulus deprivation produces activity, and there is also abundant experimental evidence, including reports of the effects of severe sensory deprivation in animals (e.g., Bexton, Heron, and Scott, 1954) and humans (e.g., Lilly, 1956; but see Orne and Scheibe, 1964). Butler (1957) found that monkeys learned to push a panel that opened the shutters of a window, the only consequence of which was a view of the outside of the opaque cage. Response frequency could be manipulated by duration of prior confinement with the shutters closed. If confinement was for only a few seconds, the mean frequency of panel presses in the succeeding hour was about 380. If confinement was for eight hours, the frequency increased to over 500 responses per hour. Thus, stimulus deprivation had the same energizing effect as food or water deprivation. There are numerous other studies of diversive exploration in animals (for reviews of this literature, see Berlyne, 1960; Fowler, 1965). Research on diversive exploration in humans is less abundant although equally in accord with the motivational hypotheses. For example, A. Jones (1961) and Jones *et al.* (1961) found diversive exploration to increase with the duration of sensory deprivation and with the uncertainty of the stimulus.

When awake, human neonates and infants are active and irritable under conditions of relative stimulus deprivation (e.g., Bartoshuk, 1962b; Birns, Blank, Bridger, and Escalona, 1965; Brackbill, Adams, Crowell, and Gray, 1966; Irwin, 1941a; Irwin and Weiss, 1934a, 1934b, 1934c), and they can be quieted by such stimuli as a monotone, a pacifier, rocking, and even insertion of a foot in warm water (Birns, Blank, and Bridger, 1966). Perhaps *any* source of stimulus variation will quiet a bored baby, provided the stimulus does not produce pain nor elicit fright and crying.[6]

---

[6] In a highly publicized study, Salk presented data suggesting that the taped sound of a human heartbeat at 72 beats per minute made infants fall asleep twice as fast as lullabies or a metronome at 72 beats per minute (Salk, 1960, 1961, 1962). It was suggested that fetal imprinting accounted for the results. In two replications, however, Brackbill *et al.* could find no evidence for such a claim. Instead, *any* sound of moderate intensity quieted the infants (and children of three to five years in one study) as compared to no sound (Brackbill *et al.,* 1966).

Child studies of the energizing property of stimulus deprivation at ages beyond infancy have not been reported. The appropriate experiment would proceed along the same lines as described to test for the drive property of any condition. That is, strength of a reference response would be measured after, say, an hour of stimulus deprivation for one group, two hours for another group, three hours for another group, etc. If a positive relation were found between strength of the reference response and duration of stimulus deprivation, the drive hypothesis would be supported. More elaborate experiments could also be carried out to determine the effects of stimulus deprivation on complex performance. It would be expected that stimulus deprivation would facilitate performance in situations in which the correct habit is dominant but would impede performance in situations in which an incorrect habit is dominant.

Several experiments in which a physiological definition of drive was used have confirmed the hypothesis. Using either a central nervous system index of drive or arousal (desynchronization of the EEG alpha rhythm) or an autonomic index (heart rate, respiration rate, basal conductance, etc.), these studies show that stimulus deprivation during the wakefulness cycle usually increases arousal (for reviews, see Berlyne, 1960; Cofer and Appley, 1964).

Turning to the final link in the chain, relating activity and stimulus variation, it might be asked whether stimulus variation is reinforcing to a subject in a state of boredom. Both anecdotal and experimental data suggest an affirmative answer. For example, numerous studies show that children and adults pay attention to and express a preference for novel stimuli more than redundant, "old" stimuli (e.g., Harris, 1965). Furthermore, responses leading to stimulus variation are often learned. It was already noted that Butler's monkeys learned a response that was followed by a peek out of the window. In a follow-up study, Haude and Ray (1967) showed that the more variable the stimulus outside the window, the faster the monkeys pushed the panel. Duration of previous stimulus deprivation, however, had no effect, contrary to the results of Butler. Rheingold showed that 6 month old infants would learn to touch a ball if each response was followed by flashes of colored light patterns on the wall (Rheingold, 1963), and she later reported similar results with older children (Rheingold et al., 1964). Friedlander (1967) found that an 11 month old infant more often pressed a button that was followed by a highly variable tape-recorded conversation between his parents than he pressed a second button followed by a recording low in variability. Odom (1964) deprived one group of 8 to 11 year olds of colored stimuli, another group of tones, another of both, and a control group of neither. After ten minutes of deprivation, a learning task was presented in which one response resulted in colors and another in tones. The control group and the group deprived of both kinds of stimuli gave the two responses about equally often, thus reflecting no development of a preference (no learning); but the color-deprived group developed a preference for the response followed by colors, and the tone-deprived group developed a preference for the response followed by tones. In addition, the previously mentioned studies with infants showed not only that stimulus deprivation increases activity, but also that subsequent stimulus variation reduces activity, much as though drive were reduced.

Summary and Implications

Berlyne's motivational explanation of specific and epistemic exploration is significant not only because it accounts for considerable data, but also because it provides developmental psychologists with a plausible overview of the conditions under which developing organisms come to experience and gain knowledge of their external environments. Berlyne is stating essentially that higher organisms attend (and respond) primarily to discrepancies of stored perceptions, symbolic responses, and schemas from present perceptions or thoughts evoked by stimuli varying along such dimensions as novelty, complexity, and uncertainty. It is these encounters with stimuli that are different but not wholly different, that spur the organism to perceptual and intellectual activity—forms of behavior that increase the probability of adaptation to the environment. Of marked interest are the findings of Berlyne and others that this striving to obtain information from the environment begins extremely early in life and remains thereafter a significant part of the behavior of higher organisms.

The boredom-drive hypothesis and the stimulus variation–reinforcement hypothesis have implications for child behavior, perhaps the most important being that much of child (and adult) behavior that previously appeared unmotivated (and led some psychologists to question the significance of the drive concept itself) appears now to be energized by boredom. Thus, we can understand the behavior of the child who gets up in the morning and, after reducing his "primary" drives, runs outside and plays all morning. Even arising from the bed is understandable, since to remain there is to suffer from the boredom of stimulus deprivation. Likewise, the interactions with toys, pets, peers, books, etc., can all be seen to produce the delights of boredom reduction. It is tempting to say the child "eats the environment" in the same way he eats food to reduce hunger.

A second implication is that much of learning that previously appeared to occur in the absence of reinforcement now appears to be reinforceable by boredom reduction. The learning of tunes, game rules, rhymes, routes, motor skills such as bicycling, skating, skiing, even academic skills such as reading, arithmetic, geography, physics—all are followed by boredom reduction for the stimulus-hungry child. And when they are not—when lessons are repetitive and predictable—then the student complains that they are "dull," and he learns little. Thus, the teacher who knows how to make a lesson "interesting" probably knows how to produce just the right amount of stimulus variation at just the right times to reinforce previous responses involved in studying. The same can be said for a good book—one that sustains attention and produces learning. "See Jane. See Jane run. See Jane run down the hill." Many reading primers go on page after page with such redundancies, until one almost dreads to turn the page, so certain are the contents. The interested reader is referred to Berlyne (1960) for a discussion of books and boredom.

A third implication follows from the fact that stimulus variation may be provided internally as well as externally. That is, new *thoughts* may provide stimulus variation, as well as new events in the outer world. Indeed, the inner source sometimes dominates the external source, and the individual is "lost in thought" or daydreaming. Infants and young children may therefore be more vulnerable to external stimulus deprivation, since they have limited inner resources to fall back upon. That is, their lack of symbols to think with, as well as a lack of interesting experiences to think *about*, would predispose them to depend more on external stimulus variation than would be the case with older children. Perhaps the physical play behavior of younger children, as compared to the more sedentary play of older children (e.g., reading) can be understood in these terms. Even individual differences may yield to such an analysis; it is commonly observed that highly intelligent children are more sedentary than children of average intelligence, perhaps as a result of a larger reservoir of thoughts and memories. The short attention span of young children may also be understood in these terms, since it would be a result of a low tolerance for external sameness—for paying attention to just one aspect of the external environment. The older child would be more able to *think* about the object of attention—to have associated thoughts—and thus to maintain a longer orientation.

Parents might therefore be well advised to recognize the dependency of their young children upon external sources of stimulus variation. Indeed, it has even been speculated that the origins of infantile love for mother, with all its benign consequences, begin with the stimulus variation provided by the attentive caretaker:

> . . . the infant soon learns that social objects have a much higher stimulating value than the inanimate part of the environment, that they are both more interesting and more responsive and thus much more satisfying. Herein, I suggest, lie the origins of attachment behavior: having learned of the special stimulating properties inherent in his human partners, the infant begins to distinguish them as a class in their own right, seeks their physical proximity in order to be exposed to their relatively high (but also accommodating) arousal value, and protests when he is prevented from achieving this end. (Schaffer, 1963, p. 194.)

Perhaps, in the last analysis, the development of such emotional attachments to others will prove to be the most important consequence of stimulus deprivation and stimulus variation.

CHAPTER 11

Perceptual Development

INTRODUCTION

Why study perception in children? Several answers may be given to this question. To begin with, the area of perceptual development may be thought of as on a par with other perhaps more obvious aspects of child behavior subject to important changes during the course of development. A complete understanding of the development of behavior in childhood requires, therefore, a concern with the processes and mechanisms underlying the development of perceptual skills and judgments, many of which are intimately related to other aspects of behavior, such as learning, thinking, and motivation.

Less obviously but no less importantly, the study of children's perception can contribute to the understanding of problems in the area of perception generally. For instance, in studying how an individual learns to identify a complex,

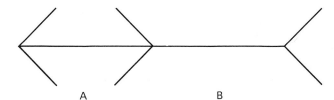

A   B

Fig. 11-1. One version of the Müller-Lyer illusion. The length of A is generally underestimated, B overestimated.

unfamiliar stimulus among other, similar ones, it is sometimes found that adults, with their extensive perceptual experience, master the problem much too quickly to provide useful information, but the learning process emerges much more clearly from an examination of younger children's performance on such a task (e.g., Gibson and Gibson, 1955). Furthermore, if on some perceptual task a particular variable has different effects at different age levels, the role played by that variable may emerge more sharply. For example, the finding that practice is ineffective in reducing the strength of one of the classical optical illusions—the Müller-Lyer (Figure 11-1)—in younger children, while it is maximally effective in adults (Noelting, 1960), points to certain plausible interpretations of the nature of such practice effects, while arguing against others that have been suggested, such as neural satiation.

A further basis for interest in the study of perceptual development originates in the nativism–empiricism controversy. The Gestalt psychologists, favoring a nativist view in their account of perceptual phenomena, generally minimized or discounted the importance of developmental changes, while those emphasizing the role of experience in perception (e.g., Brunswik, 1956) are apt to point to such changes in support of their position. But the mere demonstration of age changes in some aspect of perceptual functioning does not conclusively prove the role of experience; more importantly, it tells us nothing about the particular factors in the child's experience which may play a role in shaping or modifying his perception. Accordingly, psychologists studying perceptual development have increasingly turned away from rather sterile debate on the merits of the nativism–empiricism controversy to a detailed examination of the determinants of children's perception and the role of specific experiential factors in altering their perceptual processes.

Also not to be minimized is the potential interest of the subject of perceptual development for those in the field of education. A great many skills that the child has to acquire in school, of which reading is the most obvious and important one, involve the ability to make accurate discriminations, to recognize stimuli subjected to certain kinds of transformations, to integrate stimulus information across temporal or spatial gaps, etc. A more adequate understanding of the perceptual development of the child may thus help psychologists and teachers to devise better, more effective ways of presenting classroom materials to the child, and to facilitate his acquisition of the skills that he needs to develop.

This chapter is concerned primarily with the subject of form perception, and secondarily with some problems in the development of space perception. This treatment is thus not aimed at an exhaustive coverage of all aspects of the child's perceptual development; the topics discussed should, however, lead to an overall picture of the major changes in the child's perceptual functioning and the possible bases for these changes. This picture will have relevance and applicability to those areas, such as the perception of movement and optical illusions, that have been omitted from this account.

FORM PERCEPTION IN CHILDREN

There is little reason to doubt that from a very early age, perhaps from birth, the human being is able to perceive shape, that is, to differentiate among simple geometric forms, or to identify objects on the basis of their shape. If very young children are deficient in making finer discriminations based on shape, such as between two rectangles differing in elongation, this does not appear to reflect any basic lack of capacity for such discrimination, since it can be markedly improved by dint of extensive practice (Welch, 1939a, 1939b).

Whole versus Part Perception

There are, however, many more important questions to be asked than whether and how accurately children can perceive form. When the complex shapes which confront the child at every turn are considered, the question of *what* and *how* the child perceives becomes important. For instance, it has frequently been stated that children perceive in a diffuse or "global" manner, that is, they look at the whole configuration of a stimulus pattern, without much attention to its detail. According to this view, attention to detail appears only later, in middle childhood, and is in turn followed by an integrative mode of perception in which the parts and the whole are perceived simultaneously and in relation to one another. The early work of Claparède (1908), one of the pioneers in the field of child psychology in Europe, and more particularly the work of Werner (1940) emphasized this view of the changes in children's part–whole perception with age.

Fig. 11-2. Card 1 of the Rorschach test. (Reprinted by permission of Hans Huber, publisher, Berne.)

Evidence for this three-phase sequence was in fact obtained from developmental studies of responses to the inkblots of the Rorschach test. In several studies utilizing these materials, there was up to the age of six years a marked predominance of responses that appeared to be based on an undifferentiated perception of the whole blot; these gradually declined, in favor of responses based on small details, and subsequently of responses indicating an attempt to encompass the parts of the blot within a single, meaningful whole (Ames, Learned, Metraux, and Walker, 1953; Dworetzki, 1939; Hemmendinger, 1953). The following responses illustrate these stages with respect to the blot shown in Figure 11-2,: "A Christmas tree" (age four); "Cocks, ears, stones, and holes" (age eight); "A bat" (adult).

In interpreting such responses, however, it must be remembered that the unstructured stimulus configuration represented by a Rorschach inkblot does not correspond to any identifiable objects or things known to the child—or to anyone else. Thus, the responses reveal more about the kinds of images an individual is apt to conjure up on the basis of ambiguous stimulus information of indeterminate meaning, than about his perception of meaningful stimuli, such

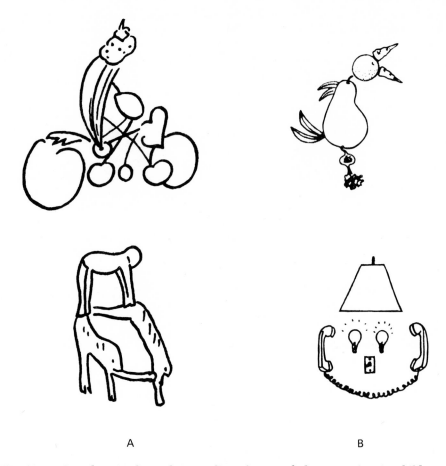

A   B

Fig. 11-3. Sample stimuli used in studies of part–whole perception in children. A. From Dworetzki (1939, Figs. 1 and 2, p. 260). (Reprinted by permission of the author and *Archives de Psychologie*, Geneva.) B. From Elkind *et al.* (1964, Fig. 1, Items 4 and 6, p. 84). (Copyright 1964 by the Society for Research in Child Development, Inc. Reprinted by permission of the authors and publisher.)

as pictorially represented objects. (This feature of the Rorschach is, of course, precisely what makes it attractive to the clinical psychologist.)

Recognizing this limitation of the Rorschach blots, Dworetzki (1939) approached this question more directly, by constructing stimulus figures made up of meaningful parts, which together make up a meaningful whole (see Figure 11-3A). Faced with this type of material, three to five year old children respond predominantly to the whole figure when asked to describe what they see. As this tendency diminishes, responses to individual parts increase, at first at the expense of the whole, but subsequently in conjunction with a recognition of the whole figure.

The results of Dworetzki's study are summarized in Table 11-1, which also presents results obtained in a subsequent study by Elkind, Koegler, and Go (1964), who tried to replicate the Dworetzki study with certain modifications. Elkind *et al.* felt that Dworetzki's figures were drawn so as to detract from the component parts, as in the lower picture in Figure 11-3A, in which it is

Table 11-1

Data on Part versus Whole Perception at Different Age Levels[a]

Mean age (years)	*Whole exclusively*		*Part exclusively*		*Whole and part*	
	Dworetzki	*Elkind*	*Dworetzki*	*Elkind*	*Dworetzki*	*Elkind*
4	80	—	10	—	3	—
$5\frac{1}{2}$	66	17	17	71	4	11
$6\frac{1}{2}$	47	19	21	50	16	32
$7\frac{1}{2}$	37	11	24	45	19	44
$8\frac{1}{2}$	31	5	28	34	21	61
$9\frac{1}{2}$	16	0	29	21	32	79

[a] Data from Dworetzki (1939) and Elkind *et al.* (1964). Percentages for Dworetzki's data add up to less than 100 percent, due to omission of "Transitional" response category. Data for Elkind *et al.* at ages $6\frac{1}{2}$, $7\frac{1}{2}$, and $8\frac{1}{2}$ represent averages over two groups of differing socioeconomic level.

admittedly difficult to recognize the arms and back of the chair as animals and a man on all fours, respectively. The stimuli used by Elkind *et al.*, illustrated in Figure 11-3B, were designed to bring the component parts into sharper relief. The results in Table 11-1 show that responses exclusively to parts did indeed strongly predominate at the youngest age level included in this study; while they exceeded the percentage of exlusively whole responses at all ages, these responses decreased rather than increased with age.

What can be concluded from these contradictory results? First, a comparison of the sample stimuli shown in Figure 11-3 suggests that in their efforts to bring out the parts more clearly, Elkind *et al.* inevitably detracted from the recognizability of the whole. Second, and more to the point, the question of whether young children focus on the part as opposed to the whole appears unanswerable in an absolute sense; it must rather be considered as depending on the nature of the stimuli presented to the child. The situation fits neatly, in fact, into a formulation proposed previously by Meili (1931) to handle similarly contradictory findings from earlier studies of part versus whole perception in children. According to Meili, the young child will respond to details in a stimulus configuration if the whole figure is complex or weakly structured, but he will favor the whole if the whole is simple or strongly structured. Admittedly, the usefulness of this formulation depends on the prior specification of criteria defining the complexity or degree of structure of a stimulus; conceivably, if these were derived from information theory principles, for example, the two dimensions of complexity and structure might turn out to represent only a single dimension.

Meili's formulation also accords nicely with evidence indicating that young children have great difficulty in isolating parts embedded in a whole—as in

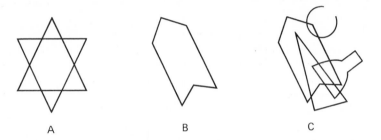

A   B   C

Fig. 11-4. Sample stimuli used in Ghent's (1956) study of perception of embedded and overlapping stimuli in children. A. Embedded figure. B. Target stimulus to be located in context of embedded and overlapping figures. C. Overlapping figure. (From Ghent, 1956, Fig. 2, Item C, and Fig. 3, Item 3, pp. 579, 580. Reprinted by permission of the author and the University of Illinois Press.)

the Gottschaldt task (Figure 11-4A and B) or in a task in which a part is hidden or camouflaged in a larger context, such as the "Find-the-duck" puzzle pictures popular with feature-page editors of newspapers and magazines (see Elkind and Scott, 1962)—while at the same time they seem to have little difficulty in perceiving shapes overlapping one another (Figure 11-4B and C). Ghent (1956) specifically compared these two perceptual tasks, utilizing the materials illustrated in Figure 11-4, and found near-perfect performance in four year old children on the overlap task, with little room for further improvement, but found a sharp improvement in performance on the embedded-figure task between the ages of four and eight. In interpreting the difference, Ghent pointed out that embedded figures share their contours with the lines of the context figures, as in Figure 11-4A, while in overlapping figures the figure to be detected only intersects the interfering ones. A principle of scanning along any available continuous path would account for the differential difficulty of these two tasks. But this may be only a special case of Meili's more general formulation, which would hold that the embedded figure is difficult to isolate from a strongly structured, cohesive whole (applying equally to the hidden-figures situation, where there may not be any shared contour lines), whereas for the overlapping figures there is no comparably structured whole to interfere with their perception.

The question of whether young children are prone to perceive in terms of parts or wholes is relevant to a controversy that erupted in the field of reading instruction some years ago. For many years, teachers of beginning reading had used the "look-say" approach, according to which the child's attention was directed at the overall outline of a word, such as *book,* and the name was then associated with that configuration of letters, usually by an intermediary picture representing the word. This approach was based on the assumption that it is somehow "natural" for young children to respond to such configurations, as opposed to the individual letters. Undue reliance on this method seems, however, to have resulted frequently in poor reading habits; this is not too surprising because an emphasis on the overall shape of the word is likely to mean a failure to differentiate between *book* and *took,* between *bed* and *bad,* etc.

The deficiencies in the "look-say" method do not, of course, prove the validity of the case made by its opponents (e.g., Flesch, 1955) for their alternative, the so-called "phonics" method, whereby the child analyzes each word into its component letter sounds. Quite apart from the notorious lack of correspondence in the English language between individual letters and the sounds associated with them, the sound of a word cannot be equated to the sum of its component phonic units. The point of bringing up this question here is rather to show how the application of erroneous assumptions about the nature of children's perception resulted in a highly inefficient, and even harmful approach to the teaching of what is probably the most important skill the school child has to acquire. Fortunately, more recent work in the field of perceptual learning and development is providing us with a firmer foundation on which to base effective reading instruction. The intricacies of the reading process are not to be minimized, and can hardly be done justice to here; the student interested in following up this topic is referred to the paper by Gibson (1965), which presents one perception psychologist's analysis of the reading problem (see also Diack, 1960; Elkind, 1969; Vernon, 1957).

The view that young children fail to perceive details in complex configurations originated in the notion of the primacy of the whole over the part, which represents a central tenet of the Gestalt theory of perception—this theory having been a highly influential force in earlier work on perceptual development, particularly in Europe. A corollary of the same principle is that the whole affects the perception of the parts, and that this should be true particularly in young children.

For all its intuitive appeal, the principle is more readily enunciated than put to an empirical test. An experimental attack was, however, devised by Lowe (1962), who presented his subjects (children between the ages of $5\frac{1}{2}$ and 10 years) with configurations of small black rectangles arranged in the pattern of a large square, or vice versa (as shown in Figure 11-5). The child's task was to reproduce the perceived shape of either the part or the whole by adjusting a variable rectangle whose shape could be changed from a square to an increas-

ingly elongated rectangle until it matched the shape of the part or whole. The
questions to which Lowe addressed himself were as follows: (a) Does the whole
literally distort the perception of the part, so that the little rectangles in Figure
11-5A are perceived as less elongated than they are, and the squares in Figure
11-5B as somewhat rectangular? (b) Conversely, is the perception of the large
rectangle in Figure 11-5B affected by the contrasting shape of the component
parts? (c) What kinds of developmental changes emerge with respect to these
questions?

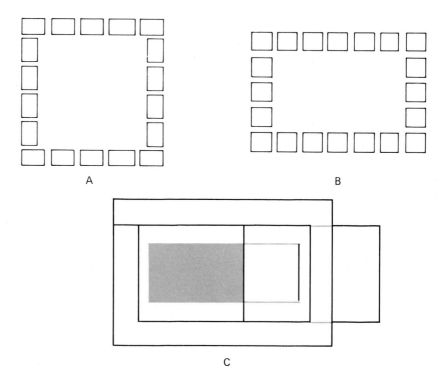

A   B

C

Fig. 11-5. Stimuli used in Lowe's (1962) investigation of the reciprocal influence
between part and whole on children's shape perception. A. Stimulus for matching
rectangular part and for matching square whole. B. Stimulus for matching square
part and for matching rectangular whole. C. Adjustable slide for shape matching.

Table 11-2 presents the results of two experiments, matching the shape of
the part appearing in a differently shaped whole, and vice versa. Data are
also shown for control conditions in which the shape of the part or of the
whole was shown in isolation to eliminate any influence of the whole or the
part, respectively. (For simplicity, differences among alternative stimulus figures
used in each experiment, varying along the rectangularity dimension, are
ignored.)

These data clearly show evidence of the expected effect of perception of
the whole on the part, particularly at the youngest age level. The effect appears,

furthermore, to decrease with age—indeed, for the matching of rectangular parts the values for Grades 2 and 4 are virtually identical with the control values, indicating simply that these children tended to underestimate the rectangularity of a small rectangle when it was matched to a larger rectangle. Lowe found a converse effect of the part on the whole. In adjusting the variable to match the shape of the whole, the kindergarten children erred in the direction of the shape of the parts, although by Grade 4 this effect had largely disappeared.

These results clearly show that the idea of a one-sided dominance of the whole over the part is fallacious, at all age levels. Apparently, young children such as the kindergartners of Lowe's study show rather a failure to perceive *either* the part *or* the whole independently of the other. This suggests, then,

Table 11-2

Mutual Influence between Part and Whole in Shape Perception[a]

| | | Whole matching | | | | Part matching | | | |
| | Mean age (years) | Square (Fig. 11-4A) | | Rectangle (Fig. 11-4B) | | Square (Fig. 11-4B) | | Rectangle (Fig. 11-4A) | |
School grade		Exptl.	Contr.	Exptl.	Contr.	Exptl.	Contr.	Exptl.	Contr.
Kindergarten	5.8	24	10	3	11	15	−1	−24	−10
Grade 2	7.8	16	6	9	14	9	4	−7	−6
Grade 4	9.7	12	8	13	14	6	−2	−8	−7

[a] Data from Lowe (1962). Exptl., experimental group; Contr., control group. Positive and negative values represent mean percentage errors in direction of rectangularity and squareness, respectively.

a general deficiency in both part and whole perception, rather than any unidirectional tendency for the whole to distort the perception of the parts.

Distinctive Features versus Prototypes

A controversy related to the one discussed in the preceding section, but raising different theoretical issues, concerns the following question: Is the improvement which children show with age in differentiating among complex forms based on increased ability to detect variables by which a set of stimuli can be discriminated, or on the ability to form more highly elaborated internal schemata of a given stimulus? For instance, on what basis does a child learn to differentiate the faces of other children? Does he pick out certain dimensional attributes by which any child may be characterized (such as high vs. low forehead, round vs. oval face), or does he pick out certain individual characteristic details for each child (e.g., a protruding chin, a mole on the cheek, slitlike eyes, etc.) which serve to define *that* child for him?

Eleanor Gibson and her associates at Cornell University maintain that the former of these two views more accurately characterizes the nature of perceptual learning in children. Their position is predicated on a "differentiation theory" of perceptual learning (Gibson and Gibson, 1955), which lays primary stress on the individual's capacity for becoming increasingly sensitized to the dimensions of variation present in a complex stimulus field, whether through specific practice or cumulative experience. Accordingly, they consider the child's primary

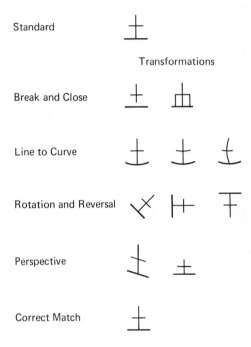

Fig. 11-6. Example of standard shape and variants presented in Gibson *et al.* (1962) study. (After Gibson *et al.*, 1962, Fig. 1, p. 898.)

task in perceptual learning situations (such as learning to read, for instance) to be one of detecting "distinctive features." This is a term borrowed from the study of phonetics, where it relates to the differentiation between, for example, the sound of the letters *c* and *g* (as in "cap" and "gap") (see Chapter 13, section entitled "Phonological Development"). To show the relevance of this concept to the development of form perception in children, and to the reading process more particularly, Gibson, Gibson, Pick, and Osser (1962) did the following experiment. They presented children a board with a standard shape at the top and with a series of 13 variants of that shape in a row below the standard shape. The series included one or more identical copies of the standards. (See Figure 11-6 for an example; in the actual display, the variants were ordered randomly.) The variants of each shape were drawn so as to represent particular types of transformations of the standard, such as closing an open figure, changing a straight line to a curve, reversing the standard up-down or left-right, rotating it 45, 90, or 180 degrees, and changing angular and linear relations by means of a geometrical perspective transformation. The child's task was to scan along the row of these variants and to pick out the ones that were "the same" as the standard.

The results of this study are shown graphically in Figure 11-7, which indicates the percentage of times a child confused a variant representing any given type of transformation with the standard. The figure shows, as one might expect, that the transformations differ in the extent to which they are discriminated by the child. Open versus closed is apparently a highly distinctive feature even for a four year old, but rotation and reversal, and straight versus curved are cues to which children do not consistently respond until somewhat later. Figure 11-7 also indicates that perspective transformations are generally not detected with any frequency even by eight year old children.

This last finding brings out a significant point. If children fail to respond to this particular transformation, it is most likely because it has lacked relevance in the prior experience of the child with such forms. Gibson *et al.* (1962) purposely constructed their stimuli to represent *letter-like* forms. In dealing with actual letters, however, it is precisely this kind of transformation that children have to ignore. The letter C may appear variously elongated or flattened, depending on the type in which it is set, yet what is important is to disregard these variations and to differentiate the generalized form from the similar closed figure O.

An analysis in terms of distinctive feature discrimination may well be a fruitful way of looking at the age changes taking place in children's form perception, but the study by Gibson *et al.* is deficient in two important respects. First, it shows nothing about the basis for the observed age changes. The study is not a learning experiment, but only shows the presumed *outcome* of a process of perceptual learning or development. Second, it does not really demonstrate the primary role which Gibson ascribes to distinctive feature discrimination as the basic process in form discrimination.

A follow-up study by Pick (1965), comprising three interrelated experiments, dealt with these points more directly. For her first experiment, with kindergartners as subjects, Pick selected six of the standard forms and six transformations of each of these standards from the original study by Gibson *et al.* (1962). Each child was shown three of these standards, and was given a pack of 15 cards containing two replicas of each of the standards, together with three transformations of each. The task was to pick out the cards that were identical to the standards. This process was repeated for several trials, until the child achieved errorless performance on one trial. After their training, the children were divided into two groups for a single transfer trial. A "distinctive features" group received a set of new standards, to be discriminated from variants that represented the same three transformations as used during training; a "prototype" group received the same standards as used during training, with a new set

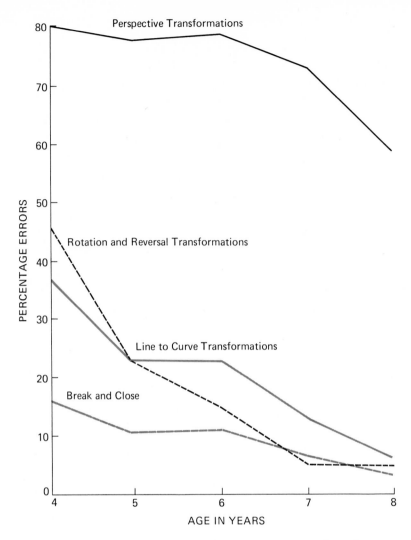

Fig. 11-7. Mean errors of children at different ages in matching from sample in Gibson *et al.* (1962) experiment. (From Gibson, 1963, Fig. 9, p. 19. Copyright 1962 by the Society for Research in Child Development, Inc. Reprinted by permission of the authors and publisher.)

of transformations of each. The results of this experiment, in terms of number of "confusion errors" (picking a transformed shape as identical to a standard), showed that both groups were far superior to a control group, which had received no preliminary training. That is, the trained groups showed a highly significant amount of transfer of their original learning. But the distinctive features group was also significantly superior to the prototype group, indicating that distinctive feature discrimination is a more effective basis for such learning than discrimination of the absolute characteristics of the standard, that is, proto-type learning.

The two succeeding experiments of Pick's investigation carried over the above design into the tactual modality; the standards and transformations were again taken from the original Gibson *et al.* study, but were adapted for tactual explora-tion. The two tactual experiments differed mainly in that in the first the children used only one hand, feeling first the standard and then the comparison form, and in the second the children used both hands, allowing exploration of the standard and comparison stimuli simultaneously. This turned out to affect very strongly the relative difficulty of the transfer tasks of the prototype group and the distinctive features group: Under successive exploration there was no differ-ence between the groups, although both were again superior to the no-practice control group. Under simultaneous exploration, however, the distinctive features group was as much superior to the prototype group as it was to the control group; that is, there was in effect no significant prototype learning under this condition.

The upshot of this study appears to be that to the extent that children have an opportunity to compare stimuli directly, they will tend to differentiate them on the basis of distinctive features, that is, on the basis of *dimensions* of stimulus variation represented in the stimuli; in the absence of such opportunity they are just as apt to learn in terms of an individual schema or prototype serving to identify a given form among other similar ones. This may be a reasonable answer, but it leaves a number of questions unresolved.

First, how do the properties of the stimulus configurations affect the relative superiority of distinctive feature versus prototype learning? The stimuli used by Pick were, after all, relatively simple, and the dimensions of variation were both relatively few and fairly obvious. Compare this situation with the one cited at the start of this section—the child learning to discriminate faces—where distinctive features might loom rather less impressively. The complexity of the total configuration and the relative subtlety of many of the attributes (e.g., curvature of the mouth, shape of the eyes) would make the attributes more difficult to detect, and thus encourage a kind of learning based more on a schema representing the total configuration, or rather its most salient characteris-tics, quite possibly dominated by one or two particularly salient ones such as a protruding chin.

Furthermore, one could argue that Pick's study was not appropriately designed to reveal the occurrence of prototype learning. *Prototype* refers to a generalized model or schema of an object, abstracted from particular instances or exemplars. Thus, the real question which one would want to examine is not whether the child is able to *differentiate* a particular standard from one of its transforma-tions, but rather how well he has learned the *class* of stimuli represented by all of the variants of a given standard. This, of course, cannot be determined from Pick's study, but it seems likely that in any given situation the child learns *both* about distinctive features differentiating a set of similar stimuli from each other *and* about general characteristics they share in common.

To find out about prototype learning, one would thus want to study how the child forms perceptual schemata based on the abstraction of common features from complex stimuli. This problem has been investigated less extensively than one might think, but two studies by a French psychologist, Èliane Vurpillot, are of interest in this connection.

STUDIES OF SCHEMA FORMATION IN CHILDREN. In one of these experiments (Vurpillot, 1962), children were simply given a deck of cards which contained schematic drawings of either a sheep or a rabbit lacking one or more of four details (for the sheep: head, horns, woolen skin, legs; for the rabbit: head, ears, bare skin, and tail), and were asked to sort these into two piles, the sheep and the rabbits. Three groups of children, 4, 7, and 11 years old, were compared. The results showed, first, that the number of cards consistently assigned to a given category by each age group increased with age. For the youngest children, 41 percent of the cards fell into a "neutral" or inconsistent category, that is, they were not assigned to either of the two animal categories by more than 60 percent of the children. In contrast, at the oldest age level only 17 percent of the cards fell into this neutral category. Second, for the 4 year olds the inconsistently sorted cards were as likely as not to be incomplete but unequivocally assignable representations of one of the two kinds of animal (e.g., a sheep lacking horns and feet), but for the 11 year olds almost all of the cards in this category were mixed "monsters," as Vurpillot called them, combining elements of both classes. Finally, even for the youngest group the inconsistently categorized cards were predominantly ones containing only one critical cue, such as the sheep's horns; virtually none of the cards containing as many as three such cues wound up in this neutral category.

These results seem to point, at least indirectly, to a process by which children come to form a schema representing a given class of concrete objects. Initially, a number of overlapping cues must all be present for the schema to be reliably activated, but as the child grows older, and presumably becomes increasingly familiar with the object, he requires progressively fewer cues, mutually interchangeable with one another. At the same time, the various details are not weighted equally; thus the presence of the ears for the rabbit, or the woolen body for the sheep, is generally sufficient at all age levels for assignment of a stimulus to its appropriate category, including the "monster" figures made up of combinations of cues from both classes.

In this connection the findings of Goldstein and Mackenberg (1966) might also be noted. They found a generally high degree of success by at least the age of 7 years in children's recognition of partially masked faces of familiar age-mates. As one might expect, performance was strongly determined by how much and what portions of the face were masked; masking the top half impaired recognition much more than masking the left half. Nevertheless, 70 percent of $6\frac{1}{2}$ year olds recognized a face showing only a quarter view (one side of the top half of the head), although at $4\frac{1}{2}$ recognition was considerably poorer. It seems likely that the child's experience in school in interacting with his classmates contributes to this age difference.

The second of Vurpillot's studies (Vurpillot and Brault, 1959) involved presenting to children replicas of common objects (a cup, a house, a doll) on a rotating turntable in front of the child. The children were then asked to choose from among a series of drawings the one they felt best represented the object itself. (Two of these series are reproduced in Figure 11-8.) One important trend apparent in the results, consistent with trends found in the earlier study, is that children between five and nine years old increasingly choose information-maximizing representations, such as the three-quarter view of the house showing both door and windows; at the same time irrelevant details (such as the ornament on the coffee cup) lose in importance.

It is worth noting that in this study the children were in fact being asked to pick two-dimensional drawings as representations of three-dimensional objects. The fact that even the youngest children did so quite readily shows that there is nothing particularly abstract or conceptual about such a task, contrary to assertions which one hears at times. Children in America have, of course, a considerable amount of experience with pictorial material, which is used effectively in preprimers and beginning readers, children's books and comic strips, etc. Many of these materials, and schematic drawings such as those shown in Figure 11-8, cannot be considered to be equivalent to photographic reproductions, but they seem nevertheless to serve as adequate representations. Related to this point is the finding of a study in which a psychologist raised his own son through infancy with a minimum of experience with pictures and photographs of objects (Hochberg and Brooks, 1962). When tested at 19 months, the child had no difficulty in recognizing objects in photographs and pictures. This finding is what one might have expected on the basis of Gibson's (1950, 1954) analysis of depth perception, which shows that two-dimensional projections of our three-dimensional world do in fact contain the information essential for perception of depth and distance. This point will be considered again in the discussion of the development of depth perception.

Yet, as Vurpillot's studies show, internalized schemata representing familiar objects do change in important ways during the course of development. Her finding that young children require relatively more overlapping cues (i.e., redundancy of information) to categorize a stimulus than do older children has been confirmed in studies in which children were asked to recognize an object on the basis of incomplete drawings (Gollin, 1960; Van der Torren, 1907); the degree of completion required for identification is generally found to decrease with age.

Gollin (1960) reported an experiment on the role of training with drawings of different degrees of completeness in the identification of minimally complete drawings. Children $3\frac{1}{2}$ to 5 years of age and adults were given practice in identifying drawings of either Type III (intermediate) or of Type V (complete), before being shown the same objects in their least complete form (Type I). (See Figure 11-9 for illustrative drawings.) Training with the intermediate type of stimuli was found to be extremely effective in leading to a high level of recognition of the Type I drawings shown subsequently, and this effect operated largely independently of both chronological age and IQ. The $3\frac{1}{2}$ year olds per-

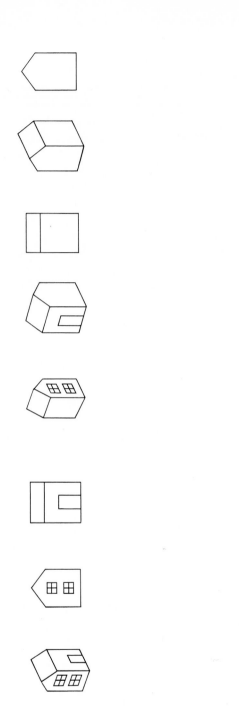

Fig. 11-8. Sample sets of drawings of objects from differing views, used by Vurpillot and Brault (1959) in study of formation of "empirical schemata." (From Vurpillot and Brault, 1959, Fig. 1, pp. 386–387. Reprinted by permission of the authors and Presses Universitaires de France.)

formed almost as well as the adults, and children of average IQ performed as well as a group with superior IQ. However, when training was with the complete (Type V) drawings, subsequent recognition of the Type I figures was much poorer, and in addition, large differences between children and adults and between average and superior IQ groups emerged.

At first blush, these findings may seem paradoxical. One might have thought that experience with the complete representations of the objects would most facilitate the recognition of the incomplete, Type I drawings, and that younger

Fig. 11-9. Sets of drawings representing objects at different levels of completion, utilized in research by Gollin (1960, 1961). (Reprinted with permission of author and publisher: Gollin, E. S. Further studies of visual recognition of incomplete objects. *Perceptual and Motor Skills*, 1961, 13, 307, Fig. 1, Items I, III, and V.)

children in particular would find such training most beneficial. But what seems to have happened is that the training with the Type III stimuli enabled the children to form more effective schemata representing the objects, and these schemata were subsequently evoked by the even more incomplete Type I drawings; in contrast, the experience with the very easy task of identifying the complete drawings of Type V led to very little schema learning. The adults, however, presumably had more effective, well-differentiated schemata already at their disposal in this type of situation, and these schemata, having been evoked by training with either type of drawings, subsequently facilitated their performance on the Type I drawings.

The Role of Stimulus Orientation in Children's Form Perception

One further question that has been the subject of considerable discussion and research concerns the sensitivity of children to differences in up-down and left-right orientation. The view of early workers on this problem, promulgated notably by the German child psychologist William Stern (1909), was that young children are totally insensitive to differences in the direction in which a stimulus faces, or the orientation in which it is presented. This view was based to some extent on observations and anecdotal evidence that young children frequently look at pictures upside down without any apparent impairment of their ability to recognize them; similarly, when they copy pictures presented to them, their drawings are apt to be mirror image or even upside-down reversals of the model.

Much of this evidence is equivocal, however. For one thing, children's drawings are by no means accurate guides to their *perceptual* abilities. Six or seven year old children frequently encounter difficulty in reproducing as simple a figure as a diamond, though they have no problem in differentiating it from any similar geometric figure, such as a square. Similarly, children's attempts to represent depth in copying a three-dimensional object lag well behind their ability to recognize adequacy of representation of depth in schematic drawings of the same object (Lewis, 1963a, 1963b). This is understandable, because copying a model demands, after all, that the child *reproduce* a perceived visual pattern on an originally blank sheet of paper, presumably through the intervention of an internalized schema linking the percept with the pattern of motor responses required for such a copy. (Alternative interpretations of the gap between perception and reproduction are possible—see Maccoby and Bee, 1965.)

Furthermore, the above-mentioned facility with which even very young children seem to be able to identify objects when looking at pictures upside down is not proof of lack of sensitivity to orientation, but possibly reflects their propensity for focusing on some salient detail (e.g., the wing of an airplane) as a basis for picture identification. (Recall Vurpillot's study of sheep vs. rabbit classification cited earlier. See also Reese, 1968, pp. 204–214.)

More recent evidence has shed fresh light on this question, and suggests that young children do indeed respond to the orientation of stimuli. But two different aspects of this question must be differentiated. One concerns the extent to which differences in orientation can be *ignored* by a child in recognizing or identifying a stimulus; the other is the converse of the first, that is, How difficult is it for children to distinguish stimuli differing only in orientation?

EASE OF DISCRIMINATING ON THE BASIS OF ORIENTATION. To start with the latter aspect of the general question, it has been found that children commonly do have difficulty in differentiating among identical stimuli presented in different orientations. This is illustrated by a difficulty familiar to teachers of beginning reading: children may not discriminate between letters that are up-down reversals of one another (M vs. W) and especially those that are left-right reversals (b vs. d). For instance, Rudel and Teuber (1963) found that up to the age of six years a large majority of children were unable to learn a discrimination between ⊏ and ⊐; with the equivalent up-down reversal the discrimination was learned by virtually all children from the age of $3\frac{1}{2}$ years in 16 to 20 trials. Such findings are in line with a hypothesis—proposed by Ghent (1961), among others—that children develop a tendency to scan stimuli downward from the top, which would yield little differential information from a left-right reversal discrimination.

Yet this still does not appear to be the whole answer. In a recent, deceptively simple study by Huttenlocher (1967), four year old children were shown a shape like the one in the above-mentioned experiment by Rudel and Teuber, and were asked to place another identical shape either next to it, by its side, or directly below it, in "exactly the same way" as the model. Huttenlocher found that when the copy was to be placed directly below the model the children's errors were limited almost exclusively to the ⊔ stimulus, but when the copy was to be placed alongside the model, the reverse was true: only the copies of the ⊏ stimulus resulted in any errors. Huttenlocher's explanation of these curious results started with the premise that young children are relatively insensitive to any mirror-image rotations of a stimulus. In some cases, such a rotation leaves the original stimulus intact—as when the ⊏ figure is rotated along the horizontal axis, or the ⊔ figure is rotated around the vertical axis—and thus the child's response is scored as correct; in other cases the rotation makes a difference, and the child thus makes an error—as when the ⊔ figure is rotated along the horizontal axis, or the ⊏ figure is rotated around the vertical axis.

Huttenlocher used a further task in which the child was asked to reproduce the order of three blocks arranged either in a pile or along a horizontal row. The latter problem proved more difficult, indicating that apart from the mirror-image reversal tendency there is still a superiority of up-down as opposed to left-right discrimination. Such a difference is hardly surprising, if we reflect on the prevalence of vertical as compared to horizontal asymmetry in everyday life (as in the case of the human body). Furthermore, even when objects are asymmetrical horizontally, they tend to be equally probable in either direction, which is not the case with vertical asymmetry: a car may be indifferently perceived facing in either direction, but rarely overturned.

If young children typically experience difficulties in discriminating between left-right reversals, or more generally mirror-image reversals, these difficulties are not to be thought of as operating in any absolute sense, but rather as relative to the demands of a given task, as well as being subject to modification through learning. First, preschool children demonstrate a fairly high degree of proficiency in differentiating even mirror-image reversals, if the task is simply to decide whether two such stimuli are or are not the same (Robinson and Higgins, 1967). The same holds true for a task in which a sample stimulus is presented with two comparison stimuli, of which one is identical to the sample and the other is an up-down or left-right reversal of it (see Figure 11-10). Using such a task, Wohlwill and Wiener (1964) found that on 16 trials involving up-down and left-right reversals, four year old children made an average of only 2.1 and 3.2 errors, respectively.

That performance on this type of task is strongly susceptible to improvement through training is indicated by the results of a study by Hendrickson and Muehl (1962). These investigators were able to get a group of kindergarten children to attach different labels to the letters *d* and *b* by having them execute opposite movements of a lever, according to the direction in which the stimulus was pointing. This finding shows the facilitative role of proprioceptive feedback

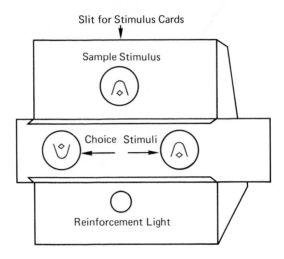

Fig. 11-10. Apparatus and sample stimuli utilized by Wohlwill and Wiener (1964) in study of discrimination of form orientation in young children. (From Wohlwill and Wiener, 1964, Fig. 1, p. 1115. Copyright 1964 by the Society for Research in Child Development, Inc. Reprinted by permission of the authors and publisher.)

from movement in perceptual discrimination—a point which will be taken up again later in this chapter.

ABILITY TO IGNORE ORIENTATION. It is time now to turn to the other side of the coin: To what extent are children affected by the spatial orientation of stimuli in recognizing an object, matching a stimulus to another identical but rotated one, etc.? Here again, the nature and conditions of the task presented to the child can make a considerable difference. For example, if preschool children are taught to pick one of two forms and are then presented an up-down rotation of the one they have been trained to choose, paired against a new stimulus not seen before, they will generally maintain their preference for the originally rewarded shape, in spite of the difference in orientation (Hunton and Hicks, 1965). Similarly, preschool children are unaffected by differences in orientation (right-left or up-down) in selecting from an array of pictures of a familiar object the one that matches a sample picture (Newhall, 1937). When the difficulty of the task is increased, however, the situation changes. For instance, under tachistoscopic presentation (brief-exposure conditions) younger children do have greater difficulty in identifying stimuli inverted in orientation than identifying those presented upright, while older children show no such impairment. This has been found to hold true whether the stimuli are meaningful objects or abstract geometric shapes (Ghent, 1960; Ghent and Bernstein, 1961). These results certainly indicate that the orientation of a stimulus is of some importance to the younger child, and do not bear out the view that he is at an actual advantage relative to older children in this type of task. Yet it is dangerous to generalize from performance under tachistoscopic exposure to perceptual functioning under normal viewing conditions; there is no reason to assume that even very young children have any particular difficulty dealing with stimuli in differing orientations, when exposure times are sufficiently long to permit effective exploration of the stimuli.

One of the problems with studies on this question is that they rely entirely on all-or-none indexes of recognition. The data are typically in terms of number of correct identifications, matches, same-different responses, or the like. Since such identifications may be based on anything from complete exploration of a stimulus shape to the detection of a small identifying cue, the results are difficult to interpret. Tampieri (1963) approached this question in a rather different fashion. Children between 5 and 11 years of age and adults were asked

Fig. 11-11. **Example of stimulus series utilized by Tampieri (1963) in study of threshold of form discrimination for stimuli in upright and rotated orientations. (Reprinted by permission of Società Editrice Universitaria.)**

to decide which of a set of geometric shapes varying by small degrees would fit into a hole, without actually being allowed to verify whether it would fit. (Figure 11-11 illustrates one of the stimulus series used.) The question was, would the degree of *precision*, that is, the smallest difference the child could detect between the shape of the hole and the comparison shape, be different when the shape was in the correct orientation with respect to the hole, as compared to when it was rotated by 45 degrees or 135 degrees? While the results are not easily summarized (in particular they varied somewhat according to the particular shapes utilized), the overall picture that emerged was of a general improvement with age in the precision of shape perception, superimposed on a decrement in performance produced by rotation, which on the whole seemed to remain fairly invariant over age.

CONCLUSIONS. The gist of the preceding, in parts rather contradictory evidence, appears to be as follows: Young children have little tendency to utilize orientation as a differentiating cue among stimuli. They are therefore apt to have difficulty in situations in which they are forced to rely on this cue, though they may be able to learn to do so, particularly through training providing differential proprioceptive feedback correlated with differences in orientation. However, where orientation has to be disregarded, they may or may not be affected by differences in orientation, depending on how this difference affects their mode of visual exploration or scanning. Older children and adults, in contrast, are more apt to relate a stimulus to a more comprehensive spatial framework, and therefore are able to differentiate stimuli differing in orientation or to abstract from this factor, whichever the situation requires.

DEVELOPMENTAL TRENDS IN SPACE PERCEPTION

One of the questions which has intrigued many philosophers and psychologists over the years is how an individual is able to perceive a three-dimensional world, given a two-dimensional retinal surface. Ever since Berkeley (1709) concerned himself with it this puzzle has been grist for the mill of the empiricists, since some kind of learning process seemed to be essential for the development of this capacity.

This question has most typically been approached through the study of size constancy. How is it possible for objects to remain nearly invariant in their perceived size, regardless of their distance from the observer? One answer is that they do not—necessarily. A five year old, embarking on his first plane flight, was heard to ask his father, as they were gaining altitude: "How come we aren't getting any littler yet?" This child had seen planes in flight seemingly lose their normal size, and imagined that he as a passenger would participate in this shrinking process. Even to an adult, a jet flying far overhead loses the appearance of gigantic size which it has on the ground; conversely, seen from a plane, houses and cars on the ground *do* look like toys. Normally, however, this is not the case; size constancy generally prevails at least as long as the object is seen across a continuous surface or stretch of terrain.

Such constancy is fairly well developed by an early age, as witnessed by the results of a classic study by Beyrl (1926) with 3 to 10 year old children and adults. This study comprised a series of judgments in which a standard square, 10 cm. on each side, or alternatively a standard disk, 7 cm. in diameter, was presented at a 1 meter distance from the subject; the subject's task was to compare a square or circle of variable size to the standard, the variable appearing at distances of 2 to 11 meters from the subject. For each distance a "point of subjective equality" was determined from each subject's judgments. (The point of subjective equality is the size of the comparison stimulus perceived as equal to the standard. More precisely, since the psychophysical method of constant stimuli was used, the point of subjective equality is the size of the comparison stimulus that a given subject judged to be larger than the standard as often as he judged it to be smaller than the standard over a series of presentations.) Figure 11-12 presents the results obtained with the square; there is a consistent age trend toward constancy (represented by the 10 cm. match) in these judgments. Furthermore, the points of subjective equality vary progressively less with the distance of the comparison stimulus as age increases; for the youngest children, there is a considerable discrepancy between the matches made with the variable at 2 and 11 meters, while for the oldest children and adults the matches are virtually the same at these distances.

One limitation of Beyrl's study is that the standard stimulus was always the near one, relative to the observer. It has been found (see Wohlwill, 1963) that judgments of this sort are subject to a systematic bias of overestimation of the standard; thus, where the standard is the near stimulus, any tendency toward underconstancy would be exaggerated through this "error of the standard." There is a good possibility, furthermore, that this error interacts with

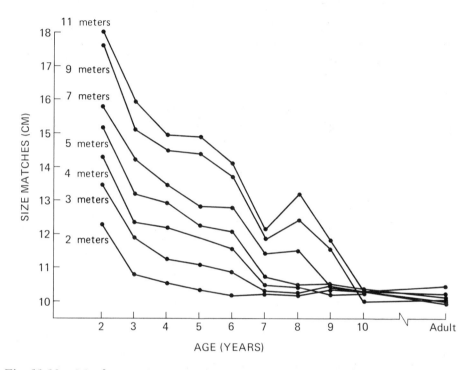

Fig. 11-12.   Matches to 10-cm. standard square at 1 meter with variables at different distances, as a function of age. (After Beyrl, 1926. Reprinted from Wohlwill, 1963, Fig. 2, p. 275, by permission of the author and Academic Press, Inc.)

age, being larger in young children than in adults. Thus, fully valid data on the size constancy problem can be obtained only by doing such a study twice, once with the standard near and once with the standard far. A series of such studies has been carried out by Piaget and Lambercier in Geneva (for a summary, see Wohlwill, 1963). These investigators found a marked error of the standard, that is, consistently more underconstancy with the standard near than with the standard far; and when the two conditions were averaged, the data revealed a steady change from only slight underconstancy in the youngest children (seven to eight years of age) to actual overconstancy in adults, that is, a tendency to judge the far stimulus as *larger* than it actually is, relative to the near one. It thus seems that the main developmental change occurring between early childhood and maturity is not the gradual establishment of size constancy. This probably takes place much earlier, quite possibly during the first year or two of life, although our information on this point is not very conclusive (see Chapter 2; and Wohlwill, 1960a). It seems, rather, that a progressively stronger overconstancy bias develops, reflecting an increasing tendency of the subject to overcompensate for the effects of distance. The phenomenon is thus an essentially judgmental error, indicative not so much of the manner in which the subject perceives the stimulus, but rather of a deliberate and frequently conscious correction imposed on his perception. It is worth noting in this connection that adult subjects show a closer approach to constancy when asked to make size matches according to the way the stimuli look to them, than when asked for "objective" judgments, that is, judgments in terms of their estimate of the true size of the stimulus; in the latter case overconstancy is the rule (see Carlson, 1960, 1962). This is not to say, however, that this is necessarily the result of a process of intellectual reasoning—at least what evidence there is concerning the relationship between tested intelligence and constancy judgments is inconclusive (e.g., Hamilton, 1966; Jenkin and Feallock, 1960).

If the perception of size is subject to increasing overconstancy as the child develops, what happens to the perception of distance itself, which presumably mediates the perception of size? Studies by Denis-Prinzhorn (1960) and Wohlwill (1963) have shown a similar change from under- to overconstancy between the ages of seven or eight and adulthood; the *perceived* midpoint of a line slanting away from the subject along the line of sight is slightly to the front of the *true* midpoint in young children, and is too far to the rear in adolescents and adults (see Figure 11-13). This phenomenon is largely independent of variation in stimulus conditions, such as the texture of the background against which the judgments are made (see Wohlwill, 1963). However, both Denis-Prinzhorn and Wohlwill have found that the overconstancy bias increases with practice; on initial exposure to the situation, adolescents and adults make judgments more nearly comparable to those of young children, but over an extended series of judgments, as they "find their bearings" in the situation, they overcompensate increasingly, and thus show a progressive heightening of their overconstancy error.

In one important respect, however, the younger children in these constancy tasks are notably deficient relative to the older subjects: they appear to be much less precise in the judgments they make, that is, their perception is less differentiated. This is shown in the *variability* of their judgments over a series of trials, for instance, as well as in the relative lack of internal consistency of the responses given to a set of variables presented in succession, from which the subject's point of subjective equality is calculated. This has a certain theoretical interest, since according to one theory of perceptual learning and development (Gibson and Gibson, 1955) the course of changes in perceptual functioning with age, experience, or practice is to be described in terms of an increase in differentiation, or increasing *specificity* of the correlation between stimulus magnitudes and perceptual judgments. Accordingly, the considerable decrease in *variable* error with age is stressed and the importance of changes in *constant* errors, such as the overconstancy bias discussed above, is minimized (e.g., Gibson and Olum, 1960).

It seems unreasonable to emphasize one type of change at the expense of the other. Increasing differentiation undoubtedly accounts for a major part of age changes in size and distance perception up to middle childhood. At the same time, for size and distance perception over larger distances, such as judgments made over a field under "natural" outdoor conditions, somewhat different results are obtained. Under these conditions children through the middle childhood years fall considerably short of constancy, to an extent increasing with

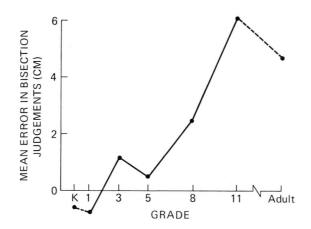

Fig. 11-13.   Age changes in errors for bisections of a 90-cm. line.   (From Wohlwill, 1963, Fig. 8, p. 298. Reprinted by permission of the author and Academic Press, Inc.)

distance, just as Beyrl's study had indicated for the younger children over shorter distances (Harway, 1963; Leibowitz, Pollard, and Dickson, 1967). Perhaps the overall picture can best be conveyed by means of an hypothetical graph indicating the way in which extents in three-dimensional space change with increasing distance at different age levels. This graph, reproduced in Figure 11-14, fails to account for all of the data in this field, but it does seem to represent adequately the main trends uncovered in the developmental research on the constancy question.

One factor that undoubtedly favors the relatively high level of constancy, and the general effectiveness of space perception attained in childhood, is the variety of cues or variables of stimulus information correlated with depth. Thus, studies of the related problems of shape and brightness constancy have generally shown a slower development for these constancies (see Wohlwill, 1960a), which is plausibly related to the greater paucity of overlapping cues available to the observer as mediators of brightness and shape information, particularly under the laboratory conditions in which these have generally been investigated.[1] Children appear to be more dependent on such redundant information than adults, as noted earlier in the discussion of form perception and the development of schemata.

The actual effects of particular sources of potential information on constancy at different age levels remain to be determined, however, even for size and distance perception, where the problem has been most extensively investigated. Binocular cues do not seem particularly critical for constancy, even over short distances, where binocular parallax would be strongest. At least this is the inference drawn from the accuracy of the distance bisections made at the younger

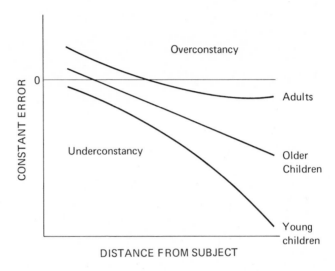

Fig. 11-14. Hypothetical function relating constancy to distance at different age levels. (From Wohlwill, 1963, Fig. 6, p. 291. Reprinted by permission of the author and Academic Press, Inc.)

age levels in Wohlwill's study (1963), in which the bisections were made under monocular conditions (see Figure 11-13). A recent report of an investigation by Leibowitz *et al.* (1967) suggests that over longer distances children's size-at-

---

[1] In one study of shape constancy, in fact, 5½ year old children showed near-perfect constancy, with a steady *decline* up to late adolescence (Meneghini and Leibowitz, 1967). In trying to account for these fairly anomalous results, the investigators suggested that possibly the older subjects may have spontaneously adopted a more analytic attitude, which would have directed their attention to projective rather than objective shape, and thus have reduced constancy. While it is difficult to assess the validity of this explanation, a possibly related finding is worth noting: Vurpillot (1964) has shown that 6 to 7 year old children fail to differentiate between instructions for projective and objective shape, exhibiting a moderate and approximately equivalent degree of constancy under both conditions; in contrast, 12 year old children are able to differentiate sharply between the two instructions, showing higher constancy than the younger children for the objective instructions and lower for the projective.

a-distance perception *is* impaired by loss of binocular cues, resulting in a greater lack of constancy, but the actual data for the various age groups were not very consistent.

In any event, there is little reason to doubt that monocular cues by themselves can provide a fairly adequate basis for size and distance perception, even in children, as evidenced by the fact that children can readily make fairly adequate distance judgments from photographic stimulus fields. This was shown in a further study by Wohlwill (1965), utilizing photographic slides of variously textured surfaces on which a toy cow and a toy horse were displayed in the

Fig. 11-15. Sample picture used in Wohlwill's (1965) developmental study of perception of distance relations in photographic slides. (From Wohlwill, 1965, Fig. 1, p. 166. Reprinted by permission of the author and Academic Press, Inc.)

foreground or background. (A sample is reproduced in Figure 11-15.) The subjects, taken from Grades 1, 4, 8, and 11, and from college, were asked to imagine themselves in the field with the cow and horse; as each slide of a series was exposed to view they were to decide whether the horse or the cow was closer to the fence. Within each set of slides, the position of the fence was varied in small steps, making it possible to determine the perceived midpoint of the distance between cow and horse.

Under these conditions the results fell in the *underconstancy* range throughout, that is, the position of the fence corresponding to the perceived midpoint was generally somewhat in front of the true midpoint (in terms of the actual three-dimensional scene as photographed). The underconstancy error was somewhat larger in the children (Grades 1, 4, and 8) than in the adolescents and adults, but age differences were comparatively small. The amount of error consistently decreased as the density of the texture elements (the black stars) in the field increased; but the role of this variable remained approximately constant at all age levels. Finally, the results of this study are notable for the marked consistency and precision of the judgments, even at the youngest age levels. This finding may be attributable to the method used in the study, calling for a series of clearly defined, two-valued decisions on the part of the subject, as opposed to the method of stopping a moving pointer, which Wohlwill used to obtain the bisections in his earlier (1963) study. But the fact that two-dimensional stimulus fields yielded judgments of distance in the third dimension of such a degree of precision, by children as young as six years of age, is noteworthy in itself.

These results provide some support for Gibson's (1950) theory of space perception, which emphasizes variables of stimulation correlated with distance, such as texture gradients, that are available in two-dimensional photographic projections, just as they are on the retina. The evidence further indicates that the ability to perceive depth in pictorial material probably develops rather early in life, and is not dependent on any advanced intellectual processes. This point is borne out by the finding that children are *more* susceptible to the influence of suggested depth in perspective drawings than adults—that is, they show more strongly an illusion of perspective, according to which the perceived midpoint of a line extending from the bottom to the top of a perspective drawing is displaced upward, in conformance with the illusion of depth conveyed by such a drawing (Wohlwill, 1962). Here again a child's perception of a feature of a stimulus field, such as depth, must be distinguished from his ability to *represent* the feature in a drawing; the latter constitutes a cognitive skill of a much more advanced order, and is undoubtedly in large measure affected by specific training and experience in art work. By the same token, utilizing drawings of a highly schematic sort, lacking in the kind of "fidelity" that a photograph or detailed perspective drawing has, one may demonstrate that variables relating to the educational and cultural experience of the child can affect to a degree his ability to perceive pictorially portrayed depth, as Hudson (1960) showed in a study of the responses of African children of greatly varying backgrounds to schematic drawings of scenes in depth.

Summary

To sum up this section on space perception, it is apparent that sensitivity to size and distance relations in three-dimensional space appears in substantially complete form well before maturity, and in many respects probably before the child reaches school. There are two exceptions to this generalization, however— the change toward overconstancy that appears in adolescence, and the increase in the span of distance over which constancy or a close approach to it is maintained (see Figure 11-14).

The period of greatest importance for this aspect of perceptual development has, however, scarcely been studied at all. This is the period from late infancy through early childhood, where precise psychophysical data, though in principle obtainable (with some degree of ingenuity and care on the part of the experimenter), are as yet virtually absent. Undoubtedly it would be found that a major respect in which perception changes during this time is in its increasing differentiation and specificity, in conformity with the views of perceptual theorists of varying theoretical persuasions, such as Gibson and Gibson (1955) on the one hand and Wapner and Werner (1957) on the other. At the same time it is safe to assume that such research would likewise bear out the relative precocity of the child's development of depth perception, that is, of his sensitivity to depth in pictorial material and material viewed monocularly. The origins of this development reside undoubtedly at an even earlier stage, the stage of sensorimotor development in infancy (see Chapter 14).

MECHANISMS OF PERCEPTUAL DEVELOPMENT

Thus far the discussion has been directed primarily at *describing* the major changes that occur in two major areas of the perceptual development of the child—form and space perception—and to note some of the variables that influence these developmental changes. *How* they occur is a very different question, and one that is much more difficult to answer. However, particularly in recent years, notable advances have been made in this regard, from which an overall picture of some consistency and scope is beginning to emerge.

A key concept in considering this question is that of "perceptual activity," a term proposed by Piaget (1969) to deal with developmental changes in perception that are not reducible to peripheral sensory mechanisms nor to primary cortical processes directly correlated with the stimulus input. The concept is intended by Piaget to refer to the child's increasingly active mode of apprehending the stimulus world, of attending to relevant aspects of it, of making comparisons between and interrelating different stimuli.

The problem that immediately arises is that of dealing with this concept in operational terms: How can "perceptual activity" be defined so as to reduce it to directly observable terms? The process of learning distinctive features or prototypes, or of judging size at a distance does not provide any direct, readily observable evidence of particular activities in which the child may be engaging. Nevertheless, a number of activities or mechanisms can be suggested as mediators of performance on a perceptual task, varying from the readily observable to ones that must be inferred from other indexes of the individual's behavior. Three of these in particular will be examined: orienting and investigatory responses, exploratory and scanning responses, and selective-attentional mechanisms.

Orienting and Investigatory Responses

In order to perceive a stimulus, it is obviously essential for the individual to orient himself so as to maximize the stimulus information impinging on his sense organs. Such behavior as turning the head in the direction of a sound or moving toward it, positioning the eyes, head, or the whole body to improve one's view of a given stimulus, reaching out to an object to explore it by touch, or sniffing to better "catch" a smell—all these activities fall in this category. There are two notable developmental trends here. First, as the child's mobility and sphere of action increase, he brings himself into contact with an increasingly larger number of stimuli—witness the toddler who "gets into everything": for the despairing mother, it may represent only mischief, but for the child himself it represents a search for new stimuli to be explored. Second, he becomes increasingly effective in adjusting his receptors, and indeed his whole body, to keep a "fix" on a stimulus. Thus, after a certain number of months he follows objects moving across his field of view, and subsequently uses his increasing motoric powers to "track" a variety of moving stimuli—such as his mother, or a ball rolling away from him.

A good illustration of this point is provided by a study by Smith, Zwerg, and Smith (1963) with children between 10 and 38 months of age. The children were placed in a rotating playpen; outside of the pen was located a television screen on which appeared either the child's own mother or a female stranger, each either reading silently or moving about. The data consisted of the number of seconds the child spent oriented toward the TV monitor, during a one-minute period, when to do so required continued motion by crawling or turning to compensate for the movement of the playpen. The results are shown in Figure 11-16. This graph clearly shows that the children are increasingly active, or perhaps increasingly effective, in maintaining their orientation toward the stimulus source (the bottom line, for a control condition with a blank screen, understandably shows no such age trend). The results further point to differences in the power of the stimuli to maintain the child's orienting activity; the movement condition was consistently above the stationary one, and the mother generally above the stranger. The fascination of young children for any moving stimulus, reflected in the superiority of the movement condition, is well known to all who are familiar with infants and toddlers; it presumably accounts for the preponderance of names of animals and vehicles in the very young child's vocabulary.

Exploratory and Scanning Activities

Probably the most important type of activity mediating perceptual development through early childhood, particularly in the perception of form, involves the exploration of the various parts of a stimulus configuration or object, through both visual scanning and tactual manipulation. First, consider touch. A two or three year old picking up an object when blindfolded, with the intent of identifying it, typically displays what Soviet psychologists have called "executive" or "catching" movements (see Zaporozhets, 1965). These are characterized by a rigid, immobile grasp that conveys little patterned information to the child regarding the overall shape of the object, variations in texture, hardness, etc.; the only information the child receives is that emanating from the few points of contact of the palm and fingers of his hand with the object. At a somewhat later stage, the child takes a more active approach, in the sense of fingering the object, moving it about in the palm of the hand, and the like. This increases the *amount* of information he receives, but it is still largely unpatterned, because of a lack of any systematic directional exploration along the edges of the object.

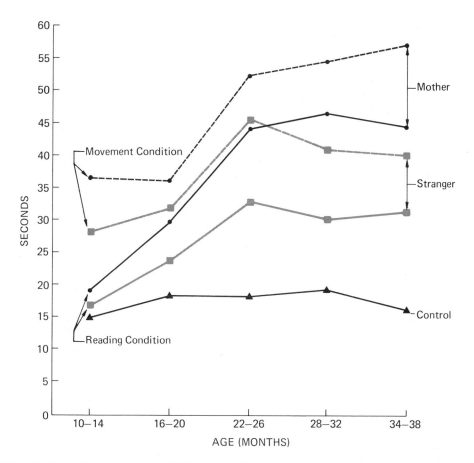

Fig. 11-16. Time spent by children of different ages in maintaining orientation to televised images of different types in moving playpen. (Reprinted with permission of authors and publisher: Smith, K. U., Zwerg, C., and Smith, N. J. Sensory-feedback analysis of infant control of the behavioral environment. *Perceptual and Motor Skills*, 1963, *16*, 730, Fig. 3.)

The latter kind of tactual exploration, tracing the outline of the figure, is generally not found until about six years of age (according to the Soviet psychologists); presumably it is itself dependent upon the establishment of generalized schemata directing the child's exploration.

The conclusions of Zaporozhets are strikingly confirmed by the findings of a recent investigation by Abravanel (1968), which dealt with the development of children's ability to integrate information from the visual and tactual modalities in making comparisons between the lengths of various kinds of stimuli. Thus, for one of his tasks, children felt a wooden bar with one hand, and had to adjust the visual length of a comparison tape to equal the length of the bar. In this and other similar tasks a marked improvement occurred in the accuracy of these judgments between the ages of 3 and 7 years. Abravanel's qualitative data further bear out Zaporozhets's observations. For instance, in the task just referred to, the most frequent form of haptic exploration of the bar at ages 3 and 4 was by means of "generalized palpation" (the child clutching the bar with the whole hand) and "cupping ends" (holding the ends of the bars passively in the palms of the hands). Between 4 and 5 years there was a sharp increase in children's using their fingers and fingertips to hold the ends of the bars, and between 5 and 14 years there was a steadily increasing tendency to span the length of the bar with the hand to get its measure. Other forms of behavior which likewise increased with age (such as aligning the bar with the tape, though the two remained separated by a screen) clearly involved a similar gain in pertinent information deriving from the activity.

A study by Klein (1963) not only corroborates the validity of the stages of haptic (i.e., tactual) exploration described by Zaporozhets and Abravanel, but also brings out some further points. Klein used a task in which the child felt a standard shape of a particular texture and then had to pick the one of two comparison shapes which he considered to be "just like the first" (the standard). In every case one of the comparison stimuli matched the standard with respect to texture, the other with respect to form. Klein found a marked shift with age from texture to form matching, and closely correlated with this shift, a progressive change from passive touching to random, unsystematic exploration of the shape and finally to controlled tracing of the outline of the shape. Yet, while this progression corresponds neatly to that described by Zaporozhets, the changes in Klein's study took place over the interval from 6 to 12 years of age; thus, Klein's youngest subjects, responding predominantly to texture for lack of active exploration of form, were of an age at which Zaporozhets had found the most advanced level of performance. The solution to this seeming paradox is probably that Klein was dealing with a situation involving spontaneous preference (the task did not *demand* any active exploration of the figures); indeed, Klein himself had found, in a control study, that even the youngest children, when forced to do so, were able to *discriminate* the shapes he was using tactually. It is important, then, to avoid drawing conclusions about a child's capacities from his spontaneous or preferential mode of behavior.

A further finding of Klein's study is significant. In one modification of his basic experimental design, he used outline cutouts rather than solid shapes. With these stimuli he found a much earlier preference for form matching, but not accompanied by any correspondingly precocious exploratory activity. Rather, many of the younger children jammed their hands into the space formed by the inside of the cutout, which provided them with sufficient information about shape to serve as a basis for a form match.

Related to the relative passivity of haptic exploration of the first graders in

Klein's study is an apparent lack of adaptiveness of haptic scanning behavior in children as compared to adults. This was seen in a study by Cirillo, Wapner, and Rand (1967), in which subjects were given a set of angular segments varying in length of sides and angular width. By tracing these with the index finger, the subjects had to find the stimulus that matched a sample in terms of either size or angular width. In contrast to the adults' performance on this task, a group of eight to ten year old children failed to modify their mode of exploration in accordance with the particular critical cue, angle or size, to which they had to respond.

The tactual modality lends itself particularly well to the observation of perceptual activity of this exploratory sort, since the movements of the hands and fingers when engaged in such exploration are readily observable. Are there any comparable changes in the field of vision, which might help account for some of the changes previously described in the area of form perception? Apparently there are, as revealed in the development of scanning of visual forms. The technical problems involved, especially in direct observation of eye movements, are of course considerably more formidable than in observation of tactual exploration. Furthermore, since the eyes are not directly "in touch" with the stimuli they are exploring, the correspondence between the path of eye movements and the visual shapes being scanned could not be expected to be as close as that found in the systematic outline tracing in the tactual modality. Similarly, since the eyes can "take in" a visual field of considerable breadth at a glance, no comparable slavish tracing of the outline of a stimulus is apt to be encountered.

In spite of these difficulties, studies of the development of eye movements in visual discrimination or recognition learning of simple geometric shapes have demonstrated a developmental progression rather similar to the progression in the tactual modality (see Zaporozhets, 1965). By superimposing the pattern of eye movements on the outline of the stimulus being examined, Zaporozhets obtained the exploration patterns shown in Figure 11-17, for three to four, four to five, and six to seven year old children. There is not only a progressive increase in activity, in the sense of more numerous changes in fixation, the eye moving from one part of the field to another, but at the same time the pattern of these eye movements becomes increasingly systematic, tracing the contour of the stimulus figure being examined. These changes are, furthermore, closely correlated with the same children's success in recognizing these stimuli from among a set of similar shapes.

A study by Vurpillot (1968) provides further evidence on changes in the way children visually explore a complex stimulus configuration. This investigator showed pictures of house fronts containing six windows, each different from the others (in the shutter, curtain, etc., as shown in Figure 11-18). These pictures were presented in pairs, in six different combinations. In half of the pairs, corresponding windows in the two houses were identical. In the remaining three pairs of houses, one, three, or five of the six pairs of corresponding windows differed. The child's task was to look the houses over and to decide whether the houses were or were not the same. The percentage correct responses, shown

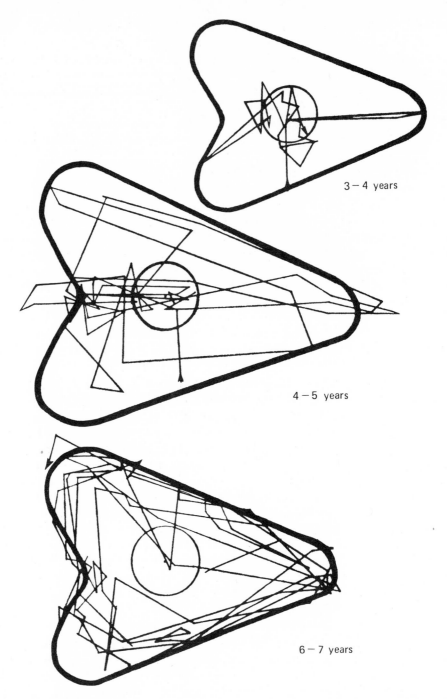

3 − 4 years

4 − 5 years

6 − 7 years

Fig. 11-17. Patterns of eye movements illustrative of scanning of visual form at different age levels. (From Zaporozhets, 1965, Figs. 1, 2, and 3, pp. 86, 87, 88. Copyright 1965 by the Society for Research in Child Development, Inc. Reprinted by permission of the publisher.)

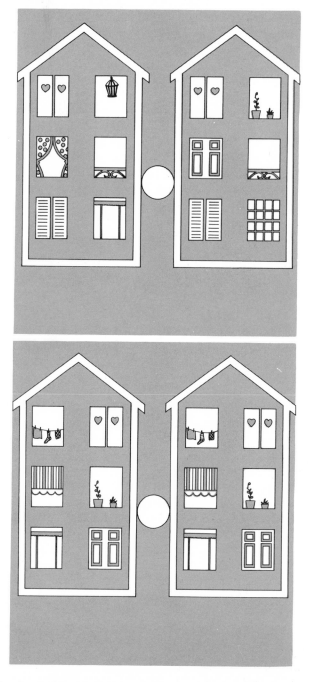

Fig. 11-18. Stimuli used by Vurpillot (1968) in study of children's eye movements in detecting differences in complex configurations. Top: "Different" pair, with differences in three corresponding window pairs. Bottom: "Identical" pair. (From Vurpillot, 1968, Fig. 1, p. 634. Reprinted by permission of the author and Academic Press, Inc.)

in Table 11-3, revealed a pattern familiar in previous perceptual-development research: The younger children had much greater success on house pairs that were in fact identical (which were rarely called different) than they had on those which differed (but which were frequently called identical). Intensive study of the children's manner of scanning these stimuli indicated that the youngest children (four to five years old) would generally limit themselves to a sample of the total set of windows (see Table 11-3); if within this sample they detected a difference, they would make a judgment of "different"; otherwise they would call them "same." In the older children, both the numbers of windows

Table 11-3

Percentage Correct Responses and Mean Number of Elements
Fixated at Different Age Levels in Comparing Paired
Six-Element Matrices[a]

	Percentage correct responses			Mean number of windows fixated		
	Number of corresponding pairs of windows showing difference			Number of corresponding pairs of windows showing difference		
Mean age (years)	0[b]	1	3 or 5	0[b]	1	3 or 5
4	73	22	52	6.5	6.8	6.7
5	95	25	72	7.1	6.7	6.8
$6\frac{1}{2}$	93	60	87	10.5	9.7	7.5
9	93	94	100	11.5	9.8	7.5

[a] Data from Vurpillot's (1968) Figures 5 and 6.
[b] Identical sets.

fixated and the number of paired comparisons of corresponding windows increased, thereby yielding increasingly accurate judgments of difference when a difference was in fact present.

The most direct and conclusive evidence about visual scanning movements obviously comes from studies such as Vurpillot's in which eye movements are recorded. For certain purposes, however, the problem can be investigated more indirectly by presenting children with a large array of discrete stimuli (e.g., pictures of familiar objects) and asking them to name them; the order in which the child does so can then be used to infer the scanning patterns he has utilized. For arrays of pictures arranged in regular rows and columns, there is a change from fairly random and unsystematic sequences to consistent scanning along rows, from left to right (Elkind and Weiss, 1967). Interestingly enough, when the stimuli are arranged along the sides of a triangle, children in the first grade still adopt this kind of left-right scanning pattern, even though the arrangement of the pictures favors rather the pattern followed by adults, of scanning along the perimeter of the imaginary triangle favored by the pictures. The onset of reading apparently produces a very marked tendency to scan from left to right, which transfers to material well removed from the province of reading.

Additional evidence on this point comes from a study by Forgays (1953), in which children were asked to report words exposed for a brief time (.15 sec.). The general pattern in this kind of situation is for subjects to be more successful in identifying material shown to the right of the fixation point than to the left, as a result of directional scanning tendencies developed through extensive practice in reading. This pattern was confirmed by Forgays at all grade levels from the second grade onward; over a certain interval, furthermore, between Grades 5 and 8, performance for words to the left of fixation actually deteriorated.

Summing up, the study of exploratory movements in the realm of visual and haptic perception shows that these become, over the course of development, increasingly active and systematic, modeling the contours of the stimuli being explored. There is every reason to consider such movements as mediating improved form discrimination during this period, as well as some of the phenomena pointed to earlier is this chapter, such as improvement in ability to perceive details embedded within a complex whole.[2]

It would be misleading to suggest, however, that all or even most changes in perceptual performance with age can be ascribed to the development of scanning movements. In fact, it appears that in the visual domain scanning movements lose this contour-tracing character after a certain time. For the older child and adult, particularly when dealing with familiar stimuli or stimuli that can be readily assimilated to relevant schemata, perception probably takes on a more economical character, with briefer glances from a fixation point within the periphery of the object sufficing for identification or even discrimination (e.g., Piaget and Vinh-Bang, 1961). Indeed, it has been found that adults do not need to explore a visual shape through eye movements in order to recognize it (Mooney, 1958) or to make judgments of qualities such as symmetry (Zusne and Michels, 1964); this holds true even for fairly complex and unfamiliar stimuli.

---

[2] The comparatively slow development of effective scanning of visual form has been emphasized in this presentation. The evidence has come largely from the Soviet research summarized by Zaporozhets (1965), and appears at variance with results of studies on infants, including even neonates, which seem to indicate that their fixation is closely determined by the contours of simple geometric patterns presented to them (see Chapter 2). The basis for this contradiction is not entirely clear. It should be noted, however, that in the infancy research the data relate chiefly to scanning of lines and angles, rather than complete outline shapes such as utilized with children. Probably more important, the infant responses studied reflect essentially reflexive, involuntary behavior, which may have a very different basis from the voluntary scanning movements involved in the context of discrimination task behavior or free visual exploration in older children. At the same time, the report of Zaporozhets should probably be interpreted with some caution, since little detail is presented concerning the precise nature of the experimental conditions, apparatus, etc.

There are, furthermore, a great many perceptual phenomena to which the notion of increasing perceptual activity could be applied, where scanning movements would be difficult to invoke. Decreases with age in a variety of illusions, for instance, appear to entail an increased ability to abstract a portion of a stimulus from a total field, such as in the Müller-Lyer illusion (Figure 11-1), which consistently shows much lower values in adults than in children (see Wohlwill, 1960a). Here, presumably, the young child is maximally subject to the influence of the arrows, since he finds it more difficult to ignore them while fixating on the lines to be compared.

Selective Attention

This brings up the notion of selective attention as a factor mediating perceptual development. Since this topic forms the subject of a separate chapter (Chapter 9), it will not be treated in any detail here; only a few examples of its applicability will be noted. Probably the best illustration comes from the marked age change, discussed earlier in this chapter, in the ability to extract shapes embedded in more complex configurations, as with the Gottschaldt figures (e.g., Figure 11-4A). In addition, decreases with age in such illusions as the Müller-Lyer illusion, just referred to, and the concentric circles illusion, among others (see Wohlwill, 1960a), are interpretable in similar terms, that is, as involving an increased ability to attend selectively to relevant portions of a stimulus configuration, so as to reduce the distorting influence of the context surrounding the stimulus being judged.

A study by Pollack (1964) throws further light on this problem. He utilized a tachistoscopic version of the Müller-Lyer illusion, and again found a substantial decrease with age; the magnitude of the illusion, furthermore, was more highly correlated with chronological age (CA) than with mental age (MA). Yet, when the situation was changed to a temporal contrast one (the arrows for Part A of the illusion, as shown in Figure 11-1, being shown first by themselves, followed by Line A by itself), a *negative* illusion developed, the line now being overestimated relative to the control line. This illusion, furthermore, increased with age—like other temporal contrast illusions—and was more highly correlated with MA than with CA. Thus, temporal contrast phenomena appear to have a strong cognitive component, presumably involving the ability to preserve in memory a stimulus no longer present, against which other stimuli shown subsequently are compared. Other evidence likewise indicates that for the younger child, a stimulus is perceived to a large extent independently of previously exposed stimuli of a similar sort, but for an older child or adult such preceding stimuli constitute a context against which the stimulus presented is evaluated (e.g., Piaget, 1969, pp. 182ff.).

With respect to the developmental changes in space perception, it is much more difficult to apply the "perceptual activity" construct with any degree of precision or concrete reference. To do so would require more intensive examination of the subject's patterns of responses to these tasks, including an analysis of scanning movements between standard and variable, fixations on different parts of the field, etc., or at least correlative information about the subjects that might have some predictive value. At this point the particular activities that might develop with age can only be guessed at—more active back-and-forth scanning, more extensive fixation on diverse parts of the visual field that could yield information as to the changing scale of the field with increasing distance, and perhaps, above all, increasing intervention of judgmental strategies deliberately aimed at adjusting for assumed distortion in the relations of size and distance as phenomenally experienced.

FEEDBACK, REINFORCEMENT, AND THE ROLE OF EXPERIENCE IN PERCEPTUAL DEVELOPMENT

Putting the problem of perceptual development in terms of the concept of increasing perceptual activity only pushes the problem back one step. It does not indicate what the basis for this increasing activity actually is. Is it simply a product of prolonged practice in perceptual tasks? If not, in what terms should one explain it?

There is no denying that specific practice, and reinforced practice in particular, can lead to improvement in children's performance in perceptual tasks. Welch's (1939a) study, discussed earlier in the chapter, showed that even two to three year old children can be trained to make rather fine shape discriminations by always being rewarded for choice of a shape arbitrarily designated as correct. Bijou and Baer (1963) have likewise utilized a method of "shaping" form discrimination, by presenting programmed sequences of stimuli designed to bring about, through selective reinforcement, discrimination of complex shapes differing in orientation.

There are several problems with a learning-through-reinforcement type of explanation to account for perceptual development in general, however. To begin with, perceptual learning is often found in the absence of any extrinsic reinforcement; furthermore, the magnitude and the occurrence of such practice effects depend on the age of the child (Wohlwill, 1960a). A good illustration comes from Noelting's study (1960) of the role of unreinforced practice in decreasing the magnitude of the Müller-Lyer illusion. Over a series of 40 trials there was a consistent, steady decline in the extent of the illusion, but this decline was not observable before approximately the age of seven years, becoming more and more pronounced with age thereafter. Presumably, practice allowed the subjects to abstract more effectively from the distracting arrows in making their judgments.

Here, as in many other instances, changes take place over age in a child's performance on stimuli or tasks that he can hardly have confronted with any frequency in his general experience. It is thus necessary to look for processes of a higher degree of generality than is entailed in the notion of specific practice, or reinforcement of correct responses. Upon closer examination, the role of reinforcement can be translated into the related role of feedback: The individual makes a response (e.g., identifies a tachistoscopically presented stimulus as a "cow"); he is then told whether his response was correct or incorrect; and this information now feeds back upon his subsequent potential judgments, enabling him to improve them by eliminating incorrect hunches, looking for further cues, etc.

But feedback of this sort is not dependent on external reinforcement. To take a perhaps obvious example, if a person scans a headline in a newspaper over the shoulders of another person, and is not sure of one of the words in the headline (perhaps the name of a public figure), because he could not see clearly enough, all he has to do is to place himself in a more advantageous position, to verify whether his guess was correct. There are many situations in which activities by the perceiver himself can mediate perceptual learning by providing him with feedback. Exploratory actions such as those involved in visual and tactual scanning are essentially of this sort. For instance, in moving along the outline of a figure, any momentary response that deviates from the outline is immediately corrected to bring the perceiver back into contact with the figure. These self-correcting mechanisms, as Zaporozhets (1961) has pointed out, have a very considerable advantage over purely external reinforcement; not only are they continually operative, without being dependent on some outside agent or other source of information, but also they allow the subject's responses to be *continually* monitored, while the information fed back from an external source is in general received after the termination of the subject's actions, and its effect on any subsequent response must therefore occur over an interval of time.

Thus, the early development of perception (e.g., through the preschool years) can be conceptualized in terms of the improved ability to utilize feedback from self-produced activity. In the early years of life such activity is almost absent, apart from orienting movements that keep the individual in touch with the stimulus in a gross sense for increasingly longer periods of time (as in the study by Smith *et al.*, 1963). Subsequently, a variety of motor actions, involving not only haptic exploration, but also active manipulation of objects in a "practical" context (inserting pegs into holes, building with blocks, handling tools in a variety of ways, as in a child's "carpentering" activities, and the like), have the effect of providing continual feedback as to the shapes and sizes of things—as brought out nicely in some of the Soviet research summarized by Zaporozhets (1965). The information involved in such feedback becomes increasingly subtle, depending on more highly organized and more finely coordinated activities. Compare, for instance, the gross motor responses involved in a child's play with a peg board, with the responses involved in his tactual exploration of the outline of a form, and finally with the highly coordinated movements demanded for the scanning of the visual stimulus. Lastly, internalized schemata take over to guide the direct visual exploration, supplanting the role of movement-produced feedback. That is, a stimulus is referred to a pre-established schema, with reinforcement being provided by the match between the input and the schema. The study by Gollin (1960) with incompletely presented familiar forms illustrates this phenomenon.

What does all this suggest with respect to the role of experience in the perceptual development of the child? The Soviet psychologists stress the value of a particular type of experience, involving "practical actions" with stimulus objects, in perfecting discrimination. The Montessori approach to early childhood education, which has recently gained new adherents in the United States (see Rambusch, 1962), is predicated on a similar principle. Such experience provides the child with the requisite feedback correlated with the visual form differences that must be learned, and, as provided by gross motor actions, this is feedback of a readily discriminable sort. Somewhat later, the mere tracing of visual forms with the fingers is sufficient; the movements of the hands are now presumably directed by corresponding scanning movements of the eyes, but reinforcing the feedback provided by the latter with additional proprioceptive feedback.

This view of the nature of perceptual learning is at variance with formulations such as Hebb's (1949), which stress the role of sheer exposure to stimulation and to variation in stimulation early in life. The importance of such stimulation has indeed been borne out in a considerable body of animal research (see Hunt, 1961, Ch. 4). For obvious reasons, evidence of this sort at the human level is difficult to come by, since it entails systematically depriving the individual of stimuli considered to be essential for normal development. Only rarely, in generally poorly documented cases of children brought up under conditions of extreme isolation and restriction (see Anastasi, 1958a), do instances occur that may be at all comparable. But apart from the unreliability of much of this evidence, it is entirely possible that the early experience of children raised under such conditions—as indeed that of rats or dogs raised under impoverished stimulus conditions in the research inspired by Hebb's theory—is likewise deficient in adequate opportunity for motor activity that could provide the requisite proprioceptive feedback to the child. (See also the discussion of cross-modal integration in Chapter 7, in section entitled "Transfer in Discrimination Tasks.")

In conclusion, consider the so-called "culturally deprived" child, who is occasionally discussed in similar terms, as reflecting a history of understimulation. This hardly seems warranted. In terms of sheer quantity of stimulation, children growing up in an urban slum undoubtedly are exposed to more than the requisite amount for normal development (see Elkind, 1969). Frequently, in fact, these children are so bombarded with intense stimuli of all kinds as to force them perhaps rather to tune out much of it from their awareness, and this may be in part what is at the root of their difficulty. More stimulation than the child knows what to do with—or how to respond to—may in fact be as deleterious for optimal development as a lack of sufficient stimulation.

THE ROLE OF MOTIVATION
IN CHILDREN'S PERCEPTION

It is commonly believed that children, with their diffuse, undifferentiated mode of responding to stimuli (Werner, 1940), are particularly susceptible to influence by motivational and affective factors in their perception. Thus, they are thought to perceive "autistically," that is, in accordance with their desires; similarly, positively valued stimuli should be seen as brighter, bigger, etc., than neutral or negatively valued objects. A certain amount of evidence in favor of such a view is indeed available (see Solley, 1966). Five to seven year old children, asked to draw a picture of Santa Claus repeatedly during the month preceding Christmas and briefly afterward, showed a marked effect of their expectations in their drawings: "As Christmas drew near, . . . their drawings of Santa became larger and larger . . . the bag with the toys and presents became more pronounced . . . . After Christmas . . . Santa was perceived as shrunken in size, plainer, and less significant" (Solley, 1966, pp. 288–289).

As mentioned before, caution must be used in interpreting children's drawings as direct reflections of their perceptions, but the same effect can be observed in a purely perceptual task. Ballin (cited by Solley, 1966) had children between five and seven years of age match a variable disk to a standard on which a picture of Santa Claus had been drawn. These size matches likewise steadily increased as Christmas approached, then decreased. The same phenomenon was shown in a situation where value was experimentally built into the stimuli. Lambert, Solomon, and Watson (1949) taught a group of nursery school children to use tokens in a "vending machine" to obtain candy. Size matches of these tokens were obtained before training, immediately following training, and after an extinction phase in which the child was no longer able to obtain candy with the tokens. Here too, perceived size following training increased from its basal level before training, and reverted to the basal level after extinction.

Murray (1933) studied the effect of emotion on perception, by having 11 year old girls rate photographs after being in a situation that presumably invoked fear and after being in neutral situations. The photographs were of men and women, and were rated on a nine-point scale from extremely good ("generous, kind, loving and tender") to extremely bad ("cruel, malicious, and wicked"); the fear-invoking situation was the game of "Murder." The majority of the girls rated most of the photographs as more malicious after the fear-invoking situation than after ordinary conditions.

A further study by Solley and Engel (1960) dealt more specifically with the role of autism and its decrease with age. They used reversible profile figures, in which either of two alternative profiles could be perceived; one of these had previously been associated with either reward or punishment. They found that in the period between 5 and 8 years of age children tend to perceive "autistically," that is, they report seeing the rewarded profile more often than the other one, and the punished profile less often. Adults, in contrast, show the reverse pattern, and 9 to 12 year old children are intermediate.

These studies are not very helpful, however, in showing *how* motivational or affective variables influence children's perceptions. A variety of factors might explain such effects. Possibly children tend to focus for a longer period of time on stimuli that are valued; this might, in line wth Piaget's (1961) centration principle, lead to overestimation. Value, whether positive or negative, may also alter scanning patterns, particularly in a situation such as the reversible profiles task used by Solley and Engel (1960). Possibly the effects reported are purely "response biases" analogous to the judgmental effects represented in the over-constancy phenomenon—that is, not based on any purely perceptual process. The information that might bear on these questions is, again, as yet lacking, although the effect of reward on directional scanning patterns has been studied with interesting results (Fisch and McNamara, 1963).

Note, finally, that the question at issue in the work just reviewed concerns the possible influence of motivational variables on children's perception. It fails to touch on the much broader, and ultimately more significant question: What is the motivational force that impels a child to perceive—to seek out and explore stimuli so as to recognize and interpret them, to assimilate them to his schemata? This question was dealt with in Chapter 10, in the section reviewing the work on motivational determinants of exploration and curiosity.

IMAGERY

The topic of imagery has been considered to be related to the topic of perception, since in traditional studies imagery was compared and contrasted with perception. Imagery and perception are similar in that both are experienced as associated with some specific sensory modality; they are unlike primarily in that perception occurs in the presence of stimulus input, and imagery occurs in the absence of or supplementary to stimulus input. For example, a person experiences auditory input as an auditory percept; later, he might recall the sound as an auditory image. A percept does not necessarily correspond closely to the stimulus input (witness, for example, the illusions described in earlier sections), but in general one might expect that the correspondence would be better than between images and original inputs. A notable exception is the *eidetic* image, which corresponds very closely to the original input. Eidetic imagery will be considered in more detail later in this concluding section.

Background

According to Aristotle, memory images "are like sense-presentations, with the exception that they are without matter" (Aristotle, p. 77 in 1902 edition). Later philosophers and psychologists proposed that there are other differences between images and sensations, such as in their intensity or vividness (e.g., Angell, 1908; Sully, 1891), but Lindworsky said, "There is no attribute of perceptions which cannot be demonstrated also for images, and vice versa" (Lindworsky, 1931, p. 135; see also Huey, 1908, p. 79). Psychologists of the eighteenth and nineteenth centuries were intensely concerned with mental images, because psychology was then defined as the study of the contents of consciousness. Interest in imagery waned among psychologists after the rise of behaviorism early in the twentieth century, probably because of a waning interest in consciousness in general (see Holt, 1964). However, although imagery received much more attention in earlier textbooks, it was discussed at least briefly in later ones, in the 1930s (e.g., Wait, 1938), the 1940s (e.g., McGeoch, 1942), the 1950s (e.g., Allport, 1955; Cameron and Magaret, 1951), and the 1960s (e.g., Bugelski, 1960; Staats and Staats, 1963; Wickens and Meyer, 1961). There has recently emerged a renewed interest in research on imagery, as Hebb (1960) had predicted there would be.

It is widely but erroneously believed that in his attack on the classical psychology of consciousness, John B. Watson—the founder of behaviorism—denied that images exist. Actually, Watson denied only that images can be studied objectively and that "imagery" is a term with demonstrated usefulness (see Watson, 1913, 1929, footnote 1, p. 362). However, even though Watson was correct when he said that images are not objectively observable, any effects they might have on behavior would be objectively observable, and if any effects were observed, then "imagery" would be a useful term. It would have the status of an "intervening variable" or "hypothetical construct."

Historically, the focus of research on imagery was primarily on the processes and contents of imagery, on the description of images, and on the classification of people into imaginal types. Now, however, almost all of the research is concerned with the ways images influence other processes, especially memory. It has long been known that images are excellent aids to memory (see Hunter, 1964), but only recently has the effect been studied experimentally.

Paired associate learning with meaningful words is easier than with nonsense syllables (see Chapter 6). Köhler (1929) said that this difference results from the greater ease with which visual images of interactions between the stimulus and response terms can be formed when the terms are meaningful than when they are nonsense syllables. According to Köhler, the image "organizes" the material, in the sense of forming a meaningful whole or Gestalt, and organized material is easier to remember than unorganized material consisting of isolated elements. Ladd and Woodworth (1911, p. 579), among others, also said that organized material is easier to remember; but this analysis, which appears to be correct as far as it goes, is incomplete because it fails to explain *why* organized material is easier to remember than unorganized material. These problems are discussed in more detail in Chapter 6 (section entitled "Variables Affecting Learning"), and will not be considered further here.

Eidetic Imagery

One definition of *image* is "a mental representation of anything not actually present to the senses" (Webster's New Collegiate Dictionary, 1953). A distinction is made between "memory images" and "imagination images" on the basis of the similarity to previously perceived objects or situations. A memory image closely approximates the original percept and the real object or situation that aroused the percept; an imagination image differs markedly from anything the person has previously perceived (McKellar, 1957, pp. 202, 203). Imagination images and, with one exception, memory images are experienced as internal or "in the mind." The exception is the "eidetic" image, which is experienced as projected, that is, as localized in space in front of the subject's eyes and usually on the plane where the original figure was seen (e.g., Allport, 1924).

In addition to the characteristic localization, eidetic images are usually extremely vivid—they have been characterized as "a half-way house to hallucination" (Drever, 1952, p. 79; see also McKellar, 1957, pp. 27, 200). They are also usually extremely persistent, lasting for a minute or more, and they can fuse, that is, the images of separately experienced figures can combine to yield an image of a new figure (e.g., Allport, 1924; Leask, Haber, and Haber, 1967).

Fig. 11-19. Silhouette hunting scene. One of pictures used by Leask *et al.* (1967) in study of eidetic imagery. (From Leask *et al.*, 1967. Reprinted by permission of the authors.)

"After images" are also experienced as projected, are often vivid, and can fuse, but they persist for only a few seconds. [After images are thought to result from continuation of activity in the sense receptors rather than from activity in the brain, and therefore the term "after sensation" has been recommended as more descriptive (Drever, 1952, p. 11; McKellar, 1957, p. 199), but "after image" seems to be the more commonly used term.] According to Allport (1928), what is called an eidetic image is often really an after image, especially in

Fig. 11-20. Indian and animals. Black and white reproduction of colored picture used by Leask *et al.* (1967) in study of eidetic imagery. (From Leask *et al.*, 1967. Reprinted by permission of the authors.)

studies in which the experimenter arranges for the subject to experience an after image before the tests for eidetic imagery are given. This procedure has often been used (e.g., Leask *et al.*, 1967).

Eidetic images can be classified as memory images, but they are more complete, more accurate, and "livelier" than other kinds of memory image (Allport, 1928). Nevertheless, the eidetic image does not necessarily retain all of the characteristics of the original impression; there is a process of selection based on the interests of the subject (Klüver, 1928).

Two examples from the report by Leask *et al.* illustrate the elaborate detail often included in reports based on eidetic images. Selectivity is also apparent in the omissions and errors. In the study, the child was seated near an easel in a small room with normal illumination. After being instructed about the nature of the task, he was shown pictures such as the ones illustrated in Figures 11-19 and 11-20. Each picture was exposed on the easel for 30 seconds, and after each was removed, the child was asked probing questions about what he could still see. The subject from whose transcript the examples are taken was a ten year old boy. He gave the following report after seeing the picture shown in Figure 11-19:

E [Examiner]: Do you see anything there?
S [Subject]: I can see the cactus—it's got three limbs and I can see the Indian, he's holding something in his hand, there's a deer beside him on his right-hand side—it looks like it's looking toward me and three birds in upper left-hand corner, one in right-hand corner, it's larger and a rabbit jumping off the little hill.
E: Can you tell me about the Indian—can you tell me about his feathers, how many are there?
S: Three or two.
E: Can you tell me about the feet of the deer?
S: They're small.
E: Are they all on the ground?
S: No.
E: Can you tell which ones aren't?
S: One of the front ones isn't.
E: Tell me if it fades.
S: I can still see the birds and the Indian. I can't see the rabbit anymore. (pause) Now it's all gone.
(Leask *et al.*, 1967, p. 16, quoted by permission.)

After seeing the picture shown in Figure 11-20, the subject gave the following report:

E: Can you see it?
S: Yes, I can see the white and blue sky and the ground has two different shades of green in it with some blue on it . . . and I can see two different squirrels, one is gray and the Indian's holding him in his hand and he's eating a nut. The one on the ground—he's red with a white stripe on him. There are three birds in the air—they're green, orange—they've got some red on them.
E: Can you see the birds' mouths?
S: No—I can see the deer and the cloth on the Indian's belt, it has many colors on it, yellow is the biggest color—and I can see his bow he's holding, it's got zigzag on it.
E: Anything else—any other animals?

S: There's three rabbits—two of them are brown and one of them is white—the one brown
  and white one are next to each other and there's another brown one in the right-hand
  corner.
E: What are they doing?
S: One over in the right-hand corner is jumping and the other two are just standing around.
E: Tell me more about the Indian.
S: Well—
E: Start at the top and move down.
S: Well, he's got a headband on—he doesn't have a shirt on, he's got a belt on with a cloth
  hanging out which is red, yellow. He's got Indian moccasins on—I think they're brown.
E: Has he got anything else on?
S: No.
E: Anything else you can tell me—and tell me if any of the parts go away.
S: The rabbits and birds are going away (pause) and the sky (pause) that's it—it's all gone.
  (Leask *et al.*, 1967, pp. 18–19, quoted by permission.)

Theoretically, stimulation in any sensory mode can give rise to eidetic
imagery. For example, the sensation of rolling movement experienced upon land-
ing from a ship may be an eidetic image of kinesthetic stimulation. However,
most of the research has dealt with eidetic visual imagery (McKellar, 1957,
pp. 25–27). Eidetic imagery is believed to be relatively common in children
and rare in adults; according to McKellar, "Jaensch established the incidence
of eidetic imagery as occurring in approximately sixty per cent of children but
only about seven per cent of adults" (McKellar, 1957, p. 26). According to Haber
and Haber, "Percentages of children said to possess some form of eidetic imagery
ranged from 30 to 90, depending upon the age and population sampled, with
a rough average of all studies around 50%. All investigators have reported zero
or near zero frequencies among adults . . ." (Haber and Haber, 1964, pp.
132–133).

Modern experimental work on eidetic imagery is still in a very preliminary
stage; but the most extensive recent work, including some 18 studies with
children ranging from 7 to 17 years of age, indicates that the occurrence of
eidetic imagery is very stable over time, is not correlated with chronological
age or mental age, and is rarer than the earlier literature indicated, occurring
in as few as about 8 percent of children (Haber and Haber, 1964, Leask *et
al.*, 1967). Haber and Haber (1964) reported that about 55 percent of the
children they studied had images of some kind, but that most were probably
after images and weak memory images. These studies also suggest that children
who are able to produce eidetic images do not use them to gain time for processing short term memory into long term storage, and in fact that this kind
of processing—active rehearsal and mnemonic coding—interferes with the adequacy and duration of the eidetic image (Leask *et al.*, 1967, pp. 77–78). Thus,
although "eidetic imagery is an exciting phenomenon in its own right and one
that clearly needs further exploration and explanation, . . . with the data at
hand we cannot yet anchor it to other cognitive or perceptual functions" (Leask
et al., 1967, p. 78).

CHAPTER 12

Emotional Development

INTRODUCTION

Emotion as State

There is perhaps no more elusive concept in all of psychology than that of emotion. The concept of emotion obviously refers to states of the organism and is usually, therefore, heavily invested with physiological connotations. In this context one often refers to "conditions" such as rage, elation, depression, excitement, anxiety, and the like, and one furthermore often describes such conditions as manifestations of activity in the autonomic nervous system. Such an account of emotion characteristically refers to Cannon's (1929) description of emergency patterns of physiological reaction which come into play under conditions of organismic threat and precipitate flight. This type of analysis of emotion is treated well in other sources (see, e.g., Hebb, 1966, pp. 234–255; Lindsley, 1951). Such considerations are more properly within the province of general or physiological psychology in that they are not unique to the study of child behavior and, moreover, there is not by any means an elaborate literature on autonomic nervous system processes of the child as such.

Explications of emotions as states or conditions often use a phenomenological language system. In this type of treatment it is said, for example, that the organism has the capacity to marshall resources for hasty flight or for quiet deliberation, and the emotions involved are *integrative*. Emotions may also be *disintegrative*, by causing the person to behave irrationally, self-destructively, or too hastily. The approach also often involves reference to some sort of hedonic scale wherein the states or conditions are regarded as varying in pleasurableness and painfulness. However, the pleasure or pain experienced by the organism is always assessed in terms of behavioral reactions (including the person's verbal report); therefore, the invocation of an hedonic explanation is often circular or, at best, adds little to the precision of delineating the causes of behavior.

Emotional Behavior

The approach taken in this chapter seeks to concentrate on emotional *behavior* rather than on emotions as states of the organism. Such an approach does not demean emotions as states, but rather attempts to make an accounting of behavior, including that which is reasonably called emotional, in terms of its antecedents. In speaking of observable and measurable response attributes of the child, such as fear or rage, an effort is made, as elsewhere in this volume, (a) to be clear about the specific behavior under observation and (b) to discover the instigating circumstances which control that behavior.

BIOGENETIC ORIGINS OF EMOTIONAL BEHAVIOR IN INFANCY

Reflexes as the Basis for Emotional Behavior

John B. Watson is sometimes seen naively or erroneously as disregarding the congenital response repertoire, and as denying individual differences in responsivity of infants, in favor of a position which asserts that all behavior is learned. However, the facts are that (a) he was one of the first to attempt detailed specification of the reflex propensities of the young infant, and (b) his views on the mechanisms underlying conditioned behavior necessitate that the infant have the capacity for *unconditioned* behavior on which all subsequent learning experience might capitalize (Watson, 1919).

Watson described three major response systems in the newborn child. One of these he called "love," which he said could be elicited through gentle stroking of the infant's skin and which would be manifested by the adoption of a quiescent demeanor. Second, Watson described a "rage" or "anger" reaction purportedly induced by physically preventing movement of the child or obstructing changes in positioning of the head and limbs. The rage reaction could be observed in fretful crying, energetic contortions, and flushing. Third, a "fear" reaction was noted to occur in response to sudden changes in position of the child, loss of support of the head, or the introduction of noxiously loud sounds.

In later research relevant to Watson's formulation, the particular responses described by Watson were not always aroused by the stimulation he specified (Sherman, 1927; Taylor, 1934). In fact, all researchers working with newborn infants now know that one of the most effective means of pacifying a fussy baby is to swaddle the infant and thus prevent agitated movement. Nevertheless, it is clear that Watson was sensitive to emotional behavior in the young child and that he was seeking to determine the experiential antecedents for different types of emotional reaction. Later it will be seen how he utilized the fear reaction as an unconditioned response in a conditioning paradigm with an older infant, and demonstrated the acquisition of a learned fear response based upon unconditioned fright in the presence of a noxious auditory stimulus.

A rather more elaborate model for the observation and understanding of emotional reactivity in infants was proposed by Bridges (1930, 1932), who started with the premise that the neonate has one basic and diffuse emotional reaction, called "excitement," which occurs in response to any intense stimulation, noxious or pleasant, and which is evidenced through general bodily reactivity, both muscular and visceral. For Bridges, like Watson, the basic emotional reaction at the start of life is a congenitally given diffuse response which through experience and learning comes to be differentiated into more specific responses. For example, Bridges postulated that "distress" as a differential emotional reaction may be observed by one month of age and that around two months of age "delight" may be observed. Thus, the condition of excitement becomes quickly bifurcated into a pleasure versus pain differentiation. With increasing age there is further differentiation. Expressions of delight become increasingly specific and can be identified behaviorally as elation, affection, and joy; and distress becomes further differentiated into specific behaviors characterized as anger, disgust, fear, and jealousy.

It is clear from both the Watson and the Bridges treatments of emotional behavior that there are some constellations of responses in early infancy that may be characterized as "avoidant behavior," in that features of the response suggest that the infant objects to the stimulation. He engages in activities which result in escape from noxious stimulation, and which tend to result in release from the offending stimulation. For example, crying behavior has the usual function of bringing aid to the relatively helpless organism. While Bridges postulated that distress does not become apparent until about one month of age, and until that time there is only undifferentiated excitement, Watson asserted that fear and anger responses are evident from the moment of birth. Similarly, while delight was presumed by Bridges to be absent until about two months of age, Watson suggested that a constellation of responses akin to approach behavior is also present from the start.

There is evidence that approach-type and avoidance-type responses are available in the repertoire of responsiveness of the newborn child. For example, if the respiratory passages of the newborn child are threatened with occlusion by the light placement of a gauze pad or cellophane over his mouth and nose he shakes his head to and fro and may even move his arms as though trying to remove the threatening object (Graham et al., 1956). Indeed, Gunther (1961) has noted that upon first exposure to the breast or bottle, neonates are often inadvertently subjected to a condition which elicits a turning away from the nipple simultaneously with the sucking experience. If the upper lip of the infant should be pushed against the nostrils at the same time that the nipple is offered, the smothering threat causes the infant to shake his head and to become otherwise agitated in the feeding situation. Gunther noted that infants may well learn to abhor the feeding situation if repetitively subjected to such an aversive experience.

With respect to approach responses that seem to represent emotional experiences, it is well known that the newborn infant has a marked "rooting reflex" whereby tactual stimulation applied to the corners of the mouth will elicit ipsilateral head-turning (Peiper, 1963, pp. 404–416). When this response occurs, particularly in the presence of hunger, it is accompanied by mouth-searching which, in the ordinary course of events, typically leads to insertion of the stimulating object in the mouth, whereupon a number of concomitant response processes are altered. For example, the crying child will stop crying and will engage in less physical movement (Kessen and Leutzendorff, 1963; Williams and Kessen, 1961), respiration will become regularized, and heart rate will usually diminish.

In general it appears that emotional quiescence is induced in newborns by tactual stimulation to the face as well as by intraoral stimulation, just as responses indicative of agitation seem to be induced by noxious stimuli such as loud noises or obstruction of the air passages. Quite possibly the Bridges conceptualization of emotional reactivity in the young human organism around the simple concept of diffuse "excitement" is a rather oversimplified version of the real state of affairs. At any rate it could be argued that, if properly operationally defined, both delight and distress are discernible even in the first days of life. Thus, even if her model for the increasing differentiation of specific emotional reactions is essentially correct, observations suggest that the infant does not wait to be one or two months old before expressing both distress and delight.

The range of stimuli that can produce distress reactions in the newborn is much greater than the range of stimuli that can produce quiescence or other responses indicative of a state of satisfaction. Distress may well have primacy over delight in this respect. Distress, in the form of crying and other agitated behavior, is produced by the application of noxious stimulation to the surface of the skin (Karelitz, Fisichelli, Costa, Karelitz, and Rosenfeld, 1964), by hunger, by loud sounds, and in general by an overload of sensory stimulation. Quiescent responsiveness is generally more difficult to evoke (as most parents know) except through oral stimulation and swaddling. The apparent primacy of distress reactions has been understood by Graham and Clifton (1966), following Sokolov (1960, 1963a), in terms of the differentiation of the so-called defensive reactions or reflexes from the orientation reaction. Presumably, defensive reactions are similar to fear responses; noxious or startling stimulation arouses the organism and produces a generalized aversive reaction, which may precipitate behavioral reactivity that terminates the offensive stimulus. The orientation reaction, in contrast, is produced by non-noxious (perhaps pleasant) stimulation and is more suited to preparation of the organism for greater intake of stimulation (see Chapter 9, section entitled "The Orientation Reaction"). According to Graham and Clifton, cardiac acceleration represents a defensive reaction to exteroceptive stimulation, and cardiac deceleration is a component of the orientation reaction. Present data indicate that most stimulation applied to the newborn results in a cardiac accelerative response and that it is quite rare to obtain heart-rate deceleration in response to specific stimulation. In adults, heart-rate deceleration is the more typical response to stimulation of moderate intensity.

In view of the above considerations, it is perhaps no accident that a good deal of attention has been directed toward the empirical investigation of crying in newborn and older infants. In one study, Gordon and Foss (1966) provided rocking stimulation to an experimental group of infants for a set period of time and noted the incidence of crying in these children relative to a control group which was not administered this rocking experience. Rather than rocking the children as a consequence of their crying behavior and looking for a reduction of crying, they recorded the temporal delay in onset of crying following the administration of intermittent rocking during quiet periods. The infants who were rocked remained quiescent for a longer period of time than the infants who were not accorded this stimulation. In a recent series of studies, DeLucia (1969) has explored the effects of rocking on the behavior of infants, using an automatic hammock that could be set to swing at various rates. In the first experiment, 24 infants with mean age of 33 days were each observed under four rocking rates—10, 20, 30, or 40 rocks per minute for four minutes at each rate. Recording amount of crying behavior, DeLucia found a descending monotonic function with increasing rocking rates. Having established that increasing rates of rocking apparently produce increased pacification, the next experiment was designed to assess the effect of an even faster rocking rate and to provide baseline data for crying under a stationary condition. The subjects were 40 infants with mean age of 35 days. Each infant was rocked at only one of the rates: 0, 10, 40, or 70 swings per minute. The number of five-second intervals during which crying occurred was recorded. Again the faster the rocking, the more was crying forestalled, almost disappearing when the baby was rocked at the rate of 70 swings per minute.

Satisfied that the more rapid rocking rate was the most effective in inducing quieting, DeLucia's next step was to utilize the rocking condition as a reinforcer in a learning paradigm with 14 infants with mean age of 45 days. Specifically, the crying response was treated as an operant to determine whether its incidence might be affected by the rocking reinforcement. The same apparatus was used, with a foot pedal making it possible for the experimenter to actuate the rocking mechanism contingent upon the baby's response. A polygraphic record of crying activity was taken, with rocking periods being superimposed on the record. All infants were tested just before a feeding period, when in an alert condition. Each infant's crying behavior was recorded during a baseline condition. The reinforcement period did not begin until the infant had cried for half of each of two minutes. At this point, contingent reinforcement was introduced, during which cessation of crying was reinforced by ten seconds of rocking at the rate of 70 rocks per minute. A second session involved the introduction of rocking on a noncontingent basis to assess the possible effects of rocking on crying cessation irrespective of the response-reinforcement contingency. In the second session, the amount and spacing of rocking was programmed to duplicate that of the first session, rather than to follow any response characteristics of the subject. The results indicate clearly that crying behavior was influenced markedly by the contingent reinforcement condition relative to the noncontingent condition. Moreover, reinstituting the contingent rocking in a third session caused a re-increase in "quiet time." It is quite clear, then, that rocking of the baby has an "unconditioned" pacification effect such that crying activity is suppressed by the rocking, but it now also appears that the rocking event may serve for infants as a reinforcer, such that the infant will learn to do something in order to have that event administered. The expression and suppression of emotional behavior obviously leads to special consequences in real life, and it is interesting to note that the baby is under the control of such contingencies at very early ages.

The inhibitory effect of rocking young infants may well be mediated by the vestibular system (Groen, 1962). Vestibular stimulation and rocking might constitute an important reinforcing event; if so, behaviors immediately preceding such rocking should be enhanced on a learning basis.

The Conditionability of Emotional Reactions

It is quite probable that the onset and perpetuation of many emotional reactions in children (and ultimately adults) are products of conditioning. While it is by no means argued here that all differentiations and nuances of emotional behavior in man are necessarily induced through learning, it is nevertheless apparent that conditioning plays an important role during ontogenesis in determining what kinds of environmental events will make a child fearful or anxious and what kinds will produce quieting. Certain kinds of fears, such as of snakes and of lightning, are rather common, but they are not universal. The absence of universality suggests that these are not congenitally dictated behavior patterns. It is therefore of value to understand their occurrence in terms of the possible conditioning antecedents that might enhance such behavior.

FEAR AND CRYING REACTIONS. A pioneering study relating to the role of conditioning in the origin of fear as one type of emotional behavior was that of Watson and Rayner (1920), who sought to condition a fear reaction in a child less than one year of age (the study is also discussed in Chapters 3 and 10). The subject, Albert, was first tested for emotional reactivity to a number of different stimuli, some of which would be subsequently used in the conditioning experiment. At the outset, he showed no withdrawal, crying, or other representation of fear to such stimuli as a wad of wool, a hairy face mask, and various animals, including a dog, rat, and rabbit. Thus, any of these stimuli could be considered as neutral but as having the capacity for becoming emotion eliciting if paired with stimulation which was initially fear evoking. As an unconditioned stimulus, the experimenters utilized a very loud sound, which unfailingly elicited crying in the child. The rat was used as the conditional stimulus, in the presence of which a bar of metal was struck near the child's ears whenever he reached toward the rat. After several such presentations of the rat and the sound, Albert was observed to cry upon the mere presentation of the rat. Albert had apparently become conditioned to fear the rat. In order to test for the possible generalization of the fear-of-rat response to other similar stimuli, Watson and Rayner later presented the previously neutral dog, ball of wool, a rabbit, and the mask. All of these stimuli were now observed to produce some component of the fear response; the presentation of other, presumably nonsimilar stimuli was ineffective. In a rather crude but nevertheless striking manner, the experimenters thus demonstrated some sort of conditioning of emotional responses, and stimulus generalization of these responses. In addition, they showed that discrimination forbids the total diffusion of fear to all aspects of the conditioning situation (such as the presence of the experimenters).

Watson and Rayner interpreted the paradigm of their study as an instance of classical conditioning, but Church (1966) reinterpreted it as conforming more with the instrumental conditioning model. He pointed out that because the so-called unconditioned stimulus—the loud sound—was presented only when the child started to reach toward the rat, the presentation of the noise was actually a contingent punishment condition and the rat was a discriminative stimulus for the presentation of this condition. According to this analysis, Watson and Rayner established operant learning in Albert under a punishment contingency rather than establishing a classically conditioned response.

It is not unlikely that particularly in the area of conditioned emotional reactivity a fusion of classical and operant conditioning processes (if indeed they are disparate in the final analysis) provides a clearer account of the true situation than either of these processes alone. A study by Hagman (1932) of fears in preschool children indicated that there is a strong relationship between the fears expressed by children and those of their mothers, suggesting that there is a heavy dose of imitative learning involved and that fear reactions of children are operantly endorsed parentally. The mother who is frightened of dogs will probably have a high likelihood of enforcing her child's withdrawal from such animals, by praising the child or fleeing with him, and saying such things as "we're safe now." From such training it can be expected that the dog as stimulus, and future presentations of such stimuli, will produce anticipatory flight responses as well as physiological concomitants such as increased respiratory and heart rate.

A pioneering investigation involving the elimination of the fear of darkness utilizing techniques of operant control and "fading in" of stimuli was that of Holmes (1936). By providing pleasant contact in association with the fear stimulation, such as darkness and height, this investigator was able to diminish or eliminate the child's aversion. The technique involved introduction of verbal reinforcement to the child for his successive approaches to the fear stimulus, simultaneously with the introduction of game activities in the presence of the feared location. For example, a dark-frightened child was engaged in a game of ball near a dark room. The experimenter secretly forced the game closer and closer to the dark room and ultimately lost the ball "accidentally," thus allowing the child to approach the feared location in the secure atmosphere of the game.

The use of operant techniques for the experimental modification of crying in infants has been well demonstrated by Etzel and Gewirtz (1967). They engaged two infants, whose species was said to be *Infans tyrannotearus*, in an extinction procedure which involved nonreinforcement of crying and the simultaneous positive reinforcement of alternative behavior. Both of the children, one 6 weeks old and the other 20 weeks old, were studied extensively at the outset and were documented to have very high base rates of crying. The crying was judged to be operant in that it consistently resulted in various caretaker attentions to the infants. The procedure involved the deliberate withholding of caretaker attention during times when the crying behavior was underway, simultaneous with the introduction of reinforcement for smiling or eye contact between the adult and infant. Both infants decreased in incidence of crying, and the incidence of smiling and eye contacting was enhanced.

SMILING AND AFFILIATIVE BEHAVIORS. Historically, there has been a great deal of attention paid to crying in the newborn child and the attachment of crying and other aversive responses to new stimulation during ontogeny, perhaps because, as Bridges assumed, distress reactions have some sort of primacy in relation to delight reactions. However, recent researchers have turned their attention increasingly toward the experimental modification of smiling and other affiliative (or approach) behaviors of the infant.

It is generally agreed that smiling and laughing are not within the behavioral repertoire of the human organism at birth but that experience soon facilitates the acquisition of these behaviors. It has been supposed that the smiling response is essentially universal in humans (Darwin, 1872) and it has been documented that smiling (a) precedes laughter in human ontogeny (Washburn, 1929), (b) is elicited earliest and most easily by the specific stimulus of the human face presented within viewing range of the infant (Spitz and Wolf, 1946), (c) has a later age of onset in institutionally reared children than in home-reared infants (Ambrose, 1961, 1963b), and (d) may become attached to specific social interactions apparently as a result of learning (Dennis, 1935).

Investigators have disagreed about the earliest age at which smiling occurs. For example, Spitz (1965) said that it is rare to find the smiling response to specific stimulation before the third month of life, while Ambrose (1961) has presented data indicating that infants reared at home first smile at about five weeks of age and those reared in institutions first smile by about ten weeks of age. Part of the discrepancy may, of course, be due to the difficulty in assessing the presence or absence of the smiling response, which is an ambiguous configuration at best. Moreover, it is possible that the type of stimulating condition imposed upon the infant may be an important determinant of whether or not the smiling response will be elicited. Wolff (1963) has presented photographic documentation of "social" smiling in an infant as young as three weeks of age. However, Wolff used rather unusual study conditions in that he observed the infants in their home setting with the mother present. Wolff said, "In some cases I have observed considerable competition of the mother with me for getting the child's attention, especially when this involves evoking 'social smiles'; in that case it has sometimes become a contest in which the mother tries to produce at least two smiles for every one that I have produced. To a degree, therefore, my presence may speed up the social responsiveness of the children I study" (Wolff, 1963, p. 114). It is very likely, then, that the particular circumstances under which infants are studied or reared may have a considerable effect upon their smiling propensities and other emotional behaviors. Wolff's comments constitute a very strong argument on behalf of the considerable role which experiential factors play in determining the onset, and perhaps social style, of smiling behavior, and Ambrose's (1961) data showing differences between home-reared and institution-reared infants provide supportive evidence.

In the previously cited study by Dennis, two infants were deliberately reared under conditions in which adult voices were not allowed to be heard in the presence of the infants' smiling behavior. The outcome was that these infants did not develop the characteristic smiling which occurs in infants when presented with the human voice. It is a reasonable possibility that this effect is based upon an operant conditioning mechanism, on the assumption that the human voice is ordinarily reinforcing of the smiling response in infants.

Ambrose has conducted rather extensive studies of the development and alteration of smiling behavior in infants, and has suggested that (a) smiling is the precursor of laughter, and (b) the full-blown laugh eventually expressed by the normal child can be understood best through the concepts of ambivalence and surprise (Ambrose, 1961, 1963a). Drawing on suggestions from both psycho-analytic theory and ethology, Ambrose suggested that the functional usefulness of smiling and crying to the human organism resides in their effects of drawing attention from adults. In a study of the elicitation of smiling and the conditions under which this response is maintained, Ambrose recorded the amount of time infants spent in smiling in the presence of an impassive adult face over a 12 minute period. He found that the response wanes considerably if it is not met with an adult response, but he also demonstrated that the response reappears some time following the end of the test period.

In an interesting study of the extent to which the smiling response of infants can be brought under stimulus control, Brackbill (1958) first conditioned two groups of four month old infants under two different reinforcement schedules, then studied the relative rates of extinction of the response when the stimulus controls were removed. During the conditioning phase, the experimenter pre-sented her face to the child; when the infant smiled, she picked the child up from the crib, smiling and making vocal sounds to him, and cuddled him. Under these conditions the smiling response to the experimenter's face was enhanced to a predetermined criterion. During extinction, the experimenter again presented her face but did not reinforce smiles of the child with the aforementioned condi-tions. The incidence of smiling diminished sharply during extinction, but not as rapidly in a group given reinforcement on an intermittent schedule during training as in a group reinforced on a continuous schedule.

Recently, Brossard and Décarie (1968) elaborated upon the Brackbill study in an attempt to determine which aspects of the reinforcing conditions used by Brackbill were most important in potentiating the smiling response. Brossard and Décarie replicated the conditioning phase of the Brackbill study, utilizing visual, auditory, tactile, and kinesthetic reinforcers in various combinations or patterns. Emphasis in this study was on the acquisition of the smiling response rather than on extinction as in the Brackbill study. The conditioning period lasted no more than 20 minutes each day and continued on successive days until 20 reinforced smiles of the infant had occurred. The results of the experi-ment suggest that the kinesthetic type of stimulation tended to be an important reinforcer of smiling; picking up the infant or providing him with rocking stimulation seemed to produce faster learning, although it must be noted that visual stimulation was often combined in this study with the kinesthetic stimula-tion and that the visual stimulus alone seemed also to produce rather rapid learning.

A behavior closely related to smiling and laughing is "attachment." Attachment in infants and an associated phenomenon called "separation-anxiety" are pre-sumed to be important in the socialization of children (Bowlby, 1958, 1969). Attachment has relevance to the development of affection, and expressions of separation-anxiety upon removal of the maternal figure have been presumed to serve as reasonable indexes of the extent to which the child has developed affiliative behavior toward the mother. In a preface to an experimental study of attachment and effects of separation in one year old infants, Ainsworth and Bell (1969) have spoken of the phenomena as follows:

> The term "attachment" refers to a class of behaviors which serve to sustain between one person and another specific person a degree of proximity, ranging from close physical contact to interaction or communication across a distance. These behaviors include active proximity- and contact-seeking behaviors, such as approaching and embracing, and signalling behaviors, such as smiling and calling. . . . It is convenient to classify all of these behaviors together as *attachment behavior,* despite their diversity.
>
> A person, whether infant or adult, does not continuously manifest attachment behavior toward those specific figures to whom he is attached, and yet the attachment is not conceived as vanishing when the attachment behavior is absent. To have an *attachment,* or, more accurately, *to be attached,* is an on-going condition of an organism and refers to its propensity to behave in ways, characteristic of that organism, which serve to maintain proximity to and interaction with a particular figure—the object of attachment.
>
> The infant is not attached at birth but becomes attached—usually first to his mother or to a substitute mother—through a process of learning, which takes place in the course of mother-infant interaction. Nevertheless, there is reason to believe that there are genetically determined biases which facilitate becoming attached. . . . If attachment is viewed within a context of evolutionary theory, it may be seen to fulfill significant biological functions—and this is clearly the case in infant-mother attachment. The long, helpless infancy of the human species occasions grave risks. For the species to have survived, the infant has required protection during this period of defenselessness. Therefore it is reasonable to infer that the genetic code makes provision for infant behaviors which have the usual outcome of bringing the infant and his mother together. (Ainsworth and Bell, 1969. Quoted by permission of the authors.)

Ainsworth and Bell conducted an exciting study in which 56 infants were introduced into a strange situation just before their first birthday. The infants were subjected to a series of eight episodes in a standard order in an experimental room. The mother and a female who was a stranger to the child were participants in some of the episodes, and both were given advance instruction as to how they were to behave. In the first episode the mother alone was present with the infant; in the second she was present with the baby but was seated distantly in a chair; in the third episode the stranger entered; and in the fourth episode the mother left the room. The mother returned to the room for the fifth episode but then made a rather hasty departure. During the sixth episode the baby was alone; in the seventh the stranger returned; and in the eighth the mother returned. Each of the episodes lasted 3 minutes and various behaviors of the infant, relating to the infant's exploratory behavior and crying (all of the measures highly reliably observed), were noted at each 15 second interval. The findings of the study indicated that the presence of the mother encouraged exploratory behavior, and her departure tended to depress such activities. The episodes in which the mother removed herself facilitated visual searching and crying behavior; reunion with the mother promoted attempts by the child to maintain proximity and contact with the mother. An interesting feature of the Ainsworth and Bell study is that they brought a widely noted naturalistic developmental phenomenon under experimental manipulative control in an infant laboratory. Their results lend credibility to the prior naturalistic and clinical observations, and at the same time they open up the possibility for further and perhaps more definitive explorations of the crucial experiential circumstances that lead to the development of such emotional behaviors as attachment and separation-anxiety.

Individual Differences in Early Reactivity

It can truly be said of the subject of individual differences in early infancy that while everyone who does research with infants knows about them, few do anything about them. One of the most striking aspects of infant behavior is that, just as with many morphological variables such as height, weight, eye color, skin color, and so on, infants vary from one another within limits, and these variations are relatively consistent from day to day. While researchers who have studied newborn children psychometrically have demonstrated the test–retest reliability of numerous psychomotor and sensory responses (e.g., Graham *et al.*, 1956; Rosenblith, 1961), few studies have dealt extensively with the persistence of early behavior over a longer period of time than a few days (see Horowitz, 1969). Studies dealing with experientially inculcated responses and their perseveration over time are rare indeed.

A pioneering research program relating to individual differences in psychophysiological attributes of human newborns was initiated by Lipton, Richmond, and Steinschneider (Lipton and Steinschneider, 1964; Richmond and Lipton, 1959; Richmond, Lipton, and Steinschneider, 1962). These researchers developed instrumentation for the careful recording and statistical analysis of various neuropsychological response indexes, such as cardiac rate, respiratory changes, skin-temperature fluctuations, and brain electric potentials. Their intent was to document stable differences with respect to such measures in infants both under conditions of exteroceptive stimulation and under resting-state conditions. As research pediatricians, they first wished to demonstrate that ". . . infants shortly after birth manifested individual traits with respect to autonomic and organ function. . . . We next investigated whether such subject-specific visceral control mechanisms continued to characterize the individual infant as he matured, and/or whether there were developmental trends" (Lipton and Steinschneider, 1964, p. 103). One of the avowed purposes of the research program was to search for constitutional characteristics of the infant that might predispose him to different psychosomatic disorders. It is obvious, however, that such an approach may also yield important insights about the influence of congenital attributes on perception, learning, and emotional expression.

In one of the studies by the Lipton group, with 16 infants between the ages of two and five days, the stimulus used was a stream of air applied to the abdomen of the child, who was swaddled during the testing and was thereby kept in a relatively quiescent state. The quiescent state is conducive both to a low heart rate prior to stimulation and, following stimulation, to an increased probability of a marked motor reaction and accelerative heart-rate response. One of the major dependent variables for this study was the amount of time the infant required to reach his peak accelerated heart rate following the imposition of the stimulus. Another measure was the peak heart rate itself, relative to the heart rate prior to stimulation. Although individual infants were reliably consistent in each measure by itself, the correlation between the time and rate measures was zero; that is, there was no relationship between the *amount* of heart-rate change that occurred in response to the stimulus and the *time* that it took for this change to occur. The infant who "does the slow take," as it were, does not necessarily respond sluggishly with respect to other autonomic indicators even within the same cardiac response system. It was also

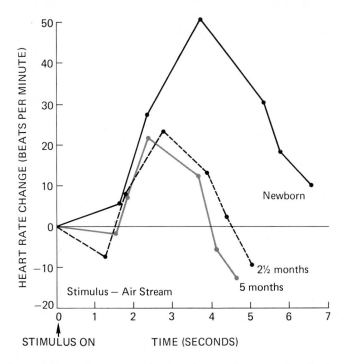

Fig. 12-1. Average response curves of one infant at three age levels. (From Lipton, Steinschneider, and Richmond, 1966, Fig. 7, p. 12. Copyright 1966 by the Society for Research in Child Development, Inc. Reprinted by permission of the authors and publisher.)

found that reliable individual differences exist with respect to the infants' return to prestimulus heart-rate level following stimulation.

The Lipton-Richmond-Steinschneider group next sought to document the possible persistence of these autonomic responses to stimulation by returning 15 infants to their laboratory at $2\frac{1}{2}$ months of age, and again at 5 months. One of their first discoveries was that the cardiac response curves were quite different from those of the newborn. By $2\frac{1}{2}$ months of age, the peak rate occurred much more quickly after the onset of the stimulus, and the peak rate was of a lesser magnitude. This may be seen in Figure 12-1. In addition, it was found that while the newborn's cardiac activity was virtually all accelerative following stimulation (with return to approximate base level after offset of the stimulus), the older infant frequently showed cardiac decelerative responses following the initial acceleratory phase, often even within the five second period. There did not seem to be any further modification in this pattern between $2\frac{1}{2}$ and 5 months of age.

These researchers also looked for a relation between the newborn measures and the same measures at the two later ages, but they found no consistency whatever between the neonatal and the $2\frac{1}{2}$ month results, although significant correlations were observed between $2\frac{1}{2}$ months and 5 months. They concluded that individual infants maintain their relative ranking within a group only *after* the newborn period. It is not possible to determine from their studies how soon after the newborn period the infants become rearranged into relatively stable rankings, nor over how prolonged a period of time these rankings might be maintained. Further explorations along such lines must surely be made to answer these questions and to determine whether the measures do indeed have pertinence for behavioral and personality functioning in later months and years.

The selection of subjects for the longitudinal study of emotional reactivity is important and probably depends upon the theoretical purposes and methodological preferences of the researchers. For example, Korner and Grobstein (1967), who have begun a longitudinal study of infants, said of their sample selection:

Since it is easy to find individual differences which are not an expression of the infant's behavioral individuality but are an artifact of pre- or post-natal complications, only completely normal, healthy, full-term babies are included. . . . Stringent selection criteria were developed to screen for prenatal maternal health, duration of labor, maternal analgesic dose, mode of delivery, and condition of the infant at birth and thereafter. (Korner and Grobstein, 1967, pp. 681–682.)

Korner and Grobstein clearly suggested that they wished to study longitudinal characteristics that may have generality for the entire continuum of "normal" behavior; they were not particularly interested, at least at this point in their research program, in the special circumstances of birth which may produce some residual deficiency or anomaly. Their suggestion that perinatal complications may produce individual differences that are relatively easy to detect and that may indeed have continuing pertinence to later behavioral deficits gains credibility from a study by Lewis, Bartels, Campbell, and Goldberg (1967a). The latter study showed that the condition of the infant at birth is related to measures of visual attentiveness throughout the first year of life. Condition at birth was assessed with the Apgar Scale, which scores such gross physiological attributes as regularity of respiration and muscular tonicity.

One of the most ambitious longitudinal studies of emotional development has been that of Kagan and Moss (1962), who had access, at the Fels Research Institute, to a vast amount of data gathered on 89 children who had been studied intensively from birth to 14 years of age. Kagan and Moss were "concerned primarily with the stability of selected motive-related behaviors, sources of anxiety, defensive responses, and modes of interpersonal interaction from earliest childhood through young adulthood" (p. 9). They supplemented the filed information on these children with results from an extensive interview and battery of tests administered to the subjects in adulthood. It is of methodological interest to note that one of the researchers did all of the adult interviewing and testing with no knowledge of the prior developmental data on any of the subjects, and the other member of the research team was entirely responsible for the personality and behavior ratings made from the historical materials. As Kagan and Moss pointed out, this separation of duties was essential to carrying out the study in an objective manner, since a major purpose of the study was to relate the childhood and adult data from the same subjects.

It is impossible to review here the large number of scales used in quantifying the thousands of pages of records on each subject of the study. Suffice it to say that many of the scales with respectable reliability tapped such attributes as passivity, dependency, tendencies toward aggression, need for achievement and recognition, and so on. Conclusions derived from the multitude of correlations conducted over the data cannot be easily summarized, but the following remarks may serve to capture the flavor and potential usefulness of such a study.

"The most dramatic and consistent finding of this study was that many of the behaviors exhibited by the child during the period 6 to 10 years of age, and a few during the age period 3 to 6, were moderately good predictors of theoretically related behaviors during early adulthood" (Kagan and Moss, 1962, p. 266). Such rated attributes as passive withdrawal from stress, dependency upon one's family, anger-arousal threshold, concern for intellectual mastery, and patterns of adult sexual behavior were related to "reasonably analogous" behavior tendencies during the early school years. But some of the non-findings of the study are perhaps as interesting as the significant correlations obtained. For example, the investigators stated: "Not all of the childhood reactions displayed long-term continuity. Compulsivity and irrational fears during childhood were not predictive of similar responses during adulthood. Moreover, task persistence and excessive irritability during the first three years of life showed no relation to phenotypically similar behaviors during later childhood" (Kagan and Moss, 1962, p. 269).

The Kagan and Moss study will probably instigate further longitudinal studies, so desperately needed for a full understanding of the possible importance of constitutional and early experience determinants of later behavior. However, greater insights into true continuities of emotional attributes of children, as well as shifts in modes of behavioral expression, will probably come in the future less from retrospective studies and more from studies which specify certain target behaviors at the outset for intensive exploration. These behaviors and their transitions would then be followed carefully and deliberately. The potpourri of data with which the researcher ends up when masses of information are collected and merely shelved for later analysis has numerous methodological and housekeeping drawbacks.

CHAPTER 13

Language Acquisition

INTRODUCTION

The study of the process by which a child acquires his native language is part of the field of psycholinguistics. While the term *psycholinguistics* has a history dating back at least to 1935 (Kantor, 1935), it has come into wide use only since 1954, when Osgood and Sebeok (1954) published a survey of theory and research in this area. Their report grew out of a conference of psychologists, linguists, and anthropologists interested in promoting a multidisciplinary attack upon the problems encountered in the understanding of the nature and function of human language. Since the publication of this report, linguistics has seen dramatic advances, stimulated by a thin volume by Chomsky, *Syntactic Structures* (1957). Although most psychologists were ignorant of the impact this book was having on linguistics, their attention was forcefully drawn to Chomsky's point of view by his very critical review (1959) of Skinner's book on verbal behavior (1957). In essence, Chomsky argued that the theoretical approaches taken by psychologists to explain language behavior are wrong and, in principle, can never account for language behavior. In the ensuing years psycholinguists have begun to separate into two groups. There are those who feel that Chomsky is wrong and that present psychological theory can, perhaps with some elaboration, be used to account for language. Others feel that Chomsky is correct and that psychologists should reorient themselves to the problems of language and even the entire subject matter of psychology.

The present chapter surveys the literature relevant to the acquisition of language. Consideration is given to research on phonological, syntactic, and semantic development, and at the end of the chapter three theoretical points of view that have been advanced to account for language acquisition are discussed. The student who is deeply interested in this area will probably adopt one of the theoretical positions, but regardless of which position he takes, he will meet opposition demanding that he defend it. He should therefore carefully evaluate the material presented, and might well bolster his position by consulting other reviews of the literature (e.g., Braine, in press; Ervin-Tripp, 1966; McCarthy, 1954; McNeill, in press; Staats and Staats, 1963).

PHONOLOGICAL DEVELOPMENT

The child does not begin to use meaningful words until about his first birthday, although he does considerable vocalizing before that time. He cries and grunts for the first two or three months of life, coos for approximately three months, babbles for about six months and then, sometimes after a short period of relative silence, begins to use true language. (The last three of these periods are sometimes referred to as the *cooing, babbling,* and *true language* or *true speech* stages.) Little is known, however, about the relation of the prelanguage utterances of the infant to the emergence of true language.

The ontogenetic emergence of speech sounds is referred to as phonological development. The early vocalizations of the child might be conceived as random sounds that are part of a developmental phase preparatory to the gaining of control over the vocal apparatus and the learning of sounds heard in the language environment. If adults react differentially to the random sounds that happen to be language-appropriate, the reactions of the adults would be expected to act as reinforcers for these sounds, increasing the frequency of these sounds relative to others that are not specific to the language in the child's environment. One study has shown that the frequency of vocalizations by three month old infants may be manipulated by the use of operant techniques (Rheingold *et al.,* 1959), and Mowrer (1960) has argued that, in addition to external reinforcement, the secondary reinforcement of hearing one's own vocalizations leads to the learning of the speech sounds of the language spoken by the parents.

However, the vocalizations of the congenitally deaf child are indistinguishable from the vocalizations of the hearing child up to about six months of age (Lenneberg, Rebelsky, and Nichols, 1965), suggesting that at least during the first half of the first year vocal development is primarily a result of maturation. Furthermore, Lenneberg (1967), in arguing for the relatively greater importance of the biological characteristics of the organism in the determination of language development, has pointed out that articulatory aspects of speech are uncorrelated with the onset of language proper. Carroll (1960, p. 746) had previously concluded that, "It is as if the child starts learning afresh when he begins to learn to utter meaningful speech."

Clearly, the role of the vocalizations of the infant during the first year of life requires a good deal more study before the basic disagreements represented by these two views can be resolved.

The Irwin Studies

Our knowledge of the character of the early vocalizations of the child is based largely upon an extensive series of studies conducted by Irwin and his colleagues (e.g., Irwin, 1947, 1948, 1951). In the early 1940s Irwin reviewed the literature on early speech sound development and found a paucity of data (Irwin, 1941b; Irwin and Chen, 1943). In these reviews it was pointed out that the usefulness of the available data was severely limited by the use of small samples, usually consisting of a single child on whom unsystematic observations had been made; lack of estimates of the reliability of the observers; failure to use standard recording procedures; minimal use of statistical analyses; and an abundance of unwarranted interpretations of the observations.

In an effort to improve the situation, Irwin first established that reliable records of infant vocalizations could be obtained using the International Phonetic Alphabet (Irwin and Chen, 1941), and then plotted the development of speech sounds during the first $2\frac{1}{2}$ years of life (Chen and Irwin, 1946). During the first 10 days of life, vocalizations are primarily vowel sounds. The most frequent sounds, as symbolized in the alphabet especially devised for recording speech sounds (see Table 13-1), are the vowels /æ/, /ɪ/, /ɛ/, and /ʌ/. (The first of these

Table 13-1

Phonemic Symbols[a]

Consonants		Vowels	
Symbol	Example	Symbol	Example
/b/	bib	/a/	papa
/d/	dub	/æ/	at
/ǰ/	jet	/ə/	sofa and about
/f/	fife	/ɛ/	let
/g/	gut	/ɪ/	it
/h/	hut	/i/	eat
/k/	cut	/o/	coke
/l/	lull	/u/	boo
/m/	mama	/ʌ/	cup
/n/	noon		
/θ/	theory		
/p/	papa		
/r/	rear		
/s/	cease		
/š/	ship		
/t/	tub		
/č/	chip		
/v/	value		
/z/	zone		
/ž/	vision		

[a] The table includes only the symbols referred to in the text. Additional symbols would be necessary for a complete transcription of English.

was the only sound uttered by all 40 of the infants observed.) Vowel sounds increase from an average of about 4.5 types at 1 to 2 months of age to about 11.4 types at 30 months. The adult English complement of vowels is approximately 14 in this system. Consonant sounds increase from about 2.7 types at 1 to 2 months of age to about 15.8 at 30 months. The adult complement of consonants is approximately 25 in this system. The frequency of vowel sound types is greater than the frequency of consonant sounds until about 1 year of age, when consonants become more frequent (as they are in adult speech). Vowels are distinguished from consonants on the basis of the characteristics of production. Vowels usually involve vibration of the vocal cords and an open vocal tract. Consonants are produced by closure, friction, or contact of tongue or lips.

The first vowel sounds uttered are those made in the front and middle of the mouth, such as the front vowels /ε/ and /ɪ/, and the middle vowel /ʌ/ (refer to Table 13-1). Later, the back vowels such as /u/ and /o/ come in, and the front and middle vowels drop in relative frequency. The consonant sounds appear in the reverse order, from back to front. Thus, the first consonants are sounds such as /k/, /g/, and /h/. Later, the consonants produced by constrictions in the middle of the vocal tract, such as /t/ and /d/, appear, and finally the consonants made by closure at the front of the vocal tract, such as /p/ and /m/, are heard.

CRITICISMS OF THE IRWIN STUDIES. The Irwin research program has provided a classic series of studies demonstrating how a systematic, carefully controlled set of observations can provide reliable answers in an unexplored area. Unfortunately, however, these studies are also subject to criticism, due in part to technological advances and in part to changes in the questions being asked about speech development. Ervin and Miller (1963) have pointed out that the full range of sounds was not reported, since the incidences of non-English types of sounds, such as rounded front vowels and clicks, were not regularly recorded. It is surprising that such sounds were omitted, because several authors have noted that nearly all the sounds heard in any language are heard in the vocalizations of the child, particularly during the latter half of the first year (e.g., Cohen, 1952; Jespersen, 1922; Tischler, 1957). Observations of vocalizations during the babbling stage suggest that there are two processes taking place, phonetic expansion and phonetic contraction (Lewis, 1936; Thompson, 1962). Brown (1958a) has referred to these phenomena as "phonetic drift" (p. 199). As the child matures he becomes capable of producing more and more different sounds, including finally all of the sounds used in all of the languages. Subsequently, his repertoire appears to contract as he learns to limit himself to the sounds relevant to the language spoken by those around him. Thus, the child who eventually acquires English (for example) appears to be capable during the babbling period of making the same sounds that may later cause him much difficulty when he tries to learn a second language.

A second criticism leveled at the Irwin studies by Ervin and Miller is that no distinction was made between the sounds uttered during the cooing, babbling, and true speech stages. Samples of sounds were taken throughout these developmental periods, but no indication was given about the nature of the larger utterance in which the sounds were occurring, and it is therefore not possible to tell whether the sounds uttered were single isolated sounds or parts of larger segments. As Lenneberg (1967) has noted, there are important changes in the acoustic characteristics of the sounds uttered during these developmental periods. The sounds heard during the cooing period are quite different from those of the preceding period; further changes occur during the babbling period; and additional changes occur when actual language begins.

Finally, the Irwin studies have been criticized by Lynip (1951) because mechanical recordings of the early speech sounds of infants indicate that there is no resemblance between the acoustic characteristics of the early vocalizations of infants and the sounds which the International Phonetic Alphabet was designed to identify in the adult language. As noted above, Lenneberg (1964, 1967) has dealt at length with the differences in the acoustic character of prelanguage vocalizations and those heard in actual language.

Analyses of Distinctive Features

Another approach to the study of the emergence of the sound system of language has been stimulated by the analysis of speech in terms of "distinctive features," as proposed by Jakobson and his colleagues (e.g., Chomsky and Halle, 1968; Jakobson and Halle, 1956; Jakobson, Fant, and Halle, 1952). The technique was applied to children's language acquisition by Jakobson (1941), but the work was originally published in German, and only since its translation, in 1968, has it begun to receive much attention in America (Jakobson, 1968). As might be expected, space limitations make it impossible to cover Jakobson's complete system here; but for present purposes the subtle details of the system can be ignored and only the salient features need be described.

More emphasis is placed upon the acoustic characteristics of sounds than in most other systems (including the International Phonetic Alphabet), which rely entirely on the point and manner of articulation to describe the sounds or *phonemes* of language. In Jakobson's system, phonemes are considered to be simultaneous actualizations of a set of attributes—not discrete individual entities but bundles of features. The emphasis is upon the features which are the components of sounds rather than upon categorizing sounds *per se*. The sound systems used in all languages can be described in terms of these features; all of the particular sounds which make up a language can be defined and differentiated in terms of the features.

There are two kinds of features, *inherent* and *prosodic*. The inherent features define a phoneme independently of the sequences in which it occurs. The prosodic features are superimposed upon the inherent features and refer to tone (voice-pitch), force (voice-loudness), and quality (subjective duration), which can be specified only in terms of the sequences of sounds in which the phoneme occurs.

INHERENT FEATURES. It is assumed that not many more than 12 to 15 inherent features are necessary to define all of the sounds in any language. The features include vocalic-nonvocalic, consonantal-nonconsonantal, diffuse-compact, tense-lax, voiced-voiceless, nasal-oral, continuant-interrupted, strident-mellow, checked-unchecked, grave-acute, flat-plain, and sharp-plain (Jakobson *et al.*, 1952). A list of the features and one or two of the characteristics used to define them are given in Table 13-2. Each of these dichotomous features is defined in terms of acoustic and articulatory characteristics. For example, a *vocalic* phoneme is characterized acoustically as having a sharply defined formant structure, articulation primarily at the glottis, and a free passage of air through the vocal

Table 13-2

Partial Description of the Attributes Defining Inherent Distinctive Features[a]

Feature	Positive	Negative
Vocalic-nonvocalic	Single harmonic structure; gradual onset	Noise structure; abrupt onset
Consonantal-nonconsonantal	Occlusion of vocal tract	Open vocal tract
Diffuse-compact	One or more noncentral formants	One central formant dominates
Tense-lax	Long sound interval; large energy	Short interval; less energy
Voiced-voiceless	Strong low frequency sound component; vibration of vocal cords	No vibration of vocal bands
Nasal-oral	Air stream bifurcated to use nasal and oral cavities as resonators	Air stream through oral cavity only
Continuant-interrupted	Gradual onset	Abrupt onset
Strident-mellow	Irregular sound waveforms	Patterned waveforms
Checked-unchecked	Abrupt decay of sound by closure of glottis	Gradual decay of sound
Grave-acute	Lower frequencies predominate	High frequencies predominate
Flat-plain	Downward shift of formants; lip rounding	No lip rounding
Sharp-plain	Rise is to second and higher formants; tongue against palate	Tongue lowered from palate

[a] After Jakobson *et al.* (1952).

tract; a *nonvocalic* phoneme is characterized acoustically as having a loose formant structure, articulation primarily at the lips or palate, and a constricted passage of air through the vocal tract. All vowels in English are vocalic and all consonants are nonvocalic (except /l/ and /r/). A *grave* phoneme has the acoustic properties of energy concentration in the lower frequencies of the sound spectrum and more ample and less compartmented resonator (mouth cavity) than *acute* phonemes. The initial phonemes in *p*ull, *b*at, *f*at, *c*ould, *g*ood, and *o*at are grave; the initial phonemes in *t*ake, *d*og, *s*it, *sh*oe, and *e*at are acute.

In practice, phonemes are characterized as possessing (+) or not possessing (−) a feature. Thus, vowels are characterized as [+vocalic] and most consonants as [−vocalic]; grave phonemes are [+grave] and acute phonemes are [−grave]. While all vowels are [+vocalic], some vowels and some consonants are [+grave]. Thus, by assigning to language sounds the appropriate features, each phoneme can be isolated as different from every other phoneme on the basis of one or more features. The greater the number of feature differences of two sounds, the more distinctive they should be (Miller and Nicely, 1955).

Considering language acquisition, Jakobson has suggested that the child begins by discriminating the features of the sounds used in the language. First, the child dichotomizes all sounds on the basis of one feature, giving him one contrast—between a group of sounds all considered alike because they are all plus on the relevant feature and a second group of sounds all of which are minus on that feature. The child then adds features to the system, progressively separating the significant sounds until all of the sounds of the language have been identified on the basis of their distinguishing features. If the child has identified the features *vocalic, consonantal, diffuse, strident, nasal, continuant,* and *voiced* but not the feature *grave*, he should correctly understand and produce the differences between *pear* and *bear*, which differ in terms of the voicing feature of the initial consonant, but he should produce and respond to *pear* and *tear* as if they were the same because the initial phonemes differ only on the basis of the grave feature.

Jakobson further argued that there is an order in which the features will appear in the child's language, corresponding to the number of languages in the world which contain the feature. The most common or universal features will appear first and the features peculiar to a specific language last. In particular, Jakobson predicted that the initial language utterance will be /pa/, which from an articulatory and acoustic analysis consists of two sound elements that are polar opposites. The two constituents consist of the /p/ phoneme, in which the vocal tract is closed at the front end, and the /a/ phoneme, in which the vocal tract is open as widely as possible at the front and narrowed at the back. The /p/ is a short burst of sound with no great concentration of energy in any frequency band; the /a/ is not limited in time and the energy is concentrated in a relatively narrow region of maximal aural sensitivity. This kind of utterance establishes the syllable which is the elementary phonemic frame. The next predicted split is a consonant division on the basis of the grave-acute feature, which leads to the appearance of /p/ contrasting with /t/. The nasal-oral feature may come in at about the same time, with /ma/ the most likely nasal syllable. The first vowel split occurs on the diffuse-compact feature, the compact /a/ contrasting with the diffuse /i/ and /u/ (refer to Table 13-1 for pronunciation). The /i/ and /u/ subsequently divide on the basis of the grave-acute feature, which comes in later for vowels than for consonants.

The development of speech sounds begins with the contrast between the optimal consonant and the optimal vowel, which is the maximal sound difference, and moves gradually to finer and finer distinctions in which the consonant sounds become more compact and more vowel-like and the vowel sounds become more diffuse and more consonant-like. The acquisition of the /l/ and /r/ sound distinction involves the finest gradations in English, in that they are composed of both the vowel-like feature [+vocalic] and the consonant-like feature [+consonantal]. The attainment of this distinction indicates the end of the phonemic acquisition process in the English language.

It should be noted that each feature is assumed to be acquired in an all-or-none fashion; when a feature is applied, it is not applied to just one sound but to all sounds for which it is relevant. Thus, when the voicing feature is acquired it should create not only the /g/ versus /k/ distinction, for example, but the /b/ versus /p/, /d/ versus /t/, and /v/ versus /f/ distinctions as well.

It should also be pointed out that this theoretical system applies only to language and therefore is not concerned with prelanguage utterances. Only when the child uses meaningful words does an active phonological system replace the unsystematic phonetic sounds that precede this stage of development. However, efforts have been made to use a distinctive features approach to analyze the prelinguistic utterances of infants (Ringwall, Reese, and Markel, 1965, 1970). The methodology is probably an advance over the International Phonetic Alphabet, but since most of the features used in this study are different from the features that are used to analyze *language*, it is not clear at this point how the results will bear upon language acquisition. Vocal development seems to be discontinuous, because the prelinguistic utterances of infants are assumed to be unsystematic and the sounds in speech are systematic, but further research of this sort may demonstrate previously undetected relationships between these two stages.

Unfortunately, there is not much evidence bearing directly on the acquisition of the sound system within the framework proposed by Jakobson. It is therefore necessary to evaluate the theory on the basis of scattered studies of the language development of individual children (e.g., Albright and Albright, 1958; Burling, 1959; Chao, 1951; Leopold, 1939–1949; Leopold, 1948; Velten, 1943; Weir, 1962). Ervin-Tripp (1966) has summarized the available data. In terms of distinctive features, these data suggest the following generalizations:

(a) The contrast between vowel and consonant—[+vocalic, −consonantal] versus [−vocalic, +consonantal]—is probably the earliest contrast to be observed.

(b) A stop-continuant contrast—[−continuant] versus [+continuant]—is quite early for all children, the continuant being a fricative [+strident] or a nasal [+nasal]. For example, the stop /p/ is contrasted with the fricative continuant /f/ and the nasal continuant /m/ at an early age.

(c) Stops precede fricatives; that is, [−continuant, −strident] precedes [+continuant, +strident].

(d) If two consonants are alike in manner of articulation (i.e., have the same markings on the features continuant and strident), one will be labial and the other alveolar or dental, that is, one will be [+grave] and the other [−grave].

For example, /p/ and /t/ are both [−continuant, −strident], but /p/ is [+grave] and /t/ is [−grave]. At this level of child development, there is no distinction between [+diffuse] and [−diffuse]; hence, the distinction between /k/ and /t/ is not present.

(e) Contrasts involving place of articulation (i.e., contrasts involving the features grave and diffuse) precede voicing contrasts. For example, the distinction between /p/ and /k/, involving [+diffuse] versus [−diffuse], precedes the distinction between /b/ and /p/, involving [+voiced] versus [−voiced].

(f) Affricates—[−continuant, +strident]—and liquids—[+vocalic, +consonantal]—usually appear later than stops and nasals. For example, the affricates /č/ as in *chip* and /ǰ/ as in *jet*, and the liquids /l/ and /r/ appear later than the stop /p/ and the nasal /m/.

(g) The vowel distinctions based on the diffuse-compact feature appear before those based on the flat-plain and grave-acute features. That is, the high versus low contrast in vowels, such as between /i/ and /æ/, precedes the front versus back distinctions, such as between /i/ and /u/.

(h) Consonant clusters or blends in which the common feature [+consonantal] is maintained across consecutive phonemes are usually late. Examples are /pl/, /bl/, and /skr/.

(i) In languages other than English (e.g., French), the distinction between oral and nasal vowels—[+vocalic, −nasal] versus [+vocalic, +nasal]—comes in relatively late, with oral vowels preceding nasal vowels.

The time period covered by these generalizations ranges from about the first birthday, when the first contrast occurs productively (although it may occur passively in terms of perception or understanding prior to production), to as late as the early grade school years, although most children seem to have completed phonological development by the time they enter school. Templin's (1957) extensive study of articulation indicates that only fricatives and some of the blends are misarticulated with any important frequency by five year old children, and by the time children are eight years old, errors on all sounds are minimal.

The predictions about the acquisition of distinctive features seem to receive some support from available data reported in studies of individual children. Burling's son Stephan and Velten's daughter Joan are presented as rather clear examples of this phenomenon (Burling, 1959; Velten, 1943). Even in these cases, however, "some phonemes seemed to be added individually and it is difficult to see any consistent pattern in their order of appearance" (Burling, 1959, p. 64).

Although there is a rough correspondence between the available data and Jakobson's predictions, there are some incongruities. In particular, some of the distinctive features that appear rather early in certain contexts are quite late in others. In addition, the child apparently acquires some sounds distinguished by a set of features before he acquires others (e.g., stops, which are marked [−continuant, −strident], precede fricatives, which are marked [+continuant, +strident]). Also, the appearance of [+nasal] is much later in combination with [+vocalic, —consonantal] (e.g., the nasal vowels in French) than with [—vocalic, +consonantal] (e.g., /n/ or /m/). In general, however, this approach to speech sound analysis promises to yield much more general insights than attempts to look at the acquisition of specific individual phonemes. It should also be pointed out that the specification of the features necessary to describe the sound system and the identification of the phonological rules specifying their interrelations are still far from complete (see Chomsky and Halle, 1968).

More difficult to verify is the hypothesis that the order of discriminating the features will reflect the relative frequency of the features in the total universe of languages. Presumably, the most frequently appearing features are the most distinctive, as in the case of the vowel-consonant contrast, and others are more subtle. The order of appearance of the features is similar in the children studied so far, but there are clear individual differences and some deviations from the expected order.

The distinctive features approach suggests that if at some developmental level the child does not yet have a particular feature, he should have some single sounds that represent many sounds in the adult system. If this is the case, then the early language of the child should include homonyms that are not homonyms in the adult language, particularly if the child's vocabulary expands more rapidly than his sound system. While Burling (1959) did not find this to be the case, Velten (1943) was struck by its occurrence and listed, for example, several meanings for /pat/ which included *pat, black, back, spot, pocket,* and several other words. Similarly, it might be expected that particular substitutions of one phoneme for another could be predicted on the basis of the features available to the child. Some data have been reported which bear on this prediction (e.g., Chao, 1951) and rules for the occurrence of substitutions can be developed (Applegate, 1961), but no effort has been made to relate substitution rules systematically to the theory of phonological development.

A somewhat different approach to the problem has been taken by Anisfeld and his students (Anisfeld and Gordon, 1968; Anisfeld, Barlow, and Frail, 1967). They have attempted to show the relationships among features by developing artificial tasks in which substitutions are forced upon the language user. Children in the first two elementary grades were asked which of two nonsense syllables best represented a plural. The syllables (e.g., NAR) were presented as singular forms and then two forms of the syllable with an additional phoneme (e.g., NARF-NARK) were presented as a choice for a plural form. The children tended to choose the plural form most similar (i.e., with fewest distinctive feature differences) to the regular /s/ or /z/ used to form plurals in English. When given a choice, the sounds with the feature [+strident] (e.g., /č/, /ǰ/, and /š/, as defined in Table 13-1) were chosen more often than chance. This feature defines the sibilants and is the distinguishing feature of the regular plural markers /s/ and /z/.

Messer (1967) has used a similar approach with three year old children. He presented his subjects with pairs of non-English words one of which followed the structural rules for English monosyllables (e.g., /frul/) and one which did not (e.g., /mrul/). The children were asked to say which of the two sounded most like a word. The children chose the words that followed the rules of English. Since the children were required to pronounce the words, the phonological changes could be noted when errors occurred. Mispronunciations of both types of words by the children were minimally distant from the correct pronunciation in terms of the number of distinctive features. These data, along with those of Anisfeld, give additional support to the psychological reality of the distinctive features analysis.

PROSODIC FEATURES. While the data relevant to inherent features are not extensive, the data bearing upon the development of prosodic features are even more sparse. Prosodic features of infant prelinguistic utterances have been investigated over the first five months of life (Lane and Sheppard, 1965). Complete and continuous recordings of all the vocalizations of two infants during the first five months of life were analyzed for fundamental frequency, amplitude, and duration. The results indicated that the mean frequency of the vocalizations began at an intermediate level at birth, dipped at about three weeks of age, rose to a higher level than at birth, and then stabilized at the higher level until the end of the study. The average pitch and variation in pitch remained about the same over the age span studied. The amplitude measures also were stable over this time period. Utterance length tended to become stable with age. Most utterances were quite short, less than half a second, but there was also a consistent tendency for a few long bursts to occur at all ages. These data do not seem to reveal any dramatic developmental trends, and their relation to language, which does not normally appear until several months after the age at which this study was discontinued, is not obvious.

Ringwall, Reese, and Markel (1970) obtained results that were not entirely consistent with those of Lane and Sheppard; for example, in the Ringwall *et al.* study, the period from birth to five months was a period of dramatic developmental changes, contrary to Lane and Sheppard's finding. However, quite different procedures and methods of analysis were used in these studies, and direct comparison of the results is probably neither justifiable nor profitable.

It has been suggested by Weir (1966), among other observers, that the infant imitates prosodic features during the babbling period before meaningful words appear. Earlier, Weir (1962) had noted that two levels of stress were used by her child, but Miller and Ervin (1964) suggested that the rising and falling intonations associated with questions and statements may come in later than had originally been supposed. Both of these latter studies dealt with children well past the babbling stage. Pike (1949) obtained some data suggesting that single word intonation patterns are learned by infants on the basis of the pattern used by the parents. It would appear that more attention needs to be paid to prosody before any clear notion of the development of the prosodic features can be developed and the possibility eliminated that the prosody heard in babbling reflects adult anthropomorphizing.

One final aspect of the acquisition of the sound system of the language should not be overlooked. An examination of the acoustic characteristics of speech sounds reveals that the relative frequencies of the formants of various phonemes remain the same for an individual speaker but the absolute frequencies vary considerably between speakers. The sounds of the male voice are lower than those of the female voice, and the female voice falls in a lower frequency range than the voice of a child. The frequencies in cycles per second of vowels uttered by the child's father are quite different from those of his mother and both are quite different from those of any siblings. The child, however, recognizes *pat* as different from *pet* whether it is spoken by father, mother, or sister. The child is not confused by the overlap in acoustic characteristics of different sounds or the acoustic differences in the same sounds when different speakers use them. Apparently the child responds to patterns of sounds rather than to the absolute characteristics of the sounds; in short, he transposes.

SYNTACTIC DEVELOPMENT

The First Words

It is difficult to establish the age at which the child utters his first word. The difficulty reflects an inability of the observer to comprehend the phonemic system of the child, a failure to recognize the referent the child may have in mind for his first word, and the unreliability of parental observers who are inclined to give their children credit for more than a trained observer might. Nevertheless, most researchers are agreed that the first birthday, or just before, is about the time that most children utter their first meaningful word (McCarthy, 1954). There follows a period of about six months during which the child gradually builds a vocabulary of words, most of which would be classified as nouns in the adult grammar. Although the words are used singly, the child appears to be trying to convey more than a single-word idea. It is difficult, however, to know what the child means except in the context of the utterance. Thus, the utterance /papa/ may be interpreted as meaning "Where is Papa?", "Come here, Papa!", "Here comes Papa," or any number of other meanings.

Usually, the first words are reduplicated syllables which seem to grow out of sounds heard in the babbling stage. These syllables are classified as words because they are used consistently in particular contexts. The most frequently reported words are *bye-bye, mama, dada, papa, bebe, tick-tick,* etc. Note that the consonant sounds are primarily those made with the front of the mouth, that is, bilabial and apico-alveolar sounds. The initial word signals the beginning of a lexicon or vocabulary which by 18 to 24 months has reached a size of about 200 to 300 words, according to one estimate (Smith, 1926), although the range of individual differences may be very large.

Syntax

During the one-word utterance stage, the child may give indications of comprehending the syntactic relations in some parental utterances, but not until the child has built a vocabulary of about a hundred words, or morphemes, is there evidence of the development of syntactic relations in the utterances of the child. A stock of available words (along with other developmental events) makes it possible for word combinations to occur, and the child begins to use two-word as well as one-word utterances. It is surprising how little attention has been paid to the structure of the initial two-word utterances and the more complex utterances that grow out of them. Some efforts have been made to classify the structures of these early utterances [see McCarthy (1954) and Templin (1957) for summaries of this literature], but simple classification systems, such as categorizing the utterances as simple, compound, and complex sentences, are not particularly useful in light of recent advances in linguistics.

Imagine the following conversation between a boy and his father who has just come home from work and is changing clothes:

"Hi Daddy."
"Hi Johnny. Did Mommy buy this truck?"
"This truck."
"Can you make it go fast?"
"Go fast. Hat off. Shirt off. Pants off. That blue."
"Yes, my pants are blue."
"Sweater on. Chair."
"Where's the kitty?"
"Kitty allgone. Here is. See Mummy. There Mummy."
"Yes, here comes Mommy."
"Here Mummy."
"I'll go out and help her carry in the groceries."
"Groceries. Bye bye. Two bag. Chicken. That red. Here kitty. Bag fall. Close it."
"I can't close the box, so we'll have pizza for dinner."
"John dinner."
"We'll make your dinner now."
"Baby dinner."
"Yes, we'll make dinner for the baby too."
"Pick glove."
"I'll pick up my glove. Say, how did your knees get so dirty?"
"Knee dirty. See knee."
"Let's wash you off before dinner."
"Wash off."
"Where's the washcloth?"
"Wash cloth. Here is. Two cloth. Dirty. Dirty allgone."

While this conversation is fictitious, most of the child's utterances have been taken from those recorded by Miller and Ervin (1964), Brown and Fraser (1964), and Braine (1963b). These are the kinds of things we might hear from a child who has begun to put words together into pairs at about 18 to 24 months of age. After collecting considerable data of this sort from a number of children, Ervin, Brown, Braine, and their collaborators were faced with the problem of making sense out of the data. Where are the consistencies? What is the child saying? What is the relation between what the child says and what the adult says?

CHILD GRAMMARS.   One possible way of analyzing such data is to count the number of words in the utterances; as the child grows older, the number of words in each utterance can be plotted as a function of age. It is also possible to classify the words by part of speech in the adult system and to show the relative growth in the use of various parts of speech as the child's age increases. It would be possible to time the responses and plot rate of speech as a function of age. One might also look at individual differences and attempt to relate these measures to sex, race, socioeconomic status, number of siblings, and related variables. In fact, a large number of such studies have been conducted. The results of this research have been carefully summarized by McCarthy (1954): In general, (a) utterances become longer (i.e., include more words) as children get older; (b) nouns and other content words (verbs and adjectives) are the most frequent words in early stages of syntactic development, and function words are used later; (c) children speak more rapidly than adults; (d) language development of girls tends to be advanced relative to language development of boys; (e) children from high socioeconomic level families develop language more rapidly than children from low socioeconomic level families; (f) singletons (only children) develop language more rapidly and twin children more slowly than others; and (g) the amount of verbal stimulation in the school and home affects rate of language development.

There are other kinds of questions that can be asked about the child's language, requiring other kinds of observations and methods of analysis. Some of these questions confront us with the nature, structure, or description of language itself. These are questions that lead us to the field of linguistics. It is the linguist who can tell us about the structure of language, that is, the nature of the system or set of rules which the child acquires when he learns to use his language. It is the linguist who can give us hints about the manner in which "This truck" or "Go fast" might be analyzed in terms of language structures and about the nature of the rules being ignored in "Two bag." The psychologist may be interested in the factors that lead to language acquisition, but he must look to the linguist for a description of the nature of the language that is being acquired.

Chomsky (1957, 1965) has provided psychology with a theory of syntax which gives some indication of the system of grammar being acquired by the child. The goal of the theory is to present a set of rules which will allow the generation of all the grammatical sentences in the language and no ungrammatical sentences. Although the theory for languages in general, or even for any specific language, is not complete, an impressive start has been made both in delineating linguistic universals (Bach and Harms, 1968; Greenberg, 1966) and in specifying the rules for specific languages. If the language of the adult reflects a rule-governed system and the child acquires this system, questions may be asked about the manner in which the system is learned. Does the child gradually acquire the whole system? Does he acquire subsystems and integrate them into a complete system? Or are there some other characteristics of his development?

In the imaginary conversation above, it is clear that there are some consistencies in the utterances of the child. Most of the utterances seem to express a complete idea or thought in the context. Frequently, it is not difficult to understand or interpret what the child means. "Dirty allgone," for example, does not resemble very closely anything an adult would say, but in the context, it is reasonable to assume that the child means that his knee has been cleaned and the dirt has been removed.

There is also some patterning in the child's utterances. He said, "Hat off," "Shirt off," "Pants off," and "Wash off"; "Kitty allgone" and "Dirty allgone"; and "Here is," "Here Mummy," and "Here Kitty." There appear to be some frequently repeated words, such as "off," "allgone" (treated as one word because *all* and *gone* never appear separately in the child's speech), and "here." These words are used with several other words but never with each other, and they seem to occur consistently in a single position in the two-word utterances.

Another kind of observation relates to the relation between what the child says and what the parent says. The child limits himself to one or two words regardless of what the parent says. When he responds to the adult, the child tends to contract what the adult says into two words and generally to pick two important words as far as the content of the message is concerned. In responding to the child, the parent expands the child's two words into a fully grammatical sentence interpreting the two words differently in different contexts.

Finally, in the child's utterances there are no indications of morphophonemic rules. The child does not inflect his verbs for tense nor does he inflect for plural or possessive forms. It can also be observed that the child does not have any way of indicating that he is asking a question.

In summary, it can be seen that as soon as the imaginary child puts two words together, there appears to be some rudimentary system or organization, which might possibly be captured with a larger sample of utterances and a larger number of children. Further, it can be seen that there are many more limitations on what the child can communicate with his system than is the case in the adult language system. The vast difference between the rudimentary system of the child and the complex system of the parents is reduced to a minimum in a matter of three to four years. By the time the child enters school, he has mastered nearly the entire syntax of his language.

Fortunately, it is not necessary to depend entirely upon imaginary children, because Ervin, Brown, Braine, and their collaborators have reported the findings of laborious efforts to record the beginnings of language in children (Braine, 1963b; Brown and Fraser, 1964; Brown, Cazden, and Bellugi, 1968; Brown, Fraser, and Bellugi, 1964; Miller, 1964a, 1964b; Miller and Ervin, 1964). These data have been supplemented by less systematic reports on other individual children, for example, Gvozdev's son [Gvozdev (1949) as reported by McNeill (1966b) and Slobin (1966a)]. The size of the available sample is not impressive, especially since most of the children have come from families with strong verbal skills; but the consistencies in the data of the relatively independent investigations are impressive and lead to greater confidence in the kinds of analyses performed despite the limitations in the samples.

Ervin's sample consisted of 5 monolingual firstborn children plus 25 other children studied less intensively (Miller and Ervin, 1964). The smaller group of children was seen from approximately the age of two years until the age of four; weekly 45 minute samples of speech were taken in the initial phases of the work and then, as the rate of change slowed down, larger amounts of material were collected at intervals of two months.

Brown's sample consisted of 13 children who were about two years old at the beginning of the data collection period. Extensive data have been presented for only four of these children—Adam, Eve, Abel, and Sarah. With the exception of Sarah, all of the children were from families with college backgrounds and professional occupations. Sarah's father was a clerk, and her parents had high school degrees.

Braine's sample of children included three boys. Observation was begun when the children had vocabularies of about 10 to 20 words, well before two-word

$$
S \to \left\{ \begin{array}{c} (P_1) + 0 \\ \\ 0 + (P_2) \end{array} \right\}
$$

Fig. 13-1.   Grammar at two-word utterance stage. See text for explanation.

utterances had begun to occur. Thus, Braine began observations at an earlier developmental level than the other two investigators.

All three investigators reported that the two-word utterance, which usually begins to occur when the child is between the ages of 18 and 24 months,[1] seems to have a characteristic structure. The child is not randomly juxtaposing two words that he has heard. There is an apparent system to his constructions which accounts for about 70 percent of the utterances heard. The system consists of using one word in a single position, and a large group of words in the other position. The child may be heard in various appropriate situations to say, for example, "There bird," "There boat," "There kitty," "There Mummy," "There reel," and so on. On other appropriate occasions the child might be heard to say, "Bird allgone," "Eyebrow allgone," "Kitty allgone," "Microphone allgone," "Reel allgone," and so on. In all of the children observed, there is a small group of words which occur fairly consistently in the first position, another smaller group of words which occur fairly consistently in the second position, and a very large group of words-which can occur in either first or second position. The grammar of this stage in the child's language development may be written as shown in Figure 13-1. That is, the sentence (S) is rewritten

[1] For the three children studied by Braine, the ages were 19, 19, and 20 months.

as *pivot* word (P_1) plus *open class* word (O) or *open class* word (O) plus *pivot* word (P_2). The pivot words are marked by a subscript because the pivot words that occur in the first position do not occur in the second position. The open class words could also be marked by subscripts but there is enough overlap in the particular words or morphemes occurring in the first and second positions that such marking would perhaps unnecessarily complicate the grammar (Brown

Table 13-3

Examples of Two-Word Utterances[a]

P-O Constructions	O-P Constructions
That truck	Hat off
That blue	Blanket off
That chicken	Pants off
That pants	Sweater off
That hat	That off
That go	
	Head on
Here brick	Fix on
Here chairs	Blanket on
Here goes	Pants on
Here Mum	Sweater on
Here is	That on
See boy	Do it
See eye	Push it
See Mummy	Close it
See radio	Buzz it
See rocker	Move it
Two Bobby	Bird allgone
Two chair	Eyebrow allgone
Two girl	Kitty allgone
Two men	Microphone allgone
Two reel	Reel allgone

[a] Taken from Miller and Ervin (1964), Brown and Fraser (1964), and Braine (1963b).

and Fraser, 1964). The pivot words are placed in parentheses in the grammar to indicate that they may be omitted and a one-word utterance of an open class word alone is possible. Table 13-3 provides some examples taken from the protocols reported by the investigators being discussed (Braine, 1963b; Brown and Fraser, 1964; Miller and Ervin, 1964).

In general, the first language constructions of the child are of the P-O or

O-P form. When the child uses single word utterances, the words tend to come from the open class. The characteristics of the pivot and open class words are difficult to specify within the framework of the adult grammar. They are grouped in this manner because of their distributional characteristics in the child's speech. *Truck, blue, chicken, pants, hat,* and *go* have been put into a category of open class words because they share a context, that is, they all occur in the presence of *that* (see Table 13-3). It can be argued that the open class of words which follow *that* is not different from the open class which follows *here* or the open class which precedes *off* because there is some overlap in the words used in these contexts. The overlap was about 20 to 40 percent for some particular words in the corpus (speech sample) of one child reported by Brown and Fraser.

If the pivot words are classified according to the adult system, several parts of speech are found, including adjectives, adverbs, pronouns, verbs, and articles. Such a classification does not seem very helpful, but a closer examination of the pairs of words suggests that these various two-word utterances reveal the beginnings of constructions that are the adult equivalents of demonstrative constructions (e.g., "that truck"), noun phrases (e.g., "two men"), verb phrases (e.g., "see boy"), and complete sentences. The child shows evidence of being able to conceptualize the relations expressed by the adult, but lacks the ability to produce a linguistically complete expression of those relations.

Although the child's language consists primarily of P-O and O-P types of constructions initially, there are exceptions for all the children studied. Some two-word utterances do not seem to fit any identifiable pattern and some utterances are several words long. In the latter case, each child seems to have a few longer utterances which he can run off as units in appropriate situations. For example, one of the children in Braine's study said "Up on there some more" during the primarily two-word utterance stage. This same child said, "Pants change" and "Papa away," which did not fit with any of his observed P-O or O-P constructions, although if a larger corpus of utterances could have been obtained, the structure might have been revealed.

Braine (1963b) noted that the next developmental stage is not a three-word utterance but an intermediate stage in which a number of O-O constructions occur. Braine suggested that these utterances consist of an open class word substitution for a P-O construction plus another open class word. In a sense, this appears to be anticipatory of the three-word utterance, which takes the form of P-O-O, O-O-P, P-O-P, or O-P-O. In the three-word utterances the child may be heard to say such things as "See baby eyebrow" when before he said "See baby" or "See eyebrow." He may say "There man coat" when before he said "There man" or "There coat." Another example is "That came off," in which "that" was a pivot word in first position earlier and "off" was a pivot in second position earlier. It might be expected that P-O-P-O four-word utterances would follow, but the grammar gets too complicated to analyze in this simple fashion as the child begins to increase the length of the utterances beyond three words.

There are problems in analyzing child grammars to study syntactic development. First, as just mentioned, the simple method of analysis is useful only with utterances shorter than four words. How the transition to more complex grammars occurs is not yet clear.

A second problem has to do with the nature of a grammar written to describe the child's language. The linguist writes a grammar that can generate all of the grammatical and none of the ungrammatical utterances in a language. The linguist can always go to an adult native speaker of the language and check to be sure that what is generated by the grammar is acceptable (grammatical) in the language. The child, however, is not a good informant in this sense, and it is therefore difficult to check on the adequacy of a child grammar. Furthermore, the child's grammar is continually changing so that a check today, if it could be established, might not be relevant to a grammar of yesterday. Brown and Fraser (1964), Brown *et al.* (1964), and Harwood (1959) all have struggled with this problem in attempting to write grammars for the children they have studied. Clearly it is not possible to write a grammar for children in the same sense as for adults. One can choose between writing a grammar that is specific enough to account for all the utterances observed in the corpus and writing a grammar that is more general. The difficulty with the former is that the grammar is too specific and will not allow prediction of many new utterances. The latter, however, may predict utterances that do not occur under any circumstances while predicting some new utterances that might occur.

Finally, writing grammars for children is difficult because presumably the child, as the adult, produces some utterances that are not fully grammatical. The grammar is a description of the person's knowledge about the language, but there are many reasons why that knowledge may not be manifest in the observable utterances of the speaker. The adult does not always speak in fully grammatical sentences (see Osgood, 1963) despite the fact that he has the competence to do so. It is likely that the child also deviates at times from his own grammar, due to a number of variables that may affect his verbal performance. When an adult makes mistakes of this sort, the linguist can exclude them from consideration because he has the opportunity of checking with an informant, that is, he can ask a native speaker of the language whether a particular string of words is grammatical. Since the child usually cannot make such judgments, there is no way to tell which utterances are grammatical and which are ungrammatical according to the child's current language state (Chomsky, 1964; Lees, 1964).

EMERGENCE OF ADULT STRUCTURES. Clearly, the problem of taking a corpus of child language and attempting to develop a grammar from it in order to understand the child's knowledge of his language and to predict the future language behavior of the child is fraught with difficulties. Another approach to the study of development toward the adult grammar is to take an adult syntactic form and study the manner in which the child proceeds to that form. This approach has been illustrated by the analysis of the emergence of the negative and interrogative structures in children's speech (Bellugi, 1964, 1965; Brown, 1968; Klima and Bellugi, 1966).

In the first of these studies, an analysis was made of the negative forms heard by the children and the developmental stages in the form of the negative sentences uttered by the two children observed. Table 13-4 presents a simplified summary of the general characteristics of the kinds of negative forms directed toward the child (Bellugi, 1964). These are the rules followed by the adult model toward which the child is progressing. It is clear from the table that parents negate sentences in several different ways. The rules in the table do not cover all the possible negative forms in English but only those which are

Table 13-4

Parental Negation Rules[a]

Rule	Examples
1. NP–Aux + $\left\{\begin{array}{c} n't \\ not \end{array}\right\}$ –VP	The boy won't run to the store. You did not do it.
2. NP–*be* + $\left\{\begin{array}{c} n't \\ not \end{array}\right\}$ – $\left\{\begin{array}{c} NP \\ adj \end{array}\right\}$	The boy isn't dirty. You're not dirty.
NP–*be* + $\left\{\begin{array}{c} n't \\ not \end{array}\right\}$ –VP (with *-ing*)	You aren't going. Daddy's not going.
3. *Do* + *n't*–VP	Don't run across the street. Don't slam the door.
4. Aux + *n't*–NP–VP–Q	Aren't you coming to dinner? Didn't you go?
Wh–Aux + *n't*–NP–VP–Q	Why didn't you go? Why aren't you coming?
5. Negation with indefinites	
NP–Aux + $\left\{\begin{array}{c} n't \\ not \end{array}\right\}$ –VP (with *any* in object position)	You shouldn't drink any more. He can't find anything.
NP–Aux–VP (with *no* as form of indefinite in any NP position)	Nobody will find you. He found no place to sit.

[a] NP: noun phrase; Aux: auxiliary verb (*do, have, will, can, may, must, need, could,* etc.); VP: verb phrase; Q: utterance with rising intonation. Brackets indicate a choice of the options within the brackets. *Wh: why, where, when, what, who, which.*

frequently used by parents in talking to their children. Note that the first and fifth rules are essentially the same except that in the latter the indefinite forms complicate the rules in order to avoid the double negative. The child has a rather complicated set of rules to learn in order to change an affirmative statement to a negative one.

The first negative constructions of the two children studied by Bellugi appeared when the mean utterance length was, respectively, 1.4 and 1.9 morphemes (excluding the negative morpheme). Table 13-5 summarizes the development

Table 13-5

Stages in Child's Development of Negation Rules[a]

Rule	Examples

Stage 1 (1.4–1.9 morphemes)

a.
$$\left\{ \begin{matrix} no \\ \\ not \end{matrix} \right\} -S$$

No wash.
No mitten.
No more
No play that.
Not fit.

b.
$$S- \left\{ \begin{matrix} no \\ \\ not \end{matrix} \right\}$$

Wear mitten no.

Why not?

Stage 2 (3.3–3.4 morphemes)

a. NP–$\left\{ \begin{matrix} can't \\ don't \end{matrix} \right\}$–VP

I can't see you.
I don't want it.

b. Demonstrative–$\left\{ \begin{matrix} no \\ not \end{matrix} \right\}$–NP

That no fish school.
That not milk.

c. *Don't*–VP

Don't leave me.
Don't push it.

d. *Why not*–NP–(*can't*)[b]–VP–Q

Why not me sleeping?
Why not me go?

Stage 3 (4.8 morphemes)

a. NP–Aux + *n't*–VP

I don't want cover on it.
I won't eat it.

b. NP–(*be*)[b]–*not*–$\left\{ \begin{matrix} NP \\ adj \end{matrix} \right\}$

That not a clown.
He is not a girl.

NP–*not*–VP (with *-ing*)

He not going.
I not crying.

c. *Don't*–VP

Same as Stage 2
Don't hit me.

d. *Why*–NP–Aux + *n't*–VP–Q

Why the kitty can't stand up?
Why it won't start?

e. NP–Aux + *n't*–VP (with *some* as form of indefinite determiner or pronoun in object position)

I didn't see something.
He won't have some.

Stage 4 (5.7 morphemes)[c]

a. NP–Aux + *n't*–VP

Same as adult and Stage 3
I doesn't know how.

b. NP–*be* + $\left\{ \begin{matrix} n't \\ not \end{matrix} \right\}$–$\left\{ \begin{matrix} NP \\ adj \end{matrix} \right\}$

He isn't happy.
Those are not your tires.

NP–(*be*)[b] + $\left\{ \begin{matrix} n't \\ not \end{matrix} \right\}$–$\left\{ \begin{matrix} VP \ (with \ \textit{-ing}) \\ adj \end{matrix} \right\}$

He isn't looking.
I not peeking.

Table 13-5 (*continued*)

Stages in Child's Development of Negation Rules[a]

Rule	Examples
c. *Don't*–VP	Same as Stage 2 Don't do it on me.
d. *Why*–NP–Aux + *n't*–VP–Q	Same as Stage 3 Why you couldn't find it?
e. NP–Aux + *n't*–VP (with indefinite determiners and pronouns containing negative element)	He can't have nothing. Nobody won't recognize us.

[a] See footnote *a* to Table 13-4. S: sentence.
[b] Optional; may be omitted.
[c] Based on only one child (Adam).

of negatives over a two year period, as Bellugi (1964) described it.[2] The first negative was formed by the simple procedure of appending a "no" or "not" to the beginning or, less frequently, to the end of an affirmative utterance. The second stage includes four negative constructions which all appear at about the same time. While the constructions of the first stage do not resemble the model (i.e., adult) language, some of the second stage negative utterances are perfectly grammatical from an adult point of view. One interesting characteristic of this stage is the use of "can't" and "don't." The children use these forms before they use "can" and "do." It appears that "can't" and "don't" operate as single unit negative morphemes at this stage, and not until the next stage does the child separate the auxiliary verb from the negative and use them independently in some of his utterances.

The third stage reflects the appearance of indefinite adjectives and pronouns and the progressive form of the verb in the child's language. Notice that the copular *be* is beginning to be used in Stage 3 but is optional, that is, sometimes it appears and sometimes it does not. In the fourth stage, *be* is obligatory in some forms and optional in others. It appears as though the child complicates his utterances a step at a time and the *be* copular verb, for example, appears first in the earlier, perhaps simpler, forms and becomes obligatory only after other aspects of the construction are well established. Later, *be* is added to other forms as they are incorporated into the child's language.

[2] The developmental levels in this table are defined in terms of mean number of morphemes per utterance, rather than age, because Brown and his colleagues (Bellugi, 1965; Brown *et al.*, 1968) have found that this measure provides a much more accurate guage of development than does age. The two children in Bellugi's study were 18, 22, and 25 months and 28, 32, and 38 months old, respectively, at the first three stages, supporting the contention that age varies considerably when utterance length and syntactic development are quite comparable.

Bellugi (1965) and Brown (1968) have also analyzed the interrogative development of the same two children plus a third child. (The third child is Sarah, whose parents did not have college backgrounds.) During the development of negative forms, the children were also learning the syntax of questions. The first three stages of development, with examples, are shown in Table 13-6.

Table 13-6

Stages in Child's Development of Interrogative[a]

Rule	Examples
Stage 1 (1.8–2.0 morphemes)	
a. S–Q	No ear?
	See hole?
	Mommy eggnog?
b. *What* NP (*doing*)[b]	What's that?
Where NP (*going*)[b]	Where Daddy going?
Stage 2 (2.3–2.9 morphemes)	
a. S–Q	You can't fix it?
	See my doggie?
	Mom pinch finger?
b. *Wh*–S	Who is it?
	What book name?
	Why not he eat?
Stage 3 (3.4–3.6 morphemes)	
a. Aux–NP–VP–Q	Can't you get it?
	Am I silly?
	Does turtles crawl?
b. *Wh*–NP–VP	Why you caught it?
	What we saw?
Wh–S (object questions; *do* optional, object NP optional and Aux is not moved)	Where my spoon goed?
Wh–VP (subject questions)	Who took this off?
	What lives in that house?

[a] See footnote *a* to Table 13-4. S: sentence; Q: utterance with rising intonation.
[b] Optional; may be omitted.

Comparing the development of the interrogative in Table 13-6 with the development of the negative in Table 13-5, it may be seen that the child is developing both syntactic structures at the same time, and there is a coordination in the development of the two structures. The child is acquiring the entire system all at once. Examining the two tables together, it can be seen that "can't" and "don't" appear in questions as well as negative declarative structures at the same stage of development. When "can" and "do" appear, they may be observed in negative, interrogative, and simple declarative affirmative sentences at about the same stage of development. Furthermore, other auxiliaries enter the system in all three types of sentences. Thus, the development of each structure may be recorded separately, but they are all coordinated in the sense that the development of all the structures is dependent upon a common core of elements. The acquisition of one element (e.g., auxiliaries or indefinite adjectives) is reflected by changes in all the larger syntactic structures or sentences.

One other point should be made about the development of these structures. The investigators noted that the responses of children to questions suggest that comprehension of interrogatives precedes or at least parallels production of interrogatives. In the first stage, for example, when the child is primarily using intonation contour, that is, a rising intonation at the end of the utterance, to indicate a question, he does not comprehend *wh* interrogatives ("why," "where," "when," "what," "who," "which"). His responses to questions such as "What are you doing?" are completely irrelevant to the question. Later, in the second stage, as he develops *wh* interrogatives in production, his answers to such questions are also appropriate, indicating comprehension. In fact, the child appears to comprehend questions of the *wh* form which are more complex than those he asks. A number of authors have suggested that a characteristic of language development is that comprehension precedes production. Some additional research relevant to this hypothesis will be presented later.

EXPANSION, REDUCTION, AND IMITATION. In the imaginary conversation between father and child which was presented earlier, the child's language can be examined from the point of view of the relation between what the child says and what the adult says when they are speaking to each other. It is obvious that the child's utterances bear some relation to those of the parent on a number of dimensions. The child's utterances are shorter, but they contain some of the same morphemes as the parent's utterances. The child appears to talk only in the present, since there is no indication of future or past tense. The parent tends to speak in relatively short and simple sentences to the child.

Brown and Bellugi (1964) have analyzed these relations in terms of the reduction of the adult utterance by the child and the expansion of the child's utterance by the adult. They pointed out that when the child imitates a parental utterance, he reduces its length but maintains the word order. This consistent preservation of word order implies that the adult sentence is processed by the child as a unitary construction and not as a list of words. A second observation is that there is no relation between length of parental utterance and length of child utterance. The child's imitative responses remain within the range of his spontaneous utterances in terms of length. If the child normally speaks in two or three morpheme lengths, then his imitations will also be about that same length regardless of the model utterance length. The child shortens the utterance of the adult in much the same way an adult shortens a message when sending a telegram. The high information or content words are retained and the functors (function words) are omitted. The nouns and verbs tend to be retained while the words with no semantic content and less stress in the sentence tend to be dropped out.

The child reduces the adult utterances; the parent in turn expands the child's utterances. The short incomplete utterances of the child are repeated with a stress contour and with the functors included. Just as the child preserves the word order in reducing the adult utterances, the adult preserves the word order in expanding the child's utterances. The parent frequently seems to be verifying his interpretation of the child's utterance when he responds by expanding. There often may be several interpretations of an utterance with respect to such things as tense of verb, prepositions, and declarative or question form. The parent seems to rely heavily upon the context in which the utterance occurs in formulating a particular expansion.

Ervin (1964) has examined the grammatical differences between the imitated utterances and the spontaneous utterances of the five children she has studied. Grammatical rules were written for the free utterances of the children, and then the children's spontaneous imitations of adult utterances were tested against the grammar to see if they were at the same or a more advanced grammatical level. While not denying that imitation may play some part in language acquisition, Ervin concluded, " . . . there is not a shred of evidence supporting a view that progress toward adult norms of grammar arises merely from practice in overt imitation of adult sentences" (p. 172).

Slobin (1965) attempted a finer analysis of children's responses to expansions to determine whether there might be circumstances under which the child does appear to be advancing his grammar through imitation of the parent. Specifically, he examined the exchanges between parent and child when the parent expanded something the child said and then the child imitated the expansion. Slobin found that under these conditions the child did expand his own previous utterance about half the time. Slobin argued that this particular type of exchange is an excellent teaching device, and that the child can advance his grammar in this manner. It seems, therefore, that Ervin's conclusion was too extreme, and that the child–parent reduction–expansion–reduction exchanges may play an important role in language acquisition.

Experimental Studies

A third approach to studying the language acquisition process consists of arranging artificial kinds of environments in which language may be used and examining the characteristics of the language children use in such situations. While not all of the studies using this procedure have been experimental, in the sense of manipulating some variable considered to be relevant to the language acquisition process, they have all provided standard situations in which the language responses of different children can be compared. These studies are artificial in a sense, but they do provide the laboratory control so necessary for the evaluation of most hypotheses and not possible with observations in the natural environment.

STUDIES OF WORD FORMS.   One of the early experimental efforts was a study conducted by Berko (1958) on the development of morphological rules. She was primarily interested in the child's acquisition of the inflections of verbs for past tense and of nouns for plural and possessive. In both cases, the adult has in English a set of three main forms, or allomorphs, which are conditioned, or determined, by the sounds that precede the inflection. For example, when you form the past tense of *punt, stop,* and *play,* you do so in three different ways, which you can hear as you say *punt* /-əd/, *stop* /-t/, and *play* /-d/. If the verb ends in /t/ or /d/ you use /-əd/, if it ends in /p k č f θ š/ you use /-t/, and for all other regular verbs you use /-d/ (see Table 13-1 for identification of the sounds symbolized). These are rules English speakers follow without usually being aware of them. The rule for plural forms in English is /-əz/ after words ending in /s z š ž č ǰ/, as in *glasses;* /-s/ after words ending in /p t k f θ/, as in *hits;* and /-z/ after all other regularly formed plurals. The possessive follows the same rules as the plural.

Berko's procedure was to present pictures of nonsense objects to children four to seven years of age and ask them to respond to questions about the pictures. For example, the child might be shown a card with pictures of three nonsense animals on it, one on top and two below. The experimenter would say to the child, "This is a niz /niz/ (or /wʌg/ or /bik/). Now there is another one. There are two of them. There are two ———." The child filled in the blank orally and the form of the response was recorded. Similar pictures and procedures were used to elicit the verb inflections for the past and progressive tenses and to elicit the possessive third person singular case. Some real words were also included to check on whether the children might have learned by rote some forms associated with particular words even if they did not know the rule and therefore could not generalize the rule to new instances.

The first thing of note about the results of this study is that the children had no trouble with the task. They knew what to do and why they were doing it; they appeared to be thinking about what endings should be used, although they were not always correct. In general, the children used appropriate inflections for all the forms examined, but there were differences in the percentage correct responses, correlated with the frequency with which the forms appear in the language. Thus, for example, the largest number of errors was made on the /-əz/ form of the plural, which is the least common form in the language. The children had the least trouble with the present progressive verb form, which is completely regular and may also reflect the child's tendency to be concerned primarily with the present. The /-t/ and /-d/ past tense forms of the verb were easiest; errors on the /-əd/ form were significantly greater. In general, percentage correct responses on all forms increased with age, although the differences between preschool and first grade children were significant on less than half the tested items. There were no sex differences on any of the measures.

It might also be noted that even though the children had most difficulty with the /-əz/ plural inflection, they made the fewest errors on the plural of the real word *glass,* which takes the /-əz/ form of plural inflection. There apparently is some rote learning involved in the development of the inflectional system prior to the actual use of the inflectional rule productively. However, the only form which not one of the preschool children (and only 25 percent of the first grade children) correctly inflected was the irregular verb *ring*, which takes *rang* as the past tense form. This finding is surprising since *ring* and *sing* are probably well known to children of this age.

In summary, the children seemed to follow a regular pattern of responding. Their responses were most likely to be correct on forms that are regular and frequent in the language. When the less frequent forms were called for, the children tended to collapse them with other forms to make a simpler version of the inflectional rule; that is, a rule with three allomorphic options in the model language was collapsed so that only two options were used rather than three.

The Berko procedure has been used by Templin (1966) as part of a larger study with kindergarten, first grade, and second grade children. Templin was primarily interested in the relation between children's articulation skills and the application of the morphological rules. Her results indicated the same kinds of developmental trends as reported by Berko. In addition, Templin found a substantial relation between scores on the Berko test and articulation scores, indicating that if articulation is poor then development of the inflectional system is likely to be poor.

Lovell and Bradbury (1967) have also used the Berko procedure, to test the morphological development of retarded children. They tested 10 boys and 10 girls, at each age from 8 to 15 years, who had IQs of 70 and were in special classes in school. Even the oldest of these children did not do as well as the first grade children in Berko's study, but the general order of difficulty of the items was the same as Berko reported. Surprisingly, there were no age trends apparent over the age range studied. However, scores on the Berko test correlated positively with IQ (.42) and reading age (.62). These results suggest that morphological rule learning of the sort evaluated by the Berko test may be complete by eight years of age and that the level of performance reached may be a function of general intellectual level. More research would be useful in evaluating such a hypothesis.

Guess, Sailor, Rutherford, and Baer (1968) showed that a morphological rule can be acquired through training on specific instances of the rule (as contrasted with training on the explicit rule). The rule was for the formation of plurals. An institutionalized mentally retarded girl, who previously had no speech (and had limited language comprehension), was taught to produce labels for objects in imitation of a model, and eventually could learn any new label in a single trial. Then she was taught labels of new objects and, at the same time, the labels for the plurals of these objects. The left portion of Figure 13-2 shows the child's progress during the plural learning stage. After the second word, she made no errors on new words; she learned each new label in a single trial and generated its plural with no prompting.

In the next phase, the reverse grammatical rule was taught, with a new set of words. In this phase, one doll (for example) was to be labeled "dolls," and two dolls were to be labeled "doll." The middle portion of Figure 13-2 shows the child's progress through this phase. As can be seen, she never achieved the same high level of mastery of this new rule as she had attained in the preceding phase, but she learned the singular of seven of the last ten words in one trial and generated their plurals with no prompting. The right portion of Figure 13-2 shows performance in the last phase of the program, in which the correct rule was again taught. The child clearly had learned to generate plurals.

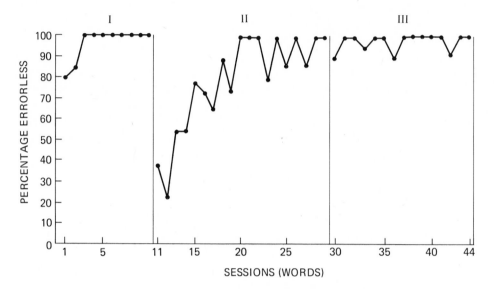

Fig. 13-2. Generation of plurals by a mentally retarded girl. One word was given in each session; the vertical axis shows the percentage errorless trials per session. I. Initial phase of learning. II. Reversal phase. III. Return to initial condition. (From Guess, Sailor, Rutherford, and Baer, *Journal of Applied Behavior Analysis*, 1968, *1*, 297–306. Fig. 1, p. 301. Copyright 1968 by the Society for the Experimental Analysis of Behavior, Inc. Reprinted by permission of the authors and publisher.)

Brown (1957) used much the same type of procedure as Berko, to evaluate children's concepts of the grammatical class of words. Brown's procedure consisted of showing pictures to children along with a verbal description of the picture. The description included a nonsense word referring to an action, a mass noun, or a count noun. The child's task was to select a second picture that depicted the referent of the nonsense word. For example, one set of pictures showed hands kneading something resembling confetti in a bowl. Depending upon whether the experimenter was referring to the kneading (verb), bowl (count noun), or confetti (mass noun), he said the picture described "someone nissing," "a niss," or "some niss." The child was then asked to identify which aspect of the picture was referred to by selecting one of the three pictures that showed the items separately.

Sixteen preschool children between the ages of three and five were tested. Of the 16, 10 correctly identified the verb, 11 the count noun, and 12 the mass noun. The results indicate that young children make use of syntactic cues when new words are presented to them in sentences. Syntactic cues cannot indicate the specific meaning of a word, but in indicating the grammatical class to which the word belongs, they can suggest the general type of meaning of the word.

Extending this general procedure further, Brown and Berko (1960) investigated the development of word class identification and its relation to responses on a word association test. They reasoned that as children gain experience with words, they learn the privileges of occurrence or grammatical class of those words in the language. This learning, they assumed, would be reflected in both the children's tendency to give words in the same grammatical class as the stimulus on a word association test and their ability to use the words correctly in their spontaneous speech.

They gave a word association test and a word usage test to 20 subjects in each of the first three grades and to a group of adults. The word association test consisted of 30 words, 5 from each of the following grammatical classes: count nouns, mass nouns, transitive verbs, intransitive verbs, adjectives, and adverbs. The usage test consisted of 12 sentences in each of which a nonsense word represented one of the 6 parts of speech. For example, a picture of a girl was shown to the subject and the experimenter said, "Do you know what a wug is? This is a girl thinking about a wug. Can you make up what that might mean?" The subjects' responses were scored on the basis of agreement of the meaning given with the part of speech represented.

There was an increase with age in the tendency to give responses in the same form class as the stimulus on the word association test and also an increase with age in the scores on the usage test. The scores on the two tests were highly correlated. The greatest number of responses in the same form class on the word association test was given to count nouns, followed in order by adjectives, intransitive verbs, transitive verbs, adverbs, and mass nouns. The order for correct responding on the usage test was very similar: Performance was best on the count nouns, followed in order by adjectives, intransitive verbs, transitive verbs, mass nouns, and adverbs. In both cases, performance on the count nouns and adjectives was far better than on the other parts of speech. It appears that the amount of experience children have with words in a particular grammatical class is a basic determinant of the degree to which that grammatical class functions in both a free association test and in natural language as measured by the usage test. Kean and Yamamoto (1965) obtained confirmatory results on a usage test for count nouns and transitive verbs in a study of kindergarten, second grade, and fourth grade children. In this experiment only two grammatical classes were used and low frequency real words were employed instead of nonsense syllables.

Finally, extending this general procedure even further, Fraser, Bellugi, and Brown (1963) examined the development of imitation, comprehension, and production in children's language development. The experiment was specifically designed to determine whether particular utterances, or features of utterances, are ordinarily understood before the same utterances are produced. Children were shown pictures about which verbal statements were made, and were asked to point to appropriate aspects of the pictures (to indicate comprehension), to repeat sentences about the pictures (to indicate ability to imitate), or to give appropriate utterances about the pictures (to indicate production ability). The test included 60 items, 6 for each of 10 contrasts not common in the spontaneous speech of children before four years of age. The contrasts included mass mouns versus count nouns, present progressive versus past tense, affirmative versus negative, subject versus object in a passive sentence, and the like. For example, the child might be shown a card with a picture of one sheep jumping over a fence on the left side and two sheep jumping over a fence on the right side. For the comprehension test, the child was asked to indicate in which picture the sheep "is" jumping over the fence and in which picture the sheep "are" jumping over the fence. The imitation test required that the child repeat both sentences correctly. In the production test, the child was given the two sentences, and then the experimenter pointed to one of the pictures and asked the child to give the appropriate sentence for that picture.

The imitation task was easiest, and comprehension was considerably better than production. These findings were consistent for individual subjects as well as consistent for all of the tasks used. The investigators suggested that imitation is a perceptual-motor task that is not dependent upon comprehension, and that sentences can be differentiated and retained without support of reference. In addition, of course, the results give support to the casual observation made by many observers of children's language development that children appear to comprehend distinctions in the language before they are able to produce these distinctions.

Palermo and Eberhart (1968) constructed a task requiring the learning of artificial rules, and designed the task to reflect performance similar to the natural acquisition of past tense inflection rules by children. When children learn the past tense inflections of verbs they learn the most frequent irregular inflections first (e.g., *was, ran, broke*), then the regular verb inflections (e.g., *walked, moved, printed*), and then they overgeneralize the regular inflection rule to the irregular forms and begin to say *runned, breaked,* etc. (Ervin, 1964). The Palermo and Eberhart study was a concept formation type of task based upon an experiment reported by Esper (1925). College sophomore subjects were required to learn a task in which there were rules with exceptions. As with children in the natural environment, the exceptions were learned first and then the rule was learned. Although the experiment was done with adults, the results were remarkably similar to those reported by Ervin (1964) for children's learning of past tense inflection of verbs; learning the rule led to overgeneralization errors in which the rule was applied to the irregular cases.

STUDIES OF SENTENCE CONSTRUCTION. The studies discussed up to this point have dealt primarily with words or parts of words. Other studies have been directly concerned with the larger units, sentences. Menyuk (1963a, 1963b, 1964a, 1964b), for example, has examined various syntactic forms in the sentence constructions of children. She obtained extensive samples of language from children in response to the Blacky Test,[3] conversations with an adult in connection with questions related to the Blacky Test, conversations with peers in a semistructured role-play situation involving three children, and recordings of spontaneous speech of the children. Her samples of children were drawn from nursery school, kindergarten, and first grade. The children ranged in age from two years and ten months to seven years and one month.

The extensive analyses performed by Menyuk are based upon an examination of the rules followed by the children in their sentence constructions relative to those used in the adult model language. She wrote grammars that described the children's utterances, and examined them to determine how the child's grammar is restricted in comparison to that of the adult speaker. In general, the results appear to parallel those of Berko (1958) in the sense that the children's constructions tend to exhibit simplified versions of the adult rules; where the adult may make several distinctions in the formulation of an utterance, the child makes only a few, with many omissions, redundancies, and substitutions apparent in his constructions. For example, the child may say such things as "that a car," in which the copular word *be* is omitted; "there is furnitures," where a redundant plural inflection occurs with the noun; or "it blowed out," in which *blowed* is substituted for *blew*. The general results indicated, however, that the three year old child uses almost all the basic syntactic structures employed by adults. Most aspects of the grammar have been acquired by the time the child is five years old; and improvement is very slow thereafter, although increasingly elaborated structures are used as the child gets older. The child appears to proceed from the most general rules to increasingly differentiated rules. Menyuk noted that the frequency of errors on particular types of constructions seems to follow a damped oscillatory function rather than a smooth growth curve to complete mastery of the grammar. The oscillations are caused by the use of increasingly complex rules in the grammar. The addition of new rules adds new errors, which are subsequently corrected before newer rules are added and cause new errors.

Words appear to be unitary for young children, in that preschool children seem to have difficulty in splitting words at the syllable boundary when asked to stop in the middle of saying a word. Huttenlocher (1964) noted that pairs of words in grammatical sequences also appear to be units for preschool children. She reasoned that if this were the case, children would have more difficulty in reversing the order of two words that form grammatical sequences, such as "he went," "pretty doll," and "I do," than in reversing a sequence of two unrelated words, letters, or numbers. Such tasks were presented to children between the ages of $4\frac{1}{2}$ and 5 years. Exactly as predicted, the children made significantly more errors in attempting to reverse the order of the grammatically related words, even when the reverse order was grammatical (e.g., "I do" to

---

[3] The Blacky Test, developed by Blum (1950), was designed as a projective personality test for children. It consists of a series of pictures of a black dog ("Blacky") in various situations, which the child is asked to describe.

"do I") than for letter pairs, number pairs, noun pairs, and anomalous word pairs such as "table goes." The latter tasks were all about equal in difficulty.

In a somewhat more extended investigation of syntax, Slobin (1966b) examined the development of the comprehension of active, passive, negative, and passive-negative sentences. His technique was to read his subjects a sentence and then present them a picture relevant to the sentence. The subject's task was to make a judgment as to whether the sentence was true or false relative to the picture. Table 13-7 gives the design of the experiment and examples of the sentences used.

The subjects in the experiment were 6, 8, 10, 12, and 20 years old, drawn from the kindergarten, second, fourth, and sixth grade, and college levels. The response measure in all cases was the amount of time taken between the exposure of the picture and the selection of one of two switches indicating congruence or incongruence between the sentence and the picture. The results indicated that if the sentences were true with respect to the pictures, the reaction times were shortest for the simple active sentences and increasingly longer for the passive, negative, and passive-negative sentences.

It had been anticipated that the negative sentences would be easier to comprehend than the passive sentences, since the grammatical derivation of the negative sentence is less complex than the passive sentence. It appeared, however, that the semantic problems associated with negative sentences were a more potent variable than the syntactic problems. Thus, the subjects had more difficulty in making a decision about the picture if the sentence contained a negative element than if the sentence was in the passive form. In general, these results were similar to results obtained with adults by Gough (1965), except that in contrast with his results, Slobin found that the children had great difficulty with true negative sentences. Some of the children would not accept any of the negative sentences as being true of the pictures.

All sentences in which the subject and object were not reversible were easier for the children than were the reversible sentences, and performance on the passive sentences was especially affected by reversibility. In fact, the passive construction was as easy as the active construction when nonreversible sentences were involved. It would appear that a part of the difficulty with passive sentences is in keeping track of which noun is the actor.

The age differences did not seem particularly important in the study. There was an improvement with age in the more complex sentence forms, but performance on the simple forms appeared to be relatively stable by the age of six.

In the Slobin study the subjects were given sentences and were asked to indicate whether the sentences correctly described a picture. Hayhurst (1967), in contrast, presented subjects with pictures and asked them to construct passive or passive-negative sentences to describe the pictures. Children of ages 5, 6, and 9.5 years were given pretraining by the experimenter in constructing the appropriate types of sentences to describe the pictures. The sentences the experimenter used were passive or passive-negative, with the subject actor of the sentence either present or absent (e.g., "The cat was chased by the dog" or "The cat was chased") and the subject and object of the sentences were either

Table 13-7

Design of Slobin Experiment and Samples of Sentences[a]

| | | Category | | |
| | | | | |
Truth	Affirmation	Grammatical type	Reversibility	Sample sentences[b]
True	Affirmative	Active	Reversible	The dog is chasing the cat.
False	Affirmative	Active	Reversible	The cat is chasing the dog.
True	Affirmative	Passive	Reversible	The cat is being chased by the dog.
False	Affirmative	Passive	Reversible	The dog is being chased by the cat.
True	Negative	Negative	Reversible	The cat is not chasing the dog.
False	Negative	Negative	Reversible	The dog is not chasing the cat.
True	Negative	Passive negative	Reversible	The dog is not being chased by the cat.
False	Negative	Passive negative	Reversible	The cat is not being chased by the dog.
True	Affirmative	Active	Nonreversible	The girl is watering the flowers.
False	Affirmative	Active	Nonreversible[c]	The flowers are watering the girl.
True	Affirmative	Passive	Nonreversible	The flowers are being watered by the girl.
False	Affirmative	Passive	Nonreversible[c]	The girl is being watered by the flowers.
True	Negative	Negative	Nonreversible[c]	The flowers are not watering the girl.
False	Negative	Negative	Nonreversible	The girl is not watering the flowers.
True	Negative	Passive negative	Nonreversible[c]	The girl is not being watered by the flowers.
False	Negative	Passive negative	Nonreversible	The flowers are not being watered by the girl.

[a] From Slobin (1966b). (Reprinted by permission of the author and Academic Press, Inc.)

[b] The picture for the reversible sentences showed a dog chasing a cat. The pictures for the nonreversible sentences showed a girl watering flowers.

[c] The sentences in these categories are anomalous.

reversible or not (e.g., "The dog was chased by the cat" is reversible because it is also sensible to say "The cat was chased by the dog").

The results, presented in Table 13-8, indicated that the children had least difficulty in constructing correct sentences in the passive form when the actor was omitted, regardless of whether they were positive or negative sentences.

If the actor was present, negative-passive sentences were too difficult for the two youngest groups to achieve any success. It was slightly easier for the oldest children to construct sentences when the actor and object were not reversible; but no differences were apparent for the youngest two groups, who did poorly in general on passives when both actor and object were present. An analysis of the errors made by the children in forming the passive sentences indicated that there was a tendency to convert the passive form into the active form of the sentence. The errors of the older children tended to be less deviant than those of the youngest children.

The results suggest a lack of comprehension of the passive form in the youngest children and a lack of ability to construct the passive form in the

Table 13-8

*Percentage Correct Replies by Age for All Sentence Types
in the Hayhurst Experiment[a]*

	Groups by mean age (years)		
Sentence type	5.0	6.2	9.5
Passive, actor not expressed	12.5	33.3	72.5
Passive-negative, actor not expressed	15.6	31.1	47.5
Passive, not reversible[b]	0.0	10.6	45.0
Passive-negative, not reversible[b]	4.2	8.3	27.5
Passive, reversible[b]	5.2	15.9	27.5
Passive-negative, reversible[b]	2.1	7.6	30.0

[a] After Hayhurst, 1967. (Reprinted by permission of the author and Academic Press, Inc.)
[b] Refers to reversibility of actor and object.

older children. The negative makes comprehension of the passive even more difficult for the youngest children to comprehend and more difficult for the older children to construct. When the subject and object of the sentence are nonreversible, this cue helps the older children to comprehend the sentences, but does not help the younger children. Omission of the actor in the sentence aids in the construction of the passive; for example, it is easier to construct the sentence "The cat is being chased" than to construct the sentence "The cat is being chased by the dog." The results of the Hayhurst and Slobin studies seem to complement each other nicely in showing the kinds of difficulty children have with passive and negative constructions.

Cazden (1965) designed an experiment to determine the influence of adult verbal responses on the development of children's language. The research focused on comparing the effectiveness of expanding the utterances of children as opposed to merely presenting a model of the language in the sense of providing samples of well-formed sentences. The subjects were 12 Negro children between the ages of 28 and 38 months attending an urban day care center. The children were divided into three groups matched on the basis of age, talkativeness, and initial level of language development measured in terms of mean length of utterance during the orientation period.

The experimenter spent 40 minutes each school day for three months with each of the four children in the expansion group, deliberately expanding the utterances of the children. A modeling group spent 30 minutes per day over the same period with the experimenter; an equal number of well-formed sentences was spoken to the child but no expansions were included. In other words, the experimenter responded to the children in the first group by expanding what they said and responded to the second group with normal conversation. A control group received no special treatment during the three month period. Tape recordings were made of the children's speech at the beginning, middle, and end of the three month period. Transcriptions of the tapes were scored on six measures of language development. The spontaneous speech of the children was coded for mean length of utterances, complexity of noun phrases, complexity of verbs, percentage of copulas included (a copula is a link verb, such as *be*), and percentage of sentences including both the subject and predicate. In addition, the children were scored on their ability to imitate sentences.

There was no evidence that expansion aids the acquisition of grammar. In contrast to the initial hypothesis, the children in the modeling group, with whom normal conversations were conducted, showed the greatest advance in language development on the measures used. To account for these results, it has been suggested that normal conversation increases the richness of the verbal stimulation, expands the ideas initiated by the child, and introduces more words and grammatical elements to express those ideas and related ideas. Expansion, however, merely repeats the same idea expressed by the child and does little more than echo what the child says (Brown *et al.*, 1968; Cazden, 1966). The results of this experiment, along with the Slobin (1965) analysis of the effects of parental expansions upon children's utterances, suggest that perhaps the ideal environment for child language development is one in which the parents expand the child's utterances both grammatically and semantically and thus provide both of the kinds of experiences necessary to the development of language.

Bandura and Harris (1966) attempted to manipulate the frequency of particular syntactic constructions in children's utterances through the use of operant conditioning techniques. Second grade children were shown nouns and induced to make up sentences; they were reinforced if the sentences were in the passive form or if the sentences included a prepositional phrase. The procedure involved obtaining a base rate for one of the syntactic constructions, followed by a period in which various reinforcement conditions were employed. The base rate for the two grammatical forms was obtained by having the children make up 20 sentences. The children were then divided into groups which differed with respect to the presence or absence of (a) an adult model who also made up sentences, (b) verbal reinforcement of the child's correct sentences, and (c) instructions designed to create a set to attend to the characteristics of the sentences which resulted in reinforcement. The children showed very low base rates for passive constructions and only a small increase as a function of the condition that included the modeling cues, reinforcement, and set. Prepositional phrases had a higher base rate and performance increased as a function of reinforcement and set conditions, although modeling cues did not contribute to performance. In the discussion of their results, Bandura and Harris implied that the acquisition of the abstract rules underlying language is brought about by similar procedures occurring in the natural interaction between children and their parents.

Brown *et al.* (1968) have provided data which suggest that the Bandura and Harris assumption may be considerably oversimplified, and perhaps false. They examined parent–child verbal interactions for occasions when the parents provided verbal reinforcement (or punishment) of the child's utterances. They found no evidence that approval or disapproval is contingent upon syntactic correctness. Instead, parental approval and disapproval tend to be contingent upon the truth value of the utterances of the child; somewhat paradoxically, "the usual product of such a training schedule is an adult whose speech is highly grammatical but not notably truthful" (Brown *et al.*, 1968).

Odom, Liebert, and Hill (1968) also provided data relevant to the Bandura and Harris hypothesis. They replicated the Bandura and Harris conditions and results, but also employed an ungrammatical control group. This group was given the combination modeling, reinforcement, and set condition for ungrammatical strings. The results showed that the children in this group could imitate the ungrammatical strings (although not quite as well as grammatical strings) but did not produce ungrammatical strings of their own. In fact, reinforcement for ungrammatical strings of the article-noun-preposition form actually increased the frequency of the grammatically correct preposition-article-noun form. As Odom *et al.* pointed out, "neither . . . [study] . . . offers a direct test of variables affecting language acquisition. . . . However, if language acquisition is to be comprehensively understood, it will become necessary to focus more on the nature and role of those internal processes which allow the child to recognize certain patterns of stimulation and, therefore, interpret what is being modeled" (p. 139).

An entirely different experimental approach to the understanding of language acquisition has been taken by Braine (1963a, 1966). His hypothesis is that children acquire grammatical structure on the basis of contextual generalization of morphemes, words, and phrases. When a child gains experience with one of these segments in a certain position and context, he will tend to place that segment in the same position in other contexts. Braine has conducted a series of experiments with artificial languages in an attempt to understand natural languages by analogy. For the most part he has conducted these experiments with fourth grade children, although he has been able to demonstrate the same phenomenon in one experiment with four year old children. The basic procedure involves teaching the child a miniature language composed of nonsense words embedded in a grammatical structure and testing for the production of new utterances not specifically taught to the child.

The most complicated of these languages (Braine, 1966) involved a structure of the form shown in Figure 13-3. The figure may be read: a sentence (S) may be constructed of an A phrase (A) preceded by a marker (f) and a PQ phrase (PQ) preceded by a marker (g) or the sentence may be constructed of the phrases in reverse order. An A phrase may be constructed of $a_1 + b_1$, $a_2 + b_2$, a_3, or a_4. A PQ phrase may be constructed as $p_1 + q_1$, $p_1 + q_2$, $p_1 + q_3$, $p_2 + q_1$, $p_2 + q_2$, etc. The brackets indicate that one of the lines within the brackets must be employed. The lower case letters refer to lexical items in the language. In the artificial language these were nonsense words, such as *yarmo* and *ged* (which were the obligatory markers of the phrases in this language). The

$$S \rightarrow \left\{ \begin{array}{c} (f\,A) + (g\,P\,Q) \\ g\,P\,Q + f\,A \end{array} \right\}$$

$$A \rightarrow \left\{ \begin{array}{c} a_1 + b_1 \\ a_2 + b_2 \\ a_3 \\ a_4 \end{array} \right\}$$

$$PQ \rightarrow \left\{ \begin{array}{cc} p_1 & q_1 \\ p_2 & q_2 \\ p_3 & q_3 \end{array} \right\}$$

$$f \rightarrow yarmo$$
$$g \rightarrow ged$$

Fig. 13-3. Form of artificial language used by Braine (1966). See text for explanation.

phrases within parentheses are optional and may be omitted; therefore, a sentence may consist of an fA phrase alone, a gPQ phrase alone, or both phrases. In contrast to natural languages, in which an infinite number of sentences is possible, this language is finite in that there is a maximum of 85 possible sentences in it, 72 long sentences and 13 short, or one-phrase, sentences.

The fourth grade children in this particular experiment were exposed to a sample of 20 long and 9 short sentences in the language. The sentences were constructed and presented in such a way that each segment in the language was presented 10 times in a total of 70 sentence presentations. (The 29 sentences were presented different numbers of times.) Following the learning phase, the children were presented with parts of sentences and three choices of words from the language to complete the sentence. For example, the child might be presented with a sentence such as f a_1 b_1 g — q_3 and asked to indicate whether

a_3, p_1, or q_1 would be the correct word for the blank in the sentence. The sentence frames presented on the test were novel—had not been seen before—and the correct choice involved the construction of a novel utterance. Correct responses, therefore, required knowledge of the rules for the internal structure of a sentence in this language.

The results of Braine's experiments clearly show that children can learn such artificial languages without great difficulty and that they understand the internal structure of the sentences in the sense that they can construct long and short sentences, recognize the markers, and distinguish the internal structure of phrases within the sentences.

SEMANTIC DEVELOPMENT

Analysis of the meaning of units within language is one of the toughest problems faced by linguist and psychologist alike. Faced with the ambiguity of the sentence, "They were entertaining speakers," it might be argued that the difference in meaning lies in the different syntactic structures associated with the two interpretations of the sentence. In one case "they" were entertaining and in the other case the "speakers" were entertaining. However, in the sentence "I stood near the bank," there is also ambiguity because "bank" may refer to a building or to the edge of a river. The problems of meaning are not simplified to any great extent by considering words or morphemes in isolation.

The linguist has often set the problem of semantics aside as outside his purview (e.g., Bloomfield, 1933), although more recently some efforts have been made to come to grips with the issues (e.g., Katz and Fodor, 1963). The psychologist has attacked the problem by attempting to analyze the connotation of words as opposed to the denotation of words, that is, the suggestive meanings of words as opposed to the direct specific meanings. Little effort has been made to deal with larger meaningful units. The development of the semantic differential scales by Osgood and his colleagues (Osgood *et al.*, 1957) has stimulated a good deal of psychological research bearing upon Osgood's theory of the acquisition of meaning through mediational processes. The theories of meaning proposed by Osgood and others (e.g., Skinner, 1957; Staats and Staats, 1963) have attempted to account for the development of the meaning of words in terms of conditioning models. These approaches have been severely criticized as being linguistically naive and theoretically inadequate (Chomsky, 1959; Fodor, 1965).

If one considers the developmental data alone, only a handful of studies bear on the problem, and they range from attempts to teach children the meanings of nonsense words by embedding them in sentences (Werner and Kaplan, 1952) to developmental investigations of the changes in word connotations as reflected by semantic differential ratings (Di Vesta, 1966). One could, of course, include all the literature on concept formation as relevant, since the acquisition of the meanings of words certainly is a concept formation task. The acquisition of meaning always involves concept formation, whether the category labeled includes a single instance (e.g., the child's "Daddy," as opposed to the larger category of "daddy"), several instances (e.g., "uncle"), many instances (e.g., "man"), or broader concepts (e.g., "animal"). Brown (1958b) discussed the category names or concepts presented to children in the course of natural language acquisition, what the child learns in terms of levels of abstractness, and how these categories and the hierarchies of abstraction may change toward concreteness or greater abstraction as the child grows older. The experimental literature on concept formation, however, has not dealt with meaning and will not be treated in this section. Only the studies dealing directly with the problem of meaning will be discussed.

Werner and Kaplan's experimental procedure consisted of presenting children a series of six sentences in which a nonsense word such as *corplum* was embedded: "A *corplum* may be used for support," "*Corplums* may be used to close off an open place," "A *corplum* may be long or short, thick or thin, strong or weak," "A wet *corplum* will not burn," etc. The child's task was to indicate after each sentence the meaning of the nonsense word (stick or piece of wood, in this case) and why he thought the word had that meaning. Twelve sets of sentences with 12 artificial words denoting either an object or an action were employed. Twenty-five children at each of five age levels from $8\frac{1}{2}$ to $13\frac{1}{2}$ years served as subjects.

As might be expected, correctness of responses increased with age, but the investigators were primarily interested in the various processes by which the children acquired the word meanings. In particular, they noted that as age increased the children gradually differentiated the meaning of the word from the sentence frames in which it appeared. The youngest children often moved a part of one sentence into the next sentence along with their interpretation of the word meaning, that is, there was a fusion of the single word with the whole sentence or parts of the sentence. In other cases, the meaning of the word was much too broad for the single sentence and the breadth of meaning changed from one sentence context to the next.

It is clear from the results of this study that the acquisition of meaning, at least through sentence contexts, is a complex process that hardly conforms to the simple view of association by pointing and labeling. The results also suggest that even though the children in the Brown and Berko (1960) study could use words in a grammatically correct manner after hearing them used in only two sentences, they may have had no clear meaning associated with the words. Recognition of grammatical class may narrow the meanings a word can have, and produce *correct* usage, but a great deal would remain to be learned before the word could be used meaningfully.

Ervin and Foster (1960) examined the difficulties children have in making distinctions among words that are frequently correlated in natural language. They chose to study aspects of the two semantic differential factors *evaluation* and *potency*. These two factors have been found in many studies, both in English and other languages, to show high loadings on the *good–bad, clean–dirty, happy–sad*, and *pretty–ugly* dimensions and the *heavy–light, strong–weak*, and *large–small* dimensions, respectively. The experimental procedure consisted of giving first and sixth grade children objects that varied from trial to trial on one of the potency dimensions—weight, strength, or size—and were constant on the other two potency dimensions. The children were asked to indicate which was heaviest, strongest, and largest. For example, the child was presented two opaque jars identical except for weight. The child was asked, "Is one of these heavier and one lighter or are they both the same?" The same question was asked for size and strength. The evaluation dimension was examined in connection with pictures of girls' faces.

The results indicated that the first graders were more likely than the sixth graders to give contaminated responses. Between 39 and 66 percent of the first grade responses and between 20 and 40 percent of the sixth grade responses indicated that if an object was big it was also strong and heavy, that is, the true physical difference led to incorrect statements about the other physical dimensions which did not vary. Very similar findings were obtained for the evaluation dimension, except that the effects were more marked in the first grade and were more likely to be reduced in the sixth grade. It appeared that 62 percent of the first grade children used *happy, good,* and *pretty* as synonyms in this situation. The investigators argued that although these words may be connotatively related for adults, they have specific denotative meanings, but for children the denotative meanings appear to be undifferentiated. The child's word concept is initially broad and many connotatively related words may be conceptualized as synonymous. Only as the words are used contrastively does the child learn to differentiate the individual denotative meanings.

Di Vesta (1964a, 1964b, 1965, 1966) has done a great deal of work investigating the development of the connotative meaning of words by use of semantic differential scales. Maltz (1963) had come to the conclusion that children's semantic space changes between Grades 2 and 6, on the basis of a limited study of the problem, but Di Vesta's extensive and careful studies suggest that the dimensions of the child's semantic space are quite stable by Grade 2. While there are some hints in the results reported by Di Vesta that connotative meaning grows from a primarily evaluative to a dual evaluative and dynamic or activity dimension, and eventuates in the three major adult dimensions of evaluation, potency, and activity, it seems clear that the three factors account for most of the variance in the meaning system of second grade children as well as adults. Di Vesta concluded that efforts to extend this work to younger children will be required before any clear picture of the development of connotative meaning will be revealed. These results are congruent with the findings of Flavell and Stedman (1961) on children's judgments of the semantic similarity of words.

In summary, there has been little headway made in determining how we acquire the meanings of words. The conditioning models proposed by Staats (e.g., Staats and Staats, 1957; Staats, Staats, and Heard, 1961) seem too simple to handle a problem of this complexity, and yet little else has been advanced even to stimulate any systematic research in this area. Other studies related to the problem of meaning have been conducted in connection with generalization (Riess, 1946) and mediation (Di Vesta and Stover, 1962; Eisman, 1955) and, in addition, studies by Luria (1961) and more recently by Birch (e.g.,

1966) on the control of motor behavior might be conceived as related to meaning. These studies, however, are not directly relevant here, and the topics are discussed elsewhere in this text.

THEORETICAL ACCOUNTS
OF LANGUAGE ACQUISITION

Relative to the amount of available data pertaining to language development, there has been no shortage of theoretical accounts of how language is acquired. Perhaps the lack of data makes it easy for those who are theoretically inclined to wax eloquent about how the process occurs without fear of running into contrary evidence. The theories proposed, however, are worth serious consideration because they suggest radically different orientations toward the field of psychology in general even though the theories are directed toward accounting for language in particular.

On one end of the range there are conditioning theories such as those proposed by Mowrer (1960) and Staats (1964). The conditioning or learning theories have been elaborated to include mediational processes to aid in accounting for meaning (Osgood, 1953) and syntax (Jenkins and Palermo, 1964; Osgood, 1963; Palermo, in press). In addition, Braine (1963a) has proposed a contextual generalization theory of syntactic acquisition which is broader in some respects than the mediation theory. All of these approaches grew out of the traditional empiricist orientation of the psychologist trained within the behavioristic scientific background. There are certainly differences among these theoretical approaches but, in general, they all accept the same basic underlying assumptions about language behavior, or any other kind of behavior, and accept the same kinds of research approaches and data as relevant to testing the theories. As Kuhn (1962) would say, in writing about the nature of scientific revolutions, all of these theorists are working within the same scientific paradigm.

In contrast, others attempting to account for the facts of language acquisition have approached the field within another paradigm. The theoretical accounts proposed by McNeill (1966a, 1966b, in press), Slobin (1966b). Lenneberg (1967), and Wales and Marshall (1966), for example, all take a rationalist rather than an empiricist position. Associated with this position is a much heavier emphasis on nativism. These theorists take a mentalistic as opposed to a behavioristic approach to language processes and behavior in general. They conceptualize the subject matter of the field within an entirely different paradigm and, as a result, the theoretical orientations are quite different, the research of interest is different, and relevant types of data are quite different.

The approach taken by these latter theorists is not entirely new to psychology for it is strongly reminiscent of Gestalt psychology, the orientation of Vygotsky (1962), and to a lesser extent the approach of Piaget to developmental psychology (see Chapter 14). Historically, it is particularly interesting to note, however, that the earlier psychologists who worked within this framework were not responsible for swaying the theorists in question. The powerful arguments for taking a new orientation toward language and the acquisition of language were brought about by the revolutionary insights presented by Chomsky (1957, 1965) in the field of linguistics. The introduction of the concept of transformational rules along with a reconceptualization of the goals of linguistics as an explanatory rather than merely a descriptive science has entirely changed the field of linguistics and may well have a marked effect upon psychology. Chomsky's (1959) review of Skinner's (1957) book on verbal behavior clearly set the stage for a conflict of paradigms within psychology. It is possible that we shall see a reorientation toward the field of psychology similar to the one that occurred when behaviorism replaced introspectionism. (It might be noted, incidentally, that the chief competition for the allegiance of psychologists at the time of the behavioristic revolution was Gestalt psychology.) It is too early to tell how important this conflict of paradigms may be to psychology, but there is little question that psychologists who are interested in language will have to give it serious thought and take a stand on the issues involved.

No effort will be made here to go into linguistics in any more detail than is necessary to present the theories. An excellent introduction to transformational linguistics may be obtained from Langacker (1968) or Jacobs and Rosenbaum (1968). Other helpful sources include Dinneen (1967), Bach (1964), Koutsoudas (1966), and Thomas (1965), as well as the original sources by Chomsky cited earlier. The philosophical background may be obtained from Katz (1966). Regardless of whether one wishes to approach the study of language acquisition within a mentalistic or behavioristic framework, it is certainly essential that one know some linguistics in order to understand the structural characteristics of the responses being acquired.

For the purposes of the present discussion, it seems sufficient to summarize three theoretical points of view on language acquisition: a theory based largely on a traditional conditioning model, a theory relying primarily on mediation and deriving from the work in the area of verbal learning, and a theory based primarily on the insights of linguistics.

Conditioning Theory

Staats has argued that language acquisition can be explained with the principles of classical and instrumental conditioning (Staats, 1961, 1968, in press; Staats and Staats, 1963). He felt that the previous efforts of learning theorists have failed because those who have attempted to use conditioning models have limited themselves to inadequate learning theories (e.g., Osgood, 1953), have failed to use the complete set of conditioning principles available (e.g., Mowrer, 1954, 1960; Skinner, 1957), and have been concerned with only limited aspects of the problem of language. Staats felt that a broad application of the principles of classical and instrumental (operant) conditioning can be applied to account for all aspects of language—speech and meaning. It is necessary to give serious consideration to both types of learning and to the interaction of the two types of learning.

Staats began by assuming that the early vocalizations of the infant are differentially reinforced such that the child more and more frequently emits the sounds associated with his particular language community and drops out the sounds of other languages. In addition, he adopted the hypothesis of Mowrer (1960) that the vocalizations of the parents in association with positive reinforcers, such as food in the feeding situation, lead to the parental voices taking on secondary reinforcing qualities. Subsequent generalization of the reinforcement value of the parents' voices to the child's own vocalizations results in the vocalizations of the child becoming reinforcing in and of themselves. Thus, the direct reinforcement by the parents for the particular speech sounds of the language and the self-reinforcement of the infant lead to the child's gradual acquisition of sounds and then syllables and, finally, words.[4]

Approximations to words are reinforced and the speech of the child is shaped through the process of differential reinforcement as the parent begins to restrict the reinforcement to better and better approximations of particular words. Once the child is saying words, the words become units and the child begins to match his behavior to that of others in the sense that if the parent says, "Say 'water,'" the child will be reinforced if he repeats the word. He does not, at this stage, have to build up the individual sounds into the unit, "water." The successive approximation is short circuited because words are now the units under the control of the appropriate speech sound stimuli of the parents. The verbal responses may also come under control of environmental stimuli that are non-verbal in nature. The child is continually reinforced for labeling objects in his environment and, thus, he learns to say "Daddy" in the presence of his father, "car" in the presence of a car, and so on. In addition, internal stimuli such as are associated with hunger or thirst can act as stimuli for verbal responses when the verbal responses are reinforced by food and water.

In such ways, many stimuli come to control many verbal responses. Any particular response occurrence is dependent upon the stimulus complex present at that time and is a function of the strength of that response to that stimulus relative to the strength of other competing responses that may be present at the time. Language itself becomes, therefore, both a stimulus and a response. The child acquires language responses that in turn act as stimuli for other language responses, and the verbal behavior of the child becomes very complex rather early in the language acquisition process.

Once the child has a repertoire of words, he begins to hook them up in two-word utterances as his learning skills improve to the extent that grammatical speech can occur. It is not a matter of maturation but rather a function of the training procedures introduced by the parents. The child may utter a single word response which the parent expands into a sentence. The child learns to construct longer utterances because the parent does not allow reinforcement to occur until the child imitates the expansion. Staats suggested that such expansions frequently take the form of adding a single word to many other single

[4] As noted in Chapter 10, most of the phenomena explained by reference to secondary reinforcement can be explained equally well by reference to other concepts, and there are certain advantages in using these other concepts. However, they could be substituted for "secondary reinforcement" in Staats's theory without changing its explanatory power.

words which the child utters. For example, the child may say "milk" or "bread" or "apple," which the parent expands by saying "Milk, please," "Bread, please," and "Apple, please," and withholds reinforcement until the child provides some approximation to the parent's two-word utterance. Thus, the parental utterances become discriminative stimuli which bring about the expansion of the child's language and, again, response hierarchies of word–word relationships are developed. In addition, after the child has learned to respond "man" to many physical *man* stimuli and, for example, "running" to many instances of *running*, seeing both a *man* and *running* simultaneously may elicit the response "man running" or "running man." Thus, the external stimuli as well as the specific training by the parents may bring about two-word utterances.

Since words have particular privileges of occurrence in sentence frames, the child learns grammatical habits which take the form of the sentence structures

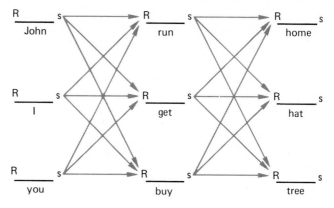

Fig. 13-4. Example of the kinds of learned interconnections that are assumed in Staats's theory to occur in strings of words.

used by adults. The child, for example, hears such things as "See the house," "Own the car," and "Walk the dog," and learns the stimulus conditions for the occurrence of the word "the." In addition, the words that follow "the" are conditioned to the word "the." In a very short period of time, words come to be interconnected with other words in rather complex ways, but since particular words have particular privileges of occurrence, only certain words get conditioned to other words. Figure 13-4 gives an example of the kinds of learned interconnections that may occur in strings of words. It may be seen that a large number of sentences can be generated as a function of the associations that have been conditioned among the words in the illustration. In addition, it will be noted that non-sentences such as "run I hat" do not occur because "run" does not have the privilege of occurring before "I," having been conditioned to occur after "I," and "hat" similarly occurs only after "run" (or one of the other verbs). As more words become conditioned to the vocabulary of the child in the appropriate grammatical environments, the interconnections become highly complex. Eventually, however, some of the two- and three-word sequences become unit responses, and they can become inserted into other grammatical sequences. The length of the children's utterances increases, not as a function of a maturational increase in memory span, but as a function of an increase in the skilled vocal responses and associations between sequences of hierarchies of responses which the child learns. Such sequences involve the conditioning of words to their inflections, words to other words, and sequences of words to other sequences of words.

While the child is learning to build up his repertoire of words and to formulate grammatical sequences, he is also learning the meanings of words. The initial contact a child has with a word is meaningless in the sense that no responses have been conditioned to that word stimulus. The originally neutral stimulus comes to have meaning through responses that are classically conditioned to it. Thus, a word such as "no" comes to stand for the actual aversive stimuli associated with it through the conditioning process. Initially, words need to be conditioned directly, but, as the child acquires the meanings of some words, these words, in turn, can be used as unconditioned stimuli for conditioning the meanings of other words. Thus, the child builds up a repertoire of meanings or responses to words, which vary as a function of responses that are conditioned to them.

In summary, Staats argued that language behavior, in all its complexity, is reducible to the simple principles of classical and instrumental conditioning which have proven so valuable in the analysis of many kinds of behaviors by all kinds of animals in various laboratory tasks. The complexity arises not from the character of speech or its meaning, but from the number of stimuli and responses involved in the control of the behavior and from the fact that several simultaneous learning principles may be operating at the same time in bringing about the behavior. Thus, the stimuli for language (Staats was more inclined to call it "speech") may be the speech of others, the overt and the covert speech of the person speaking, internal physiological responses, written words, meanings of verbal responses, stimuli produced by motor behaviors, and all other stimuli that may be present at the time of the speech act. The responses include emotional and sensory reactions that define meaning, sounds produced, syllables, inflectional parts of words, words, phrases, and sentences. The reinforcement comes from external primary reinforcers, parental approval and disapproval, and the self-reinforcement of speech *per se*. All of these stimuli and responses are being conditioned at the same time by classical conditioning, instrumental conditioning, and the interactions of these processes. Herein lies the complexity of language. Staats argued that language can be explained only within the general framework that provides an analysis of the stimuli and responses and establishes causal relations between the two.

Mediation Theory

While Staats's theoretical account is basically a learning theory, it draws primarily from a tradition of animal learning with an effort to take principles from both the Hullian (Hull, 1943) and Skinnerian (Skinner, 1957) positions to form an amalgamation that will account for language. The mediation theories advanced to account for language also grew out of a learning orientation that was influenced by the same roots, but these theoretical accounts have drawn much more heavily upon the verbal learning field of psychology, emphasizing the kinds of research surveyed in Chapter 6 and in the sections on mediation in Chapter 7. Thus, Osgood, Jenkins, Palermo, and others associated with this theoretical orientation have as their background a long association with research in the verbal learning area.

JENKINS AND PALERMO.   Jenkins and Palermo (1964) and Palermo (in press) have attempted to account for the acquisition of syntax within this general orientation.[5] They have argued that language acquisition is basically not different from the learning of any other kind of behavior. One needs to analyze the environment of the developing child for the potential contextual and linguistic stimuli that are impinging on the receptors of the organism and determine which of those potential stimuli are functional stimuli. Analysis of language development will involve establishing lawful relations between the functional stimuli and the linguistic responses of the child. Such relations will resemble the kinds of learning studied in the paired associate task. Thus, in the pairing of environmental stimuli, whether they be visual, auditory, or of other kinds, with the verbal responses of the child, at least the appropriate contiguous relationships in time must be maintained in order for learning to occur. It will be necessary for the initially meaningless auditory sounds to be integrated into word units, which in turn will be easier to learn as they become more meaningful to the child. Once response integration has occurred, the child will be able to associate these word responses with the appropriate stimuli just as in the paired associate task in the experimental laboratory.

It is assumed that the child begins language learning by imitation with appropriate reinforcements. Gradually, the child builds a repertoire of simple stimulus-response connections between verbal labels and salient features of the environment. The parent places objects before the child and labels them, indicating the observable characteristics of the objects in adjective, noun, and verb forms. Thus, the single-word utterances of the child tend to be content words such as "ball," "Mommy," "big," "go," "allgone," and so on. These are labels and descriptions of objects and events that have clearly observable correlates.

When the child has acquired a small vocabulary of word responses to appropriate stimuli, he begins to attach words to other words in sequences, and the ordering or structuring of language begins. It is assumed that some of the single word utterances of the child occur under the same or similar stimulus conditions. Under these circumstances the child is assumed to form classes of words through mediational processes directly related to the stimulus and response equivalence paradigms studied in paired associate learning. For example,

_____
[5] It should be noted that the mediation theoretical model presented here has been abandoned by both Jenkins and Palermo as inadequate to the explanation of language behavior (e.g., see Palermo, 1970).

the child may obtain a ball which is on the shelf by saying "want" or he may obtain the ball by saying "ball." Sometimes he says "want" and sometimes he says "ball," and both utterances may bring about the desired results. The situation is directly analogous to the response equivalence paradigm in which two different responses are learned to the same stimulus, leading to the establishment of associations between the two responses. Thus, the occurrence of both responses in this situation will lead to an increase in the probability that "ball" will occur to "want" and the child will begin to utter the two-word utterance "Want ball." Once this utterance has been established, the child may say such things as "Want truck," "Want milk," and "Want Mommy," which will lead to the establishment of a pivot-open type of construction in which "want" is the pivot word and "ball," "truck," "milk," and "Mommy" all become an open class of words with similar privileges of occurrence and may be substituted for each other under the appropriate stimulus conditions. Subsequently, if the child learns "Allgone truck" it would be predicted, according to mediation theory, that the child would also be likely to say such things as "Allgone milk," "Allgone Mommy," and so on. Thus, new utterances may occur without prior training by the substitution of previously acquired equivalences.

Once the child has built a number of two-word utterances, these in turn may become integrated units and occur in the presence of other words so that the child may build longer and longer sentence structures. Such elaborations of the grammatical structures of the child, of course, do not occur independently of the verbalizations of the other people around the child. The parents, for example, are continually talking to the child, and their speech emphasizes some words more than others. The stressed words in the parents' language are the ones the child is most likely to learn first, and only when the less stressed or function words make a difference in the communication process will they be emphasized and pointed out to the child. Thus, the first words the child learns are most likely to be the content words, which include nouns, adjectives, and verbs. At this stage in the child's development, he speaks what has been referred to as "telegraphic speech." The function words will come in later as the child learns that such words as "the," "and," "of," and "under," for example, make a difference in the communication process.

As the child's syntax develops, he begins to ask questions, negate sentences, embed sentences in other sentences, and so on, and in general his syntax gets more complex. Such complexities involve transformational rules, according to the linguists. It is assumed in mediation theory that such transformations are initially learned independently and are facilitated by semantic mediation. Thus, the child learns to append the word "no" to a sentence unit and develops a new equivalence of responses based upon the semantic concept of negation. The basic adult classes of structure will be acquired on the basis of more specific equivalences. In particular, the child will begin with broad conceptual categories developed on the basis of mediation, and subsequently he will make finer and finer differentiations within categories based upon discriminations that limit or subdivide the broader categories which were initially established.

In summary, it is assumed that the child begins with those aspects of the language which are more salient to him and learns individual words followed by the grouping of those words into classes and the subsequent grouping of classes into larger units which also become classes. The process of acquiring the complete adult syntax is a matter of expanding and contracting constructions by this process on the basis of discriminations and generalizations which occur as the child learns those utterances which lead to efficient communication relative to other utterances which are followed by confusion.

Osgood. The theoretical efforts by Jenkins and Palermo have focused primarily upon grammatical development; Osgood has used a similar mediational

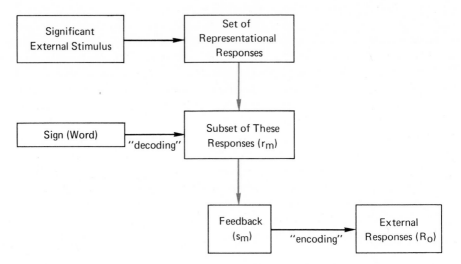

Fig. 13-5. Outline of Osgood's theory of the development of meaning. See text for explanation.

theory to account for the development of meaning in language. Osgood (1968) has argued that the mediating processes invoked by Jenkins and Palermo need to be expanded to include a representational mediating response to account for the symbolic processes. The representational mediating response is not a single reaction based upon a single word response but is, rather, a multicomponent affair. Thus, the representational mediating response consists of a complex of mediators, including affective, motor, verbal, and physiological responses. The young child makes a total set of responses to a significant (external stimulus) in his environment and some proper subset of these responses is made to the signs, or words, associated with the significant. These mediating responses may in turn have their own stimulus properties to which a whole host of new responses may become conditioned.

Thus, as shown in Figure 13-5, meaning begins with the establishment of implicit nonlinguistic responses (r_m), with their consequent automatic motor-sensory feedback (s_m), and the establishment of additional responses (R_o) to the latter stimuli. In Osgood's terms, the sign–r_m aspect of the conditioning represents the decoding aspect of language and the s_m–R_o aspect is the encoding aspect of language. The mediators may consist of minimal, difficult-to-observe reactions of the peripheral system, along with feedback, or they may consist of purely central representations of what were originally peripheral events. (In addition, Osgood postulated an integration level which includes s-s and r-r learning based upon frequency, redundancy, and contiguity principles which do not require reinforcement. This level was introduced so that the theory could account for Gestalt data on perception and the linguistics notion of words as psychological units of meaning.)

Mentalistic Theory

A quite different theoretical point of view on language acquisition has been articulated by McNeill (1966a, 1966b, 1968, in press). He argued that learning theories such as those just discussed are inadequate in principle to account for language acquisition because the process of acquiring language involves the discovery of the relations between the surface structures, or overt manifestations of language, and the underlying abstract, or deep, structures of language. The underlying structures of language are assumed to be universal in all languages and to represent the innate capacities of all children.

Clearly, such a point of view is unfamiliar to most psychologists, because it rejects the orientation toward the subject matter of the field which has been dominant since the days of John B. Watson. Hence, it will be necessary to try to make clear just what is being claimed and what it may mean for research in the psycholinguistics area if this point of view is accepted.

The acquisition of the native language, McNeill maintained, is an interaction between the linguistic experience of the child and his innate linguistic capacities. In other words, the child has some capabilities or predispositions with respect to language which are biologically determined. In addition, the child must have some interaction with the language in his environment in order to acquire a particular language. This claim is not particularly unusual, in the sense that most learning theorists would agree that the biological characteristics of the organism are, in some way, related to the experiences that the organism has and, therefore, the interaction of the two determines behavior. The difference is that learning theorists have focused primarily upon the environmental variables in attempting to account for language acquisition, while McNeill has placed a much heavier emphasis on the biological characteristics of the organism in determining the language behavior of the child. Thus, McNeill argued that any theory of language acquisition should describe the innate capacities of the child and how they interact with experience to bring about the automatic, natural, effortless, and very rapid acquisition of the native language.

McNeill felt that such an orientation has been forced upon any theory of language acquisition by the recent analyses of language precipitated by the transformational generative grammar advanced by Chomsky (1957, 1965). Many linguists have argued for some time that one must postulate an underlying abstract structure for language which is different from the actual manifestations of language in the speech of those who use the language. The postulation of an underlying abstract system, or set of relations among the concepts expressed in a sentence, is required by paraphrase and ambiguity. Since all speakers of English know that the sentence "John ran the race" means the same thing as "The race was run by John," there must be some underlying abstract relation between the two sentences. Similarly, "Elmer selected a tie" is a paraphrase of "Elmer picked out a tie." In the first case, the underlying abstract relations involve syntax; in the second case, the abstract relations involve semantics. In both cases, linguists have made some progress in demonstrating that there are abstract structures underlying such sentences and that there are rules that can be applied to show the relation between the two structures.

The rules are general, in the sense that they apply to an infinite number of sentences, so that the same rule is applied to show the relation between "John ran the race" and "The race was run by John," for example, and between "Horatio's wife, who works in the zoo, sent the package" and "The package was sent by Horatio's wife, who works in the zoo." Thus, in the case of paraphrase, two different language expressions may be shown to have the same underlying abstract structure with rules which specify the relations between the two different manifestations. The abstract underlying structures are referred to as *deep structures,* the manifestations are referred to as *surface structures,* and the rules relating the two kinds of structures are called *transformational* rules.

In the case of ambiguity, two different deep structures are associated with the same surface structure. For example, "They were entertaining speakers" may be interpreted as having the underlying structure in which "entertaining" modifies "speakers," or it may have the underlying structure in which "entertaining" is the main verb with "they" as the subject. Only by postulating an underlying abstract structure for each of the two different interpretations can these two different sentences be distinguished.

The linguistic analysis of language makes it clear that all sentences are composed of a manifest part and an abstract part. The deep structure contains the description of the syntactic and semantic relations which, by means of transformational rules, are converted to a surface structure which, in turn, may be converted into an actual utterance by means of phonological rules. The phonological rules specify the sound combinations and stress patterns to be used in uttering the sentence. When a person can speak the language, he has, therefore, a knowledge of the semantic rules, syntactic rules, and phonological rules of that language. It is this knowledge that has been referred to as the speaker's *competence* with respect to his language. Competence is contrasted with *performance,* which refers to speech, because speakers of the language do not always demonstrate their competence in their performance. A professor lecturing in class, for example, deviates from the underlying structure of his language by doing such things as failing to speak in complete sentences or failing to have his subject and predicate agree in all sentences. This does not mean that he lacks the knowledge of what a sentence is or what the agreement rules are. He knows these rules, but he does not always follow them because many psychological variables may influence his performance.

This analysis of language behavior, as McNeill argued, requires an entirely different theoretical approach to account for language acquisition. Since the deep, or abstract, aspect of language is never presented in the surface structure, it can never be a stimulus. It is for this reason that a learning theory cannot be applied to language acquisition; learning theories argue that language is a response acquired in the presence of particular stimuli. McNeill argued instead that the development of linguistic abstraction is a mental and not a behavioral phenomenon. The child must take the language he hears and construct a theory of the grammar or underlying structure which is appropriate to the language he hears. Since the child is able to do this in a matter of two or three years and since both dull and bright children appear to learn any language that may happen to be presented to them in their environment, whether Swahili, Japanese, Russian, or English, there must be some universal characteristics of language that correspond to the native abilities of the child. Thus, the child is assumed to be predisposed to look for, analyze, or abstract some aspect of the incoming speech of other people and fail to focus on other aspects of it.

It is this predisposition which McNeill referred to as the child's native capacities. The child responds to the universal aspects of language and ignores other aspects of language. He discovers the universal features of language because he is predisposed to do so. He will discover that the phonological system is made up of vowels and consonants and a limited set of distinctive features which distinguish sounds. He will be constrained with respect to semantic concepts. He will conceptualize noun phrases in particular relations to verb phrases. He will consider only certain transformational relations between the abstract or deep structure and the surface structure. These universal categories and relations will be evident in his language because they are innate to the human organism. Language acquisition, then, consists of relating the universal characteristics of language—that is, the things that are true of all languages—to the particular language the child is learning. The child learns transformational rules which convert the universal aspects of all languages to the specific aspects of his language.

Since this is assumed to be the case, the child should begin with utterances that manifest the universals and, as he learns the transformations, he should modify the abstract universals to conform to the specific language being acquired. The study of language acquisition is, therefore, the study of transformational-rule learning. Such rule learning may take place by the progressive differentiation of gross generic categories or by the progressive identification of the features that determine how the surface aspects of language are related to the deep structures of language. Which of these latter two alternatives may be correct will be revealed by an examination of the characteristics of the language observed in the developing child. At the present time no one really knows how, why, or when these discoveries of the relations between surface and deep structures are made by the child. McNeill suggested, however, that acquisition probably occurs in a stepwise manner as the child notices successive relations. Certainly no practice is needed but, instead, the child develops hypotheses about the relations which tie surface to deep structures. Once these hypotheses are verified, they are applied in the child's comprehension and production of language. The child moves from one stage to another as the relations are noticed, rather than gradually acquiring a response as a learning approach might imply.

Research strategy within this theoretical framework would be quite different from that suggested by the two previously discussed theoretical points of view. Experiments on how the child is able to learn new combinations of already known relations should be the focus, rather than the typical learning experiment in which the learning of new arbitrary relations is studied. In addition, the syntax of language should be examined to determine the kinds of relations that might be of interest. Such relations are not arbitrary as in the typical learning experiment. The relations observed in syntax are natural and therefore lead to much more rapid learning than is seen in the typical laboratory experiment. In addition, of course, the examination of the language acquisition process itself, the characterization of the rules learned, and the identification of the variables that may influence the discovery of these rules would be of particular interest.

SUMMARY

Language is a highly complex form of behavior entailing systems of sounds, grammar, and meaning, which in combination allow man to communicate with man. The process by which the child changes from an inarticulate organism, much like many other kinds of animal, to the unique, highly articulate organism that is an adult human has long defied understanding. The phenomenon has seemed so complex that few scientists have exerted any significant effort toward attempting an understanding, although some have naively tried to account for it within rather simple theoretical systems based upon research little related to language. At this moment in scientific history, however, there appears to be a serious, concerted effort by individuals in a number of disciplines to examine the multifaceted puzzle of language. Linguists have presented a challenge, and psychologists, anthropologists, sociologists, speech scientists, educators, and many others are taking up the challenge from their varying points of view. There is an optimism and excitement in the field which foretells insights unsuspected up to now.

The field of linguistics is moving particularly rapidly. The phonologists are delving more deeply into the characteristics of the distinctive features and the rules that apply to the phonological component, or sound system, of language. The grammarians are not satisfied with the early analyses of the underlying structure of sentences and the relation of that structure to semantics. Advances in semantics lag behind, as is traditional, but there seems to be some agreement about the general form that a semantic theory might take.

The behavioral scientist, however, is often in a quandary about where to begin. What kind of research is relevant? How can one contrive experiments that will take into account the linguistically relevant variables and yet produce nontrivial results? The fact that the child acquires so much of the complex language system—sound, syntax, and semantics—in such a short time is strong support for the argument that there is something about the child which makes him especially "tuned," "wired," or "built" to do the job. But what research will answer questions related to this uniqueness of the child? The field is ripe for new ideas, and as they come the study of language should become even more exciting.

The subfield of developmental psycholinguistics is in a turmoil. Traditional research techniques and theories are being challenged and new approaches to the problems are being advanced. It seems clear that some background in linguistics is required to understand what language is and in order to be able to work on the relevant problems. There is little question that the study of language behavior will be a central concern of many psychologists in the near future, and if some form of the theoretical position espoused by McNeill proves fruitful, there will be marked conceptual changes in the field. Furthermore, it is likely that these changes will spill over into the rest of psychology and lead to a new orientation toward the entire science. Only history will tell whether the new challenges being advanced today will have such widespread effects on the field.

CHAPTER 14

Cognitive Development

INTRODUCTION

Cognition has to do with the processes of knowing and with the product of these processes, knowledge itself. From a developmental point of view, the problem of cognition is to describe the growth of concepts in the child and to detail the processes by which these concepts are acquired and put to use. Although there was widespread interest in children's thinking early in this century, it subsequently diminished, and only within the past decade has a developmental psychology of cognition become a substantive area of research within psychology. Indeed, the research literature in this area has already become so vast that only a limited segment of it can be surveyed here.

To a large extent the renaissance of interest and research in cognitive development is attributable to the monumental work of Jean Piaget, the Swiss psychologist. Although Piaget began his investigations into children's thinking in the 1920s, the work went almost unrecognized until the middle 1950s. At that time public schools came under attack for failing to teach children how to think; the attack led to the discovery of Piaget's writings or, better, rediscovery since there had been a quickly melted flurry of interest in the 1930s. It was Piaget's long standing concern with the development of children's mathematical and scientific concepts and with the processes involved in their acquisition that attracted the attention of those concerned with designing new curricula for the schools.

As psychologists became aware of Piaget's studies, the novelty of the methods and the unexpected nature of the results led others to begin replicating, refining, and extending his research. Over the past decade there has thus been a burgeoning literature on the development of cognition in children which has very largely been attributable to Piaget's influence. Accordingly, this chapter will begin with a review of Piaget's general theory of cognitive growth, and then proceed to a survey of some of his findings on the growth of concepts of quantity, class, and relation. A final section will review studies by other investigators on one or another of the many issues raised by Piaget's research and theory.

PIAGET'S DEVELOPMENTAL THEORY OF INTELLIGENCE

In the course of almost half a century of continuous research on children's thinking Piaget has evolved a general theory of mental growth. According to the theory, adult intelligence (adaptive thinking and action) is derived from the earliest sensorimotor coordination of infants, in a series of stages that are related to age. Piaget recognized that there are wide individual differences in the age at which any particular stage emerges, but he believed that the sequence in which the stages appear is necessary and invariant for all children. Piaget's theory is thus a "nature" theory in the sense that the sequence of stages is determined by maturational factors, but it is also a "nurture theory" in the sense that the age at which any particular stage is achieved depends upon individual differ-

Table 14-1

Stages of Cognitive Growth in Piaget's Theory

Stage	Approximate age range (years)	Major characteristic
Sensorimotor period	0 to 2	Object permanence, elementary causality
Pre-operational period	2 to 6	Symbolic function
Period of concrete operations	6 or 7 to 11 or 12	Concrete operations (see Table 14-2), "age of reason"
Period of formal operations	11 or 12 on	Formal operations (see text), complex reasoning, metaphor

ences in ability, background, and experience. The developmental stages are listed in Table 14-1, and are briefly described below.

Sensorimotor Period

During the first two years of life the infant is transformed from a relatively helpless organism with limited motility, powers of expression, and social awareness to a highly mobile, verbal, relatively socially adept child. Corresponding to these remarkable changes in motility, expression, and socialization are equally significant changes in cognitive awareness and capacity.

During the early months of life, to illustrate, the young infant behaves as if the world about him were a kind of motion picture, a continuously changing panorama of events no one of which has any permanence. If an adult is playing with a three month old and suddenly ducks out of sight, the infant may not look after him and may attend to something else. Despite the fact that the infant appeared totally engrossed in the adult a moment before, after the adult disappears the infant behaves as if he never existed. For the infant, it is literally true that "out of sight is out of mind."[1]

---

[1] The point here is that the young infant gives no sign of "remembering" an absent stimulus; he may, however, "recognize" it when it reappears, as demonstrated by the occurrence of conditioning in infants (see Chapters 3 and 4).

Toward the end of the first year, however, the infant begins to seek after objects that have disappeared and thus gives evidence that he now attaches permanence to objects that are no longer present to his senses. It is only toward the end of the first year, for example, that infants begin to cry at the disappearance of the mother and sometimes to display a fear of strangers. Likewise, if an infant less than six months old is removed from the home (say for a minor operation) he shows no vexatious signs after his return. If, however, the infant is eight to nine months old, his return home is marked by crying, tantrums, and clinging to mother (Schaffer, 1958). Other evidence (Charlesworth, 1966; White, 1969) also attests to the validity of Piaget's (1964) observation that a major achievement of the sensorimotor period is the construction of the concept of a permanent object, one that is believed to exist even when it is outside the child's immediate psychological world.

Other cognitive accomplishments during the sensorimotor period are equally striking and significant. During this period the infant acquires an elementary notion of causality and begins to anticipate the results of his actions. He will, for example, push his cereal off the tray of the high chair and then look at the floor where it has fallen. Toward the end of the second year his spatial concepts are also well elaborated and he usually knows the floor plan of his home quite well and can get where he wants to go (and sometimes where he is not supposed to go) with ease. All in all, then, the remarkable achievements made by the infant in the realms of motility, expression, and socialization are coupled with equally remarkable achievements with respect to his conception of objects, space, and causality.

The Pre-Operational Period

In Piaget's view, the pre-operational period (usually two to six years of age) is marked by the emergence of what he calls the *symbolic function,* or true systems of representation such as language. The symbols of the pre-operational period must not be confused with the more primitive representations of the sensorimotor stage. The infant can use both *signals*—stimuli which through conditioning come to elicit particular behaviors, like the sight of the bottle which *signals* sucking—and *signs,* which are part of the object represented (e.g., the tail of the dog is a *sign* of the dog; mother's voice is a *sign* of mother). Neither signs nor signals are true symbols because they cannot be produced by the subject.

Evidence for the presence of the symbolic function during the preschool period comes from a variety of sources. First, the acquisition of language increases rapidly during the third year. Further, symbolic play appears. A child engages in symbolic play when, for example, he puts two sticks together and calls them an airplane or he calls a stone a turtle. Such designations are true symbols because they are produced by the subject and are not simply imposed upon him. In addition, the first evidence of dreams and night terrors, which suggest active symbolic activity, is obtained. Finally, "deferred imitation" begins; the child becomes able to see an action and to repeat or mimic it hours later.

Here again the suggestion is that the delay is bridged by some form of internalized representation. The attainment and development of the symbolic function is thus one of the central accomplishments of the pre-operational period of cognitive development.

Period of Concrete Operations

Although children in the pre-operational stage make remarkable progress in symbolic activities, particularly language expression, their ability to deal with classes, relations, and numbers is quite limited. For example, pre-operational children have difficulty in distinguishing between "some" and "all" (Sinclair-DeZwart, 1967) and between use of a class term to represent a single member of the class and use of it to represent the class as a whole. When a pre-operational child calls his pet "doggie," he uses the term both as a proper name (e.g., as a substitute for "Spot") and as a class name ("dog") without clearly differentiating between the two uses. In the realm of number, the pre-operational child can usually discriminate up to three or four objects and may be able to count to twenty, but he cannot coordinate his verbal counting with the enumeration of elements.

Toward the age of six or seven years, however, the child gradually attains what Piaget (1950) called *concrete operations*, internalized actions that operate in a manner analogous to elementary arithmetic operations. These operations fall into groupings such that if one operation in a grouping is present, all are present. One of the groupings that appear in this period is described in Table 14-2.

The emergence of these concrete operations permits achievements not possible in the pre-operational period. With respect to classes, for example, the child can now deal with their combinations. He can now say that boys and girls are children and that children minus boys is equal to girls (Elkind, 1961a; Wohlwill, 1968). He is thus, in Piagetian terms, able to *nest* classes. In a like manner, concrete operations enable children to arrive at a true concept of number and to perform the elementary operations of arithmetic. The acquisition of the number concept will be discussed in more detail later.

In short, the emergence of concrete operations, usually during the period from 6 or 7 to 11 or 12 years of age, enables the child to engage in elementary reasoning of the syllogistic variety. That is why the age of 6 to 7 has traditionally been called the "age of reason." During the elementary school period, concrete operations enable the child to elaborate his conceptions of time to include clock and historical time and to elaborate his conceptions of space to include geographical and geometrical space. Likewise, his conception of causality is expanded to include complex cause and effect sequences such as those found in mystery stories, which begin to be appreciated toward the end of childhood. Moreover, since concrete operations are internalized, the child can now solve in his head problems which as a pre-operational child he had to solve by means of trial and error actions.

Table 14-2

One of the Groupings of Concrete Operations

Operation	Description
Composition	A class (A) combined with its complement (A') gives rise to the total class (B): $A + A' = B$. E.g., boys (A) and ($+$) girls (A') are ($=$) children (B).
Inversion	A class (A) subtracted from the total class (B) gives rise to its complement (A'): $B - A = A'$. E.g., children (B) who are not ($-$) boys (A) are girls (A').
Identity	For every class there is another that when combined with it gives rise to the identity element, 0: $A - A = 0$. E.g., the class of boys minus the class of boys equals the null or identity class.
Tautology	For every class there is another that when combined with it gives rise to the class itself: $A + A = A$. E.g., the class of boys plus the class of boys equals the class of boys.
Partial associativity	In some cases the order in which a set of classes is combined has no effect upon the result: $A + A' + B' = A + (A' + B')$; but $(A + A) - A \neq A + (A - A)$, since $(A + A) - A = 0$ and $A + (A - A) = A$.

Period of Formal Operations

The concrete operations of childhood enable the child to deal with the concrete reality about him in a logical way, but they have certain limitations. For one thing, even though the child can reason about concrete objects, he has difficulty in reasoning about verbal propositions. For example, if a child is first shown two different-sized dolls, A and B (where $A > B$) and then another two, B and C (where $B > C$), he can deduce that A is bigger than C without having compared the two directly. He has much more difficulty, however, if the problem is posed verbally, for example, "Helen is taller than Jane and Jane is taller than Mary. Who is the tallest of the three?" (Glick and Wapner, 1968; Piaget, 1950).

The child with concrete operations is limited in still another respect. He is limited, for the most part, to dealing with at most two classes or relations at a time. A child with *formal operations*, however, can deal with many variables simultaneously. Inhelder and Piaget (1958), for example, showed children and adolescents a variety of experimental setups, such as the experimental determination of what combination of four colorless liquids (diluted sulfuric acid, water, oxygenated water, and thiosulfate) and a reagent (potassium chloride) would turn the liquid in one container yellow. Adolescents were able to solve the problem (which required the combination of three liquids) in a systematic manner, but children combined two of the liquids at a time, often without arriving at a solution. Formal operations thus permit the adolescent to engage in the kind of thinking that is characteristic of scientific experimentation. The period of formal operations usually begins at 11 or 12 to 15 years of age.

Formal operations also make possible other achievements. For example, adolescents can conceptualize their own thoughts and think about thinking. To illustrate, if a child is asked, "Can a dog or cat be a Protestant?", he is likely to say, "No, because they won't let him into church"; but the adolescent is likely to say, "No, because dogs wouldn't understand things like that." In addition, formal operations enable adolescents to think about ideal or counterfactual situations and to understand metaphorical expressions. If a child is asked to suppose that coal is white, he is likely to reply that "coal is black," but the adolescent can accept the counterfactual premise and reason from it.

The attainment of formal operations, in contrast with the attainment of concrete operations, does not appear to be universal, and may therefore be much more dependent upon culture (Goodnow and Bethon, 1966) and perhaps competence in symbolic skills such as reading (Elkind, Barocas, and Rosenthal, 1968).

A Final Note

This brief sketch of Piaget's theory of intellectual development is meant merely to convey the general trend of development of cognitive abilities and does not begin to touch upon the wealth of evidence Piaget has provided nor does it touch upon the many complex issues that his work has raised (see Flavell, 1963; Kessen and Kuhlman, 1962). The next section will take up in more detail some of his findings and conclusions with respect to particular conceptions.

THE DEVELOPMENT OF CONCEPTS OF QUANTITY, RELATION, AND CLASS

Introduction

Before Piaget's work on the development of particular concepts is discussed, it might be well to deal with the psychology of concepts in general, since Piaget's approach to this problem has been quite different from the approach of most psychologists. One of the definitions most frequently encountered in the literature on concept formation is to the effect that a concept is "a common response to dissimilar stimuli" (e.g., Kendler, 1961, p. 447). According to this definition a child has a concept when, say, he calls both a poodle and a spaniel "dog." The trouble with this definition is that it deals with but one aspect of what is usually meant by "concepts"; it omits reference to the evocative aspect. For example, if a child is asked to point to a dog and he does so, it can be said that he "knows what *dog* means," or has a concept of dog; or if a child is asked to define the word "dog" and he says, "it barks," it can also be said that the child has a concept of dog. The difficulty arises because the child is able to recognize dogs, usually by the age of two, long before he can give a verbal definition of dog. If only the verbal criterion is used, it will have to be said that the child of two does not have a concept of dog; and if only the behavioral criterion is used, it will have to be said that the two year old has a concept of dog even though he cannot define it.

What seems to be wrong is that neither the behavioral criterion nor the verbal definition is sufficient by itself to identify what people usually talk about and what psychologists study as concepts. In other words, a concept is not only a common response to dissimilar stimuli, but also is capable of evoking other appropriate responses, gestural or verbal. Neither the common response nor the other responses evoked by it need be verbal. From this point of view, a concept is a mediator, and therefore the study of cognitive processes (the use of concepts) is the study of mediation. Studies of mediation and mediation theories are discussed in detail in other chapters (especially in Chapter 7, sections entitled "Transfer in Paired Associate Tasks" and "Age Trend in Efficiency of Mediation"; Chapter 8, section entitled "Perceptual Set"; Chapter 9, section entitled "Attention"; and Chapter 13, section entitled "Theoretical Accounts of Language Acquisition"). Therefore, these need not be considered here, but the interested student should also consult the work of the Kendlers (e.g., Kendler and Kendler, 1967), Berlyne (e.g., 1965), Reese (1968, especially·pp. 146–159 and 254–271), and Jeffrey (1968).

The Piagetian approach to concepts is similar in that every concept is assumed to have two components, corresponding roughly to the common response and the responses evoked by it. However, the correspondence is not exact, because the first component is assumed to be a *figurative* or perceptual component and the second a *cognitive* component. The figurative component corresponds to what Woodworth (1938) has called a kind of "composite photograph" of all the exemplars of a class with the differences "washed out." Thus, after seeing a variety of dogs the child builds up a kind of general picture of dogs—four legs, furriness, barking, etc.—which like stretch-hose can fit any size or shape of dog. The figurative components of concepts are built up quite early and the young child of two or three has a remarkable store of them.[2]

The cognitive component of concepts corresponds to the *actions*, at first real and later mental, that the child can perform with respect to the group of things represented by the figurative component. The young child says, for example, "a hole is to dig" and "a bike is to ride." However, he does not recognize

[2] Two points should be noted here. First, the figurative component is not directly observable in the young child (it can be observed only introspectively, and only the adult has the requisite verbal skills to give reliable introspective reports). Therefore, the footnoted statement in the text is not a report of *data,* in Pepper's (1942) sense, but rather is a theoretical statement supported by "circumstantial evidence" (or, to use Pepper's term, it is a *dandum*). Second, the concept of a "figurative component" is probably better characterized as a theoretical term than as a descriptive term, because even adults who are well trained in giving introspective reports have seldom found such a component in their own mental concepts (see Titchener, 1909, pp. 14–19).

either the hole or the bicycle in terms of these actions but rather in terms of the figurative picture. Figuratively, a hole is an empty place in the ground and a bike has two wheels, etc. The figurative component is thus separate from the cognitive component. For simplicity, one might think of the figurative component as permitting the child to recognize new instances of the concept, and the cognitive component as permitting him to understand what to do with what he has recognized. Every concept thus has both a figurative and a cognitive *meaning* or significance.

The developmental patterns of these two aspects or components of a concept are not the same. The child's figurative concepts improve with age, but they are probably never radically different from the figurative components of adult concepts. Children are just about as good at recognizing dogs, makes of cars, etc., as are adults. In contrast, the cognitive component of concepts does undergo a radical change with age. At first the cognitive meaning of a concept is limited to the real actions that can be performed with it; with increasing age this meaning becomes the understanding of the *mental actions* that can be performed with it. Thus, the young child might say that a dog is to play with, and the older child might say that the dog is an animal or a canine. These latter definitions imply that for the older child the cognitive meaning of the concept is the understanding of the broader classes into which the concept can be put. Classifying a dog into the class of animals is simply an action on the mental plane that corresponds to playing with the dog on the plane of real action.

In general, Piaget has been concerned with the evolution of the cognitive components of concepts as these evolve from their figurative forerunners. This is an important point because in the development of concepts the child is seldom in the position of either having or not having a concept. In the more usual case, he is moving from one level of conceptualization to another. As will be seen, even young children have a concept of number, of right and left, and so on, *but these concepts are different from the concepts of number and of right and left that are held by adults.* It is the transformation of the cognitive component of concepts as the child grows older that has been the particular concern of Piaget.

The Conservation Problems

Perhaps no aspect of Piaget's work has attracted so much attention as his "conservation" problems. Conservation problems all have to do with the assessment of the child's understanding that a quantity remains unchanged across changes in its appearance. A major reason for the interest in these problems is that they elicit responses in young children that tend to astound and mystify adults. Many of Piaget's studies with conservation problems have now been replicated by investigators all over the world with essentially comparable results. The *facts* of children's performance on these problems are thus no longer in dispute. How to account for these behaviors is, however, quite another matter, and many investigators have challenged Piaget's interpretations of the findings.

In this section of the chapter the results of some of Piaget's most well known studies of conservation will be reported together with some of his interpretations. The last section of the chapter will survey the research of other investigators on conservation and other problems, and alternative interpretations of the phenomena.

CONSERVATION OF NUMBER. In considering the development of number concepts, one must keep in mind the distinction between the figurative and the cognitive components of these concepts. Animals, for example, have been assumed to have a figurative concept of number (Dantzig, 1956) because they can distinguish between two and three objects. By the same reasoning children two years of age also have a figurative concept of number; they are usually able to distinguish and use correctly the notions of "one" and "two," although beyond that they seem to have some difficulty (Terman and Merrill, 1960). It is only at the age of about six years that children attain a cognitive conception of number in the sense of being able to perform elementary arithmetic operations.

Table 14-3

Stages in the Development of Number Concepts

Stage	Age (years)	Characteristic behavior
1	4	Incorrectly matches model perceptually, responding to one figurative dimension and ignoring the other
2	5	Matches model perceptually, but without conservation
3	6	"Matches" model cognitively, with conservation

Some of the steps in the development from the figurative to the cognitive conception of number have been shown by Long and Welch (1941) in a study with children from 3½ to 7 years of age. The children were given three tasks: to select on demand two to ten marbles, to choose the larger and the smaller of two groups of marbles among four groups of marbles, and to match groups of two to ten marbles. The investigators found that the ability to select a given number of marbles on demand was achieved first, that is by the youngest children; the selection of number groups was achieved next; and the matching of number groups was achieved only by the oldest children in the sample. In a somewhat different type of study, Wohlwill (1960b) also found that discrimination of number precedes ability to match numbers.

In studies by Piaget and his colleagues, the development of the cognitive concept of number from its figurative forerunner has been demonstrated in dramatic form (Piaget, 1952a). They found three fairly distinct age-related stages in the development of the operational concept of number. These are discussed below and are summarized in Table 14-3.

In the first stage, usually at four years of age, Piaget's subjects had only a figurative or global conception of number as shown by their matching behavior. When the four year olds were asked to match a set of six pennies (lined up in a row with regular spacing) with other pennies from a pile of coins, they proceeded in one of two ways. Some children matched the length of the row but ignored the size of the intervals between the pennies and so put in too many or too few. Other children ignored the length of the row and focused on the spaces between the pennies and continued to space the pennies at regular intervals until all the pennies were used or until the row reached the end of the table. Thus, when four year old children had to break down their figurative conception of number and coordinate the length and the density of the row, they responded to one figurative dimension and ignored the other.

At about the age of five years, a second stage in the development of the operational conception of number was observed. Children at this stage correctly matched the model of six pennies, although this often involved considerable trial and error. The ability to match did not really indicate a logical conception of number, however, as was readily demonstrated by the conservation procedure. After the two rows were matched, the investigators proceeded to elongate one row by increasing the spacing between the pennies. When the five year olds were asked whether the two rows had the same number of pennies (an equality they themselves had constructed) the children often replied, "No, the longer row has more." This reply was found even among children who had correctly counted the pennies! The explanation seems to be that as long as the five year old has a model, he is able to coordinate the length of the row and the spacing within it. When the model is destroyed (by spreading one row apart), he reverts to judging number on the basis of a single dimension, just as in the first stage.

In the third stage, around the age of six years, children usually displayed a truly operational conception of number. The behavior in this stage was quite in contrast to that observed in the previous stages. For example, six year olds often did not bother to match the sample. When they were asked to take the same number as in the model, they simply counted out the correct number and held the coins in their hands. They no longer needed a perceptual model to match number. Their response to the conservation problem was also different. Confronted with the two rows of pennies equal in number but unequal in length, these children replied that "of course" they were the same. Three types of explanation were usually given: "Nothing was added or taken away"; "one row is longer but the pennies aren't as close together"; and "if you put them back like they were before (in one-to-one correspondence) they will be the same again."

In Piaget's (1952a) view the child attains a true notion of number when he is able to coordinate two dimensions simultaneously, in this case length and density. More generally, Piaget argued that the concept of number is based on the concept of a unit, which is essentially the coordination of relations of similarity and difference. A child attains a true (adult) conception of number when he can recognize that a given element (say a penny) can be like every other element (other pennies) and yet different in its order of enumeration.

It is only when the child combines these two ideas simultaneously that a true or mathematical conception of number is attained. Accordingly, the child's ability to coordinate length and density in the number conservation task is but an instance of a more general ability to deal with two dimensions, relations, or classes at one and the same time.

Several investigators have replicated Piaget's studies, and have reported generally comparable results (e.g., Almy, Chittenden, and Miller, 1966; Churchill, 1958; Dodwell, 1960, 1961; Elkind, 1961d; Wohlwill, 1960b). The observations that Piaget reported on children's performance on number conservation tasks therefore appear to be substantiated. However, the interpretation of these facts, given above, has been questioned. Some of these questions will be dealt with later.

THE CONSERVATION OF MASS, WEIGHT, AND VOLUME.   Piaget and his colleague, Bärbel Inhelder, also explored children's understanding of the concepts of continuous quantities such as solids and liquids (Piaget and Inhelder, 1962). They were concerned, as in the case of number, with the steps by which children are able to judge that a continuous quantity has not been altered in amount by a change in its appearance, that is, that quantity is conserved.

A variety of techniques was employed, but present purposes can be served by consideration of results obtained with clay figures. The procedure was to present the child two balls of clay (equivalent in every respect) and then to ask him whether they contained the same amount of clay. Then, after the child had judged that the two balls did indeed contain the same amount of clay, one of the balls was transformed (before the child's eyes) into a "sausage" or a "pancake" or a number of little pellets. At this point the child was again asked whether there was the same amount of clay.

Three levels of response were noted. Among the youngest children the response most frequently obtained was that the ball and the sausage did not contain the same amount of clay because the sausage was "longer" or because the ball was "fatter." Even when the sausage was rolled back into a ball these children insisted that while there was an equal amount of clay in the two balls, when one was made into a sausage there was more clay in the ball or the sausage.

At a somewhat more advanced level (usually five to six years of age), an intermediate type of response was obtained. Children at this level generally said that there was the same amount of clay in the ball and the sausage, but not when the sausage was much elongated nor when it was broken into a number of small pieces. Put differently, at this level of response children judged that the amount of clay was the same across small transformations but not across large ones.

At the third level (usually six to seven years of age), some children said that the amount of clay in the ball and in the sausage, pellets, or pancake was the same across any and all transformations. These children gave three types of explanation for their response: (a) nothing was added or taken away so the amounts are the same; (b) if the sausage (pellets, and so on) were made back into a ball, the two amounts of clay would be the same; and (c) what the sausage gained in length, it lost in thickness, and therefore the two amounts are the same. Moreover, to these children the equality of the two amounts of clay, despite their difference in appearance, seemed to be self-evident and they accepted the equality as if they had always known that this was true. Once a child attains conservation, he is not aware of his own part in the process and treats his judgment as if it were rooted in the materials themselves.

The conservation of mass, then, makes its appearance, on the average, at about the age of six or seven years. However, when the same procedure is employed with a child of six or seven who has the conservation of mass, but is now asked about weight, a rather remarkable phenomenon occurs. The child now says that the ball and sausage do not weigh the same and gives the same reasons as given by four or five year old children for the non-conservation of mass. Such behavior is all the more remarkable because the child could give as the explanation for the conservation of weight the same explanation he had previously given for the conservation of mass. It is not, however, until the age of about nine years that the majority of children say that the weights of the ball and sausage are the same.

If now the same procedure is repeated with the 9 year old, who has just given an explanation for the conservation of weight, but the question of equality is posed with respect to volume, the response is again unexpected. The child who knows that changing the ball into a sausage does not alter the amount and weight of clay nonetheless says that the volume has been changed. Again the explanations given for the conservation of mass and weight would serve equally well for the conservation of volume, but the child does not utilize them. It is only at about the age of 11 or 12 years that the majority of children say that the ball and sausage have the same volume.

Piaget labeled this separation between the attainment of mass, weight, and volume conservation as a horizontal *décalage* (separation). He believed that although the attainment of these three conservations rests upon concrete operations, already present at the age of six or seven, the difference in difficulty resides in the nature of the concepts themselves. That is, mass is the most primitive or undifferentiated concept, from which the notion of weight must be abstracted, and volume is even more abstract than weight. The *décalage*, accordingly, derives from two facts: (a) volume presupposes a concept of weight, and weight presupposes a concept of mass; and (b) it takes time for the child to move from one level of abstraction to another.

As in the case of Piaget's number experiments, the studies of mass, weight, and volume conservation have been repeated by many other investigators with essentially comparable results (e.g., Elkind, 1961b; Lovell and Ogilvie, 1961a, 1961b; Uzgiris, 1964). The facts of these conservations are thus established, as are the *décalages* reported by Piaget. Whether the *décalage* is necessary, however, and whether these conservations, like number conservation, necessitate the logical structures postulated by Piaget has been questioned by other investigators.

OTHER CONSERVATION PROBLEMS. In addition to studying number and mass, weight, and volume conservation, Piaget and his colleagues have also studied the conservation of other concepts, such as length and area (Piaget, Inhelder, and Szeminska, 1960). In these investigations, as in those just described, the attainment of conservation occurred at or after the age of six or seven years, the age at which Piaget said most children attain concrete operations (see Table 14-4).

To explore length conservation, the child was presented two rods of equal length. Initially, the two rods were placed in spatial correspondence with their ends parallel, and the child was asked whether they were equally long. After the child made his judgment, one of the rods was displaced several inches to the right or left of the other. Once again the question of their equality was posed to the child. Young children (four to five years old) usually said that now one of the rods was longer, and justified this statement by pointing to the ends of the rods where one jutted out beyond the other. Toward the

Table 14-4

Approximate Ages for Various Conservations

Concept	Age (years)
Number	6
Mass	6–7
Length	6–7
Area	6–7
Weight	9
Volume	11–12

age of six or seven, however, children said that the two rods were equally long and that moving one did not change the length. This conservation of length is usually attained about a year later than the conservation of number.

In Piaget's view the conservation of length comes about when the child can attend to both the right and left ends of the rods. When he does this, he observes that the segment of rod A which extends beyond rod B on the left is just equal to the segment of B which extends beyond A on the right. It is by the coordination of these two segments that the child recognizes that what the displaced rod gained in length at one end, it lost at the other and so remained the same length. Here again Piaget attributed the coordination of the two segments to the activity of concrete operations.

The procedure used to study area conservation was as follows. Two green boards of equal area were used to represent fields upon which two cows were grazing. On each field the examiner successively put down a number of houses (like those used in *Monopoly*), the same number on each field. On one field, however, the houses were placed together in a square, and on the other field they were placed at random. Confronted with this situation, the child was asked, "Have the two cows got the same amount of grass to eat?"

The responses to this problem varied with age. Young children (four to five years old) said that the field with the closely packed houses provided the cows with more area than the field with the widely scattered houses. Toward the age of six or seven, however, children discounted the apparent difference in area and based their judgment on enumeration of the houses. At this stage they said that it "looks like more green there . . . but it isn't true because there are the same number of houses" (Piaget *et al.*, 1960, p. 271).

Piaget's explanation of this developmental change in the child's ability to conserve area was that the older child is able to take both the field and the houses into account simultaneously. If the child responds simply to the field, the one with the closely packed houses appears to have more field area. If he takes the houses into account, however, he is able to deduce that if the number of houses is the same, the area taken up is the same and hence the amount of grass to eat is the same on the two fields.

Replication studies of length conservation (e.g., Braine, 1959; Elkind, 1966; Smedslund, 1963) and area conservation (Beilin and Franklin, 1962; Lovell, 1961) have at least roughly confirmed Piaget's findings, but some investigators found much more variability in the age of attaining length and area conservation than did Piaget *et al.* (1960).

Relational Concepts

Concrete operations, in Piaget's view, not only enable the child to conserve quantities, but also enable him to combine relations and arrive at adultlike, or true relational concepts. Piaget's work on relations can be illustrated by presenting his findings on series relations and on simple positional relations.

CONCEPTION OF A SERIES. Young children, sometimes as early as three years of age, already have a figurative conception of a series. It is not unusual to find, for example, that preschoolers can stack a size-graded set of colored plastic rings upon a stick. The presence of this figurative conception, however, does not indicate the presence of a true or relational conception of a series; the latter conception develops much more gradually.

To study the child's conception of series relations, Piaget (1952a) used the following procedure. Sticks graded in size were presented to the child, and he was first asked to pick the largest and the smallest to ascertain his ability to make these gross, figurative discriminations. Next, the experimenter constructed a "staircase" with the sticks, then broke it up and asked the child to reconstruct the "staircase." If the child succeeded in constructing the staircase, he was presented a second series of sticks, intermediate in size relative to the first set, and was asked to insert these within the series. Thus, if the members of the initial series were *A, B, C, D,* and *E,* and the second set was *a, b, c, d,* and *e,* the combined series would be *Aa, Bb, Cc, Dd,* and *Ee.*

The patterns of performance observed on these tasks were as follows. Young children (about four to five years of age) were usually able to select the smallest and the largest sticks, but were unable to reconstruct the entire series (of ten sticks). Instead, they built small series of three or four sticks. Somewhat older children arranged all the sticks so that each successive one extended above the preceding one. These children, however, ignored the lengths of the sticks so that the bottom of the series did not form a straight line but rather a jagged edge. They created the staircase effect but did not order the sticks with respect to size.

Toward the age of five or six, children were usually able to reconstruct the staircase. However, their method of construction was tedious, and they made many mistakes which they either corrected spontaneously or at the prompting of the examiner. They often appeared to be trying to construct the series from a mental picture of what the series looked like rather than on the basis of the size relations among the sticks. That this was probably the case was suggested by their performance once the staircase was completed and they were given the second set of sticks to insert within the first. Their performance was quite surprising in the sense that they made what, to the adult, seemed like glaring errors. To illustrate, a child might alter the series to yield Ac, Bd, Ca, De, and so on. Other children were reluctant to alter the constructed series even after the examiner had demonstrated how the second series was to be inserted. Such children tended to construct a second series alongside the first.

Toward the age of six or seven a new pattern of behavior emerged. At this age level, children reconstructed the series with dispatch. They appeared to know what they were doing and did not make errors. When they were given the second set of sticks they inserted these without difficulty. Indeed, if one had not observed the behavior of the younger children struggling with the problem, it would appear from the performance of the older children that it was a very simple problem that required hardly any thought or concentration.

In accounting for these results (replicated by Elkind, 1964), Piaget argued that the young children had a purely figurative notion of a series, as a kind of picture, but they could not reproduce the series either because they could not keep the picture in mind or because they could not keep both the top and the bottom of the series in mind at the same time.

The intermediate children also had a figurative conception of a series and were beginning to be able to coordinate relations, although on a purely perceptual level. In constructing the series, they always selected from the pile of sticks the smallest or largest, thus reducing the problem of successive selection to a simple size discrimination. That these children did not have a true relational conception of a series was shown by their performance with the inserts. To these children the intact series was a complete picture and the second set of elements to be added made no sense. It was as if they had completed a jigsaw puzzle and were suddenly given additional pieces to insert. This accounts for the building of the second series and for the egregious errors.

What enabled the older children to succeed on all parts of the tests was their ability to deal with the elements in relational terms. The older children recognized that in a series each element (B) is both larger than its predecessor $(B > A)$ and smaller than its successor $(B < C)$ or that one and the same element can be in two relations at once. This awareness of the relational character of the series and of the fact that one element can be in two relations derives from concrete operations and makes possible a true or adult conception of a series as a set of elements in relation to one another.

CONCEPTIONS OF RIGHT AND LEFT.   As with the other concepts that have been discussed so far, it is necessary to distinguish between the figurative and the

Table 14-5

The Six Tests in the Study of Right and Left Conceptions

Test	Content
1	Show me your right hand. Your left. Show me your right leg. Now your left.
2	Show me my right hand. Now my left. Show me my right leg. Now my left. (During this test the examiner sits opposite the child facing him.)
3	(A coin is placed on the table to the left of a pencil, from the point of view of the child.) Is the pencil to the right or to the left? And the penny?
4	(The child is opposite to and facing the examiner, who has a coin in his right hand and a bracelet on his left arm.) You see the penny. Have I got it in my right hand or my left? And the bracelet?
5	(The child is opposite three objects in a row: a pencil to the left, a key in the middle, and a coin to the right.) Is the pencil to the left or to the right of the key? And of the penny? Is the key to the left or to the right of the penny? And of the pencil? Is the penny to the left or the right of the pencil? And of the key?
6	(The child is opposite three objects in a row: a key to the left, a piece of paper in the middle, and a pencil to the right. The objects are shown for 30 seconds and are then covered.) Now listen; I am going to show you three things only for a moment. You must look carefully and then afterwards tell me by heart how the things are arranged. Look carefully. (Questions analogous to those in Test 5 are asked after the objects are covered.)

cognitive or operational concepts of *right* and *left*. Even as early as four years of age, many children know their right and left hands. However, at this stage *right* and *left* are not true relations but rather are simple discriminations in the sense that the child believes that "right" and "left" are properties of things in the same way that "redness" or "roundness" are properties of things. Piaget's (1951b) work on conceptions of right and left demonstrates the gradual transition from this figurative conception of right and left to a relational conception of these terms.

In his study of right and left conceptions, Piaget employed the six tests described in Table 14-5. The results are summarized in Table 14-6, where a clear increase in performance level with increasing age can be seen. The results suggested that the attainment of a true relational conception of right and left evolved in three stages. In the first stage (usually at 5 to 8 years of age), the child considered right and left only from his own point of view; when asked to label the right and left hands of an examiner standing opposite him, the child said that the examiner's right and left are opposite his own right and left. That is, he identified the other's right and left as mirror images of his own right and left.

Table 14-6

Performance on the Six Tests as a Function of Age Level

Age (years)	Tests passed[a]
4	None
5	1
6	1
7	1, 3
8	1, 2, 3, 4
9	1, 2, 3, 4
10	1, 2, 3, 4
11	1, 2, 3, 4, 5
12	1, 2, 3, 4, 5, 6

[a] A test is "passed" at a given age level if at least 75 percent of the children at that age level pass it.

In the second stage (usually at 8 to 11 years of age), these relations came to be viewed from the standpoint of another person; the child could correctly identify the right and left arms and legs of the examiner standing opposite him. He could also deal with the right-left relation between two objects, provided they were related to another person. It was only in the third stage (usually at 11 to 12 years of age) that children considered right and left from the standpoint of objects. This was suggested by the observation that it was not until the third stage that the child recognized that with three objects in a row the middle object is *both* on the right *and* on the left of its two boundary objects. Prior to this stage, the child when asked whether the middle object is on the right or the left of its accompanying objects would simply say that it "is in the middle."

Accordingly, the conception of right and left as having to do with relative positions of objects rather than with their properties comes about gradually as the child becomes able to put himself in the position of other people and then in the position of objects. Again, these findings have been replicated with comparable results (Elkind, 1961c; Wapner and Cirillo, 1968).

Class Concepts

In traditional psychology, even before the time of Hull's (1920) early work, the most frequently studied concepts have been *class* concepts, such as *dog, horse,* and the like. The interest has been in the processes by which such classifications are formed; the method used to study the formation of class concepts was generally a discrimination procedure in which the subject was trained by selective reinforcement to respond to stimuli that were alike or identical in certain ways. Piaget's method was derived from a more clinical tradition (Goldstein and Sheerer, 1941; Reichard, Schneider, and Rapaport, 1944), and was designed to "diagnose" how the child constructs classes and how he moves from a figurative to an operational classification.

In one of his investigations with Inhelder (Piaget and Inhelder, 1959), the materials used were pieces of wood or plastic of different shapes (squares, triangles, and arches) and of different colors. The children were instructed simply to "put together those that are alike." With these materials Piaget and Inhelder again found three stages in the age range from $2\frac{1}{2}$ to 7 or 8 years.

In the first stage (usually $2\frac{1}{2}$ to $4\frac{1}{2}$) Piaget and Inhelder observed what they called "figural" groupings. Several different types of reaction were observed, but all of them were apparently attempts by the child to construct some figure or form. For example, some children selected one square and then put another next to it in a row; when all the squares had been used, these children continued building the row with the triangles and then the arches. Apparently, the grouping on the basis of similarity of shape became secondary to establishing a particular figure, in this case a straight line. In this stage, in short, children seemed incapable of grouping the materials without making them into some kind of figure, which took precedence over the class relations. Similar findings have been reported by Vygotsky (1962) and by Bruner and Olver (1963).

In the second stage (usually $4\frac{1}{2}$ to 6 or 7) children demonstrated what Piaget called *quasi* classifications. The characteristics of the quasi classification are that it is incomplete and often inconsistent. For example, the child might group the materials into several piles, one on the basis of color, another on the basis of form, and another on the basis of size. Because of the nature of the materials, this procedure left some elements ungrouped. A somewhat more advanced form of classification in this stage was a grouping on the basis of a single dimension such as color or form. In using this basis, the children simply ignored the other dimensions of the stimulus materials.

Finally, in the third stage (usually 7 or 8) children spontaneously formed class hierarchies. For example, the child would first separate all the curved pieces from the noncurved pieces and then subdivide these into subgroups according to color and form (e.g., triangles vs. squares in the noncurved grouping).

These children were demonstrating an ability to deal with several classificatory dimensions at once, as well as the ability to form class hierarchies. It is only when the child is able to form classifications of this kind that Piaget would speak of the child as having a true or operational understanding of classes.

In some earlier studies Piaget (1952a) demonstrated that the child's difficulty with class inclusions holds equally well on the verbal plane. In one study, children were shown a box with 20 white and 2 brown wooden beads. After the child had acknowledged that all the beads were wooden and that there were more white than brown beads, he was asked, "Are there more white than wooden beads?" Prior to about the age of six or seven most children replied that there were "more white than brown beads" and ignored the "wooden" part of the question. For these children a class and its members were still concrete elements which existed in time and space. When the child thought of a bead as being in the "white place," he could not think of it as being in the "wooden place" at the same time because a bead cannot be in two places at the same time. Hence, he equated the "brown" with the "wooden" beads. It is only when the child can think of properties apart from the elements in which they inhere that he can successfully *nest* classes and, as previously indicated, grasp the true relational quality of terms such as right and left.

General Considerations

The foregoing paragraphs have described a selected sample of the many research investigations carried out by Piaget and his colleagues. Unfortunately, there is not space to convey the full range of his investigations, which include studies of children's conceptions of space (Piaget and Inhelder, 1956), time (Piaget, 1946a), speed (Piaget, 1946b), chance (Piaget and Inhelder, 1951), physical causality (Piaget, 1951a), and moral judgment (Piaget, 1948). The studies described, however, will perhaps convey the general tenor of the research and of Piaget's approach to the interpretation of his findings.

Before turning to questions about the reliability, generalizability, and validity of these findings, several general considerations about Piaget's work need to be discussed.

Role of the Subject. In all of his work, Piaget has sought to demonstrate that the product of cognitive activity—knowledge—is never a simple copy of some external reality. Put differently, Piaget argued that all our knowledge of the external world, even such aspects of it as chairs and tables which seem so clearly "out there," always depends at least in part upon our own activity. Our cognitive activity is, moreover, always logical in character. Knowledge, as illustrated by the concepts already discussed, thus derives not from perception alone but also from reason. We learn about the external world not by copying it ever more exactly but rather by reasoning about it ever more correctly.

The role of reason in the origination of knowledge is easy to demonstrate even outside the Piagetian research described above. For example, the earth was long regarded as flat because to the eye it indeed appears to be so. It was only when men began to reason from observations such as the disappearance of a ship on the horizon and the shape of the earth's shadow on the moon that the roundness of the earth was *deduced*. The idea that the earth revolves around the sun is still another example of how what is apparent, that the sun revolves around the earth, is in fact not correct. True knowledge about the revolution of planets was deduced from mathematical calculations.

In the studies described earlier a similar progression could be observed. The child who judged numerosity on the basis of the density or length of the row, and the child who regarded right and left as properties of things, were responding in a manner analogous to that of prescientific men who thought the earth was flat and that the sun revolved around the earth. Children who attain true numerical and relational concepts with the aid of reason are analogous to men who have deduced the true shape of the earth and its motion with respect to other stars and planets. Mental activity, or reason, therefore plays a role in the origination of all true knowledge.[3] If this position is correct, why then are we not aware of the part we play in knowing and why does the external world seem so independent of our mental activities? This raises the question of consciousness, which is discussed next.

ROLE OF CONSCIOUSNESS.   Why, if Piaget is correct and we play such a large part in constructing our knowledge about the world, are we not aware of the fact? One explanation has to do with a law of consciousness which Claparède (1951) laid down and which he termed *prix de conscience*. In essence this law states that we are conscious of our own mental activity whenever we are forced to accommodate or adapt to reality.[4] According to this view we are more conscious of our mental activities when we are confronted with problems, conflicts, and contradictions than after they are resolved. From this point of view, the child is aware of discrepancy between what he sees and what he knows in the conservation problem, and this awareness is part of the process of working toward its resolution. Once the difficulty is resolved, however, the child is no longer aware of his role in arriving at conservation and takes it to be a perceptually given property of the object.

The situation is not unlike the learning of a motor skill. Initially, we are fully aware of all the coordinations required in driving a car or in skiing. Later, after the skills are mastered, we are no longer aware of the coordinations and usually think about anything but the actions of driving or skiing as we perform effortlessly and unconsciously. Apparently, something similar happens in the cognitive plane; after we attain a particular concept, we are no longer aware of the difficulties encountered in its acquisition.

ROLE OF LANGUAGE.   The third consideration in attempting to comprehend the Piagetian position is the relation between language and thought. For Piaget,

---

[3] "True knowledge" is, in Pepper's analysis, a *dandum* (Pepper, 1942).

[4] Claparède's law can be deduced from a more general principle: Mental activities are engaged only when difficulties are encountered; otherwise, behavior is habitual and mechanical (Uznadze, 1966, pp. 112–119).

language and thought are independent but closely related systems, each with its own unique developmental progressions. During the preschool years, the child masters not only a huge vocabulary but also the grammatical rules for generating a variety of utterances (see Chapter 13). However, during this period language growth far outstrips the growth of thought, and young children therefore speak with a sophistication that is far beyond their level of comprehension.

The major mechanisms of language mature during the preschool period, but mental growth continues until adolescence, when thought finally catches up with language. That is, it is only during adolescence that the child can fully appreciate the metaphorical subtleties of the language he has been using and can comprehend stories such as *Gulliver's Travels* on a new plane more subtle than attainable from reading it as a child. Hence, although Piaget used the child's language to diagnose the child's mental operations, he made it clear that it is an error to *equate* thought with language.

EVALUATION OF PIAGET'S WORK

Investigators other than Piaget and his colleagues have dealt with four main issues about Piaget's research and theory. (a) *Reliability:* Several investigators have explored the reliability or reproducibility of Piaget's findings. Studies of this kind have already been cited in the discussions of Piaget's specific investigations, and since the general consensus is that the findings are reliable, the research on this issue need not be further considered here. (b) *Generalizability:* There have been studies of the generalizability of Piaget's findings to children from different social classes and cultures, and to children with sensory deficits and limited intelligence. (c) *Interpretation:* Some investigators have questioned Piaget's interpretations of the findings and have tested alternative hypotheses. This has led, in some cases, to concern with the modifiability of the child's performance in the kinds of tasks used by Piaget. (d) *Relation to Other Variables:* One group of researchers has studied the relation of performance on these kinds of tasks to other aspects of the child's behavior and thought, such as intelligence test performance and personality.

In the rest of the present section a summary of selected research on each of the last three issues will be presented, together with conclusions as to what the results seem to suggest so far.

Generalizability of the Findings

Researchers have asked to what extent the results obtained by Piaget with white middle class Western European children are generalizable to children of other races and cultures. Perhaps in no other area of psychology is there so much cross-cultural and cross-social-class information available as on the Piagetian tasks. For example, conservation problems have been given to children in Canada (Dodwell, 1960, 1961; Laurendeau and Pinard, 1962), England (Lovell, 1961), Hong Kong (Goodnow and Bethon, 1966), Italy (Peluffo, 1962),

Jamaica (Vernon, 1965), Prince Edward County, Virginia (Mermelstein and Shulman, 1967), and Senegal (Greenfield, 1966).

There are problems in interpreting results from cross-cultural studies, however, because of the differences in language, experience, and cultural values. If similar results are obtained cross-culturally, there is no problem; but if differences are observed, it is not easy to interpret or account for the cause of the differences.

To illustrate the kinds of issues that come up in cross-cultural research, a study by Greenfield (1966) is instructive. Greenfield worked in Senegal, French Africa, with Wolof children, who are Moslem and represent the dominant population. The subjects were from three age levels and were grouped according to residence and school—urban-school, bush-school, and bush-unschooled. They were tested on the liquid conservation task, in their native language. The results showed that no more than 50 percent of the unschooled bush children attained conservation by the age of 11 to 13 years. Both urban (Dakar) and bush school children, however, showed 100 percent conservation by the same age level. A secondary finding of this study was that when bush children rather than the experimenter poured the liquid, many more children showed conservation both immediately and on a delayed posttest. Greenfield interpreted this result as due to the child's attributing less magic to himself than to the adult.

In a comprehensive summary of the findings of the cross-cultural studies, Goodnow (1969) arrived at the following conclusions: (a) Some tasks are more vulnerable than others to departures from urban, Western schooling. The most hardy of the tasks appears to be the conservation of number, and the most vulnerable tasks appear to be those requiring "words, drawings, visual imagery" (Goodnow, 1969, p. 453). (b) The tasks that are less vulnerable to cultural differences may be those for which the child has action models. In societies where children have many measurement and measuring experiences, concepts of length and time may be more fully developed than in cultures where such experiences are less frequent. (c) "The critical skill may be versatility in the use of different sources of information and different models" (Goodnow, 1969, p. 454).

In summary, then, it is not possible to make any sweeping statements about the cross-cultural replication of Piaget's findings. Some tasks appear to be more hardy than others, and the differences that do appear seem to revolve around the ages at which the tasks are passed rather than the sequence of their acquisition. It is not known, however, whether the *processes* by which children of other cultural groups attain conservation are the same as for urban Western children. What cross-cultural studies do unequivocally show is that the "naturalness" of conservation as known in Western culture is probably a product, in part at least, of direct or indirect physical and social experience.

Tests of Piagetian Interpretations

One of the most active areas of research now current has to do with testing Piaget's interpretations of his findings, namely, that the age differences in performance are attributable to age differences in cognitive structures or mental operations. Some investigators have attempted to show that the child's performance on the conservation task is a result of misleading perceptual cues rather than a result of a cognitive deficit; others have argued that the failure to conserve has to do with language misunderstandings; and still others have attempted to show that non-conservation is due to a lack of instruction or learning.

PERCEPTUAL INTERPRETATIONS. Several investigators (e.g., Bruner, 1966; Gelman, 1969; Mehler and Bever, 1967) have argued that the conservation problem presents children with misleading perceptual cues, and that conservation involves learning to ignore such misleading perceptual information. Such a position is not really contrary to Piaget's views, since he too believed that the child must

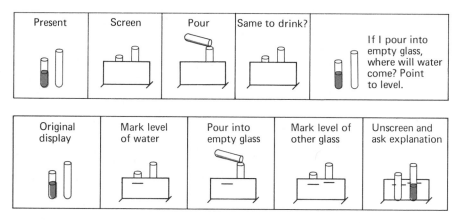

Fig. 14-1. The three tasks used by Frank. Task 1 is at the upper left, Task 2 at the upper right, and Task 3 across the bottom of the figure. (From Bruner, 1966, Fig. 3, p. 195. Reprinted by permission of the author and John Wiley & Sons, Inc., publisher.)

overcome misleading perceptual cues if he is to attain conservation. A conflict in interpretation arises over *how* the misleading perceptual cues are to be overcome. For Bruner (1966), it appears that a verbal formula shields the child from the illusion of non-conservation; for others, such as Mehler and Bever (1967) and Gelman (1969), what is required is a more sophisticated perceptual discrimination.

To illustrate the research on which these alternative interpretations are based, consider a study by Frank (reported by Bruner, 1966, pp. 193–202). In this investigation four to seven year old children were exposed to three tasks (see Figure 14-1). In the first, they observed two beakers that were either the same or different in width, height, or both width and height. One was half filled with colored water. After the child had observed the two beakers, they were placed behind a screen so that only their tops were visible; the liquid was then poured from one beaker into the other, and the child was asked whether there was still the same amount of water as before. In the second task, the same beakers were used, and the child had to predict the outcome of the pouring by pointing to the level the water would reach if it were poured into the second beaker. The third task was a combination of the first and second in that the pouring was actually carried out behind the screen but the child had to predict, by marking upon the screen, the level to which he expected the water to come in the second container. Pre- and posttests of conservation of liquid quantities were also employed.

The results showed that young children, who did not exhibit conservation on the standard test, nonetheless said that the amount of liquid was unchanged when it was poured into a wider container, but only when they could not actually see the level reached (first-task condition). They also predicted that the height reached by liquid poured from a narrow container into a wide one would be the same in the wide one as it had been in the narrow one (second-task condition). Thus, their judgment that the amount of liquid would be the same when poured into a wide container was based on the false premise that the level would not change with the width of the container. This interpretation of the apparent "conservation" was corroborated when, in the third task, the screen was removed and virtually all of the four year old children changed their judgment and said that the amount of water was not the same because the level was different.

Another finding, which according to Bruner demonstrates the role of misleading cues, was that after experiencing the three screening procedures, many children who were non-conservers in the pretest became conservers in the posttest. Apparently, the screening procedures had the effect of inducing conservation, at least in some children. This result supports a perceptual interpretation of conservation, but the support might be more convincing if the children who attained conservation in this way were shown *not* to be about to attain conservation spontaneously, through the utilization of operational thought. Other studies (e.g., Wallach, Wall, and Anderson, 1967) have shown the importance of determining the child's precise level of conservation before assessing the effectiveness of a particular training procedure.

The level of development of conservation can be assessed by determining if there are any circumstances under which a child will say that a quantity is conserved across a transformation of its appearance. For example, if the child says that the ball and the sausage of clay (in the test of conservation of mass) contain different amounts of clay but that they will both contain the same amount of clay if one is rolled back into a ball, he is more advanced than a child who says that the transformation is completely irreversible. Likewise, the child who judges a quantity as conserved across a relatively small alteration in its appearance but not across a relatively large one is more advanced than a child who will not acknowledge conservation under any circumstances.

Another study of the same type was reported by Mehler and Bever (1967). These investigators gave conservation problems to children as young as two years of age. The children were shown unequal numbers of elements in different arrays. In one array the more numerous elements were close together, and the less numerous were farther apart. The two and three year olds correctly judged the more numerous but shorter row to have more elements, but somewhat older children made the opposite judgment. Mehler and Bever argued that the child originally has conservation but later gets misled as he becomes more attentive to perceptual cues. Alternative interpretations can be made, however, particularly because the actual inequality of the two sets provided immediate perceptual cues to the solution. It is possible, for example, that the young children were responding on an undifferentiated basis of sheer numerosity and the older children were responding to a more differentiated perceptual impression of length. If so, the response of the two year olds would be analogous to the pseudo-conservation responses in Frank's investigation in the sense that they would be correct judgments made for reasons that, in the adult view, are wrong.

Still another example of this kind of study is the work of Gelman (1969). Gelman taught her subjects a large number of oddity problems (which require determining which one of three elements is different from the other two); the relevant dimension was size or number, but irrelevant dimensions such as color were also present. For example, in one problem there were three sticks, two of the same length and one shorter, but all the same color. Color was thus irrelevant to the problem, and the children had to focus upon size to attain the solution. Gelman found that a large proportion of her non-conserving children became conservers after the oddity problem training. She did not, however, diagnose how close these children were to attaining conservation prior to the training. Nevertheless, this study provides the most powerful evidence yet obtained for a perceptual as opposed to an operational interpretation of conservation.

LANGUAGE INTERPRETATIONS. The role of language in the solution of Piaget-type tasks has been explored from a number of different points of view, including direct tutelage on the correct verbal responses to the Piaget items (Kohnstamm, 1967; Sinclair-DeZwart, 1967). In general, the role of language seems to vary with the nature of the particular task used. Deaf children, without language competence, attain conservation at about the same age as hearing subjects (Furth, 1966). [Use of nonverbal procedures with normal children does not appear to make conservation easier (Wohlwill and Lowe, 1962).] Sinclair-DeZwart (1967) found that children who spontaneously described objects as tall *and* narrow or short *and* fat were conservers, and children who simply described objects as "big" or "little" did not conserve. However, training children to use the operational verbal formulas ("longer and narrower") did not affect their success on the conservation task. In contrast, Almy et al. (1966) reported that conservation was attained a year later in lower class children than in middle class children; this might be attributable to language deficit.

In classification problems, however, the situation is more dramatic. With such problems, which often include pictorial materials, children from culturally deprived or disadvantaged homes usually do much more poorly than middle class children. Sigel, Anderson, and Shapiro (1966a) and Sigel and McBane (1967) found that lower class Negro children were inferior to middle class Negro children in the ability to label pictorial materials. When content is important on a Piaget-type task, socioeconomic and cultural differences will probably be greater than when content is not important. This effect will be attributable at least in part to the great variations in linguistic training between, say, lower class Negro children and middle class white children (Bernstein, 1961).

LEARNING INTERPRETATIONS. Piaget (1967) held that the attainment of concrete operations and the attendant conservation, classification, and seriation concepts have an "optimal" time of development. Furthermore, although he believed that acceleration is possible, he also felt that the price paid for such acceleration may be too high. Acceleration is one goal of trying to train children to succeed on Piaget-type tasks, but it is not the only one nor the most important one. Many investigators who have carried out training studies have been concerned about whether or not such concepts as conservation can be taught in the traditional manner. If they can, then there would be no need to appeal to logical operations or "optimal periods of development."

In considering this kind of training or teaching study, however, the difference between what Flavell and Wohlwill (1969) called "performance" and "competence" must be made clear. Performance is the child's behavior in particular situations, and can be affected by a host of different factors. For example, a child who is unsure of his response on the conservation problem may look to the examiner for clues. If he finds such clues his performance may be successful, but it would not be a true index of his competence in conservation (it would be more an index of his competence in reading the examiner's clues). Obviously, it is easier to change a child's performance than his competence, and controls such as delayed posttests and tests for the generalizability and transfer of the training effects are required to determine whether training has genuinely altered the child's competence.

Unfortunately, not many of the training studies have taken this distinction seriously into account. Even so, many of the early attempts to train children on Piaget-type tasks were largely unsuccessful. In a study by Wohlwill and Lowe (1962) on number conservation, four groups of children were trained. One group was given trials in which they counted equal sets of elements in different spatial arrays. Another group had additional practice that illustrated that adding or taking away elements did indeed change the numerical quantity. A third group was trained to see that a set of elements spaced farther apart or closer together did not change in number. The fourth group was a nontraining control. Results showed that although all children made progress on a nonverbal measure of conservation of number, there was virtually no improvement on a verbal test of number conservation.

Perhaps the most extensive series of early training studies was carried out by Smedslund (1961a, 1961b, 1961c) on weight conservation. One of these experiments is of particular interest because it clearly exemplifies the competence-performance distinction mentioned above. Smedslund tested a group of children who demonstrated weight conservation on a pretest, and a group of children who did not manifest weight conservation on the pretest but who did do so after two training sessions. After this initial training and testing phase, the two groups participated in a modification of the training procedure, with two clay balls one of which was made into a sausage. In this procedure, children were allowed to verify the equal weights on a scale. Smedslund, however, surreptitiously removed a piece of the clay as he rolled it into a sausage. The children who had demonstrated conservation on the pretest tended to continue to maintain that the weights were equal, even when the scales did not confirm this, but most of the children who had acquired conservation in the training sessions reverted to perceptual explanations of the nonequivalence of the ball and sausage.

Although the results of these early studies were largely negative, more recent investigators have reported more positive results (Brison, 1965; Gelman, 1969; Kingsley and Hall, 1967; Sigel, Roeper, and Hooper, 1966b; I. D. Smith, 1968; Zimiles, 1966). However, not all of these investigators controlled for how advanced the children were before training. The work of Brison and Zimiles is of particular interest because motivation was manipulated. In the Brison study, the child's task was to get the most juice for himself after the juice was poured into containers of different sizes. This experience seemed to facilitate conservation. Motivation or *need* to conserve may turn out to be one of the most important variables in conservation performance.

In classification problems, which have been the concern of recent investigations, the effects of training are much more clear-cut. In a carefully controlled study of children's ability to deal with class inclusions ($A + A' = B$, $B - A' = A$, where A might be boys, A' girls, and B children), Kohnstamm concluded:

Briefly, the subjects to whom the standard inclusion problem had to be taught were *as a group* inferior in three ways to the groups who either discovered the solution immediately or after a series of related problems in *durability, resistance to counter suggestion and composition of a good inclusion item*. However, there were many taught subjects who performed as well as the non-taught subjects in the first two of these criteria and some who did as well in all three. (Kohnstamm, 1967, p. 144.)

Recently, Inhelder (1968) has reported that she and other co-workers of Piaget have also been concerned with instruction and have carried out extended training experiments. They have tried to devise procedures that would engage the child's interest and that would bring about spontaneous discrimination and coordination of relations. Although they have had some success, the amount of improvement is always relative to the child's level of development at the time training was undertaken. Older children move more quickly and with less training than do younger children.

In general, the training studies emphasize that success on Piagetian tasks is a complex matter and that the success of training will vary with at least (a) the child's level of development at the start of training, (b) the training method employed, (c) the particular tasks used, (d) the amount of training, and (e) the criteria used to evaluate success (e.g., delayed posttests and tests of generalization, transfer, and resistance to extinction). It is therefore not yet possible to make any general statements about the teachability of the concepts assessed by the Piagetian tests.

Relation of Performance on Piagetian Tasks to Other Variables

INTELLIGENCE. Piaget's tests are avowedly concerned with intelligence, but with a kind of intelligence different from that assessed with standard intelligence tests (IQ tests). Many IQ tests, such as the Stanford-Binet and the Wechsler scales (see Chapter 15, section entitled "Intelligence Testing"), contain tests of many different abilities, including perception, language skills, and sensori-motor coordination. For Piaget, however, intelligence refers exclusively to rational processes such as reasoning, problem solving, and concept formation. Not surprisingly, therefore, the correlations between performance on Piaget-type tests and performance on IQ tests are not exceptionally high.

Several investigators have reported correlations between Piaget-type tasks and IQ measures. Using a concept test, based in part upon Piaget-type tests, Beard (1960) obtained a correlation of .38 between performance and Stanford-Binet MA (mental age). Elkind (1961d) quantified several of Piaget's conservation tests (number, continuous and discontinuous quantity) and obtained a correlation of .43 with full-scale IQ on the Wechsler Intelligence Scale for Children. Correlations with various subtest IQs seemed to vary with the cognitive content of the subtest. Similarly, Dodwell (1961) used a Piagetian test of logical classification, and obtained a correlation of .34 with IQ. With a somewhat different approach, Hood (1962) observed that children with MA of less than five years almost never showed conservation, but children with MA of eight or nine years were almost always conservers. Goldschmid (1967) reported similar results.

In short, the Piagetian tests and IQ tests overlap to a certain extent but do not tap the same range of mental abilities. By and large, the Piagetian tests are more narrow and are limited to the assessment of cognitive processes, and IQ tests measure much else besides. In practical terms, what this probably means is that the Piagetian tests would predict general IQ well at the extremes—the very bright or very dull—but would be much less diagnostic of general intelligence in the middle range of mental ability.

PERSONALITY. The relation between performance on Piagetian tests and personality variables has only recently begun to attract the attention of researchers. For example, Inhelder (1968) reported results on Piagetian tests with psychotic children, and American work of this kind was recently reported by Goldschmid (1967, 1968). In one investigation (Goldschmid, 1967), a battery of Piagetian tests was given to normal children and to emotionally disturbed children; the emotionally disturbed children, who were on the average two years older than the normal children, were at about the same level of conservation behavior. This result was not clear-cut, however, because the emotionally disturbed children also had lower IQs, which could have been the critical variable.

In another study, Goldschmid (1968) gave a large battery of Piagetian tests and personality measures to children of middle class background. Goldschmid reported: "children with a high level of conservation tend to be (1) more objective in their self-evaluation, (2) described more favorably by their teachers, (3) preferred by their peers, (4) less dominated by their mothers, and (5) seen as more attractive and passive, than children with a low level of conservation" (Goldschmid, 1968, p. 579). In interpreting these results, the problem of IQ is again a factor because the same kinds of differences are found between high IQ and low IQ children (see Chapter 16, section entitled "Correlates of IQ"). The results are suggestive, however, and much more work of this kind is to be expected in the future.

SUMMARY

The present chapter has briefly outlined Piaget's developmental theory of intelligence, summarized some of the studies most representative of his work, and presented the research of other investigators who have taken Piaget's investigations and theory as a starting point for their own investigations. To a considerable extent the results Piaget has reported have been confirmed by other investigators all over the world. However, his interpretations of these findings, attributing the age changes in conservation, class concepts, and relation logic to the unfolding of mental operations, have been challenged by other workers. At present, there is no really clear-cut evidence that Piaget was wrong nor that he was right. His theories and research have, however, been tremendously fruitful and have produced a renaissance of the study of cognition. Whatever the fate of Piaget's theory of mental growth, the facts he has discovered about children's thinking are now a fundamental part of contemporary child psychology.

CHAPTER 15

Intelligence: Theory and Assessment

In the following pages, an area traditionally falling under the general heading of "intelligence" will be discussed. In this chapter general considerations will be emphasized—definitions of concepts, theories of intelligence, and characteristics of intelligence tests—and in Chapters 16 and part of 18 specific research findings on the development and correlates of intelligent behavior will be emphasized. Wherever relevant, problems of interpretation that have particularly beset this area will be pointed out, especially problems stemming from disagreement about how most appropriately to define "intelligence," from a tendency to regard intelligence tests as something more than they are, and from the close relation between research and certain controversial social issues.

PROBLEMS OF DEFINITION

A fundamental point is that, in practice, not "intelligence" but intelligent behavior is dealt with. Abstract verbal definitions of intelligence abound, but when practically meaningful statements are called for, these definitions must yield to behavioral ones.

Students in introductory psychology courses readily respond when asked, "What does it mean when you say someone is intelligent?" Common answers include, "He learns rapidly," "He knows a lot," "He can use past experience well," and "He's creative." However, these students would find the problem of arranging a group of people in order of increasing "intelligence" more difficult. Reference to verbal definitions alone would not help. The most likely solution would be to see how the people acted—to set them certain tasks and, on the basis of their performance on these tasks, arrange them in order of "intelligence." The tasks selected by each student would vary with his own preferred verbal definition, since there is no clearly delimited set of behaviors that all members of a given culture designate as intelligent. If our group of students included members of various cultural groups, the behavioral tasks chosen to represent intelligent behavior would vary still more widely. American students, for example, might wish to include a vocabulary test while Samoan students might wish to include a test of fishing and diving skill.

The situation is in some respects similar in scientific psychology. Numerous verbal definitions of intelligence have been offered. For example, Terman (1921) wrote, "An individual is intelligent in proportion as he is able to carry on abstract thinking" (p. 128). Wechsler (1944) maintained, "Intelligence is the aggregate or global capacity of the individual to act purposefully, to think rationally and to deal effectively with his environment" (p. 3), and the English psychologist, Burt (1955), defined intelligence as "innate, general, cognitive ability" (p. 162). For these psychologists, as for the students, however, the task of arranging people in order of "intelligence" could not be met by direct reference to their verbal definitions. They would either have to devise tasks or samples of behavior or use previously devised ones. When such tasks are formally assembled in ways to be discussed later, they are known as intelligence tests. The particular tasks that go into each test vary as widely as do the psychologists' verbal definitions.

The verbal definitions referred to in the preceding paragraph, and many others that cannot be included because of space limitations, have been valuable; they have stimulated the thinking and research efforts of individual psychologists and have led to the development of a host of useful tests. None, however, gives the concept of intelligence an *operational definition*—a criterion that is widely held to be essential by those viewing psychology as a scientific discipline logically akin to the older physical sciences. This viewpoint has been clearly and cogently set forth by Spiker and McCandless (1954), and their analyses underlie many discussions in these chapters. However, the interested student who wishes exposure to a somewhat different viewpoint, one that advocates defining intelligence as an hypothetical construct, may refer to papers by Jessor and Hammond (1947) and Cronbach and Meehl (1955).

Briefly, Spiker and McCandless (1954) held that to be scientifically meaningful, the concept of intelligence, like all other concepts in science, must be defined in terms of ultimately observable objects and events. To define intelligence, one specifies the observable conditions that must exist when the word is used. Each intelligence test and the behavior of the subject taking it constitute a separate, formally correct, operational definition of the concept. In this view, when one speaks of "John's intelligence" one means John's score on a particular test and the kind of nontest behavior that has been demonstrated to be associated with such a score.

Many psychologists today advocate defining intelligence in terms of a variety of laboratory and real life learning and problem-solving behaviors that go beyond those incorporated into traditional intelligence tests. Technically, this is a perfectly legitimate proposal. There is no necessary logical connection between the word "intelligence" and the kinds of tasks that are found in current tests. Also, expanding the use of the term in this way might help to break down popular misconceptions about the special status of traditional intelligence tests. However, any new definitions should be as subject to the operational requirements discussed above as are the old ones.

A more radical proposal is that because the word has come to refer to so many different complex sets of behaviors, it should be dropped completely as an explanatory concept. According to Liverant (1960), for example, the behaviors now subsumed under the term could be dealt with, with less confusion, in terms of the concepts of modern learning theory. This proposal seems to have great merit, but tradition militates against its acceptance in the forseeable future. It is important, therefore, that the student be aware of the great variety of ways in which the word is used in the literature.

Often, students find it hard to accept the notion that there is no one absolute definition of intelligence. They want to know how to evaluate the relative merits of the alternative definitions. The solution to this problem requires some elaboration.

Some people construe the question "Which is the best definition of intelligence?" to mean "Which is the *correct* definition?" Miles (1957) has suggested that these people are asking for a "real" definition, one that will reveal the "essential nature of the thing." Behind this quest lies an assumption that there is an entity—a thing—that *is* the "intelligence." It may be hidden, inaccessible to direct observation like an appendix, but it is there and the definition that most accurately describes it is the most correct one.

The fruitlessness of such a quest becomes apparent upon examination of the underlying assumption. If a number of people gave a definition of the word "appendix," it could be determined who gave the most accurate descriptive definition by surgically removing an appendix and looking at it, since it actually exists as an entity. The same could not be done for "intelligence." No one has ever seen an "intelligence," because no such entity exists. In other words, in the case of an appendix independent procedures can be specified through which the correctness of a "real" definition can be evaluated; in the case of "intelligence" this cannot be done. In recognition of this distinction Miles (1957) cautioned, "Any sentence starting 'intelligence is . . .' justifiably arouses one's suspicions" (p. 155).

In fairness, however, it should be pointed out that some who take the "entity approach" may simply be asserting their belief that there are physical correlates of intelligent behavior, events within the organism intervening between stimulating conditions and overt responses. With this interpretation there is no disagreement. Most psychologists believe that there are physiological structures and events relating to intellectual behavior, as well as to every other kind of behavior. Eventually, it is hoped, it will be possible to specify these relations and take account of them in the understanding and prediction of behavior.

The clearest criterion that can be applied in evaluating alternative definitions of intelligence is that of *usefulness,* in the sense of permitting reliable predictions about other behavior. Any operational definition of intelligence necessarily refers to some sample of behavior. Sometimes this sample takes the form of a standardized test, sometimes it does not. In any case, the investigator chooses a certain kind of sample because he assumes that it is representative of, or is related to, some larger domain of behavior. If it turns out, through empirical verification, that his assumption is correct, his definition can be said to be a good one. It is useful.

Consider, for example, the evaluation of alternative test definitions of intelligence. One is interested not in any intelligence test performance *per se,* but rather in whether this gives useful information about other areas of the subject's behavior that are of interest. Intelligence tests have always been used for practical purposes (Goodenough, 1954), such as placing children in adoptive homes, studying the correlates of delinquency, diagnosing behavioral disorders, and, especially, predicting success in scholastic and vocational endeavors. It has also been of interest to study the relation of intelligence test performance to various experimental learning tasks and to such status variables as personal popularity or membership in given socioeconomic, racial, or ethnic groups. Some intelligence tests are better than others in the sense of correlating more highly with other variables, but a given test may be good for one purpose and not for another. Therefore, it can never be said absolutely, "This test constitutes the best definition of intelligence." However, it is always possible to state the purpose for which a test will be used and to select the one best suited for that purpose. The same is true for any other behavioral definition of intelligence.

In summary, throughout these chapters "intelligence" will be taken to mean one or another variety of behaviors that members of our culture call intelligent. References to such things as its underlying nature will be taken to refer to the as yet unspecified physiological correlates of intelligent behavior.

THEORIES OF INTELLIGENCE

From the ancient Greeks onward through history, men have tried to formulate general theories concerning the nature and development of intelligent behavior. In this section a few twentieth century formulations that have attracted particular attention will be described.

Piaget: A Developmental Theory

In the United States there has been a recent resurgence of interest in the work of the Swiss psychologist, Jean Piaget. Previously known in America only through a few early works, Piaget has written voluminously. Flavell's (1963) comprehensive summary of his writings included an extensive bibliography of both his work and studies stimulated by it. Other useful summaries have been published by Hunt (1961), Maier (1965), and contributors to a monograph edited by Kessen and Kuhlman (1962). The theory is discussed in Chapter 14 (section entitled "Piaget's Developmental Theory of Intelligence"), and need be reviewed only briefly here.

Piaget viewed intelligence as a continuous process of adaptation to the environment. Intellectual development consists basically of changes in the way this adaptation is accomplished. The successive developmental stages—the sensorimotor period, pre-operational period, period of concrete operations, and period of formal operations—emerge gradually from babyhood onward as a result of the interaction of the maturing organism with its environment, and are hierarchical in nature. Each is built upon and incorporates the preceding one. Children vary in the ages at which they pass through each stage as a function of the richness of their environments, but the order of emergence is always the same. In each stage, there is a characteristic mode of cognition, which determines how the child adapts to his environment. In general, the child's progress through the stages is marked by decreasing dependence on subjective interpretations of his immediately perceivable environment and increasing ability to deal logically with abstract propositions about the world of the possible.

Despite the fact that Piaget has liberally illustrated his ideas with concrete behavioral observations, many behavioristic psychologists consider his research techniques to be quite imprecise (e.g., Braine, 1962). Another criticism is that there is evidence that neither the order nor the age levels of the developmental stages are always as he described them (Davies, 1965; Kofsky, 1966). Nevertheless, his acute descriptions of the qualitative dimensions of intellectual development make sense to many who work with children and it is likely that there will be a continuation of current research repeating his studies, and testing their educational implications, with more carefully controlled conditions and more objective methods of observation.

Hebb: A Physiological Theory

D. O. Hebb (1949, 1959) has been concerned with the physiological correlates of intelligent behavior. Along with many others, he was dissatisfied with a strict stimulus-response psychology that appeared to posit an empty, passive organism. He felt that an active, participating organism intervenes between observable stimuli and responses and that the crucial problem for psychology is the problem of *thought*. "In mammals even as low as the rat it has turned out to be impossible to describe behavior as an interaction directly between sensory and motor processes. Something like thinking intervenes" (Hebb, 1949, p. xviii).

For Hebb, thinking is identified with central neural processes. Specifically, he posited the existence of "cell assemblies" and "phase sequences" in the brain. Space does not permit description of the hypothesized neurological details, but the basic notions can be summarized. A cell assembly is "a brain process which corresponds to a particular sensory event, or a common aspect of a number of sensory events. This assembly is a closed system in which activity can 're-verberate' and thus continue after the sensory event which started it has ceased. . . . The assembly activity is the simplest case of an image or an idea: a representative process." The phase sequence is "a temporally integrated series of assembly activities: it amounts to one current in the stream of thought." (See Hebb, 1959, p. 629.)

The importance of early environmental stimulation is heavily stressed. Cell assemblies are built up slowly in infancy as a result of many repetitions of stimulating conditions, such as "exposure to a particular vowel sound," "an optical contour of a particular slope falling in the central foveal area," and "a series of tactual stimulations as the infant's hand touches a rattle, a bar of his crib, the milk bottle, and so forth" (Hebb, 1959, p. 628).

There is a great deal of evidence on the animal level, summarized by Hunt (1961), that organisms deprived of environmental stimulation in infancy later show impaired problem solving ability as compared to animals not so deprived. Presumably, this is attributable to failure to develop appropriate cell assemblies during critical periods in infancy. Many psychologists feel that similar explanations may account for poor intellectual performances in human children whose earliest months and years are characterized by extreme lack of environmental stimulation. Some relevant data will be considered later.

Transfer plays a central role in Hebb's system. All learning beyond that occurring in the earliest years involves transfer from prior learning. Individuals who suffer early deprivation do not build up an adequate repertoire of skills and concepts that can then transfer to new situations.

Hebb's emphasis on early experience stemmed not only from the results of animal experiments, but also from findings that some adult humans who underwent extensive brain surgery did not show subsequent deterioration on the kinds of intelligence test items that rely heavily on abstract verbal skills. He was led by such findings to hypothesize that the presence of intact brain tissue during the early years of cell assembly growth is essential, but that once the cell assemblies and phase sequences have been established, considerable brain tissue can be lost without functional loss in familiar problem solving situations. The surgical data, and observations on infant sensory stimulation, underscore the provocative notion that early learning experiences may be more important determinants of adult intellectual functioning than later ones.

Finally, as background for later discussions of the effects of heredity and environment, it is important to note Hebb's distinction between "Intelligence A" and "Intelligence B." The first is innate potential that "amounts to the possession of a good brain and neural metabolism"; the second refers to "the functioning of a brain in which development has gone on, determining an average level of performance or comprehension by the partly grown or mature person" (Hebb, 1949, p. 294). Intelligence A is no guarantee of the development of Intelligence B, which depends on experience, although A may set upper limits on B. Test scores are primarily related to B. As Hebb put it,

> The I.Q. can be trusted as an index of A only when the social backgrounds of the subjects compared are identical; and this adds up to the proposition that we cannot in any rigorous sense measure a subject's innate endowment, for no two social backgrounds are identical and we do not know what the important environmental variables are in the development of intellectual functions. (Hebb, 1949, p. 300.)

Ferguson: A Learning Theory

G. A. Ferguson (1954, 1956) was strongly influenced by Hebb, but his approach to the problem of intelligence was a general attempt to integrate the traditionally separate fields of individual differences (ability description) and learning. He maintained that the only useful meaning that can be given the term intelligence is that of a collection of distinguishable learned abilities. Specifically, he referred to abilities that have been thoroughly overlearned under intermittent reinforcement and have thereby achieved relative stability. In the adult they are assumed to be stable over long periods of time; in the child they have at least considerable stability at any given age. Examples of these abilities include what Thurstone (1938) called perceptual, spatial, number, and reasoning abilities.

Abilities are acquired through the individual's experiences with his environment. Biological factors are important in determining ultimate level, but which particular abilities are learned depends upon the cultural milieu. In each culture certain abilities are necessary for effective adaptation and, indeed, survival. These abilities are valued; they are learned and show increments with age because their occurrence is rewarded by parents or other agents who reflect the values of the culture. Since cultures differ widely, they demand the learning of different abilities at different ages. As an illustration of this principle, Ferguson referred to Burnett's (1955) finding that children growing up in isolated Newfoundland outport communities develop perceptual and motor abilities to a high level, while the verbal and reasoning skills less essential for survival in that setting are not highly developed. Similarly, on standard intelligence tests which rely heavily on abstract verbal abilities, the IQs of children in such nonurban milieus as English canal boats and remote American mountain communities decline with age. Ferguson also strongly agreed with the Hebbian view that the age at which environmental experiences occur is crucial. Unless children receive stimulation conducive to the acquisition of, say, verbal ability early in life, they are likely never to attain a high level of proficiency in that ability.

Ferguson went beyond Hebb in the emphasis on the concept of transfer. Transfer is assumed to operate, first of all, in the course of acquisition of abilities. "The distinctive abilities which emerge in the adult in any culture [are] those that tend to facilitate rather than inhibit each other" (Ferguson, 1956, p. 121). Moreover, abilities transfer, either positively or negatively, in the course of all new learning. "The role of human ability in subsequent learning, for example, intelligence in relation to scholastic performance, can be viewed as a problem in transfer" (Ferguson, 1954, p. 110). However, transfer is differential. Abilities that transfer at an early stage of learning may be quite different from those that transfer at a later stage of learning. It is also quite likely that transfer of abilities varies with cultural background: " . . . through learning, individuals in diverse cultures may bring different abilities to bear on the solution of an identical problem" (Ferguson, 1954, p. 108). In view of the above considerations, the same intellectual task presented to subjects with varying degrees and kinds of past experience may present very different problems.

In short, Ferguson viewed intelligence as a collection of overlearned abilities. Transfer is important both in the acquisition and later effects of these abilities. Since cultural demands vary, the abilities acquired by individuals in different cultures vary. There is, accordingly, not one "intelligence" but many, corresponding to the diversity of cultural demands. This general viewpoint provides a background that is especially pertinent to the evaluation of data on group differences in intelligence test performance, which will be presented later.

Statistical Theories

THE METHOD OF FACTOR ANALYSIS. Several formulations about the nature of intelligence have been based on statistical analyses of the test responses of subjects. In particular, use has been made of various correlational techniques known as *factor analysis*. Although the technicalities of factor analysis are complicated and beyond the scope of this text, the basic logic is fairly simple.

Briefly, when factor analysis is to be used, a group of subjects is given a large number of tasks. The tasks may be all the items in a particular test or, more commonly, all the items in a large number of separate tests. Correlations are computed between scores on all the possible combinations of the tasks. When this is done, the tasks are found to fall into clusters; each cluster includes tasks that are highly correlated with each other and not highly correlated with tasks forming other clusters. Tasks that are highly correlated (that is, tasks on which subjects show a high degree of consistency of performance) define a "factor"; in other words, each factor is defined as a cluster of intercorrelated tasks. The factors obtained vary with the tasks that are used, the subjects who are tested, and the computational technique that is employed.

Factors, operationally defined, refer simply to a given pattern of intertask correlations. However, most investigators go beyond this. They look at the various tasks that define a factor, try to judge what skills are involved, and name the factor by referring to these skills. For example, factors have been given such names as "verbal comprehension," "numerical ability," and "spatial relations ability." As Anastasi has pointed out, "This step calls for psychological insight rather than statistical training" (Anastasi, 1961, p. 342).

To counteract a common tendency to make unwarranted assumptions about what factors "really" represent, it is important to keep in mind that factors are "discovered" statistically and named subjectively. It is possible that there are unique physiological systems underlying at least some of the factors that have been identified, but what they are is an empirical question, the answer to which cannot be given at the present stage of knowledge.

With this background, a survey of some of the influential statistical formulations that have been offered in this century can be given. It will be apparent that the major trend has been toward increased proliferation of factors.

SPEARMAN'S THEORY. The English statistician, Charles Spearman (1904, 1927), was the first to make major use of the technique of factor analysis. He found sufficient intercorrelation among the tasks he used to maintain that there was operating in all intellectual tasks a general or g factor, which he thought of as a general mental energy. In addition, he identified a number of specific or s factors that were unique to separate tasks. Performance on any task was, thus, based on a certain amount of the universal factor g and a certain amount of s unique to that task. This principle is known as the two-factor theory of intelligence. As Spearman and his students continued their work, it became apparent that some of the specific factors overlapped and that the correlations between them were too large to be explained on the basis of the amount of g in each. Thus, it was necessary to introduce, reluctantly, "group" factors less universal than g but less specific than s.

THURSTONE'S THEORY. In the late 1930s and 1940s L. L. Thurstone refined and elaborated factor analytic procedures to make them suitable for the analysis of many factors at once (e.g., Thurstone, 1947). Thurstone began with the belief that intelligent behavior can best be described in terms of a series of relatively distinct factors, and he and his co-workers did succeed in identifying a number of such "primary mental abilities." However, Thurstone and Thurstone (1941) analyzed the scores of a large number of school children on 21 tests and identified seven factors that have come to be the ones most often associated with Thurstone's name. The seven factors are *perceptual speed, number, word fluency, verbal comprehension, space, associative memory,* and *induction* or *general reasoning.* Thurstone (1948) eventually included a general factor somewhat analogous to Spearman's g, but he did not consider it to be as important as the primary mental abilities for purposes of describing an individual's intellectual skills.

Thurstone (1948) was strongly of the opinion that factor analysis should be regarded as a tool for psychological understanding rather than as a mathematical exercise. "If we have no psychological ideas, we are not likely to discover anything interesting because even if the factorial results are clear and clean, the interpretation must be as subjective as in any other scientific work" (Thurstone, 1948, p. 402). He also believed that his technique of multiple factor analysis would eventually result in the breakdown of the traditional line of demarcation between intellect and temperament because it would enable psychologists to study the effects of both kinds of factors in the performance of intellectual tasks. This is a viewpoint that is becoming increasingly popular, and it will be discussed in more detail in a later section ("Correlates of IQ," in Chapter 16).

GUILFORD'S THEORY. J. P. Guilford's theory of human intellect is known as *SI* or *Structure of Intellect* (Guilford, 1956, 1957, 1959, 1966). Beginning with a thoughtful examination of 37 factors that had already been identified, Guilford conceived the idea that human intellectual activities could be described in terms of the subdivisions of three major dimensions—operations, products, and contents. As presently conceived, this three-dimensional model postulates some 120 separate factors. Guilford (1966) reported that 80 of these had already been demonstrated and that a great deal of research was underway with the aim of demonstrating the others.

This theory, which is referred to again in the discussion of gifted children in Chapter 16, is of major significance in the United States today. It exemplifies the current tendency to expand the definition of intelligence beyond the limits of traditional tests. As Sarason and Gladwin put it, "Guilford's description and discussion of these factors represent a systematic attempt to observe in a test situation intellectual processes which heretofore had been noted as important in the non-test problem solving behavior of people" (Sarason and Gladwin, 1958, p. 55). Because the theory is currently attracting so much attention, it is important to understand at least the basic principles, which are brought out in the following extensive descriptive quotation from Guilford, and are diagrammed in Figure 15-1.

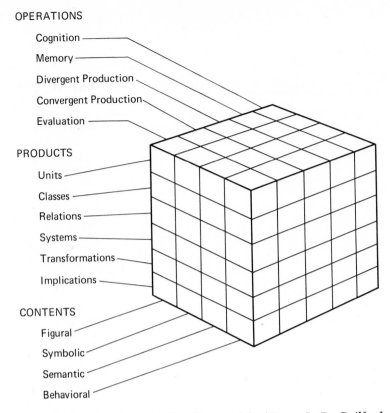

Fig. 15-1. Guilford's Structure of Intellect model. (From J. P. Guilford, "Intelligence: 1965 model," *American Psychologist*, 1966, *21*, 20–26. Fig. 1, p. 21. Copyright 1966 by the American Psychological Association, and reprinted by permission of the author and publisher.)

One basis of classification is according to the basic kind of process or operation performed. This kind of classification gives us five major groups of intellectual abilities: factors of cognition, memory, convergent thinking, divergent thinking and evaluation.

Cognition means discovery or rediscovery or recognition. Memory means retention of what is cognized. Two kinds of productive-thinking operations generate new information from known information and remembered information. In divergent-thinking operations we think in different directions, sometimes searching, sometimes seeking variety. In convergent thinking the information leads to one right answer or to a recognized best or conventional answer. In evaluation we reach decisions as to goodness, correctness, suitability, or adequacy of what we know, what we remember, and what we produce in productive thinking.

A second way of classifying the intellectual factors is according to the kind of material or content involved. The factors known thus far involve three kinds of material or content: the content may be figural, symbolic or semantic. Figural content is concrete material such as is perceived through the senses. It does not represent anything except itself. Visual material has properties such as size, form, color, location, or texture. Things we hear or feel provide other examples of figural material. Symbolic content is composed of letters, digits, and other conventional signs, usually organized in general systems, such as the alphabet or the number system. Semantic content is in the form of verbal meanings or ideas, for which no examples are necessary. . . . Along the dimension of content a fourth category has been added, its kind of content being designated as "behavioral." This category has been added on a purely theoretical basis to represent the general area sometimes called "social intelligence."

When a certain operation is applied to a certain kind of content, as many as six general kinds of products may be involved. There is enough evidence available to suggest that, regardless of the combinations of operations and content, the same six kinds of products may be found associated. The six kinds of products are units, classes, relations, systems, transformations and implications. (Guilford, 1959, pp. 470–471. Quoted by permission.)

Concluding Remarks

The trend is away from general toward multifactor conceptions of intelligence. There is, however, certainly no universal agreement as to the desirability of this trend. Despite growing advocacy of the use of batteries of tests that yield many separate scores, tests based on the notion of g continue to be widely used. These include the Stanford-Binet (Terman and Merrill, 1960) and the Progressive Matrices (Raven, 1956, 1958) tests. McNemar (1964) is a particularly staunch advocate of general, single-score tests, maintaining that they continue to be better predictors of nontest behavior than any available battery. Garrett's (1946) position, which is similar to that of Burt (1954) and Lienert and Crott (1964), may perhaps be regarded as a middle ground. He studied the correlations between factors as a function of age and concluded that overall ability or g looms large in the elementary school years but is less in evidence at the high school and college levels, when "general ability dissolves into more specialized talents . . ." (Garrett, 1946, p. 376). Clearly, there is need for further research. Particularly, data are needed on the predictive value of special-ability batteries used to test young children.

INTELLIGENCE TESTING

Since so much of the data on intellectual development has come from intelligence tests, it is important for the student to be aware of the nature of these instruments. Accordingly, in the following sections a brief overview of the major aspects of a highly technical field is given.

Construction and Standardization Procedures

The potential test constructor begins by deciding what he wants his test to do. Often, this involves simply listing the nontest criteria that he wants to be able to predict. Sometimes, however, a constructor wants his test to constitute a small behavioral sample of a kind of activity believed on theoretical grounds to be important. For example, Guilford and his co-workers attempt to devise tests of the various postulated factors in the "structure of intellect" model (e.g., Guilford, 1966).

In either case, the constructor must amass a large pool of items judged to be suitable for his purpose. Sometimes he uses or adapts items that have been used in other tests; sometimes he devises new ones. This initial pool of items is then tried out on subjects of the sort for whom the final test is intended. Administration and scoring procedures are refined, awkward items eliminated, and the difficulty level of each item determined by the percentages of tryout subjects who pass and fail it. After one or several tryouts, the constructor makes a final selection of items. He retains the ones that meet his needs for ease and efficiency of administering and scoring, and that cover what he feels to be a suitable range of difficulty.

The constructor is then ready to amass performance averages or norms to publish with his test. He does this by administering the test to a standardization sample—a group, preferably a large one, representative of the total population for whom the test is intended. If, for example, he is constructing a group intelligence test for American high school students, a suitable standardization sample would consist of a large group of American high school students representative of all American high school students in terms of geographical distribution, socioeconomic status, sex, race, and kind of school attended. The distribution of scores earned by this sample would establish the general norms for the test.

After the test and its norms are published, the performance of anyone who takes it is usually compared with the norms from the general standardization sample. Sometimes, however, the constructor amasses and publishes norms for various circumscribed groups, and sometimes an administrator builds up his own set of norms to use for the specific groups with which he must deal. Always, however, an individual score is evaluated with reference to the performance of some standardization sample.

Several different kinds of norms have been used, including age, grade, percentile, and standard score norms. It is important to remember that norms are not universal facts, but come from some particular standardization population, which may differ in many ways from other populations of interest. *Age* and *grade norms* are obtained by computing the average raw score of children in the standardization sample at selected age or grade levels, and are utilized by converting an examinee's raw score into the equivalent age or grade level. For example, if eight year old children in the standardization sample obtained an average raw score of 25 on some test, then an examinee who obtained a raw score of 25 would be said to have a mental age of eight years (or he is said to show typical eight year old ability). *Percentile norms* indicate what percentage of the standardization group obtained raw scores less than a particular score. For example, if 75 percent of the group obtained scores less than 30 on some test, then an examinee who obtained a score of 30 would be said to score at the 75th percentile. *Standard score norms* express each raw score in terms of its distance from the mean in standard deviation units.[1] Standard

---

[1] The equation for computing a standard score is

$$Z = \frac{b(X - M)}{SD} + a$$

where Z is the standard score, X is the raw score, M and SD are the mean and standard deviation of the raw scores, b is to be the standard deviation of the standard scores, and a is to be the mean of the standard scores.

score norms have certain technical advantages over the other kinds of norms, and are becoming increasingly popular, but they are probably harder to understand intuitively.

It has become conventional to refer to any score on an intelligence test as an IQ (Intelligence Quotient), and this will be done throughout these chapters even though, as has just been seen, such scores actually take a variety of forms. Historically, IQ referred to the kind of scoring first used widely in the United States with the 1916 Stanford-Binet. It involved calculating the child's mental age (MA), by using age norms, then dividing his MA by his chronological age (CA), and multiplying by 100 to yield the IQ. Thus, the traditional age ratio formula was: $IQ = 100 \times MA/CA$. The average child's MA equalled his CA, yielding an IQ of 100; the slow child's MA was less than his CA, yielding an IQ below 100; and the bright child attained an IQ greater than 100 since his MA exceeded his CA.

Over the years it became apparent that the traditional age ratio IQ had serious weaknesses, and very few of the tests in use today still utilize it. A major fault lay in the fact that identical IQs represented different degrees of inferiority or superiority at different age levels, because the variability of IQ was not constant at all ages in the standardization samples. If at one age the standard deviation were 10, an IQ of 110 would indicate that the examinee had surpassed 84 percent of the standardization sample. If at another age the standard deviation were 16, this examinee would need an IQ of 116 to maintain the same relative degree of superiority. Because of this difficulty, in the 1960 revision of the Stanford-Binet, which is described later, the traditional age ratio IQ was abandoned and replaced by a score called a *deviation IQ,* which is essentially a standard score that is transformed to have a mean of 100 and a standard deviation of 16 at all ages. A given deviation IQ therefore indicates the same relative placement at all ages.

Many parents and some professionals have built up rather rigid views about what to expect of children with various IQs. To some extent this can be traced to indiscriminate popular dissemination of such descriptive terms as "superior," "normal," "dull," etc., ascribed to various Stanford-Binet IQ categories. For reasons that will be explained below, however, it is now more widely recognized that a given IQ has no universal significance, and therefore many administrators are reluctant to reveal to subjects or their parents the exact score earned on any intelligence test.

As already noted, the same score, even on one instrument, may indicate different relative levels of performance at different ages. It is not surprising, therefore, that the same score often indicates different relative levels of performance on different instruments. Several studies clearly demonstrate that the same individual can earn very different IQs on different tests (e.g., Dreger, 1953; Heil and Horn, 1950), and data from the Harvard Growth Study show a wide range of equivalent IQ norms for a number of group intelligence tests (Dearborn and Rothney, 1963). For example, in the Harvard Growth Study the 75th percentile on four widely used tests (the Dearborn, Otis, Haggerty, and Terman tests) was represented by IQs of 109, 117, 122, and 133. The discrepancy between

IQs on different tests results in part from the use of different standardization populations, and in part from the sampling of different skills in different tests. An individual who performs one set of skills well seldom performs another set of skills exactly as well. The amount of expected discrepancy varies, of course, with the correlation between the two tests. Also, in interpreting any IQ it is necessary to keep in mind the characteristics of the examinee in relation to the characteristics of the standardization population. If a college freshman takes a test standardized for graduate students, he is apt to do more poorly than if he takes a test standardized for high school students.

Any IQ should be regarded simply as a score on a specific test. Its interpretation varies with the type of items involved and the nature and variability of the standardization sample. It should never be regarded as a permanent characteristic of an individual indicating a general level of superiority in all intellectual activities. These and other points concerning the nature of IQs have been ably discussed in greater detail by Cautela (1958, 1959) and Dyer (1960).

Reliability and Validity

If a test is to be useful at all, it must have both reliability and validity.

RELIABILITY. *Reliability* is usually defined as *consistency*—the extent to which a score earned by an individual is repeatable, at least over short periods of time. A test is reliable if the variation among individuals does not result from the operation of chance variables irrelevant to the purpose of the test; more technically, a test is reliable if the amount of error variance is minimal.

Error variance can stem from any one or a combination of various sources. On a given administration of a test, temporary factors operating in either the subject or the environment may influence performance. Examples include illness or fatigue and poor lighting or distracting noises. Error variance can also result from poor selection of test items out of the population of all possible relevant test items, or from poor techniques of administering or scoring. The last-named source is especially important when scoring involves subjective judgments. Sources of error operating in one administration of a test affect the subject's earned score, and if these sources of error are not operating in a subsequent administration of the same test or an equivalent test, the subject is likely to earn a very different score. Note, however, that if the temporal separation between the two administrations is extreme, it may be reasonable to assume that a change in score reflects a change in the basic skill.[2] (For a more detailed discussion of these kinds of variables, see Jones, 1954, pp. 643–645.)

Several statistical techniques are available to estimate how much of the total test variance is attributable to the various sources of error. Without going into detail, it can be said that each involves the calculation of a correlation coefficient. The higher the correlation, the higher the reliability. Test users

---

[2] "Basic skill" is a theoretical concept, but not a particularly rigorous one. It refers to the subject's level of test performance under error-free conditions plus related nontest performance.

typically demand reliability of at least .85.[3] Preliminary calculations of reliability may be based on the performance of the standardization sample. Additional data are, of course, accumulated over the years as the test is put to practical use.

VALIDITY. There has been disagreement about what constitutes *validity* of a test, stemming from disagreement about what constitutes proper definition of a concept. For those who adhere to a strictly operational approach, the issue is clear. The essential principles of this approach have already been discussed in the section on definition, but bear elaboration in the present context. A test is valid if it is useful in the sense of entering into relations with other variables. If scores on a test correlate with other measures, such as clinicians' or teachers' judgments, the test is said to be valid. If the criterion measures are obtained at about the same time as the test scores, the test has *concurrent validity;* and if the criterion measures are obtained at some later date, such as posttest scholastic or vocational success, the test has *predictive validity.* In a sense, the amount of criterion-based validity of any test is open-ended, because it is always possible, in principle at least, to demonstrate a relation between the test and some new criterion measure.

For those who prefer not to rely entirely on operational definitions, validity has a different meaning. Some, for example, view intelligence as a "theoretical construct"—a postulated trait assumed to have certain properties. A test is considered to be valid if it "measures what it is supposed to measure," if scores on the test conform to theoretical expectations. This kind of validity is called *construct validity.* For example, one might incorporate into one's theoretical construct of intelligence the idea that it is related to "achievement motivation." In this case a test that showed the predicted relation with a given measure of achievement motivation would be said to show construct validity.[4]

There is considerable disagreement in the literature over the scientific legitimacy of the concept of construct validity (Bechtoldt, 1959; Clark, 1959). Nevertheless, the student should be aware of what is meant by it and should be able to distinguish between the different kinds of validity data reported for various instruments. A comprehensive discussion of both reliability and validity is available in the *Technical Recommendations for Psychological Tests and Diagnostic Techniques,* published by the American Psychological Association (1954).

Some Widely Used Tests

Available intelligence tests for children can be classified in various ways. Some are suitable only for restricted age levels; some can be administered in

[3] A correlation of .85 would mean than 72.25 percent of the variability in the second test can be predicted from scores on the first test; the other 27.75 percent is attributed to error. The proportion that is predicted is equal to the square of the correlation coefficient.

[4] Many test constructors consider intelligence to be a general trait that increases with age, and when they succeed in constructing a test that shows increments in scores with increasing age, they offer this as evidence of construct validity. However, since test constructors eliminate items that in preliminary testing fail to show an increment with age, the increment with age is built into the test and therefore provides no real evidence of construct validity.

groups, and others require individual administration; most rely heavily on verbal skills, requiring the child to respond with or to spoken or written words, but a few, intended for use with children who have speech, hearing, or language handicaps, minimize the use of verbal skills. These last, the so-called performance tests, use manipulative or purely visual materials, and often use pantomimic techniques of administration. Buro's (1965) *Mental Measurements Yearbook* is an excellent source of descriptions and critiques of currently available tests. In this section a few widely used tests from different categories will be described.

AN INFANT INTELLIGENCE TEST. The Cattell Infant Intelligence Scale (Cattell, 1960) was standardized on a sample of 274 lower-middle class white infants in the Boston area. The scale covers the range from 2 to 30 months of age and was intended to be a downward extension of the Stanford-Binet. As is true in all infant scales, items at the early age levels are entirely sensory or motor in content. At 3 months, for instance, the infant is given credit for following a moving ring with his eyes, inspecting his own fingers, and holding his head erect without wobbling. At 6 months he gets credit for lifting an aluminum cup and reaching out to and fingering his reflection in a mirror. Increasingly complex perceptual and motor responses are required throughout the remaining age levels. However, rudimentary verbal skills are considered at later ages, beginning at 11 months when the child is given credit if the mother reports a one-word vocabulary. At 18 months the child must point out various body parts on a doll, and later he must identify pictures of objects by name. Scoring involves the calculation of a traditional age ratio IQ.

It is difficult to hold the attention of a very young infant and to interpret his fleeting responses. This is reflected by very low reliability at the earliest age levels. After 6 months, however, reliability is satisfactory. Construct validity in the sense of increasing percentage passing with age was built into the scale. Predictive validity in the sense of correlations with IQs earned later in childhood is poor, as it also is for the other infant tests. This is not surprising when the nature of the items is considered. Late in the nineteenth century, there were unsuccessful attempts to develop formal tests of intelligence using the same kinds of items with older children and adults. The items assessed simple sensory and motor abilities such as acuteness of color vision, judgment of absolute pitch, reaction time, and dynamometer pressure (Cattell, 1890). It was found that performance was unrelated to estimates of intellectual level based on teachers' ratings and on academic grades (see Anastasi, 1954, pp. 8–10; Goodenough, 1949, pp. 40–42).

A PERFORMANCE TEST. The Progressive Matrices (Raven, 1956, 1958) are performance tests which have been fairly widely used in both the United States and England. They require subjects to educe relations among abstract items, and were designed as measures of *g*. The items consist of sets of geometrical designs of increasing complexity, from each of which a piece has been cut out. The subject's task is to select the missing part from a number of alternatives. The

Coloured Progressive Matrices (Raven, 1958) were standardized on a sample of 608 Scottish children and were intended for use with children between the ages of 5 and 11 years, with mental patients, and with senescents. Norms are expressed in percentile form. The most recent review of research on this test reveals that data on reliability and validity are quite sparse (Burke, 1958).

A GROUP TEST. The latest edition of the Lorge-Thorndike tests (Lorge, Thorndike, and Hagen, 1964) is usable from the third grade to the college freshman level. It includes verbal tests, such as vocabulary, verbal classification, sentence completion, arithmetic reasoning, and verbal analogy, and nonverbal tests, such as pictorial classification, pictorial analogy, and numerical relations. The scale was standardized on a very large representative sample of 180,000 pupils in 70 school systems in 42 states. Four types of norms were developed: deviation IQs, grade percentiles, grade equivalents, and age equivalents. Reliability is high.

Members of the standardization sample also furnished the norms for two achievement batteries, the Iowa Tests of Basic Skills and the Tests of Academic Progress. Correlations between Lorge-Thorndike scores and scores on the achievement batteries give evidence of concurrent validity. Specifically, correlations between the Lorge-Thorndike verbal battery and total achievement on the Iowa tests range from .79 in Grade 3 to .88 in Grade 8, with most of the values in the middle and upper .80s. For the nonverbal battery correlations range from .65 in Grade 3 to .77 in Grade 8, with most of the values in the middle to upper .70s. Scores on the verbal and nonverbal batteries correlate about .88 and .77, respectively, with total achievement scores on the Tests of Academic Progress. Additional reliability and validity information is clearly reported in the technical manual (Lorge, Thorndike, and Hagen, 1966).

THE STANFORD-BINET. The successive revisions of the Stanford-Binet published by Terman and his associates (Terman and Merrill, 1960) have long been widely used and highly regarded both in the United States and abroad. In recent years the Wechsler Intelligence Scale for Children (Wechsler, 1949) has offered real competition, but to many the term IQ is still synonymous with Stanford-Binet IQ.

The Stanford-Binet is individually administered and yields a single score presumably indicative of g. The first version was published in 1916 and was followed in 1937 by the publication of a revision with two equivalent forms, Form L and Form M. The 1937 standardization sample consisted of 3184 native-born white children. The sample was approximately representative of the United States in terms of geographical, rural-urban, and socioeconomic distribution, although urban residents and members of the higher socioeconomic classes were somewhat overrepresented. Table 15-1 shows the approximate distribution of traditional age ratio IQ scores in the 1937 standardization sample; for example, about 2.65 percent obtained scores below 70, and were therefore in the range usually identified as "mentally retarded," and about 1.35 percent scored 140 or above, thus falling in the "very superior" range. (The labels are not always appropriate, because criteria other than IQ are also important in classifying individuals.)

The latest revision (Terman and Merrill, 1960) is a single form made up of the best items from the 1937 forms arranged in levels from two years of age through superior adult. In the 1960 version, some items from the 1937 forms

Table 15-1

Approximate Percentile Ranks of Selected IQ Scores[a]

IQ	Percentage below
30	.02
40	.05
50	.25
60	.65
70	2.65
80	8.25
90	22.75
100	45.75
110	69.25
120	87.35
130	95.55
140	98.65
150	99.75
160	99.95
170	99.98
180	99.99+

[a] Age ratio IQs from 1937 standardization of the Stanford-Binet. (Adapted from Merrill, 1938, Table VII, p. 650.)

were reallocated to different age levels since over the years their difficulty levels had changed. Also, as previously mentioned, the traditional age ratio IQ was abandoned in favor of the deviation IQ. However, there was not complete re-standardization. The norms are still based on the performance of the previously described 1937 standardization sample.

At the preschool levels, the Stanford-Binet includes many performance items. At the Year 3 level, for example, the child must string beads, build a block tower, and copy a printed circle. However, at later levels there is a heavy verbal emphasis, represented, for example, in picture vocabulary items in which the child must identify pictures of common objects. Throughout the school years, verbal items predominate. At Year 6 the child must define words, tell the difference between pairs of common objects, name the missing parts in mutilated pictures, count blocks, give antonyms, and trace a simple maze. At Year 14 he must again define words, deduce a rule stating how many holes will appear when folded paper is cut, and reason out the solution to a simple mystery. He must also solve some fairly complicated arithmetic problems, demonstrate knowledge of directions, and come up with a verbal concept integrating pairs of words of opposite meanings.

Reliability of the 1937 scale was determined by correlating performance on the equivalent forms. While it is not possible to do this with the single-form 1960 revision, many are willing to accept the old figures since, presumably, the improved version would have at least as high reliability as the old one. Reliability of the 1937 scales was high, especially for older subjects and those in the lower IQ ranges.

Terman and Merrill (1960) themselves relied heavily on construct validity claims. They pointed out that the test was constructed in such a way that there is a regular increase in MA from one age to the next and that each item correlates with performance on the total scale. Both these elements are demanded by their view that intelligence is a general trait that increases with age. Evidence for concurrent and predictive validity of the Stanford-Binet scales abounds in the literature of five decades. Only the relation to scholastic performance will be considered here, as illustrative of this literature.

According to Anastasi (1961, p. 205) the correlations between Stanford-Binet IQs and school grades, teachers' ratings, and achievement test scores are typically between .40 and .75. The strength of the relation varies with the subject matter; it is strongest for highly verbal areas such as reading comprehension, less strong for quantitative areas such as arithmetic. Working with fourth, fifth, and sixth graders, Clelland and Toussaint (1962) found a correlation of .61 with reading ability and one of only .21 with arithmetic achievement. Bond (1940) tested tenth graders and found correlations of .73 with reading comprehension, .59 with history, .54 with biology, and .48 with geometry. Sartain (1946) found a correlation of .58 with first year college grades.

LIMITATIONS ON VALIDITY. The discussions of both the Lorge-Thorndike and the Stanford-Binet have shown that standardized intelligence tests administered during the school years have substantial correlations with academic performance. Such tests are, in fact, widely used in educational settings as a basis for classroom groupings and for educational guidance. It must be remembered, however, that none of the correlations is perfect, and that many things besides the skills sampled by intelligence tests determine academic performance.

Both anxiety and scholastic motivation as defined by standardized tests have been shown to have significant relations to school success (Feldhausen and Klausmeier, 1962; Keller and Rowley, 1962; McBee and Duke, 1960; McCandless and Castaneda, 1956; Sarason, Hill, and Zimbardo, 1964). Also, Dave (1963) found a correlation of .80 between educational achievement and ratings on a home environment scale. Moreover, many subtle motivational factors associated with parental attitudes and membership in various socioeconomic or racial groups affect school performance. Clearly, then, whenever important educational decisions are to be made about individual children, intelligence test scores should be just one of the variables taken into account.

CHAPTER 16

Intelligence: Development and Correlates

With the enormous growth of the testing movement in the twentieth century, a large body of data has been amassed relating intelligence test performance to a host of other variables. In this chapter some of the most important relations will be explored. It will become clearly apparent that far too few of the studies were aimed at theory testing; the vast majority were almost entirely empirical, designed to gather normative data.

GROWTH TRENDS

Most of the data on changes in intelligence test performance with age have come from longitudinal studies, in which the same children were repeatedly observed over a number of years. There are certain inherent difficulties in the use of the longitudinal method. It is never possible, for example, to assess precisely the practice effects resulting from repeated testing. Moreover, there is inevitable attrition of the sample as subjects move or for other reasons drop out of the study. If the attrition is selective, it may be quite damaging to the usefulness of the study. In general, however, the disadvantages of the method are far outweighed by the fact that it is only through repeated measurement of the same individual that patterns of individual as well as group development can be discovered.

Brief descriptions of two major projects will illustrate the variations among longitudinal studies in the size and representativeness of the samples, the length of time involved, and the testing instruments used.

The Berkeley Growth Study began with a sample of 74 one month old children in the Berkeley, California area. The last round of adult tests was given at the age of 36 years to 54 members of the original group—a quite remarkable feat in view of the age span involved. Although there was considerable range in IQ, this sample was a somewhat superior one. The children's parents were above average in education, occupation, and income, and the group was above average in intelligence test performance. The sample was in many ways similar to samples used in two other longitudinal studies, the Berkeley Guidance Study (Honzik, 1938, 1967; Honzik, Macfarlane, and Allen, 1948) and the Fels Study (Baker, Sontag, and Nelson, 1958; Sontag and Baker, 1958). Individual intelligence tests were used throughout the study. Findings from the Berkeley Growth Study have been reported by Bayley (1933, 1940a, 1940b, 1949, 1954, 1955, 1968),

Bayley and Schaefer (1964), Bloom (1964), and Pinneau (1961), among others.

The Harvard Growth Study (Dearborn and Rothney, 1963) had a very large sample and, unlike most of the longitudinal studies in the literature, included many children from lower socioeconomic levels. It began in 1922 with 3500 children who were entering the first grade of three cities in the Boston metropolitan area. Most were 6, 7, or 8 years of age at the start of the study. Over a period of 12 years annual physical and mental measurements were taken on as many of these children as remained in school. The original large sample was severely decimated over the years, but according to the authors, unpublished data indicated that even the mutilated samples met the statistical assumptions required for many analyses. Except for a few selected cases, the testing was done with group tests. The great masses of data accumulated in this study are still being analyzed, the most recent analysis being reported by R. L. Thorndike (1966).

Other longitudinal studies of intelligence have been reported by Freeman and Flory (1937), Ebert and Simmons (1943), Hilden (1949), and Bradway and Thompson (1962), and in addition there have been numerous cross-sectional studies. The salient findings of all these studies will be discussed in the rest of this chapter.

Average Mental Growth

Over the years many investigators have drawn general mental growth curves, which have sometimes been enthusiastically interpreted as yielding a picture of the "true" course of mental development. They are more realistically seen, however, simply as records of the average performances of groups of individuals of different ages on standardized intelligence tests. The exact form of the curves varies with the units plotted, the nature of the sample, and the tests involved. Most of them represent performance on general intelligence tests: curves for the separate skills that enter into these complex scores would no doubt show varying forms.

Gesell (1928) presented a logarithmic curve derived from repeated application of his Developmental Schedule to a group of preschool children; and E. L. Thorndike (1926) drew a parabolic curve to represent the performance of groups of adult imbeciles, school children, and army recruits on his test (the CAVD). Scores from the group tests administered to the children in the Harvard Growth Study were subjected to Thurstone's technique of "absolute scaling," which is presumed to yield equivalent units all along the mental age range. The curve in Figure 16-1 represents these data and mathematically extrapolated extensions above and below the actual ages studied (Dearborn and Rothney, 1963, p. 215). The curve in Figure 16-2 shows both the average performance and the variability of the children in the Berkeley Growth Study from infancy to 21 years of age (Bayley, 1955). To obtain this curve different tests used at various ages were made comparable by transforming all scores into "16D" units, expressing "each child's scores at all ages in terms of the 16 year standard deviation from the mean score at 16 years" (Bayley, 1955, p. 811).

The overall picture that emerges from a study of general mental growth curves in childhood shows a period of very rapid increase in early childhood, followed by a period of less rapid increase in middle childhood, and finally a period of still less rapid increase into the teens and early twenties.

Statements in the literature about mental maturity rest partly on mathematical extrapolation and partly on empirical observation and must be interpreted with caution. For example, in a recent widely quoted study, Bloom re-examined the data from a large number of longitudinal studies and concluded that "in terms of intelligence measured at age 17, at least 20% is developed by age 1, 50%

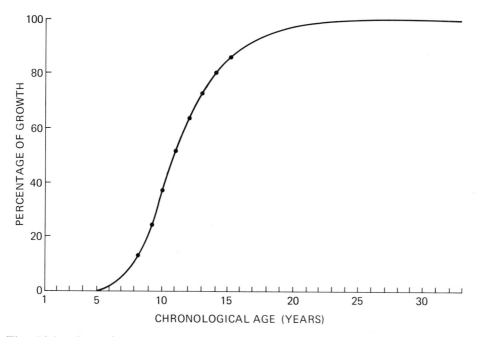

Fig. 16-1. General mental growth curve from the Harvard Growth Study based on absolute scale units. (From Dearborn and Rothney, 1963. Reprinted by permission of the author and Sci-Art Publishers.)

by about age 4, 80% by about age 8 and 92% by age 13" (Bloom, 1964, p. 88). It is important to note, however, that he made these statements relative to intelligence measured at the age of 17 years, not relative to any assumed absolute age of full maturity.

The data on maturity are not conclusive. Early studies indicated that average mental performance typically peaked in the early twenties and then began a period of gradual decline (Foulds and Raven, 1948; Jones and Conrad, 1933; Miles, 1942; Wechsler, 1944). However, more recent studies on a wide range of adult populations reveal a picture of either continued improvement or at least maintenance of general intellectual level in adulthood, in some cases well into middle age (Bayley and Oden, 1955; Bradway and Thompson, 1962; Corsini

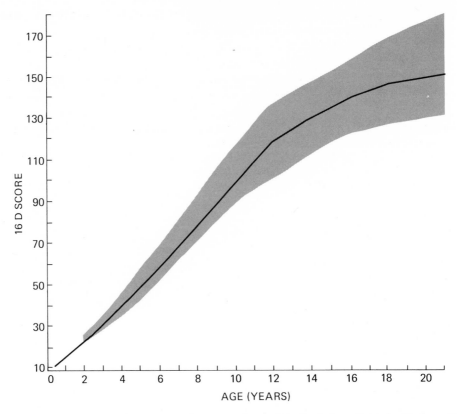

Fig. 16-2. General mental growth curve from the Berkeley Growth Study with average scores and standard deviations in 16D units. (From N. Bayley, "On the growth of intelligence," *American Psychologist*, 1955, *10*, 805–818. Copyright 1955 by the American Psychological Association, and reprinted by permission of the author and publisher.)

and Fassett, 1953; Nisbet, 1957; Owens, 1953, 1966). It seems plausible, although it has not been proved, that the discrepancies between newer and older studies reflect better and more widespread educational opportunities.

Individual Mental Growth

The data discussed so far, based as they are on average group performance, completely mask the enormous variety of individual growth patterns that have been revealed in every major longitudinal study and that must be considered whenever practical judgments about individuals are required.

Cornell and Armstrong (1955) reanalyzed 1100 cases from the Harvard Growth Study and concluded that there were essentially four basic patterns of development with some subclasses in each. In summarizing this analysis, Armstrong (1955) maintained that the most significant differences in growth patterns seem to revolve around the relative rate of growth before and after puberty. The first type of curve is characterized by continuous growth over the whole range with no major change at puberty. The second shows slow advance until puberty and then a shift to a more rapid advance. The third involves rapid growth until puberty, followed by a sudden shift to a slower rate of advance. [Bayley (1966, p. 387) noted that both she and Freeman and Flory (1937) found a period of acceleration for boys just before the adolescent spurt in physical growth that accompanies puberty.] Finally, the fourth type of growth pattern shows advances in a series of steps, with the top of the

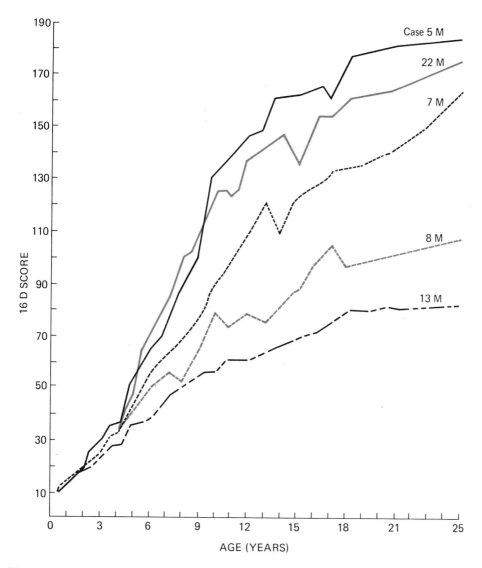

Fig. 16-3. Individual mental growth curves from the Berkeley Growth Study in 16D units. (From N. Bayley, 1955, *op. cit.* Copyright 1955 by the American Psychological Association, and reprinted by permission of the author and publisher.)

steps falling into one of the three other patterns. Armstrong (1955) urged educators to be aware of this variety of mental growth patterns and not to assume one universal course of development.

Because of the difficulty of finding appropriate units in which to express the data, there are relatively few individual growth curves in the literature depicting absolute score changes with age. Bayley (1955), however, presented individual curves from the Berkeley Growth Study. Figure 16-3 shows scores

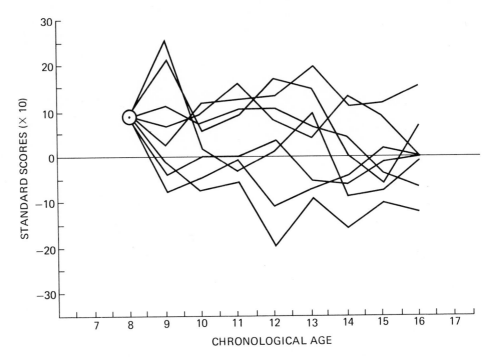

Fig. 16-4. Individual mental growth curves from the Harvard Growth Study in standard score units: Curves of eight girls initially high in IQ and subsequently variable. (From Dearborn and Rothney, 1963. Reprinted by permission of the author and Sci-Art Publishers.)

converted to 16D units for five boys over the age period from 1 month to 25 years. It is immediately apparent that each of these subjects had his own pattern and rate of development. None followed exactly the curve in Figure 16-2, which shows the average performance of the group of which they were members.

Many investigators have plotted individual growth curves showing relative rather than absolute scores. The scores are standard scores, which express the individual's performance at each age relative to the mean and standard deviation of the group. This procedure masks absolute score changes, but emphasizes shifts in relative placement. Figures 16-4 and 16-5 show such curves from the

Harvard Growth Study (Dearborn and Rothney, 1963). Figure 16-4 shows the change in relative placement from age 8 to 16 of eight girls all of whom initially ranked .9 standard deviation above the mean of the total group but showed marked divergence over the years. The girls represented in Figure 16-5 showed great variability over the childhood years, but all attained the same rank, .5 standard deviation above the mean, at age 16.

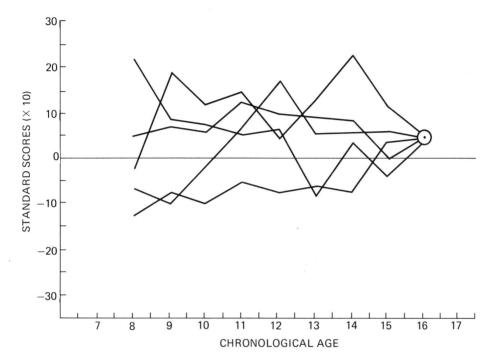

Fig. 16-5. Individual mental growth curves from the Harvard Growth Study in standard score units: Curves of five girls initially variable and subsequently high in IQ. (From Dearborn and Rothney, 1963. Reprinted by permission of the author and Sci-Art Publishers.)

Other individual growth curves show that while some children do remain quite stable in their absolute and relative intelligence test performance throughout childhood, many others show great variability (Baker *et al.*, 1958; Hilden, 1949; Honzik *et al.*, 1948).

Predictive Value of Tests at Different Ages

Since many children show changes in their relative placement over the years, it follows that age to age correlations between IQs will not be perfect nor, consequently, will age to age predictions be perfect.

Most of the studies involving infant intelligence tests have revealed that they are of little value for predicting later intelligence, particularly if the first test is administered during the first year of life. L. D. Anderson (1939) administered items from three infant tests (the Gesell, Bühler, and Linfert-Hierholzer scales) to a group of 91 infants. Scores obtained at 3, 6, 9, 12, 18, and 24 months of age were correlated with Stanford-Binet IQs at 5 years of age. The respective correlations were .008, —.065, —.001, .055, .231, and .450. A number of other early studies, summarized by Thorndike (1940), and a more recent one by Cavanaugh, Cohen, Dunphy, Ringwall, and Goldberg (1957) confirmed the poor predictive power of infant intelligence tests.

However, some investigators have maintained that valuable information can be secured from available infant tests if they are utilized in conjunction with qualitative clinical appraisals of the infant's performance. MacRae (1955), for example, reported a study in which 102 infants were given either of two tests (the Gesell or the Cattell Scale). Examiners did not compute numerical scores but on the basis of clinical judgment assigned each infant to one of five categories ranging from definitely deficient to definitely superior. Ratings were made for groups of infants aged 0 to 11 months, 12 to 23 months, and 24 to 35 months. These descriptive ratings correlated .56, .55, and .82, for the respective age groups, with scores on either the Wechsler Intelligence Scale for Children or Stanford-Binet secured at a median age of 9.2 years. (See also Escalona and Moriarity, 1961; Gallagher, 1953, Illingworth, 1961; Knobloch and Pasamanick, 1963.)

It should be pointed out that marked success has been achieved in this kind of study only with reference to the low end of the IQ scale; it has been possible to make fairly good predictions of future low intellectual status, especially when organic damage was apparent in infancy, but it has not been possible to make good predictions within the normal or superior ranges. Also, while reliance on intuitive, qualitative judgments may work well for individual skillful clinicians, the difficulty of communicating such skills to the average test user limits their usefulness.

Several investigators reported attempts to improve the predictive power of infant scales by basing prediction on only certain selected items from the scales (L. D. Anderson, 1939; Nelson and Richards, 1938, 1939). These efforts met with no notable success. More recently, there have been suggestions that infant verbal behavior may be a useful predictor of later intelligence. Catalano and McCarthy (1954) reported that a combination of three infant vocalization measures correlated .52 with IQ at about four years of age; and data from the Berkeley Growth Study showed that, for girls, infant vocalization measures yielded correlations ranging between .40 and .60 with IQs obtained between 13 and 26 years of age (Cameron, Livson, and Bayley, 1967). This whole area certainly merits further investigation since so many of our operational definitions of intelligence are heavily loaded with linguistic skills.

In general, it may be said that existing infant intelligence scales are useful in revealing an infant's level of sensory and motor development relative to his peers. The skills they sample, however, seem to be very different from those sampled by later intelligence tests, and it is therefore not surprising that except in cases of extreme retardation, they are poor predictors of later intelligence test performance.[1]

From about the age of four years onward, standardized test scores become more useful predictors of later intelligence. Many longitudinal studies have revealed the same pattern of test–retest correlations (Baker *et al.*, 1958; Bayley, 1949; Ebert and Simmons, 1943; Honzik *et al.*, 1948). For tests administered to children from the preschool period through the late teens, predictability varies with the size of the interval between tests and with the age at the initial test. Test–retest correlations decrease as the interval between tests increases. For example, Honzik *et al.* (1948) found that the correlations of scores obtained at 6 years of age with scores obtained at 7, 9, 14, and 18 years were .82, .80, .67, and .61, respectively. With test–retest interval constant, correlations increase with the age at which the initial test is administered. Again referring to the data of Honzik *et al.* (1948), correlations between tests administered at 4 and 6 years, 8 and 10 years, and 12 and 14 years were .62, .88, and .92, respectively. Figure 16-6, which summarizes the findings from a number of studies, graphically illustrates this increase in predictability with age.

The concept of "overlap" (J. E. Anderson, 1939) is often invoked to account for the fact that correlations between successive tests increase with age. Only a small proportion of the skills sampled in a test at 4 years of age is sampled in a test at 2 years of age; tests at 2 years are almost entirely sensorimotor in content, but tests at 4 years contain both sensorimotor and verbal items. A much larger proportion of the skills sampled in a test at 12 years is sampled in a test at 10 years; typically, both are almost exclusively verbal. The greater amount of overlap of sampled skills at the higher age level is said to produce the higher correlations.

In short, the correlational data show that as children grow older they show an increasing, although never absolute, tendency to maintain their relative placement in a group. As a cautionary note, it should be kept in mind that even if the correlation between an earlier and later test is as high as .90, a very rare occurrence except for very brief time intervals, only 81 percent of the variance on the second test is accounted for. Prediction of any individual child's performance on a later test can never rest entirely on knowledge of his performance on an earlier test.

IQ Changes

A discussion of the amount of IQ change occurring in children between successive testings will complete the picture of growth trends. Such data are of particular interest in view of the once widely held belief, still occasionally expressed, that "most studies comparing I.Q.s obtained after the preschool age have found an average fluctuation of less than 5 points . . ." (Ruch, 1967, p. 161). The

---

[1] An analysis by Hofstaetter (1954) is usually cited as evidence for the change in skills sampled at different age levels (see also Bayley, 1955), but Cronbach has convincingly argued on statistical grounds that "Students of child development should drop the Hofstaetter analysis from further consideration" (Cronbach, 1967, p. 289).

data simply do not bear this out (Baker *et al.*, 1958; Bayley, 1949; Bradway, 1944; Dearborn and Rothney, 1963; Ebert and Simmons, 1943; Honzik *et al.*, 1948). For example, Baker *et al.* (1958), reporting on 50 children from the Fels population for whom complete Stanford-Binet records were available, found that 62 percent changed more than 15 points between the ages of 3 and 10 years. Honzik *et al.* (1948) found that 75 percent of their Berkeley

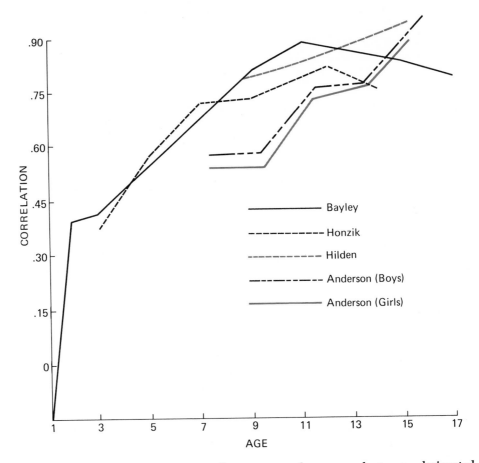

Fig. 16-6. Correlations between intelligence at early ages and at ages designated "maturity." (From Bloom, 1964. Fig. 2, p. 54. Reprinted by permission of the author and John Wiley and Sons.)

Guidance Study sample changed more than 9 points on the Stanford-Binet between the ages of 6 and 18 years and 47 percent showed changes of 20 or more points.

Pinneau (1961) has made the point that it is more useful to study changes in terms of deviation IQs rather than age ratio IQs, since only the former accurately reflect changes in relative placement. He accordingly reanalyzed the data from the Berkeley Growth Study after converting all scores into deviation IQs, and presented charts showing age to age changes from 3 months to 17 years. While the absolute amounts of change were sometimes greater and sometimes smaller than with age ratio IQs, the expected pattern emerged. Change was greater in the earlier years and across the longer time intervals. In all but a very few cases involving short intervals in the older age brackets, the median deviation IQ change was greater than 5 points. For example, the chart showing changes for children tested at 5 years and at subsequent ages up to 17 years, reveals median changes ranging from 6 to 12 points. The range of absolute individual changes is from 0 to 40 points.

In summary, study of individual growth curves, test–retest correlations, and absolute score changes demonstrates conclusively that the IQ is not constant. While most children do not show gross changes in relative placement after the preschool years, smaller changes are the rule rather than the exception. An IQ is not a fixed attribute of an individual in the way that blood type is. It is, to repeat a point made earlier, a score on a test. As such, it is subject to change from a variety of influences, some of which will be discussed in the next section.

CORRELATES OF IQ

This section deals with personal and environmental variables that have been shown to correlate with intelligence test performance. In the discussion of each variable, data on its effect on IQ changes, if available, will be summarized first, then data on its effect on group averages.

General Considerations Concerning iQ Change

When a child shows a marked change in IQ from one occasion to another, it becomes important to ask why the change occurred. The answer is not always easy to pinpoint. It is always possible that some drastic change in the child's life caused general improvement or regression in the behaviors being sampled, but the factors that have already been discussed in the section on test reliability (in Chapter 15) must also be considered. These include temporary conditions in the child and his surroundings and characteristics of the test instrument itself. R. L. Thorndike (1966) has recently raised another relevant point. On the basis of a reanalysis of data from the Harvard Growth Study he concluded that IQ change scores are extremely susceptible to errors of measurement. Although this conclusion was based on group-test data and most of the data referred to below are from individual tests, it is well to keep Thorndike's note of caution in mind.

Parental Behaviors and Attitudes

It has by now become more or less a truism that parents influence their children's behavior. Presumably, this is as true of intellectual behavior as it is of social and emotional behavior, although the emphasis until recently has been on the latter areas.

Research in this area is not easy to conduct. Parental behaviors and attitudes are complex, multidimensional, and to some extent confounded with socioeconomic variables. It is therefore not surprising that of the literally thousands of correlation coefficients that have been reported, most are statistically nonsignificant. Of those that are significant, the great majority are low to moderate in magnitude. The field is further complicated by the fact that different investigators have focused on different parental variables. Even when the names of the variables in different studies are similar, it does not necessarily follow that the behaviors involved were. Moreover, one cannot be sure that parental behavior ratings secured through interview or brief observation are typical of the everyday "on-the-job" practices that they are often assumed to represent. Nevertheless, this is a field of potential practical significance and some suggestive findings have been accumulated.

Because of space limitations discussion here is confined to data relating parental behaviors and attitudes to their children's intelligence test performance. The interested student may also wish to consult a recent review paper by Freeberg and Payne (1967) which includes additional material on nontest cognitive behavior.

Sontag and Baker (1958), dealing with the Fels population, studied a number of parental behavior variables to determine whether any distinguished between children showing marked increases and decreases in Stanford-Binet IQs. The only significant finding was at the elementary school level, where a tendency to deal with discipline in a rational manner and a tendency to push or accelerate the child's development were found to be characteristic of parents of children in the "increase" group.

Moss and Kagan (1958) also used members of the Fels population to study the influence of early maternal encouragement of intellectual development on IQs at three and at six years of age. Maternal behavior was not significantly related to IQ in either sex at six; but at three, maternal acceleration correlated significantly with boys' IQs, and maternal restrictiveness had a significant *negative* correlation with girls' IQs.

Honzik (1967) used records from the Berkeley Guidance Study to explore the relation between a variety of home behaviors and attitudes rated when the children were 21 months old and their intelligence test scores between the ages of 21 months and 30 years. Boys whose mothers were tense, worrisome, active, energetic, and concerned over health and achievement tended to have high scores. In addition, after the very earliest years, a close affectional bond between mother and son was positively correlated with IQ. There were relatively few significant relations between father and son variables. For girls, higher IQs were associated with a heterogeneous set of parental variables, including concern of both parents over health, a tendency for both parents to favor sex instruction, friendliness of the parents to each other, and friendliness of the father to the daughter.

In the Berkeley Growth Study, maternal behaviors were rated when the children were between birth and 3 years of age and when they were between 9 and 14 years of age. Bayley and Schaefer (1964) studied the relation between these ratings and the children's IQs from infancy to 18 years of age. As in the Honzik (1967) study, boys' scores were significantly related to the affectional relation with the mothers. In the first year or so, boys with hostile mothers earned high scores, but thereafter high scores tended to be associated with loving, positively evaluating mothers. These early maternal influences persisted well into adulthood; scores on the Wechsler Adult Intelligence Scale obtained at 36 years of age correlated —.60 with the early maternal hostility behaviors and .49 with early maternal love and understanding (Bayley, 1968). The pattern for girls was quite different. In infancy, girls who had loving, controlling mothers had high scores; but after the age of 3 years, girls' scores showed little relation to maternal behavior except, as in the Moss and Kagan study, a negative relation to maternal restrictiveness.

Wolf (1964) found significant relations between the IQs of fifth grade children and their parents' intellectual expectations for the child, the amount of information the mother had about the child's intellectual development, the opportunities provided for enlarging the child's vocabulary, the extent to which the parents created situations for learning in the home, and the extent of assistance given in learning situations related to school and nonschool activities. The correlation between the children's IQs and the total score on the parental rating instrument was a quite impressive .69.

In connection with Wolf's finding that parental expectations correlated with children's scores, it is of interest to note another study not directly concerned with parents. Rosenthal and Jacobson (1966) studied teachers' expectancies, and found that when teachers were told that a given group of children had unusual potential for intellectual gains, these children gained significantly more in IQ than a control group.

Kent and Davis (1957) found relations between the Stanford-Binet IQs of British children tested at eight years of age and various kinds of parental discipline. The highest scores were earned by children of demanding parents who provided a stimulating home environment together with rather rigid high standards for the children; the lowest IQs were earned by children of unconcerned parents who made no demands and showed very little interest in their children's behavior. These findings are at least in partial contrast to earlier ones reported by Baldwin, Kalhorn, and Breese (1945), who found high intelligence associated with acceptant, democratic, and indulgent homes, and low intelligence associated with autocratic, rejectant homes. It is difficult to know whether the discrepancies reflect differences in the samples involved or the particular parental behaviors rated. At any rate, the question of whether permissive or nonpermissive child rearing practices foster high intellectual performance remains open (Hurley, 1959).

In general, the data relating parental behavior to children's intelligence are still fragmentary and suggestive rather than conclusive. Several studies, however, indicate that parents, especially mothers, who are concerned and to some extent pushy about intellectual achievement have children who do well on intelligence tests. Also of potential importance is the tentative finding that the scores of boys are more influenced by early interpersonal relations, again especially with the mother, than are the scores of girls.

Personal Behaviors and Attitudes

The relation between intellectual functioning and various noncognitive traits has been receiving increasing attention. As indicated in Chapter 15, Thurstone (1948) hoped that factor analysis would prove useful in integrating the study of intellectual and emotional behaviors. Various theorists, with a variety of orientations, have maintained that there is a close, perhaps inextricable relation between intellectual behaviors and emotional behaviors or motivational tendencies (Fromm and Hartman, 1955; Hayes, 1962; Wechsler, 1944; see also discussion of exploratory behavior, especially "epistemic curiosity," in Chapter 10). Beyond this, as will be seen in later sections, there is a growing tendency to account for socioeconomic and racial group differences in terms of variations in motivational systems. In this tradition Haggard wrote of growing evidence "that mental functioning does not exist in a vacuum but that the individual's motivational and personality structure, his attitudes, interests, needs and goals are intimately related to, and in a large measure determine his mental processes" (Haggard, 1953, pp. 115–116).

Sontag and Baker (1958) explored the relation between Stanford-Binet IQ change and ratings on a variety of personality traits. Using the data of children from the Fels population who had been repeatedly observed in home and school settings, they identified subgroups who showed marked increase or decrease in IQ between $4\frac{1}{2}$ and 6 years of age or between 6 and 10 years of age. In the younger group, only ratings on independence significantly favored the gainers, while for the older group a definite cluster of traits differentiated gainers from losers. Gainers had significantly higher ratings on independence, self-initiative, anticipation of reward (ability to tolerate delay of reward), general competitiveness with peers, scholastic competitiveness, and independence in scholastic achievement. All these ratings were closely interrelated, leading the authors to hypothesize an achievement motive as a common dimension.

This hypothesis was explored and to an extent substantiated in a study by Kagan, Sontag, Baker, and Nelson (1958), in which achievement motivation was defined in terms of projective test responses. From a group of 140 Fels children, they selected the 25 percent showing the highest Stanford-Binet gain and the 25 percent showing the greatest loss between six and ten years of age, and administered to them two projective tests (the TAT and the Rorschach). Protocol ratings, which were reported to be highly reliable, revealed significant differences between the groups. The gainers of both sexes showed significantly more need for achievement and intellectual curiosity and less passivity. Boys who were gainers also tended toward higher ratings on aggression, which was taken to be an index of general competitive striving. While emphasizing that their findings may hold only for groups of initially high ability from homes in which intellectual achievement is valued, the authors contended that "high need achievement, competitive strivings and curiosity about nature are correlated with gain in I.Q. score because they may facilitate the acquisition of skills that are measured by the intelligence test" (Kagan *et al.*, 1958, p. 266).

The projective test results of the previous study contrast with those reported by Crandall, Katkovsky, and Preston (1962), who focused on typical performance rather than IQ change. In a group of relatively superior first, second, and third graders they found that need achievement (defined by TAT responses) was not correlated with Stanford-Binet IQ. They also failed to find an expected correlation with scores on the Children's Manifest Anxiety Scale (see section entitled "Anxiety," Chapter 10, for a description of this test). However, a number of other motivational attitudes were significantly related to IQ. Boys who set themselves higher intellectual achievement standards, who accepted personal responsibility for success and failure, and who had realistic expectations of success in intellectual achievement situations tended to have high IQs. For girls, however, the only significant finding was a negative correlation between IQ and realistic expectations of success in intellectual achievement situations.

Bayley and Schaefer (1964) presented a vast array of correlations between various childhood personality traits, rated at five age levels from infancy through adolescence, and IQs earned over the period from 1 month to 18 years by members of the Berkeley Growth Study. It is difficult to do justice to this major undertaking in a few summary sentences. In general, however, it can be said that for both sexes there was a rather persistent tendency for IQ to be associated with intellectually oriented behaviors such as those designated "attentiveness," "facility," and "swift comprehension." Also, for boys far more than for girls, there were persistent correlations with behaviors that are ordinarily thought of as social and emotional, such as "happy," "positive behavior," "friendly," "independent," and "social." This sex difference was particularly apparent in late childhood and adolescence.

Sex

Despite cherished beliefs to the contrary, there is no evidence that either sex is in general very much brighter than the other.

In the construction of some general intelligence tests, such as the Stanford-Binet, items on which there were large sex differences were either eliminated or counterbalanced. Such tests can therefore provide no information about sex differences in intelligence. However, in the construction of some other general intelligence tests no effort was made to eliminate or counterbalance items showing sex differences; with these tests the most common finding is a very slight female superiority. When large numbers of subjects are involved, the sex differences are statistically significant, but they are small and there is always a great deal of overlap between the distributions of boys' and girls' scores.

There are sex differences, in American culture, on *specific* intellectual abilities. Girls tend to excel on verbal and memory items, boys on numerical items and items involving spatial relations. It seems plausible that the slight female superiority on general intelligence tests is attributable to the heavy verbal content of these instruments.

Typical results were reported by Hobson (1947) in a study including data on both general and specific ability performance in eighth and ninth grade children. On the Kuhlmann-Anderson Group IQ test, which is a general intelligence test with the usual heavy concentration of verbal items, he got the typical result of a slight but significant female superiority. In the eighth grade, for example, the average IQ of boys was 111.0 and of girls 114.5. He also administered the Tests of Primary Mental Abilities, which yield separate scores for specific abilities. On these tests, the girls exceeded the boys significantly on word fluency, reasoning, and rote memory; boys were markedly superior on space. There was also a tendency for boys to excel in verbal comprehension, indicating that girls are not necessarily superior in all verbal skills. Herzberg and Lepkin (1954) used a later version of the Tests of Primary Mental Abilities with a sample of high school students, and obtained similar results.

The rather consistent finding of sex differences on specific abilities can reasonably be explained in terms of cultural practices. From babyhood on, boys and girls are treated differently, expected to adopt different roles, and differentially rewarded for early displays of interest and ability. To cite just one example, boys are more likely to be given mechanical toys and blocks and encouraged to manipulate them skillfully, girls are more likely to be given dolls and dishes and generally encouraged in the kind of "playing house" role-taking that entails considerable verbal interplay. It seems quite likely that the skills each sex develops reflect these kinds of early experiences.

Family Resemblance

Children's IQs are related to the IQs of members of their families, both natural and adoptive. Erlenmeyer-Kimling and Jarvik (1963) summarized the findings of 52 studies conducted in eight countries over a period spanning two generations. As shown in Figure 16-7 the median reported correlation on "tests of intellectual functioning" was .50 for parent and child, .49 for nontwin siblings, .53 for fraternal twins, .87 for identical twins reared together, .75 for identical twins reared apart, and .20 for foster parents and children.

There has been heated debate about such data, and they have been interpreted and reinterpreted over the years. Hereditarians have emphasized the direct relation between degree of genetic similarity and the size of the correlation. Identical twins, for example, whether reared together or apart have scores that are more closely correlated than are the scores of fraternal twins (Burt, 1966; Newman, Freeman, and Holzinger, 1937). Also, the correlation between children and their true parents is higher than between children and foster parents (Burks, 1928; Leahy, 1935), and there is some evidence that the correlation between the scores of child and true parents exhibits the same age changes whether the child is reared by his true parents or by foster parents, further suggesting a genetic basis (Honzik, 1957).

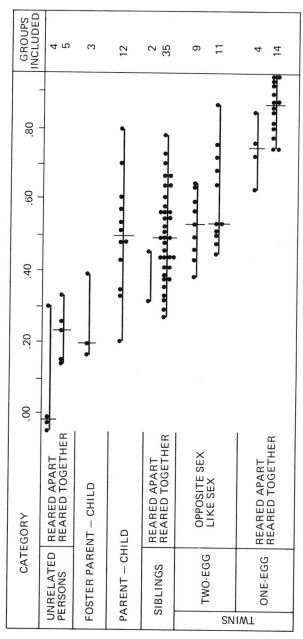

Fig. 16-7. Correlations between IQs of individuals showing different degrees of genetic resemblance and experiencing different degrees of environmental similarity. Data from 52 studies. Median findings are represented by vertical lines intersecting the horizontal lines, which represent the range of reported correlations. (From Erlenmeyer-Kimling and Jarvik, *Science*, 1963, *142*, 1477–1479. Fig. 1, p. 1478. Copyright 1963 by the American Association for the Advancement of Science. Reproduced by permission of the authors and the publisher.)

Environmentalists have emphasized that the correlations for fraternal twins are higher than for ordinary siblings, even though there is no difference in degree of genetic relationship. They have also pointed out that there is a significant relation between scores of children and genetically unrelated foster parents and that the use of correlational data obscures the fact that foster children often attain absolute levels of performance far above what would be expected on the basis of the characteristics of their true parents (Skodak and Skeels, 1949).

Actually, unequivocal interpretations have not been possible in any of the studies on family resemblance. The identical twin studies illustrate typical ambiguities of experimental design; but similar objections have been raised about all of the kinds of studies that yielded the data of Figure 16-7.

Newman, Freeman, and Holzinger (1937) found a correlation of .73 between the IQs of 19 pairs of identical twins who had been reared apart, compared to .92 for 50 pairs of identical twins reared together and .62 for 51 pairs of fraternal twins reared together. More recently, Burt (1966) reported a correlation of .86 for 53 pairs of identical twins reared apart, compared to .92 for 95 pairs of identical twins reared together and .53 for 127 pairs of fraternal twins reared together. On the face of it, these data seem to indicate an overriding importance of genetic factors in intelligence test performance.

An early discussion of the data of Newman *et al.* by Neff, however, made the point that an environmental interpretation is as plausible as the genetic interpretation: "It should be quite obvious, although it apparently has not been so, that one cannot speak of individuals being reared in differing environments merely because they were brought up in different homes" (Neff, 1938, p. 749). In five cases in which the environments of the separated twins were judged to be quite different in the educational opportunities provided, there were considerable differences in IQ, amounting to 24 points in one case. Moreover, the correlation between Stanford-Binet IQ and judged difference in educational opportunity was a substantial .79. Neff (1938) further maintained that at least some of the similarity of IQs in the other pairs of twins may have reflected similarity in their environments in areas other than educational opportunity. Lewis (1966) has raised similar objections with reference to Burt's (1966) study. In addition, Stott (1966) has criticized the identical twin studies on the grounds that it is not possible to assess adequately the relevance of the common prenatal environment experienced by these individuals to their later intellectual development.

Several attempts have been made to partition the observed variance in intelligence test performance into the proportion attributable to heredity and the proportion attributable to environment. Leahy (1935) found a correlation of .20 between the intelligence of foster parents and children; the correlation could reflect only environmental influences since these were genetically unrelated individuals, and she therefore concluded that environmental influences account for only 4 percent of the observed variation in intellectual performance (4 percent represents the square of the correlation coefficient; see footnote 3, Chapter 15). More recently, Burt (1958) used assessments of intelligence secured from surveys of the entire school population of a representative London borough and calculated that 12 percent of observed variation is attributable to nongenetic influences and 88 percent is attributable to the operation of a complex set of major genes that contribute a general intellectual factor and polygenes that contribute specific factors.

Attempts to quantify in absolute terms the proportional contribution of hereditary and environmental factors involve two basic assumptions: (a) it is possible to hold one set of factors constant while varying the other, and (b) the two kinds of factors combine additively to determine behavior. Both of these assumptions have been attacked as untenable (Anastasi, 1958b; Maddox, 1957).

In the United States, both hereditary and environmental influences on behavior continue to be explored, but the controversy has abated. Many writers, including Anastasi (1958b) and Patin (1965), have pointed out the fruitlessness of traditional attempts to determine which of the two factors produced a behavior or the relative contribution of each. It simply has not been possible to design studies that could yield unequivocal answers. Instead, attention is now being centered on the various ways in which hereditary and environmental factors can interact to produce behavior. According to Anastasi, greater progress will be made through ". . . the gradual replacement of the questions, 'Which one?' and 'How much?' by the more basic and appropriate question, 'How?'" (Anastasi, 1958b, p. 206). Typically, all behavior is now viewed as a function of the interaction of genetic and nongenetic factors. This interaction begins at conception and it is not possible, at least with currently available techniques, to isolate experimentally the two kinds of influences in human subjects. Given genes may lead ultimately to any of a wide variety of behaviors, depending on the occurrence of any of a wide variety of environmental situations. This viewpoint applies to intelligence test behavior as well as to all other kinds of behavior shown by biological organisms, even though the connections between genes and test behavior are very indirect indeed. A. Gordon succinctly reported the present day consensus when he wrote, "Any extreme view in the nature-nurture controversy appears to be unjustified at the present time. The most useful hypothesis is neither of those hypotheses of a generation ago that considered one or the other influence alone but a hypothesis that assumes undetermined contributions from both" (Gordon, 1961, p. 378).

Finally, it should be pointed out that the modern approach to heredity and environment is not incompatible with scientifically or socially inspired attempts to change behavior. As Bijou and Baer have pointed out, ". . . it should be assumed that any behavior, genetically influenced or not, is nevertheless modifiable by experience." Failure to produce modification with one technique should merely stimulate the search for other techniques. "Neither the suspicion nor the affirmation of genetic influence in any pattern of development must ever produce an aura of hopelessness, especially when the development is an undesirable one" (Bijou and Baer, 1967, p. 111).

Special Restricted Environments

It is commonly assumed that experiences in the earliest years of childhood are crucial determinants of later intellectual development (e.g., Ferguson, 1954,

1956; Hebb, 1949, 1959; Hunt, 1961; Piaget, 1952b; Sarason and Gladwin, 1958).
While it is not possible, of course, to subject children deliberately to presumably
damaging early experiences, it is instructive to study those who, through natural
circumstances, spend their early lives in restricted environments.

INSTITUTIONALIZATION.   Studies on the effects of early institutionalization are
relevant. It is true, of course, that the caliber of institutions varies widely. However, it seems reasonable to assume that in most cases they provide a less stimulating environment than is available in private homes where there is more opportunity for the formation of a close personal attachment to a single adult and
for the varied sensory stimulation that Hebb (1959) thought to be so important.[2]

While most studies of institutionalization have stressed its relation to social,
emotional, and motor development, there are some data relevant to intelligence
test performance. Levy (1947) gave a battery of tests to infants in an institution
and to a comparable group being raised in private boarding homes. At each
age level studied—under 6 months, 6 to 12 months, and over 12 months—the
institution children scored lower than the others. Goldfarb (1943, 1945) has
compared groups of children who spent several years in institutions before being
placed in foster homes and carefully matched control groups who were placed
in homes early in infancy. In the series of studies, with groups whose average
ages were roughly $3\frac{1}{2}$, 7, $8\frac{1}{2}$, and 12 years at the time of testing, intelligence
and general language development were lower in the groups whose early years
were spent in institutions than in those who had had continuous foster home
care. Goldfarb adopted a view similar to Hebb's (1949) when he interpreted
his findings as indicating that "extreme psychological deprivation in infancy
produces a lag in mental growth which is maintained even under new conditions
of environmental stimulation" (Goldfarb, 1945, p. 3). However, in the absence
of conclusive longitudinal data relating specific kinds of early deprivation to
specific kinds of subsequent enrichment experiences, this pessimistic conclusion
seems to be premature. In fact, a recent report (Skeels, 1966) gives at least
tentative support to the view that the damaging effects of very early deprivation
can be successfully counteracted if remedial measures are instituted early
enough. Skeels (1966) reported on a group of 13 subjects who, as infants, resided
in an extremely impoverished orphanage setting and who were, at the time,
diagnosed as mentally retarded. At a median age of 17.1 months these children
were transferred to a more stimulating institutional setting in which each received warm individual attention. Eleven of the children were subsequently
adopted by private families. Although no data are available on adult intelligence
test performance, Skeels' (1966) follow-up of the subjects as adults revealed
that educationally the group had completed a median of 12 grades of schooling,
all were self-supporting, and 10 were involved in apparently stable, permanent
marriages.

[2] There is some very suggestive evidence that the deficit in environmental stimulation is a
much more important source of the intellectual deficit than is the lack of a close attachment
to a single adult (see Casler, 1961; Gardner, Hawkes, and Burchinal, 1961; Rheingold and
Bayley, 1959).

CULTURAL ISOLATION. Several studies have dealt with the intelligence test performance of children living in areas characterized not only by severe economic and educational deprivation, but also by isolation from the larger cultural setting. The latest of these dealt with children living in isolated Newfoundland outport villages (Burnett, Beach, and Sullivan, 1963). The average IQs on two predominantly verbal tests were 80.5 (Otis Intermediate Group Intelligence Test) and 86 (Wechsler Bellevue, Full Scale), which are, of course, below normal. However, on a test of spatial rather than verbal abilities (Progressive Matrices), they earned an average score equivalent to normal (median) performance. These findings fit nicely with Ferguson's view that different cultures reward and thus facilitate the development of different sets of skills (see section entitled "Theories of Intelligence," Chapter 15).

Earlier studies dealt with English canal boat and gypsy children (Gordon, 1923) and children in remote mountain areas of the southern United States (Asher, 1935; Chapanis and Williams, 1945; Sherman and Key, 1932; Wheeler, 1942). Utilizing traditional intelligence tests, all these studies revealed average IQs far below the general norms. Moreover, all revealed a negative relation between age and IQ; older children had lower IQs than younger children.

There is some disagreement as to how to interpret the negative correlation of IQ with age in these isolated groups. Many have seen it as an indication of the cumulative depressing effect of continued residence in restricted environments, while others have maintained that it is an artifact of the different test items used with younger and older children. Still another interpretation is that it is a "secular" trend, that is, it reflects differences in the environment as a function of time rather than differences in age. This interpretation is possible because all of the studies were cross-sectional. Had they been longitudinal, the group would consist of children all born in the same year. Since they were cross-sectional, each age group was born in a different year, and therefore the observed group differences could as plausibly be attributed to environmental differences (such as gradually improving educational facilities, which would benefit the younger children) as to age differences.

No matter what causes it, however, it is a widespread phenomenon, found not only in children living in isolated areas, but also in children from other kinds of impoverished backgrounds. Jordan (1933) found it in the children of millworkers in North Carolina, and Skeels and Fillmore (1937) found it in children committed to an Iowa orphanage after varying periods of residence in substandard homes. Very recently, Kennedy, Van de Reitt, and White (1963) found it in their large sample of southern Negro school children; 5 year olds had a mean Stanford-Binet IQ of 86, 13 year olds a mean of 65. However, Schaefer (1965) has recently presented a convincing argument that these last findings may reflect the sampling procedure used. The sample of 5 year olds was relatively small, and may have included only the brighter children who entered school early; the sample of 13 year olds may have already lost the brighter pupils through completion of elementary school.

It should be noted that in all of these studies, single-score tests were used. It would be interesting in view of Ferguson's ideas (1954, 1956) to see if the negative correlation with age in restricted environments shows up on all test items or only certain kinds of items.

Despite the frequency of the finding of a negative relation between age and IQ in restricted environments, a hopeful note is sounded by the results of a study by Wheeler (1942). He tested groups of East Tennessee mountain children in 1930 and 1940, and although there was a decline in test score with age both times, the absolute scores were considerably higher in the later testing, as shown in Table 16-1. Wheeler interpreted this as a secular trend reflecting a decade of improvement in roads, schools, and agricultural and economic life.

Table 16-1

Mean IQs of East Tennessee
Mountain Children[a]

		Age	
Year of testing	*6*	*10*	*16*
1930	95	84	75
1940	103	91	80

[a] Representative data from Wheeler (1942).

A more detailed discussion of the possibility of raising the intelligence level of children through environmental enrichment will be given later.

Socioeconomic Class

One of the most reliable findings in the psychological literature is that of a direct relation between socioeconomic status and intelligence test performance. Socioeconomic status has been defined in terms of parental occupation, income, or education, characteristics of the home and neighborhood, and various combinations of these. The same basic relation—low socioeconomic status, low intelligence—has been obtained whichever definition is used. It has also been obtained with both group and individual intelligence tests. If low socioeconomic status is viewed as a kind of restricted environment, this whole section may be considered an extension of the preceding one.

Wiener, Rider, and Oppel (1963) reported data on the relation between socioeconomic class and IQ change. Following a technique suggested by Warner, they combined ratings on parents' income, education, employment, and residence into a Social Class index and related this to IQ change scores of two and of children who were given the Stanford-Binet between the ages of two and five years and again between the ages of six and seven years. Change was significantly related to social class; upper class background was associated with rising IQ, and lower class background with declining IQ.

Because of space limitations only a few of the dozens of studies that have related socioeconomic status to average performance are mentioned here. Reviews of many of the earliest studies may be found in reports by Neff (1938) and Loevinger (1940).

Relevant data have been accumulated in the major longitudinal studies. For example, Shuttleworth (1940) analyzed data from the Harvard Growth Study and found that at each half-yearly age level from 8 to 18 the average IQ of children whose fathers had high occupational status (professional, semiprofessional, managerial, and large business) exceeded the average IQ of children whose fathers had low occupational status (semiskilled and unskilled labor). Differences ranged from 9.9 to 14.2 points, with no consistent tendency for the differences to change with age. In the Berkeley Growth Study positive correlations were reported for both sexes, from about 2 to 18 years of age, between a number of socioeconomic variables and scores on individual intelligence tests (Bayley, 1954; Bayley and Schaefer, 1964). The scores of girls more often showed significant correlations with parental status than did the scores of boys. Highest correlations were with parental education. From 2 to 10 years they ranged from .35 to .59, and from 11 to 15 years they ranged from .59 to .62.

In the standardization samples of the two most widely used individual intelligence tests for children—the Stanford-Binet (McNemar, 1942) and the Wechsler Intelligence Scale for Children (Seashore, Wesman, and Doppelt, 1950)—essentially the same relation was found between IQ and father's occupational level. On the Stanford-Binet, for instance, children of professional workers had an average IQ of 115; children of skilled tradesmen and retail business workers, 108; and children of both urban and rural day laborers, 94. Findings with the 1960 revision of the Stanford-Binet corroborate the findings with the 1937 edition (Kennedy et al., 1963; Tiber and Kennedy, 1964).

Herrick (1951) concluded that in the United States there is typically a 15 to 25 point difference between the scores of children of professional parents and those of laborers, and that correlations between socioeconomic status and IQ range around a typical value of .35. Anastasi indicated that findings similar to those observed in the United States have been reported for many other countries (Anastasi, 1958a, p. 518).

As pointed out before, data on average group differences obscure overlap between groups. Many lower class children earn scores higher than many upper class children (Eells, Davis, Havighurst, Herrick, and Tyler, 1951, p. 53). This point was clearly demonstrated in an early study by McGehee and Lewis (1942) which utilized data from a sample of 45,000 children in Grades 4 to 8 in 36 states who had been given the Kuhlmann-Anderson Intelligence Tests. In most cases ratings of parental occupation, on a five point scale, were also available. Children who scored in the top 10 percent on the intelligence test were *on the average* higher in social class than children who scored in the bottom 10 percent; but as shown in Table 16-2, there was considerable overlap between the distributions. Children from both ends of the IQ range were found at all occupational levels, and in terms of absolute figures, the greatest number of both groups came from the middle occupational level.

Though the data are clear, the interpretation is not. Laird (1957) felt that previously reported class differences resulted from failure to control a number of relevant variables. He divided a sample of 11 year old boys into high and low socioeconomic groups on the basis of parental occupation, education, and income, then carefully equated the groups for age, residence, school attendance, family unit, race, nationality, physical status, and health. Despite this procedure, typical social class differences were found on the Wechsler Intelligence Scale for Children. Average IQ for the high status children on the verbal, performance, and total scales were 120, 107, and 115, respectively; corresponding figures for the lower class children were 105, 101, and 103. In interpreting his data Laird

Table 16-2

Relation of Children's IQ Level to Parental Occupational Level[a,b]

IQ level	Occupational level[c]				
	I	II	III	IV	V
Top 10%	10.3	35.9	37.4	10.3	5.9
Bottom 10%	.6	10.9	41.6	15.6	28.9

[a] After McGehee and Lewis (1942, Table 2, p. 377).
[b] Body of table gives percentage in each occupational level who fell into each IQ level.
[c] I, Professional; II, semiprofessional and business; III, skilled labor; IV, semiskilled and slightly skilled labor; V, common labor.

suggested that the results might reflect failure to control the possibly crucial factor of the child's perception of himself and the world he lives in.[3]

Some see in the test score data an indication of inherent differences in intellectual capacity among the various socioeconomic classes. Since the methodological difficulties of genetic interpretations have already been discussed, they need not be repeated here, although they are, of course, relevant to the view under consideration. Briefly, this view is that genetically superior individuals show greater upward social mobility; because of their intellectual superiority they rise to the higher classes and, once there, marry within the higher classes and

[3] The impossibility of unambiguous interpretation of the data of this study illustrates the major drawback of all correlational studies, as opposed to experimental manipulative studies. In principle, correlational data would be unambiguously interpretable if all irrelevant variables were controlled, but it seems to be impossible to ensure even that all have been *indentified*, much less controlled.

pass on superior intelligence to their children. Those of inherently lower intellectual capacity remain and reproduce in the lower classes. With greater or less modification, this view has been expressed by such American psychologists as Goodenough (1940, p. 329), Jones (1954, p. 649), and Thompson (1962, p. 429). It is a particularly popular view in England, where it has been vigorously defended in the writings of Burt (1959, 1961), Conway (1959), and Warburton (1959), and equally vigorously attacked by Halsey (1958) and Floud and Halsey (1958). The last-named authors seem to accept the Hebbian distinction between Intelligence A and Intelligence B (see section entitled "Theories of Intelligence," Chapter 15). They agreed that individual intelligence has a large innate component, conceived as some quality of the central nervous system, but they maintained that this genetic component is randomly distributed across social classes and, moreover, that the skills sampled by intelligence tests do not represent inherited potential but rather a set of acquired behaviors.

In the United States a very articulate and eloquent group loosely known as the "Chicago school" (Davis and Havighurst, 1948; Eells, 1953; Eells et al., 1951; Haggard, 1953; Warner, Havighurst, and Loeb, 1946) has been vitally concerned with the findings on intelligence and socioeconomic status. Their writings, which include the general topic of intelligence testing in relation to educational practice, have strongly influenced the thinking of those presently working with underprivileged children and will accordingly be summarized in some detail.

These writers felt that the commonly used standardized intelligence tests should be regarded simply as tests of scholastic aptitude for schools as presently constituted, and not as measures of any general basic intellectual ability. They pointed out, however, that many users adopt the latter interpretation, and consequently, a child, particularly a lower class child, who performs badly on one of these tests is often written off as worthless and given no further attention.

This group held, further, that the relatively poor performance of lower class children is attributable largely, perhaps entirely, to cultural bias in the test items. By this they meant that many items have relevance to the out of school experiences of middle class children but not of lower class children. This was seen as an inevitable outcome of the fact that for many tests, items were deliberately selected on the basis of their ability to discriminate between children who did well or poorly in school. The typical American school is described as an institutionalized manifestation of middle class values, run by middle class administrators and teachers. Naturally, test items that relate to such a criterion would be biased in favor of middle class children.

This argument has been bolstered by data on the actual differences between middle and lower class children on different test items. In the most ambitious study, by Eells et al. (1951), a series of widely used group intelligence tests was administered to a large sample of middle and lower socioeconomic status children in a Midwestern community. On the tests used with 9 and 10 year old subjects, about 50 percent of the items showed significant differences between middle and lower class children; for 13 and 14 year old subjects about 85 percent of the items showed significant differences. Class differences were largest on verbal items and smallest on picture, geometric design, and stylized drawing items. In addition, almost all the items showing large class differences were couched in academic or bookish vocabulary—words, objects, or concepts with which middle class children would be more familiar. One such item, for example, required an understanding of the word "sonata." Items with small class differences were couched in very simple words and dealt either with "noncultural" subject matter or subject matter common to the experience of all groups. An example of this kind of item is one that required the children to select a cutting tool from a number of tools that can be used for other purposes.

Members of the Chicago school maintained that to build an unbiased intelligence test one should utilize only items common to the experience of all groups in the culture. They held that such a "culture fair" test, sampling a wide variety of skills and not only those involved in academic success, could be considered a test of basic intelligence in the sense of general ability to solve important life problems.

Several published tests have been designated as culture fair (Cattell and Cattell, 1950–1959; Davis and Eells, 1953; Goodenough, 1926; Raven, 1956, 1958). However, results from most studies utilizing them have not confirmed the expectation that class differences would be eliminated. For example, Angelino and Shedd (1955) administered the Davis-Eells Games to groups of upper and lower socioeconomic class elementary school children in a large urban area. This test, which is presented to the children as a game, consists entirely of a set of pictures presumably dealing with general problems common to all groups in the American culture. Nevertheless, typical class differences were found. Except in the first grade, the scores of the upper class children were clearly above those of the lower class children. Further evidence of the failure to eliminate class differences can be found in studies by Knief and Stroud (1959) and Marquart and Bailey (1955). In fact, one former proponent of the use of culture fair intelligence tests, Florence Goodenough, eventually came to the conclusion that "the search for a culture-free test, whether of intelligence, artistic ability, personal-social characteristics, or any other measurable trait is illusory" (Goodenough and Harris, 1950, p. 399). It seems likely that the persistent finding of class differences may be attributable to failure to identify and control a host of subtle relevant motivational variables.

Despite negative results so far, the possibility remains, of course, that it will eventually be possible to devise a test that will not show socioeconomic class differences. It is difficult to imagine, however, any useful criterion that could be predicted by such a test. Eells, for one, has been quite aware of this possibility. He observed that if, as he advocated, tests are made up only of items common to the cultural backgrounds of lower and upper class children

. . . it may be that some of the most important kinds of problems—when judged in terms of their importance within the culture—may have to be eliminated. The result would be an estimate of intelligence which, while unbiased so far as the cultural comparison is concerned, might be quite unrepresentative of various kinds of abilities—some of which might be much more important for the well-being of the child, and of his society, than those selected on the basis of their cultural communality. (Eells et al., 1951, p. 75.)

Lorge (1953), who has been quite critical of the attempt to eliminate cultural differences from tests, felt that knowledge of such differences is intrinsically valuable. As tests are developed to measure mastery of different skills, evidence about inequalities of opportunity for maximal development will be obtained; such information can then be used to ameliorate conditions. "When differences are reduced by the advantages of opportunity the credit will be to tests that showed their existence" (Lorge, 1953, p. 83).

The Chicago viewpoint seems to offer a good example of several of the methodological pitfalls that have beset research on intelligence, specifically, the intermixture of fact and value and unrealistic conceptions about the nature of psychological tests.

It is true that lower class children, as a group, do relatively poorly on the widely used conventional intelligence tests. Also, it seems likely from anecdotal evidence that many users view the tests as measures of "intelligence," as that value-laden term is loosely used in everyday language, and conclude from their test scores that lower class children are basically inferior. The fact that any scientific instrument is popularly misused, however, does not in itself render it useless for the purposes for which it was intended. It simply underscores the fact that many test users have not been adequately trained.

It may also be true that test performance is largely a function of cultural bias in test items, although other interpretations are possible. The zeal with which the interpretation of cultural bias is promoted, however, and the vigor of the attack on conventional intelligence tests stem, it seems, from the critics' commitment to a democratic value system which holds that all men are equally worthwhile or, at least, that their personal worth has nothing to do with how much money they have. There is also a commitment to the idea that ability should be sought and developed wherever it exists and that not to do so constitutes a waste of a valuable national resource as well as a serious personal injustice. Moreover, it is felt that the schools, as presently constituted, are not doing a good job of realizing these democratic values. One can agree with all these sentiments, yet argue that they should be recognized as such and kept separate from the search for factual relationships. Social reform is one area of human endeavor. The accumulation of a body of scientific information is another. Fortunately, the fruits of scientific endeavor may often be applied to social reform. Sometimes they cannot. Nothing is gained, however, by failing to make a clear distinction between the roles of social reformer and scientific investigator. It therefore seems futile to condemn conventional intelligence tests for failing to promote democratic goals; as scientific research instruments they should not be expected to do so.

The attempt to develop culture fair intelligence tests seems to have been motivated, at least in part, by a desire to confirm the democratic expectation that the socially desirable trait "intelligence" or "general problem-solving ability" is equitably distributed. The attempt seems doomed to failure, because it rests on the unrealistic hope that any test can usefully sample such a vaguely defined, all inclusive domain as "general problem-solving ability." Conventional intelligence tests do not do this, but neither could any other test. It would seem to be in the best interests of both science and social welfare if this impossible goal were abandoned and efforts were concentrated on improving tests that sample particular kinds of problem-solving abilities and relate to clearly defined criteria.

The ability to succeed in schools as they are currently set up is fairly well predicted by existing tests. Children who do badly on these tests tend to do badly in school. It is certainly true, however, that a good deal of damaging misinterpretation could be avoided if conventional intelligence tests were simply called scholastic aptitude tests.

If the schools were reorganized in line with proposals that have at various times been made by the Chicago group, it is possible that existing tests would no longer be very effective predictors. New tests, with less cultural bias, might do a better job. They would still, however, be tests of scholastic aptitude.

The Chicago writers, however, wanted to be able to predict more than success in school. They wanted to be able to predict a child's ability to solve any life problem that is important to him. Presumably, this might include such problems as making and keeping friends, avoiding difficulties with the law, and selecting a vocation and learning the skills essential for success in it. All of these are meaningful problems. Perhaps tests can be devised that relate to each of them. If so, a series of specific problem-solving tests would be available and they could be appropriately named for the specific criterion they predict. On some of these, socioeconomic background might still be a factor; on others it might not. In any event, such an approach would probably be of greater practical value and would certainly avoid the controversies and ambiguities inherent in the attempt to devise culture fair tests of intelligence.

Race

Before considering the data on Negro–white differences in intelligence test performance, it is necessary to comment on a relevant methodological issue. It has often been pointed out that many of the widely used intelligence tests on which racial comparisons have been based did not include Negroes in their standardization populations. Many have questioned the validity of the use of such tests, but it depends on the use that is to be made of the test score.

It is sometimes desirable to evaluate an individual's test performance in relation to his peers within a circumscribed environmental setting. If the individual and his peers are not represented in the standardization norms of the test and if, in addition, little is known about the relation between scores on the test and criterional performance in that environment, the whole procedure is essentially meaningless. This is the situation that has prevailed for years in the southern United States.

While it is common practice for professional workers to build up special test norms to enable them to make particular intragroup comparisons in the absence of suitable published norms, until very recently this had not been done on any large scale for southern Negro school children. Kennedy *et al.* (1963) summed up the problem quite succinctly in writing, "There is no test of individual intelligence or achievement which has been standardized on both white and Negro populations. There is no test of individual intelligence which has been validated against achievement tests or scholastic ratings on this large population" (Kennedy *et al.*, 1963, p. 9). Clinicians and school psychologists concerned with guiding Negro children within their own restricted educational settings have used standard test instruments along with vague, rule of thumb qualifications. Because of the generally poor performance of Negro children on such tests it has been assumed, for instance, that any Negro child who attains an IQ of 100 is indeed superior. It has not been possible, however, in the absence of appropriate norms, to state exactly what percentage of his peers such a child exceeds, nor have there been any concrete data available for educational counseling purposes.

Kennedy *et al.* (1963) have recently ameliorated this situation. By testing Negro children in five southeastern states, they have amassed a set of norms for the 1960 Stanford-Binet and the California Achievement Tests and have determined the relation between them. In doing so they have provided "a broad sample study that would enable professional workers when examining a child to know where this child stands relevant to the school setting from which he comes" (Kennedy *et al.*, 1963, p. 10).

However, as indicated in the discussion of culture fair tests, when the relation between original test norms and a specific criterion has been firmly established, then it is perfectly meaningful to use the test with any individual who will be performing the criterion task. This can be done whether or not he was represented in the standardization sample.

Prothro (1955) stressed this point with reference to cross-cultural comparisons. He administered a group test of verbal intelligence (modeled after the American Henmon-Nelson Test of Mental Abilities) to Arabian students at the American University of Beirut. They had not, of course, been represented in the standardization sample. Nevertheless, he found a significant correlation of .58 between scores on this test and first semester grade averages, and concluded that it is both possible and valid to do cross-cultural testing when the criterion of intelligent behavior is shared by the cultures.

This same point applies to racial comparisons within a culture. A southern Negro child with a low IQ on any of the widely used intelligence tests is quite likely to show poor criterional performance in a predominantly white school in, for instance, a suburban midwestern community. Such a prediction could be made from knowledge of the relationship between IQs on that test and success in that kind of school setting even if the standardization sample contained no southern Negro children. This prediction says nothing at all about why the child earned the low IQ nor what could be done to improve both it and his school performance. These are important but separate questions. The fact that they arise does not invalidate the use of the test.

The extensive literature on Negro–white differences in intelligence test performance has been reviewed in great detail by Shuey (1958) and in less detail by Dreger and Miller (1960) and Kennedy *et al.* (1963).

With the exception of one early study by McGraw (1931), there is no evidence for white superiority in infancy nor in the early preschool years. Gilliland (1951) reported that one group of Negro infants in the 4 to 12 month age bracket obtained a mean score of 110 (on the Northwestern Infant Intelligence Test), significantly above the white infants with whom they were compared. In another group in the same age bracket and one in the 3 to 9 month age bracket, there were no significant racial differences. Pasamanick and Knobloch (1955) found no significant differences between Negro and white babies (on the Gesell Developmental Schedule) during the first 18 months and in a follow up at 2 years. These and similar results are not surprising in view of the low correlations between infant tests and later tests.

From the late preschool years on, the average performance of groups of Negro children on traditional IQ tests is, typically, significantly below that of white children. Klineberg (1963) estimated the median Negro IQ to be 85, and Shuey (1958) estimated 86. The white median is 100. Osborne (1960) found mean IQs (California Mental Maturity Scale) for white children 6, 8, and 10 years of age to be 101, 100, and 102, respectively; corresponding Negro means were 79, 84, and 79. Similarly, Semler and Iscoe (1966) found white IQ (Wechsler Intelligence Scale for Children) to be 105 at both 6 and 8 years of age; corresponding means for Negro children were 83 and 97. Findings from tests designed to minimize the effect of cultural background are more variable. Anastasi and D'Angelo (1952) found no Negro–white difference on the Goodenough Draw-a-Man Test in a sample of 5 year olds; and Semler and Iscoe (1966), using Raven's Coloured Progressive Matrices, found white children scoring significantly higher at 7 years of age but not at 8 and 9 years of age. Love and Beach (1957) reported significantly higher scores for white subjects on the Davis-Eells Games, and McGurk (1953, 1956), using a specially constructed test with high school students, reported racial differences favoring whites to be greater on noncultural items than on cultural items.

As in all cases of group comparisons, there is great within-group variation and a good deal of overlap between distributions. Anastasi maintained that 30 percent overlap is "close to that usually found between psychological test scores of Negroes and Whites in the U.S." (Anastasi, 1958a, p. 549). This means that 30 percent of the Negro children attain higher scores than the average white child, and as Anastasi pointed out, "the implications of overlapping make it abundantly clear that differences between group means even when statistically significant may be of little practical value for dealing with individuals" (Anastasi, 1958a, p. 550).

As shown in the preceding section, socioeconomic status is related to intelligence test performance. Since a disproportionate number of Negroes in American society come from the lower socioeconomic levels, several investigators attempted to equate Negro and white groups on socioeconomic variables before comparing their IQs. However, even when this was done, racial differences were still found. Bruce (1940) matched the home backgrounds of groups of southern Negro and white rural children, and reported the average Stanford-Binet IQ of the Negroes to be 77, significantly below the average white IQ of 86. Critics of this study have pointed out, however, that the children attended segregated schools, thus leaving the important variable of equality of educational opportunity uncontrolled. McGurk (1953, 1956) equated 213 white and Negro high school seniors for age, school attendance, school curriculum, and socioeconomic background. Nevertheless, the average score of the Negroes was significantly lower than the average of the whites. Further analyses of his data, in comparison with the data of studies reported during World War I, led McGurk to conclude, ". . . when the Negro is given better social and economic opportunity the differences between Negroes and Whites actually increase" (McGurk, 1956, p. 96). This conclusion was widely publicized and generated a storm of controversy and several well-documented rebuttals. McCord and Demerath (1958), for instance, pointed out severe methodological flaws in the studies on which McGurk had based his conclusions, and Long (1957) convincingly refuted McGurk's contention that the social and economic position of Negroes in the United States had improved more than had the position of whites in the period between the two world wars.

Two studies frequently cited in opposition to McGurk's viewpoint are those of Klineberg (1938) and Lee (1951). Both demonstrated that change to a more stimulating environment is associated with a rise in IQ for Negro children and that the longer the exposure continues, the greater is the rise. In the methodologically sounder of the two studies, Lee repeatedly tested groups of Negro children who had migrated from the South to Philadelphia, where the educational environment was presumably more stimulating. There was a steady improvement in test performance as each of the migrant groups increased its length of residence in Philadelphia. Migrant children entering the first grade were definitely inferior in test performance to those born in the Northern city, but by the time they reached sixth grade there was no significant difference between them.

The belief that Northern environments are "superior" has recently been questioned by Scott (1966). He reported that the mean IQ of a group of Negro students in a Negro public school in Chicago dropped significantly from 93 in the first grade to 90 in the ninth grade. While he failed to consider the possibility that the finding may have been an artifact of the use of different tests in the first and ninth grades, Scott's interpretation of his finding is thought provoking. He wrote, "Possibly as a result of social factors such as flight of whites to the suburbs, larger families of lower-class Negroes, growing congestion within Negro neighborhoods and rising indices of crime, the northern environment once was, but is no longer, 'superior' " (Scott, 1966, p. 160).

The interpretation of observed racial differences has been hotly debated because of its obvious relevance to social and political decisions. A minority has pointed to the consistency of results in various studies as evidence of innate racial differences (Garrett, 1947; Jensen, 1969; McGurk, 1956; Shuey, 1958). The majority view, expressed by 18 prominent social scientists (see Klineberg, 1957), is that intelligence tests do not differentiate between innate capacity and environmental influences and, moreover, that if any innate racial differences do exist they have not been demonstrated.

It is often assumed that if all relevant nongenetic influences are controlled by equating groups, any residual differences in intelligence test performance can be attributed to genetic factors. The catch, of course, is in the assumption that one can identify and control all relevant nongenetic influences.

Tangible socioeconomic differences between Negroes and whites were controlled in several studies, and still racial differences in IQ were found. The environmentalists are quick to point out that this is not conclusive. Other differences, in more subtle factors such as generalized personality traits (Pettigrew, 1964), motivation (Katz, 1967), self-concept (Gibby and Gabler, 1967), stability of home background (Deutsch and Brown, 1964), linguistic skill, and poor rapport with examiners of a different race (Pasamanick and Knobloch, 1955), may contribute to the inferiority of the test performance of Negro children. More and more writers have been expressing doubt that any group of Negroes and whites can really be equated under existing social conditions (e.g., Deutsch and Brown, 1964). Dreger and Miller (1960) pointed out that in the United States today Negroes are differentiated from whites by caste as well as class. It may be possible to equate class, but it is probably impossible to equate caste. They pointed out that in their own state

. . . there are a number of Negroes whose social and economic statuses exceed those of most white persons. These Negroes, however, cannot yet sit in the same seats on public transportation (in most places), go to the same hotel, restaurant, club, school, church, social events, or even restrooms. Although some of these strictures do not hold in Northern states, attitudes regarding intermarriage and the more personal forms of social intercourse do not appear greatly different from those in the South. (Dreger and Miller, 1960, p. 367.)

In short, there are many environmental influences on the lives of Negroes today that simply are not found in the lives of whites. Under these circumstances it is not possible to achieve any complete equating of Negro and white groups on nongenetic factors relevant to test performance and, therefore, score differences cannot be unequivocally ascribed to genetic factors. The question of innate racial differences underlying the abilities sampled by intelligence tests must remain open.

Stimulating Environments

In the 1930s and 1940s in the United States, the question of whether stimulating environments could affect IQ was part and parcel of an acrimonious debate concerning the constancy of the IQ. Those committed to the belief in a constant IQ unaffected by anything except measurement errors, aligned themselves against those committed to the belief that stimulating experiences could raise IQ and, by implication, more general intellectual behavior.

To a large extent, the debate centered around the interpretation of a series of studies in which IQ was measured before and after a period of attendance at nursery school. Of close to 50 studies reviewed by Wellman (1945), 22 utilized some version of the Binet scales as the testing instrument. All but one of these studies showed IQ increases in groups of children attending nursery school for periods ranging from 5 to 14 months. The mean reported change was 5.4

points, with a range of —.6 to +12.5. In only 9 studies, however, were the changes in the preschoolers compared with changes in suitable control groups. Of these, 3 showed significant changes in favor of the preschoolers, 2 showed differences in the same direction that approached significance, and 4 reported no significant difference. The question of what factors in the groups, schools, or testing conditions accounted for these discrepant results was never adequately answered.

The bitterly debated question of whether the observed differences in these studies were artifactual or were a genuine consequence of nursery school stimulation was, to the participants, of great theoretical significance, even though the differences were so small as to be of little practical value. Most of the children involved were of rather high initial IQ level and somewhat superior socioeconomic status. It does not seem likely that a five point increase in IQ for these children would have materially affected their futures.

Today, when evidence from various sources has undermined the notion of IQ constancy, these early studies recede to largely historical interest. Attention is now focused on determining exactly what experiences can improve intellectual performance, particularly among the large numbers of children with deprived backgrounds. This research has assumed great social significance now that there is little room left in society for those whose intellectual skills prepare them only for jobs as unskilled laborers. Numerous studies are in progress involving nursery school programs, such as Project Head Start, and special enrichment curricula in elementary and high schools. Data are being accumulated not only on changes in IQ but also on changes in language skills, academic performance, and social and emotional adjustment. Because of space limitations only studies concerning the effect of preschool experiences on intelligence test performance will be discussed here. However, extensive bibliographies, discussions of methodological problems, and reviews of relevant research may be found in several recent publications (Bloom, Davis, and Hess, 1965; White, 1966; Witty, 1967).

One early study that attracted a great deal of attention dealt with preschool-aged children residing in an orphanage that offered virtually no opportunity for intellectual stimulation (Skeels, Updegraff, Wellman, and Williams, 1938). A nursery school was set up in the orphanage and a group of children selected for attendance at this nursery was carefully matched with a nonattending control group. It was found that for children who had resided in the orphanage less than 400 days, there was no significant difference in Stanford-Binet IQ change between the preschool and control groups. However, for children who had resided in the orphanage more than 400 days, preschoolers with 50 percent or better attendance gained 6.8 points as contrasted with a loss for the control group of 6.1 points. The final IQ difference between these preschoolers and their controls was a significant 14.8 points. The investigators' conclusion that continued residence in an impoverished environment is associated with a decrease in IQ is consistent with the results of the studies described previously. The investigators further concluded that extended attendance at the stimulating nursery school counteracted these losses. Both conclusions were severely criticized on statistical grounds by McNemar (1940); but Wellman and Pegram (1944) reanalyzed the data using more appropriate statistical techniques and reached essentially the same conclusions.

Recent attempts at preschool enrichment have yielded varying results. Gray and Klaus (1965), while pointing out that the ultimate criterion of success is a demonstration of long term effects, reported initial success with a sample of culturally deprived Negro children. In an experimental group who experienced three summer school preschool sessions and whose homes were regularly visited throughout the year, the mean Stanford-Binet IQ rose from 86 to 95. Over the same period of time two control groups lost 4 and 6 IQ points, respectively.

Blank and Solomon (1968) found that socioeconomically deprived preschoolers who were given a special language program improved in verbal IQ (Stanford-Binet) and, to a lesser extent, performance IQ (Leiter). Incidental observations suggested that there was also improvement in nontest cognitive behaviors.

Seidel, Barkley, and Stith (1967) found no significant IQ increase on either of two nonverbal intelligence tests in a group of North Carolina youngsters who experienced seven or eight weeks of attendance at a Head Start preschool. Also, Blatt and Garfunkel (1967) reported no significant effect of preschool enrichment over a two year period in a group of urban deprived children. On a battery of cognitive tests which included the Stanford-Binet there was no more difference between the experimental and control groups at the end of the study than at the beginning. Blatt and Garfunkel felt that their failure to obtain an effect might have resulted from a failure to influence the families from which the children came. One writer (Jensen, 1969) has expressed the controversial viewpoint that all compensatory educational attempts are doomed to failure to the extent that they do not consider innate unmodifiable cognitive differences between groups of children.

Several enrichment studies have been specifically concerned with the mentally retarded. Spicker, Hodges, and McCandless (1966) dealt with a group of mentally retarded children whose initial Stanford-Binet IQs ranged from 50 to 85 and who had particularly deprived backgrounds. One group attended a special experimental preschool in which an attempt was made to diagnose each child's special areas of weakness and to find compensatory educational techniques for dealing with them. At the end of the first year, the IQs of this experimental group had increased from 74.9 to 92.8. This increase was significantly greater than the increase shown by two "regular" control groups that had not attended any school, but not greater than the increase in a control group that had attended an ordinary school kindergarten. One year later, after all groups had gone through first grade, the experimental group was still relatively the highest in IQ, but it was no longer significantly above the regular control groups, whose IQs had continued to rise during first grade. These results are in some ways similar to results obtained by Kirk (1958): A group of noninstitutionalized mentally defective children gained an average of 11.2 Stanford-Binet IQ points after attending a special nursery school, while a control group of nonattenders lost .6 point; but after one year during which all the children attended regular school, the experimental subjects showed no further increase while the controls increased 7.5 points. As Kirk pointed out, "if these results are corroborated by later studies, it could mean that preschools for mentally handicapped children are not necessary since the children will accelerate their rate of development after entering school at the usual age of six" (Kirk, 1958, p. 209). This viewpoint contrasts with that expressed by writers who, extrapolating from animal studies on the effects of infantile deprivation, maintain that compensatory enrichment techniques have not been instituted early enough to be maximally beneficial.

In summary, it has been demonstrated in several studies that special stimulating environments are associated with improved intelligence test performance. More systematic data are needed, however, to determine whether there are certain critical periods during which such experiences are maximally effective and whether the effects are permanent and are related to important nontest behavior.

Mentally Retarded Children

According to the official definition by the American Association of Mental Deficiency, "Mental retardation refers to subaverage general intellectual functioning which originates during the development period and is associated with impairment in one or more of the following: (1) maturation, (2) learning, and (3) social adjustment [i.e., adaptive behavior]" (Heber, 1959, p. 3).

No matter how it is defined, the problem of mental retardation is a large and unhappy one. A typical estimate of the incidence of mental retardation in the United States, given by Benda, Squires, Ogonik, and Wise (1963), is that there are 180,000 severely retarded, 540,000 moderately retarded, and a staggering 5,000,000 mildly retarded individuals in this country. The severely retarded typically have IQs between 0 and 25 and require custodial care in institutions throughout their lives. The moderately retarded, who are designated "trainable," generally have IQs between 25 and 50. Most of them are institutionalized but can be taught a variety of simple social and self-help skills. The mildly retarded, or "educable," most often have IQs between 50 and 70. Only about one percent of the educable group is institutionalized on any long range basis; the rest function with varying degrees of success in society.

Although IQs are used above in connection with the classifications of mental retardation, they do not establish hard and fast boundaries. It is common practice to consider various measures of social competence and subjective clinical impressions as well as IQ in classifying these people. When this is done, some with IQs below 70 are not classified as retarded while some above 70 are.

In the two lower groupings and in about 15 percent of the mildly retarded, behavioral symptoms can clearly be related to physical pathology including central nervous system defects and disorders of the metabolic and endocrine systems. Some of these defects are genetic in origin; others are traceable to pre- or postnatal disease or accidents or to injuries associated with birth. These defects are discussed in Chapter 18 (section entitled "Mental Impairment").

By far the largest group is made up of mildly retarded people who show no obvious physical pathology. This group has been variously labeled subcultural, simple, familial, or garden variety retarded. Because of space limitations, the rest of this section will deal only with the noninstitutionalized subcultural retarded group. For a good summary of the entire field of retardation, the student is referred to a recent comprehensive review of research edited by Stevens and Heber (1964).

The more severe forms of mental retardation are normally distributed throughout the various socioeconomic levels. However, there is general agreement among workers in the field that subcultural mental retardation is most heavily concentrated in the lowest socioeconomic classes, and there is some empirical evidence to support this view (Bradway, 1935; Kennedy, 1948; Meyerowitz, 1967; Solomons, Cushna, Opitz, and Greene, 1966). These children often come from homes characterized not only by low income, but also by broken marriage, high crime rate, and a general social value system that deviates markedly from the dominant middle class values of American society. To the extent that subcultural mental retardation is associated with lower class status, all the material covered in the section on class differences is relevant here also.

In the past 15 years or so, there has been a shift in thinking about the causes of subcultural mental retardation. Earlier formulations attributed it to hereditary physical defects that were simply not detectable with available diagnostic tools. Nowadays, however, according to Clausen (1967), most psychologists believe that subcultural retardation is a function of environmental experiences. Sarason (1953) and Sarason and Gladwin (1958) stressed the importance of the social and psychological deprivation that characterizes the home backgrounds of so many mildly retarded children. McCandless maintained that the behavior of the mildly retarded can be understood in terms of two learning hypotheses:

> First, the environment from which the subcultural mentally defective person comes is one providing minimal opportunity for the learning of the skills which are subsumed under the term intelligence. Second, the environment . . . is one in which he has maximum opportunity to learn self-defeating techniques—e.g., loosely defined, expectancies of failure, absolute as opposed to relative thinking, concrete as opposed to abstract thinking, belief in his essential worthlessness, etc. (McCandless, 1952, p. 684.)

Others who have stressed the role of experiential factors in the etiology of subcultural mental retardation include Cromwell (1961), Bijou (1963), Zimmerman (1965), and Zigler (1966).

The personal-social experiences of subcultural mentally retarded children are unhappy. Other children do not pick them as friends and often actively reject them because of such antisocial behavior patterns as "he bothers us," "he fights," "he talks back to the teacher," etc. (Baldwin, 1958, p. 108; see also Johnson, 1950; Jordan, 1959; Turner, 1958).

In view of the home backgrounds and poor social acceptance of subcultural retardates, it seems reasonable to assume a high incidence of personal emotional maladjustment. This assumption is, in fact, very often made, although as W. I. Gardner (1966) pointed out in a recent review article, there is a dearth of solid, systematic evidence to support it. Several studies do, however, support the assumption. Chazan (1964) reported that a group of "educationally subnormal" pupils showed significantly more depression, hostility toward adults, inhibitions, and symptoms of emotional tensions than did a control group. Several investigators using the California Test of Personality as a measure of adjustment found that retarded children obtained very low scores in comparison to the test norms (Blatt, 1958; G. O. Johnson, 1961; Kern and Pfaeffle, 1963). In partial contrast to these data, however, are those reported by Enos (1961), who studied emotional adjustment in a group of mildly retarded children and groups with average and superior IQ. Emotional adjustment was defined in terms of ratings by experienced psychologists. The retarded girls showed the most maladjustment, but the retarded boys showed the least. It would seem, in short, that a great deal more definitive information is needed on the nature and incidence of various kinds of emotional problems in the subcultural retardate.

The subcultural mental defective is most conspicuously inadequate during the elementary school years. Follow-up studies of individuals diagnosed as mildly retarded in childhood are almost unanimous in finding that the majority make adequate, though low level, postschool adjustments (Charles, 1953; Hegge, 1944; Jastak and Whiteman, 1957; Muench, 1944; see also Skeels, 1966). Sarason and Gladwin summed up the relevent data as follows:

> Compared to individuals earlier judged "normal" who were used as controls, the formerly retarded persons have slightly higher divorce and minor civil offense rates and somewhat lower grades of occupations with lower standards of living. They are therefore not spectacularly successful, but can scarcely be called failures, inadequate to cope with the requirements of social living. (Sarason and Gladwin, 1958, p. 171.)

The Gifted

As the complexity of modern civilization increases, so does the recognition that the intellectually gifted constitute a most precious national resource. Recent years have witnessed an unprecedented increase in research aimed at the identification, description, and training of the gifted child. Such enterprises as the National Merit Scholarships (Stalnaker, 1961), Project Talent (Flanagan and Dailey, 1960; Shaycoft, Dailey, and Orr, 1963), and the New York City Intellectually Gifted Classes (Krugman, 1960) are but a few of the major projects undertaken in pursuit of these goals. (A more complete listing is given by K. E. Anderson, 1961.)

Although the upsurge of interest in the gifted is fairly recent, the most comprehensive study in the area remains that of Terman, who set out in 1921 to determine "What are the physical, mental and personality traits characteristic of intellectually superior children and what sort of adult does the typical gifted child become?" (Terman and Oden, 1947, p. 2).

This study began with a total of 1528 cases. Slightly more than two-thirds had Stanford-Binet IQs of 135 or over, placing them in the top two percent of the population, and the rest had group intelligence test scores that placed them in the top one percent of the norms. The majority of the subjects were drawn from a population of children nominated by teachers for final screening through tests. This sampling technique has been criticized on the grounds that it may have led to underrepresentation of high IQ children who, for various reasons, failed to attract a teacher's attention or who were members of less-favored socioeconomic or racial groups (Hughes and Converse, 1962). While not minimizing the importance of Terman's contribution, these criticisms do underscore the desirability of other longitudinal studies utilizing better sampling procedures.

Terman's gifted children, as a group, proved to be fortunate in many ways. They tended to come from homes of above average occupational and educational status. Nearly one-half had learned to read before starting school. On standardized achievement tests given in school, the average educational age of the gifted children was 44 percent above their chronological age, and there was evidence that more than half "had already mastered the scholastic curriculum to a point two full grades beyond the one in which they were enrolled, and some of them as much as four grades beyond" (Terman and Oden, 1947, p. 28). The incidence of physical defects and abnormal conditions of every kind was below that usually reported by school doctors. These children displayed a wide range of social and play interests, and on a series of character tests administered between 10 and 14 years of age they scored well above control groups. This overall picture of the characteristics of high IQ children, as a group, has been repeatedly confirmed in later studies (see Durr, 1960). Clearly the once prevalent belief that the highly intelligent child must be a physical or social freak can be laid to rest.

In adulthood the gifted individuals remained highly superior on standardized intelligence tests, despite a slight regression toward the mean (Terman and Oden, 1947). The percentage that entered and finished college was eight times that of the general California population. Adult occupational level and earned income were far higher than in the general population, and mortality rate, incidence of mental illness, and divorce rate were slightly lower (Terman and Oden, 1947, 1959).

Several psychologists have been particularly interested in those extremely rare children with IQs over 170.[4] Terman and Oden (1947) reported on 81 such cases from Terman's gifted sample. In childhood they showed greater scholastic acceleration than their less-gifted peers, but the quality of their academic achievement through the high school years was not markedly superior. In college a greater percentage of the highly gifted earned the top grades and honors, but about 25 percent had college records that were only fair, or even poor. Men of the highly gifted group surpassed the total group in adult occupational status, but women did not. As Terman and Oden put it, "Regardless of intellectual level, women as a rule accept whatever employment is at hand to bridge the gap between school and marriage" (Terman and Oden, 1947, p. 291).

Hollingworth (1942) studied 12 children in the New York City area with IQs over 180 and found that most of them had early school problems, either because their superiority was resented or because they were bored with ordinary

---

[4] According to Terman and Oden (1947, p. 282), "It is doubtful whether more than 3 children in 10,000 of the general population would score this high."

curricula. Those who were very accelerated in grade placement in school had problems stemming from differences in the size and strength of their classmates. She felt that because of the disparity between physical immaturity and intellectual superiority, many children with IQs above 160 find themselves socially isolated, and she maintained that the optimal IQ range for personality development was between 125 and 155. This picture of relative social isolation of the very high IQ person, at least in childhood, has received some confirmation in later studies. Gallagher (1958) found that a sample of elementary school children with IQs over 165 had greater difficulty achieving social acceptance than those in the 150 to 164 bracket, and Sheldon (1959) reported that out of 28 children under 12 years of age with IQs over 170, 15 felt themselves to be isolated and 21 nearly always played alone. This was true even though a variety of observations, interviews, and sociometric studies revealed that 3 of them were popular with their peers, 19 were accepted, and only 6 were rejected.

Although the majority of high IQ children do very well academically and, later on, vocationally, there is a substantial number who do not. This group, the underachievers, has been the object of several hundred investigations, the great majority conducted after 1955. Relatively few of the studies have dealt with elementary school children, since underachievement most typically does not become clearly apparent until the junior high school level.

The many reports on the characteristics and backgrounds of underachieving children are not all in agreement. However, the extensive review of the literature by Raph, Goldberg, and Passow (1966) reveals that the weight of the evidence favors the following description. The underachieving child is more apt to be a boy than a girl, to have poor work habits and study skills, and to come from a home of relatively low socioeconomic or educational level. His home is also apt to be characterized by a generally poor emotional climate. Personally, he is apt "to be somewhat impulsive, to lack independence and initiative with respect to school work, to have more negative attitudes toward himself and others and to resist assuming responsibility for his own behavior" (Raph et al., 1966, p. 29).

Efforts have been made to improve the academic performance of underachievers through counseling, homogeneous groupings, special teaching, family casework, etc. Results have been mixed, but predominantly negative. Their review of these studies led Raph et al. to state, "For many of the students, underachievement seems to have become a deeply rooted way of life, unamenable to change through school efforts. . . . Early identification of the potential underachiever, in terms of cognitive as well as sociopersonal factors, might enable schools to engage in preventative rather than curative programs for these gifted students" (Raph et al., 1966, p. 179).

In recent years, the study of the gifted has assumed new dimensions. Several influential writers have argued for expanding the definition of giftedness to include not only those with high IQ, but also those who earn high scores on various creativity tests (Getzels and Jackson, 1962; Guilford, 1962; Torrance, 1962). It is held that in terms of its potential value for society, creativity is at least as important an asset as intelligence, but that many, perhaps as many as 70 percent, of the most highly creative children are not identified through traditional intelligence tests.

Numerous creativity tests have been devised. They vary widely, but most involve tasks that seem to fit Guilford's (1959) description of divergent thinking—requiring subjects to produce new or varied solutions to problems. In this they contrast with traditional intelligence tests, which emphasize convergent thinking—requiring subjects to reproduce from memory a single correct solution. One creativity test requires subjects to give as many uses as possible for common objects such as bricks (Guilford, 1959); another requires the composition of a moralistic, a humorous, and a sad ending to each of four fables (Getzels and Jackson, 1962); still another calls for the creation of a picture from standardized shapes of colored paper (Torrance, 1962). Thorndike has sounded a cautionary note with reference to these and similar creativity tests. He maintained that the correlations among them are typically very low, lower than among traditional intelligence tests, and that "We should be most circumspect in using such a global value laden term as 'creative'" (Thorndike, 1963, p. 424).

A recent collection of papers edited by Gowan, Demos, and Torrance (1967) and an earlier review paper by Golann (1963) reveal the multidimensionality of this burgeoning field. Various investigators are exploring the nature of creative processes and products while others are concentrating on the characteristics and problems of creative children. Still others are working on techniques through which parents, teachers, and guidance counselors can most effectively deal with these children.

A great many studies have explored the relationship among intelligence, creativity, and scholastic achievement. The consensus is that the correlation between traditional IQs and creativity is nonlinear, being higher for subjects with IQs below 120 than for those above that point. Yamamoto (1964c) maintained that the correlation is almost zero in selected (high IQ) populations and that it ranges between .20 and .40 in unselected populations. Ripple and May (1962), however, working with a very wide range, reported correlations with various creativity tests ranging between .11 and .73. Torrance (1967), whose summary of many studies revealed a median correlation of .20, pointed out that the nature of both kinds of measures, the sex and age of the subjects, the range of IQ, and motivational factors all contribute to the reported correlations. Clearly, however, there are many high IQ children who do not score high on creativity, and vice versa. As McNemar put it, "Having a high IQ is not a guarantee of being creative; having a low IQ means creativity is impossible" (McNemar, 1964, p. 879).

Over the whole IQ range, intelligence is a far better predictor of academic success than is creativity (Yamamoto and Chimbidis, 1966). However, for children with IQs over 120 there is considerable evidence that highly creative children do as well as their less creative but more intelligent peers (Getzels and Jackson, 1962; Torrance, 1962; Yamamoto, 1964a, 1964b, 1964c, 1965). This phenomenon, known as the Getzels-Jackson effect, has not, however, always been confirmed (e.g., Edwards and Tyler, 1965; Flescher, 1963).

Although many highly creative children do well in school, teachers seem to prefer those who are gifted only in terms of high IQ (Getzels and Jackson, 1962; Torrance, 1963). It is easy to see that the creative child would constitute quite a challenge to the average teacher, in view of Guilford's description of such a child as one who is

. . . less bound by what we agree to as reality; he is ready to reinterpret it and to change it to suit his purposes. . . . He does things that appear odd in the context of the behavior of other children. He takes liberties with what he observes and knows. He has a playful attitude toward his experiences. His thinking goes off in unusual directions. He is sometimes referred to as a rebel. . . . (Guilford, 1962, p. 90.)

The accumulating material on the creatively gifted child makes provocative reading. Its ultimate significance, however, rests on the yet to be determined relations between childhood creativity and valued adult behavior.

SUMMARY

Chapters 15 and 16 have covered a variety of behaviors that members of American culture designate intelligent. The viewpoint stressed is that these behaviors develop as a result of the continuous interaction of the biological organism with its environment. Level of performance changes as life conditions change, but there is a growing belief that the very earliest life experiences are particularly important determinants of later performance.

Most of the data reviewed pertained to the abstract, predominantly verbal skills sampled by traditional intelligence tests. These skills, which in American culture predict academic and vocational achievement, tend to develop best in the living conditions experienced by middle and upper class white citizens.

There are several major current trends. These include efforts to define intelligence in terms of problem solving behaviors that are likely to develop in all, not just some, groups in a society, attempts to define giftedness in terms of a wide variety of creative behaviors, and increased emphasis on the subtle interactions of motivational and intellectual behaviors.

CHAPTER 17

Socialization

INTRODUCTION

Socialization is a descriptive, value ridden, culturally and developmentally relativistic lay term that ill meets the requirements for rigorous definition demanded by science. To use the colloquial, however, "we are stuck with it," and an attempt to define it for purposes of the present chapter must be made. Of necessity, the present chapter is more speculative and less data-bound than some other chapters in this volume.

In the descriptive sense, socialization is a class name for all the behaviors of the child that concern other people, directly or indirectly. If a child is delinquent, a fault in socialization is said to be present. If he is withdrawn or unpopular, he is considered to be inadequately socialized. If a little boy plays exclusively with little girls, one worries about his socialization. The list of behaviors and attributes included under socialization is as extensive as the possible range of social relations and characteristics that go into the product.

The term is also clearly value tinged. Too much competitiveness is judged to be "bad," while too little is contrary to the American way of life. Under the heading of personality adjustment (and socialization and personality cannot be considered separately), it is considered desirable for a child to be comfortable with himself and reasonably self-accepting. But under the heading of character, the judgment as to "good or bad character" is almost entirely made in social value terms. A self-accepting gang member who steals with his group is not considered (by "outsiders") to be of good character.

Almost no one, scientist or layman, uses the terms *personality* and *character* without explicit or implicit value judgments couched in such terms as *good, bad, ineffective, effective, authoritarian,* and so on; therefore, since it is assumed that personality and character are partial products of socialization, it is impossible to discuss socialization entirely outside a value framework. This chapter, then, is not only more theoretical and speculative than others, but is unavoidably developed according to a value system. Such value systems are undoubtedly unique to individual writers, although an attempt has been made here to anchor to "national" or United States or Western or industrialized cultural values. As will be seen, this has not been a simple task.

A scientist does not need to apologize for holding values, and a study of values is a legitimate scientific enterprise. A scientist must be extremely careful, however, at points where his values may influence the way in which he gathers, analyzes, interprets, and generalizes from his data.

That cultural and developmental relativism operate importantly in evaluating socialization is clear: The get-up-and-go considered desirable in a United States 10 year old female would be considered, at the very best, as being in bad taste for a well-reared girl in a conventional middle class Japanese family. The openness of heterosexual behavior permitted in Margaret Mead's (1928) Samoa would, if detected, put a United States boy or girl in Juvenile Court. The curious, questioning, spontaneously vocal third grader in a progressive demonstration school will be considered intolerably aggressive and out of line in a conventional, authoritarian school system. The angry physical encounters considered normal in a group of two year olds will be severely put down among fifth grade children. The vigorous verbal sexiness of a lower class elementary school boy constitutes disturbed behavior if shown by a middle class girl.

In sum, no absolute definition, but only a relativistic definition of socialization can be provided. To evaluate any child's socialization on a good–bad or effective–ineffective dimension, one must consider at the very minimum the following variables:

(a) The generally accepted ways of behaving within the child's *effective* culture (i.e., his school, community and, in a loose sense, his national residence).

(b) Sex.

(c) Chronological, mental, and physical age.

(d) Social class.

In the United States, for example, social class is commonly divided into *upper class*—the aristocrats of a community or nation; *middle class*—respectable, solid citizens who range from upper middle class families headed by men in such occupations as medicine, education, and industrial management through lower middle class, such as small tradesmen and white collar clerks; and *lower class*. Upper lower social class is commonly considered to consist of skilled workers and their families, while lower lower social class is made up of unskilled workers, usually very poorly educated and at or near the poverty line in family income. The sharpest "socialization cleavage" exists between lower lower class families (at least one-fourth of the nation's families) and all the other social classes, which hold more common than different values.

Some consider that a fifth dimension, race, is an important element in socialization. They may be correct, but until more evidence is forthcoming, race differences in the United States may be presumed to result chiefly from forces such as socioeconomic and educational status. Hence, for present purposes, racial variables are included under the social class heading.

An important social action point should be made in this connection, however. It is important, if a child's socialization is to proceed benignly, that he develop at least a moderately positive self-concept (i.e., that he esteem himself realistically, that he be able to accept himself within the normal limits of "wishing to be better," and that he be moderately optimistic). To the degree that society militates against such self-concept development for any group of children, the characteristics of that group, be it racial, religious, or other, must be considered as a basic variable in its members' socialization. If a child considers that "To be black is to be bad," then countermeasures must be taken if his socialization is to proceed normally. The United States is currently in agonizing throes as its white majority begins to realize the often insuperable hurdles it has set up to block the constructive socialization of the 11 percent or more of the nation's population that classifies as black. Such built-in hurdles exist for other minority groups, among them the *Hispaños* (most notably Puerto Ricans and Mexican-Americans), American Indians, and the Appalachian co-culture.[1] Other minority groups have their troubles on the mainland United States, but with the leverage of education, succeed as well as or better than the so-called core culture majority. Chinese- and Japanese-Americans seem, on the whole, to manage about as well as anyone else. Jews (a religious grouping that carries with it ethnic connotations), when judged in statistical socioeconomic terms, probably fare better than the average core culture. Members of distinctly "different" religious groups, such as Catholics, Mormons, Unitarians, Quakers, Seventh Day Adventists (and many others) may, under special circumstances, face problems in their social interactions with the core culture. But most members of such groups believe that their social cohesiveness provides advantages that more than compensate for the disadvantages.

Ideally, then, racial differences in socialization in the United States *should* be most parsimoniously treated only as they interact with social class, which they do to a very large extent. *Practically*, it is necessary to consider race and often religion as important socialization modifiers.

Definition

What, then, is adequate socialization? The well-socialized child is one who, in his current life within his effective culture, is above average in the major areas of social behavior according to that culture. His behavior will typically include (if he is old enough) having at least some good friends, occasionally assuming a role of leadership, being able to follow when the occasion is appropriate, adjusting to school at an appropriate age, being within the masculine or feminine range of behavior acceptable for his biological sex (by three to five years of age, earlier in the United States for boys than for girls), and living without undue discomfort within his family. His contribution in a social situation should be at least moderately positive, not neutral or negative.

This definition raises at least two questions. The first and most important concerns social adjustment within the lowest socioeconomic class, as defined in the preceding section in the list of variables against which social adjustment must be judged. As a group, lower lower social class children have been commonly found to be more physically aggressive, more openly sexual in their be-

---

[1] The term *co-culture* is used rather than the more commonly employed *subculture* because subculture vaguely implies condescension, while co-culture carries with it a (perhaps entirely subjective) connotation that different groups on the American scene are of equal worth, and that each has things it can profitably learn from the others.

havior, less planful and more impulsive in action, and relatively unambitious in achieving for achievement's sake when compared with middle class children (McKee and Leader, 1955; Silberman, 1964; Tulkin, 1968). This last characteristic is essential for success in school, among other things. However, many consider that lower class people, and particularly their children, find more fun in life, experience their sensations more fully, are freer in their use of their bodies, and enter more spontaneously, more genuinely, and with more emotion into their interpersonal relations.

These differences in socialization characteristics to some degree parallel the philosophical streams of Apollonian and Judeo-Christian thought, which characterize the middle class, and Dionysian and Hellenic thought and behavior, which characterize the lower lower class. There are real socialization virtues in either type of adjustment. It may be that in American society, the two traditions cannot be reconciled. At present, as embodied in the official sanctions of society and the goals of the average school, middle class values for socialization are considered correct, lower class values suspect. Herein lies one of the most important questions for those who assist in socializing children. There is no ready answer to it, although evidence begins to suggest that under certain conditions the "civilized virtues" of the middle class can coexist with the freedom and spontaneity that characterize many lower lower class children (lower lower class adults have usually lost these qualities as a result of the multiple frustrations they meet in a society the rules of which are set by the middle class).

The second question raised by the definition of adequate socialization is allied with the first: What of the well-adjusted but delinquent child, adolescent, or adult? Such individuals may be self-accepting, may be above average in their adjustment to their effective culture, may have good friends, exert leadership and, within the rules of their society, follow constructively. They may be appropriately masculine or feminine, and live moderately easily with their families. They may even do relatively well in school, although family and school adjustment are usually unsatisfactory.

The question about such children is easier to answer than is the one about the different socialization value systems of the middle and lower social classes. The assumption, which has been found tenable in practice although the research evidence is not tight, is that such children, if and when shifted from their allegiance to their delinquent effective society, are good candidates for healthy *non*delinquent socialization. In an orderly society, there can be little argument that allegiance to a delinquent subsociety must whenever possible be broken down or that, as has been done successfully in a few cases in the past few years, the goals of the delinquent society—the gang—must be shifted in a direction that is acceptable to a society of established law. Shore, Massimo, and Ricks (1965) demonstrated that this can be done, although they worked with only 20 boys (15 to 17 years old). Their findings relate to the Cloward and Ohlin (1960) hypothesis of legitimate and illegitimate community opportunities, and to Tallman's (1966) experimental test of it: Delinquency (in Tallman's study, cheating) occurs only where there are very few or no opportunities for a person to "go straight."

A general, rather abstract, and not altogether satisfactory definition of socialization has been given in the preceding paragraphs. But how does one put this definition to work? How can one say in some functional way that a child is or is not satisfactorily socialized?

For children from perhaps three and definitely four years of age on, sociometric techniques supply a rough working definition of conventionally acceptable socialization. Thompson (1960) has provided excellent coverage of sociometric techniques and their associated research literature. A method for measuring friendship status (a sociometric) of preschool-aged children is described by McCandless and Marshall (1957).

Sociometric Techniques

When a child is a member of a clearly defined group—a given third grade, for example—the following sociometric information provides a useful working picture of his adjustment.

Each child in the group is asked to nominate his three (or five) best friends. The investigator usually asks boys to choose only from the boys in the group, and girls only from the girls, because elementary school children typically choose friends and to some degree "enemies" almost solely within their own sex group. However, the use of this technique overlooks the occasional child (who clearly has socialization problems in American culture) who is chosen by and chooses friends only from the opposite sex. Unless a school administration objects (and it sometimes does), each child is also asked to choose the three (or five) children whom he likes least in the class.

These two measures, taken together, give a clear, reliable, and stable picture of a child's popularity in the group. Almost all children who are chosen by at least one or two others in the group are adequately socialized *according to the standards of that group*. Interestingly enough, the standards of the group are typically standards that are quite acceptable to the group leader (the teacher) and the community, except when one is working within a delinquent culture. Isolates (children chosen by no one), rejects (children rejected by a great majority), and sometimes extreme leaders or "popularity stars" are usually found on further investigation to have problems in socialization in addition to their dubious status in the group. No clear cause and effect relation can be demonstrated; their dubious status in the group may be caused by their socialization (and personality) problems, or the problems may result from their status in the group, or both.

Popularity and leadership (or status) are highly correlated [$r = .74$ to $.82$ (Harvey and Rutherford, 1960)], but are not always equally related to other variables. For example, popularity is not related to influencibility; but status is, in that low status children are more influencible than high status children (Harvey and Rutherford, 1960).

Some leaders are suspect, because it is sometimes found that a child will sacrifice almost everything else for popularity and/or a leadership role. This, too, is a fault in socialization. However, experience suggests that this condition is an exception rather than a rule, at least during childhood. Leadership and popularity striving may become pathological in high schools and colleges, where the BMOC (Big Man On Campus) syndrome strikes a sophisticated observer as being sick.

A simple measure of popularity, however, does not satisfy the definition of socialization given above. An additional sociometric measure, designed to tap children's preferences for workmates in constructive, on-going activities, provides a useful and necessary supplement to the popularity sociometric: With whom would you rather work together on your homework? With whom would you rather plan the class party? These are work preference (or rejection, when phrased in the negative) sociometric questions. A child who is both well liked and also desired as a companion in the on-going business of childhood—school—is likely to be well socialized across the board. A child who is not chosen in either role is almost bound to have socialization problems.

Finally, it is often necessary to obtain working or research definitions of socialization in specific areas. For example, in all industrialized societies, adequate sex role socialization is highly valued (appropriate masculinity or femininity, in keeping with the child's chronological age). In the *Buddy Rating* or *Guess Who* technique, children may be asked who fits the cultural stereotypes of "all boy" or "all girl," for example, "Tell me who is always in the middle of the tough games?" (male) or "Who is almost always neat and clean?" (female). Extremely aggressive, or shy, or furtive children may also be picked out using such techniques, usually much more accurately than can be done by even the most socially sensitive teacher (although good teachers agree moderately well with classmate choices).

These techniques must be used with full regard for children's right of privacy, however, and should be administered and used only according to the most scrupulous professional ethics. The investigator should obtain parents' permission in addition to school administration permission and must excuse all children who do not wish to participate. (When confidentiality is guaranteed and maintained, and the children are told the potential usefulness of the techniques, they rarely decline to take part in such evaluations.)

The social and work relationship lines within a group of up to 40 or 50 children are firmly laid down within a few weeks after the formation of the group, although, of course, children entirely new to the group are penalized. Additionally, certain children who from a long range point of view may prove to be constructively socialized emerge as isolates or even rejects—the extremely creative child, for example, or the child who is much brighter than anyone else in his group, or the child who holds loyally to parental standards that differ sharply from those of the group, as is true for children from, for example, minority religions and families that have immigrated but hold to the ways of their mother country.

But for practical work, including research with groups of children, the sociometric techniques are invaluable in assessing socialization. It should be restressed that they provide only a rough working measure and that, in any sort of class or individual manipulation, close attention must be paid to the individual case.

SOCIALIZATION AND INTRAINDIVIDUAL CHARACTERISTICS

While socialization seems principally to be the result of learning, relatively unchangeable characteristics of a given child make socialization easier or more difficult for him.

Intelligence

Consensus from the data about intellectual development is that intelligence is a combined function of genetic, congenital, and environmental or learning opportunity factors. Since the two former cannot be controlled in a free society, the attention of action-oriented psychologists and educators is currently directed intensively toward the role of environment and learning. Data suggest that severely disadvantaged learning environments may depress a child's IQ into the retardation range, while optimal learning environments may raise it to the "very bright" level (the literature on the subject is reviewed in detail in Chapter 16).

In any event and whatever the determinants, once a stable level of intellectual functioning is reached (including the child's predictable and cooperative participation in its measurement), the IQ for groups remains remarkably stable and plays a major but as yet not well documented role in socialization. Evidence abounds that socialization problems accompany low intelligence if for no other reason than that society is so complex that considerable intelligence is required to cope with even the everyday problems of social living. The evidence is less clear about the socialization advantages or disadvantages of an IQ that is conspicuously higher than those of the other children in a child's social reference group. In such cases, high intelligence may "put the child on a different plane" and make it difficult for him to function as an integral member of his peer group.

However, within these limits, intelligence is moderately and positively correlated with adequate socialization.

Body Build

Effects of body build on socialization are fairly well documented. Staffieri (1967) and Hassan (1967) found that mesomorphic and ectomorphic boys and girls are better accepted at age levels from four years on than endomorphic boys and girls.[2] Mesomorphs are more realistic about their own body builds and thus, by extrapolation, perhaps about themselves than ectomorphs or endo-

---

[2] These are terms made well known in the literature by Sheldon (1940), and more clearly defined in terms of measurement by Parnell (1958). The ectomorph is the lean, "string bean" child; the mesomorph the brawny, muscular child; the endomorph the barrel-bodied, often fat child.

morphs; and the mesomorphic body build is consistently preferred to either the ectomorphic or the endomorphic. While there is little difference in the social acceptance given to the ectomorph and the mesomorph, the traits ascribed to them are very different. Mesomorphs are given almost all possible desirable social traits—they are rated as leaders, withstand pain easily, are good sports, and so on. But ectomorphs are given attributes of tenderness, vulnerability, and self-indrawnness. They seem to be thought of as harmless, even likable and socially constructive, self-punishing neurotics like those so common in society. An expectation of delinquency, poor sportsmanship, and general poor socialization is given to endomorphs, quite in contradiction to the stereotype of the "jolly fat boy—or girl."

There is little reason to agree with Sheldon (1942) that temperament automatically varies according to body build; but body build may *mediate* temperament, because there is a tendency for each of us to behave as he is expected to behave. If mesomorphs are expected always to be leaders and good sports, perhaps they inevitably learn the role. If ectomorphs are seen as brittle and vulnerable, perhaps they learn to fracture easily and to suffer deeply.

Time of Sexual Maturation

There may be other accompaniments of body build. Mesomorphs reach sexual maturity earlier than children with other body builds (Tanner, 1962). At least for boys, there are for a number of years following sexual maturation (puberty) many social advantages associated with early maturity, accompanied by an equal number of indexes of good social-personal adjustment (Jones, 1957, 1965; Jones and Bayley, 1950; Mussen and Jones, 1957, 1958). Early maturing boys, tending as they do to possess the mesomorphic characteristics so admired in United States society, are taller and stronger during adolescence than their later maturing counterparts. This gives them an advantage in the esteemed area of sports, and helps them to assume positions of leadership and to become popular. Adults view them favorably and open doors for them that lead to autonomy and exercise of responsibility. They do not suffer during a long growth period when they are shorter than the average girl of the same age.

A casual visit to sixth through tenth grade classes in any school shows that many boys are shorter than girls of the same age. Since some courtship pairing off and dating usually occur at least by the ninth grade, the short (usually late maturing) boy and the tall, early maturing girl may be placed in a socially embarrassing situation if they date. Often, instead of continuing to mix in groups that become increasingly heterosexual in their interests, they withdraw socially. Early maturity makes it easier for boys to gain competence and confidence in the heterosexual, courtship area earlier and more easily than later maturing boys. Early maturing boys also find earlier sexual outlet than late maturing boys, and have more frequent outlets. The effects of this early and enduring superiority in the primal male function may be mixed; in middle class America, pressure for regular sexual outlet other than within the framework of marriage may lead to social, personal, and legal complications, and may add to one's level of frustration, but sexual prowess is valued as an important aspect of masculinity, and masculinity ranks high in the socialization hierarchy. Thus, it may be conjectured that, while not unmixed in its effects, the overall result of early, frequent, and prolonged demonstration of sexual prowess should contribute to the American male's feeling of self-worth.

A cautionary note should be added about the studies that lead to these conclusions (as well as the conclusions about girls that are summarized below). The results come from a small sample heavily weighted with middle class people. Consequently, generalization across social class lines cannot be made. It is conceivable, for example, that a mesomorphic body build and early maturity are advantages for a middle class boy, but disadvantages for a lower class boy. The former comes from an environment rich in positive opportunities for developing socially approved competence. His family is solid, his schools usually adequate, his intelligence normal to superior. His strong, active physique is simply another tool he can use to master an environment that, like a tree full of ripening apples, is ready to be plucked. A lower lower class boy from the urban ghetto or isolated rural area may find few or no legitimate opportunities in his environment which may, however, abound with illegitimate opportunities (see, e.g., Cloward and Ohlin, 1960). In this environment, his physique may also help him master this environment, but in ways that are antisocial. Hence, depending on his environmental opportunities, the body build that is an asset to a boy from an advantaged social class may destroy the boy from another. The same argument can be applied to girls although, as will be seen below, the evidence for the interaction of body build, time of physical maturation, and socialization is unclear for girls.

As Mary Cover Jones (1965) followed her samples of early and late maturing boys into early middle age, many of the advantages that had characterized the early maturers well into their thirties had begun to disappear, and in some respects this group had begun to show less adequate socialization than late maturers. Perhaps the early maturing boys, for whom almost everything had come relatively easily, had not learned to use their inner resources. As middle age proceeds, with the primacy of the body beginning to wane and sexual prowess losing its glamor, the individual without inner resources faces social difficulty. A tendency toward outerdirectedness, already evident in Jones's early maturing boys in their early teens, may be no great virtue in the middle and later years when one is expected more and more to live by his own personal resources.

The effects of early sexual maturity in girls are not clearly directional (H. E. Jones, 1949; M. C. Jones and Mussen, 1958). Neither definite advantages nor disadvantages have been demonstrated for groups of girls, although individuals who differ markedly from the average are likely, at least for a time, to suffer some difficulties in their adjustment. This finding illustrates a point that occurs periodically in the literature, although it is not frequently clearly stated. Girls' socialization seems to be determined more by the environmental forces within which they live, while boys' socialization seems to be more subject to their own characteristics. Girls' futures seem to be at least as much and perhaps more influenced, for example, by the man they marry than by their own personal qualities (Bijou, Ainsworth, and Stockey, 1943). Girls incorporate their past into their self-concepts in terms more of what their current living situation is and less according to the documented facts of the past than boys (Rosenthal, 1963). Girls seek a role that is suitable for them as women, stressing interpersonal relations, while boys seek autonomy and seem to devote much of their socialization effort to becoming their own man (Douvan and Adelson, 1966). Girls with high autonomy needs who strive to master their objective environment in an active way (as illustrated, e.g., by increases in IQ) are less well adjusted than girls who take the world as it comes, while the opposite is true for boys (Haan, 1963).

Activity Level

Activity level is an important human variable, easily demonstrable from birth, but has been little studied even though it obviously has great importance in socialization. It may be related to body build, as discussed above, mesomorphic children being more active than ectomorphs and endomorphs. Given a benign environment (i.e., one where there is opportunity to move around widely without meeting frustration and rejection), a high activity and energy level would seem to be an asset in socialization. The active, energetic youngster will make contact with a wider spectrum of his environment, will meet more people, will do more things. If he is generally competent, this greatly expands his range of environmental mastery, increases his sense of self-sufficiency, enriches his techniques of socializing, perhaps increases his intellectual power and, on the whole, benefits him enormously. The opposite, of course, may occur if he lives in a malign environment in which the more he explores, the more he meets frustration, rejection, and defeat.

Cuddling

Infants differ greatly in their propensity for bodily contact with others. Some are cuddlers, some are not. Girls, clinical observation suggests, may be more cuddly than boys. Other things being equal, the cuddly infant can expect a better "social reception" than the infant who resists cuddling. He is more appealing to his mother, handling him is simpler and thus, it would be predicted, he will be handled more, thus have more opportunity to acquire the early reward systems that underlie socialization. There is corroborative evidence for part of this sequence: Male infant monkeys initiate more negative contacts with their mothers than do female infants, and are embraced and handled by their mothers *less* frequently than are female infants (Mitchell, 1968).

This important dimension, probably congenital and perhaps genetic, has received little careful scrutiny by developmental psychologists, although Schaffer and Emerson (1964) have opened the field for study.

Sensory Modalities

From birth, individual differences in sensitivity to stimulation of all sorts are evident. The slightest stimulation causes vigorous response in some infants, little in others. The relations between sensitivity to stimulation and activity level are not known, but it is logical to believe that they are related. One baby will sleep through a violent thunder storm or a large noisy party; another will go into something resembling a panic state over the sound of crumpled paper.

If, as Hebb (1949) among others suggested, the human organism seeks stimulation—if curiosity and the desire for novelty are attributes of the human species (e.g., Berlyne, 1960)—then the child who is relatively insensitive to stimuli should actively seek out new stimuli; whereas the child who is hypersensitive may well withdraw to reduce stimulus input so as to avoid being overwhelmed. Socialization implications of such differential sensory sensitivity are obvious.

Cultural Impacts on Socialization

If, on the one hand, individual differences related to sex, congenital factors, and genetics affect the socialization process of any given child, then on the other hand common values and learning opportunities within a given culture should have some effect on all members of the culture, regardless of individual differences. As suggested in Chapter 1 of this book, cross-cultural studies suffer from imprecision and incompleteness of data, and few are rigorously comparable with each other. Within these limits, however, cross-cultural studies and cultural anthropological studies offer interesting suggestions about how the socialization process occurs.

Three studies have been arbitrarily selected to illustrate cultural impacts on socialization. The first concerns the development of sex differences in behavior (Barry, Bacon, and Child, 1957). The investigators used as their data cultural anthropologists' records for 110 different cultures, and concentrated on sex differences in five different personal characteristics: (a) *nurturance,* tending or desiring to look after and help others; (b) *responsibility,* assuming the burden of regular duties, being dependable; (c) *obedience,* conforming to the wishes of the elders; (d) *achievement,* valuing *doing* and *accomplishing* things; and (e) *self-reliance,* depending on oneself to get things done.

The incompleteness and unreliability of the data made it impossible to determine sex differences in child rearing for any of these characteristic ways of behaving for all 110 cultures, but data were found for numbers of cultures ranging from 31 in which measurement of *achievement* could be satisfactorily made to 84 in which *responsibility* could be determined.

Girls more than boys were trained to be *nurturant* and *responsible* in a majority of the cultures where measurement was possible; *achievement* and *self-reliance* were stressed more for boys than girls in a majority of the cultures. *Obedience* training could be estimated for 69 cultures, of which a majority did not put differential emphasis in the child training of boys and girls. However, 35 percent of the cultures stressed obedience more for girls, only 3 percent stressed it more for boys.

Evidence from United States culture suggests that it stresses training in sex differences strongly, and along the lines depicted by Barry, Bacon, and Child. Girls are encouraged to be nurturant, responsible, and obedient; boys achievement oriented and self-reliant. Douvan and Adelson (1966) portrayed these differences vividly in their study of a cross section of American children in their early and middle teens.

In the second study selected for this section, Berry (1967) employed direct measurement with carefully specified samples of Baffin Island Eskimos and the Temne people of Sierra Leone. He was interested in conformity, which he judged by the Asch (1956) technique—assessing how much an individual will change his estimate of the length of a line in the direction of what has been falsely reported to him as the consensual judgment of his fellows. From previous anthropological data, Berry made a plausible case for the Eskimo's great stress on independence, venturesomeness, self-reliance, competence, and individualism. The Temne, in contrast, annually harvest only a single crop of rice, which must be meted out in daily units until the next harvest; lack of conformity to the rules of the culture is strongly punished. Both cultures, however, are subsistence cultures.

Berry's prediction of much more conformity for the Temne than for the Eskimo was borne out by his results. On the average, the traditional Temne changed his estimate more than 9 units in the direction of the false group consensus, while the traditional Eskimo changed his estimate only 2.8 units. Comparison groups of relatively industrialized (or "Westernized") Eskimo and Temne showed similar results which, Berry suggested, indicates the staying power of cultural norms even when the old ways of life are changing. Berry also tested a comparison group of rural and urban Scots and found them to be more individualistic than the Temne, but more conforming than the Eskimo. They were closer to the latter than to the former. This fits well with the stereotype of the rugged Scot.

In the third study illustrating cultural impact on socialization, Berkowitz and Friedman (1967) experimented with the important social variable of helping behavior. As subjects, they used 345 13- to 16-year-old midwestern white boys. They determined the type of employment the boys' fathers had, and divided the boys into two groups, *entrepreneurial* and *bureaucratic*. Boys' fathers were called entrepreneurs if they owned businesses (excluding self-employed laborers) or were sales people or professionals working either for themselves or in partnership. Bureaucratic fathers worked for someone else, typically in a multilevel organization. For Berkowitz and Friedman's sample, the bureaucratic fathers averaged somewhat higher occupational prestige than the entrepreneurial fathers. This fact must be considered in interpreting the findings.

The investigators employed an elaborate but careful and ingenious experimental design. The boys were seen singly, told that this was a study of their supervisory ability, that they would have to supervise their "employee" (who was actually not present) by writing notes, and that a special reward went to those who were particularly effective supervisors. The mythical pairings were between boys of different social classes and father's employment patterns. In some cases, the hypothetical partner "helped," in others he hindered the "supervisor" in receiving a rating of "excellent." Retesting involved each boy's later "helping" an equally mythical supervisor.

Briefly, the boys from the entrepreneurial more than the bureaucratic group gave help to their work partners to the degree to which they themselves received previous help; the bureaucratic boys seemed to be more responsive to social responsibility ideals, allowing their attitudes toward their working partner-supervisor to affect their helping behavior less than the entrepreneurial boys did. Middle class boys from both groups were prejudiced against working class boys, but the bureaucratic boys "did their duty anyway," while the entrepreneurial boys tended to slack off when they were helping working class boys.

THEORIES OF SOCIALIZATION

Stage Theory of Socialization

Chapter 1 of this volume has introduced the reader to stage theories. Such theories have the virtue of convenience and neatness, but they are usually descriptive rather than explanatory. Their very neatness and appearance of permanence often retard scientific inquiry, particularly into the phenomenon of change—the very important emerging behavior that moves an individual from one type or stage of development to another. In a sense, a stage theory is not a developmental theory, which demands an assumption of continuity.

Stages are useful in description, however, and since much of our knowledge of socialization is still at the descriptive level, it is appropriate to discuss at least one stage theory in some detail. The one chosen is neopsychoanalytic theory; its foundations were suggested by Freudian, psychoanalytic psychology, but it has been extensively modified by social learning theory and twentieth century research, therapy, and observation of children, adolescents, and adults from more than one social class. This is in contrast to the usual psychoanalytic data, which are typically drawn from a middle (usually upper) class population. Erikson (1963) believed that the socialization process is made up of eight stages, each of which he considered to be a psychosocial crisis that must be resolved before the individual can move constructively and effectively on to the next stage. Erikson, as has been implied, anchored his theory much less than Freud on the organs of the human body, and talked little of instincts. His major variables are social forces as they operate on the human organism at different stages of biological and physical maturity.

Each of Erikson's stages is described as bipolar. Extremely good socialization is presumed to characterize one end of the population distribution, and bad socialization the other end. However, the distribution for each stage is presumably normal, and very few individuals will fall at either end of the graphed population. Progressively more will be located as one moves from either end toward the maximum concentration in the middle. This is the familiar normal or bell-shaped curve into which so many human characteristics group themselves whenever a large population is examined.

Erikson's eight stages of man are as follows:

(1) *Trust versus mistrust.* This basic tendency toward optimism or pessimism is thought by Erikson to develop in the first year or two of life. Thus, from a learning point of view, it may be thought of as belonging to the classical conditioning family of learning concepts (see next section).

(2) *Autonomy versus shame.* This stage occurs between $1\frac{1}{2}$ or 2 and $3\frac{1}{2}$ or 4 years of age. It corresponds generally to Freud's anal stages of psychosexual development. During it, in American culture, a major emphasis in child training is to establish bowel and bladder control. Erikson believed that gentle handling of this process results in the child's learning self-sufficiency and pride in himself, while unwise handling produces a child who is ashamed or afraid of the way society regards him. Parenthetically, *autonomy* in a two year old often resembles wilfulness, but is probably a necessary rehearsal stage for later independence and self-sufficiency.

(3) *Initiative versus guilt.* This is the play age; the child learns to interact with his environment with reasonable confidence of being able to cope with it, or he is immobilized and withdraws. The period is thought to extend from about $3\frac{1}{2}$ years of age until the time a child enters formal school.

(4) *Industry versus inferiority.* This stage characterizes the school child up to adolescence. Well-socialized children realistically and energetically tackle the job of learning the skills necessary to live in their society. Ill-socialized children may, for example, retreat into underachievement in school or show other manifestations of self-perceptions of inferiority.

The remaining stages concern adolescents and adults, and are therefore beyond the purview of this book. They are included here only to complete the list.

(5) *Identity versus identity diffusion.* This is the adolescent stage.

(6) *Intimacy versus isolation.* This stage characterizes young adulthood.

(7) *Generativity versus self-absorption.* This is the stage of maturity.

(8) *Integrity versus despair.* This stage occurs in later middle and old age.

As one reads through Erikson's stages, it is evident that with each successive psychosocial crisis, primary rewards and classical conditioning play less and less a role in shaping behavior, while secondary rewards (relations with people) and instrumental learning play a more and more important role. A possible exception to this is the fifth stage, *identity versus identity diffusion,* during which the individual's mature adjustment to his sexuality, including provision for its outlet, must usually be made. Here, the old classical conditioning family of responses often interferes or, more rarely in American society (where sex is an uneasy topic), facilitates. Much of the child's learning about his genitals and their function has occurred during toilet training, when modesty training is also accomplished. During this period, most children have had masturbation responses eliminated (or suppressed), and have picked up considerable anxiety about handling their genitals in any fashion more elaborate than that involved in urination. They have also frequently acquired distaste responses for the odors and secretory textures and products associated later with consummatory sex behavior. Rewarding sexual experiences usually overcome these earlier avoidance responses, fortunately. But guilt may continue to be indefinitely associated with sexual behavior, particularly if it is outside the realm of socially sanctioned actions, as in the case of masturbation (which few boys can avoid) or homosexual responses. The necessary linkage of affection and interpersonal intimacy with the biological aspects of sex is a very difficult one. Boys and young men in our culture tend, particularly at the beginning of their sexual careers, to concentrate on the biology of sex, cheating both themselves and their partners of the interpersonal affection and intimacy that should be a part of mature sexuality. Girls are more likely to want the affection and intimacy, but shy away from the biological aspects of sex. However, disturbances in mechanical sexuality such as frigidity, impotence, and premature ejaculation are common enough that they present a major socialization problem in the sexual-affectional area. Eroticism toward members of one's own sex is also an important socialization problem in most Western societies, being probably more frequent and more serious, in terms of its social consequences, among boys and men than girls and women.

This section on stages of socialization illustrates the difficulties of theory building in the area. Erikson had the beginnings of a theory. He predicted that if some unspecified set of experiences occurs, then a conflict described in rather general terms will be resolved, opening the way for the resolution of a conflict that, because of the structure of society and the necessities of the growing organism, will necessarily occur next. He also predicted that unless preceeding psychosocial stage crises are resolved, succeeding ones cannot be satisfactorily handled.

Before Erikson can be thought to have any sort of complete theory, his terms must be much more clearly specified, and the training or learning opportunity portions of his equations must be filled in in detail. It will be many years before this can be accomplished, and only the bare beginnings of data are now available for filling it in. The final theoretical schema is likely to be much different from Erikson's, although his theory is interesting and potentially constructive.

Socialization and the Theories of Learning

Social learning theories are founded on the two conceptualizations of conditioning discussed in detail earlier in this volume, particularly in Chapters 3 and 4. As pointed out at the beginning of the present chapter, *socialization* is not a good scientific term, and its dimensions are so broad that no elegant and precise socialization learning theory can be constructed. Learning principles must be applied to socialization by analogy. While analogies may contribute to science (e.g., by suggesting research strategies, as has already been done in the previous sections of this chapter), they are *not* science. However, as they are made public and become specific, and are interrelated systematically with each other, they may not only contribute to new knowledge but actually become science. Glibly advanced and taken as explanations, reasoning by analogy often hinders scientific progress (see Black, 1962, Ch. XIII; Ferré, 1963).

The foundation of socialization is discussed in this section by analogy with classical and instrumental or operant conditioning. The basic definitions of classical and operant conditioning are those advanced in Chapters 3 and 4 but, analogically, the terms as used in this chapter may be thought of as *process families*.

By the classical conditioning family is meant that class of socialization learning that happens *automatically* to the child, usually in infancy before he can apply appropriate verbal labels or classifications to his learning. Such "automatic" or involuntary learning after infancy is probably relatively rare. As children grow older, they seem almost to resist the process of classical conditioning, perhaps because they are seeking autonomy. Classical conditioning, after speech is well established, is largely confined to responses over which the child does not have voluntary control.

By the instrumental conditioning family is meant more or less voluntary and—after language is developed—usually cognized behavior designed to help an individual reach goals and solve problems. The instrumentally conditioned response typically has little or no resemblance to the unconditioned response that might be made to the evoking stimulus. For present purposes, responses belonging to this family are considered to be goal directed, although there are certainly many instances that, judging from appearances, cannot readily be so described.

There are many points of view about the origins of socialization, and which point of view an author or student adopts is to some degree a matter of his own preference. The preference adopted in the present chapter is traditional, and fits under the heading of social learning theories.

Freud spoke of the socialization process as a change from the *pleasure principle,* under which the infant seeks immediate gratification of primary or biological needs, to the *reality principle,* under which the child adjusts his behavior to the realities of his total life situation. The reality principle, in contrast to the pleasure principle, is *foresighted* rather than *immediate;* it posits that many immediate gratifications are foregone for larger future gratifications, and that, by and large, the immediate pleasures of the senses are often better served by and thus best subordinated to the rules of social intercourse. In other words, it is better to be loved, or at least accepted, than to have exactly what you want, in great quantity, exactly when you want it (which is always, of course, *now*). Living according to the reality principle may postpone gratification, but often maximizes and guarantees it. The distinction between the middle and the lower lower social class discussed earlier parallels to some extent the present distinction between the reality and the pleasure principles.

The theory is accepted here that very young infants learn through classical conditioning applied to biological drives that are satisfied by primary or unconditioned rewards. The biological drives that are most influential in early socialization are those that demand social interaction between the helpless infant and the caretaking adult for their satisfaction. Air hunger, for example, demands no social interaction since, if a child were dependent on someone else for breathing, he would almost certainly die. The drives that best fit the social interaction criterion appear plausibly to be hunger, elimination (which is closely linked to cleanliness, modesty, and sexual training), sex, and probably aggression and curiosity (for discussion of these "drives," see Chapter 10).

Dependency, which in older children is partially transformed into love, seems to be the most plausible mechanism by which socialization is accomplished. The caretaking adult, at first through classical and later through instrumental conditioning, comes to be associated with the primary rewards essential to the infant's well-being, and indeed his very life. Presently, the infant's caretakers come to have secondary reinforcement or reward stimulus value in and of themselves (see Chapter 10). The infant (and young child) signifies this value by *depending* on his caretakers, responding to their approval and disapproval as well as their tangible rewards and punishments. Eventually, he governs his behavior to a large degree by standards that he has accepted and made automatic, that have been taught to him by people whom he *loves*. Such people, of course, constantly give him primary as well as social reinforcements. Gewirtz and Stingle (1968) have prepared an excellent review of this process.

This process is endlessly complicated by the infant's enormous potential for symbolic development, and none of the material dealing with cognitive development, concept formation, and language behavior treated earlier in this book is irrelevant to the present discussion of socialization. Increases in physical size and skill also modify socialization. People are the agents of socialization. Early socialization most probably consists very simply of learning that people are important and, ideally, well disposed to the infant. Later socialization depends on the complex interaction of the child's liking for and dependency on people with his modifying his behavior according to his perceptions of how others can affect his behavior, directly or indirectly, through learning from them techniques for problem solving that work for them. This interaction is discussed more fully in the next section.

POWER AND SOCIALIZATION

The point has been made earlier in this chapter that socialization proceeds in two major ways. First, a child modifies his behavior because people are important to him. He loves them and depends on them. Second, as he observes them, he sees that others possess important sources of power and competence that may or do affect him, or that enable them to reach goals that he too wishes to reach. This power may and indeed usually does include the power of others to reward or punish him in tangible ways (as contrasted to psychological ways, such as giving him love and approval).

The analysis of sources of power that follows is adapted in part from Wolowitz (1965). As with other aspects of socialization, power must be considered not only in terms of its type, but in terms of the child's effective culture (including his social class), and his age and sex.

Definition of Power

One has *power* if he possesses something someone else wants or fears, and if he is known to be willing and/or able to share it or dispense it. In other words, one is powerless if he has nothing that anyone else wants or is afraid of, or if it has been made clear that he cannot or will not share it, or is unable to dispense it, or if the potential recipient does not know that he has the power and the willingness to share or dispense it.

In order to acquire the attributes of power, the stranger may make known to a new group his background, often manufacturing a more prestigious one than he actually possesses. Power cannot be exercised over an alienated child or subpopulation because the child or the group no longer wants (or fears) the power of the would-be dispenser. Power is lost over the desperate man who no longer cares whether he lives or dies.

Types of Power

COMFORT GIVING.   The first major category of power is the ability to nurture, or take care of, or give comfort. The term *comfort giving* is used in this chapter because it is the most adequately descriptive. Comfort giving is unquestionably important for the first of the two types of socialization (producing change in the child because he wants to please), but it also fits well with the second or modeling induction aspect of socialization. Comfort giving is traditionally ascribed more to mothers than to fathers (e.g., Parsons, 1955), although research does not bear out the assumption very clearly (e.g., Moulton, Liberty, Burnstein, and Altucher, 1966; Mussen and Distler, 1959).

The research literature abounds with evidence that comfort giving is effective in shaping behavior, although there is disagreement about such issues as the differential effect of comfort giving according to the child's age and sex, the sex of the person giving the comfort as it interacts with the child's sex, and so on.

For example, Wahler (1967) demonstrated that mothers, following a prescribed schedule of positive reinforcement, quickly increased the frequency with which their three month old babies responded to them by smiling; but young women who were strangers to the babies (i.e., who had no history of previous comfort giving to the baby) were not successful in increasing the smiling rate. Hartup and Coates (1967) found that when placed in an experimental situation, preschool-aged children whose histories showed that they characteristically received much comfort (friendship behavior) from their peers, imitated generous peer models more than children with histories of having received relatively little comfort from the members of their peer group. In a study by Hartup, Glazer, and Charlesworth (1967), the children in nursery school who gave the most comfort to others were the most popular. By "comfort" the authors meant attention and approval, affection and personal acceptance, submissions, and tokens. Grusec (1966) showed that kindergartners handled nurturantly, particularly when the disciplinary technique used with them was "withdrawal of love," were more likely to show "internalized control"—self-blame—than kindergartners not handled nurturantly and disciplined in a "thing-oriented" way.

Rubenstein (1967) found that six month old babies of highly attentive mothers were significantly more curious (did more looking at, manipulating, and vocalizing in response to novel objects) than babies of medium or low attentive mothers. There was also a significant tendency for mothers of firstborns to be more attentive than mothers of later born infants. Rubenstein's definition of attention was the frequency with which a mother looked at, touched, held, or talked to her baby during specified observational times.

Parke (1967) worked with first and second graders, and used a male and female experimenter. Some of his children had been given continuous nurturance, while others had experienced interruption and, presumably, had learned that nurturance was a sometime thing that could be gained or lost. After Parke had manipulated the nurturance condition, he placed each child in a temptation situation. The child knew that resistance to temptation would lead to the opportunity to interact again with the experimenter. Girls were more responsive than boys (i.e., deviated less), suggesting possibly that a nurturance that they knew was conditional was more important to them than it was to boys; and girls were much more responsive to the female experimenter than to the male experimenter. However, boys too modified their behavior in the direction of resisting temptation, and showed some tendency (not statistically significant) to be more responsive to the male experimenter than to the female experimenter. Gewirtz (1969) demonstrated that with boys in the first three years of school, comfort giving in the form of praise acts much like more tangible rewards such as candy. Too much praise "satiates" the child; he ceases to regard it as rewarding. However, a period of time spent without praise whets his appetite, as it were, so that he will again begin to modify his behavior to gain praise.

In short, there is no question but that comfort giving modifies social behavior of many types at many ages. The specific parameters of this modification remain to be filled in by further research.

The literature is in fair agreement that comfort giving varies widely along dimensions of social class, sex, and age. Lower lower class children receive less than children from higher socioeconomic levels, at least from their parents. Parenthetically, it should be added that little is known about the upper social classes. Psychologists and sociologists, themselves middle class, seem to lack the temerity to penetrate the homes of the rich, famous, and aristocratic; and exclusive private schools do not welcome tampering with their pedigreed charges. The child rearing practices of the upper class may not be at all upper class if, as is frequently the case, the children are turned over almost entirely to servants who come from the lower socioeconomic class. Hence, very little information is available; but the child rearing practices may be much less patterned in upper than in middle or lower class homes, since more people from more varied social backgrounds are likely to be involved.

Boys receive less comfort giving behavior than girls; and older children less than younger children. The evidence is not at all clear about the important question of cross-sex comfort giving: Do mothers give more comfort to their sons than to their daughters, fathers more comfort to their daughters than to their sons?

PHYSICAL POWER. The second type of power is *physical*. This, too, varies by social class, sex, and age. To the very young child, male or female, the parent of either sex is all-powerful. With advancing age, he begins to see his mother as less powerful than his father. By late adolescence, it is probable that the boy is more powerful than his father, and by then both boys and girls have moved beyond the stage where their mothers can safely count on physical power to discipline them. Hence, discipline by physical power is, in a sense, a short term investment. There is little in the literature to suggest that it has any long term advantages, and most evidence suggests that physical discipline has more disadvantageous outcomes than it has advantages. It is, however, parsimonious, in that it is quick and usually, unless too often employed, effective at a particular moment in time.

Little children, then, are more likely to be managed by physical power than older children, although many people use physical force on their children as long as they are able to. It is a rare parent, regardless of his dislike for physical force, who has not used it now and again with his young children, at least "until they are old enough to reason with."

Boys are more likely than girls to be handled by means of physical power, and are also more likely to esteem it in themselves. "To be strong is to be masculine." All boys admire a bulging bicep.

Physical power is more frequently used and probably more esteemed as a source of prestige and power among the disadvantaged than among the advantaged. For many lower lower class men, their only source of power (and esteem) with their children is their physical power. When they lose it or when their children catch up to or exceed them in strength, they lose all effective power.

SEXUAL POWER. The third source of power is *sexual*. Perhaps typically in lower lower class society sexual power of the male is an important *overt* variable, explicitly recognized as conferring prestige. It seems to be agreed that among *Hispaño* populations, *machismo*—as manifested by fathering many children by a number of different women—is a highly regarded masculine characteristic. Boys, young men, and often older men acquire much prestige from demonstrated sexual prowess; the more girls and women seduced, the better. It is almost universal for male youth of high school age and older to brag about sexual conquests, particularly as a result of casual encounters. Sexual interactions with steady girls or fiancees seem to be little discussed (Kirkendall, 1961). Gang leaders typically excel in sexual behavior as well as in physical power and leadership qualities, and their leadership position usually confers on them substantial sexual prerogatives. In matricentric, lower lower class Negro co-cultures, often the only sources of power older boys and men have is their physical and sexual power, and promiscuous sexual conquests often seem to be the major way in which a boy may shore up his shaky masculine self-concept. This is, of course, by no means confined to Negro society, but it is thought to be more frequent there than among white lower lower class groups (see, e.g., Reiss, 1968). Nor is crude sexual power a minor matter among the middle class.

Sexual power for girls and women, except for the vanished breed of the *cocotte*, is typically manifested by the number of boys or men who can be attracted but *not* allowed to have intercourse. In extreme forms, even this results in rejection of a girl by her feminine peers and, often, by males with serious intentions. However, there are, particularly in lower class groups, clubs whose membership is denied to virgins or, in many cases, to girls who are not illegitimately pregnant. In the latter case, one suspects the exclusiveness of the membership is defensive, but this is not certain.

Prepubescent boys are just as proud of sexual exploits, although not as driven toward them, as postpubescent boys. Sexual play seems not to be taken as seriously by prepubescent girls as by postpubescent girls.

As suggested above, the role of sexual power differs sharply between the sexes. Conquest is a matter of prestige for men, perhaps (and only *perhaps*) to a greater degree in lower than in middle class society; while successful flirtation without succumbing is a matter (within limits) of prestige for girls. This is perhaps (but again only *perhaps*) more true in middle than in lower class societies in the United States.

One can only conjecture about the role of sexual power in the socialization of very young children. Psychoanalytic theory has been too often proved right for one to reject out of hand such conceptions as penis envy, castration threat, and the fantasy (or actuality) of the child as witness to the primal scene. Yet there are almost no sound data concerning the part such concepts, fantasies, or exposures play in the developing identity and socialization of children. Certainly, children living in very close quarters with their parents are likely to have been witness, at least auditorily, to their parents' intercourse and to have seen and heard about explicit courtship and open mating behavior in their crowded neighborhoods. Pornography is widely peddled to children of both sexes. The mass media leave few nuances of sexual power to the imagination of any child old enough to interpret a picture and certainly not to any child who reads at the third or fourth grade level. For the nonreader, universally available television becomes more and more explicit, particularly in the hours after which children are presumed to be asleep.

Adolescent and adult genitalia are regarded with a certain amount of awe and envy by small boys and, probably less openly, by small girls. The envy of the latter, however, is more likely to be elicited by her older counterpart's breasts. Large penises and large breasts (short of grotesque) are esteemed as symbols of sexual power in many societies, and certainly in United States society. The same appears to be true of hairy chests and profuse pubic hair, particularly for Caucasian males.

Even though solid data are nearly impossible to find concerning this source of power, and one is helpless in describing its differential importance as a function of age, there is no question about the important role it plays in socialization toward masculinity and femininity. One is inclined to say, although hesitantly, that as far as the central values are concerned—the things that *count*—physical and sexual power are less important in shaping children's socialization than are such categories as omniscience (knowledge, expertness) and status or prestige. It may be that advancing this tentative conclusion is simply an expression of middle class bias.

Expertness. The fourth class of power that seems importantly to shape children's socialization is omniscience, or knowledge, or perhaps better, *expertness*.

This type of power does not vary in its impact by social class, although the importance of particular kinds of expertness does. But all the world loves a winner, whether he is a basketball star or a computer wizard. The middle and upper classes, while enthusiastic about the sports and arts, tend more to value professional expertness, whether this be law, journalism, or economics. Small boys revere athletic prowess, small girls still seem to be bowled over by the actress and chanteuse. The expert at his trade is more esteemed by the skilled and unskilled tradesman than by the middle class man. Certain types of expertness carry minimal prestige: Male ballet dancers, of high prestige in the Soviet Union, are often denigrated in the United States. Salesmen seem always to carry with them a self-apology and a behest to their sons, either directly or mediated through their wives, "Do not follow in my footsteps." Willie Loman in *Death of a Salesman* has become an American classic.

Boys model on expertness that the society considers appropriately masculine, girls on expertness that is designated as feminine (although there are many individual variations). With increasing age, children's evaluations of expertness approach their parents' standards.

In a task-oriented society, expertness at one's job is likely to be the most important source of a father's or mother's power *if* society esteems the job. Many "just a housewife" women do not convey to their daughters the prestige that should accompany being a wife and mother, although almost any housewife quickly sets herself up a notch over the unmarried woman. In general, the prestige of workaday jobs is a direct function of the level of education demanded to train for them, plus the power over the lives of others the position is judged to carry with it (as in medicine and the judiciary) plus, at least to some degree, the returns in money from the job. In today's society, wealth alone is not sufficient to confer on its holder or earner the full kudos of expertness. However, it helps.

The power of expertness does not diminish as a child grows older, as is likely to be the case for physical and sexual power. If anything, expertness is more highly valued by older than younger children; and the "success before retirement" of their father remains a source of pride to the middle-aged son and daughter. In contrast, the man with the unskilled job, or the man who is unsuccessful at his job, rapidly loses power in the eyes of his children as they grow older. This is probably a major problem in the masculine socialization of lower lower class boys. The problem is particularly acute when their fathers are not only unskilled, but also discriminated against, as is true for lower lower class Negro men. The *middle class* Negro male also suffers from discrimination, but may gain additional prestige in his children's eyes by having "succeeded in spite of whitey." There is no doubt, however, that discrimination hinders masculine socialization.

Upper class children whose parents were born to the purple, as it were, face peculiar problems in the expertness-competence area. McArthur (1955), one of the few who has conducted research with such groups, believed that upper class people, when compared to middle class, substitute "becoming a good person" for expertness, and concentrate more on the present and past than on the future, discipline themselves more strictly, and are more selflessly interested in their fellow man. *Noblesse oblige.*

PRESTIGE. The fifth and final class of power refers to status, prestige, or influence. An eloquent descriptive term taken from the argot is *clout*. Like expertness, clout is independent of social class, but takes different forms from one social class to another. The ways in which clout operates have been discussed, at least implicitly, in the preceding discussion of expertness, since to separate the two is artificial. Expertness *plus* prestige or clout are much more influential on a child's social development than either expertness or clout taken alone. However, although expertness and clout are positively correlated, the correlation is by no means perfect. An expert embalmer does not have the prestige in middle class society that an expert judge has. Old but inexpert and nonaffluent families have more clout, it is said, in Boston or Savannah than they have in Los Angeles or Chicago. The mobsman may have high clout in the urban ghetto, none in the suburbs.

As with expertness, adult prestige or clout is more clearly perceived by and thus is more influential with older children than younger ones. Girls and boys appear equally susceptible to the influence of clout, although the effectiveness of different types of clout will vary between the sexes. "A nice family" usually carries more impact for a girl than for a boy, for example.

Children who come from families very high on the expertness and prestige scales may actually have more difficulty with socialization than those from more humble families. It is a middle class virtue, mediated by both mothers and fathers, for the son to succeed more than the father, and the daughter to marry better than her mother did. This poses great problems for the children of exceptionally expert and prestigeful parents.

The Mediators of Power

To influence children's socialization, power must be mediated to children. The following seem to be the variables that are most relevant to effective mediation in the *process* of socialization.

PREDICTABILITY. First, power is likely to be ineffective unless it is meted out or demonstrated in a predictable fashion. No matter how expert, or physically powerful, or full of sexual prowess a parent may be, unless his child can predict the exercise—and the success—of the parent's power behaviors, the child will not (because he cannot) model on him. Complete consistency in the exercise and results of power is impossible in the complex interrelations of parents and their children, or of parents and children together in a complex world. But children soon detect a pattern so that, given appropriate circumstances, if parental (or other model) power is exerted most of the time, and succeeds most of the time, then it is effective in shaping behavior. If probability is above chance, a predictor pattern can be established. Rosekrans and Hartup (1967) provide buttressing data for this point.

EQUITABILITY. Second, the exercise of power needs to be equitable or fair. Festinger and his students have presented a theoretical rationale and have provided some research data that support the point (Festinger, 1957, 1964). Exercise of overwhelming power is likely to leave the child feeling without volition, so that he does not commit himself to behavior that has been so influenced. Overwhelming punishment for moderate crime is also likely to be ineffective, because it arouses resentment instead of compliance and may even be seen as being so extreme as to be ridiculous. Similarly, overwhelming reward is likely to be construed as arbitrary, thus unpredictable, thus ineffective.

PERCEIVED SIMILARITIES. Third, power exercised by those seen by the child to have similarities to himself seems to be more effective than power exercised by those with whom the child perceives no similarities. Studies by Byrne and his students (e.g., Byrne and Clore, 1967; Byrne and Griffitt, 1966) and Rosekrans (1967), among others, strongly suggest an important influence of perceived similarities in producing attitudes of attraction and actual modeling behavior in human subjects from at least nine years of age through college. Reiss (1968) suggested that in the area of sexual attitudes and behavior, individuals place themselves intermediate between their parents' standards and the standards of their best friends, seeing themselves as less conservative than their parents but less liberal or permissive than their best friends. However, as would be expected from a theory of perceived similarity, 89 percent of his sample reported being closer to their best friends than to their parents. Reiss also presented evidence for a relatively strong relation between sexual attitudes and sexual practices, about two-thirds of his subjects reporting that they actually behaved as they believed. Reiss's subjects were high school students, college students, and adults, and their ages ranged upward from 16 years.

Like Byrne and his colleagues, McCandless and Hoyt (1961) have also demonstrated the phenomenon of perceived similarity as a factor in social preferences. This was judged by the actual group play associations of 59 three and four year old Hawaii children, about half of whom were *haole* (Caucasoid) and half of whom were non-*haole* (mostly of Chinese or Japanese ancestry). Regardless of ethnicity, boys played significantly more with boys than with girls, and vice versa; and regardless of sex, *haole* children played more with *haoles*, non-*haoles* with non-*haoles*. No conventional evidence of ethnic prejudice, however, was observed in the children at any time. This led the investigators to conclude that this latter cleavage "was not due to prejudice in any conventional sense, but possibly to differential 'comfort' due to more common backgrounds among the members of a given group" (McCandless and Hoyt, p. 685). Preference for their own ethnic group was as strong in *haole* children as in non-*haole* children; but boys preferred boys more than girls preferred girls.

In a study of elementary school-aged children in a summer camp, Davitz (1955) found that sociometric choices were correlated with perceived similarity, but not with actual similarity. However, as with any correlational study, there is no way to tell whether the perceptual distortion led to social acceptance or social acceptance led to the perceptual distortion.

COMMUNICATION THAT POWER IS POSSESSED. Fourth, the mere possession of power is not enough to make it effective. The potential modeler or learner must *know* that his model has power. To a child living with his parents, this is made abundantly clear from his earliest years for comfort giving, physical, and possibly sexual power. In the specific sense of doing things for the child and answering his questions, expertness is also conveyed to the child at a very early age. His awareness of his parents' clout or lack of it comes later as the youngster moves into the wider community, compares his home with the homes of his friends, his father's job status with that of other fathers, his family income with the incomes of his friends' families, and so on. In other words, the child must be exposed to and assimilate the norms, first of his particular small co-culture and later the wider culture in order for clout and, in a sophisticated way, expertness to show their greatest effects.

With increasing age, as has been suggested, physical power and probably sexual power decrease in effectiveness as child motivators, while expertness and prestige loom ever more important. The role of comfort giving is less clear. Certainly, with older children, it takes less obvious forms (particularly for boys) than for little children, but it may be no less important for the teenager than for the two year old. In adolescence and adulthood, of course, other sources of comfort giving than the parents are sought, and this is a progressive development from the time the child first begins to interact with his peers and teachers.

A child learns about his model's power, and forms his perceptions of similarity to the model, through direct interaction with the model—demonstration, observation, direct communication (perhaps the last is relatively ineffective, particularly when construed as bragging)—and through communication from other persons about the model.

WILLINGNESS TO SHARE POWER AND ABILITY TO INFLICT PUNISHMENT. Fifth, the child must be aware that the model is willing to share with him the things the child wants from the model. These rewards may range all the way from tangibles such as candy or money, through affection (if the child wants it, he knows the model will give it to him), to formally taught skills (the model is willing to teach the child *how* to do something the child wants to do). However, models often influence children without any intent on the part of the model. If the child sees that the model is able to do something the child also wants to do, the child is likely to copy the model. Girls adopt the hair styles of their feminine heroes, boys the speech or stance of their favorite television or screen hero. Boyd R. McCandless, a "twiddler," once set half the population of a school for delinquents to twirling keys on the ends of their key chains because this was a conspicuous action pattern of his own and he was an important source of power to the boys. A current antismoking television segment shows a small boy modeling on his father in activity sequence after activity sequence, and ends with the open but clearly answerable question of what the boy will do following seeing his father sit down to relax by having a cigarette.

Freud early coined the theory of "identification with the aggressor," which has received sufficient research support that it deserves serious attention (see, e.g., Hartup and Coates, 1967; Hetherington and Frankie, 1967). This may be paraphrased by the colloquial expression, "If you can't lick them, join them," and is one of Freud's central theories to account for appropriate sex identification in boys. The boy, fearful of the power of his father (the concept of castration threat), incorporates the father's image so as to be like him, thus presumably to be safe from his threatening power. Presumably, when there is no possible escape from threat, the threatened child or person in self-defense takes on the characteristics of the oppressor. This mechanism has frequently been used to account for the behavior of prisoners in concentration camps in World War II, or the identification with the majority group that discriminates against them in the case of minority groups such as Jews and Negroes.

Something like identification with the aggressor seems to occur often when children grow up in authoritarian and punishing circumstances from which they have no escape. It may be a mechanism for many lower lower class children who, as a group, seem to be meted out less comfort, more physical punishment and verbal castigation, and who are handled in a more authoritarian fashion than middle class children (see, e.g., Bowerman and Elder, 1964).

Hetherington and Frankie (1967) detected something resembling defensive identification in a carefully conducted study of midwestern small town 4 to 6½ year olds (although their finding did not quite meet the usual .05 level of significance). In highly stressful homes with high conflict, there was more imitation of the dominant parent than was found in homes with low conflict. It might be said that in such homes conflict is a way of life, the winner is seen as having all the goodies and, in the absence of any escape, indentification is made with him. However, Hetherington and Frankie also found that if the nondominant parent is warm or if conflict is reduced, there is a trend toward less imitation of the aggressive parent. In other words, an escape hatch is provided by the warm parent, or the tension produced by the conflict which forces the child to identify differentially is reduced in low conflict homes.

Hopefully, relatively few children live in such harsh environments, however, and the power of punishment in shaping socialization is typically more straightforward and less pervasive than it is in circumstances where identification with the aggressor occurs. For most children, it is likely that the model's capacity to punish is simply one aspect of his total power—the logical other side of the coin from his ability to reward. For such children, punishment probably serves as a straightforward reinforcement that tells them *not* to do what they were punished for, or to do it another way (see, e.g., Blum and Kennedy, 1967). There is considerable evidence that modeling in moral development, that is, in the direction of conscience development and inner control of behavior, is more likely to occur under circumstances of reasonably democratic handling and psychological techniques of control than under authoritarian conditions with harsh, "thing-oriented" punishment, such as physical discipline (see Grusec, 1966; Hoffman and Saltzstein, 1967). However, hard data are scarce in this complex field.

Models may lose their effectiveness when they do not communicate with children. It is common clinical experience that parents, more often fathers than mothers, fail to communicate to their children that they love them (love is one dimension of comfort giving power). Americans are shy about tender emotions, and the "strong silent" masculine stereotype militates against men's communicating the love they feel for their children (or spouses, or friends). This may operate more between fathers and sons than between fathers and daughters, although such a statement is speculative. While the evidence is by no means clear, it is plausible that mutual affection is the "leaven" within which the other dimensions of power operate most benignly in the modeling process. Moulton *et al.* (1966) presented evidence that for sons, the parent after whom the son is most likely to model is both dominant and loving. Among the group of parents of the college men whom Moulton *et al.* studied, the fathers were judged by their sons to be the dominant parent in about 70 percent of the cases. In these father-dominant families, 55 percent of the fathers were seen as high in affection by their sons; where the mother was dominant, the percentage of high affection fathers dropped to 44 percent. This is probably a higher percentage of loving fathers than would be found in less highly selected families, although this judgment is made by extrapolating from other studies with different techniques of assessing paternal affection, a topic that has actually been little studied even though its great importance is granted by all. Bronson (1959), working with 9 to 13 year old boys, and Mussen and Distler (1959), working with kindergarten boys, obtained data that agree closely with the Moulton *et al.* results.

RATIO OF POSITIVE TO NEGATIVE REINFORCEMENT. The sixth and final mediator of power is the ratio of positive to negative reinforcement (reward to punishment). McCandless (1967, p. 424) has conjectured that power is more effective in producing modeling behavior when it is exerted in an overall learning situation where the ratio of reward to punishment is greater than 1, that is, where reward is more frequent than punishment. However, modeling of the "identification with the aggressor" type is a clear exception to this hypothesis. The hypothesis should be rephrased to include a concept of good or happy personal adjustment and creative socialization, cloudy though these terms may be. It can be hypothesized that modeling that occurs in a setting where the reward–punishment ratio is more than 1 will be accompanied by less anxiety, will be more flexible and adaptive, and will be accompanied more by hope of success (optimism?) and less by fear of failure (pessimism?).

An Illustrative Study of Modeling and Power

Bandura, Grusec, and Menlove (1967a) have published a study that embodies many of the dimensions of power and its mediation that have been discussed in general terms in the preceding pages. These investigators were interested in an analogue of conscience, which they called "self-monitoring reinforcement systems." By this, they meant that a child will, in private, exhibit conscientious behavior that has been publicly modeled for him by models differing in power styles.

A bowling alley type of game was used in this experiment. The game had been previously rigged so that a pattern of low and high scores emerged, although the children who took part in the study did not know this. The adult model, a young man, rewarded himself only for high scores. When he received a low score, he commented (making his criterion of expertness totally explicit), "A score like that doesn't deserve a chip"; when he attained his self-imposed standard, he said approvingly of himself, "That's a good score, I deserve a chip for that"; and when he was substantially above his self-imposed and rigorous schedule, he said, "That was a really good score. I deserve two chips for that." The children were given to understand that they could exchange their chips for prizes at the end of the game, and that the more chips they had, the more valuable would be the prize they received.

The children who took part in the study ranged in age from 7 to 11 years. The experimental design was a $2 \times 2 \times 2 \times 2$ factorial design. The first factor was *sex*, equal numbers of boys and girls being exposed to each of the conditions described below. It was necessary to control for the sex, since sex differences have so often been found in modeling behavior and "moral" development; but the investigators actually found few sex differences, and were able partially to ignore this factor in their later analysis.

The second factor consisted of two levels of comfort giving or *nurturance*, low and high. The experimenter introduced each child to the model, then excused herself to prepare the equipment. Under the low nurturance condition, which was used for half of all the children and equal numbers of boys and girls, the model simply announced that he would read his newspaper while the children waited, and that as far as he knew, the toys on the table in the trailer where the study was conducted were there for the child to play with. The model then read the newspaper for 15 minutes, taking part in no social interaction with the child. Under the high nurturance condition, the model said, after the experimenter had departed, that since the child was there the two of them might as well play together. The model got more toys from an adjoining room and played actively with the child for the 15 minutes during which they waited for the equipment to be readied. "During the high level of social interaction, the model responded in a consistently warm, friendly, and generously rewarding manner" (Bandura *et al.*, 1967a, p. 451). This difference in comfort giving, as will be seen, produced marked differences in the child's later scheduling of rewards for himself.

The third factor was *conflict*. In the high conflict condition, the reward pattern of the adult model, who never rewarded himself for a score less than 60, was contrasted with a relaxed, "low expertness" reward pattern of a child who served as a confederate. This confederate rewarded himself for any score above 20. The adult model and child confederate alternated blocks of 5 trials for a total of 20 games each. In the low conflict condition, the child confederate was not present; the subject experienced the stringent reward pattern of the adult model, but not the lenient reward pattern of the child confederate. Half the children in each of these conflict conditions came from the low nurturance group and the other half in each conflict condition came from the high nurturance group.

The subjects were again symmetrically split into groups for exposure to the fourth factor, *power feedback*. This consisted of explicit feedback, to half the children in each of the previous conditions, about the social desirability of the behavior of the model (social recognition of excellence, thus an explicit recognition of a type of prestige). No feedback about the model was provided for the other half of the children. Under the condition of feedback, the experimenter returned at the end of the modeling trials and praised the adult model in the presence of the subject, making approving comments to the effect that the model was the sort of person who set high standards of achievement for himself and thought well of himself only when he had done an excellent job. In the situation where the model had been working with the confederate child, the experimenter waited until the confederate child was gone to give this praise, so as to avoid any connotation of criticizing the confederate. In the situation with no feedback, the experimenter on her return merely thanked the model for his assistance, but gave him no social recognition.

At this time, the model left and the experimenter excused herself, ostensibly leaving the child alone to play another 36 games on the bowling alley. Again, the game was rigged and, without his awareness, the child's behavior was observed and recorded to determine what his pattern of self-reinforcement would be.

High conflict (exposure to the child confederate) caused the subjects to be more lenient in their self-rewards than low conflict (exposure only to the adult model). Extrapolating, this might be generalized by saying that when the peer is more lenient than the adult, the child moves in the direction of the peer's standards. This relates to the earlier discussion about the modeling effectiveness of perceived similarity: The child subject sees himself as similar to the child confederate and thus tends to embrace his standards. (It would be interesting to reverse the condition to see what happens when a child confederate is more stringent than the adult model.) The finding fits with the earlier mentioned Reiss data about sex attitudes and behavior.

A second finding in the Bandura, Grusec, and Menlove study was that the children modeled significantly more after the adult model when he was praised (the direct power feedback condition) than when he was not praised.

In general, the children modeled *less* after the model when he was high in nurturance (comfort giving), particularly when he was nurturant *and* working with the child confederate. Then the children were more inclined to relax their self-reward standards than when the model was non-nurturant. The most faithful modeling occurred when the model was non-nurturant, when he worked alone without the peer confederate, and when he received praise (feedback about his high self-standards).

The results of this study illustrate and support some of the hypotheses advanced in the preceding discussion of the principles of power and its mediation: model expertness and feedback concerning the model's prestige, and the influence of perceived similarities. However, the hypothesis concerning comfort giving is not supported. Indeed, the evidence suggests that less modeling, at least under some circumstances, occurs with nurturant models than with non-nurturant models. It is necessary to look more closely at the conditions of the experiment to evaluate this finding.

In every case, the experimenter took the child away from activities connected with an elementary school summer recreation program. It is probable that many if not most children participate in such programs tepidly, at best. The children moved from a group situation to one where they received individual attention. Additionally, the novelty of a trailer, new toys, and an interesting game with contingent rewards were available to them. They were also interacting with a young man, an experience that is welcomed by most elementary school children, as they see little of young men. The children were from Palo Alto, California, and were thus probably from middle to high socioeconomic class. It is possible that for them, a model who accepted them as they were in an enjoyable situation, and who left them amiably alone while he (like their fathers?) read his paper was perceived as friendly, rewarding, and a source of power and acceptance; but a model who, perhaps surprisingly, got out still more toys to play with and attempted to interact as a peer was perceived as an incongruous, atypical adult who "really did not count" and thus was not worth modeling on. For the children, then, it may be that the nurturance contrast was not "really" a contrast between non-nurturance and nurturance, but between natural matter-of-fact acceptance and "loss of dignity." It would be interesting to repeat this experiment with variations on the nurturance conditions employed by Bandura, Grusec, and Menlove. This critique also illustrates that it is potentially useful to look from experimental conditions and results to "real life" before attempting (and even then very cautiously) to generalize the results to "real life." A constant validating, checking back and forth between the laboratory and the free (not scientifically controlled) social situation is essential both in devising experiments and applying their findings. This is particularly true for research on socialization which, to say the least, is a most complex process.

IDENTIFICATION

Distinction between Modeling and Identification

As the summary of the Bandura, Grusec, and Menlove study indicates, it is possible to construct a clear and potentially useful scientific definition of modeling. It has been questioned (e.g., Sanford, 1955) whether such a definition of *identification* is possible. However, the concept is so much discussed and so plausible that it is necessary first to define the term, then to distinguish it from modeling.

The following several pages on the distinction between modeling and identification are not referenced in the same detail as the preceding and following sections of this chapter. The reason for this is that the concepts are drawn from so many sources—theoretical, research, and clinical-personal experience—that detailed referencing would serve more to confuse than to orient the reader. Two general references may be used to supplement this section: (a) a theoretical treatment by Gewirtz and Stingle (1968), who cut refreshingly through and eliminate many of the turgid concepts by which the term *identification* is plagued; and (b) McCandless (1967, Chs. 6, 10, and 11). The McCandless review is relatively traditional; the present treatment brings it up to date and, hopefully, improves upon it.

In Gewirtz and Stingle's (1968) theoretical treatment, generalized imitation, which they regarded as the basis for identification, refers to copying (exact or approximate) of many of a model's responses, in many different types of situations, and often when no observable outside reward (or punishment) can be detected. Like McCandless (1967), they pointed out that identification, as the term is used in the literature, often includes—and confuses—process, source, and product; that unmeasurable concepts such as introjection are involved in it; that it mixes up modeling and dependency; and, in sum, that it is not a satisfactory construct. Gewirtz and Stingle's position seems to be as follows: A child has identified with a model when he imitates a broad range of the model's behaviors, and at a high level of abstraction and generalization. These behaviors include attitudes and beliefs.

A child learns to identify in exactly the same way he learns to imitate: Behaviors (including attitudes) that work—that is, that secure for the child what he wants—are learned by him from the significant power figures in his environment. The models' effectiveness follows the principles of learning theory, of which power and power style are an integral part.

Gewirtz and Stingle, in other words, made no real distinction between imitation or modeling and identification. Their simplistic position, whether or not it is fully accepted, serves the purpose of forcing authors in the field to think more clearly.

However, totally adopting their position—to which many will object strongly—forces one to restructure the entire topic of identification. While such restructuring is desirable, the present volume is not the place to undertake so technical, controversial, and complex a process. For present purposes, then, an eclectic point of view about identification is taken in the pages that follow. Readers are urged to become familiar with the detailed Gewirtz and Stingle treatment, and to make their own applications to the discussion presented here.

Modeling, as usually defined for experimental purposes, is imitation. Thus, Bandura, Grusec, and Menlove considered that their child subjects modeled when they refused to reward themselves for game performances below the model's minimum standard for rewarding himself. This is not necessarily *exact* imitation, but is the copying of the model's rules for behavior (see Aronfreed, 1969). Nothing "unseen" is inferred from modeling, other than that the modeler has observed and learned. Of course, as the reader knows by the time he has read this far in this book, saying that someone has observed and learned requires many inferences. However, for observing and learning, the rules governing inference are better known than for socialization.

Identification is an inferred construct, not directly observable. Like an intelligence quotient (but far less precisely), it is said to exist at a low, intermediate, or high level when certain criterion behaviors occur. Identification implies internalization. This means that the individual who has identified with some model is self-activating. He behaves according to his identification because of what he has inside himself—his *self*-stimuli—rather than because of changing conditions in his environment. It is assumed, of course, that "what is inside himself" was originally learned but, once learned, it is largely self-perpetuating regardless of later environmental changes. In this, also, *identification* resembles *intelligence*.

Moral and Sex Role Identification

The present section concerns itself with two types of identification, conscience or moral identification and sex role identification (Gewirtz and Stingle would make no distinction between these). Identification must also be followed by *with:* identification *with* father, identification *with* mother, identification *with* the masculine or feminine sex role.

The most commonly agreed upon criterion behavior from which moral or conscience identification is inferred is guilt. Guilt is self-punishment—punishment that occurs regardless of how the external world reacts to the public or private behavior that evokes the guilt. Shame is "fear of losing face"; guilt is self-inflicted punishment. One is at least mildly ashamed if he appears with his fly open or her blouse unbuttoned. One is guilty if he harbors angry and rejecting thoughts toward his well-loved and lovable parents. It is quite possible to be both ashamed and guilty about the same things and it may be that guilt develops from shame. However, some evidence exists linking shame to thing-oriented punishments and guilt to psychologically oriented punishments.

One is identified with a sex role if it is automatic, stable, and consistent at all levels of behavior, whether the motives behind these behaviors are fully cognized or not. Thus, the male is appropriately sex role identified if his dreams, his fantasies, his purposeful thinking, his gestures, his sexual preferences, and his vocational and avocational interests are all male. Additionally, it may be posited, not only is he masculine but he is glad of it and takes some pride in it. He would not have it any other way. The same kinds of attributes characterize feminine sex role identification.

Qualifiers must be added to some of the characteristics listed in the preceding paragraph. There is a very wide latitude of socially acceptable masculinity and femininity in, for example, masculine and feminine vocational and avocational interests. The social judgment about masculinity and femininity of such interests may change with time. A few years ago in Atlanta, Georgia, for example, the sale of residential real estate was handled almost entirely by men. Today, most of it is handled by women. Math is considered something of a masculine domain, but many thoroughly feminine girls and women both like math and are good at it. Before World War II, almost no men went into elementary school teaching. Currently, in states where elementary school teachers' salaries are high (such as New York and California), there are many male elementary teachers and teachers in training. A liking for professional football and good painting may coexist comfortably in the same boy or girl.

The "she doth protest too much" syndrome has considerable plausibility in inferring identification. Is the man who constantly protests his honesty *truly* and genuinely honest? Is the girl or woman who is contemptuous of any masculine pursuit or interest genuinely and consistently feminine in her identification?

These paragraphs illustrate the difficulty of inferring masculine and feminine sex role identification. Under some circumstances, a liking for football may lead to an inference of masculine identification. Under other circumstances, it may be construed as defensive and thought to cover an underlying femininity. The conclusion must necessarily follow that much distance remains to be traveled before scientifically acceptable definitions of sex role identification are constructed. Careful individual evaluation of a boy or a girl, if the boy or girl (or adolescent or adult) is open and honest, usually leads to an approximately correct evaluation of sex role identification, but objective measurement of either individuals or groups is as yet inexact.

Useful approximations are made by several of the current pencil and paper tests of masculinity and femininity, but these are subject to conscious distortion and to cultural influence. For example, college-educated men score more feminine on such scales, college-educated women more masculine, than less well educated men and women. The reasons are simple: College, by exposing the boy to art, music, and the humanities, has induced in him a (highly desirable) interest in and often liking for such things. But for the culture as a whole and according to the standardization of the tests, such preferences increase his femininity score. By the same token, the well-educated woman has come to know and be interested in math and science. As measured by current tests, her liking for such areas "makes her more masculine." There is no reason to think that the sex role identifications of the well-educated are any shakier than those of the ill-educated. If anything, there is some reason to believe the opposite.

Measurement of sex role identification in young children has not progressed even as far as for adolescents and adults, although sensitive teachers and clinicians seem to be able to spot children who are having difficulty. This is an important field for study, since the social sanctions against inappropriate sex role identification are extreme in most Western cultures and, hopefully, young children can be directionally changed more readily than adolescents or adults. This is particularly true when sexual relations with the same sex have occurred at a mature level of release. However, sexual relations with the same sex constitute no clear commitment to inappropriate sex role identification, as Kinsey fully documented, although they may tip the balance inappropriately for those whose sex role identification is already precarious. Thus, a real danger exists for a youth who moves into a sexual interaction with someone of his own sex.

While many refinements remain to be made, the measurement of moral or conscience identification seems to be closer to scientific acceptability than the measurement of sex role identification. However, the social relativism of "good" and "bad" values, behaviors, and beliefs seriously complicates socialization research.

SEX TYPING.   The concept of *sex typing* is simpler than sex role identification (except in Gewirtz and Stingle's analysis, where sex typing would be simply one aspect of sex role identification). An individual is appropriately sex typed if his behavior fits the norm of his particular effective culture. There is considerable variation in acceptable sex typing behavior by social class. Typically, sex differences are more accentuated in lower than in middle and upper socioeconomic classes. The lower class boy may be thought "vulgarly male" and crude when he moves into middle class society, and the neat, well-behaved, and mannerly middle class boy may be considered a sissy if he ventures into lower class society. Middle class girls and women are more likely to admit masculine interests and tastes than their lower class sisters. But, regardless of social class, the differences between the sexes in patterns of behavior and interest are as unmistakably clear as the biological differences. The differences can easily be seen by casual observation of a group of two year olds.

There is no satisfactory evidence relating physical characteristics either to sex typing or sex role identification, although the path toward either is probably easier for boys with masculine physiques and girls with feminine physiques. It is surely more difficult for short, hippy, and nonmuscular boys to overcome negative social expectations about their masculinity than it is for tall, broad-shouldered, and muscular boys to be accepted as masculine. The petite but bosomy girl undoubtedly has an easier time of it than her tall, rawboned sister. However, research does not bear out this relation of differential body builds to differential success in reaching appropriate sex roles.

THE RELATION BETWEEN MORAL AND SEX ROLE IDENTIFICATION.   In a society with strong sanctions against inappropriate sex role identification, it can be predicted that there will be a moderate positive correlation between moral or conscience identification and appropriate sex role identification, just as there is a moderate positive correlation between appropriate sex typing and appropriate sex role identification. The youngster or adult who is inappropriately sex role identified, unless he is inordinately skilled at concealing his identification, is brutally handled in most Western societies. His life is so beleaguered that it is almost inevitable for him to develop extreme anxieties, to be in constant conflict, and to suffer continuous frustration and fear. His fears, in American society, are realistically founded. Doidge and Holtzman (1960) tested four groups of young service men, a quite unsophisticated population. One group was homosexual both in practice and preference. Another was heterosexual in preference, but its members had had some homosexual experience. A third group was heterosexual but its members had encountered disciplinary difficulty in the establishment; and the fourth group was both heterosexual and free from discipline problems. The different tests of personal-social adjustment all pointed to significant maladjustment of the first group compared to the other three groups. Other investigators, such as Chang and Block (1960), have worked with older groups of homosexuals, usually successful and well-educated males who had volunteered as research subjects, and found them psychologically healthy. It must be concluded, then, that it is possible to be happy, possessed of socially constructive moral-conscience identification, and inappropriately sex role identified. But the sanctions society puts on the homosexual are such that it is more difficult for him than for the appropriately sex role identified person to achieve a constructive and happy moral identification. Moral identification is difficult to achieve in circumstances that evoke anxiety, fear, shame, conflict, and frustration.

Parental Power and Identification

Farina (1960) devised a set of ingenious indexes based on observed behavior and designed to measure dominance and conflict in the relations between husband and wife. He used it to test the hypothesis that father-dominated families produced better adjusted sons than mother-dominated families. This hypothesis has its roots in the paternalistic, father-centered family structure of Victorian society, but fits well with some of the previous discussion in this chapter. The population Farina worked with was made up of parents of good and poor premorbid schizophrenic men, and parents of male patients hospitalized with tuberculosis. The last-named were used as controls. A poor premorbid schizophrenic man is one whose illness has had a long onset, whose courting and sexual behavior have been defective, and who in general has never been an adequate member of society. A good premorbid schizophrenic male has mixed with other people and had friends prior to his illness, has courted normally and has typically been married, and his illness has usually come on suddenly. Farina found, not quite according to his prediction, that his control subjects fell between his good and poor premorbid groups in family father dominance; that is, if father dominance is a good thing, then the controls should have come from the most extremely father dominated families, the good premorbids should have been intermediate, and the poor premorbids should have been found to have the weakest fathers and the strongest mothers.

Farina's finding is not surprising if one analyzes the structure of United States society, which is nominally an equalitarian society. If there is anything to its avowed equalitarianism between sexes, then the prediction would be exactly what Farina found: The psychologically healthiest men should come from families where there was no strong imbalance of power in favor of one or the other parent, the unhealthiest from families that departed furthest from the United States norm. This norm is still Victorian enough that, if one parent is to be dominant, it should be the father.

That American homes are likely to be equalitarian in actuality is suggested by Bowerman and Elder (1964). They reported data from nearly 20,000 white seventh to twelfth graders from intact homes who lived in central Ohio and central North Carolina, and nearly 1600 tenth graders from Florida. For various breakdowns (i.e., into older and younger boys and girls, and for different regions), from a minimum of one-third to a maximum of almost two-thirds of the youngsters reported that their homes were equalitarian. Over all, for the large sample, 45.6 percent reported equalitarianism, 34.3 percent father dominance, and only 20.1 percent mother dominance. Boys were more likely to report father dominance than girls, and older children of both sexes were more likely to report father dominance than younger children. Significantly, and in line with earlier discussions of the role of the lower class male, middle class children were significantly more likely to report their fathers as dominant (powerful) than were lower class children. For the older boys in the large sample, the difference between lower and middle class boys reporting father dominance was 13 percent (50.2 percent of the middle class boys and 37.3 percent of the lower class boys said that their fathers were dominant).

Before proceeding to a discussion of the theory of cross-identification and equalitarianism, it is useful to introduce more data.

Another very clear finding of Farina's was that the parents of his control subjects were least in conflict with each other. The parents of his good premorbid schizophrenic men were intermediate, and the most conflict existed between the parents of the poor premorbid men. This relates to style of mediating power: Any modeling or identification is likely to be difficult in the midst of a power struggle, the outcome of which is difficult for the child to predict, although Hetherington and Frankie (1967) reported high modeling with the clearly dominant parent in high conflict homes.

Reference should be made again to Moulton et al. (1966). These investigators found that college-age men most frequently made an appropriate sex role identification when their fathers were both dominant and high in comfort giving. Hetherington (1965) studied 4 to 11 year old boys and girls, and reported that the appropriate sex typing (and presumably identification) of boys was weakest in homes where the mother was dominant, strongest in homes where the father was dominant, and that this tendency was stronger for older than younger boys. Her findings were comparable to Farina's, whose techniques she used. Unfortunately, she did not report data for parental conflict. In her study, the boys but not the girls were disturbed in sex role identification when the parent of the opposite sex was dominant. Hetherington stated, "Since normal identification for girls involves sustaining and intensifying the mother-child relationship, father dominance may contribute only to cross-sex identification and do little to disrupt the girls' primary identification" (Hetherington, 1965, p. 193). Hetherington, like many other investigators, added that the feminine role in American society, and particularly for middle class children, is less clear than the masculine role. Thus, a girl's patterning on her father behaviorally will put her under less duress than a boy's patterning on his mother. This leads to a prediction, apparently as yet untested, that boys of exceptionally masterful mothers—particularly in situations where there is little mother–father conflict—may turn out all right in sex typing and sex role identification.

These data lead to a theory of developmental and cross-sex identification. Where the parent of the appropriate sex is both suitably powerful, in terms of cultural expectations, and comfort giving, and where respective parental power roles are played out according to an equalitarian model, the child will make comfortable identifications and modelings that will be appropriate to his sex (within the limits of the social norms), flexible, and neither defensively masculine nor feminine. However, boys will be strongly masculine identified and appropriately but perhaps not extremely masculine modeled. Girls, for whom the feminine model in the core society is less clear and perhaps less highly valued, will be strongly feminine identified and at least acceptably feminine modeled.

Payne and Mussen (1956) provided data for adolescent boys that support this point. Boys whose scores on a personality inventory were much more like their fathers' than their mothers' were assumed by Payne and Mussen to be father identified. According to tests, the highly identified boys had masculinity scores substantially higher than those of boys with little father identification. They also saw their fathers as rewarders, not punishers and, in addition, reported that their fathers were relatively more rewarding than their mothers. They also said that their entire family constellation was a happy one (this perhaps corresponds to Farina's finding of low conflict being associated with good adjustment).

Fitting with the prediction of flexibility in sex role modeling made above, Payne and Mussen reported that there was no relation between the masculinity test scores of highly identified boys and those of their fathers. This finding is congruent with the notion of developmental identification: The boy well identified with his father is flexible, and if his father does not provide an appropriate behavior model for his needs, then the boy is free to seek other and more effective models. As McCandless has said in another context, "a ruggedly masculine but highly adequate father can rear a son with somewhat effeminate behavior, but with appropriate sex-role identification; or a rather effeminate but good father can rear a son who is ruggedly masculine in behavior as well as appropriately sex-identified" (McCandless, 1967, p. 463). It would be predicted, further, that such a flexible adjustment does not occur in defensive identification (a concept discussed earlier in the present chapter). A defensively identified boy or girl—in American culture, it is probably more likely to be a boy than a girl—would be predicted to be rigidly sex typed, imitative of his same-sex parent regardless of the adaptiveness of the imitated behavior, and probably relatively weakly sex role identified. Such a child, if he deviates from the behavior of his same-sex parent, may feel intolerably anxious because, as the child sees it, he is betraying the parent and risking his wrath. When Freud spoke of infantile and ego identification, he probably had such a distinction in mind.

Finally, in the equalitarian, warm, and low conflict home, children should be able to cross-model and cross-identify (in the moral sense) in whatever way best serves their personal-social needs. For a daughter, it will then be possible to incorporate those of her father's adjustments that are clearly superior to certain of her mother's attitudes or behaviors. A son can pattern himself in like manner.

A soundly cross-identified girl should be a more appreciative and better wife, and mother to her sons; an appropriately cross-identified boy a better husband, and father to his daughters. Additionally, such individuals could without uneasiness enjoy those aspects of culture that are stereotypically reserved for the opposite sex but which, free from stereotypes, can be equally enjoyable and rewarding for either sex. Men so identified might well feel freer to express their emotions and communicate about things other than the tangible world, thus, perhaps, becoming more relaxed and living longer. Women so identified could feel more at ease about efforts toward autonomy and self-sufficiency that seem to trouble so many modern women. Johnson (1963) summarized evidence for girls, and concluded that a degree of father identification is perhaps as important for girls as for boys.[3]

Need for Achievement, Impulse Control, and Delay of Gratification

Our capitalistic, democratic, competitive, cooperative, and task-oriented society demands that its members value achievement for its own sake: Achievement is a virtue in and of itself, according to the core culture. To compete effectively, to "save," and to live in a predominantly urban society, it is essential to control many impulses, particularly those that are aggressive, sexual, and dependent in nature. It is also necessary to plan ahead and in so doing to give up many immediate gratifications for future and, hopefully, more substantial rewards.

The attributes of need for achievement, impulse control, and delay of gratification, for American society, are central components of moral-conscience development.[4] Thus, their determinants are similar to the determinants of moral and sex role identification that have been discussed earlier in this chapter, and little further discussion is required. However, the work of Mischel (e.g., Mischel and Grusec, 1967) has not previously been mentioned. He has contributed substantially to the literature on impulse control and delay of gratification. He and his students have demonstrated that these are positive functions of age and intelligence, that trusting and optimistic children are more likely to manifest them than untrusting children, and that certainty of reward—which theoretically is one aspect of trust or optimism—promotes delay of gratification.

This relates to the opportunities a culture provides for its citizens. Cloward and Ohlin (1960), who have previously been mentioned, advanced the hypothesis that children given legitimate opportunities for achievement will not become delinquent, but children in an environment that makes available only illegitimate opportunities (or possibly, a vast preponderance of illegitimate over legitimate opportunities) will become delinquent. This hypothesis has been tested experimentally and strongly supported in a study of advantaged college youth (rather than the slum youth concerning whom it was originally advanced) by Tallman (1966).

---

[3] Biller and Borstelmann (1967) have provided an exhaustive review of the sex typing and identification literature for males.

[4] The term "need for achievement" as used here is descriptive; the *theoretical* use of the term is criticized in Chapter 10.

To conclude this section, it need only be said that the discussion of power and the style in which it is manifested can be predicted to apply as felicitously to need for achievement, impulse control, and delay of gratification as to sex role and moral identification. Where data exist (and many data have been cited), they fit the predictions rather well—indeed, in many cases the predictions were suggested from the data.

SOCIAL INFLUENCES

Role of the Peer Group

Evidence already presented in the present chapter—the influence of perceived similarity and power, for example—demonstrates the important effects of peers on children's behavior. This influence seems steadily to increase from the time the child first begins to interact socially with his peers until adolescence. While clear data are not available, observation suggests that the influence of the peer group peaks in late adolescence and probably declines thereafter, when young people marry and set up standards for their own families. However, in the sense that it represents peer influence, "keeping up with the Joneses" is very much a part of United States culture for adults.

While Coleman's research techniques in *The Adolescent Society* (1961) maximize the apparent independence of adolescent and adult society, the evidence of conflicting influences of peers and parent-adults is seen so plainly all around us that it would be ostrich-like to deny the phenomenon. For example, McDill and Coleman (1965) studied parental and peer influence on plans for attending college. In the freshman year of high school, the relative influence of parents compared with peers was in a ratio of almost 5 to 1; but by the time the students in the sample had reached their senior year of high school, parental and peer influences were almost equal, although the parents still had a slight edge. As has been pointed out, Reiss (1968) found that his sample of adolescents and adults held sexual attitudes (by which most of them apparently also governed their behavior) that were more like their best friends' than like their parents'. It should be pointed out that Reiss's sample (and presumably most samples, judging from a consensus of the literature) choose friends who are actually rather like their parents. For example, Reiss's students with liberal sex attitudes came from homes with such attitudes. Their friends were also liberal, but more so than the parents, and the respondents fell between their parents and their best friends, but closer to the latter. This similarity between friends and parents operates to close the "generation gap." Such authors as Douvan and Adelson (1966) are frankly skeptical about the existence of any true generation gap, and maintain that the tendency to choose friends who hold to the same standards as parents simply reinforces the parents' basic codes, although perhaps liberalizing them to some degree. However, Douvan and Adelson studied children in their early teens. It may be that differences between parents and children grow more acute as youngsters reach the latter half of the teens. The McDill and Coleman data suggest this.

The Hartup and Coates (1967) data demonstrate that peer models can influence young children to be altruistic or selfish; Bandura *et al.* (1967a) showed that a self-lenient peer can significantly dilute the influence of a young adult model with high standards; Bandura *et al.* (1967b) presented findings that illustrate how peer models can help children to overcome fear of dogs. In the Hartup and Coates study, nursery school children with histories showing few friendships were (rather pathetically) more likely to model their nonrewarding peers than children with histories of plentiful friendships. Is this a socially rather unrealistic effort to placate and win friends?

Undoubtedly, the peer group provides a necessary setting in which children can practice the skills essential to development beyond childish dependence on parents and other adults, and to development of autonomy.

The McCandless and Hoyt (1961) study mentioned earlier perhaps illustrates the role of the peer group in giving a child opportunity to rehearse his important life roles. The tendency for boys to prefer boys and girls girls in free play may be an instance of seeking models for appropriate masculine and feminine behavior, as well as due to attraction based on perceived similarity. Some force is lent to this observation by the fact that boys prefer boys more strongly, even at the ages of three and four years, than girls prefer girls. It has been noted earlier in this chapter that urgency toward appropriate sex role behavior (as well as the clarity and desirability of the sex role) is greater for boys than girls. Such sex cleavage in friendship choices is increasingly strongly manifested up through pubescence in most coeducational groups.

Reese (1962b, 1966) also found that children, in Grades 5 through 8, give higher sociometric ratings to members of their own sex, but boys give higher ratings to girls than girls give to boys. Since Reese used a rating scale, rather than direct observation of interactions, his findings are probably best interpreted as reflecting *attitudes* rather than actual choices. If so, the greater rejection of the opposite sex by girls than by boys could result from hostility in the girls arising from a recognition of the greater prestige of the male role. However, acceptance by the same sex was positively correlated with acceptance by the opposite sex, indicating that the variables determining popularity are, to some extent at least, not sex linked and can attenuate the effects of hostility.

Where parental warmth is lacking, the peer group may provide the comfort giving that all children seem to seek. This may be particularly important in the lower lower social classes. Hoffman and Saltzstein (1967), for example, found considerable moral-conscience modeling by middle class children on their parents, but almost none by lower class children. While Hoffman and Saltzstein did not report on peer modeling, it is plausible to suggest that the peer group has provided the models for the lower class children studied.

Charlesworth and Hartup (1967) documented the comfort giving process among nursery school children in an elaborate observational study of children functioning in groups. They reported that children in older groups, between four and five years of age, reinforce their peers more often than those in three year old groups, and younger boys give more reinforcements than younger girls. When reinforcement was defined as giving positive attention and approval, affection and personal acceptance, submitting, imitating, sharing, accepting another's idea or help, or giving "gifts," the average four year old boy gave 23 reinforcements during 12 three minute periods during which he was observed, the average four year old girl 21, the average three year old boy 18, and the average three year old girl 10 (three year olds' figures are extrapolated to match the longer observation of the older groups). Interestingly, boys gave more submissive reinforcements than girls. However, the investigators' definition of submissive behavior was "passive acceptance, imitation, sharing, accepting another's idea or help, allowing another child to play, compromise, following an order or request with pleasure and cooperation" (Charlesworth and Hartup, 1967, p. 995). These are behaviors that take place in on-going activities where the activity rather than the social relation is the important thing, and where the boy's great task mindedness, compared with the girl's, is likely to lead him into so-called submissive behavior so that "he can get on with the job." Instead of "submission," one might prefer a term such as "instrumental positive reinforcement," which implies that the child is agreeable in order that the task may be continued. McCandless, Bilous, and Bennett (1961) have demonstrated that boys are likely to make more such instrumental socialization responses (or to have greater "instrumental dependency," to use their term) than girls.

As might be expected, older children reinforced a significantly greater number of other children than did younger children. About half of the reinforcements given were spontaneous, the other half in response to an overture from another child. Dramatic play provided the setting for the most frequent social reinforcement. This constitutes an argument (with which few would disagree) for free play as a valuable training setting for peer socialization.

These studies provide the merest sample of studies of the influence of the peer group, and its style of influence. The effective style seems to be one where the amount of positive reinforcement rather than the amount of negative reinforcement is the important thing. This fits well with the discussions earlier in this chapter about reinforcement ratio and comfort giving. However, Hartup *et al.* (1967) reported that a child's popularity is related to the amount of positive reinforcement but *not* the amount of negative reinforcement he gives to his peers, although active rejection of a child by his peers is related to the amount of negative reinforcement and *not* the amount of positive reinforcement he provides for his peers. Nor was there a significant correlation between a child's tendency to give positive and negative reinforcement. It might be predicted that socially very active children would give more of both types of reinforcement. In the four year old groups that provided the data for this study, there was an average of 60.4 positive reinforcements during the 30 minutes each child was observed, and only 8.0 negative reinforcements administered to peers during the same observational period, but the investigators did not report actual ratio data for administering or receiving positive and negative reinforcement for highly accepted and rejected children. Thus, it cannot be said that their study fits precisely with the reinforcement ratio hypothesis advanced in the present chapter, nor can it be said that it contradicts it.

Campbell (1964) provided an excellent summary of the literature on peer influences. The contemporary literature deliberately selected for this section of the present chapter offers conclusions in no important way different from those emerging in Campbell's treatment of the topic, based principally on research dated 1962 and earlier.

Roles of Social Institutions

Solid research information about the effects of such institutions as the school, the church, boys' and girls' groups (such as Scouts), and the mass media is startlingly scarce, especially when the amount of social action and investment, not to include fulmination and pronouncements, is considered.

THE INFLUENCE OF THE SCHOOL, THE CHURCH, AND FORMAL CHILDREN'S GROUPS. The school, the church, and formal children's groups are superficially very different types of social institutions but are grouped together because, upon analysis of the dynamics of their operation, they are more similar than different. They represent the core culture, and are organized according to middle class values. These values run the gamut from some of the more intolerable priggishness, materialism, and rigidity of the *petite bourgeoisie* (the lower middle class) to values that stress such socially useful, even necessary, concepts as need for achievement, impulse control, and willingness to delay gratification. These latter, it is obvious, are central to the concept of moral-conscience development as it has been defined in this chapter.

A child's socialization is materially shaped by institutions in which he spends a considerable amount of his time. Thus, it would be expected that of the three types of institution included in this section, the school will be most influential, the church next, and formal children's groups third.

The social psychology of the classroom is a relatively new area for study. Kounin has been one of the pioneers in this field (e.g., Kounin, Gump, and Ryan, 1961). The area of study is so new that few firm conclusions are available, even in the area of academic achievement, which is by definition the first and most imperative task of the school. If, as many believe, competence is requisite for good socialization in American culture, if adequate academic achievement represents competence to a child, and if schools succeed in developing academic competence in all their pupils, the schools might be the *major* socialization influence for children. However, academic achievement is only one type of competence. It is differentially variable by social class (less the lower the social class), by age (less for younger children), and sex (more for younger girls and older boys—with obvious exceptions—and less for older girls and younger boys). The failure of the schools in the rural areas and inner city ghettos is so glaring and so widely publicized as to require little further discussion here [see, e.g., the so-called Coleman Report, *Equality of Educational Opportunity* (Coleman and committee, 1966); or almost any current issue of either the popular or the "highbrow" magazines; or your daily newspaper].

As far as competence is concerned, then, schools typically deal with only one important but circumscribed aspect, and rather inefficiently with that aspect for a large proportion of the students enrolled. Lower lower class children, who make up between a fifth and a third of the typical school population, suffer particularly.

Glidewell, Kantor, Smith, and Stronger (1966) have reviewed the literature on social structure in the classroom and its influence on socialization. Diffused social structures apparently spread social acceptance around better than extremely centralized structures. Research supports the conclusion that a democratic organization with clear structure promotes more constructive socialization than repressive and authoritarian organizations, whether these be in the classroom or the family. The fact that socialization is more constructively shaped in free than in tightly organized activity has already been pointed out in an earlier section. Teachers who are aware of individual differences, who convey a sense of accountability to their pupils, who are able to hold their instructional goals in mind, who leave the child free to pursue a clearly defined task, who pace their activities variably, and who are generally well organized produce more attentive work (and thus presumably greater competence) in their classes than teachers with opposite management techniques (Kounin, unpublished work; McCandless, unpublished work).

The Coleman Report startled its readers by a conclusion, perhaps unfairly oversimplified here, that schools contribute relatively little to the academic and social development of their pupils. The overwhelming influence, it was concluded, is exerted by the families and the communities from which the children come. Later critical logical and statistical analyses of the Coleman et al. data show that the conclusions were in part due to the methods by which the data were gathered, and in part to the statistical analyses used. The fact that the nature of its clientele dictates the nature of a school was partially overlooked in the Coleman Report. In no way do the Coleman et al. data answer the question of what would happen, for example, to inner city slum children if their schools were organized according to the rigorous standards demanded by the upper middle class suburbs, and if an influential infusion of high achieving, conventionally socialized upper middle class students (and teachers) were integrated functionally into slum schools. It is true that bussing inner city children to the suburbs has had little effect on the academic achievement of the children so bussed, on the children in the schools they entered, or on the children in the schools they left. It is probable that the children who were bussed out of the inner city were those who were already relatively high achievers. Going into high achievement situations, they effected little change in the behavior of the children and teachers already there. Their going removed some portion of the "model of excellence" they provided for their old classmates so that, if anything, their absence reduced the achievement level of the students remaining in the slum classes. In this context, it is well to think back to the discussion of modeling and power presented earlier in this chapter. Certainly, good academic models may upgrade the academic achievement of a class and probably the teaching effectiveness of the teachers.

The differential effects of schools by sex and social class deserve special attention here, and substantial data exist to buttress the arguments that will be advanced. Since schools (and churches and formal groups for children) represent "The Establishment," it may be predicted that they deal less equitably, more abrasively, and less effectively with boys than girls, and with lower than middle class children. The Establishment, as already noted, fosters nurturance, responsibility, and obedience for girls but encourages, at least as an end result, achievement and self-reliance for boys. That it is successful in this is clearly suggested by such data as Douvan and Adelson's (1966).

At least through elementary school, schools are feminine organizations. The aggressive little boy, the innovative (and thus probably not very obedient) child, and the ruggedly self-reliant child are out of place in a nurturant setting that stresses responsibility and obedience, often at the cost of individualized achievement and autonomy. Schools are also remarkably authoritarian, and it has been demonstrated that lower class children identify poorly, at best, with adult authority figures. Sgan (1967), for example, found this particularly true for her lower class first grade boys. Thus, it may be predicted that boys will have more difficulty in school than girls, and that lower class children will experience more trouble than middle class children. Data abound to support these predictions. More boys than girls drop out of school and do it earlier. Lower class children achieve more dramatically below their potential than middle class children. Boys are the trouble makers, the discipline problems, the stutterers, and the nonreaders much more frequently than girls. Teachers' grades predict girls' actual achievement on standardized tests more accurately than boys'—and so on and on.

Concerning churches and formal children's organizations, little can be added to what has been said above. Hodges, McCandless, and Spicker (1967), studying hard core Appalachian poor in the Bible Belt of central and southern Indiana—where it is axiomatic that every family belongs to and attends a church—found that only about 50 percent of the mothers and 25 percent of the fathers of the children with whom they were working even belonged to a church, let alone attended it. This is simply one segment of data to illustrate the well-documented point that the churches do not reach the lower lower class poor. If the churches do not reach them, obviously they have little influence on them. Once in a church, boys are less likely than girls to find the atmosphere congenial. The reasons for this state of affairs are identical to those already advanced for the American school.

Church youth groups, however, give certain children a feeling of being needed and welcomed that is not provided for them by their schools, particularly when the schools are very large and there is little opportunity for all children to participate in activities. The difficulties faced in a large school system by marginal children are well illustrated by a research study conducted by Willems (1967). He selected two groups of eleventh grade boys and girls whose characteristics were such that they were predicted to be high school dropouts; their IQs were below 99, they had received two grades of D or lower the previous semester, their fathers had not finished tenth grade and were in a nonprofessional or nonmanagerial occupation, and their mothers had not finished twelfth grade. The two large schools he studied included 702 and 794 juniors; the average of his several small high schools included only about 25 juniors. There were almost 10 times as many available students per activity in the large schools as in the small schools. Willems predicted that less urgency for activity participation, including attendance, would be conveyed to the marginal student in the large school than in the small school, because more students per activity were available. His prediction was strongly supported: The small school attenders reported significantly more sense of obligation (thus, perhaps, of belongingness) to the school's activities than did students in the large schools. In the small schools, the borderline subjects of the study felt as much of a sense of obligation to support school activities as the regular students, "while marginal students in large schools reported little, if any" (Willems, 1967, p. 1247).

The factor of alienation implicitly present for the marginal students in these large schools must necessarily be a strong deterrent to taking advantage of the socialization opportunities provided by the school. It is as a remedy for such alienation that church youth groups seem to serve many boys and girls.

Leaders for formal children's and youth groups (such as Scouts) are rare in isolated rural areas and urban ghettos. The activities of the group are often alien to the surroundings of children living isolatedly or in a ghetto. In the latter, the jugular blood of the street is likely to offer more drama and validity than the program of the youth group. Finally, the youth group almost always demands dues and, typically, uniforms. Ghetto and poor country children cannot afford such luxuries. In sum, the advantages of youth groups for children are neither more nor less than the advantages of belonging to an advantaged social class.

THE INFLUENCE OF THE MASS MEDIA. The picture for the mass media is equally depressing. Evidence exists that children will model on depictions of violence (see Maccoby, 1964b, for a review of the rather sparse literature). Television is full of violence. Television also forcefully reminds the poor that they do not have the things the middle class has. This, logically, adds to their frustration and bitterness. The level of intellectual challenge of television is immediately apparent to the most casual viewer. About the only thing that can be said about the mass media, as now employed, is that they seem to harm only a small proportion of those exposed to them, and this proportion was already vulnerable before its exposure to mass media (Bailyn, 1959).

Maccoby summarized the situation: "The findings . . . have been predominantly negative in their implications concerning mass media effects" (Maccoby, 1964b, p. 345). It is also significant that she was able to report only 29 references for her comprehensive review of the subject, of which 4 were her own and several others were general discussions rather than research papers.

SUMMARY

While socialization is at best an unsatisfactory scientific term, attempts to define it must be made and, if science is to serve society, determinants of ade-

quate (socially useful) and inadequate (personally and socially harmful) socialization must be investigated by research workers.

A child is usually considered to be "well-adjusted" socially if he is at least
moderately well accepted by his immediate reference group. Sociometric techniques, while they are unfair to some children, have proved to be a useful
tool in defining socialization. It is impossible to talk about socialization without
using value terms, being culturally relativistic, and taking into account a child's
social reference group, his age, his sex, his socioeconomic class and, in many
instances, his race.

While socialization is partially a function of learning opportunities, intraindividual characteristics such as intelligence, body build, age at which the child
matures sexually (particularly for boys), activity level, propensity for bodily
contact in infancy, and probably sensitivity to stimulation exert profound but
as yet insufficiently studied influences on socialization.

United States culture places great stress on sex differences. It emphasizes
nurturance, responsibility, and obedience for girls; and achievement and self-
reliance for boys. Since such social institutions as schools, churches, and formal
youth groups reflect the middle class establishment, they interact more abrasively
with boys and lower class children than with girls and middle class children.

Stage theories of socialization often obscure the study of social development,
if uncritically accepted. They may be helpful, however, in describing and classifying behavior. "Transition" behaviors are likely to be overlooked by stage
theorists.

Current research suggests that variables of power (possession of something
someone wants or fears, and communicated ability and willingness to share
it or dispense it), and the styles in which power is administered are central
to modeling theory (a social learning theory). Modeling theory, in turn, is a
promising approach to understanding socialization. A convenient classification
of types of power includes *comfort giving*, *physical* power, *sexual* power, *expertness*, and *prestige*. A classification of styles of administering or dispensing power
includes *predictability, equitability, perceived similarities, communication that
power is possessed, willingness to share power, ability to inflict punishment,*
and *ratio of reward to punishment*.

It may be that there is no clear logical reason to make a distinction between
modeling (or generalized imitation) and *identification*, but making such a distinction is conventional. Modeling is imitation; identification is an inferred construct that applies either to sex role identification or moral-conscience development. Like the IQ, it is pervasive and relatively little influenced by any but
the most major environmental changes. Measures of "guilt" seem to provide
the best inference for moral-conscience identification. Sex role identification remains a concept with great "face validity," but the most accurate approach
to its measurement at present is extensive and intensive individual study of
a child or adult. However, although existing tests of masculinity and femininity
must be used with caution, they are, at the very least, useful research tools
for studying this socially crucial area of socialization. Since society lays down
strong sanctions against inappropriate sex role identification, it is probable that

the inappropriately sex identified boy or girl, placed in great conflict as he is, experiences more difficulty in achieving acceptable moral-conscience development than his appropriately sex role identified peer.

While the evidence is by no means conclusive, power dimensions of dominance and comfort giving seem to be the most crucial determiners of sex role identification. The evidence is rather clear that in order for boys to be adequately sex typed, they should have a dominant but nurturant father. The male sex role seems to be clearer and more desirable in our society, and greater pressure to achieve appropriate sex typing and identification is exerted on boys than girls. Recent evidence suggests that fathers are as important in social development for girls as for boys. Dominance and comfort giving need not be linked to the same-sex parent for adequate moral-conscience development, as they are for appropriate sex role identification. However, greater problems undoubtedly exist for the inappropriately sex role identified child in establishing a viable moral-conscience identification.

The characteristics of need for achievement, impulse control, and delay of gratification are greatly esteemed by the core (middle class) United States culture. They also form the foundation of moral-conscience identification, and their determinants seem, as far as evidence is available, to be similar to the determinants of the latter (power and the styles of its administration).

As children grow older, the peer group seems steadily to approach the parents in degree of influence in shaping socialization, although the peer group effects may not be as profound (i.e., they may not shape personality and basic life style). A child chooses as his best friends other children who rather resemble the child's own parents, but who typically are seen as somewhat more extreme in their values than the child's parents. Prevailing evidence suggests that the generation gap is not a major social problem, primarily because of the child's tendency to choose friends who are like his parents, although more liberal (or extreme in the other direction, as far as is known). Children's popularity is closely related to the degree to which they positively reinforce other children; and the degree to which they negatively reinforce other children relates closely to their being rejected by the group. There is little relation between a child's giving positive and negative reinforcements to his peers.

Evidence about the effects of mass media on children's socialization is scanty. What there is suggests that the cumulative effect ranges from neutral to negative.

CHAPTER 18

Biogenetic Factors in Development

INTRODUCTION

Study of the brain is one of the basic experimental approaches to the analysis of psychological function. Sensation and perception are based on specialized receptors and their connections with the brain. Movement and posture are mediated by nerve cells in the brain and spinal cord which receive sensory inputs and control the ordered contraction of muscles. Indeed, motives and feelings, as well as the ability to learn and remember, are ultimately based on the functioning of the brain. In some cases the causes of mental impairment can be traced to brain dysfunction either genetically determined or acquired after birth.

In this chapter some biological principles that are important for developmental psychology will be introduced. It will be seen that the immaturity of the brain at birth may have important consequences for development. Because of limitations in space, these subjects must be presented cursorily. The reader is referred to other texts for more detailed accounts of the physiology and anatomy of the nervous system (e.g., Crosby, Humphrey, and Lauer, 1962; Ruch and Patton, 1965; Stevens, 1966). Some of the major organic determinants of mental impairment will also be reviewed, and it will be shown that in some cases even a genetically based dysfunction is reversible if treatment is instituted early enough.

It must be made clear at the outset that understanding of the functioning of the nervous system is far from complete. Although a great deal is known about the physical basis of nerve conduction and the organization of a few simple reflex pathways, relatively little is known about more complex processes. For example, while some of the mechanisms involved in the regulation of posture are rather well understood, there is as yet no adequate account of how the brain learns and remembers. While some knowledge of the location of brain structures associated with biological drives has been acquired, many details of interconnections and functioning of these structures are poorly understood. While something of the biochemical disorders that may impair intelligence is understood, nothing is known about how normal variations in intelligence might be related to brain structure.

In this chapter, techniques for the anatomical study of the nervous system will be described and the appearance of representative structures illustrated. Then the ionic basis of nerve activity will be discussed and an example given of how nerve cells are interconnected in a simple reflex pathway. These concepts of structure and function will then be related to certain aspects of neurological development. Evidence will be presented to show that the human nervous system is structurally incomplete at birth, and that the lack of completeness may impose some limitations on the sensory and behavioral capacities of the very young.

In addition to their applicability to normal function, the concepts of brain anatomy and physiology are often useful for the understanding of developmental defects that are associated with the nervous system. Such defects may be determined by genetic or prenatal factors or may be caused at birth or in early infancy. The nature of biologically based impairment, both directly structural as well as metabolic and biochemical, will be discussed.

The study of young organisms has also revealed a paradox that bears on the general problem of interpreting the effects of lesions of the brain. Specifically, there is a rather surprising degree of plasticity of brain function in young mammals. Brain lesions appear to cause relatively less permanent impairment when they are sustained in early life than when they occur during the adult period. The evidence for this conclusion will be considered in the last section of this chapter.

STRUCTURE AND FUNCTION OF THE NERVOUS SYSTEM

Anatomical Structure

The nervous system in mammals includes the brain and spinal cord as well as the nerves that emerge from these structures to connect with sense organs, muscles, and glands. The microscopic structure of the brain and spinal cord is described in terms of the types of cells of which they are composed. The basic unit of the nervous system is a highly specialized type of cell called the nerve cell, or neuron. The central nervous system also has a particularly rich blood supply, and a great number of cells, called glia, which support and help nourish the neurons.

Nerve cells vary enormously in their shape and function. There are, however, certain common elements that permit description of a typical neuron. In addition to a cell body, or soma, which may be spherical, pyramidal, or spindle shaped, the neuron has long fiberlike extensions emerging from the cell body. Typically, there is a single long fiber, called the axon, which transmits information away from the neuron. Axons are often specialized for conducting information over long distances, and may reach a length of several feet. While the typical nerve cell has only a single axon arising from the cell body, it usually has many dendrites, which are specialized fibers for receiving information. Dendrites and their many branches typically do not extend far from the cell body.

In preparing brain tissue for detailed study of its structure, the brain is first immersed in a fluid which preserves and hardens it, after which it is embedded in a relatively firm substance or is frozen. The hardening and embedding processes permit very thin slices to be made by a specially constructed knife. The thin sections so obtained are then stained to bring out some desired structural detail for study. In some special procedures the tissue may have been stained before being cut. The stained tissue is mounted on a glass slide and covered with a thin glass cover slip.

Much of what is seen in a slide will be determined by the type of stain used. For example, one might choose to stain only myelin—a fatlike coating that surrounds many of the axons in the nervous system. With myelin stains, however, the nerve cells themselves would be seen only poorly. Other techniques selectively stain the cell bodies of neurons and the nuclei of glial cells. Certain methods developed in the last century by Camillo Golgi permit entire nerve cells, with all of their processes, to be stained. Because of the remarkable, but fortunate, fact that only a small percentage of neurons take up the stain, the Golgi technique is especially valuable. Since only a small percentage are stained, one can see the true shape of an individual neuron without its being hidden by its neighbors. When brain tissue is stained with the Golgi technique, a beautiful and detailed picture of the structure of many individual nerve cells can be seen. One such Golgi-stained preparation from the brain of a cat is shown in Figure 18-1. The figure shows typical cells from the cerebral cortex, the great mass of neurons that forms most of the outermost covering of the mammalian brain. Note that most of the neurons stained have a roughly pyramidal shape. A single long dendritic process, the apical dendrite, emerges from the top of each pyramidal cell and extends toward the surface of the brain, branching in its course. Another class of dendrites, the so-called basal dendrites, emerge from the base of the cell bodies and extend in a plane roughly parallel to the surface of the brain. The axons of pyramidal cells usually emerge from the bottom of each cell as a single thin strand travelling in a direction away from the cortical surface. When Golgi-stained cells are studied with high magnification the dendrites are seen to be profusely covered with tiny spine-like processes. Electron microscopic study of dendritic spines suggests that they are sites of contact between the dendrite and incoming axons.

In contrast to spine-covered dendrites, axons are smooth. Some extend only a very short distance before terminating on nearby neurons, while others travel great distances to connect with other neurons or with the muscles, glands, or sense organs.

The long fibers connecting sensory receptors in the skin and deeper structures to the central nervous system may actually be classed as dendrites since they conduct activity toward the neuron. Such long dendrites are also specialized for conduction over long distances; hence the distinction between axons and dendrites breaks down in this case. As a convention such fibers will be referred to as sensory axons.

The functioning of the nervous system is based on connection of neurons to sensory structures, muscles, and glands as well as interconnections among the nerves themselves. A connection between two neurons is called a synapse. Synapses usually involve an axon of one neuron terminating on the cell body or dendrite of another neuron, although there are also instances of connections between axons (axo-axonal connections).

When nerve cells are packed together in great numbers the tissue has a charac-

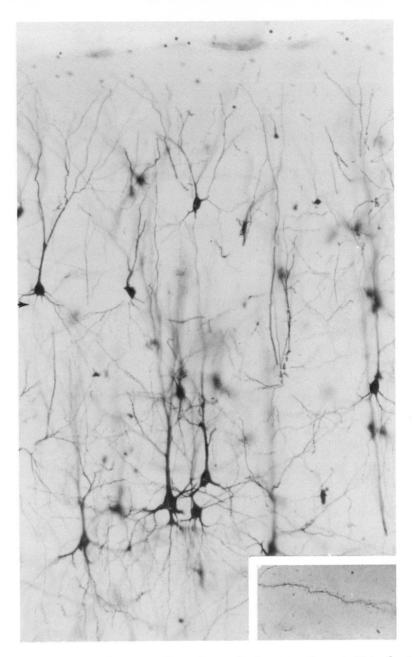

Fig. 18-1.   Golgi-stained neurons from the cerebral cortex of a cat. Note the typical pyramidal-shaped cell body with apical and basal dendrites (see text). Although in this variant of the Golgi stain axons are usually poorly impregnated, the arrow at left points to an axon which has been stained. The insert is a higher magnification view of a single dendritic shaft, to show the dense dendritic spines.

teristic gray color. It is the unstained appearance of brain tissue which gives us the expression "gray matter." In addition to predominantly gray regions, large portions of the brain and spinal cord have a glistening white appearance. White matter of the brain and spinal cord is an area containing mostly axons, the white appearance deriving from the many small cylinders of myelin, each of which surrounds an individual axon. Axons may be coated with myelin whether they are found in the white matter of the central nervous system, or in the sensory and motor nerves that travel out to the skin, muscles, and glands.

Simple staining procedures can reveal the distribution of myelin in the nervous system. With appropriate sections viewed at high magnification, myelin is seen

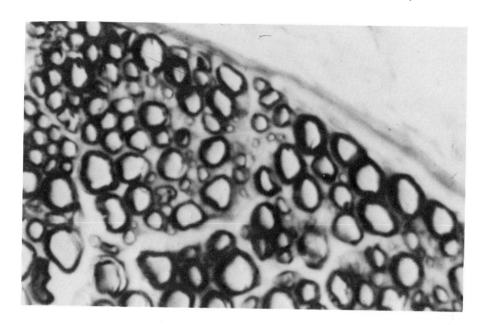

Fig. 18-2. Cat peripheral nerve: osmic acid stain. Note dark-staining rings of myelin surrounding an unstained axon. Note also great variability in size typical of peripheral nerves.

as dark-staining rings surrounding individual axons. Figure 18-2 shows the myelin coatings of axons in a peripheral nerve from a section cut at right angles to the nerve and stained with osmic acid.

At lower magnification the individual myelin sheaths would not be seen. Rather, regions of the brain containing great amounts of myelin, such as subcortical white matter, would stain uniformly dark.

Ionic Basis of Nerve Conduction

It has been known for hundreds of years that the action of nerves is in some way electrical, but details of nerve function have become clear only in recent years. If a small electrode is inserted inside a nerve cell at rest, a negative potential can be recorded across the cell membrane, with the inside of the cell electrically negative. The resting negative potential is due to a relatively greater concentration of sodium ions, which are positively charged, outside the nerve cell membrane. Two mechanisms are important for maintaining the inequality in distribution of sodium ions and the consequent resting potential: (a) the membrane is relatively impermeable to sodium ions in the resting state, and (b) the sodium ions that do diffuse across the membrane into the cell are being constantly pumped out. At rest sodium ions leak in at a low rate matched by outward pumping across the membrane.

Excitation of the cell is accomplished by changing the permeability of the cell to sodium ions. As a result of increased permeability, sodium ions enter the cell and hence the potential across the membrane is lowered.

When excited, the cell body of a neuron and its dendrites respond with relatively small graded changes of voltage. Axons, in contrast, are also capable of a larger, self-propagating voltage change. When the resting potential across the axon membrane is reduced below a critical threshold voltage, the axon membrane is activated and fires a "spike" in which a sequence of changes in membrane permeability permits a large number of sodium ions to flow across the membrane, followed after a slight delay by a comparable outflow of potassium ions, which are also positively charged. The spike discharge starts at the point of origin of the axon and is carried along the axon all the way to its end. Conduction along an axon resembles conduction of heat in a firecracker fuse; the heat applied at the end is not instantaneously conducted to the firecracker. Rather, the fire at one end burns the next patch of fuse which in turn ignites the next, until the firecracker is reached. The change in potential across the axon's membrane associated with the spike discharge triggers the next patch of membrane to respond, and in this way the spike potential is propagated to the very end of the axon. In sharp contrast to electrical transmission through wires, the ionic nature of axonal conduction is associated with relatively slow conduction speeds of from 1 to 100 meters per second. In more familiar terms, the fastest that a nerve can transmit impulses is around 250 miles an hour.

Actually, nerve conduction would be slower if it were not for the action of the myelin coating around nerve fibers. Myelin functions primarily as an insulator. However, within each millimeter or so there is an interruption of the myelin sheath known as the node of Ranvier. Physiologists believe that the presence of myelin and its periodic nodes provide a means for increasing the speed of the nerve impulse. The spike discharge does not have to pass through each point in the axon membrane but can leap from node to node. Since myelin has a role in regulating the velocity of propagation of the spike potential along an axon, it will determine the time at which the spike reaches a synapse. In the discussion of reflex functioning it will be seen that the timing of inputs is inportant for normal functioning of the synapse. Indirect evidence that such precise timing is absent in most synapses of the newborn infant will be presented. The consequences of lack of myelinization can be readily seen in premature infants, in whom not only the central nervous system but peripheral nerves as well are incompletely myelinated. As a consequence, premature infants show a slower rate of nerve conduction and smaller reflex response to muscle-stretch than do full term infants (Schülte, Michaelis, Linke, and Nolte, 1968).

Information transfer from place to place in the nervous system is accomplished by the firing of impulses along axons. Because spike discharges in a given axon do not vary in size, *details* of the information are signaled by two variables: which axon responded and how frequently it responded.

Nerve Function in a Simple Reflex Pathway

One way to get an idea about functional connections between neurons is to consider how the nervous system is organized to control a simple form of behavior like the reflex. In reflexes a definite stimulus tends to evoke the same response repeatedly. Reflexes do not require learning and are relatively less affected by the state of the organism than spontaneous behavior is. Physiological analysis has revealed the structural basis for a number of reflexes, in turn providing indirect evidence about functions of the nervous system in general. Simple reflexes can provide an example of the way in which a behavioral observation can be analyzed and understood in physiological terms.

One of the most familiar and clinically important reflexes is the knee-jerk. When the knee is tapped just below the knee cap, the leg swings upward. Because of the simplicity of its structural organization, the knee-jerk can serve as a model for the analysis of reflex mechanisms in general.

The first step toward such an analysis would be to translate the behavioral observation into anatomical and physiological terms. The first questions to be asked are, What anatomical structures are activated by the tap on the knee, and how are the muscles reflexively activated? The tap on the knee vigorously stretches a tendon (the patellar tendon), which in turn stretches a muscle group located on the front surface of the thigh. Extension of the knee is brought about by active contraction of that muscle group. To restate the observation, stretching of a muscle group leads to contraction of that same muscle group.

The next problem is to establish that the observed effect is indeed a reflex— that it is mediated by the nervous system, rather than mediated locally by the muscle itself. The reflex nature of contraction to stretch is demonstrated by the fact that if the sensory or motor nerves to the stretched muscle are cut the reflex is abolished.

In pursuing the analysis, the next questions are, What sensory mechanisms are activated by the muscle stretch, and where are these receptors located? In parallel with the cells which are responsible for actual contraction of muscle, there are modified muscle cells to which are connected endings of relatively thick sensory axons. These endings are especially sensitive to the stretch of muscles. A pull on the muscle causes the sensory endings to initiate a train of spikes in the sensory axons, the rate of spike firing being determined by the degree of stretch placed upon the muscle. The cell bodies of these sensory fibers are located near the spinal cord, and their axons continue past the cell body to enter the cord. When the muscle receptor endings are activated, the stretch is coded by spike firing and is conducted all the way to the spinal cord where some of the axons end directly on motor nerve cells.

As noted earlier, functional connections between the axon of one neuron and the dendrite or cell body of another neuron are called synapses. Each incoming sensory axon synapses on many motor neurons, and each motor neuron receives synaptic inputs from many incoming sensory fibers. Despite convergence and divergence, however, the stretch reflex involves only a single interposed synapse between the sensory and motor neuron and, hence, is an example of a mono-synaptic reflex. When the motor neuron is activated, spike discharges are carried down the motor axons to end on muscle cells, causing the muscle to contract.

The stretch reflex acts to shorten a muscle after it has been stretched. In normal functioning, stretch is seldom applied abruptly as when a tendon is tapped. Rather, during standing, there is a continuous stretch on extensor muscles and these graded stretches are continuously being compensated by reflex shortening of the muscles. The stretch reflex works toward maintaining the muscle at a relatively constant length and is an important component of the ability to remain upright.

Nerve cells are seldom activated by the isolated synaptic input from a single incoming axon. In the stretch reflex, for example, each sensory spike which arrives at the synapse causes a small depolarization in the motor neuron, but a motor neuron must receive more than one impulse before its axon will fire. There are two ways in which neurons combine the effects of incoming impulses: spatial and temporal summation. If several incoming axons which synapse on the same motor neuron are activated simultaneously, the excitatory effects might summate spatially to activate the motor neuron. Alternatively, if an incoming axon were to fire repetitively, the successive incoming spikes might add to the effective excitatory input to the motor neuron. This latter mechanism is termed temporal summation.

Summation is an extremely important principle in synaptic activation; but for summation to work, incoming impulses must be rather close together in time. As pointed out above, myelin acts to regulate the rate of propagation of impulses along axons within the nervous system. If synaptic activation were dependent upon precise timing of incoming nerve impulses, the absence of myelin from axons might be expected to have important functional consequences.

The Infant Nervous System

One of the most striking characteristics of the infant nervous system is the relative absence of myelin. Indeed, the characteristic color, "white matter," is almost entirely lacking in the brain of the newborn. Figure 18-3 shows sections through the brains of rhesus monkeys; the upper figure is from the brain of a neonate, the lower figure is from a nearby area in a mature brain. Note the rich dark-staining myelin in subcortical white matter and fiber tracts of the adult, and the poorly myelinated brain of the neonate. The same general pattern of myelinization is seen in the developing human brain. Myelinization

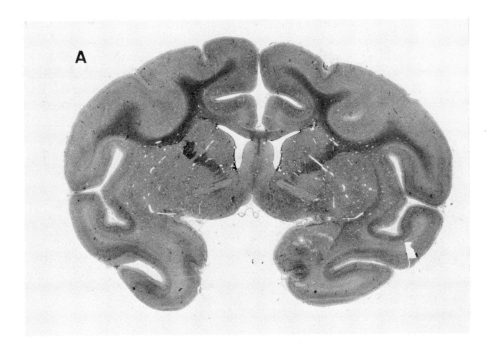

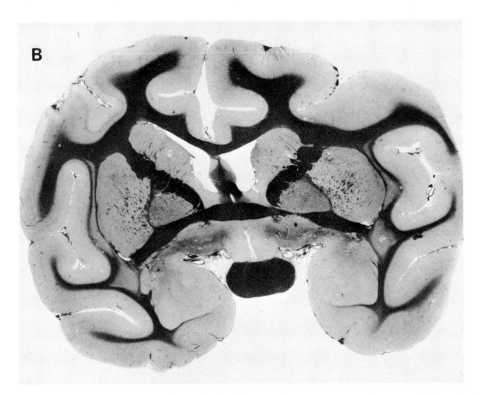

Fig. 18-3.   Cross sections through the brains of macaque monkeys, myelin-stained.
A. Brain of a newborn. Note the relative uniformity in the staining due to absence of
myelin. B. Slightly more caudal section through the brain of an adult macaque. Note
rich dark-staining subcortical white matter and fiber tracts. (Photograph courtesy of
Dr. Paul Yakovlev, Department of Neurology and Warren Anatomical Museum, Harvard Medical School.)

takes place slowly after birth and is not fully completed until the human infant is over one year old (Dekaban, 1959). The question might then be raised as to how much of the behavior of an infant is limited by the relative immaturity of his nervous system. Traditionally, many workers have assumed that absence of myelin is a sign of complete inability of a portion of the nervous system to function. While learning is possible in the neonate (see Chapters 3 to 5) the scientific problem remains as to the functional limitations which are imposed on newborns by the relative absence of myelin. To what extent are perceptual, cognitive, and motor skills dependent on the maturation of the brain? Answers to such questions will be forthcoming only when the full behavioral repertoire of the infant is known through systematic studies of sensory and learning processes.

The consequences of the absence of myelin are not always clearly understood. One might gain some insight into the role of myelin in normal function by observing developmental changes in reflex function and attempting to relate those changes to the myelinization of specific pathways in the brain. There are some hazards to this procedure, since the fact that two observations covary does not necessarily imply that one is caused by the other. If such correlations are considered along with other more direct evidence, however, the approach can be a fruitful one.

One reflex that has a clear-cut relation to a definite fiber pathway is the Babinski reflex (see below), the manifestations of which are closely tied to the presence or absence of the pyramidal tract.

The pyramidal tract is one of the major fiber tracts in the spinal cord of man and the other higher primates. Cell bodies giving rise to the pyramidal tract are in the cortex, and their axons descend through the brainstem to the spinal cord. In man some of these corticospinal fibers end directly on motor neurons. The so-called "pathological" Babinski reflex is a definite consequence of interruption of the pyramidal tract.

The Babinski reflex is elicited by stroking the sole of the foot. In the normal adult the toes may flex downward; but in patients with interruption of the pyramidal tract, and in monkeys and chimpanzees in which the pyramidal tract has been cut (Tower, 1949), the toes extend backwards.

Since the pyramidal tract is among the last of the nervous system pathways to become myelinated, the study of the maturation of the Babinski reflex might illustrate a possible role of myelin in the normal functioning of the pyramidal tract. When infants are tested in the first year of life, prior to complete development of myelin in the pyramidal tract, the Babinski reflex is predominantly extensor, similar to the response seen in patients with destruction of the pyramidal tract. Parallel with myelinization of the pyramidal tract, the Babinski reflex becomes flexor (Dekaban, 1959). Although the axons of the pyramidal tract are present in the neonate, they are unmyelinated (Dekaban, 1959). The presence of an abnormal Babinski reflex suggests that this tract functions poorly before its axons are myelinated. Tentatively this observation might be generalized as follows: Few fiber tracts in the brain of the newborn are myelinated, hence limitations of the infant's behavioral repertoire might exist until maturation is complete. However, a note of caution is necessary. The evidence for the role of the pyramidal tract in the Babinski reflex of infants is still circumstantial. An alternative explanation, for example, might be that the cells of origin of the pyramidal tract are not completely mature in the neonate or do not yet receive tonic synaptic input from other brain structures.

Parallel to the relative absence of myelin from the brain of the newborn child is the incomplete development of dendritic branching and fine dendritic spines on cortical nerve cells (Scheibel and Scheibel, 1964). The typical dendrites of cortical pyramidal cells in the neonate, for example, have few branches and few spines. Since dendrites are believed to be major sites of synaptic contact with cortical neurons, the lack of dendritic development might suggest that cortical cells would not begin to function normally until the dendrites were fully developed. Indirect physiological evidence lends support for the view that activity is not yet mature in the cortex of very young animals. For example, if one records the spontaneous electrical activity (electroencephalogram) from the time of birth to adulthood, one can see that the pattern of brain activity changes reliably and predictably with age (Dekaban, 1959; Ellingson, 1967). In the newborn the electroencephalogram may have a very low frequency or even be completely flat. There is a rather clear developmental sequence from a stage of relative absence of measurable electrical activity in the neonate through stages of increasing frequency of the dominant rhythm. Although they cannot be related directly to behavioral capacity, developmental changes in the electroencephalogram constitute indirect evidence for functional maturation, probably associated with the normal postnatal development of dendrites.

Many studies of nervous system structure and function can be carried out on animals. Anomalies occurring in the natural course of human development also provide the opportunity to determine relationships between structure and behavior. Very often, laboratory techniques permit the determination of the site of a brain injury or a metabolic impairment; such information can often be related to specific behavioral aberrations in children.

MENTAL IMPAIRMENT

Introduction

The term "mental impairment" is used here instead of "mental retardation." Over the years mental retardation has come to be rather rigidly defined by conventional intelligence tests and thus is not so useful for the purposes of this chapter. By mental impairment is meant any defect in intellectual function leading to impaired adaptive behavior during the developmental period (for reviews, see Carter, 1965; Masland, Sarason, and Gladwin, 1958; Stevens and Heber, 1964). Not all mental impairment is caused by biogenetic factors nor are these the only factors influencing the growth of normal, adaptive intellectual function. As should be evident from other sections of this book, many psychological, social, economic, and cultural factors, not germane to the considerations of this chapter, are also important. In general, such "environmental" determinants are contrasted with biogenetic factors, which are classified as "organic." The distinction between environmental and organic causes is not mutually exclusive, of course; in many individuals mental impairment is the result of a complex interaction of both. In addition, many children exhibit mental impairment without evident abnormality in either the environmental or the organic spheres, and these raise several problems. Methods for determining both organic and environmental abnormalities are still insensitive in many respects, and continuing advances are required to understand the underlying mechanism in all children with impaired intellectual function. With respect to adaptive function, moreover,

Table 18-1

Diagnoses in Patients Admitted to State Schools for the Mentally Retarded in New York in 1957[a]

Diagnosis	Percent of admissions
Familial mental retardation	23.4
Mongolism	10.1
Developmental defects of the brain	5.8
With cerebral palsy	4.3
With epilepsy	3.3
With endocrine disorders	0.6
Secondary to prenatal or postnatal infections	3.8
Secondary to cerebral trauma	10.2
With other organic nervous system disease	4.6
Without diagnosis	31.2
Not mentally defective	2.7

[a] Modified from Gruenberg (1964).

the definition of impairment is undergoing continual change in our rapidly advancing technological society.

Environmental factors predisposing to mental impairment are considered in Chapter 16. The present section reviews some of the better known or more exemplary types of biogenetically determined mental impairment to show the range of factors that may be important in the biological determination of intelligence. Such organic factors may be considered in two categories: genetically determined impairment and acquired impairment. The incidence of mental impairment is difficult to assess accurately for a number of reasons, some of which are evident from the preceding paragraphs. General figures from several sources indicate that about 1 to 4 percent of the population exhibits significant functional impairment. Most of this cannot be attributed to organic determinants and, even within the organically determined group, relative frequencies are uncertain. Entities such as mongolism (see below), however, are recognized with relative ease and the frequency with which mongolism occurs is known to be about .15 percent in the population. To appreciate the frequency with which other organic determinants result in severe mental impairment, one can compare their incidence in a system of state schools for the mentally retarded (see Table 18-1) with the incidence of mongols in the same system. Taken as individual causes of mental impairment, none of these has a truly "high" incidence, yet each is important to the affected person, his family, and society. A discussion of organic factors which cause mental impairment follows.

Genetically Determined Mental Impairment

The principal determinant of the normal development of intellectual function is the development of the central nervous system. Without this, no adaptive interaction with the environment is possible. Genetic defects in the central nervous system may appear as anatomical, or structural abnormalities; they may appear as derangements in metabolism or chemical composition of nerve cells without structural changes; or they may appear as metabolic abnormalities with subsequent secondary structural changes. The association of mental impairment with structural changes has been recognized for many years. In contrast, understanding of biochemical changes producing mental impairment is more recent. Knowledge has advanced rapidly in the last 30 years, paralleling the advance of modern biochemistry.

STRUCTURAL ABNORMALITIES. The central nervous system forms first as a long plate of cells. Subsequently, this plate becomes folded and the sides fuse to make a long tube (the neural tube). Although much distorted in development, this fundamental pattern can be perceived even in the adult brain. At the head of the individual, the multiplication and growth of cells in the neural tube is rapid and this part becomes the brain. In the human, growth is most rapid at the front of the brain and this part becomes the cerebral hemispheres. Each cerebral hemisphere has a greatly convoluted outer part, largely made up of nerve cells. This part is cerebral cortex, or gray matter. Inside it is the white matter, which contains axons of nerve cells going to and from the gray matter. Within the white matter is a cavity, the ventricle, which is a continuation of the cavity that was present in the neural tube. The ventricles contain the watery cerebrospinal fluid, which is continually being formed and removed from them.

Structural changes resulting from genetic developmental defects and producing mental impairment generally occur in the cerebral hemispheres (Norman, 1966). There are many kinds of defects in the formation of the hemispheres and many degrees of severity of defect. The most severe is absence of most or all of the cerebral hemispheres. With this defect there may be normal development of the bones of the skull so that the infant is not unusual in appearance at birth. Commonly the infant also behaves normally, even though he has no cerebral hemispheres, because most of the activities of the newborn infant are reflexive in nature and maintained by the spinal cord and brainstem. In only a short time, however, the infant's failure to develop becomes evident. Diagnosis of absence of the cerebral hemispheres can often be made simply by shining a bright light through the skull. Unlike the normal infant, whose cerebral hemispheres fill the skull and are opaque, the child with absence of the cerebral hemispheres has a skull filled largely with cerebrospinal fluid, and light transilluminates it, as it does one's tightly clenched fingers. These children rarely survive for long periods.

Less severe defects in development of the cerebral hemispheres are more common and are not infrequently the cause of mental impairment. Many deformed states of the cerebral hemispheres have been described, ranging in severity from a complete or partial absence of convolutions (lissencephaly, or smooth brain) to deformation of the convolutions in restricted areas. Sometimes there are many small, deformed convolutions in a particular region or over much of the cerebral hemisphere. In other instances the abnormal convolutions are much too large. Occasionally there is no gross defect in the convolutional pattern but abnormalities in the number and distribution of nerve cells in the cerebral cortex that can be seen only upon microscopic examination.

The function and structure of the cerebral hemispheres can also be altered by genetically determined anatomical defects in other parts of the central nervous system and its surrounding tissues. A common example is the enlargement of the cerebral ventricles (hydrocephalus) resulting from a block in the circulation of cerebrospinal fluid at some critical point. There is an increasing expansion of the ventricles with compression of the surrounding white and gray matter against the skull. If the condition is not treated, severe mental impairment occurs.

Despite the long interest in structural changes producing mental impairment, only rudimentary understanding of the mechanisms that underlie the structural anomalies and the ways they produce functional changes has been achieved. An example of a recent advance of this understanding can be drawn from mongolism, a well-known and frequent cause of mental impairment (Penrose, 1961). Recently, it has been found that individuals with mongolism have a chromosomal abnormality. Instead of the usual human complement of 46 chromosomes, most mongols have 47, with 3 rather than the usual pair of chromosome number 21. (In some mongols there is a slightly different abnormality.) The structural disorders in mongolism are numerous and involve many organs and tissues. Defects are often present in the brain, bones, teeth, thyroid gland, skeletal muscles, skin, eyes, gonads, and heart. When the chromosomal abnormality was discovered in 1959, many thought that it would not be a difficult step to elucidate the basic defect underlying the manifestations of mongolism. This has not proved so easy. The brain abnormality is of interest, however, because it represents a different kind of structural problem from those described previously. The severe mental impairment of mongolism is associated with a brain that appears immature at birth and is subsequently unable to make up for the retarded maturation occurring during fetal life. The detailed mechanisms that lead to structural abnormality are still a mystery, but the discovery of the chromosomal abnormality points the appropriate direction for further studies of the precise cause of mongolism.

BIOCHEMICAL ABNORMALITIES. In contrast to the structural abnormalities, the genetically determined biochemical abnormalities resulting in mental impairment are becoming increasingly well understood (see Stanbury, Wyngaarden, and Frederickson, 1966, for review). Biochemical defects are usually transmitted as recessive traits. The abnormality is expressed as the absence of a single critical enzyme in a metabolic pathway. The absence of the enzyme may have two effects: accumulation of large amounts of the chemical ordinarily metabolized by the enzyme, or deficiency of a critical product of the reaction normally catalyzed by the enzyme. In some instances both factors are important.

The consequences of such defects can be illustrated by using a simple analogy. The enzyme is like the gate of a dam on a river. If the gate works properly, the appropriate amount of water is let through and the regions below prosper. If the dam has no gate, or the gate is blocked, water accumulates above the dam and eventually fills the tributaries of the river, causing disastrous floods above the dam; at the same time, there is a drought below the dam. Treatment is carried out by bringing in a new source of water below the blocked dam or by bypassing the dam. The analogy is not entirely appropriate nor accurate, but perhaps it permits one to visualize the defects in these "inborn errors of metabolism."

Phenylketonuria (PKU) is the classical example of a genetically determined form of mental impairment resulting from the absence of a single enzyme and accumulation of the substrate for the enzyme. In this disease the missing enzyme is phenylalanine hydroxylase, which normally converts the essential amino acid phenylalanine to another amino acid, tyrosine (Mitoma, Auld, and Udenfriend, 1957).[1] The enzymatic defect in PKU results in high blood levels of phenylalanine and the metabolism of some of this by alternative pathways into toxic metabolites, phenylketones and phenyl acids. Although the precise mechanism is not well understood, phenylketones and phenyl acids appear to alter brain metabolism in an important way during its development. Early diagnosis and treatment is therefore necessary, and in many states it is now mandatory to test newborn infants for PKU in order to ensure that the diagnosis will be made and dietary management (restriction of phenylalanine) can be instituted before irreparable damage is done. An experimental model of PKU has recently been found in rats, permitting further laboratory study of many aspects of this disease.

There are numerous examples of genetically determined enzyme defects resulting in a deficiency state and consequent mental impairment. A few examples will give some view of the spectrum of these diseases. The typical example is cretinism. Absence of the thyroid hormone in adult life leads to a number of symptoms, but not mental impairment (mental processes are slow but within normal limits). Lack of thyroid hormone in infancy, however, leads to severe and permanent mental impairment if it is not replaced in the first few months

---

[1] In passing it might be mentioned that defects of this kind do not always lead to mental impairment. Tyrosine, for example, is a critical component of the pigment, melanin, which is found in the skin of all pigmented individuals. In albinos the enzyme that converts tyrosine to melanin is absent, but the albino is not necessarily mentally impaired.

of life. The lack of thyroid hormone production may be due to the absence of single enzymes. It has been shown in the last few years that there are several types of cretinism, each due to the absence of a different single enzyme in the metabolic pathway for the production of thyroid hormone (Stanbury, 1966). The effect of each is to prevent normal development of the brain because of a failure of its stimulation by thyroid hormone (Gelber, Campbell, Deibler, and Sokoloff, 1964).

Another defect of this type occurs in the metabolism of a sugar found in milk, galactose. The symptoms begin as soon as the child is fed milk. Here the genetic defect is the absence of the enzyme, galactose 1-phosphate uridyl transferase, which participates in the conversion of galactose to glucose (Isselbacher, Anderson, Kurahashi, and Kalckar, 1956). Glucose is the only carbohydrate that the brain can use for production of energy. The absence of glucose results in seizures and mental impairment. In addition to being converted to glucose, galactose is an essential component of certain complex compounds, cerebrosides, which form part of the structure of membranes in brain and other tissues.

Another example is a type of gout occurring in children and termed the Lesch-Nyhan syndrome. This disease differs from the more usual type of gout in that it appears in infancy and is due to the absence of an enzyme, hypoxanthine-guanine phosphoribosyl transferase, which participates in the metabolism of nucleotides (Seegmiller, Rosenbloom, and Kelley, 1967). In affected infants, the enzyme is absent in the brain as well as other tissues. Affected individuals exhibit the typical arthritis and kidney stones found in gout, severe cerebral palsy, and mental impairment, and are prone to self-mutilation. Cerebral palsy is a broad term referring to any developmental defect in an individual's ability to move.[2] The self-mutilation observed in these children is uncommon in other forms of mental impairment. Children so affected appear to be under a sort of compulsion to place their fingers or toes in their mouths, and, upon doing so, they actually cannibalize themselves. For this reason they require continuous restraint, but even so almost all are missing one or more fingers and an upper or lower lip (see Bland, 1968). There are individuals with the characteristic biochemical abnormality who show only gout and no mental nor motor impairment. In these individuals the enzyme defect is nearly, but not quite, complete. Apparently in this, as in other similar diseases, the production of very small amounts of the enzyme is sufficient to protect the individual from the full manifestation of the disease.

Not all inborn errors of metabolism present symptoms in infancy. One class of these diseases is characterized by a defect in the complex lipid and lipoprotein compounds that form structural elements in the brain. These, as the others, are due to simple enzyme defects but, tragically for many families, the children often develop normally for a time before going into a slow decline in mental function.

---

[2] There are several forms of cerebral palsy; it may vary in severity, in different forms, from mild weakness to nearly complete paralysis. As in the Lesch-Nyhan syndrome, some cerebral palsy is related to congenital defect; in other types the defect is acquired. It is not always associated with mental impairment.

Instances of genetically determined biochemical defects of metabolism are being discovered at an amazing rate. Many of these defects are like PKU in that they involve metabolism of amino acids. The brain is exquisitely sensitive to metabolic derangements in the developmental period, and many of these diseases result in mental impairment which is apparent soon after birth as the child fails to achieve normal developmental milestones. Until recently, certain cases of some of the diseases were inexplicable in that the individuals appeared to have the metabolic defect but did not show mental impairment. New methods in enzyme measurement have demonstrated, however, that such individuals are protected by low levels of the enzyme. Thus, the defect is symptomatic only if it is complete.

Acquired Mental Impairment

PRENATAL AND PERINATAL CAUSES. It is commonly known that impairment of mental function, or of other functions of the human organism, may be acquired during the period of gestation or around the time of birth. Examples of well-known forms of impairment are the complications of maternal German measles when acquired in the first three months of pregnancy (cataracts, deafness, and heart defects), and the abnormalities of limbs associated with thalidomide treatment in pregnancy. In addition to these well-advertised complications, there are a number of other conditions that may affect the nervous system of an infant either during uterine development or around the time of birth and that result in mental impairment.

The process of producing malformations during intrauterine life is called teratogenesis (see Wilson and Warkany, 1965, for review). A number of experimental models of this process are available in animals and are under exhaustive study. One of the most effective of these is ionizing radiation. This can produce severe abnormalities of the nervous system, as can some drugs. The teratogenic agents in animals, and probably similar conditions in humans, are effective because immature or dividing cells are more susceptible to alteration than mature cells are. In the nervous system nearly all cell division takes place during embryonic life. The mature nervous system is unable to initiate division among nerve cells and, consequently, is far less susceptible to injury from ionizing radiation or teratogenic (and carcinogenic) drugs.

As has been suggested, the causes of acquired mental impairment are many. An uncommon but still important cause even in these days of antibiotics is maternal infection transmitted to the fetus. In past years, the most common infection of this kind was the venereal infection, syphilis. The mother with a syphilitic infection usually has one or more abortions (the technical term for "miscarriage") and then a stillbirth. Subsequent children often have congenital syphilis, acquired from the mother, and may show severe mental impairment. During the last few decades the incidence of congenital syphilis has fallen markedly because of the requirement in most states that expectant mothers have serological tests for syphilis and receive treatment if tests are positive. Treatment of the maternal infection with penicillin is cheap, simple, and effective for both mother and child. It is to be hoped, though, that the recent upsurge in the incidence of venereal disease among individuals of childbearing age, particularly in ghetto areas of large cities where medical care is not as easily available as elsewhere, does not cause a marked increase in congenital syphilis.

Maternal infections with a few viruses and with at least one protozoan organism may also be transmitted to the fetus with sequelae of developmental retardation, convulsions, and severe mental impairment. No treatment is available for these infections and current efforts are directed toward their prevention.

The development and normal functioning of the fetus's and infant's brain is dependent not only upon freedom from infection, but also upon large supplies of oxygen, brought to it by the blood. Although the brain makes up only about one-fiftieth of the total body weight of the adult, it is about one-fifth of the body weight of a newborn infant, and receives a comparable proportion of the total output of oxygenated blood from the heart. A reduction in the blood supply to the brain, or in the oxygen content of the blood, results in a deficiency of the required oxygen to maintain the metabolism of the brain, because unlike muscles and some other tissues, the brain cannot carry on its metabolism without oxygen.

Lack or deficiency of oxygen (anoxia) just before or at the time of birth may have disastrous results. If the period of anoxia is brief, there is only a transient depression and then restitution of function. If the period of anoxia is prolonged, structural changes take place in the affected nerve cells and recovery is no longer possible. The developing nervous system is more resistant to anoxic insult than the mature nervous system, but anoxia in the perinatal period (i.e., around the time of birth) is frequently severe enough to cause permanent damage and mental impairment. The causes of perinatal anoxia are many and cannot be detailed here. Sometimes there are brief, intermittent periods of severe anoxia, as may be associated with the rhythmic uterine contractions of labor. Sometimes the anoxia is not severe but is exceptionally prolonged, as may occur with partial, premature separation of the placenta. And sometimes the anoxia may be relatively brief, but very severe, as with complete placental separation, massive maternal blood loss, or other complications of labor and delivery.

Anoxia resulting from different causes may have different sequelae. The regions of the brain affected may vary and, because separate regions of the brain are more important for some functions than for others, the effects may differ. On some occasions the cerebral cortex is principally affected. If areas important for the elaboration of movement are affected, the child will have motor impairment (cerebral palsy). If the damage is more widespread and involves the temporal lobes particularly, there is more chance of mental impairment. This is especially true if a primitive part of the cerebral cortex, the hippocampus, is damaged. Unfortunately, the hippocampus is one of the most sensitive parts of the brain, and it is frequently damaged by both anoxia and head injury. Research in the last few years has suggested the possibility that normal function of the hippocampus may be necessary for the establishment of a continuing record of memories. Removal of the structure produces an individual who experiences great difficulties in acquiring memories and in some instances is nearly unable to do so. The effects this would have on the intellectual development of a child are obvious. Everyone is dependent upon the continual laying down of new memories to adapt to the environment, and the inability to do so presents a formidable impairment.

Direct injury to the brain is another important cause of mental impairment in childhood. About 95 percent of all children are born head first. During labor and delivery the head is the part most exposed to the forces attendant upon the expulsion of the infant from the uterus. In most instances, of course, the head and brain do not suffer injury, regardless of the trauma to which they are exposed in labor and delivery. Also, modern obstetrical technique has greatly reduced the dangers associated with birth. Nevertheless, an unusually long labor, abnormal positioning of the infant, a severe disproportion between the infant's size and the dimensions of the mother's birth canal, and other factors may cause trauma and injury to the infant's brain. There may be direct damage of the cerebral hemispheres, the largest and most exposed part of the brain, or the trauma may result in hemorrhage with secondary compression and damage of the cerebral hemispheres. In either case the results are the same—impaired function. As with anoxia, the type of impairment depends upon the particular regions damaged. Unlike anoxia, there is a greater tendency for birth injury to result in restricted damage to motor areas and, hence, cerebral palsy, but mental impairment does occur with distressing frequency.

PREMATURITY.   The advances in obstetrical technique and in the care of new-born infants in this century have brought about an increasing survival of premature infants. Prematurity is variously defined in terms of weight, gestational age, or both. The normal, full term infant weighs around 3000 grams (about 6.6 pounds). Often, infants weighing less than 2300 grams (about 4.1 pounds) are categorically viewed as premature, but low birth weight is not always attributable to prematurity. In any event, the near term premature appears to be at little disadvantage. However, premature infants weighing between 500 and 1500 grams (about 1.1 to 3.3 pounds) do poorly. Their survival rate is low (about 50 percent) and they exhibit frequent abnormalities if they survive the immediate newborn period. Prominent among these abnormalities are cerebral palsy and mental impairment. Estimates of the frequency of such disorders vary and studies are often not comparable. Control groups have usually not been analyzed and the examination for defects has often not been carried out in a manner designed to lead to conclusions free of bias.

A group of prematures (birth weight 500 to 1500 grams) born at the Chicago Lying-In Hospital between 1954 and 1956 has been studied (Wright et al., 1968). The circumstances of prenatal care, birth, delivery, and postnatal care were known for each, as well as for a group of carefully matched full term controls born at the same hospital. Among other examinations, each premature and each control was given a group of psychological tests (including IQ determination) and a complete neurological examination. These examinations were carried out without the examiner's knowing whether the child belonged to the control group or the premature group. The incidence of neurological abnormalities, particularly cerebral palsy, and mental impairment was much higher in the premature group than in the control group. Of the children born prematurely, 44 percent had IQs below 90, but only 8 percent of the control group showed such low scores. Conversely, only 11 percent of the prematures had IQ scores above 110, compared to 46 percent of the controls. Similar data have been obtained by others (Harper, Fischer, and Rider, 1959). These differences between the two groups demonstrate a significant deleterious concomitant of prematurity.

The cause of these and the more gross effects of prematurity is unknown. The premature infant may be born too early because he is defective, or the circumstances leading to the premature birth and the birth itself may result in the defects observed. In all probability both factors are important and the exact interplay of factors varies from one child to another. Premature birth is common, and as advances in pediatric care lead to more frequent survival of premature infants, this cause of mental impairment may raise important problems requiring solution. Among these are the consequences of the kind of medical care the premature often experiences (Rothschild, 1967; Solkoff, Yaffe, Weintraub, and Blase, 1969).

POSTNATAL CAUSES. The acquisition of mental impairment after birth is less common than before birth. The most frequent causes after birth are infection and brain injury. Meningitis and encephalitis are fairly widespread infections in childhood and may leave a residual of permanent mental impairment. The greatest hazard to the health of a child today is accident. Head injury is frequent and many children suffer lasting brain damage that impairs mental function. The most successful way of dealing with such head injury is to introduce programs to prevent accidents.

There are also rare diseases resulting in degeneration of parts of the brain and some instances of impairment of function resulting from exposure to toxins. The most important toxin of this type is lead. Although lead is used less often than in past years, this heavy metal is still found in many paints. Not infrequently, children will eat paint from walls, particularly in ghetto areas, where hunger is common and many layers of flaking, old paint are present. If the ingestion is chronic and the paint contains lead, unfortunate complications may arise. The continuing accumulation of lead in the body results in a massive swelling of the brain, widespread damage of nerve cells, and convulsions. The resultant acute illness, called lead encephalopathy, is frequently fatal. When it is not, the affected child is usually left with severe mental impairment and requires continuing custodial care.

Minimal Brain Damage and Minimal Brain Dysfunction

A little more than 25 years ago a new concept was adopted to explain certain behavioral abnormalities in the developmental period. This was the concept of minimal brain damage. Basically, the idea was that when certain behavior patterns similar to those which are attributed to known brain injury in children and adults are observed in children who have no known history of brain damage, they are attributable to "minimal" brain damage (see Birch, 1964). It has become apparent since then that the evidence for even minimal brain *damage* in these children is equivocal, and in some writings the term has been discarded in favor of the less concrete "minimal brain *dysfunction.*"

Over the years the concept has been broadened greatly and the neurologist specializing in children's problems is often asked to find some objective evidence of brain dysfunction in children with a wide variety of manifestations. Some view of the difficulty in dealing with this can be gleaned from a review of the problems presented by the children classified in this way. The children should have normal or borderline IQ. They are said to show impairment of perception (the so-called "perceptual handicap") and concept formation. They may have poor spatial orientation, time orientation, and judgment of distance, difficulty in telling right from left, reversals in reading and writing letters and numbers, and poor discrimination of figure from ground. Such children may also show disorders of speech and communication, varying from a minor impairment of hearing or slow language development to a full-blown aphasic syndrome (the inability to use words as symbols). Frequently, children with difficulties in academic adjustment—reading disabilities, difficulties in drawing or writing, variability in school performance, problems in organizing work, and confusion about the exact intent of instructions—have been classified as minimally brain damaged, with little else to suggest any organic defect. Children classified as having minimal brain damage are often described as being overly distractable, having a short attention span, and being hyperactive and difficult to manage. Their emotional stability is said to be poor and they are thought to be impulsive and to have poor emotional control. The social behavior of such children is considered impaired; they develop poor peer relationships, participate poorly in play, and exhibit inappropriate social behavior. Many other features have been described, but these are the main ones. Symptoms may occur singly or in groups.

The organic nature of the brain dysfunction diagnosis is predicated on four types of information. The first is the features of the syndrome and their similarity to known symptoms which may be associated with brain damage (or dysfunction). Regrettably, the same symptoms may, for the most part, equally well be those of psychological disturbance. The symptoms are not specific and cannot be considered so. Second, certain psychological tests are said to show evidence of organic disturbance. With all due respect to the originators of these tests, they do no such thing. Again, there is an invalid argument by analogy, as the tests are unable to distinguish well between organically and environmentally determined dysfunction. Third, these children are said to show, on exhaustive neurological examination, a number of "soft" neurologic signs. To most reputable neurologists, such as the head of child neurology at the Mayo Clinic (Gomez, 1967), such signs are less than dependable as indicators of organic disease and cannot be used, with or without other evidence, as unequivocal evidence for brain damage or dysfunction. Fourth, many of these children are said to show electroencephalographic abnormalities. Despite the feelings of some educators and physicians to the contrary, the electroencephalogram is not an all-or-none test for organic disorders, and is particularly difficult of interpretation in children. The difficulties raised by using such indicators for brain damage, particularly in relation to behavior problems, have been summarized aptly by D. A. Pond, Professor of Child Psychiatry at the University of London, who specializes in problems of behavioral disturbance and brain damage. In a recent review he stated, "There are . . . no absolutely unequivocal clinical signs, physiological tests or psychological tests, that prove a relationship between brain damage and any particular aspect of disturbed behavior" (Pond, 1967, p. 127).

The concept, and hence diagnosis, of minimal brain damage or dysfunction should probably be discarded. It serves no useful medical or educational purpose. Some children unhappily classed in this group do have a specific neurological (organic) problem. To a child with total dyslexia, the written word will be forever meaningless. As Gomez has so forcefully indicated, there is nothing minimal about his handicap. He does, however, require special training and there is nothing to be gained from throwing him into a school class with children having borderline intelligence, seizures, hyperactivity, or other perceptual handicaps.

In many instances of so-called minimal brain damage there is nothing to suggest that the brain is any more involved in the process than it is, for example, in the functional neuroses. The critical distinction that needs to be made is whether the impairment shown by the child is due to an abnormality of his nervous system as such or to an abnormality of his interaction with his environment. In many instances it will not be possible to make the distinction because of the limitations of our understanding and diagnostic methods. In others it will not be possible to make it because both factors are inextricably interwoven in providing the problem (Abrams, 1968). The task is to work at understanding the problems, the antecedents of their occurrence, and the remedial techniques that seem to facilitate intellectual gains in such children. Much information is required about both the psychology and neurology of children to understand school problems and behavior problems.

NERVOUS SYSTEM DAMAGE AND AGE

Lesions of the brain are brought about by a number of causes. Some are the direct result of head injury, others may be caused more indirectly, for example, by interference with the blood supply in a region of the brain. The nature and severity of the deficit produced varies with the location and extent of the brain damage. Some large brain lesions may produce no detectable impairment, while a relatively small amount of damage to other regions in the brain may lead to profound dysfunction.

A surprising property of the deficits caused by brain lesion is that they may be partially reversible. Despite the fact that the central nervous system of mammals cannot regenerate, recovery of sensory-motor or intellectual function may be possible after injury. The degree of recovery appears to vary with age. For some as yet unexplained reason, damage to the brain of a young organism is likely to be followed by far greater recovery than equivalent damage sustained by an adult. Two examples of the relative plasticity of young organisms will be discussed. Speech is not as lastingly disrupted following brain injury in children as in adults. Also, experimental studies of brain lesions in mammals show that many functions are less impaired or recover more quickly when lesions are sustained at an early age.

Speech and Brain Lesions

The left hemisphere of a man weighs as much as the right hemisphere, almost to the gram. Surprisingly, although no clear structural differences have yet been established by anatomical study, there are great functional differences between the two hemispheres. Equivalent damage of cerebral cortex on the left and right side is not equivalent in the deficit produced. Large lesions of certain regions of the cortex on the left side almost always cause a loss in expression or understanding of speech, a disability called aphasia. Aphasia rarely follows lesions to the right hemisphere. Despite the regularity with which aphasia is produced by lesions of the left cortex, the severity of the initial symptoms and the degree of recovery are related to the age at which the damage is sustained (Lenneberg, 1967). Initially, aphasic symptoms may be present in such young patients, but speech may be recovered if the lesion is sustained before the patient reaches adolescence. Eventually, the young patient with damage to the left hemisphere may recover the complete ability to speak and understand language. In contrast, aphasia produced by large lesions of left association cortex in adults almost always leaves a residual degree of language impairment. It appears that the child's brain possesses the capacity to reestablish normal language independent of the structure that might have been damaged. Since damage to neurons in the central nervous system of humans is irreversible, this indicates that the undamaged part of the brain in the child has sufficient functional plasticity to establish and maintain language despite the damage to the primary speech center.

Animal Experiments

The relatively milder effect of brain lesions on speech in children is paralleled with rather convincing uniformity by studies of lesions placed in various brain structures of immature animals. For example, if one makes a lesion in the so-called motor cortex, adult animals show a profound and immediate impairment of motor function. Some recovery might eventually be observed but the typical immediate postoperative picture is one of great weakness, to the point of inability of the animal to stand or walk in a normal fashion. In sharp contrast, when a similar lesion was made in the brain of a three week old monkey (Kennard, 1942), no postoperative deficits in movement or posture were observed. These results may be generalized. Many experimental studies have revealed far less deficit in sensory (Benjamin and Thompson, 1959; Scharlock, Tucker, and Strominger, 1963) and cognitive (Akert, Orth, Harlow, and Schlitz, 1960) as well as motor functions in organisms that sustained injury at an early age.

CHAPTER 19

Behavior Modification:
Clinical and Educational Applications

"Behavior modification" has recently come to serve as a label for a distinctive approach to child behavior problems. The phrase implies that the essence of the child's problem is simply his behavior—what he should do but does not, and what he should not do but does. If indeed the child's problem is his behavior, then techniques that can change his behavior can thereby solve his problem, provided they are applied to him.

The techniques that can change a child's behavior have been described in preceding chapters of this book. The most basic of them are repeated here, as a summary of techniques now to be regarded as clinical tools, as a gathering together of essential terms, and as a statement of organization for the bulk of this chapter.

BASIC PRINCIPLES

Behaviors are commonly given one of two available labels, simply to denote which of two basic formulas describes the way in which the behavior is determined by environmental events. One such label is *respondent;* the other is *operant.*

Respondents

Respondents are behaviors that are determined by the pattern of stimulation preceding them in the environment, but are unaffected by the pattern of stimulation following them. Dilation of the pupil of the eye is a classical example: when the level of light intensity falling on the eye is increased, the pupil constricts; when the level is decreased, the pupil dilates. Giving rewards for either response has no known effect on the response; similarly, attempting punishment for either response has no known effect on the response. Thus, environmental control seems restricted to the antecedent side of the response, and lies in specific stimuli which have the power to elicit the response. Other notable examples of such behaviors are blushing, crying (tearing), and the knee jerk (patellar reflex).

Some respondents prove modifiable through environmental events. Obvious mechanisms that can affect these behaviors include injury and fatigue of the relevant body structures. Not quite so obvious is the mechanism of conditioning, credited to Pavlov for its discovery and variously labeled Pavlovian, classical, Type S, and respondent conditioning (see Chapter 3). Respondent conditioning is a mechanism whereby the range of stimuli capable of eliciting a respondent sometimes can be expanded to include new stimuli, chosen fairly arbitrarily. Pavlov provided one of the most celebrated demonstrations of this technique by showing successful conditioning of the respondent, salivation, in the dog (Pavlov, 1927). A dog, like many other animals, will salivate when food is placed in its mouth. Pavlov devised a convenient method of eliciting the respondent: he presented food to the dog, and thereby reliably elicited salivation, measurable by the drop. Subsequently, he presented the dog with a modified stimulus: preceding the delivery of food by a few seconds, he began the ticking of a metronome. Metronome ticks are a stimulus to which the ordinary dog may turn his head and lift his ears, but is hardly likely to salivate. However, after a series of experiences in which the metronome ticks consistently preceded the food presentation, the dog began to salivate to the ticks themselves, and the food then could be discontinued. The dog's behavior, thereby, could be considered newly elaborated: whereas previously he would salivate to food but not to metronome ticks, now he would salivate to either. He was probably the only dog in all Russia of whom this was true; if so, respondent conditioning can be seen as a mechanism leading to individual differences, and thus, personality. If a child turns white and trembles in the presence of cats, it may be guessed that for this child, cats have played the same role that Pavlov's metronome ticks played for his dog: cats have preceded some stimulus which in itself could elicit paling and trembling. Perhaps this child was once bitten by a cat. The bite of the cat could well elicit those responses, and the appearance of the cat was to its bite as the tick of the metronome was to food powder.

Pavlov's dog, if presented with metronome ticks alone very often, eventually stopped salivating in answer to them. Thus, their conditioned eliciting power was lost, through use. This loss of conditioned eliciting function is termed *respondent extinction*. It occurs, of course, because the responsible correlation between ticks and food is discontinued, yet the ticks continue to occur. If those correlations are resumed (i.e., if ticks again precede food) the conditioned eliciting function of the ticks can be recovered, and they may then be used alone (for a while) to elicit salivation again. Similarly, the pale and trembling child, if presented sufficiently often with a cat who does not bite him, eventually should lose these behaviors, through a similar process of extinction. If such response to the cats of his environment is considered maladaptive, troublesome, and predictive of future constrictions in his ability to enjoy his environment, then that response may be considered a "problem" and its extinction thereby becomes "therapy"—or, in this context, behavior modification: deliberate structuring of environmental correlations to produce behavior change in the service of clinical goals.

A behavior therapy for this particular problem would proceed, as indicated, by extinction of the troublesome respondents of trembling, paling, etc. That would leave a child with no maladaptive responses to cats, but with no particular other responses to them, either. Partly so as not to leave a response gap toward a familiar stimulus of children's worlds, and partly because it may well cause extinction of the problem respondents to go faster, a typical behavior therapy program would probably establish positive responses toward cats at the same time. A typical program also conducts extinction in a systematically progressive manner. This it accomplishes by first exposing the child to stimuli only faintly resembling cats, perhaps statements about cats or pictures of cats far away. Gradually, these stimuli are changed so that they more and more closely resemble the problem stimuli, until finally the child is presented live cats at close range. How quickly this sequence proceeds is ordinarily guided by the current intensity of the troublesome respondents throughout the sequence; as such responding is reduced at a given level of stimulation, a closer approach to the final stimulus forms can be made; if the responding remains strong, that advance is delayed, or a retreat toward less effective stimuli can be made, and the desired advance then can proceed again, but probably more slowly.

A possible example is seen in an early study by Jones (1924). In this study a young boy, Peter, exhibited crying and other fear responses (presumably respondents) to fuzzy objects such as cotton, feathers, fur, rats, and rabbits. The first procedure employed was to allow Peter to play with other children while one of these stimuli (a rabbit) was present in the playroom. During this procedure, Peter stopped exhibiting crying and fear responses to the rabbit and at one point touched it (this aspect of the study was discussed in Chapter 10, as an example of "social inhibition" of anxiety). However, after a two month illness Peter returned to the experimental situation and again exhibited fear reactions when the rabbit was present. A second procedure, termed "direct conditioning," was then employed. In this procedure, the child was fed food which he liked, while the experimenter brought a caged rabbit as close as possible without producing crying or fear responses, which would interfere with eating. Gradually the rabbit was brought closer and closer to the child until he touched it without crying. It was then found that the other fuzzy stimuli had lost much of their eliciting function for crying.

A technique similar to that used by Jones has been developed by Wolpe to eliminate fear responses (Wolpe, 1958; see also Wolpe and Lazarus, 1966). This technique has been termed reciprocal inhibition; it is used in cases where an "anxiety" is assumed to produce fear responses. In reciprocal inhibition, various methods are employed to establish responses that are presumably incompatible with anxiety. The most commonly used method is to teach the patient relaxation responses. Then stimuli that elicit the fear responses are presented, beginning with the least fearful and proceeding to the most fearful, until the patient no longer exhibits or reports fear responses to any of the stimuli. In many cases the stimuli presented to patients are verbal: the therapist simply tells the patient to imagine a fearful situation. In other cases (e.g., Clark, 1963) the patient is instructed to come gradually into actual contact with previously fearful situations—as long as he does not become fearful. The procedures of reciprocal inhibition have been used more often with adults than with children.

With adults the ease of verbal control of the client's behavior allows the therapist to establish, practice, and maintain relaxation responses in the client. With young children such verbal control is often impractical, and therefore other techniques of evoking responses presumably incompatible with anxiety are employed. For example, in a study by Lazarus (1960) a child who apparently feared automobiles was first asked to talk about them and was given chocolate for any positive comments he made about them; later, he was presented with toy autos and was given chocolate for playing with them; finally, he was given chocolate for riding in real automobiles.

The study by Jones, and the reciprocal inhibition procedures employed by Wolpe and by Lazarus, contain at least two possible functional components: (a) simple respondent extinction of fear responses, and (b) establishment of positive behavior to previously fearful stimuli by instructions or rewards. But in the examples cited, the two components were applied in combination and not separately; therefore it cannot be determined whether both were functional. Remediation might have proceeded entirely because of one rather than the other; or, perhaps, either might have been effective alone, yet their combination need not have achieved any better outcome than either could have produced alone. This failure to analyze, experimentally, the separate contributions of the procedures involved has unfortunately been characteristic of such behavior therapies. As a consequence, it has typically remained unclear which parts of the procedure are functional and which are not. However, it is encouraging to note that experimental examination of the separate roles of respondent extinction and the establishment of incompatible responses like relaxation is beginning (Davison, 1968).

Only some respondents prove modifiable by conditioning techniques; others, like the knee jerk, apparently are difficult to condition reliably to arbitrarily chosen stimuli (Schlosberg, 1928). If a given respondent is not conditionable, there is little point in attempting its extinction, as though it were a conditioned respondent. However, if it is not conditionable, then there will be no cases of its attachment to unique and unfortunate stimuli which constitute a problem for some individual, comparable to a child's fear of cats. Consequently, they will not require clinical effort. (The knee jerk, although perhaps embarrassing in certain social situations, is not considered a behavior problem; it is a uniform affliction.)

Operants

CONTINGENCIES.   Operants, unlike respondents, are behaviors which are determined primarily by the pattern of stimulation following them in the environment. That is, operants are controlled by their environmental consequences (see Chapter 4). A response can have consequences in environmental action in only two basic ways: new stimuli may be added to the environment as a result of the response, or stimuli previously present may be subtracted from the environment. Some stimuli, when consistently added to the environment following a response, produce a strengthening of that response in the future. Such stimuli are termed *positive reinforcers*. Other stimuli, when consistently subtracted from the environment following a response, strengthen that response for the future. These stimuli are called *negative reinforcers*, or, alternatively, *aversive stimuli*. Both processes—strengthening a response through its adding of stimuli, and strengthening a response through its subtraction of stimuli—are referred to as *reinforcement contingencies*.

These definitions depend on the strengthening function of the stimuli in question. But certain stimulus consequences of behavior obviously are capable of weakening rather than strengthening behavior. Stimuli that weaken a response when added to the environment following the response are called *punishing stimuli*. But, parallel to the case of reinforcement, there is a second way to weaken behavior, through the subtraction of certain stimuli from the environment following a response. Such stimuli may be termed *response costs*. The term *response cost* is not in wide use, but there appear to be few other terms which unfailingly can be used to label the stimuli in this contingency. Weiner (1962) has used the term in a simple but descriptive manner for these purposes, and it is extended to the general case here, as elsewhere (Sherman and Baer, 1969). Both processes—weakening a response through the addition of stimuli following the response, and weakening a response through the subtraction of stimuli following a response—are referred to as *punishment contingencies*.

Some simplicity can be discerned in these four contingencies (two of reinforcement, two of punishment) when it is recognized that positive reinforcers typically will function as effective response costs, and that negative reinforcers typically will function as punishing stimuli. But the operative word is "typically," and the two equations:

$$\text{positive reinforcer} = \text{response cost,}$$
$$\text{negative reinforcer} = \text{punishing stimulus,}$$

are only statements of high probability.

In summary, then, there are two reinforcement and two punishment contingencies which may be used to alter behavior in specified directions. When that alteration has been accomplished, however, if the responsible contingency is discontinued, the behavior often will revert to its original form or rate prior to alteration. This process is termed *operant extinction*. Extinction may be quick or slow after the previous contingency has been discontinued (depending mainly on the nature and pattern over time of the previous contingency), but typically extinction will be seen, such that the effects of the previous contingency will be undone.

To the extent that a child's behavior problems are identical to the behaviors which comprise them, there are five basic clinical tools for the remediation of operant problem behavior: two reinforcement contingencies, two punishment contingencies, and extinction. Thus, behavior modification, applied to operant behavior, consists first of an analysis of what behaviors are involved in the problem. Subsequently, depending on whether these behaviors are desirable ones too low in strength at present, or undesirable ones too high in strength at present, one or more of the applications described in Table 19-1 is appropriate.

Table 19-1

*Contingencies for the Remediation of Operant Responses
Involved in Behavior Problems*

Nature of problem behavior	Contingency
Desirable response too low in strength	Reinforce the response: rearrange the environment so that available reinforcers occur as consequences of the response; or introduce new reinforcers into the environment as consequences of the response; or rearrange the environment so that available negative reinforcers are subtracted as a consequence of the response; or introduce new negative reinforcers into the environment and subtract them as consequences of the response. Extinguish or punish (as detailed below) any incompatible responses that interfere with, or compete with, the response.
Undesirable response too high in strength	Extinguish the response: determine which reinforcers in the environment are maintaining it, and either remove or rearrange these. If rearranging so that they occur at other times, choose a desirable response counterpart to reinforce with them. Punish the response: rearrange the environment so that available punishing stimuli occur as consequences of the response; or bring new punishing stimuli into the environment as consequences of the response; or rearrange the environment so that available response costs are subtracted as a consequence of the response; or bring new response costs into the environment and subtract them as consequences of the response. Reinforce specific desirable or acceptable behavior incompatible with the response; or strongly reinforce any acceptable behavior other than the response (i.e., reinforce only when the response has not occurred for a criterion length of time).

DISCRIMINATION. The action of reinforcement, punishment, or extinction contingencies is almost never universal—they rarely operate uniformly in all environments, or at all times within a given environment. Thus, the question arises: Will their effects be seen everywhere, even though the contingencies producing these effects do not operate everywhere? The typical answer to this question is *no*. The effects of reinforcement, punishment, and extinction contingencies are seen primarily in those environments where they operate, and are seen to a lesser extent, if at all, elsewhere or at other times. This typical observation is referred to as the phenomenon of *discrimination*. Discrimination implies that behavior will have different forms in different stimulus settings, because the contingencies responsible for the form are not the same in all settings. The distinctive stimuli of such settings thus are called *discriminative stimuli*, when they exert environmental control over the behaviors in question. Consequently, operants, like respondents, will answer to certain antecedent stimuli; but operants are responsive to these stimuli only because the stimuli set the occasion for the consequences which the response usually produces. In effect, discriminative stimuli signal what the effects of a given response are. Thus, stimuli discriminative for reinforcement of a response will evoke the response; stimuli discriminative for punishment of the response will suppress it; and stimuli discriminative for neither reinforcement nor punishment of a response will produce the level characteristic of the response before reinforcement or punishment was applied to it.

A child may have a behavior problem simply because his behavior has come under the control of inappropriate discriminative stimuli, or has failed to come under the control of appropriate discriminative stimuli. For example, running away is in itself not an inappropriate or troublesome operant: little children should run away from many dangerous situations. However, it is not appropriate that children run away from rides in their parents' automobile; this can cause considerable trouble for the family in a mobile society. Thus, it is not the existence of the response which is the problem in this case, but the stimulus control of the response. Adequate behavior modification may require nothing more than elimination of this particular stimulus function of automobiles for the child in question. Another child, by contrast, may not show avoidance behavior to busy streets, which he should if his life is to be preserved. Thus, it is an absence of appropriate stimulus control which is at issue, especially if it is clear that the child is perfectly capable of such avoidance behavior in other settings. In this case, behavior modification may require nothing more than establishment of discriminative stimulus control by streets for avoidance responses.

In principle, problems with such elementary stimulus objects as automobiles and streets are no different from problems with such psychologically complex stimulus arrays as mothers and fathers. Behavior modification for a girl who runs away from her father but not from her mother may proceed by exactly the same logic as it would in establishing appropriate stimulus control by automobiles or streets: if staying with father is desired, then the father must be given discriminative stimulus function for reinforcement of operants directed toward him. Reference to Table 19-1 will display the general options available. (Some of these may need to be applied to the father, too, since his behavior also is at issue; probably he must begin reinforcing his daughter for staying with him, and this is a behavior of his which may be low in strength and, thus, will require development.)

SHAPING AND FADING. Two procedures of operant technology need specification at this point, if a reasonable armamentarium of behavioral tools for clinical purposes is to become apparent. One involves the differential use of contingencies to change behavior; it is called *response differentiation,* or *shaping.* The other involves a similarly differential use of stimuli to achieve discriminative stimulus control of behavior; it is called *fading.*

Table 19-1 suggests that to strengthen a desirable but weak response, it should be reinforced. But if the response is so weak that it never or rarely occurs, it may well prove impractical or impossible to reinforce. What then? Almost certainly, there will exist other responses which occur often enough to be practical targets of reinforcement, and of these, surely some will resemble the response that is eventually to be developed. These remote relatives of the final response *are* reinforced, therefore, and the typical observation is that as they are strengthened, new responses are seen, some of which resemble the desired response more closely than their predecessors. The emergence of these new responses is referred to as *response induction,* or *response generalization.* The high probability of this process is capitalized on in shaping; as the new responses appear, those which more closely resemble the desired final behavior are reinforced, and reinforcement of their predecessors is discontinued. With the strengthening of these better approximations to the desired response, still newer responses will appear, and some of these almost certainly will resemble the desired response even more closely. Reinforcement is transferred to these new and better approximations, and they are strengthened until still better approximations result. The process can thus be continued until the desired behavior itself begins to appear with enough frequency to be practical for direct reinforcement. At that point, it alone is reinforced until it develops to the desired level of strength.

An example is seen in a study conducted by Wolf, Risley, and Mees (1964). The case in point was a young boy who had recently had the lenses of his eyes removed because of cataracts. His behavior was generally described as "autistic"; he appeared to be under very little control by other people, including his parents. One aspect of this failure of control was his refusal to wear the new glasses which optically would serve as substitutes for his own missing lenses. Because medical opinion was that the boy would permanently lose his macular vision unless he began to wear his glasses, that behavior was shaped by successive approximations, using food at mealtimes as the basic reinforcer. Initially, the boy was reinforced merely for contacting a pair of empty glasses frames left around the experimental room. Subsequently, lenses were inserted in the frames and the boy was reinforced for carrying the glasses, and then only for responses which lifted them toward his head. As these responses became very frequent, only those which involved placing the ear pieces straight over the ears and looking through the lenses were reinforced. Thus, over a span of weeks, a glasses-wearing performance was shaped from a literally zero level to dependable daylong durations. Glasses-wearing later was reinforced by such everyday reinforcers as being eligible for a walk (as long as his glasses were on), and eventually the behavior was reinforced (it would be presumed) simply by the child's ability to see better with them than without them.

Whereas shaping is primarily an operation on responses, *fading* is mainly an operation on stimuli, and a highly analogous one. Fading is a technique for establishing new stimulus control over behavior, that is, for giving some important new stimulus discriminative function for that behavior. Fading is used primarily when it will apparently prove difficult to achieve such stimulus control by more ordinary means. The behavior modifier starts with a stimulus that already controls the response in question. Gradually, as the child responds under the control of this stimulus, the stimulus is changed so that it more and more closely resembles the stimulus which is desired as the controlling stimulus. Elements of the new stimulus gradually appear; elements of the former stimulus gradually disappear—hence, the descriptive term, fading. Reinforcement is still involved in that as the response occurs in the stimulus circumstances, it is reinforced.

An example is seen in the work of Risley and Wolf (1967). These experimenters developed language behavior in retarded and autistic children. The children were already under one form of stimulus control: they mimicked sounds they heard from the experimenter. However, the stimulus control desired was that appropriate to labeling rather than mimicking. The object itself, rather than the word supplied by the experimenter, should have discriminative function for the verbalizations of the children if these verbalizations were to serve as labels in the children's speech. A transfer of discriminative control, from the sounds presented by the experimenter to objects and pictures of objects, was achieved by fading in the following way: First the experimenter held up an object, for example, a picture of a train, asked "What is this?" and then provided a prompt by saying "train." When the child imitated this prompt he was reinforced. After this step was repeated several times, the experimenter held up the picture, asked "What is this?" and waited. If the child did not reply, he was given a partial prompt. This consisted of only a soft enunciation of the first sounds of the word "train." When the child said "train," reinforcement was delivered and the sequence was repeated. Gradually, the partial prompts were said more and more quietly until the experimenter was merely "mouthing" the prompt; finally, he provided no prompt at all. During this sequence, all correct responses of the children were reinforced. At the last step in the series the children were essentially labeling the object, rather than imitating the experimenter's sound (which now was no longer present). This technique could be repeated with many objects and their names, such that the children developed a repertoire of labels which were reliably correct at all times, with no necessity of vocal prompting by the questioner. In essence, the technique involved the fading out of *imitative* control, leaving *object* control as the discriminative stimulus controlling the children's vocalization. The same development of object control might have been achieved by simply presenting a picture of a train and waiting for a correct vocalization from the child to reinforce, but the probability of such a response, of course, would be extremely low, and the possibility of making a useful contribution to the child's labeling repertoire would be virtually zero without the fading technique.

Fading can have one other major application. It may be used, not because other methods would be virtually impossible, but because other methods would involve a certain number of errors (responses in inappropriate stimulus circumstances). Error is sometimes disruptive in itself to learning organisms, and perhaps especially so to those children who become the subjects of behavior modification applications. Error, after all, means either extinction or punishment for the child, and both of these conditions may produce a flurry of behavior, some of it resulting in escape from the situation, some of it simply labeled "emotional." Fading, if conducted appropriately, typically will involve very little error. The behavior modifier usually will be guided in his rate of fading by the ease with which discriminative stimulus control is being transferred (as evidenced by the child's behavior); thus, he will fade no faster than the child can continue to respond correctly, and errors will be almost completely avoided. Indeed, practice may confer upon the behavior modifier an "artfulness" that will allow him to avoid errors completely.

Avoidance of errors in developing new stimulus control of behavior may have yet another significance. Suppose that a child comes under discriminative stimulus control, making errors in the process. The errors obviously represent occasions when the current control of his behavior is incomplete; the disappearance of errors indicates that correct control has finally been achieved. However, observers of his learning cannot tell which of the differences between the correct and incorrect stimuli control the discrimination. Furthermore, errors indicate that *our* efforts to teach the child have failed; presumably, he is engaged in solving the stimulus problem himself. To some extent, that solution will be private and within him, where it cannot be observed. Thus, since the task of anyone attempting to shift control of behavior from one stimulus to another is to understand all steps in the process, if possible, the occurrence of errors makes the experimenter's task more difficult. When new discriminations are managed in an errorless manner, the experimenter believes that he understands more of the basic steps in that discrimination process than he might if errors occur.

The argument in the preceding paragraph emphasizes value to the experimenter, rather than to the learner. However, it might be argued that the experience in solving his own problems, necessitated by errors in a learning program, may be of value to the learner. Possibly, the occurrence of errors teaches him skills in analysis that may be useful for future problems. This possibility awaits empirical evaluation.

Current work in child behavior modification is based primarily on the operant techniques outlined so far: two contingencies of reinforcement, two of punishment, and extinction, in conjunction with shaping and fading (which, of course, include discrimination). Thus, the preceding description of these techniques, which by no means exhaust the technology of operant behavior, represents a fairly complete picture of current practice. That it is the simplest core of operant technology which is finding application may follow from the fact that this is a new endeavor in clinical application. It may also represent the possibility that most of the problem behaviors of children dealt with so far are in fact relatively simple affairs not requiring the elaborate techniques which laboratory investigations of the subtleties of behavior often involve.

CONTRAST WITH TRADITIONAL
CHILD PSYCHOTHERAPY

Behavior modification (or behavior therapy) represents a distinctive departure from the more traditional forms of psychotherapy that have been applied to child behavior problems. [For descriptions of traditional psychotherapies applied to children, see A. Freud (1928), Levy (1939), Axline (1947), Slavson (1952), and Kanner (1957).] That this is so would seem to require (a) that any exposition of behavior modification techniques make the contrast to the traditional techniques as clear as possible, and (b) that the newer technique be assumed to require comprehensive documentation with reliable data before it is considered valid and useful. This section of the chapter is intended to serve the first goal; the subsequent sections are meant to display examples of the kinds of data that have so far been produced in the interests of documentation.

Perhaps the most basic contrast between behavior modification and psychotherapy lies in the role of the child's behavior. In behavior modification, as has been seen, the child's behavior *is* his problem. In the psychotherapeutic approach, a child's behavior more likely is only an expression, or symptom, of his problem; his problem is assumed to involve a central organization of the total behavioral repertoire, an organization having the status of a maladaptive personality state. The central mechanism operating within this personality state is typically postulated to be anxiety (or some derivative concept, such as insecurity or inadequacy).

If behavior is merely a manifestation, or symbol, of the underlying maladaptive organization, then changing the behavior will generally leave the underlying cause untouched. Indeed, it is sometimes assumed that an actual disservice will have been performed, in that a signal of internal trouble will have been removed and consequently the child may not attract the more fundamental help which his problem requires. A favorite analogy cites appendicitis: the apparent characteristics of appendicitis are soreness in the abdomen, headache, possible nausea, and fever. Aspirin will usually suppress most of these, but clearly that is no cure; the central inflammation is untreated, and presently will kill the patient through peritonitis, despite the current absence of headache, soreness, and fever (removed by the aspirin). Proper treatment is to remove the infected appendix, not to remove the soreness, headache, and fever. Indeed, when the central problem has been treated, the soreness, headache, and fever will disappear automatically.

Psychotherapy has typically proceeded as if behavior problems were analogous to appendicitis. Behavioral aberrations are seen as clues to the underlying problem, and efforts are directed toward alleviation of the underlying problem, assuming that a consequence of successful treatment is correction of the behavioral signs. In psychotherapy with children, it has often been assumed that the child's problem grows out of the fundamental relation between him and his parents, and much psychotherapeutic effort has thus been directed toward the child's parents, even though the referring complaint centers on the child, and even though the child's behavioral organization is the ultimate target of the therapist.

Another point of strong contrast between the approaches lies in the assumptions about the developmental history of the child's behavior problem. In psychotherapy, the causes of behavioral disturbance are generally seen as emanating from incorrect and very early interpersonal relations, typically between child and parents. In behavior modification, there is frequently only mild interest in the prior history of a behavior problem. Past events may explain how the current pattern of behavior originated, but only current events are likely to explain why that same pattern still exists. If only the past events were at issue, extinction would either have occurred, or at least be on its way, and the problem would be a simple one indeed. Remediation will involve manipulation of the current environment, of course, as that is the only environment available. Very often, the behavior modifier's manipulations of that environment will be the same when he knows the history of the problem behavior as when he does not. Thus, for behavior modification, history often is almost without function, especially distant history; for psychotherapy, history—and especially distant history—is considered of central importance in knowing what to do now.

Still another point of important contrast centers on the concept of "relationship." Psychotherapy is assumed to be effective only when therapist and client have entered into a mutual relationship, such that the therapist has become a person of sufficient value to the client to be effective in contributing to a reorganization of his personality. The therapist is likely to assume that the client himself will accomplish this reorganization. The therapist will prompt it, help to direct it, perhaps, but not determine it. However, the behavior modifier will not see such a "relationship" as the essential variable determining his success or failure in dealing with problem behavior. He will require control of the salient aspects of the client's environment, most probably control of an effective reinforcer for his behavior. Only if he plans to use his own social reinforcers to modify that behavior will anything approximating their "relationship" be at issue; but those, of course, are only a few of the reinforcers that might be used, not the exclusive ones. The behavior modifier naturally will require cooperation from the child's parents, teacher, guardian, and other caretakers, and that cooperation may be more likely if his relationship to these people is good. But this is a matter of practicality, not the central theoretical necessity that it appears to be in psychotherapeutic approaches.

A final point of contrast involves style, rather than theoretical orientation. Psychotherapy, perhaps because it is assumed to deal with very basic and very deep processes and in addition must proceed on a basis of personal relationship, is generally a relatively slow process. The psychotherapist often appears to be willing to continue without objectively measured evidence of progress, and often without prompt changes in the symptomatic behaviors, which indeed may sometimes be seen as the last ones to change, if therapy succeeds. Behavior modification, in contrast, is likely to proceed relatively rapidly; it is typically assumed that if an effective environmental contingency has been applied to behavior, change will be seen promptly. If there are many behaviors to change, then the total program may well require a lengthy period of time, but each component of the program is expected to go quickly. When directly measurable behavior change does not go quickly, it is typical in behavior modification enterprises to assume that the current technique is ineffective, and therefore to apply another.

In summary, the contrasts between psychotherapy and behavior modification involve the role of behavior, as a symptom of the problem or as the essence of it; the role of past history, as essential to understanding the current problem or as of only mild relevance to it; the role of the therapist–patient relationship, as essential to the therapy or as only one of many ways in which to apply reinforcers; and the role of quickness of change, as an unrealistic index of effectiveness or as the prime criterion of it.

THE PROBLEM OF PROOF

When the contrast between what is traditional and what is new is both extreme and comprehensive, then the burden of proof surely lies with what is new. Presumably, this should be especially true in science. Although it is not thoroughly clear that the principles of traditional psychotherapy are matters of science, it is probably safer nevertheless to assume that any challenge to them should proceed on a firm basis of demonstration, rather than logic, intuition, or rhetoric. Consequently, what follows in this chapter has been selected because of its design as convincing research as well as remediation of some problem behavior.

Measurement

The essence of behavior modification is the identification of a child's problem in terms of what he does and does not do. It follows that a convincing demonstration of the effectiveness of behavior modification techniques in alleviating the problem will require direct measurement of the behavior at issue. Directness of measurement implies that the behavior most directly constituting the problem of the child be measured, rather than some indirect, or only presumably related, response. Thus, if a child's problem is his fear of dogs, it is more convincing to be able to produce approach responses to dogs, touching of them, and playing with them, than it is merely to bring a child to the point of saying that he no longer fears dogs. What a child says need not correlate with what he will do. If a child's problem is lack of a verbal repertoire, it is more compelling to count the number and diversity of objects he can label, the questions he can answer, and the sentences he can generate, than to collect his teacher's rating of his improvement in language arts. The former are *his* behaviors; the latter is his teacher's. If there is any interest in her behavior at all, it is in her language-teaching behavior, not her rating behavior. But her teaching behavior can be evaluated only in terms of how well it produces language behavior in the child.

This is not to imply that behavior is not to be measured by human observers. However, it does argue very strongly that the human observer should do nothing more interpretive than count explicitly describable behaviors. When the observer is asked to rate, interpret, or evaluate the child's behaviors, then the result is certainly a study of behavior modification in the observer, and possibly, but not certainly, of behavior modification in the child as well. Probably it is impossible to describe behavior so explicitly that an observer can count it without any interpretation, but the closest approach possible to this goal is the prime criterion of behavior modification as an exercise in proof of how behavior works, as well as in remediation of the problems that behavior causes. Thus, in a study of the experimental development of cooperative behavior in a preschool child, Hart, Reynolds, Baer, Brawley, and Harris (1968) did not ask their observers to judge when the child was playing cooperatively, which would typically mean to interpret the child's intent. Instead, they defined cooperation as follows:

> . . . any of the following activities: pulling a child or being pulled by a child in a wagon; handing an object to a child, or pouring into his hands or into a container held by him; helping a child by supporting him physically, or bringing, putting away, or building something verbalized as expressly for him; sharing something with the child by digging in the same hole, carrying the same object, painting on the same paper or from the same paint pot, or adding to some structure or construction (such as a chain of manipulative toys, or a block house). (Hart *et al.*, 1968, p. 74.)

This definition is not devoid of interpretation, clearly, but attempts to minimize it, and to eliminate guesses about the child's motives. Conceivably, it will prevent the observer from counting certain choice episodes of cooperation which simply do not fit the categories defined. However, it will also prevent the study from becoming one of the observer's autisms.

The standard way of showing that a behavioral definition is indeed explicit and objective is to show that two observers, watching the same child simultaneously, will produce substantially similar counts of the behavior over a lengthy span of time. This demonstration is most impressive when the second observer, simply after reading the behavioral definition, immediately achieves agreement with the first. Correspondingly, it is less impressive when two observers achieve agreement only after some practice in observing the behavior; it still attests to reliability, albeit not in its most desirable form.

Design

Two designs are typically cited as adequate to produce a convincing experimental analysis of behavioral processes that are also problem behaviors. The fact that they are problem behaviors usually militates against the usual group designs of experimental psychology, in which the means of an experimental group and a control group are compared for statistical significance. It is difficult to amass adequate numbers of children with sufficiently similar problem behaviors at one time to constitute these groups, although it has been accomplished on occasion. [For example, Lovibond (1963) reported on the average differences among three different ways of eliminating bed-wetting.] However, typical clinical practice deals with one child at a time, and attempts to discover the dynamics of his behavior, rather than the actuarial characteristics of the general class of children with problem behaviors. Therefore, the introduction of experimental design into clinical practice will emphasize single-subject designs. There are, of course, other reasons which recommend single-subject designs, having to do with the reliability and generality of the data produced (Sidman, 1960).

The more frequently used of the two designs most often cited is sometimes called the "reversal" design (see Sherman and Baer, 1969). In this design, the child's behavior is observed and measured over time, to display the baseline magnitude and stability of his problem. Then, an experimental variable is applied. If the variable produces a clear behavioral change of the type desired, it is either discontinued, modified, or reversed, to see if the behavioral change just produced will be correspondingly altered, lost, or reversed. If so, that begins to show that it is unlikely that the behavioral development was mere coincidence. The variable is then reapplied; if the desired behavioral change is recovered, the possibility of coincidence is diminished still further. Repeated "reversals" with similar outcomes can add their weight to the improbability of coincidence, although they are seldom performed. This is understandable, of course, when the behavior under study is a problem behavior, and every period of reversal is thereby likely to be a period of difficulty for the child and his associates. When the experimental technique is reinforcement, for example, the reversal technique may consist of discontinuation of reinforcement (e.g., Birnbrauer, Wolf, Kidder, and Tague, 1965b), noncontingent reinforcement (e.g., Risley and Wolf, 1967), or reinforcement of any behavior other than the one just developed by reinforcement (e.g., Sherman, 1965). Occasionally, two or more types of reversals or baselines may be compared in the same study (e.g., Hart *et al.*, 1968). Graphic examples of reversal designs are presented in later portions of this chapter.

The second design typically cited, but infrequently applied, may be called the "multiple baseline" (Baer, Wolf, and Risley, 1968) or "sequential analysis" design (Sherman and Baer, 1969). To apply this design, it is necessary to distinguish at least two, and preferably more, separate on-going behaviors in the child, all or some of which are suitable behaviors for application of the experimental variable under study. The variable is applied to these behaviors, one behavior at a time. Each time, the experimenter waits until the effect of the variable on that baseline is clear, and then applies it to the next. If each baseline changes in the appropriate direction only after the variable is applied to it, and if the variable is applied to different behaviors at different times, then it becomes clear that these changes cannot all be coincidental, and thus some must represent a functional relationship between the behaviors and the variable. One difficulty in the multiple baseline design is that at least some of the behaviors chosen for study must be sufficiently independent of one another that not all change when the variable is applied to only one of them. (If all do change at one time, the result may well be beneficial for the child, but the possibility of showing that the variable was responsible for this change is lost.) A compensating advantage is that no desirable behavioral change need be reversed, even briefly. However, certain desirable behavioral changes must be delayed later than they might have been accomplished, although only briefly so. A graphic example of a multiple baseline design is seen in Figure 19-1, taken from a study by Martin and Siegel (1966).

Sherman and Baer (1969) have argued that the inclusion of some kind of

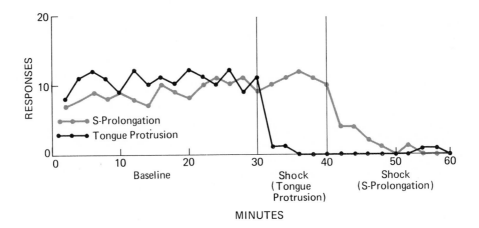

Fig. 19-1. Number of tongue protrusions and of prolongations in the stuttering be- havior of a subject during successive 2-minute periods of speech. One observer recorded tongue protrusion responses and a second observer recorded /s/–prolongation re- sponses. For the first 30 minutes there were no contingencies for either response. For the next 10 minutes, a shock was delivered through wrist electrodes following tongue protrusion responses, whereupon these responses decreased markedly. Then, during the last 20 minutes, shock was presented following /s/–prolongation responses and these responses decreased. Meanwhile, tongue protrusion responses remained low. (From Martin and Siegel, 1966, Fig. 9. Reprinted by permission of the authors and the *Journal of Speech and Hearing Research.*)

experimental design is extremely important in any application of behavior modi- fication techniques. Part of their argument follows:

. . . short term subservience to the apparent and most proximate therapeutic goal may in fact accomplish a long-term antitherapeutic outcome. The therapist may have just accomplished only one of a number of behavioral changes which his client requires. Unless he investigates the functional nature of the technique which has just apparently worked, he is failing to achieve the potential efficiency for the future work that this demonstration can give him. A good part of that technique may be irrelevant to the behavioral changes desired (indeed, the whole technique may be irrelevant—coincidence is no rarity in clinical work). Experimental manipulation of the technique could show whether or not it does contain truly functioning elements; further experimentation could narrow down those elements to their functional core (and thereby probably increase the efficiency of their application).

Furthermore, the therapist using a novel technique needs to be able to convince not only himself, but also other therapists that it is an effective technique; similarly, he needs to con- vince his client, or his client's parents, or his client's caretakers. These are primarily clinical goals rather than research goals; they are likely to be served best by experimental investiga- tions of novel therapies as they are ongoing in particular cases.

There is thorough precedent for such clinical practice in medical applications. The well trained allergist, for example, when he suspects a certain allergen as the critical offender of his patient, will remove that allergen from the patient's environment, and hope to note a decrease in allergic symptoms. If this decrease is found, the allergist nevertheless is quite likely to reintroduce the allergen into the environment, to see if the allergic symptoms will be recovered. He is, of course, merely checking against the possibility of coincidence: allergic symptoms (like problem behaviors) do occasionally decrease for unknown reasons, and reappear later. Thus, the allergist is making his patient worse, briefly, after he had succeeded in making him better. But it is hardly likely that the allergist would be accused of antitherapeutic practice. He means to advise his patient to rearrange his environment so as to minimize all future contact with the allergen. Such rearrangements typically are difficult, drastic, and expensive. The allergist wishes not to advise such a difficult course until he is certain that it will be a functional course. The analogy to behavior therapy [behavior modification] is close; thus, temporary manipulation of behavioral change, even for the worse, is not antitherapeutic if it leads the therapist to take wise action in the future for the client-subject and for other client-subjects with similar problems. (Sherman and Baer, 1969, pp. 217–218. Quoted by permission of the authors and McGraw-Hill Book Company.)

EXAMPLES OF EXPERIMENTAL BEHAVIOR MODIFICATION

Desirable Behaviors Too Low in Strength

POSITIVE REINFORCEMENT. Perhaps the simplest way to accomplish strengthening of desirable behavior currently too weak is to rearrange the positive reinforcers already existing in the child's present environment. This technique, of course, requires identifying these reinforcers; but this is often accomplished in the process of successful behavior modification, rather than before the modification is attempted. Thus, success in such efforts makes clear that the stimuli were reinforcing, the behaviors treated were operant, and the contingencies were efficient. Failure, by contrast, establishes almost nothing, because the reason for failure could lie in any one of these three areas, or in others.

Examples of the use of existing positive reinforcers to increase *desirable behaviors* are seen in a series of studies reported by Harris, Wolf, and Baer (1964) and Baer and Wolf (1968). These were studies of relatively mild problem behaviors in preschool children. The basic technique of remediation was social reinforcement; the source of this reinforcement was the attending behavior of preschool teachers. After measuring the baseline rate of the child's problem behavior, the teachers carefully attended to virtually all instances of the behavior they wished to strengthen, and typically produced an increase in its rate; then they briefly discontinued their reinforcement to demonstrate experimental control and thus rule out the possibility of coincidence. A typical instance is the recent study by Hart *et al.* (1968), in which an uncooperative young girl was reinforced for various categories of cooperative play with other children. There were five phases in the study. (a) The teachers first measured her rate of cooperative behavior for 10 days and found it stable, occurring on the average about 3 percent of the time. (b) They then applied frequent social reinforcement in a noncontingent manner for 7 days, and noted no change in the girl's typical

rate of cooperative play. (c) Subsequently, they applied much less social reinforcement, but contingent on instances of cooperative play (or approximations
to it), and in 12 days produced a markedly higher average rate of cooperation,
reaching an average of approximately 20 percent during the last 6 days of this
reinforcement. (d) Next they briefly discontinued the contingent reinforcement
by reinstating the condition of frequent noncontingent reinforcement which had
previously failed to produce any change in cooperative play. In this phase,

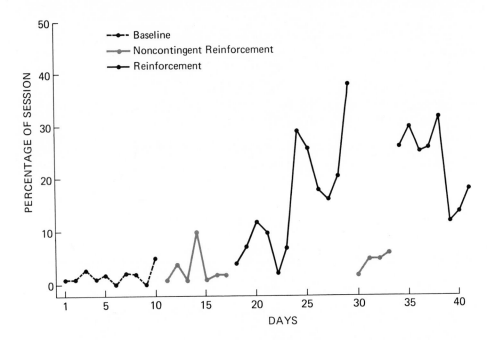

Fig. 19-2. Daily percentages of a preschool child's playtime spent in proximity to
other children and cooperative play with them. Data were collected daily in consecutive
ten-second intervals by an observer in a preschool setting. Experimental manipulations are noted on the figure. (From B. M. Hart, N. J. Reynolds, D. M. Baer, E. R.
Brawley, and F. R. Harris, *Journal of Applied Behavior Analysis*, 1968, *1*, 73–76.
Copyright 1968 by the Society for the Experimental Analysis of Behavior, Inc. Reprinted by permission of the authors and publisher.)

the noncontingent reinforcement did not support the high rate of cooperation
just built up by contingent reinforcement; during the 4 days of this condition,
the rate of cooperative play averaged about 5 percent. (e) Finally, resumption
of less frequent but contingent reinforcement immediately recovered a suitably
high rate of cooperative play in the child. Figure 19-2 presents these data
graphically.

One purpose of the brief discontinuations of a variable like reinforcement
in such studies can be to examine the possible independence of the behavior
being developed from the technique originally responsible for its increase. A
study in Ingram (reported by Baer and Wolf, in press) showed this usage. Ingram

was developing the class of social interaction skills in an asocial preschool boy. During the course of a relatively long condition of systematic teacher reinforcement for play with other children, the independence of the child's rates of various forms of such play was examined repeatedly, by brief discontinuations of systematic reinforcement (in favor of noncontingent, intermittent rein-

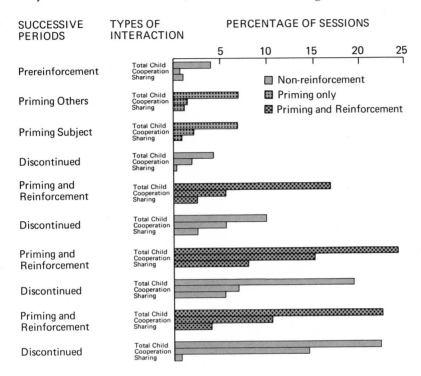

Fig. 19-3.   Measures of a preschool child's social interaction with other children, including two significant components of that interaction (cooperation and sharing), across ten consecutive conditions of an experiment. The bars represent mean percentages of playtime spent in each category of behavior, per condition, recorded daily in consecutive ten-second intervals by an observer. "Priming" was an operation in which suggestions were made either to other children, or to the subject child, or to both, about mutual play; these suggestions were often accompanied by the giving of materials appropriate to the suggested play. The figure shows a small effect resulting from priming alone; a larger effect resulting from the addition of social reinforcement to the priming procedure; and a gradual loss of experimental control of this effect as these procedures were repeated over several months of the study. (From Baer and Wolf, in press. Reprinted by permission of the authors and Appleton-Century-Crofts, Inc.)

forcement—the "natural" condition for most preschool child behavior). As shown in Figure 19-3, in the course of four spaced discontinuations of the techniques, the child's developing social skills decreased less and less with each successive discontinuation. The next-to-last discontinuation produced only a slight decrease in the child's total rate of social interaction, but a marked decrease in one of its components, cooperation. Consequently, reinforcement was resumed again. During the next discontinuation of reinforcement, no appreciable loss was seen in either the total rate or its important cooperative component, and the study was terminated. Repeated discontinuations, or reversals, thus can serve as a guide for termination of systematic behavior modification efforts.

Very similar applications have been made to behavior problems of children in school classrooms, using basically the existing potential for reinforcement inherent in the teacher's pattern of attending to, or ignoring, the children in the class (Hall, Lund, and Jackson, 1968; Zimmerman and Zimmerman, 1962). Wahler, Winkel, Peterson, and Morrison (1965) showed a similar potential for reinforcement in the attention of mothers, given to their children (paradoxically) for the very behaviors they hoped to reduce. These experimenters brought mothers and children to a clinic playroom and recorded the typical patterns of mother–child interaction which emerged there. These interactions frequently showed mothers attending to undesirable behaviors coupled with ignoring of desirable ones. The mothers were then trained to attend to the desired behaviors and to ignore the undesirable behaviors. The mothers were both cued to respond and reinforced for responding correctly by a light flash, operated by the experimenters from behind one-way viewing screens. Brief discontinuations of maternal reinforcement showed experimental control of behaviors such as excessive dependency, demanding responses, and opposition to the mother. The experimenters thus succeeded in teaching mothers behavior modification techniques not requiring that any new reinforcers be brought into the setting. The experimenters themselves presumably were capitalizing on the already existing reinforcement value their advice and instructions, as clinical psychologists, had for these troubled mothers. The light flash thus was merely a token for that reinforcement, and had function only for the mothers in the playroom, not for their children. However, the light flash clearly could control the mothers' attending behaviors, and that attention, it was shown, did have powerful function for the children's behaviors.

Among the reinforcers naturally existing within the child's environment are the primary ones of food and water. Particularly with institutionalized children, these stimuli have been used repeatedly in the service of behavior modification. Baer, Peterson, and Sherman (1967) developed widely generalized imitation in three retarded children, by working with them at mealtimes, feeding them spoonfuls of food as reinforcement. The children were taken at mealtimes to a special room by the experimenter, who had also picked up their meal at the kitchen. Thus, mealtimes became training sessions. During these sessions, the child was shown simple motor responses demonstrated by the experimenter, prefaced by the statement, "Do this." After a baseline of no response, imitative behaviors were shaped, one after another, until new demonstrations began to be imitated without direct training in the specific acts involved in them. Training continued until all new demonstrations were imitated on their first presentation, and continued to be imitated thereafter, even though some of these imitations were never reinforced. When reinforcement was given consistently only for behaviors other than imitations, however, the child's tendency to imitate experimenter demonstrations was greatly reduced. Imitation was recovered by resumption of reinforcement for it (rather than for any behavior other than it), and was elaborated into reliable vocal imitation (which had not existed previously).

Probably the most monumental use of a child's meals as reinforcers is exemplified by the work of Lovaas (1967). Dealing with autistic children institutionalized in a neuropsychiatric hospital, Lovaas set up extraordinarily extensive and comprehensive programs in motor and vocal imitation, language development, self-care, and academic skills. The great bulk of this development was accomplished over a span of months in autistic children generally considered nearly impossible to change through typical therapeutic means; much of it was brought about by an unusually thorough use of the food and drink reinforcers normally served from the kitchens of the institution. However, rather than serving these foods at relatively brief training sessions (as in the Baer *et al.* study, and most others), Lovaas and his colleagues extended the feeding sessions of each child for many hours throughout the day, broken by frequent but brief periods for vigorous outdoor play, or rest. Shifts of personnel made these reinforcement programs constitute nearly the majority of the child's waking hours; thus, thousands of hours, and hundreds of thousands of contingencies were invested in the behavioral development of each child. The results of the program constitute one of the outstanding demonstrations of comprehensive behavior modification so far available. These children displayed minimal repertoires at the outset of the program, as they had for a period of years. Yet in the program they steadily developed into social, verbal, self-caring individuals who answered questions, described their experiences, asked for what they wanted, read books, and began finally to relate to their parents. In the process, Lovaas and his associates displayed experimental control at many points in their application of techniques, thus establishing with good confidence that the fundamental aspects of their program were indeed functional, and not superstitious. In particular, their demonstrations repeatedly make it clear that good will, devotion, and effort do not bring about such behavior change without contingent reinforcement.

When the environment does not contain adequate reinforcers which may be reprogrammed for behavior modification, then they must be imported. Sometimes they will be imported simply because the experimenter does not have the time or capability to analyze the current environment for its usable existing reinforcers. Sometimes they will be imported because the experimenter estimates that the program of modification planned will require durably powerful reinforcers unlikely to be found in the present environment. In the simplest form of importation, the experimenter merely appears with toys, trinkets, or candies that the child does not ordinarily encounter, and relies upon them. Thus Risley and Wolf (1967), in their previously described study of language development, used ice cream as a reinforcer, and arranged to see children at times when they had not eaten for several hours.

However, the most comprehensive way to import reinforcers seems to be to introduce the so-called *token system*. A token, conceptually, is simply a generalized discriminative stimulus for some variety of reinforcer. In practice, however, the discriminative stimulus must be one which can be dispensed easily, can be kept in some way by each child operating within the system, and can be exchanged for the reinforcers it symbolizes. These reinforcers, typically called "back-up" reinforcers, are chosen for maximal power as such, but also for variety. It is clear that different children will be best reinforced by different stimuli at different times. Rather than try constantly to diagnose what a particular child's best reinforcer is on a given day, it is simpler and more effective to have such a wide variety available to him that he can always find an effective one available (if only he responds properly).

One of the first applications of this system was made by Ferster and DeMyer (1962) in their study of the possibility of operant conditioning in autistic children. Their experimental situation involved a number of devices which could be operated by inserting a coin in a slot. Thus, the coin became the stimulus discriminative for whatever reinforcement was afforded by these devices, which included a food and trinket vendor, pinball machine, color wheel, picture viewer, candy vendor, television set, performing monkey, phonograph, electric train, telephone set playing music, slide viewer, and electric organ. Most of these back-up reinforcers were used by the end of a lengthy study of two children, although certain reinforcers were used much less than others by a given child. With the token reinforcement (the coin), Ferster and DeMyer were able to demonstrate the acquisition of both simple and complex (stimulus matching) operant performances in autistic children, who at that date were still frequently considered incapable of responding to their environment in an adaptive way.

The autistic children of the Ferster and DeMyer study were, in effect, studied within a store, in which they could "buy" reinforeers of their own choice with the coins earned by learned behavior. Token systems in general require some such store, and the system will reinforce no better than will the items in the store. Thus, the token system, to achieve its potential, burdens the experimenter with the task of stocking such a store appropriately, maintaining it, and giving his subjects access to it at frequent enough intervals to maintain the reinforcement value of the tokens. Some experimenters, when possible, solve this problem by using money as the token, allowing their subjects access to the everyday world of stores, theaters, swimming pools, and other such commercially available reinforcers. Failing that possibility, they do indeed stock stores within the children's environment. (Most readers will recognize the money system as the familiar token system under which they operate. Although this system is most often studied as a phenomenon in areas such as economics and business administration, it still clearly qualifies as a behavior modification technique.)

The prime advantage of the token system, as already stated, is its uniform effectiveness across children and across time; but a second advantage nearly as great is the convenience of dispensing tokens, compared to the inconvenience of dispensing the back-up reinforcers that may be most effective for the child that day. Food is generally not easy to administer cleanly and promptly, and usually requires that the subject be seated at a table or in front of a vending machine. Thus, behavior modification is not easy to extend throughout the child's total environment if the reinforcer available is limited to such commodities. The ubiquitous M&M chocolate candy does represent a technological achievement of the food industry which obviates some of these disadvantages, in that training personnel can carry it about with them and dispense it fairly readily on all sorts of occasions—but the M&M is neither a universal nor a durably effective reinforcer. And when the child's best reinforcer is an event that takes place else-where—like a movie, field trip, swim, or walk—then it is simply impossible to dispense directly at the moments when the behavior to be strengthened occurs.

By contrast, poker chips, coins, plastic chips, points marked on a child's card, or holes punched in his card, are easy to dispense at virtually any moment or any place in a child's environment by training personnel. As soon as their discriminative function is established for a durably effective stock of back-up reinforcers, then correspondingly durable but much more convenient reinforce-ment can permeate all aspects of the child's situation, if desired.

It is a common observation in research on conditioned reinforcement that to make a stimulus discriminative for a reinforcer is to confer upon it, to some degree, the function of that reinforcer (Kelleher and Gollub, 1962). Thus it, too, will reinforce. It has also been shown that giving a stimulus discriminative func-tion is neither necessary nor always sufficient to give it reinforcing function; never-theless, this method remains the most reliable technique so far known for creating new reinforcers. The token system is exactly that: giving generalized discrimina-tive status to the token, and thus expecting generalized reinforcing function to accrue to it.[1]

A token system may well require shaping exercises, simply to become func-tional. This is more likely with retarded, autistic, or disturbed children; with other children, simple instructions often suffice. When shaping is required, a method suggested by Murray Sidman[2] can be used. It requires two experimenters to approach a group of children, one carrying tokens and the other, reinforcers. One experimenter places a token in a child's hand, and the second experimenter quickly approaches, takes the token from the child's hand, and gives him the reinforcer (perhaps a candy). Other children, seeing this, probably will approach the experimenter with the reinforcers, but are refused unless they have a token for the exchange. The first experimenter, noting those who were so refused, approaches them after a few seconds to give them a token, and the second experimenter, watching for this, then takes their token and offers them candy. Presently all children in the group are likely to be streaming back and forth between the two experimenters, who then may gradually increase their distance from each other, so as to provide the children with longer and longer periods of holding their tokens before exchange. The techniques for quickly extending this system to one in which the children collect tokens as reinforcers, and hold them for long periods before having an opportunity to exchange them, are obvious enough.

Birnbrauer and his associates (Birnbrauer, Bijou, Wolf, and Kidder, 1965a; Birnbrauer et al., 1965b) described a token system applied to the problem of academic instruction within a classroom setting for retardates. The tokens were exchangeable for food, drinks, toys, and school supplies. They were used in conjunction with programming techniques (based largely on fading procedures)

[1] As noted in Chapter 10, it may be possible to explain some of the effects of discriminative stimuli without assuming any conditioned reinforcing function.

[2] Personal communication to D. M. Baer and J. A. Sherman, 1968.

to develop and maintain basic academic skills such as writing, reading, following complex written instructions, and simple arithmetic. The children's progress was relatively rapid under these conditions. When token reinforcement for academic behaviors was discontinued in an experimental probe of the independence of these behaviors, it was found that of the 15 children in the class, 10 showed decreased accuracy in their work, and 4 of these began to display increasing rates of disruptive behaviors.

Wolf, Giles, and Hall (1968) applied token reinforcement to special classes of low-achieving fifth and sixth grade children from a poverty area of a large city. All of the children had scored at least two years below the norms for their grade level on a standardized reading test. The experimenters engaged the children (during summers and after school hours) for a "job"; the job consisted of doing school work and work from the usual academic workbooks available, scaled according to grade level. Pay for the job was given in the form of "points" marked on each child's card by a teacher of the class. Points were exchanged at the end of each day, or later, in four different exchange systems: money (which could be spent anywhere) or small items available in the classroom store; snacks available at the classroom store; larger items purchasable from the store (such as models, watches, cameras, radios, bicycles); and field trips (circus, swimming, zoo, sporting events, movies, etc.). Different colors of points operated for different exchange systems. Under this system, children showed marked gains on a standardized reading test, and their school grades advanced from the D and F level to a C average. A comparable control group not in this program showed less gain during the year required for the study. Within the experimental classroom, the child's preference for work in any given topic area could be controlled by manipulation of the number of points that could be earned by correct work completed in that area, permitting the experimenters to adjust the amounts of time invested by the child in areas of work such as reading, writing, and arithmetic in accordance with the child's relative deficits at the time.

Both of these examples emphasize the use of tokens in a specialized setting, the classroom. However, it should be clear that a token system can operate throughout a child's living environment, and that the tokens can be used not only by teachers, but also by parents, ward aides, nurses, social workers, etc.

NEGATIVE REINFORCEMENT.   There are negative reinforcers normally present in a child's environment. Just as the positive reinforcers already there may be rearranged for behavior modification, so may the negative ones, in principle. However, there are few experimental examples of this possibility, probably because of the natural preference for positive methods. When a child learns to avoid a negative reinforcer, he is likely to undergo punishment in the early stages, before efficient avoidance behavior develops. Punishment is rarely used as a systematic technique, for obvious reasons (but not always for good reasons: see Baer, in press).

A study by Gelber and Meyer (1965) provides one possibly illustrative example, although it did not involve experimental analysis of the process presumably operating. They developed appropriate toilet training in an institutionalized boy, simply by allowing him a brief period of time away from his ward whenever he defecated in the toilet, or when, at random moments of inspection, his pants were found to be clean. The possibility that the development of toilet training at that time resulted from other causes was not ruled out experimentally, but since the boy had gone some 13 years without developing the skill prior to the introduction of the experimental contingency, there may be some reason for crediting his sudden development to this contingency. At any rate, the study illustrates the possibility of using the child's current environment as a negative reinforcer [or, alternatively, of interpreting environments other than his present one as positive reinforcers, as Sherman and Baer (1969) implicitly did in discussing this study elsewhere]. Although it is not clear how this study should be classified, the possibility of using time away from the child's institutional, classroom, or home environment as a behavior-modifying contingency is certainly worth consideration.

Lovaas, Schaeffer, and Simmons (1965) presented a case that involved bringing new negative reinforcers into the environment and removing them contingent upon the social behavior of two autistic children. Autistic children, in their extremes, represent a thorough absence of social control. They sometimes appear to be selectively blind, deaf, and anesthetic to social objects (although they usually are properly in touch with their physical environment, in that they do not walk into walls, fall down stairs, or trip over objects more than is normal). Lovaas and his colleagues produced a very rapid change in this characteristic by placing the child barefoot on a floor that could be electrified at the experimenter's option. First, the experimenter asked the child to come to him periodically. A complete lack of response was observed. The experimenter then continued to ask the child to come to him, but the shock was turned on. It was removed only when the child moved toward the experimenter (if the child did not move within a short period of time, a second experimenter pushed the child toward the first experimenter and the shock was terminated). In subsequent sessions the shock was withheld if the child approached an experimenter within a short time following the experimenters' request. Within three sessions of this procedure, the children responded quickly to the experimenters' requests; this behavior was maintained for a nine month period during which no shocks were delivered. Lovaas and his colleagues also reported that the children showed more behavior than simple approach to the experimenter, in that they seemed more affectionate and seeking of the experimenters' company in the experimental room. This type of behavior was evaluated in a second part of the experiment. When the children were requested to hug or kiss the experimenter in the room in which the shock escape and avoidance trials had occurred, they showed a high proportion of appropriate responses to these requests. However, when these requests were given in a different room, the children displayed a low proportion of appropriate responses. The children were then given five shock-escape trials in the second room for approaching the experimenter when he requested them to do so. Following this the children displayed a high proportion of appropriate responses to the experimenter's requests to hug and kiss him, even though no further shocks were delivered.

The basic way to strengthen desirable behavior clearly is to reinforce it. However, it may sometimes prove profitable, or even necessary, to weaken incompatible behavior which competes with the desired response. Risley (1968), for example, found that in order to begin a program of speech development with an autistic girl living at home, he first had to suppress her extremely high rates of climbing furniture, door jambs, ledges, etc. This he accomplished by direct punishment of the climbing behavior, using electric shock.[3] The suppression of this behavior was important, not only because of the value of language development, which apparently could not proceed in this girl while the climbing behavior was prepotent, but also because the climbing had proven both costly and dangerous to the girl, resulting in broken teeth and other injuries in the recent past. Risley accomplished experimental analyses of certain aspects of the girl's behavior and the process of suppression, and also noted an absence of the usually expected side effects of punishment (such as the emergence of other, equally undesirable behaviors in replacement of the punished one). Given effective and durable suppression of the incompatible climbing behavior, Risley was then able to proceed with initial language development, using techniques described previously in this chapter. Thus, suppression of the girl's climbing behavior, while it did not in itself immediately produce the vocalizations desired, was important to the ability of another, concurrent program to accomplish that development. This is a typical pattern of application of such techniques in aid of desirable behavioral development.

Undesirable Behaviors Too High in Strength

EXTINCTION.   The classic method for reducing undesirable behavior is to identify its maintaining reinforcers, and rearrange the environment to prevent these from reinforcing the behavior. In the preschool behavior modification programs described previously (e.g., Harris et al., 1964), this technique was occasionally the central one in use, but more often figured as an incidental technique, as when extinction was applied to incompatible behaviors while social reinforcement was applied to the desired behavior. One study in which extinction was the central technique was done by Hart, Allen, Buell, Harris, and Wolf (1964), and concerned excessive rates of crying in two preschool children. In one case, the teachers simply discontinued attending to the boy when he cried, after observing a ten day baseline during which crying occurred about five to ten times per session. In the course of ten days of extinction, his crying rate declined. Attending to crying was then resumed, and crying recovered its previous high rate. It was then, of course, extinguished once again, with good success. The second case proceeded similarly, but the recovery of crying was not so clear-cut when crying

---

[3] Research has shown that electric shock is an extremely efficient negative reinforcer and/or punishing stimulus, in that it produces the desired learning rapidly; consequently, it minimizes the cumulative amount of aversive stimulation experienced by the child. Furthermore, the shock intensities used, though sometimes painful, are not physically harmful; and it has been demonstrated that undesirable emotional responses need not develop. Finally, its use is often demanded by a need to produce results rapidly, as in the treatment of self-destructive behaviors.

was again attended to after initial extinction. The study ended with low crying rates in both cases.

Lovaas (1967) has suggested that certain undesirable behaviors such as tantrums and self-destructive responses may have the operant function of escaping increased demands placed on the child, and thus can be decreased by ignoring them and maintaining the demands. This possibility was examined by Sailor, Guess, Rutherford, and Baer (1968). In the course of developing vocal imitations in a retarded girl, these experimenters were increasingly plagued by tantrums from her, which effectively subtracted much of the time available for language development. They dealt with these tantrums by rearranging the materials of their program. In one condition, whenever the girl had a tantrum, the next two phrases presented for imitation would be easier than the current level of imitation. Tantrums occurred at a rate of almost one per minute. Then, the experimenters reversed the contingency, such that following a tantrum the next two items for imitation would be more difficult than the current level. (The contingency would be more clearly extinction if the difficulty level were maintained following each tantrum; increasing the difficulty level after tantrums could be interpreted as a mild punishment contingency.) Tantrums declined markedly in frequency. Both conditions were repeated to demonstrate experimental control, and the language development program was able to proceed to labeling and simple grammatical development.

PUNISHMENT. Bed-wetting (nocturnal enuresis) is a frequent behavior problem in children, and certainly represents an undesirable behavior too high in strength. However, it should be recognized that the essence of this problem is lack of appropriate stimulus control. Urination must, of course, occur periodically in every child, but parents and caretakers prefer that it not occur at night in the child's bed. For some years, there has been a technique available which decreases bed-wetting with fair reliability, but which is difficult to classify. Its essential contingencies are mediated by an apparatus placed under the child in bed. This apparatus electrically senses the conductive urine and turns on a bell or buzzer to awaken him when he urinates. Observations indicate that children consistently awakened in this manner begin to awaken prior to wetting the bed, and thus often are able to go to the toilet first and thereby keep the bed dry (see Munn, 1954, pp. 386–387).

Early users of this technique, notably Mowrer and Mowrer (1938), analyzed it as a case of respondent conditioning. The child has already acquired daytime control, and therefore the problem is to train him to awaken (and hence exert control) before urination occurs during sleep. The bell, according to the theoretical analysis, is an unconditioned stimulus eliciting an unconditioned awakening response; bladder tension typically builds up in stimulation before urination occurs, and hence before the bell occurs, and thus functions as a conditional stimulus which eventually comes to elicit the waking response in time to prevent urination. Going to the toilet then becomes possible. (Later, the child will become able to stay dry while asleep; how he learns to do this is not at issue here, but it might be noted that since awakening is reliably followed by contraction of the urethral sphincter, the contraction is *functionally* an unconditioned response and can become conditioned to the bladder tension present during sleep.)

Lovibond (1963) argued that the technique could be interpreted as a case of operant avoidance conditioning. He suggested that the bell is a negative reinforcer (aversive stimulus), and that awakening and sphincter contraction are responses that can avoid the bell. Thus, after conditioning, the child should either awaken and go to the toilet or should maintain sphincter contraction throughout the night. Lovibond attempted to support this hypothesis by a study in which three different methods of training were compared. One method was the same as the one used by the Mowrers; when the child urinated, he was awakened by a bell. In a second method, electric shock was used instead of the bell, presumably both to awaken the child and to provide a negative reinforcer to be avoided by earlier (preurination) awakening. In the third method, a loud blast of sound from a car horn was presented when the child urinated. This blast was timed to last just long enough so that contraction of the sphincter would occur as the sound ended, thus making sphincter contraction an "escape" response. (The "escape" depended upon the accuracy of Lovibond's estimates of the time relations involved, and their stability from trial to trial.) The first method required the largest number of trials to produce continence. The second method required fewer trials to achieve the same outcome. The third method produced continence in the least number of trials, however, and Lovibond therefore argued that escape conditioning (or avoidance conditioning, or a mixture of the two) was the better interpretation of the processes involved.

Another, simpler interpretation of the technique is that it involves only punishment. According to Lovibond's interpretation, awakening and sphincter contraction are strengthened through avoidance or escape conditioning. According to a punishment interpretation, sphincter *relaxation* is weakened through punishment. (The weakening of sphincter relaxation necessarily results in relative strengthening of sphincter contraction, but sphincter contraction *per se* is not assumed to be conditioned in the punishment interpretation.) Being awakened by a bell is less punishing than being awakened by electric shock; and being awakened by a loud sound that lasts only as long as the relaxation of the sphincter lasts is both punishing and more efficient than being awakened by a shock that lasts until it is turned off, because the shock may punish both the sphincter relaxation which allows the voiding of urine, *and* the subsequent sphincter contraction (a desired response in this context) which promptly follows the stimulus presentation. Bell, shock, and car horn blast all meet the definition of punishing stimuli, in that after they were applied as consequences of the bed-wetting response, its frequency diminished.

Risley's (1968) use of a shock contingency to reduce the frequency of undesirable behaviors has already been described. Lovaas *et al.* (1965) have also used shock contingencies to reduce the frequency of self-stimulatory and tantrum behaviors in two autistic children. This reduction was maintained for a number of months, in which no shock was delivered, before the frequency of the behaviors began to increase. One noncontingent shock again suppressed the behavior to a zero frequency.

RESPONSE COST. A use of response costs was made by Baer (1962a). He studied three young thumbsuckers, who were engaged in watching movie cartoons. For an experimental application of costs, whenever a child placed his thumb in his mouth, the cartoons were discontinued; whenever the thumb was removed from the mouth, the cartoons were resumed. Thumbsucking was greatly decreased under this condition, and recovered when the condition was discontinued, across several replications. Children receiving noncontingent withdrawal of cartoons, at the same times when thumbsucking children had theirs withdrawn, were unaffected in their thumbsucking rate. The modification of thumbsucking was effective only within the laboratory setting where it took place; no attempt was made to generalize the control to other environments.

One complex form of response cost is the classic "time-out." Time-out refers either to the withdrawal of the child from the relevant aspects of his current environment, or the withdrawal of those aspects of the environment from him. In behavior modification applications, however, it tends to be a complicated operation difficult to analyze into components. For example, Wolf *et al.* (1964) markedly reduced tantrums and self-destructive behaviors in a temporarily institutionalized boy, simply by having him placed in his room on the occasion of each such response. Apart from the lack of experimental manipulation of this process (which was discouraged by the grave nature of the child's problems and the need for rapid, steady progress), it is extremely difficult to interpret. At least four interpretations are possible, each depending on assumptions about the stimulus functions of various aspects of the child's environment.

(a) To the extent that the current environment contained positive reinforcers, the time-out from it was a loss of these reinforcers contingent on the tantrum behavior. Thus, the mechanism of response cost would describe the weakening of the behaviors.

(b) The child was returned to the previous environment only after his tantrums and self-destructive behaviors had stopped for ten minutes. If the environment contained positive reinforcers, then return to it reinforced behaviors other than tantrums, and thereby competed with them.

(c) Time-out meant a lack of social contact. Thus, if his behaviors were socially maintained, they were now cut off from that maintenance, and extinction would have operated to reduce them.

(d) If the child's room, or isolation in the room, were a punishing stimulus, then the reduction could be attributed to a simple punishment contingency.

Time-out in practical situations is typically that complex; and its usual power in reducing undesirable behaviors may be due to the combination of two or more of these mechanisms into what appears to be a simple procedure.

Risley and Wolf (1967) used a somewhat simpler version of time-out in reducing tantrums, autisms, and responses of leaving the chair, in children undergoing language development. On the occasions of these behaviors (which greatly interfered with the progress of the training), the experimenter simply looked away (in extreme cases, however, he left the room). Looking back (or returning to the room) occurred only when the child had ceased the undesired behavior for a criterion span of seconds.

Reinforcement of Incompatible Behavior. One of the few applications of reinforcement of incompatible behaviors as a means of reducing undesirable behavior is found in a study by Wolf and Risley (1967) in the previously described use of tokens to establish academic skill in underachieving children. The single class of disruptive behavior evident in the classroom was a high rate of out-of-seat behavior, involving wandering about the classroom, overly long stays in the bathroom or at the pencil sharpener, and too frequent social interaction. Consequently, with an average class rate of about 17 such incidents per hour, a contingency was applied. At random intervals, averaging every 20 minutes, a timer rang audibly throughout the classroom. On each such occasion, extra token reinforcers were given to all children who were in their seats. The average rate of out-of-seat behavior declined to about 2 per hour. Experimental discontinuation of the contingency recovered the original rate rather promptly. For one subject in the group (a girl) the clock contingency was not completely effective. In this case the procedure was modified so that each of her peers working near her also earned token reinforcement when she was in her seat on the occasions of inspection. The modified procedure was effective, and experimental control of its effects was demonstrated. This procedure probably involved social reinforcement by peers for the subject's in-seat behavior, in addition to the token reinforcement.

The study demonstrates the feasibility of suppressing undesirable behavior with positive reinforcement for incompatible, desirable behaviors. The technical term, from the technology of operant conditioning and its schedules of reinforcement, is "differential reinforcement of behavior other than the one under examination," or, more briefly, differential reinforcement of other (DRO). When punishment is undesirable, and extinction is either impractical, dangerous, or not clearly applicable (because the maintaining reinforcers have not been identified), DRO may well prove the technique of choice. It should be clear, however, that successful application of DRO requires that the occasions when the incompatible behavior may be reinforced will not be discriminated by the child. If these occasions are discriminated, then all other occasions become stimulus conditions in which the original undesirable behavior may as well occur.

SUMMARY

The examples presented in this chapter represent a highly selected sample of behavior modification techniques applied to child behavior problems. Most were chosen because they embody an experimental analysis of their effectiveness, and this is important because behavior modification techniques represent a novel approach to child behavior, at least in their systematic application. Others were chosen because of their historical importance to this field, or because they illustrate an important point (even if they do not prove it in their own cases). All were chosen because they exemplify environmental influence, through specifiable contingencies with the child's behavior, as the most basic approach possible in accomplishing remediation of his problem.

References

Abrams, A. L. Delayed and irregular maturation versus minimal brain injury. *Clinical Pediatrics,* 1968, **7,** 344–349.

Abravanel, E. The development of intersensory patterning with regard to selected spatial dimensions. *Monographs of the Society for Research in Child Development,* 1968, 33(2, Whole No. 118).

Adamson, K., and Towell, M. E. Thermal homeostasis in the fetus and newborn. *Anesthesiology,* 1965, **26,** 531–548.

Adrian, E. D. Electrical responses of the human eye. *Journal of Physiology (London),* 1945, **104,** 84–104.

Ainsworth, M. D. S., and Bell, S. M. Attachment, exploration, and separation: Illustrated by the behavior of one-year-olds in a strange situation. Unpublished manuscript, 1969.

Akert, K., Orth, O. S., Harlow, H. F., and Schlitz, K. A. Learned behavior of rhesus monkeys following neonatal bilateral prefrontal lobotomy. *Science,* 1960, **132,** 1944–1945.

Albright, R. W., and Albright, J. B. Application of descriptive linguistics to child language. *Journal of Speech Research,* 1958, **1,** 257–261.

Alexander, P. *Sensationalism and scientific explanation.* London: Routledge & Kegan Paul, 1963.

Allport, F. H. *Theories of perception and the concept of structure.* New York: Wiley, 1955.

Allport, G. Eidetic imagery. *British Journal of Psychology,* 1924, **15,** 99–120.

Allport, G. The eidetic image and the after-image. *American Journal of Psychology,* 1928, **40,** 418–425.

Almy, M., Chittenden, E., and Miller, P. *Young children's thinking.* New York: Teachers College, Columbia University, Bureau of Publications, 1966.

Alsop, A. A conversation with Catfish. *Saturday Evening Post,* 1968, February 24, p. 18.

Ambrose, J. A. The development of the smiling response in early infancy. In B. M. Foss (Ed.), *Determinants of infant behavior.* Vol. I. London: Methuen (New York: Wiley), 1961. Pp. 179–201.

Ambrose, J. A. The age of onset of ambivalence in early infancy: Indications from the study of laughing. *Journal of Child Psychology and Psychiatry,* 1963, **4,** 167–181. (a)

Ambrose, J. A. The concept of a critical period for the development of social responsiveness in early human infancy. In B. M. Foss (Ed.), *Determinants of infant behavior.* Vol. II. London: Methuen (New York: Wiley), 1963. Pp. 201–225. (b)

American Psychological Association. Technical recommendations for psychological tests and diagnostic techniques. *Psychological Bulletin* (Supplement), 1954, **51,** No. 2, Part 2.

Ames, E. W., and Silfen, C. K. Methodological issues in the study of age differences in infants: Attention to stimuli varying in movement and complexity. Paper presented at the meeting of the Society for Research in Child Development, Minneapolis, March 1965.

Ames, L. B., Learned, J., Metraux, R., and Walker, R. Development of perception in the young child as observed in responses to the Rorschach test blots. *Journal of Genetic Psychology,* 1953, **82,** 183–204.

Amsel, A. The role of frustrative nonreward in noncontinuous reward situations. *Psychological Bulletin,* 1958, **55,** 102–119.

Amsel, A. Frustrative nonreward in partial reinforcement and discrimination learning: Some recent history and a theoretical extension. *Psychological Review,* 1962, **69,** 306–328.

Amsel, A. Secondary reinforcement and frustration. *Psychological Bulletin,* 1968, **69,** 278.

Amsel, A., and Roussel, J. Motivational properties of frustration: I. Effect on a running response of the addition of frustration to the motivational complex. *Journal of Experimental Psychology,* 1952, **43,** 363–368.

Anastasi, A. *Psychological testing.* New York: Macmillan, 1954.

Anastasi, A. *Differential psychology.* (3rd ed.) New York: Macmillan, 1958. (a)

Anastasi, A. Heredity, environment, and the question, "How?" *Psychological Review,* 1958, **65,** 197–208. (b)

Anastasi, A. *Psychological testing.* (2nd ed.) New York: Macmillan, 1961.

Anastasi, A., and D'Angelo, R. Y. A comparison of Negro and white preschool children in language development and Goodenough Draw-a-Man I.Q. *Journal of Genetic Psychology,* 1952, **81,** 147–165.

Anderson, J. E. The limitations of infant and preschool tests in the measurement of intelligence. *Journal of Psychology,* 1939, **8,** 351–379.

Anderson, K. E. *Research on the academically talented.* Washington, D.C.: National Education Association, 1961.

Anderson, L. D. The predictive value of infancy tests in relation to intelligence at five years. *Child Development,* 1939, **10,** 203–212.

Angelino, H., and Shedd, C. L. An initial report of a validation study of the Davis-Eels tests of general intelligence or problem solving ability. *Journal of Psychology,* 1955, **40,** 35–38.

Angell, J. R. *Psychology.* (4th ed.) New York: Holt, 1908.

Anisfeld, M., Barlow, J., and Frail, C. M. Distinctive features in the pluralization rules of English speakers. Paper presented at the meeting of the Eastern Psychological Association, Boston, April 1967.

Anisfeld, M., and Gordon, M. Phonological features in morphological rules of English. Paper presented at the meeting of the Eastern Psychological Association, Washington, D.C., April 1968.

Applegate, J. R. Phonological rules of a subdialect of English. *Word,* 1961, **17,** 186–193.

Archer, E. J. Re-evaluation of the meaningfulness of all possible CVC trigrams. *Psychological Monographs,* 1960, **74**(10, Whole No. 497).

Arey, L. B. *Developmental anatomy.* (7th ed.) Philadelphia: Saunders, 1965.

Aristotle. *Psychology.* (Translated by W. A. Hammond.) London: Swan Sonnenschein, 1902.

Armington, J., and Biersdorf, W. R. Flicker color adaptation in the human electroretinogram. *Journal of the Optical Society of America,* 1956, **46,** 393–400.

Armstrong, C. How do children grow? *New York State Education,* 1955, **43,** 181–183.

Aronfreed, J. The problem of imitation. In L. P. Lipsitt and H. W. Reese (Eds.), *Advances in child development and behavior.* Vol. 4. New York: Academic Press, 1969. Pp. 209–319.

Asch, S. E. Studies of independence and conformity: I. A minority of one against a unanimous majority. *Psychological Monographs*, 1956, **70**(9, Whole No. 416).

Asch, S. E., and Ebenholtz, S. M. The principle of associative symmetry. *Proceedings of the American Philosophical Society*, 1962, **106**, 135–163.

Asher, E. J. The inadequacy of current intelligence tests for testing Kentucky mountain children. *Journal of Genetic Psychology*, 1935, **46**, 480–486.

Atkinson, R. C., Hansen, D. N., and Bernbach, H. A. Short-term memory with young children. *Psychonomic Science*, 1964, **1**, 255–256.

Attneave, F., and Arnoult, M. D. The quantitative study of shape and pattern perception. *Psychological Bulletin*, 1956, **53**, 452–471.

Avery, M. E., and Normand, C. Respiratory physiology in the newborn infant. *Anesthesiology*, 1965, **26**, 510–521.

Axline, V. M. *Play therapy.* Boston: Houghton Mifflin, 1947.

Babb, H. Transfer from a stimulus complex to differentially discriminable components. *Journal of Comparative and Physiological Psychology*, 1957, **50**, 288–291.

Bach, E. *An introduction to transformational grammars.* New York: Holt, Rinehart & Winston, 1964.

Bach, E., and Harms, R. T. *Universals in linguistic theory.* New York: Holt, Rinehart & Winston, 1968.

Bacon, W. E., and Bindra, D. The generality of the incentive-motivational effects of classically conditioned stimuli in instrumental learning. *Acta Biologiae Experimentalis,* 1967, **27**, No. 2, 185–197.

Baer, D. M. Escape and avoidance responses of preschool children to two schedules of reinforcement withdrawal. *Journal of the Experimental Analysis of Behavior,* 1960, **3**, 155–159.

Baer, D. M. Effect of withdrawal of positive reinforcement on an extinguishing response in young children. *Child Development,* 1961, **32**, 67–75.

Baer, D. M. Laboratory control of thumbsucking by withdrawal and re-presentation of reinforcement. *Journal of the Experimental Analysis of Behavior,* 1962, **5**, 525–528. (a)

Baer, D. M. A technique of social reinforcement for the study of child behavior: Behavior avoiding reinforcement withdrawal. *Child Development,* 1962, **33**, 847–858. (b)

Baer, D. M. A case for the selective reinforcement of punishment. In C. Neuringer and J. L. Michael (Eds.), *Behavior modification in clinical psychology.* New York: Appleton-Century-Crofts, 1970, in press.

Baer, D. M., Peterson, R. F., and Sherman, J. A. The development of imitation by reinforcing behavioral similarity to a model. *Journal of the Experimental Analysis of Behavior,* 1967, **10**, 405–416.

Baer, D. M., and Wolf, M. M. The reinforcement contingency in preschool and remedial education. In R. D. Hess and R. M. Baer (Eds.), *Early education.* Chicago: Aldine, 1968. Pp. 119–129.

Baer, D. M., and Wolf, M. M. Some recent examples of behavior modification in preschool settings. In C. Neuringer and J. L. Michael (Eds.), *Behavior modification in clinical psychology.* New York: Appleton-Century-Crofts, 1970, in press.

Baer, D. M., Wolf, M. M., and Risley, T. R. Some current dimensions of applied behavior analysis. *Journal of Applied Behavior Analysis,* 1968, **1**, 91–97.

Bailyn, L. Mass media and children: A study of exposure habits and cognitive effects. *Psychological Monographs*, 1959, **73**(1, Whole No. 471).

Bakan, P. *Attention.* Princeton, N.J.: Van Nostrand, 1966.

Baker, C. T., Sontag, L. W., and Nelson, V. L. Individual and group differences in the longitudinal measurement of change in mental ability. In L. W. Sontag, C. T. Baker, and V. L. Nelson (Eds.), Mental growth personality development: A longitudinal study. *Monographs of the Society for Research in Child Development,* 1958, **23,** No. 2. Pp. 11–83.

Baker, R. A., and Osgood, S. W. Discrimination transfer along a pitch continuum. *Journal of Experimental Psychology,* 1954, **48,** 241–246.

Baldwin, A. L., Kalhorn, J., and Breese, F. H. Patterns of parent behavior. *Psychological Monographs,* 1945, **58,** No. 3.

Baldwin, K. C. The social position of the educable mentally retarded child in the regular grades in the public schools. *Exceptional Children,* 1958, **25,** 106–108, 112.

Bandura, A., Grusec, J. E., and Menlove, F. L. Some determinants of self-monitoring reinforcement systems. *Journal of Personality and Social Psychology,* 1967, **5,** 449–455. (a)

Bandura, A., Grusec, J. E., and Menlove, F. L. Vicarious extinction of avoidance behavior. *Journal of Personality and Social Psychology,* 1967, **5,** 16–23. (b)

Bandura, A., and Harris, M. B. Modification of syntactic style. *Journal of Experimental Child Psychology,* 1966, **4,** 341–352.

Bandura, A., and Menlove, F. L. Factors determining vicarious extinction of avoidance behavior through symbolic modeling. *Journal of Personality and Social Psychology,* 1968, **8,** 99–108.

Barker, R. G., and Wright, H. F. Psychological ecology and the problem of psychosocial development. *Child Development,* 1949, **20,** 131–143.

Barker, R. G., and Wright, H. F. *One boy's day: A specimen record of behavior.* New York: Harper, 1951.

Barnett, A. B., and Goodwin, R. S. Averaged evoked electroencephalographic responses to clicks in the human newborn. *Electroencephalography and Clinical Neurophysiology,* 1965, **18,** 441–450.

Barnett, A. B., Lodge, A., and Armington, J. C. Electroretinogram in newborn human infants. *Science,* 1965, **148,** 651–654.

Barnett, C. D., and Cantor, G. N. Discrimination set in defectives. *American Journal of Mental Deficiency,* 1957, **62,** 334–337.

Barry, H., III, Bacon, M. K., and Child, I. L. A cross-cultural survey of some sex differences in socialization. *Journal of Abnormal and Social Psychology,* 1957, **55,** 327–332.

Bartoshuk, A. K. Human neonatal cardiac acceleration to sound: Habituation and dishabituation. *Perceptual and Motor Skills,* 1962, **15,** 15–27. (a)

Bartoshuk, A. K. Response decrement with repeated elicitation of human neonatal cardiac acceleration to sound. *Journal of Comparative and Physiological Psychology,* 1962, **55,** 9–13. (b)

Bartoshuk, A. K. Human neonatal cardiac responses to sound: A power function. *Psychonomic Science,* 1964, **1,** 151–152.

Battig, W. F. Facilitation and interference. In E. A. Bilodeau (Ed.), *Acquisition of skill.* New York: Academic Press, 1966. Pp. 215–244.

Bayley, N. Mental growth in the first three years. *Genetic Psychology Monographs,* 1933, **14,** No. 1, 1–92.

Bayley, N. Factors influencing the growth of intelligence in young children. *Yearbook of the National Society for the Study of Education,* 1940, **39,** Part II, 49–79. (a)

Bayley, N. Mental growth in young children. *Yearbook of the National Society for the Study of Education,* 1940, **39,** Part II, 11–47. (b)

Bayley, N. Consistency and variability in the growth of intelligence from birth to eighteen years. *Journal of Genetic Psychology*, 1949, **75**, 165–196.

Bayley, N. Some increasing parent-child similarities during the growth of children. *Journal of Educational Psychology*, 1954, **45**, 1–21.

Bayley, N. On the growth of intelligence. *American Psychologist*, 1955, **10**, 805–818.

Bayley, N. A new look at the curve of intelligence. In A. Anastasi (Ed.), *Testing problems in perspective*. Washington, D.C.: American Council on Education, 1966. Pp. 384–399.

Bayley, N. Behavioral correlates of mental growth: Birth to thirty-six years. *American Psychologist*, 1968, **23**, 1–17.

Bayley, N., and Oden, M. H. The maintenance of intellectual ability in gifted adults. *Journal of Gerontology*, 1955, **10**, 91–107.

Bayley, N., and Schaefer, E. S. Correlations of maternal and child behaviors with the development of mental abilities: Data from the Berkeley Growth Study. *Monographs of the Society for Research in Child Development*, 1964, **29**(6, Whole No. 97).

Beach, F. A. The descent of instinct. *Psychological Review*, 1955, **62**, 401–410.

Beard, R. M. The nature and development of concepts. *Educational Review*, 1960, **13**, 12–26.

Bechtoldt, H. P. Construct validity: A critique. *American Psychologist*, 1959, **14**, 619–629.

Beilin, H., and Franklin, I. C. Logical operations in area and length measurement: Age and training effects. *Child Development*, 1962, **33**, 607–618.

Bekhterev, V. M. *La psychologie objective*. Paris: Alcan, 1913.

Bell, R. Q. Some factors to be controlled in studies of the behavior of newborns. *Biologia Neonatorum*, 1963, **5**, 200–214.

Bell, R. Q., and Costello, N. S. Three tests for sex differences in tactile sensitivity in the newborn. *Biologia Neonatorum*, 1965, **7**, 335–347.

Bellugi, U. The emergence of inflection and negation systems in the speech of two children. Paper presented at the meeting of the New England Psychological Association, Chicopee, Mass., November 1964.

Bellugi, U. The development of interrogative structures in children's speech. In K. F. Riegel (Ed.), *The development of language functions*. Rept. No. 8. Ann Arbor, Mich.: Center for Human Growth and Development, University of Michigan, 1965. Pp. 103–137.

Belmont, J. M., and Butterfield, E. C. The relations of short-term memory to development and intelligence. In L. P. Lipsitt and H. W. Reese (Eds.), *Advances in child development and behavior*. Vol. 4. New York: Academic Press, 1969. Pp. 29–82.

Benda, C. E., Squires, N. D., Ogonik, J., and Wise, R. Personality factors in mild mental retardation. Part I. Family background and sociocultural patterns. *American Journal of Mental Deficiency*, 1963, **68**, 24–40.

Benjamin, R. M., and Thompson, R. F. Differential effects of cortical lesions in infants and adult cats on brightness discrimination. *Experimental Neurology*, 1959, **1**, 305–321.

Bensberg, G. J., Jr. Concept learning in mental defectives as a function of appropriate and inappropriate "attention sets." *Journal of Educational Psychology*, 1958, **49**, 137–143.

Berger, S. M. Conditioning through vicarious instigation. *Psychological Review*, 1962, **69**, 450–466.

Bergmann, G. *Philosophy of science*. Madison, Wis.: University of Wisconsin Press, 1957.

Berkeley, G. *An essay toward a new theory of vision*. Dublin, 1709.

Berko, J. The child's learning of English morphology. *Word*, 1958, **14**, 150–177.

Berkowitz, L., and Friedman, P. Some social class differences in helping behavior. *Journal of Personality and Social Psychology*, 1967, **5**, 217–225.

Berkson, G., and Cantor, G. N. A study of mediation in mentally retarded and normal school children. *Journal of Educational Psychology*, 1960, **51**, 82–86.

Berlyne, D. E. Conflict and choice time. *British Journal of Psychology*, 1957, **48**, 106–118. (a)

Berlyne, D. E. Conflict and information theory variables as determinants of human perceptual curiosity. *Journal of Experimental Psychology*, 1957, **53**, 399–404. (b)

Berlyne, D. E. The influence of the albedo and complexity of stimuli on visual fixation in the human infant. *British Journal of Psychology*, 1958, **49**, 318–319. (a)

Berlyne, D. E. The influence of complexity and novelty in visual figures on orienting responses. *Journal of Experimental Psychology*, 1958, **55**, 289–296. (b)

Berlyne, D. E. *Conflict, arousal, and curiosity*. New York: McGraw-Hill, 1960.

Berlyne, D. E. Conflict and the orientation reaction. *Journal of Experimental Psychology*, 1961, **62**, 476–483.

Berlyne, D. E. Uncertainty and epistemic curiosity. *British Journal of Psychology*, 1962, **53**, 27–34.

Berlyne, D. E. Motivational problems raised by exploratory and epistemic behavior. In S. Koch (Ed.), *Psychology: A study of a science*. Vol. 5. New York: McGraw-Hill, 1963. Pp. 284–364.

Berlyne, D. E. *Structure and direction in thinking*. New York: Wiley, 1965.

Berlyne, D. E. Curiosity and exploration. *Science*, 1966, **153**, 25–33.

Berlyne, D. E., and Frommer, F. D. Some determinants of the incidence and content of children's questions. *Child Development*, 1966, **37**, 175–190.

Berlyne, D. E., and Lawrence, G. H., Jr. Effects of complexity and incongruity variables on GSR, investigatory behavior, and verbally expressed preference. *Journal of General Psychology*, 1964, **71**, 21–45.

Bernstein, B. Social structure, language and learning. *Educational Research*, 1961, **3**, 163–176.

Berry, J. W. Independence and conformity in subsistence-level societies. *Journal of Personality and Social Psychology*, 1967, **7**, 415–418.

Best, C. H., and Taylor, N. B. *The physiological basis of medical practice*. (6th ed.) Baltimore: Williams & Wilkins, 1955.

Bexton, W. A., Heron, W., and Scott, T. H. Effects of decreased variation in the sensory environment. *Canadian Journal of Psychology*, 1954, **8**, 70–76.

Beyrl, F. Über die Grössenauffassung bei Kindern. *Zeitschrift für Psychologie*, 1926, **100**, 344–371.

Bijou, S. W. A systematic approach to an experimental analysis of young children. *Child Development*, 1955, **26**, 161–168.

Bijou, S. W. Methodology for an experimental analysis of child behavior. *Psychological Reports*, 1957, **3**, 243–250. (a)

Bijou, S. W. Patterns of reinforcement and resistance to extinction in young children. *Child Development*, 1957, **28**, 47–55. (b)

Bijou, S. W. Operant extinction after fixed-interval schedules with young children. *Journal of the Experimental Analysis of Behavior*, 1958, **1**, 25–29.

Bijou, S. W. Discrimination performance as a baseline for individual analysis of young children. *Child Development*, 1961, **32**, 163–170.

Bijou, S. W. Theory and research in mental (developmental) retardation. *Psychological Record*, 1963, **13**, 95–110.

Bijou, S. W., Ainsworth, M. H., and Stockey, M. R. The social adjustment of mentally retarded girls paroled from the Wayne County Training School. *American Journal of Mental Deficiency*, 1943, **47**, 422–428.

Bijou, S. W., and Baer, D. M. Some methodological contributions from a functional analysis of child development. In L. P. Lipsitt and C. C. Spiker (Eds.), *Advances in child development and behavior.* Vol. 1. New York: Academic Press, 1963. Pp. 197–231.

Bijou, S. W., and Baer, D. M. *Child development.* Vol. 2. *Universal stage of infancy.* New York: Appleton-Century-Crofts, 1965.

Bijou, S. W., and Baer, D. M. (Eds.) *Child development: Readings in experimental analysis.* New York: Appleton-Century-Crofts, 1967.

Bijou, S. W., and Orlando, R. Rapid development of multiple-schedule performances with retarded children. *Journal of the Experimental Analysis of Behavior*, 1961, **4**, 7–16.

Bijou, S. W., Peterson, R. F., and Ault, M. H. A method to integrate descriptive and experimental field studies at the level of data and empirical concepts. *Journal of Applied Behavior Analysis*, 1968, **1**, 175–191.

Biller, H. B., and Borstelmann, L. J. Masculine development: An integrative review. *Merrill-Palmer Quarterly*, 1967, **13**, 253–294.

Bindra, D. Neuropsychological interpretation of the effects of drive and incentive-motivation on general activity and instrumental behavior. *Psychological Review*, 1968, **75**, 1–22.

Binet, A., and Simon, T. Upon the necessity of establishing a scientific diagnosis of inferior states of intelligence. *Année Psychologique*, 1905, **11**, 163–190.

Birch, D. Verbal control of nonverbal behavior. *Journal of Experimental Child Psychology*, 1966, **4**, 266–275.

Birch, H. G. *Brain damage in children. The biological and social aspects.* Baltimore: Williams & Wilkins, 1964.

Birge, J. S. The role of verbal responses in transfer. Unpublished doctoral dissertation, Yale University, 1941.

Birnbrauer, J. S., Bijou, S. W., Wolf, M. M., and Kidder, J. D. Programmed instruction in the classroom. In L. P. Ullman and L. Krasner (Eds.), *Case studies in behavior modification.* New York: Holt, Rinehart & Winston, 1965. Pp. 358–363. (a)

Birnbrauer, J. S., Wolf, M. M., Kidder, J. D., and Tague, C. E. Classroom behavior of retarded pupils with token reinforcement. *Journal of Experimental Child Psychology*, 1965, **2**, 219–235. (b)

Birns, B., Blank, M., and Bridger, W. H. The effectiveness of various soothing techniques on human neonates. *Psychosomatic Medicine*, 1966, **28**, 316–322.

Birns, B., Blank, M., Bridger, W. H., and Escalona, S. K. Behavioral inhibition in neonates produced by auditory stimuli. *Child Development*, 1965, **36**, 639–645.

Bisett, B. M., and Rieber, M. The effects of age and incentive value on discrimination learning. *Journal of Experimental Child Psychology*, 1966, **3**, 199–206.

Bitterman, M. E. Toward a comparative psychology of learning. *American Psychologist*, 1960, **15**, 704–712.

Bitterman, M. E., Fedderson, W. E., and Tyler, D. W. Secondary reinforcement and the discrimination hypothesis. *American Journal of Psychology*, 1953, **66**, 456–464.

Bitterman, M. E., and McConnell, J. V. The role of set in successive discrimination. *American Journal of Psychology*, 1954, **67**, 129–132.

Black, M. *Models and metaphors.* Ithaca, N.Y.: Cornell University Press, 1962.

Bland, J. H. (Chm.) Proceedings of the seminars on the Lesch-Nyhan syndrome. *Federation Proceedings*, 1968, **27**, 1017–1112.

Blank, M., and Bridger, W. H. Cross-modal transfer in nursery-school children. *Journal of Comparative and Physiological Psychology*, 1964, **58**, 277–282.

Blank, M., and Solomon, F. A tutorial language program to develop thinking in socially disadvantaged preschool children. *Child Development*, 1968, **39**, 379–389.

Blatt, B. The physical, personality and academic status of children who are mentally retarded attending special classes as compared with children who are mentally retarded attending regular classes. *American Journal of Mental Deficiency*, 1958, **62**, 810–818.

Blatt, B., and Garfunkel, F. Educating intelligence: Determinants of school performance of disadvantaged children. *Exceptional Children*, 1967, **33**, 601–608.

Blau, T. H., and Blau, L. R. The sucking reflex: The effects of long feeding vs. short feeding on the behavior of a human infant. *Journal of Abnormal and Social Psychology*, 1955, **51**, 123–125.

Bloom, B. S. *Stability and change in human characteristics.* New York: Wiley, 1964.

Bloom, B. S., Davis, A., and Hess, R. *Compensatory education for cultural deprivation.* New York: Holt, Rinehart & Winston, 1965.

Bloomfield, L. *Language.* New York: Holt, Rinehart & Winston, 1933.

Blum, E. R., and Kennedy, W. A. Modification of dominant behavior in school children. *Journal of Personality and Social Psychology*, 1967, **7**, 275–281.

Blum, G. S. *The Blacky Pictures.* New York: Psychological Corporation, 1950.

Blum, R. A., and Blum, J. S. Factual issues in the "continuity" controversy. *Psychological Review*, 1949, **56**, 33–50.

Boat, B. M., and Clifton, C., Jr. Verbal mediation in four-year-old children. *Child Development*, 1968, **39**, 505–514.

Bogartz, R. S., and Witte, K. L. On the locus of the stimulus familiarization effect in young children. *Journal of Experimental Child Psychology*, 1966, **4**, 317–331.

Bond, E. A. Tenth grade abilities and achievements. *Teachers College Contributions to Education*, 1940, No. 813.

Boneau, C. A. The interstimulus interval and latency of the conditioned eyelid response. *Journal of Experimental Psychology*, 1958, **56**, 456–460.

Bousfield, W. A., and Cohen, B. H. The occurrence of clustering in the recall of randomly arranged words of different frequencies of usage. *Journal of General Psychology*, 1955, **52**, 83–95.

Bousfield, W. A., Esterson, S., and Whitmarsh, G. A. A study of developmental changes in conceptual and perceptual associative clustering. *Journal of Genetic Psychology*, 1958, **92**, 95–102.

Bower, T. G. R. Discrimination of depth in premature infants. *Psychonomic Science*, 1964, **1**, 368.

Bower, T. G. R. The determinants of perceptual unity in infancy. *Psychonomic Science*, 1965, 3, 323–324. (a)

Bower, T. G. R. Stimulus variables determining space perception in infants. *Science*, 1965, **149**, 88–89. (b)

Bower, T. G. R. Slant perception and shape constancy in infants. *Science*, 1966, **151**, 832–834. (a)

Bower, T. G. R. The visual world of infants. *Scientific American*, 1966, **215**, 80–93. (b)

Bower, T. G. R. Phenomenal identity and form perception in an infant. *Perception & Psychophysics,* 1967, **2,** 74–76.

Bowerman, C. E., and Elder, G. H. Variations in adolescent perception of family power structure. *American Sociological Review,* 1964, **29,** 551–567.

Bowlby, J. The nature of the child's tie to his mother. *International Journal of Psychoanalysis,* 1958, **39,** 350–373.

Bowlby, J. *Attachment and loss.* Vol. 1. *Attachment.* London: Hogarth (New York: Basic Books), 1969.

Brackbill, Y. Extinction of the smiling response in infants as a function of reinforcement schedule. *Child Development,* 1958, **29,** 115–124.

Brackbill, Y. Research and clinical work with children. In R. A. Bower (Ed.), *Some views on Soviet psychology.* Washington, D.C.: American Psychological Association, 1962. Pp. 99–164.

Brackbill, Y. (Ed.) *Infancy and early childhood.* New York: Free Press, 1967.

Brackbill, Y., Adams, G., Crowell, D. H., and Gray, M. L. Arousal level in neonates and preschool children under continuous auditory stimulation. *Journal of Experimental Child Psychology,* 1966, **4,** 178–188.

Brackbill, Y., Bravos, A., and Starr, R. H. Delay-improved retention of a difficult task. *Journal of Comparative and Physiological Psychology,* 1962, **55,** 947–952. (a)

Brackbill, Y., Fitzgerald, H. E., and Lintz, L. M. A developmental study of classical conditioning. *Monographs of the Society for Research in Child Development,* 1967, **32,** No. 8.

Brackbill, Y., and Kappy, M. S. Delay of reinforcement and retention. *Journal of Comparative and Physiological Psychology,* 1962, **55,** 14–18.

Brackbill, Y., Kappy, M. S., and Starr, R. H. Magnitude of reward and probability learning. *Journal of Experimental Psychology,* 1962, **63,** 32–35. (b)

Brackbill, Y., and Koltsova, M. M. Conditioning and learning. In Y. Brackbill (Ed.), *Infancy and early childhood.* New York: Free Press, 1967. Pp. 207–286.

Brackbill, Y., and O'Hara, J. The relative effectiveness of reward and punishment for discrimination learning in children. *Journal of Comparative and Physiological Psychology,* 1958, **51,** 747–751.

Bradway, K. P. Paternal occupational intelligence and mental deficiency. *Journal of Applied Psychology,* 1935, **19,** 527–542.

Bradway, K. P. I.Q. constancy on the revised Stanford-Binet from the preschool to the junior high school level. *Journal of Genetic Psychology,* 1944, **65,** 197–217.

Bradway, K. P., and Thompson, C. W. Intelligence at adulthood: A twenty-five year follow-up. *Journal of Educational Psychology,* 1962, **53,** 1–14.

Braine, L. G. Age changes in the mode of perceiving geometric forms. *Psychonomic Science,* 1965, **2,** 155–156.

Braine, M. D. S. The ontogeny of certain logical operations: Piaget's formulations examined by non-verbal methods. *Psychological Monographs,* 1959, **73**(5, Whole No. 475).

Braine, M. D. S. Piaget on reasoning: A methodological critique and alternative proposals. In W. Kessen and C. Kuhlman (Eds.), Thought in the young child. *Monographs of the Society for Research in Child Development,* 1962, **27,** No. 2. Pp. 41–63.

Braine, M. D. S. On learning the grammatical order of words. *Psychological Review,* 1963, **70,** 323–348. (a)

Braine, M. D. S. The ontogeny of English phrase structure: The first phase. *Language,* 1963, **39,** 1–13. (b)

Braine, M. D. S. Learning the positions of words relative to a marker element. *Journal of Experimental Psychology,* 1966, **72,** 532–540.

Braine, M. D. S. The acquisition of language in infant and child. In C. Reed (Ed.), *The learning of language.* In press.

Braley, L. S. Some conditions influencing the acquisition and utilization of cues. *Journal of Experimental Psychology,* 1962, **64,** 62–66.

Braley, L. S., and Johnson, D. M. Novelty effects in cue acquisition and utilization. *Journal of Experimental Psychology,* 1963, **66,** 421–422.

Bridger, W. H. Sensory discrimination and autonomic function in the newborn. *Journal of the American Academy of Child Psychiatry,* 1962, **1,** 67–82.

Bridges, K. M. B. A genetic theory of emotions. *Journal of Genetic Psychology,* 1930, **37,** 514–527.

Bridges, K. M. B. Emotional development in early infancy. *Child Development,* 1932, **3,** 324–341.

Brison, D. W. Acquisition of conservation of substance in a group situation. Unpublished doctoral dissertation, University of Illinois, 1965.

Brodbeck, A. J. The effect of three feeding variables on nonnutritive sucking of newborn infants. *American Psychologist,* 1950, **5,** 292–293.

Bronshtein, A. I., Antonova, T. G., Kamenetskaya, A. G., Luppova, N. N., and Syrova, V. A. On the development of the functions of analyzers in infants and some animals at the early stage of ontogenesis. In *Problems of evolution of physiological functions.* Washington, D.C.: Office of Tech. Serv. Rep. No. 60-61066, 1960.

Bronshtein, A. I., and Petrova, E. P. An investigation of the auditory analyzer in neonates and young infants. *Zhurnal Vysshei Nervnoi Deyatel'nosti imeni I. P. Pavlova,* 1952, **2,** 333–343. [Translated and reprinted as "The auditory analyzer in young infants" in Y. Brackbill and G. G. Thompson (Eds.), *Behavior in infancy and early childhood: A book of readings.* New York: Free Press, 1967. Pp. 163–172.]

Bronson, W. C. Dimensions of ego and infantile identification. *Journal of Personality,* 1959, **27,** 532–545.

Brooks, L. R. The suppression of visualization by reading. *Quarterly Journal of Experimental Psychology,* 1967, **19,** Part 4, 289–299.

Brossard, L. M., and Décarie, T. G. Comparative reinforcing effect of eight stimulations on the smiling response of infants. *Journal of Child Psychology and Psychiatry,* 1968, **9,** 51–59.

Brown, J. L., and Mueller, C. G. Brightness discrimination and brightness contrast. In C. H. Graham, N. R. Bartlett, J. L. Brown, Y. Hsia, C. G. Mueller, and L. A. Riggs (Eds.), *Vision and visual perception.* New York: Wiley, 1965. Pp. 208–250.

Brown, J. S. Problems presented by the concept of acquired drives. In *Current theory and research in motivation.* Lincoln, Neb.: University of Nebraska Press, 1953. Pp. 1–21.

Brown, J. S., and Farber, I. E. Emotions conceptualized as intervening variables—with suggestions toward a theory of frustration. *Psychological Bulletin,* 1951, **48,** 465–495.

Brown, J. S., and Farber, I. E. Secondary motivational systems. *Annual Review of Psychology,* 1968, **19,** 99–134.

Brown, R. W. Linguistic determinism and the part of speech. *Journal of Abnormal and Social Psychology,* 1957, **55,** 1–5.

Brown, R. W. How shall a thing be called? *Psychological Review,* 1958, **65,** 14–21. (a)

Brown, R. W. *Words and things.* Glencoe, Ill.: Free Press, 1958. (b)

Brown R. [W.] The development of Wh questions in child speech. *Journal of Verbal Learning and Verbal Behavior,* 1968, **7,** 279–290.

Brown, R. W., and Bellugi, U. Three processes in the child's acquisition of syntax. *Harvard Educational Review*, 1964, **34**, 133–151.

Brown, R. W., and Berko, J. Word association and the acquisition of grammar. *Child Development*, 1960, **31**, 1–14.

Brown, R. W., Cazden, C., and Bellugi, U. The child's grammar from I to III. In J. P. Hill (Ed.), *Minnesota symposium on child psychology*. Vol. II. Minneapolis: University of Minnesota Press, 1968. Pp. 28–73.

Brown, R. [W.], and Fraser, C. The acquisition of syntax. In U. Bellugi and R. Brown (Eds.), The acquisition of language. *Monographs of the Society for Research in Child Development*, 1964, **29**(1, Whole No. 92). Pp. 43–79.

Brown, R. [W.], Fraser, C., and Bellugi, U. Explorations in grammar evaluation. In U. Bellugi and R. Brown (Eds.), The acquisition of language. *Monographs of the Society for Research in Child Development*, 1964, **29**(1, Whole No. 92). Pp. 79–92.

Bruce, M. Factors affecting intelligence test performance of whites and Negroes in the rural south. *Archives of Psychology*, 1940, **36**, No. 252.

Bruck, K. Temperature regulation in the newborn infant. *Biologia Neonatorum*, 1961, **3**, 65–119.

Bruck, K., Parmelee, A. H., and Bruck, M. Neutral temperature range and range of "thermal comfort" in premature infants. *Biologia Neonatorum*, 1962, **4**, 32–51.

Bruner, J. S. The course of cognitive growth. *American Psychologist*, 1964, **19**, 1–15.

Bruner, J. S. On the conservation of liquids. In J. S. Bruner, R. R. Olver, P. M. Greenfield *et al.*, *Studies in cognitive growth*. New York: Wiley, 1966. Pp. 183–207.

Bruner, J. S., and Olver, R. R. Development of equivalence transformations in children. In J. C. Wright and J. Kagan (Eds.), Basic cognitive processes in children: Report of the second conference on intellective development. *Monographs of the Society for Research in Child Development*, 1963, **28**(2, Whole No. 86). Pp. 125–140.

Bruning, J. L. The effects of magnitude of reward and percentage of reinforcement on a lever movement response. *Child Development*, 1964, **35**, 281–285.

Brunswik, E. *Perception and the representative design of psychological experiments*. Berkeley: University of California Press, 1956.

Budoff, M., and Quinlan, D. Auditory and visual learning in primary grade children. *Child Development*, 1964, **35**, 583–586.

Bugelski, B. R. Extinction with and without sub-goal reinforcement. *Journal of Comparative Psychology*, 1938, **26**, 121–134.

Bugelski, B. R. *The psychology of learning*. New York: Holt, 1956.

Bugelski, B. R. *An introduction to the principles of psychology*. New York: Holt, Rinehart & Winston, 1960.

Bugelski, B. R. Presentation time, total time, and mediation in paired-associate learning. *Journal of Experimental Psychology*, 1962, **63**, 409–412.

Bugelski, B. R. Learning theory and the reading process. Paper presented at the 23rd Annual Conference on Reading, University of Pittsburgh, July 1968.

Bugelski, B. R. Images as mediators in one-trial paired-associate learning—II: Self-timing in successive lists. *Journal of Experimental Psychology*, 1969, in press.

Bugelski, B. R., and Alampay, D. A. The role of frequency in developing perceptual sets. *Canadian Journal of Psychology*, 1961, **15**, 205–211.

Bugelski, B. R., Kidd, E., and Segmen, J. Image as a mediator in one-trial paired-associate learning. *Journal of Experimental Psychology*, 1968, **76**, 69–73.

Bugelski, B. R., and Rickwood, J. Presentation time, total time, and mediation in paired-associate learning: Self pacing. *Journal of Experimental Psychology*, 1963, **65**, 616–617.

Burke, H. R. Raven's Progressive Matrices: A review and critical evaluation. *Journal of Genetic Psychology*, 1958, **93**, 199–228.

Burks, B. S. The relative influence of nature and nurture upon mental development: A comparative study of foster parent-foster child resemblance and true parent-true child resemblance. *Yearbook of the National Society for the Study of Education*, 1928, **27**, Part I, 219–316.

Burling, R. Language development of a Garo and English speaking child. *Word*, 1959, **15**, 45–68.

Burnett, A. Assessment of intelligence in a restricted environment. Unpublished doctoral dissertation, McGill University, 1955. (Cited in Ferguson, 1956.)

Burnett, A., Beach, H. D., and Sullivan, A. M. Intelligence in a restricted environment. *Canadian Psychologist*, 1963, **4a**, 126–136.

Buros, O. K. (Ed.) *The sixth mental measurements yearbook.* Highland Park, N.J.: Gryphon Press, 1965.

Burt, C. The differentiation of intellectual ability. *British Journal of Educational Psychology*, 1954, **24**, 76–90.

Burt, C. The evidence for the concept of intelligence. *British Journal of Educational Psychology*, 1955, **25**, 158–177.

Burt, C. The inheritance of mental ability. *American Psychologist*, 1958, **13**, 1–15.

Burt, C. Class differences in general intelligence III. *British Journal of Statistical Psychology*, 1959, **12**, 15–33.

Burt, C. Intelligence and social mobility. *British Journal of Statistical Psychology*, 1961, **14**, 3–24.

Burt, C. Genetic determination of intelligence: A study of monozygotic twins reared together and apart. *British Journal of Psychology*, 1966, **57**, 137–153.

Butler, R. A. The effect of deprivation of visual incentives on visual exploration motivation in monkeys. *Journal of Comparative and Physiological Psychology*, 1957, **50**, 177–179.

Butterfield, G., and Butterfield, E. C. Acquisition of a learning set is independent of interproblem interval. *Journal of Experimental Child Psychology*, 1967, **5**, 318–323.

Bykov, V. D. The rapidity of conditioned reflex formation as an index of the development of higher nervous activity in the course of ontogenetic development. *Pavlov Journal of Higher Nervous Activity*, 1960, **10**, 107–117.

Byrne, D., and Clore, G. L., Jr. Effectance arousal and attraction. *Journal of Personality and Social Psychology Monographs*, 1967, **7**, Part 2 (Whole No. 638).

Bryne, D., and Griffitt, W. A developmental investigation of the law of attraction. *Journal of Personality and Social Psychology*, 1966, **4**, 699–702.

Bystroletova, G. N. The formation in neonates of a conditioned reflex to time in connection with daily feeding rhythm. *Zhurnal Vysshei Nervnoi Deyatel'nosti imeni I. P. Pavlova*, 1954, **4**, 601–609.

Cakmak, M. B. Extinction vs. reversal of a position discrimination with differing amounts of reward in alternative goal boxes. Paper presented at the meeting of the Eastern Psychological Association, Atlantic City, April 1965.

Calvin, A. D. Configurational learning in children. *Journal of Educational Psychology*, 1955, **46**, 117–120.

Calvin, A. D., and Clifford, L. T. The relative efficiency of various types of stimulus-objects in discriminative learning by children. *American Journal of Psychology*, 1956, **69**, 103–106.

Calvin, A. D., Clancy, J. J., and Fuller, J. B. A further investigation of various stimulus-objects in discriminative learning by children. *American Journal of Psychology*, 1956, **69**, 647–649.

Cameron, J., Livson, N., and Bayley, N. Infant vocalizations and their relation to mature intelligence. *Science*, 1967, **157**, 331–333.

Cameron, N., and Magaret, A. *Behavior pathology.* Boston: Houghton Mifflin, 1951.

Campbell, B. A. Developmental studies of learning and motivation in infra-primate mammals. In H. W. Stevenson, E. H. Hess, and H. L. Rheingold (Eds.), *Early behavior: Comparative and developmental approaches.* New York: Wiley, 1967. Pp. 43–71.

Campbell, B. A., and Cicala, G. A. Studies of water deprivation in rats as a function of age. *Journal of Comparative and Physiological Psychology*, 1962, **55**, 763–769.

Campbell, J. D. Peer relations in childhood. In M. L. Hoffman and L. W. Hoffman (Eds.), *Review of child development research.* Vol. 1. New York: Russell Sage Foundation, 1964. Pp. 289–322.

Campione, J., Hyman, L., and Zeaman, D. Dimensional shifts and reversals in retardate discrimination learning. *Journal of Experimental Child Psychology*, 1965, **2**, 255–263.

Canestrini, S. Über das Sinnesleben des Neugeborenen. (Sensations of the Neonate.) *Monographien aus dem Gesamtgebiet der Neurologie und Psychiatrie*, No. 5. Berlin: Springer, 1913. (Cited by Carmichael, 1954b.)

Cannon, W. B. *Bodily changes in pain, hunger, fear, and rage.* New York: Appleton, 1929.

Cantor, G. N. Effects of three types of pretraining on discrimination learning in preschool children. *Journal of Experimental Psychology*, 1955, **49**, 339–342.

Cantor, G. N. Basic learning research and mental retardation. In E. P. Trapp and P. Himelstein (Eds.), *Readings on the exceptional child.* New York: Appleton-Century-Crofts, 1962. Pp. 170–180.

Cantor, G. N., and Cantor, J. H. Effects of conditioned-stimulus familiarization on instrumental learning in children. *Journal of Experimental Child Psychology*, 1964, **1**, 71–78.

Cantor, G. N., and Cantor, J. H. Discriminative reaction time performance in preschool children as related to stimulus familiarization. *Journal of Experimental Child Psychology*, 1965, **2**, 1–9.

Cantor, G. N., and Cantor, J. H. Discriminative reaction time in children as related to stimulus familiarization. *Journal of Experimental Child Psychology*, 1966, **4**, 150–157.

Cantor, G. N., and Ryan, T. J. Retention of verbal paired-associates in normals and retardates. *American Journal of Mental Deficiency*, 1962, **66**, 861–865.

Cantor, J. H. Amount of pretraining as a factor in stimulus predifferentiation and performance set. *Journal of Experimental Psychology*, 1955, **50**, 180–184.

Cantor, J. H. Transfer of stimulus pretraining. In L. P. Lipsitt and C. C. Spiker (Eds.), *Advances in child development and behavior.* Vol. 2. New York: Academic Press, 1965. Pp. 19–58.

Capaldi, E. J., and Stevenson, H. W. Response reversal following different amounts of training. *Journal of Comparative and Physiological Psychology*, 1957, **50**, 195–198.

Carlson, V. R. Overestimation in size-constancy judgments. *American Journal of Psychology*, 1960, **73**, 199–213.

Carlson, V. R. Size-constancy judgments and perceptual compromise. *Journal of Experimental Psychology*, 1962, **63**, 68–73.

Carment, O. W., and Miles, C. G. Resistance to extinction and rate of lever-pulling as a function of percentage of reinforcement and number of acquisition trials. *Canadian Journal of Psychology*, 1962, **64**, 249–252.

Carmichael, L. (Ed.) *Manual of child psychology.* (2nd ed.) New York: Wiley, 1954. (a)

Carmichael, L. The onset and early development of behavior. In L. Carmichael (Ed.), *Manual of child psychology.* (2nd ed.) New York: Wiley, 1954. Pp. 60–185. (b)

Caron, R. F. Visual reinforcement in young infants. *Journal of Experimental Child Psychology*, 1967, **5**, 489–511.

Carroll, J. B. Language development in children. In C. W. Harris (Ed.), *Encyclopedia of educational research.* New York: Macmillan, 1960. Pp. 744–752.

Carroll, W. R. Response availability and percentage of occurrence of response members in children's paired-associate learning. *Journal of Experimental Child Psychology*, 1966, **4**, 232–241.

Carroll, W. R., and Penney, R. K. Percentage of occurrence of response members, associative strength, and competition in paired-associate learning in children. *Journal of Experimental Child Psychology*, 1966, **3**, 258–266.

Carter, C. H. *Medical aspects of mental retardation.* Springfield, Ill.: Thomas, 1965.

Casler, L. Maternal deprivation: A critical review of the literature. *Monographs of the Society for Research in Child Development*, 1961, **26**(2, Whole No. 80).

Cassell, R. L. Serial verbal learning and retroactive inhibition in aments and children. *Journal of Clinical Psychology*, 1957, **13**, 369–372.

Castaneda, A. Supplementary report: Differential position habits and anxiety in children as determinants of performance in learning. *Journal of Experimental Psychology*, 1961, **61**, 257–258.

Castaneda, A. The paired-associates method and the study of conflict. In L. P. Lipsitt and C. C. Spiker (Eds.), *Advances in child development and behavior.* Vol. 2. New York: Academic Press, 1965. Pp. 1–18.

Castaneda, A., Fahel, L., and Odom, R. Associative characteristics of sixty-three adjectives and their relation to verbal paired-associate learning in children. *Child Development*, 1961, **32**, 297–304.

Castaneda, A., McCandless, B. R., and Palermo, D. S. The children's form of the manifest anxiety scale. *Child Development*, 1956, **27**, 317–326. (a)

Castaneda, A., Palermo, D. S., and McCandless, B. R. Complex learning and performance as a function of anxiety in children and task difficulty. *Child Development*, 1956, **27**, 327–332. (b)

Catalano, F. L., and McCarthy, D. Infant speech as a possible predictor of later intelligence. *Journal of Psychology*, 1954, **38**, 203–209.

Cattell, J. McK. Mental tests and measurements. *Mind*, 1890, **15**, 373–380.

Cattell, P. *The measurement of intelligence in young children.* (Rev. ed.) New York: Psychological Corporation, 1960.

Cattell, R. B., and Cattell, A. K. S. *IPAT Culture Free Intelligence Test.* Champaign, Ill.: Institute of Personality and Ability Testing, 1950–1959.

Caul, W. F., and Ludvigson, H. W. The effect of overlearning on response shifting. *Psychonomic Science*, 1964, **1**, 159–160.

Cautela, J. R. Misconceptions: Intelligence and the I.Q. *Education*, 1958, **78**, 300–303.

Cautela, J. R. Meaningless questions concerning "intelligence." *Education*, 1959, **80**, 33–36.

Cavanaugh, M. C., Cohen, I., Dunphy, D., Ringwall, E. A., and Goldberg, I. D. Prediction from the Cattell Infant Intelligence Scale. *Journal of Consulting Psychology*, 1957, **21**, 33–37.

Cazden, C. B. Environmental assistance to the child's acquisition of grammar. Unpublished doctoral dissertation, Harvard University, 1965.

Cazden, C. B. Subcultural differences in child language: An interdisciplinary review. *Merrill-Palmer Quarterly*, 1966, **12**, 185–220.

Chang, J., and Block, J. A study of identification in male homosexuals. *Journal of Consulting Psychology*, 1960, **24**, 307–310.

Chao, Y. R. The Cantian idiolect: An analysis of the Chinese spoken by a twenty-eight-months-old child. In W. I. Fischel (Ed.), Semitic and Oriental studies. *University of California Publications in Semitic Philology*, 1951, **11**, 27–44.

Chapanis, A., and Williams, W. C. Results of a mental survey with the Kuhlmann-Anderson Intelligence Tests in Williamson County, Tenn. *Journal of Genetic Psychology*, 1945, **67**, 27–55.

Charles, D. C. Ability and accomplishment of persons earlier judged mentally deficient. *Genetic Psychology Monographs*, 1953, **47**, first half, 3–71.

Charlesworth, R., and Hartup, W. W. Positive social reinforcement in the nursery school peer group. *Child Development*, 1967, **38**, 993–1002.

Charlesworth, W. R. The development of the object concept: A methodological concept. Paper presented at the meeting of the American Psychological Association, New York, September 1966.

Chazan, M. The incidence and nature of maladjustment among children in schools for the educationally subnormal. *British Journal of Educational Psychology*, 1964, **34**, 292–304.

Chen, H. P., and Irwin, O. C. Infant speech vowel and consonant types. *Journal of Speech Disorders*, 1946, **11**, 27–29.

Chiles, W. D. Effects of shock-induced stress on verbal performance. *Journal of Experimental Psychology*, 1958, **56**, 159–165.

Chomsky, N. *Syntactic structures*. The Hague: Mouton, 1957.

Chomsky, N. Review of *Verbal behavior* by B. F. Skinner. *Language*, 1959, **35**, 26–58.

Chomsky, N. Formal discussion. In U. Bellugi and R. Brown (Eds.) The acquisition of language. *Monographs of the Society for Research in Child Development*, 1964, **29**(1, Whole No. 92). Pp. 35–39.

Chomsky, N. *Aspects of the theory of syntax*. Cambridge, Mass.: M.I.T. Press, 1965.

Chomsky, N., and Halle, M. *The sound pattern of English*. New York: Harper & Row, 1968.

Church, R. M. The role of fear in punishment. In J. R. Braun (Chm.), The effects of punishment on behavior. Symposium presented at the meeting of the American Psychological Association, New York, September 1966.

Church, R. M., LoLordo, V. M., Overmier, J. B., Solomon, R. L., and Turner, L. H. Cardiac responses to shock in curarized dogs. *Journal of Comparative and Physiological Psychology*, 1966, **62**, 1–7.

Churchill, E. M. *The number concepts of children: Researches and studies I & II*. Leeds: Leeds University Publication, 1958.

Cirillo, L., Wapner, S., and Rand, G. Differentiation of haptic exploration in two age groups. *Psychonomic Science*, 1967, **9**, 467–468.

Claparède, E. Exemple de perception syncrétique chez un enfant. *Archives de Psychologie*, 1908, **7**, 195–198.

Claparède, E. *Le développement mental.* Neuchatel: Delachaux & Niestlé, 1951.

Clark, C. A. Developments and applications in the area of construct validity. *Review of Educational Research,* 1959, **29,** 84–105.

Clark, D. F. The treatment of monosymptomatic phobia by systematic desensitization. *Behaviour Research and Therapy,* 1963, **1,** 63–68.

Clausen, J. Mental deficiency: Development of a concept. *American Journal of Mental Deficiency,* 1967, **7,** 727–745.

Clayton, K. N. The overlearning-reversal-effect: Dependent on a confound with drive? Paper presented at the meeting of the Southeastern Psychological Association, Atlanta, April 1965.

Clelland, D. L., and Toussaint, I. The interrelationships of reading, listening, arithmetic computation and intelligence. *Reading Teacher,* 1962, **15,** 228–231.

Clifton, C., Jr. Initial transfer in the mediation of paired associates. *Journal of Experimental Psychology,* 1966, **71,** 758–763.

Cloward, R. A., and Ohlin, L. E. *Delinquency and opportunity.* New York: Free Press of Glencoe, 1960.

Cofer, C. N., and Appley, M. H. *Motivation: Theory and research.* New York: Wiley, 1964.

Cohen, L. D., Kipnis, D., Kunkle, E. C., and Kubzansky, P. E. Observations of a person with congenital insensitivity to pain. *Journal of Abnormal and Social Psychology,* 1955, **51,** 333–338.

Cohen, M. Sur l'etude du language enfantin. *Enfance,* 1952, **5,** 181–249.

Cole, M., Sharp, D. W., Glick, J., and Kessen, W. Conceptual and mnemonic factors in paired-associate learning. *Journal of Experimental Child Psychology,* 1968, **6,** 120–130.

Coleman, J. S. *The adolescent society.* New York: Free Press of Glencoe, 1961.

Coleman, J. S., and committee. *Equality of educational opportunity.* Washington, D.C.: U.S. Office of Education, 1966.

Conway, A. H. Class differences in general intelligence. *British Journal of Statistical Psychology,* 1959, **12,** 5–14.

Cook, W. M. Ability of children in color discrimination. *Child Development,* 1931, **2,** 303–320.

Cornell, E. L., and Armstrong, C. M. Forms of mental growth patterns revealed by reanalysis of the Harvard Growth Data. *Child Development,* 1955, **26,** 169–204.

Cornwell, A. C., and Fuller, J. L. Conditioned responses in young puppies. *Journal of Comparative and Physiological Psychology,* 1961, **54,** 13–15.

Corsini, D. A., Pick, A. D., and Flavell, J. H. Production deficiency of nonverbal mediators in young children. *Child Development,* 1968, **39,** 53–58.

Corsini, R. J., and Fassett, K. K. Intelligence and aging. *Journal of Genetic Psychology,* 1953, **83,** 249–264.

Cottrell, N. B. The effect of dissonance between expected and obtained performance upon task proficiency and self-estimates of task proficiency. *Journal of Social Psychology,* 1967, **72,** 275–284.

Cowan, P. A., and Walters, R. H. Studies of reinforcement of aggression: I. Effects of scheduling. *Child Development,* 1963, **34,** 543–551.

Crandall, V. J., Katkovsky, W., and Preston, A. Motivational and ability determinants of young children's intellectual achievement behaviors. *Child Development,* 1962, **33,** 643–661.

Crane, N. L., and Ross, L. E. A developmental study of attention to cue redundancy introduced following discrimination learning. *Journal of Experimental Child Psychology*, 1967, **5**, 1–15.

Cromwell, R. L. Selective aspects of personality development in mentally retarded children. *Exceptional Children*, 1961, **28**, 44–51.

Cronbach, L. J. Year-to-year correlations of mental tests: A review of the Hofstaetter analysis. *Child Development*, 1967, **38**, 283–289.

Cronbach, L. J., and Meehl, P. E. Construct validity in psychological tests. *Psychological Bulletin*, 1955, **52**, 281–302.

Crosby, E., Humphrey, T., and Lauer, E. *Correlative anatomy of the nervous system.* New York: Macmillan, 1962.

Cross, H. A., and Tyer, Z. E. The overlearning reversal effect in preschool children as a function of age. *Psychonomic Science*, 1966, **6**, 175–176.

Crowell, D. H., Davis, C. M., Chun, B. J., and Spellacy, F. J. Galvanic skin reflex in newborn humans. *Science*, 1965, **148**, 1108–1111.

Curry, C. The effects of verbal reinforcement combinations on learning in children. *Journal of Experimental Psychology*, 1960, **59**, 434.

Daehler, M. W., and Wright, J. C. Visual prompting in a paired-associates mediation paradigm. *Journal of Verbal Learning and Verbal Behavior*, 1968, **7**, 148–153.

Dallenbach, K. M. Two pronounced cases of verbal imagery. *American Journal of Psychology*, 1927, **38**, 667–669.

Damianopoulos, E. N. S-R contiguity and delay of reinforcement as critical parameters in classical aversive conditioning. *Psychological Review*, 1967, **74**, 420–427.

Dantzig, T. *Number: The language of science.* Garden City, N.Y.: Doubleday, 1956.

Darwin, C. *Expression of the emotions in man and animals.* London: Murray, 1872.

Dave, R. H. The identification and measurement of educational process variables that are related to educational achievement. Unpublished doctoral dissertation, University of Chicago, 1963.

Davies, C. Development of the probability concept in children. *Child Development*, 1965, **36**, 779–788.

Davis, A., and Eells, K. *Davis-Eells Games: Davis-Eells Test of General Intelligence or Problem Solving Ability.* Tarrytown-on-Hudson, N.Y.: World Book, 1953.

Davis, A., and Havighurst, R. J. The measurement of mental systems. *Scientific Monthly*, 1948, **66**, 301–316.

Davis, H. V., Sears, R. R., Miller, H. C., and Brodbeck, A. J. Effects of cup, bottle, and breast feeding on oral activities of newborn infants. *Pediatrics*, 1948, **3**, 549–558.

Davison, G. C. Systematic desensitization as a counterconditioning process. *Journal of Abnormal Psychology*, 1968, **73**, 91–99.

Davitz, J. R. Social perception and sociometric choice of children. *Journal of Abnormal and Social Psychology*, 1955, **50**, 173–176.

Davson, H. (Ed.) *The eye.* New York: Academic Press, 1962.

Dayton, G. O., Jr., Jones, M. H., Aiu, P., Rawson, R. A., Steele, B., and Rose, M. Developmental study of coordinated eye movements in the human infant. I. Visual acuity in the newborn human. *Archives of Ophthalmology*, 1964, **71**, 865–870. (a)

Dayton, G. O., Jr., Jones, M. H., Steele, B., and Rose, M. Developmental study of coordinated eye movements in the human infant. II. An electrooculographic study of the fixation reflex in the newborn. *Archives of Ophthalmology*, 1964, **71**, 871–875. (b)

Dearborn, W. F., and Rothney, J. W. M. *Predicting the child's development.* (2nd ed.) Cambridge, Mass.: Sci-Art, 1963.

Dekaban, A. *Neurology of infancy.* Baltimore: Williams & Wilkins, 1959.

DeLucia, C. A. A system for response measurement and reinforcement delivery for infant sucking-behavior research. *Journal of Experimental Child Psychology*, 1967, **5**, 518–521.

DeLucia, L. D. The influence of rocking stimulation on the crying behavior of infants. In preparation, 1969.

Denis-Prinzhorn, M. Perception des distances et constance des grandeurs (étude génétique). *Archives de Psychologie*, 1960, **37**, 181–309.

Denisova, M. P., and Figurin, N. L. [An investigation of the first combinative feeding reflexes in young infants.] *Voprosy Geneticheskoi Refleksologii i Pedologii Mladenchestva*, 1929, **1**, 81–88.

Dennis, W. An experimental test of two theories of social smiling in infants. *Journal of Social Psychology*, 1935, **6**, 214–223.

Deutsch, M., and Brown, B. Social influences on Negro-white intelligence differences. *Journal of Social Issues*, 1964, **20**, 24–35.

Diack, H. *Reading and the psychology of perception*. New York: Philosophical Library, 1960.

Dickerson, D. J. Performance of preschool children on three discrimination shifts. *Psychonomic Science*, 1966, **4**, 417–418.

Dickerson, D. J. Irrelevant stimulus dimensions and dimensional transfer in the discrimination learning of children. *Journal of Experimental Child Psychology*, 1967, **5**, 228–236.

Dilley, M. G., and Paivio, A. Pictures and words as stimulus and response items in paired-associate learning of young children. *Journal of Experimental Child Psychology*, 1968, **6**, 231–240.

Dinneen, F. P. *An introduction to general linguistics*. New York: Holt, Rinehart & Winston, 1967.

Di Vesta, F. J. Effects of mediated generalization on the development of children's preferences for figures. *Child Development*, 1962, **33**, 209–220.

Di Vesta, F. J. The distribution of modifiers used by children in a word-association task. *Journal of Verbal Learning and Verbal Behavior*, 1964, **3**, 421–427. (a)

Di Vesta, F. J. A simplex analysis of changes with age in responses to a restricted word-association task. *Journal of Verbal Learning and Verbal Behavior*, 1964, **3**, 505–510. (b)

Di Vesta, F. J. Developmental patterns in the use of modifiers as modes of conceptualization. *Child Development*, 1965, **36**, 185–214.

Di Vesta, F. J. A developmental study of the semantic structures of children. *Journal of Verbal Learning and Verbal Behavior*, 1966, **5**, 249–259.

Di Vesta, F. J., and Stover, D. O. The semantic mediation of evaluative meaning. *Journal of Experimental Psychology*, 1962, **64**, 467–475.

Dockeray, F. C., and Rice, C. Responses of newborn infants to pain stimulation. *Ohio State University Studies*, 1934, **12**, 82–93.

Dodwell, P. C. Children's understanding of number and related concepts. *Canadian Journal of Psychology*, 1960, **14**, 191–205.

Dodwell, P. C. Children's understanding of number and related concepts: Characteristics of an individual and of a group test. *Canadian Journal of Psychology*, 1961, **15**, 29–36.

Doidge, W. T., and Holtzman, W. H. Implications of homosexuality among Air Force trainees. *Journal of Consulting Psychology*, 1960, **24**, 9–13.

Dollard, J., and Miller, N. E. *Personality and psychotherapy*. New York: McGraw-Hill, 1950.

Donaldson, T. E. Secondary reinforcement vs other stimulus effects in extinction and learning of a new response. Unpublished doctoral dissertation, Purdue University, 1961.

Doris, J., Casper, M., and Poresky, R. Differential brightness thresholds in infancy. *Journal of Experimental Child Psychology,* 1967, **5,** 522–535.

Doris, J., and Cooper, L. Brightness discrimination in infancy. *Journal of Experimental Child Psychology,* 1966, **3,** 31–39.

Douvan, E., and Adelson, J. *The adolescent experience.* New York: Wiley, 1966.

Dreger, R. M. Different I.Q.s for the same individual associated with different intelligence tests. *Science,* 1953, **118,** 594–595.

Dreger, R. M., and Miller, K. S. Comparative psychological studies of Negroes and whites in the United States. *Psychological Bulletin,* 1960, **57,** 361–402.

Drever, J. *A dictionary of psychology.* Harmondsworth, Middlesex: Penguin, 1952.

Duncan, C. P. Description of learning to learn in human subjects. *American Journal of Psychology,* 1960, **73,** 108–114.

Dunlap, K. Are there any instincts? *Journal of Abnormal Psychology,* 1919, **14,** 35–50.

Durr, W. K. Characteristics of gifted children: Ten years of research. *Gifted Child Quarterly,* 1960, **4,** 75–80.

Dworetzki, G. Le test de Rorschach et l'évolution de la perception. *Archives de Psychologie,* 1939, **27,** 233–396. [Summarized in G. Meili-Dworetzki, The development of perception in the Rorschach. In B. Klopfer (Ed.), *Developments in the Rorschach technique.* Vol. 2. *Fields of application.* Yonkers, N.Y.: World Book, 1956. Pp. 104–176.]

Dyer, H. S. A psychometrician views human ability. *Teachers College Record,* 1960, **61,** 394–403.

Dysinger, D. An investigation of stimulus predifferentiation in a choice discrimination problem. Unpublished doctoral dissertation, State University of Iowa, 1951.

Easterbrook, J. A. The effect of emotion on cue utilization and the organization of behavior. *Psychological Review,* 1959, **66,** 183–201.

Ebbinghaus, H. *Memory: A contribution to experimental psychology.* (Orig. publ. 1885.) (Translated by H. A. Ruger and C. E. Bussenius.) New York: Dover, 1964.

Ebert, E., and Simmons, K. The Brush Foundation study of child growth and development. I. Psychometric tests. *Monographs of the Society for Research in Child Development,* 1943, **8,** No. 2.

Edwards, M. P., and Tyler, L. E. Intelligence, creativity and achievement in a nonselective public junior high school. *Journal of Educational Psychology,* 1965, **56,** 96–99.

Eells, K. Some implications for school practice of the Chicago studies of cultural bias in intelligence tests. *Harvard Educational Review,* 1953, **23,** 284–297.

Eells, K., Davis, A., Havighurst, R. J., Herrick, V. E., and Tyler, R. W. *Intelligence and cultural differences.* Chicago: University of Chicago Press, 1951.

Eimas, P. D. Components and compounds in the discrimination learning of retarded children. *Journal of Experimental Child Psychology,* 1964, **1,** 301–310.

Eimas, P. D. Stimulus compounding in the discrimination learning of kindergarten children. *Journal of Experimental Child Psychology,* 1965, **2,** 178–185.

Eimas, P. D. Effects of overtraining and age on intradimensional and extradimensional shifts in children. *Journal of Experimental Child Psychology,* 1966, **3,** 348–355. (a)

Eimas, P. D. Effects of overtraining, irrelevant stimuli, and training task on reversal discrimination learning in children. *Journal of Experimental Child Psychology*, 1966, **3**, 315–323. (b)

Eimas, P. D. Optional shift behavior in children as a function of overtraining, irrelevant stimuli, and age. *Journal of Experimental Child Psychology*, 1967, **5**, 332–340.

Eimas, P. D. Multiple-cue discrimination learning in children. *Psychological Record*, 1969, **19**, 417–424. (a)

Eimas, P. D. Observing response, attention, and the overtraining reversal effect. *Journal of Experimental Psychology*, 1969, **82**, in press. (b)

Eisenberg, R. B. Auditory behavior in the human neonate: Functional properties of sound and their ontogenetic implications. Paper presented at the meeting of the American Speech and Hearing Association, Washington, D.C., November 1966.

Eisenberg, R. B., Coursin, D. B., and Rupp, N. R. Habituation to an acoustic pattern as an index of differences among human neonates. *Journal of Auditory Research*, 1966, **6**, 239–248.

Eisman, B. S. Attitude formation: The development of a color preference response through mediated generalization. *Journal of Abnormal and Social Psychology*, 1955, **50**, 321–326.

Elkind, D. The additive composition of classes in the child. *Journal of Genetic Psychology*, 1961, **99**, 51–57. (a)

Elkind, D. Children's discovery of the conservation of mass, weight and volume. *Journal of Genetic Psychology*, 1961, **98**, 219–227. (b)

Elkind, D. The child's conception of right and left. *Journal of Genetic Psychology*, 1961, **99**, 269–276. (c)

Elkind, D. The development of quantitative thinking. *Journal of Genetic Psychology*, 1961, **98**, 37–46. (d)

Elkind, D. Discrimination, seriation and numeration of size differences in young children. *Journal of Genetic Psychology*, 1964, **104**, 275–296.

Elkind, D. Conservation across illusory transformations. *Acta Psychologica*, 1966, **25**, 389–400.

Elkind, D. Developmental studies of figurative perception. In L. P. Lipsitt and H. W. Reese (Eds.), *Advances in child development and behavior*. Vol. 4. New York: Academic Press, 1969. Pp. 1–28.

Elkind, D., Barocas, R., and Rosenthal, R. Concept production in adolescents from graded and ungraded classrooms. *Perceptual and Motor Skills*, 1968, **27**, 1015–1018.

Elkind, D., Koegler, R. R., and Go, E. Studies in perceptual development: II. Part-whole perception. *Child Development*, 1964, **35**, 81–90.

Elkind, D., and Scott, L. Studies in perceptual development: I. The decentering of perception. *Child Development*, 1962, **33**, 619–630.

Elkind, D., and Weiss, J. Studies in perceptual development: III. Perceptual exploration. *Child Development*, 1967, **38**, 553–562.

Ellingson, R. J. The study of brain electrical activity in infants. In L. P. Lipsitt and C. C. Spiker (Eds.), *Advances in child development and behavior*. Vol. 3. New York: Academic Press, 1967. Pp. 53–97.

Ellis, N. R. (Ed.) *Handbook of mental deficiency*. New York: McGraw-Hill, 1963.

Ellison, G. D. Differential salivary conditioning to traces. *Journal of Comparative and Physiological Psychology*, 1964, **57**, 373–380.

Engen, T. Psychophysical scaling of odor intensity and quality. *Annals of the New York Academy of Sciences*, 1964, **116**, 504–516.

Engen, T. Psychophysical analysis of the odor intensity of homologous alcohols. *Journal of Experimental Psychology*, 1965, **70**, 611–616.

Engen, T., and Lipsitt, L. P. Decrement and recovery of responses to olfactory stimuli in the human neonate. *Journal of Comparative and Physiological Psychology*, 1965, **59**, 312–316.

Engen, T., Lipsitt, L. P., and Kaye, H. Olfactory responses and adaptation in the human neonate. *Journal of Comparative and Physiological Psychology*, 1963, **56**, 73–77.

Enos, F. A. Emotional adjustment of mentally retarded children. *American Journal of Mental Deficiency*, 1961, **65**, 606–609.

Entwisle, D. R. *Word associations of young children*. Baltimore: Johns Hopkins Press, 1966.

Erickson, M. T. Effects of delayed reward, anxiety, and intelligence on simultaneous and successive discrimination learning in children. Unpublished master's thesis, Brown University, 1959.

Erickson, M. T. Effects of social deprivation and satiation on verbal conditioning in children. *Journal of Comparative and Physiological Psychology*, 1962, **55**, 953–957.

Erickson, M. T., and Lipsitt, L. P. Effects of delayed reward on simultaneous and successive discrimination learning in children. *Journal of Comparative and Physiological Psychology*, 1960, **53**, 256–260.

Erikson, E. H. *Childhood and society*. (2nd ed.) New York: Norton, 1963.

Erlenmeyer-Kimling, L., and Jarvik, L. F. Genetics and intelligence: A review. *Science*, 1963, **142**, 1477–1479.

Ervin, S. M. Imitation and structural change in children's language. In E. H. Lenneberg (Ed.), *New directions in the study of language*. Cambridge, Mass.: M.I.T. Press, 1964. Pp. 163–189.

Ervin, S. M. Language development. In M. L. Hoffman and L. W. Hoffman (Eds.), *Review of child development research*. Vol. 2. Ann Arbor, Mich.: University of Michigan Press, 1966. Pp. 55–105.

Ervin, S. M., and Foster, G. The development of meaning in children's descriptive terms. *Journal of Abnormal and Social Psychology*, 1960, **61**, 271–275.

Ervin, S. M., and Miller, W. Language development. *Yearbook of the National Society for the Study of Education*, 1963, **62**, Part I, 108–143.

Escalona, S. K., and Moriarity, A. Prediction of school age intelligence from infant tests. *Child Development*, 1961, **32**, 597–605.

Esper, E. A. A technique for the experimental investigation of associative interference in artificial linguistic material. *Language Monographs*, 1925, No. 1.

Estes, R. E. Number of training trials and variations in stimulus cues as factors affecting extinction in children. Unpublished master's thesis, University of Southern California, 1960.

Estes, R. E. The effect of constant and varied delay of reward on the speed of an instrumental response. Unpublished doctoral dissertation, State University of Iowa, 1963.

Etzel, B. C., and Gewirtz, J. L. Experimental modification of caretaker-maintained high-rate operant crying in a 6- and a 20-week-old infant (*Infans tyrannotearus*): Extinction of crying with reinforcement of eye contact and smiling. *Journal of Experimental Child Psychology*, 1967, **5**, 303–317.

Etzel, B. C., and Wright, E. S. Effects of delayed reinforcement on response latency and acquisition learning under simultaneous and successive discrimination learning in children. *Journal of Experimental Child Psychology*, 1964, **1**, 281–293.

Fagan, J. F., and Witryol, S. L. The effects of instructional set and delay of reward on children's learning in a simultaneous discrimination task. *Child Development*, 1966, **37**, 433–438.

Fantz, R. L. Pattern vision in young infants. *Psychological Record*, 1958, **8**, 43–47.

Fantz, R. L. Ontogeny of perception. In A. M. Schrier, H. F. Harlow, and F. Stollnitz (Eds.), *Behavior of nonhuman primates*. Vol. II. New York: Academic Press, 1965. Pp. 365–403.

Fantz, R. L. Visual perception and experience in early infancy: A look at the hidden side of behavior development. In H. W. Stevenson, E. H. Hess, and H. L. Rheingold (Eds.), *Early behavior: Comparative and developmental approaches*. New York: Wiley, 1967. Pp. 181–224.

Fantz, R. L., Ordy, J. M., and Udelf, M. S. Maturation of pattern vision in infants during the first six months. *Journal of Comparative and Physiological Psychology*, 1962, **55**, 907–917.

Farina, A. Patterns of role dominance and conflict in parents of schizophrenic patients. *Journal of Abnormal and Social Psychology*, 1960, **61**, 31–38.

Feather, N. T. Effects of prior success and failure on expectations for success and subsequent performance. *Journal of Personality and Social Psychology*, 1966, **3**, 287–298.

Feather, N. T., and Saville, M. R. Effects of amount of prior success and failure on expectations of success and subsequent task performance. *Journal of Personality and Social Psychology*, 1967, **5**, 226–232.

Feldhausen, J. F., and Klausmeier, H. J. Anxiety, intelligence and achievement in children of low, average and high intelligence. *Child Development*, 1962, **33**, 403–409.

Feldstone, C. S. Effects of correlated reinforcement on response amplitude in children. *Journal of Experimental Child Psychology*, 1966, **3**, 244–257.

Ferguson, G. A. On learning and human ability. *Canadian Journal of Psychology*, 1954, **8**, 95–112.

Ferguson, G. A. On transfer and the abilities of man. *Canadian Journal of Psychology*, 1956, **10**, 121–131.

Ferré, F. Mapping the logic of models in science and theology. *Christian Scholar*, 1963, **46**(Spring), 9–39.

Ferster, C. B. The use of the free operant in the analysis of behavior. *Psychological Bulletin*, 1953, **50**, 263–274.

Ferster, C. B. Positive reinforcement and behavioral deficits of autistic children. *Child Development*, 1961, **32**, 437–456.

Ferster, C. B., and DeMyer, M. K. A method for the experimental analysis of the behavior of autistic children. *American Journal of Orthopsychiatry*, 1962, **32**, 89–98.

Ferster, C. B., and Skinner, B. F. *Schedules of reinforcement*. New York: Appleton, 1957.

Festinger, L. *Theory of cognitive dissonance*. Evanston, Ill.: Row, Peterson, 1957.

Festinger, L. *Conflict, decision, and dissonance*. Stanford: Stanford University Press, 1964.

Fisch, R. I., and McNamara, H. J. Conditioning of attention as a factor in perceptual learning. *Perceptual and Motor Skills*, 1963, **17**, 891–907.

Fiske, D. W., and Maddi, S. R. *Functions of varied experience*. Homewood, Ill.: Dorsey Press, 1961.

Flamer, G. B. Conditions of positive and negative transfer in children's verbal learning. Unpublished doctoral dissertation, University of Minnesota, 1965.

Flanagan, J. C., and Dailey, J. T. Project Talent: The identification, development, and utilization of human talent. *Personnel Guidance Journal,* 1960, **38,** 504–505.

Flavell, J. H. *The developmental psychology of Jean Piaget.* Princeton, N.J.: Van Nostrand, 1963.

Flavell, J. H. Developmental studies of mediated memory (tentative title). In H. W. Reese and L. P. Lipsitt (Eds.), *Advances in child development and behavior.* Vol. 5. New York: Academic Press, 1970, in press.

Flavell, J. H., Beach, D. R., and Chinsky, J. M. Spontaneous verbal rehearsal in a memory task as a function of age. *Child Development,* 1966, **37,** 283–299.

Flavell, J. H., and Stedman, D. J. A developmental study of judgments of semantic similarity. *Journal of Genetic Psychology,* 1961, **98,** 279–293.

Flavell, J. H., and Wohlwill, J. F. Formal and functional aspects of cognitive development. In D. Elkind and J. H. Flavell (Eds.), *Studies in cognitive development: Essays in honor of Jean Piaget.* New York: Oxford University Press, 1969. Pp. 67–120.

Flesch, R. *Why Johnny can't read.* New York: Harper & Row, 1955.

Flescher, I. Anxiety and achievement of intellectually gifted and creatively gifted children. *Journal of Psychology,* 1963, **56,** 251–268.

Floud, J. E., and Halsey, A. H. Measured intelligence is largely an acquired characteristic. *British Journal of Educational Psychology,* 1958, **28,** 290–291.

Fodor, J. A. Could meaning be an r_m? *Journal of Verbal Learning and Verbal Behavior,* 1965, **4,** 73–81.

Ford, L. H., Jr. Reaction to failure as a function of expectancy for success. *Journal of Abnormal and Social Psychology,* 1963, **67,** 340–348.

Forgays, D. G. The development of differential word recognition. *Journal of Experimental Psychology,* 1953, **45,** 165–168.

Fort, J. G. Secondary reinforcement with preschool children. *Child Development,* 1961, **32,** 755–764.

Fort, J. G. Discrimination based on secondary reinforcement. *Child Development,* 1965, **36,** 481–490.

Foster, W. S. The effect of practice upon visualization and upon reproduction of visual impression. *Journal of Educational Psychology,* 1911, **2,** 11–22.

Foulds, G. A., and Raven, J. C. Normal changes in the mental abilities of adults as age advances. *Journal of Mental Science,* 1948, **94,** 133–142.

Fowler, H. *Curiosity and exploratory behavior.* New York: Macmillan, 1965.

Fraser, C., Bellugi, U., and Brown, R. W. Control of grammar in imitation, comprehension, and production. *Journal of Verbal Learning and Verbal Behavior,* 1963, **2,** 121–135.

Freeberg, N. E., and Payne, D. T. Parental influence on cognitive development in early childhood: A review. *Child Development,* 1967, **38,** 65–87.

Freeman, F. N., and Flory, C. D. Growth in intellectual abilities as measured by repeated tests. *Monographs of the Society for Research in Child Development.* 1937, **2,** No. 2.

Freud, A. Introduction to the technique of child analysis. *Nervous and Mental Disorders Monographs,* 1928, No. 48.

Friedlander, B. Z. The effect of speaker identity, voice inflection, vocabulary, and message redundancy on infants' selection of vocal reinforcers. Paper presented at the meeting of the Society for Research in Child Development, New York, March 1967.

Fritz, B., and Blank, M. Role of the irrelevant cue in rapid reversal learning in nursery school children. *Journal of Comparative and Physiological Psychology,* 1968, **65,** 375–378.

Fromm, E., and Hartman, L. D. *Intelligence: A dynamic approach.* Garden City, N.Y.: Doubleday, 1955.

Fuller, J. L., Easler, C. A., and Banks, E. M. Formation of conditioned avoidance responses in young puppies. *American Journal of Physiology,* 1950, **160,** 462–466.

Furth, H. G. *Thinking without language: Psychological implications of deafness.* New York: Free Press, 1966.

Furth, H. G., and Youniss, J. The effect of overtraining on three discrimination shifts in children. *Journal of Comparative and Physiological Psychology,* 1964, **57,** 290–293.

Gaeth, J. H., and Allen, D. V. Association values for selected trigrams with children. *Journal of Verbal Learning and Verbal Behavior,* 1966, **5,** 473–477. (a)

Gaeth, J. H., and Allen, D. V. Effect of similarity upon learning in children. *Journal of Experimental Child Psychology,* 1966, **4,** 381–390. (b)

Gaeth, J. H., and Cooper, J. C., Jr. A note on performance as a function of association value. *Journal of Verbal Learning and Verbal Behavior,* 1967, **6,** 682–684.

Gagné, R. M., and Baker, K. E. Stimulus pre-differentiation as a factor in transfer of training. *Journal of Experimental Psychology,* 1950, **40,** 439–451.

Gallagher, J. Clinical judgement and the Cattell Infant Intelligence Scale. *Journal of Consulting Psychology,* 1953, **17,** 303–305.

Gallagher, J. Peer acceptance of highly gifted children in elementary school. *Elementary School Journal,* 1958, **58,** 465–470.

Gallagher, J., and Palermo, D. S. The effect of type of associative relationship on word recognition times. *Child Development,* 1967, **38,** 849–855.

Gardner, D. B., Hawkes, G. R., and Burchinal, L. G. Noncontinuous mothering in infancy and development in later childhood. *Child Development,* 1961, **32,** 225–234.

Gardner, R. A. On box score methodology as illustrated by three reviews of overtraining reversal effects. *Psychological Bulletin,* 1966, **66,** 416–418.

Gardner, W. I. Social and emotional adjustment of mildly retarded children and adolescents: Critical review. *Exceptional Children,* 1966, **33,** 97–105.

Garrett, H. E. A developmental theory of intelligence. *American Psychologist,* 1946, **1,** 372–378.

Garrett, H. E. Negro-white differences in mental ability in the United States. *Scientific Monthly,* 1947, **65,** 329–333.

Geber, M. The psychomotor development of African children in the first year, and the influence of maternal behavior. *Journal of Social Psychology,* 1958, **47,** 185–195.

Geber, M., and Dean, R. F. A. Gesell tests on African children. *Pediatrics,* 1957, **20,** 1055–1065.

Gelber, H., and Meyer, V. Behaviour therapy and encopresis: The complexities involved in treatment. *Behaviour Research and Therapy,* 1965, **2,** 227–231.

Gelber, S., Campbell, P. L., Deibler, G. E., and Sokoloff, L. Effects of L-thyroxine on amino acid incorporation into protein in mature and immature rat brain. *Journal of Neurochemistry,* 1964, **11,** 221–229.

Gellermann, L. W. Chance orders of alternating stimuli in visual discrimination experiments. *Pedagogical Seminary,* 1933, **42,** 206–208. (a)

Gellermann, L. W. Form discrimination in chimpanzees and two-year-old children: I. Form (triangularity) *per se. Pedagogical Seminary,* 1933, **42,** 3–27. (b)

Gellermann, L. W. Form discrimination in chimpanzees and two-year-old children: II. Form versus background. *Pedagogical Seminary,* 1933, **42,** 28–50. (c)

Gelman, R. Conservation acquisition: A problem of learning to attend to relevant attributes. *Journal of Experimental Child Psychology*, 1969, 7, 167–187.

Gerjuoy, I. R., and Spitz, H. H. Associative clustering in free recall: Intellectual and developmental variables. *American Journal of Mental Deficiency*, 1966, **70**, 918–927.

Gesell, A. *Infancy and human growth*. New York: Macmillan, 1928.

Gesell, A. *An atlas of infant behavior*. New Haven: Yale University Press, 1934.

Gesell, A. The genesis of behavior form in fetus and infant: The growth of the mind from the standpoint of developmental morphology. *Proceedings of the American Philosophical Society*, 1941, **84**, 471–488.

Getzels, J. W., and Jackson, P. W. *Creativity and intelligence*. New York: Wiley, 1962.

Gewirtz, J. L. Potency of a social reinforcer as a function of satiation and recovery. *Developmental Psychology*, 1969, **1**, 2–13.

Gewirtz, J. L., and Baer, D. M. Deprivation and satiation of social reinforcers as drive conditions. *Journal of Abnormal and Social Psychology*, 1958, **57**, 165–172. (a)

Gewirtz, J. L., and Baer, D. M. The effect of brief social deprivation on behaviors for a social reinforcer. *Journal of Abnormal and Social Psychology*, 1958, **56**, 49–56. (b)

Gewirtz, J. L., Baer, D. M., and Roth, C. H. A note on the similar effects of low social availability of an adult and brief social deprivation on young children's behavior. *Child Development*, 1958, **29**, 149–152.

Gewirtz, J. L., and Stingle, K. G. The learning of generalized imitation as the basis for identification. *Psychological Review*, 1968, **75**, 374–397.

Ghent, L. Perception of overlapping and embedded figures by children of different ages. *American Journal of Psychology*, 1956, **69**, 575–587.

Ghent, L. Recognition by children of realistic figures presented in various orientations. *Canadian Journal of Psychology*, 1960, **14**, 249–256.

Ghent, L. Form and its orientation: A child's eye view. *American Journal of Psychology*, 1961, **74**, 177–190.

Ghent, L., and Bernstein, L. Influence of the orientation of geometric forms on their recognition by children. *Perceptual and Motor Skills*, 1961, **12**, 95–101.

Gibby, R. G., and Gabler, R. The self concept of Negro and white children. *Journal of Clinical Psychology*, 1967, **23**, 144–148.

Gibson, E. J. A systematic application of the concepts of generalization and differentiation to verbal learning. *Psychological Review*, 1940, **47**, 196–229.

Gibson, E. J. Improvement in perceptual judgement as a function of controlled practice or training. *Psychological Bulletin*, 1953, **50**, 401–431.

Gibson, E. J. Development of perception. In J. C. Wright and J. Kagan (Eds.), Basic cognitive processes in children. *Monographs of the Society for Research in Child Development*, 1963, **28**(2, Whole No. 86). Pp. 5–32.

Gibson, E. J. Learning to read. *Science*, 1965, **148**, 1066–1072.

Gibson, E. J., Gibson, J. J., Pick, A. D., and Osser, H. A developmental study of the discrimination of letter-like forms. *Journal of Comparative and Physiological Psychology*, 1962, **55**, 897–906.

Gibson, E. J., and Olum, V. Experimental methods of studying perception in children. In P. H. Mussen (Ed.), *Handbook of research methods in child development*. New York: Wiley, 1960. Pp. 311–373.

Gibson, J. J. *The perception of the visual world*. Boston: Houghton Mifflin, 1950.

Gibson, J. J. A theory of pictorial perception. *Audio-Visual Communication Review,* 1954, **1**, 3–23.

Gibson, J. J., and Gibson, E. J. Perceptual learning: Differentiation or enrichment? *Psychological Review,* 1955, **62**, 32–41.

Gilbert, D. H. Reward expectancy strength as related to the magnitude of frustration in children. Unpublished doctoral dissertation, University of Southern California, 1968.

Gilliland, A. R. Socio-economic status and race as factors in infant intelligence test scores. *Child Development,* 1951, **22**, 271–273.

Gladis, M. Grade differences in transfer as a function of the time interval between learning tasks. *Journal of Educational Psychology,* 1960, **51**, 191–194.

Glanzer, M. Grammatical category: A rote learning and word association analysis. *Journal of Verbal Learning and Verbal Behavior,* 1962, **1**, 31–41.

Glick, J., and Wapner, S. Development of transitivity: Some findings and problems of analysis. *Child Development,* 1968, **39**, 621–638.

Glidewell, J. C., Kantor, M. B., Smith, L. M., and Stronger, L. A. Socialization and social structure in the classroom. In M. L. Hoffman and L. W. Hoffman (Eds.), *Review of child development research.* Vol. 2. New York: Russell Sage Foundation, 1966. Pp. 221–256.

Glucksberg, S. The influence of strength of drive on functional fixedness and perceptual recognition. *Journal of Experimental Psychology,* 1962, **63**, 36–41.

Golann, S. E. Psychological study of creativity. *Psychological Bulletin,* 1963, **60**, 548–565.

Gold, N. Complex performance in rats as a function of conflict. Unpublished master's thesis, University of Southern California, 1960.

Goldfarb, W. The effects of early institutional care on adolescent personality. *Journal of Experimental Education,* 1943, **12**, 106–129.

Goldfarb, W. Effects of psychological deprivation in infancy and subsequent stimulation. *American Journal of Psychiatry,* 1945, **102**, 18–33.

Goldschmid, M. L. Different types of conservation and nonconservation and their relation to age, sex, IQ, MA and vocabulary. *Child Development,* 1967, **38**, 1229–1246.

Goldschmid, M. L. The relation of conservation to emotional and environmental aspects of development. *Child Development,* 1968, **39**, 579–589.

Goldstein, A. G., and Mackenberg, E. Recognition of human faces from isolated facial features: A developmental study. *Psychonomic Science,* 1966, **6**, 149–150.

Goldstein, K., and Sheerer, M. Abstract and concrete behavior: An experimental study with special tests. *Psychological Monographs,* 1941, **53**, No. 239.

Gollin, E. S. Developmental studies of visual recognition of incomplete objects. *Perceptual and Motor Skills,* 1960, **11**, 289–298.

Gollin, E. S. Further studies of visual recognition of incomplete objects. *Perceptual and Motor Skills,* 1961, **13**, 307–314.

Gollin, E. S. A developmental approach to learning and cognition. In L. P. Lipsitt and C. C. Spiker (Eds.), *Advances in child development and behavior.* Vol. 2. New York: Academic Press, 1965. Pp. 159–186.

Gomez, M. R. Minimal cerebral dysfunction (maximal neurologic confusion). *Clinical Pediatrics,* 1967, **10**, 589–591.

Gonzalez, R. C., Eskin, R. M., and Bitterman, M. E. Extinction in the fish after partial and consistent reinforcement with number of reinforcements equated. *Journal of Comparative and Physiological Psychology,* 1962, **55**, 381–386.

Gonzalez, R. C., Eskin, R. M., and Bitterman, M. E. Further experiments on partial reinforcement in the fish. *American Journal of Psychology*, 1963, **76**, 366–375.

Goodenough, F. L. *Measurement of intelligence by drawings.* Tarrytown-on-Hudson, N.Y.: World Book, 1926.

Goodenough, F. L. New evidence on environmental influence on intelligence. *Yearbook of the National Society for the Study of Education*, 1940, **39**, Part I, 307–365.

Goodenough, F. L. *Mental testing.* New York: Rinehart, 1949.

Goodenough, F. L. The measurement of mental growth in childhood. In L. Carmichael (Ed.), *Manual of child psychology.* (2nd ed.) New York: Wiley, 1954. Pp. 459–491.

Goodenough, F. L., and Harris, D. B. Studies on the psychology of children's drawings: II 1928–1949. *Psychological Bulletin*, 1950, **47**, 369–433.

Goodnow, J. Problems in research on culture and thought. In D. Elkind and J. H. Flavell (Eds.), *Studies in cognitive development: Essays in honor of Jean Piaget.* New York: Oxford University Press, 1969. Pp. 440–462.

Goodnow, J., and Bethon, G. Piaget's tasks: The effects of schooling and intelligence. *Child Development*, 1966, **37**, 573–582.

Goodwin, J., Long, L., and Welch, L. Generalization in memory. *Journal of Experimental Psychology*, 1945, **35**, 71–75.

Goodwin, W. R., and Lawrence, D. H. The functional independence of two discrimination habits associated with a constant stimulus situation. *Journal of Comparative and Physiological Psychology*, 1955, **48**, 437–443.

Gordon, A. Intellectual potential and heredity. *Science*, 1961, **133**, 378–379.

Gordon, H. *Mental and scholastic tests among retarded children: An enquiry into the effects of schooling on the various tests.* Education Pamphlets, No. 44. London: Board of Education, 1923.

Gordon, T., and Foss, B. M. The role of stimulation in the delay of onset of crying in the newborn infant. *Quarterly Journal of Experimental Psychology*, 1966, **18**, 79–81.

Gorman, J. J., Cogan, D. C., and Gellis, S. S. An apparatus for grading the visual acuity of infants on the basis of opticokinetic nystagmus. *Pediatrics*, 1957, **19**, 1088–1092.

Goss, A. E. Verbal mediating responses and concept formation. *Psychological Review*, 1961, **68**, 248–274.

Goss, A. E. Paired-associate learning by young children as functions of initial associative strength and percentage of occurrence of response members. *Journal of Experimental Child Psychology*, 1966, **4**, 398–407.

Goss, A. E., Morgan, C. H., and Golin, S. J. Paired-associates learning as a function of percentage of occurrence of response members (reinforcement). *Journal of Experimental Psychology*, 1959, **57**, 96–104.

Goss, A. E., and Nodine, C. F. *Paired-associates learning.* New York: Academic Press, 1965.

Gough, P. B. Grammatical transformations and speed of understanding. *Journal of Verbal Learning and Verbal Behavior*, 1965, **4**, 107–111.

Goulet, L. R. Anxiety (drive) and verbal learning: Implications for research and some methodological considerations. *Psychological Bulletin*, 1968, **69**, 235–247. (a)

Goulet, L. R. Verbal learning in children: Implications for developmental research. *Psychological Bulletin*, 1968, **69**, 359–376. (b)

Gowan, J. C., Demos, G. D., and Torrance, E. P. *Creativity: Its educational implications.* New York: Wiley, 1967.

Graham, C. H., Bartlett, N. R., Brown, J. L., Hsia, Y., Mueller, C. G., and Riggs, L. A. (Eds.) *Vision and visual perception.* New York: Wiley, 1965.

Graham, F. K. Behavioral differences between normal and traumatized newborns. I. The test procedures. *Psychological Monographs,* 1956, **70**(20, Whole No. 427).

Graham, F. K., and Clifton, R. K. Heart-rate change as a component of the orienting response. *Psychological Bulletin,* 1966, **65**, 305–320.

Graham, F. K., Clifton, R. K., and Hatton, H. M. Habituation of heart rate response to repeated auditory stimulation during the first five days of life. *Child Development,* 1968, **39**, 35–52.

Graham, F. K., Ernhart, C. B., Craft, M., and Berman, P. W. Learning of relative and absolute size concepts in preschool children. *Journal of Experimental Child Psychology,* 1964, **1**, 26–36.

Graham, F. K., Matarazzo, R. G., and Caldwell, B. M. Behavioral differences between normal and traumatized newborns: II. Standardization, reliability, and validity. *Psychological Monographs,* 1956, **70**(21, Whole No. 428).

Grant, D. A. Classical and operant conditioning. In A. W. Melton (Ed.), *Categories of human learning.* New York: Academic Press, 1964. Pp. 1–31.

Grant, D. A., and Dittmer, D. G. A tactile generalization gradient for a pseudo-conditioned response. *Journal of Experimental Psychology,* 1940, **26**, 404–412.

Gray, S. W., and Klaus, R. A. An experimental preschool program for culturally deprived children. *Child Development,* 1965, **36**, 887–898.

Green, P. C. Learning, estimation, and generalization of conditioned responses by young monkeys. *Psychological Reports,* 1962, **10**, 731.

Greenberg, J. H. (Ed.) *Universals of language.* (2nd ed.) Cambridge, Mass.: M.I.T. Press, 1966.

Greenfield, P. M. On culture and conservation. In J. S. Bruner, R. R. Olver, P. M. Greenfield *et al.,* *Studies in cognitive growth.* New York: Wiley, 1966. Pp. 225–256.

Greenfield, P. M., Reich, L. C., and Olver, R. R. On culture and equivalence: II. In J. S. Bruner, R. R. Olver, P. M. Greenfield *et al.,* *Studies in cognitive growth.* New York: Wiley, 1966. Pp. 270–318.

Griffiths, J. A., Shantz, C. A., and Sigel, I. E. A methodological problem in conservation studies: The use of relational terms. *Child Development,* 1967, **38**, 841–848.

Grings, W. W., Lockhart, R. A., and Dameron, L. E. Conditioning autonomic responses of mentally subnormal individuals. *Psychological Monographs,* 1962, **76**(39, Whole No. 558).

Groen, J. J. Inhibitory mechanism of the vestibular system in man in comparison with hearing. *Journal of the Acoustical Society of America,* 1962, **34**, 1497–1503.

Gruenberg, E. M. Epidemiology. In H. A. Stevens and R. Heber (Eds.), *Mental retardation: A review of research.* Chicago: University of Chicago Press, 1964. Pp. 259–306.

Grusec, J. Some antecedents of self-criticism. *Journal of Personality and Social Psychology,* 1966, **4**, 244–252.

Guess, D., Sailor, W., Rutherford, G., and Baer, D. M. An experimental analysis of linguistic development: The productive use of the plural morpheme. *Journal of Applied Behavior Analysis,* 1968, **1**, 297–306.

Guilford, J. P. The structure of the intellect. *Psychological Bulletin,* 1956, **53**, 267–293.

Guilford, J. P. A revised structure of intellect. *University of Southern California Psychological Laboratory Report,* 1957, No. 19.

Guilford, J. P. Three faces of intellect. *American Psychologist,* 1959, **14**, 469–479.

Guilford, J. P. Potentiality for creativity. *Gifted Child Quarterly,* 1962, **6**, 87–90.

Guilford, J. P. Intelligence: 1965 model. *American Psychologist,* 1966, **21**, 20–26.

Gullickson, G. R., and Crowell, D. H. Neonatal habituation to electrotactual stimulation. *Journal of Experimental Child Psychology,* 1964, **1**, 388–396.

Gunther, M. Infant behavior at the breast. In B. M. Foss (Ed.), *Determinants of infant behavior.* Vol. I. London: Methuen (New York: Wiley), 1961. Pp. 37–44.

Guttman, N., and Kalish, H. I. Discriminability and stimulus generalization. *Journal of Experimental Psychology,* 1956, **51**, 79–88.

Guy, D. E., Van Fleet, F. M., and Bourne, L. E., Jr. Effects of adding a stimulus dimension prior to a nonreversal shift. *Journal of Experimental Psychology,* 1966, **72**, 161–168.

Gvozdev, A. N. *Formirovanie u rebenka grammaticheskogo stroya russkogo yazyka* (Formation in the child of the grammatical structure of the Russian language). Parts I & II. Moscow: Akademiia Pedagogicheskikh Nauk RSFSR, 1949.

Haan, N. Proposed model of ego functioning: Coping and defense mechanisms in relationship to IQ change. *Psychological Monographs,* 1963, **77**(8, Whole No. 571).

Haber, R. N. Nature of the effect of set on perception. *Psychological Review,* 1966, **73**, 335–351.

Haber, R. N., and Haber, R. B. Eidetic imagery: I. Frequency. *Perceptual and Motor Skills,* 1964, **19**, 131–138.

Hagen, J. W., and Kingsley, P. R. Labeling effects in short-term memory. *Child Development,* 1968, **39**, 113–121.

Haggard, E. A. Techniques for the development of unbiased tests. In *Proceedings of the 1952 conference on testing problems.* Princeton, N.J.: Educational Testing Service, 1953. Pp. 93–117.

Hagman, R. R. A study of fears of children of preschool age. *Journal of Experimental Education,* 1932, **1**, 110–130.

Haith, M. M. The response of the human newborn to visual movement. *Journal of Experimental Child Psychology,* 1966, **3**, 235–243.

Haith, M. M. Unpublished manuscript, Harvard University, 1968.

Hake, H. W. Form discrimination and the invariance of form. In L. Uhr (Ed.), *Pattern recognition.* New York: Wiley, 1966. Pp. 142–173.

Hall, J. F. Learning as a function of word frequency. *American Journal of Psychology,* 1954, **67**, 138–140.

Hall, J. R. *The psychology of learning.* Philadelphia: Lippincott, 1966.

Hall, J. W. Secondary reinforcement or frustration? Unpublished doctoral dissertation, University of Southern California, 1964.

Hall, J. W., and Ware, W. B. Implicit associative responses and false recognition by young children. *Journal of Experimental Child Psychology,* 1968, **6**, 52–60.

Hall, R. V., Lund, D., and Jackson, D. Effects of teacher attention on study behavior. *Journal of Applied Behavior Analysis,* 1968, **1**, 1–12.

Haller, M. The reactions of infants to changes in the intensity and pitch of pure tone. *Journal of Genetic Psychology,* 1932, **40**, 162–180.

Halsey, A. H. Genetics, social structure and intelligence. *British Journal of Sociology,* 1958, **9**, 15–28.

Halverson, H. M. Genital and sphincter behavior of the male infant. *Journal of Genetic Psychology,* 1940, **56**, 95–136.

Hamilton, V. Size-constancy and intelligence: A re-examination. *British Journal of Psychology,* 1966, **57**, 319–328.

Haner, C. F., and Brown, P. A. Clarification of the instigation to action concept in the frustration-aggression hypothesis. *Journal of Abnormal and Social Psychology,* 1955, **51**, 204–206.

Harlow, H. F. The formation of learning sets. *Psychological Review,* 1949, **56**, 51–65.

Harlow, H. F. Analysis of discrimination learning by monkeys. *Journal of Experimental Psychology,* 1950, **40**, 26–39.

Harlow, H. F. Motivation as a factor in the acquisition of new responses. In *Current theory and research in motivation.* Lincoln, Neb.: University of Nebraska Press, 1953. Pp. 24–49.

Harlow, H. F. Learning set and error factor theory. In S. Koch (Ed.), *Psychology: A study of a science.* Vol. 2. New York: McGraw-Hill, 1959. Pp. 492–537.

Harlow, H. F. The development of affectional patterns in infant monkeys. In B. M. Foss (Ed.), *Determinants of infant behavior.* Vol. I. London: Methuen (New York: Wiley), 1961. Pp. 75–88.

Harlow, H. F., and Harlow, M. K. Learning to think. *Scientific American,* 1949, **181**, 36–39.

Harper, P. A., Fischer, L. K., and Rider, R. V. Neurologic and intellectual status of prematures at three to five years of age. *Journal of Pediatrics,* 1959, **55**, 679–690.

Harris, D. B. Child psychology and the concept of development. Presidential address, Division on Developmental Psychology, presented at the meeting of the American Psychological Association, September 1956. [In D. S. Palermo and L. P. Lipsitt (Eds.), *Research readings in child psychology.* New York: Holt, Rinehart & Winston, 1963. Pp. 21–31.]

Harris, D. B. Problems in formulating a scientific concept of development. In *The concept of development,* D. B. Harris (Ed.). Minneapolis: University of Minnesota Press, 1957. Pp. 3–14.

Harris, F. R., Wolf, M. M., and Baer, D. M. Effects of adult social reinforcement on child behavior. *Young Children,* 1964, **20**, 8–17.

Harris, L. The effects of relative novelty on children's choice behavior. *Journal of Experimental Child Psychology,* 1965, **2**, 297–305.

Harrow, A., and Friedman, G. B. Comparing reversal and nonreversal shifts in concept formation with partial reinforcement . *Journal of Experimental Psychology,* 1958, **55**, 592–598.

Hart, B. M., Allen, K. E., Buell, J. S., Harris, F. R., and Wolf, M. M. Effects of social reinforcement on operant crying. *Journal of Experimental Child Psychology,* 1964, **1**, 145–153.

Hart, B. M., Reynolds, N. J., Baer, D. M., Brawley, E. R., and Harris, F. R. Effects of contingent and non-contingent social reinforcement on the cooperative play of a preschool child. *Journal of Applied Behavior Analysis,* 1968, **1**, 73–76.

Harter, S. Discrimination learning set in children as a function of IQ and MA. *Journal of Experimental Child Psychology,* 1965, **2**, 31–43.

Harter, S. Mental age, IQ, and motivational factors in the discrimination learning set performance of normal and retarded children. *Journal of Experimental Child Psychology,* 1967, **5**, 123–141.

Hartmann, G. W. The field theory of learning and its educational consequences. *Yearbook of the National Society for the Study of Education,* 1942, **41**, Part II, 165–214.

Hartup, W. W., and Coates, B. Imitation of a peer as a function of reinforcement from the peer group and rewardingness of the model. *Child Development,* 1967, **38**, 1003–1016.

Hartup, W. W., Glazer, J. A., and Charlesworth, R. Peer reinforcement and sociometric status. *Child Development,* 1967, **38**, 1017–1024.

Harvey, O. J., and Rutherford, J. Status in the informal group: Influence and influencibility at differing age levels. *Child Development*, 1960, **31**, 377–385.

Harway, N. I. Judgment of distance in children and adults. *Journal of Experimental Psychology*, 1963, **65**, 385–390.

Harwood, F. W. Quantitative study of the syntax of the speech of Australian children. *Language and Speech*, 1959, **2**, 236–271.

Hassan, I. N. The body image and personality correlates of body type stereotypes. Unpublished doctoral dissertation, Indiana University, 1967.

Haude, R. H., and Ray, O. S. Visual exploration in monkeys as a function of visual incentive duration and sensory deprivation. *Journal of Comparative and Physiological Psychology*, 1967, **64**, 332–336.

Hayes, K. J. The backward curve: A method for the study of learning. *Psychological Review*, 1953, **60**, 269–275.

Hayes, K. J. Genes, drives and intellect. *Psychological Reports*, 1962, **10**, 299–342.

Hayes, K. J., and Pereboom, A. C. Artifacts in criterion-reference learning curves. *Psychological Review*, 1959, **66**, 23–26.

Hayhurst, H. Some errors of young children in producing passive sentences. *Journal of Verbal Learning and Verbal Behavior*, 1967, **6**, 634–640.

Haynes, H., White, B. L., and Held, R. Visual accommodation in human infants. *Science*, 1965, **148**, 528–530.

Heal, L. W. The role of cue value, cue novelty, and overtraining in the discrimination shift performance of retardates and normal children of comparable discrimination ability. *Journal of Experimental Child Psychology*, 1966, **4**, 126–142.

Heal, L. W., Bransky, M. L., and Mankinen, R. L. The role of dimension preference in reversal and non-reversal shifts of retardates. *Psychonomic Science*, 1966, **6**, 509–510.

Hebb, D. O. *The organization of behavior.* New York: Wiley, 1949.

Hebb, D. O. A neuropsychological theory. In S. Koch (Ed.), *Psychology: A study of a science.* Vol. 1. New York: McGraw-Hill, 1959. Pp. 622–643.

Hebb, D. O. The American revolution. *American Psychologist*, 1960, **15**, 735–745.

Hebb, D. O. *A textbook of psychology.* Philadelphia: Saunders, 1966.

Heber, R. A manual on terminology and classification in mental retardation. *American Journal of Mental Deficiency*, 1959, **64** (Monogr. Suppl. 2).

Heckman, B. Varied exposure duration in paired-associate learning in normal and retarded children. *American Journal of Mental Deficiency*, 1966, **70**, 709–713.

Hegge, T. G. The occupational status of higher-grade mental defectives in the present emergency: A study of parolees from the Wayne County Training School at Northville, Michigan. *American Journal of Mental Deficiency*, 1944, **49**, 86–98.

Heid, N. L. An operant analysis of behavior of an infant (from 10 days to 4 months). Unpublished doctoral dissertation, University of Washington, 1965.

Heidbreder, E. F. Problem solving in children and adults. *Journal of Genetic Psychology*, 1928, **35**, 522–545.

Heil, W. G., and Horn, A. *A comparative study of the data for five different intelligence tests administered to 284 twelfth grade students at South Gate High School, Los Angeles.* Los Angeles: Los Angeles City School Districts, Curriculum Division, 1950.

Held, R., and Hein, A. Movement-produced stimulation in the development of visually guided behavior. *Journal of Comparative and Physiological Psychology*, 1963, **56**, 872–876.

Hemmendinger, L. Perceptual organization and development as reflected in the structure of Rorschach test responses. *Journal of Projective Techniques*, 1953, **17**, 162–170.

Hempel, C. G., and Oppenheim, P. Studies in the logic of explanation. *Philosophy of Science,* 1948, **15,** 135–175.

Hendrickson, L. N., and Muehl, S. The effect of attention and motor response pretraining on learning to discriminate b and d in kindergarten children. *Journal of Educational Psychology,* 1962, **53,** 236–241.

Henning, L. B., and Hayweiser, L. J. Abstract form discrimination learning by young children in a T-maze. Paper presented at the meeting of the Eastern Psychological Association, Washington, D.C., April 1968.

Hermelin, B., and O'Connor, N. Short term memory in normal and subnormal children. *American Journal of Mental Deficiency,* 1964, **69,** 121–125.

Hernández-Peón, R., Scherrer, H., and Jouvet, M. Modification of electric activity in cochlear nucleus during "attention" in unanaesthetised cats. *Science,* 1956, **123,** 331–332.

Herrick, V. E. What is already known about the relation of the I.Q. to cultural background? In K. Eels, A. Davis, R. J. Havighurst, V. E. Herrick, and R. W. Tyler (Eds.), *Intelligence and cultural differences.* Chicago: University of Chicago Press, 1951. Pp. 10–15.

Herrnstein, R. J., and Loveland, D. H. Complex visual concept in the pigeon. *Science,* 1964, **146,** 549–551.

Hershenson, M. Visual discrimination in the human newborn. *Journal of Comparative and Physiological Psychology,* 1964, **58,** 270–276.

Hershenson, M. Form perception in the human newborn. Paper presented at the Second Annual Symposium, Center for Visual Science, University of Rochester, June 1965.

Hershenson, M. Development of the perception of form. *Psychological Bulletin,* 1967, **67,** 326–336.

Herzberg, F., and Lepkin, M. A study of sex differences and the Primary Mental Abilities Test. *Educational and Psychological Measurement,* 1954, **14,** 687–689.

Hetherington, E. M. A developmental study of the effects of sex of the dominant parent on sex-role preference, identification, and imitation in children. *Journal of Personality and Social Psychology,* 1965, **2,** 188–194.

Hetherington, E. M., and Frankie, G. Effects of parental dominance, warmth, and conflict on imitation in children. *Journal of Personality and Social Psychology,* 1967, **6,** 119–125.

Hetherington, E. M., and Ross, L. E. Discrimination learning by normal and retarded children under delay of reward and interpolated task conditions. *Child Development,* 1967, **38,** 639–647.

Hetherington, E. M., Ross, L. E., and Pick, H. L. Delay of reward and learning in mentally retarded and normal children. *Child Development,* 1964, **35,** 653–659.

Hicks, J. A., and Stewart, F. D. The learning of abstract concepts of size. *Child Development,* 1930, **1,** 195–203.

Hicks, L. H. An analysis of number-concept formation in the rhesus monkey. *Journal of Comparative and Physiological Psychology,* 1956, **49,** 212–218.

Hilden, A. H. A longitudinal study of intellectual development. *Journal of Psychology,* 1949, **28,** 187–214.

Hilgard, E. R. Methods and procedures in the study of learning. In S. S. Stevens (Ed.), *Handbook of experimental psychology.* New York: Wiley, 1951. Pp. 517–567.

Hilgard, E. R. *Theories of learning.* (2nd ed.) New York: Appleton-Century-Crofts, 1956.

Hilgard, E. R., and Marquis, D. G. *Conditioning and learning.* New York: Appleton-Century-Crofts, 1940.

Hill, K. T., and Sarason, S. B. The relation of test anxiety and defensiveness to test and school performance over the elementary school years: A further longitudinal study. *Monographs of the Society for Research in Child Development,* 1966, **31**(2, Whole No. 104).

Hill, K. T., and Stevenson, H. W. The effectiveness of social reinforcement following social and sensory deprivation. *Journal of Abnormal and Social Psychology,* 1964, **68**, 579–584.

Hill, S. D. Chronological age at which children solve three problems varying in complexity. *Perceptual and Motor Skills,* 1962, **14**, 254–258.

Hill, S. D. The performance of young children on three discrimination-learning tasks. *Child Development,* 1965, **36**, 425–435.

Hinde, R. A. *Animal behavior: A synthesis of ethological and comparative psychology.* New York: McGraw-Hill, 1966.

Hobson, J. R. Sex differences in Primary Mental Abilities. *Journal of Educational Research,* 1947, **41**, 126–132.

Hochberg, J., and Brooks, V. Pictorial recognition as an unlearned ability: A study of one child's performance. *American Journal of Psychology,* 1962, **75**, 624–628.

Hockman, C. H., and Lipsitt, L. P. Delay-of-reward gradients in discrimination learning with children for two levels of difficulty. *Journal of Comparative and Physiological Psychology,* 1961, **54**, 24–27.

Hodges, W. L., McCandless, B. R., and Spicker, H. H. *The development and application of a diagnostically-based curriculum for culturally deprived preschool children.* Washington, D.C.: U.S. Office of Education, 1967.

Hoffman, M. L., and Saltzstein, H. D. Parent discipline and the child's moral development. *Journal of Personality and Social Psychology,* 1967, **5**, 45–57.

Hofstaetter, P. R. The changing composition of "intelligence": A study of the T-technique. *Journal of Genetic Psychology,* 1954, **85**, 159–164.

Hollingworth, L. S. *Children above 180 I.Q.* New York: World Book, 1942.

Holmes, F. B. An experimental investigation of a method of overcoming children's fears. *Child Development,* 1936, **7**, 6–30.

Holt, E. B. *Animal drive and the learning process.* New York: Holt, 1931.

Holt, R. R. Imagery: The return of the ostracized. *American Psychologist,* 1964, **19**, 254–264.

Holton, R. B. Amplitude of an instrumental response following the cessation of reward. *Child Development,* 1961, **32**, 107–116.

Honig, W. K., Boneau, C. A., Burstein, K. R., and Pennypacker, H. S. Positive and negative generalization gradients obtained after equivalent training conditions. *Journal of Comparative and Physiological Psychology,* 1959, **56**, 111–116.

Honzik, M. P. The constancy of mental test performance during the preschool period. *Journal of Genetic Psychology,* 1938, **52**, 285–302.

Honzik, M. P. Developmental studies of parent child resemblance in intelligence. *Child Development,* 1957, **28**, 215–228.

Honzik, M. P. Environmental correlates of mental growth: Prediction from the family setting at 21 months. *Child Development,* 1967, **38**, 337–364.

Honzik, M. P., Macfarlane, J. W., and Allen, L. The stability of mental test performance between 2 and 18 years. *Journal of Experimental Education,* 1948, **18**, 309–324.

Hood, B. H. An experimental study of Piaget's theory of the development of number in children. *British Journal of Psychology,* 1962, **53,** 273–286.

Horowitz, F. D. Developmental studies of simultaneous and successive discrimination learning in normal and retarded children. Paper presented at the meeting of the Society for Research in Child Development, Minneapolis, March 1965.

Horowitz, F. D. Learning, developmental research, and individual differences. In L. P. Lipsitt and H. W. Reese (Eds.), *Advances in child development and behavior.* Vol. 4. New York: Academic Press, 1969. Pp. 83–126.

Horowitz, F. D., and Armentrout, J. Discrimination-learning, manifest anxiety, and effects of reinforcement. *Child Development,* 1965, **36,** 731–748.

Horsten, G. P. M., and Winkelman, J. E. Electrical activity of the retina in relation to the histological differentiation in infants born prematurely and at full-term. *Vision Research,* 1962, **2,** 269–276.

Horton, D. L., and Kjeldergaard, P. M. An experimental analysis of associative factors in mediated generalizations. *Psychological Monographs,* 1961, **75**(11, Whole No. 515).

Houlahan, F. J. Retroactive inhibition as affected by the temporal position of interpolated learning activities in elementary school children. *Catholic University of America Educational Research Monographs,* 1937, **10,** No. 3.

House, B. J., Smith, M., and Zeaman, D. Verbal learning and retention as a function of number of lists in retardates. *American Journal of Mental Deficiency,* 1964, **69,** 239–243.

House, B. J., and Zeaman, D. Transfer of a discrimination from objects to patterns. *Journal of Experimental Psychology,* 1960, **59,** 298–302.

House, B. J., and Zeaman, D. Reversal and nonreversal shifts in discrimination learning in retardates. *Journal of Experimental Psychology,* 1962, **63,** 444–451.

House, B. J., and Zeaman, D. Miniature experiments in the discrimination learning of retardates. In L. P. Lipsitt and C. C. Spiker (Eds.), *Advances in child development and behavior.* Vol. 1. New York: Academic Press, 1963. Pp. 313–374.

Hudson, W. Pictorial depth perception in sub-culture groups in Africa. *Journal of Social Psychology,* 1960, **52,** 183–208.

Huey, E. B. *The psychology and pedagogy of reading.* New York: Macmillan, 1908.

Hughes, H., and Converse, H. D. Characteristics of the gifted: A case for a sequel to Terman's study. *Exceptional Children,* 1962, **29,** 179–183.

Hull, C. L. Quantitative aspects of the evolution of concepts. *Psychological Monographs,* 1920, **28,** No. 123.

Hull, C. L. *Principles of behavior.* New York: Appleton-Century-Crofts, 1943.

Hull, C. L. *A behavior system.* New Haven: Yale University Press, 1952.

Hunt, J. McV. *Intelligence and experience.* New York: Ronald Press, 1961.

Hunter, I. M. L. An experimental investigation of absolute and relative theories of transpositional behaviour in children. *British Journal of Psychology,* 1952, **43,** 113–128.

Hunter, I. M. L. *Memory.* (Rev. ed.) Baltimore: Penguin, 1964.

Hunter, W. S. The delayed reaction in animals and children. *Behavior Monographs,* 1913, **2,** No. 1, 52–62.

Hunter, W. S. The delayed reaction in a child. *Psychological Review,* 1917, **24,** 74–87.

Hunter, W. S., and Bartlett, S. C. Double alternation behavior in young children. *Journal of Experimental Psychology,* 1948, **38,** 558–567.

Hunton, V. D., and Hicks, L. H. Discrimination of figural orientation by monkeys and children. *Perceptual and Motor Skills,* 1965, **21,** 55–59.

Hurley, J. R. Maternal attitudes and children's intelligence. *Journal of Clinical Psychology*, 1959, **15**, 291–292.

Hurlock, E. B. *Child development.* (4th ed.) New York: McGraw-Hill, 1964.

Hutt, C. Exploration and play in children. In P. A. Jewell and C. Loizos (Eds.), *Play, exploration, and territory in mammals.* London: Academic Press, 1966. Pp. 61–81.

Huttenlocher, J. Children's language: Word-phrase relationship. *Science*, 1964, **143**, 264–265.

Huttenlocher, J. Children's ability to order and orient objects. *Child Development*, 1967, **38**, 1169–1176.

Illingworth, R. S. Predictive value of developmental tests in the 1st year. *Journal of Child Psychology and Psychiatry*, 1961, **2**, 210–215.

Inhelder, B. Recent trends in Genevan research. Paper presented at Temple University, Fall 1968.

Inhelder, B., and Piaget, J. *The growth of logical thinking from childhood to adolescence.* New York: Basic Books, 1958.

Irion, A. L. The relation of "set" to retention. *Psychological Review*, 1948, **55**, 336–341.

Irwin, O. C. Effect of strong light on the body activity of newborns. *Journal of Comparative Psychology*, 1941, **32**, 233–236. (a)

Irwin, O. C. Research on speech sounds for the first six months of life. *Psychological Bulletin*, 1941, **38**, 277–285. (b)

Irwin, O. C. Infant speech: Consonantal sounds according to place of articulation. *Journal of Speech Disorders*, 1947, **12**, 397–401.

Irwin, O. C. Development of vowel sounds. *Journal of Speech and Hearing Disorders*, 1948, **13**, 31–34.

Irwin, O. C. Infant speech: Consonantal position. *Journal of Speech and Hearing Disorders*, 1951, **16**, 159–161.

Irwin, O. C., and Chen, H. P. A reliability study of speech sounds observed in the crying of newborn infants. *Child Development*, 1941, **12**, 351–368.

Irwin, O. C., and Chen, H. P. Speech sound elements during the first year of life: A review of the literature. *Journal of Speech Disorders*, 1943, **8**, 109–121.

Irwin, O. C., and Weiss, L. A. Differential variations in the activity and crying of the newborn infant under different intensities of light: A comparison of observational with polygraph findings. *University of Iowa Studies in Child Welfare*, 1934, **9**, No. 4, 139–147. (a)

Irwin, O. C., and Weiss, L. A. The effect of clothing on the general vocal activity of the newborn infant. *University of Iowa Studies in Child Welfare*, 1934, **9**, No. 4, 151–162. (b)

Irwin, O. C., and Weiss, L. A. The effect of darkness on the activity of newborn infants. *University of Iowa Studies in Child Welfare*, 1934, **9**, No. 4, 163–175. (c)

Isaacs, I. D., and Duncan, C. P. Reversal and nonreversal shifts within and between dimensions in concept formation. *Journal of Experimental Psychology*, 1962, **64**, 580–585.

Iscoe, I., and Semler, I. J. Paired-associate learning in normal and mentally retarded children as a function of four experimental conditions. *Journal of Comparative and Physiological Psychology*, 1964, **57**, 387–392.

Isselbacher, K. J., Anderson, E. P., Kurahashi, K., and Kalckar, H. M. Congenital galactosemia, a single enzymatic block in galactose metabolism. *Science*, 1956, **123**, 635–636.

Jackson, T. A., and Jerome, E. Studies in the transposition of learning by children:

IV. A preliminary study of patternedness in discrimination learning. *Journal of Experimental Psychology*, 1940, **26**, 432–439.

Jackson, T. A., and Jerome, E. A. Studies in the transposition of learning by children. VI. Simultaneous vs. successive presentation of stimuli to bright and dull children. *Journal of Experimental Psychology*, 1943, **33**, 431–439.

Jackson, T. A., Stonex, E., Lane, E., and Dominguez, K. Studies in the transposition of learning by children. I. Relative vs. absolute response as a function of amount of training. *Journal of Experimental Psychology*, 1938, **23**, 578–600.

Jacobs, R. A., and Rosenbaum, P. S. *English transformational grammar.* New York: Random House (Blaisdell), 1968.

Jakobson, R. *Kindersprache, Aphasie, und allgemeine Lautgesetze.* Uppsala: Almqvist & Wiksell, 1941.

Jakobson, R. *Child language aphasia and phonological universals.* (Translated by A. R. Keiler.) The Hague: Mouton, 1968.

Jakobson, R., Fant, C. G. M., and Halle, M. *Preliminaries to speech analysis. The distinctive features and their correlates.* Cambridge, Mass.: M.I.T. Press, 1952.

Jakobson, R., and Halle, M. *Fundamentals of language.* The Hague: Mouton, 1956.

James, W. *The principles of psychology.* New York: Holt, 1890. 2 vols.

Janos, O. Development of higher nervous activity in premature infants. *Pavlov Journal of Higher Nervous Activity*, 1959, **9**, 760–767.

Janos, O. Age and individual differences in higher nervous activity in infants. *Halek's Collection of Studies in Pediatrics*, 1965, No. 8.

Jarrett, R. F., and Scheibe, K. E. Association chains and paired-associate learning. *Journal of Verbal Learning and Verbal Behavior*, 1963, **1**, 264–268.

Jarvik, M. E. Discrimination of colored food and food signs by primates. *Journal of Comparative and Physiological Psychology*, 1953, **46**, 390–392.

Jastak, J., and Whiteman, M. The prevalence of mental retardation in Delaware. Preliminary report on a state-wide survey. In *The nature and transmission of the genetic and cultural characteristics of human populations.* New York: Millbank Memorial Fund, 1957.

Jeffrey, W. E. The effects of verbal and nonverbal responses in mediating an instrumental act. *Journal of Experimental Psychology*, 1953, **45**, 327–333.

Jeffrey, W. E. Variables in early discrimination learning: I. Motor responses in the training of a left-right discrimination. *Child Development*, 1958, **29**, 270–275. (a)

Jeffrey, W. E. Variables in early discrimination learning: II. Mode of response and stimulus difference in the discrimination of tonal frequencies. *Child Development*, 1958, **29**, 531–538. (b)

Jeffrey, W. E. Variables in early discrimination learning: III. Simultaneous vs. successive stimulus presentation. *Child Development*, 1961, **32**, 305–310.

Jeffrey, W. E. Variables affecting reversal-shifts in young children. *American Journal of Psychology*, 1965, **78**, 589–595.

Jeffrey, W. E. Discrimination of oblique lines by children. *Journal of Comparative and Physiological Psychology*, 1966, **62**, 154–156.

Jeffrey, W. E. The orienting reflex and attention in cognitive development. *Psychological Review*, 1968, **75**, 323–334.

Jeffrey, W. E., and Cohen, L. B. Response tendencies of children in a two choice situation. *Journal of Experimental Child Psychology*, 1965, **2**, 248–254.

Jenkin, A. M. Imagery and learning. *British Journal of Psychology*, 1935, **26**, 149–164.

Jenkin, N., and Feallock, S. M. Developmental and intellectual processes in size-distance judgment. *American Journal of Psychology*, 1960, **73**, 268–273.

Jenkins, H. M. Generalization gradients and the concept of inhibition. In D. I. Mostofsky (Ed.), *Stimulus generalization*. Stanford: Stanford University Press, 1965. Pp. 55–61. (a)

Jenkins, H. M. Measurement of stimulus control during operant conditioning. *Psychological Bulletin*, 1965, **64**, 365–376. (b)

Jenkins, H. M., and Harrison, R. H. Generalization gradients of inhibition following auditory discrimination learning. *Journal of the Experimental Analysis of Behavior*, 1962, **5**, 435–441.

Jenkins, J. J. Mediated associations: Paradigms and situations. In C. N. Cofer and B. S. Musgrave (Eds.), *Verbal behavior and learning: Problems and processes*. New York: McGraw-Hill, 1963. Pp. 210–245.

Jenkins, J. J., Foss, D. J., and Odom, P. B. Associative mediation in paired-associate learning with multiple controls. *Journal of Verbal Learning and Verbal Behavior*, 1965, **4**, 141–147.

Jenkins, J. J., Mink, W. D., and Russell, W. A. Associative clustering as a function of verbal association strength. *Psychological Reports*, 1958, **4**, 127–136.

Jenkins, J. J., and Palermo, D. S. Mediation processes and the acquisition of linguistic structure. In U. Bellugi and R. Brown (Eds.), The acquisition of language. *Monographs of the Society for Research in Child Development*, 1964, **29**(1, Whole No. 92). Pp. 141–169.

Jensen, A. R. How much can we boost I.Q. and scholastic achievement? *Harvard Educational Review*, 1969, **39**, 1–123.

Jensen, A. R., and Rohwer, W. D., Jr. The effect of verbal mediation on the learning and retention of paired-associates by retarded adults. *American Journal of Mental Deficiency*, 1963, **68**, 80–84. (a)

Jensen, A. R., and Rohwer, W. D., Jr. Verbal mediation in paired-associate and serial learning. *Journal of Verbal Learning and Verbal Behavior*, 1963, **1**, 346–352. (b)

Jensen, A. R., and Rohwer, W. D., Jr. Syntactic mediation of serial and paired-associate learning as a function of age. *Child Development*, 1965, **36**, 601–608.

Jensen, D. D. Operationism and the question "Is this behavior learned or innate?" *Behaviour*, 1961, **17**, 1–8.

Jensen, G. D. Preference for bar pressing over "freeloading" as a function of number of rewarded presses. *Journal of Experimental Psychology*, 1963, **65**, 451–454.

Jensen, K. Differential reactions to taste and temperature stimuli in newborn infants. *Psychological Monographs*, 1932, **12**, 363–479.

Jersild, A. T., and Holmes, F. B. Children's fears. *Monographs of the Society for Research in Child Development*, 1935, **6**, No. 20.

Jespersen, J. O. H. *Language: Its nature, development, and origin*. London: Allen & Unwin, 1922.

Jessor, R., and Hammond, K. R. Construct validity and the Taylor Anxiety Scale. *Psychological Bulletin*, 1947, **54**, 161–170.

Johnson, B. M. Reward schedules and instrumental conditioning in normal and retarded children. *Child Development*, 1966, **37**, 633–644.

Johnson, D. M. Formulation and reformulation of figure-concepts. *American Journal of Psychology*, 1961, **74**, 418–424.

Johnson, G. O. A study of the social position of mentally handicapped children in the regular grades. *American Journal of Mental Deficiency*, 1950, **55**, 60–89.

Johnson, G. O. *A comparative study of the personal and social adjustment of mentally handicapped children placed in special classes with mentally handicapped children who remain in regular classes*. Syracuse, N.Y.: Syracuse University Press, 1961.

Johnson, J. I., Jr., and Michels, K. M. Learning sets and object-size effects in visual discrimination learning by raccoons. *Journal of Comparative and Physiological Psychology*, 1958, **51**, 376–379.

Johnson, M. M. Sex-role learning in the nuclear family. *Child Development*, 1963, **34**, 319–333.

Jones, A. Information deprivation and irrelevant drive as determiners of an instrumental response. *Journal of Experimental Psychology*, 1961, **62**, 310–311.

Jones, A., Wilkinson, H. J., and Braden, I. Information deprivation as a motivational variable. *Journal of Experimental Psychology*, 1961, **62**, 126–137.

Jones, H. E. The galvanic skin reflex in infancy. *Child Development*, 1930, **1**, 106–110.

Jones, H. E. Adolescence in our society. In G. Emerson (Chm.), *The family in a democratic society*. New York: Columbia University Press, 1949. Pp. 70–84.

Jones, H. E. The environment and mental development. In L. Carmichael (Ed.), *Manual of child psychology*. (2nd ed.) New York: Wiley, 1954. Pp. 631–696.

Jones, H. E., and Conrad, H. S. The growth and decline of intelligence: A study of a homogeneous group between the ages of ten and sixty. *Genetic Psychology Monographs*, 1933, **13**, No. 3, 233–294.

Jones, J. E. The CS-UCS interval in conditioning short- and long-latency responses. *Journal of Experimental Psychology*, 1961, **62**, 612–617.

Jones, M. C. A laboratory study of fear: The case of Peter. *Pedagogical Seminary and Journal of Genetic Psychology*, 1924, **31**, 308–315.

Jones, M. C. The later careers of boys who were early- or late-maturing. *Child Development*, 1957, **28**, 113–128.

Jones, M. C. Psychological correlates of somatic development. *Child Development*, 1965, **36**, 899–911.

Jones, M. C., and Bayley, N. Physical maturing among boys as related to behavior. *Journal of Educational Psychology*, 1950, **41**, 129–148.

Jones, M. C., and Mussen, P. H. Self-conceptions, motivations, and interpersonal attitudes of early- and late-maturing girls. *Child Development*, 1958, **29**, 491–502.

Jordan, A. M. Parental occupations and children's intelligence scores. *Journal of Applied Psychology*, 1933, **17**, 103–119.

Jordan, A. M. Personal social traits of mentally handicapped children. In T. G. Thurstone (Ed.), *An evaluation of educating mentally handicapped children in special classes and in regular classes*. Chapel Hill, N.C.: University of North Carolina Press, 1959.

Kagan, J., and Moss, H. A. *Birth to maturity: A study in psychological development*. New York: Wiley, 1962.

Kagan, J., Moss, H. A., and Sigel, I. E. Psychological significance of styles of conceptualization. In J. C. Wright and J. Kagan (Eds.), Basic cognitive processes in children. *Monographs of the Society for Research in Child Development*, 1963, **28**, No. 2. Pp. 73–112.

Kagan, J., Sontag, L. W., Baker, C. T., and Nelson, V. L. Personality and I.Q. change. *Journal of Abnormal and Social Psychology*, 1958, **56**, 261–266.

Kamin, L. J. Temporal and intensity characteristics of the conditioned stimulus. In W. F. Prokasy (Ed.), *Classical conditioning: A symposium*. New York: Appleton-Century-Crofts, 1965. Pp. 118–147.

Kanner, L. *Child psychiatry*. Springfield, Ill.: Thomas, 1957.

Kantor, J. R. *An objective psychology of grammar*. Bloomington, Ind.: Principia Press, 1935.

Kantrow, R. W. An investigation of conditioned feeding responses and concomitant adaptive behavior in young infants. *University of Iowa Studies in Child Welfare*, 1937, **13**, No. 3.

Karelitz, S., Fisichelli, V. R., Costa, J., Karelitz, R., and Rosenfeld, L. Relation of crying activity in early infancy to speech and intellectual development at age three years. *Child Development*, 1964, **35**, 769–777.

Kasatkin, N. I. Rannie uslovnye refleksy rebenka. (Early conditioned reflexes in human ontogenesis.) Moscow: Izdatelstvo Akad. Med. Nauk S.S.S.R., 1948.

Kasatkin, N. I. Early conditioned reflexes in the child. *Pavlov Journal of Higher Nervous Activity*, 1952, **2**, 572–581.

Kasatkin, N. I. Early ontogenesis of reflex activity in the child. *Zhurnal Vysshei Nervnoi Deyatel'nosti imeni I. P. Pavlova*, 1957, **7**, 805–818. (Translated by National Institutes of Health, U.S. Public Health Service, February 1960.)

Kasatkin, N. I., and Levikova, A. M. On the development of early conditioned reflexes and differentiations of auditory stimuli in infants. *Journal of Experimental Psychology*, 1935, **18**, 1–19. (a)

Kasatkin, N. I., and Levikova, A. M. The formation of visual conditioned reflexes and their differentiation in infants. *Journal of General Psychology*, 1935, **12**, 416–435. (b)

Kasatkin, N. I., Mirzoiants, N. S., and Khokhitva, A. Conditioned orienting responses in children in the first year of life. *Zhurnal Vysshei Nervnoi Deyatel'nosti imeni I. P. Pavlova*, 1953, **3**, 192–202. [Republished: In *The central nervous system and behavior, translations from the Russian medical literature for the third Macy conference on the central nervous system and behavior*. Princeton, N.J.: Josiah Macy, Jr., Foundation, 1960. Pp. 343–358.]

Kass, N. Resistance to extinction as a function of age and schedules of reinforcement. *Journal of Experimental Psychology*, 1962, **64**, 249–252.

Kass, N., and Wilson, H. Resistance to extinction as a function of percentage of reinforcement, number of training trials, and conditioned reinforcement. *Journal of Experimental Psychology*, 1966, **71**, 355–357.

Kass, N., Wilson, H., and Sidowski, J. B. Effects of number of training trials upon the development of a secondary reinforcer with children. *American Psychologist*, 1964, **19**, 451. (Abstract)

Katona, G. Imagery. *American Psychologist*, 1964, **19**, 773–774.

Katz, I. Some motivational determinants of racial differences in intellectual achievement. *International Journal of Psychology*, 1967, **2**, 1–12.

Katz, J. J. *The philosophy of language*. New York: Harper & Row, 1966.

Katz, J. J., and Fodor, J. A. The structure of a semantic theory. *Language*, 1963, **39**, 170–210.

Kaye, H. Skin conductance and electro-tactual threshold in the newborn. Unpublished master's thesis, Brown University, 1962.

Kaye, H. Skin conductance in the human neonate. *Child Development*, 1964, **35**, 1297–1305.

Kaye, H. The conditioned Babkin reflex in human newborns. *Psychonomic Science*, 1965, **2**, 287–288.

Kaye, H. The effects of feeding and tonal stimulation on non-nutritive sucking in the human newborn. *Journal of Experimental Child Psychology*, 1966, **3**, 131–145.

Kaye, H. Infant sucking behavior and its modification. In L. P. Lipsitt and C. C. Spiker (Eds.), *Advances in child development and behavior*. Vol. 3. New York: Academic Press, 1967. Pp. 1–52.

Kaye, H. The effect of tone length and intertone interval on habituation of the startle response in human newborns. Unpublished manuscript, Emory University, 1968. (a)

Kaye, H. Tonal suppression of sucking movements in newborns. Unpublished manuscript, Emory University, 1968. (b)

Kaye, H., and Brown, J. Habituation and dishabituation as a function of tonal frequency. Unpublished manuscript, Emory University, 1968.

Kaye, H., Brown, J., and Jones, E. Habituation of the startle response in newborns as a function of preceding activity level. Unpublished manuscript, Emory University, 1968.

Kaye, H., and Karp, E. Tactile threshold in the human neonate. Unpublished manuscript, Emory University, 1968.

Kaye, H., and Levin, G. R. Two attempts to demonstrate tonal suppression of non-nutritive sucking in neonates. *Perceptual and Motor Skills*, 1963, **17**, 521–522.

Kaye, H., and Lipsitt, L. P. Relation of electrotactual threshold to basal skin conductance. *Child Development*, 1964, **35**, 1307–1312.

Kean, J. M., and Yamamoto, K. Grammar signals and assignment of words to parts of speech among young children: An exploration. *Journal of Verbal Learning and Verbal Behavior*, 1965, **4**, 323–326.

Keen, R. E., Chase, H. H., and Graham, F. K. Twenty-four hour retention by neonates of an habituated heart response. *Psychonomic Science*, 1965, **2**, 265–266.

Keeney, T. J., Cannizzo, S. R., and Flavell, J. H. Spontaneous and induced verbal rehearsal in a recall task. *Child Development*, 1967, **38**, 953–966.

Kelleher, R. T. Discrimination learning as a function of reversal and nonreversal shifts. *Journal of Experimental Psychology*, 1956, **51**, 379–384.

Kelleher, R. T., and Gollub, L. R. A review of positive conditioned reinforcement. *Journal of the Experimental Analysis of Behavior*, 1962, **5**, 543–597.

Keller, E. D., and Rowley, V. M. Anxiety, intelligence and scholastic achievement in elementary school children. *Psychological Reports*, 1962, **11**, 19–22.

Kellogg, W. N., and Kellogg, L. A. *The ape and the child: A study of environmental influence upon early behavior.* New York: McGraw-Hill, 1933.

Kendler, H. H. *Basic psychology.* New York: Appleton-Century-Crofts, 1963.

Kendler, H. H., and Kendler, T. S. Vertical and horizontal processes in problem solving. *Psychological Review*, 1962, **69**, 1–16.

Kendler, H. H., and Kendler, T. S. Selective attention versus mediation: Some comments on Mackintosh's analysis of two-stage models of discrimination learning. *Psychological Bulletin*, 1966, **66**, 282–288.

Kendler, T. S. Concept formation. *Annual Review of Psychology*, 1961, **12**, 447–472.

Kendler, T. S. Verbalization and optional reversal shifts among kindergarten children. *Journal of Verbal Learning and Verbal Behavior*, 1964, **3**, 428–436.

Kendler, T. S., and Kendler, H. H. Reversal and nonreversal shifts in kindergarten children. *Journal of Experimental Psychology*, 1959, **58**, 56–60.

Kendler, T. S., and Kendler, H. H. Optional shifts of children as a function of number of training trials on the initial discrimination. *Journal of Experimental Child Psychology*, 1966, **3**, 216–224.

Kendler, T. S., and Kendler, H. H. Experimental analysis of inferential behavior in children. In L. P. Lipsitt and C. C. Spiker (Eds.), *Advances in child development and behavior.* Vol. 3. New York: Academic Press, 1967. Pp. 157–190.

Kendler, T. S., Kendler, H. H., and Learnard, B. Mediated responses to size and brightness as a function of age. *American Journal of Psychology*, 1962, **75**, 571–586.

Kendler, T. S., Kendler, H. H., and Wells, D. Reversal and nonreversal shifts in nursery school children. *Journal of Comparative and Physiological Psychology*, 1960, **53**, 83–88.

Kennard, M. Cortical reorganization of motor function: Studies on a series of monkeys of various ages from infancy to maturity. *Archives of Neurology and Psychiatry*, 1942, **48**, 227–240.

Kennedy, R. J. R. *The social adjustment of morons in a Connecticut city*. Hartford, Conn.: Mansfield-Southbury Social Service, 1948.

Kennedy, W. A., Van de Reitt, V., and White, J. C. A normative sample of intelligence and achievement of Negro elementary school children in the Southeastern United States. *Monographs of the Society for Research in Child Development*, 1963, **28**(6, Whole No. 90).

Kent, N., and Davis, D. R. Discipline in the home and intellectual development. *British Journal of Medical Psychology*, 1957, **30**, 27–34.

Keppel, G. Verbal learning in children. *Psychological Bulletin*, 1964, **61**, 428–435.

Keppel, G., and Rehula, R. J. Rate of presentation in serial learning. *Journal of Experimental Psychology*, 1965, **69**, 121–125.

Kern, W. H., and Pfaeffle, H. A comparison of social adjustment of mentally retarded children in various educational settings. *American Journal of Mental Deficiency*, 1963, **67**, 407–413.

Kessen, W. "Stage" and "structure" in the study of children. In W. Kessen and C. Kuhlman (Eds.), Thought in the young child. *Monographs of the Society for Research in Child Development*, 1962, **27**, No. 2. Pp. 65–82.

Kessen, W. Research in the psychological development of infants: An overview. *Merrill-Palmer Quarterly*, 1963, **9**, 83–94.

Kessen, W. Sucking and looking: Two organized congenital patterns of behavior in the human newborn. In H. W. Stevenson, E. H. Hess, and H. L. Rheingold (Eds.), *Early behavior: Comparative and developmental approaches*. New York: Wiley, 1967. Pp. 147–179.

Kessen, W., and Hershenson, M. Ocular orientation in the human newborn infant. Paper presented at the meeting of the American Psychological Association, Philadelphia, August 1963.

Kessen, W., and Kuhlman, C. (Eds.) Thought in the young child. *Monographs of the Society for Research in Child Development*, 1962, **27**(2, Whole No. 83).

Kessen, W., and Leutzendorff, A.-M. The effect of non-nutritive sucking on movement in the human newborn. *Journal of Comparative and Physiological Psychology*, 1963, **56**, 69–72.

Kimble, G. A. *Principles of general psychology*. New York: Ronald Press, 1956.

Kimble, G. A. *Hilgard and Marquis' conditioning and learning*. New York: Appleton-Century-Crofts, 1961.

Kimble, G. A., and Posnick, G. M. Anxiety? *Journal of Personality and Social Psychology*, 1967, **7**, 108–110.

Kimmel, H. D. Instrumental inhibitory factors in classical conditioning. In W. F. Prokasy (Ed.), *Classical conditioning*. New York: Appleton-Century-Crofts, 1965. Pp. 148–171.

Kingsley, R. C., and Hall, V. C. Training conservation through the use of learning sets. *Child Development*, 1967, **38**, 1111–1126.

Kirk, S. A. *Early education of the mentally retarded*. Urbana, Ill.: University of Illinois Press, 1958.

Kirkendall, L. A. *Premarital intercourse and interpersonal relationships*. New York: Julian Press, 1961.

Kitchell, R. L. Neural response patterns in taste. In M. R. Kare and B. L. Halpern (Eds.), *Physiological and behavioral aspects of taste.* Chicago: University of Chicago Press, 1961. Pp. 39–48.

Kjeldergaard, P. M. Transfer and mediation in verbal learning. In T. H. Dixon and D. L. Horton (Eds.), *Verbal behavior and general behavior theory.* New York: Prentice-Hall, 1968. Pp. 67–96.

Klein, S. D. A developmental study of tactual perception. Unpublished doctoral dissertation, Clark University, 1963. (See *Dissertation Abstracts,* 1964, **24,** 2977.)

Klima, E. S., and Bellugi, U. Syntactic regularities in the speech of children. In J. Lyons and R. J. Wales (Eds.), *Psycholinguistics papers.* Edinburgh: Edinburgh University Press, 1966. Pp. 183–208.

Klineberg, O. The intelligence of migrants. *American Sociological Review,* 1938, **3,** 218–224.

Klineberg, O. On race and intelligence: A joint statement. *American Journal of Orthopsychiatry,* 1957, **27,** 420–422.

Klineberg, O. Negro-white differences in intelligence test performance. *American Psychologist,* 1963, **18,** 198–203.

Klinger, N. N., and Palermo, D. S. Aural paired-associate learning in children as a function of free-associative strength. *Child Development,* 1967, **38,** 1143–1152.

Klüver, H. Studies on the eidetic type and on eidetic imagery. *Psychological Bulletin,* 1928, **25,** 69–104.

Klüver, H. *Behavior mechanisms in monkeys.* Chicago: University of Chicago Press, 1933.

Knief, L. M., and Stroud, J. B. Intercorrelations among various intelligence, achievement and social class scores. *Journal of Educational Psychology,* 1959, **50,** 117–120.

Knobloch, H., and Pasamanick, B. Predicting intellectual potential in infancy. *American Journal of Diseases of Children,* 1963, **106,** 43–51.

Koch, J. The development of the conditioned orienting reaction to humans in 2–3 month infants. *Activitas Nervosa Superior,* 1965, **7,** No. 2, 141–142.

Koff, R. H. Systematic changes in children's word-association norms. *Child Development,* 1965, **36,** 299–305.

Kofsky, E. A scalogram study of classificatory development. *Child Development,* 1966, **37,** 191–204.

Köhler, W. *The mentality of apes.* (Translated from 2nd Rev. ed. by E. Winter.) New York: Harcourt, 1925.

Köhler, W. *Gestalt psychology.* New York: Liveright, 1929.

Kohnstamm, G. A. *Teaching children to solve a Piagetian problem of class inclusion.* The Hague: Mouton, 1967.

Konorski, J. *Conditioned reflexes and neuron organization.* Cambridge, Eng.: Cambridge University Press, 1948.

Koopman, P. R., and Ames, E. W. Infants' preferences for facial arrangements: A failure to replicate. *Child Development,* 1968, **39,** 481–488.

Koppenaal, R. J., Krull, A., and Katz, H. Age, interference, and forgetting. *Journal of Experimental Child Psychology,* 1964, **1,** 360–375.

Korner, A. F., and Grobstein, R. Individual differences at birth: Implications for mother-infant relationship and later development. *Journal of Child Psychiatry,* 1967, **6,** 676–690.

Koronakos, C., and Arnold, W. J. The formation of learning sets in rats. *Journal of Comparative and Physiological Psychology,* 1957, **50,** 11–14.

Kounin, J., Gump, P. V., and Ryan, J. J., III. Explorations in classroom management. *Journal of Teacher Education*, 1961, **12**, 235–246.

Koutsoudas, A. *Writing transformational grammars: An introduction.* New York: McGraw-Hill, 1966.

Krachkovskaia, M. V. Reflex changes in the leukocyte count of newborn infants in relation to food intake. *Pavlov Journal of Higher Nervous Activity*, 1959, **9**, 193–199.

Krasnogorski, N. I. The formation of artificial conditioned reflexes in young children. *Russkii Vrach*, 1907, **36**, 1245–1246. [Translated and republished: In Y. Brackbill and G. G. Thompson (Eds.), *Behavior in infancy and early childhood: A book of readings.* New York: Free Press, 1967. Pp. 237–239.]

Krasnogorski, N. I. Über die Grundmechanismen der Arbeit der Grosshernrunde bei Kindern. *Jahrbuch für Kinderheilkunde*, 1913, **78**, 373–389.

Kruger, L., Feldzmen, A. N., and Miles, W. R. Comparative olfactory intensities of the aliphatic alcohols in man. *American Journal of Psychology*, 1955, **68**, 386–395.

Krugman, M. Identification and preservation of talent. *Teachers College Record*, 1960, **61**, 459–463.

Kuenne, M. R. Experimental investigation of the relation of language to transposition behavior in young children. *Journal of Experimental Psychology*, 1946, **36**, 471–490.

Kuhn, T. S. *The structure of scientific revolutions.* Chicago: University of Chicago Press, 1962.

Kuo, Z. Y. A psychology without heredity. *Psychological Review*, 1924, **31**, 427–451.

Kurtz, K. H. Discrimination of complex stimuli: The relationship of training and test stimuli in the transfer of discrimination. *Journal of Experimental Psychology*, 1955, **50**, 283–292.

Kurtz, K. H., and Hovland, C. I. The effect of verbalization during observation of stimulus objects upon accuracy of recognition and recall. *Journal of Experimental Psychology*, 1953, **45**, 157–164.

Lacey, J. I. The evaluation of autonomic responses: Toward a general solution. *Annals of the New York Academy of Science*, 1956, **67**, 123–164.

Lachman, R. The model in theory construction. *Psychological Review*, 1960, **67**, 113–129.

Ladd, G. T., and Woodworth, R. S. *Elements of physiological psychology.* (Rev. ed.) New York: Scribner, 1911.

Lahey, M. F. L. Retroactive inhibition as a function of age, intelligence, and the duration of the interpolated activity. *Catholic University of America Educational Research Monographs*, 1937, **10**, No. 2.

Laidlaw, R. G. N. Appreciate or perish. *Ontario Psychological Association Quarterly*, 1960, **13**, 53–57.

Laird, D. S. The performance of two groups of 11 year old boys on the Wechsler Intelligence Scale for Children. *Journal of Educational Research*, 1957, **51**, 101–107.

Lambert, W. E., and Paivio, A. The influence of noun-adjective order on learning. *Canadian Journal of Psychology*, 1956, **10**, 9–12.

Lambert, W. W., Solomon, R. L., and Watson, P. D. Reinforcement and extinction as factors in size estimation. *Journal of Experimental Psychology*, 1949, **39**, 637–641.

Landau, R., and Gewirtz, J. L. Differential satiation for a social reinforcing stimulus as a determinant of its efficiency in conditioning. *Journal of Experimental Child Psychology*, 1967, **5**, 391–405.

Lane, H., and Sheppard, W. Development of the prosodic features of infants' vocalizing. In K. F. Riegel (Ed.), *The development of language functions.* Rept. No. 8.

Ann Arbor, Mich.: Center for Human Growth and Development, University of Michigan, 1965. Pp. 79–90.

Langacker, R. W. *Language and its structure: Some fundamental linguistic concepts.* New York: Harcourt, Brace & World, 1968.

Laurence, M. W. Age differences in performance and subjective organization in the free-recall learning of pictorial material. *Canadian Journal of Psychology,* 1966, **20,** 388–399.

Laurence, M. W. A developmental look at the usefulness of list categorization as an aid to free recall. *Canadian Journal of Psychology,* 1967, **21,** 153–165.

Laurendeau, M., and Pinard, A. *La pensée causale.* Paris: Presses Universitaires de France, 1962.

Lawrence, D. H. Acquired distinctiveness of cues: I. Transfer between discriminations on the basis of familiarity with the stimulus. *Journal of Experimental Psychology,* 1949, **39,** 770–784.

Lawrence, D. H. Acquired distinctiveness of cues: II. Selective association in a constant stimulus situation. *Journal of Experimental Psychology,* 1950, **40,** 175–188.

Lawrence, D. H. The transfer of a discrimination along a continuum. *Journal of Comparative and Physiological Psychology,* 1952, **45,** 511–516.

Lazarus, A. A. The elimination of children's phobias by deconditioning. In H. J. Eysenck (Ed.), *Behaviour therapy and the neuroses.* New York: Macmillan (Pergamon), 1960. Pp. 114–122.

Leahy, A. M. Nature-nurture and intelligence. *Genetic Psychology Monographs,* 1935, **17,** No. 4, 235–308.

Leask, J., Haber, R. N., and Haber, R. B. Eidetic imagery in children: II. Longitudinal and experimental results. Unpublished manuscript, University of Rochester, 1967.

Lee, E. S. Negro intelligence and selective migration: A Philadelphia test of the Klineberg hypothesis. *American Sociological Review,* 1951, **61,** 227–233.

Lee, L. C. Concept utilization in preschool children. *Child Development,* 1965, **36,** 221–227.

Lees, R. Formal discussion. In U. Bellugi and R. Brown (Eds.), The acquisition of language. *Monographs of the Society for Research in Child Development,* 1964, **29**(1, Whole No. 92). Pp. 92–98.

Leibowitz, H., Pollard, S. W., and Dickson, D. Monocular and binocular size matching as a function of distance at various age levels. *American Journal of Psychology,* 1967, **80,** 263–268.

Leiman, A. J., Myers, J. L., and Myers, N. A. Secondary reinforcement in a discrimination problem with children. *Child Development,* 1961, **32,** 349–353.

Lele, P. P., and Weddell, G. The relationship between neurohistology and corneal sensibility. *Brain,* 1956, **79,** 119–154.

Lenneberg, E. H. Speech as a motor skill with special reference to non-aphasic disorders. In U. Bellugi and R. Brown (Eds.), The acquisition of language. *Monographs of the Society for Research in Child Development,* 1964, **29**(1, Whole No. 92). Pp. 115–127.

Lenneberg, E. H. *Biological foundations of language.* New York: Wiley, 1967.

Lenneberg, E. H., Rebelsky, F. G., and Nichols, I. A. The vocalization of infants born to deaf and to hearing parents. *Vita Humana,* 1965, **8,** 23–37.

Leopold, W. F. *Speech development of a bilingual child: A linguist's record.* Evanston, Ill.: Northwestern University Studies in the Humanities, 1939–1949. 4 vols.

Leopold, W. F. The study of child language and infant bilingualism. *Word,* 1948, **4,** 1–17.

Leventhal, A., and Lipsitt, L. P. Adaptation, pitch discrimination, and sound localization in the neonate. *Child Development*, 1964, **35,** 759–768.

Levine, M. A model of hypothesis behavior in discrimination learning set. *Psychological Review*, 1959, **66,** 353–366.

Levine, M. Mediating processes in humans at the outset of discrimination learning. *Psychological Review*, 1963, **70,** 254–276.

Levinson, B., and Reese, H. W. Patterns of discrimination learning set in preschool children, fifth-graders, college freshmen, and the aged. *Monographs of the Society for Research in Child Development*, 1967, **32**(7, Whole No. 115).

Levinson, C., and Levinson, P. Operant conditioning of headturning for visual reinforcement in three month old infants. *Psychonomic Science*, 1967, **8,** 529–530.

Levy, D. M. Release therapy. *American Journal of Orthopsychiatry*, 1939, **9,** 913–936.

Levy, R. J. Effects of institutional vs. boarding home care on a group of infants. *Journal of Personality*, 1947, **15,** 233–241.

Lewis, D. G. Commentary on "The genetic determination of intelligence: A study of monozygotic twins reared together and apart" by Cyril Burt. *British Journal of Psychology*, 1966, **57,** 431–433.

Lewis, D. J. Partial reinforcement in a gambling situation. *Journal of Experimental Psychology*, 1952, **43,** 447–450.

Lewis, D. J. Partial reinforcement: A selective review of the literature since 1950. *Psychological Bulletin*, 1960, **57,** 1–28.

Lewis, H. P. The relationship of picture preference to developmental status in drawing. *Journal of Educational Research*, 1963, **57,** 43–46. (a)

Lewis, H. P. Spatial representation in drawing as a correlate of development and a basis for picture preference. *Journal of Genetic Psychology*, 1963, **102,** 95–107. (b)

Lewis, M. Social isolation: A parametric study of its effect on social reinforcement. *Journal of Experimental Child Psychology*, 1965, **2,** 205–218.

Lewis, M., Bartels, B., Campbell, H., and Goldberg, S. Individual differences in attention: The relation between infants' condition at birth and attention distribution within the first year. *American Journal of Diseases of Children*, 1967, **113,** 461–465. (a)

Lewis, M., Goldberg, S., and Dodd, C. Cardiac responsivity to tactile stimulation in waking and sleeping infants. Unpublished manuscript, Fels Research Institute, 1967. (b)

Lewis, M. M. *Infant speech: A study of the beginnings of language.* New York: Harcourt, Brace, 1936.

Licklider, J. C. R. Three auditory theories. In S. Koch (Ed.), *Psychology: A study of a science.* Vol. I. New York: McGraw-Hill, 1959. Pp. 41–144.

Lieberman, S. M. A study of secondary reinforcement. Unpublished master's thesis, University of Southern California, 1967.

Lienert, G. A., and Crott, H. W. Studies on the factor structure of intelligence in children, adolescents and adults. *Vita Humana*, 1964, **7,** 147–163.

Lilly, J. C. Mental effects of reduction of ordinary levels of physical stimuli on intact, healthy persons. *Psychiatric Research Reports*, 1956, **5,** 1–9.

Li Lollo, V., and Berger, S. M. Effects of apparent pain in others on observers' reaction time. *Journal of Personality and Social Psychology*, 1965, **2,** 573–575.

Lindsley, D. B. Emotion. In S. S. Stevens (Ed.), *Handbook of experimental psychology.* New York: Wiley, 1951. Pp. 473–516.

Lindsley, O. R. Experimental analysis of social reinforcement: Terms and methods. *American Journal of Orthopsychiatry*, 1963, **33,** 624–633.

Lindsley, O. R., Hobika, J. Y., and Etsten, B. E. Operant behavior during anesthesia recovery: A continuous and objective method. *Anesthesiology,* 1961, **22,** 937–946.

Lindworsky, J. *Experimental psychology.* (Translated from the 4th German ed. by H. R. DeSilva.) New York: Macmillan, 1931.

Ling, B.-C. Form discrimination as a learning cue in infants. *Comparative Psychology Monographs,* 1941, **17,** No. 2, 66.

Ling, B.-C. I. A genetic study of sustained visual fixation and associated behavior in the human infant from birth to six months. *Journal of Genetic Psychology,* 1942, **61,** 227–277.

Lintz, L. M., and Fitzgerald, H. E. Apparatus for eyeblink conditioning in infants. *Journal of Experimental Child Psychology,* 1966, **4,** 276–279.

Lintz, L. M., Fitzgerald, H. E., and Brackbill, Y. Conditioning the eyeblink response to sound in infants. *Psychonomic Science,* 1967, **7,** 405–406.

Lipsitt, L. P. A self-concept scale for children and its relationship to the children's form of the Manifest Anxiety Scale. *Child Development,* 1958, **29,** 463–472.

Lipsitt, L. P. Simultaneous and successive discrimination learning in children. *Child Development,* 1961, **32,** 337–347.

Lipsitt, L. P. Learning in the first year of life. In L. P. Lipsitt and C. C. Spiker (Eds.), *Advances in child development and behavior.* Vol. 1. New York: Academic Press, 1963. Pp. 147–194.

Lipsitt, L. P. Learning processes of human newborns. *Merrill-Palmer Quarterly,* 1966, **12,** 45–71.

Lipsitt, L. P., and Ambrose, J. A. A preliminary report of temporal conditioning to three types of neonatal stimulation. Paper presented at the meeting of the Society for Research in Child Development, New York, March 1967.

Lipsitt, L. P., and DeLucia, C. An apparatus for the measurement of specific responses and general activity of the human neonate. *American Journal of Psychology,* 1960, **73,** 630–632.

Lipsitt, L. P., Engen, T., and Kaye, H. Developmental changes in the olfactory threshold of the neonate. *Child Development,* 1963, **34,** 371–376.

Lipsitt, L. P., and Kaye, H. Conditioned sucking in the human newborn. *Psychonomic Science,* 1964, **1,** 29–30.

Lipsitt, L. P., Kaye, H., and Bosack, T. N. Enhancement of neonatal sucking through reinforcement. *Journal of Experimental Child Psychology,* 1966, **4,** 163–168. (a)

Lipsitt, L. P., and Levy, N. Electrotactual threshold in the neonate. *Child Development,* 1959, **30,** 547–554.

Lipsitt, L. P., Pederson, L. J., and DeLucia, C. A. Conjugate reinforcement of operant responding in infants. *Psychonomic Science,* 1966, **4,** 67–68. (b)

Lipton, E. L., and Steinschneider, A. Studies on the psychophysiology of infancy. *Merrill-Palmer Quarterly,* 1964, **10,** 102–117.

Lipton, E. L., Steinschneider, A., and Richmond, J. B. Autonomic function in the neonate: VII. Maturational changes in cardiac control. *Child Development,* 1966, **37,** 1–16.

Liverant, S. Intelligence: A concept in need of re-examination. *Journal of Consulting Psychology,* 1960, **24,** 101–110.

Loeb, J. The incentive value of cartoon faces to children. *Journal of Experimental Child Psychology,* 1964, **1,** 99–107.

Loess, H. B., and Duncan, C. P. Human discrimination learning with simultaneous and successive presentation of stimuli. *Journal of Experimental Psychology,* 1952, **44,** 215–221.

Loevinger, J. Intelligence as related to socio-economic factors. *Yearbook of the National Society for the Study of Education,* 1940, **39,** Part I, 159–210.

Long, E. R. Multiple scheduling in children. *Journal of the Experimental Analysis of Behavior,* 1959, **2,** 268.

Long, E. R. Additional techniques for producing multiple schedule control in children. *Journal of the Experimental Analysis of Behavior,* 1962, **5,** 443–455.

Long, E. R. Chained and tandem scheduling in children. *Journal of the Experimental Analysis of Behavior,* 1963, **6,** 459–472.

Long, E. R., Hammack, J. T., May, F., and Campbell, B. J. Intermittent reinforcement of operant behavior in children. *Journal of the Experimental Analysis of Behavior,* 1958, **1,** 315–340.

Long, H. The relative learning capacity of Negroes and whites. *Journal of Negro Education,* 1957, **26,** 121–134.

Long, I., and Welch, L. The development of the ability to discriminate and match numbers. *Journal of Genetic Psychology,* 1941, **59,** 377–387.

Longstreth, L. E. The relationship between expectations and frustration in children. *Child Development,* 1960, **31,** 667–671.

Longstreth, L. E. Incentive stimuli as determinants of instrumental response strength in children. *Journal of Comparative and Physiological Psychology,* 1962, **55,** 398–401.

Longstreth, L. E. An operational distinction between secondary reinforcement and frustration. *American Psychologist,* 1964, **19,** 452. (Abstract)

Longstreth, L. E. Unconditioned and conditioned frustration in retardates. *American Psychological Association Proceedings,* 1965, **1,** 1–2.

Longstreth, L. E. Frustration and secondary reinforcement concepts as applied to human instrumental conditioning and extinction. *Psychological Monographs,* 1966, **80**(11, Whole No. 619). (a)

Longstreth, L. E. Frustration rather than Sr effects in children. *Psychonomic Science,* 1966, **4,** 425–426. (b)

Longstreth, L. E. Secondary reinforcement and frustration. Paper presented at the meeting of the Society for Research in Child Development, New York, March 1967.

Longstreth, L. E. *Psychological development of the child.* New York: Ronald Press, 1968.

Lorge, I. Difference of bias in tests of intelligence. In *Proceedings of the 1952 conference on testing problems.* Princeton, N.J.: Educational Testing Service, 1953. Pp. 76–82.

Lorge, I., Thorndike, R. L., and Hagen, E. *The Lorge-Thorndike Intelligence Tests— Multi-Level Edition.* Boston: Houghton Mifflin, 1964.

Lorge, I., Thorndike, R. L., and Hagen, E. *Technical manual—Lorge-Thorndike Intelligence Tests—Multi-Level Edition.* Boston: Houghton Mifflin, 1966.

Loth, G. Neurologische Untersuchungen an Fruhgeborenen und jungen Sauglingen (Neurological examinations of premature and young infants). *Zeitschrift für Kinderheilkunde,* 1952, **72,** 42.

Lott, D. F. Secondary reinforcement and frustration: A conceptual paradox. *Psychological Bulletin,* 1967, **67,** 197–198.

Lovaas, O. I. Interaction between verbal and nonverbal behavior. *Child Development,* 1961, **32,** 329–336.

Lovaas, O. I. A behavior therapy approach to the treatment of childhood schizophrenia. In J. P. Hill (Ed.), *Minnesota symposium on child psychology.* Vol. 1. Minneapolis: University of Minnesota Press, 1967. Pp. 108–159.

Lovaas, O. I., Schaeffer, B., and Simmons, J. Q. Building social behavior in autistic children by use of electric shock. *Journal of Experimental Research in Personality,* 1965, **1**, 99–109.

Love, M. I., and Beach, S. Performance of children on the Davis-Eels and other measures of ability. *Journal of Consulting Psychology,* 1957, **21**, 29–32.

Lovejoy, E. Analysis of the overlearning reversal effect. *Psychological Review,* 1966, **73**, 87–103.

Lovell, K. *The growth of basic mathematical and scientific concepts in children.* London: University of London Press, 1961.

Lovell, K., and Bradbury, B. The learning of English morphology in educationally subnormal special school children. *American Journal of Mental Deficiency,* 1967, **71**, 609–615.

Lovell, K., and Ogilvie, E. A study of the conservation of substance in the junior school child. *Journal of Child Psychology and Psychiatry,* 1961, **2**, 118–126. (a)

Lovell, K., and Ogilvie, E. A study of the conservation of weight in the junior school child. *British Journal of Educational Psychology,* 1961, **31**, 138–144. (b)

Lovibond, S. H. The mechanism of conditioning treatment of enuresis. *Behaviour Research and Therapy,* 1963, **1**, 17–21.

Lowe, R. C., Jr. A developmental study of part-whole relations in visual perception. Unpublished doctoral dissertation, Clark University, 1962.

Lubker, B. J., and Spiker, C. C. The effects of irrelevant stimulus dimensions on children's oddity-problem learning. *Journal of Experimental Child Psychology,* 1966, **3**, 207–215.

Lundgren, J. B. The effect of grades upon achievement level of children. Unpublished master's thesis, University of Southern California, 1968.

Lunneborg, P. W. Relations among social desirability, achievement, and anxiety measures in children. *Child Development,* 1964, **35**, 169–182.

Luria, A. R. The role of language in the formation of temporary connections. In B. Simon (Ed.), *Psychology in the Soviet Union.* Stanford: Stanford University Press, 1957. Pp. 115–129.

Luria, A. R. *The role of speech in the regulation of normal and abnormal behaviour.* New York: Liveright, 1961.

Lynip, A. W. The use of magnetic devices in the collection and analysis of the preverbal utterances of an infant. *Genetic Psychology Monographs,* 1951, **44**, 221–262.

Lynn, R. *Attention, arousal and the orientation reaction.* New York: Macmillan (Pergamon), 1966.

McAllister, D. E. The effects of various kinds of relevant verbal pretraining on subsequent motor performance. *Journal of Experimental Psychology,* 1953, **46**, 329–336.

McArthur, C. Personality differences between middle and upper classes. *Journal of Abnormal and Social Psychology,* 1955, **50**, 247–254.

McBee, G., and Duke, L. Relationship between intelligence, scholastic motivation and academic achievement. *Psychological Reports,* 1960, **6**, 3–8.

McCandless, B. Environment and intelligence. *American Journal of Mental Deficiency,* 1952, **56**, 674–691.

McCandless, B. R. *Children: Behavior and development.* (2nd ed.) Holt, Rinehart & Winston, 1967.

McCandless, B. R., Bilous, C. B., and Bennett, H. L. The relation between peer-popularity and dependence on adults in preschool-age socialization. *Child Development,* 1961, **32**, 511–518.

McCandless, B. R., and Castaneda, A. Anxiety in children, school achievement and intelligence. *Child Development,* 1956, **27**, 379–382.

McCandless, B. R., and Hoyt, J. M. Sex, ethnicity, and play preferences of preschool children. *Journal of Abnormal and Social Psychology*, 1961, **62**, 683–685.

McCandless, B. R., and Marshall, H. R. A picture sociometric technique for preschool children and its relation to teacher judgments of friendship. *Child Development*, 1957, **28**, 139–147.

McCarthy, D. Language development in children. In L. Carmichael (Ed.), *Manual of child psychology*. (2nd ed.) New York: Wiley, 1954. Pp. 492–630.

McClelland, D., Atkinson, J. W., Clark, R. A., and Lowell, E. L. *The achievement motive*. New York: Appleton-Century-Crofts, 1953.

Maccoby, E. E. Developmental psychology. *Annual Review of Psychology*, 1964, **15**, 203–250. (a)

Maccoby, E. E. Effects of the mass media. In M. L. Hoffman and L. W. Hoffman (Eds.), *Review of child development research*. Vol. 1. New York: Russell Sage Foundation, 1964. Pp. 323–348. (b)

Maccoby, E. E., and Bee, H. L. Some speculations concerning the lag between perceiving and performing. *Child Development*, 1965, **36**, 367–378.

Maccoby, E. E., and Hagen, J. W. Effects of distraction upon central versus incidental recall: Developmental trends. *Journal of Experimental Child Psychology*, 1965, **2**, 280–289.

Maccoby, E. E., and Konrad, K. W. The effect of preparatory set on selective listening: Developmental trends. *Monographs of the Society for Research in Child Development*, 1967, **32**, No. 4.

McCord, W. M., and Demerath, N. J. Negro vs. white intelligence: Continuing controversy. *Harvard Educational Review*, 1958, **28**, 120–135.

McCormack, P. D. Negative transfer in motor performance following a critical amount of verbal pretraining. *Perceptual and Motor Skills*, 1958, **8**, 27–31.

McCullers, J. C. Effects of associative strength, grade level, and interpair interval in verbal paired-associate learning. *Child Development*, 1961, **32**, 773–778.

McCullers, J. C. An analysis of some factors underlying intralist associative transfer in paired-associate learning. *Journal of Experimental Psychology*, 1963, **65**, 163–168.

McCullers, J. C. Correlates of verbal paired-associate learning in children. *Psychological Reports*, 1965, **17**, 747–752.

McCullers, J. C. Associative strength and degree of interference in children's verbal paired-associate learning. *Journal of Experimental Child Psychology*, 1967, **5**, 58–68.

McDill, E. L., and Coleman, J. Family and peer influences in college plans of high school students. *Sociology of Education*, 1965, **38**, 112–126.

McDougall, W. *Outline of psychology*. New York: Scribner, 1923.

McGehee, W., and Lewis, W. D. The socio-economic status of the homes of mentally superior and retarded children and the occupational rank of their parents. *Journal of Genetic Psychology*, 1942, **60**, 375–380.

McGeoch, J. A. *The psychology of human learning*. New York: Longmans, Green, 1942.

McGinnis, J. M. Eye movements and optic nystagmus in early infancy. *Genetic Psychology Monographs*, 1930, **8**, 321–430.

McGraw, M. B. A comparative study of a group of southern white and Negro infants. *Genetic Psychology Monographs*, 1931, **10**, 1–105.

McGurk, F. C. On white and Negro test performance and socio-economic factors. *Journal of Abnormal and Social Psychology*, 1953, **48**, 448–450.

McGurk, F. C. A scientist's report on race differences. *U.S. News and World Report*, 1956, **41**, No. 12, Sept. 21, 92–96.

Mach, E. *The analysis of sensations and the relation of the physical to the psychical.* (Translated by C. M. Williams from 1st ed., orig. publ. 1886; Rev. and suppl. by S. Waterlow from 5th ed., orig. publ. 1907.) Chicago: Open Court, 1914. (Republished: New introduction by T. S. Szasz. New York: Dover, 1959.)

McKee, J. P., and Leader, F. B. The relationship of socioeconomic status and aggression to the competitive behavior of preschool children. *Child Development,* 1955, **26,** 135–142.

McKellar, P. *Imagination and thinking. A psychological analysis.* New York: Basic Books, 1957.

Mackintosh, N. J. The effects of overtraining on a reversal and a nonreversal shift. *Journal of Comparative and Physiological Psychology,* 1962, **55,** 555–559.

Mackintosh, N. J. The effect of irrelevant cues on reversal learning in the rat. *British Journal of Psychology,* 1963, **54,** 127–134.

Mackintosh, N. J. Overtraining, reversal, and extinction in rats and chicks. *Journal of Comparative and Physiological Psychology,* 1965, **59,** 31–36. (a)

Mackintosh, N. J. Selective attention in animal discrimination learning. *Psychological Bulletin,* 1965, **64,** 124–150. (b)

McManis, D. L. Retroactive inhibition in paired-associate learning by normals and retardates. *American Journal of Mental Deficiency,* 1967, **71,** 931–936.

McMurray, G. A. Experimental study of a case of insensitivity to pain. *A.M.A. Archives of Neurology and Psychiatry,* 1950, **64,** 333–338.

McNamara, H. J., and Fisch, R. I. Effect of high and low motivation on two aspects of attention. *Perceptual and Motor Skills,* 1964, **19,** 571–578.

McNeil, E. G. *The concept of human development.* Belmont, Calif.: Wadsworth, 1966.

McNeill, D. The creation of language by children. In J. Lyons and R. J. Wales (Eds.), *Psycholinguistics papers.* Edinburgh: Edinburgh University Press, 1966. Pp. 99–115. (a)

McNeill, D. Developmental psycholinguistics. In F. Smith and G. A. Miller (Eds.), *The genesis of language: A psycholinguistic approach.* Cambridge, Mass.: M.I.T. Press, 1966. Pp. 15–84. (b)

McNeill, D. On theories of language acquisition. In T. R. Dixon and D. L. Horton (Eds.), *Verbal behavior and general behavior theory.* Englewood Cliffs, N.J.: Prentice-Hall, 1968. Pp. 406–420.

McNeill, D. The capacity for grammatical development in children. In D. Slobin (Ed.), *The ontogenesis of grammar: Some facts and several theories.* New York: Academic Press, in press. (a)

McNeill, D. Language development in children. In P. Mussen (Ed.), *Handbook of child psychology.* New York: Wiley, in press. (b)

McNemar, Q. A critical examination of the University of Iowa studies of environmental influences upon the I.Q. *Psychological Bulletin,* 1940, **37,** 63–92.

McNemar, Q. *The revision of the Stanford-Binet scale: An analysis of the standardization data.* Boston: Houghton Mifflin, 1942.

McNemar, Q. Lost: Our intelligence? Why? *American Psychologist,* 1964, **19,** 871–882.

MacRae, J. M. Retests of children given mental tests as infants. *Journal of Genetic Psychology,* 1955, **87,** 111–119.

Maddox, H. Symposium: Contributions on the theory of intelligence. II. Nature-nurture balance sheets. *British Journal of Educational Psychology,* 1957, **27,** 166–175.

Maier, H. W. *Three theories of child development.* New York: Harper & Row, 1965.

Maier, S. F., Seligman, E. P., and Solomon R. L. Pavlovian fear conditioning and learned helplessness In B. A. Campbell, and R. M. Church, (Eds.),

Punishment and Aversive Behaviour New York: Appleton-Century-Crofts, 1968.

Maltz, H. E. Ontogenetic change in the meaning of concepts as measured by the sematic differential. *Child Development*, 1963, **34**, 667–674.

Mandler, G. From association to structure. *Psychological Review*, 1962, **69**, 415–427.

Mandler, G., and Stephens, D. The development of free and constrained conceptualization and subsequent verbal memory. *Journal of Experimental Child Psychology*, 1967, **5**, 86–93.

Manis, M. *Cognitive processes*. Belmont, Calif.: Wadsworth, 1966.

Mann, I. *The development of the human eye*. (3rd ed.) New York: Grune & Stratton, 1964.

Marinesco, G., and Kreindler, A. Des reflexes conditionnels: L'organization des reflexes conditionnels chez l'enfant. *Journal de Psychologie*, 1933, **30**, 855–886.

Marquart, D. I., and Bailey, L. L. An evaluation of the culture free test of intelligence. *Journal of Genetic Psychology*, 1955, **86**, 353–358.

Marquis, D. P. Can conditioned responses be established in the newborn infant? *Journal of Genetic Psychology*, 1931, **39**, 479–492.

Marsh, G. Effect of overtraining on reversal and nonreversal shifts in nursery school children. *Child Development*, 1964, **35**, 1367–1372.

Marsh, G. Intradimensional transfer of discrimination along the hue continuum. *Psychonomic Science*, 1967, **8**, 411–412.

Marsh, G., and Sherman, M. Verbal mediation of transposition as a function of age level. *Journal of Experimental Child Psychology*, 1966, **4**, 90–98.

Martin, C. J., Cox, D. L., and Bulgarella, R. Verbalization of associative strategies at three developmental levels. Paper prepared for the American Psychological Association Convention, New York, 1966.

Martin, E. Transfer of verbal paired associates. *Psychological Review*, 1965, **72**, 327–343.

Martin, J. G. Associative strength and word frequency in paired-associate learning. *Journal of Verbal Learning and Verbal Behavior*, 1963, **2**, 317–320.

Martin, R. R., and Siegel, G. M. The effects of response contingent shock on stuttering. *Journal of Speech and Hearing Research*, 1966, **9**, 340–352.

Martin, W. E., and Blum, A. Intertest generalization and learning in mentally normal and subnormal children. *Journal of Comparative and Physiological Psychology*, 1961, **54**, 28–32.

Marum, K. D. A study of classical conditioning in the human infant. Unpublished master's thesis, Brown University, 1962.

Marx, M. H., and Murphy, W. W. Resistance to extinction as a function of the presentation of a motivating cue in the startbox. *Journal of Comparative and Physiological Psychology*, 1961, **54**, 207–210.

Masland, R., Sarason, S., and Gladwin, T. *Mental subnormality*. New York: Basic Books, 1958.

Mateer, F. *Child behavior: A critical and experimental study of young children by the method of conditioned reflexes*. Boston: R. G. Badger, 1918.

Matousek, M. A. Reproductive and retroactive inhibition as a function of similarity in the recall and recognition of paired associates. *Catholic University of America Educational Research Monographs*, 1939, **12**, No. 1.

Mead, M. *Coming of age in Samoa*. New York: Morrow, 1928.

Mead, M. Research on primitive children. In L. Carmichael (Ed.), *Manual of child psychology*. New York: Wiley, 1946. Pp. 667–706.

Mednick, S. A., and Lehtinen, L. E. Stimulus generalization as a function of age in children. *Journal of Experimental Psychology*, 1957, **53**, 180–183.

Mehler, J., and Bever, T. J. Cognitive capacity of very young children. *Science*, 1967, **158**, 141–142.

Meili, R. Les perceptions des enfants et la psychologie de la Gestalt. *Archives de Psychologie*, 1931, **23**, 25–44.

Menaker, S. L. Heteromodal facilitation in perceptual development. Paper presented at the meeting of the American Psychological Association, New York, September 1966. (Abstracted in *American Psychologist*, 1966, **21**, 649–650.)

Meneghini, K. A., and Leibowitz, H. The effect of stimulus distance and age on shape constancy. *Journal of Experimental Psychology*, 1967, **74**, 241–248.

Menyuk, P. A preliminary evaluation of grammatical capacity in children. *Journal of Verbal Learning and Verbal Behavior*, 1963, **2**, 429–439. (a)

Menyuk, P. Syntactic structure in the language of children. *Child Development*, 1963, **34**, 407–422. (b)

Menyuk, P. Alternation of rules in children's grammars. *Journal of Verbal Learning and Verbal Behavior*, 1964, **3**, 480–488. (a)

Menyuk, P. Syntactic rules used by children from preschool through first grade. *Child Development*, 1964, **35**, 533–546. (b)

Meredith, H. V. Selected anatomic variables analyzed for interage relationships of the size-size, size-gain, and gain-gain varieties. In L. P. Lipsitt and C. C. Spiker (Eds.), *Advances in child development and behavior*. Vol. 2. New York: Academic Press, 1965. Pp. 221–256.

Mermelstein, E., and Shulman, L. S. Lack of formal schooling and the acquisition of conservation. *Child Development*, 1967, **38**, 39–52.

Merrill, M. A. The significance of IQ's on the revised Stanford-Binet Scales. *Journal of Educational Psychology*, 1938, **29**, 641–651.

Meryman, J. J. The magnitude of an unconditioned GSR as a function of fear conditioned at a long CS-UCS interval. Unpublished doctoral dissertation, State University of Iowa, 1953.

Messer, S. Implicit phonology in children. *Journal of Verbal Learning and Verbal Behavior*, 1967, **6**, 609–613.

Meyer, W. J., and Seidman, S. B. Age differences in the effectiveness of different reinforcement combinations on the acquisition and extinction of a simple concept learning problem. *Child Development*, 1960, **31**, 419–429.

Meyerowitz, J. Environmental variation and education retardation. *Journal of Health and Social Behavior*, 1967, **8**, 141–146.

Meyers, C. S. Some observations on the development of colour sense. *British Journal of Psychology*, 1908, **2**, 353–362.

Meyers, W. J., McQuiston, M. D., and Miles, R. C. Delayed-response and learning-set performance of cats. *Journal of Comparative and Physiological Psychology*, 1962, **55**, 515–517.

Michels, K. M., Pustek, J. J., Jr., and Johnson, J. I., Jr. The solution of patterned-strings problems by raccoons. *Journal of Comparative and Physiological Psychology*, 1961, **54**, 439–441.

Milerian, E. A. Involuntary and voluntary attention. (Translated by J. Ellis and M. Ellis from *Sovetskaya Pedagogika*, 1954, **2**, 55–67.) In B. Simon (Ed.), *Psychology in the Soviet Union*. Stanford, Calif.: Stanford University Press, 1957. Pp. 84–91.

Miles, T. R. Contributions to intelligence testing and the theory of intelligence: I. On defining intelligence. *British Journal of Educational Psychology,* 1957, **27**, 153–165.

Miles, W. R. Psychological aspects of ageing. In E. V. Cowdry (Ed.), *Problems of ageing: Biological and medical aspects.* (2nd ed.) Baltimore: Williams & Wilkins, 1942. Pp. 756–784.

Milgram, N. A. Retention of mediation set in paired-associate learning of normal children and retardates. *Journal of Experimental Child Psychology,* 1967, **5**, 341–349. (a)

Milgram, N. A. Verbal context versus visual compound in paired-associate learning by children. *Journal of Experimental Child Psychology,* 1967, **5**, 597–603. (b)

Miller, G. A., Galanter, E., and Pribram, K. H. *Plans and the structure of behavior.* New York: Holt, Rinehart & Winston, 1960.

Miller, G. A., and Nicely, P. E. Analysis of perceptual confusions among some English consonants. *Journal of the Acoustical Society of America,* 1955, **27**, 338–352.

Miller, L. B., and Estes, B. W. Monetary reward and motivation in discrimination learning. *Journal of Experimental Psychology,* 1961, **61**, 501–504.

Miller, N. E. Experimental studies of conflict. In J. McV. Hunt (Ed.), *Personality and the behavior disorders.* New York: Ronald Press, 1944. Pp. 431–465.

Miller, N. E. Theory and experiment relating psychoanalytic displacement to stimulus-response generalization. *Journal of Abnormal and Social Psychology,* 1948, **43**, 155–178.

Miller, N. E. Learnable drives and rewards. In S. S. Stevens (Ed.), *Handbook of experimental psychology.* New York: Wiley, 1951. Pp. 435–472.

Miller, N. E., and Dollard, J. *Social learning and imitation.* New Haven, Conn.: Yale University Press, 1941.

Miller, W. R. The acquisition of grammatical rules by children. Paper presented at the meeting of the Linguistic Society of America, New York, December 1964. (a)

Miller, W. R. Patterns of grammatical development in child language. In C. Mohrmann (Ed.), *Proceedings of the 9th International Congress of Linguistics.* The Hague: Mouton, 1964. Pp. 511–516. (b)

Miller, W., and Ervin, S. The development of grammar in child language. In U. Bellugi and R. Brown (Eds.), The acquisition of language. *Monographs of the Society for Research in Child Development,* 1964, **29**(1, Whole No. 92). Pp. 9–34.

Mink, W. D. Semantic generalization as related to word association. *Psychological Reports,* 1963, **12**, 59–67.

Mirzoiants, N. S. The conditioned orienting reflex and its differentiation in the child. *Zhurnal Vysshei Nervnoi Deyatel'nosti imeni I. P. Pavlova,* 1954, **4**, 616–619.

Mischel, W., and Grusec, J. Waiting for rewards and punishments: Effects of time and probability on choice. *Journal of Personality and Social Psychology,* 1967, **5**, 24–31.

Mitchell, G. D. Attachment differences in male and female infant monkeys. *Child Development,* 1968, **39**, 611–620.

Mitoma, C., Auld, R. M., and Udenfriend, S. On the nature of the enzymatic defect in phenylpyruvic oligophrenia. *Proceedings of the Society for Experimental Biology and Medicine,* 1957, **94**, 634–635.

Mitrano, A. J. Principles of conditioning in human goal behavior. *Psychological Monographs,* 1939, **51**(14, Whole No. 230).

Moffitt, A. R., and Ryan, T. J. The frustration effect in normal and retarded children using a one-trial-a-day procedure. Research Bulletin No. 15, Department of Psychology, University of Western Ontario, 1966.

Mooney, C. H. Recognition of novel visual configurations with and without eye movements. *Journal of Experimental Psychology*, 1958, **56**, 133–138.

Morgan, J. J. B., and Morgan, S. S. Infant learning as a developmental index. *Journal of Genetic Psychology*, 1944, **65**, 281–289.

Morse, P. A., and Shepp, B. E. The effects of overt verbalization and overtraining on dimensional shifts. In B. E. Shepp, *Studies of discriminative learning and transfer in normal and retarded children*. Progress Report No. 1, Research Grant HD–01349, National Institute of Child Health and Human Development, U.S. Public Health Service, 1967. Pp. 95–121.

Moss, H. A., and Kagan, J. Maternal influences on early I.Q. scores. *Psychological Reports*, 1958, **4**, 655–661.

Moulton, R. W., Liberty, P. G., Jr., Burnstein, E., and Altucher, N. Patterning of parental affection and disciplinary dominance as a determinant of guilt and sex-typing. *Journal of Personality and Social Psychology*, 1966, **4**, 356–363.

Mowrer, O. H. The psychologist looks at language. *American Psychologist*, 1954, **9**, 660–694.

Mowrer, O. H. *Learning theory and the symbolic process*. New York: Wiley, 1960.

Mowrer, O. H., and Mowrer, W. M. Enuresis: A method for its study and treatment. *American Journal of Orthopsychiatry*, 1938, **8**, 436–459.

Muench, G. A. A follow up of mental defectives after eighteen years. *Journal of Abnormal and Social Psychology*, 1944, **39**, 407–418.

Mumbauer, C. C., and Odom, R. D. Variables affecting the performance of preschool children in intradimensional, reversal, and extradimensional shifts. *Journal of Experimental Psychology*, 1967, **75**, 180–187.

Munn, N. L. Learning in children. In L. Carmichael (Ed.), *Manual of child psychology*. (2nd ed.) New York: Wiley, 1954. Pp. 374–458.

Munn, N. L. *The evolution and growth of human behavior*. (2nd ed.) Boston: Houghton Mifflin, 1965.

Munn, N. L., and Stiening, B. R. The relative efficacy of form and background in a child's discrimination of visual patterns. *Pedagogical Seminary*, 1931, **39**, 73–90.

Murdock, B. B., Jr. Direction of recall in short-term memory. *Journal of Verbal Learning and Verbal Behavior*, 1962, **1**, 119–124.

Murdock, B. B., Jr. Forward and backward associations in paired associates. *Journal of Experimental Psychology*, 1966, **71**, 732–737.

Murray, H. A., The effect of fear upon estimates of the maliciousness of other personalities. *Journal of Social Psychology*, 1933, **4**, 310–329.

Murray, H. A. *Explorations in personality: A clinical and experimental study of fifty men of college age*. London and New York: Oxford University Press, 1938.

Mussen, P. H., Conger, J. J., and Kagan, J. *Child development and personality*. New York: Harper & Row, 1963.

Mussen, P. H., and Distler, L. Masculinity, identification, and father-son relationships. *Journal of Abnormal and Social Psychology*, 1959, **59**, 350–356.

Mussen, P. H., and Jones, M. C. Self-conceptions, motivations, and interpersonal attitudes of late- and early-maturing boys. *Child Development*, 1957, **28**, 242–256.

Mussen, P. H., and Jones, M. C. The behavior-inferred motivations of late- and early-maturing boys. *Child Development*, 1958, **29**, 61–68.

Myers, C. S. Some observations on the development of color sense. *British Journal of Psychology*, 1908, **2**, 353–362.

Myers, J. L. Secondary reinforcement: A review of recent experimentation. *Psychological Bulletin*, 1958, **55**, 284–301.

Myers, J. L., and Myers, N. A. Effects of schedules of primary and secondary reinforcement on extinction behavior. *Child Development*, 1963, **34**, 1057–1063. (a)

Myers, J. L., and Myers, N. A. Secondary reinforcement in children as a function of conditioning associations, extinction percentages and stimulus types. *Journal of Experimental Psychology*, 1963, **65**, 455–459. (b)

Myers, J. L., and Myers, N. A. Secondary reinforcement in children as a function of conditioning association and extinction percentages. *Journal of Experimental Psychology*, 1964, **68**, 611–612.

Myers, N. A. Extinction following partial and continuous primary and secondary reinforcement. *Journal of Experimental Psychology*, 1960, **60**, 172–179.

Myers, N. A., Craig, G. J., and Myers, J. L. Secondary reinforcement as a function of the number of reinforced trials. *Child Development*, 1961, **32**, 765–772.

Myers, N. A., and Myers, J. L. Effects of secondary reinforcement schedules in extinction on children's responding. *Journal of Experimental Psychology*, 1962, **64**, 586–588.

Myers, N. A., and Myers, J. L. A test of a discrimination hypothesis of secondary reinforcement. *Journal of Experimental Psychology*, 1965, **70**, 98–101.

Nagel, E. Determinism and development. In D. B. Harris (Ed.), *The concept of development*. Minneapolis: University of Minnesota Press, 1957. Pp. 15–24.

Naunton, R. F. The measurement of hearing by bone conduction. In J. Jerger (Ed.), *Modern developments in audiology*. New York: Academic Press, 1963. Pp. 1–29.

Neff, W. S. Socioeconomic status and intelligence: A critical survey. *Psychological Bulletin*, 1938, **35**, 727–757.

Nelson, A. K. A study of taste, smell and temperature reactions in infants. Unpublished doctoral dissertation, Ohio State University, 1928.

Nelson, V. L., and Richards, T. W. Studies in mental development. I. Performance on Gesell items at six months and its predictive value for performance on mental tests at two and three years. *Journal of Genetic Psychology*, 1938, **52**, 303–325.

Nelson, V. L., and Richards, T. W. Studies in mental development: III. Performance of twelve months old children on the Gesell Schedule and its predictive value for mental status at two and three years. *Journal of Genetic Psychology*, 1939, **54**, 181–191.

Newhall, S. M. Identification by young children of differently oriented visual forms. *Child Development*, 1937, **8**, 105–111.

Newman, H. H., Freeman, F. N., and Holzinger, K. J. *Twins: A study of heredity and environment*. Chicago: University of Chicago Press, 1937.

Newsletter, American Psychological Association, Division on Developmental Psychology, Spring 1968.

Nichaeva, I. P. K. Funktsionalnoi kharakteristike slukhogo analizatora rebenka rannego vozrosta. (The functional character of the auditory analyzer in the young child.) *Zhurnal Vysshei Nervoni Deyatel'nosti imeni I. P. Pavlova*, 1954, **4**, 610–615.

Nikkel, N., and Palermo, D. S. Effects of mediated associations in paired-associate learning of children. *Journal of Experimental Child Psychology*, 1965, **2**, 92–102.

Nisbet, J. D. Symposium: Contributions to intelligence testing and the theory of intelligence. IV. Intelligence and age-retesting with 24 year interval. *British Journal of Educational Psychology*, 1957, **27**, 190–198.

Noble, C. E. Measurements of association value (*a*) rated associations (*a'*) and scaled meaningfulness (*m'*) for the 2100 CVC combinations of the English alphabet. *Psychological Reports*, 1961, **8**, 487–521.

Noble, C. E. Reply to comments on the measurement of CVC trigrams. *Psychological Reports*, 1962, **10**, 547–550.

Noble, C. E., Stockwell, F. E., and Pryer, M. W. Meaningfulness (*m'*) and association value (*a*) in paired-associate syllable learning. *Psychological Reports*, 1957, **3**, 441–452.

Noelting, G. La structuration progressive de la figure de Müller-Lyer in fonction de la répétition chez l'enfant et l'adulte. *Archives de Psychologie*, 1960, **37**, 311–413.

Norcross, K. J., and Spiker, C. C. The effects of type of stimulus pretraining on discrimination performance in preschool children. *Child Development*, 1957, **28**, 79–84.

Norcross, K. J., and Spiker, C. C. The effects of mediated associations on transfer in paired-associate learning. *Journal of Experimental Psychology*, 1958, **55**, 129–134.

Norman, R. M. Malformations of the nervous system, birth injury and diseases of early life. In W. Blackwood *et al.* (Eds.), *Greenfield's neuropathology*. London: Arnold, 1966. Pp. 324–440.

Nunnally, J. C., Duchnowski, A. J., and Knott, P. D. Association of neutral objects with rewards: Effects of massed versus distributed practice, delay of testing, age, and sex. *Journal of Experimental Child Psychology*, 1967, **5**, 152–163. (a)

Nunnally, J. C., Duchnowski, A. J., and Parker, R. K. Association of neutral objects with rewards: Effect on verbal evaluation, reward expectancy, and selective attention. *Journal of Personality and Social Psychology*, 1965, **1**, 270–274. (a)

Nunnally, J. C., and Faw, T. T. The acquisition of conditioned reward value in discrimination learning. *Child Development*, 1968, **39**, 159–166.

Nunnally, J. C., Knott, P. D., and Duchnowski, A. J. Association of neutral objects with rewards: Effects of different numbers of conditioning trials and of anticipated reward versus actual reward. *Journal of Experimental Child Psychology*, 1967, **5**, 249–262. (b)

Nunnally, J. C., Stevens, D. A., and Hall, G. F. Association of neutral objects with rewards: Effect on verbal evaluation and eye movements. *Journal of Experimental Child Psychology*, 1965, **2**, 44–57. (b)

Odom, R. D. Effects of auditory and visual stimulus deprivation and satiation on children's performance in an operant task. *Journal of Experimental Child Psychology*, 1964, **1**, 16–25.

Odom, R. D. A method for studying the effects of mediated associations in the paired-associate learning of children. *Psychonomic Science*, 1965, **2**, 1–2.

Odom, R. D., Liebert, R. M., and Hill, J. H. The effects of modeling cues, reward, and attentional set on the production of grammatical and ungrammatical syntactic constructions. *Journal of Experimental Child Psychology*, 1968, **6**, 131–140.

Offenbach, S. I. Bibliography of learning in children. Unpublished manuscript, Purdue University, 1966.

Ohlrich, E. S., and Ross, L. E. Reversal and nonreversal shift learning in retardates as a function of overtraining. *Journal of Experimental Psychology*, 1966, **72**, 621–624.

Orlando, R. Shaping multiple schedule performances in retardates: Establishment of baselines by systematic and special procedures. *Journal of Experimental Child Psychology*, 1965, **2**, 135–153.

Orlando, R., and Bijou, S. W. Single and multiple schedules of reinforcement in developmentally retarded children. *Journal of the Experimental Analysis of Behavior*, 1960, **4**, 339–348.

Orne, M. T., and Scheibe, K. E. The contribution of nondeprivation factors in the production of sensory deprivation effects: The psychology of the panic button. *Journal of Abnormal and Social Psychology,* 1964, **68,** 3–12.

Osborn, W. J. Associative clustering in organic and familial retardates. *American Journal of Mental Deficiency,* 1960, **65,** 351–357.

Osborne, R. T. Racial differences in mental growth and school achievement: A longitudinal study. *Psychological Reports,* 1960, **7,** 232–239.

Osgood, C. E. *Method and theory in experimental psychology.* London and New York: Oxford University Press, 1953.

Osgood, C. E. On understanding and creating sentences. *American Psychologist,* 1963, **18,** 735–751.

Osgood, C. E. Toward a wedding of insufficiencies. In T. R. Dixon and D. L. Horton (Eds.), *Verbal behavior and general behavior theory.* Englewood Cliffs, N. J.; Prentice-Hall, 1968. Pp. 495–519.

Osgood, C. E., and Sebeok, T. A. (Eds.) Psycholinguistics: A survey of theory and research. *Journal of Abnormal and Social Psychology,* 1954, Part 2 (Suppl.).

Osgood, C. E., Suci, G. J., and Tannenbaum, P. H. *The measurement of meaning.* Urbana, Ill.; University of Illinois Press, 1957.

Osler, S. F., and Trautman, G. E. Concept attainment: II. Effect of stimulus complexity upon concept attainment at two levels of intelligence. *Journal of Experimental Psychology,* 1961, **62,** 9–13.

Otto, W. The acquisition and retention of paired-associates by good, average, and poor readers. *Journal of Educational Psychology,* 1961, **52,** 241–248.

Overmier, J. B. Instrumental and cardiac indices of Pavlovian fear conditioning as a function of US duration. *Journal of Comparative and Physiological Psychology,* 1966, **62,** 15–20.

Owens, W. A., Jr. Age and mental abilities: A longitudinal study. *Genetic Psychology Monographs,* 1953, **48,** first half, 3–54.

Owens, W. A., Jr. Age and mental abilities: A second adult follow up. *Journal of Educational Psychology,* 1966, **57,** 311–325.

Paivio, A. Learning of adjective-noun paired associates as a function of adjective-noun word order and noun abstractness. *Canadian Journal of Psychology,* 1963, **17,** 370–379.

Paivio, A. Abstractness, imagery, and meaningfulness in paired-associate learning. *Journal of Verbal Learning and Verbal Behavior,* 1965, **4,** 32–38.

Paivio, A. Meaning, mediation, and memory. Research Bulletin No. 48, Department of Psychology, University of Western Ontario, July 1967. (a)

Paivio, A. Paired-associate learning and free recall of nouns as a function of concreteness, specificity, imagery, and meaningfulness. *Psychological Reports,* 1967, **20,** 239–245. (b)

Paivio, A. Mental imagery in associative learning and memory. *Psychological Review,* 1969, **76,** 241–263.

Paivio, A., and Yarmey, A. D. Pictures versus words as stimuli and responses in paired-associate learning. *Psychonomic Science,* 1966, **5,** 235–236.

Paivio, A., and Yuille, J. C. Word abstractness and meaningfulness, and paired-associate learning in children. *Journal of Experimental Child Psychology,* 1966, **4,** 81–89.

Paivio, A., and Yuille, J. C. Changes in associative strategies and paired-associate learning over trials as a function of word imagery and type of learning set. Research Bulletin No. 81, Department of Psychology, University of Western Ontario, June 1968.

Paivio, A., Yuille, J. C., and Smythe, P. C. Stimulus and response abstractness, imagery, and meaningfulness, and reported mediators in paired-associate learning. *Canadian Journal of Psychology*, 1966, **20**, 362–377.

Palermo, D. S. Backward associations in the paired-associate learning of fourth and sixth grade children. *Psychological Reports*, 1961, **9**, 227–233.

Palermo, D. S. Mediated association in a paired-associate transfer task. *Journal of Experimental Psychology*, 1962, **64**, 234–238.

Palermo, D. S. Word associations and children's verbal behavior. In L. P. Lipsitt and C. C. Spiker (Eds.), *Advances in child development and behavior*. Vol. 1. New York: Academic Press, 1963. Pp. 31–68.

Palermo, D. S. Characteristics of word association responses obtained from children in grades one through four. Paper presented at the meeting of the Society for Research in Child Development, Minneapolis, March 1965.

Palermo, D. S. Mediated association in the paired-associate learning of children using heterogeneous and homogeneous lists. *Journal of Experimental Psychology*, 1966, **71**, 711–717.

Palermo, D. S. Research on language acquisition: Do we know where we are going? In L. R. Goulet and P. B. Baltes (Eds.), *Theory and research in life-span developmental psychology*. New York: Academic Press, 1970.

Palermo, D. S. On learning to talk: Are principles derived from the learning laboratory applicable? In D. I. Slobin (Ed.), *The ontogenesis of grammar: Some facts and several theories*. New York: Academic Press, in press.

Palermo, D. S., and Eberhart, V. L. On the learning of morphological rules: An experimental analogy. *Journal of Verbal Learning and Verbal Behavior*, 1968, **7**, 337–344.

Palermo, D. S., Flamer, G. B., and Jenkins, J. J. Association value of responses in the paired-associate learning of children and adults. *Journal of Verbal Learning and Verbal Behavior*, 1964, **3**, 171–175.

Palermo, D. S., and Jenkins, J. J. Frequency of superordinate responses to a word association test as a function of age. *Journal of Verbal Learning and Verbal Behavior*, 1963, **1**, 378–383.

Palermo, D. S., and Jenkins, J. J. Paired-associate learning as a function of the strength of links in the associative chain. *Journal of Verbal Learning and Verbal Behavior*, 1964, **3**, 406–412. (a)

Palermo, D. S., and Jenkins, J. J. *Word association norms: Grade school through college*. Minneapolis: University of Minnesota Press, 1964. (b)

Palermo, D. S., and Jenkins, J. J. Changes in the word associations of fourth- and fifth-grade children from 1916 to 1961. *Journal of Verbal Learning and Verbal Behavior*, 1965, **4**, 180–187.

Palermo, D. S., and Jenkins, J. J. Oral word association norms for children in grades one through four. Research Bulletin No. 60, Department of Psychology, Pennsylvania State University, 1966.

Palermo, D. S., and Ullrich, J. R. Verbal discrimination learning as a function of associative strength between the word pair members. *Journal of Verbal Learning and Verbal Behavior*, 1968, **7**, 945–952.

Papoušek, H. A method of studying conditioned food reflexes in young children up to the age of six months. *Pavlov Journal of Higher Nervous Activity*, 1959, **9**, 136–140.

Papoušek, H. Conditioned head rotation reflexes in infants in the first months of life. *Acta Paediatrica*, 1961, **50**, 565–576.

Papoušek, H. Conditioning during postnatal development. In Y. Brackbill and G. G. Thompson (Eds.), *Behavior in infancy and early childhood: A book of readings.* New York: Free Press, 1967. Pp. 259–274. (a)

Papoušek, H. Experimental studies of appetitional behavior in human newborns. In H. W. Stevenson, E. H. Hess, and H. L. Rheingold (Eds.), *Early behavior: Comparative and developmental approaches.* New York: Wiley, 1967. Pp. 249–277. (b)

Parke, R. D. Nurturance, nurturance withdrawal, and resistance to deviation. *Child Development,* 1967, **38,** 1101–1110.

Parker, R. K., and Nunnally, J. C. Association of neutral objects with rewards: Effects of reward schedule on reward expectancy, verbal evaluation, and selective attention. *Journal of Experimental Child Psychology,* 1966, **3,** 324–332.

Parmelee, A. H., The hand-mouth reflex of Babkin in premature infants. *Pediatrics,* 1963, **31,** 734–740.

Parnell, R. W. *Behaviour and physique: An introduction to practical and applied somatrometry.* London: Arnold, 1958.

Parsons, T. Family structure and the socialization of the child. In T. Parsons and R. F. Bales (Eds.), *Family, socialization, and interaction process.* Glencoe, Ill.: Free Press of Glencoe, 1955. Pp. 35–131.

Pasamanick, B., and Knobloch, H. Early language behavior in Negro children and the testing of intelligence. *Journal of Abnormal and Social Psychology,* 1955, **50,** 401–402.

Patin, H. A. Intelligence and education. *School Review,* 1965, **73,** 359–373.

Paul, C. Effects of overlearning upon single habit reversal in rats. *Psychological Bulletin,* 1965, **63,** 65–72. (a)

Paul, C. Verbal discrimination reversal as a function of overlearning and percent of items reversed. Paper presented at the meeting of the Eastern Psychological Association, Atlantic City, April 1965. (b)

Pavlov, I. P. *Conditioned reflexes.* (Translated by G. V. Anrep.) London: Oxford University Press, 1927.

Payne, D. E., and Mussen, P. H. Parent-child relations and father identification among adolescent boys. *Journal of Personality and Abnormal Psychology,* 1956, **52,** 358–362.

Pederson, D. R. Associative versus motivational interpretations of reward percentage effects on children's performance. *Psychonomic Science,* 1967, **8,** 139–140.

Peiper, A. *Cerebral function in infancy and childhood.* (Translated by B. Nagler and H. Nagler from the 3rd German ed., orig. publ. 1961.) New York: Consultants Bureau, 1963.

Peluffo, N. Les notions de conservation et de causalité chez les infants prevenant de differents milieux physiques et socio-culturels. *Archives de Psychologie,* 1962, **38,** 75–90.

Penney, R. K. On a distinction between fact versus value in child psychology. *Ontario Psychological Association Quarterly,* 1960, **13,** 92–94. (a)

Penney, R. K. The effects of nonreinforcement on response strength as a function of number of previous reinforcements. *Canadian Journal of Psychology,* 1960, **14,** 206–215. (b)

Penney, R. K. A recent trend in child psychology. *Ontario Psychological Association Quarterly,* 1960, **12,** 80–85. (c)

Penney, R. K., and Croskery, J. Instrumental avoidance conditioning of anxious and nonanxious children. *Journal of Comparative and Physiological Psychology,* 1962, **55,** 847–849.

Penney, R. K., and Kirwin, P. M. Differential adaptation of anxious and nonanxious children in instrumental escape conditioning. *Journal of Experimental Psychology,* 1965, **70,** 539–549.

Penney, R. K., and Lupton, A. A. Children's discrimination learning as a function of reward and punishment. *Journal of Comparative and Physiological Psychology,* 1961, **54,** 449–451.

Penney, R. K., and McCann, B. The instrumental escape conditioning of anxious and nonanxious children. *Journal of Abnormal and Social Psychology,* 1962, **65,** 351–354.

Penrose, L. S. Mongolism. *British Medical Bulletin,* 1961, **17,** 184–189.

Pepper, S. C. *World hypotheses. A study in evidence.* Berkeley, Calif.: University of California Press, 1942.

Perkins, M. J., Banks, H. P., and Calvin, A. D. The effect of delay on simultaneous and successive discrimination in children. *Journal of Experimental Psychology,* 1954, **48,** 416–418.

Pettigrew, J. F. Negro American intelligence: A new look at an old controversy. *Journal of Negro Education,* 1964, **33,** 6–25.

Pfaffmann, C. Preface. In M. R. Kare and B. P. Halpern (Eds.), *Physiological and behavioral aspects of taste.* Chicago: University of Chicago Press, 1961. Pp. vii–xi.

Phillips, B. N., and DeVault, M. V. Relation of positive and negative sociometric valuations to social and personal adjustment of school children. *Journal of Applied Psychology,* 1955, **39,** 409–412.

Piaget, J. *Le développement de la notion de temps chez l'enfant.* Paris: Presses Universitaires de France, 1946. (a)

Piaget, J. *Les notions de mouvement et de vitesse chez l'enfant.* Paris: Presses Universitaires de France, 1946. (b)

Piaget, J. *The moral judgment of the child.* Glencoe, Ill.: Free Press, 1948.

Piaget, J. *The psychology of intelligence.* London: Routledge & Kegan Paul, 1950.

Piaget, J. *The child's conception of physical causality.* London: Routledge & Kegan Paul, 1951. (a)

Piaget, J. *Judgment and reasoning in the child.* London: Routledge & Kegan Paul, 1951. (b)

Piaget, J. *The child's conception of number.* London: Routledge & Kegan Paul, 1952. (a)

Piaget, J. *The origins of intelligence in children.* New York: International Universities Press, 1952. (Republished: New York, Norton, 1963.) (b)

Piaget, J. *The construction of reality in the child.* New York: Basic Books, 1964.

Piaget, J. Notes on learning. Lecture delivered at New York University, Winter 1967.

Piaget, J. *The mechanism of perception.* (Translated by G. N. Seagrim.) New York: Basic Books, 1969.

Piaget, J., and Inhelder, B. *La genèse de l'idée de hasard chez l'enfant.* Paris: Presses Universitaires de France, 1951.

Piaget, J., and Inhelder, B. *The child's conception of space.* London: Routledge & Kegan Paul, 1956.

Piaget, J., and Inhelder, B. *La genèse des structures logiques elementaires.* Neuchatel: Delachaux & Nistle, 1959.

Piaget, J., and Inhelder, B. *Le développement des quantités physiques chez l'enfant.* Neuchatel: Delachaux & Niestle, 1962.

Piaget, J., Inhelder, B., and Szeminska, A. *The child's conception of geometry.* New York: Basic Books, 1960.

Piaget, J., and Vinh-Bang. Comparaisons des mouvements oculaires et des centrations du regard chez l'enfant et chez l'adulte. *Archives de Psychologie*, 1961, **38**, 167–200.

Pick, A. D. Improvement of visual and tactual form discrimination. *Journal of Experimental Psychology*, 1965, **69**, 331–339.

Pick, H. L., Pick, A. D., and Klein, R. E. Perceptual integration in children. In L. P. Lipsitt and C. C. Spiker (Eds.), *Advances in child development and behavior*. Vol. 3. New York: Academic Press, 1967. Pp. 191–223.

Pike, E. G. Controlled infant intonation. *Language Learning*, 1949, **2**, 21–24.

Pillsbury, W. B. *The fundamentals of psychology*. (3rd ed.) New York: Macmillan, 1934.

Pinneau, S. R. *Changes in intelligence quotient*. Boston: Houghton Mifflin, 1961.

Polikanina, R. I. The relationship between autonomic and somatic components of a defensive conditioned reflex in premature children. *Pavlov Journal of Higher Nervous Activity*, 1961, **11**, 72–82.

Pollack, R. H. Contour detectability thresholds as a function of chronological age. *Perceptual and Motor Skills*, 1963, **17**, 411–417.

Pollack, R. H. Simultaneous and successive presentation of elements of the Müller-Lyer figure and chronological age. *Perceptual and Motor Skills*, 1964, **19**, 303–310.

Pollack, R. H. Hue detectability thresholds as a function of chronological age. *Psychonomic Science*, 1965, **3**, 351–352.

Pond, D. A. Behavior disorders in brain-damaged children. In D. Williams (Ed.), *Modern trends in neurology*. (Series 4.) London and Washington, D.C.: Butterworth, 1967. Pp. 125–134.

Postman, L. The present status of interference theory. In C. N. Cofer (Ed.), *Verbal learning and verbal behavior*. New York: McGraw-Hill, 1961. Pp. 152–179.

Postman, L. The effects of language habits on the acquisition and retention of verbal associations. *Journal of Experimental Psychology*, 1962, **64**, 7–19.

Potts, M. The effects of a morphological cue and of distinctive verbal labels on the transposition responses of three-, four-, and five-year olds. *Journal of Experimental Child Psychology*, 1968, **6**, 75–86.

Pratt, K. C. The neonate. In L. Carmichael (Ed.), *Manual of child psychology*. (2nd ed.) New York: Wiley, 1954. Pp. 215–291.

Prechtl, H., and Beintema, D. *The neurological examination of the full-term newborn infant*. Lavenham, Eng.: Lavenham Press, 1964.

Premack, D. Reinforcement theory. In D. Levine (Ed.), *Nebraska symposium on motivation*. Vol. 13. Lincoln, Neb.: University of Nebraska Press, 1965. Pp. 123–180.

Price, L. E. Learning and performance in a verbal paired-associate task with pre-school children. *Psychological Reports*, 1963, **12**, 847–850.

Price, L. E., and Spiker, C. C. Effect of similarity of irrelevant stimuli on performance in discrimination learning problems. *Journal of Experimental Child Psychology*, 1967, **5**, 324–331.

Prokasy, W. F. Classical eyelid conditioning: Experimenter operations, task demands, and response shaping. In W. F. Prokasy (Ed.), *Classical conditioning: A symposium*. New York: Appleton-Century-Crofts, 1965. Pp. 208–225.

Prothro, E. An alternative approach in cross-cultural intelligence testing. *Journal of Psychology*, 1955, **39**, 247–251.

Pumroy, D. K., and Pumroy, S. S. Effect of amount and percentage of reinforcement on resistance to extinction in preschool children. *Journal of Genetic Psychology*, 1961, **98**, 55–62.

Rabinowitz, M. F. Conditioned stimulus duration and delay of reward as variables in a lever pulling situation. *Journal of Experimental Child Psychology*, 1966, **3,** 225–234.

Rambusch, N. M. *Learning how to learn.* Baltimore: Helicon Press, 1962.

Rank, L. An investigation of two different response contingencies on sucking in three to four month old infants using auditory reinforcement. Unpublished master's thesis, Brown University, 1968.

Raph, J. B., Goldberg, M. L., and Passow, A. *Bright underachievers.* New York: Teachers College, Columbia University, Bureau of Publications, 1966.

Raven, J. C. *Guide to using Progressive Matrices (1938).* London: Lewis, 1956. (U.S. distributor: Psychological Corporation.)

Raven, J. C. *Guide to using the Coloured Progressive Matrices (1947). Sets, A, Ab, B.* London: Lewis, 1958. (U.S. distributor: Psychological Corporation.)

Razran, G. H. S. Conditioned responses in children: A behavioral and quantitative review of experimental studies. *Archives of Psychology*, 1933, **23,** No. 148, 120.

Reese, H. W. Transfer to a discrimination task as a function of amount of stimulus pretraining and similarity of stimulus names. Unpublished doctoral dissertation, State University of Iowa, 1958.

Reese, H. W. Motor paired-associate learning and stimulus pretraining. *Child Development* 1960, **31,** 505–513.

Reese, H. W. Level of stimulus pretraining and paired-associate learning. *Child Development*, 1961, **32,** 89–93. (a)

Reese, H. W. Manifest anxiety and achievement test performance. *Journal of Educational Psychology*, 1961, **52,** 132–135. (b)

Reese, H. W. Transposition in the intermediate-size problem by preschool children. *Child Development*, 1961, **32,** 311–314. (c)

Reese, H. W. The distance effect in transposition in the intermediate size problem. *Journal of Comparative and Physiological Psychology*, 1962, **55,** 528–531. (a)

Reese, H. W. Sociometric choices of the same and opposite sex in late childhood. *Merrill-Palmer Quarterly*, 1962, **8,** 173–174. (b)

Reese, H. W. Verbal mediation as a function of age level. *Psychological Bulletin*, 1962, **59,** 502–509. (c)

Reese, H. W. Discrimination learning set in children. In L. P. Lipsitt and C. C. Spiker (Eds.), *Advances in child development and behavior.* Vol. 1. New York: Academic Press, 1963. Pp. 115–145. (a)

Reese, H. W. "Perceptual set" in young children. *Child Development*, 1963, **34,** 151–159. (b)

Reese, H. W. "Perceptual set" in young children: II. *Child Development*, 1963, **34,** 451–454. (c)

Reese, H. W. A reply to Youniss and Furth. *Psychological Bulletin*, 1963, **60,** 503–504. (d)

Reese, H. W. Discrimination learning set in rhesus monkeys. *Psychological Bulletin*, 1964, **61,** 321–340.

Reese, H. W. Discrimination learning set and perceptual set in young children. *Child Development*, 1965, **36,** 153–161. (a)

Reese, H. W. Imagery in paired-associate learning in children. *Journal of Experimental Child Psychology*, 1965, **2,** 290–296. (b)

Reese, H. W. Attitudes toward the opposite sex in late childhood. *Merrill-Palmer Quarterly*, 1966, **12,** 157–163.

Reese, H. W. *The perception of stimulus relations. Discrimination learning and transposition.* New York: Academic Press, 1968.

Reese, H. W. (Chm.) Imagery in children's learning: A symposium. *Psychological Bulletin,* in press.

Reese, H. W., and Ford, L. H., Jr. Expectancy and perception of an ambiguous figure in preschool children. *Journal of Verbal Learning and Verbal Behavior,* 1962, **1,** 188–191.

Reese, H. W., and Overton, W. F. Models of development and theories of development. In L. R. Goulet and P. B. Baltes (Eds.), *Theory and research in life-span developmental psychology.* New York: Academic Press, in press.

Reichard, S., Schneider, M., and Rapaport, D. The development of concept formation in children. *American Journal of Orthopsychiatry,* 1944, **14,** 156–162.

Reid, L. S. The development of noncontinuity behavior through continuity learning. *Journal of Experimental Psychology,* 1953, **46,** 107–112.

Reiss, I. L. America's sex standards—how and why they're changing. *Trans-Action,* 1968, **5,** 26–32.

Rendle-Short, J. The puff test. *Archives of Disease in Childhood,* 1961, **36,** 50–57.

Renshaw, S. The errors of cutaneous localization and the effect of practice on the localizing of movement in children and adults. *Journal of General Psychology,* 1930, **38,** 223–238.

Rescorla, R. A. Pavlovian conditioning and its proper control procedures. *Psychological Review,* 1967, **74,** 71–80.

Restle, F. Toward a quantitative description of learning set data. *Psychological Review,* 1958, **65,** 77–91.

Restle, F. Note on the "hypothesis" theory of discrimination learning. *Psychological Reports,* 1960, **7,** 194.

Restle, F. The selection of strategies in cue learning. *Psychological Review,* 1962, **69,** 329–343.

Reynolds, G. S. Attention in the pigeon. *Journal of the Experimental Analysis of Behavior,* 1961, **4,** 203–208.

Reynolds, G. S. *A primer of operant conditioning.* Glenview, Ill.: Scott, Foresman, 1968.

Rheingold, H. L. Controlling the infant's exploratory behavior. In B. M. Foss (Ed.), *Determinants of infant behavior.* Vol. II. London: Methuen (New York: Wiley), 1963. Pp. 171–175.

Rheingold, H. L., and Bayley, N. The later effects of an experimental modification of mothering. *Child Development,* 1959, **30,** 363–372.

Rheingold, H. L., Gewirtz, J. L., and Ross, H. W. Social conditioning of vocalizations in the infant. *Journal of Comparative and Physiological Psychology,* 1959, **52,** 68–73.

Rheingold, H. L., Stanley, W. C., and Cooley, J. A. A method for studying exploratory behavior in infants. *Science,* 1962, **136,** 1054–1055.

Rheingold, H. L., Stanley, W. C., and Doyle, G. A. Visual and auditory reinforcement of a manipulatory response in the young child. *Journal of Experimental Child Psychology,* 1964, **1,** 316–326.

Rice, U. M., and Di Vesta, F. J. A developmental study of semantic and phonetic generalization in paired-association learning. *Child Development,* 1965, **36,** 721–730.

Richmond, J. B., Grossman, H. J., and Lustman, S. L. A hearing test for newborn infants. *Pediatrics,* 1953, **11,** 634–638.

Richmond, J. B., and Lipton, E. L. Some aspects of the neurophysiology of the newborn and their implications for child development. In L. Jessner and E. Pavenstedt (Eds.), *Psychopathology in children.* New York: Grune & Stratton, 1959.

Richmond, J. B., Lipton, E. L., and Steinschneider, A. Observations on differences in autonomic nervous system function between and within individuals during early infancy. *American Academy of Child Psychiatry Journal*, 1962, **1**, 83–91.

Richter, C. P. High electrical skin resistance of newborn infants and its significance. *American Journal of Diseases of Children*, 1930, **40**, 18–26.

Rie, H. E. An exploratory study of the CMAS lie scale. *Child Development*, 1963, **34**, 1003–1017.

Rieber, M. The effect of CS presence during delay of reward on the speed of an instrumental response. *Journal of Experimental Psychology*, 1961, **61**, 290–294. (a)

Rieber, M. Shifts in response-reward interval and its effect upon response speed. *Psychological Reports*, 1961, **9**, 393–398. (b)

Rieber, M. Delay of reward and discrimination learning in children. *Child Development*, 1964, **35**, 559–568. (a)

Rieber, M. Verbal mediation in normal and retarded children. *American Journal of Mental Deficiency*, 1964, **68**, 634–641. (b)

Rieber, M. Response alternation of children under different schedules of reinforcement. *Psychonomic Science*, 1966, **4**, 149–150. (a)

Rieber, M. The role of stimulus comparison in children's discrimination learning. *Journal of Experimental Psychology*, 1966, **72**, 263–270. (b)

Rieber, M., and Johnson, B. M. The relative effects of alternating delayed reinforcement and alternating nonreinforcement on response speeds of children. *Journal of Experimental Child Psychology*, 1964, **1**, 174–181.

Riegel, K. F. The Michigan restricted association norms. (Mimeographed report.) Ann Arbor, Mich.: Office of Research Administration, University of Michigan, April 10, 1965.

Riess, B. Genetic changes in semantic conditioning. *Journal of Experimental Psychology*, 1946, **36**, 143–152.

Riggs, L. A. Visual acuity. In C. H. Graham, N. R. Bartlett, J. L. Brown, Y. Hsia, C. G. Mueller, and L. A. Riggs (Eds.), *Vision and visual perception*. New York: Wiley, 1965. Pp. 321–349.

Riley, D. A. *Discrimination learning*. Boston: Allyn & Bacon, 1968.

Ring, E. M. The effect of anticipation interval on paired-associate learning in retarded and normal children. *American Journal of Mental Deficiency*, 1965, **70**, 466–470.

Ring, E. M., and Palermo, D. S. Paired-associate learning of retarded and normal children. *American Journal of Mental Deficiency*, 1961, **66**, 100–107.

Ringwall, E. A., Reese, H. W., and Markel, N. N. A distinctive features analysis of pre-linguistic infant vocalizations. In K. F. Riegel (Ed.), *The development of language functions*. Report No. 8. Ann Arbor, Mich.: Center for Human Growth and Development, University of Michigan, 1965. Pp. 69–78.

Ringwall, E. A., Reese, H. W., and Markel, N. N. Behavioral correlates of infant vocalizations. Final Report, United States Public Health Service Grant No. NB 04923-01, 1970.

Rinsland, H. D. *A basic vocabulary of elementary school children*. New York: Macmillan, 1945.

Ripple, R. E., and May, F. B. Caution in comparing creativity and I.Q. *Psychological Reports*, 1962, **10**, 229–230.

Risley, T. R. The effects and side effects of punishing the autistic behaviors of an autistic child. *Journal of Applied Behavior Analysis*, 1968, **1**, 21–34.

Risley, T., and Wolf, M. M. Establishing functional speech in echolalic children. *Behaviour Research and Therapy*, 1967, **5**, 73–88.

Robinson, J. S., and Higgins, K. E. The young child's ability to see a difference between mirror-image forms. *Perceptual and Motor Skills*, 1967, **22**, 893–897.

Robinson, N. M., and Robinson, H. B. A method for the study of instrumental avoidance conditioning with children. *Journal of Comparative and Physiological Psychology*, 1961, **54**, 20–23.

Rohwer, W. D., Jr. Social class differences in the role of linguistic structures in paired-associate learning: Elaboration and learning proficiency. Final Report, 1967, Project No. 5–0605, Contract No. OE–6–10–273, U.S. Department of Health, Education and Welfare, Office of Education.

Rohwer, W. D., Jr., and Lynch, S. Form class and intralist similarity in paired-associate learning. *Journal of Verbal Learning and Verbal Behavior*, 1967, **6**, 551–554.

Rohwer, W. D., Jr., Lynch, S., Levin, J. R., and Suzuki, N. Pictorial and verbal factors in the efficient learning of paired associates. *Journal of Educational Psychology*, 1967, **58**, 278–284. (a)

Rohwer, W. D., Jr., Lynch, S., Suzuki, N., and Levin, J. R. Verbal and pictorial facilitation of paired-associate learning. *Journal of Experimental Child Psychology*, 1967, **5**, 294–302. (b)

Rosekrans, M. A. Imitation in children as a function of perceived similarity to a social model and vicarious reinforcement. *Journal of Personality and Social Psychology*, 1967, **7**, 307–315.

Rosekrans, M. A., and Hartup, W. W. Imitative influences of consistent and inconsistent response consequences to a model on aggressive behavior in children. *Journal of Personality and Social Psychology*, 1967, **7**, 429–434.

Rosenbaum, M. E., and Bruning, J. L. Direct and vicarious experience of variations in percentage of reinforcement. *Child Development*, 1966, **37**, 959–966.

Rosenblith, J. F. The modified Graham Behavior Test for neonates: Test-retest reliability, normative data and hypotheses for future work. *Biologia Neonatorum*, 1961, **3**, 174–192.

Rosenhan, D. Aloneness and togetherness as drive conditions in children. *Journal of Experimental Research in Personality*, 1967, **2**, 32–40.

Rosenthal, I. Reliability of retrospective reports of adolescence. *Journal of Consulting Psychology*, 1963, **27**, 189–198.

Rosenthal, R., and Jacobson, L. Teacher's expectancies: Determinants of pupils' I.Q. gains. *Psychological Reports*, 1966, **19**, 115–118.

Ross, L. E. Conditioned fear as a function of CS-UCS and probe stimulus intervals. *Journal of Experimental Psychology*, 1961, **61**, 265–273.

Ross, L. E., Hetherington, E. M., and Wray, N. P. Delay of reward and the learning of a size problem by normal and retarded children. *Child Development*, 1965, **36**, 509–518.

Rossi, E. L. Associative clustering in normal and retarded children. *American Journal of Mental Deficiency*, 1963, **67**, 691–699.

Rossi, E. L. Development of classificatory behavior. *Child Development*, 1964, **35**, 137–142.

Rossi, E. L., and Rossi, S. I. Concept utilization, serial order and recall in nursery school children. *Child Development*, 1965, **36**, 771–779.

Rossi, S. I., and Wittrock, M. C. Clustering versus serial ordering in recall by four-year-old children. *Child Development*, 1967, **38**, 1139–1142.

Rothblat, L. A. Intradimensional and extradimensional shifts in the monkey within and across sensory modalities. Paper presented at the meeting of the Eastern Psychological Association, Boston, April 1967.

Rothschild, R. Incubator isolation as a possible contributing factor to the high incidence of emotional disturbance among prematurely born persons. *Journal of Genetic Psychology*, 1967, **110**, 287–304.

Rovee, C. K. Psychophysical scaling of olfactory response to the aliphatic alcohols in human neonates. Unpublished doctoral dissertation, Brown University, 1966.

Rovee, C. K., and Levin, G. R. Oral "pacification" and arousal in the human newborn. *Journal of Experimental Child Psychology*, 1966, **3**, 1–18.

Rubenstein, J. Maternal attentiveness and subsequent exploratory behavior in the infant. *Child Development*, 1967, **38**, 1089–1100.

Ruch, F. L. *Psychology and life*. (7th ed.) Chicago: Scott, Foresman, 1967.

Ruch, T. C., and Patton, H. D. *Physiology and biophysics*. Philadelphia: Saunders, 1965.

Rudel, R. G., and Teuber, H.-L. Discrimination of direction of line in children. *Journal of Comparative and Physiological Psychology*, 1963, **56**, 892–898.

Russell, W. A. An experimental psychology of development: Pipe dream or possibility? In D. B. Harris (Ed.), *The concept of development*. Minneapolis: University of Minnesota Press, 1957. Pp. 162–174.

Russell, W. A., and Storms, L. H. Implicit verbal chaining in paired-associate learning. *Journal of Experimental Psychology*, 1955, **49**, 287–293.

Ryan, T. J. The effects of nonreinforcement and incentive value on response speed. *Child Development*, 1965, **36**, 1067–1081.

Ryan, T. J. Instrumental performance related to several reward schedules and age. *Journal of Experimental Child Psychology*, 1966, **3**, 398–404.

Ryan, T. J., and Moffitt, A. R. Response speed as a function of age, incentive value, and reinforcement schedule. *Child Development*, 1966, **37**, 103–113.

Ryan, T. J., Orton, C., and Pimm, J. B. Discrete-trial instrumental performance related to reward schedule and developmental level. *Journal of Experimental Psychology*, 1968, **78**, 31–37.

Ryan, T. J., and Voorhoeve, A. C. A parametric investigation of reinforcement schedule and sex of S as related to acquisition and extinction of an instrumental response. *Journal of Experimental Child Psychology*, 1966, **4**, 189–197.

Ryan, T. J., and Watson, P. Frustrative nonreward theory applied to children's behavior. *Psychological Bulletin*, 1968, **69**, 111–125.

Sadowsky, S. Discrimination learning as a function of stimulus location along an auditory intensity continuum. *Journal of the Experimental Analysis of Behavior*, 1966, **9**, 219–225.

Sailor, W., Guess, D., Rutherford, G., and Baer, D. M. Control of tantrum behavior by operant techniques during experimental verbal training. *Journal of Applied Behavior Analysis*, 1968, **1**, 237–243.

Salapatek, P., and Kessen, W. Visual scanning of triangles by the human newborn. *Journal of Experimental Child Psychology*, 1966, **3**, 155–167.

Salapatek, P. H., and Kessen, W. Prolonged investigation of a plane geometric triangle by the human newborn. Paper presented at the meeting of the Society for Research in Child Development, Santa Monica, March 1969.

Salk, L. The effects of the normal heartbeat sound on the behavior of the newborn infant: Implications for mental health. *World Mental Health*, 1960, **12**, 168–175.

Salk, L. The importance of heartbeat rhythm to human nature: Theoretical, clinical, and experimental observations. *Proceedings of the Third World Congress of Psychiatry*, 1961, **1**, 740–746. (Montreal: McGill University Press.)

Salk, L. Mothers' heartbeat as an imprinting stimulus. *Transactions of the New York Academy of Science*, 1962, **24**, 753–763.

Saltzman, I. J. Maze learning in the absence of primary reinforcement: A study of secondary reinforcement. *Journal of Comparative and Physiological Psychology,* 1949, **42,** 161–173.

Sameroff, A. J. An apparatus for recording sucking and controlling feeding in the first days of life. *Psychonomic Science,* 1965, **2,** 355–356.

Sameroff, A. J. Can conditioned responses be established in the newborn infant? Paper presented at the Eastern regional meeting of the Society for Research in Child Development, Worcester, Mass., March 1968. (a)

Sameroff, A. J. The components of sucking in the human newborn. *Journal of Experimental Child Psychology,* 1968, **6,** 607–623. (b)

Sanford, R. N. The dynamics of identification. *Psychological Review,* 1955, **62,** 106–118.

Sarason, S. B. *Psychological problems in mental deficiency.* (2nd ed.) New York: Harper, 1953.

Sarason, S. B., and Gladwin, T. Psychological and cultural problems in mental subnormality: A review of research. *Genetic Psychology Monographs,* 1958, **57,** first half, 3–289.

Sarason, S. B., Hill, K., and Zimbardo, P. G. A longitudinal study of the relation of test anxiety to performance on intelligence and achievement tests. *Monographs of the Society for Research in Child Development,* 1964, **29**(7, Whole No. 98).

Saravo, A. Effect of number of variable dimensions on reversal and nonreversal shifts. *Journal of Comparative and Physiological Psychology,* 1967, **64,** 93–97.

Sartain, A. Q. A comparison of the new Revised Stanford-Binet, the Bellevue Scale and certain group tests of intelligence. *Journal of Social Psychology,* 1946, **23,** 237–239.

Schaefer, E. S. Does the sampling method produce the negative correlation of mean I.Q. with age reported by Kennedy, Van de Reitt and White? *Child Development,* 1965, **36,** 257–259.

Schaffer, H. R. Objective observations of personality development in early infancy. *British Journal of Medical Psychology,* 1958, **31,** 174–183.

Schaffer, H. R. Some issues for research in the study of attachment behavior. In B. M. Foss (Ed.), *Determinants of infant behavior.* Vol. II. London: Methuen (New York: Wiley), 1963. Pp. 179–198.

Schaffer, H. R., and Emerson, P. E. Patterns of response to physical contact in early human development. *Journal of Child Psychology and Psychiatry,* 1964, **5,** 1–13.

Scharlock, D. P., Tucker, T. J., and Strominger, N. L. Auditory discrimination by the cat after neonatal ablation of temporal cortex. *Science,* 1963, **141,** 1197–1198.

Scheibel, M. E., and Scheibel, A. B. Some neural substrates of postnatal development. In M. L. Hoffman and L. W. Hoffman (Eds.), *Review of child development research.* Vol. 1. New York: Russell Sage Foundation, 1964. Pp. 481–519.

Schiller, P. Interrelation of different senses in perception. *British Journal of Psychology (General Section),* 1935, **25,** 465–469.

Schiller, P. H. Delayed detour response in the octopus. *Journal of Comparative and Physiological Psychology,* 1949, **42,** 220–225.

Schlosberg, H. A study of the conditioned patellar reflex. *Journal of Experimental Psychology,* 1928, **11,** 468–494.

Schneirla, T. C. The concept of development in comparative psychology. In D. B. Harris (Ed.), *The concept of development.* Minneapolis: University of Minnesota Press, 1957. Pp. 78–108.

Schülte, F. J., Michaelis, R., Linke, I., and Nolte, R. Motor nerve conduction velocity in term, preterm, and small-for-dates infants. *Pediatrics,* 1968, **42,** 17–26.

Schulz, R. W., and Martin, E. Aural paired-associate learning: Stimulus familiarization, response familiarization, and pronunciability. *Journal of Verbal Learning and Verbal Behavior,* 1964, **3,** 139–145.

Scott, R. First to ninth grade I.Q. changes of northern Negro students. *Psychology in the Schools,* 1966, **3,** 159–160.

Seashore, H., Wesman, A., and Doppelt, J. The standardization of the Wechsler Intelligence Scale for Children. *Journal of Consulting Psychology,* 1950, **14,** 99–110.

Seegmiller, J. E., Rosenbloom, F. M., and Kelley, W. N. Enzyme defect associated with a sex-linked human neurologic disorder and excessive purine synthesis. *Science,* 1967, **155,** 1682–1684.

Seidel, H. E., Jr., Barkley, M. J., and Stith, D. Evaluation of a program for Project Head Start. *Journal of Genetic Psychology,* 1967, **110,** 185–197.

Seltzer, R. J. Effects of reinforcement and deprivation on the development of non-nutritive sucking in monkeys and humans. Unpublished doctoral dissertation, Brown University, 1968.

Semb, G., and Lipsitt, L. P. The effects of acoustic stimulation on cessation and initiation of non-nutritive sucking in neonates. *Journal of Experimental Child Psychology,* 1968, **6,** 585–597.

Semler, I. J., and Iscoe, I. Structure of intelligence in Negro and white children. *Journal of Educational Psychology,* 1966, **57,** 326–336.

Semler, I. J., and Pederson, D. R. Children's reactions to nonreward: Partial vs. continuous reinforcement using a within-subjects design. *Psychonomic Science,* 1968, **10,** 285–286.

Setterington, R. G., and Walters, R. H. Effects of concurrent delays of material rewards and punishments on problem-solving in children. *Child Development,* 1964, **35,** 275–280.

Seward, J. P., Pereboom, A. C., Butler, B., and Jones, R. B. The role of prefeeding in an apparent frustration effect. *Journal of Experimental Psychology,* 1957, **54,** 445–450.

Sgan, M. L. Social reinforcement, socioeconomic status, and susceptibility to experimenter influence. *Journal of Personality and Social Psychology,* 1967, **5,** 202–210.

Shapiro, M. M., and Miller, T. M. On the relationship between conditioned and discriminative stimuli and between instrumental and consummatory responses. In W. F. Prokasy (Ed.), *Classical conditioning: A symposium.* New York: Appleton-Century-Crofts, 1965. Pp. 269–301.

Shapiro, S. I. Paired-associate response latencies as a function of free association strength. *Journal of Experimental Psychology,* 1968, **77,** 223–231.

Shapiro, S. I., and Palermo, D. S. The influence of part of speech on paired-associate learning. *Psychonomic Science,* 1967, **8,** 445–446.

Shapiro, S. I., and Palermo, D. S. Mediation in children's aural paired-associate learning. *Child Development,* 1968, **39,** 569–577.

Shapiro, S. S. Meaningfulness values for 52 CVCs for grade-school-aged children. *Psychonomic Science,* 1964, **1,** 127–128. (a)

Shapiro, S. S. Word associations and meaningfulness values for grade-school children. *Psychological Reports,* 1964, **15,** 447–455. (b)

Shapiro, S. S. Paired-associate learning in children. *Journal of Verbal Learning and Verbal Behavior,* 1965, **4,** 170–174.

Shapiro, S. S. Aural paired associates learning in grade-school children. *Child Development,* 1966, **37,** 417–424.

Shapiro, S. S. Paired-associate learning in children: Length of list, initial associative strength, presentation time, and grade level. *Psychological Reports,* 1967, **20,** 903–908.

Shaycoft, M. F., Dailey, J. T., and Orr, D. B. *Project Talent: Studies of a complete age group: Age 15.* Pittsburgh: University of Pittsburgh Press, 1963.

Shearn, D. Does the heart learn? *Psychological Bulletin,* 1961, **58,** 452–458.

Sheffield, F. D. Relation between classical conditioning and instrumental learning. In W. F. Prokasy (Ed.), *Classical conditioning: A symposium.* New York: Appleton-Century-Crofts, 1965. Pp. 302–322.

Sheffield, V. F. Extinction as a function of partial reinforcement and distribution of practice. *Journal of Experimental Psychology,* 1949, **39,** 511–526.

Sheikh, A. A. Response speed as a function of different reinforcement conditions and a ready signal. *Child Development,* 1967, **38,** 857–867.

Sheldon, P. M. Isolation as a characteristic of highly gifted children. *Journal of Educational Sociology,* 1959, **32,** 215–221.

Sheldon, W. H. *The varieties of human physique.* New York: Harper, 1940.

Sheldon, W. H. *The varieties of temperament.* New York: Harper, 1942.

Shell, W. F., and Riopelle, A. J. Multiple discrimination learning in raccoons. *Journal of Comparative and Physiological Psychology,* 1957, **50,** 585–587.

Shepp, B. E. Some cue properties of anticipated rewards in discrimination learning of retardates. *Journal of Comparative and Physiological Psychology,* 1962, **55,** 856–859.

Shepp, B. E., and Eimas, P. D. Intradimensional and extradimensional shifts in the rat. *Journal of Comparative and Physiological Psychology,* 1964, **57,** 357–361.

Shepp, B. E., and Schrier, A. M. Consecutive intradimensional and extradimensional shifts in monkeys. *Journal of Comparative and Physiological Psychology,* 1969, **67,** 199–203.

Shepp, B. E., and Turrisi, F. D. Learning and transfer of mediating responses in discriminative learning. In N. R. Ellis (Ed.), *International review of research in mental retardation.* Vol. 2. New York: Academic Press, 1966. Pp. 86–120.

Shepp, B. E., and Turrisi, F. D. Effects of overtraining on the acquisition of intradimensional and extradimensional shifts. *Journal of Experimental Psychology,* 1969, **82,** 46–51.

Shepp, B. E., and Zeaman, D. Discrimination learning of size and brightness by retardates. *Journal of Comparative and Physiological Psychology,* 1966, **62,** 55–59.

Sheppard, W. C. The analysis and control of infant vocal and motor behavior. Unpublished doctoral dissertation, University of Michigan, 1967.

Sherman, J. A. Use of reinforcement and imitation to reinstate verbal behavior in mute psychotics. *Journal of Abnormal Psychology,* 1965, **70,** 155–164.

Sherman, J. A., and Baer, D. M. Appraisal of operant techniques with children and adults. In C. M. Franks (Ed.), *Assessment and status of the behavior therapies and associated developments.* New York: McGraw-Hill, 1969. Pp. 192–219.

Sherman, M. The differentiation of emotional responses in infants: II. The ability of observers to judge the emotional characteristics of the crying of infants, and of the voice of an adult. *Journal of Comparative Psychology,* 1927, **7,** 335–351.

Sherman, M., and Key, C. B. The intelligence of isolated mountain children. *Child Development,* 1932, **3,** 279–290.

Sherman, M., and Sherman, I. C. Sensorimotor responses in infants. *Journal of Comparative Psychology,* 1925, **5,** 53–68.

Sherman, M., Sherman, I., and Flory, C. D. Infant behavior. *Comparative Psychology Monographs,* 1936, **12,** 1–107.

Shirley, M. M. *The first two years: A study of twenty-five babies.* Vol. II. *Intellectual development.* Institute of Child Welfare Monograph Series No. 7. Minneapolis: University of Minnesota Press, 1933.

Shore, M. F., Massimo, J. L., and Ricks, D. F. A factor analytic study of psychotherapeutic change in delinquent boys. *Journal of Clinical Psychology,* 1965, **21**, 208–212.

Shuey, A. *The testing of Negro intelligence.* Lynchburg, Va.: J. P. Bell, 1958.

Shusterman, R. J. The use of strategies in two-choice behavior of children and chimpanzees. *Journal of Comparative and Physiological Psychology,* 1963, **56**, 96–100.

Shuttleworth, F. K. The cumulative influence on intelligence of socio-economic differentials operating on the same children over a period of ten years. *Yearbook of the National Society for the Study of Education,* 1940, **39**, Part II, 275–280.

Sidman, M. *Tactics of scientific research.* New York: Basic Books, 1960.

Sidowski, J. B., Kass, N., and Wilson, H. Cue and secondary reinforcement effects with children. *Journal of Experimental Psychology,* 1965, **69**, 340–342.

Siegel, A. E. Editorial: State of the journal. *Child Development,* 1967, **38**, 901–907.

Siegel, H. Observations on electrical measurements of threshold sensibility of the skin with square-wave current. *Journal of Investigative Dermatology,* 1955, **25**, 55–62.

Siegel, P. S., and Foshee, J. G. The law of primary reinforcement in children. *Journal of Experimental Psychology,* 1953, **45**, 12–14.

Sigel, I. E., Anderson, L. M., and Shapiro, H. Categorization behavior in lower and middle class Negro preschool children: Differences in dealing with representation of common objects. *Journal of Negro Education,* 1966, *Summer,* 218–229. (a)

Sigel, I. E., and McBane, B. Cognitive competence and level of symbolization among five year old children. In J. Hellmuth (Ed.), *The disadvantaged child.* Seattle: Special Child Publications, 1967. Pp. 433–453.

Sigel, I. E., and Mermelstein, E. Effects of nonschooling on Piagetian tasks of conservation. Paper presented at the meeting of the American Psychological Association, Chicago, September 1965.

Sigel, I. E., Roeper, A., and Hooper, F. H. A training procedure for acquisition of Piaget's conservation of quantity: A pilot study and its replication. *British Journal of Educational Psychology,* 1966, **36**(3), 301–311. (b)

Silberman, C. E. *Crisis in black and white.* New York: Random House, 1964.

Silverman, I. W. Effect of verbalization on reversal shifts in children: Additional data. *Journal of Experimental Child Psychology,* 1966, **4**, 1–8.

Simmons, M. W. Operant discrimination learning in human infants. *Child Development,* 1964, **35**, 737–748.

Simmons, M. W., and Lipsitt, L. P. An operant-discrimination apparatus for infants. *Journal of the Experimental Analysis of Behavior,* 1961, **4**, 233–235.

Simon, H. A., and Newell, A. Computer simulation of human thinking and problem solving. In W. Kessen and C. Kuhlman (Eds.), Thought in the young child. *Monographs of the Society for Research in Child Development,* 1962, **27**, No. 2. Pp. 137–150.

Sinclair-DeZwart, H. *Acquisition du language et développement de la pensée.* Paris: Dunod, 1967.

Siqueland, E. R. Operant conditioning of headturning in four month infants. *Psychonomic Science,* 1964, **1**, 223–224.

Siqueland, E. R. Two experimental procedures for the analyses of learning processes in human infants. Paper presented at the meeting of the Eastern Psychological Association, New York, April 1966.

Siqueland, E. R. Reinforcement patterns and extinction in human newborns. *Journal of Experimental Child Psychology*, 1968, **6**, 431–442. (a)

Siqueland, E. R. Visual reinforcement and exploratory behavior in infants. Paper presented at the Eastern regional meeting of the Society for Research in Child Development, Worcester, Mass., March 1968. (b)

Siqueland, E. R., and DeLucia, C. A. Visual reinforcement of nonnutritive sucking in human infants. *Science*, 1969, **165**, 1144–1146.

Siqueland, E. R., and Lipsitt, L. P. Conditioned headturning in human newborns. *Journal of Experimental Child Psychology*, 1966, **3**, 356–376.

Skeels, H. M. The use of conditioning techniques in the study of form discrimination of young children. *Journal of Experimental Education*, 1933, **2**, 127–137.

Skeels, H. M. Adult status of children with contrasting early life experiences. *Monographs of the Society for Research in Child Development*, 1966, **31**(3, Whole No. 105).

Skeels, H. M., and Fillmore, E. A. Mental development of children from underprivileged homes. *Journal of Genetic Psychology*, 1937, **50**, 427–439.

Skeels, H. M., Updegraff, R., Wellman, B. L., and Williams, H. M. A study of environmental stimulation. *University of Iowa Studies in Child Welfare*, 1938, **15**, No. 4.

Skinner, B. F. Two types of conditioned reflex: A reply to Konorski and Miller. *Journal of General Psychology*, 1937, **16**, 272–279.

Skinner, B. F. *The behavior of organisms: An experimental approach.* New York: Appleton-Century, 1938.

Skinner, B. F. *Verbal behavior.* New York: Appleton-Century-Crofts, 1957.

Skodak, M., and Skeels, H. M. A final follow up study of one hundred adopted children. *Journal of Genetic Psychology*, 1949, **75**, 85–125.

Slamecka, N. J. A methodological analysis of shift paradigms in human discrimination learning. *Psychological Bulletin*, 1968, **69**, 423–438.

Slavson, S. R. *Child psychotherapy.* New York: Columbia University Press, 1952.

Slobin, D. I. The role of imitation in early language learning. Paper presented at the meeting of the Society for Research in Child Development, Minneapolis, March 1965.

Slobin, D. I. The acquisition of Russian as a native language. In F. Smith and G. A. Miller (Eds.), *The genesis of language: A psycholinguistic approach.* Cambridge, Mass.: M.I.T. Press, 1966. Pp. 129–148. (a)

Slobin, D. I. Grammatical transformations and sentence comprehension in childhood and adulthood. *Journal of Verbal Learning and Verbal Behavior*, 1966, **5**, 219–227. (b)

Smedslund, J. The acquisition of conservation of substance and weight in children. II. External reinforcement of conservation of weight and of the operations of addition and subtraction. *Scandinavian Journal of Psychology*, 1961, **2**, 71–84. (a)

Smedslund, J. The acquisition of conservation of substance and weight in children. III. Extinction of conservation of weight acquired "normally" and by means of empirical controls on a balance scale. *Scandinavian Journal of Psychology*, 1961, **2**, 85–87. (b)

Smedslund, J. The acquisition of the conservation of substance and weight in children. IV. An attempt at extinction of the visual components of the weight concept. *Scandinavian Journal of Psychology*, 1961, **2**, 153–155. (c)

Smedslund, J. Development of concrete transitivity of length in children. *Child Development*, 1963, **34**, 389–405.

Smiley, S. S., and Weir, M. W. Role of dimensional dominance in reversal and nonreversal shift behavior. *Journal of Experimental Child Psychology*, 1966, **4**, 296–307.

Smith, I. D. The effects of training procedures upon the acquisition of conservation of weight. *Child Development,* 1968, **39,** 515–526.

Smith, K. U., and Smith, W. M. *Perception and motion.* Philadelphia: Sanders, 1962.

Smith, K. U., Zwerg, C., and Smith, N. J. Sensory-feedback analysis of infant control of the behavioral environment. *Perceptual and Motor Skills,* 1963, **16,** 725–732.

Smith, M. E. An investigation of the development of the sentence and the extent of vocabulary in young children. *University of Iowa Studies in Child Welfare,* 1926, **3,** No. 5.

Smock, C. D., and Rubin, B. M. Utilization of visual information in children as a function of incentive motivation. *Child Development,* 1964, **35,** 109–117.

Sokolov, E. N. Higher nervous activity and the problem of perception. (Translated in the U.S.S.R. from *Voprosy Psikhologii,* 1955, **1,** 58–66.) In B. Simon (Ed.), *Psychology in the Soviet Union.* Stanford, Calif.: Stanford University Press, 1957. Pp. 92–99.

Sokolov, E. N. Neuronal models and the orienting reflex. In M. A. B. Brazier (Ed.), *The central nervous system and behavior. Transactions of the third conference.* New York: Josiah Macy, Jr., Foundation, 1960. Pp. 187–276.

Sokolov, E. N. Higher nervous functions: The orienting reflex. *Annual Review of Physiology,* 1963, **25,** 545–580. (a)

Sokolov, E. N. *Perception and the conditioned reflex.* New York: Macmillan (Pergamon), 1963. (b)

Solenkova, E. G., and Nikitina, G. M. The initial formation and development of conditioned defensive reflexes in the young monkeys. *Pavlov Journal of Higher Nervous Activity,* 1960, **10,** 220.

Solkoff, N., Yaffe, S., Weintraub, D., and Blase, B. Effects of handling on the subsequent developments of premature infants. *Developmental Psychology,* 1969, **1,** 765–768.

Solley, C. M. Affective processes in perceptual development. In A. H. Kidd and J. L. Rivoire (Eds.), *Perceptual development in children.* New York: International Universities Press, 1966. Pp. 275–304.

Solley, C. M., and Engel, M. Perceptual autism in children: The effects of reward, punishment, and neutral conditions upon perceptual learning. *Journal of Genetic Psychology,* 1960, **97,** 77–91.

Solomons, G., Cushna, B., Opitz, E., and Greene, M. An investigation of social status differences among educable and trainable children. *American Journal of Mental Deficiency,* 1966, **71,** 207–212.

Sontag, L. W., and Baker, C. T. Personality, familial and physical correlates of change in mental ability. In L. W. Sontag, C. T. Baker, and V. L. Nelson (Eds.), Mental growth and personality development: A longitudinal study. *Monographs of the Society for Research in Child Development,* 1958, **23,** No. 2. Pp. 87–143.

Spearman, C. "General intelligence" objectively determined and measured. *American Journal of Psychology,* 1904, **15,** 201–293.

Spearman, C. *The abilities of man.* New York: Macmillan, 1927.

Spearman, C. *Psychology down the ages.* Vol. I. London: Macmillan, 1937.

Spears, W. C. Assessment of visual preference and discrimination in the four-month-old infant. *Journal of Comparative and Physiological Psychology,* 1964, **57,** 381–386.

Spears, W. C., and Hohle, R. H. Sensory and perceptual processes in infants. In Y. Brackbill (Ed.), *Infancy and early childhood.* New York: Free Press, 1967. Pp. 51–121.

Spelt, D. K. The conditioning of the human fetus in utero. *Journal of Experimental Psychology*, 1948, **38**, 375–376.

Spence, J. T. Verbal-discrimination performance as a function of instructions and verbal-reinforcement combination in normal and retarded children. *Child Development*, 1966, **37**, 269–281.

Spence, J. T., and Segner, L. L. Verbal versus nonverbal reinforcement combinations in the discrimination learning of middle and lower class children. *Child Development*, 1967, **38**, 29–38.

Spence, K. W. The nature of discrimination learning in animals. *Psychological Review*, 1936, **43**, 427–449.

Spence, K. W. The differential response in animals to stimuli varying within a single dimension. *Psychological Review*, 1937, **44**, 430–444.

Spence, K. W. The basis of solution by chimpanzees of the intermediate size problem. *Journal of Experimental Psychology*, 1942, **31**, 257–271.

Spence, K. W. *Behavior theory and conditioning.* New Haven, Conn.: Yale University Press, 1956.

Spence, K. W. *Behavior theory and learning.* Englewood Cliffs, N.J.: Prentice-Hall, 1960.

Spence, K. W. Anxiety (drive) level and performance in eyelid conditioning. *Psychological Bulletin*, 1964, **61**, 129–139.

Spence, K. W., and Runquist, W. N. Temporal effects of conditioned fear on the eyelid reflex. *Journal of Experimental Psychology*, 1958, **55**, 613–616.

Sperling, S. E. Reversal learning and resistance to extinction: A review of the rat literature. *Psychological Bulletin*, 1965, **63**, 281–297. (a)

Sperling, S. E. Reversal learning and resistance to extinction: A supplementary report. *Psychological Bulletin*, 1965, **64**, 310–312. (b)

Spicker, H. H., Hodges, W. L., and McCandless, B. R. A diagnostically based curriculum for psychosocially deprived preschool mentally retarded children: Interim report. *Exceptional Children*, 1966, **33**, 215–220.

Spiker, C. C. The effects of number of reinforcements on the strength of a generalized instrumental response. *Child Development*, 1956, **27**, 37–44. (a)

Spiker, C. C. Effects of stimulus similarity on discrimination learning. *Journal of Experimental Psychology*, 1956, **51**, 393–395. (b)

Spiker, C. C. Experiments with children on the hypothesis of acquired distinctiveness and equivalence of cues. *Child Development*, 1956, **27**, 253–263. (c)

Spiker, C. C. The stimulus generalization gradient as a function of the intensity of stimulus lights. *Child Development*, 1956, **27**, 85–98. (d)

Spiker, C. C. Stimulus pretraining and subsequent performance in the delayed reaction experiment. *Journal of Experimental Psychology*, 1956, **52**, 107–111. (e)

Spiker, C. C. Performance on a difficult discrimination following pretraining with distinctive stimuli. *Child Development*, 1959, **30**, 513–521.

Spiker, C. C. Associative transfer in verbal paired-associate learning. *Child Development*, 1960, **31**, 73–87.

Spiker, C. C. The hypothesis of stimulus interaction and an explanation of stimulus compounding. In L. P. Lipsitt and C. C. Spiker (Eds.), *Advances in child development and behavior.* Vol. 1. New York: Academic Press, 1963. Pp. 233–264. (a)

Spiker, C. C. Verbal factors in the discrimination learning of children. In J. C. Wright and J. Kagan (Eds.), Basic cognitive processes in children. *Monographs of the Society for Research in Child Development*, 1963, **28**, No. 2 (Whole No. 86). Pp. 53–69. (b)

Spiker, C. C. The concept of development: Relevant and irrelevant issues. In H. W. Stevenson (Ed.), Concept of development. *Monographs of the Society for Research in Child Development,* 1966, **31,** No. 5. Pp. 40–54.

Spiker, C. C., and Holton, R. B. Similarity of stimuli and of responses in the successive discrimination problem. *Child Development,* 1959, **30,** 471–480.

Spiker, C. C., and McCandless, B. R. The concept of intelligence and the philosophy of science. *Psychological Review,* 1954, **61,** 255–266.

Spiker, C. C., and Norcross, K. J. Effects of previously acquired stimulus names on discrimination performance. *Child Development,* 1962, **33,** 859–864.

Spitz, R. A. *The first year of life.* New York: International Universities Press, 1965.

Spitz, R. A., and Wolf, K. M. The smiling response: A contribution to the ontogenesis of social relations. *Genetic Psychology Monographs,* 1946, **34,** 57–125.

Spradlin, J. E., Girardeau, F. L., and Corte, E. Fixed ratio and fixed interval behavior of severely and profoundly retarded subjects. *Journal of Experimental Child Psychology,* 1965, **2,** 340–353.

Spradlin, J. E., Girardeau, F. L., and Horn, G. L. Stimulus properties of reinforcement during extinction of a free operant response. *Journal of Experimental Child Psychology,* 1966, **4,** 369–380.

Staats, A. W. Verbal habit-families, concepts, and operant conditioning of word classes. *Psychological Review,* 1961, **68,** 190–204.

Staats, A. W. *Human learning.* New York: Holt, Rinehart & Winston, 1964.

Staats, A. W. *Learning, language, and cognition.* New York: Holt, Rinehart & Winston, 1968.

Staats, A. W. Integrated-functional learning theory and language development. In D. Slobin (Ed.), *The ontogenesis of grammar: Some facts and several theories.* New York: Academic Press, in press.

Staats, A. W., and Staats, C. K. *Complex human behavior: A systematic extension of learning principles.* New York: Holt, Rinehart & Winston, 1963.

Staats, A. W., Staats, C. K. and Heard, W. G. Denotative meaning established by classical conditioning. *Journal of Experimental Psychology,* 1961, **61,** 300–303.

Staats, C. K., and Staats, A. W. Meaning established by classical conditioning. *Journal of Experimental Psychology,* 1957, **54,** 74–80.

Staffieri, J. R. A study of social stereotypes of body image in children. *Journal of Personality and Social Psychology,* 1967, **7,** 101–103.

Stalnaker, J. M. Recognizing and encouraging talent. *American Psychologist,* 1961, **16,** 513–522.

Stanbury, J. B. Familial goiter. In J. B. Stanbury, J. B. Wyngaarden, and D. S. Frederickson (Eds.), *The metabolic basis of inherited disease.* New York: McGraw-Hill, 1966. Pp. 273–320.

Stanbury, J. B., Wyngaarden, J. B., and Frederickson, D. S. (Eds.) *The metabolic basis of inherited disease.* New York: McGraw-Hill, 1966.

Stanley, W. C., Cornwell, A. C., Poggiani, C., and Trattner, A. Conditioning in the neonatal puppy. *Journal of Comparative and Physiological Psychology,* 1963, **56,** 211–214.

Staples, R. The responses of infants to color. *Journal of Experimental Psychology,* 1932, **15,** 119–141.

Steigman, M. J. Effect of discrimination conflict upon drive level as manifested in children's performance. *Child Development,* 1964, **35,** 1385–1390.

Steigman, M. J., and Stevenson, H. W. The effect of pretraining reinforcement schedules on children's learning. *Child Development,* 1960, **31,** 53–58.

Steinschneider, A. Developmental psychophysiology. In Y. Brackbill (Ed.), *Infancy and early childhood.* New York: Free Press, 1967. Pp. 3–47.

Steinschneider, A., Lipton, E. L., and Richmond, J. B. Auditory sensitivity in the infant: Effect of intensity on cardiac and motor activity. *Child Development,* 1966, **37**, 233–252.

Stern, C., and Stern, W. *Die Kindersprache: Eine psychologische und sprachtheoretische Untersuchung.* Leipzig: Barth, 1907.

Stern, E. R., and Jeffrey, W. E. Operant conditioning of non-nutritive sucking in the neonate. Paper presented at the meeting of the Society for Research in Child Development, Minneapolis, March 1965.

Stern, W. Über verlagerte Raumformen. *Zeitschrift für angewandte Psychologie,* 1909, **2**, 498–526.

Stevens, C. *Neurophysiology: A primer.* New York: Wiley, 1966.

Stevens, H. A., and Heber, R. *Mental retardation: A review of research from all the major disciplines.* Chicago: University of Chicago Press, 1964.

Stevens, S. S. The attributes of tones. *Proceedings of the National Academy of Science, U.S.,* 1934, **20**, 457–459.

Stevenson, H. W. Piaget, behavior theory and intelligence. In W. Kessen and C. Kuhlman (Eds.), Thought in the young child. *Monographs of the Society for Research in Child Development,* 1962, **27**, No. 2. Pp. 113–126.

Stevenson, H. W. Social reinforcement of children's behavior. In L. P. Lipsitt and C. C. Spiker (Eds.), *Advances in child development and behavior.* Vol. 2. New York: Academic Press, 1965. Pp. 97–126.

Stevenson, H. W., and Bitterman, M. E. The distance-effect in the transposition of intermediate-size by children. *American Journal of Psychology,* 1955, **68**, 274–279.

Stevenson, H. W., and Hoving, K. L. Probability learning as a function of age and incentive. *Journal of Experimental Child Psychology,* 1964, **1**, 64–70.

Stevenson, H. W., and Knights, R. M. Effect of visual reinforcement in the performance of normal and retarded children. *Perceptual and Motor Skills,* 1961, **13**, 119–126.

Stevenson, H. W., and McBee, G. The learning of object and pattern discriminations by children. *Journal of Comparative and Physiological Psychology,* 1958, **51**, 752–754.

Stevenson, H. W., and Odom, R. D. Effects of pretraining on the reinforcing value of visual stimuli. *Child Development,* 1961, **32**, 739–744.

Stevenson, H. W., and Odom, R. D. The effectiveness of social reinforcement following two conditions of social deprivation. *Journal of Abnormal and Social Psychology,* 1962, **65**, 429–431.

Stevenson, H. W., and Pirojnikoff, L. A. Discrimination learning as a function of pretraining reinforcement schedules. *Journal of Experimental Psychology,* 1958, **56**, 41–44.

Stevenson, H. W., and Weir, M. W. Response shift as a function of overtraining and delay. *Journal of Comparative and Physiological Psychology,* 1959, **52**, 327–329. (a)

Stevenson, H. W., and Weir, M. W. Variables affecting children's performance in a probability learning task. *Journal of Experimental Psychology,* 1959, **57**, 403–412. (b)

Stoddard, L. T. Operant conditioning of timing behavior in children. Unpublished doctoral dissertation, Columbia University, 1962.

Stollnitz, F. Spatial variables, observing responses, and discrimination learning sets. *Psychological Review,* 1965, **72**, 247–261.

Stolz, S. B., and Lott, D. F. Establishment in rats of a persistent response producing a net loss of reinforcement. *Journal of Comparative and Physiological Psychology,* 1964, **57,** 147–149.

Stone, G. C. Attainment of color, form, and size concepts by rhesus monkeys. *Journal of Comparative and Physiological Psychology,* 1961, **54,** 38–42.

Stott, D. H. Commentary on "The genetic determination of differences in intelligence: A study of monozygotic twins reared together and apart" by Cyril Burt: Congenital influences on the development of twins. *British Journal of Psychology,* 1966, **57,** 423–429.

Strong, C. A. A sketch of the history of psychology among the Greeks. *American Journal of Psychology,* 1891, **4,** 177–197.

Stubbs, E. M. The effect of the factors of duration, intensity, and pitch of sound stimuli on the responses of newborn infants. *University of Iowa Studies in Child Welfare,* 1934, **9,** No. 4, 75–135.

Suchman, R. G., and Trabasso, T. Color and form preferences in young children. *Journal of Experimental Child Psychology,* 1966, **3,** 177–187. (a)

Suchman, R. G., and Trabasso, T. Stimulus preference and cue function in young children's concept attainment. *Journal of Experimental Child Psychology,* 1966, **3,** 188–198. (b)

Sullivan, J. P., and Moran, L. J. Association structures of bright children at age six. *Child Development,* 1967, **38,** 793–800.

Sully, J. *Outlines of psychology with special reference to the theory of education.* New York: Appleton, 1891.

Sutherland, N. S. Stimulus analyzing mechanisms. In *Proceedings of a symposium on the mechanization of thought processes.* Vol. 2. London: H. M. Stationery Office, 1959. Pp. 575–609.

Sutherland, N. S. The learning of discriminations by animals. *Endeavour,* 1964, **23,** 148–152. (a)

Sutherland, N. S. Visual discrimination in animals. *British Medical Bulletin,* 1964, **20,** 54–59. (b)

Sutherland, N. S., and Holgate, V. Two-cue discrimination learning in rats. *Journal of Comparative and Physiological Psychology,* 1966, **61,** 198–207.

Sutherland, N. S., Mackintosh, N. J., and Mackintosh, J. Simultaneous discrimination of *Octopus* and transfer of discrimination along a continuum. *Journal of Comparative and Physiological Psychology,* 1963, **56,** 150–156.

Tallman, I. Adaptation to blocked opportunity: An experimental study. *Sociometry,* 1966, **29,** 121–134.

Tampieri, G. Il problema dell'indifferenze infantile per l'orientamento nello spazio visivo. *Rivista di Psicologia,* 1963, **57,** 125–177.

Tanner, J. M. *Growth at adolescence.* Oxford, Eng.: Blackwell, 1962.

Taylor, J. A. The relationship of anxiety to the conditioned eyelid response. *Journal of Experimental Psychology,* 1951, **41,** 81–92.

Taylor, J. A. A personality scale of manifest anxiety. *Journal of Abnormal and Social Psychology,* 1953, **48,** 285–290.

Taylor, J. A. Drive theory and manifest anxiety. *Psychological Bulletin,* 1956, **53,** 303–320.

Taylor, J. H. Innate emotional responses in infants. *Ohio State University Studies,* 1934, **12,** 69–81.

Templin, M. C. *Certain language skills in children: Their development and interrela-*

tionships. Institute of Child Welfare Monograph Series No. 26. Minneapolis: University of Minnesota Press, 1957.

Templin, M. C. The study of articulation and language development during the early school years. In F. Smith and G. A. Miller (Eds.), *The genesis of language: A psycholinguistic approach.* Cambridge, Mass.: M.I.T. Press, 1966. Pp. 173–180.

Tempone, V. J. Stimulus generalization as a function of mental age. *Child Development,* 1965, **36,** 229–235.

Terman, L. M. In Symposium: Intelligence and its measurement. *Journal of Educational Psychology,* 1921, **12,** 127–133.

Terman, L. M., and Merrill, M. A. *Stanford-Binet Intelligence Scale: Manual for the third revision, Form L-M.* Boston: Houghton Mifflin, 1960.

Terman, L. M., and Oden, M. H. *The gifted child grows up.* Stanford, Calif.: Stanford University Press, 1947.

Terman, L. M., and Oden, M. H. *The gifted group at mid-life: Thirty-five years' follow-up of the superior child.* Stanford, Calif.: Stanford University Press, 1959.

Terrace, H. S. Errorless transfer of discrimination across two continua. *Journal of the Experimental Analysis of Behavior,* 1963, **6,** 223–232.

Terrace, H. S. Wavelength generalization after discrimination learning with and without errors. *Science,* 1964, **144,** 78–80.

Terrace, H. S. Stimulus control. In W. K. Honig (Ed.), *Operant behavior: Areas of research and application.* New York: Meredith, 1966. Pp. 271–344.

Terrell, G. The incentive in discrimination learning in children. *Child Development,* 1958, **29,** 231–236.

Terrell, G. Delayed reinforcement effects. In L. P. Lipsitt and C. C. Spiker (Eds.), *Advances in child development and behavior.* Vol. 2. New York: Academic Press, 1965. Pp. 127–158.

Terrell, G., Durkin, K., and Weisley, M. Social class and the nature of the incentive in discrimination learning. *Journal of Abnormal and Social Psychology,* 1959, **59,** 270–272.

Terrell, G., and Kennedy, W. A. Discrimination learning and transposition in children as a function of the nature of the reward. *Journal of Experimental Psychology,* 1957, **52,** 257–260.

Terrell, G., and Ware, R. Role of delay of reward in speed of size and form discrimination learning in childhood. *Child Development,* 1961, **32,** 409–415.

Terrell, G., and Ware, R. Emotionally as a function of delay of reward. *Child Development,* 1963, **34,** 495–501.

Theios, J., and Blosser, D. Overlearning reversal effect and magnitude of reward. *Journal of Comparative and Physiological Psychology,* 1965, **59,** 252–257.

Theios, J., and Brelsford, J. Overlearning-extinction effect as an incentive phenomenon. *Journal of Experimental Psychology,* 1964, **67,** 463–467.

Thomas, O. *Transformational grammar and the teacher of English.* New York: Holt, Rinehart & Winston, 1965.

Thompson, G. G. Children's groups. In P. H. Mussen (Ed.), *Handbook of research methods in child development.* New York: Wiley, 1960. Pp. 821–853.

Thompson, G. G. *Child psychology.* (2nd ed.) Boston: Houghton Mifflin, 1962.

Thorndike, E. L. *Animal intelligence. Experimental studies.* New York: Macmillan, 1911.

Thorndike, E. L. *The measurement of intelligence.* New York: Teachers College, Columbia University, Bureau of Publications, 1926.

Thorndike, E. L., and Lorge, I. *The teacher's word book of 30,000 words.* New York: Columbia University Press, 1944.

Thorndike, R. L. "Constancy" of the I.Q. *Psychological Bulletin,* 1940, **37,** 167–186.

Thorndike, R. L. The measurement of creativity. *Teachers College Record,* 1963, **64,** 422–424.

Thorndike, R. L. Intellectual status and intellectual growth. *Journal of Educational Psychology,* 1966, **57,** 121–127.

Thorpe, W. H. *Learning and instinct in animals.* London: Methuen, 1956.

Thrum, M. E. The development of concepts of magnitude. *Child Development,* 1935, **6,** 120–140.

Thune, L. E. The effect of different types of preliminary activities on subsequent learning of paired-associate material. *Journal of Experimental Psychology,* 1950, **40,** 423–438.

Thurstone, L. L. *Primary mental abilities.* Chicago: University of Chicago Press, 1938.

Thurstone, L. L. *Multiple factor analysis.* Chicago: University of Chicago Press, 1947.

Thurstone, L. L. Psychological implications of factor analysis. *American Psychologist,* 1948, **3,** 402–408.

Thurstone, L. L. and Thurstone. T. G. Factorial studies of intelligence. *Psychometric Monograph,* 1941, No. 2.

Tiber, N., and Kennedy, W. A. The effects of incentives on the intelligence test performance of different social groups. *Journal of Consulting Psychology,* 1964, **28,** 187.

Tighe, L. S., and Tighe, T. J. Overtraining and discrimination shift behavior in children. *Psychonomic Science,* 1965, **2,** 365–366.

Tighe, T. J., and Tighe, L. S. Overtraining and optional shift behavior in rats and children. *Journal of Comparative and Physiological Psychology,* 1966, **62,** 49–54.

Tinklepaugh, O. L. Multiple delayed reaction with chimpanzees and monkeys. *Journal of Comparative Psychology,* 1932, **13,** 207–243.

Tischler, H. Schreien, Lallen und erstes Sprechen in der Entwicklung Sauglings. *Zeitschrift für Psychologie,* 1957, **160,** 210–263.

Titchener, E. G. *Lectures on the experimental psychology of the thought-processes.* New York: Macmillan, 1909.

Torrance, E. P. *Guiding creative talent.* Englewood Cliffs, N.J.: Prentice-Hall, 1962.

Torrance, E. P. The creative personality and the ideal pupil. *Teachers College Record,* 1963, **63,** 220–226.

Torrance, E. P. The Minnesota studies of creative behavior: National and international extensions. *Journal of Creative Behavior,* 1967, **1,** 137–154.

Toulmin, S. *The philosophy of science. An introduction.* (6th Printing.) London: Hutchinson, 1962.

Tower, S. S. The pyramidal tract. In P. C. Bucy (Ed.), *The precentral motor cortex.* (2nd ed.) Urbana, Ill.: University of Illinois Press, 1949. Pp. 149–172.

Trabasso, T., Deutsch, J. A., and Gelman, R. Attention in discrimination learning of young children. *Journal of Experimental Child Psychology,* 1966, **4,** 9–19.

Travers, R. M. W. *Essentials of learning.* New York: Macmillan, 1963.

Trincker, D., and Trincker, I. Die ontogenetische Entwicklung des Helligkeitsund Farbensehens beim Menschen. I. Die Entwicklung des Helligkeitssehens. (The ontogenetic development of brightness and color vision in man. I. The development of brightness.) *Graefe's Archiv. für Ophthalmologie,* 1955, **156,** 519–534. [Translated and reprinted in Y. Brackbill and G. G. Thompson (Eds.), *Behavior in in-*

fancy and early childhood: A book of readings. New York: Free Press, 1967. Pp. 179–188.]

Tulkin, S. R. Race, class, family, and school achievement. *Journal of Personality and Social Psychology,* 1968, **9,** 31–37.

Tulving, E. Subjective organization in free recall of "unrelated" words. *Psychological Review,* 1962, **69,** 344–354.

Turkewitz, G., Gordon, E. W., and Birch, H. G. Head-turning in the human neonate: Effect of prandial condition and lateral preference. *Journal of Comparative and Physiological Psychology,* 1965, **59,** 189–192.

Turkewitz, G., Moreau, T., and Birch, H. G. Head position and receptor organization in the human neonate. *Journal of Experimental Child Psychology,* 1966, **4,** 169–177.

Turner, M. W. A comparison of the social status of mentally retarded children enrolled in special classes. Unpublished doctoral dissertation, University of Indiana, 1958.

Twedt, H. M., and Underwood, B. J. Mixed vs. unmixed lists in transfer studies. *Journal of Experimental Psychology,* 1959, **58,** 111–116.

Underwood, B. J. *Experimental psychology.* New York: Appleton-Century-Crofts, 1949.

Underwood, B. J. Stimulus selection in verbal learning. In C. N. Cofer and B. S. Musgrave (Eds.), *Verbal behavior and learning.* New York: McGraw-Hill, 1963. Pp. 33–48.

Underwood, B. J., and Erlebacher, A. H. Studies of coding in verbal learning. *Psychological Monographs,* 1965, **79**(13, Whole No. 606).

Underwood, B. J., and Postman, L. Extra-experimental sources of interference in forgetting. *Psychological Review,* 1960, **67,** 73–95.

Underwood, B. J., and Richardson, J. Some verbal materials for the study of concept formation. *Psychological Bulletin,* 1956, **53,** 84–95.

Underwood, B. J., and Schulz, R. W. *Meaningfulness and verbal learning.* Philadelphia: Lippincott, 1960. (a)

Underwood, B. J., and Schulz, R. W. Response dominance and rate of learning paired associates. *Journal of General Psychology,* 1960, **62,** 153–158. (b)

Uzgiris, I. C. Situational generality of conservation. *Child Development,* 1964, **35,** 831–841.

Uznadze, D. N. *The psychology of set.* (Translated from the Russian by B. Haigh.) New York: Plenum Press (Consultants Bureau), 1966.

Vakhrameeva, I. A. Osobennosti obrazovaniia i protekanniia bilateralnykh uslovnykh dvigatelnykh refleksov u detei rannego vozrasta. (Characteristics of the formation and development of bilateral conditioned movement reflexes in young children.) In N. I. Kasatkin (Ed.), *From the simple to the complex.* Leningrad: Izdatel'stvo "Nauka," 1964. Pp. 115–126.

Valentine, C. W. The colour perception and colour preferences of an infant during its fourth and eighth month. *British Journal of Psychology,* 1914, **6,** 363–386.

Valentine, C. W. The psychology of imitation with special reference to early childhood. *British Journal of Psychology,* 1930, **21,** 105–132.

Van der Torren, J. Über das Auffassungstund Unterscheidungsvermogen für optische Bilder bei Kindern. *Zeitschrift für angewandte Psychologie,* 1907, **1,** 189–232.

Velten, H. V. The growth of phonemic and lexical pattern in infant language. *Language,* 1943, **19,** 281–292.

Vergason, G. A. Retention in retarded and normal subjects as a function of amount of original training. *American Journal of Mental Deficiency,* 1964, **68,** 623–629.

Vernon, M. D. *Backwardness in reading.* London and New York: Cambridge University Press, 1957.

Vernon, P. E. Environmental handicaps and intellectual development. Part I and Part II. *British Journal of Educational Psychology*, 1965, **35**, 9–20, 117–126.

Vincent, S. B. The function of the vibrissae in the behavior of the white rat. *Behavior Monographs*, 1912, **1**, No. 5.

von Békésy, G. *Experiments in hearing*. New York: McGraw-Hill, 1960.

Voronin, L. G., and Sokolov, E. N. Cortical mechanisms of the orienting reflex and its relation to the conditioned reflex. *Electroencephalography and Clinical Neurophysiology*, 1960, No. 13(suppl.), 335–344.

Vurpillot, E. Détails caractéristiques et reconnaissance de formes familières. *Psychologie Française*, 1962, **7**, 147–155.

Vurpillot, E. Perception et representation dans la constance de la forme. *Année Psychologique*, 1964, **64**, 61–82.

Vurpillot, E. The development of scanning strategies and their relationship to visual differentiation. *Journal of Experimental Child Psychology*, 1968, **6**, 632–650.

Vulpillot, E., and Brault, H. Etude expérimentale sur la formation des schèmes empiriques. *Année Psychologique*, 1959, **59**, 381–394.

Vygotsky, L. S. *Thought and speech*. Cambridge, Mass: M.I.T. Press, 1962.

Wagner, A. R. The role of reinforcement and nonreinforcement in an "apparent frustration effect." *Journal of Experimental Psychology*, 1959, **57**, 130–136.

Wagner, A. R., Logan, F. A., Haberlandt, K., and Price, T. Stimulus selection in animal discrimination learning. *Journal of Experimental Psychology*, 1968, **76**, 171–180.

Wahler, R. G. Infant social attachments: A reinforcement theory interpretation and investigation. *Child Development*, 1967, **4**, 1079–1088.

Wahler, R. G., Winkel, G. H., Peterson, R. F., and Morrison, D. C. Mothers as behavior therapists for their own children. *Behaviour Research and Therapy*, 1965, **3**, 113–124.

Wait, W. T. *The science of human behavior*. New York: Ronald Press, 1938.

Wales, R. J., and Marshall, J. C. The organization of linguistic performance. In J. Lyons and R. J. Wales (Eds.), *Psycholinguistics papers*. Edinburgh: Edinburgh University Press, 1966. Pp. 29–95.

Walk, R. D. Monocular compared to binocular depth perception in human infants. *Science*, 1968, **162**, 473–475.

Walk, R. D., and Gibson, E. J. A comparative and analytical study of visual depth perception. *Psychological Monographs*, 1961, **75** (15, Whole No. 519).

Wallach, L., Wall, J., and Anderson, L. Number conservation: The roles of reversibility, addition, subtraction, and misleading perceptual clues. *Child Development*, 1967, **38**, 425–442.

Walters, R. H., and Karal, P. Social deprivation and verbal behavior. *Journal of Personality*, 1960, **28**, 89–107.

Walters, R. H., and Parke, R. D. Emotional arousal, isolation and discrimination learning in children. *Journal of Experimental Child Psychology*, 1964, **1**, 163–173.

Walters, R. H., and Ray, E. Anxiety, social isolation, and reinforcer effectiveness. *Journal of Personality*, 1960, **28**, 358–367.

Wapner, S., and Cirillo, L. Imitation of a model's hand movements: Age changes in transposition of left-right relations. *Child Development*, 1968, **39**, 887–894.

Wapner, S., and Werner, H. *Perceptual development: An investigation within the framework of sensory-tonic field theory*. Worcester, Mass.: Clark University Press, 1957.

Warburton, F. W. Reply to "Measured intelligence is largely an acquired characteristic." *British Journal of Statistical Psychology*, 1959, **12**, 291–292.

Ware, R., and Terrell, G. Effects of delayed reinforcement on associative and incentive factors. *Child Development*, 1961, **32**, 789–793.

Warner, W. L., Havighurst, R. J., and Loeb, M. B. *Who shall be educated?* New York: Harper, 1946.

Warren, A. B., and Brown, R. H. Conditioned operant response phenomena in children. *Journal of General Psychology*, 1943, **38**, 181–207.

Warren, J. M. Stimulus perseveration in discrimination learning by cats. *Journal of Comparative and Physiological Psychology*, 1959, **52**, 99–101.

Warren, J. M. The comparative psychology of learning. *Annual Review of Psychology*, 1965, **16**, 95–118.

Warren, J. M., and Baron, A. The formation of learning sets by cats. *Journal of Comparative and Physiological Psychology*, 1956, **49**, 227–231.

Warren, J. M., and Kimball, H. Transfer relations in discrimination learning by cats. *Journal of Comparative and Physiological Psychology*, 1959, **52**, 336–338.

Washburn, M. F. *The animal mind.* (3rd ed.) New York: Macmillan, 1926.

Washburn, R. W. A study of the smiling and laughing of infants in the first year of life. *Genetic Psychology Monographs*, 1929, **6**, 397–537.

Watson, J. B. Psychology as the behaviorist views it. *Psychological Review*, 1913, **20**, 158–177.

Watson, J. B. *Psychology from the standpoint of a behaviorist.* Philadelphia: Lippincott, 1919.

Watson, J. B. *Behaviorism.* New York: Norton, 1924. (a)

Watson, J. B. *Psychology from the standpoint of a behaviorist.* (2nd ed.) Philadelphia: Lippincott, 1924. (b)

Watson, J. B. *Psychology from the standpoint of a behaviorist.* (3rd ed.) Philadelphia: Lippincott, 1929.

Watson, J. B., and Rayner, R. Conditioned emotional reactions. *Journal of Experimental Psychology*, 1920, **3**, 1–14.

Watson, J. S. Evidence of discriminative operant learning within thirty seconds by infants 7 to 26 weeks of age. Paper presented at the meeting of the Society for Research in Child Development, Minneapolis, March 1965.

Watson, J. S. The development and generalization of "contingency awareness" in early infancy: Some hypotheses. *Merrill-Palmer Quarterly*, 1966, **12**, 123–136.

Watson, P., and Ryan, T. J. Duration of the frustration effect in children. *Journal of Experimental Child Psychology*, 1966, **4**, 242–247.

Webster's new collegiate dictionary. Springfield, Mass.: Merriam, 1953.

Wechsler, D. *The measurement of adult intelligence.* (3rd ed.) Baltimore: Williams & Wilkins, 1944.

Wechsler, D. *Wechsler intelligence scale for children.* New York: Psychological Corporation, 1949.

Weiner, H. Some effects of response cost upon human operant behavior. *Journal of the Experimental Analysis of Behavior*, 1962, **5**, 201–208.

Weinrich, W. W., Cahoon, D. D., Ambrose, G., and Laplace, R. Secondary stimulus control of a "new" operant incompatible with "running to the food magazine." *Psychonomic Science*, 1966, **5**, 189–190.

Weinstock, S. Acquisition and extinction of a partially reinforced running response at a 24-hr. intertrial interval. *Journal of Experimental Psychology*, 1958, **56**, 151–158.

Weir, M. W. Children's behavior in probabilistic tasks. In W. W. Hartup and N. L. Smothergill (Eds.), *The young child: Reviews of research.* Washington, D.C.: National Association for the Education of Young Children, 1967. Pp. 136–154.

Weir, R. H. *Language in the crib*. The Hague: Mouton, 1962.

Weir, R. H. Some questions on the child's learning of phonology. In F. Smith and G. A. Miller (Eds.), *The genesis of language: A psycholinguistic approach*. Cambridge, Mass.: M.I.T. Press, 1966. Pp. 153–168.

Weisberg, P. Social and nonsocial conditioning of infant vocalizations. *Child Development*, 1963, **34**, 377–388.

Weisberg, P. Operant procedures for establishment of stimulus control in two-year-old infants. Unpublished manuscript, Brown University, 1968.

Weisberg, P., and Fink, E. Fixed ratio and extinction performance of infants in the second year of life. *Journal of the Experimental Analysis of Behavior*, 1966, **9**, 105–109.

Weisberg, P., and Simmons, M. W. A modified WGTA for infants in their second year of life. *Journal of Psychology*, 1966, **63**, 99–104.

Weisberg, P., and Tragakis, C. J. Analysis of DRL behavior in young children. *Psychological Reports*, 1967, **21**, 709–715.

Weitzman, E. D., Fishbein, W., and Graziani, L. Auditory evoked responses obtained from the scalp electroencephalogram of the full-term human neonate during sleep. *Pediatrics*, 1965, **35**, 458–462.

Welch, L. The development of discrimination of form and area. *Journal of Psychology*, 1939, **7**, 37–54. (a)

Welch, L. The development of size discrimination between the ages of 12 and 40 months. *Journal of Genetic Psychology*, 1939, **55**, 243–268. (b)

Wellman, B. L. I.Q. changes of preschool and non-preschool groups during the preschool years: A summary of the literature. *Journal of Psychology*, 1945, **20**, 347–368.

Wellman, B. L., and Pegram, E. L. Binet I.Q. changes of orphanage preschool children: A reanalysis. *Journal of Genetic Psychology*, 1944, **65**, 239–263.

Wenger, M. A. An investigation of conditioned responses in human infants. *University of Iowa Studies in Child Welfare*, 1936, **12**, No. 1.

Werner, H. *Comparative psychology of mental development*. New York: Harper, 1940. (Republished: New York, Science Editions, 1961.)

Werner, H. *Comparative psychology of mental development*. (Rev. ed.) Chicago: Follett, 1948.

Werner, H., and Kaplan, E. The acquisition of word meaning: A developmental study. *Monographs of the Society for Research in Child Development*, 1952, **15**, No. 51.

Wertheimer, M. Psychomotor coordination of auditory and visual space at birth. *Science*, 1961, **134**, 1832.

Wheeler, L. R. A comparative study of the intelligence of East Tennessee mountain children. *Journal of Educational Psychology*, 1942, **33**, 312–334.

White, B. L. The initial coordination of sensorimotor schemas in human infants: Piaget's ideas and the role of experience. In D. Elkind and J. H. Flavell (Eds.), *Studies in cognitive development: Essays in honor of Jean Piaget*. London and New York: Oxford University Press, 1969. Pp. 237–256.

White, M. A. (Ed.) Compensatory education and school psychology. *Journal of School Psychology*, 1966, **3**, 1–82.

White, S. H. Bibliography: Psychological studies of learning in children. Unpublished manuscript, Harvard University, 1962.

White, S. H. Age differences in reaction to stimulus variation. Paper presented at the Office of Naval Research Conference on Adaptation to Complex and Changing Environments, Boulder, Colorado, March 1964.

White, S. H. Evidence for a hierarchical arrangement of learning processes. In

L. P. Lipsitt and C. C. Spiker (Eds.), *Advances in child development and behavior.* Vol. 2. New York: Academic Press, 1965. Pp. 187–220.

White, S. H., and Plum, G. E. Eye movement photography during children's discrimination learning. *Journal of Experimental Child Psychology,* 1964, **1**, 327–338.

Wickens, D. D., and Meyer, D. R. *Psychology.* (Rev. ed.) New York: Holt, Rinehart & Winston, 1961.

Wickens, D. D., and Wickens, C. D. A study of conditioning in the neonate. *Journal of Experimental Psychology,* 1940, **26**, 94–102.

Wickens, D. D., and Wickens, C. D. Some factors related to pseudoconditioning. *Journal of Experimental Psychology,* 1942, **31**, 518–526.

Wicklund, D. A. Paired-associate learning in children as a function of free association strength and type of associative response hierarchy at four grade levels. Unpublished doctoral dissertation, University of Minnesota, 1964.

Wicklund, D. A., Palermo, D. S., and Jenkins, J. J. The effects of associative strength and response hierarchy on paired-associate learning. *Journal of Verbal Learning and Verbal Behavior,* 1964, **3**, 413–420.

Wicklund, D. A., Palermo, D. S., and Jenkins, J. J. Associative clustering in the recall of children as a function of verbal association strength. *Journal of Experimental Child Psychology,* 1965, **2**, 58–66.

Wiener, G., Rider, R. V., and Oppel, W. Some correlates of I.Q. change in children. *Child Development,* 1963, **34**, 61–67.

Willems, E. P. Sense of obligation to high school activities as related to school size and marginality of student. *Child Development,* 1967, **38**, 1247–1260.

Williams, J. P., and Kessen, W. Effect of hand-mouth contacting on neonatal movement. *Child Development,* 1961, **32**, 243–249.

Williams, R. A., and Campbell, B. A. Weight loss and quinine-milk ingestion as measures of "hunger" in infant and adult rats. *Journal of Comparative and Physiological Psychology,* 1961, **54**, 220–222.

Willmann, R. R. An experimental investigation of the creative process in music: The transposability of visual design stimuli to musical themes. *Psychological Monographs,* 1944, **57**(1, Whole No. 261).

Willner, A. E. Associative neighborhoods and developmental changes in the conceptual organization of recall. *Child Development,* 1967, **38**, 1127–1138.

Wilson, J. G., and Warkany, J. *Teratology: Principles and techniques.* Chicago: University of Chicago Press, 1965.

Wismer, B., and Lipsitt, L. P. Verbal mediation in paired-associate learning. *Journal of Experimental Psychology,* 1964, **68**, 441–448.

Witryol, S. L., Lowden, L. M., and Fagan, J. F. Incentive effects upon attention in children's discrimination learning. *Journal of Experimental Child Psychology,* 1967, **5**, 94–108.

Witte, K. L. Children's response speeds to familiarized stimuli. *Psychonomic Science,* 1967, **7**, 153–154.

Witte, K. L., and Cantor, G. N. Children's response speeds to the offset of novel and familiar stimuli. *Journal of Experimental Child Psychology,* 1967, **5**, 372–380.

Witty, P. E. (Ed.) The educationally retarded and disadvantaged. *Yearbook of the National Society for the Study of Education,* 1967, **66**, Part I.

Wohlwill, J. F. Developmental studies of perception. *Psychological Bulletin,* 1960, **57**, 249–288. (a)

Wohlwill, J. F. A study of the development of the number concept by scalogram analysis. *Journal of Genetic Psychology,* 1960, **97**, 345–377. (b)

Wohlwill, J. F. The perspective illusion: Perceived size and distance in fields varying in suggested depth, in children and adults. *Journal of Experimental Psychology*, 1962, **64**, 300–310.

Wohlwill, J. F. The development of "overconstancy" in space perception. In L. P. Lipsitt and C. C. Spiker (Eds.), *Advances in child development and behavior*. Vol. 1. New York: Academic Press, 1963. Pp. 266–312.

Wohlwill, J. F. Texture of the stimulus field and age as variables in the perception of relative distance in photographic slides. *Journal of Experimental Child Psychology*, 1965, **2**, 163–177.

Wohlwill, J. F. Responses to class inclusion questions for verbally and pictorially presented items. *Child Development*, 1968, **39**, 449–466.

Wohlwill, J. F., and Lowe, R. C. Experimental analysis of the conservation of number. *Child Development*, 1962, **33**, 153–167.

Wohlwill, J. F., and Wiener, M. Discrimination of form orientation in young children. *Child Development*, 1964, **35**, 1113–1127.

Wolf, M. M., Giles, D. K., and Hall, R. V. Experiments with token reinforcement in a remedial classroom. *Behaviour Research and Therapy*, 1968, **6**, 51–64.

Wolf, M. M., and Risley, T. Analysis and modification of deviant child behavior. Paper presented at the meeting of the American Psychological Association, Washington, D.C., September 1967.

Wolf, M. M., Risley, T., and Mees, H. Application of operant conditioning procedures to the behaviour problems of an autistic child. *Behaviour Research and Therapy*, 1964, **1**, 305–312.

Wolf, R. M. The identification and measurement of environmental process variables related to intelligence. Unpublished doctoral dissertation, University of Chicago, 1964.

Wolff, P. Observations on the early development of smiling. In B. M. Foss (Ed.), *Determinants of infant behaviour*. Vol. II. London: Methuen (New York: Wiley), 1963. Pp. 113–134.

Wolford, G., and Bower, G. H. Continuity theory revisited: Rejected for the wrong reasons? *Psychological Review*, 1969, **76**, 515–518.

Wolner, M., and Pyle, W. H. An experiment in individual training of pitch deficient children. *Journal of Educational Psychology*, 1933, **24**, 602–608.

Wolowitz, H. M. Attraction and aversion to power: A psychoanalytic conflict theory of homosexuality in male paranoids. *Journal of Abnormal Psychology*, 1965, **70**, 360–370.

Wolpe, J. *Psychotherapy by reciprocal inhibition*. Stanford, Calif.: Stanford University Press, 1958.

Wolpe, J., and Lazarus, A. A. *Behavior therapy techniques: A guide to the treatment of neuroses*. New York: Macmillan (Pergamon), 1966.

Wood, G. Mnemonic systems in recall. *Journal of Educational Psychology Monograph*, 1967, **58**(6, Part 2, Whole No. 645).

Woodrow, H., and Lowell, F. Children's association frequency tables. *Psychological Monographs*, 1916, **22**(5, Whole No. 97).

Woodworth, R. S. *Experimental psychology*. New York: Holt, 1938.

Woodworth, R. S., and Schlosberg, H. *Experimental psychology*. New York: Holt, 1954.

Worell, L., and Castaneda, A. Response to conflict as a function of response-defined anxiety. *Journal of Personality*, 1961, **29**, 10–29.

Wright, F. H., Naunton, R. F., Newell, F. W., Halstead, W. C., and Moore, R. Y. Unpublished report to the Children's Bureau, University of Chicago, 1968.

Wright, H. F., Barker, R. G., Koppe, W., Myerson, B., and Nall, J. Children at home in midwest. *Progressive Education*, 1951, **28**, 137–143.

Wright, J. C., and Smothergill, D. Observing behavior and children's discrimination learning under delayed reinforcement. *Journal of Experimental Child Psychology*, 1967, **5**, 430–440.

Wright, P. L., Kay, H., and Sime, M. E. The establishment of learning sets in rats. *Journal of Comparative and Physiological Psychology*, 1963, **56**, 200–203.

Wu, C. J., and Lipsitt, L. P. Effects of anxiety and stress on verbal mediation in children. *Psychonomic Science*, 1965, **2**, 13–14.

Wyckoff, L. B., Jr. The role of observing responses in discrimination learning. *Psychological Review*, 1952, **59**, 431–442.

Yamamoto, K. A further analysis of the role of creative thinking in high school achievement. *Journal of Psychology*, 1964, **58**, 277–283. (a)

Yamamoto, K. Role of creative thinking and intelligence in high school achievement. *Psychological Reports*, 1964, **14**, 783–789. (b)

Yamamoto, K. Threshold of intelligence in academic achievement of highly creative students. *Journal of Experimental Education*, 1964, **32**, 401–405. (c)

Yamamoto, K. Multiple achievement battery and repeated measurement: A postscript to three studies of creative thinking. *Psychological Reports*, 1965, **16**, 367–375.

Yamamoto, K., and Chimbidis, M. F. Achievement, intelligence and creative thinking in fifth grade. *Merrill-Palmer Quarterly*, 1966, **12**, 233–241.

Young, F. A. Classical conditioning of autonomic functions. In W. F. Prokasy (Ed.), *Classical conditioning: A symposium*. New York: Appleton-Century-Crofts, 1965. Pp. 358–377.

Youniss, J. Concept transfer as a function of shifts, age, and deafness. *Child Development*, 1964, **35**, 695–700.

Youniss, J., and Furth, H. G. Reaction to a placebo: The mediational deficiency hypothesis. *Psychological Bulletin*, 1963, **60**, 499–502.

Youniss, J., and Furth, H. G. Reversal learning in children as a function of overtraining and delayed transfer. *Journal of Comparative and Physiological Psychology*, 1964, **57**, 155–157. (a)

Youniss, J., and Furth, H. G. Reversal performance in children as a function of overtraining and response conditions. *Journal of Experimental Child Psychology*, 1964, **1**, 182–188. (b)

Zaporozhets, A. V. The development of voluntary movements. (Translated in the U.S.S.R. from *Voprosy Psikhologii*, 1955, **1**, 42–49.) In B. Simon (Ed.), *Psychology in the Soviet Union*. Stanford, Calif.: Stanford University Press, 1957. Pp. 108–114.

Zaporozhets, A. V. The origin and development of the conscious control of movements in man. In N. O'Connor (Ed.), *Recent Soviet psychology*. New York: Macmillan (Pergamon), 1961. Pp. 273–289.

Zaporozhets, A. V. The development of perception in the preschool child. In P. H. Mussen (Ed.), European research in cognitive development. *Monographs of the Society for Research in Child Development*, 1965, **30**(2, Whole No. 100). Pp. 82–101.

Zeaman, D., and House, B. J. The role of attention in retardate discrimination learning. In N. R. Ellis (Ed.), *Handbook of mental deficiency*. New York: McGraw-Hill, 1963. Pp. 159–223.

Zeaman, D., and House, B. J. The relation of I.Q. and learning. In R. M. Gagne

(Ed.), *Learning and individual differences*. Columbus, Ohio: Merrill, 1967. Pp. 192–212.

Zeaman, D., House, B. J., and Orlando, R. Use of special training conditions in visual discrimination learning with imbeciles. *American Journal of Mental Deficiency*, 1958, **63**, 453–459.

Zeigler, H. P. Learning-set formation in pigeons. *Journal of Comparative and Physiological Psychology*, 1961, **54**, 252–254.

Zeiler, M. D. The ratio theory of intermediate size discrimination. *Psychological Review*, 1963, **70**, 516–533.

Zeiler, M. D. Stimulus definition and choice. In L. P. Lipsitt and C. C. Spiker (Eds.), *Advances in child development and behavior*. Vol. 3. New York: Academic Press, 1967. Pp. 125–156.

Zetterström, B. The ERG in children during the first year of life. *Acta Ophthalmologica*, 1951, **29**, 295.

Zetterström, B. The electroretinogram in prematurely (born) children. *Acta Ophthalmologica*, 1952, **30**, 405–408.

Zetterström, B. Flicker electroretinography in newborn infants. *Acta Ophthalmologica*, 1955, **33**, 157–166.

Zigler, E. Metatheoretical issues in developmental psychology. In M. H. Marx (Ed.), *Theories in contemporary psychology*. New York: Macmillan, 1963. Pp. 341–369.

Zigler, E. Motivational determinants in the performance of retarded children. *American Journal of Orthopsychiatry*, 1966, **36**, 848–856.

Zimiles, H. The development of conservation and differentiation of number. *Monographs of the Society for Research in Child Development*, 1966, **31**, No. 6.

Zimmerman, D. W. A conceptual approach to some problems in mental retardation. *Psychological Record*, 1965, **15**, 175–183.

Zimmerman, E. H., and Zimmerman, J. The alteration of behavior in a special classroom situation. *Journal of the Experimental Analysis of Behavior*, 1962, **5**, 59–60.

Zimmerman, R. R., and Torrey, C. C. Ontogeny of learning. In A. M. Schrier, H. F. Harlow, and F. Stollnitz (Eds.), *Behavior of nonhuman primates: Modern research trends*. Vol. 2. New York: Academic Press, 1965. Pp. 405–447.

Zusne, L., and Michels, K. M. Nonrepresentational shapes and eye movements. *Perceptual and Motor Skills*, 1964, **18**, 11–20.

Author Index

Numbers in italics refer to the pages on which the complete references are listed.

A

Abrams, A. L., 640, *673*
Abravanel, E., 393, *673*
Adams, G., 359, *681*
Adamson, K., 56, *673*
Adelson, J., 580, 582, 609, 614, *691*
Adrian, E. D., 38, *673*
Ainsworth, M. D. S., 30, 420, *673*
Ainsworth, M. H., 580, *679*
Aiu, P., 40, 44, *689*
Akert, K., 642, *673*
Alampay, D. A., 264, 265, *683*
Albright, J. B., 432, *673*
Albright, R. W., 432, *673*
Alexander, P., 9, *673*
Allen, D. V., 199, 217, *696*
Allen, K. E., 668, *702*
Allen, L., 529, 535, 537, 538, *705*
Allport, F. H., 406, *673*
Allport, G., 406, 407, 409, *673*
Almy, M., 489, *673*
Alsop, A. A., 358, *673*
Altucher, N., 588, 597, 606, *726*
Ambrose, G., 321, *753*
Ambrose, J. A., 70, 74, 83, 418, 419, *673*, *718*
Ames, E. W., 39, 43, *673*, *714*
Ames, L. B., 365, *673*
Amsel, A., 330, 332, 335, *674*
Anastasi, A., 403, 516, 524, 527, 547, 551, 558, *674*
Anderson, E. P., 634, *707*
Anderson, J. E., 537, *674*
Anderson, K. E., 565, *674*
Anderson, L., 502, *752*
Anderson, L. D., 536, *674*
Anderson, L. M., 503, *742*
Angelino, H., 554, *674*
Angell, J. R., 405, *674*
Anisfeld, M., 434, *674*
Antonova, T. G., 37, 39, 51, *682*
Applegate, J. R., 434, *674*
Appley, M. H., 49, 316, 350, 360, *688*
Archer, E. J., 199, 217, *674*

Arey, L. B., 47, *674*
Aristotle, 405, *674*
Armentrout, J., 185, 186, 352, *706*
Armington, J. C., 38, *674*, *676*
Armstrong, C. M., 532, 534, *674*, *688*
Arnold, W. J., 274, *714*
Arnoult, M. D., 41, *675*
Aronfreed, J., 602, *674*
Asch, S. E., 216, 582, *675*
Asher, E. J., 549, *675*
Atkinson, J. W., 354, *721*
Atkinson, R. C., 218, *675*
Attneave, F., 41, *675*
Auld, R. M., 633, *725*
Ault, M. H., 28, *679*
Avery, M. E., 58, *675*
Axline, V. M., 653, *675*

B

Babb, H., 308, *675*
Bach, E., 438, 466, *675*
Bacon, M. K., 581, *676*
Bacon, W. E., 321, *675*
Baer, D. M., 4, 75, 84, 108, 120, 134, 135, 139, 354, 401, 451, 452, 547, 647, 656, 657, 658, 659, 660, 662, 667, 668, 669, 671, *675*, *679*, *697*, *700*, *702*, *738*, *741*
Bailey, L. L., 554, *723*
Bailyn, L., 615, *675*
Bakan, P., 280, *675*
Baker, C. T., 529, 535, 537, 538, 540, 542, 543, *676*, *710*, *744*
Baker, K. E., 228, *696*
Baker, R. A., 295, *676*
Baldwin, A. L., 541, *676*
Baldwin, K. C., 564, *676*
Bandura, A., 345, 347, 459, 598, 610, *676*
Banks, E. M., 73, *696*
Banks, H. P., 185, *732*
Barker, R. G., 20, 26, *676*, *757*
Barkley, M. J., 562, *740*
Barlow, J., 434, *674*
Barnet, A. B., 38, 48, *676*

Barnett, C. D., 269, *676*
Barocas, R., 484, *692*
Baron, A., 274, *753*
Barry, H., III, 581, *676*
Bartels, B., 423, *717*
Bartlett, N. R., 38, *700*
Bartlett, S. C., 152, *706*
Bartoshuk, A. K., 48, 49, 51, 52, 359, *676*
Battig, W. F., 250, *676*
Bayley, N., 529, 530, 532, 533, 534, 536, 537, 538, 541, 543, 548, 551, 578, *676, 677, 685, 710, 735*
Beach, D. R., 232, 258, 261, *695*
Beach, F. A., 314, *677*
Beach, H. D., 549, *684*
Beach, S., 558, *720*
Beard, R. M., 506, *677*
Bechtoldt, H. P., 2, 523, *677*
Bee, H. L., 380, *721*
Beilin, H., 492, *677*
Beintema, D., 54, *733*
Bekhterev, V. M., 86, *677*
Bell, R. Q., 54, 55, *677*
Bell, S. M., 30, 420, *673*
Bellugi, U., 439, 443, 444, 446, 447, 448, 453, 459, 460, *677, 683, 695, 714*
Belmont, J. M., 218, *677*
Benda, C. E., 563, *677*
Benjamin, R. M., 642, *677*
Bennett, H. L., 611, *720*
Bensberg, G. J., Jr., 270, *677*
Berger, S. M., 344, 345, *677, 717*
Bergmann, G., 4, 7, *678*
Berkeley, G., 384, *678*
Berko, J., 450, 453, 455, 463, *678, 683*
Berkowitz, L., 582, *678*
Berkson, G., 256, *678*
Berlyne, D. E., 107, 280, 281, 285, 287, 313, 339, 355, 356, 357, 358, 359, 360, 361, 485, 581, *678*
Berman, P. W., 180, 182, *700*
Bernbach, H. A., 218, *675*
Bernstein, B., 504, *678*
Bernstein, L., 383, *697*
Berry, J. W., 582, *678*
Best, C. H., 38, 48, 58, 59, *678*
Bethon, G., 484, 499, *699*
Bever, T. J., 501, 502, *724*
Bexton, W. A., 359, *678*
Beyrl, F., 384, 385, *678*
Biersdorf, W. R., 38, *674*
Bijou, S. W., 4, 75, 84, 103, 108, 116, 120, 122, 124, 126, 127, 128, 129, 131, 137, 138, 401, 547, 564, 580, 665, *678, 679, 728*

Biller, H. B., 608, *679*
Bilous, C. B., 611, *720*
Bindra, D., 321, 325, 337, *675, 379*
Binet, A., 21, *679*
Birch, D., 261, 465, *679*
Birch, H. G., 52, 54, 109, 639, *679, 751*
Birge, J. S., 226, 227, *679*
Birnbrauer, J. S., 657, 665, *679*
Birns, B., 359, *679*
Bisett, B. M., 190, 191, *679*
Bitterman, M. E., 68, 122, 148, 168, 242, *679, 680, 698, 699, 747*
Black, M., 10, 586, *680*
Bland, J. H., 634, *680*
Blank, M., 247, 250, 305, 359, 562, *679, 680, 695*
Blase, B., 638, *744*
Blatt, B., 562, 565, *680*
Blau, L. R., 114, *680*
Blau, T. H., 114, *680*
Block, J., 605, *687*
Bloom, B. S., 530, 531, 538, 561, *680*
Bloomfield, L., 462, *680*
Blosser, D., 300, *749*
Blum, A., 152, 277, *723*
Blum, E. R., 597, *680*
Blum, G. S., 455, *680*
Blum, J. S., 300, *680*
Blum, R. A., 300, *680*
Boat, B. M., 252, 256, 261, *680*
Bogartz, R. S., 286, *680*
Bond, E. A., 527, *680*
Boneau, C. A., 84, 159, *680, 705*
Borstelmann, L. J., 608, *679*
Bosack, T. N., 55, 71, 74, 75, 78, 80, 83, *718*
Bourne, L. E., Jr., 300, 308, *701*
Bousfield, W. A., 218, *680*
Bower, G. H., 304, *756*
Bower, T. G. R., 45, 116, 169, 170, 171, 172, *680, 681*
Bowerman, C. E., 596, 605, *681*
Bowlby, J., 419, *681*
Brackbill, Y., 39, 70, 71, 81, 89, 91, 92, 93, 94, 103, 115, 122, 152, 159, 187, 188, 189, 359, 419, *681, 718*
Bradbury, B., 451, *720*
Braden, I., 359, *710*
Bradway, K. P., 530, 531, 538, 564, *681*
Braine, L. G., 192, *681*
Braine, M. D. S., 425, 437, 439, 441, 442, *460*, 461, 465, 492, 513, *681, 682*
Braley, L. S., 308, *682*
Bransky, M. L., 184, *703*
Brault, H., 377, 378, *752*
Bravos, A., 188, 189, *681*

Brawley, E. R., 656, 657, 659, 660, *702*
Breese, F. H., 541, *676*
Brelsford, J., 300, *749*
Bridger, W. H., 49, 247, 250, 359, *679, 680, 682*
Bridges, K. M. B., 412, *682*
Brison, D. W., 505, *682*
Brodbeck, A. J., 114, *682, 689*
Bronshtein, A. I., 37, 39, 51, 78, *682*
Bronson, W. C., 597, *682*
Brooks, L. R., 204, 206, *682*
Brooks, V., 377, *705*
Brossard, L. M., 419, *682*
Brown, B., 560, *690*
Brown, J., 50, 52, *712*
Brown, J. L., 37, 38, *682, 700*
Brown, J. S., 311, 315, 340, 353, *682*
Brown, P. A., 330, *702*
Brown, R. H., 103, 116, 121, 123, 124, 136, *753*
Brown, R. W., 428, 437, 439, 441, 443, 446, 447, 448, 452, 453, 459, 460, 463, *682, 683, 695*
Bruce, M., 558, *683*
Bruck, K., 56, *683*
Bruck, M., 56, *683*
Bruner, J. S., 210, 496, 501, *683*
Bruning, J. L., 140, 148, *683, 737*
Brunswik, E., 364, *683*
Bryne, D., 594, *684*
Budoff, M., 200, *683*
Buell, J. S., 668, *702*
Bugelski, B. R., 200, 201, 205, 206, 211, 264, 265, 268, 318, 406, *683*
Bulgarella, R., 205, *723*
Burchinal, L. G., 548, *696*
Burke, H. R., 525, *684*
Burks, B. S., 544, *684*
Burling, R., 432, 433, 434, *684*
Burnett, A., 515, 549, *684*
Burnstein, E., 588, 597, 606, *726*
Buros, O. K., 524, *684*
Burstein, K. R., 159, *705*
Burt, C., 510, 519, 544, 546, 553, *684*
Butler, B., 330, *740*
Butler, R. A., 359, *684*
Butterfield, E. C., 218, 277, *677, 684*
Butterfield, G., 277, *684*
Bykov, V. D., 73, *684*
Bystroletova, G. N., 70, *684*

C

Cahoon, D. D., 321, *753*
Cakmak, M. B., 300, *684*

Caldwell, B. M., 37, 413, 421, *700*
Calvin, A. D., 153, 184, 185, 260, *684, 685, 732*
Cameron, J., 536, *685*
Cameron, N., 210, 406, *685*
Campbell, B. A., 66, 67, 94, *685, 755*
Campbell, B. J., 125, 126, 127, 129, *719*
Campbell, H., 423, *717*
Campbell, J. D., 611, *685*
Campbell, P. L., 634, *696*
Campione, J., 298, 301, 302, *685*
Canestrini, S., 57, *685*
Cannizzo, S. R., 261, *712*
Cannon, W. B., 411, *685*
Cantor, G. N., 104, 217, 230, 233, 256, 263, 269 285, 286, *676, 678, 685, 755*
Cantor, J. H., 104, 233, 235, 285
Capaldi, E. J., 300, *685*
Carlson, V. R., 386, *685, 686*
Carment, O. W., 122, *686*
Carmichael, L., 3, 36, *686*
Caron, R. F., 104, 105, 116, 119, 120, 167, 169, *686*
Carroll, J. B., 426, *686*
Carroll, W. R., 216, *686*
Carter, C. H., 629, *686*
Casler, L., 548, *686*
Casper, M., 37, *691*
Cassell, R. L., 253, *686*
Castaneda, A., 198, 203, 338, 339, 340, 349, 350, 351, 527, *686, 720, 756*
Catalano, F. L., 536, *686*
Cattell, A. K. S., 554, *686*
Cattell, J. McK., 524, *686*
Cattell, P., 524, *686*
Cattell, R. B., 554, *686*
Caul, W. F., 300, *686*
Cautela, J. R., 522, *686*
Cavanaugh, M. C., 536, *687*
Cazden, C. B., 439, 446, 458, 459, 460, *683, 687*
Chang, J., 605, *687*
Chao, Y. R., 432, 434, *687*
Chapanis, A., 549, *687*
Charles, D. C., 565, *687*
Charlesworth, R., 588, 610, 611, *687, 702*
Charlesworth, W. R., 481, *687*
Chase, H. H., 51, *712*
Chazan, M., 564, *687*
Chen, H. P., 426, 427, *687, 707*
Child, I. L., 581, *676*
Chiles, W. D., 344, *687*
Chimbidis, M. F., 568, *757*
Chinsky, J. M., 232, 258, 261, *695*
Chittenden, E., 489, 503, *673*

Chomsky, N., 425, 429, 434, **438**, 443, **462**, 466, 473, *687*
Chun, B. J., 48, *689*
Church, R. M., 85, 86, 416, *687*
Churchill, E. M., 489, *687*
Cicala, G. A., 94, *685*
Cirillo, L., 395, 496, *687, 752*
Clancy, J. J., 260, *685*
Claparède, E., 365, 498, *687, 688*
Clark, C. A., 523, *688*
Clark, D. F., 645, *688*
Clark, R. A., 354, *721*
Clausen, J., 564, *688*
Clayton, K. N., 300, *688*
Clelland, D. L., 527, *688*
Clifford, L. T., 153, 260, *684*
Clifton, C., Jr., 252, 256, 261, *680, 688*
Clifton, R. K., 47, 49, 51, 414, *700*
Clore, G. L., Jr., 594, *684*
Cloward, R. A., 574, 579, 608, *688*
Coates, B., 588, 596, 610, *702*
Cofer, C. N., 49, 316, 350, 360, *688*
Cogan, D. C., 39, 40, *699*
Cohen, B. H., 218, *680*
Cohen, I., 536, *687*
Cohen, L. B., 161, 192, *708*
Cohen, L. D., 355, *688*
Cohen, M., 428, *688*
Cole, M., 204, *688*
Coleman, J. S., 609, 612, *688, 721*
Conger, J. J., 315, *726*
Conrad, H. S., 531, *710*
Converse, H. D., 566, *706*
Conway, A. H., 553, *688*
Cook, W. M., 152, *688*
Cooley, J. A., 104, 115, 116, 119, *735*
Cooper, J. C., Jr., 217, *696*
Cooper, L., 37, *691*
Cornell, E. L., 532, *688*
Cornwell, A. C., 73, *688, 746*
Corsini, D. A., 261, *688*
Corsini, R. J., 532, *688*
Corte, E., 126, 127, *746*
Costa, J., 414, *711*
Costello, N. S., 54, *677*
Cottrell, N. B., 329, *688*
Coursin, D. B., 52, *692*
Cowan, P. A., 137, *688*
Cox, D. L., 205, *723*
Craft, M., 180, 182, *700*
Craig, G. J., 319, 320, *727*
Crandall, V. J., 543, *688*
Crane, N. L., 308, *688*
Cromwell, R. L., 564, *689*
Cronbach, L. J., 510, 537, *689*

Crosby, E., 619, *689*
Croskery, J., 146, *731*
Cross, H. A., 302, *689*
Crott, H. W., 519, *717*
Crowell, D. H., 48, 55, 359, *681, 689, 701*
Curry, C., 187, *689*
Cushna, B., 564, *744*

D

Daehler, M. W., 252, 256, *689*
Dailey, J. T., 565, *695, 741*
Dallenbach, K. M., 206, *689*
Dameron, L. E., *343, 700*
Damianopoulos, E. N., 74, *689*
D'Angelo, R. Y., 558, *674*
Dantzig, T., 487, *689*
Darwin, C., 418, *689*
Dave, R. H., 527, *689*
Davies, C., 513, *689*
Davis, A., 551, 553, 554, 561, *680, 689, 691*
Davis, C. M., 48, *689*
Davis, D. R., 541, *713*
Davis, H. V., 114, *689*
Davison, G. C., 646, *689*
Davitz, J. R., 595, *689*
Davson, H., 35, *689*
Dayton, G. O., Jr., 40, 44, *689*
Dean, R. F. A., 26, *696*
Dearborn, W. F., 521, 530, 531, 534, 535, 538, *689*
Décarie, T. G., 419, *682*
Deibler, G. E., 634, *696*
Dekaban, A., 628, 629, *689*
DeLucia, C. A., 57, 60, 104, 105, 112, 115, *690, 718, 743*
DeLucia, L. D., 415, *690*
Demerath, N. J., 559, *721*
Demos, G. D., 568, *699*
DeMyer, M. K., 664, *694*
Denisova, M. P., 55, 73, 80, 81, 82, 84, 167, *690*
Denis-Prinzhorn, M., 386, *690*
Dennis, W., 418, *690*
Deutsch, J. A., 298, 299, *750*
Deutsch, M., 560, *690*
DeVault, M. V., 353, *732*
Diack, H., 369, *690*
Dickerson, D. J., 298, 303, 304, *690*
Dickson, D., 387, 388, *716*
Dilley, M. G., 210, *690*
Dinneen, F. P., 466, *690*
Distler, L., 588, 597, *726*
Dittmer, D. G., 88, *700*
Di Vesta, F. J., 199, 252, 257, **462**, 464, *735*

Dockeray, F. C., 54, *690*
Dodd, C., 55, *717*
Dodwell, P. C., 489, 499, 506, *690*
Doidge, W. T., 604, *690*
Dollard, J., 29, 224, 227, *690, 725*
Dominguez, K., 103, *708*
Donaldson, T. E., 319, *691*
Doppelt, J., 551, *740*
Doris, J., 37, *691*
Douvan, E., 580, 582, 609, 614, *691*
Doyle, G. A., 104, 116, 120, 121, 360, *735*
Dreger, R. M., 521, 557, 560, *691*
Drever, J. A., 407, *691*
Duchnowski, A. J., 327, *728*
Duke, L., 527, *720*
Duncan, C. P., 185, 277, 299, *691, 707, 718*
Dunlap, K., 314, *691*
Dunphy, D., 536, *687*
Durkin, K., 187, 189, *749*
Durr, W. K., 566, *691*
Dworetzki, G., 365, 366, 367, *691*
Dyer, H. S., 522, *691*
Dysinger, D., 233, *691*

E

Easler, C. A., 73, *696*
Easterbrook, J. A., 190, *691*
Ebbinghaus, H., 195, *691*
Ebenholtz, S. M., 216, *675*
Eberhart, V. L., 454, *730*
Ebert, E., 530, 537, 538, *691*
Edwards, M. P., 568, *691*
Eells, K., 551, 553, 554, *689, 691*
Eimas, P. D., 299, 300, 301, 302, 306, 307, 308, *691, 692, 741*
Eisenberg, R. B., 52, *692*
Eisman, B. S., 257, 464, *692*
Elder, G. H., 596, 605, *681*
Elkind, D., 366, 367, 368, 369, 398, 403, 482, 484, 489, 490, 492, 493, 496, 506, *692*
Ellingson, R. J., 629, *692*
Ellis, N. R., *692*
Ellison, G. D., 337, *692*
Emerson, P. E., 580, *739*
Engel, M., 404, *744*
Engen, T., 59, 60, 61, 90, 94, *692, 693, 718*
Enos, F. A., 565, *693*
Entwisle, D. R., 198, 199, *693*
Erickson, M. T., 185, 186, 188, 354, *693*
Erikson, E. H., 583, *693*
Erlebacher, A. H., 197, *751*
Erlenmeyer-Kimling, L., 544, 545, *693*
Ernhardt, C. B., 180, 182, *700*

Ervin, S. M., 425, 428, **432**, 435, 437, 439, 440, 441, 449, 454, 463, *693, 725*
Escalona, S. K., 359, 536, *679, 693*
Eskin, R. M., 122, *698, 699*
Esper, E. A., 454, *693*
Esterson, S., 218, *680*
Estes, B. W., 190, *725*
Estes, R. E., 144, 319, *693*
Etsten, B. E., 105, *718*
Etzel, B. C., 103, 115, 120, 188, 417, *693*

F

Fagan, J. F., 188, 189, 329, *694, 755*
Fahel, L., 198, 203, *686*
Fant, C. G. N., 429, 430, *708*
Fantz, R. L., 40, 41, 44, *694*
Farber, I. E., 311, 340, *682*
Farina, A., 605, *694*
Fassett, K. K., 532, *688*
Faw, T. T., 327, *728*
Feallock, S. M., 386, *708*
Feather, N. T., 329, *694*
Fedderson, W. E., 148, *679*
Feldhausen, J. F., 527, *694*
Feldstone, C. S., 99, *694*
Feldsmen, A. N., 61, *715*
Ferguson, G. A., 514, 515, 547, 548, 549, *694*
Ferré, F., 10, 586, *694*
Ferster, C. B., 99, 102, 317, 664, *694*
Festinger, L., 594, *694*
Figurin, N. L., 55, 73, 80, 81, 82, 84, 167, *690*
Fillmore, E. A., 549, *743*
Fink, E., 103, 116, 120, 122, *754*
Fisch, R. I., 287, 405, *694, 722*
Fischer, L. K., 638, *702*
Fishbein, W., 49, *754*
Fisichelli, V. R., 414, *711*
Fiske, D. W., *694*
Fitzgerald, H. E., 70, 71, 93, 94, *681, 718*
Flamer, G. B., 217, 256, *694, 730*
Flanagan, J. C., 565, *695*
Flavell, J. H., 21, 232, 258, 261, 464, 484, 504, 512, *688, 695, 712*
Flesch, R., 369, *695*
Flescher, I., 568, *695*
Flory, C. D., 36, 530, 533, *695, 741*
Floud, J. E., 553, *695*
Fodor, J. A., 462, *695, 711*
Ford, L. H., Jr., 260, 266, 331, 339, *695, 735*
Forgays, D. G., 399, *695*
Fort, J. G., 319, 320, *695*
Foshee, J. G., 122, 138, *742*
Foss, B. M., 414, *699*
Foss, D. J., 257, *709*

Foster, G., 463, *693*
Foster, W. S., 205, *695*
Foulds, G. A., 531, *695*
Fowler, H., 359, *695*
Frail, C. M., 434, *674*
Frankie, G., 596, 606, *704*
Franklin, I. C., 492, *677*
Fraser, C., 437, 439, 441, 443, 453, *683, 695*
Frederickson, D. S., 633, *746*
Freeberg, N. E., 540, *695*
Freeman, F. N., 530, 533, 544, 546, *695, 727*
Freud, A., 653, *695*
Friedlander, B. Z., 104, 115, 119, 360, *695*
Fritz, B., 305, *695*
Fromm, E., 542, *696*
Frommer, F. D., 358, *678*
Fuller, J. B., 260, *685*
Fuller, J. L., 73, *688, 696*
Furth, H. G., 260, 299, 300, 302, 503, *696, 757*

G

Gabler, R., 560, *697*
Gaeth, J. H., 199, 217, *696*
Gagné, R. M., 228, *696*
Galanter, E., 205, 215, *725*
Gallagher, J., 204, 536, 567, *696*
Gardner, D. B., 548, *696*
Gardner, R. A., 13, 300, *696*
Gardner, W. I., 564, *696*
Garfunkel, F., 562, *680*
Garrett, H. E., 519, 559, *696*
Geber, M., 26, *696*
Gelber, H., 666, *696*
Gelber, S., 634, *696*
Gellermann, L. W., 103, 153, 155, 178, *696*
Gellis, S. S., 39, 40, *699*
Gelman, R., 298, 299, 501, 503, 505, *697, 750*
Gerjuoy, I. R., 219, *697*
Gesell, A., 22, 37, 530, *697*
Getzels, J. W., 567, 568, 569, *697*
Gewirtz, J. L., 103, 115, 116, 117, 120, 354, 417, 426, 587, 589, 601, *693, 697, 715, 735*
Ghent, L., 368, 381, 383, *697*
Gibby, R. G., 560, *697*
Gibson, E. J., 45, 47, 152, 157, 223, 228, 363, 369, 372, 373, 374, 386, 387, 391, *697, 698, 752*
Gibson, J. J., 44, 363, 372, 373, 374, 377, 386, 390, 391, *697, 698*
Gilbert, D. H., 325, 330, 331, *698*
Giles, D. K., 666, *756*
Gilliland, A. R., 558, *698*

Girardeau, F. L., 126, 127, 318, *746*
Gladis, M., 252, *698*
Gladwin, T., 517, 548, 564, 565, 629, *723, 739*
Glanzer, M., 215, *698*
Glazer, J. A., 588, 611, *702*
Glick, J., 204, 483, *688, 698*
Glidewell, J. C., 613, *698*
Glucksberg, S., 342, *698*
Go, E., 366, 367, *692*
Golann, S. E., 568, *698*
Gold, N., 342, *698*
Goldberg, I. D., 536, *687*
Goldberg, M. L., 567, *734*
Goldberg, S., 55, 423, *717*
Goldfarb, W., 548, *698*
Goldschmid, M. L., 506, 507, *698*
Goldstein, A. G., 376, *698*
Goldstein, K., 496, *698*
Golin, S. J., 216, *699*
Gollin, E. S., 3, 68, 377, 379, 402, *698*
Gollub, L. R., 665, *712*
Gomez, M. R., 639, *698*
Gonzalez, R. C., 122, *698, 699*
Goodenough, F. L., 512, 524, 553, 554, *699*
Goodnow, J., 484, 499, 500, *699*
Goodwin, J., 219, *699*
Goodwin, R. S., 48, *676*
Goodwin, W. R., 287, *699*
Gordon, A., 547, *699*
Gordon, E. W., 109, *751*
Gordon, H., 549, *699*
Gordon, M., 434, *674*
Gordon, T., 414, *699*
Gorman, J. J., 39, 40, *699*
Goss, A. E., 200, 216, 254, 257, *699*
Gough, P. B., 456, *699*
Goulet, L. R., 195, 221, 252, 350, *699*
Gowan, J. C., 568, *699*
Graham, C. H., 38, *700*
Graham, F. K., 37, 47, 49, 51, 54, 180, 182, 413, 414, 421, *700, 712*
Grant, D. A., 66, 67, 72, 88, *700*
Gray, M. L., 359, *681*
Gray, S. W., 562, *700*
Graziani, L., 49, *754*
Green, P. C., 73, 95, *700*
Greenberg, J. H., 438, *700*
Greene, M., 564, *744*
Greenfield, P. M., 184, 500, *700*
Griffiths, J. A., 261, *700*
Griffitt, W., 594, *684*
Grings, W. W., 343, *700*
Grobstein, R., 423, *714*
Groen, J. J., *700*
Grossman, H. J., 47, *735*

Gruenberg, E. M., 630, *700*

Grusec, J. E., 347, 588, 597, 598, 608, 610, *676, 700, 725*

Guess, D., 451, 452, 669, *700, 738*

Guilford, J. P., 517, 518, 519, 567, 568, 569, *700, 701*

Gullickson, G. R., 55, *701*

Gump, P. V., 612, *715*

Gunther, M., 413, *701*

Guttman, N., 156, *701*

Guy, D. E., 300, 308, *701*

Gvozdev, A. N., 439, *701*

H

Haan, N., 580, *701*

Haber, R. B., 407, 408, 409, 410, *701, 716*

Haber, R. N., 264, 265, 267, 407, 408, 409, 410, *701, 716*

Haberlandt, K., 237, 304, *752*

Hagen, E., 525, *719*

Hagen, J. W., 218, 261, *701, 721*

Haggard, E. A., 542, 553, *701*

Hagman, R. R., 345, 417, *701*

Haith, M. M., 37, 41, *701*

Hake, H. W., 41, *701*

Hall, G. F., 327, *728*

Hall, J. F., 198, *701*

Hall, J. R., 65, 86, 90, 316, 318, *701*

Hall, J. W., 204, 319, *701*

Hall, R. V., 662, *701*

Hall, V. C., 505, *713*

Hall, V. R., 666, *756*

Halle, M., 429, 430, 434, *687, 708*

Haller, M., 52, *701*

Halsey, A. H., 553, *695, 701*

Halstead, W. C., 637, *757*

Halverson, H. M., 316, *701*

Hamilton, V., 386, *701*

Hammack, J. T., 125, 126, 127, 129, *719*

Hammond, K. R., 510, *709*

Haner, C. F., 330, *702*

Hansen, D. N., 218, *675*

Harlow, H. F., 24, 53, 274, 276, 277, 313, 642, *673, 702*

Harlow, M. K., 24, *702*

Harms, R. T., 438, *675*

Harper, P. A., 638, *702*

Harris, D. B., 2, 3, 5, 9, 29, 554, *699, 702*

Harris, F. R., 656, 657, 659, 660 668, *702*

Harris, L., 360, *702*

Harris, M. B., 459, *676*

Harrison, R. H., 159, 181, 182, *709*

Hart, B. M., 656, 657, 659, 660, 668, *702*

Harter, S., 273, *702*

Hartman, L. D., 542, *696*

Hartmann, G. W., 250, *702*

Hartup, W. W., 588, 594, 596, 610, 611, *687, 702, 737*

Harvey, O. J., 575, *702*

Harway, N. I., 387, *703*

Harwood, F. W., 443, *703*

Hassan, I. N., 577, *703*

Hatton, H. M., 47, 49, 51, *700*

Haude, R. H., 360, *703*

Havighurst, R. J., 551, 553, 554, *689, 691, 753*

Hawkes, G. R., 548, *696*

Hayes, K. J., 18, 292, 294, 542, *703*

Hayhurst, H., 456, 458, *703*

Haynes, H., 44, *703*

Hayweiser, L. J., 178, *704*

Heal, L. W., 184, 300, *703*

Heard, W. G., 464, *746*

Hebb, D. O., 42, 403, 406, 411, 513, 514, 548, 581, *703*

Heber, R., 563, 564, 629, *703, 747*

Heckman, B., 200, *703*

Hegge, T. G., 565, *703*

Heid, N. L., 118, 181, *703*

Heidbreder, E. F., 184, 191, *703*

Heil, W. G., 521, *703*

Hein, A., 250, *703*

Held, R., 44, 250, *703*

Hemmendinger, L., 365, *703*

Hempel, C. G., 7, *704*

Hendrickson, L. N., 382, *704*

Henning, L. B., 178, *704*

Hermelin, B., 217, *704*

Hernández-Peón, R., 280, *704*

Heron, W., 359, *678*

Herrick, V. E., 551, 553, 554, *691, 704*

Herrnstein, R. J., 275, *704*

Hershenson, M., 41, 44, *704, 713*

Herzberg, F., 544, *704*

Hess, R., 561, *680*

Hetherington, E. M., 188, 189, 596, 606, *704, 737*

Hicks, J. A., 180, *704*

Hicks, L. H., 275, 382, *704, 706*

Higgins, K. E., 381, *736*

Hilden, A. H., 530, 535, *704*

Hilgard, E. R., 65, 97, 277, *704, 705*

Hill, J. H., 460, *728*

Hill, K., 527, *739*

Hill, K. T., 349, 354, *705*

Hill, S. D., 153, 173, 182, 273, *705*

Hinde, R. A., 27, *705*

Hobika, J. Y., 105, *718*

Hobson, J. R., 544, *705*

Hochberg, J., 377, *705*

Hockman, C. H., 185, 188, 189, *705*
Hodges, W. L., 562, 614, *705, 745*
Hoffman, M. L., 597, 610, *705*
Hofstaetter, P. R., 537, *705*
Hohle, R. H., 35, 62, *744*
Holgate, V., 308, *748*
Hollingworth, L. S., 566, *705*
Holmes, F. B., 345, 417, *705, 709*
Holt, E. B., 314, *705*
Holt, R. R., 206, 405, *705*
Holton, R. B., 185, 330, *705, 746*
Holtzman, W. H., 604, *690*
Holzinger, K. J., 544, 546, *727*
Honig, W. K., 159, *705*
Honzik, M. P., 529, 535, 537, 538, 540, 541, 544, *705*
Hood, B. H., 506, *706*
Hooper, F. H., 505, *742*
Horn, A., 521, *703*
Horn, G. L., 318, *746*
Horowitz, F. D., 185, 186, 187, 352, 421, *706*
Horstein, G. P. M., 36, 38, *706*
Horton, D. L., 255, *706*
Houlahan, F. J., 253, *706*
House, B. J., 193, 237, 252, 277, 280, 287, 288, *289, 292, 293, 294,* 297, 298, 299, 304, 305, 308, 310, 355, *706, 757, 758*
Hoving, K. L., 190, *747*
Hovland, C. I., 205, *715*
Hoyt, J. M., 594, 595, 610, *721*
Hsia, Y., 38, *700*
Hudson, W., 390, *706*
Huey, E. B., 211, 405, *706*
Hughes, H., 566, *706*
Hull, C. L., 311, 315, 316, 470, 496, *706*
Humphrey, T., 619, *689*
Hunt, J. McV., 24, 403, 512, 513, 548, *706*
Hunter, I. M. L., 180, 205, 206, 406, *706*
Hunter, W. S., 25, 152, *706*
Hunton, V. D., 382, *706*
Hurley, J. R., 541, *707*
Hurlock, E. B., 8, *707*
Hutt, C., 28, *707*
Huttenlocher, J., 381, 455, *707*
Hyman, L., 298, 301, 302, *685*

I

Illingworth, R. S., 536, *707*
Inhelder, B., 483, 489, 491, 492, 496, 497, 505, 506, *707, 732*
Irion, A. L., 268, *707*
Irwin, O. C., 37, 359, 426, 427, *687, 707*
Isaacs, I. D., 299, *707*

Iscoe, I., 217, 558, *707, 740*
Isselbacher, K. J., 634, *707*

J

Jackson, D., 662, *701*
Jackson, P. W., 567, 568, 569, *697*
Jackson, T. A., 103, 185, *707, 708*
Jacobs, R. A., 466, *708*
Jacobson, L., 541, *737*
Jakobson, R., 429, 430, *708*
James, W., 279, 314, *708*
Janos, O., 91, 94, 159, *708*
Jarrett, R. F., 203, *708*
Jarvik, L. F., 544, 545, *693*
Jarvik, M. E., 278, *708*
Jastak, J., 565, *708*
Jeffrey, W. E., 105, 161, 185, 192, 228, 229, 260, 281, 307, 309, 485, *708, 747*
Jenkin A. M., 205, *708*
Jenkin, N., 386, *708*
Jenkins, H. M., 156, 159, 170, 181, 182, 318, *709*
Jenkins, J. J., 198, 199, 203, 204, 217, 219, 220, 254, 257, 465, 470, *709, 730, 755*
Jensen, A. R., 211, 559, 562, *709*
Jensen, D. D., 70, *709*
Jensen, G. D., 337, *709*
Jensen, K., 54, 56, 57, *709*
Jerome, E. A., 185, *707, 708*
Jersild, A. T., 345, *709*
Jespersen, J. O. H., 428, *709*
Jessor, R., 510, *709*
Johnson, B. M., 141, 149, *709, 736*
Johnson, D. M., 268, 308, *682, 709*
Johnson, G. O., 564, 565, *709*
Johnson, J. I., Jr., 274, *710, 724*
Johnson, M. M., 608, *710*
Jones, A., 359, *710*
Jones, H. E., 50, 86, 522, 531, 553, 579, *710, 712*
Jones, J. E., 84, *710*
Jones, M. C., 346, 578, 579, 645, *710, 726*
Jones, M. H., 40, 44, *689*
Jones, R. B., 330, *740*
Jordan, A. M., 549, 564, *710*
Jouvet, M., 280, *704*

K

Kagan, J., 21, 260, 315, 345, 423, 424, 540, 542, 543, *710, 726*
Kalckar, H. M., 634, *707*
Kalhorn, J., 541, *676*
Kalish, H. I., 156, *701*

Kamenetskaya, A. G., 37, 39, 51, *682*
Kamin, L. J., 81, *710*
Kanner, L., 653, *710*
Kantor, J. R., 425, *710*
Kantor, M. B., 613, *698*
Kantrow, R. W., 82, 83, *711*
Kaplan, E., 462, *754*
Kappy, M. S., 152, 188, 189, *681*
Karal, P., 354, *752*
Karelitz, R., 414, *711*
Karelitz, S., 414, *711*
Karp, E., 55, *712*
Kasatkin, N. I., 39, 73, 81, 82, 83, 84, 94, 159, *711*
Kass, N., 122, 137, 138, 148, 319, 320, *711, 742*
Katkovsky, W., 543, *688*
Katona, G., 206, *711*
Katz, H., 222, 253, *714*
Katz, I., 560, *711*
Katz, J. J., 462, *711*
Kay, H., 274, *757*
Kaye, H., 37, 48, 49, 50, 51, 52, 54, 55, 57, 59, 60, 71, 74, 75, 77, 78, 79, 80, 82, 83, 90, 94, *693, 711, 712, 718*
Kean, J. M., 453, *712*
Keen, R. E., 51, *712*
Keeney, T. J., 261, *712*
Kelleher, R. T., 304, 665, *712*
Keller, E. D., 527, *712*
Kelley, W. N., 634, *740*
Kellogg, L. A., 24, *712*
Kellogg, W. N., 24, *712*
Kendler, H. H., 3, 192, 268, 287, 302, 304, 307, 359, 485, *712*
Kendler, T. S., 3, 192, 260, 268, 287, 302, 304, 307, 484, 485, *712*
Kennard, M., 642, *713*
Kennedy, R. J. R., 564, *713*
Kennedy, W. A., 189, 549, 551, 556, 557, 597, *680, 713, 749, 750*
Kent, N., 541, *713*
Keppel, G., 195, 200, 252, 253, *713*
Kern, W. H., 565, *713*
Kessen, W., 8, 11, 41, 42, 65, 204, 414, 484, 512, *686, 713, 738, 755*
Key, C. B., 549, *741*
Khokhitva, A., 81, 83, *711*
Kidd, E., 205, *683*
Kidder, J. D., 657, 665, *679*
Kimball, H., 274, *753*
Kimble, G. A., 65, 66, 86, 90, 93, 97, 268, 316, 318, 352, *713*
Kimmel, H. D., 67, 74, 84, *713*
Kingsley, P. R., 261, *701*
Kingsley, R. C., 505, *713*

Kipnis, D., 355, *688*
Kirk, S. A., 562, 563, *713*
Kirkendall, L. A., 590, *713*
Kirwin, P. M., 147, *731*
Kitchell, R. L., 57, *714*
Kjeldergaard, P. M., 250, 255, *706, 714*
Klaus, R. A., 562, *700*
Klausmeier, H. J., 527, *694*
Klein, R. E., 247, *733*
Klein, S. D., 394, *714*
Klima, E. S., 443, *714*
Klineberg, O., 558, 559, *714*
Klinger, N. N., 200, *714*
Klüver, H., 275, 409, *714*
Knief, L. M., 554, *714*
Knights, R. M., 104, *747*
Knobloch, H., 536, 558, 560, *714, 731*
Knott, P. D., 327, *728*
Koch, J., 83, 105, *714*
Koegler, R. R., 366, 367, *692*
Köhler, W., 247, 271, 406, *714*
Koff, R. H., 198, *714*
Kofsky, E., 513, *714*
Kohnstamm, G. A., 503, 505, *714*
Koltsova, M. M., 81, 91, 93, 159, *681*
Konorski, J., 69, *714*
Konrad, K. W., 268, *721*
Koopman, P. R., 43, *714*
Koppe, W., 26, *757*
Koppenaal, R. J., 222, 253, *714*
Korner, A. F., 423, *714*
Koronakos, C., 274, *714*
Kounin, J., 612, *715*
Koutsoudas, A., 466, *715*
Krachkovskaia, M. V., 70, *715*
Krasnogorski, N. I., 73, *715*
Kreindler, A., 86, 89, *723*
Kruger, L., 61, *715*
Krugman,, M., 565, *715*
Krull, A., 222, 253, *714*
Kubzansky, P. E., 355, *688*
Kuenne, M. R., 225, 242, 307, *715*
Kuhlman, C., 484, 512, *713*
Kuhn, T. S., 465, *715*
Kunkle, E. C., 355, *688*
Kuo, Z. Y., 314, *715*
Kurahashi, K., 634, *707*
Kurtz, K. H., 205, 237, 238, 270, *715*

L

Lacey, J. I., 49, *715*
Lachman, R., 10, *715*
Ladd, G. T., 406, *715*
Lahey, M. F. L., 253, *715*

Laidlaw, R. G. N., 3, *715*
Laird, D. S., 552, *715*
Lambert, W. E., 214, *715*
Lambert, W. W., 404, *715*
Landau, R., 354, *715*
Lane, E., 103, *708*
Lane, H., 435, *715*
Langacker, R. W., 466, *716*
Laplace, R., 321, *753*
Lauer, E., 619, *689*
Laurence, M. W., 219, 220, *716*
Laurendeau, M., 499, *716*
Lawrence, D. H., 236, 274, 287, 295, *699, 716*
Lawrence, G. H., Jr., 357, *678*
Lazarus, A. A., 645, 646, *716, 756*
Leader, F. B., 574, *722*
Leahy, A. M., 544, 546, *716*
Learnard, B., 268, 302, 307, *712*
Learned, J., 365, *673*
Leask, J., 407, 408, 409, 410, *716*
Lee, E. S., 559, *716*
Lee, L. C., 183, *716*
Lees, R., 443, *716*
Lehtinen, L. E., 88, *724*
Leibowitz, H., 387, 388, *716, 724*
Leiman, A. J., 320, *716*
Lele, P. P., 53, *716*
Lenneberg, E. H., 426, 428, 429, 465, 641, *716*
Leopold, W. F., 432, *716*
Lepkin, M., 544, *704*
Leutzendorff, A.-M., 414, *713*
Leventhal, A., 52, *717*
Levikova, A. M., 39, 73, 81, 82, 94, 159, *711*
Levin, G. R., 37, 51, *712, 738*
Levin, J. R., 204, 213, *737*
Levine, M., 275, 276, *717*
Levinson, B., 18, 19, 271, 272, 273, 275, 276, *717*
Levinson, C., 104, 105, 106, *717*
Levinson, P., 104, 105, 116, *717*
Levy, D. M., 653, *717*
Levy, N., 54, 59, 89, 94, *718*
Levy, R. J., 548, *717*
Lewis, D. G., 546, *717*
Lewis, D. J., 122, 148, *717*
Lewis, H. P., 380, *717*
Lewis, M., 55, 354, 423, *717*
Lewis, M. M., 428, *717*
Lewis, W. D., 551, 552, *721*
Liberty, P. G., Jr., 588, 597, 606, *726*
Licklider, J. C. R., 47, *717*
Lieberman, S. M., 318, *717*
Liebert, R. M., 460, *728*
Lienert, G. A., 519, *717*

Lilly, J. C., 359, *717*
Li Lollo, V., 345, *717*
Lindsley, D. B., 411, *717*
Lindsley, O. R., 105, 115, *717, 718*
Lindworsky, J., 248, 405, *718*
Ling, B.-C., 41, 103, 152, 172, *718*
Linke, I., 625, *739*
Lintz, L. M., 70, 71, 92, 93, 94, *681, 718*
Lipsitt, L. P., 23, 24, 37, 38, 51, 52, 54, 55, 59, 60, 70, 71, 74, 75, 77, 78, 80, 83, 84, 86, 89, 90, 94, 103, 104, 105, 108, 109, 111, 112, 113, 114, 115, 116, 118, 119, 120, 162, 163, 164, 165, 166, 167, 174, 175, 176, 177, 182, 184, 185, 186, 188, 189, 256, 352, *693, 705, 712, 717, 718, 740, 742, 743, 755, 757*
Lipton, E. L., 48, 421, 422, *718, 735, 747*
Liverant, S., 510, *718*
Livson, N., 536, *685*
Lockhart, R. A., *343, 700*
Lodge, A., 38, *676*
Loeb, J., 320, *718*
Loeb, M. B., 553, *753*
Loess, H. B., 185, *718*
Loevinger, J., 551, *719*
Logan, F. A., 237, 304, *752*
LoLordo, V. M., 85, 86, *687*
Long, E. R., 125, 126, 127, 129, 130, 131, 132, 133, *719*
Long, H., 559, *719*
Long, I., 487, *719*
Long, L., 219, *699*
Longstreth, L. E., 142, 317, 320, 322, 323, *324*, 328, 330, *332*, 333, *334*, 336, 337, 339, 354, *719*
Lorge, I., 198, 525, 555, *719, 750*
Loth, G., 36, *719*
Lott, D. F., 335, 336, *719, 748*
Lovaas, O. I., 116, 119, 663, 667, 669, 670, *719*
Love, M. I., 558, *720*
Lovejoy, E., 287, 300, *720*
Loveland, D. H., 275, *704*
Lovell, K., 451, 490, 492, 499, *720*
Lovibond, S. H., 656, 670, *720*
Lowden, L. M., 329, *755*
Lowe, R. C., 369, 370, 371, 503, 504, *720, 756*
Lowell, E. L., 354, *721*
Lowell, F., 198, *756*
Lubker, B. J., 277, *720*
Ludvigson, H. W., 300, *686*
Lund, D., 662, *701*
Lundgren, J. B., 329, *720*
Lunneborg, P. W., *720*

Luppova, M. N., 37, 39, 51, *682*
Lupton, A. A., 187, *732*
Luria, A. R., 71, 159, 181, 192, 260, 268, 307, 464, *720*
Lustman, S. L., 47, *735*
Lynch, S., 204, 213, *737*
Lynip, A. W., 429, *720*
Lynn, R., 283, *720*

M

McAllister, D. E., 233, *720*
McArthur, C., 593, *720*
McBane, B., 503, *742*
McBee, G., 297, 527, *720, 747*
McCandless, B. R., 14, 349, 510, 527, 562, 575, 594, 595, 597, 601, 607, 610, 611, 614, *686, 705, 720, 721, 745, 746*
McCann, B., 147, *732*
McCarthy, D., 245, 425, 436, 437, 438, 536, *686, 721*
McClelland, D., 354, *721*
Maccoby, E. E., 218, 258, 260, 268, 380, 615, *721*
McConnell, J. V., 186, *680*
McCord, W. M., 559, *721*
McCormack, P. D., 233, *721*
McCullers, J. C., 203, 217, 218, *721*
McDill, E. L., 609, *721*
McDougall, W., 314, *721*
Macfarlane, J. W., 529, 535, 537, 538, *705*
McGehee, W., 551, 552, *721*
McGeoch, J. A., 205, 206, 405, *721*
McGinnis, J. M., 39, *721*
McGraw, M. B., 557, *721*
McGurk, F. C., 558, 559, *721*
McKee, J. P., 574, *722*
McKellar, P., 248, 406, 407, 410, *722*
Mackenberg, E., 376, *698*
Mackintosh, J., 287, *748*
Mackintosh, N. J., 287, 300, 302, 304, 308, *722, 748*
McManis, D. L., 253, *722*
McMurray, G. A., 355, *722*
McNamara, H. J., 287, 405, *694, 722*
McNeil, E. G., 3, *722*
McNeill, D., 425, 439, 465, 473, *722*
McNemar, Q., 519, 551, 561, 568, *722*
McQuiston, M. D., 274, *724*
MacRae, J. M., 536, *722*
Mach, E., 279, *722*
Maddi, S. R., *694*
Maddox, H., 547, *722*
Maier, H. W., 512, *722*
Maltz, H. E., 464, *723*

Mandler, G., 221, 287, *723*
Manis, M., 205, *723*
Mankinen, R. L., 184, *703*
Mann, I., 35, *723*
Margaret, A., 210, 406, *685*
Marinesco, G., 86, 89, *723*
Markel, N. N., 432, 435, *736*
Marquart, D. I., 554, *723*
Marquis, D. G., 97, *705*
Marquis, D. P., 70, 71, 74, 75, 76, 83, *723*
Marsh, G., 260, 295, 300, *723*
Marshall, H. R., 575, *721*
Marshall, J. C., 465, *752*
Martin, C. J., 205, *723*
Martin, E., 199, 251, *723, 740*
Martin, J. G., 202, *723*
Martin, R. R., 658, *723*
Martin, W. E., 152, 277, *723*
Marum, K. D., 71, 89, 90, 91, 107, *723*
Marx, M. H., 321, *723*
Masland, R., 629, *723*
Massimo, J. L., 574, *742*
Matarazzo, R. G., 37, 413, 421, *700*
Mateer, F., 55, 83, 94, *723*
Matousek, M. A., 253, *723*
May, F., 125, 126, 127, 129, *719*
May, F. B., 568, *736*
Mead, M., 25, 572, *723*
Mednick, S. A., 88, *724*
Meehl, P. E., 510, *689*
Mees, H., 650, 671, *756*
Mehler, J., 501, 502, *724*
Meili, R., 368, *724*
Menaker, S. L., 250, *724*
Meneghini, K. A., 388, *724*
Menlove, F. L., 345, 347, 598, 610, *676*
Menyuk, P., 454, *724*
Meredith, H. V., 23, *724*
Mermelstein, E., 500, *724, 742*
Merrill, M. A., 487, 519, 525, 526, 527, *724, 749*
Meryman, J. J., 344, *724*
Messer, S., 434, *724*
Metraux, R., 365, *673*
Meyer, D. R., 406, *755*
Meyer, V., 666, *696*
Meyer, W. J., 187, *724*
Meyerowitz, J., 564, *724*
Meyers, C. S., 172, *724*
Meyers, W. J., 274, *724*
Michaelis, R., 625, *739*
Michels, K. M., 274, 399, *710, 724, 758*
Milerian, E. A., 281, *724*
Miles, C. G., 122, *686*
Miles, R. C., 274, *724*

Miles, T. R., 511, *725*
Miles, W. R., 61, 531, *715*, *725*
Milgram, N. A., 206, 209, 210, 261, 269, *725*
Miller, G. A., 205, 215, 431, *725*
Miller, H. C., 114, *689*
Miller, K. S., 557, 560, *691*
Miller, L. B., 190, *725*
Miller, N. E., 29, 224, 227, 268, 332, 338, 343, 690, *725*
Miller, P., 489, 503, *673*
Miller, T. M., 337, *740*
Miller, W. R., 428, 435, 437, 439, 440, 441, *693*, *725*
Mink, W. D., 204, 219, *709*, *725*
Mirzoiants, N. S., 81, 82, 83, *711*, *725*
Mischel, W., 608, *725*
Mitchell, G. D., 580, *725*
Mitoma, C., 633, *725*
Mitrano, A. J., 320, *725*
Moffitt, A. R., 140, 330, *725*, *738*
Mooney, C. H., 399, *726*
Moore, R. Y., 637, *757*
Moran, L. J., 199, *748*
Morgan, C. H., 216, *699*
Morgan, J. J. B., 86, 94, *726*
Morgan, S. S., 86, 94, *726*
Moriarity, A., 536, *693*
Morrison, D. C., 662, *752*
Morse, P. A., 299, *726*
Moss, H. A., 21, 260, 345, 423, 424, 540, *710*, *726*
Moulton, R. W., 588, 597, 606, *726*
Mowrer, O. H., 426, 465, 466, 467, 669, *726*
Mowrer, W. M., 669, *726*
Muehl, S., 382, *704*
Mueller, C. G., 37, 38, *682*, *700*
Muench, G. A., 565, *726*
Mumbauer, C. C., 298, *726*
Munn, N. L., 2, 3, 103, 178, 669, *726*
Murdock, B. B., Jr., 217, *726*
Murphy, W. W., 321, *723*
Murray, H. A., 315, 404, *726*
Mussen, P. H., 315, 578, 579, 588, 597, 607, *710*, *726*, *731*
Myers, C. S., 103, *726*
Myers, J. L., 318, 319, 320, *716*, *726*, *727*
Myers, N. A., 319, 320, *716*, *727*
Myerson, B., 26, *757*

N

Nagel, E., 2, *727*
Nall, J., 26, *757*
Naunton, R. F., 47, 637, *727*, *757*

Neff, W. S., 546, 551, *727*
Nelson, A. K., 57, *727*
Nelson, V. L., 529, 535, 536, 537, 538, 542, 543, *676*, *710*, *727*
Newell, A., 268, 277, *742*
Newell, F. W., 637, *757*
Newhall, S. M., 382, *727*
Newman, H. H., 544, 546, *727*
Nicely, P. E., 431, *725*
Nichaeva, I. P. K., 159, *727*
Nichols, I. A., 426, *716*
Nikitina, G. M., 73, *744*
Nikkel, N., 200, 256, *727*
Nisbet, J. D., 532, *727*
Noble, C. E., 198, 199, *727*, *728*
Nodine, C. F., 200, 216, *699*
Noelting, G., 363, 401, *728*
Nolte, R., 625, *739*
Norcross, K. J., 230, 231, 232, 234, 256, *728*, *746*
Norman, R. M., 631, *728*
Normand, C., 58, *675*
Nunnally, J. C., 327, *728*, *731*

O

O'Connor, N., 217, *704*
Oden, M. H., 531, 565, 566, *677*, *749*
Odom, P. B., 257, *709*
Odom, R. D., 104, 198, 203, 256, 298, 354, 360, 460, *686*, *726*, *728*, *747*
Offenbach, S. I., 65, *728*
Ogilvie, E. A., 490, *720*
Ogonik, J., 563, *677*
O'Hara, J., 187, *681*
Ohlin, L. E., 574, 579, 608, *688*
Ohlrich, E. S., 300, 304, *728*
Olum, V., 387, *697*
Olver, R. R., 184, 496, *683*, *700*
Opitz, E., 564, *744*
Oppel, W., 550, *755*
Oppenheim, P., 7, *704*
Ordy, J. M., 40, 44, *694*
Orlando, R., 126, 127, 128, 129, 131, 310, *679*, *728*, *758*
Orne, M. T., 359, *728*
Orr, D. B., 565, *741*
Orth, O. S., 642, *673*
Orton, C., 141, *738*
Osborn, W. J., 219, *729*
Osborne, R. T., 558, *729*
Osgood, C. E., 247, 249, 425, 443, 462, 465, 466, 472, *729*
Osgood, S. W., 295, *676*

Osler, S. F., 193, *729*
Osser, H., 372, 373, 374, *697*
Otto, W., 218, *729*
Overmier, J. B., 85, 86, *687, 729*
Overton, W. F., 10, 11, 43, *735*
Owens, W. A., Jr., 532, *729*

P

Paivo, A., 198, 204, 205, 206, 210, 214, 215, 216, *690, 715, 729, 730*
Palermo, D. S., 198, 199, 200, 203, 204, 215, 216, 217, 220, 256, 257, 349, 454, 465, 470, *686, 696, 709, 714, 727, 730, 736, 740, 755*
Papoušek, H., 53, 83, 99, 103, 108, 109, 160, 161, 182, *730, 731*
Parke, R. D., 354, 589, *731, 752*
Parker, R. K., 327, *728, 731*
Parmelee, A. H., 54, 56, *683, 731*
Parnell, R. W., 577, *731*
Parsons, T., 588, *731*
Pasamanick, B., 536, 558, 560, *714, 731*
Passow, A., 567, *734*
Patin, H. A., 547, *731*
Patton, H. D., 619, *738*
Paul, C., 300, *731*
Pavlov, I. P., 66, 74, 86, 158, 311, 337, 644, *731*
Payne, D. E., 607, *731*
Payne, D. T., 540, *695*
Pederson, D. R., 140, *731, 740*
Pederson, L. J., 104, 105, 115, *718*
Pegram, E. L., 561, *754*
Peiper, A., 36, 38, 47, 48, 54, 56, 413, *731*
Peluffo, N., 499, *731*
Penney, R. K., 3, 5, 141, 146, 147, 187, 216, *686, 731, 732*
Pennypacker, H. S., 159, *705*
Penrose, L. S., 632, *732*
Pepper, S. C., 43, 485, 498, *732*
Pereboom, A. C., 18, 294, 330, *703, 740*
Perkins, M. J., 185, *732*
Peterson, R. F., 28, 662, *675, 679, 752*
Petrova, E. P., 78, *682*
Pettigrew, J. F., 560, *732*
Pfaeffle, H., 565, *713*
Pfaffmann, C., 57, *732*
Phillips, B. N., 353, *732*
Piaget, J., 21, 391, 399, 400, 404, 481, 482, 483, 487, 488, 489, 491, 492, 494, 496, 497, 504, 548, *707, 732, 733*

Pick, A. D., 247, 261, 372, 373, 374, *688, 697, 733*
Pick, H. L., 247, *704, 733*
Pike, E. G., 435, *733*
Pillsbury, W. B., 249, *733*
Pimm, J. B., 141, *738*
Pinard, A., 499, *716*
Pinneau, S. R., 530, 538, *733*
Pirojnikoff, L. A., 269, *747*
Plum, G. E., 280, *755*
Poggiani, C., 73, *746*
Polikanina, R. I., 91, 107, *733*
Pollack, R. H., 192, 400, *733*
Pollard, S. W., 387, 388, *716*
Pond, D. A., 640, *733*
Poresky, R., 37, *691*
Posnick, G. M., 352, *713*
Postman, L., 198, 202, 253, *733, 751*
Potts, M., 260, 261, *733*
Pratt, K. C., 56, *733*
Prechtl, H., 54, *733*
Premack, D., 72, *733*
Preston, A., 543, *688*
Pribram, K. H., 205, 215, *725*
Price, L. E., 185, 186, 200, *733*
Price, T., 237, 304, *752*
Prokasy, W. F., 67, 70, 72, 84, *733*
Prothro, E., 557, *733*
Pryer, M. W., 198, *728*
Pumroy, D. K., 116, 122, 136, 138, *733*
Pumroy, S. S., 116, 122, 136, 138, *733*
Pustek, J. J., Jr., 274, *724*
Pyle, W. H., 152, *756*

Q

Quinlan, D., 200, *683*

R

Rabinowitz, M. F., 144, *733*
Rambusch, N. M., 403, *734*
Rand, G., 395, *687*
Rank, L., 171, *734*
Rapaport, D., 496, *735*
Raph, J. B., 567, *734*
Raven, J. C., 519, 524, 525, 531, 554, *695, 734*
Rawson, R. A., 40 44, *689*
Ray, E., 354, *752*
Ray, O. S., 360, *703*
Rayner, R., 85, 108, 343, 416, *753*
Razran, G. H. S., 73, *734*
Rebelsky, F. G., 426, *716*

Reese, H. W., 10, 11, 13, 18, 19, 43, 152, 184,
    192, 206, 207, 208, 209, 232, 233, 234,
    235, 238, 239, 240, 241, 242, 243, 244,
    247, 258, 260, 261, 265, 266, 267, 268,
    269, 271, 272, 273, 275, 276, 280, 307,
    308, 352, 380, 432, 435, 485, 610, *717*,
    734, 735, 736
Rehula, R. J., 200, *713*
Reich, L. C., 184, *700*
Reichard, S., 496, *735*
Reid, L. S., 287, 300, *735*
Reiss, I. L., 591, 594, 609, *735*
Rendle-Short, J., 86, 94, 159, *735*
Renshaw, S., 81, *735*
Rescorla, R. A., 70, *735*
Restle, F., 275, *735*
Reynolds, G. S., 102, 129, 170, *735*
Reynolds, N. J., 656, 657, 659, 660, *702*
Rheingold, H. L., 104, 115, 116, 117, 119, 120,
    121, 360, 426, 548, *735*
Rice, C., 54, *690*
Rice, U. M., 252, *735*
Richards, T. W., 536, *727*
Richardson, J., 202, *751*
Richmond, J. B., 47, 48, 421, 422, *718, 735,
    747*
Richter, C. P., 54, *736*
Ricks, D. F., 574, *742*
Rickwood, J., 200, *683*
Rider, R. V., 550, 638, *702, 755*
Rie, H. E., 352, *736*
Rieber, M., 141, 143, 144, 145, 184, 185, 186,
    189, 190, 191, 192, 256, *679, 736*
Riegel, K. F., 202, *736*
Riess, B., 464, *736*
Riggs, L. A., 38, 39, *700, 736*
Riley, D. A., 239, *736*
Ring, E. M., 200, 217, *736*
Ringwall, E. A., 432, 435, 536, *687, 736*
Rinsland, H. D., 198, *736*
Riopelle, A. J., 274, *741*
Ripple, R. E., 568, *736*
Risley, T. R., 650, 651, 657, 663, 668, 670,
    671, 672, *675, 736, 756*
Robinson, H. B., 145, 146, *737*
Robinson, J. S., 381, *736*
Robinson, N. M., 145, 146, *737*
Roeper, A., 505, *742*
Rohwer, W. D., Jr., 204, 205, 206, 211, 212,
    213, 214, *709, 737*
Rose, M., 40, 44, *689*
Rosekrans, M. A., 594, *737*
Rosenbaum, M. E., 148, *737*
Rosenbaum, P. S., 466, *708*
Rosenblith, J. F., 37, 421, *737*

Rosenbloom, F. M., 634, *740*
Rosenfeld, L., 414, *711*
Rosenhan, D., 354, *737*
Rosenthal, I., 580, *737*
Rosenthal, R., 484, 541, *692, 737*
Ross, H. W., 115, 116, 117, 426, *735*
Ross, L. E., 188, 189, 300, 304, 308, 344, *688,
    704, 728, 737*
Rossi, E. L., 219, *737*
Rossi, S. I., 219, *737*
Roth, C. H., 354, *697*
Rothblat, L. A., 299, *737*
Rothney, J. W. M., 521, 530, 531, 534, 535,
    538, *689*
Rothschild, R., 638, *737*
Roussel, J., 330, *674*
Rovee, C. K., 51, 61, *738*
Rowley, V. M., 527, *712*
Rubenstein, J., 589, *738*
Rubin, B. M., 190, *744*
Ruch, F. L., 537, *738*
Ruch, T. C., 619, *738*
Rudel, R. G., 380, *738*
Runquist, W. N., 344, *745*
Rupp, N. R., 52, *692*
Russell, W. A., 6, 219, 255, *709, 738*
Rutherford, G., 451, 452, 669, *700, 738*
Rutherford, J., 575, *702*
Ryan, J. J., III, 612, *715*
Ryan, T. J., 140, 141, 142, 149, 217, 330, *685,
    725, 738, 753*

                                S

Sadowsky, S., 181, *738*
Sailor, W., 451, 452, 669, *700, 738*
Salapatek, P. H., 41, 42, *738*
Salk, L., 359, *738*
Saltzman, I. J., 318, *738*
Saltzstein, H. D., 597, 610, *705*
Sameroff, A. J., 51, 57, 84, 85, 89, 110, 119,
    739
Sanford, R. N., 600, *739*
Sarason, S. B., 349, 517, 527, 548, 564, 565,
    629, *705, 723, 739*
Saravo, A., 305, *739*
Sartain, A., 527, *739*
Saville, M. R., 329, *694*
Schaefer, E. S., 530, 541, 543, 549, 551, *677,
    739*
Schaeffer, B., 667, 670, *719*
Schaffer, H. R., 362, 481, 580, *739*
Scharlock, D. P., 642, *739*
Scheibe, K. E., 203, 359, *708, 728*
Scheibel, A. B., 629, *739*

Scheibel, M. E., 629, *739*
Scherrer, H., 280, *704*
Schiller, P., 247, *739*
Schiller, P. H., 246, *739*
Schlitz, K. A., 642, *673*
Schlosberg, H., 66, 97, 646, *739, 756*
Schneider, M., 496, *735*
Schneirla, T. C., 2, *739*
Schrier, A. M., 299, *741*
Schülte, F. J., 625, *739*
Schulz, R. W., 197, 198, 199, 202, *740, 751*
Scott, L., 368, *692*
Scott, R., 559, *740*
Scott, T. H., 359, *678*
Sears, R. R., 114, *689*
Seashore, H., 551, *740*
Sebeok, T. A., 425, *729*
Seegmiller, J. E., 634, *740*
Segman, J., 205, *683*
Segner, L. L., 187, *745*
Seidel, H. E., Jr., 562, *740*
Seidman, S. B., 187, *724*
Seltzer, R. J., 103, 112, 115, 119, 122, *740*
Semb, G., 37, 51, *740*
Semler, I. J., 140, 217, 558, *707, 740*
Setterington, R. G., 188, *740*
Seward, J. P., 330, *740*
Sgan, M. L., 614, *740*
Shantz, C. A., 261, *700*
Shapiro, H., 503, *742*
Shapiro, M. M., 337, *740*
Shapiro, S. I., 200, 203, 215, 257, *740*
Shapiro, S. S., 198, 199, 200, 203, 216, 217, *740*
Sharp, D. W., 204, *688*
Shaycoft, M. F., 565, *741*
Shearn, D., 72, *741*
Shedd, C. L., 554, *674*
Sheerer, M., 496, *698*
Sheffield, F. D., 85, 337, *741*
Sheffield, V. F., 148, *741*
Sheikh, A. A., 144, *741*
Sheldon, P. M., 567, *741*
Sheldon, W. H., 577, 578, *741*
Shell, W. F., 274, *741*
Shepp, B. E., 183, 185, 186, 295, *297*, 298, 299, 300, 302, 303, 304, *726, 741*
Sheppard, W. C., 118, 121, 181, 182, 435, *715, 741*
Sherman, I. C., 36, 54, *741*
Sherman, J. A., 647, 657, 658, 659, 662, 667, *675, 741*
Sherman, M., 36, 54, 260, 412, 549, *723, 741*
Shirley, M. M., 21, 22, *742*
Shore, M. F., 574, *742*

Shuey, A., 557, 558, 559, *742*
Shulman, L. S., 500, *724*
Shusterman, R. J., 192, *742*
Shuttleworth, F. K., 551, *742*
Sidman, M., 16, 657, *742*
Sidowski, J. B., 320, *711, 742*
Siegel, A. E., 178, *742*
Siegel, G. M., 658, *723*
Siegel, H., 55, *742*
Siegel, P. S., 122, 138, *742*
Sigel, I. E., 260, 261, 503, 505, *700, 710, 742*
Silberman, C. E., 574, *742*
Silfen, C. K., 39, *673*
Silverman, I. W., 260, *742*
Sime, M. E., 274, *757*
Simmons, J. Q., 667, 670, *719*
Simmons, K., 530, 537, 538, *691*
Simmons, M. W., 104, 115, 116, 119, 173, 174, 175, 182, *742, 754*
Simon, H. A., 268, 277, *742*
Simon, T., 21, *679*
Sinclair-DeZwart, H., 482, 503, *742*
Siqueland, E. R., 43, 103, 104, 105, 106, 108, 109, 110, 111, 112, 113, 115, 118, 119, 120, 122, 162, 163, 164, 165, 166, 167, 168, 171, *742, 743*
Skeels, H. M., 103, 179, 546, 548, 549, 561, 565, *743*
Skinner, B. F., 66, 97, 102, 315, 316, 425, 462, 466, 470, *694, 743*
Skodak M., 546, *743*
Slamecka, N. J., 298, *743*
Slavson, S. R., 653, *743*
Slobin, D. I., 439, 449, 456, 457, 459, 465, *743*
Smedslund, J., 492, 504, *743*
Smiley, S. S., 307, *743*
Smith, I. D., 505, *744*
Smith, K. U., 104, 392, 393, 402, *744*
Smith, L. M., 613, *698*
Smith, M., 252, 277, *706*
Smith, M. E., 22, 436, *744*
Smith, N. J., 392, 393, 402, *744*
Smith, W. M., 104, *744*
Smock, C. D., 190, *744*
Smothergill, D., 188, *757*
Smythe, P. C., 215, *730*
Sokoloff, L., 634, *696*
Sokolov, E. N., 280, 281, 282, 284, 414, *744, 752*
Solenkova, E. G., 73, *744*
Solkoff, N., 638, *744*
Solley, C. M., 404, *744*
Solomon, F., 562, *680*
Solomon, R. L., 85, 86, 404, *687, 715*
Solomons, G., 564, *744*

Sontag, L. W., 529, 535, 537, 538, 540, 542, 543, *676, 710, 744*
Spearman, C., 279, 516, *744*
Spears, W. C., 35, 39, 62, *744*
Spellacy, F. J., 48, *689*
Spelt, D. K., 85, *745*
Spence, J. T., 187, *745*
Spence, K. W., 18, 19, 141, 142, 144, 239, 240, 241, 268, 269, 287, 292, 304, 344, 350, *745*
Sperling, S. E., 300, *745*
Spicker, H. H., 562, 614, *705, 745*
Spiker, C. C., 2, 3, 6, 99, 185, 186, 201, 205, 230, 231, 232, 233, 234, 235, 246, 252, 256, 263, 269, 277, 295, 510, *720, 728, 733, 745, 746*
Spitz, H. H., 219, *697*
Spitz, R. A., 418, *746*
Spradlin, J. E., 126, 127, 318, *746*
Squires, N. D., 563, *677*
Staats, A. W., 317, 406, 425, 462, 464, 465, 466, *746*
Staats, C. K., 406, 425, 462, 464, 466, *746*
Staffieri, J. R., 577, *746*
Stalnaker, J. M., 565, *746*
Stanbury, J. B., 633, 634, *746*
Stanley, W. C., 73, 104, 115, 116, 119, 120, 121, 360, *735, 746*
Staples, R., 39, *746*
Starr, R. H., 152, 188, 189, *681*
Stedman, D. J., 464, *695*
Steele, B., 40, 44, *689*
Steigman, M. J., 269, 339, *746*
Steinschneider, A., 48, 421, 422, *718, 735, 747*
Stephens, D., 221, *723*
Stern, C., 21, *747*
Stern, E. R., 105, *747*
Stern, W., 21, 380, *747*
Stevens, C., 619, *747*
Stevens, D. A., 327, *728*
Stevens, H. A., 564, 629, *747*
Stevens, S. S., 47, *747*
Stevenson, H. W., 5, 104, 130, 190, 242, 269, 297, 300, 302, 354, *685, 705, 746, 747*
Stewart, F. D., 180, *704*
Stiening, B. R., 103, 178, *726*
Stingle, K. G., 587, 601, *697*
Stith, D., 562, *740*
Stockey, M. R., 580, *679*
Stockwell, F. E., 198, *728*
Stoddard, L. T., 121, *747*
Stollnitz, F., 287, *747*
Stolz, S. B., 336, *748*
Stone, G. C., 275, *748*
Stonex, E., 103, *708*

Storms, L. H., 255, *738*
Stott, D. H., 546, *748*
Stover, D. O., 257, 464, *690*
Strominger, N. L., 642, *739*
Strong, C. A., 249, *748*
Stronger, L. A., 613, *698*
Stroud, J. B., 554, *714*
Stubbs, E. M., 48, 52, *748*
Suchman, R. G., 153, 174, 183, 184, 192, *748*
Suci, G. J., 247, 462, *729*
Sullivan, A. M., 549, *684*
Sullivan, J. P., 199, *748*
Sully, J., 405, *748*
Sutherland, N. S., 287, 308, *748*
Suzuki, N., 204, 213, *737*
Syrova, V. A., 37, 39, 51, *682*
Szeminska, A., 491, 492, *732*

T

Tague, C. E., 657, 665, *679*
Tallman, I., 574, 608, *748*
Tampieri, G., 383, *748*
Tannenbaum, P. H., 247, 462, *729*
Tanner, J. M., 578, *748*
Taylor, J. A., 349, 350, *748*
Taylor, J. H., 412, *748*
Taylor, N. B., 38, 48, 58, 59, *678*
Templin, M. C., 433, 437, 451, *748, 749*
Tempone, V. J., 88, *749*
Terman, L. M., 487, 509, 519, 525, 526, 527, 565, 566, *749*
Terrace, H. S., 159, 166, 171, 181, 308, *749*
Terrell, G., 144, 187, 188, 189, *749, 753*
Teuber, H.-L., 380, *738*
Theios, J., 300, *749*
Thomas, O., 466, *749*
Thompson, C. W., 530, 531, *681*
Thompson, G. G., 23, 428, 553, 575, *749*
Thompson, R. F., 642, *677*
Thorndike, E. L., 66, 198, 530, *749, 750*
Thorndike, R. L., 525, 530, 536, 539, 568, *719, 750*
Thorpe, W. H., 27, *750*
Thrum, M. E., 180, *750*
Thune, L. E., 268, *750*
Thurstone, L. L., 514, 517, 542, *750*
Thurstone, T. G., 517, *750*
Tiber, N., 551, *750*
Tighe, L. S., 300, 304, 307, *750*
Tighe, T. J., 300, 304, 307, *750*
Tinklepaugh, O. L., 246, *750*
Tischler, H., 428, *750*
Titchener, E. G., 485, *750*

Torrance, E. P., 567, 568, 569, *699, 750*
Torrey, C. C., 73, *758*
Toulmin, S., 7, 8, 9, 10, *750*
Toussaint, I., 527, *688*
Towell, M. E., 56, *673*
Tower, S. S., 628, *750*
Trabasso, T., 153, 174, 183, 184, 192, 298, 299, *748, 750*
Tragakis, C. J., 116, 121, 122, *754*
Trattner, A., 73, *746*
Trautman, G. E., 193, *729*
Travers, R. M., 317, *750*
Trincker, D., 38, *750*
Trinker, I., 38, *750*
Tucker, T. J., 642, *739*
Tulkin, S. R., 574, *751*
Tulving, E., 220, *751*
Turkewitz, G., 52, 54, 109, *751*
Turner, L. H., 85, 86, *687*
Turner, M. W., 564, *751*
Turrisi, F. D., 298, 299, 300, 302, 303, 304, *741*
Twedt, H. M., 251, *751*
Tyer, Z. E., 302, *689*
Tyler, D. W., 148, *679*
Tyler, L. E., 568, *691*
Tyler, R. W., 551, 553, 554, *691*

U

Udelf, M. S., 40, 44, *694*
Udenfriend, S., 633, *725*
Ullrich, J. R., 204, *730*
Underwood, B. J., 197, 198, 202, 217, 223, 251, 253, *751*
Updegraff, R., 561, *743*
Uzgiris, I. C., 490, *751*
Uznadze, D. N., 206, 260, 264, 285, 498, *751*

V

Vakhrameeva, I. A., 159, *751*
Valentine, C. W., 103, 108, 172, *751*
Van de Reitt, V., 549, 551, 556, 557, *713*
Van der Torren, J., 377, *751*
Van Fleet, F. M., 300, 308, *701*
Velten, H. V., 432, 433, 434, *751*
Vergason, G. A., 217, *751*
Vernon, M. D., 369, *751*
Vernon, P. E., 500, *752*
Vincent, S. B., 17, *752*
Vinh-Bang, 399, *733*
von Békésy, G., 47, *752*
Voorhoeve, A. C., 141, 142, 149, *738*
Voronin, L. G., 284, *752*

Vurpillot, E., 376, 377, 378, 388, 395, 397, 398, *752*
Vygotsky, L. S., 465, 496, *752*

W

Wagner, A. R., 237, 304, 330, *752*
Wahler, R. G., 103, 115, 588, 662, *752*
Wait, W. T., 405, *752*
Wales, R. J., 465, *752*
Walk, R. D., 45, 47, *752*
Walker, R., 365, *673*
Wall, J., 502, *752*
Wallach, L., 502, *752*
Walters, R. H., 137, 188, 354, *688, 740, 752*
Wapner, S., 391, 395, 483, 496, *687, 698, 752*
Warburton, F. W., 553, *752*
Ware, R., 144, 188, 189, *749, 753*
Ware, W. B., 204, *701*
Warkany, J., 635, *755*
Warner, W. L., 553, *753*
Warren, A. B., 103, 116, 121, 123, 124, 136, *753*
Warren, J. M., 274, 300, *753*
Washburn, M. F., 242, *753*
Washburn, R. W., 418, *753*
Watson, J. B., 37, 85, 108, 314, 343, 406, 412, 416, *753*
Watson, J. S., 43, 104, 115, 119, 160, *753*
Watson, P., 141, 330, *738, 753*
Watson, P. D., 404, *715*
Wechsler, D., 510, 525, 531, 542, *753*
Weddell, G., 53, *716*
Weiner, H., 647, *753*
Weinrich, W. W., 321, *753*
Weinstock, S., 141, 142, *753*
Weintraub, D., 638, *744*
Weir, M. W., 190, 192, 302, 307, *743, 747, 753*
Weir, R. H., 432, 435, *754*
Weisberg, P., 99, 103, 104, 115, 116, 117, 118, 120, 121, 122, 173, 180, 182, *754*
Weisley, M., 187, 189, *749*
Weiss, J., 398, *692*
Weiss, L. A., 37, 359, *707*
Weitzman, E. D., 49, *754*
Welch, L., 152, 180, 219, 364, 401, 487, *699, 719, 754*
Wellman, B. L., 560, 561, *743, 754*
Wells, D., 304, *712*
Wenger, M. A., 38, 71, 74, 75, 86, 87, *754*
Werner, H., 248, 249, 365, 391, 403, 462, *752, 754*
Wertheimer, M., 52, *754*
Wesman, A., 551, *740*
Wheeler, L. R., 549, 550, *754*

White, B. L., 44, 481, *703*, *754*
White, J. C., 549, 551, 556, 557, *713*
White, M. A., 461, *754*
White, S. H., 11, 65, 81, 159, 161, 183, 192, 259, 260, 280, *754*, *755*
Whiteman, M., 565, *708*
Whitmarsh, G. A., 218, *680*
Wickens, C. D., 71, 86, 87, 88, *755*
Wickens, D. D., 71, 86, 87, 88, 406, *755*
Wicklund, D. A., 203, 220, *755*
Wiener, G., 550, *755*
Wiener, M., 381, 382, *756*
Wilkinson, H. J., 359, *710*
Willems, E. P., 614, 615, *755*
Williams, H. M., 561, *743*
Williams, J. P., 414, *755*
Williams, R. A., 94, *755*
Williams, W. C., 549, *687*
Willmann, R. R., 247, *755*
Willner, A. E., 220, *755*
Wilson, H., 122, 137, 138, 319, 320, *711*, *742*
Wilson, J. G., 635, *755*
Winkel, G. H., 662, *752*
Winkelman, J. E., 36, 38, *706*
Wise, R., 563, *677*
Wismer, B., 256, *755*
Witryol, S. L., 188, 189, 329, *694*, *755*
Witte, K. L., 286, *680*, *755*
Wittrock, M. C., 219, *737*
Witty, P. E., 561, *755*
Wohlwill, J. F., 381, 382, 385, 386, 387, 388, 389, 390, 400, 401, 482, 487, 489, 503, 504, *695*, *755*, *756*
Wolf, K. M., 418, *746*
Wolf, M. M., 650, 651, 657, 659, 660, 661, 662, 663, 665, 666, 668, 671, 672, *675*, *679*, *702*, *736*, *756*
Wolf, R. M., 541, *756*
Wolff, P., 418, *756*
Wolford, G., 304, *756*
Wolner, M., 152, *756*
Wolowitz, H. M., 587, *756*
Wolpe, J., 645, *756*
Wood, G., 205, *756*

Woodrow, H., 198, *756*
Woodworth, R. S., 66, 97, 208, 406, 485, *715*, *756*
Worell, L., 338, 339, *756*
Wray, N. P., 188, 189, *737*
Wright, E. S., 188, *693*
Wright, F. H., 637, *757*
Wright, H. F., 20, 26, *676*, *757*
Wright, J. C., 188, 252, 256, *689*, *757*
Wright, P. L., 274, *757*
Wu, C. J., 256, *757*
Wyckoff, L. B., Jr., 287, *757*
Wyngaarden, J. B., 633, *746*

Y

Yaffe, S., 638, *744*
Yamamoto, K., 453, 568, *712*, *757*
Yarmey, A. D., 204, *729*
Young, F. A., 93, *757*
Youniss, J., 260, 298, 299, 300, 302, *696*, *757*
Yuille, J. C., 210, 215, 216, *729*, *730*

Z

Zaporozhets, A. V., 81, 281, 284, 309, 392, 395, 396, 399, 402, *757*
Zeaman, D., 183, 193, 237, 252, 277, 280, 287, 288, *289*, *292*, *293*, *294*, 295, *297*, 298, 299, 301, 302, 304, 305, 308, 310, 355, *685*, *706*, *741*, *757*, *758*
Zeigler, H. P., 274, *758*
Zeiler, M. D., 243, 258, *758*
Zetterström, B., 36, *758·*
Zigler, E., 7, 10, 564, *758*
Zimbardo, P. G., 527, *739*
Zimiles, H., 505, *758*
Zimmerman, D. W., 564, *758*
Zimmerman, E. H., 662, *758*
Zimmerman, J., 662, *758*
Zimmerman, R. R., 73, *758*
Zusne, L., 399, *758*
Zwerg, C., 392, 393, 402, *744*

Subject Index

A

Absolute scaling, 530
Abstraction, 275
Achievement, 581, 608–609
Acquired distinctiveness, 29, 226–236
Acquired equivalence, 226–234
Activation, 37
Activity level, 580
Adjustment, 616
Affiliative behavior, 419
African children, 26, 500
Age effects, 191–194, 307–308
   on conditioning, 109
   in mediation, 257–261
Aggression, 424
Ahistorical studies, 14
Alternation learning, 152
Ambivalence, 30, 419
Anatomical considerations, 619–629
Anecdotal method, 21
Anger, 30, 412
Anoxia, 636–637
Anthropology, 25–26
Anxiety, 342–354, 645–646
Appetitional reinforcer, 103
Approach behavior, 413, 418
Area conservation, 490–492
Arousal, 356–357, 414
Association strength, word, 202–204
Associative symmetry, 216
Atheoretical studies, 15
Attachment behavior, 30, 362, 419–421
Attention, 107, 154, 230–233, 268, 269, 274,
   279–310, 400–401, 589
   theory, 286–308
Attitudes, 539–543, 601
Auditory perception, 47–53
Auditory reinforcers, 104–107
Autistic children, 664–666
Autonomic responses, 91, 107
Aversive conditioning, 85–94

Avoidance behavior, 97, 145–147, 413
Avoidance conditioning, 97, 134–136

B

Babinski reflex, 628–629
Babkin reflex, 82–83
Backward conditioning, 69
Backward learning curves, 18, 293–295
Basic vs. applied research, 15
Bed-wetting, 669–670
Behavior modification, 643–672
Behaviorism, 6, 279, 314, 406
Berkeley Growth Study, 529–530
Biogenetic factors, 619–642
Body build, 577–578
Boredom, 358–360
Brain lesions, 640–642
Breast feeding, 73
Brightness discrimination, 295

C

Cardiac response, 72, 107, 360, 414, 421–422
Cerebral palsy, 634
Character, 571
Child-rearing, 354
Church and socialization, 612–615
Class, social, 550–556
Class concepts, 496–497
Classical conditioning, 65–95, 643–646
Clustering, word, 218–221
Cognition, 479–507
Comparative psychology, 3, 24–25
Concept formation, 288, 639
Conceptual behavior, 484–486, 496–497
Conceptual learning, 151, 152–153
Concrete operations stage, 482–483
Conditioning, 11, 33–35, 37–38, 39, 40, 51, 53,
   55, 65–149, 416
   age differences, 94–95
   in language development, 466–469

Conflict, 338–342, 356–357, 598–599
Conjugate reinforcement, 105–107
Consciousness, 498
Conservation problems, 486–492
Constancy, 387–390
Cooperation, 660–661
Correlational studies, 23–24
Creativity, 568–569
Cross-cultural approach, 25–26
Cross-modal transfer, 247–250
Cross-sectional studies, 20–24
Crying, 30, 54, 413–415
Cuddling, 580
Cue-producing responses, 224–227
Cultural effects, 581–583
Cultural isolation, 549–550
Culture-free tests, 553–556
Curiosity, epistemic, 358
Curve plotting, 15–19

D

Dark adaptation, 36–37
Deduction, 7–8
Delay
    of gratification, 608–609
    of reinforcement, 142–145, 188–189
Delayed conditioning, 69
Delayed reaction, 245–247
Delayed response, 25
Delinquency, 574
Dependency, 362, 424, 587
Deprivation, 359–360, 547–550
Depth perception, 43–47
Development
    classification of studies, 2–5
    concept of, 2, 20–24
Developmental norms, 23
Developmental schedules, 530
Differential conditioning, infant, 158–160
Differentiation theory, 372–376
Dimensional learning, 151, 153
Dimensional preferences, 183–184
Dimensional responding, 287–292
Direction conceptions, 494–496
Discrete-trial training, 98
Discrimination learning set, 269–277
Discrimination performance, 648–649
Discriminative learning, 151–194, 224, 237–238
    in infants, 157–182
Distress, 414
Diversive exploration, 358–360
Drive effects, 311–362

E

Early stimulation, 513–514
Ecological approach, 26–28
Education, 364
Eidetic imagery, 406–410
Electroencephalography, 281, 284, 360
Electroretinogram, 36, 38
Emotion, 67, 269, 274, 277, 411–424, 652
Enuresis, 669–670
Environmental stimulation, 560–563
Escape behavior, 145–147
Escape training, 97, 134–136
Esthesiometer, 54–55
Ethics in research, 30–32
Ethology, 26–28, 419
Experimental approach, 28–30
Experimental child psychology, definition, 5–7
Expertness and socialization, 592–593
Explanation, 7–11
Exploratory behavior, 14, 280, 281–286, 355–360, 392–400
Extinction, 69, 136–139, 147–149, 647, 668–669
Extradimensional shifts, 297–300
Eyelid conditioning, 91–92

F

Fact, definition, 12–13
Factor analysis, 515–519
Fading, 649–652
Familial influences, 544–547
Fantasy, 30
Fear, 85, 346–349, 412, 417, 645–646
Femininity, 576
Form discrimination, 178–179
Form perception, 40–43, 364–384
Formal operations stage, 483–484
Free operant conditioning, 98, 123–139, 167–172, 174–177
Free-operant discrimination, 180–182
Freudian theory, 586, 591
Frustration, 30, 330–338
    theory, 332–334

G

Games, 26–27
Generalization, 240
Genetic determinants, 631–635
Genetic effects, 544–547
Genetic psychology, 3
Gesell's developmental schedules, 22, 530
Gestalt theory, 239, 364
Gifted children, 565–569

Grammar, 438–448
Group research, 15
Gustatory perception, 56–58

H

Habituation, 33–35, 37, 39, 40, 49–52, 55,
    59–62, 281–284
Haptic exploration, 394–395
Harvard Growth Study, 530
Head-turning behavior, 83, 107–112, 162–167
Heart-rate, 107, 281, 360, 414, 421–422
Hebbian theory, 513–514
Hedonic scale, 411
Heredity, 24, 544–547
Historical studies, 14
Hostility, 30
Hunger, 413
Hypothetical construct, 510

I

Identification, 346, 596–597, 600–609
Imagery, 204–215, 405–410
Imitation, 30, 346–349, 417, 448–449, 600–
    609
Incentive effects, 189–191, 327–329
Incentive motivation, 320–327, 334–338
Incongruity, 357
Individual differences, 19, 421–422
Infant discrimination learning, 157–182
Infant nervous system, 626–629
Infant sensation, 33–63
Inhibition, 222, 241, 346–349, 645
    conditioned, 70–72
Instinct, 314
Institutionalization, 117, 418, 548
Instrumental conditioning, 97–149
Intelligence, 193–194, 377–379, 479–484, 506,
    509–569, 577, 639
    correlates, 539–569
    growth trends, 529–539
    quotient, 521
    scales, 21–22
    tests, 523–527
    theories, 512–519
Intelligence changes, 537–539
Interference, 251–254
Intradimensional shifts, 297–300
Investigatory responses, 391–392
Isolation, 353–354, 549–550

K

Kicking response, infant, 115
Kymograph, 82

L

Language, 425–477, 498–499, 503–504, 651
    acquisition theory, 465–476
    brain lesions and, 641
Latency, response, 98
Laughing, 419
Law of effect, 66
Leadership, 573
Learned needs, 313
Learning
    discrimination, 151–194
    in intelligence, 514–515
    paradigms and processes, 65–95, 97–149
    in Piaget, 504–505
Learning to learn, 270–278
Learning set, 270–278
Learning theory and socialization, 585–587
Length conservation, 490–492
Level of aspiration, 329
Linguistics, 425–477
Localization, 52–53
Longitudinal studies, 20–24, 423–424
Lorge–Thorndike test, 525
Love, 412, 587

M

Manifest anxiety, 349–352
Manipulative studies, 14
Masculinity, 576, 590–592
Mass conservation, 489–490
Mass media, 615
Maturation, 24
Mediation, 12, 25, 29, 254–257, 303–305,
    469–473
    motor, 229–230
    verbal, 224–230
Mediational deficiency, 257–261, 265–268
Memory, 66, 195–222, 267
Mental growth, 532–535
Mental impairment, 451–452, 562–565, 619,
    629–640
Mentalistic theory, 473–476
Metabolism, 633–635
Methodology, general comments, 4
Minimal brain dysfunction, 638–640
Mnemonic devices, 206, 211
Modeling, 9–11, 600–609
Mongolism, 630
Moral development, 597, 602–605
Motivation, 186–187, 311–362, 403–405
Müller–Lyer illusion, 363, 400–401
Myelination, 626–629

N

Nativism–empiricism, 364
Naturalistic studies, 14
Needs, 353–354
  learned, 313
Negative reinforcement, 97, 107–108, 187–188, 666–668
Nerve conduction, 619–629
Nervous system, 620–629
  autonomic, 411, 421
Neural model, 283–284
Nonreversal shifts, 297–308
Nonspecific transfer, 263
Normative studies, 14
Novelty, 283–284, 286, 356, 357
Number conservation, 487–489
Nurturance, 581, 598
Nystagmus, 36–37, 39, 40

O

Observing responses, 268–269
Oddity learning, 152, 277
Olfaction, 58–62
Ontogenesis, 2, 62, 72, 426
Operant behavior, 97, 415, 417, 418, 646–653
Operational definition, 510, 523
Optical illusions, 363–364
Orientation reaction, 281–286, 414
Orienting behavior, 281–286, 391–392, 414
Overtraining reversal effect, 300–302

P

Pain, 53–56
Paired associate learning, 195, 202–218
Parental behavior, 539–542
Parental control, 605–608
Passivity, 424
Peer groups, 609–612
Percentiles, 520
Perception, 33–63, 363–410
  infant, 421–422
Perceptual learning, 151, 152
Perceptual set, 263–268
Performance set, 268–270
Perinatal factors, 635–637
  complications, 423
Personality, 506–507, 571
Personality disturbance, 506
Phenylketonuria, 633
Phonics, 369
Phonology, 425–436

Phylogenesis, 2
Physiological psychology, 1, 343, 360, 411, 619–642
Piagetian theory, 479–484, 512–513
Play behavior, 566, 611
Pleasure principle, 586
Polygraph, 60, 108
Positive reinforcement, 97, 123–130, 187–188, 659–666
Power and socialization, 587–600
Prediction, 7–11
Prematurity, 637–638
Prenatal conditioning, 85–86
Prenatal factors, 635–637
Preoperational stage, 481–482
Preschool effects on intelligence, 560–563
Prestige, 593
Primary research, 13
Probability learning, 152
Production deficiency, 258
Projective tests, 542–543
Pseudoconditioning, 70, 75, 77, 82
Psychoanalytic theory, 419, 586, 591
Psycholinguistics, 425–477
Psychological theory, 29
Psychosis, 506
Psychotherapy, 643–672
Punishment, 66–67, 97, 108, 416–417, 595–597, 647, 669–670
Pupillary conditioning, 92–94

Q

Quieting, 37

R

Race, 572, 590
  intelligence and, 556–560
Rage, 412
Ratings, behavioral, 424
Reading, 369, 484, 566
Reality principle, 586
Reciprocal inhibition, 645–646
Reflexes, 33–35, 38–39, 41–43, 48–49, 53–55, 59, 412–416, 421, 619–629
Reinforcement, 401–403, 415, 586–587, 647–649, 672
  amount, 138–139
  definition, 66–67
  positive, 123–130
  schedules, 112–114, 136–137, 139–142, 147–149, 216, 419
  secondary, 313–320, 325–327, 334–338
  socialization and, 597
  withdrawal, 108

Relational concepts, 492–494
Reliability, 522
Respiration, 107, 281, 413
Respondent behavior, 643–646
Respondent learning, definition, 97
Response differentiation, 650
Response measurement in therapy, 655–656
Response-produced cues, 224–227
Response speed, 141–142
Response-suppression, 135–136
Restricted operant training, 98
Retardation, 304–305
Retention learning, 66
Reversal learning, 277
Reversal shifts, 297–308
Reward training, 97
Rocking, 414–415, 419
Rooting reflex, 413

S

Salivation, conditioned, 73
Schedules of reinforcement, 100–102, 120–
    122, 130–134, 136–137, 147–149, 216
Schema formation, 376–379
Schizophrenia, 605
School and socialization, 612–615
Secondary reinforcement, 97, 313–320, 325–
    327, 334–338
Secondary research, 13
Self-concepts, 572, 590
Semantics, 462–465
Sensitization, 49, 70, 77
Sensorimotor stage, 480–481
Sensory processes, 33–63
Sentence construction, 454–462
Separation-anxiety, 419
Set, 263–278
Sex differences, 54, 543–544
Sex-role identification, 603–605
Sexual behavior, 424
Sexual control, 590–592
Sexual maturation, 578–580
Shaping behavior, 649–652
Simultaneous discrimination learning, 155,
    184–187
Single-subject research, 15
Size discrimination, 180, 295
Smiling, 417–419, 588–589
    conditioned, 120
Social adjustment, 571–617
Social disapproval, 353–354
Social institutions, 612–615
Social isolation, 353–354
Social reinforcement, 103, 104, 610–611, 660

Socialization, 419, 571–617
    theory, 583–587
Socioeconomic effects, 550–556
Sociometric techniques, 575–577
Somatotyping, 577–578
Somesthesis, 53–56
Soviet studies, 81–82, 92, 94, 264, 281–285
Space perception, 384–391
Specific transfer, 263
Speech, 641
Stabilimeter, 60
Stages of development, 11–12
Standard scores, 520
Standardization, 519–522
Stanford–Binet Scales, 21, 525–527
Startle reaction, 414
Stat-children, 291–292
State variables, 63, 116, 411
Statistical analysis, 16–19
Stimulation
    oral, 414
    tactual, 413
    vestibular, 415
Stimulus deprivation, 359–360
Stimulus familiarization, 285–286
Stimulus orientation, 380–384
Stimulus predifferentiation, 227–230, 236–238
Successive discrimination learning, 155, 184–
    187
Sucking behavior, infant, 51, 56, 57, 105–107,
    110–111
    conditioned, 73–82
Swaddling, 412, 421
Symbolic functions, 481–482
Synesthesia, 248–250
Syntax, 222, 425, 436–462

T

Tachistoscope, 382
Tactile stimulation, 53–56, 108, 413
Taste, 56–58
Temporal conditioning, 69, 83, 92–93
Test anxiety, 349–352
Testing, 519–528
Theory
    discrimination learning, 237–238
    general comments, 4–5, 15
Thermal sensitivity, 56
Topography, response, 119
Touch, 53–56
Trace conditioning, 69
Transfer of training, 205, 223–262, 295–297,
    515
Transposition, 238–245

U

Uncertainty, 357
Underachievement, 567–568, 672
Underconstancy, 389–390

V

Validity, 523, 527–528
Values, 571
Verbal learning, 195–222
Verbal mediation, 224–230
Vestibular stimulation, 415
Vincent curves, 17–19
Visual acuity, 39–40
Visual processes, 35–47

Visual reinforcers, 104–107
Vocabulary, 22
Vocalization, 117–118, 425–436
Volume conservation, 489–490

W

Warm-up, 268
Weight conservation, 489–490
Word association strength, 202–204
Word development, 436–438

Y

Yoked-control procedure, 115, 118